Political Corruption

Political Corruption

Concepts & Contexts

Third Edition

Arnold J. Heidenheimer
Michael Johnston
editors

Transaction Publishers
New Brunswick (U.S.A.) and London (U.K.)

Library of Congress Catalog Number: 2001041596
ISBN: 0-7658-0761-2
Printed in the United States of America

Library of Congress Cataloging-in-Publication Data

Political Corruption : concepts and contexts / Arnold J. Heidenheimer and
    Michael Johnston, editors—3rd ed.
        p. cm.
    Includes bibliographical references.
    Contents: v. 1. Newspaper culture.
    ISBN 0-7658-0761-0 (pbk. : alk. paper)
    1. Political corruption. I. Heidenheimer, Arnold J. II. Johnston,
    Michael, 1949-

JF1525.C66 P65 2001
364.1' 323—dc21   2001041596

Contents

Preface

Corruption in Space and Time

Probably no period has witnessed the birth of more publications on political corruption than the closing decade of the twentieth century. The 1990s have also seen unprecedented expansion in relevant efforts at the measurement and monitoring, as well as mobilization efforts to control corruption. The latter activity in particular involved the mobilization of significant new forces in both the policy world and in academe. This volume presents a context for examining how this frenzy of activity has affected issues of definition, causation, and consequences of corruption. Thus it explores whether startling "awakenings" and crusades—after a generation during which corruption received relatively little attention—have exposed yet greater empirical and theoretical complexities for students of the subject.

As one of few volumes on corruption that can trace its genealogy to the period "before Watergate," this compendium has been assembled in the belief that improved comprehension can be induced by understanding a broad range of manifestations over *both* time and space. Thus the contexts which are treated in our articles fall within a chronological dimension that commences in the early modern period, and also relate to geopolitical cases drawn from virtually all continents. Hence, we can clarify for the reader why in some Western countries corruption incidence declined between the eighteenth and the twentieth centuries, while in others it seems to have increased. Similarly, we can help readers understand why in 1960 corruption was seen in some West European countries as neither a problem nor an issue, and why such perceptions were radically altered in the 1990s, at a time when corruption practices were also changing in post-Communist Eastern Europe. Contrasts between corruption in Africa and Asia, which raise major questions about the social networks sustaining corruption as well as about its consequences, should likewise be made clearer, both by selections discussing those regions and others linking corruption to more deeply embedded aspects of development.

Corruption and Measurement

For some groups of scholars, the global corruption landscape has come to be even more radically transfigured. This is exemplified by the observation that where, in the 1980s, most transnational comparisons were largely impressionistic, the 1990s saw the dispersion of methodology which seemed to allow objective quantification of corruption incidence and perception in various national settings. But these breakthroughs were accomplished in the face of bypassing crucial conceptual hurdles, such as the definition of basic terms. Moreover, they reflected a range of interests and outlooks that, while bringing new energy to the study of corruption, also tended to "flatten out" the variations among cases, rather than probing more subtle historical, cultural, and linguistic issues. In a way the dominant measurement efforts became focused on examining the extent to which various test tubes were more or less full than others, while ignoring variations in their shapes, and in what they contained.

In addition to assessing the new methodologies, we seek to enhance insight by presenting more qualitative contrasts among small groups of contiguous countries. Thus, one chapter explores why corruption became more pervasive in Italy than in France or Spain, while another compares the corruption control efforts of Singapore with those of Thailand and the Philippines.

One of the ways in which we seek to couple comparative emphasis with the exploration of new ground is in the way we explore the relationships between party finance and political corruption. Previous academic studies have been hesitant to examine the interpretation of these arenas, but we believe that the time has come to face such challenges more directly. We must identify definitional problems, but not let them restrain us so as to allow the terms of debates to be set solely by publicists.

It is significant that the definitional discussion as to how closely corruption should be linked to the legality of electoral and other practices is being diminished at a time when the national legal frameworks are themselves being partially replaced or augmented by rules adopted at other levels of government, such as the OECD convention.

In the midst of those developments, European leaders have found their reputations entrapped in the shifting sands of judicial and public opinions. Thus the echoes of praise for national and European icons like François Mitterand and Helmut Kohl were still reverberating when new revelations led them to be condemned for having abused their dominant positions by directing corrupt side payments from cross-border economic transactions to subsidize party favorites. Several comparative articles examine in greater detail how the unmasking of corrupt party finance patterns in these and other countries led both to divergent national aftermaths, and to the inducement of similar corrective endeavors in neighboring countries.

Disciplinary or Multidisciplinary Approaches

Some of the extensive corruption literature published by social scientists in the 1990s has been mono-disciplinary, as in the case of most publications by international lending and development agencies. Other parts of that literature have been so directed toward policy lessons that key conceptual and definitional questions have been largely ignored, as in many of the publications produced or sponsored by reform groups.

By contrast, political scientists like ourselves and many others have continued to rely on multidisciplinary sources in our studies of corruption. Ever since its inception in 1970, this series of compendia has pursued a policy of drawing upon the contributions of authors affiliated with any one of the range of disciplines extending from history, economics, and sociology, to law, anthropology, and political science.

Analytical Logic and Sequential Emphasis

The analytical, conceptual, and descriptive contents in each of the book's fourteen parts have been assembled with a view towards maximizing coherence and complementarity for purposes of teaching and research. But, the reader will quickly recognize that there is method both behind our grouping of topics and also the sequence in which they are presented.

Broadly speaking, the first six parts of our book constitute explorations of conceptual and definitional questions across broad temporal and spatial dimensions. Our purpose here is to inform the reader about how structural and ideational developments have culminated in the modern definitions of corrupt practices, and why, as it has at times appeared to some, contemporary reformers seek to impose these on obstreperous outliers.

Then follow parts 7 through 10, in which we seek to demonstrate that deeper understanding is best served by grouping analytic and descriptive concepts as data according to geo-political and regime-type categories. Here the reader will find that the way in which material is assessed to answer questions of causation and effect is somewhat different in part seven on Africa than for Asia in part 8, or for the United States in part 10. For the eclectic reader, this organization could provide options for how to bundle chapters in diverse sections of the book in the course of an initial exploratory sampling of the volume.

Finally, in parts 11 through 14, we pursue mixed strategies. The geopolitical dimension is present, but more variable. For the discussion of the connections between party finance and political finance we refer almost exclusively to developed Western countries, whereas the sections devoted to the analysis of transitional systems in part 12 draw on more variables found in countries with more disparate societies and political traditions.

The final two parts then tackle the broad range of intellectual and conceptual problems that arise when issues such as the incidence of bribery and corruption are elevated from the local and national levels—the locus of almost all previous studies—to the level of international debate and policy formulation. Here the authors contrast the ways the new impetus affected traditional structures like the leading national print media, and how the newly coined statistical artifacts were utilized to link local, national, and international opinion groups. The volume concludes with selections intended to give some preliminary perspective on the events of the past decade, such as the causes and consequences of major scandals and reform efforts, and the roles both of corruption in the global economy and of globalization as a force reshaping our view of corruption. What issues might prove most noteworthy a decade from now, we can only guess, but the trends and events analyzed in this final part help define the starting point from which this decade's events will unfold.

Ancestral Archive

Regarded in alignment with its two predecessor volumes, originally published in 1970 and 1989, *Political Corruption* constitutes a distinctive combination of serial and originative publication. The editors designed this volume to augment some selected previous articles by soliciting, adapting, and translating new contributions. Among articles included in the two preceding editions, some have been retained, while the majority have been replaced under our system of rotating editorial content.

The roster of those who served honorably and well in previous intellectual exposures is an extensive one. It is not carved into stone, but it is recalled in the compilation of titles of the nearly four score previous contributions to the predecessor volumes which can be found in Appendix A. Classified by topic, this listing may prove helpful to some of our readers who are interested in observations by earlier cohorts of scholars.

Acknowledgements

Leading off the list of colleagues and students whose assistance we would like to acknowledge are Jean-François Médard and Holger Moroff, who from their home bases in Bordeaux and Bochum, as well as in meetings in St. Louis, Bergerac, and Paris, played crucial roles in helping us to translate broad goals into editorial reality. Their assistance made it possible for us to include the work of authors publishing in German and French, which on this account played a larger role than in previous editions. They combined these roles with those of authors and co-authors of several articles, following the example set by our esteemed colleague Victor T. LeVine, our co-editor of the preceding volume.

Considerable thanks are also due to another group of colleagues who helped to organize diverse formal and informal conferences at which concepts and ideas were vigorously discussed. Important among these was Yves Mény, the director of the Robert Schuman Center, who encouraged Donatella Della Porta to help set up the conference on political parties and corruption at the European University Institute in Fiesole in 1999. Another sponsor was Antoine Garapon of the École Nationale de la Magistrature, who hosted an initial meeting in Paris in 1997.

Valuable contributions at these and other meetings were also made by Ulrich von Alemann, University of Düsseldorf; Paul Heywood, University of Nottingham; Christina Landfried, University of Hamburg; Susan Pharr, Harvard University; Jean Cartier-Bresson, University of Reims; Leo Huberts, Free University of Amsterdam; and Mushtaq Khan, University of London, as well as French corruption specialist Laurence Giovacchini, and Irene Hors of the Organization for Economic Cooperation and Development.

Also very stimulating for pursuit of this endeavor were discussions with our students in courses on political corruption. At Washington University in St. Louis, particularly good critical discussion of various manuscripts were provided by Leora Addison, Michael Apfel, Paul Frederiksen, Omar McLaughlin, and Paul Sonderegger. At Colgate University, a dozen years' experience of teaching and debating the contents of the previous volume with very able undergraduates shaped this book in a variety of ways; Michael Johnston also thanks the Colgate Division of Social Sciences for funding enabling him to participate in the workshops noted above.

Critical discussion of several of the articles was also provided at a panel on modes of comparison in the study of political corruption, at the World Congress of the International Political Science Association, held in Quebec in August 2000. Participating in that discussion were contributors to this book like Verena Blechinger, Tokyo; Eva Etzioni-Halevy, Bar Ilan University; and

Maryvonne Genaux, Paris, and the two editors. Valuable commentaries were also provided by Linda Dolive, Northern Kentucky University, Also very helpful in St. Louis were two students at Washington University, Noah Evans and Bryan Brody. To all, and to many others who have contributed to this work over the years, our thanks.

ARNOLD J. HEIDENHEIMER
St. Louis, MO

MICHAEL JOHNSTON
Hamilton, NY

June, 2000

Part I

TERMS, CONCEPTS, AND DEFINITIONS

Introduction to Part I

Aristotle wrote that "there are three kinds of constitution, or an equal number of deviations, or, as it were, corruptions of these three kinds...The deviation or corruption of kingship is tyranny. Both kingship and tyranny are forms of government by a single person, but...the tyrant studies his own advantage...the king looks to that of his subjects."

Was Aristotle, when he described tyranny as a corrupt form of monarchy, using the concept of corruption much as we would apply it today to an official who secretly accepts a bribe to decide a policy issue differently than he otherwise would have?

Carl Friedrich, following Aristotle, holds that both applications derive from the basic core meaning, which he formulates as "deviant behavior associated with a particular motivation, namely that of private gain at public expense" (chapter 1).

However, today this attempt sacrifices clarity to brevity, insofar as it leaves too implicit how or why behavior is deviant from which norms for those whose conceptions are not based on Aristotelian ideal types. Some institutional framework seems a definitional prerequisite. We have less disagreement with Friedrich's formulation that corruption exists, "whenever a power holder who is charged with doing certain things, that is a responsible functionary or office holder, is by monetary or other rewards, such as the expectation of a job in the future, induced to take actions which favor whoever provides the reward and therefore damage the group or organization to which the functionary belongs, more specifically the government."

How prevalent has corruption thus defined been in various countries over recent times? His answer is:

> That corruption is endemic in all government is practically certain. That there are striking differences in the extent of corruption between governments which are formally similar such as Great Britain, Switzerland and the United States, all functioning constitutional democracies, is equally patent.

It is possible that a law could be stated that would say that the degree of corruption varies inversely to the degree that power is consensual.

Switzerland can be taken as an example of a political system where consensual power was maintained into the period of industrialization and mass suffrage, so that in the nineteenth and twentieth centuries, that country has reported very few cases of corruption. The Scandinavian countries of Sweden and Denmark have used different techniques to inhibit corruption, even in recent periods when the same political party has remained in control of local and national power over many decades.

How time-bound are these perceptions? If, for instance, we turn back to the eighteenth century, how were these countries ranked on corruption by Americans in the decades preceding the American Revolution?

We are not surprised to find that eighteenth century Americans regarded the British system of that period as "corrupt." At the time Robert Walpole and his friends ruled Britain by assembling majorities in parliament, which they largely recruited through money payments and the trading of patronage favors. But the traditional English concept of "corruption" on which the eighteenth century writers built related not only to means, but to the ends of politics. It was the encroachment of the executive power on that of the legislature and of the elites it then represented, which constituted the core of the definition of corruption used by many Englishmen as early as 1700:

> The executive possesses means of distracting parliament from its proper functions; it seduces members by the offer of places and pensions, by retaining them to follow ministers and ministers' rivals, by persuading them to support measures.-standing armies, national debts, excise schemes-whereby the activities of administration grow beyond Parliament's control. These means of subversion are known collectively as corruption.

In the period in which American protest boiled up to culminate in the revolution, Americans echoed and escalated such charges against George III and his ministers. But how did they rank Sweden and Switzerland, countries not particularly allied with Britain or involved in North America?

Very differently from each other. Switzerland was regarded as a country which had not only maintained local direct democracy usages similar to those employed in New England towns, but had protected its local institutions and effectively resisted the encroachment of potential political centralizes or 'despots.' Denmark and Sweden, by sharp contrast, were seen as systems which had become corrupted because their estates had allowed the powers of their parliaments to be undermined by centralizing monarchs who deprived the nobility and citizens of legislative rights which they had earlier enjoyed. Their people and elites had failed to maintain effective checks on the wielders of power. The Americans believed that it had been lack of vigilance

> that had brought liberty in Denmark to its knees, for there is a corrupt nobility, more interested in using its privileges for self-indulgence than for service to the state, had dropped its guard and allowed in a standing army which quickly destroyed the constitution and the liberties protected by it.

Sweden was a subsequent case in point.

> The colonists themselves could remember when the Swedish people had enjoyed liberty to the full; but now, in the 1760s, they were known to "rejoice at being subject to the caprice and arbitrary power of a tyrant, and kiss their chains.

The concepts of corruption employed by the American colonists partly anticipated the manner in which concepts and terms were employed in some subsequent American crises, but also relate to concepts employed by such founding fathers of western political thought as Thucydides, Plato, and Aristotle. They and some modern political theorists have employed the notion of the "corruption of the bad polity," to characterize situations which they perceived as marked by the decay of the moral and political order. As Friedrich writes about one of them: "Rousseau was deeply concerned with what he believed to be the corruption of his age, and he looked upon himself as the wise man who must raise a warning voice:...Rousseau's concern with corruption is primarily with moral corruption, and only indirectly with political corruption, as providing the setting for moral corruption." Another writer notes that, "The arguments about corruption are scattered throughout the Western political tradition but a coherent theory of corruption has never been fully articulated."

As some of the above examples illustrate, there may be some overlap between the broader 'institutional decay' concept of corruption, and the more delineated one which defines corruption in terms of the acceptance of money or money's worth by public officials for misusing official powers. But analytically the two concepts are fairly clearly distinguishable. There will tend to be some "corrupt" public officials in most political systems which are not widely believed to be becoming corrupt in the sense of the decay of their vital moral or constitutional rules of behavior. But by and large even radical critics have come *not* to link the establishment of standing armies and the growth of national debts as indicators of political system corruption in the way that eighteenth century critics did.

At times shocking revelations about the misuse of political, and especially executive powers, have tended to revive the associations and partly archaicized usages linked with the concept of institutional decay. Watergate was a marked instance of that. When it became apparent that President Nixon and his White House aides had boldly abused the powers of their offices to undermine their opponents, the issue of corruption reappeared starkly on the American national scene.

The Watergate revelations revealed clear violations of political rules in the shape of a television drama, which seemed to come, "straight out of the American Christian literary tradition...revealing naked ambition, Christian piety, lust for power and tragic betrayal." Americans watching it got the overwhelming impression that "all the president's men were satanic minions, that the president himself was villainy incarnate, and that the highest office in the land had been lamentably stained." (Eisenstadt, 1990) In its drama and consequence the Watergate revelations, leading as they did to the near-impeachment and resignation of the president and the imprisonment of many of his closest advisers, far exceeded both the drama and political import of such "normal" American scandals of earlier days, like Teapot Dome and Credit Mobilier.

Yet the prevailing definitions of political corruption by recent political scientists have fairly consistently defined corruption in terms of transactions between the private and public sectors such that collective goods are illegitimately converted into private-regarding payoffs.

The intrigues and plots which composed portions of the illegal chain in which operatives of the Nixon White House abused executive powers did not clearly conform to such and similar definitions of corruption. By contrast to the typical patterns of bribery, nepotism, patronage, misappropriation of funds, sale of office, and the like, Watergate did *not* involve primarily private-regarding payoffs, the president's tax returns and home remodeling notwithstanding. All the President's Men were not interested in private gain. Watergate thus differed from such cash-oriented scandals as Teapot Dome, Credit Mobilier, or the Agnew affair.

> Many political scientists whose attention to political corruption phenomena antedated the Nixon/Watergate period reacted critically to these proposed, more broadened definitions. We are inclined to agree with a British colleague that the looseness of contemporary definitions provides infinite scope for argument. Unethical behavior or behavior which violates "the norms of the system of public order" may include almost anything. The danger here seems to be that clarity and consistency in analysis may have been sacrificed for comprehensiveness. The fundamental weakness of the recent literature on corruption lies in the use of vague criteria and inappropriate perspectives which distort, exaggerate or otherwise over-simply explanations of corruption in the United States.

Varieties of Meanings

A careful examination of what past and present writers seem to have intended when they employed the term *corruption* in political contexts reveals an even broader catalog of usages and potential ambiguities. Some reasons for this become more apparent by referring to the *Oxford English Dictionary* (OED), where we find that only one of nine commonly accepted definitions for the term is applicable to political contexts: "Perversion or destruction of integrity in the discharge of public duties by bribery or favor; the use or existence of corrupt practices, especially in a state, public corporation, etc."

The OED categorizes the nine meanings of corruption as follows:

1. *Physical*—for example, "the destruction or spoiling of anything, especially by disintegration or by decomposition with its attendant unwholesomeness and loathsomeness; putrefaction."
2. *Moral*—the "political" definition already given comes under this category. Another definition in this category is: "a making or becoming morally corrupt; the fact or condition of being corrupt; moral deterioration or decay; depravity."
3. *The perversion of anything from an original state of purity*—for example, "the perversion of an institution, custom, and so forth from its primitive purity; an instance of this perversion."

The present usage of the term corruption in political contexts has obviously been colored by the meanings in the "moral" category, and in earlier times usage was frequently colored by the meanings in the two other categories, especially by those in the third category. Thus the author of a nineteenth-century encyclopedia article entitled "Corruption in Politics" developed his discussion essentially in terms of meanings derived by way of Montesquieu from Aristotle, who, for instance, conceived of tyranny as a "corrupted" variant of monarchy.

Contemporary Social Science Definitions

The variety of definitions employed by contemporary social scientists interested in corruption fortunately does not cover as wide a span as those given in the OED. Among them we can identify usages that seek to define corruption in terms of one of three kinds of basic models or concepts. The largest group of social science writers follow the OED definition and relate their definitions of corruption essentially to concepts concerning the duties of the public office. A smaller group develop definitions that are primarily related to demand, supply, and exchange concepts derived from economic theory; while a third group discuss corruption more with regard to the concept of the public interest.

Public-Office-Centered Definitions

Definitions of corruption that relate most essentially to the concept of the public office and to deviations from norms binding upon its incumbents are well illustrated in the work of three authors—David H. Bayley, G. Myrdal, and J.S. Nye—who have concerned themselves with the problems of development in various continents.

> Corruption, while being tied particularly to the act of bribery, is a general term covering misuse of authority as a result of considerations of personal gain, which need not be monetary.

Examining the wording of American statutes relating to bribery, Lowenstein (*Handbook*, 1990) finds that one of five elements generally mentioned, that relating to the involvement of a public official, is least ambiguous. More open to interpretation are conditions that

  i. the defendant must have a corrupt intent;
  ii. that benefits of value must accrue to the public official;
  iii. that there must be a relationship between the thing of value and an official act; and,
  iv. that the relationship must involve the intent to influence or be influenced in the carrying out of an official act.

J.S. Nye (chapter 17) defines corruption as

> . . . behavior which deviates from the normal duties of a public role because of private-regarding (family, close private clique), pecuniary or status gains; or violates rules against the exercise of certain types of private-regarding influence. This includes such behavior as bribery (use of reward to pervert the judgement of a person in a position of trust); nepotism (bestowal of patronage by reason of ascriptive relationship rather than merit); and misappropriation (illegal appropriation of public resources for private-regarding uses).

Market-Centered Definitions

Definitions in terms of the theory of the market have been developed particularly by those authors dealing with earlier Western and contemporary non-Western societies, in which the norms governing public officeholders are not clearly articulated or are nonexistent. Thus Van Klaveren (chapter 5) states that

> A corrupt civil servant regards his public office as a business, the income of which he will...seek to maximize. The office then becomes a—maximizing unit." The size of his income depends...upon the market situation and his talents for finding the point of maximal gain on the public's demand curve.

Also pertinent is the statement by Nathaniel Leff (chapter 18).

> Corruption is an extra-legal institution used by individuals or groups to gain influence over the actions of the bureaucracy. As such the existence of corruption *per se* indicates only that these groups participate in the decision-making process to a greater extent than would otherwise be the case.

Public-Interest-Centered Definitions

Some writers feel that the first set of definitions is too narrowly conceived and the second set too broadly conceived. They tend to maintain that the embattled concept of "public interest" is not only still useful but necessary to illustrate the essence of concepts like corruption. Carl Friedrich, for instance, contends that

> The pattern of corruption can be said to exist whenever a powerholder who is charged with doing certain things, i.e., who is a responsible functionary or office-holder, is by monetary or other rewards not legally provided for, induced to take actions which favor whoever provides the rewards and thereby does damage to the public and its interests.

Since the concept of the public interest is open to broad interpretation, it has been suggested that determination of whether a political policy-influencing action is or is not corrupt will depend on the observer's judgment as to whether a particular policy is or is not desirable. But Lowenstein argues that acts that "are made according to the wishes of the highest bidder," may be regarded as contrary to the public interest, without regard to the substantive direction of its influence on public policy" (*Handbook*, 1990).

In the 1980s there has been a revival of attempts to employ the public interest concept to delegitimate particularly large-scale business financing of political activity by attaching the label of corruption to legal or quasi-legal activities. Accordingly, distinctions are made between "public interest groups," which represent "the community at large" and whose focus is on "non-pecuniary interests," and "special interest groups," which have a narrow base and represent primarily pecuniary interests. Thus the financial allocations of political action committees have in the American context, been attacked, by Amitai Etzioni as exercising power through so-called "legalized corruption."

Plutocrats in a democracy work by corrupting public life. They seek to turn a government of, by and for the people into one of the wealthy....Political corruption is typically perpetrated by private interests seeking illicit public favors and finding quite willing public officials.[10]

In West Germany, where similar payments evaded disclosure requirements, similar charges have been made by members of the Green party. For political analysts this raises the question of whether they should blur the distinctions between exchanges that are implicit rather than explicit, and between those that are channeled through legalized organizations rather than through back-door contacts. Should "undue influence" become labeled as "corruption" when the means are used by a group that is seen as working less in the public interest than others? Arguments about whether social scientists should endorse or employ such broadened definitions continue to be vehement in both America and Europe.

Whose Norms Set the Criteria?

The definitions employed in the first and third of the categories just discussed directly raise the question encountered in all normative analysis: Which norms are the ones that will be used to distinguish corrupt from noncorrupt acts? If the definitions are public-office-centered, then which statement of the rules and norms governing public officeholders is to be employed? If the definitions are public-interest-centered, then whose evaluation of the public's interest is to be operationalized? Definitions couched in terms of market theory appear to bypass this problem, but in fact they do not. They too imply that somewhere there is an authority that distinguishes between the rules applicable to public officials and those applicable to businessmen operating in the free market, or that there are certain characteristics that distinguish a "black market" from the free market.

Political scientists of an earlier generation tried to deal with the problem of norm setting with reference to the legal rules provided by statute books and court decisions. Thus behavior was judged by James Bryce to be either permissible or corrupt in accordance with the criteria established by legislators and judges:

> Corruption may be taken to include those modes of employing money to attain private ends by political means which are criminal or at least illegal, because they induce persons charged with a public duty to transgress that duty and misuse the functions assigned to them.

But the author of the article on "Corruption, Political," in the *Encyclopedia of the Social Sciences* argued that "the question of formal legality...is not the essence of the concept." The normative judgments that should be used as criteria, he thought, were the judgments of the elite: "Where the best opinion and morality of the time, examining the intent and setting of an act, judge it to represent a sacrifice of public for private benefit, then it must be held to be corrupt."

Senturia's particularistic emphasis would require that this fairly large body of elites serve as a jury for each particular case. Their findings, in effect, would relate only to their society of that particular era. A consensus of the "best opinion" in a time and place, such as Britain in 1960, could presumably establish criteria beyond which private-regarding behavior would be considered corrupt in the contemporary setting. However, it would then be impossible to compare either the extent or the verities of political corruption between the situations prevailing of Britain in 1960 and in 1860 because of the uniqueness of the suggested definition. This difficulty would apply equally to attempts to compare, say, bureaucratic corruption in nineteenth-century Russia and twentieth-century Chicago.

Is there a term which political scientists could use as a synonym for corruption, which would include the meanings most relevant for them, while screening out some of those that create ambiguity, such as the one associated with the broader meaning linked with system decay? The term *graft* is put forward as one possible candidate. Although the exact origins of the term are not known, it is clearly of American origins and was long regarded as an Americanism, as the OED *Supplement* records. Terms very similar to corruption have been taken over from Latin into most established languages, and this constitutes an advantage from the comparative perspective. (See Moroff & Blechinger, chapter 44.)

Although corruption is often exemplified with examples of bribery, it is generally recognized that corruption is a broader and more embracing concept. Bribery is regarded by many lawyers as a concept with relatively fixed boundaries, whose definitions centered around quid-pro-quo relationships. In American jurisprudence, the bribery concept has generally been held to be broader than that of a lesser offence like 'giving or receiving an unlawful gratuity (FN). The distinction between corruption and bribery which is found in English can also be identified in most of the languages, with some exceptions. For a more extensive description of terminological differences among major languages, and how these are reflected in journalistic usage, see the article by Holger Moroff and Verena Blechinger (chapter 44).

* * *

Several articles in the next section elaborate different perspectives on the problem of defining corruption and related concepts and terms. In his article on defining corruption Gardiner underlines the distinction between misuse of public office and outright forms of corruption. For instance, if a legislator votes for a bill which gives tax concessions to a company he owns stock in this would best be labeled as legislative conflict of interest, rather than necessarily of corruption. He also criticizes attempts to base definitions of corruption on legality and evaluates tendencies to attach the corruption label to legislation which one-sidedly benefits entrenched social interests, but notes that some people "feel uncomfortable using the term corruption in all situations where the political process produces policies which do not benefit everyone equally." He also provides an initial overview of survey based and other empirical studies concerning perceptions of corruption which are contained in this book.

Philp's article identifies five criteria of a core definition of corruption and identifies difficulties which are raised by their application. He critically examines the attempts to distinguish additional categories of defining corruption and tends to be critical of efforts to distinguish either a definition based on public opinion, or Thompson's attempt to crystallize a category of institutional corruption.

Philp's deconstructionist efforts are also directed at classical Greek terms, which he finds did not adequately distinguish between bribery and gift giving or receiving. This he attributes to the lack in the ancient Greek world of a fully developed concept of public office and trust.

Did the criteria of personal gain also apply to the extortion of sexual favors in places like seventeenth-century England? Philp explores this question with reference to the revelations in the famous diary of Samuel Pepys. Finally the author also cautions us not to apply the corruption concept indiscriminately, and in particular asserts that public office mal-functions like incompetence and favoritism should not be subsumed under the umbrella term of corruption.

The four chapters exemplify how discussion of definitional issues progressed since about 1970. Friedrich's article constitutes an early comment on the presentation developed in the Introduction, as it appeared in the first edition. Gardiner's chapter then synthesizes much of the academic discussion of the 1970s and 1980s. Philp in turn deals with some new contributions from the 1990s and broadens the theoretical format of the analysis in cross-cultural and cross-national terms. The Leys article, finally, reminds the reader what the state of play was like before corruption issues drew broader academic attention.

Western Versus Non-Western Standards

If one does not accept the criteria established by law or the norms of a small elite group as delimiting political corruption, how far can one go in delineating the relevant norms with reference to the standards of a more diverse set of reference groups and codes? At present this problem presents itself most directly for those social scientists who have sought to analyze corruption in developing countries where mores rooted in two very distinct milieu govern the standards of political and bureaucratic behavior.

> It not infrequently happens...in developing non-Western societies that existing moral codes do not agree with Western norms as to what kinds of behavior by Public servants should be condemned. The Western observer is faced with an uncomfortable choice. He can adhere to the Western definition, in which case he lays himself open to the charge of being censorious and he finds that he is condemning not abhorrent behavior, but normal acceptable operating procedure. On the other hand, he may face up to the fact that corruption, if it requires moral censure, is culturally conditioned. He then argues that an act is corrupt if the surrounding society condemns it. This usage, however, muddies communication, for it may be necessary then to assert in the same breath that an official accepts gratuities but is not corrupt.

The problem of applying the concept and standards of corruption to developing countries is exhaustively discussed by Colin Leys (chapter 4), who builds on the analysis of the literature as it had developed by the 1960s, to raise and answer questions both of conceptual and empirical relevance. He criticizes some of the parallels drawn by earlier writers between developments in Britain and Africa. The British ruling class of the Victorian period is seen by him as having a clear if tenuous conception of the public interest and the duty they owed to it through their use of public offices. In Africa, by contrast, "the idea contained in the phrase noblesse oblige scarcely applies. There is no previous experience, and so no prior ideology, of the rules of public offices and institutions in relation to the public interest, in terms of which the private exploitation of public office could be rationalized." This illustrates how developing countries, where definitions of corruption were rather peremptorily incorporated into new legal codes, differed from western countries, where changes in the moral and legal connotation of corruption evolved gradually along, with other processes of societal change.

Corruption Contestation

Analysts of political corruption over the past decades might tend to agree that "corruption" is a contested concept. Whether it is a *basically* contested concept is less evident. There is considerable overlap between various components of proposed definitions. Of the three definitional types suggested above, some have been candidates for deletion, while other writers have proposed additional definitional types.

Thus the 1970s witnessed persuasive arguments for recognition of a fourth definitional type, based on *public opinion*. The inflation of conceptual types has partly been buttressed by the argument that the needs of dealing with the theoretically difficult interface between political party finance abuses involving kickbacks is not served well enough through use of the three-pronged typology. The question, however is, whether acceptance of additional types of corruption definitions would contribute to solutions, rather than adding further complexity to the analytical problem. In retrospect it seems that the case for a distinct public opinion-based definition has not been irrevocably established.

The presumption that twenty-five years of varied corruption research could call for a reformulation of the three-pronged typology is reasonable. On the other hand, not much research has been both conceptually self-conscious and oriented toward coping with broader cross-language challenges. Most optimal in the new millennium might be an attempt to resynthesize the typology. Conceivably the typology might be reformulated while not expanding the numbers. Although there is no inherent virtue in small numbers, in this case the advocates of conceptual multiplication might be asked to shoulder the burden proving "need."

Forthcoming typologies might also seek to incorporate elements of the directness or indirectness of the relation between exchanges and their policy outcomes. This dimension would apply particularly where donors are groups and where recipients are collective political actors like parties. The traditional quid-pro quo criterion applicable to bribery convictions of individuals could find their equivalents where recipients are parties. But donations to parties might also be found corrupt if they indirectly lead to policy outcomes that would shortcut or distort democratic processes of decision-making. Here judgment calls are of course much more difficult as an analysis of jurisprudence of the U.S. and German Supreme and constitutional courts has borne out (Burke, chapter 34; Moroff, chapter 36).

Notes

1. *The Politics of Aristotle,* translated and edited by Ernest Barker (Oxford: Clarendon Press, 1946), p. 373.
2. Carl J. Friedrich, "Corruption Concepts," chapter 1, this volume.
3. J.G.A. Pocock, "Machiavelli, Harrington and English Political Ideologiesin the Eighteenth Century," *William and Mary Quarterly,* 3d ser., 22 (1965), p. 565.
4. Bernard Bailyn, *The Ideological Origins of the American Revolution* (Cambridge, Mass.: Harvard University Press, 1967), p. 65.
5. Ibid., p. 64.
6. Patrick Dobel, "The Corruption of a State," *American Political Science Review,* (1978), p. 959.
7. Larry L. Berg, H. Hahn, and J. R. Schmidhauser, *Corruption in the American Political System,* Morristown, N.J.: General Learning Press, 1976. George C. S. Benson, S. A. Maaranen, and A. Heslop, *Political Corruption in America,* Lexington, Mass.: Lexington Books, 1978.
8. Robert J. Williams, "Political Corruption in the United States," *Political Studies, XXXIX, I* (March 1981), 126–29.
9. Friedrich, *loc. cit.*
10. Amitai Etzioni, *Capital Corruption: The New Attack on American Democracy* (New York: Harcourt, Brace Jovanovich, 1984), pp. 3–4, 201.
11. James Bryce, *Modern Democracies, 11.* New York: St. Martins, 1921, 524.
12. Joseph A. Senturia, "Corruption, Political," *Encyclopedia of the Social Sciences,* IV. New York: Crowell-Collier-Macmillian, 1930–1935, 449. FN. Daniel H. Lowenstein "Legal Efforts to Define Political Bribery." *Political Corruption: A Handbook* New Brunswick: Transaction, 1989. 29–38. John T. Noonan *Bribes* New York: Macmillan, 1984.

1

Corruption Concepts in Historical Perspective

Carl J. Friedrich

"Any attempt to analyze the concept of corruption must contend with the fact that in English and other languages the word *corruption* has a history of vastly different meanings and connotations."[1] This is very true; but a core meaning readily emerges from an analysis of these different meanings. Corruption is a kind of behavior which deviates from the norm actually prevalent or believed to prevail in a given context, such as the political. It is deviant behavior associated with a particular motivation, namely that of private gain at public expense. But whether this was the motivation or not, it is the fact that private gain was secured at public expense that matters. Such private gain may be a monetary one, and in the minds of the general public it usually is, but it may take other forms. It may be a rapid promotion, an order, decorations, and the like, and the gain may not be personal, but benefit a family or other group. The pattern of corruption may therefore be said to exist whenever a power holder who is charged with doing certain things, that is a responsible functionary or office holder, is by monetary or other rewards, such as the expectation of a job in the future, induced to take actions which favor whoever provides the reward and thereby damage the group or organization to which the functionary belongs, more specifically the government. It is preferable for our purposes to state the concept of corruption thus, rather

Source: Carl J. Friedrich. *The Pathology of Politics: Violence, Betrayal Corruption, Secrecy and Propaganda*. New York: Harper & Row, 1972, pp. 127–41. Copyright ©1972 by Carl J. Friedrich. Reprinted by permission of Harper & Row, Publishers, Inc.

than as the use of public power for private profit, preferment, or prestige, or for the benefit of a group or class, in a way that constitutes a breach of law or of standards of high moral conduct; for while such breaches constitute some sort of damage, they are not necessarily involved. But there is typically gain for corrupter and corrupted, and loss for others, involved in such a situation.[2]

This kind of corruption is the specific kind related to the notion of administrative service which the modern bureaucracy conceived as meritocracy has fostered.[3] But there is a much broader notion of political corruption which is implied in judgments such as that expressed by Lord Acton in his famous dictum that all power tends to corrupt and absolute power corrupts absolutely.[4] For while the specific kind of corruption may be involved here too, the meaning of Lord Acton is focused on the moral depravity which power is believed to cause in men; they no longer think about what is right action or conduct, but only about what is expedient action or conduct. Such deep suspicion of power has, it would seem, a religious root, and is typically Western and Christian. It harks back to the notion of the two kingdoms and to the contrast between the earthly and the heavenly city.[5] In this broad and imprecise sense, corruption cannot by definition be "functional." For such corruption, being in fact a decomposition of the body politic through moral decay, is a general category to include all kinds of practices which are believed to be dysfunctional and hence morally corrupt.

Acton's famous statement touches the paradox of power and morals. Systematically, corruption is a form of coercion, namely economic coercion. Not only the buying of votes and actual monetary rewards, but all the more indirect forms, such as gifts, or otherwise influencing the judgment of those who exercise governmental functions, are instrumentalities in this sphere. Here it is a question of the degree of corruption. For that such corruption is endemic in all forms of government is practically certain. But that there are striking differences in the extent of corruption between governments which are formally similar, such as Great Britain, Switzerland, and the United States, all functioning constitutional democracies, is equally patent. It is possible to state a "law" or general regularity by saying that the degree of corruption varies inversely to the degree that power is consensual. Corruption is a corrective of coercive power and its abuse, when it is functional. Many complications arise from the fact that power often appears to be consensual when it actually is not; or it may be consensual for Anglo-Saxon, Protestant whites, whereas it is not for immigrants or blacks.

. . . It would appear that in those situations where a semblance of consent hides the coercive reality, corruption is rife. The power which is believed to be consensual, having to a considerable extent become coercive, lends itself to corruption. Tammany Hall is a sort of example of this situation.[6] As Willie Stark puts it in *All the King's Men,* "Graft is what he calls it when the fellows do it who don't know which fork to use."[7] There is and always has been a tendency on the part of critics of democracy to assert that developments of this kind are typical of democracy. Historical studies have shown that such a judgment is untenable.[8] In monarchial England, Prussia, and Russia corruption was ubiquitous. The real difference is that in open societies corruption is often uncovered by the opposition and brought to public notice by a free press, whereas in autocratic regimes it remains largely hidden. The extensive corruption in totalitarian dictatorships is evident in the now available documents of the fascist and national socialist regimes. Reports from the Soviet Union suggest similar conditions.[9] To give a couple of illustrations let me cite Hermann Goering, Hitler's field marshal: "I have seen terrible things. Chauffeurs of District leaders have enriched themselves to the extent of half a million. The gentlemen know this? It is true? (Assent) These are things which are impossible. I shall not hesitate to proceed ruthlessly." This happened in a meeting on November 12, 1938, and treated such corruption as widespread and generally known.[10] Trotsky reported such corruption on a great scale as proof of his contention that the Soviet Union was utterly bureaucratized.[11] These bits of evidence could readily be multiplied. If it had not been for such corruption, many more would have perished under the terror whom corrupt officials allowed to escape.

Corruption in totalitarian regimes may also be of the broader unspecific kind. Thus the ideology has been undergoing what critics have described as corruption, namely a disintegration of the belief system upon which a particular political system rests. Such corruption will often take the form of a perversion of legal rules by misinterpretation. Such perversion, like a breach, challenges the intended generality of the rule: when exceptions multiply, they become the rule. It is obvious that they may thus become the basis of a revision of a basic ideological position which to the true believer appears as a corruption. There can be little doubt that this sort of "moral corruption" is what concerned political philosophers in the past. Aristotle, and after him Machiavelli particularly, but basically Plato in his theory of the "corrupted" or "perverted" constitutions-democracy, oligarchy, and tyranny-stressed the point that these regimes instead of being guided by the law (we would say the public interest) were serving the interest of the rulers. They were, we might say, exploitative, and thus corrupt. Aristotle followed Plato's notions, but substituted the happiness of the ruled, that is to say their well-being, for the law; such general happiness is, of course, closely akin to what is customarily in modern times referred to as the public or general interest. These fundamental general notions of corruption all practically define corruption as dysfunctional; for it is seen as destructive of a particular political order, be it monarchy, aristocracy, or polity, the latter a constitutionally limited popular rule, and thus by definition devoid of any function within a political order.

This classic conception of corruption as a general disease of the body politic persisted into modern times, and is central to the political thought of

Machiavelli, Montesquieu and Rousseau. For Machiavelli corruption was the process by which the *virtú* of the citizen was undermined and eventually destroyed. Since most men are weak and lacking in the *virtú* of the good citizen except when inspired by a great leader, the process of corruption is ever threatening. And when *virtú* has been corrupted, a heroic leader must appear who in rebuilding the political order infuses his *virtú* into the entire citizenry. Thus the miserable creatures that human beings ordinarily are or become when not properly guided are thereby transformed into patriotic citizens, capable of sacrifice, self-exertion, and other patriotic virtues. But such a leader must not be a Caesar. Machiavelli was sharply critical of the great Roman. He described him as one of the worst figures in Roman history; for he had destroyed the venerable Roman constitution instead of regenerating it.[12] He was, we might say, himself corrupted. In our time, a similar misunderstanding aided Hitler in seizing power. Instead of proving the heroic benefactor who would reconstitute Germany, he proved to be a corrupted destroyer of the German values and beliefs. The evidence we have on the thought of the resistance brings this out very clearly; men like Pastor Niemoeller offer instances of this original misunderstanding and eventual reversal.

Francis Bacon was generally believed to be a Machiavellian. He certainly shows Machiavelli's influence. Yet he was a corrupt man, perhaps the most famous instance of a high English dignitary brought down by his corruption. As High Chancellor he accepted bribes in order to favor certain parties before the court. The complexities of the case are considerable[13] and they are of no particular interest for our purpose. But what is of interest is that he and his friends essentially defended his case on the ground that he was not doing anything that was not generally done. It is a defense that has persisted to this day; he was the unlucky one who got caught. In the functional perspective, the matter may be stated differently; Bacon's case indicated that corruption had gone too far, that the limit of what might be allowed for purposes of moderating the regime's injustices was here exceeded and caused a reaction. . . .

The Roman Republic also had its trials of corruption, and men like Cicero who were interested in regenerating the Republic addressed themselves to the task of unearthing and bringing to trial extreme cases of corruption, especially in provincial administration.[14] But these efforts came too late. The Republic's public ethic was already too generally corrupted, and the limits had by that time been greatly transgressed. Corruption had become so general that corrupt practices rather than the strict morals of the forefathers had become the accepted mode of behavior. This Roman case was a primary instance in the theory of Montesquieu.[15] This nobleman and believer in the aristocracy, or a monarchy moderated by a nobility, devoted a major work to *Grandeur des Romains et de leur Decadence,* a work in which he described the process of corruption which he attributed to the imperial enterprise of the Romans. Their *virtù* gave them the victories over the other regimes of the Mediterranean and the extension of their city from *urbs* to *orbs* corrupted their moral fiber and eventually destroyed the constitutional order which had won them the empire. Some may anxiously ask today whether the Americans are not undergoing the same process. Be that as it may, Montesquieu again saw corruption as the dysfunctional process *par excellence* by which a good political order or system is perverted into an evil one, a monarchy into a despotism.

This global concept was pushed to its extreme and thereby to its *reductio ad absurdum* by Rousseau, who argued at one point that man had been corrupted by social and political life, and this notion was elaborated by the anarchists of the nineteenth century from Godwin to Bakunin. It is not the corruption of men which destroys the political system but the political system which corrupts and destroys man. Beyond this, Rousseau was deeply concerned with what he believed to be the corruption of his age, and he looked upon himself as the wise man who must raise a warning voice; for he believed that the right kind of guidance could shape public opinion to avoid such corruption. He believed in the manipulation of opinion as it was practiced in Sparta as a proper defense against corruption.[16] Artists, scientists, and literary men are "both the victims and the promoters of social conditions which necessarily caused them to corrupt their fellow men . . . The *corps littéraire* only cheers on princes when they oppress their peoples.[17] In short, Rousseau's concern with corruption is primarily with moral corruption, and only indirectly with political corruption, as providing the setting for moral corruption. Political corruption is seen by Rousseau as a necessary consequence of the struggle for power, and he could have agreed with Acton that all power tends to corrupt. According to Rousseau, equality is natural and good laws are directed toward maintaining this equality against the corrupting influence of power-hungry individuals.[18]

Although this preoccupation with equality may he reduced and refined to an equality before the law, Rousseau's outlook provides the setting for the modern and specific sense of corruption. The abuse of power, which constitutionalism is primarily concerned with preventing through the application of the rule of law to public officers (*Rechtsstaat*), is at the heart of corruption. Corruption was widespread, as mentioned before, under monarchies, absolute and other, and more particularly in England. In fact, the system which Walpole built is perhaps the most striking instance of corruption functioning effectively to transform a political system and establish a new one; for it is well known that the parliamentary system of government in which the ruling party rests upon majority support in the House of Commons was first organized by Walpole. In a celebrated, if somewhat controversial study, Professor Namier has analyzed this system.[18] Each party, but more particularly the Whig party under Walpole and Pelham (1715–1760) sought to secure for itself a solid majority in Parliament; for such a majority greatly facilitated the realization of policies and the enactment of necessary legislation. Walpole proceeded to secure such a parliamentary majority for himself and his cabinet by a carefully worked-out system which to his contemporaries, more especially the leader of the opposition, Lord Bolingbroke, appeared to be a system of corruption. Wraxall tells us in his *Memoirs* that the government under Pelham handed each of its partisans in Parliament from five hundred to eight hundred pounds at the end of a session, the amount varying according to the services rendered. These payments were official enough to be entered on a record kept in the Treasury (which has enabled recent researchers to elucidate the actual practice of corruption involved). These investigations have shown that the Whigs had worked out a very elaborate system of governmental favors, ranging from direct payments to voters and members of parliament, to patronage and the various favors available in foreign trade and the privileged trading companies. All this is well enough known, and was intimately bound up with what caused the Americans to rebel. If they had been better informed, they would have attacked this corruption rather than King George in their Declaration of Independence. In fact, Walpole once remarked that he and Lord Townsend constituted the "firm" to which the king had entrusted the government of the country.[20]

The argument of Bolingbroke and his friends that this system constituted corruption of the old constitution was, of course, sound. It was radically dysfunctional in one sense, but in another it actually helped a system which had become antiquated to function and to be transformed into a preferable one. An economist might say that a kind of market of the services of government officials had been substituted for monocratic (monopolistic) control. Such an arrangement was at variance with the requirements of a responsible public service, a rational bureaucracy in which ideally the official is paid from the public treasury for precisely defined legal duties, and must not have any other interests.[21] In Germany, all attempts at bribery on the part of private persons or groups are made crimes and punished. Such bribery is considered the most pernicious crime, an attack upon the very foundations of the state, and comparable to treason, in fact a form of treason. These are views by no means restricted to Germany,[22] but are found also in Switzerland, the Low Countries, and Scandinavia. They are logical consequences of the rationalized bureaucracy as developed in modern government and economics. For a large business concern will just as rigorously insist upon this approach to personal favors as will a responsible government.

Corruption, then, has become a particular form of political pathology rather than a global degeneration. As such it can be defined in behavioral terms, and the activities objected to can be outlawed. Institutions like the Comptroller's Office can be and have been set up in all advanced countries to watch the expenditure of public funds, and civil service commissions and the like have been established to inhibit and prevent patronage outside the official merit system. In this sense, modern bureaucracy spells the end of aristocratic privilege. Under absolutism, it was quite common that offices could be bought and sold. But to speak here of corruption is anachronistic, for the kings were not subject to any legal rules. Such sales were regulated and the proceeds went to the public treasury to be employed for such purposes as the king and his council decided upon. Thus, the sale of public offices was considered a "check on corruption" because it benefited the public weal, instead of some personal favorites of the king.[23] Reform-minded writers, such as Montesquieu and Bentham, openly advocated the buying and selling of offices because the service would thereby be improved. It is remarkable that Bentham of all thinkers should have taken this position: for it was the utilitarians and the reform movement they sparked which put an end to the venality of public offices in Britain. In fact, the process by which the British pulled themselves out of the morass of corruption which had made a Burke defend the "rotten borough"[24] as a sound political institution and developed what is, in the opinion of many, the most thoroughly honest public service ever organized is little short of miraculous. It shows that pathological phenomena are not necessarily destined to go from bad to worse and the corrective for them is often quite readily at hand. By the second half of the nineteenth century what had been considered "normal behavior" had become corruption sharply condemned by the majority of Britons.[25] Similar, though less dramatic, reforms were achieved in Prussia, Bavaria, and France; in all of which a properly trained bureaucracy, a responsible public service, was developed in this period.[26] It is not here possible to explore the problem of "bureaucracy" and its development, to which this transformation in the concept of corruption is linked.[27] The socialist movement, and more especially Marxism, developed their revolutionary ideology without any stress on the corruption of the social and political order they proposed to supersede. Only in recent years have the rulers of the Soviet Union and other socialist states had to acknowledge the growth of corruption in their own regimes, and to seek to combat it by vigorous countermeasures, not especially successfully. In view of the corrupt behavior of the tsarist bureaucracy, notorious at the turn of the century, the original thrust was in the direction of developing an honest public service, thereby catching up with the bourgeois societies of the West. In this connection, these regimes have added yet another dimension to the unfolding concept of corruption. As mentioned above, their conceit is that most corruption in socialist countries is traceable to a preceding ideological corruption of which it is the result. The total bureaucratization which the socialist ideology has tended to promote in practice has made the problem of corruption particularly central to these regimes, and each case is apt to appear as a flagrant case of betrayal of the trust that had been placed in the offending functionary.

Thus treason and corruption become intertwined and the language of the Soviet criminal code demonstrates it.[28]

Notes

1. Arnold J. Heidenheimer, ed., *Political Corruption: Readings in Comparative Analysis,* 1970, p.3.
2. Joseph J. Senturia, "Corruption, Political," *International Encyclopedia of the Social Sciences,* 1968; and Charles Aiken, "Corruption" in *Dictionary of the Social Sciences.*
3. On bureaucracy cf. Carl J. Friedrich and Taylor Cole, *Responsible Bureaucracy: A Study of the Swiss Civil Service,* 1933; Max Weber's classical treatment in *Wirtschaft und Gesellschaft,* 1922, 2d ed., 1925, and the comments in *Reader on Bureaucracy,* Robert K. Merton, ed., 1952 (includes a critique by Friedrich); and Friedrich, *Man and His Government,* 1963, ch. 18. which has extensive further references, as has Friedrich, *Constitutional Government and Democracy,* 4th ed., 1968, ch. 2.
4. The statement is found not in one of Lord Acton's major writings but in a letter in which he criticizes another scholar for "the canon that we are to judge Pope and King unlike other men, with a favorable presumption that they did no wrong." The text of Acton's remark is given in context in John E. E. Dalberg Acton, *Essays on Freedom and Power,* G. Himmelreich, ed., 1948. p.364.
5. Especially as developed by St. Augustine in *City of God.* Cf. Carl J. Friedrich, *Transcendent Justice,* 1964. pp.11 ff.; and Herbert A. Deane, *The Political and Social Ideas of Saint Augustine,* 1956; as well as Friedrich. *The Philosophy of Law in Historical Perspective,* 2d ed., 1965. ch. 5.
6. M. R. Werner, *Tammany Hall,* 1928; and V. O. Key, Jr., *Politics, Parties and Pressure Groups,* 4th ed., 1958, ch. 13, gives a scholarly analysis of a phenomenon which Bryce had emphasized in his *Modern Democracies* and *The American Commonwealth;* Werner's is a detailed descriptive account of Tammany's workings at the time, soon to be superseded by the impact of La Guardia's welfare state operations and the New Deal's social security legislation.
7. Robert Penn Warren, *All the King's Men,* 1946, p.134.
8. Walter L. Dorn, "The Prussian Bureaucracy in the Eighteenth Century," *Political Science Quarterly,* vol. 46, pp. 403 ff.: vol.47, pp.75 ff.; and vol. 49, pp. 259 ff., 1931–1932. Lewis B. Namier, *The Structure of Politics at the Accession of George III,* 1929; Norman Gash, *Politics in the Age of Peel,* 1953; Holden Furber, *Henry Dundas, First Viscount Melville, 1742–1811,* 1931.
9. Merle Fainsod, *How Russia is Ruled,* rev. ed., 1963. For the comparable situation in Hitler's Germany cf. my *Totalitarian Dictatorship and Autocracy* (with Z. K. Brzezinski), rev. ed., 1965, pp.241 ff., on the intermingling of government and business. A study is in preparation by Assessor Nebelung at Heidelberg which will soon appear, it is hoped. Soviet publications provide ample proof in their own articles against corrupt practices.
10. "Stenographisehe Niederschrift von einem Teil der Besprechung ueber die Judenfrage unter Vorsitz von Feldmarschal Goering im RLM am 12. November, 1938," to be found in *Der Prozess gegen die Hauptkriegsverbrecher vor dem internationalen Militaergerichtshof Nuernberg,* 1948, vol. XXVIII, p. 502 ff.
11. Leon Trotsky, *Die Verratene Revolution (Revolution Betrayed),* 1937, *p.* 120; cf. also the works cited in note 9, above.

12. Cf. Friedrich, *Introduction to Political Theory,* 1967, p.138. The discussion on Caesar is found in Machiavelli's *Discourses,* bk. I, ch. 10.
13. C. D. Bowen, *Adventures of a Biographer,* 1946.
14. John Dickinson, *Death of a Republic: Politics and Political Thought at Rome, 59–44 B.C.,* G. L. Haskins, ed., 1963.
15. Montesquieu, *Considérations sur les causes de la Grandeur des Romains et de leur Décadence,* 1734; cf. also the bicentenary collection of papers on Montesquieu edited by Mirkine-Guetzevitch and Henri Puget, *La Pensée Politique et Constitutionelle,* Paris, 1948.
16. Rousseau, *Contrat Social;* see also the comments by Dita Shklar, *Men and Citizens-A Study of Rousseau's Theory,* 1969, esp. pp. 100, 103, and 110; Mario Emaudi's interesting *The Early Rousseau,* 1967, does not especially address itself to the problem, but of. his pp. 114 ff.
17. Shklar. *op. cit.,* p. III.
18. Friedrich, *op. cit,* (note 12, above), pp.164 ff. dealing with equality.
19. Namier, *op. cit.* (note 8, above).
20. Friedrich, *Constitutional Government and Democracy,* 4th ed.. 1968, pp. 431–432; Namier, *op. cit.* (note 8, above), and more recently Samuel E. Finer, "Patronage and Public Service: Jeffersonian Bureaucracy and the British Tradition." *Public Administration,* vol.30, 1952. pp.333 ff., and reprinted in Heidenheimer, *op. cit.* (note 1 above), pp. 106 ff. Cf. also Harvey C. Mansfield, Jr., *Statemanship and Party Government: A Study of Burke and Bolingbroke,* 1965, esp. comments on pp. 66ff. Concerning Bolingbroke, cf. Isaac Kramnick, *Lord Bolingbroke and His Circle: The Politics of Nostalgia in the Age of Walpole.* 1968.
21. On bureaucracy see the works cited above in note 3
22. Rotteck-Welcker, the typical liberal progressive (cf. the study by Ursula Herdt [Albrecht] on Rotteck, Ph.D. thesis, Heidelberg), in his *Staatslexikon,* on p. 454.
23. Heidenheimer, *op. cit.* (note 1, above), in his Introduction, p. 13. There references are given to Montesquieu's *The Spirit of the Laws,* 1748, and Bentham's "The Rationale of Rewards," in his *Works,* vol, V. pp. 246–248.
24. For Burke see reference given in footnote 7, ch. 10. Cf. also in general E. and A. G. Porritt, *The Unreformed House of Commons,* 1901, ch. III; cf. also Karl Loewenstein's *Staatsrecht und Staatspraxis von Grossbritannien,* vol. 1., 1965, pp. 95 ff. At one point. this author echoes Burke's argument when he writes: "Without the rotten and pocket borough the British parliament would not have been that incomparable gathering of the political and social elite which let England rise to the rank of the leading world power." Who knows? Like all arguments from history, it is inconclusive.
25. This instance incidentally shows how risky it is, and how misleading, to treat such conditions as stable, unalterable features of a "political culture." Cf. Samuel E. Finer's study, *op. cit.* (note 20, above).
26. On Prussia, Hans W. Rosenberg, *Bureaucracy, Aristocracy, and Autocracy: The Prussian Experience, 1600–1815,* 1958, is valuable, in spite of its Marxist slant; cf. also Dorn's paper,. cited above, in note 8,; on France see W. A. Robson, *The Civil Service in Britain and France,* 1956, and Walter R. Sharp, *The French Civil Service: Bureaucracy in Transition,* 1931.
27. Friedrich and Brzezinski, op. *cit.* (note 9. above), chs. 16 and 18 and the literature cited there.
28. Harold J. Berman, *Justice in the USSR: An Interpretation of Soviet Law,* 1950, 2d ed., 1963, and John N. Hazard, *The Soviet System of Government,* 1964, who gives special attention to the legal aspect.

2

Defining Corruption

John Gardiner

Introduction

There are several major problems in attempting to define "corruption."
First, there are in fact several distinct but related problems. Second, there are
important differences among "corruption" as it is defined in the official laws
of nations, "corruption" as it affects the public, and "corruption" as it is
defined by public opinion, by the people who are both the ultimate authorities
in democratic nations and the ones who by their complacency and their
collusion may contribute to corruption taking place or who by their vigilance
and integrity may assist authorities in monitoring public officials. Finally,
there are important differences among nations in how these problems are
defined.

1. Corruption and Related Public Problems

A series of problems are often linked in public discussions of corruption.
Government investigation and prosecution agencies may have the responsibility to deal with all of them together, and they may occur together, but they
have different causes and may have different solutions.

Source: John Gardiner, "Defining Corruption." Ch. 3 (pp. 21–38) in Maurice Punch,
Emile Kolthoff, Kees van der Vijver, and Bram van Vliet, eds., *Coping with Corruption in a Borderless World: Proceedings of the Fifth International Anti-Corruption
Conference*. Deventer and Boston: Kluwer Law and Taxation Publishers, 1993. Reprinted by permission.

1.1. Corruption by Public Officials

The first problem is "Corruption by Public Officials." The definition of corruption most often used by social scientists has been provided by Harvard political scientist Joseph S. Nye. Nye says corruption is "behaviour which deviates from the normal duties of a public role because of private-regarding (family, close private clique), pecuniary or status gains; or violates rules against the exercise of certain types of private-regarding influence. This includes such behaviour as bribery (use of rewards to pervert the judgment of a person in a position of trust); nepotism (bestowal of patronage by reason of ascriptive relationship rather than merit); and misappropriation (illegal appropriation of public resources for private-regarding uses)" (Nye, 1967: 966).

Several parts of Nye's definition are particularly important. All probably would agree with Nye's emphasis on public roles. If an official fights with a lover or abuses a child, that may be assault but it is not corruption: corruption only involves the behaviour of an official in his or her public role. But what about Nye's requirement of personal gain—his focus on abuses for "private-regarding (family, close private clique) pecuniary or status gains"? This definition certainly covers situations where money winds up in the pockets of the official or a relative, but it does not cover situations where the goal of the abuse is to benefit the official's political party, ethnic group, etc., rather than the official or the official's family. The Watergate abuses in the United States, for example, certainly involved extensive illegality, but most of the illegal acts were intended to benefit the President's party—to insure that the Republicans would win in the 1972 presidential election, and later to prevent the embarrassing disclosure of the Nixon Administration's role in arranging the cover-up of the original burglary. While Richard Nixon frequently did abuse his office for personal gain (for example, by remodeling his California mansion at government expense, and by padding his tax returns), the basic Watergate episode itself was not intended to enrich the President or his advisors.

A second very important limitation comes from Nye's requirement that the behaviour deviate from normal duties or violate rules. As will be seen later, this part of the definition leads to major variations in what different nations see as corruption: some governments do not have formal rules about official conduct, and in some nations it may be taken for granted that elected officials and bureaucrats will mix their official duties and their private business affairs. In other words, the "normal duties" of an official in one country may include accepting "gifts" or making a decision even if it involves a conflict of interest.

For example, the answers to "Is it acceptable for a contractor to take the government purchasing officer and his family on a two-week vacation on the

Riviera?" or "Can the Minister for Highways award a construction contract to a company of which he is part owner?" often depend on where the events take place. In some nations, the government may not have rules forbidding these acts; or public expectations may be that they are 'normal' in that society. If that is true, then the acts would fall outside Nye's formal definition of corruption in those nations even though the acts would be labeled corrupt in other nations.

1.2. Abuse of Office by Public Officials

A second major category is abuse of office by public officials. Here, a precise definition is impossible: the dictionary says only that "to abuse" means "to misuse" or "to do something improper," and misuse and improper are as vague as abuse. Canadian political scientist Kenneth Gibbons suggests a number of actions which some people may label "abuse of office" (adapted from Gibbons, 1985: 778):

- A civil servant gives a position in his office to a relative rather than to a better-qualified applicant. *(Nepotism)*
- A political party wins an election and then removes all office-holders who supported the opposition party. *(Patronage)*
- A legislator owns stock in a mining company, and votes for a bill which will give tax concessions to the company. *(Legislative conflict of interest)*
- Government bureaucrats use their knowledge and contacts to establish a part-time consulting firm which gives advice to private clients. *(Bureaucratic conflict of interest)*

To Gibbons' list might be added the *awarding of government contracts* to favoured friends or political supporters, *lying* to the media and the public, and many forms of *campaign finance;* all raise similar problems of abuse of office.

Before leaving this category of abuse of office, the definitional ambiguity which is present here should be stressed: some forms of these abuses may be prohibited by statutes in some nations. Where this is true, they might be equated with other forms of "corruption" if Nye's second requirement is met, that the official is deriving a personal gain from the act. Even where they are not illegal, however, all of these actions are at least unethical—offensive to widely shared views as to how an official should act and how democratic governments should operate.

1.3. Business Corruption, Fraud, Theft, Abuse, Error and Waste

These improprieties differ from official corruption and abuse of office primarily because they are committed by someone who is not an office-holder. Probably the most frequent activity under this category concerns business corruption or "kickbacks." For example, a sales representative may offer a prospective buyer an extra payment if his or her product is selected, or a buyer may offer a manufacturer a payment if the shipment is "expedited" (delivered faster) or if it contains more or better goods than are required under the contract, etc. In both cases, whether the payment is proper or improper depends on whether a law specifies some other procedure, and who receives the extra payment. If the corporation has a policy of offering discounts or of charging extra for fast service, then the payments are probably not improper. If the money is kept by the individual salesman or buyer, however, it can be assumed that the company—the employer—is being cheated, and thus that ordinary principles of agency law (that everything earned by an agent belongs to the principal) are being violated.

A second form of private misconduct is fraud. A government official who takes unauthorized funds from the treasury, is committing "embezzlement" or "corruption." Private citizens or corporations, however, which intentionally use deception to take excessive or unauthorized government benefits or contracts from the treasury, are committing fraud. Examples of fraud might involve a welfare recipient providing incorrect facts (saying "I have three children" when in fact the recipient only has one child) or failing to provide correct facts (for example, correctly stating that she has lost her job but falling to state that she receives child support). A contractor might overstate the costs of materials or the number of items delivered to the purchaser, or submit a bill for quality materials when substandard or defective materials have been used. All of these deceptive acts are fraudulent.

Several other forms of misconduct by corporations or private citizens should be noted here. If there is no deception when unauthorized benefits are intentionally taken, it should probably be called simple theft. As was true with misconduct by public officials, there are also forms of misconduct by private citizens which are not illegal. Abuse occurs [when] "benefits are obtained or used in ways which are not intended by those who design or administer programs, but which are not specifically prohibited by law or regulation" (Lange and Bowers, 1979: 15). For example, it might be legal for a student—depending on the rules of a program—to use funds from a government education loan program to buy a car rather than to pay her tuition. If it is not illegal, there could not be prosecution, but since it is not consistent with the intended use of the program, it would be an abuse.

The terms error and waste often arise in discussions of some government programs. "Errors involve program decisions which violate relevant rules, and may be intentional or unintentional, substantial or technical, and may be caused by the official (e.g., not knowing the rules, or incorrectly applying the rules to the facts) or the client. Waste is a concept even more vague than abuse. In general it refers either to ineffective expenditures (expenditures which do not accomplish programmatic goals) or to inefficiencies, things which cost more than is necessary" (Gardiner and Lyman, 1984: 3).

1.4. Organized Crime and Racketeering

The final public problem which should be mentioned is "Organized Crime and Racketeering." Crime syndicates and racketeers can and do corrupt public officials to nullify law enforcement. However, while corruption is a tool of crime syndicates and racketeers, it is not the same thing. Many forms of official corruption are unrelated to crime syndicates and racketeering, and crime syndicates are sometimes able to operate even where officials are completely honest.

2. Definitions of Corruption: Legal, Public Interest, and Public Opinion Criteria

The discussion thus far has separated corruption from the related problems of abuse, fraud, and organized crime. Fraud and organized crime are clearly different from corruption, since they are not themselves the acts of public officials. Official corruption and official abuse, however, have many similarities.

In turning to the different sources which can be used in forming a definition of corruption, there is a much more serious problem. Yale University political scientist James C. Scott has stated this problem very clearly: "Corruption, we would all agree, involves a deviation from certain standards of behaviour. The first question which arises is, what criteria shall we use to establish those standards?" (Scott, 1972: 3).

2.1. Legal Definitions of Corruption

To answer Professor Scott's question, one thought would naturally be to use the criteria set forth in official statutes. These criteria are very straightforward: if an official's act is prohibited by laws established by the government, it is corrupt; if it is not prohibited, it is not corrupt even if it is abusive or unethical. Lawyers will appreciate the virtues of this formal or positivist definition: it is clear, and officials, government employees, and ordinary citizens can be expected to know the requirements and prohibitions spelled out in statutes. These conditions justify punishing violators. In public education as well as enforcement efforts, the fact that something is illegal as well as unethical provides something firm—something tangible—to focus on. Even if the corruption laws are not perfect, the legislature can amend the laws to deal with new problems.

While the legal or statutory definition of corruption may be convenient and unambiguous, Professor Scott stresses a major problem with this type of definition:

> Our conception of corruption does not cover political systems that are, in Aristotelian terms, "corrupt" in that they systematically serve the interests of special groups or sectors. A given regime may be biased or repressive; it may consistently favour the interests, say, of the aristocracy, big business, a single ethnic group, or a single region while it represses other demands, but it is not ipso facto corrupt unless these ends are accomplished by breaching the formal norms of office. (Scott, 1972: 5)

Professor Scott concludes his analysis of the legalistic definition of corruption by warning us of three problems:

1. The danger of implicitly giving normative value to whatever standards of official conduct happen to prevail and thereby failing to treat corruption as an integral part of politics. Here, in other words, Professor Scott warns us of the danger of assuming that everything legal is always ethical.
2. Professor Scott next warns us of "the difficulty of comparing nations (or a single nation at two points in time) when their formal norms of office are quite divergent." In other words, Professor Scott points to the danger that an identical action in two nations will be labeled differently because of differences in laws.
3. Finally, Professor Scott notes "the distortion introduced when we compare a nation with a small public sector with one with a large public sector." A nation where almost everyone is a government employee, he tells us, can't easily be compared with one where most people work for private corporations (Scott, 1972: 5).

2.2. Public Interest Definitions of Corruption

The problems involved in comparing corruption in different nations—the last two issues raised by Professor Scott—will be discussed later. With regard to the issue of legal definitions, however, two examples will illustrate the problem:

- In Nazi Germany during World War II, Jews were forbidden by law to emigrate. If a passport inspector took 1000 DM from a Jewish family and approved its departure, could his act be called "corruption"? Certainly the inspector took money to "pervert his judgment," in Nye's terminology, but should it be called corruption or does the evil of the Anti-Jewish laws justify the inspector's action? In this situation, most people would probably say that the legal act (enforcing the Jewish laws) would be evil and that evading the laws (letting the family escape) would be the ethical thing to do.

- If the first example shows that an illegal act may not be corrupt, a second example may show the opposite situation, one in which a legal action may be corrupt. This example occurred often in the United States in the 1950s and 1960s. To combat widespread decay in its central cities, the United States Congress created a program called urban renewal. In this program, government agencies condemned land in "blighted" areas, cleared buildings on the land, and resold the land to developers. Much of the land which was condemned under the urban renewal program, in cities throughout the United States, was occupied by poor people; often the occupants were racial minorities. After land was condemned and cleared, many urban renewal projects produced luxury apartment complexes and office buildings. Now consider the action of an official who destroys an old apartment building housing poor black families, and then constructs a new building with luxury housing for white executives. Assume that the official follows required procedures in every step of the process, that the old buildings met all statutory requirements for demolition, and that the luxury housing was an eligible development under the urban renewal statute. In this situation, the official's actions were legal, but weren't they also corrupt? In Scott's language, the urban renewal program "systematically served the interests" of America's middle and upper-middle classes at the expense of the poor and minorities. Whether or not America's urban renewal program was an appropriate way to deal with cities' economic problems (the costs and benefits of the program were very complex and the net effects may have been very good), it is clear that people who are suspicious of programs in which poor people suffer and rich people become richer will argue that a program like urban renewal epitomizes the "corruption" of the American political process. On the other hand, others probably feel uncomfortable using the term corruption in all situations where the political process produces policies which do not benefit everyone equally. In comparison with the example of the Nazi immigration inspector, where most probably agree on the issues of ethics, people probably have mixed views of the "corruptness" of the urban renewal example.

What do these examples say about definitions of corruption? The limitations built into the statutory or legalistic definition have led some scholars to focus on the effects of an act rather than on its legal status. Simply stated, this definition says: if an act is harmful to the public interest, it is corrupt even if it is legal; if it is beneficial to the public, it is not corrupt even if it violates the law. Returning to the two examples offered earlier—the inspector who allows Jews to escape Nazi Germany and the urban renewal officer who destroys low-income housing—the effects of the two officials' acts could be analyzed both at the level of the individuals involved (for example, the families trying to emigrate, the residents of the housing which was destroyed and of the new housing built) and at the level of the broader society.

The differences of opinion which will arise here are obvious. Trying to analyze a concept as broad as "the public interest" involves both very serious measurement problems and conflicts over the values which should be considered in the analysis. Supporters of the Nazi movement would say that the effort to "purify the Aryan race" justified the Jewish laws, and therefore that the inspector hurt the public interest; supporters of the urban renewal program would say that the harm suffered by individual residents of old buildings was outweighed by improvements in the total supply of housing, in the economy of the city, etc. In short, the effects of corruption on the public interest cannot be analyzed without considering the many, many views people have about public goals.

Finally, thinking about corruption requires thinking about the political process. A belief that anything the legislature decides is good, requires condemnation as corruption of any actions which nullify the legislature's intent. Acceptance of the possibility that the legislature can create a bad policy, however—especially if the legislative process in a nation systematically excludes the views of some parts of the society—creates the possibility that some corruption may be necessary or even good. This leads to a mixed assessment of the public interest approach to defining corruption: it is inevitably broad and ambiguous, and will rarely give one answer that everyone accepts. However, it may raise important questions to consider in judging some situations.

2.3. Public Opinion Definitions of Corruption

A third source of criteria to define standards of official integrity, in addition to official statutes and the public interest, is public opinion—how the people in a nation define corruption. Why should public opinion be used to define corruption? If there are significant differences between what a nation's laws say and how most citizens define corruption, it is likely that officials and government employees will be guided more by local culture than by the words of a law, and thus will be more likely to violate the law. In addition, effective action against corruption will be difficult or impossible if public opinion does not correspond to the statute's definitions. Investigators and prosecutors know that if citizens are concerned about corruption—if they demand the strictest honesty—they will be more likely to report crimes, to assist in investigations, and to vote for convictions when they serve as jurors. As voters, citizens sensitive to corruption may be more likely to elect officials with similar views and to throw out the rascals. Finally, citizens' values about corruption are likely to affect how they behave themselves—whether they will offer bribes or will abide by the requirements of the law. For all of these reasons, understanding public opinion about corruption will provide a basis for effective law enforcement efforts.

Illustrating how public opinion may vary, American political scientist Arnold Heidenheimer advises us to focus our attention on differences between "black," "grey," and "white" corruption. The evaluation "black corruption," Heidenheimer says, "indicates that in that setting that particular action is one which a majority consensus of both elite and mass opinion would condemn and would want to see punished as a matter of principle." "Grey corruption" indicates that some elements, usually elites, may want to see the action punished, others not, and the majority may well be ambivalent. "White corruption" signifies that the majority of both elite and mass opinion probably would not vigorously support an attempt to punish a form of corruption that they regard as tolerable. This implies that they attach less value to the maintenance of the values involved than they do to the costs that might be generated as the result of a change in rule enforcement (Heidenheimer, 1989:161).

What is known about these variations? Colgate University Professor Michael Johnston warns us of a number of problems involved in trying to measure these differences in public opinion. First, public opinion polls taken over a period of time show that attitudes can and do fluctuate—about corruption as about other issues (Erskine,1973). During and after Watergate, for example, public opinion polls in the U.S. showed a much stronger concern about official integrity than was seen in earlier polls, and the level of concern fell off several years after President Nixon resigned. This fluctuation raises the question: which time provides the best measure of the public's sentiments: is the higher percent expressing anger during a scandal more accurate than the lower figures at other times? The higher figure may suggest how many people can become angry, but the lower figures show that other issues are usually more important to them.

Johnston also points to an even more troublesome problem, "the problem of deciding who 'the public' is." Johnston asks, "is it everyone, or just adults, or just registered voters? Is it only those who are knowledgeable about issues and events, or only those with a direct interest in a given area of politics and decision-making? Or do we regard 'the public' as those who respond to surveys? There are, after all, many 'publics', and they rarely agree on anything of importance" (Johnston, 1982: 7).

Two examples will show the importance of Johnston's point that there are many publics with different opinions. Chicago is just reaching the end of a ten-year federal investigation of its court system. "Operation Greylord" has led to the conviction of more than 100 judges, attorneys, and courtroom staff for various forms of corruption. In the state of Maryland in the 1970s, a federal investigation of the awarding of state construction contracts documented a system where all contractors kicked back about 5 percent of the contract amount to elected officials. The investigation led to the conviction of contractors, state officials, and the Vice President of the United States! Whose "public opinion" should be looked at in Chicago and Maryland? There is no data on how the general public felt about corruption, but in both cases, the system of corruption was well-known and accepted by insiders—by lawyers and workers in the court system in Chicago, and by construction firms, politicians, and bureaucrats in Maryland. There were no complaints from the insiders, and the voters did not throw out the rascals; in both cases, reform came about only because federal investigators and prosecutors invested enormous resources to destroy the system.

Accepting Johnston's warnings that public attitudes will change over time and that different groups will have different attitudes, what is known about public opinion about corruption? Over the last twenty years, several research projects have developed very important scientific insights into the question "how does the public define corruption?"

In 1966, I studied a city in the United States which had been the home of a crime syndicate for over forty years, a city whose elected officials and senior police officials had been personally picked by the syndicate. I was particularly interested in the politics of corruption—in whether the citizens wanted corrupt officials. A survey of city residents did not show that they wanted corruption per se, or that they opposed law enforcement efforts, but the survey clearly showed a widespread tolerance of gambling (the chief source of the syndicate's revenues), and it showed that substantial numbers of respondents were tolerant of minor forms of corruption such as conflicts of interest and accepting gifts from companies doing business with the city (these might correspond with Professor Heidenheimer's "white corruption"). I concluded the report by saying, "the survey clearly shows that the residents did not tolerate corruption per se. Whenever symbols of law enforcement and official morality were brought into survey questions, most respondents chose public norms of morality. While some of the survey respondents were slow to perceive that corruption might arise from relationships between officials and persons doing business with the city, they clearly chose honesty and law enforcement when they recognized the nature of the relationship" (Gardiner, 1970: 55–56).

The second opinion survey was conducted by American political scientists John Peters and Susan Welch. They asked over 400 American state legislators to judge ten hypothetical situations. In each case, they asked whether the respondent would consider it corrupt, whether "most public officials" would consider it corrupt, and whether "most of the public" would consider it corrupt. Analyzing variances in responses about corruptness, Peters and Welch concluded that variations related to four components of the situation: the public official, the donor, the favor rendered by the public official, and the payoff involved. An act was likely to be judged as more corrupt, they concluded, if the official who took the money held a nonpolitical position (for example, if the official was a judge rather than a politician) and if the official was acting in his or her public role when the act occurred (i.e., if the act was part of his job rather than if he was acting as a private citizen).

With regard to the donor in each of their hypothetical situations, Peters and Welch found that the act was viewed as less corrupt if a legislator received funds from a constituent (someone from the legislator's district) than if the donor was a nonconstituent or if the donor was the official himself.

Several characteristics of the favor rendered affected how the situation was judged. The situation was more corrupt if the benefits were private rather than public, if the recipient was a nonconstituent rather than a constituent, and if the act was nonroutine rather than routine (in other words, if the official departed from normal routines to provide the favor). Finally, several characteristics of the payoff in each situation affected whether it was judged to be more or less corrupt. Respondents were more likely to see the situation as corrupt if the payoff was large, if its benefits were short-range (immediate rather than in the distant future), if it was specific rather than general, and if it was unrelated to an election campaign rather than a campaign contribution (Peters and Welch, 1978: 976). The conclusions reached by Peters and Welch based on the opinions of American state legislators are almost identical with the findings of Michael Atkinson and Maureen Mancuso after interviewing members of the Canadian Parliament (Atkinson and Mancuso, 1985: 468–469).

A final set of surveys seeking to identify public definitions of corruption was conducted by Michael Johnston. He also used hypothetical situations to identity what makes acts more or less corrupt in the eyes of the general public. Johnston's respondents were more likely to label as corrupt acts involving larger sums of money, involving public officials rather than private citizens, involving direct rather than indirect taking, involving the official keeping the money rather than passing it on (for example to a political party), and situations in which the rule-breaker is prominent rather than an average citizen (Johnston, 1986a).

What do these public opinion surveys say about the problem of defining corruption? Certainly they confirm Arnold Heidenheimer's distinction between "black" and "white" corruption: small-scale payments to low-level officials to alter routine decisions are viewed as being less serious than large payments to major officials. Similarly, while the survey respondents condemn non-political officials such as judges who act improperly, they seem to expect that "political" officials will do favors for campaign contributors and constituents. In short, the public is making distinctions based on which official is involved, what decisions were involved, and what payoffs were involved.

These studies clearly show that there are wide variations in how citizens define corruption, but there is also evidence that public opinion changes over time. Scandals by definition increase public awareness of corruption issues, and at least for a short time increase public outrage at violations of their expectations. What is especially important is that public awareness and concern can be increased by public education programs, so it is possible to change the ways citizens define corruption.

The most extensive anti-corruption public education program in the world is being conducted by Hong Kong's Independent Commission Against Corruption. ICAC uses a wide variety of techniques to increase public awareness and change attitudes: liaison with community organizations, public education in the schools, and television public service announcements. Summarizing the first ten years of ICAC's public education activities, Professor David Clark concluded that the Hong Kong public has become more aware of corruption problems and of ICAC's mission, is aware of the Prevention of Bribery Statute and (in general) its provisions, and thinks positively of corruption control (Clark, 1987. See also Clark, 1989, and Gardiner and Malec, 1989).

3. Variations among Nations

Variations in definitions among nations guarantee that no definition of corruption will be equally accepted in every nation. These variations can be found whether definitions are based on statutory criteria, on the impact of corruption on the public interest, or on public opinion.

First, different nations have different legal definitions of corruption. As already discussed, it is difficult to compare socialist and capitalist nations: many activities which are performed by government employees in socialist nations are performed by employees of private corporations in capitalist societies, and different standards often apply in the two situations. A second variation can be seen in the scope of corruption laws. In some nations, laws deal only with the most blatant bribery; other nations however have added laws to regulate nepotism, conflicts of interest, election campaign contributions, etc. Some nations feel that "gift-giving" or "dash" payments are acceptable while other nations have very detailed codes of conduct regulating both legislators and bureaucrats. In some nations, prosecutors must be able to prove that the official intended to violate the laws; other prosecutors only are required to prove that a prohibited act has occurred, or that an official has wealth which cannot be explained by the income reported on past tax returns.

The second criterion presented earlier defined corruption by its effects on the public interest. Once again, looking at different nations can show a different conclusion about the effects of similar acts. Corruption often has very dangerous effects, but there are some nations where corruption is relatively harmless or even healthy. Several examples may show how this can happen.

Students of socialist, planned economies have often noted that bribes or illegal side-payments are essential to making the system work—to getting anything done despite the inefficiencies and disincentives of the legal, official system. Russian social scientist Aron Katsenelinbogen noted in 1983, "in the USSR, where bureaucracy has permeated all aspects of life, there is a wide spectrum that characterizes the extent of illegality. There one encounters a wide variety of semi-legal activities because on the one hand the government does not want to legalize them (since they contradict the predominant ideological principles of the system) but on the other hand finds itself compelled to take account of its own best interests" (Katsenelinbogen, 1983: 236).

In a different setting, analysts of rapidly developing third world nations have reached a variety of conclusions about the effects of corruption. David H. Bayley suggests that corruption diverts scarce national resources, frustrates the implementation of national policies, and erodes the status of elites. However, he also notes that in some nations corruption also can attract to public service able administrators who would not accept low official salaries, and it opens a door to groups excluded from the official political process (Bayley, 1966). In a parallel vein, a study of political corruption in West Africa concluded that it simply reflected maladministration of government in general—that corruption was simply a way to get around the incompetence of inefficient government bureaucracies (Riley, 1987).

Michael Johnston, reviewing the literature on the consequences of corruption, concludes that its effects in a particular nation will depend on the scale of corruption relative to the overall economy, and on alternative opportunities to get ahead. Corruption will be more harmful, Johnston concludes, if it pervades the entire society and if the "boundaries of a disintegrative form of corruption correspond with existing class, racial, ethnic and factional cleavages in society"(Johnston, 1986b: 1003). By comparison, corruption would be less harmful in a nation if it is limited in scope or if it gives a fringe group a unique chance to get ahead.

There are no simple answers to the issue of effects. British scholar Michael Clarke, summarizing a series of studies of corruption in capitalist and socialist, industrialized and developing nations, explicitly cautions against such generalizations. Prof. Clarke points out that there are "constantly changing opportunities for and pressures towards corruption even within the same political economies. However, none of this should, I think, make us unduly pessimistic about understanding corruption, and thereby understanding its consequences and the means necessary to control it" (Clarke, 1983: xviii-xix).

One final indication of differences among nations in their definitions of corruption comes from variations in public opinion about corruption issues. There are nations where official corruption has been widespread for many years with no visible signs of public outrage. However, there are also nations where the smallest violation leads to scandals, investigations, and swift punishment. Similarly, conflicting attitudes exist within nations. Sometimes, these internal variations are primarily geographical. Daniel J. Elazar, for example, has argued that the United States contains at least three political cultures. "Moralistic," "individualistic" and "traditionalistic" attitudes about official integrity, Elazar believes, have been dominant in different states depending on patterns of immigration as the U.S. grew in the nineteenth century (Elazar, 1972).

Similar variations in attitudes appear in former colonies where a European legal system was superimposed on the traditional codes and values of the native population: official practices accepted by everyone in pre-colonial days only became "improper" when colonial values were introduced. As a senior official of a Pacific nation said at the Third International Anti-Corruption Conference in Hong Kong, "we did not have corruption in my nation until the British legal system was brought in. The British introduced us to the concept of corruption!"

This does not necessarily mean that there is no consistency in attitudes about corruption among nations. As already mentioned, Michael Atkinson and Maureen Mancuso (1985) found that Canadian members of parliament ranked hypothetical corruption incidents in about the same order of corruptness that John Peters and Susan Welch (1978) found in their survey of American state legislators. Michael Johnston has adapted the questions be has asked in the United States to situations common in Britain, and has found substantial similarities in the outcomes of opinion surveys: law-breaking such as petty bribery is condemned more than simply unethical practices, and government officials are judged more strictly than ordinary citizens. However, the British survey respondents showed greater consistency in their comments, while the Americans were slightly more individualistic, tending to treat officials and citizens equally. The Americans emphasize formal laws and codes to deal with corruption problems, but "Britain relies more upon culture and the 'etiquette' associated with important roles" (Johnston, 1989: 428). As a result, Johnston argues, the British are more likely to settle problems informally while the Americans have more public scandals and extended lawsuits.

4. Implications of the Definitions for the Attack on Corruption

Corruption has many definitions, and these variations affect the work of enforcement agencies. Many legal systems are very limited, and do not address important problems. Their laws may include definitions of corruption or procedures which make prosecution and conviction very difficult. The discussion about the public interest suggests that under certain circumstances, citizens may reasonably feel that an act which is legally defined as corruption is nevertheless a necessary tool to survive. This is especially likely to occur in nations with extreme poverty, discriminatory access to advancement, or repressive laws. Finally, public opinion surveys remind us that citizens are not equally concerned about all actions which violate the law.

References

Atkinson, M. and M. Mancuso (1985) "Do We Need a Code of Conduct for Politicians? The Search for an Elite Political Corruption in Canada" *Canadian Journal of Political Science* XVIII (September): 459–479.

Bayley, D. H. (1966) "The Effects of Corruption in a Developing Nation" *Western Political Quarterly* XIX (December): 719–732.

Clark, D. (1987) "A Community Relations Approach to Corruption: the Case of Hong Kong" *Corruption and Reform* 2 (3): 235–257.

Clark, D. (1989) "Mobilizing Public Opinion against Corruption: A Commentary" *Corruption and Reform* 4 (2): 123–129.

Clarke, M. (1983) (ed.) *Corruption: Causes, Consequences, and Control.* New York: St. Martin's.

Elazar, D. (1972) *American Federalism: A View from the States.* New York: Crowell.

Erskine, H. (1973) "The Polls: Corruption in Government" *Public Opinion Quarterly* 37. Winter, 1973–1974: 628–644.

Gardiner, J. A. (1970) *The Politics of Corruption: Organized Crime in an American City.* New York: Russell Sage.

Gardiner, J. A. and T. R. Lyman (1984) *The Fraud Control Game: State Responses to Fraud and Abuse in AFDC and Medicaid.* Bloomington: Indiana University Press.

Gardiner, J. A, and K. L. Malec (1989) "Mobilizing Public Opinion against Corruption: A Report to the Chicago Ethics Project" *Corruption and Reform* 4 (2): 107–121.

Gibbons, K. M. (1985) "Variations in Attitudes toward Corruption in Canada" in A. J. Heidenheimer, M. Johnston, and V. T. LeVine, eds., *Political Corruption: A Handbook.* New Brunswick: Transaction, 1989, pp. 763–788.

Heidenheimer, A. J. (1989) "Perspectives on the Perception of Corruption," in A. J. Heidenheimer, M. Johnston, and V. T. LeVine, eds., *Political Corruption: A Handbook.* New Brunswick: Transaction, 1989, pp. 149–163.

Johnston, M. (1982) *Political Corruption and Public Policy in America.* Monterey: Brooks/Cole.

Johnston, M. (1986a) "Right and Wrong in American Politics: Popular Conceptions of Corruption" *Polity* 18 (Spring): 367–391.

Johnston, M. (1986b) "The Political Consequences of Corruption: A Reassessment" in

A. J. Heidenheimer, M. Johnston, and V. T. Levine, eds., *Political Corruption: A Handbook.* New Brunswick: Transaction, 1989, pp.985–1006.

Johnston,M. (1989) "Corruption and Political Culture in Britain and the United States" *Innovation* 2: 417–436.

Katsenelinbogen, A. (1983) "Corruption in the USSR: Some Methodological Notes," in M. Clarke, ed., *Corruption: Causes, Consequences, and Control.* New York: St. Martin's, pp. 220–238.

Lange, A., and R. Bowers (1979) *Fraud and Abuse in Government Benefit Programs.* Washington, D. C.: Government Printing Office.

Nye, J.S. (1967) "Corruption and Political Development: A Cost Benefit Analysis" in A. J. Heidenheimer, M. Johnston, and V. T. Levine, eds., *Political Corruption: A Handbook.* New Brunswick: Transaction, 1989, pp. 963–983.

Peters, J., and S. Welch (1978) "Political Corruption in America: A Search for Definitions and a Theory" *American Political Science Review* 72 (September): 974–984

Riley, S. (1987) "Public-Office Corruption in West Africa: Political Culture, Context, and Control" (unpublished).

Scott, J.C. (1972) *Comparative Political Corruption.* Englewood Cliffs: Prentice-Hall.

3

Conceptualizing Political Corruption

Mark Philp

I

Is a politician or public official acting corruptly by accepting financial and other inducements from someone seeking a piece of legislation or bidding for a government contract, if the understanding is that the official will work to ensure that the legislative initiative or bid is successful against its competitors? Is it corrupt for a politician to accept money from an organisation in return for defending its interests within the legislature? Is a politician who accepts campaign contributions from an interest group and who subsequently presses their interests in the legislature, acting corruptly? In the first of these cases, few people would doubt that we are dealing with political corruption. The second case does not look much different from the first, although it is less detailed in its specification. The third case does not differ greatly from at least one possible interpretation of the second case, yet if such transactions constitute corruption it is doubtful that any democratic systems in the western world could be pronounced clean. The ease with which we move from clear cut to ambiguous cases underlines the importance of reaching a clear definition of political corruption, even as it suggests the difficulties associated in so doing. In this essay I identify a set of core criteria for political corruption and discuss the difficulties associated with each of the major existing definitions of corruption. I go on to examine why the definition of political corruption raises such difficulties for political science and political theory and I conclude by indicating ways in which political corruption can be distinguished from other forms of political failure, such as incompetence.

Despite the substantial problems raised in the definition of political corruption, there are cases which seem incontestably corrupt. We can recognise political corruption where:

1. a public official (A),
2. in violation of the trust placed in him by the public (B),
3. and in a manner which harms the public interest,
4. knowingly engages in conduct which exploits the office for clear personal and private gain in a way which runs contrary to the accepted rules and standards for the conduct of public office within the political culture,[1]
5. so as to benefit a third party (C) by providing C with access to a good or service C would not otherwise obtain.[2]

As we shall see in section II, there are substantial difficulties in filling in the detail of these different components, but in at least some cases we can see how to do so and in such cases they allow us to recognise a core group of cases of political corruption. Unfortunately, a great many cases are not clear cut and do not unequivocally meet each of these criteria. The boundaries between an agent's persona as a public official as against his or her standing as a private person are often blurred; the exact character of the trust in which he or she acts is often undefined; the public interest is not always obvious, nor do we always condone acts which by happenstance turn out to be in the public interest; many public officials convicted of corrupt practices deny that they acted with corrupt intent; and A can use his or her control of a resource to extort money from C, where C ends up being allocated that to which he was originally entitled. Even in more straightforward cases, each of the five criteria are intelligible only against the background of a political culture in which there are clear, shared norms and rules governing the conduct both of public officials and of members of the public in their dealings with these officials. In less ordered contexts the identification of political corruption becomes correspondingly difficult.

We can add both to these difficulties and to the sophistication of our definition, following the work of Dennis F. Thompson, by distinguishing between individual and institutional corruption. Individual corruption can be identified using the above criteria. "Institutional corruption" is differentiated by the nature of the gain to the public official, the service to the private citizen, and the tendency of the act, rather than its intention. Individual corruption benefits the office holder personally; institutional corruption produces gains for A within the political process—so A gains in a way which benefits him in his capacity as a politician or public official rather than as a private individual. Cases of individual corruption, where the service C receives is undeserved, can also be distinguished from those of institutional corruption, where what matters is less whether the service is deserved, and more how the service is provided—the institutions may allow the promotion of one's constituents' interests, but without endorsing every possible means to promote them. What links the nature of the gain to the manner of provision of the service in a way which further defines institutional corruption, is the "institutional appearance" or "institutional tendency" of the act. "We have to show only that a legislator accepted the gain and provided the service under institutional conditions that tend to cause such services to be provided in exchange for gains."[3] The cost, then, of institutional corruption, is the damage done to the purposes of the democratic process—to the institutional fabric of the political culture.

These costs are put in the broadest terms. For example, Thompson suggests that favours in return for campaign contributions are corrupt if they undermine the legislative or democratic process more generally. As long as politicians acquire political advantages, such as contributions, endorsements, leadership positions etc, in ways that promote the purposes of the democratic process then they are legitimate; "when the pursuit of political gain undermines those purposes, politicians not only fail to do their job, they disgrace it."[4] Thompson gives, as a major example of institutional corruption, the case of the Keating Five, which was the subject of extensive investigation by the Senate Ethics Committee, concluding in January 1992.

The Keating Five were five senators—Dennis DeConcini (Dem., Arizona), Alan Cranston (Dem., California), John Glenn (Dem., Ohio), Donald Riegle (Dem., Michigan), and John McCain (Rep., Arizona)—who collectively and, in some cases, individually, brought pressure and influence to bear on the political system in the interests of one of their constituents, Charles Keating who was being investigated for his role in the collapse of a Savings and Loan company in California in 1988. Each senator benefited politically (but not personally) from campaign contributions made by Keating, and each senator performed services for Keating, by representing his interests in the political and investigatory process. The inquiry recognised differences in the way in which the Senators acted, with Cranston being singled out for the strongest rebuke on the grounds of his having taken large campaign contributions during the height of his activity on Keating's behalf, but a problem remained in knowing how to categorize Cranston's conduct. In his defence, Cranston insisted that he had done nothing which the vast majority of other senators had not done on previous occasions, and that his activity was nothing more than the normal process of politics in which campaign support is traded for a willingness to help contributors with their problems. The difficulty facing those wishing to condemn his activity is that a charge of individual corruption is too strong, because of the political character of the gains, while to condemn all such political gain threatens the whole process of electoral finance and constituency representation in the United States. The alternative which Thompson advocates is to recognise political gain as a distinct form of gain and to ask whether the way they sought to render Keating service—putting pressure on officials entrusted with responsibility for investigating his affairs, lobbying, and meeting secretly to press his case—was legitimate. Seeking to bring influence to bear on quasi-judicial hearings, or by covert pressure, could be regarded as damaging the legislative process. Moreover, for both the Senate committee and for Thompson, the *appearance* of a corrupt connection between A's service to B and B's gain justified the accusation of institutional corruption—political rectitude needs both to be done, and to be seen to be done if the institutions of politics are to sustain their public legitimacy. The appearance or tendency of the Keating Five activities (especially Cranston) was to create the impression of a link between service and gain in the behaviour of the institution in a way that undermines public confidence in the legitimacy of the political and investigatory process.[5] Despite the fact that the charge of corruption is a very strong form of condemnation, the criterion for identifying a link between the service to C and the gain to A is a weak one: we have only to show that a legislator accepted the gain and provided the service under "institutional conditions that *tend to cause such services to be provided in exchange for such gains.*" [6]

Both the five basic components of corruption outlined above, and Thompson's attempt to move beyond and identify a distinct category of institutional corruption, rely heavily on appeals to such standards as the public interest, the norms and rules of public office, and the nature and purpose of the democratic political process. Each of these involves highly contestable claims. Moreover, it is precisely upon such standards that more traditional definitions of political corruption have relied, and have foundered. To see the difficulties which the core criteria raise, and the still greater problems faced by Thompson's account of institutional corruption, we must turn to an evaluation of the three definitions of political corruption which have dominated discussion of the concept for the last thirty years.

II

The three most commonly cited definitions are public-interest centered, public office centered, and market definitions. (Public opinion and legal norms have also been cited, but they can be subsumed under the other cases and are dealt with in this manner below). In the two works which have framed the study of corruption over the last twenty-five years, Heidenheimer's *Political Corruption* (1970), and its successor volume edited by Heidenheimer, Johnston and Levine (1989), these three definitions are proposed as different ways of identifying the scope of the concept of political corruption. The public office conception of corruption is exemplified by Nye:

Corruption is behavior which deviates from the formal duties of a public role because of private regarding (personal, close family, private clique) pecuniary or status gains; or violates rules against the exercise of certain types of private regarding influence. This includes such behaviour as bribery (use of reward to pervert the judgement of a person in a position of trust); nepotism (bestowal of patronage by reason of ascriptive relationship rather than merit); and misappropriation (illegal appropriation of public resources for private-regarding uses)[7]

Nye explicitly excludes considerations of the public interest so as to avoid confusing the phenomenon with its effects. Others, however, have sought to define political corruption precisely in terms of a conception of the public interest. Carl Friedrich, for example argues that:

> . . . corruption can be said to exist whenever a power-holder who is charged with doing certain things, i.e., who is a responsible functionary or office holder, is by monetary or other rewards not legally provided for, induced to take actions which favour whoever provides the rewards *and thereby does damage to the public and its interests.*[8]

Although there is an issue, as Nye recognises, about confusing the phenomenon with its consequences, the view that corruption involves the subversion of the public interest or common good by private interests is one with an impeccable historical pedigree. Machiavelli is hardly alone in understanding corruption as the decay of the capacity of the citizens and officials of a state to subordinate the pursuit of private interests to the demands of the common good or public interest. Indeed, even Nye's public office account, in which corruption deviates from the formal duties of the public role, implicitly recognises the public interest dimension by insisting that the deviation must be for private regarding gains—thereby covertly introducing the distinction between public and private interests.

Both public office and public interest definitions of corruption, however, face the issue of which view of the character and scope of public office or public interest should be accepted, and it is not immediately obvious which norms we should use to flesh out these subsidiary concepts. The potential sources are manifold but they share the range of difficulties which can be identified with the three main candidates: public opinion; legal norms; and the norms derived from western views of politics.

Public opinion is an important element in the identification and understanding of political corruption but it raises a number of difficulties. To whose opinion do we give most weight when opinions differ over the appropriate standards? The norms of a local community may differ from those insisted on by a central authority or a political élite and they may differ between sections of the local population, either vertically [e.g., between different classes] or horizontally [different ethnic groups or segmented communities] or both. More damagingly, we need to recognise that opinion may be disjoint from behaviour—that is, people may say one thing and do another.

Moreover, relying on public opinion means that we risk omitting cases where the casualty of corruption is the capacity of the citizenry to recognise a distinct set of public norms or a conception of the public interest. This possibility is a central feature of the classical republican tradition and its view that corruption involves the decay of the citizenry's capacity to recognise and commit themselves to the pursuit of the comon good.[9] On this view, public opinion is not an independent variable which we can use to identify corruption, since it will itself be a symptom of the extent to which the state has become corrupt. Nor is this merely a scholarly point about past conceptions of corruption: the presence of an appropriate political culture which legitimates and supports sound standards of public office remains an essential precondition for a clean political system. Moreover, it is something which is widely recognised in public life, with , for example, the Hong Kong and New South Wales Independent Commissions Against Corruption sharing the view that a central part of their mission is precisely public education and the eradication of a corrupt public culture.[10]

Appeal to the law is equally fraught with difficulty. In few states does the law define a category of acts as "political corruption"—the issue of the defining features of the general set tend to be evaded by focusing on the definition of various sub-sets—such as bribery, fraud, electoral malpractice, etc. But even here, the law is an inadequate guide—not only because it may not cover cases which are widely perceived as corrupt (such as the conduct of the Keating Five, or of those British MPs who received cash payments or favours for asking Parliamentary questions), but also because the law can itself originate in corrupt practices—that an act is legal does not always mean that it is not corrupt. Moreover, laws regulating political conduct rest on prior assumptions about the character of political office and the appropriate rules for its conduct. At best, laws express such principles, and it is this normative or principled structure which must be regarded as the baseline from which we should work to flesh out definitions of public office or public interest— although these principles are open to very similar questions to those raised in the case of norms. The final objection to taking law as the sole and determining standard for conduct is that the actions of those engaged in politics cannot be exhaustively settled by systems of rules. There is inevitable indeterminacy in politics, both for bureaucrats in the conduct of their administrative offices and for politicians in the conduct of their political ones, and many public scandals are prompted by cases where, although the law does not prohibit an action, the action violates the public's sense of appropriate conduct for public officials.

Because the identification of the norms and principles which give a determinate content to the concept of the public interest or which govern the exercise of public office is fraught with difficulty, many political scientists in the 1960s and 70s came to the view that there was no alternative but to plump for a definition which was clear and could be applied with a degree of objectivity—even if it meant they had to fall back on assumptions about politics and its corruption which rested heavily on Western views of the central values of democratic societies. More recently, in reaction to such earlier positivism and despite recognising the substantial problems in identifying and endorsing local norms, many modern political analysts have sought to avoid imposing the cultural prejudices of Western democratic systems by arguing that what counts as a wrongful exercise of public duty must have some reference to accepted standards of behaviour within a community. The net result is that the analysis of political corruption has been left caught between the equally repugnant options of stipulative definition following Western norms, or a relativist appeal to local norms or standards.

The relativism that we risk is not simply moral relativism. That might seem like a price worth paying to avoid western stipulation—we simply accept the normative judgments of each culture as to what is or is not acceptable practice. But the danger of this move is that the damage to one's analysis spreads beyond moral relativism and extends to a conceptual relativism.

Consider, for example, the case of bribery. In most Western cultures bribery is defined in terms similar to those used by Nye—"the use of reward to pervert the judgment of a person in a position of trust." In different western cultures, different understandings will exist as to when something meets these criteria—what things count as rewards, what sorts of influence are held to pervert judgment (rather than being things which an office-holder should take into account), what defines what counts as positions of trust, and how far other components of an individual's life are held to be constrained by the responsibilities associated with that trust. But, while such differences are tolerable, it would be another matter entirely if a culture claimed to have the concept of bribery without believing that there was anything wrong with it. On the modern view, if it is bribery, then there is something wrong with it. To believe otherwise verges on incoherence. It has been claimed that "The (ancient) Greeks did not have a word for bribes because all gifts are bribes. All gifts are given by way of reciprocation for favors past or to come." [11] In fact, the Greeks did have terms (*d ron, lemma, chresmasi peithein*) for bribes but they were terms which also meant gift-giving or receiving, or persuasion and the existence of a number of neutral terms for giving, receiving and persuading in ancient Greek literature implies a tolerance for much that we would now regard as bribery. But do these terms recognisably denote bribery? They do not imply that someone's judgment has been perverted, even where they recognise that it has been influenced; and since it is not perverted, but influenced, it is difficult to see them as indicating that a trust has been betrayed. If these were the only terms for bribery in the Ancient Greek world we would, I think, have to take the view that there is a basic untranslatability of the terms between us and them—that they not only failed to distinguish gifts and bribes, but that they also had no real concept of public office or trust.

In fact, as David Harvey has pointed out, although there were a number of terms for bribery which were essentially neutral and reveal an attitude to bribery which was initially relatively lenient, there were also powerfully negative terms, such as *diaphtheirein,* which implied the destruction of a person's independent judgment and action—which was seen as reducing the person to a non-entity.[12] There is also ample evidence that the Greeks could recognise both the concept of a public trust, and the use of gifts to subvert the ends of that trust. There was a general law in Athens concerning bribery which laid down penalties for giving or taking bribes to the detriment of the interests of the people, and "cata-political bribery" was accorded the most powerful condemnatory adjective in Greek, namely *aischorn* or, shameful.[13] Although this means that there are common elements between modern and ancient understandings of bribery, we should recognise the implication of the thought that there might not have been. Namely, that if we rely wholly on local norms we end up risking a fundamental incommensurability between ourselves and the local normative and conceptual vocabulary.

The use of local norms and judgments must, then, be handled with care. Clearly, they have a role in identifying what types of activity are understood as corrupt, but they cannot be accepted as the only criteria, since this would be to embrace a conceptual relativism which renders any cross-cultural analysis of corruption incoherent. Consider, for example, the entry for 20 August 1664, in Samuel Pepys' Diary in which he reports that he went to his office "where I took in with me Bagwell's wife; and there I caressed her, and find her every day more and more coming, with good words and promise of getting her husband a place, which I will do." Mrs. Bagwell makes frequent appearances in the Diary in pursuit of a career for her husband, which lies in Pepys' disposal—an objective she failed to achieve despite Pepys raping her in her own home. Nor is she alone, a similar fate befalls Mrs. Robins, Mrs. Daniel, and Deb Willett also in search of patronage from Pepys. Pepys does occasionally show qualms about his treatment of Mrs. Bagwell, but it is unclear how far this arises from a sense that he is exploiting her, and how far there is some residual guilt about his adultery. Is Pepys acting corruptly?

It is certainly not difficult to find his behaviour abhorrent (although scholars have been astonishingly tolerant towards him), and although some part of this reaction arises from Pepys' transgression of norms of sexual conduct which it may be anachronistic to apply to the late seventeenth century, there remains a sense that he was exploiting a position of power and influence for personal gain, at the expense of others. The same has also to be said of the way Pepys gleaned a fortune from back-handers and gifts from provisioners of the navy. His use of his office was not especially remiss compared to that made by others, and there was clearly some partly shared understanding that certain types of public office were a form of property which could be used to generate financial or other forms of personal gain (judgeships, on the other hand, could not). As such, Pepys was, in a relatively benign way, given how some of his contemporaries behaved, simply exacting an "income" from his office. But in both cases Pepys was fully aware that his conduct could not withstand public scrutiny. Even if we believe that Pepys did not think there was anything corrupt about his conduct, and even if many of his contemporaries would have agreed, this does not mean we have to endorse that judgment in full. While local norms provide evidence about what people accept and reject, they should not be permitted to impinge upon the deeper sense of corruption, which Pepys and his contemporaries certainly recognised, involving the violation of the norms of public office for private and personal gain. Indeed, Pepys himself believed that corruption was an evil and was full of praise for the 1618 commission on the provisioning of the Navy which had sought to reduce corruption in the earlier Stuart reign.[14] Where they differ from us is not on what it is about corruption which makes it corrupt, but on what particular activities are identified as corrupting—that is, they differ in their judgment of what is ruled in and out by those norms, but they do not differ fundamentally on what it is for there to be a norm and for it to be violated in a corrupt way.[15]

Market-centered definitions have sometimes offered themselves as a morally neutral way of avoiding the kind of complexities involved in this delicate balancing of objective or universalist components with local and relative standards. The term "market-centered" is not entirely felicitous. What such theorists broadly share is the application of social or public choice methods to the analysis of corruption—or, more crudely, the use of economic methods and models for the analysis of politics. Not all theorists who use rational choice methods claim a distinctive rational choice definition of political corruption,[16] but a significant number do. Consider for example, the definition offered by Leff:

> Corruption is an extralegal institution used by individuals or groups to gain influence over the actions of the bureaucracy. As such the existence of corruption *per se* indicates only that these groups participate in the decision making process to a greater extent than would otherwise be the case." [17]

Van Klaveren is also cited as advancing a market-centered conception:

> . . . corruption means that a civil servant abuses his authority in order to obtain an extra income from the public . . . Thus we will conceive of corruption in terms of a civil servant who regards his office as a business, the income of which he will . . . seek to maximize. The office then becomes a "maximising unit." [18]

Although such accounts seem dedicated to the task of conceptual clarification, the view that they can offer an alternative definition of political corruption is itself conceptually muddled. Market-centered definitions are certainly one way of *understanding* corruption, they may also provide a fruitful model for the explanation of the incidence of corruption, but they are not a way of defining it. Indeed, Van Klaveren's analysis starts from the view that the occurrence of corruption is contingent on the development of a system in which the people are subject to the control of officials, where there exists a "regulating principle which gives to the officials and other intermediary groups a public existence with a purpose of their own."[19] Thus, what defines an act as corrupt is not that it is income maximising, but that it is income maximising in a context where prior conceptions of public office and the principles for its conduct define income-maximising as corrupt. Which means that Van Klaveren, at least, cannot be identified with a market-centered definition.

Leff, however, is similarly vulnerable. Despite his impressive commitment to nominalism in the identification of corruption, Leff's account is also predicated on a prior conception of public office and the norms for its exercise. The very identification of the extra-legal character of corruption is enough to introduce into the definition a conception of public office and its principles of conduct which acts as the standard from which corruption deviates. Both Leff and Von Klaveren, then, are implicitly appealing to publicoffice conceptions of corruption in defining corruption, even if their subsequent accounts of the conditions for its emergence and persistence might differ substantially from other public-office centered accounts.

This conclusion is of more general applicability to economic definitions of corruption, and can be generalised also to accounts which rely upon modeling public office in principal-agent terms or in terms of rent seeking.[20] To ask if a civil servant or politician is acting corruptly when he or she acts in an income or interest-maximising way, we have to show what it is that makes this use of office a member of a distinct set of cases identifiable as corrupt, as opposed to non-corrupt. Not all cases of income or interest maximising need be corrupt (as witness cases where office is understood as a certain type of property). To be able to point to those cases of interest/income maximising which are also politically corrupt, one has to appeal to constructions of public office and the public-interest which draw on norms and values which are external to the market model. For example, it needs to appeal to that set of normative constraints on income or interest maximising which picks out the full set of politically corrupt acts. Market-based accounts might well be able to show under what conditions it becomes more or less likely that people will break those constraints, but it has to take those constraints as a given—and it is these which distinguish corrupt from non-corrupt behaviour.

On this account, we are reduced to the alternatives of public-office and public-interest definitions of political corruption. There is, however, some pressure towards further reduction. There are two major sources of this pressure. The first comes from the recognition of the open-ended character of much public office. Some civil servants may have tightly defined and constrained activities permitting little substantive discretion, but many do not. Similarly, politicians do not act simply as functionaries to fulfil promises made to an electorate which is fully cognisant of its interests. On the contrary, politics is in part about the contestation and projection of conceptions of the public interest. Part of the conception of the role of leaders is precisely to lead, not to act as wholly impartial mechanisms for the adjudication of interests and the production of the social optimum. Public office and public interest are, then, intimately connected. The open character of much public office is structured by principles and expectations that demand of office holders that they be guided by considerations of the public interest. To ask whether a politician acts corruptly we must be aware that the characterisation of public office will inevitably point beyond the compliance with rules to the principles underlying those rules—principles which come into play to cover cases on which formal rules are silent.

The second pressure comes from the recognition that the definitional disputes concerning political corruption have obscured the basic point that the term corruption is not in itself problematic. As the OED reiterates throughout its entry on the term: it is rooted in the sense of a thing being changed from its naturally sound condition, into something unsound, impure, debased, infected, tainted, adulterated, depraved, perverted, etc. The problem arises in the application of this to politics. Definitional problems are legion because there is hardly a general consensus on the "naturally sound condition of politics." Public office and public interest definitions focus on different aspects of the political, and may be derived from different conceptions of the nature of politics, but the contest between them is not over what corruption is, so much as over how to derive the standard for identifying the naturally sound condition from which corrupt politicians deviate—which is a problem which applies equally to individual and institutional corruption, the later of which is premised on norms about the ethical standards inherent in democratic decision-making.

We should not mistake the nature of this pressure towards reduction. It does not mean that there is a single, adequate definition of political corruption which identifies it with the exercise of public office in violation of the public interest for private gain. These pressures towards reduction do not allow us further to refine and delimit the definition of political corruption so as to pick out a core conception. At best we might identify core criteria such as those with which we began, where people break the rules, and do so knowingly, while subverting the public interest in the search for private gain and to the benefit of a third party, in ways which run directly counter to accepted standards of practice within the political culture. But few of these conditions are absolutely necessary, and in most cases we are forced us to recognise that what counts as political corruption depends on commitments to conceptions of the nature of politics and the form of the public interest. One line definitions of political corruption are inherently misleading because they generally obscure the extent to which the concept and its components are rooted in ways of thinking about the distinctive character of public office and the distinctive ends to which political activity is directed.

There should be little surprising in this. Few if any concepts in social and political science or theory can claim a wholly factual content, and given the core meaning of the term "corruption" it should not be surprising to find that identifying its political form will implicate us in a range of commitments about the nature and ends of the political domain. Moreover, this recognition must also be tied to an acknowledgement that the perspective on politics from which we generate our conception of political corruption will play a major role in shaping the explanations we offer. The philosophical and practical upshot of all this is that while the original trinity of definitions collapses under a little pressure to a single core set of concerns, these concerns (such as the nature and ends of the political) themselves generate a wide range of views as to the nature (and causes) of political corruption.

III

Definitional disputes about political corruption are linked directly to arguments about the nature of the healthy or normal condition of politics. And because these arguments cut across a range of issues and can draw on dramatically divergent social, economic, anthropological and philosophical theories they cannot be ranged along a single axis—for example from the more to the less restrictive. Faced with these difficulties with the definition of corruption it is not surprising to find political scientists willing to forego the niceties of philosophical and methodological disputes by stipulatively defining a class of events for study as politically corrupt. This is a prudent move, with considerably utility for studies of phenomena within a single culture or political system. But even studies with such moderate ambitions will find it difficult to avoid moving from identification of cases of rule infraction to more general questions about what such infractions mean within that political culture—and, thereafter to questions about the character of politics. Small questions have a way of leading to big ones—and, however laudable the search for scientific objectivity in the study of political phenomena, the broader questions almost inevitably raise deeper normative and ethical issues. Moreover, claims about political corruption are not ethically neutral. They condemn people's actions, and challenge the legitimacy of distributions or policies. It is, then, extremely important that we get it right and that those who are investigated, publicly criticised or prosecuted can recognise that their fate

Superficially, because it can have similar results, incompetence may seem like a type of corruption, but it does not put into question this distinction between the public and the private—it may lead to conflict, but it does not introduce it at the heart of the political system. What is taken to be central to sustaining that distinction will vary between political systems, and may be vigorously contested. Moreover, a great many activities enjoined by law, or not prohibited by it, may lead to the erosion of that distinction and the collapse of the political order into open conflict, so we need to distinguish a core set of cases of corruption, in which intentionality, illegality, the triadic relations of A, B, and C, and the substitution of private for public interests are all present, and a set of penumbra cases where more complex judgments have to be made about whether and to what extent these different criteria are met.[25] But both this core and the extensions from it must be informed by the recognition that what distinguishes corruption from other forms of destructive political behaviour is that it works by eroding the distinction between private and public concerns and interests. Extreme incompetence may lead to the collapse of political authority, but it does so because of its consequences, not because public officials actively suborn that authority so as to pursue interests in a manner which that order is expressly designed to resist.

This is why terrorist movements, although they may exacerbate conflict or war, are not corrupt. Although they deny the validity of the existing political system, they implicitly project a conception of a political solution in which the distinction between the public and their private concerns is sustained. Similarly, authoritarian regimes, such as Hitler's Fascist state, may come to pursue goals which are so grandiose, so evil, and so appalling in their consequences, that we may be tempted to describe them as corrupt. But, while many individuals within such states may be corrupt, not all are. For many there remains a clear sense that in accepting office they are accepting certain public responsibilities. It is, however, another issue as to whether these men and women, by refusing to ask questions about what was happening elsewhere in the state, by putting their self-protection above a broader sense of public responsibilities, or, by allowing themselves unreflectingly to indulge their prejudices and passions, increasingly sacrificed the integrity which public office requires, resulting in the eventual corruption of the entire political order. We need to distinguish carefully between the question as to whether or not a type of political authority (with an associated conception of public office) is being preserved, and the question of whether there is any ethical standing left attached to that authority. Many things may erode the ethical force of political authority, without that authority being corrupt. Bad government is one thing, corrupt government another, and it is only when the conduct of public office becomes subordinate to interests it is intended to exclude or regulate that we should talk of corruption.

Notes

1. The core of this fourth condition is the intention to act for private gain (one is not less corrupt for being unsuccessful) The other elements of this condition are paraphrases of conditions 1, 2, and 3.
2. The five features: the public official (A); his/her trust to the public (B); the existence of formal rules or standards associated with public office; the knowledge of A and the intention to gain; and the presence of a third party (C), who gains when A responds to incentives and/or opportunities (which may be provided by C) to act in ways which run contrary to his trust to B, are derived from a variety of sources, on which see the more detailed discussions of definitions below. The emphasis on the triadic relationships between A, B, and C is neatly expressed in Diego Gambetta's "What is Corruption" Mimeo, 24.9.98.
3. Dennis F. Thompson, *Ethics in Congress: From Individual to Institutional Corruption* (Brookings, Washington, 1995) p. 30.
4. Thompson, p. 31.
5. See Thompson, pp.37–42, and "Mediated Corruption: The Case of the Keating Five " *American Political Science Review* 87, 2 (1993) pp. 369–81.
6. Thompson, p. 31, emphasis added.
7. A.J. Heidenheimer, M. Johnston and V. LeVine, *Political Corruption: A Handbook* (Transaction, New Brunswick, 1989) p. 966.
8. Heidenheimer et al., *Political Corruption,* p. 10, emphasis added.
9. See, for example, Maurizio Viroli, *Machiavelli* (Oxford University Press, Oxford, 1998), p. 131. "The corruption that destroys civil and political life is the corruption of the customs, of the habits of citizens, their unwillingness to put the common good above private or factional interest."
10. See for example, *An Introduction to the Independent Commission Against Corruption* (Hong Kong, 1983, 1987, 1989), and *Second Report on Investigation into the Metherall Resignation and Appointment* (ICAC, Sydney, September 1992).
11. A claim cited and refuted by J. T. Noonan, *Bribes* (Berkeley, University of California Press, 1984), and commented on by Jon Elster, *The Cement of Society* (Cambridge, Cambridge University Press, 1989), p. 267.
12. David Harvey, "Dona Ferentes: Some Aspects of Bribery in Greek Politics", *History of Political Thought,* Vol VI (1/2), 1985, 76–117, p. 86.
13. Harvey, p. 111, and 109.
14. Cf., Linda Levy Peck, *Court Patronage and Corruption in Eary Stuart England* (Routledge, London, 1993), p. 111.
15. Pepys is a very complex case—as is made clear in the discussion by Noonan, *Bribes* , pp.366–391.
16. See, e.g., Susan Rose-Ackerman, *Corruption* (New York, Academic Press, 1978), p. 7, or the work of Jens Chr. Andvig, "The Economics of Corruption" *Studi economici* 43, 1, (1991) p.57–94 and, with Karl Ove Moene, "How corruption may corrupt" *Journal of Economic Behaviour and Organisation* 13 (1990), pp. 63–76. See also Francis T. Lui, "A dynamic model of corruption deterrence" *Journal of Public Economics* 31 (1986) 215–36, and Oliver Cadot, "Corruption as a gamble" *Journal of Public Economics* 33 (1987) 223–44.
17. Heidenheimer et al., p. 389.
18. Heidenheimer et al.,pp. 25–6.
19. Heidenheimer et al., p. 75.
20. See for example, Edward Banfield, "Corruption as a feature of Governmental Organisation" *Journal of Law and Economics* 18 (1975) pp 587–605, who uses

principal-agent terminology to explore corruption, as do Andrei Shleifer and Robert W. Vishny, "Corruption" *Quarterly Journal of Economics* August 1993, pp. 599–617. On "rent-seeking" see, Gordon Tullock, *Rent-Seeking* (The Locke Institute, Edward Elgar, Aldershot, 1993). Both principal-agent accounts and those drawing on rent-seeking theory presume an account of the end which public officials serve—but they must both draw on further assumptions to distinguish between corrupt deviations from that end as against those arising from, for example, incompetence or idleness.

21. ICAC, *Report on Investigation into . . . Metherall*, p. 92–3.
22. The final three sections of the original paper discuss the nature of politics and its "ethical pull" at greater length.
23. Which is not to say that it necessarily has such appeal—it is not always the best way of handling matters (it would usually, for example, be inappropriate to solve family disputes).
24. The Court of Appeal majority judgment was that the Commissioner went beyond his jurisdiction in finding Greiner's behaviour "reasonable grounds for dismissal" because the grounds for such a judgment must be legal and objective. The dissenting opinion was that the conduct could constitute reasonable grounds for dismissal. So the disagreement was not over whether the distinction should be drawn, nor over whether Greiner's conduct violated that distinction, but over whether the appropriate standards for judging reasonable grounds must be objective legal standards or can be more subjective and intuitive in character.
25. With respect to Thompson's category of institutional corruption, this proposes that beneath all types of political corruption lies a deeper and more significant set of issues about the character of political activity which must be articulated if we are to apply the various criteria.

4

What is the Problem about Corruption?

Colin Leys

The "Moralistic Approach"

The systematic investigation of corruption is overdue. There are three main types of literature in English on the subject: historical studies of corrupt practice in Britain; inquisitional studies, mainly of the United States and the English-speaking West African and Asian countries; and sociological studies which deal with corruption incidentally. So far as I know no general study in English has appeared.[1] One reason for this seems to be a widespread feeling that the facts cannot be discovered, or that if they can, they cannot be proved, or that if they can be proved, the proof cannot be published. All these notions seem dubious. There are nearly always sources of information, some of them-such as court records-systematic in their way, and some of them very circumstantial (like privileged parliamentary debates). Many of the people involved are quite willing to talk. And commissions of inquiry have published large amounts of evidence, obtained by unusual powers of compulsion.

I doubt if it would really be as hard to discover the facts about corruption in most countries as it would be to find out the facts about some legitimate political matters which those involved really want to keep secret. One could even find ways of measuring, within broad limits, the scale and economic effects of some forms of corruption. Publishing the results might present difficulties, but these would only be acute if naming persons were essential to

Source: Colin Leys, "What Is the Problem about Corruption?" *Journal of Modern African Studies,* 3: 2 (1965), pp. 215–230. By permission of the publisher, Cambridge University Press.

the object of publishing, which is not ordinarily the case in scientific inquiry, even in the social sciences. As anyone who has written on contemporary issues is aware, there are adequate conventions which enable events and incidents to be described anonymously or obliquely without reducing their credibility or value as evidence.

But so far very few people have approached the subject of corruption in this spirit, aiming to describe, measure, analyze, and explain the *phenomena* involved.[2] This is curious when one considers the *word* itself (corruption means to change from good to bad; to debase: to pervert); it denotes patterns of action which derive their significance from the role of value-systems in social behavior. Similar phenomena, such as suicide, crime, or religious fanaticism, have intrigued sociologists greatly. However, the question of corruption in the contemporary world has so far been taken up almost solely by moralists.

The recent book by Ronald Wraith and Edgar Simpkins on *Corruption in Developing Countries* is of this *genre.* They are concerned with "the scarlet thread of bribery and corruption," with corruption which "flourishes as luxuriantly as the bush and weeds which it so much resembles, taking the goodness from the soil and suffocating the growth of plants which have been carefully, and expensively, bred and tended." It is a "jungle of nepotism and temptation," a "dangerous and tragic situation" in which the enthusiasm of the young African civil servant turns to cynicism, and where there are "not the attitudes of progress and development."[3]

They are aware that the "moralizing approach" (their own term) involves a difficulty, namely that their standpoint may differ from that of those who do the things which they regard as corrupt. For instance, they can see that since any African who is so fortunately placed as to be able to get jobs for his relatives is felt (by the relatives at least) to be under an obligation to do so, it is peculiar to call this corrupt: "an act is presumably only corrupt if society condemns it as such, and if the doer is afflicted with a sense of guilt when he does it: neither of these apply to a great deal of African nepotism."[4]

However, they are convinced (no evidence is adduced) that the results of nepotism and all other forms of what they call corruption ("in the strict sense . . . in the context of the *mores* of Great Britain") are serious and bad; and they take courage from the fact that a small minority in most developing countries shares their ethical viewpoint. Consequently they conceive the problem as one of seeking in British history the causes which led to the triumph in Britain of this point of view, with its attendant advantages, in the hope that African and other developing countries might profit from the experience of Britain. (Over half the book is devoted to this inquiry.)

The results are, as they recognize, inconclusive, which is not surprising when one considers that this formulation of the problem ("Why does the public morality of African states not conform to the British?") contains an obvious enough answer: because they have a different social, economic and political system, and a different historical experience. The approach is not as bad as it sounds, for Wraith and Simpkins have observed the Nigerian scene with discrimination and sympathy. But the basis of the whole book is a simple faith, that corruption is what it is, namely what has been known as corruption in Britain for a long time; and it has at bottom a "simple cause"-avarice: "the wrong that is done is done in the full knowledge that it is wrong, for the concept of theft does not vary as between Christian and Muslim, African and European, or primitive man and Minister of the Crown."[5]

Emotionally and intellectually, this seems to be in a direct line of descent from the viewpoint of those missionaries who were dedicated to the suppression of native dancing. The subject seems to deserve a more systematic and open-minded approach.[6]

What is Corruption?

Under what circumstances are actions called corrupt? It seems best to start from some examples.

1. In the spring of 1964 the (Republican) secretary of state of Illinois died. Under the state constitution the (Democratic) governor temporarily filled his place by appointing a young (Democratic) official to the office. Within a few weeks a substantial number of state civil servants appointed by the late secretary of state were dismissed, and their jobs were filled by Democratic Party supporters.
2. In Chicago about the same time a controversy was taking place concerning school desegregation. Active desegregationists alleged that they were prevented from attending in force a meeting of the city council as part of their campaign, because all the public seating was filled by council employees who had for this purpose been given a holiday by the city administration.
3. In Kampala, Uganda, in August 1963 the city council decided to award a petrol station site to a majority-party member of the council, who offered the lowest price. £4,000: the highest offer was for £11,000. It was alleged in the National Assembly that the successful purchaser resold the plot to an oil company at a profit of £8,000.[7]
4. In Port Harcourt, Nigeria, in 1955, there were people in the Town Hall drawing laborers' salaries not provided for in the estimates; they were employed on the personal recommendation of individual councillors.[8]
5. In New York City, in 1951, it was estimated that over $1 million per annum was paid to policemen (for overlooking illegalities) by a bookmaking syndicate.[9]
6. In Lagos, Nigeria, in 1952, the practice of giving an unofficial cash gift

or a fee for services rendered was fairly authoritatively stated to be found

in hospitals where the nurses require a fee from every in-patient before the pre-scribed medicine is given, and even the ward servants must have their "dash" before bringing the bed-pan; it is known to be rife in the Police Motor Traffic Unit, which has unrivalled opportunities on account of the common practice of over-loading vehicles; pay clerks made a deduction from the wages of daily paid staff; produce examiners exact a fee from the produce buyer for every bag that is graded and sealed; domestic servants pay a proportion of their wages to the senior of them, besides often having paid a lump sum to buy the job.[10]

One thing which all these events have in common is that someone regards each of them as a bad thing. Equally, however, it is clear that at least some-one else—i.e., those involved in the acts in question—regards each of them as a good thing. Writers of the moralist school accept this, but they are convinced that such behavior is always against the "public interest." But what is the "public interest"? Some substantial arguments have been put forward to suggest that the public interest may sometimes *require* some of these prac-tices. The most famous of these is probably the American defense of patron-age, as in case (1) above, and "honest graft."[11] This argument turns essen-tially on the view that democratic politics in "mass" societies can only be insured by the integration of a multitude of interests and groups into political parties, capable of furnishing leadership and coherent policies;[12] this involves organization and inducements, both of which cost money; therefore, politics must be made to pay. From this point of view the political role of money is to serve as a cement—"a *hyphen* which joins, a *buckle* which fastens" the other-wise separate and conflicting elements of a society into a body politic; "the greater the corruption, the greater the harmony between corruptor and corruptee," as one candid critic recognized.[13] And Professor Hoselitz has argued that the early years of the life of a nation are dominated by these "persistent integrative needs of the society," and that

Much of the alleged corruption that Western technical advisers on administrative services of Asian and African stages encounter, and against which they inveigh in their technical reports with so little genuine success, is nothing but the prevalence of these non-rational norms on the basis of which these administrations operate.[14]

This can be taken a stage further. The moralist school of thought may recognize that some of the activities recorded above indirectly serve these broadly beneficial purposes. But they generally assume that the economic price paid is a heavy one. For instance: "The sums involved in some of the proved cases of corruption in Africa would have brought considerable ben-efits to people for whom 'under-privileged' is too mild a word, if they had been properly spent."[15]

But spending public money properly does not guarantee that it will benefit the poor.[16] The Uganda Minister of Information was much criticized for giving a lucrative and unusual monopoly of television set sales to an American contractor, in return for building a transmission station at cut rates: even had corruption been involved, the policy did produce a television station much more quickly and cheaply than the policy adopted in neighboring Kenya.[17] To take another example, one may ask whether the Russian consumer would be better off without the operations of the illegal contact men who derive illegal incomes in return for their aid in overcoming bottlenecks in the supply of materials for production.[18] Even in the case of petty bribery or extortion, it is relevant to ask, What is the alternative? Could an equally efficient and socially-useful administration be carried on if effective means of eliminating perquisites were found and all concerned were required to live on their salaries? Would the pressure for higher salaries be no greater? Could it be resisted? If it could not, would increased taxation fall on those most able to pay and would this, or reduced services, be in the public interest? To ask these questions is to realize that the answers call for research and analysis which is seldom undertaken, and that they are likely to vary according to circumstances. One also becomes aware that near the heart of the moralists' concern is the idea that the public interest is opposed to anything that heightens *inequality*. But we also have to ask how far equality and development are themselves compatible ideals. The regime most committed to both of them— the USSR—found it necessary to postpone its concern with equality in order to achieve development.[19] This is not to say that all kinds of inequality promoted by all kinds of corruption are beneficial from the point of view of development; it is merely to challenge the assumption that they are invariably bad.

But we still have not answered the question, Under what circumstances are actions called corrupt? What is at issue in all the cases cited above is the existence of a standard of behavior according to which the action in question breaks some rule, written or unwritten, about the proper purposes to which a public office or a public institution may be put. The moralist has his own idea of what the rule should be. The actors in the situations concerned have theirs. It may be the same as the moralists' (they may regard themselves as corrupt); or quite different (they may regard themselves as behaving honorably according to their standards, and regard their critics' standards as irrelevant); or they may be "men of two worlds," partly adhering to two standards which are incompatible and ending up exasperated and indifferent (they may recognize no particular moral implications of the acts in question at all—this is fairly obviously quite common). And in addition to the actors there are the other members—more or less directly affected—of their own society; all these positions are possible for them too.[20]

The Analysis of Corruption

The following questions suggest themselves as a reasonable basis for the analysis of any case in which corrupt is alleged:

1. What is being called corrupt and does it really happen? In the case of the African Continental Bank it became clear that no one was able to formulate a clear enough allegation against Dr. N. Azikiwe showing precisely what was the rule which he had broken.[21] A precise statement is required of the rule and the sense in which it is said to have been perverted. It may turn out, as in the case of the African Continental Bank, that there is really no clear idea of what the rule is; or that there is a clear rule but that it has not clearly been broken (this was Lord Denning's verdict on the Profumo case).[22]

2. Who regards the purpose which is being perverted as the proper or "official" purpose? It may be so regarded by most people in the society, including those who pervert it; or it may be so regarded by only a few people (e.g., state political patronage is regarded as corrupt by only a relatively small group of American reformers).[23]

3. Who regards the allegedly corrupt action as perverting the official purpose? This is not necessarily the same question as question (2) above. For example, in a subsequent debate in the Uganda National Assembly on the petrol station site mentioned above, the Minister of Regional Administrations accepted the principle that the council ought not to accept offers lower than the official valuer's valuation of the property, but held that they were by no means obliged to accept the highest offer and that the council were justified in preferring to give a "stake" in the city to a poor man rather than to a rich one.[24] The opposition took the view that it was the man's politics rather than his poverty which actuated the majority on the council, and that the loss to the public revenue was too high a price to pay for assisting one individual member of the public. They also took the view that the official object should be to accept the highest bid, unless circumstances of public importance not present in this case dictated otherwise. Thus the nature of the rule was also a matter of controversy, but both sides to the dispute to some extent made the distinction between the rule on the one hand, and the question of what amounted to breaking it on the other.

4. What are the short-term and long-term consequences of the behavior in question, both of each particular case and of such behavior generally? The answer might usefully, if roughly, be broken into two parts: (a) objective consequences, and (b) subjective consequences. Under (a) will come such questions as, What resources are directed from what

applications to what other applications? What are the real as opposed to the theoretical opportunity costs of the alleged corruption? What are the effects for income distribution? And what consequential effects are there on the pattern of loyalties, the scope of party activities, the incentives to economic activity? etc. etc. Under (b) will come such questions as e.g., What effect does behaving in this way have on the work of civil servants who regard themselves as behaving corruptly? and, What effect does observing such behavior have on the attitudes and/or behavior of others? etc. etc.

It is natural but wrong to assume that the results of corruption are always both bad and important. For instance it is usually assumed that a corrupt civil service is an impediment to the establishment of foreign private enterprise, which has enough difficulties to contend with without in addition having to pay bribes. This may be clearly the case, but sometimes also the reverse appears to be true. Where bureaucracy is both elaborate and inefficient, the provision of strong personal incentives to bureaucrats to cut red tape may by the only way of speeding the establishment of the new firm. In such a case it is certainly reasonable to wish that the bureaucracy were simpler and more efficient, but not to argue that bribery *per se* is an obstacle to private economic initiative.[25] On the other hand the results may be unimportant from any practical standpoint, even if they are not particularly nice.

From such questions one may go on to pose another which is clearly the central one for the scientific study of the problem: In any society, under what conditions is behavior most likely to occur which a significant section of the population will regard as corrupt? Some obviously relevant points are:

1. *The "standing" of the "official purpose" of each public office or institution in the society.* This involves the diffusion of understanding of the idea generally, and within particular relevant groups (e.g., civil servants or police); how strongly supported this conception is, generally, and within particular groups; and what effect distance and scale have on both these dimensions. For example, ordinary people in England did not immediately condemn the Ferranti company for wanting to keep over £4 million windfall profits on a defense contract, because it was an incomprehensibly vast sum gained in highly unfamiliar circumstances; but the same people would instantly condemn a local contractor who made a windfall profit of £40,000 on laying a drainpipe for the Rural District Council. And the "standing" of the "official purpose" of anything is also affected by the "standing" of other rival conceptions of its purpose, e.g., the competing moral claims of relatives on a civil servant who is making junior appointments.

2. *The extent to which action which perverts or contravenes such official purposes is seen as doing so*-another complex problem of research into attitudes.
3. *The incentives and disincentives to corrupt the official purposes of an office or institution.* For instance, the size of the profits to be made by bribery, or the losses liable to be incurred by refraining from it, compared with the penalties attached to being caught and exposed.
4. *The ease with which corruption (once defined) can be carried on.* This involves such things as the case of a particular type of corruption, and the extent to which ordinary people are exposed to opportunities for it (which is among other things affected very much by the range of the activities of the state).[26]

All these aspects clearly interact with each other.

New States and the Concept of Corruption

It is clear that new states are very likely to be the scene of a great deal of behavior that will be called corrupt. Neither attitudes nor material conditions in these countries are focused on the support of a single concept of the national interest or of the official purposes of state and local officers and institutions which would promote that interest. We can consider this under the headings outlined above:

1. The idea of the national interest is weak because the idea of a nation is new. And the institutions and offices of the states are, for most people, remote and perplexing. Even to the civil servants and politicians directly involved in them they are new; they are aware of the "official purposes" which are attached to them by importation, but they scarcely regard them as "hallowed" and hence they do not necessarily regard them as sacrosanct.[27] On the contrary, their Western origin makes them suspect. To many people the "state" and its organs were identified with alien rule and were proper objects of plunder,[28] and they have not yet been reidentified fully as instruments for the promotion of common interests. Meanwhile to the illiterate peasant the "state" and its organs continue to be the source of a web of largely unknowable and complicated regulations, and hence of a permanent threat of punishment: against this threat it is very reasonable to take any available precaution, such as offering bribes. Some official purposes of public office are challenged by strongly supported counter-conceptions, especially the strong obligations of family, tribe, and district in the matter of awarding jobs, scholarships, or other scarce commodities in the gift of the state. Neither politicians nor civil servants are usually drawn from a class brought

up for public service from an early age, or insulated from corrupting pressures by the established aloofness of a mandarin class. And to the extent that the rules of public morality lean ultimately on the strength of the rules of private morality, they are weakened by the hammer blows delivered to all moral rules by rapid social and economic change.

2. The incentive to corrupt whatever official purposes public institutions are agreed to have is especially great in conditions of extreme inequality and considerable absolute poverty. The benefits of holding an office—any office—are relatively enormous; by comparison the penalties for attempting to obtain one by bribery are fairly modest, in relation to the low standard of living of the would-be office holder, or in relation to the pressure of relatives' claims on his existing standard of living. Generally, corruption seems likely to be inseparable from great inequality.

3. Corruption is relatively easy to conceal in the new states. Partly this is because people are generally not too clear about what the official rules are, or what *(really)* constitutes breaking them; or if they are clear, it may be because they do not greatly resent their being broken, and so are not zealous to prevent corruption. Partly it is because the law is ineffectively enforced and the police themselves may not be immune from corruption. And while traditional gift-giving can be distinguished from a bribe of money, it is quite obvious that from the point of view of the giver the one has shaded into the other, so that although the practice has taken on a new significance, as the open gift of a chicken is replaced by a more furtive gift of a pound note, it is nevertheless an established fact of life, in which the precise nature of the rule-infringement is partially concealed by continuity with an older custom.[29]

To say all this is only to explain, however, why there is likely to be much behavior in new states that will be called corrupt. It is not to say anything about the "level" of morality of the citizens of these countries. It is only to say that, poised as they are between the inherited public morality of the western nation-state and the disappearing public morality of the tribe, they are subject to very considerable cross-pressures which make it unlikely that the western state morality at least in its refined and detailed forms, will emerge as the new public morality of these countries; meantime, however, the criteria of the West have sufficient standing in some quarters to ensure that the accusation of corruption is freely leveled against all behavior which does not conform to them. To go much beyond this is, in the apt words of Lucy Mair, to ignore

> the kind of social pressure that is in fact responsible for the practice of the virtues that are cherished in any given society. Good men do not practice . . . industry in circumstances where this would lead to a reduction in piece-rates.[30]

What is the Problem in New States?

Of course there are ample grounds for *concern,* if not for moralizing, about corruption in new states. The most important of them can probably be best isolated by making the comparison with Britain again, but from a different point of view.

Wraith and Simpkins tend to present a picture of Britain, for instance, as having been—around 1800—the scene of great corruption, which was then quite remarkably eliminated. However, the prevalence and the robustness, so to speak, of the practices which they, following the Victorian reformers, regard as corrupt, suggests a rather different interpretation; namely that according to the previously obtaining moral code many of these practices were not corrupt, but either had no moral significance, or indeed were actually quite right and desirable. For instance, the average landlord thought it quite natural, and to that extent desirable, that his tenants should use their votes on behalf of his favored candidate and did not hesitate to put pressure on them to this end. Jobbery, sinecures, rotten boroughs, treating, and other colorful political practices of the period were practiced with an openness that shows that they were not regarded as improper by those whose opinions mattered.[31] What is really remarkable is the rapidity and completeness of the reformers' victory during the nineteenth century.

What seems to have happened is that the ruling classes were induced to accept an altered perception of the nature of the public interest and so to redefine the purposes of the public offices and state institutions which remained, during most of this period, still under their control. It was precisely because they already had a clear notion of the public interest that the assertion of the new notion was established with such completeness. What was involved was not the establishment for the first time of a set of ideas about how public offices and institutions were to serve the public interest, but the adaptation of an established set. Britain did not, in other words, pass from a corrupt condition to a very pure one: rather it passed from one set of standards to another, *through* a period in which behavior patterns which were acceptable by the old standards came to be regarded as corrupt according to the new. It is arguable that, at the height of this experience, public life in Britain was not much less "pure" than it is today. Certainly the records of so-called corruption in the early nineteenth century have about them an air of innocence which is largely lacking in the literature on the same subject in America.

Such innocence is also absent from the portrait of corruption in modern Nigeria drawn in the novels of, for instance, Chinua Achebe and Cyprian Ekwensi, and no doubt this partly explains the compulsive moralism of so many commentators on it. In Britain the corruption of public office was by a ruling class who *had* had a clear conception, even if in the end it was rather tenuous, of the public interest and the duty they owed to it by their use of the public offices and institutions under their control, a conception which complemented their frank exploitation of those offices and institutions for personal gain. In the era of reform they eventually accepted a redefinition of the principles governing the use of those offices and institutions and this, together with the other adaptations on their part, in large measure ensured their survival as a ruling class.

By contrast the ruling classes of Africa are new classes, exercising a new rule. Only a minority have been brought up in ruling-class circles. The idea contained in the phrase, *noblesse oblige,* scarcely applies. There is no previous experience, and so no prior ideology, of the roles of public offices and institutions in relation to the public interest, in terms of which the private exploitation of public office could be rationalized. There *is* a prevailing conception of the national interest and dedication to popular welfare. But it is precisely this idea that may be called into question by the way in which public office is actually exploited by those who occupy it. They have publicly accepted, at least by implication, the official purposes officially attached to public offices and institutions by the colonial powers. If their practice is indefensible by any standards which they are publicly prepared to defend, it robs the whole business of any air of innocence, and this is what provoked Dumont's reluctant protest against the creation in Africa of "a bourgeoisie of a new type, which Karl Marx could scarcely have foreseen, a bourgeoisie of the public service."[32]

The contrast between this contemporary phenomenon and the English scene in the early nineteenth century can be exaggerated. But it would not be hard to sharpen it further. Before the era of reform there were, as well as sinecures worth thousands of pounds, exacting civil service jobs which were not paid enough to induce anyone competent to occupy them, and which consequently were made attractive only by perquisites. Government-provided services, too, tended to be needed primarily by the relatively affluent sections of the population. And the idea was broadly accepted that well-born young men had some sort of entitlement to be maintained in one capacity or another in the public service. By contrast, in contemporary Africa public service is not merely paid well, in relation to local income levels, but lavishly;[33] government services affect the ordinary citizen in numerous ways, not as a luxury but as a conventional (or even an actual) necessity; and there is no accepted "natural" ruling elite. In any case, these eighteenth-century ideas do not seem to have been invoked in defense of "corruption" by those engaged in it today.

This is, perhaps, the main reason for the automatic condemnation of these widespread behavior patterns by most contemporary commentators, and it seems rather reasonable. For to the extent that the official public morality of a society is more or less systematically subverted, especially if the leadership is involved in it, it becomes useless as a tool for getting things done, and this is expensive in any society where other resources are scarce. What is involved here is the idea of a "corrupted society."

It seems impossible to declare that a society without an effective public morality *cannot* develop economically. On the other hand, there do seem to be reasons for doubting whether in African conditions this is likely to happen. In the first place, most African states are extremely dependent upon government action for their development. Their development prospects largely depend on attaining the targets chartered in development plans, and by very fine margins. This requires single-minded hard work from all holders of public office. If the top political elite of a country consumes its time and energy in trying to get rich by corrupt means, it is not likely that the development plans will be fulfilled.

Secondly, if this is the pattern of behavior of the elite and if this is fairly well known, it is likely to rob them of much of their authority both with subordinates in the government and with political followers in the countryside. The country will be apt to forfeit whatever benefits can be derived by the output of effort not solely motivated by the hope of personal gain.

Thirdly, the wealth improperly accumulated by the top elite may be modest by world standards, but still large in relation to the level of investment on which the economic development of the country depends. In this case much will turn on how such wealth is redeployed. If political leaders try to buy security by depositing their wealth in numbered accounts in Swiss banks it represents a wholly negative drain on the economy.[34] (But perhaps they will buy farms and make them very productive.) Fourthly, if the top elite flout the public moral code which is cherished by "donor" nations the supply of foreign aid may diminish.

The likelihood of the last two developments seems remote. The possibility which seems most solid and even obvious is the first; there are perfectly plain differences to be seen between one developing nation and another in terms of the amount of public spirit and devotion to duty shown by their elites, and the idea of a society economically stagnating in the grip of a self-seeking and corrupt elite is not a pure fantasy. The line of escape from such a situation is also fairly clear. Typically, a nucleus of "puritans"—drawn from groups such as an independent business class, professional groups, or small farmers—begins to exercise effective pressure to apply the official but disregarded public code of ethics.

By and large this was the experience of the reform movement in America. The moral vulnerability of the ruling groups was very great, and so piecemeal advance was possible. Distinctions were gradually insisted upon which narrowed the area of operation of self-interest and widened that of the public interest; it came to be held, for instance, that "private profit by public servants at the expense of the public welfare was corrupt; but private profit by public servants obtained as a *concomitant* to service in the general welfare was quite proper."[35] (A similar distinction was drawn by Achebe's hero when he took to accepting bribes: "But Obi stoutly refused to countenance anyone who did not possess the minimum educational and other requirements. On that he was unshakeable.")[36] The result in America is a patchwork: the scope of political patronage has been greatly reduced and the cash bribery of higher public servants largely eliminated. At the same time, large areas of public life have so far remained more or less immune to reform, and practices that in one sphere would be regarded as corrupt are almost taken for granted in another.

The question is where the puritans are to come from in the new states, with their prevailing lack of economically independent professional and middle classes and the corresponding weakness of the puritan ethos; and whether the puritans in new states can succeed by gradualist means, rather than by revolution.

Notes

1. The best known English study is perhaps Norman Gash's *Politics in the Age of Peel* (London, 1953). Much of the American literature is reviewed in V.O. Key, *Politics, Parties and Pressure Groups* (New York. 1955), chap. 13, "Party Machine as Interest Group." See also *The Annals of the American Academy Of Political and Social Science* (Philadelphia), March 1952, special number on "Ethical Standards in American Public Life." The wide range of reports of commissions of enquiry into colonial malpractice is indicated in the footnotes to Ronald Wraith and Edgar Simpkins' recent work *Corruption in Developing Countries* (London, 1963). While the bulk of this material is from West Africa and deals with local government, there are valuable reports from East Africa, and also from India and Malaya and elsewhere. Unfortunately I have not had an opportunity to study Professor Van Klaveren's series of articles in *Vierteljahrschrift für Sozial and Wirtschaftsgeschichte* since 1957, referred to in his comments on M.G. Smith's "Historical and Cultural Conditions of Political Corruption among the Hausa," in *Comparative Studies in Society and History* (The Hague), January 1964, pp.164–198.
2. An interesting and ably written exception is M. McMullan, "A Theory of Corruption," *A Sociological Review* (Keele), July 1961; pp. 181–201. The author has, however, a rather restricted conception of what corruption is, and a number of unwarrantable assumptions about the results.
3. Wraith and Simpkins, *Corruption in Developing Countries*. pp. 12–13 and 172.
4. Wraith and Simpkins, p. 35.
5. Wraith and Simpkins, p. 45.
6. The authors display a militant ignorance of sociological theory and research, which may be partly a consequence of their reluctance to abandon their ethical absolutism, but seems more a part of the settled philistinism on this matter which is still so depressingly common in Britain. "It is always unwise" (they write of social anthropology) "to argue with exponents of this formidable science, since they have their own vocabulary, which differs from that of the ordinary man, and their own concepts, which are not readily understood" (p. 172), and they proceed to represent the main burden of the social anthropologist's contributions on the

72   **Political Corruption**

subject as being to the effect that all corruption in their sense is the African's idea
of a customary gift. One is provoked to echo Campbell-Bannerman's exasperated
reply to the outmoded dialectics of Balfour: "Enough of this foolery."

7. *Uganda Parliamentary Debates,* 27 September 1963, pp. 179–200, and 3 October
   1963, pp. 411–21. The Uganda government subsequently denied that any such
   sale had taken place.
8. *Report of the Commission of Enquiry into the Working of Port Harcourt Town
   Council, 1955;* quoted in Wraith and Simpkins, p. 22.
9. *Third Interim Report of the Senate Committee* to Investigate *Organized Crime in
   Interstate Commerce, 1951* (Kefauver Committee), quoted in H.A. Turner, *Politics in the United States* (New York, 1955), p.412.
10. From the Storey Report, *Commission of Inquiry into the Administration of Lagos
    Town Council, 1953* (Lagos, 1954).
11. William Turner, "In Defence of Patronage," in *The Annals Of the American
    Academy of Political and Social Science,* January 1937, pp. 22–8, and William J.
    Riordan, *Plunkitt of Tammany Hall* (New York, 1958). Plunkitt coined the phrase
    "honest graft" in a famous passage:
      There's an honest graft, and I'm an example of how it works. I might sum up
    the whole thing by sayin': "I seen my opportunities and I took 'em." Just let me
    explain by examples. My party's in power in the city and it's goin' to undertake a
    lot of public improvements. Well, I'm tipped off, say, that they're going to lay out
    a new park at a certain place and I buy up all the land I can in the neighborhood.
    Then the board of this or that makes its plan public and there is a rush to get that
    land which nobody cared particular for before. Ain't it perfectly right to charge a
    good profit and make a profit on my investment and foresight? Of course it is.
    Well, that's honest graft.
12. V. O. Key, pp. 395–98.
13. M. McMullan, p.197.
14. Bert F. Hoselitz. "Levels of Economic Performance and Bureaucratic Structures,"
    in La Palombara (ed.), *Bureaucracy and Political Development* (Princeton, 1963),
    p. 190.
15. Wraith and Simpkins, p. 172; although previously they do say "The economic
    effects of all this [corruption] on a country may not be very considerable."
    McMullan also believes the economic costs are high, but his definition of eco-
    nomic cost appears to be somewhat Gladstonian, "A Theory of Corruption," p.
    182.
16. For an interesting discussion of the general question, see C. C. Wrigley. *Crops
    and Wealth in Uganda* (Kampala, 1959), pp. 70–73.
17. *Uganda Parliamentary Debates,* 8 November 1963, pp. 108–12, and 11 Novem-
    ber 1963, pp. 137–42. Corruption was alleged by the opposition.
18. M. Fainsod, *How Russia Is Ruled* (Cambridge, Mass, 1958), p. 437.
19. For a brief but penetrating comment on this see W. Arthur Lewis, *The Theory of
    Economic Growth* (London, 1955), pp. 428–29.
20. Chinua Achebe provides a fascinating selection in *No Longer at Ease* (London,
    1960), pp. 5–6 and 87–88. See also E. C. Banfield, *The Moral Basis of a Back-
    ward Society* (Chicago, 1958), ch. 5.
21. *Report of the Tribunal Appointed to Inquire into Allegations Reflecting on the
    Official Conduct of the Premier of, and Certain Persons Holding Ministerial and
    other Public Offices in, the Eastern Region of Nigeria* (London, 1957).
22. *Lord Denning's Report* (London, 1963).
23. Wraith and Simpkins ally themselves with the analogous minority in West Africa

whom they identify as "the most eminent and responsible citizens" of these countries, p. 173. It appears that Chinua Achebe should be included among these, and to this extent it is permissible to wonder how typical are the reactions of his hero in *No Longer at Ease,* who has an ultimate and profound revulsion against his own acceptance of bribes.

24. *Uganda Parliamentary Debates,* 27 September 1963, p. 187.
25. McMullan, p.182, takes the orthodox view: "Investors and entrepreneurs are frustrated and dismayed and may find that the unofficial cost of starting an enterprise is too great for it to be profitable." Another view is that this is one method of reducing excess profits. In the case of extractive industries this has some plausibility. McMullan points out (p. 197) that "a group under harsh disability but still possessed of considerable wealth" provides the "optimum conditions for corruption" and that it is perhaps another "useful" function of corruption to enable economically energetic ethnic minorities to protect themselves.
26. An official study of civil service corruption in Malaya in the 1950s found much more corruption in those departments of government which provide extensive services than in those which do not.
27. Dr. Lucy Mair has put this excellently: "They cast for a play in which the *dramatis personae* are enumerated but the lines are not written. The new African governments are recruited from new men. . . . The relationship of the leader with his followers, of ministers with their colleagues, with bureaucrats, with the general public, are new relationships." *The New Nations* (London, 1963), p.123.
28. Senator Kefauver's comment on the attitude of Americans to colonial administration before the American Revolution: "In a sense the whole populace engaged in the profitable process of mulcting the government-which was after all a hated tyrant-of every possible penny"; *The Annals of the American Academy of Political anal Social Science,* March 1952, p. 2.
29. See the interesting and detailed discussion of this in A.W. Southall and P.C.W. Gutkind, *Townsmen in the Making* (Kampala. 1957), p. 189–94.
30. Lucy Mair, pp. 124–25.
31. "In the latter half of the eighteenth century *it was taken for granted* that the purpose for going into parliament or holding any public office was to make or repair a man's personal fortune." R.M. Jackson, *The Machinery of Local Government* (London, 1958), p. 345. (Italics mine.) It seems clear that during this period there was a tendency for this attitude to become more widespread and the consequences more extensive and expensive, and that this in turn aided the development of the reform movement. However, the use of public office for private gain was a recognized public practice going back to a period in English history when these distinctions were still imperfectly worked out.
32. R. Dumont, *L'Afrique noire est mal porte* (Paris, 1962), p.66.
33. Cf. Dumont's notorious comparison: "A deputy works (?) for three months a year, but receives from 120,000 to 165,000 CFA per month. In six months of salary— i.e., in one and a half months' work—he makes as much as the average African peasant in 36 years, in a whole life of hard labor."
34. See. e.g., Frantz Fanon, *Les Damnés de la terre,* quoted by Dumont, pp. 67–68.
35. Kefauver, Ref. 2, p.3.
36. Chinua Achebe, *No Longer at Ease* (London, 1960), p.169.

Part II

COMPARING ACROSS TIME
AND COUNTRIES

Introduction to Part II

The approach emphasized in part two centers on the public office concept and attempts to trace how in the process of modernization and bureaucratization in Western societies the holders of public offices came to be subject to norms and rules that were scarcely applicable to their predecessors. The selection of articles is guided by the aim of illustrating how, in the process of modernization, distinct public responsibilities were gradually built into the public-office concept, how earlier property claims to office were gradually disappropriated, and how bureaucratic concepts of the office were introduced in varying ways in European and American political systems.

Public Offices in Pre-Bureaucratic Systems

In framing his definition of the public official's position within modern bureaucratic systems, Max Weber stressed contrasts to practices in pre-bureaucratic systems, which serve as a key take-off point for this discussion:

> Legally and actually, officeholding is not considered ownership of a source of income, to be exploited for rents or emoluments in exchange for the rendering of certain services, as was normally the case in the Middle Ages....Rather entrance into an office...is considered an acceptance of a specific duty or fealty to the purpose of the office in return for the grant of a secure existence. It is decisive for the modern loyalty to an office that, in the pure type, it does not establish a relationship to a person, like the vassal's or disciple's faith under feudal or patrimonial authority, but rather is devoted to impersonal and functional purposes.[1]

Among the varieties of premodern, pre-bureaucratic systems the most important was that based upon patrimonial domination. The Inca society, discussed by Jacob van Klavern in chapter 6, clearly fits into the category. Under patrimonial systems a ruler could legitimately engage in a self—or family-centered distribution of the national income to the extreme of the Inca model, but whether or not he tried to do so, no one could seek to challenge his decision making as illegitimate or corrupt.[2] One can therefore agree with Van Klaveren that "by definition, corruption does not occur" in the Inca and other systems based upon pure patrimonial domination.

In feudal Europe the problem was not that all constitutional and economic power was centralized in one ruler but rather that offices had come to be perceived as properties rather than being associated with assigned duties. As the "appropriation" of offices progressed, the ruler's power fell apart into various powers, which became the property of various privileged individuals. As Weber argued, "Whatever traces of an objectively defined official duty there are disappear altogether with the treatment of the office as benefice or property."[3]

Public Office as Benefice or Property

The appropriation of benefices to officeholders was seen by Weber as characteristic both of the feudal system and of the early modern patrimonial-bureaucratic state. The feudal period was most strongly associated with landed benefices, which assigned office land for the incumbent's own use in the manner of a fief, thus giving the benefice holder and his heirs great autonomy from the ruler. Under early modern patrimonialism there was some reassertion of the ruler's control, but this period was characterized by the widespread and continued use of fee benefices, under which the ruler assigned to a favorite or to a purchaser the right to receive certain fees due him from his subjects. Thus the office could also become hereditary in the family of the original favorite or turn into the patrimonial possession of the purchaser.

In the early patrimonial-bureaucratic state the practice of remunerating officials by means of fees had the effect of making the officials' income largely dependent upon his "rapacity and ingenuity." It is thus seen by Koenraad W. Swart (chapter 7) and others to have been "very irrational" from the perspective of developing a responsible administrative instrument. However, says Swart, "the system...had great advantages in a society in which it was difficult to check on local officials because of a widespread dishonesty, relatively large distances, and a primitive administrative technique. In this way much accounting and transferring of money was avoided, and the official was interested in the execution of his duties."

As a matter of fact, in early modern history one does not have much choice. Apart from general models—which have already been elaborated and convincingly state the causes, effects and functions of corruption in pre-bureaucratic societies—it is very difficult, not to say impossible—to apprehend the reality or the degree of political corruption in pre-bureaucratic societies. But it seems possible to study some of the political impacts of corruption through an analysis of the representations that surrounded the notion of corruption in those days and, in doing so, to reach another level of reality. And this includes terminological studies of the kind I sent you which are only one of the ways—maybe the first one that has to be followed—opened to track down the articulations and meanings of all these representations.

The Growth of a Permanent Officialdom

The Sale of Offices

In many parts of continental Europe the reemergence of a powerful merchant class and the growing importance of a highly developed money economy soon resulted in something like a "refeudalization" of large parts of the career officialdom. For in order to meet pressing financial demands, rulers adopted, to varying degrees, the practice of selling office (venalite des offices), which became objects of trade and exchange. The purchasers of these offices served in them as a matter of right, and thus the king was prevented from choosing his officials on the basis of their ability or reliability.

Royal rulers during this period of absolution were still not subject to any significant constitutional rules that limited their choice of alternative techniques for achieving the goals of the state. Had they been subject to such rules, they would have run as much chance of being accused of corruption for selling judgeships as do contemporary American presidents for appointing large campaign contributors to ambassadorial positions. For once the sale of offices became officially regulated so that the proceeds flowed into the treasuries of the king and the state, they ceased to constitute a drain of public resources toward private-regarding ends. The king used the proceeds from the sale of offices to meet the costs of military campaigns, just as contemporary parties use financial contributions to meet the costs of election campaigns, and both procedures are seen as goals asserted to be related to the public interest.

Van Klaveren perceives that excessive private-regarding resource extraction during this period can be conceived of in terms of "corruption." From this perspective the main question is: Which group of officeholders would tend to be relatively more conscientious and relatively less greedy-those who received their office because they were favorites of the king or those who purchased their office from the king? Montesquieu was one of a number of reform-minded writers of the time who actually supported the sale of p°ublic office over other methods of appointment because "change will furnish better subjects than the prince's choice.[4] Thus, whereas today the venality of office is considered a form of political corruption, it was then perceived as a check on corruption. Jeremy Bentham, who saw the British aristocracy as being particularly prone to self-indulgence, also favored the sale-of-office principle, because he believed that it would allow more of the wealthier and more moral middle-class types to have access to high government posts.[5]

Appointments in Exchange for Parliamentary Support

By comparison with contemporaneous practices in France, fewer offices were sold and more were given away by the crown in eighteenth-century Britain. This was primarily due to the fact that the British monarch's ministers had an overriding concern that their French equivalents did not have to face up to: they had to maintain pro-government majorities in an elected parliament. In Britain it was not so much administrative posts as seats in the House of Commons that had acquired a quasi-proprietary character: "they were a valuable inheritance or a costly acquisition from which proper returns were expected.[6] Some members ensured their reelection through tiny electorates by personal favors or family influence; others felt themselves primarily responsible to small cliques of powerful patrons in their respective constituencies. By the early eighteenth century the promise of government jobs had become a main means through which pro-government members of Parliament rounded up marginal voters in their boroughs. By the time of the accession of George III, in many boroughs "few extensive electoral interests could be maintained except with the help of Government patronage lavished at the recommendation of the borough patron."[7] These practices were long legitimatized by "a universal belief that the politically active portion of the community had a legitimate claim to maintenance by the State, just as the medieval knight had a claim to maintenance by the lord."[8]

Public-Office Conceptions in Britain and France

Whereas the Continental code-law countries could easily remodel their legal systems through the adoption of comprehensive codes, norms in the English-speaking countries had to be operationalized in terms of a more complex sequence of legislative and judicial acts and precedents. Thus, even in the twentieth-century discussions of public officers and their duties have had to be very circuitous because "the terminology and the precedents relied upon in interpretation developed before public administration had developed its present scope and complexity."[9]

In Britain judicial decisions that serve as important precedent date back to the beginning of the civil service reform movement there, especially a 1783 decision which held that "a man accepting an office of trust concerning the public, especially if attended with profit, is answerable criminally to the king for misbehavior in his office." American and English courts have followed the same rule that the public officer, occupying a position of trust, is bound by the duties of a fiduciary.

In her study of the application of the corruption label in the early modern English and French discourse, Maryvonne Genaux finds that efforts to define corruption are particularly difficult because of contemporary understanding of public service carry many meanings. She demonstrates how the concept of public service was articulated with such diverse variables as the Prince's service, social harmony, the law, divine vengeance. Lacking a fixed vocabulary, the author draws on diverse application of related terms in French and English encyclopedia's of the period. Thus, her methodology bears some similarity with that employed by Moroff and Blechinger in their analysis of the use of corruption terminology in major newspapers (see chapter 45).

Genaux's comparative analysis of how application of negatively loaded terms developed as these two monarchial states adapted their means of political controversy. Since the charge of corruption came to be the easiest to make and the most difficult to refute, the study of relevant vocabulary is utilized to "read a society and trace the rise of the modern state."

How can one compare practices that are illegal in terms of legal standards which non-western countries have imported from the West, with similar behaviors that were tolerated by both legal and moral standards in western countries some centuries ago? This problem is addressed by James C. Scott in an excerpt from a longer study which concentrates on contrasts between corrupt practices in Tudor and Stuart England and contemporary developing countries like Thailand.

He makes a case for comparing practices that are corrupt only by modern standards so as to facilitate inquiry into their causes in different periods and locales, as well as their effect on the composition of elites. "If nepotism or bribery have similar causes and consequences in early France as in contemporary India, that is an important subject for analysis, notwithstanding the fact that legal codes and public standards have changed so much that what was tolerated (not corrupt) in early France is now forbidden by law (corrupt) in India?"

Scott proposes that earlier practices that anticipate behaviors, later stigmatized as corrupt, be labeled examples of "protocorruption." Such a terminological usage would in some ways parallel the manner in which historians distinguish between the parliamentary factions which are seen as constituting "proto-parties" in the eighteenth century House of Commons before the development of fully fledged political parties in the nineteenth century. However, the suitability of this label in European settings has been called into question by historians and others, among them, Maryvonne Genaux, in chapter seven .

Scott's approach to destigmatizing the study of corruption is to regard it as one form of influence among others—such as those more legitimately based considerations of ideology and equity. He suggests that enhancing the analytical capacity of social scientists should take precedence over their role as labeling agents on behalf of a particular set of moral values. He argues that his approach highlights "the functional equivalence of a variety of acts of political influence—some of which violate all standards of community ethics and some of which are totally beyond reproach."

Scott also cautions social scientists and historians to be aware of how their attitudes toward regimes in which corruption occurs can affect their implicit attitudes. He points out that present-day observers can find corruption in earlier systems, which involved the subversion of an aristocratic monopoly of government, ideologically less unacceptable than they might in instances of corruption in liberal democratic or socialist regimes, where wealth may be used to undermine egalitarian values which they themselves might be inclined to share.

Notes

1. Max Weber, *Economy and Society*, 111, New York: Bedminster Press, 1968, p. 959.
2. Weber, *Economy and Society*, p. 1007.
3. Weber, *Economy and Society*, p. 1040.
4. Charles Secondat de Montesquieu, *The Spirit of the Laws*, New York: Hafner, 1949, p. 69.
5. Jeremy Bentham, "The Rationale of Reward," *Works*, vol. 5, Edinburgh, 1863, pp. 246–248.
6. Donald Kingsley, *Representative Democracy*, Yellow Springs, OH: Antioch Press, 1944, p. 26.
7. Sir Lewis B. Namier, *The Structure of Politics of the Accession of George III*, 2d ed. New York: St. Martin's, 1957, p. 169.
8. Kingsley, *Representative Democracy*, p. 26.
9. Arthur W. MacMahon, "Public Office," *Encyclopedia of the Social Sciences*, VI, p. 665.

5

Corruption as a Historical Phenomenon

Jacob van Klaveren

Corruption as a historical phenomenon is, to the best of my knowledge, a problem that has never been dealt with systematically. The reason probably is that corruption has not been regarded as a problem. This point of view is completely justified as long as corruption is only perceived as a series of accidental acts of dishonesty on the part of civil servants. He who examines this subject more carefully, however, recognizes that the phenomenon occurred much more frequently prior to the French Revolution and that it was almost constitutionally determined. In this paper, too, corruption shall be examined as an [unwritten] part of a political constitution.

Constitutions[1] and Corruption

There are two types of constitutions under which corruption, by definition, does not occur—namely in the case of monarchy when interpreted as absolute one-man rule, and in the case of constitutions built upon the idea of popular sovereignty. Thus in this respect one could say *les extrèmes se touchent.*
First we shall discuss the Inca state as the closest approximation to the model of absolute monarchy. Here all the resources of the country were claimed for an economic plan that served the glorification of the ruler and the

Source: Jacob van Klaveren, "Die historische Erscheinung der Korruption, in ihrem Zusammenhang mit der Staats—und Gesellschaftsstruktur betrachtet." *Viertaljahresschrift für Sozial—und Wirtschaftsgeschichte,* 44:4 (December 1957), pp. 294–302, 312–318. By permission of the publisher, Franz Steiner Verlag. Translated by Peggy Hofmann and Karl Kurtz.

sun cult. Since there were no productive factors left untapped, it was impossible for civil servants to divert more revenues than were already allocated to them by the king in the economic plan. The incomes of civil servants and the people were precisely determined according to social position. This even affected nutrition patterns, number of wives, and the quality of the clothes that were distributed. A governor of the Inca caste received vicuña clothes from the public storehouses, while the people's clothes were made from llama wool. The people walked: the Sapa Inca and the high civil servants of Inca origin were carried in sedan chairs.[2] Thus everyone received an appropriate income, and to claim more constituted an offense against the Sapa Inca and the sun cult. This distribution of the national income to the furthering of the commonweal was based on ethical and religious values, but was centripetally oriented toward the glorification of the Sapa Inca and the sun.

It will be intelligible without more ado that this *ex-ante* distribution of the national income by means of an economic plan in a natural economy . . . could be realized rather easily. This task becomes more complicated in a money economy. The presence of money is a symptom of the existence of an exchange economy, which is not to say that an exchange economy could not also exist without money. In an exchange or market economy, quasi-anonymous forces determine the extent of employment and the distribution of the national income. It could only be confirmed afterward, but not regulated in advance whether all productive forces of a nation were really utilized fully and for what ends, and whether every social group obtained the income deemed appropriate on ethical grounds. Only through the techniques of modern economic policy is it possible nowadays to determine in advance not only the size of the national product but its distribution. In this process the market economy is regulated and the functions of money are to a large extent eliminated or at least influenced into a desired direction through a public monetary policy.

These modern possibilities were still unknown at the beginning of the twentieth century and are even nowadays not available for the less-developed countries. Thus if we posit an absolute monarchy existing simultaneously with a money economy, we could assume for the above-mentioned reason that it would be impossible to carry out a patriarchal distribution of income on the Inca model. The monarch could obtain from the people through taxes what he deems necessary for himself and the public civil service, but he would always be lagging behind developments by one phase. Although he is not able to dictate to his subjects what constitutes appropriate income, he can compellingly prescribe the income appropriate to the civil servants and penalize all cases of corruption. To this extent the monarchy has a beneficial effect on the broad mass of the population. This is not to say, however, that the monarch will always act in this manner. It is possible that he might allow his civil servants to maximize their income in dealing with the public.[3] However, this would loosen the relationship between the civil servants and the monarch's decision-making power. The civil service hierarchy would disintegrate into a number of "maximizing units," each with its own interests, and would thus become unreliable for the execution of the national policy.[4] The more developed the monarchy, the greater its corruption-checking tendency, to the point that corruption disappears completely in an absolute monarchy, as in the case of the Inca state.

We shall now discuss the other polar situation. Let us assume that the common good is not found in an almost metaphysical way by a sovereign prince in the sense similar to Rousseau's *volonté générale* but is ascertained by an expression of opinion by the people. Let us assume further that the popular will is genuinely reflected in the nation's policy. Thus there incontestably exists a situation of popular sovereignty, and the civil servants are only executive instruments of the people's will. It goes without saying that it can never be the people's will to be exploited by the civil servants and this is just the inevitable consequence of corruption. Therefore, the people will precisely prescribe the income appropriate to the civil servants and will not tolerate corruption. As a result corruption can never be rooted in the constitution and can only occur as occasional acts of dishonesty.[5]

What we have described here are two extreme ideal types, which will never be fully realized. However, the contrast between them should make evident which circumstances determine whether corruption is built into the constitution. Corruption is built on the underlying principle that the people are subjected to the control of officials. Thus there exists a regulating principle, which gives to the officials and other intermediary groups a public existence with a purpose of their own. We divide these intermediary groups into those that are created by the monarch, that is, the public officials, and those which have autonomous origins, that is, the traditional intermediary groups. Among the latter are the landlords but also the urban patricians. Without a monarchy there would be no royal civil servants but only the civil servants who serve traditional intermediary groups. These have, however, been historically less significant than the royal civil servants; therefore, we shall pass them by. Similarly, among the traditional intermediary groups we will consider only the urban patricians.

These intermediary groups have rights of their own. The people exist not only for the king, but also for the intermediary group. The monarch may adjust to letting these intermediary groups claim what they regard as their due portion of the national income. It is obvious that relevant opinions may diverge, in which case tensions may occur. There may ensue a struggle around the distribution of the national income, which takes place in a field encompassed by a conflict triangle whose pillars are the monarch, the civil service, and the urban oligarchy. The intermediary forces tend to nurture corruption, whereas the monarchy tends to check corruption. However, the intermediate groups do not necessarily stick together; on the contrary, quite often the civil service is created by the monarch during the struggle with the traditional intermediary groups. There then tends to ensue a rechanneling of corruption incomes in favor of civil servants and courtiers, although the total amount of corruption incomes may well decrease.

In his study *Deutsches Städtleben in der älteren Zeit (German City Life)* Gustav Schmoller[6] emphasized the corruption-checking effect of the monarchy. However, he exhaustively discussed the tendency of intermediary groups to further corruption only where blame was attached to the city oligarchy. This, of course, is due to the topic of his study but is also significant for his mentality. Corruption by civil servants is only mentioned where an honest historiography cannot avoid it. It is his major concern to correct those historians who, influenced by the Enlightenment, had viewed the "free" cities as "democratic" communities whose character had supposedly been aborted by the encroachment of the Prussian princes. Schmoller is perfectly right to correct this widely prevalent but erroneous idea and to point out that these very cities were breeding places of oligarchic despotism and corruption and had no claim to being considered democratic.[7]

This error is, by the way, very widespread, and is reflected in the title of a study by Pirenne, dealing with *Les anciennes démocraties des Pays Bas* (Paris, 1922). At the end of the eighteenth century there were in the Netherlands several thinkers influenced by the Enlightenment, who praised "grand pensionaries" Johann van Oldenbarneveldt and Johann de Witt, who fell victims to the hostility of the House of Orange, as martyrs in the struggle against tyranny. In reality, however, these proud patricians were the last to be concerned with the promotion of popular influence.[8] Even Cunningham falls into this error in his thorough and learned study *The Growth of English Industry and Commerce,* in which he asserts that democracies are more often corrupt and inefficient than are autocratic governments.[9] This, however, is impossible since democracy-as we have seen-is without corruption by definition. If, on the other hand one recognizes that Cunningham identifies democracy with the rule of parliament, then this statement carries more truth. One sees here that the conception of "democracy" was already completely diffuse by the end of the nineteenth century, although its identifying characteristics can be precisely determined on the basis of an exact analysis of the ideas of the Enlightenment.[10] Therefore, we prefer to avoid this expression as far as possible, and to speak instead of constitutions that honestly reflect the people's will. If one identifies democracy with the government of parliament, as Cunningham does, then the Magna Carta, which the English nobility extracted from John Lackland in 1215, could be regarded as the beginning of English democracy, since parliament was founded then. That would be incorrect. While correcting Cunningham in this regard, one may otherwise agree with him since he is stating only what has been extrapolated above, namely that intermediary groups tend to further corruption. His reference is primarily to the rural squires that were then dominant in Parliament, so that particularly for the period after 1688 one may speak of a "squirearchy." However, for Prussia, which is examined by Schmoller, and with respect to the Netherlands, the city oligarchies are more significant. Schmoller maintains that the kings, by integrating the cities into the Prussian national state, rid them of "oligarchic corruption" and extended to them an "honest and well-regulated administration." However, he feels forced to admit some reservations, particularly for the age of the soldier-king Frederick William I (1730–1740). Schmoller admits that the groups from which the civil service was recruited were not at all "ethically pure," and that a decay of the civil servants' morality must be noted during the reigns of Frederick the Great and Frederick Wilhelm II, although this did not lead back to the nadir marked during the reign of the Great Elector (1640–1688).[11]

We must contradict Schmoller as well if he thinks that his description of the situation explains a gradual transition from an "oligarchic corruption" to the—in our sense—"honest" city regulation of 1808.[12] The later reform is, in our view, rooted in the Enlightenment, which penetrated Prussia after the defeats of Jena and Auerstaedt, even though the intellectual instruments of the reform, the "educated bourgeoisie" which had grown considerably during the eighteenth century, could not participate in the country's government to a great extent until after 1848. Thus it becomes clear that Schmoller's benevolent monarchy and his spontaneous rises and declines of morality will not carry us very far. These are not accidental events; we are concerned with a new epoch of intellectual and cultural history, the age of the Enlightenment, which affected the constitutions of Europe.[13]

Such an optical illusion could not arise with regard to the Netherlands, where the Orange Stadtholder had to flee to England in 1795. The democratic reform party, the "Patriots," had already carried out a type of French Revolution in 1786. However, they were defeated by the hurriedly summoned Prussian forces in 1787, causing their leadership to flee to France. Strongly influenced by Jacobin thought, the exiles returned with the French troops in 1795, took over the government, and established the Republic on modern foundations.[14] One of their leaders, the lawyer Herman Willem Daendels, went as governor to Java and accomplished there what he described as the "sincere and honest political rule of the Netherlands." He established good official salary levels and forbade all forms of corruption, whether at the expense of the state or of the natives. One European civil servant who did not take the sudden reversal seriously and continued to extort from the natives was executed; thus was "honest" administration established.[15]

Monarchy as a Check to Corruption

This section maintains that the tendency of monarchy to check corruption was little developed in Europe during the *ancien régime,* perhaps least of all in England. . . .

The Tendency of the Intermediary Groups to Encourage Corruption

As we have already pointed out, "corruption lay," so to speak, "in the middle."[16] The intermediary groups were the breeding places for corruption. This is generally true for both the traditional intermediary groups and the civil-servant class created by the prince. This distinction gradually disappeared, especially when the civil service was mixed with representatives of the traditional intermediary layers, as was the case inmost countries. The only remaining distinction was that the city oligarchies to which we limited ourselves were organized in a collegial manner, whereas the civil servants' underlying structure was hierarchical. Therefore, the internal relations were not quite the same. Of course, the civil servants were quite often organized collegially in "boards," but this was only true for each step of the hierarchy. To begin with we shall overlook the differences and concentrate on the general conditions that are true of both groups.

Every intermediary group has the tendency to set itself apart from the lower ones, thus developing a specific social and economic consciousness. It regards itself as a specific entity of a higher social order that has the right to place itself on a higher economic level than the masses, not on the basis of any specific service to the community but because of its mere existence. But even when its members indulge in notions of their own usefulness to the community, they think of a more or less metaphysically based common good and are inclined to consider their privileged position as a requisite for the divine order. This kind of "service" is not exactly what is demanded by a truly sovereign people.

This was the mentality of Tolstoi's Count Vronsky, who supported the principle of promptly paying a gambling debt to a friend, but thought that one should kick a tailor out the door for his boldness when he time and again appeared to claim payment for his work. He would complain bitterly if this tailor asserted his legal rights; equality before the law was anathema to these strata. In 1768 this same opinion was expressed by the Scottish nobleman who called the businessmen who reclaimed Lady Caithness' furniture "a set of low-lifed creatures."[17]

Of course, these *were* noblemen, but the intermediary groups of lower origin were no different. The Dutch city patricians were always on the same level as the hereditary nobility, and they were truly convinced that they ruled by divine right.[18] John Evelyn noted with satisfaction in his diary one day that on the previous Sunday the priest had praised the differences of rank and position as being divinely ordered.[19] This mentality is evidenced by many other references. But the remarkable thing is that those civil servants who advanced by virtue of their own skills, but who were not of noble origin, assumed this view. For example, Samuel Pepys[20] succeeded in gradually achieving a more or less equal position among the members of the Naval Board of which he was the secretary. He proudly noted that day when he, like the others, kept his hat on during a conference without any objection from the other gentlemen. Soon he brought himself a sword and a carriage with two beautiful horses.[21]

Thus the intermediary groups were not totally closed, particularly not the civil service, since the work had often to be done by an ambitious member of humble origin like Pepys. Nevertheless, it can be regarded as closed, since such outsiders were assimilated at once. This mentality of the middle groups gradually led its members to believe that they were entitled to a certain conventionally conditioned way of life and the corresponding incomes. It is important for us to note here that the already mentioned standards were rather vague. Even among contemporaries and colleagues there must have been some uncertainty about the rights due to them because of their position. This uncertainty had the effect—and this is what concerns us here—of continuously increasing the demands but never of decreasing them. The tendency of the demands to spiral—and thereby the corruption, too—can be observed among both the civil servants and the city oligarchy. No one wanted to fall behind his colleagues either in his outwardly visible way of life or in the less noticeable size of his income. Thus, even when corruption was thoroughly accepted, there was an astonishing amount of secretiveness, with the result that only little material can be found for these periods as well.

The demands of the intermediary groups were sometimes pushed to a higher level by the shock-like effect of external conditions, for example, by the spread of French fashion during the era of Louis XIV or by the growing acquaintance with Oriental luxury goods. Chinese porcelain, japanned goods, or art objects made out of ivory spread more rapidly the more one believed that he had to keep pace with everyone else. There is no need to emphasize that the women were primarily responsible for this. A comparison between the way of life of the Dutch patricians and the English gentry during the seventeenth and the eighteenth centuries shows a very significant increase of demands as well as of income gained by corruption.[22] On close inspection this would certainly be found to be the case in every country. Schmoller[23] has already pointed to an increasing closure in Prussia of the civil service, which became a caste at the same time, as well as an increase in corruption after the death of the simple soldier-king Frederick William I (1713–1740). Undoubtedly, the predominance of French and courtly culture during the reign of Frederick the Great influenced this development. It is clear that the king's way of life had great influence. The courtiers all tried to copy this way of life in miniature, but they had to make sure that they kept their distance, just as it was generally between inferiors and superiors. What was considered an "appropriate" distance was not clear and depended on the superior.[24]

It will be obvious that not even high salaries were a prophylactic against corruption in view of these spiraling demands and the prevailing attitudes. This was particularly true because it was not just *income* that was at stake but the building of a *fortune* in a relatively short period of time in order to allow one's descendants to live the life of gentlemen without having to work.[25] It is hard for us to imagine the high demands made by the intermediary groups of that time. From our point of view, the salaries cannot be considered low. That is, they were rather average by our standards for the lower civil servants; for the higher officials they were nominally almost as high as today's but, of course, much higher in purchasing power.[26] Samuel Pepys made £350 a year. It should be realized that an excellent cook earned £4 a year with room and board, or that a clever widow got by on £6 a year and was still able to give alms.[27] With an income of £350 a year Pepys' fortune increased annually by about £1,000.[28] The many figures he notes in his diary show, furthermore, that he was only one of the smaller officials. A high income in itself did not serve the purpose: there had to be some pressure for honesty, which increased at the same rate that the morals and opinions of the time increased in favor of corruption. Only a tyrant could provide order here.

The Forms of Corruption

This section establishes two broad categories of practices: (1) fraud or graft at the expense of the treasury and (2) extortion of the subjects. It is argued that once corruption is tolerated both forms must come into existence. . . .

The Instability of the System of Corruption

This section tries to ascertain how the profits of corruption were divided: (a) between the colleagues of oligarchical bodies and (b) within the official hierarchy. The lack of precise standards led to frictions and generally unstable equilibria of corruptional systems. . . .

Notes

1. Of course, we do conceptualize "constitutions" as referring not only to written constitutions or to those that were framed by a deliberate act of legislation, as many adopted since 1789 have been. Administrative principles are of far more importance, particularly during the *ancien régime*, when they were never devel-

oped *ad hoc.* Numerous Asian and Latin American states today possess written constitutions that tolerate corruption no more than do our own constitutions. Yet corruption in these countries is systematized and goes back to superordinate, unwritten principles of administration. The author had the opportunity to observe the functioning of such a political system during his stay as university lecturer at Chulalongkorn University in Siam in 1950–1953.

2. For a discussion of the Inca state's economic system see particularly P. A. Means, *Ancient Civilizations of the Andes.* New York, 1931, chap, VIII, and Louis Baudin, *L'Empire socialiste des Inka.* Paris, 1928.

3. This tended to be the case in the Muslim states, which is partly explained by the fact that the emirs, the caliphs, and the dignitaries recruited from the upper social classes were Arabs, whereas the people had been conquered by force of arms and had then turned to Islam. However, the distinctions persisted, even though the conquerors, as the result of mingling with harem women of all nationalities, ceased to remain pure Arabs. At any rate, a close union between people and princes proved infeasible, so that the intermediary castes, originally also of Arab origin, were able to prevent the establishment of an absolute monarchy. They formed an intermediary group with a goal of its own, which to a large extent succeeded in making its offices hereditary but which also fell apart into cliques and parties whom the emir could use for his own purposes. Domestic politics were thus complex and difficult to keep track of. The emir let his governors and civil servants largely go their own ways, but when they had sucked themselves full, he pressed them like a sponge. To illustrate this we refer to a dialogue that took place between Emir Abdurrhaman II of Cordoba (822–852) and a high official, as noted in an Arab chronicle. Emir: 'je voudrais couper la tête de celui quil sais avoir une grosse fortune a notre détriment et qui n'en verse rien au tresor." Mohammed-ben-Said (turning pale since he felt that the reference was to himself): "Ma fortune, je l'ai acquise par l'économie!" The outcome was that Mohammed donated part or his fortune to the emir, thus saving his own life. For this interesting dialogue see Louis Bertrand, *Histoire d'Espagne,* Paris, 1932, p. 82. These were the prevailing conditions in the entire area from Morocco to Yemen, which can be learned of Dimacqui's vade mecum for merchants as well. See G. H. Bousquet, "L'économie politique non européano-chretienne: L'exemple de Dimachqui," *Revue d'histoire economique et sociale,* 1957, p. 15.

4. One may speak of feudalism as a horizontal decomposition of the state, which disintegrates into a number of quasi-independent territories. Corruption, on the other hand, leads to a vertical decomposition of the civil service, which was created precisely to centralize state powers. The colonial policy of Charles V of Spain provides a good example. Shortly after the Conquest the *conquistadores* tended to develop into a powerful landed caste, which to a large extent threatened to isolate the native population from the monarch. Charles now endeavored, with more energy than caution, to inhibit the distribution of these estates, the so-called *encomiendas.* This led to the uprising of the Pizarro brothers in Peru in 1544, and the attempt to dissolve the *encomiendas* failed. However, the still undistributed parts of the country now came under the supervision of civil servants the *corregidores.* Soon the emperor realized that he did not have command over the colonies by these means either, since the *corregidores* intercepted the natives' tributes without penalty and blackmailed them in every possible way. To put an end to the thievery from the treasury Charles at last sent royal treasury officials to the colonies in 1550, but they converted themselves as well into quasi-owners of their offices. Thus Charles had to recognize that even with the help of civil

servants he was unable to maintain tight control over the colonies. Under Philip II the aggressive policy toward the *encomiendas* ceased altogether. See Silvio Zavala, *La encomienda indiana.* Madrid, 1935, pp. 54, 63. 173, and L. Simpson, *The Economienda in New Spain, 1492–1550.* Berkeley, 1929, p. 112.

5. Act XII of the Declaration on Human and Citizen Rights of the French Revolution says: cette force [publique] est donc instituée pour l'avantage de tous et non pour l'utilité particuliere de ceux a qui elle est confiée."

6. Gustav Schmoller, *Deutsches Städtleben in der älteren Zeit,* Bonn and Leipzig, 1922.

7. Gustav Schmoller, p.232. See also his *Umrisse und Untersuchungen zur Verfassungs-, Verwaltungs-, und Wirtschaftsgeschichte,* Leipzig, 1898, p. 250.

8. See P.J. Blok, *Geschichte der Niederlande (Ubers.).* Gotha, 1910, VI, p. 387.

9. See William Cunningham, *The Growth of English Industry and Commerce,* II, 5th ed. Cambridge, 1912, p.19.

10. This was brilliantly done by Leonard Woolf in his not-well-enough-known study, *After the Deluge.* London: Pelican, 1937.

11. Gustav Schmoller, *Deutsches Städtleben,* p.232; Derselbe, *Umrisse und Untersuchungen,* pp.250, 308.

12. Gustav Schmoller, *Deutsches Städtleben,* p.232.

13. Likewise, the "honest" administration in Bavaria was only installed after the French successes. Sec Hans Schmelze, *Der Staatshaushalt des Herzzogtums Bayerns In 18, Jahrhundert,* Stuttgart, 1900, p. 186. Schmelze tends to attribute the corruption that was widespread before this time to the nonexistence of an established salary and pension system. But this point of view is a naive one. High salaries and pensions are in themselves insufficient for the establishment of an honest administration, as shall be shown below. Likewise, Lawrence Stone, who generally has a good understanding for phenomena of corruption does not comprehend this decisive point when he writes about the government of Queen Elizabeth: "Lacking the financial resources or the educational media to produce an honest and efficient bureaucracy." See Lawrence Stone, *Sir Horatio Palavicino.* Oxford, 1956, p. XV. Precisely the higher civil servants, who generally derived the biggest advantages from corruption, normally received pensions the size of which was determined by the king on the basis of varying considerations. Thus Edmond-Jean Francois Barbier, *Chronique de la Regence,* II. Paris, 1857, p. 16, with respect to such a case: " . . . on retranche a cent pauvres familles des rentes viagères . . . ; on donne . . . de pension à gens qui ont été dans grands postes, dans lesquelles ils ont amassés des biens considérables, toujours au depens du peuple. . . . "

14. See I . T. Brugmans, *Sociaal-economische Geschiedenis von Nederland, 1795–1940.* The Hague, 1961, p.16.

15. Details maybe found in the study by the veteran director of the archives of the Dutch East India Company in Batavia. F. de Haan, *Priangan,* 4 vols. Batavia, 1910–1912, particularly vol. I, p.461. See also J. van Klaveren, *The Dutch Colonial System in the East Indies.* The Hague, 1953, chaps. X, XI, XII. In Europe the conversion to "honest" administration cannot be precisely identified; but in the colonies corruption occurred quite openly precisely for the reason that it occurred at the cost of foreign people who had been conquered for exploitation. Hence the conversion was most obvious here. More details and also a summary may be found in my forthcoming textbook *General Economic History 200–1760,* esp. in chap. 25.

16. Wilhelm Roscher, *Naturgeschichte der Monarchie, Aristokratie, Demokratie,*

Munich, 1933 (1892), p.147, describes the aristocracy as "the most self-serving of all three forms of government." It is striking that this important economist never examined the effects the forms of government have on the distribution of income. The above quotation, however, shows a latent understanding for the relationship. In my view the physiocrats' preference for absolute monarchy can only be explained because they realized the tendency of the intermediary strata to encourage corruption. This fact is generally known, although not yet explained. Sismondi comes close to an explanation when be writes: "Ils révéloient les abus effroyables sous lesquelles le peuple était écrasé; mais en général, plus ennemis des corps privilegiés que de l'autorité royale, ils sembloient, par leurs principes, favoriser le despotisme." See H.C.L. Simonde de Sismondi, *Histoire des Français,* XXVIII. Paris, 1821, 1844, p. 483.

17. We quote this passage at some length because it is so characteristic of the spirit of the *ancien régime:* "My Lady Caithness is harassed in a most barbarous and inhumane way by a set of low-lifed creatures she has had the misfortune to have dealings with. Upon Saturday last her Ladyship's furniture was all sequestrated and carried away by one Pett an upholsterer, for a debt due him." The letter has been published by Leonard Woolf, *After the Deluge,* p. 75.

18. See P. J. Blok, VI, pp. 199, 203 ff.

19. See John Evelyn, *Diary II,* p.47. Evelyn's opinions were clearly revealed in the following incident. As he was returning from Italy through Switzerland to the North with a number of gentlemen, a dog belonging to one of his companions killed a goat. When the poor shepherd asked for compensation, he was refused out of hand as being ridiculous. However, at the next village the company was stopped and forced to compensate for the loss and to pay a small fine as well, Evelyn called this "an affront" and complained about the "ill-treatment we had received for killing a wretched goat." See John Evelyn. *Diary I,* pp.231, 233 f. It should be pointed out here that Evelyn had an honest, humane, and even noble character.

20. Samuel Pepys came from a family of estate managers in Cambridgeshire. After the Black Death these "villici" appeared as tenants (farmers). See Sir John Clapham, A *Concise Economic History of Britain.* Cambridge, 1951, p.115, 202. Pepys' father was a tailor in London.

21. See Samuel Pepys, *Diary I,* pp. 128, 132.

22. At the beginning of the seventeenth century the way of life of the Dutch patricians was not much different from that of the petty bourgeoisie. A hundred years later, however, they owned villas, saloons, and gardens in the style of Le Notre, and often married into the hereditary nobility, who receded in the background. See P. J. Blok, IV, p. 112 and VI, pp. 101, 199. For England we refer to the cases of the Duke of Marlborough and Lord Chancellor Somer, which we will discuss further below. Thus two contradictory developments are to be observed: on the one hand an increasing degree of corruption and on the other a significant growth of the educated bourgeoisie, the carriers of the Enlightenment, who insisted on an "honest" administration. This inevitably led to a shock-like confrontation which took place during the French period. The transition is difficult to recognize in England, where—from my point of view—it had already taken place prior to the French Revolution during the financial reforms of Pitt the Younger (1784). However, I am still trying to prove this assumption.

23. See Gustav Schmoller, *Deutsches Städtleben,* p.232.

24. Compare the careful manner in which Samuel Pepys imitated the gentlemen's habits and the satisfaction he got when he succeeded. History noted some transgression of the proper distance, particularly in the case of important persons. This

aroused both the envy of colleagues and the wrath of princes. The "colleagues" ruined Lord Chancellor Hyde, whose magnificent Dunkirk House supposedly caused him to make the prophetic statement: "This house will one day be my ruin." See Samuel Pepys, *Diary II,* p.233, notation of the editor. In France the splendid palace of the superintendent Nicholas Fouquet invoked the wrath of the young Louis XIV, which led to his own overthrow, although the skids were greased by Colbert.

25. We want to illustrate this with only a few examples. Thus Lawrence Stone, *Sir Horatio Palavicino,* Oxford, 1956, p.271, mentions that Palavicino had bought the estate Babraham from a Robert Taylor. He was a protégé of Lord Chancellor Burghley (also spelled Burleigh) and "had made a handsome fortune as teller in the Exchequer." John Evelyn. *Diary II,* p. 118, reports that in passing he once visited Viscount Hereford, who had fallen out of favor in Ipswich, and he says, "Whilst he was Secretary of State and Prime Minister he had gotten vastly. but spent as hastily, even before he had established a fund to maintain his greatness." Of Will Hewer, Samuel Pepys' friend and dependent, John Evelyn, p. 323, reports: " . . . Mr. Hewer, who got a considerable estate in the Navy. . . . "

26. This is a widespread phenomenon. See Wilhelm Roscher, *Naturgeschichte der Monarchie, Aristokratie, Demokratie,* new ed. Munich, 1933 (1892), p. 311.

27. For these figures see Samuel Pepys, *Diary I,* p.352, and John Evelyn, *Diary II,* p.244, From this it appears that the civil servants' salaries were so high that large amounts could be saved for old-age pensions. Naturally, Pepys did not have to live like a cook. Note, however, that households with an income of £50 or an estate of £600 were classified as "substantial households" according to a census taken in London in 1695. See Roger Mols S.J., *Introduction à la Démographie historique des villes d'Europe du XIVe au XVIIIe siècle,* II. Louvain, 1954–1956, p. 94. However, Pepys was able to make the £600 necessary for a comfortable existence in less than a year because his fortune increased by £1000 annually. We must remember that Pepys, who did not belong to high society, did not have high expenses. Nevertheless, he spent more than his salary, that is, more than £350 per year. Even though the salaries were sufficient to build up considerable reserves while living quite well, the high officials often received lifetime salaries. Thus Admiral Lord Sandwich received £4000 a year for his entire life. Corruption, however, was flourishing among the highest classes. Thus it is clear that high salaries and pensions in themselves are not sufficient to inhibit corruption.

28. John Evelyn's remark in 1703 shows how differently corruption was looked upon then: "This day died Mr. Samuel Pepys, a very worthy, industrious and curious person, none in England exceeding him in knowledge of the navy, in which he had passed through all the most considerable offices . . . all of which he performed with great integrity." See John Evelyn, *Diary II,* p. .371 f. Of course, it must he considered that Pepys insisted on delivery of good quality and correct amounts by the suppliers Though he certainly cheated the Treasury by way of padded accounts, This can be discovered from his own notes as well. He deprecated other officers of the Navy Board who collaborated in the supply of bad materials to the shipyards. John Evelyn, *Diary II,* pp. 152, 167, writes of Sir Stephen Fox, a paymaster general in time of war, who was allowed to keep "a moderate allowance" of the soldiers' pay thanks to the prompt payment " . . . an able and honest man" and describes his fortune of £200,000 as "honestly got"!

6

The Sale of Public Offices

Koenraad W. Swart

Sale of offices was a phenomenon which was common to many countries in Europe, Asia, America and Africa, but which was not prevalent everywhere in the same forms or to an equal degree. Sometimes offices were sold for only a few years, in other cases for lifetime, or even as inheritable property. Offices could be sold by the governments, as in despotic countries, by ministers or other prominent people, as in the English departments, or by the officials themselves, as in the English army. Offices were also sold both by the government and the officials, as was the case in France. In most countries sale of offices was a more or less official institution, but there was a considerable difference between countries, such as France, England and Spain, in which the buyer of an office acquired a piece of property almost as secure as real estate, and states, such as China and the Ottoman Empire, in which every official could be deprived of his office by a caprice of the prince. The legal aspect of sale of offices was most pronounced in France where offices were regarded as immovable property.

In France, sale of offices also penetrated in more departments of government than anywhere else: in Spain, for example, the system was not followed with regard to the more important posts of government; in the Curia Romana, where the highest positions were sold, the total number of offices was small compared with that in France; in China the status of the mandarins bore much similarity to that of the French officials, but offices were normally acquired

Source: Koenraad Walter Swart, *Sale of Offices in the Seventeenth Century*. The Hague: Martinus Nijhoff, 1949, pp.112–27. By permission of the author and the publisher.

here by passing competitive examinations, and only in exceptional cases could be bought.

The similarities between sale of offices in the various countries are as important as the differences. The origin of the institution everywhere dated back to the Middle Ages if not to earlier periods. The peak was generally reached in the seventeenth or eighteenth century. It was in all countries abolished when modern political institutions became powerful. This historical phenomenon, occurring on a world-wide scale, had everywhere similar causes and similar effects. This will be evident when this institution is examined in its political, social and economic setting.

The most widespread of all factors contributing to sale of offices was the practice of remunerating officials by means of fees, or other payments made by the population. Until recently it was very common for officials to receive no salary, or only a small one. Instead, the judicial official demanded fees, the financial agent imposed taxes, and the military commanders held the population for ransom. The size of the income of the official, therefore, largely depended on his rapacity and ingenuity. He was financially almost independent from the central government.

The system of remunerating officials by means of fees is very irrational. All the proceeds from the offices should be accounted for by the official, and sent to the central government, which pays the official according to the importance of the duties he performs. The system, however, had great advantages in a society in which it was difficult to check on local officials because of a widespread dishonesty, relatively large distances, and a primitive administrative technique. In this way much accounting and transferring of money was avoided, and the official was interested in the execution of his duties.

It is obvious how this system easily changed into farming, or selling offices. If the fees increased, the remuneration of the official would become so large that it was fair that he should pay a part of it to the government or to the person who had nominated him. The only prerequisite was a certain degree of economic prosperity. Offices could not be sold unless people existed who were willing and able to buy them. If trade and commerce flourished, the fees from the offices would increase and this would in its turn, influence the degree of eagerness of the place-hunting. Moreover, people would not be able to pay sizeable sums for offices if a considerable degree of capital forming had not taken place. In societies with a primitive economy, therefore, sale of offices did not develop.

The same conditions were the basis for the system of farming out taxes, which was followed in so many countries in the past centuries. It is not a mere coincidence that in countries in which sale of offices was general, such as France, Spain, Turkey and China, farming of taxes was also a firmly established practice.[1]

In some states, notably in the Ottoman Empire, remuneration of officials by means of fees was the main cause of the sale or farming of offices. In these countries, however, an element was lacking which largely contributed to the development of sale of offices elsewhere, i.e., the conception of public office as private property. Offices could only be considered as freeholds if the official had a more or less permanent status and was independent in a political as well as in a financial respect.

The conception of public office as private property is typical of rather primitive societies,[2] and generally does not develop in bureaucracies, in which the officials are usually dependent on their superiors. However, [in] the societies in which the possibilities of control were limited and aristocratic forces powerful, the officials often succeeded in extending their rights. It was common for officials, who were originally instituted as dependable agents, soon to become appointed for life, and almost independent of the prince. This trend went farthest in the feudal system in which officials developed into sovereigns, but a certain feudal character was inherent in many offices, secular as well as ecclesiastical, which were created by the princes in the later centuries of the Middle Ages. The aristocratic society of this age did not yet draw the distinction between public office and private property as sharply as today.

The officials of a bureaucracy ruled by aristocratic principles were often no longer appointed by the prince. Sometimes the officials themselves had the right to nominate their successors, or their offices had become entirely hereditary. In other cases courtiers or high noblemen had a decisive voice in granting offices, or the patronage of offices belonged to ministers or superiors in office.

Offices of this kind were sought because they brought prestige and honor or because they were very lucrative. True ability was not required for the execution of these offices and the nomination was made according to criteria which had little to do with the merit of the candidates. These offices were often held by deputies and could, therefore, easily be cumulated. These types of officials were not always held responsible for the performance of their duties. Many of them looked upon public service as a commercial enterprise and shamelessly extorted the population.

The freehold conception of public office developed in a combination of bureaucratic and aristocratic forms of government, which was typical of the Western European kingdoms during the later Middle Ages. The civil services of France and Spain, which were organized during a period in which the feudal forces were still powerful, showed all the characteristics of an aristocratic bureaucracy; in England this type of official lingered on well into the nineteenth century. These conditions also existed, to a certain extent, in China, at the moment when the feudal society was replaced by a state governed by officials (300–200 B.C.) and in the Curia Romana at the beginning of the fifteenth century.[3]

If offices are considered as private property, it is natural for them to be sold, but under the rule of aristocracies sale of offices often occurred to only a limited extent, because the number of offices was small and many other forms of jobbery were preferred. The aristocratic bureaucracies, however, in developing the freehold conception of public office, paved the way to the systematic sale of offices by absolute princes.

We have seen how the rise of absolutism was often connected with the introduction of sale of offices: in China sale of offices was embarked upon by the absolute princes of the Ch'in and Han dynasties; in Rome it became firmly established under the despotism of the later Roman Empire; in England it was introduced by the powerful kings of the twelfth century; and above all it flourished during the European absolutism of the sixteenth, seventeenth and eighteenth centuries.

On the other hand, the representatives of the people, the parliament, the Cortes, and the States-General, usually opposed this policy, and in the Dutch Republic and in England, where absolutism did not triumph, sale of offices was practiced on a much smaller scale.

Yet, as has already been argued, absolutism was in principle more opposed to than in favor of the medieval, or aristocratic conception of public office, on which sale of offices was based. Absolute rulers whose policy was more or less consistent, such as Philip II of Spain, Colbert, and King Frederick II, have, therefore, attempted to abolish sale of offices.

Absolute governments exploited an institution, which was in essence incompatible with their ideal of a reliable body of officials, only because of financial or political necessity. Lack of means to defray urgent expenses, especially those in connection with wars, was the main cause leading to sale of offices. In France, sale of offices was introduced during the wars in Italy, and was practiced on the largest scale during the wars of the seventeenth century. In Spain, sale of offices was embarked upon during a war against the Moors and was most frequently resorted to during the many wars against France. One war, that of the Spanish Succession, led to sale of offices in such different countries as France, Savoy, Prussia, Austria and the Dutch Republic. Also in China wars were one of the mainsprings of sale of offices.

The princes would have preferred to use methods less damaging for their authority, but the possibilities which the rulers of the seventeenth century had at their disposal were still very limited. Their greatest drawback was that unlike governments in modern times, they could not issue loans without assigning a special part of their income as security for the interest. The Dutch Republic was probably the only state of the seventeenth century in which public debts in their modern form were already common.[4] In other countries sale of offices was one of the expedients which had to fill this need. The difference was in many cases nominal rather than actual, because the offices had often an entirely honorary character; but people who were not willing to subscribe to loans, were sometimes very eager to buy an office.

In introducing sale of offices as a systematic policy, princes were also motivated by political considerations. Sale of offices put an end to favoritism and intrigue inherent in oligarchies; in fifteenth century Spain, for example, sale of offices was used to restrict the corrupt power of the urban aristocracies and in France, the *Paulette* was said to have been introduced in order to prevent political appointments by the nobility.[5]

The middle classes often supported the royal policy, because they looked askance at the aristocracy granting all offices, and they obtained a fairer share of the spoils of office under the new system. Moreover, offices could never be sold on a large scale without the existence of a rich class who was willing to buy them. In many cases, notably in city governments, the initiative to introduce sale of offices came from this part of the population. They introduced the system into the French, Flemish and Zeeland cities during the Middle Ages, and into Hamburg in 1684. It was the same part of the people who pressed for public sale of offices in the towns of Holland in 1747 and 1748.

Many factors were influential in bringing about systematic sale of offices: a bureaucracy ruled by aristocratic principles, remuneration by means of fees, a flourishing of trade and commerce, a powerful middle class, an absolutist government which had no other means of meeting its financial emergencies than that of resorting to desperate expedients. These circumstances did not exist to the same degree in all countries which I have discussed; in Germany, the middle classes were not powerful and the economic life was only slightly developed; in Spain, the government was not entirely centralized and the economic life was not very prosperous; in the Dutch Republic and in England, the social and economic conditions were favorable to the development of sale of offices, but in these countries absolutism was thwarted and no large bureaucracies existed; in the Ottoman Empire, and to a less extent also in China, the aristocratic principle was not represented.

Only in France were all the factors which furthered sale of offices strongly developed. There existed no other European state of the size of France in which absolutism was so firmly established; on the other hand, as early as the fifteenth century French officials were much less dependent upon the king than elsewhere, even than in an aristocratic country like England.[6] The economic life of France was one of the most prosperous of Europe and the French middle class was rich and numerous. Finally, as a result of the many wars in which France was involved, its financial system was entirely disrupted and all types of financial expedients had to be used. It is, therefore, no wonder that in France sale of offices reached a greater extent than anywhere else.

Whereas sale of offices has come into being under the influence of certain political, social and economic factors, it has, in its turn, also influenced the political, social and economic development. This influence was naturally much greater in countries in which sale of offices prevailed to a large extent (France, the United States and China) than in states in which the habit was more sporadically indulged in (England and the Dutch Republic). The effects of sale of offices have always been the subject of much speculation by contemporaries. Publicists who condemned sale of offices held it responsible for all sorts of evils, whereas defenders tried to discover wholesome consequences. The passionate point of view of both groups was generally a hindrance to a correct analysis of the question.

One of the most important consequences was hardly noticed by these publicists. This was the weakening of the same royal power which had so greatly contributed to the development of sale of offices. If the king sold offices, he could no longer choose his servants according to their capacities or reliability. In France, for instance, people whose only contact with the university had consisted in the buying of a degree, became judges at a very young age. We have seen that in other countries the inability of many officials also was notorious; in many countries these officials could not be discharged. In introducing sale of offices the princes had called into existence a power which they could not check on.[7] Princes who wanted to retain control of their administration were forced to institute new officials. The French kings created the offices of intendants, officials who had not bought their offices and to whom most of the administrative functions of the *parlements, bureaux de finances,* and *baillis* were gradually transferred.[8] Similar dependent agents were appointed by the kings of Spain and Prussia in the eighteenth century.

The strengthening of the independence of the officials has sometimes been considered as a wholesome consequence of sale of offices. It has been pointed out, for example, that in France the judiciary of the *ancien régime* could not easily be influenced by politicians and that the country enjoyed a considerable degree of self-government.[9] The independence of the officials found also expression in the opposition of the *parlements* against many measures of the government.[10] It should not be forgotten, however, that the many small potentates seldom used their power for the public good. On the whole the officials were conservative and opposed to any reform of abuses which could interfere with their privileges. They were also afraid that by showing too much disobedience to the royal power they would forfeit the valuable property invested in their offices. Sale of offices fostered the revolutionary spirit outside, but not inside the body of officials.

The bureaucratic abuses resulting from sale of offices were numerous; the number of offices multiplied without any relation to the increased task of the government; many of these offices were sinecures, *offices imaginaires;* other offices were held by deputies; some people cumulated many offices; the administration of justice was slow, as the officials could in this way exact more fees. One should beware, however, of attributing all these evils merely to sale of offices. It should not be forgotten that the aristocratic bureaucracies had already suffered under the same sorts of abuses before the systematic sale of offices by the princes had started.

The relationship between political corruption and sale of offices is likewise more subtle than often assumed. Sale of offices is an aspect of corruption as long as it is not officially regulated and not all the proceeds flow into the treasury of the prince or the state, but this jobbery came to an end when sale of offices had become a legal institution. Sale of offices was defended by writers like Barclay and Montesquieu for the very reason that it had eliminated the favoritism and intrigue of courtiers and ministers.[12] Even a radical thinker like Jeremy Bentham defended his proposal for the introduction of sale of offices by this argument.[13]

Whereas public sale of offices eliminated corrupt practices as far as they concerned the *appointment* to office, the same cannot be said with regard to the *execution* of offices which had been bought. It has always been argued that people who had bought public authority would feel themselves entitled to sell it.[14] This generalization, however, is not true for all officials. There were many who had bought their offices because they wanted to enrich themselves. People who had inherited offices were likewise not much tempted to exploit their offices. The standards of the French judiciary compare favorably with those of England and Spain, although in the latter countries the judgeships never became freeholds. The most notorious case of bribery in France was committed by a judge who was member of the reformed Parliament of Maupeou (1771–1774) and who had not bought his office.[15] It was a different matter if officials regarded the purchase of an office purely as a commercial enterprise. Extortion, bribery and peculation were the usual characteristics of their administrations.

Sale of offices also introduced some useful innovations into the bureaucracies. Elderly officials who were allowed to sell their offices obtained in this way a sort of old-age pension. The purchase price paid by financial officials fulfilled at the same time the function of security for the finances under their control.

The effect of sale of offices on the financial system of a country can be compared either with that of farming taxes or with that of issuing of loans. Sale of offices was similar to farming of taxes if the offices were sold, or rather farmed, for a short period. This method might have been financially profitable to the government, although it generally increased the tax burden.[16] Sale of offices resembled issuing of loans in its result if the officials were entitled to transfer the offices to third persons or if the offices were entirely hereditary. In this case, the financial problems of the present were solved at the expense of future generations. Sale of offices, as part of an irresponsible financial policy, often contributed to the disruption of the financial system of a country.

The effect of sale of offices on the social structure of a country has not always been the same. Shortly after its introduction, sale of offices opened the public service to classes which had been excluded under the rule of oligarchies, and furthered the social mobility. This was the case in France in the sixteenth and seventeenth centuries, when by means of purchase of offices the *bourgeoisie* replaced the nobility in the government of the state. The farming out of offices in the Mohammedan countries had a similar consequence. This effect disappeared, however, when sale of offices developed into heritability of offices and new offices were no longer sold. In the eighteenth century the *noblesse de robe* in France was as closed to newcomers as any other oligarchy.[17] Moreover, sale of offices has an undemocratic feature of its own, because it confines office holding to people of means. The purchase system in the English army was advocated for the very reason that in this way the aristocratic selection of officers was guaranteed. By excluding many capable people from public office, sale of offices called into being a group of discontented intellectuals who sometimes, as in France and China, played an important part in revolutionary movements.

The economic development was also affected by sale of offices. In China, where grain was the medium of exchange, it was argued that sale of offices would promote agriculture, because people would be eager to possess grain with which they could acquire public office.[18] A similar opinion was held by Montesquieu, who maintained that sale of offices would stimulate the economic activity as the possession of money opened the road to honorable positions.[19] Actually, the influence was rather the reverse. Sale of offices stirred up the place-hunting and caused a decrease of interest in commerce and industry. In France a great part of the capital that might have been invested in branches of industry was used for buying offices and the government used the funds which it received in this way not for promoting the economic development, but for waging wars. On the other hand, groups which were excluded from holding office, such as the Protestants in France in the seventeenth century, and Jews in general, have often advanced the economic life of a country.

The conclusion from the examination of the causes and effects of sale of offices is that this institution is a product of still primitive forms of administration as long as it occurs in an undeveloped form, but is a mark of decay when it is exploited by absolute, irresponsible governments because of fiscal motives. In this latter form it is a typical characteristic of politically declining societies, such as the Byzantine Empire, the Caliphate of the tenth century, the *anciens régimes* in France and Spain, and China in the nineteenth century. Systematic sale of offices deprived the government of an efficient and reliable body of officials, strengthened the oligarchic tendencies, created a discontented *élite* and disrupted the financial system. The consequence was that the political instability of the country was increased and the outbreak of revolutions furthered.

Only few publicists who discussed sale of offices defended this institution. Among them were some statesmen, such as Richelieu, wanting to justify the course of their policy, and a few financial projectors hoping to profit by the introduction of this system. Other people who upheld sale of offices were distinguished officials, like Montesquieu and Wellington, who pleaded more or less their own cause.[20] Finally, there were critics of the aristocratic society, like Jeremy Bentham, who hoped that the introduction of sale of offices would have a wholesome influence on a political system in which the patronage of offices belonged to an oligarchy.[21]

The great majority of writers were opposed to sale of offices. They can also be divided into different groups. First, the nobility and their spokesmen, who argued that "merit," *i.e.,* gentle birth, and not money, should be the decisive factor in appointments. This opinion was voiced in France by Le Vassor, Boulainvilliers, Fénelon and Saint-Simon,[22] in Spain by Davila and Bovadilla. Most publicists who condemned sale of offices were jurists or literates: out of the numerous writers I mention only Bodin, Pasquier and Voltaire in France,[23] Francisco de Vitoria, Las Casas and Martinez de Mata in Spain, Edward Coke, Sir Walter Raleigh and Sir Matthew Hale in England, Botero in Italy,[24] Erasmus, Hugo Grotius and Jacob van Heemskerck in the Netherlands,[25] Breckling, Moser and Justi in Germany,[26] Kochi Bey in the Ottoman Empire[27] and Wang Ghi in China. Their opinions were inspired partly by resentment against an institution which had excluded many of them from public office, partly by the conviction that sale of offices was nefarious for the State.

Another category, which had many ties with the preceding one, consisted of dissatisfied officials. They especially denounced a certain aspect of the institution, namely, the sale of new offices by the king, because this measure lessened the proceeds from the existing offices. The representative assemblies were opposed to sale of offices largely because of this consideration, although they sometimes expressed the grievances of lower classes, who suffered more than any other group under the increasing number of officials.[28] A last group of opponents of sale of offices were the princes themselves. Edward VI of England, Philip II of Spain and Frederick II of Prussia are the best known of the monarchs who condemned the institution since it was at variance with their ideal of a reliable body of officials.

This verdict of the overwhelming majority of writers against sale of offices did not achieve any result until the most important factors which had caused sale of offices ceased to exist in the eighteenth and nineteenth centuries. As early as the beginning of the eighteenth century, governments which were in urgent need of money no longer resorted to such expedients as sale of offices, but issued loans. At the same time, the system of remuneration of officials by means of fees fell into disuse as a result of the prevalence of more rational administrative habits. Finally, in the nineteenth century, when the more democratic form of government limited the influence of the aristocracy, and the modern idea of the State came into existence, the conception of public office as private property disappeared. The State became considered as a moral entity and the exercising of public authority as a duty. The official of the *ancien régime,* the *officier,* was replaced by his modern colleague, the *fonctionnaire.* One of the outstanding representatives of the philosophy of this new conception of the state, Hegel, called the sale of government rights the most barbarous trait of a people who constitute a state.[29]

The actual abolishment of sale of offices was the easiest in those states, like the Ottoman Empire where the institution was mainly based on the remuneration of officials by means of fees. In countries where the proprietary rights on offices were firmly established, the abolishment of sale of offices [was] complicated by the problem of the compensation of the proprietors. At the end of the eighteenth century the following objection was raised, for example, by Edmund Burke against a too hasty reform of the English bureau-cracy:

> These places, and others of the same kind which are held for life, have been considered as property. They have been given as a provision for children; they have been the subject of family settlements; they have been the security of creditors. . . . If the discretion of power is once let loose upon property, we can be at no loss to determine whose power and what discretion it is that will prevail at last.[30]

The old system, therefore, often lingered on long after the mainspring of sale of offices had disappeared. In England it was not until the end of the nineteenth century that the *ancien régime* was liquidated. In most countries sale of offices came to an end only after the outbreak of a revolution. It was the French Revolution which abolished sale of offices in France and gave a great impetus to the reform movements of most continental European states (for example, the Netherlands, Savoy, Naples, Rome the Palatinate, Bavaria and Hamburg). Sale of offices in some Oriental states, such as Persia and China, was likewise abolished as a result of revolutionary movements.

Important factors which caused sale of offices in the past have ceased to exist. On the other hand, there are today conditions, unknown to older societ-ies, which may lead to a revival of this institution. The increased power of the State has placed into the hands of officials greater possibilities for abusing the public authority for their own profit than ever before. Naturally the eager-ness to hold these offices is great so that many people may be willing to pay for them. Even more important is the increase in power of political parties which are influential in conferring offices in many states. Their position is comparable with that of ancient oligarchies. Sale of offices, if occurring in modern society, would no longer be carried on for the benefit of the State, which has other means of obtaining funds at its disposal, but for that of political parties. In this form it was practiced until recently in the United States, where candidates for office often had to pay sizeable "assessments" either to the party treasury or to bosses.[31] On the whole, however, no systematic and legal sale of offices has developed in the modern state. In this respect our society, in which many other forms of political corruption are prevalent, compares favorably with those of the past.

Notes

1. W. Lotz, *Studien uber Steuerverpachtung. Sitzungsberichte der Bayerischen Akademie der Wissenschaften*, Phil.-hist. Abt. 1935, 4; W. Lotz, "Revenue Farming," *Encyclopaedia of the Social Sciences*, XIII (1934), 359; K. Brauer, "Steuerverpachtung, Steuersubmission," *Handwörterbuch der Staatswissenschaften*, 4th ed. VII, 1126; P. Roux, *Les fermes d'impôts sous l'ancien régime* (Paris, 1916); H. Sieveking, *Genueser Finanzwesen. Volkswirtschaftliche Abhandlungen der Badischen Hochschule*, vol.1, no.3 (1898), 41.
2. R.H. Lowie, *Primitive Society* (London, 1921), 230–231, 263–265, 310–313.
3. Göller, "Hadrian VI und der Aemterkauf an der päpstlichen kurie," *Vorreformationsgeschichtliche Forschungen*. Suppl. bd., Munster, 1925, 376.
4. W. Lotz, "Staatsschulden," *Handwörterbuch der Staatswissenschaften*, 4th ed. (1926), 824–825; E. Baasch, *Holländische Wirtschaftgeschichte* (Jena, 1927), 188 ff.
5. Richelieu and the Marquis of Fontenay-Mareuil, cited by Ch. Normand, *La bourgeoisie française au XVIIe Siècle*, 34–35.
6. Cf. E.F. Churchill, "The Crown and Its Servants," *Law Quarterly Journal*, XLII (1926).
7. Emperior Anastasius made the Empire into a kind of aristocracy by selling all offices, according to Suidas, *Lexicon*, ed. by A. Adler (Lipsiae, 1928), s.v. "Anastasius."
8. Godard, *Les pouvoirs des intendants* (Paris, 1902), 439–41.
9. Homais, *De la venalité des offices sous l'ancien regime* (Paris, 1903), 174–75; G. Page's, "La venalité des offices sous l'ancien regime," *Revue historique*, CLXIX (1932), 493.
10. Ch. Normand, 266–69; Göhring, *Die Aemterkauflichkeit im Ancien Regime* (Berlin, 1938), 88, 290, 306–9; Homais, 47, 125.
11. Loyseau, *Cinq livres du droit des offices*, III, chap. I, no. 101; Ch. Normand, 17–18.
12. J. Barclay, *Icon animarum* (Francofurti, 1668), chap. 3; Montesquieu, *Esprit des lois*, V, 19 (Paris, n.d.) 61–63; Montesquieu, *Cahiers (1716–1755)*, B. Grasset, ed. (Paris, 1941), 120–121.
13. *The Rationale of Reward*, II, chap. IX. Works ed. Bowring, II, 246–48.
14. Seneca, *De Beneficiis*, I, 9, Ed. by J.W. Basore in the Loeb Classical Library, CCCX (London, 1935), 30; *cf.* J. Bentham, and *Constitutional Code*, Works, IX, 31–32, 286 ff.

106   Political Corruption

15. H. Carré', *Le règne de Louis XV (1715–1774) (Histoire de France* . . . E. Lavisse, ed., VIII²) (Paris, 1909), 416–17.
16. Cf. places referred to in note 1.
17. Normand, 132; M. Kolabinska, *La circulation des élites en France* . . . (Lausanne, 1912), 95,104–105, 109–10; P. Boiteau, *Etat de France en 1789* (Paris, 1861), 328.
18. J.J.L. Duyvendak, trans., *The Book of Lord Shang* (London, 1928), 64–65, 236, 253, 304; L. Wieges, *Rudiments: Textes historiques* (Paris, 1905), 421–24.
19. *Esprit des lois,* V, 19.
20. Montesquieu, *Esprit des lois,* V, 19; *Report from Select Committee on Army and Navy Appointments 1833,* 273–74.
21. Among the many works by Bentham concerning his plans of pecuniary competition see especially: *Draught of a Code for the Organization of the Judicial Establishment in France, March 1790. Works* IV, 285ff., 354; *The Rationale of Reward,* first published in French in 1810. *Works* V, 246–48; *Constitutional Code,* Book II, chap. IX, section 16, 17, chap. X, section 10, art. 63, *Works* IX, 271 ff., 380–81; cf. Also *Works* V, 278ff., 302ff., 363 ff., IX 31–32; about similar plans by J. Sinclair, see his work *The History of the Public Revenue of the British Empire* (London, 1790), III, 219, 229.
22. Cf. Göhring, 299–304.
23. Cf. Göhring, 69–73, 80–81; Homais, 168–77; ante.
24. G. Botero, *Della ragione di stato libri deici con tre libri delle cause della grandezza e magnificenza delle citta'* (Venezia, 1589), libro I, cap. 16.
25. Erasmus Encomium morias, L.V.P. de Holhac and M. Rat, eds. (Paris, 1936), 142–43; H. Grotius, *Parallelon rerum publicarum, liber tertius; De moribus ingenioque populorum Atheniensium, Romanorum Batavorum* (Haarlem, 1801–1803), II, 8, 9, Johan van Heemskerck, *Batavische Arcadia,* 4th ed. (Amsterdam, 1663), 485.
26. J.H.G. van Justi, *System des Finanzwesens* . . . (Halle, 1766), 528.
27. E. Tyan, *Histoire de l'organisation judiciaire en pays d'Islam* (Paris, 1938), 429–30, 450–51.
28. Cf. Göhring, 61 ff.; Marion, *Dictionnaire des institutions de la France* (Paris, 1925) s.v., "Venalité."
29. G.W.F. Hegel. *Die Verfassung des Deutschen Reichs. Eme politische Flugschrift.* 1801/1802. G. Mollat, ed. (Stuttgart, 1935), 35.
30. *Works,* II, 101, cited by Holdsworth, *History of English Law,* X, 504.
31. M. Ostrogorski, *Democracy and the Organization of Political Parties* (London, 1902), II, 148, 157, 343–45, 352.

7

Early Modern Corruption in English and French Fields of Vision[1]

Maryvonne Génaux

Historians and social scientists have sought to discern the parameters of corruption in the early modern period, arguing that some standards of public behavior existed.[2] Jean-Claude Waquet has highlighted the existence of administrative legal norms in late Medicean Tuscany. According to Jeffrey Sawyer, the French Estates General in Paris (1614–1615) complained about abuses and sought extensive reforms in the administration of justice. Robert Harding and Linda Levy Peck have clearly shown that English and French grandees spoke of corruption when favorites—i.e., brokers that did not belong to well-established families—used gift, patronage and venality to build factions through the diversion of royal grants. In this volume Koenraad Swart explains that a vast majority of early modern European writers held the sale of offices to be "responsible for all sorts of evils."[3]

Despite this evidence of the perception of corrupt practices, historians argue that early modern definitions of corruption differed from ours. British and French aristocrats did not think that gift, patronage, and venality were inherently corrupt. They might complain that favoritism filled the state machinery with second-rate men, but what they really objected to was the fact that "obscure" newcomers were taking over the practice of patronage thus threatening traditional clientele networks.

Closer examination of opinions in the early modern period reveals, however, what specialists of the modern period have also shown : the understanding of corruption varied from individual to individual. Moreover, efforts to define corruption in abstract terms pose specific problems for studies of Europe from the sixteenth to eighteenth century because the contemporary understanding of public service carried a multiplicity of meanings. The conceptions of public service varied widely among the major political actors and were often in conflict with each other at a moment when the state was taking shape. In addition, for the most part these competing definitions have vanished from our cultural horizons.

Prior to the end of the eighteenth century, the term "public" referred to the idea of community, but this community did not have the political weight that it holds today in western democracies. Either it held no political legitimacy at all or, according to the theory of the mediate devolution of power, it had received the authority to administer public goods[4] from God and transferred it to the prince. The prince was liable only to God, except when he applied his authority tyrannically. Under these conditions, the concept of "public service" did not directly reflect abstract ideals. Instead, it was articulated with reference to a number of variables: the prince's service, social harmony, the law, and divine vengeance. These four variables—which were ways of structuring society—can then be traced back to the main models of behavior that were proposed to French and English early modern administrators[5].

The prince's agents served the public good by preserving the kingdom's prosperity and enhancing the legitimacy of his power. In other words, the prince's interests took priority. From his viewpoint public service was inscribed in the personal logic of clientelism which also dominated in the medieval relationships of vassalage. Honor, fidelity and duty were bound up in moral obligations of reciprocity toward a patron who held a position of authority.

Humanists advocated another code of behavior which also had broad implications because it concerned all forms of civic commitment: that of the *vir bonus*, borrowed from the Roman republic and the Italian city-states of the Renaissance.[6] This model promoted an ideal of public virtue which was associated, in the language of "republican humanism," with that of liberty. It was based on a very Ciceronian sense of honor, fidelity or duty that was far more *social* than moral to the extent that these values were intended to ensure social cohesion.[7]

A new understanding of administrative service emerged, as well, after the Hundred Year's War. Jurists developed an organicist vision of public service for their colleagues, the king's servants. In this vision, which also resumed the Roman values, justice underpinned society and became the principle of all administrative activity. The just society was represented as a body with the king's agents acting to perpetuate it harmoniously.[8]

For jurists, honor, fidelity and duty were partially understood along the same lines as in the two previous examples. These terms continued to vehicle a *social* dimension to the extent they guaranteed the *solidarity* necessary to ensure collective survival. In addition, they continued to be expressed in feudal language which emphasized relationships of clientelism. But jurists insisted on the transcendence of their profession and on their *direct* link to divine justice.[9] In other words, they emphasized their independence with respect to men. The juridical understanding of fidelity, honor and duty was positioned at another level than that of common social values.

Paradoxically, the elaboration of a behavioral code *just* for the king's agents contributed to the *secularization* of understandings of the administrative function. The concern to recognize the prince's agents created a "fourth state," to borrow Montaigne's phrase[10], and valorized this state compared to the other three traditional orders of society whose functions were praying, fighting and nourishing. This evolution brought into question the theoretical validity of a social hierarchy that reflected God's will.

This tendency toward the secularization of public service developed in the second half of the seventeenth century as statecraft and historical sensibilities became more materially oriented[11]. The parameters of wise government became a way to read an entire society as well as its historical future. Law and politics increasingly imposed their logic in the definition of those virtues expected in public servants. Political and administrative activities were still judged with respect to the moral values of earlier systems, but also according to the more pragmatic considerations underlying the theory of the "reason of state"[12]. The rise of liberalism that reasoned in terms of rights—both those of the prince and those of his citizens—definitively inscribed law at the heart of modern thought.[13]

The weight of older frames of reference prevented, however, the emergence of an autonomous and universal deontology of public service over the course of the eighteenth century.[14] As the English case suggests, despite the progress of rational values, the secularization of public service did not necessarily imply its laicization. The ability of Protestantism to present itself as an earthly *ecclesia*, furthered the former while also limiting the latter. In England, "civil liberty" remained synonymous for a long period of time with "religious liberty": as a result, civic virtue was primarily understood as a necessary condition for salvation.

In France, laicization was also limited. In part this stemmed from the influence of English reasoning which appeared in France at the end of the seventeenth century with the writings of the Huguenots and in the eighteenth century thanks to the Anglomania common among the—often deist—philosophers of the Enlightenment. Above all, however, the English model was initially applied in France in a political context that made it difficult to envision an autonomous public service. This model was used in the conflicts between the *parlements* and the king (from the 1750s to the 1770s) and became associated with former values : the understanding of public service that each group used to advocate, that is the juridical organicist version or the king's quasi-domestic version.

The very reality of these many conceptions makes James Scott's underlying hypotheses no longer acceptable. The comparative study of the practices is not to be put into question, yet the concept as James Scott coined it, no longer can be used: "this convention [proto-corruption] will allow us to analyze the comparative causes and effects of similar behavior while recognizing that such earlier practices *did not contravene existing norms of official conduct* and thus cannot be considered corruption as we have chosen to use the term." [15]

Conversely, the behaviors condemned by the Old Regime perfectly fit in Joseph Nye's definition of corruption: "corruption is a behavior which deviates from the normal duties of a public role." [16] Yet, these behaviors varied depending on the diverse definitions of public service and they were expressed with different vocabularies.

The prince particularly dreaded that the oath of fidelity could be broken. The failure to acquit a personal commitment went through the lexicon of treason, which led to the use of the high treason notion (*crime de lèse-majesté*). The mistakes of the king's servants fell under the sway and the categories of penal law.

If the word "corruption" did not belong to this royal way of thinking, the organicist thinkers and the humanists knew and used it. In their discourses, "corruption" could refer to public agents' misbehaviors. [17]

Late Middle Age publicists' aim was to keep society riotless and preserve the body and unity of the kingdom. The desertion, the fault of any member of the body was synonymous with sickness and putrefaction. This kind of physical impairing was, according to Aristotelian physics, true "corruption."

In humanist circles the influence of Aristotelian physics led to the belief in the inevitable "corruption" of *sublunary* [earthly] objects because of their particular, finite and unstable character. The humanist definition of the *res publica* sought to counteract this evolution through an effort to achieve universality, understood as stability and liberty. The quest for universality initially involved associating individuals in this task in order to prevent their becoming corrupted through their own isolation, their own *particularity*. Then they had to submit their individual interests to those of the general good. "Corruption" represented any failure of these efforts, the victory of the particular over the universal; in other words, it represented the invasion of the public domain by private interests.

For the secularized thought of the eighteenth-century, resuming the language of civic humanism, the word "corruption" worked to point out the subjection of public authorities to private financial interest as well as the deregulation of the political machine. John Pocock has shown how, in England, a world, based on exchange, commerce and "neo-Harringtonian" thought, reaffirmed and redefined around the 1710s-1730s, the principals of classical republicanism in order to confront the "Whig commercial regime." This latter was depending on patronage, public debt and mutual dependence with a "monied interested" elite of stockholders and officeholders.[18] Keith Michael Baker has, more recently, pointed out how 1770s France was described as a corrupted society through this very language.[19]

Although this last definition of the concept and of the word "corruption" is familiar to us, it should not obscure the essential for those interested in exploring corruption in the Old Regime: corruption was expressed through a variety of different languages and vocabularies. Linda Levy Peck has argued along similar lines by showing that in early seventeenth-century England the languages of corruption drew on religious, judicial and curial traditions.[20] In her documents the word "corruption" does not indicate public agents' misbehaviors but social disorders. It contends that the language of civic humanism was not on its own responsible for making the concept of corruption shift. Linda Levy Peck consequently criticizes Pocock's periodization : in England the king's servants' abuses were denounced before the emergence of the language of civic humanism in the 1710s-1730s.

As a result, no established list of "corrupt" practices existed : the acts that some complained about were accepted by others and contemporaries could not draw on a fixed vocabulary of corruption. This article seeks to illustrate the diversity of these understandings of corruption. But in order to encompass the condemned practices and avoid confusion with the actual approach based on the Weberian bureaucratic rules, I will speak here of *early modern corruption*.

Drawing on an analysis of the historical meaning of words, this article is using French language dictionaries that appeared between the sixteenth and the eighteenth century[21] as well as English repertories.[22] While dictionaries present problems for lexicologists seeking to uncover linguistic realities, this type of source is an extremely useful source for the historian of representations. Although editors were unable to avoid the pressure to standardize articles and at times had to accept the intervention of their patrons, in general they remained far more in charge of the internal logic of their repertory than editors today. These dictionaries offer, as a result, the range of their opinions about the meaning and the significance of words.

Although dictionaries recognized multiple perspectives concerning public service, they principally conveyed the royal viewpoint. To this extent it is significant that this type of criminality was not conceived of as "corruption," since the word did not encompass a generic range of practices in this type of sources as it does today. Corruption carried weighty political implications : it was far too dangerous to apply it to the deviant behavior of those servants who served the king.

Consequently, this paper seeks to show that the choice of vocabulary used when speaking of *early modern corruption* represented a political stance. We go here beyond the lexicographical analysis. Joel Hurstfield clearly stated that the word "corruption" had "quite understandably, become the stock-in-trade of political controversy." Besides, "either by direct accusation or by innuendo, it is the easiest charge to make and the most difficult charge to refute."[23] It enables one to get rid of any political adversary. These uses of the word and the concept put corruption at the center of the political game. Indeed, under the Old Regime what was at stake in political issues was the state construction and the exercise of power. The study of the vocabulary, and through it, of the making of *early modern corruption* allows not only to "read a society"[24] but also to enter the debates about the rise of the modern state.

*   *   *

Between 1539 and 1788 three words in particular emerge in French and English lexicons to designate the variety of ways that the king's servants enriched themselves: "péculat/peculate," "exaction," "concussion."

In both countries the definitions were very similar. For Randle Cotgrave, the French word "*péculat*" meant "a robbing of the Princes, or publicke treasure; a converting it unto his private use by theeverie, userie." The English word "peculation," which only appeared in 1658, according to *The Oxford English Dictionary*, had a similar meaning: "a robbing of the Prince or Common-Wealth." "*Péculat*," "peculation" or "peculate" (a term that appeared in the eighteenth century) was used to describe a financial officer who discretely pocketed the kingdom's money without resort to violence.

"Exaction" and "concussion," words that dated back to the end of the Middle Ages, were more complex; in seventeenth-century dictionaries they are used to describe financial, judicial and police officers who employ force to extort goods from individuals. Cotgrave describes an "*exacteur*" in the following terms: "an exactor, extortioner, hard dealer, mercilesse collector; severe corrector; one that takes, or looks for the utmost, or extremitie of a debt or dutie"; while "concussion" is translated in this fashion: "concussion, publicke extorsion, close rapine; an extorting of gifts by a false show of authoritie, or imposition of crimes; any violent, any uniust procurement of bribes. . . ." By the middle of the eighteenth century, however, Samuel Johnson no longer offered a technical meaning for "concussion": it had vanished from English vocabulary.

These terms were then associated with three broader categories: abus/abuse, prévarication/prevarication and malversation. This last word, in particular, was a term that in French was applied specifically to the world of public servants. An examination of how this vocabulary became structured over time then shows that lexicographers relatively quickly attempted to make clear the ways that words could be linked to forms of misconduct in public service. But their efforts were heavily influenced by the princely conception of public service which was personal and domestic in its orientation.

The princely influence is clear in the way lexicographers specified the status of both the actors and victims of deviant practices. Actors were given a professional status: concussion, peculate, exaction, malversation were used more and more frequently only to designate the actions of the king's agents. At the same time, the "public" was presented as the victim of malversations. This did not refer, however, to our contemporary understanding of the public interest. Lexicographers made little effort to differentiate the "king" from the "public" while they were careful to distinguish this same "public" from "individual persons."[25] When the concept of public interest was used, its meaning was largely identified with that of the king. Moreover, abuses and malversations in general were increasingly perceived of as crimes and presented as such in the repertories. This process of criminalization led to "forfaiture/forfeit," that is to say treason, *lèse-majesté*. Finally, if one considers the problem of venality, which was particularly rampant in France, it becomes clear that it too was considered mainly in relationship with the king's domestic vision of public service.

None of these dictionaries defined venality as a crime; to this extent they simply conformed to the king's law which officially authorized the sale of offices and the farming of princely finances.[26] French repertories clearly illustrate, however, that such practices were perceived negatively. In 1694, members of the Academy declared that the "venality of public charges has opened the door to all sorts of chicanery and abuses."[27] The second edition of Furetière's *Dictionnaire* (1701), *s. v.* charge, complained that "incompetent people" *(personnes incapables)* increasingly invade the tribunals, but it also recognized that venality was a "necessary evil" *(mal nécessaire)*. One of Boileau's phrases appeared in this edition as well as that of Richelet's in 1728: "In the *Palais* (i.e., the Parlement of Paris, which functioned as a tribunal) money alone makes the magistrate"[28].

French lexicographers thus recognized that venality could entail abuses. In their opinion, however, the problem did not stem from the fact that offices were a form of *private property* : the dictionaries did not openly present the argument from Seneca's *De Beneficiis* (I, ix, 5), that a venal officer adjudicates more than he judges, "since it is the law of nations that you can sell what you have bought"[29] . Problems arose from changes in the nature of *service* for the king, once money had replaced merit in the selection process.

As a result of this evolution, the traditional links of fidelity between the king and his officers became more distant and impersonal. Although the royal power sought to conceal this change, men no longer owed much either to royal patronage or to the intervention of brokers. This newly acquired independence was consolidated through permanent appointments for judicial charges (1467) and through inherited offices (in 1604 with the establishment of the *Paulette* tax); this served to throw into doubt the loyalty of these *individuals* who served the king. Venality in itself did not represent a form of *early modern corruption*, but it served to undermine the whole series of values—fidelity, loyalty, honor and obligation—that had structured those relationships of hierarchy and dependence that guaranteed the order (l'*ordre*) of the king. By undermining the administrative machinery, it potentially threatened its very coherence and reliability. Venality, then, introduced the new possibilities of misbehavior on the part of the king's ministers. Abuses, as a result of these historical changes, were contrary to the king's *ordre*.

The king's administrative policies were not completely spared in this criticism of venal practices. Indeed, this may have reflected humanist and juridical hostility to the systematic sale of offices. Lexicographers knew about and at times shared attitudes which were not those of the king. The dictionaries of Trévoux and Furetière both contained completely negative articles about "commissions," those temporary contracts that linked public servants to the king's political person. Moreover, Furetière's 1701 edition established a parallel between the condition of a "commis" and that of a slave, thus implicitly recognizing the weight of Italian republican culture which associated the loss of liberty with citizen's "corruption."[30]

*   *   *

In this respect, dictionaries were strikingly able to register the diverse meanings of the word "corruption" while carefully avoiding definitions that acknowledged its political overtones. In particular, lexicographers avoided making too explicit connections between corrupt practices and the criminality of king's agents.

The word "corruption" occupied an unusual position in this vocabulary. In French its technical sense remained very restricted in the sixteenth, seventeenth, and eighteenth centuries since it only applied to judges. Corruption implied the presence of an agent of the king's justice, a corruptor, and a litigant where the magistrate sold his judgement to an individual. The latter then intervened in the judicial process to the detriment of the third party. In English the noun "corruption" did not have this technical meaning until the Victorian period. Only the verb "to corrupt" carried such a meaning when it meant "to bribe."[31] As in France, it was generally applied in the judicial arena—for Johnson, "bribe" meant "a reward given to pervert the judgment"— but its meaning remained very allusive.

In the end, it is difficult to pin down the technical meaning of "corruption" in dictionaries of the period, since it is not used as a generic term to indicate the deviance of the king's agents. This confirms Joël Hurtsfield's and Jean-Claude Waquet's argument that "corruption" is not the appropriate term to investigate this subject prior to the eighteenth century.[32] For lexicographers of the early modern period, "corruption," in its technical meaning, was situated at another level from other practices of *early modern corruption*. Certainly, it upset traditional social values but its impact far exceeded that of other malversations. Moreover, it did not position itself solely with respect to penal logic.

In the article "corruption" of the *Dictionnaire de l'Académie française* the word is understood in the following sense: "figuratively, concerning all moral depravations and especially those with regard to justice, fidelity and modesty. The corruption of morals, the corruption of the century. The corruption of youth. The corruption of men's hearts. Sin has left the seed of corruption within human nature. The world is but corruption. A judge is suspected of corruption."[33] By associating judicial corruption with moral corruption, the Immortals vastly magnified the consequences of the former.

This definition suggests that a venal judge violated his pledge, sold his loyalty and lost his incorruptibility, that is to say his integrity and, consequently, his honesty. He abdicated then his accountability as a judge and became a criminal. By selling his judgement he committed perjury but also "forfeiture," hence was guilty of betrayal and treachery. This accumulation of crimes amounted logically to lese-majesty, since the selling of justice implied giving up what was considered the essence of royal and godly prerogatives. In this fashion the corruption of magistrates attacked not only the legitimacy of the judicial machinery but also the figure of the king, the monarchy and divine right. Yet, the evil went beyond this. "Justice," like fidelity, faith, and loyalty, was considered one of the foundational values of early modern society and one that constituted human relationships. The "Queen of Virtues" was indeed the supreme value, that "which rendered unto others that which belonged to them."[34]

In this vision, when a corrupt judge disrupted the judicial process, he sacrificed an innocent person but also betrayed his king in three separate ways : he sold the duties that were part of his function, he compromised the image of royal justice, and shattered the social order. These consequences far outweighed those of peculation when the guilty party merely robbed the State's assets, or the effects of concussion and exaction where perpetrators misused the authority of their function to their own advantage thus betraying the king's confidence.

The image of "corruption" that emerges from the Academy's definition was structured around two levels of understanding. Judicial corruption was understood as one aspect of moral corruption while moral corruption emanated from the original and physical understanding of the term.

This understanding is found more succinctly in all French and English dictionaries. Samuel Johnson, for example, began his definition like this:

Corruption,
1. the principle by which bodies tend to the separation of their parts.
2. Wickedness; perversion of principles.

Lexicographers in this way referred back to Aristotelian physics and transposed into the vernacular meanings derived from the old Latin vocabulary. The terms *corrumpere, pervertere, violare, vitiare* combined both obviously negative meanings with a more figurative dimension that included the concepts of dishonor and profanation. "Corruption" was both a physical process that implied transformation and was thus frequently associated semantically with rotting and stench, as well as a moral degradation as a result of those human passions whose existence stemmed from the Fall.

Judicial corruption was understood as one of the possible results of general corruption; little by little then all false actions of public ministers were seen as evidence of mankind's general corruption. In this way *early modern corruption* was inscribed in the discussion of corruption, but the latter nonetheless was not presented in the dictionaries as the moral *category* in which all administrative misbehaviors were subsumed.

The very construction of the definition implied physical changes in matter which introduced an understanding of corruption as an *irreversible* process. In other words, neither corrupt men nor institutions could be saved. In contrast the rest of the vocabulary of *early modern corruption* was presented within a dialectic perspective that implied "abuse" and "reform." A generic word for the criminality of the king's agents, "abuse/abus" was systematically related in French to the words "réforme" or "réformation." The glorified master of reform was the king, the all-powerful leader who could correct all disorders. The regenerative logic of this cycle of abuse and reform served royal power, particularly since it inverted aspects of the Protestant discourse of abuse and reform in favor of the Catholic king. On the contrary, incurable corruption threatened royal legitimacy at its very core.

*   *   *

These conclusions raise a number of questions since there is widespread evidence of the use of the word "corruption" in English and French political and religious disputes.[35] In this context the term's unquestionable power was used to denounce the depravity and the despotism of power and, by the way, those acts of *early modern corruption* which were seen as the irrefutable evidence of the State's disarray. In the eyes of critics, this corruption-deviance brought about the regime's decadence before heralding the birth of a new regime, following a line of reasoning commonly adopted since Polybius. This Greek historian had turned the Aristotelian political classification—monarchy, tyranny; aristocracy, oligarchy; democracy, anarchy—into a circle of birth, growth and death led by corruption: "any state, unless prevented, must pass through each of these forms in turn and in the order stated, and from anarchy must return back to monarchy."[36]

French lexicographers, however, while recognizing in their definitions of "corruption" the cyclical principle of corruption/generation never openly applied it to the political domain. In their minds, the realm was not doomed to fall into the malignant cycle of constitutions just by the fault of its corruption. Yet, "corruption" could deeply undermine the foundations of the State and poison the social and civil life of the kingdom. Already remote from the royal domestic vision of public service, "corruption" was also too dangerous a word to be linked with the vocabulary of *early modern corruption*. Given that lexicographers associated the latter in a dialectic relationship to the king's glory, one can legitimately wonder whether the whole structure of the vocabulary was not a *deliberate* decision to protect his power and legitimacy.

The succinctness of English dictionaries definitions does not reveal a similar logic, but the brevity of these classifications does not necessarily explain this silence. Certainly the dialectic of abuse/reformation was also present in judicial sources of the early Stuart period, and one cannot help wondering whether the English king and head of the English church did not also need to affirm his position as the master of reform while casting from his body and that of his servants any hint of "political"—that is Polybian – corruption.[37]

One must keep in mind, however, that English lexicographical work in the eighteenth century took place in a profoundly reconfigured intellectual context. In liberal thought, the wheel of fortune no longer represented the passage of time : anxiety was rather generated by the perverse effects of exchange and transaction. The struggle to counter "corruption"—in the current understanding of the word—was no longer accomplished through periodic reformations, but instead through the establishment of the principle of equilibrium at all levels.[38] Progress, not stability, became the goal, and progress depended on the active participation of particular interests, especially those of public servants who played such a critical role in the kingdom. It may be at this moment that the term "corruption" was definitively applied directly to public agents' misbehaviors, understood by then as the triumph of private interests in the public sphere.

"Corruption" continued to carry political connotations: it designated any disruptions of the English parliamentary edifice. By the eighteenth century, however, the kingdom's representatives guaranteed the system and not the king. The effort to combat corruption no longer belonged to royal prerogative but rather to the arbitrating powers of the Parliament. It remains difficult to determine whether the fear of corruption precipitated the emergence of a new mode of political operation,[39] or whether it simply accompanied these changes. In either case, nonetheless, the eradication of corruption had become by the end of the eighteenth century the necessary condition for the liberal State to function. This eradication was doubly "political" both in its stakes and in its ability to encompass the deviant practices of the State's agents.

Notes

1. This article has greatly benefited from the suggestions of Arlette Jouanna, Robert Descimon, Arnold Heidenheimer, Michael Johnston, Adrien Lherm, Rebecca Rogers and Jean-Claude Waquet. My thanks to all of them and to Rebecca Rogers for translating this text.
2. J. C. Scott, "Proto-Corruption in Early Stuart England," in *Comparative Political Corruption*, Englewood Cliffs, NJ, 1972, p. 36–55; J. Hurstfield, *Freedom, Corruption and Government in Elizabethan England*, Cambridge, MA, 1973; J. G. A. Pocock, *The Machiavellian Moment*, Princeton, 1975; R. Harding, "Corruption and the Moral Boundaries of Patronage in the Renaissance," in G. Fitch Lytle and S. Orgel eds., *Patronage in the Renaissance*, Princeton, 1981, p. 47–64; J.—C. Waquet, *De la corruption: morale et pouvoir à Florence aux XVIIe et XVIIIe siècles*, Paris, 1984; *Id.*, "Some Considerations on Corruption, Politics and Society in Sixteenth and Seventeenth-Century Italy," W. Litle, E. Posada Carbo eds., *Political Corruption in Europe and Latin America*, London, 1996; J. Sawyer, "Judicial Corruption and Legal Reform in Early Seventeenth-Century France," *Law and History Review*, VI, 1988, p. 95–117; L. Levy Peck, *Court Patronage and Corruption in Early Stuart England*, London, 1990; F. Bayard, "Malversations et corruption dans les finances françaises de la première moitié du XVIIe siècle," *Papers of the symposium "Venality and Corruption,"* Leyde, December 1990; "De la corruption: officiers, fonctionnaires et idéal administratif," in J. Imbert, J. Meyer, J. Nagle, *Du XVIe au XVIIIe siècle*, Paris, 1993, (*Histoire de la fonction publique en France*, dir. M. Pinet), p. 389–407. See also, V. Groebner, "Angebote die man ablehnen kann. Institutionen, Verwaltung und die Definition von Korruption am Ende des Mittelalters," in R. Blänkner, B. Jussen eds., *Institutionen und Ereignis : über historiche Praktiken und Vorstellungen gesellschaftlichen Ordnens*, Göttingen, 1998, p. 163–184.
3. In this volume, see chapter 6.
4. For a discussion about the public good, cf. A. Jouanna, *Le devoir de révolte. La noblesse française et la gestation de l'Etat moderne, 1559–1661*, Paris, 1989, p. 279–312.
5. For more information about ethical problems and the weight of the theological-juridical culture, cf. B. Clavero, *Antidora. Antropologia catolica de la economia moderna*, Milano, 1991 (trans. in French, *La grâce du don. Anthropologie catholique de l'économie moderne*, J.-F. Schaub, Paris, 1996).
6. Cf. Q. Skinner, *The Foundations of Modern Political Thought*, vol. 1, *The Renaissance*, Cambridge, 1996 (1978), p. 88–101. On the many meanings of "virtue," cf. J. A. G. Pocock, *Virtue, Commerce, and History. Essays on Political Thought and History, Chiefly in the Eighteenth Century*, Cambridge, 1986 (1st ed. 1985), p. 41–2.
7. Cf. J. Helegouarch, *Le vocabulaire latin des relations et des partis politiques sous la république*, Paris, 1972 (1963), p. 23–5, 30–7, 152–63, 259–86, 383–410.
8. E. Kantorowicz, *The King's two Bodies; a Study in Medieval Political Theology*, Princeton, 1957, R. E. Giesey, *The Royal Funeral Ceremony in Renaissance France*, Genève, 1960, W. F. Church, *Constitutional Thought in Sixteenth-Century France*, Cambridge (Conn.), London, 1941 and, from the same, "The Decline of French Jurists as Political Theorists," *French Historical Studies*, 1967 (5), p.1–40, J. Krynen, *L'empire du roi, idées et croyances politiques en France XIIIe-XVe siècle*, Paris, 1993; J. Barbey, *La fonction royale, essence et légitimité d'après les tractatus de Jean de Terrevermeille*, Paris, 1983.

9. Cf. R. Descimon, "La royauté française entre féodalité et sacerdoce. Roi seigneur ou roi magistrat?," *Revue de Synthèse*, 1991, IV (3–4), 455–473.
10. "Un quatriesme estat," M. de Montaigne, *Les Essais*, bk. I, chap. XXIII, p. 116, in *Oeuvres Complètes*, M. Rat ed., Paris, 1962.
11. Cf. J. G. A Pocock, *The Machiavellian Moment . . .*, p. 423–506 and from the same, "Virtues, rights, and manners. A model for historians of political thought," *Virtue, Commerce and History. . . .*, Cambridge, 1986 (1st ed. 1985), p. 37–50. For the French case, see D. R. Kelley, *Foundations of Modern Historical Scholarship. Language, Law, and History in the French Renaissance*, New York, London, 1970 and J.-M. Goulemot, *Le règne de l'histoire. Discours historiques et révolutions XVIIe-XVIIIe siècle*, Paris, 1996, esp. p. 295–344 dealing with the impact of the English model. On the same topic, cf. also K. M. Baker, *Inventing the French Revolution: Essays on French Political Culture in the Eighteenth Century*, Cambridge, 1990, chap. 6, p. 128–152.
12. Cf. M. Viroll, *From Politics to Reason of State. The Acquisition and Transformation of the Language of Politics 1250–1600*, Cambridge, 1992, also P. Burke, "Tacitism, sceptisism, and reason of state," in J. H. Burns ed., *The Cambridge History of Political Thought, 1450–1700*, Cambridge, 1991, esp. p. 489–484. On how Scepticism, Stoicism and reason of state went together, cf. R. Tuck, *Philosophy and Government 1572–1651*, Cambridge, 1993.
13. On the role of liberalism on the modern understanding of history, cf. R. Tuck, *Natural Rights Theories : Their Origins and Development*, Cambridge, 1980.
14. For further discussion of the subject, cf. R. Descimon, J. F. Schaub, B. Vincent dir., *Les figures de l'administrateur. Institutions, réseaux, pouvoirs en Espagne, en France et au Portugal 16e-19e siècles*, Paris, 1997.
15. J.C. Scott, *Comparative . . .*, p. 8. Italics are mine.
16. J. S. Nye, "Corruption and Political Development: A Cost-Benefit Analysis," *Political Corruption: Readings in . . .*, p. 565 (also in this volume).
17. On the technical use of the word "corruption" in early modern times but also on its philosophical and political implications in France, see D. Gembicki, "Corruption, Décadence," in R. Reichardt and E. Schmitt eds., *Handbuch politisch-sozialer Grundbegriffe in Frankreich, 1680–1820*, München, Oldenbourg, 1994, p. 9–60.
18. Cf. J. A. G. Pocock, *op. cit.,* and also W. D. Rubinstein, "The End of 'Old Corruption' in Britain 1780–1860," *Past and Present*, 1983 (101), p. 55–86.
19. K. M. Baker, *Inventing . . .*, p. 128–152.
20. L. L. Peck, *Court Patronage . . .*, p. 163–179.
21. Reeditions are indicated in abbreviated form—place, editor, date. This article bases its analysis on seven types of French dictionaries :
    • the French-Latin "humanist" dictionaries : R. Estienne, *Dictionnaire françois latin*, Paris, 1539 and 1549; J. Nicot, *Thresor de la langue françoyse*, Paris, Douceur, 1606 (1st ed. 1604); *Le Grand dictionnaire françois-latin*, Paris, N. Buon, 1614, Lyon; C. Larjot, 1625; Rouen, J. Osmont, 1628.
    • the French-Latin Jesuit dictionaries : P. Monet, *Invantaire . . .* Lyon, Vve C. Rigaud, 1635; C. Pajot, *Dictionnaire nouveau . . .*, La Flèche, G. Griveau, 1644; P. Delbrun, *Grand apparat françois . . .*, Toulouse, Jean Boyde, 1658 (1st ed. 1657); F. Pomey, *Le dictionnaire royal..*, Lyon, Antoine Molin, 1671 (1st ed. 1667); G. Tachard, *Dictionnaire nouveau . . .*, Paris, A. Pralard, 1689.
    • P. Richelet, *Dictionnaire françois contenant les mots et les choses . . .* Genève, Widerhold, 1680, 2 vols.; Genève, Ritter, 1693, 2 vols.; Genève, G. de Tournes, 1710, 2 vols.; Lyon, Girin, 1719, 2 vol.; Lyon, vendu à Paris chez J. Estienne,

1728, 3 vols.; Amsterdam, aux dépens de la Compagnie, 1732, 2 vols.; Lyon, Duplain, 1759, 3 vols.
- A. Furetiere, *Dictionnaire universel* . . . ,Rotterdam, Leers, 1690, 3 vols.; La Haye, Rotterdam, Leers, 1701, 3 vols.; Rotterdam, Leers, 1708, 3 vols.; La Haye, Husson, 1727, 4 vols.; et pour le Trévoux qui copie grandement le Furetière: *Dictionnaire universel françois et latin* . . . , Trévoux, Ganneau, 1704, 2 vols.; Trévoux, vendu à Paris chez F. Delaulne, 1721, 5 vols.; Trévoux, F. Delaulne, 1732, 4 vols.; Nancy, Antoine, 1740, 5 vols.; Paris, Delaulne, Gandoin, 1763 (reimpression of the 1752 reedition), 6 vols.; Paris, Cie des libraires associés, 1771, 8 vol.
- *Dictionnaire de l'Académie françoise dédié au Roi*, Genève, 1981, (reproduction of the 1st ed., Paris, 1694), 2 vols.; Paris, 1718, 2 vols.; Paris, 1740, 2 vols.; Paris, 1762, 2 vols.
- I have also used three texts that were published for the first time in the second half of the eighteenth century: *Encyclopédie ou Dictionnaire raisonné des sciences, des arts et des métiers, par une société de gens de lettres* . . . , Paris, Le Breton, Briasson, David, Durand, 1751–1765, 17 vols.; *Le Grand Vocabulaire françois contenant l'explication de chaque mot* . . . *par une société de gens de lettre*, Paris, Hôtel de Thou, 1778, 30 vols.; J.-F. Feraud, *Dictionnaire critique de la langue françoise*, Marseille, Mossy père et fils, 1787–1788, 3 vols.
- dictionaries of synonymes : G. Girard, *Synonymes François*, Leide, J. de Wetstein, 1762 (réimpression de l'édition de 1736); N. Beauzee, *Dictionnaire universel des synonymes françois*, Paris, Lesguilliez, 1801 (réimpression de l'édition de 1770); P. Roubaud, *Nouveaux synonymes François*, Liège, C. Plomteux, 1786 (1st ed. Paris, 1785), 4 vols.

22. A complete dictionary of the English language only appeared tardily and the definitions were to remain short compared to those in French dictionaries. Samuel Johnson explained in the preface of his dictionary : "I have . . . attempted a dictionary of the English language, which, while it was employed in the cultivation of every species of literature, has itself been hitherto neglected," *A Dictionary of the English Language,* London, J. Knapton, 1756, 2 vols., 1, p. 3. There are a few anglo-saxon dictionaries (for example those of G. Somner (1659) or Th. Benson (1701)), but most of the lexicons which appeared prior to 1756 seem, in fact, to have imitated French models. Robert Estienne's *Thesaurus* apparently inspired the bishop of Winchester, Thomas Cooper's, reeditions of the *Bibliotheca Eliotae* of Sir Thomas Elyot (1538). The polyglot and bilingual English-French dictionaries which were the most common lexicographic genre in the British kingdom before the nineteenth century, recycled French advances in these genres. Since the issue of corruption has been well studied in early modern England, deeper insight concerning the brief lexicographic references can be found in the bibliography and, in certain cases, in the lengthier passages of French dictionaries. In addition to Johnson's dictionary, I have used the following : R. Cotgrave, *A dictionary of the French and English tongues*, London, A. Islip, 1611 and 1632; G. Miege, *A New dictionary French and English*, London, Basset, 1679 (1st ed. 1677); A. Boyer, *Dictionnaire anglais-français*, La Haye,1702, 2 vols.; T. Deletenville, *A New French Dictionary in two part*, London, Nourse, 1779 (1st ed. 1711); T. Dyche, *A New General Dictionary* . . . London, R. Ware, 1787.

23. J. Hurstfield, *Freedom, Corruption* . . . , p. 139.

24. According to Robert Darnton's method depicted in *The Great Cat Massacre and Other Episodes in French Cultural History,* New York, 1984.

25. This is particularly evident in Furetière, 1694–1771, *s. v.* public : "public, a relative and collective term that is opposed to particular. What encompasses the

general in citizens and men. Morality defends the love of the public good, the conservation of the public good or the Republic .." ("public, terme relatif et collectif opposé à particulier. Le général des citoyens ou des hommes. La morale ne prêche autre chose que l'amour du bien public, la conservation de la chose publique ou Republique . . . ").

26. For the practice of venality in France, see K. Swart, in this volume, and also R. Mousnier, *La vénalité des offices en France sous la monarchie absolue*, Rouen, 1945; D. Bien, "The Use of Venal Offices," K. M. Baker ed., *The Political Culture of the Old Regime*, (*The French Revolution and the Creation of Modern Political Culture*, t. 1), Oxford, New York, 1987, 89–115; R. Descimon, "Il mercato degli uffici regi a Parigi (1604–1665): Economia politica ed economia privata della funzione pubblica di antico regime," *Quaderni storici*, 1997 (32), 685–716; R. E. Giesey, "State-Building in Early Modern France: The Role of Royal Officialdom," *Journal of Modern History*, 1983 (55), 191–207.

27. *Dictionnaire de l'Académie . . .*, 1694–1762, *s. v.* vénalité : "la vénalité des charges a ouvert la porte aux chicaneries et aux abus."

28. Furetière, 1701–1771 and Richelet, 1728–1759, *s. v.* charge : "l'argent seul au Palais peut faire un magistrat."

29. The exact sentence is : "That the provinces are plundered, that the judgement-seat is for sale, and, when two bids have been made, is knocked down to one of the bidders is of course not surprising, since it is the law of nations that you can sell what you have bought!," Seneca, *Moral Essays, with an English Translation by John W. Basore*, vol. 3, *De Beneficiis*, The Loeb Classical Library, London, Cambridge (Mass.), 1964 (1935), p. 30–31. Cf. also K. Swart, . . . p. 93 and note 14 p. 98.

30. Furetière, 1701–1727, *s. v.* servitude.

31. In France the word "corruption" offers the only equivalent to "bribe" que "corruption." "Pot de vin" does not have the same meaning and, moreover, had no negative connotations in the Old Regime.

32. J. Hurstfield, *Freedom, Corruption . . .*, pp. 159–160 and J.—C. Waquet, *De la corruption . . .*, pp. 108–120.

33. *Dictionnaire de l'Académie . . .*, 1694–1762, *s. v.* corruption : "figurément, de toute dépravation dans les moeurs, et principalement de celles qui regardent la justice, la fidélité, la pudicité. La corruption des moeurs, la corruption du siècle. La corruption de la jeunesse. La corruption du coeur de l'homme. Le péché a laissé un fond de corruption dans toute la nature humaine. Le monde n'est que corruption. Un juge soupçonné de corruption."

34. *Dictionnaire de l'Académie . . .*, 1694–1762, *s. v.* justice: "la reine des vertus, . . . qui rend à chacun ce qui luy appartient."

35. Cf. the works of J. G. A Pocock, L. Levy Peck and D. Crouzet, *op. cit.*

36. J. G. A Pocock, *op. cit.*, p. 78.

37. See for instance the chapter L. L. Peck dedicated to reformation in the navy and her conclusion, *Court Patronage . . .*, p. 106–133 et p. 203–4.

38. For an understanding of the way passion and reason ceased to be opposed in the eighteenth century, cf. A. O. Hirschman, *The Passions and the Interests. Political Arguments for Capitalism before its Triumph*, Princeton, 1976 and M. M. Goldsmith, *Private Vices, Public Benefits: Bernard Mandeville's Social and Political Thought*, Cambridge, 1985, esp. chap. 2.

39. As John Pocock has suggested: "We are looking at the origins of the doctrine of the separation of powers, and it should be observed both how far these origins lay in the fear of corruption, and how little a role was played by any clear theory of a democratic mode of understanding," *The Machiavellian . . .*, p. 288.

8

Handling Historical Comparisons
Cross-Nationally

James C. Scott

If the study of corruption teaches us anything at all, it teaches us not to take a political system or a particular regime at its face value. Corruption, after all, may be seen as an informal political system. Whereas party manifestos, general legislation, and policy declarations are the formal façade of the political structure, corruption stands in sharp contrast to these features as an informal political system in its own right. Here coalitions that could not survive the light of day, government decisions that would set off a public outcry, elite behavior that would destroy many a political career are all located. For a few nations this hidden arena is only of marginal importance and, although worthy of study, would not appreciably change an evaluation based on what takes place in public. For most nations at some point in their history, and for many nations today, however, the surreptitious politics of this arena is so decisive that an analysis which ignored it would be not simply inaccurate but completely misleading. How for example, could we have adequately explained the rule of Boss Tweed in New York of the 1890s, the structure of Chiang Kai-shek's Kuomintang Party, the methods of "Papa Doc" Duvalier in Haiti, or the failure of the parliamentary system in Indonesia without examining corruption? These are perhaps dramatic examples but they alert us to the fact that corruption is frequently an integral part of the political system—a part which we ignore only at our great peril . . .

Source: James C. Scott, *Comparative Political Corruption*. Englewood Cliffs, N.J.: Prentice Hall, 1972, pp.2–8, 21–35. By permission of the author and copyright-holder.

A closely related problem in the comparative study of corruption involves not so much a question of formal analysis as a question of our scope of inquiry. As much as possible, we shall try to view corruption as a special case of political influence—a case that must be seen in the context of the distribution of power in society and the character of regime institutions. When we examine specific regimes such as England under the early Stuarts, or India under the Congress party, we will attempt to show how the pattern of corruption is related in each case to the values and institutions of both the elite and the society as a whole. In concrete terms, this means treating an American urban political "machine," in which corruption is commonly rife, *as part of an entire system* of electoral and financial influence in which legal patronage, pork-barrel legislation, and lax regulation of city-based business interests are also important features. Thus, because an adequate understanding of corruption generally requires a grasp of an entire network of influence, we shall try to deal with corruption in a way that embeds it contextually in a broader analysis of a regime's political dynamics.

Comparing Norms

The second, and most serious, difficulty arising from the use of formal norms to define corruption is that it seems to rule out some historical comparisons. An example will illustrate the dilemma. If we wanted to compare corruption in seventeenth-century France with corruption in twentieth-century France, a legal perspective would make our task difficult. The sale of state offices in seventeenth-century France would not come under our definition of corruption, whereas the same act in twentieth-century France—or the United States—would. The behavior seems the same; only the legal context has changed. Nor would the use of a "public opinion" criterion here instead of the legal standard solve the dilemma, inasmuch as the sale of office in seventeenth-century France was neither illegal nor frowned upon, except by the old nobility who resented the nouveau riche office holder. In a similar vein, the alarm among the Dutch at increased corruption in colonial Indonesia in the nineteenth century did not result from a change in what colonial officials were doing, but rather from a shift in the values and public law being applied to such behavior in Holland.

We face the same problem in comparing practices in eighteenth-century Europe with identical practices in new states today. The new states, for the most part, have adopted the full panoply of laws that emerged from the long political struggle for reform in the west. Considering only political patronage jobs, the Indian, Malaysian, or Nigerian politician finds himself denied by law many of the spoils that legally aided the growth of political parties in England and America. The 1964 *Report of the Committee on Prevention of Corruption,* an official Indian report, explicitly recognizes the difficulty of comparing the severity of bureaucratic corruption in India with that of eighteenth-century England because the legal framework under which India operates was not yet established in England at that time. Patronage in contemporary India and in eighteenth-century England may seem to serve much the same purpose but from the legal perspective the former is corruption whereas the latter is not.

The difficulty here simply serves to highlight the fact that much corruption is in a real sense a product of the late eighteenth and nineteenth centuries. Only the rise of the modern nation-state, with its mass participation, broadly representative bodies, and elaborate civil service codes, signaled the transformation of the view of government office, and even kingship, from a private right into a public responsibility.

How, then, can we handle historical comparisons? If, for example, we wanted to compare the practice of bribing to gain appointment to the bureaucracy in traditional England with the same practice in modern England, we could classify such an act as corrupt in the modern period but not in the traditional period, where it often occurred openly and legally. We will want, nonetheless, to compare *practices* that are corrupt only by modern standards and ask what their causes are in different periods, how they affect the composition of the elite, and so forth. If nepotism or bribery have similar causes and consequences in early France as in contemporary India, that is an important subject for analysis, notwithstanding the fact that legal codes and public standards have changed so much that what was tolerated (not corrupt) in early France is now forbidden by law (corrupt) in India. For our comparative purposes, then, we will refer to pre-nineteenth-century practices which only became "corrupt" in the nineteenth century as *"proto-corruption."* This convention will allow us to analyze the comparative causes and effects of similar behavior while recognizing that such earlier practices did not contravene the existing norms of official conduct and thus cannot be considered corruption as we have chosen to use the term . . .

Means of Persuasion in Different Political Systems

Our central concern here is with the political significance of corrupt actions. Most acts we call corrupt are transactions in which one party exchanges wealth—or more durable assets such as kinship or friendship—for influence over the decisions of government. Whether the "buyer" seeks an honorary title (status), a post of some authority (power), or a large supply contract (wealth), the essential characteristics of the transaction fit this pattern.

Corruption may then be seen as just one of many ways a person can persuade someone who exercises public authority to act as he wishes—that is, as a kind of influence. Other sorts of influence, such as appealing to regulations, to ideology, or to equity, are quite legitimate means of persuasion so long as the power-holder acts within the rules. When we say that influence is corrupt we imply that without the special consideration of kinship, bribery, or friendship the public official could not have made the same decision.

Although not every corrupt act can be interpreted in this fashion, analyzing most forms of corruption in terms of a process of political influence allows us to examine corruption as part of a larger mosaic of political influence. This approach highlights the functional equivalence of a variety of acts of political influence-some of which violate all standards of community ethics and some of which are totally beyond reproach.

Were it not for the fact that a host of government decisions represent valuable commodities to some citizens, there would be little corruption. Nor would there be much corruption if the valuable things a state had at its disposal were simply sold at auction to the highest bidder. No modern government, however, sells civil service jobs or allots public health service and education only to those who can bid highest. Using the price system to allocate such services would violate shared standards or justice and equity. The problem, of course, is that demand for many government dispensations far outstrips their limited supply, and because the state makes no charge, or only a nominal one, the price for such services does not begin to reflect the supply-demand situation. In this context, the effort by many citizens to circumvent government non-price criteria for the award of these valuables takes the form of what Tilman has aptly called a "black-market bureaucracy." Such attempts to influence government decisions are naturally more frequent where state activities are more pervasive. The legitimate influence of political pressure on legislatures, and ideological or ethical appeals compete against the illegitimate influence of wealth, kinship, and "connections."

Three instances of the use of wealth to sway state decisions will illustrate the expressly political perspective of viewing corruption as a form of influence. Each case exemplifies, in a different manner, what is likely to occur when wealth and power elites are separate. All are cases of influence, but in Thailand the political influence of wealth was achieved by corruption, in Japan by quite unexceptionable means, and in seventeenth—and eighteenth-century England by devices that are questionable but not illegal.

In England throughout the seventeenth and eighteenth centuries the lesser, wealthy gentry and the new commercial elite were able to buy positions of political authority either through the purchase of public office and peerages from the crown or, especially later, through the purchase of parliamentary boroughs. In this way, the new classes began to replace the older nobility in the affairs of state. Objections were raised to all these practices but they were not illegal until well into the nineteenth century.

In contemporary Thailand, by contrast, the business elite is largely Chinese, not Thai, and thus for ethnic reasons formal positions of authority are seldom open to them. Instead, members of the Chinese commercial community have established fairly stable relations with individual clique leaders in the Thai military and bureaucracy in order to protect and advance their entrepreneurial concerns. Many of the transactions that provide the cement for this informal coalition are quite illegal, but the relationships are, of course, enormously rewarding for members of the Thai bureaucratic elite who oversee the licensing and taxing of enterprises. Deprived of the privilege of outright office-holding, Chinese businessmen in Thailand have nevertheless managed quite well—albeit through corruption—to share quite fulsomely in the decisions which affect them.

Wealthy business elites in Japan, finally, operating in a very different fashion from Thai entrepreneurs, have also managed to wield great political influence. Working through the factions—particularly the "main current" faction of the Liberal Democratic party (LDP) that has dominated elections in the postwar era—businessmen have provided the lion's share of this party's huge electoral war chest. Rather than having each firm work out its own arrangements, as in the Thai case, Japanese businessmen functioned for a time collectively through an industry-wide association that assessed member firms according to their assets and annual profits and passed on these funds to factions of the LDP. Japanese industrialists have thus had a large, and quite legal, hand in determining which clique would prevail within the LDP. The legislative program of the LDP has, of course, consistently reflected the support it has received from large business concerns.

These three illustrations are all cases in which wealthy elites attempt, more or less successfully, to influence government actions. In the Thai case, much of what occurs meets the definition of corruption; the English case belongs in the category of "proto-corruption"; and the Japanese case would be difficult to construe as corruption in any sense. Using divergent strategies in each nation, wealthy elites have achieved strikingly similar ends by bending government actions to their needs. The sale of office and parliamentary seats in Britain made the direct pursuit of office by the nouveau riche a common pattern. The ethnic background of wealthy elites in Thailand severely circumscribed formal avenues to power and thereby promoted more corrupt practices. But in Japan the existence of an organized party system allows businessmen to contribute openly and legally to the ruling party in order to gain their policy ends. Such factors as whether a nation has an electoral system, whether wealth elites are organized, whether there are ethnic or religious barriers that prevent wealth elites from formally holding office will thus partly determine the kind or amount of corruption in a political system. Each political system has distinctive routes by which wealth, as a political resource, influences government policies. The availability of some channels for influence and the exclusion of others set boundaries on the channels available to wealthy elites for influencing formal power-holders, thereby affecting both the incidence and style of corruption.

Influence at the Output Stage

Corruption, like other forms of political influence, often arises from the claims and demands people make on government. The study of how claims and demands are made on government in the industrialized west has for the most part focused on interest groups and the process by which such groups affect the content of legislation. If we distinguish between influence at the "input" stage (influence on lawmakers) and influence at the "output" stage (influence on enforcers after rules and laws have been promulgated), we can see that the "input" process has occupied the center of scholarly attention.

Students of politics in the new states of Asia and Africa, however, have been struck by the relative weakness both of the interest structures that might organize demands and of institutionalized channels through which such demands, once organized, might be communicated to the political decision-makers. The open clash of organized interests, so common in the west, is often conspicuously absent during the formulation of policy and legislation in these nations. To conclude from this fact, however, that the public has little or no effect on the eventual "output" of government would be completely unwarranted. Between the passage of legislation and its actual implementation lies an entirely different political arena that, in spite of its informality and particularism, has great effect on the execution of policy.

Much of the expression of political interests in the new states has been disregarded simply because western scholars, accustomed to their own contemporary politics, have been looking in the wrong place. A large portion of individual demands, and even group demands, in developing nations reaches the political system, not before laws are passed, but rather at the enforcement stage.[1] Influence before legislation is passed often takes the form of "pressure-group politics"; *influence at the enforcement stage often takes the form of "corruption" and has seldom been analyzed as the alternative means of interest articulation which in fact it is.*[2]

The peasants who avoid their land taxes by making a smaller and illegal contribution to the income of the assistant revenue officer are as surely influencing the outcome of government policy as if they formed a peasant union and agitated collectively for the reduction of land taxes. In a similar fashion, businessmen who protect their black-market sales by buying protection from the appropriate civil servants are changing the outcome of policy as effectively as if they had worked collectively through chambers of commerce for an end to government price controls. A strong case can be made that it may often be more "efficient" (and here the term "efficient" is used in the sense of minimizing the costs involved in attaining a given objective) to advance one's interests when policy is being implemented rather than when it is still being debated in the cabinet or in parliament. Three typical examples of situations in which corruption may help minimize costs for would-be influencers are suggested below.

1. Where the narrowness of loyalties or the scarcity of organizational skills inhibits the formation of political interest groups, the corruption of law enforcement may be the most efficient means of affecting changes in *de facto* policy.[3] The divisive loyalties of many peasants to their kinship, ethnic, village, religious, or caste groupings create social barriers that may preclude their organizing a common association that would advance their interests *qua* peasants. Given this fact, it is more efficient for the individual peasant to bribe local government officials, and thereby avoid the application of laws that may disadvantage him than for him to attempt to alter those laws.

2. Where legislative acts tend to be formalistic—where the administration of law is so loose and erratic that existing law bears little relationship to administrative behavior—it may be more efficient to make demands known at the enforcement stage than at the legislative stage. Even though interest groups exist, businessmen in developing nations may realize that the administration of even the most favorable tax laws will have little or no resemblance to what is called for in the statutes. That is, they may have to bribe as much to secure enforcement of a favorable law as to escape the provisions of an unfavorable one. Under the circumstances, then, it may make more sense for each enterprise to quietly "buy" precisely what it needs in terms of enforcement or non-enforcement, rather than to finance an open campaign for a new law that would be as formalistic as the existing one.[4]

3. Where a minority is discriminated against and its political demands are regarded as illegitimate by the governing elite and the general population, its members may feel that open pressure-group action would expose them to attacks from more powerful groups. Therefore, they may turn to the corruption of politicians and/or civil servants in order to safeguard their interests. Throughout much of Southeast Asia and East Africa, a large portion of commerce and small industry is in the hands of Indian or Chinese minority groups which, even if they have managed to acquire local citizenship, are considered as aliens by most of the local population. It would be foolish, even suicidal, for these so-called "pariah" capitalists to seek influence openly as an organized pressure group. A healthy regard for their property and skin alike impels them to rely on payments and favors to strategically placed power-holders.

Each of the three situations described, in which influence at the enforcement stage minimizes costs, are quite typical of the less developed nations.

The relative absence of organized interest-group activity in new nations is in part due to the fact that group loyalties are still centered at the family, village, or ethnic-group level. The peasant thinks of himself first a member of his extended family, then perhaps as a member of his village or tribal/ethnic group; he hardly ever sees himself as a peasant with interests similar to others who work the land. If he has political demands, they are not likely to be demands that embrace the entire peasantry, but instead will center either on his family's needs or on some small group to which he has direct links.

Implicit in this reasoning is the fundamental fact that the nature of most political demands in transitional nations is such that they are simply not amenable to the legislative process. Family-centered demands—e.g., a family's desire to secure a civil service post for its eldest son—are generally not expressible in legislative terms. When demands occasionally are made on behalf of wider groupings, they are likely to refer to ethnic, linguistic, or village units and only seldom can they be given general legislative form.[5] The problem thus lies less with the weakness *per se* of interest structures at the legislative stage than with the very character of loyalties in transitional nations and the kinds of demands fostered by such loyalty patterns. Couched, as it generally is, in universalistic language, legislation is often not a suitable vehicle for the expression of particularistic interests.[6] Influence at the enforcement level, on the other hand, is almost exclusively particularistic. It is scarcely surprising, then, that many of the narrow, parochial demands characteristic of new nations should make their weight felt when laws are being implemented rather than when they are being passed. Appropriate though it may be for organized groups in the modern sector, the modern legislative machinery of new nations is less effective in coping with the host of special pleadings coming from outside the modern sector.

The illustrations given above were, moreover, designed to show how potential political demands might be channeled along corrupt paths *even* in a functioning parliamentary system. For the majority of Afro-Asian nations, however, military rule has meant that interest group pressure on parliaments is no longer an alternative means of gaining political ends. In the absence of such open institutionalized procedures for influence, informal—often corrupt—channels have become all the more decisive.

Seen as a process of informal political influence, then, corruption might be expected to flourish most in a period when the formal political system, for whatever reasons, is unable to cope with the scale or the nature of the demands being made on it. Samuel Huntington, in his analysis of what he calls "political decay" in the new states, views corruption from virtually the same vantage point. Rapid social mobilization—urbanization, politicization, etc.— he argues, has placed an impossible burden on the frail political institutions of new nations, thereby leading to the decline of political competition and to political instability, institutional decay, and corruption.[7] But corruption in this sense not only reflects the failure of the formal political system to meet demands from important sectors, but also represents a kind of subversive effort by a host of individuals and groups to bend the political system to their wishes. Those who feel that their essential interests are ignored or considered illegitimate in the formal political system will gravitate to the informal channel of influence represented by corruption. It is possible, as in the case of the American urban "machine," that while the formal political process may seem restrictive and rigid, corruption and other informal arrangements may add substantial openness and flexibility to ultimate policies. Thus important political interests that seem unrepresented in the formal structure may enter unobtrusively through the back door.

An empirical assessment of the interests served by state action would be inadequate, then, if it stopped at the content of laws or decrees and failed to ask in what direction and to what extent corruption altered the implementation of policy. Table 8.1 represents an effort to distinguish between those

TABLE 8.1
Groups and their Means of Access to the Political System in
Less Developed Nations

Generally Easy Access to Formal Political System	Groups Often Securing Access Primarily by Means of Corruption Because Denied Formal Access by Virtue of:		
	Ideological Reasons	Parochial Reasons	Lack of Organization
1. Political elite commercial and industrial groups	1. Indigenous religious, or linguistic groups	1. Minority ethnic, peasants and other rural interests	1. Unorganized
2. Cadre and branches of ruling party	2. Foreign business interests	2. Unorganized urban lower classes	
3. Civil servants' associations	3. Political opposition		
4. Professional associations			
5. Trade unions (especially those dominated by ruling party)			

groups that usually achieve direct access to the formal political system in new nations and those groups that, for a variety of reasons, enter the competition for influence at a more informal level.

This rather sketchy composite cannot do complete justice to the situation in any single developing nation; it is, however, sufficiently descriptive of the situation in enough cases to alert one to the variety of interests that may seek to gain a surreptitious hearing. Aside from those groups that are blocked from formal participation for ideological reasons—for they are frequently in the modern sector and relatively well organized—the formal political system is *par excellence* the domain—virtually the monopoly—of the modern social sector. Minorities and the unorganized are placed at a distinct disadvantage since they face a formal political system that is simply not designed to accommodate them.

While a wide variety of groups may gain access to the political system through corruption, it is clearly those with substantial wealth who have the greatest capacity to bend government policy in their direction. Except for favors done from motives of kinship or friendship, it is the wealthy who are involved in most of the larger "deals" and whose influence is likely to overshadow that of smaller claimants. The reasons such powerful groups may operate corruptly rather than openly will be examined next.

Patterns of Access and Exclusion

Any set of political arrangement creates its own distinct pattern of access and influence. When we call a given regime oligarchic or aristocratic we are essentially making a judgment about the size and nature of those groups in the society which exercise the most influence over public policy; we are describing a particular pattern of access.

The dominant forces in a political system usually have no reason to resort to corruption or revolution to make their influence felt, for the state is institutionalized to serve their purposes. If we look at local government in mid-nineteenth-century Prussia, for example, we find that government was tailored entirely to the needs and interests of local landed elites. Exploitation of the rural lower classes was built into the political system; it was carried on legally and openly through preferential taxation and expenditure of public funds. Being virtually the owners of the state, landed elites had little reason to corrupt local officials.

Groups which may have engaged in bribery to advance their interests may cease to corrupt public officials once they have achieved greater formal access to power. Dutch business interests in colonial Indonesia follow this pattern. Prior to 1920 they tended to bribe colonial administrators in Batavia to secure, on a piecemeal basis, the advantages they desired for their enterprises. Later, however, they became organized and their businesses became profitable enough to achieve many of their goals directly through legislation back in Holland. Thus, throughout the 1920s and 1930s there was no export duty on oil from Indonesia and little or no tax on rubber. The need for colonial financial interests to bribe agents of the state diminished in proportion as their open influence over the state increased.

The pattern of formal access to influence in any political system provides preferential treatment to some kinds of interests while slighting or even excluding others. Occasionally the excluded groups are without resources to back their claims (e.g., small, oppressed minorities such as Indians in the United States, aborigines in Australia) and cannot improve their position without powerful allies. More often, however, excluded groups possess political resources such as wealth, organization, numbers, or armed force that provide them with the potential for enhancing their influence. If the resources of the disadvantaged groups center around organization or armed force, they may well choose to engineer a revolution or coup that would refashion the political structure to give them greater formal power. If, on the other hand, the disadvantaged groups control wealth and property, they may seek an informal adjustment of their influence through corruption.

Broadly speaking, there are two situations in which important and powerful groups are likely to have less access to formal influence than one would anticipate on the basis of the resources they command. First is the common historical case of a pattern of formal access established in the past which has been gradually undermined by rapid social change that has yet to find formal expression in institutional changes or legislation. The formal rules, in this case, no longer reflect the new distribution of potential power in society. This situation was, of course, typical in much of Europe in the early industrial revolution when traditional aristocratic rule made little allowance for the new social forces then emerging. The second situation in which the gap between formal access and informal power potential is likely to be great is when there has been a *sudden political transformation* that diminishes or cuts off the access of groups that still command potent political resources. Recently independent nations with socialist ruling parties fall into this category, inasmuch as the new regime has often formally excluded such powerful groups as commercial and business elites and traditional chiefs and headmen who still command significant resources for influence.[8] The gap between formal access and potential for influence is thus widened both when the pace of social change outruns traditional political arrangements and when abrupt political changes suddenly displace groups that still have some weight to throw around. Excluded groups in both instances are a threat to the regime either by the violence of which they are capable—whether revolutionary or counterrevolutionary—or by their ability to corrupt the agents of the existing order.

To illustrate, we may compare the strains created by the gap between formal access and potential for influence in seventeenth-century England and in Ghana after independence. In the former case large landowning families and well-placed nobility enjoyed preferential access to positions of power and influence under the monarchy. The rapid pace of commercialization had even by this time, however, created a commercial elite of considerable wealth whose formal influence did not yet reflect their newly acquired power in the economy. As this new elite had interests that often clashed with those of the older landowning magnates, they employed their wealth to influence state policy informally. Some bought seats in parliament by bribing small electorates or by advancing loans to impecunious notables who controlled a constituency. Other sought, by means of loaning money to the Crown, to assure themselves a lucrative franchise or a strategic post in the king's administration. These activities were not illegal at the time, although older elites complained loudly against the steady infiltration of new men. The commercial elites were not, of course, the only excluded group since both the new urban mass and the increasingly destitute rural wage-laborers had no influence till late in the nineteenth century. But these latter groups had few resources and little organization with which to press their demands save by occasional riots that generally lacked both leadership and direction. Until they acquired the force of organization, their exclusion could be enforced without greatly threatening the system. Wealth elites, by contrast, had the resources to make their way informally to power.

In England at this time, then, we have an example of a formal political system that has not kept pace with momentous changes occurring in the society. A new wealth elite whose resource position is growing steadily more powerful has little formal influence while the older nobility, whose position has declined, still enjoys preferential access. The adjustment, to the extent one has been made, has not taken place formally but has occurred through informal, often corrupt means.

Ghana in 1960 presents a somewhat different situation in terms of formal and informal access. Nkrumah's Convention People's party had become the dominant institution in structuring patterns of access and exclusion. The groups under the umbrella of the CPP that enjoyed preferential access to influence were the new, lower middle class of teachers, journalists, and government clerks, the so-called "veranda boys" representing the young urban unemployed who flocked to the CPP, party-dominated trade union leadership, a large number of petty traders, and, of course, the party branches. A number of other groups, many of which had enjoyed greater access to influence in the colonial order, were placed at a disadvantage under the new regime, although they were not without resources. Wealthy Ghanaian traders and large expatriate firms that dominated the export-import sector were foremost among the groups now largely excluded from formal access. In addition, many of the traditional leaders (particularly in Ashanti areas but elsewhere as well), some smaller, upcountry minority communities like the Tiv, and the older professional and bureaucratic elites were not relatively disadvantaged by the CPP. The excluded groups each sought to improve its situation with the resources it had at hand. Many wealthy Ghanaian owners of construction firms and traders joined the CPP and contributed lavishly to its coffers and/or bribed administrators or politicians to acquire the needed licenses and permits and to win government contracts. For the expatriate firms the formal difficulties were somewhat greater since such businesses were in a legal sense outside the Ghanaian political system. But if their difficulties were greater, so were their resources for illegal influence. Foreign firms doing business with Ghana quietly contributed 5 to 10 percent of their overpriced supply contracts to the CPP; they did a lucrative business and became the financial mainstay of the party. Thus the interests of foreign business—and the CPP—were amply served by an informal system of highly priced corruption.

Other disadvantaged groups under the new regime—such as the Ashanti, Tiv, and the professional class—by and large lacked the resources to attain their ends corruptly. Consequently, the Ashanti and Tiv regions became hotbeds of opposition activity and incipient revolt that became significant only when the military and the trade unions became alienated from the Nkrumah regime. Much of the professional class was also in opposition, but it lacked the broad following that made the Ashanti and Tiv a more palpable threat.

In Ghana during this period, then, we have an example of a new regime— a sudden political change—that has abruptly displaced groups that had enjoyed formal avenues to influence in the last years of the colonial regime. The formal pattern of access has, in a sense, shot ahead of the rate of social change, pushing aside groups that still have significant political resources. Those groups that control wealth or property have resorted to corruption to repair their position while those without wealth have turned to nonviolent or violent political opposition . . .

Our feeling about corruption often depends on whether this "uninstitutionalized" influence of wealth is undermining a formal system of which we approve or disapprove. Thus, corruption in eighteenth and early nineteenth-century England seems less contemptible to us than modern corruption since it involves the subversion of an aristocratic or status-based monopoly of government. Corruption in modern liberal democratic or socialist regimes, on the other hand, seems especially damaging since it undermines both the egalitarian assumptions of majority rule and the principles of even distribution of civil and social rights of which we normally approve. Under liberal democratic regimes, corruption represents an additional and *illegal* advantage of wealthy interests over and above the *legal* advantages they ordinarily enjoy by virtue of large campaign contributions, muscle in the courts, and so forth. Wealth, in this sense, is doubly conservative in such regimes . . .

Notes

1. It seems also that western scholars have perhaps underemphasized the importance of administrative politics in their own political systems, where both particularistic and organized interests can undo the effects of legislation or secure a favorable application of the law in their own case.

2. Although not all corruption occurs at the enforcement stage and not all "influence at the enforcement stage" is corrupt, the empirical referents of the two terms overlap considerably. A striking exception, of course, is the legitimate arena of "regulatory politics" in the West—an area that largely involves contending interpretations of statutes governing private-sector activity.

3. Here we are assuming, of course, that there are few compunctions about corruption and few costs (e.g., probably of arrest) attached to such an act. Whether the bureaucrat "sells" influence—given a fixed reward—depends as well on the probability of his being caught, the penalty if caught, and his scruples.

4. Occasionally politicians even may pass legislation that restricts the private sector so as to maintain the proper ideological stance while, at the same time, permitting private firms to operate unimpeded through corruption in which the politicians may share.

5. "Pork-barrel" legislation catering to regional interests and legislation about languages of instruction in school or about local rule for minorities are exceptions to this statement. India has legislated preferential treatment for its *harijan* castes as has Malaysia for its Malay population.

6. There is a history of "special legislation" and, in England, "private member bills" that attempted to meet particularistic demands or redress specific grievances at the legislative stage. The kinds of demands represented by this type of legislation have tended increasingly to shift to the administrative or judicial arenas.

7. Samuel P. Huntington, *Political Order in Changing Societies*. New Haven: Yale University Press, 1968, pp. 59–71. The frailty of such institutions is often due to the fact that they have been tailored to the demands and requirements of narrow oligarchies.

8. Postrevolutionary France might fit this category too, inasmuch as the nobility was still a powerful force in the countryside despite the formal liquidation of the *ancien régime*.

Part III

PERCEPTIONS AND DISTINCTIONS

Introduction to Part III

These selections complement the institutional focus of the preceding one by analyzing how the cultural and social contexts in which the powers of political office are exercised affect perceptions of whether and how much corrupt behavior (as previously defined above) is morally and legally condemned. Altogether these are intellectual exercises in relativity because they develop, from various theoretical perspectives, how dependent is the perception of corruption on various contextual influences. If we ask what is required to reduce or eliminate these ambiguities, the answer probably would be the existence of a universal bureaucracy with total control to impose and adjudicate norms across all societies.

Black, Grey and White Corruption

In the absence of such a universal authority, real-life situations tend rather to reflect differences such as those discussed by Arnold J. Heidenheimer in chapter 9. From the welter of relevant literature he distills four models of community structure found in the contemporary world. He then in an elementary way characterizes how they differ from each other with regard to prototypes for political exchange relations, and the relative strength of family and community regarding norms. Are obligations to sustain and help members of one's family perceived as having a claim on the officeholder that are superior to those of the formal rules that regulate the use of the office? In two cases the answer is yes, and in others it is no, and the reasons for these and similar differences emerge from the descriptive analyses of the four types of communities.

If various forms of behavior classified as corrupt by some universal schema occur more in some types of communities, what does this imply about the degree of severity with which various kinds of corruption are morally condemned by the citizens of these communities? To illustrate a hypothetical answer to this problem, the author lists on one dimension a scale of kinds of political corruption classified, as they might be in a legal code, from petty to aggravated. He then records whether these forms of corrupt behavior are coded tolerantly (white), with some opprobrium (grey), or regarded as severe violations of community moral and legal norms (black). The suggestion is that, as one moves from the traditional to the modern, and from the boss to the civic culture-based communities, actions and exchanges that are objectively similar come to be more severely coded and often punished.

Public Conceptions and Corruption Distinctions

Any discussion of the political consequences of corruption must take into consideration the perceptions of both elites and ordinary citizens, and must recognize that their judgments—while often vague, contradictory, and at variance with more formal standards—will influence what is regarded as unacceptable behavior, and what responses (if any) are likely to occur in specific instances. Two studies present these social conceptions of corruption, analyzing the judgments of American elites and ordinary citizens and comparing them.

In the second chapter of this section, John G. Peters and Susan Welch present the results of a survey of legislators in several American states. Like the people they represent, these officials perceive many shadings and gradients of right and wrong. While their judgments are influenced by the legality or illegality of a hypothetical action, a variety of other considerations are taken into account as well—some of which, of course, reflect these elites' greater experience in politics. However, even for these politically experienced individuals, there are many "gray zones" of behavior, and many kinds of misconduct which are seen as more or less "wrong" than others depending upon characteristics of situations and of the people involved.

Subtly shaded judgments are also found in Michael Johnston's survey of ordinary citizens in a major metropolitan area. No clear boundary between right and wrong emerges in judgments of a diverse set of hypothetical actions. Instead, there is a spectrum of finely graded relative judgments, with formal standards being tempered by commonsense rationalizations, equivocations, and standards of fairness learned in everyday life. Judgments of misconduct tend to cluster into perceived categories of wrongdoing, with different class status groups varying significantly in their reactions to them.

9

Perspectives on the Perception of Corruption

Arnold J. Heidenheimer

Most actions that are considered corrupt by norm enforcers within or critics outside a political system are basically varieties of exchange transactions. Depending on the technique employed, the transactions create varying degrees of specificity of obligation on the parts of the exchangers. Bribery is the most frequently cited technique of corruption, because it creates a very specific obligation on the part of the officeholder. The more that political exchange transactions engender specific obligations, the more they resemble the prototype of an economic transaction, which rests on a formal contract stipulating the exact quantities to be exchanged. The bribed official typically agrees to undertake or to forego a designated action in return for a designated compensation.

Other kinds of corrupt political exchange agreements are based on obligations that are more vague and that involve less specific quantities.[1] Officials may tacitly agree to extend unspecified forms of future preferment to office seekers or contractors in return for accepting extensive services that have a large but deliberately unspecific value. The more developed the economy, the less specific the benefit is likely to be. A tip-off leading to purchase of stock or real estate holdings that are likely to increase sharply in value will benefit the office-holder much more than will cash presents. Indeed, the more that political exchange resembles social exchange, the more unspecific and the more difficult to classify in terms of corruption it becomes. The more com-

Source: Arnold J. Heidenheimer, *Political Corruption: Readings in Comparative Analysis,* 1970, pp. 18–28.

plex the network of social interaction and the more complicated and diverse the ways that tangible benefits can be exchanged, the less likely it is that particular actions can clearly be labeled corrupt. To the extent that their exchange transactions tend to be more direct, the citizens of less-developed countries are indeed somewhat one-sidedly exposed to the easy moral judgments of citizens of more developed societies.

Insofar as more politically developed societies are also more highly integrated societies, they tend to socialize their citizens against the temptations of material gain in ways that are organically related to the basic, supracultural definitions of corruption. If their strong civic and other social norms are effectively internalized by their members, they tend to give a greater subjective reality to "community interests" in terms of the preferences of their citizens. Thus sanctions in terms of guilt feelings and social disapproval may constitute costs that under certain circumstances may cause commitment to a proposed exchange relationship to appear irrational rather than rational from the perspective of the individual's self-interest.[2] By contrast, in a community like Montegrano no community interest or norms to enforce it are perceived to exist, hence the value of a bribe received would be discounted neither by guilt feelings nor by fear of moral condemnation.[3] It is expected that an officeholder will accept bribes when he can get away with it, and indeed community lore ascribes corruptibility to officials almost *ex officio*.

Communities at various levels of sociopolitical development may be related to various prototypical types of exchange relations. In a culture that contains a money economy but where most individuals relate only to collectivities like the family or the tribe, exchanges with other groups closely follow the economic exchange model, since there is limited precedent that might have created trust that nonspecific obligations will ever be repaid. Because the gradual expansion of mutual interaction is accompanied by a parallel growth of mutual trust, there will be a tendency to enter into more exchanges that entail unspecified obligations to well-known clients and patrons whose reliability has been established. Trust in neighbors and identification with the community certainly does not increase monotonically with modernization! As the former peasant becomes an immigrant to an urban environment, whether in his own country or abroad, his environment seems very untrustworthy and he seeks relationships resembling those he has known. Gradually, then, he and his children develop greater faith in their neighbors and greater identification with the community, because the processes of social exchange generate trust in social relations through their recurrent and gradually expanding character.[4]

It is from this conceptual background that we may attempt to approach the "central question for the scientific study of the problem of corruption," which Colin Leys suggests . . . should be posed as follows: "In any society, under what conditions is behavior most likely to occur which a significant section of the population will regard as corrupt?" However, because Leys's formulation appears overly ambitious and general at this stage of research and assessment, the following, more modest form is suggested: "Which of the various forms of behavior that a significant portion of the population regards as corrupt are more likely to be more pervasive in one society than another, and why?"

Four Types of Political Obligation Relationships

Our analysis will be developed in terms of four types of political obligation relationships characteristic of communities (see table 9.1). For each type of community we will seek to show:

1. The relative prevalence of varieties of political behavior which are considered corrupt in terms of Western elite norms regarding office-holding and civic participation.
2. The severity or tolerance with which elite and mass opinions in that community regard the varieties of behavior which are corrupt by official definition.

The Traditional Familist (Kinship) Based System

The community that comes closest to illustrating the familist-based system is Montegrano, as described by Edward C. Banfield.[5] The "amoral familists" who populate this community distinguish it from kinship-based systems in underdeveloped countries around the globe in that the absence of the "extended family" traditions emphasizes the especially narrow bases of group interests. Here loyalty to the nuclear family is the only loyalty that counts. In contrast to other Mediterranean communities, upper-class inhabitants avoid entering into patron-client relationships with the poorer families. Families are jealous of their neighbors' good fortune even if it has occurred at no cost to themselves. There is not enough trust to support the kind of "political machine" characteristic of American cities, because the voters do not believe in the promises of potential bosses, and the latter have no faith that bribed voters will stay bought. Among appointed officials there is a decided lack of any sense of duty or calling.

The Traditional Patron-Client-Based Systems

Illustrative of the patron-client-based type are the Sicilian and Greek communities studied by anthropologists Jeremy Boissevain and J.K. Campbell. They exist in the twentieth century but are still the captives of belief and authority patterns rooted in the distant past. Protection is sought outside the

Table 9.1
Types of Community and Political Exchange

Characteristic	Traditional Familist (Kinship) Based Systems		Traditional Patron-Client Based System	Modern Boss-Follower-Based System	Civic-Culture-Based System
	Within Families	Between Families			
Archetypal protector	Family head		Patron Saint	Political Boss	State (constitution and courts)
Prototype for political exchange relations	Family obligation	Economic exchange	Social and Economic exchange	Economic and social exchange	Social (indirect) exchange
Strength of community-regarding norms	—	Nil	Weak	Weak	Strong
Denotation of "patron"	—	—	Moral ideal, protector, intermediary	Protector, intermediary	Benefactor of community (art and education)
Strong reciprocal basis of obligations between chief patron and client	No	—	Yes	Yes	—

Table 9.1 (*cont.*)

Kinship/friendship network open enough to permit independent "contacts" by client	No	Yes	No (depends)	Yes (depends)	Yes
Collective (family) obligation for favors to its members	—	Yes	Yes	Yes (depends)	No
Clients directly follow patron-chief in political behavior	Yes	—	Yes	Yes	—
Family obligations perceived as having primary claim on officeholder	Yes	—	Yes	No	No

family; but in the minds of the simpler peasants the powers of supernatural patron saints and of upper-class patrons blur into one another. Ties to powerful protectors are strong, identification with the general community still quite weak. Through the patron-client relationships, which unlike the kinship relationship is based upon voluntary choice of both parties, a strong sense of reciprocal obligation develops. Friendship ties and those to the patron in particular are viewed as the "throwing stick" that gives the extended family greater range when dealing with established authority. Out of reciprocity the family head pledges his own voting support and that of his entire family to the patron's discretion. The client maintains the dependency tie to the patron because he senses a need for protection that neither the family nor the state is able to provide. In terms of social distance the lowest officials of the state are so far above him that he needs to work through the patron in order to establish favorable contact with it.

The Modern Boss-Follower-Based System

Two types of situations illustrate the boss-patronage-based system. The first is the operation of American big-city political machines in normal (that is, not excessively scandalous) times during most periods in the first half of this century. The second situation is that of a chronically corrupt town, Wincanton, as analyzed by John Gardiner[6] where the incidence of "dirty graft" has been a paramount issue for half a century. These communities differ from those in the preceding category by virtue of the fact that they are "wide-open" urban centers based upon highly differentiated economies in which even the greenest immigrant differentiates very clearly between a patron saint and the political boss. Traditionally legitimated social and bureaucratic elites have little direct influence here, for the machine makes the political decisions and the only important question is whether it is headed by a "game politician" or a "gain politician." Nonetheless, many aspects of the boss-follower relationship are modeled on that of the patron-client relationship in the traditional setting. One of the few differences in the client's situation is that, due to the greater diversity of direct links to the larger society, he has somewhat more discretion as to which mediator to attach himself to, although he may have to move to another ward to effect the change. And most importantly, since these communities are "modern," they foster and adapt to change. Thus, whereas in the traditional patron-client setting, political exchange relationships tend to be based primarily on the social exchange model and secondarily on that of economic exchange, in these modern settings it is the more flexible and adaptable economic exchange model that tends to be dominant.

The Civic-Culture-Based System

The civic-culture-based system of political exchange relationship prevails in "clean," medium-sized towns or suburbs in America or Britain. The citizens do not feel they need to work through an influential intermediary in order to get the benefit of the laws and administrative programs. They have developed strong community-regarding norms, which are supported by viable voluntary associations who repay their volunteer activists in tokens of moral satisfaction rather than money or money's worth. Political exchange relations follow a model of diversified and indirect social exchange. Crude political reciprocity in economic terms, such as the bribe, occurs very rarely. Political obligations insofar as they are still undergirded by economic exchange techniques, assume sophisticated and respectable new forms, such as testimonial dinners, lawyer's fees, consultant contracts, and campaign funds. These communities are "clean" because the political leaders are not bound by reciprocity agreements with lower-class followers, which the latter could utilize as channels for forcing their styles of competition on the more "respectable" strata. In this setting the "patron" still exists, but only in a very attenuated and generalized function. The object of his patronage, directly or indirectly, is the community at large. It may benefit directly from his philanthropy or indirectly from his patronage of creative artists, the value of whose work to the community some rank higher than market prices recognize.

Corrupt Behavior Incidence in the Four Types of Communities

All ten types of corrupt behavior listed in table 9.2 would be defined corrupt by a scrupulous upholder of Western administrative norms and civic behavior rules, and could be prosecuted in almost any North American or European country by an able public prosecutor who does not mind making enemies or appearing slightly ridiculous among his peers. What we shall attempt to show with reference to these types of corrupt behavior is their varying incidence in the four types of situations, as suggested by a loose form of content analysis of the relevant literature. Behaviors coded SOP are believed to be "standard operating procedure" in the respective locality. Behaviors coded FI are believed to occur with "frequent incidence." Those coded OI are thought to occur with only "occasional incidence." Finally, those coded OO are thought to occur without any regular pattern of incidence, with individual acts of official turpitude being no more frequent than they are in any large organization employing fallible human beings. For convenience in discussion the corrupt behaviors are arbitrarily grouped into three categories, those involving "petty," "routine," and "aggravated" corruption.

Table 9.2
Incidence and Evaluation of Corrupt Practices

Type of Behavior	Traditional Familist (Kinship) Based System		Traditional Patron-Client Based System		Modern Boss-Patronage-Based System		Modern Civic-Culture-Based System	
	Incidence	Evaluation	Incidence	Evaluation	Incidence	Eval	Inc	Eval
Petty Corruption Officials deviate from rules in minor ways for benefit of friends	SOP	W	SOP	W	SOP	W	FI	G
Routine Corruption Gifts accepted by public officials (or parties) for generalized good will	SOP	W	SOP	W	SOP	W	OI if collectivized	B G
Nepotism practices in official appointments and contract awarding	SOP	W	SOP	W	SOP	G	OI if collectivized	B G
Officials profit from public decisions through sideline occupations (clean graft)	SOP	W	SOP	W	FI SOP: Wincanton	G	OI	B
Clients pledge votes according to patron's direction	SOP	W	SOP	W	FI	G	OO	B

Table 9.2 (cont.)

Aggravated Corruption							
Clients need patron intervention to get administrative "due process"	SOP	W	FI	G	OI	B	OO	B
Gifts (kickbacks) expected by officials as prerequisite for extending "due process"	SOP	W	FI	G	OI SOP: Wincanton	B	OO	B
Officials tolerate organized crime in return for payoffs	FI	W	FI	G	OI SOP: Wincanton	B	OO	B
Activists suddenly change party allegiance for pecuniary reasons	FI	W	OI	B	OI	B	OO	B
Officials and citizens ignore clear proof of corruption	FI	W	OI	B	OI	B	OO	B

Key: SOP = Standard Operating Procedure; FI = Frequent Incidence; OI = Occasional Incidence; OO = Rare Incidence, Without Regular Pattern

B = Black Corruption; G = Gray Corruption; W = White Corruption

Petty Corruption

Petty corruption refers to the bending of official rules in favor of friends, as manifested in the somewhat untruthful reporting of details, the ignoring of cut-off dates, the "fixing" of parking tickets, and so on. It occurs widely in all four settings, although it is not standard practice in the civic-culture town, where it is likely to be frowned upon by purists, but taken advantage of by practical businessmen. In the boss-patronage community it is a widely engaged in practice, even among all recipients of the "newspaper wards."

Routine Corruption

Some of the practices listed in the category of routine corruption do occur to some extent in civic-culture towns, but usually only in forms where they are sanitized through the "collectivization of the receiver." Thus campaign contributors to political party funds may win some degree of preference as contract bidders or appointive office candidates. In the boss-patronage city, on the other hand, most of these practices were either standard or widely practiced operating procedures, with most material benefits accruing to individuals. Thus, the wealth through which many of the Irish elevated themselves to middle-class status in American cities was to a large degree accumulated in construction, trucking, and waterfront industries, in which prosperity was largely dependent upon favoritism in city contracts. Favoritism, or the guarantee of unequal access, is of course the main lever through which the machine generated the stock of resources from which it diverted the "economic" component of the rewards extended to ward leaders and voters. The boss also used patronage powers to pay colleagues for obeying orders and to bribe elected officials to follow leads.

In the *traditional patron-client* settings many of the gifts received by public officials are less clearly related to specific obligations, but are standard practice in the sense that they recur almost seasonally. Thus, some Greek shepherd families give the village president each spring a gift of cheese, butter, or meat in the hope that this may "moderate his general attitude towards them in the coming months." In return for helping them when they are in trouble, the lawyer-patron, who acts in the general role of a professional fixer, is able to promise the political support of his clients during local and national elections. The assistance of patrons is as essential in applying for a government job as it was some decades ago in Chicago, even though there is no party machine. In Sicily a former municipal employee who sought to regain his job had to mobilize two higher-class patrons before his application was given due consideration. In this setting, therefore, all the activities that would be considered "routine corruption" by official Western standards are standard procedures deeply rooted in more general social relationships and obligations.

Of course, all the syndromes noted above are also standard procedure in the amoral familist community of Montegrano. Because families in Montegrano are nuclear rather than extended, and because of the lack of the patron as mediating agent, the exchanges are more nakedly specific and the contracts more short-term in duration. A poor peasant votes for the Christian Democrats because the party has given him a "few days work on the roads each year. . . . If it ceased to give him work and if there were no advantage to be had for voting for another party, he would be a monarchist again."[7]

Aggravated Corruption

In the civic-culture-based community instances of aggravated corruption occur very rarely, if at all.

Among boss-patronage-based communities it is precisely the frequency of incidence of aggravated corruption that distinguishes "reform" periods from "scandal-ridden" ones, or "corrupt cities" from "machine cities." Thus, most of the varieties of corrupt behavior occur occasionally in the better-run "machine cities" of twentieth century America, but they were standard practice in the town that John A. Gardiner calls Wincanton.[8] Whereas in Chicago crime operators could intermittently purchase toleration from various police officials, in Wincanton the syndicate head controlled the police to the extent that he could use it to run rivals out of town. Corrupt mayors made it a standard practice to demand $75 gifts for the approval of building permits and $2,000 kickbacks for the awarding of city contracts. The crooked police chief had to pay the mayor $10,000 for his appointment, and was allowed to recoup through payoffs from organized crime. In Wincanton, therefore, the varieties of "dirty graft" and aggravated corruption were as widespread as in any traditional community, except that the more developed state of the economy caused the amounts involved in the corrupt transactions to be much larger.

The incidence pattern of aggravated corruption in the patron-client society seems to differ in two interesting ways from the same pattern in the two other communities. It differs from the boss-patronage community in that the properly connected client can use it to tap a wider variety of services. It is unlikely that anyone in the Wincanton machine would have been of much help in establishing contact with a particular university professor, who would be far less likely to offer the client a thesis that he could hand in as his own. (In the Sicilian context these acts did constitute *political* corruption.) On the other hand, this setting appears to differ from the familist society in that some of the techniques of aggravated corruption are less widely employed. The Greek shepherds conceded that "eating money" (the acceptance of small bribes) was one of the rights of office that the village president needed to exercise in order to support his family. However, they were cautious about offering bribes to higher officials; and if they pledged their votes to a patron, they usually maintained their agreements for a decent period of time. In Montegrano, on the other hand, most of the inhabitants were sure that not only the local officials, but also those up the line to the national government, were corrupt and completely without a sense of obligation to office. This belief encouraged an almost universal tendency among both officials and citizens to ignore proof of corrupt behavior even when it was directly observed and to undertake no initiatives to cooperate with established authority to invoke sanctions.

The Tolerance and Evaluation of Corrupt Practices

Although behavior fitting into any one of the forty categories in table 9.2 could be considered corrupt by some citizen who was particularly conscious of official norms, his interpretations would obviously be shared to a very widely varying degree by his fellow citizens. Indeed, it has been argued that if 99 percent of the community disagrees, then, although one's viewpoint is well-grounded in the applicable legal codes, the action is not considered "corrupt" in that community. It is this problem of normative evaluation that we seek to approach in terms of the shorthand notations of black, gray, or white corruption in table 9.2. The evaluation "black corruption" indicates that in that setting that particular action is one which a majority consensus of both elite and mass opinion would condemn and would want to see punished on grounds of principle. "Gray corruption" indicates that some elements, usually elites, may want to see the action punished, others not, and the majority may well be ambiguous. "White corruption" signifies that the majority of both elite and mass opinion probably would not vigorously support an attempt to punish a form of corruption that they regard as tolerable. This implies that they attach less value to the maintenance of the values involved than they do to the costs that might be generated as the result of a change in rule enforcement.

One of the subtler characteristics of norm patterns in the civic-culture community relates to the "grayness" of attitudes toward petty corruption. The general elite disapproval of favoritism would tend to contain its extent, even though some forms of "giving consideration" persist. This would be in contrast to the boss-patronage city, where even the reform-minded elements would tend to think that practices such as ticket fixing have to be tolerated. Attitudes toward several forms of "routine" corruption might also tend to be "gray" in the civic-culture setting, with the degree of toleration related essentially to important questions of form. The giving of gifts to public officials and nepotism may be regarded as "black," or punishable, if favors are exchanged at the level of the individual official or firm, but their equivalents are likely to be tolerated if the funds in question are "collectivized" through devices such as party campaign treasuries. Investigations often reveal that individual politicians surreptitiously cross the indistinct line differentiating "gray" from "black" behavior. Thus, in 1967, Senator Thomas Dodd of Connecticut was shown to have diverted to private use funds allegedly raised for his campaign treasury, and this revelation was instrumental in causing his colleagues to levy censure upon him.

In boss-patronage communities much of the "grayness" characterizing attitudes toward forms of "routine" corruption is likely to be associated with sharp differences between attitudes in the poorer, or "river," wards and those in the more well-to-do, or "newspaper," wards. Robert Lane and others have found that the attitude of working-class residents of large cities to reports of governmental corruption is "generally speaking a tolerant one, certainly not indignant, not moralistic, possibly insufficiently censorious."[9] Corrupt practices localized in the poorer sections are likely to be tolerated by middle-class opinion and to be strenuously resisted only when they spread into, or more directly affect, the "respectable" areas of the city. In Wincanton, surveys showed that very significant minorities were willing to be tolerant of varieties of favoritism and "clean graft," which were technically illegal; thus 35 percent thought it all right for city officials to accept presents from companies, and 27 percent had no objections if the mayor profited financially from municipal land purchases as long as the price charged was "fair." The "grayness" of attitudes in the boss-patronage city makes possible a higher threshold of enforcement beneath which multiple forms of "clean graft" and favoritism are tolerated. It is when rings of politicians and contractors expand their practices to include forms of aggravated corruption which do run counter to the values of the vast majority of the population that a "clean-up" campaign will sooner or later ensue, as John Gardiner illustrates in the Wincanton case.

In the traditional patronage-client community the attitudes toward the various forms of corruption are several shades "lighter" and more tolerant. Thus, most of the routine forms of corruption regarded as "gray" in the American city setting are viewed as "white," or quite acceptable, in this environment. The strength of informal social obligations is too great to permit significant criticism of the widely prevalent practices of nepotism and the purchase of influence. In the words of a local informant, the perception that "in Sicily all friendships are political," leads to acceptance of the fact of life that all politics involves giving preference to one's friends. There the patronage system, which Boissevain likens to "a parasitic vine," weakens the rule of law to the point where many cases of aggravated corruption are considered as falling into the "gray" rather than "black" area. In Sicily, as in Greece, it is regarded as legitimate for officials to require bribes or patron intervention in order to give the peasant what should be his due according to the law. In contrast to the modern setting, where even lower-class citizens are infused with some measure of egalitarian ideology, the peasants in this kind of community accept the arrogance of officials as an almost legitimate function of their higher social status and regard it as natural that their sympathy can only be aroused through gifts and bribes.

In the familist-based system all of the types of behavior that are considered corrupt by the standards of Western legal norms are considered "white," or acceptable, by the bulk of the population. As effective community-regarding norms are lacking, attitudes will be determined in individual cases in relation to who is doing the corrupting on whose behalf. Since public affairs are conceived to be the exclusive concern of those public officials who are paid to look after them, the latter can expect little citizen cooperation, which would be a prerequisite for norm enforcement. In the face of such total apathy they, too, will incline to ignore evidence of obvious corruption, and thus join the conspiracy of silence that permits most forms of corrupt activity to have a frequent incidence or to become standard operating procedure.

Notes

1. Harold D. Lasswell, "Bribery." *Encyclopedia of the Social Sciences,* vol. I. New York: Crowell-Collier-Macmillan, 1930, pp.690–92.
2. Peter M. Blau, *Exchange and Power in Social Life.* New York: Wiley, 1964, p. 258.
3. Edward C. Banfield, *The Moral Basis of a Backward Society.* New York: The Free Press, 1958.
4. Blau, *op. cit.,* p.94.
5. Banfield, *op. cit.*
6. John A. Gardiner, "The Politics of Corruption in an American City." In Arnold J. Heidenheimer. ed., *Political Corruption: Readings in Comparative Analysis,* New Brunswick. N.J.: Transaction Publishers, 1978. pp. 167–75.
7. Banfield, *op. cit.*
8. Gardiner, *op. cit.*
9. Robert E. Lane, *Political Ideology.* New York: Free Press. 1962, p.335.

10

Gradients of Corruption in Perceptions of American Public Life

John G. Peters and Susan Welch

Though corruption has been an ever-present part of American political life (cf. Tocqueville, 1861), analysts of American politics have not studied it systematically (for exceptions, see Greenstein, 1964; Gardiner, 1970; Wolfinger, 1972). This chapter offers a conceptual scheme which circumvents definitional problems that have posed such a roadblock to the systematic study of corruption. We also provide some attitudinal data about corrupt acts gathered from state senators across the United States and show how our scheme contributes to the analysis of this data. Finally, some reasonable future research directions for the study of corruption are briefly discussed.

Definitions of Political Corruption

The attention devoted to a serious examination of corruption in America occurs largely at those times when particularly venal acts have been exposed. Thus, the post-Watergate period has brought with it a renewed interest in the study of political corruption, especially among political scientists (cf. Rundquist et al., 1977; Scoble, 1973; Gardiner, 1970, Berg et al., 1976). In all of these studies it becomes immediately apparent that no matter what aspect of American politics is examined, the systematic study of corruption is hampered by

Source: John G. Peters and Susan Welch, "Political Corruption in America: A Search for Definitions and a Theory." *American Political Science Review, 78* (September 1978), 974–84. By permission of the publisher.

the lack of an adequate definition. What may be "corrupt" to one citizen, scholar, or public official is "just politics" to another, or "indiscretion" to a third. Several definitions of political corruption have been proposed and generally can be classified according to three criteria: definitions based on legality, definitions based on the public interest and definitions based on public opinion (Scott, 1972).

The definition of political corruption based on legalistic criteria assumes that political behavior is corrupt when it violates some formal standard or rule of behavior set down by a political system for its public officials. Perhaps the clearest statement of this definition has been given by J.S. Nye when he stated that a political act is corrupt when it "deviates from the formal duties of a public role (elective or appointive) because of private-regarding (personal, close family, private clique) wealth or status gains: or violates rules against the exercise of certain types of private-regarding influence" (Nye, 1967, p. 416). While such a definition of corruption is useful to the researcher in that it is generally clear-cut and can be operationalized, when the behavior in question allegedly deviates from a legal norm or standard which is not tied to a specific statute or court ruling, this definition of political corruption becomes less useful as the formal duties of office or the appropriate rules of influence become ambiguous. Moreover, this definition suffers from being simultaneously too narrow and too broad in scope; all illegal acts are not necessarily corrupt and all corrupt acts are not necessarily illegal.[1]

Definitions of political corruption based on notions of the public or common interest significantly broaden the range of behavior one might investigate. Consider the definition proposed by Arnold Rogow and Harold Lasswell: "A corrupt act violates responsibility toward at least one system of public or civic order and is in fact incompatible with (destructive of) any such system" (Rogow and Lasswell, 1966, pp. 132–33). While this definition focuses our attention on any act or set of acts which threaten to destroy a political system, the researcher has the responsibility of determining what the public or common interest is before assessing whether a particular act is corrupt. The possibility exists that a behavior may be proscribed by law as corrupt but be beneficial for the common good, such as "fixing" the papers of an illegal alien who contributed his labor and skills to a rapidly expanding economy. Furthermore, this definition enables a politician to justify almost any act by claiming that it is in the public interest.

A third approach to the definitional problem suggests that a political act is corrupt when the weight of public opinion determines it so (see, for example, Rundquist and Hansen, 1976). This conception of political corruption harbors the same limitations as the public interest focus. Studies of public opinion have revealed that on many issues public sentiments are either ambiguous (significant portions of the public hold no opinion or hold those of low intensity) or are divided in their opinions. Additionally, a definition of corruption based on public opinion must consider the differences which may exist between the public and political elites in their assessment of appropriate standards of public conduct.

This approach to political corruption is probably best illustrated in the work of Arnold J. Heidenheimer (1970). In his view the corruptness of political acts is determined by the interaction between the judgment of a particular act by the public and by political elites or public officials. According to this scheme, behavior is judged particularly heinous or corrupt if *both* public officials and the public judge it corrupt *and* both wish it restricted. This type of behavior is referred to as "black" corruption. An act such as "a public official involved in heroin trafficking" would most likely fit this category in that both groups find the act reprehensible and would demand punishment for the guilty public official. At the other end of the corruption spectrum might be categorized political acts judged corrupt by both public officials and the people, but which neither feel are severe enough to warrant sanction. Quite possibly such acts of "white" or petty corruption as a city council member fixing a parking ticket for a constituent fall into this category. Between these two extremes of corruption acts lie the forms of behavior which are the most difficult to define and detect, and consequently are potentially most destructive to a political system organized along democratic principles. Heidenheimer refers to these political acts as "gray corruption" when either public officials or the people want to see an action punished, while the other group does not, or it may well be that one group is intense about the issue and the other ambivalent or unconcerned.[2] Heidenheimer's work in this area, therefore, points to the existence of a scale or dimension of corruption that can be used to classify political behaviors according to their degree of corruptness from "black" to "gray" to "white." It does not, however, account very well for those acts seen as corrupt by only one group, nor does it seek to explain *why* some groups may see an act as corrupt but other groups see it as less corrupt. Although this conception of political corruption is based on the criterion of opinion (both public and elite), the assessment of a specific political act may rest on violation of a legal norm or a threat to the public interest. In other words, definitions of corruption are not mutually exclusive: elements of the public interest and public opinion criteria are embedded in legal norms which sanction certain political behaviors as corrupt.

Although the Heidenheimer scheme enables us to classify politically corrupt acts in a general way, a more detailed scheme seems required if we are to classify adequately the many variations of corrupt acts, and if we are to develop an explanation of why some acts are judged corrupt and others not. We propose to analyze potentially corrupt acts according to the component elements apparently involved with every political act or exchange. We believe this process can meaningfully be partitioned into the "public official" involved, the actual "favor" provided by the public official, the "payoff" gained by the public official, and the "donor" of the payoff and/or "recipient" of the "favor" act. Although at this early stage in the development of a theory of political corruption it would be too much to claim to be able to specify the exact nature of each of these components and its relation to the others, we do believe that examining acts of political corruption in this manner might hold the key to a better understanding of why public officials perceive some acts as corrupt and others as "just politics," and why public officials and the public may differ in their assessment.

When discussing the subdimensions of each component of a potentially corrupt act, we will be stating some propositions about what acts will be seen as corrupt. Those propositions will be discussed in some detail later. When examining a "public official" involved in an alleged act of corruption, we are particularly interested in whether the act was entered into in the performance of the official's *political* duties. Presumably, an act which is considered mal-feasance, misfeasance, or nonfeasance of public duty is *more* corrupt than a behavior engaged in outside of one's official political role. In other words, misusing one's political office for private gain is more objectionable than engaging in questionable behavior outside of one's official duties.[3]

A second characteristic of the public official that seems to determine whether behavior is to be judged corrupt is the political nature of the public official's role. If a public official is in a judicial or other nonpolitical post, certain acts are more likely to be seen as corrupt than if the public official holds a political post. For example, judges have traditionally been held to higher standards with regard to conflict-of-interest situations than legislators. With the new congressional actions to regulate conflict of interest, it is possible that this situation may be changing at the national level, however.

The second component of a politically corrupt act is the "donor" of the payoff or "recipient" of the political favor. It is most important to determine if the "donor" is a *constituent*, broadly defined, or a nonconstituent. If the donor is a constituent, then a "favor" given is more likely to be perceived as *less* corrupt than if the favor is rendered to a nonconstituent. The reason is obvious: acts which are performed under the rubric of "constituency service," no matter how questionable, have a certain legitimacy. Of two similar, poten-tially corrupt acts, the odds are that the constituency-related act will be judged less corrupt than the service rendered to the nonconstituent. Beard and Horn (1975) offer two examples supporting this proposition. In one case, members of congress were asked about the legitimacy of putting favorable articles about campaign donors in the *Congressional Record,* as a "thank you" to donors. This was seen as more legitimate if the donor were a constituent rather than a firm outside the district. A second example involved accepting rides to and from one's congressional district on a national firm's private plane. If the firm had ties to the constituency, accepting such favors was seen as more legitimate than if the firm had no such ties. Probably the most corrupt situation is when the donor is the public official himself. If the public official can directly enrich himself by tapping the public till, he himself is the donor. Examples of this include padding the expense account, using public funds for personal travel, using money allocated for office expenses for personal activities, and so on.

Another characteristic to be considered is whether the "donor" of the payoff (recipient of the "favor") is more than one private individual or firm. We argue that the single donor will be perceived as making an action more corrupt than if the donor is a large group of individuals or firms.

A third component to consider is the "favor" provided by the public official. We can surmise that the corruptness of the favor will vary in some ways as does the nature of the donor. Private favors and nonconstituency favors will be seen as more corrupt than those with large public benefit or those done for a constituent.[4] Finally, if the favor is done in routine performance of duty rather than extraordinary activity, it is less likely to be seen as corrupt. For example, a member of congress who makes a routine phone call to a federal agency to check on a federal contract of a firm whose officers supported the congress member in an election campaign is less likely to be viewed as performing a corrupt act than one who makes threats or acts in a way that the federal bureaucrat perceives as non-routine.

The fourth component of a potentially corrupt act, the "payoff" given to the public official, is possibly the most important determinant of its perceived corruptness. The obvious fact to consider is, of course, the size of the payoff. It should come as no surprise that the larger the payoff, the greater the perceived degree of corruptness in the act, although as we shall see later on, just what is "large" can be difficult to agree upon. The payoff can also vary according to the long- versus short-range nature of the benefit to the public official. We would assume that a short-range benefit would be perceived as more corrupt than a payoff that will yield benefits at a much later date, because the long-range payoff is separated in time from the favor done. Consider, for instance, an official of a regulatory agency who takes a lucrative position in a regulated corporation after leaving government service. Presumably the official looked with some benevolence on the activities of the corporation while in public office; if that official had been given an immediate tangible payoff, for example a gift of money, we think most people would charge corruption. But the later payoff probably is seen by many as legitimate.[5]

In a similar vein, the payoff can be distinguished as to whether it is specific or general. If a payoff takes specific form, such as money or a service rendered, it will likely be perceived as more corrupt than a general payoff, such as future electoral support or good will. Although this is a rather special case of payoff, it is also important to determine if a gift is related to a political campaign. Payoffs in the form of campaign contributions have a legitimacy not rendered to other forms of material payoffs. A $1,000 cash donation to a campaign is perfectly acceptable, while an equal amount offered as a personal gift to a public official subjects the donor and official to possible legal penalties.

In table 10.1, we have summarized the basic components of a politically corrupt act, and indicated the dimensions in each component which can vary according to perceived corruptness. In outlining these components and their salient characteristics, we have articulated a large number of testable propositions about the conditions under which an act can and will be viewed as corrupt. We have only outlined propositions at the first level, i.e., dealing with each subdimension singly, and have not defined propositions dealing with more than one subdivision at a time. Certainly an act having most or all of the characteristics listed on the left side is considered more corrupt than one having only characteristics on the right. Which components are most important in determining corruptness is a researchable question not answered here. Yet taking a broader view, our rudimentary scheme offers a conceptual framework for analyzing and comparing potentially corrupt political acts. This framework allows us to circumvent the definitional problems surrounding the meaning of "corruption."

The Study Design

Our study was designed specifically to ascertain information on attitudes about corruption held by a large group of public officials. We mailed questionnaires to all 978 state senators in 24 states.[6] After three mailings, 441 senators had responded with completed questionnaires.[7] Response rate by state ranged from only 21 percent in California to over 78 percent from North Dakota. Generally, response rate was slightly higher in the rural states than in the industrialized ones.[8]

The major focus of the questionnaire was a series of items concerning ten actions by public officials that might or might not be considered corrupt. As sometimes happens, we have since found problems and lack of clarity in some of the items These problems will be discussed later. The items are as follows (in the order listed on the questionnaire):

1. A presidential candidate who promises an ambassadorship in exchange for campaign contributions (AMBASSADOR);
2. A member of congress using seniority to obtain a weapons contract for a firm in his or her district (WEAPONS);
3. A public official using public funds for personal travel (TRAVEL);
4. A secretary of defense who owns $50,000 in stock in a company with which the Defense Department has a million-dollar contract (DEFENSE STOCK);

5. A public official using influence to get a friend or relative admitted to law school (LAW SCHOOL);
6. The driveway of the mayor's home being paved by the city crew (DRIVEWAY);
7 A state assembly member while chairperson of the public roads committee authorizing the purchase of land s/he had recently acquired (LAND SALE);
8. A judge with $50,000 worth of stock in a corporation hearing a case concerning that firm (JUDGE):
9. A legislator accepting a large campaign contribution in return for voting "the right way" on a legislative bill (RIGHT WAY);
10. A member of congress who holds a large amount of stock (about $50,000 worth) in Standard Oil of New Jersey working to maintain the oil depletion allowance (OIL).

We omitted items on which we felt there would be near total consensus, either because they were so serious or because they were so trivial; at one extreme, for example, a public official engaging in heroin traffic, and at the other, a policeman taking a free cup of coffee from a local cafe. We asked several questions about each item, with five degrees of response. In this article we will examine responses to the question as to whether the act was believed to be corrupt or not.

Findings

We do not have enough items to explore systematically a number of propositions that could be generated by our work, but we will use these data in ways that indicate the usefulness of our scheme in analyzing corruption. We first ranked the items according to the proportion agreeing that the act was corrupt or very corrupt (table 10.1). In table 10.2 we have sketched the most salient characteristics of each act, according to our fourfold scheme; we have also outlined the characteristics of a hypothetical act in which a member of congress in a district with a large percentage of minority population votes in favor of the civil rights act (CIVIL RIGHTS). In return, members of civil rights groups in the district support the member of congress in a reelection bid. We judge that few would see anything corrupt in this sequence of events.

The first conclusion from table 10.3 is that the acts considered corrupt by most people have many characteristics starred (where starred characteristics indicate more corrupt features, i.e.. features on the left-hand side of table 10.1). Clusters of stars are particularly apparent in the "payoff" boxes. Acts considered by few to be corrupt

Table 10.1
Components of a Potentially Corrupt Act and some Salient Characteristics

Component	More Corrupt	Less Corrupt
Public official		
Type of position	"Nonpolitical," i.e., the official is a judge	Political
Role when act performed	Public role, i.e., act is done as part of official's public duties	Private role, i.e., act is performed by public official acting as a private citizen
Donor's relation to public official	Nonconstituent pays official Public official pays self	Constituent pays official
Favor rendered by public official		
Type of benefit	Private	Public
Type of recipient	Nonconstituent	Constituent
Nature of act providing favor	Nonroutine, i.e., official departs from normal routine to provide favor	Routine, i.e., favor is performed as routine part of job
Payoff		
Size	Large	Small
Time when benefits accrue to donor	Short-range benefit	Long-range benefit
Substance	Specific	General
Relation to campaign	Noncampaign	Campaign

have few stars; CIVIL RIGHTS has only one. Those acts whose corruptness is most disputed have an intermediate number of characteristics starred. We can also immediately see that any one attribute, in isolation, probably does not determine corruptness. For example, an act performed in one's public role may lead to corruption, but simply knowing that an official performed an act as part of a public role tells us nothing by itself. Unfortunately not enough information was given to classify fully some of the acts on our four components. Greater specificity may have changed the public officials' responses, and would also have made the pattern of classification clearer.

Four acts were perceived as corrupt by over 90 percent of our sample: RIGHT WAY, DRIVEWAY, TRAVEL, and LAND SALE. While two of these acts involve minor sums of money, all are illegal and all result in personal financial gain for the public official. In terms of our four components we can say that three of the four acts are characterized by the merger of the donor and the public official role. That is, in the cases of DRIVEWAY, TRAVEL, and LAND SALE, the public official is in the position of personally ensuring direct financial gain. Of our ten examples, these are the only three where such a merger is the case, and are the instances of highest con-

Table 10.2
Characteristics of Ten Potentially Corrupt Acts

Act	Public Official	Donor	Favor	Payoff
DRIVEWAY	Political, public role*	Self*	Private*	Large(?)* Specific* Short-range* Noncampaign*
TRAVEL	Political, public role*	Self*	Private*	Large* Specific* Short-range* Noncampaign*
LAND SALE	Political, public role*	Self*	Private*	Large* Specific* Short-range* Noncampaign*
RIGHT WAY	Political, public role*	Unclear ?	Unclear ?	Large* Specific* Short-range* Campaign
JUDGE	Nonpolitical,* public role*	Unclear ? (in part) Self*	Unclear Potential Private* Routine act	Indeterminate size Specific* Long-range Noncampaign
AMBASSADOR	Political, public role*	Constituent	Private* Constituent	Large* Specific*

Table 10.2 (*cont.*)

DEFENSE STOCK	Political, public role* (?)	Unclear, in part self*	Routine act Unclear Potential Private* Routine	Short-range* Campaign Indeterminate size Specific* Long-range Noncampaign*
OIL	Political, public role*	Unclear, in part self*	Unclear Potential Private* Routine	Indeterminate size Specific* Long-range Noncampaign*
WEAPONS CONTRACT	Political, public role*	Unclear, possibly Constituent	Unclear, possibly nonroutine*	Small Nonspecific Long-range Noncampaign
LAW SCHOOL	Political, unclear	Unclear, possibly Constituent	Unclear, possibly nonroutine*	Small Nonspecific Long-range Noncampaign
CIVIL RIGHTS	Political, public role*	Constituent	Routine Constituent Public	Small Nonspecific Long-range Possibly campaign

Table 10.3
Percent Agreeing Act is Corrupt

	Percent of Respondents Viewing This Act as Corrupt	Percent of Respondents Believing Most Public Officials Would Condemn This Act	Percent of Respondents Believing Most of Public Would Condemn This Act
Driveway	95.9	92.2	97.5
Travel	95.2	80.4	96.5
Land Sale	95.1	92.1	97.5
Right Way	91.9	82.2	94.3
Judge	78.8	82.3	91.0
Ambassador	71.1	44.5	81.2
Defense Stock	58.3	62.1	84.4
Oil	54.9	55.1	81.2
Weapons Contract	31.6	20.9	34.4
Law School	23.7	15.5	35.9

sensus. The fourth case perceived as corrupt by over 90 percent is RIGHT WAY. Here the donor is not the public official but an unspecified second party. However, the payoff is very direct and immediate, though in the context of a campaign contribution. We assume that if a campaign contribution were not involved, almost all would have seen the act as corrupt. RIGHT WAY might be compared with another example, OIL, where the payoff from voting a certain way is much more indirect and long-range (i.e., the possible increase in the value of the legislator's stock), and fewer see this type of payoff as corrupt. In sum, from these four examples, we infer that these illegal acts are judged highly corrupt because of the merger of the donor and public official role in three cases, and because of the direct and monetary gain in exchange for a vote in the fourth.

At the other end of the continuum, less than 40 percent of the sample found LAW SCHOOL and the WEAPONS examples corrupt. These acts might be characterized as rather minor forms of influence peddling. In both cases, the payoff is indirect and long-range: good will that perhaps increases the possibility of future campaign support. In both cases the donor is presumably a constituent. The acts themselves obviously are seen by most as routine kinds of favors that public officials try to do for constituents, and thus only a minority are willing to call the acts corrupt.

Our fourfold typology also sheds some light on why there is some ambiguity about these acts. While the payoff is long-range, and the donor a constituent, it is implied that doing the favor takes the legislator outside the narrow performance of legislative duty. While the question is unfortunately silent about some aspects of the transaction, it can be presumed that the legislator is calling the law school dean or members of the admissions committee in the one instance, and perhaps putting undue pressure on a bureaucrat in the other. These acts would be considered by some to be overstepping the normal scope of a legislator's activity, but by others as routinely trying to provide a constituent service. Perhaps a clarification of the item would allow a better interpretation.

The acts where there is the least consensus are conflict of interest activities: OIL, DEFENSE STOCK, JUDGE, and AMBASSADOR. In each case, public officials are in the position of furthering personal financial interests while making a decision in their public role. In the case of DEFENSE STOCK, OIL and JUDGE, public officials are in the position of performing a favor (i.e., casting a favorable vote or awarding a contract) for which the payoff is an increase in the value of their own stock. Unlike the DRIVEWAY, TRAVEL or LANDSALE instances, legislators are not the sole donors, although they are in the position of being past donors. Public officials, by their acts, cannot convert favors directly into payoffs. Other events might have an impact on the stock's value, regardless of a public official's favor. And, the payoff is much less direct than a cash grant or immediate service rendered. The government contract, the favorable court ruling, the increased oil depletion allowance may or may not increase stockholders' dividends. On the other hand, the payoff is more tangible than the generalized "good will" engendered by the WEAPONS or LAW SCHOOL acts.

Other factors are also involved in comparing conflict-of-interest acts to the others previously discussed. The size of the payoff as well as its immediacy influences an official's perception of corruption. We cannot demonstrate that with our data, as all involve $50,000 worth of stock. Beard and Horn (1975), however, offer a relevant example. More congress members believe it more corrupt for a legislator to cast a vote for benefits to the savings and loan industry when the legislator owns $100,000 worth of stock rather than only $5,000 (1975, p.22). In our own data, several people indicated that if instead of owning $50,000 of stock, the secretary of defense were a "major" stockholder, then the taint of corruption might be greater.

Finally, in these four items we can see that the nature of the public office is also relevant. The conflict of interest involving a judge was believed more odious than that involving either a bureaucrat or a member of congress. A judge, in a nonpolitical role, is held to higher standards than are legislators.

The AMBASSADOR items differ from the OIL, DEFENSE and JUDGE acts. The payoff, a campaign donation, is much more immediate. The donor, however, is providing a campaign contribution rather than funds to be used simply for personal enrichment. To us, the AMBASSADOR and RIGHT WAY cases seem parallel. In one case, the favor is a vote, in another, an appointment. Why the former is seen as more corrupt is undoubtedly because the "spoils system" of appointment has a residue of legitimacy that the practice of "voting for pay" has not.

Our typology of corrupt acts helps explain why these conflict-of-interest behaviors are often ambiguous. As the payoff becomes more and more long-range, and the donor and favors are constituency-oriented, it is easy to argue that an act is not corrupt. Most public officials hope that all acts have some positive payoff for them, principally reelection (Mayhew, 1975), and doing constituency-oriented favors is one way to increase the probability of reelection.[9] When the "favor" done for a constituent coincides with personal enrichment, then the charge of conflict of interest is relevant. Clearly our sample is ambivalent and divided about the propriety of these acts.

In sum, the simple rank ordering of our ten examples shows at one end of the continuum a clustering of acts that are clearly illegal or represent a direct financial gain, at the other, acts that are minor influence peddling, and in between a set of acts representing a variety of conflict of interest situations. A Guttman scaling procedure revealed that this set of acts was unidimensional. They scaled in the same order as discussed, and produced a coefficient of reproducibility of .95, as shown in table 10.4.[10]

Our categorization of the components of a corrupt act aided in pinpointing some of the reasons for differential perceptions of the corruptness of various acts. The nature of the favor, the donor, the public official, and particularly the payoff were all useful in analyzing these perceptions. Acts more perceived as corrupt tended to have different characteristics from those few perceived as corrupt. And, where there was near-unanimity about the corruptness of an act, more components of the act were regarded as corrupt than where there were divided sentiments. Using only these ten acts, it could not be determined which (if any) components, or combinations of components, were crucial in influencing perceptions. More research on that point is necessary. We have only explored reasons why some acts are perceived as more corrupt than others; we have not yet tried to analyze why there are intergroup differences in perception of corruption, particularly differences between elites and the public.[11]

Discussion

Political corruption has not been subjected to the sort of rigorous analysis received by other phenomena in American politics. In large measure, the difficulty of defining "political corruption" accounts for this neglect. The present analysis develops a fourfold classification scheme composed of what we consider the essential ingredients of every act of political corruption. While this scheme is not a "theory," it does offer a conceptual framework helpful in comparing and analyzing potentially corrupt acts. In doing that it allows us to avoid the definitional pitfalls which have stalemated the study of corruption for so long. These problems can be avoided because the components of our conceptual scheme allow one to analyze acts classified as corrupt according to any of the corruption definitions described earlier: the public opinion, public interest, and legalistic definitions.

The scheme, for instance, renders the "public opinion" definition more usable by refining it in such a way as to allow gradients of corruptness in an act and to assist in finding reasons why public officials and elites hold similar or divergent beliefs about a particular corrupt act. This can be accomplished by systematically varying each component of our scheme over a wide variety of acts. The result should enable researchers to pinpoint differences between elites and the mass public, and thus to infer why there are divergent areas— "gray areas of political corruption." Might it be because the two groups view the "payoff" differently: what is seen as small or petty by public officials may be viewed as large and serious to citizens? Or, does the divergence lie in the perception of what is extraordinary in the act providing the favor? Many similar explanations could be posited and tested.

Moreover, the opportunity now exists to explore possible differences in corruption perceptions based on social class and other subgroups in the population such as race, region, and sex (see Welch and Peters, 1977b). Corruption may also be related to psychological or attitudinal predispositions. For example, "private" vs. "public-regarding" distinctions sometimes used to explain corrupt behavior can be encompassed within our scheme. For instance, are citizens and elites whose approach to political life is considered "private-regarding" inclined to be less severe in their condemnation of certain political acts than those displaying a "public-regarding" disposition? In this manner, the study of political corruption can be integrated into the broader propositions about the social and attitudinal bases of political behavior.

The scheme can also be related to the definitions of corruption based on

Table 10.4
Correlation Matrix of Perceived Corruption Items

	TRVL	LDSL	RTWY	JUDG	AMB	DFST	OIL	WPNS	LAWS
Driveway	.19	.28	.28	.06	.12	.13	.02	.03	.09
Travel	—	.29	.35	.07	.15	.08	.10	.10	.10
Land Sale		—	.33	.16	.15	.16	.06	.08	.10
Right Way			—	.16	.20	.14	.10	.14	.06
Judge				—	.16	.45	.31	.11	.20
Ambassador					—	.19	.23	.15	.22
Defense Stock						—	.46	.07	.18
Oil							—	.12	.12
Weapons Contract								—	.12

"illegal acts" or violations of the "public interest." Are all corrupt acts viewed similarly which are proscribed by law because they deviate from the formal duties of public office for personal gain? If so, the explanation for the common belief may lie in the components of illegal acts such as the payoff, favor, public official or donor. One can view acts considered to be against the public interest or order in a similar way. An act of political corruption may or may not be viewed by all public officials and citizens as violating a responsibility to maintain civic order or as destroying a political system. Given the wide and varying opinions about the "public interest," one would expect they would not. And the four elements, public official, donor, favor, and payoff, allow us to compare and analyze a wide variety of political acts, whether their potential corruptness is based on illegality, violation of the public interest, or condemnation by public opinion. Our approach is also compatible with the "systemic view" of political corruption. If a large part of political corruption in the United States can be attributed to inherent weaknesses in certain offices, situations, or processes, then more honest government will only come about when those weaknesses are identified and eradicated by public officials and concerned citizens. Thus an understanding of individual attitudes is important even when considering the systemic view of corruption.

Inherent weaknesses are difficult to identify. But once exposed they can be analyzed according to our conceptual scheme. Patterns may emerge which would help one predict those offices, institutions or processes susceptible to political corruption. In this manner the sources of political corruption can be systematically identified.[12]

Our approach to defining corruption, then, is offered as a way to integrate research on corruption with the mainstream of research in American politics, a way of integrating theories about corruption to a well-grounded literature in American political beliefs and behavior. This approach also offers a way to study political corruption from the comparative and international perspective. Again the four components are common to every potentially corrupt act. Different hypotheses might be suggested in the cross-national or international study of corruption, but our scheme offers a framework for such a study. For example, a hypothesis might specify that one type of political culture views a certain type of payoff as a routine part of a public official's perquisites, while another culture views the payoff quite differently. Thus our understanding of differential views toward potentially corrupt acts is enhanced. The citizens of one country may condemn a specific political act as corrupt because it violates the norms of public office holding, while the citizens of another country condone the same act because it does not. The scheme can help us understand why the leaders of a foreign country consider it proper to expect monetary kickbacks from large U.S. corporations in exchange for a government contract, or to offer bribes to key members of the U.S. congress in exchange for favorable treatment. Moreover, it may well be that stages of economic development, modernization, social infrastructure, and so forth, bear systematic relationship to the components of our conceptual framework. It provides us with another way of demonstrating how political corruption is related to political development.

This approach can also be linked to the more traditional approach of studying corruption only when a significant local or national scandal has occurred. One can monitor public and elite attitudes over time in an attempt to link public attitudes to the situational context.

For too long the systematic study of political corruption has been neglected by serious students of American politics. That this should be so is understandable, considering not only the imposing conceptual problems but also the lack of intellectual respectability about the concept itself. But it has become increasingly evident to citizens, public officials, and scholars alike that "corruption in politics" is just too prevalent a phenomenon not to be subjected to rigorous study. Our chapter has attempted to demonstrate one approach, but by no means the only approach, to the systematic study of political corruption.

Notes

1. Berg, Hahn, and Schmidhauser (1976, p. 170) discuss seminars being conducted for large campaign donors on how to use the loopholes in the new campaign fund laws.
2. Harry Scoble (1973) refers to the situation (gray corruption) where public officials tolerate a corrupt act or practice and citizens are unaware or ignorant of the act but would condemn it if they knew about it as "systemic corruption." Moreover, this view of political corruption is useful and important in that it leads to an emphasis on the basic defects and weaknesses in the political system which may be responsible for corruption (see Berg, Hahn, and Schmidhauser, 1976). Therefore, rather than attributing such phenomena as "Watergate" to the weaknesses and foibles of individual political actors, the "systemic view" of corruption would lead to a search for the sources of "Watergate" in the defects of the political process itself.
3. The recent example of Congressman Allan Howe's (D-Utah) alleged solicitation of a prostitute might be a good example. He committed an illegal act, but it would hardly be called the misuse of public office. This is not to say that the voters in his district judged him any less harshly. The other recent "congressional sex scandal," that of Congressman Wayne Hayes, who allegedly put Elizabeth Ray on the payroll only because she was his mistress, more rightly fits into the misuse of public office category, and thus would be judged more potentially corrupt.
4. Even though the dimensions of "favor" are similar to those outlined for the "donor," there are some differences. For example, it is conceivable that a private donor might pay for a favor having public benefit.
5. President Carter, however, has extracted pledges from his high-level appointees that they will not take jobs with firms doing business with or regulated by their agency for a period of two years.
6. All of our mailings, sent in October, December and January, 1975–76 were sent to

the senators' home addresses, in order to minimize the possibility that the senator would delegate filling out the questionnaire to a staff member or legislative intern. The states surveyed were ALABAMA, California, Connecticut, Florida, Georgia, Illinois, IOWA, Kansas, Kentucky, Maine, Massachusetts, MICHIGAN, Minnesota, MISSOURI, Nevada, New Jersey, New York, NORTH DAKOTA, Oregon, PENNSYLVANIA, TEXAS, Utah, West Virginia, and Wyoming. These states were picked randomly, with a few substitutions to assure geographic dispersion (after our initial random selection, we had eight southern states but no states from the industrial Middle West). Only some of the nonrespondents,   those from   the states listed in capital letters, were sent a third-wave questionnaire.

7. For a discussion of the rationale behind the shorter, third-wave questionnaire, see Welch and Peters (1977a).

8. In addition to California, only New York (25 percent) had a response rate of less than 30 percent. Three more had response rates of less than 40 percent: Massachusetts (30 percent), Illinois (32 percent), and Minnesota (32 percent). On the other hand, eight states had a response rate of more than 50 percent: North Dakota (78 percent), Utah (62 percent), Iowa (62 percent), Alabama (60 percent), Maine (58 percent), Kansas (53 percent), Wyoming (53 percent), and Oregon (53 percent),

9. Jack Anderson commented on this point in a recent "exposé" of congressional misbehavior: "Favors are part of a politician's stock in trade. He is expected to produce government jobs, public works projects, appointments to military academies and government contracts which can be arranged within the constraints of the law and ethics. But some legislators are not content to wait until election day to bask in the gratitude of the voters.

10. This correlation matrix of the ten items partially confirms the clustering into three groups though the correlation between the two influence-peddling items is very small.

11. We have no public opinion data to test hypotheses about elite-mass differences. We do, however, have data on how our respondents think citizens feel about these acts. While the rank ordering of legislators' perceptions of citizens' beliefs of corrupt acts is similar to the respondents' belief that most citizens would see every conflict-of-interest act as corrupt (Table 3). The only acts the majority of our respondents believe citizens would not condemn are the WEAPONS and LAW SCHOOL acts. Unfortunately, these data do not test our propositions. They are only suggestive. The respondents' views of citizens' reactions to these potentially corrupt acts also form an acceptable Guttman scale, with a CR of .94 and with no items having more than 10 percent error.
One study that surveyed public opinion about corrupt acts was that of John Gardiner (1970), who assessed the attitudes of citizens about political corruption in their community. While he examined tolerance of corruption as it related to several socioeconomic attributes, he did not compare public and elite attitudes. He did find, however, that more educated people were less tolerant of corruption than those with less education.

12. In our own sample, 35.5 percent believed that there were no specific offices particularly susceptible to corruption; rather, it was a few susceptible individuals (the "rotten apple" view). Of the remaining 64.5 percent, there was little apparent agreement as to which offices were more susceptible to corruption. Most frequently mentioned were offices handling a lot of money, named by 7.3 percent.

References

Anderson, Jack (1976). "A Citizens' Committee is Needed to Crack Down on Congressmen who Cheat." *Parade,* 1 November 1976, 4–5.

Banfield, Edward and James Q. Wilson (1963). *City Politics.* New York: Vintage.

Beard, Edmund and Stephen Horn (1975). *Congressional Ethics: A View from the House.* Washington: Brookings.

Berg, Larry L., Harlan Hahn, and John R. Schmidhauser (1976). *Corruption in the American Political System.* Morristown.N.J.: General Learning Press.

Cohen, Richard M., and Jules Witcover (1974). *A Heartbeat Away.* New York: Viking.

Edelman, Murray (1964). *The Symbolic Uses of Politics.* Urbana: University of Illinois Press.

Elazar. Daniel (1966). *American Federalism: A View from the States.* New York: Crowell.

Gardiner, John (1970). *The Politics of Corruption.* New York: Sage.

Getz, Robert S. (1966). *Congressional Ethics: The Conflict of Interest Issue.* Princeton, N.J.: Van Nostrand.

Greenstein, Fred I. (1964). "The Changing Pattern of Urban Party Politics." *Annals of the American Academy of Political and Social Science* 353: 1–13.

Heidenheimer, A. J., ed. (1970). *Political Corruption: Readings in Comparative Analysis.* New York: Holt.

Lippman, Walter (1970; first published 1930). "A Theory about Corruption." In Arnold Heidenheimer (ed.). *Political Corruption.* New York: Holt, pp. 294–97.

Nye. J. S. (1967). "Corruption and Political Development: A Cost-Benefit Analysis." *American Political Science Review* 61: 417–27.

Pinto-Duschinsky, Michael (1976). "Theories of Corruption in American Politics," paper presented at the annual meeting of the American Political Science Association, Chicago, 1976.

Rogow. Arnold A. and Harold Lasswell (1963). *Power, Corruption and Rectitude.* Englewood Cliffs, N.J.: Prentice-Hall.

Rundquist, Barry S. and Susan Hansen (1976). "On Controlling Official Corruption: Elections vs. Laws." Unpublished manuscript.

Rundquist, Barry S., Gerald S. Strom and John G. Peters (1977). "Corrupt Politicians and Their Electoral Support: Some Theoretical and Empirical Observations." *American Political Science Review* 71: 954–63.

Scoble, Harry (1973). "Systemic Corruption," a paper presented at the annual meeting of the American Political Science Association, New Orleans, September, 1973.

Scott, James (1972). *Comparative Political Corruption.* Englewood Cliffs, N.J.: Prentice-Hall,

De Tocqueville, Alexis (1961). *Democracy in America,* Vols. 1–2. New York: Schocken.

Welch, Susan and John G. Peters (1977a). "Some Problems of Stimulating Responses to Mail Questionnaires: Controllable and Non Controllable Aspects." *Political Methodology* 4: 139–52.

———. (1977b). "Attitudes of U.S. State Legislators Toward Political Corruption." *Legislative Studies Quarterly* 2: 445–64.

Wilson, James Q. (1966). "Corruption: The Shame of the States," *The Public Interest* 2: 28–38.

Wolfinger, R. E. (1972). "Why Machine Politics Have Not Withered Away and Other Revisionist Thoughts." *Journal of Politics* 34: 365–98.

11

Right and Wrong in American Politics: Popular Conceptions of Corruption

Michael Johnston

> *"A great part of both the strength and weakness of our national existence lies in the fact that Americans do not abide very quietly the evils of life. We are forever restlessly pitting ourselves against them, demanding changes, improvements, remedies, but not often with sufficient sense of the limits that the human condition will in the end impose on us."*
>
> —Richard Hofstadter,
> *The Age of Reform*[1]

Political corruption and ethics in public life were important concerns during the "age of reform" of which Hofstadter wrote. They remain so today. But what do Americans consider to be corrupt? How do people apply or withhold their judgments of right and wrong in politics? My purpose here is to examine important political perceptions which, as Gunnar Myrdal once observed, constitute the "folklore of corruption."[2] This inquiry is based on a 1983 survey of the greater Pittsburgh metropolitan area in which respondents were asked, among other things, to describe their reactions to perceived corruption, and to judge the "corruptness" of a set of hypothetical examples of

Source: Michael Johnston, "Right and Wrong in American Politics: Popular Conceptions of Corruption." *Polity XVIII*, 3 (Spring 1986), 367–91. By permission of the publisher.

behavior. People apply the term "corruption" to a wide variety of activities; their reactions range from anger to amusement to cynicism and resignation. Judgments are complex and seemingly contradictory: on one hand, they involve the invocation of values and traditions deeply rooted in the American political culture; on the other, they include processes of rationalization, equivocation, and attribution of motives, growing out of everyday problems and experience. The result is not a set of clear-cut distinctions, but rather a spectrum of finely graded judgments reflecting multiple standards of right and wrong.

Social conceptions of corruption and misconduct in politics are of interest for several reasons. They have much to do with popular trust (or distrust) of elites and institutions, and they also affect one's own choices as to participation or nonparticipation in politics. Moreover, anyone undertaking reforms would be well advised to consider popular standards of right and wrong before devising anticorruption measures or asking for political support. This line of inquiry also has implications for the study of corruption itself, for there has been much debate over "objective" versus "subjective" definitions of corruption.[3] Do social perceptions of corruption offer standards and distinctions sharp enough to be built into basic analytical definitions? Or do they produce subtle judgments, categories differing only by small degree, and norms that apply to various situations in different, even contradictory ways? If the latter is the case, we might best treat popular conceptions of corruption as factors influencing political responses (or non-responses) to it. I will return to this issue in the concluding section.

Policymaking is typically a time-consuming and complex process, characterized by stiff (and often expensive) competition over important decisions and valuable public goods. Opportunities and incentives to short circuit established rules and procedures through the use of corrupt influence will frequently be present in such circumstances, both for public and private participants. Thus it is not surprising that corruption has proven such a persistent political phenomenon, nor that ethical issues have been an important continuing theme in American politics.[4] But the emotions which corruption elicits derive in part from the fact that perceived corruption runs contrary to some of the fundamental ideals and myths in our political culture. In this idealized picture, the United States is a republic in which power flows from the governed. Elites are merely temporary trustees; short terms and the principle of rotation in office suggest an officialdom made up of citizen-politicians, not of political careerists. Politics is supposed to be an endeavor of service, not a game of self-enrichment. Even when this "government of commoners" does not act on the policy demands of citizens, it is expected to abide by their basic values and rules. Closely related to republicanism is a fear of concentrated power, be it elite power or the clout of runaway majorities. The Constitution, and especially our federal system, were devised to fragment power, making it hard to win and even more difficult to hold. Lord Acton's often-misquoted observation that "power tends to corrupt, and absolute power corrupts absolutely," may not hold true as a positive proposition,[5] but as a statement of widely held political apprehensions, it retains great appeal.

It is clear that perceived corruption is difficult to reconcile with this idealized image: one does not expect a government of citizen-trustees to abuse public roles and resources for their own enrichment. Corruption can also be seen as a way to amass power despite the checks and balances of our institutions. Political wrongdoing can conflict with ideals of equality. Those who abide by the rules may be angered when they see others rise in the world through less legitimate channels; indeed, they may conclude that most of those who succeed do so through corrupt means. As Tocqueville once cautioned:

> what is to be feared is not so much the immorality of the great as the fact that immorality may lead to greatness. In a democracy, private citizens see a man of their own rank in life who rises from that obscure position in a few years to riches and power; the spectacle excites their surprise and envy, and they are led to inquire how a person who was yesterday their equal today is their ruler. To attribute his rise to his talents or his virtues is unpleasant, for it is tacitly to acknowledge that they are themselves less virtuous or less talented than he was. They are therefore led, and often rightly, to impute his success mainly to some of his vices; and an odious connection is thus formed between the ideas of turpitude and power, unworthiness and success, utility and dishonor.[6]

Revelations of scandal, or the belief that wrongdoing is common even if it never comes to light, can upset one's general image of the way politics works, of who wins and loses and how, and of one's own ability to influence government. While idealized pictures of American politics have never fully corresponded with reality, they can still be matters of great emotional investment. This is not to say that everyone starts out with these ideals in mind, only to suffer some loss of political innocence later. But for those who hold at least a few of these perceptions, corruption can strike a heavy blow.

Public Rules, Private Equivocations

Idealized pictures of the political process are not the only influences upon a "social definition" of corruption. Politics and policymaking are, after all, complex, distant and unfamiliar worlds to most people. It is unlikely that most citizens have a clear or consistent idea of the rules governing these activities. Indeed, when questionable deeds come to light, they may fall back upon everyday experience and home truths in forming their judgments. A belief that government should be made up of "people like us" may make them willing to relax their judgments in cases where the behavior in question seems understandable in terms of exigencies of everyday life.

Chibnall and Saunders have discussed these concerns in connection with cases of corruption in Britain.[7] They observe that both elites and ordinary citizens engage in the "social construction of reality,"[8] devising their own conceptions of political ethics. These incorporate not only notions of legality, but also such concerns as the secrecy of an action, exchanges of gifts and favors, the actor's intentions, and whether or not an action has become general practice. Not surprisingly, Chibnall and Saunders conclude that private citizens' "rules" differ markedly from those of elites. Citizens, they suggest, are apt to see secrecy as evidence of wrongdoing ("why keep it a secret if you have nothing to hide?"), while elites defend secrecy as a necessary part of policymaking. Gifts and favors are likewise seen by citizens as evidence of corrupt dealings, while elites claim a right to develop private friendships with people they encounter in public life. Elites are more willing to accept the notion of breaking the rules in pursuit of worthwhile goals, and to defend an action with the argument that "everyone else does it," or that while an action is forbidden in public life it has become routine in private business.

The survey data at hand do not include a sample of elites, so we cannot put these contrasts to a direct test. Chibnall and Saunders' study does suggest, however, that popular conceptions will not conform to formal definitions of corruption. Those definitions employ relatively strict formal rules of behavior, and draw important distinctions between public and private roles, resources, and relationships. We can lay the groundwork for some hypotheses about social conceptions of corruption by examining the ways these two aspects of formal definitions—rules, and distinctions between the public and the private—might be translated into popular perceptions.

Rules and Rationalizations

Stuart Henry's study of the sale of stolen goods in Britain's "hidden economy" tells us much about the fuzzy nature of social rules.[9] He describes the elaborate "excuses and justifications" people offer for their own actions, and for those of others like them. These include mitigating circumstances— that one's wages are low, or that one is in need, at least temporarily; that others have much more, or that one is constantly being tricked and "done" by big business and government. Finally, there is the oldest justification of all- "everyone else does it."[10]

Accompanying these mitigating claims are a set of equivocations that serve to "neutralize" formal standards of behavior. A person selling stolen radios, for example, would never explicitly describe them as such. Instead, the goods would be offered as "something cheap," which "fell off the back of a lorry," or as damaged goods, leftovers, or part of a "bulk purchase." These terms provide "neutral" reasons for offering goods informally and at low prices; all avoid explicitly labeling the goods as "stolen."[11]

These private equivocations are of interest to us because of their implications for the process of rationalization itself.[12] We would expect social judgments of corruptness to reflect a variety of rationalizations, equivocations, and attributions of motives—the more so if the situations and persons involved are familiar in everyday life. Smigel suggests that most people's ethical systems are better suited for judging familiar, private dealings, than they are for judging public situations, because moral systems, and the religions upon which they were often based, developed in small communities at times when great impersonal organizations did not exist.[13] As far as possible, people will judge the corruptness of public actions, as well as that of private deeds, in terms of "social ethics" worked out in everyday life. This notion helps account for Chibnall and Saunders' suggestion that citizens use such criteria as secrecy and gift-giving, in addition to, or even instead of, less familiar legal notions, to judge official conduct. It also suggests that while we might expect public figures to be judged more harshly than private citizens, we should not expect to find clear-cut and consistent distinctions between what is considered public, and what is private.

Hypotheses

It follows that we should not expect to find a sharp social distinction between corrupt and noncorrupt actions. Instead, we will find fine gradations of judgment, reflecting a variety of equivocations, mitigating circumstances, and attributed motives. But we can still compare more—and less-harshly judged examples of behavior in order to understand the implicit distinctions among them, and to draw inferences about general social conceptions of corruptness. Specifically, we might expect the following contrasts to emerge:

1. Actions which are clearly corrupt by more formal definitions will be judged as more corrupt than those of more doubtful status.
2. (a) The larger the stakes or "take," the more harsh the judgment;
   (b) similarly, the more direct the method of "taking," the harsher the judgment.
3. Actions by public figures will be judged more harshly than those of private citizens.
4. (a) Mitigating motives and circumstances will reduce the severity of judgments;
   (b) this effect should be greater when the mitigating factors fit into the realm of private equivocations than when they do not.
5. Social distance, and the contrasts between public standards and private

rationalizations, will mean that judgments will depend upon the nature of the perpetrator, and that of the victim.[14] Specifically,

(a) when a prominent person takes from a large organization, judgments should be relatively harsh;
(b) when a prominent person or organization takes from ordinary citizens, judgments should also be harsh;
(c) when ordinary citizens take from a large organization, judgments should be more lenient.

The survey data will not conclusively settle the question of what Americans regard as corruption, but with these hypotheses in mind it should yield an understanding of some of the important distinctions people make in applying, mitigating, or withholding their judgments of corruptness.

The Data

The questionnaire included several types of items. After a series probing general political attitudes, we asked respondents whether they were typically surprised or angered by revelations of corruption, and how serious a problem they felt corruption posed for the nation. Then came a set of twenty hypothetical examples of behavior, drawn from both public and private life, in which some kind of rule-breaking was arguably taking place. Respondents were asked to judge each of these actions as extremely, somewhat, slightly, or not at all corrupt. Six political information questions came next, followed by questions on the respondent's own political participation, media use, and personal characteristics. This analysis will focus primarily upon the respondents' judgments of the twenty examples of behavior.

Conceptions of Corruption

Our respondents were concerned about corruption. Some 61.8 percent responded that corruption is an "extremely serious" problem in America today, and another 35.3 percent saw it as a "somewhat serious" problem. To some extent, corruption seems to have become a part of politics as usual: only about a third responded that they were "very surprised" (2.9 percent) or "somewhat surprised" (30.7 percent) at revelations of corruption. Still, corruption can be upsetting: 45.2 percent responded that corruption tended to make them "very angry," and another 49.4 percent described their reactions as "somewhat angry." Corruption thus seems to be an important concern, and the notion that perceived corruption can engage one's emotional investment in politics receives some support.

As I have already pointed out, "corruption" in this sense is what people think it is. Thus, we need to describe the major components of their judgments of corruptness in order to understand just what it is about which they are (or are not) getting angry. We can turn to the hypothetical examples of rule-breaking to see how respondents tended to apply or withhold the label of corruption.[15] Table 11.1 presents these twenty items, rank-ordered in terms of the severity with which they were judged.

Our respondents' notions of corruption do encompass most of what would be defined as corrupt by an analyst. Rule-breaking by public officials was judged rather harshly: the mean judgment for actions initiated by public figures was 2.314 on a zero-to-three scale, versus a mean of 1.580 for private citizens' actions $(T = 21.56; p .000)$. So was behavior involving money or tangible benefits. Moreover, there seemed to be strong consensus regarding the five most corrupt actions, as suggested by their small standard deviations. Analysts and citizens seem to agree that clear-cut abuse of a public role for private benefit is corruption.

But the social definition of corruption also includes behavior which most analytical definitions would not. As shown in table 11.1, five actions were seen as clearly more corrupt than the rest, while another cluster of eight were regarded as at least moderately corrupt. A supermarket's raising prices on welfare-check days ranked in the first cluster. While such an action is reprehensible, and in some places illegal, it would not be corrupt by most formal definitions. Similarly, a purchasing agent's accepting gifts, and an individual's bouncing a check, are included in the second, "moderately corrupt," cluster. So too is a public official's false claim of holding a management degree, an action which (as Chibnall and Saunders might point out) involves secrecy and deception. While this would certainly be dishonest in a public role, it is not clearly corrupt in the sense implied by a definition such as Nye's.

The Hypotheses Revisited

Table 11.1 thus reveals no precise division between corrupt and noncorrupt actions. Comparisons among items, however, can shed some light on our hypotheses (all inter-item comparisons below are statistically significant at at least the .01 level, unless noted otherwise).

1. *Formally corrupt actions should be judged as more corrupt.* This hypothesis is supported: actions involving theft of public resources, in the view of our respondents, are definitely corrupt. Even where such an action is accompanied by rather strong mitigating circumstances (an official's taking a "cut" in order to pay a child's hospital bills), the mean judgment was more harsh than the mean for all twenty cases. But the issue does not seem to be illegality alone; in fact, the two "least corrupt" actions—a babysitter's asking for cash, and a cafe owner's giving free food to the police—are violations of federal, and of state and local laws, respectively. Perhaps many people are

Table 11.1
Mean Judgments of Examples of Behavior
(Rank-Ordered by Severity of Judgment)

0= "Not at all corrupt"
I = "Slightly corrupt"
2 = "Somewhat corrupt"
3 = "Extremely corrupt"
Grand mean for all examples: 1.930

	Mean	Std. Dev.
Treasurer embezzles $10,000	2.967	.240
Official keeps 5 percent cut for self	2.892	.361
Treasurer embezzles $500	2.795	.489
Official takes 5 percent cut, gives to party	2.591	.705
Higher supermarket prices on welfare days	2.529	.828
Official falsely claims management degree	2.227	.851
Driver offers cop $20	2.121	.914
Officer asks driver for $20	2.117	.890
Official takes 5 percent, pays child's hospital bills	2.029	1.025
Purchasing agent accepts gifts	1.870	1.000
Councilman gives city job to political supporter	1.776	1.002
Long-distance calls on office phone	1.733	.957
Person bounces a check	1.644	1.002
Councilman gives city job to son	1.463	1.022
Concealing remodeling from tax assessor	1.418	.991
Bouncing check to buy kids' clothes	1.343	1.008
Employee calls in sick, goes to game	1.180	1.036
Offer trash collectors $20	1.155	.930
Babysitter asks for cash	.882	.995
Free food for cops	.632	.893

NOTE: Missing observations were deleted on an item-by-item basis; one item had five missing observations, two had four, and all others had three or less.

not aware that the cafe owner is breaking the law; the data cannot tell us about that. it seems more likely, though, that the most corrupt actions involve an element of public trust (and/or social distance) in addition to illegality. In the private realm, by contrast, there seem to be some illegal actions which are not "really wrong."

2.a. *The larger the stakes or "take," the more harsh the judgment.* This hypothesis is supported as well. A public official's embezzlement of $10,000 was regarded as significantly more corrupt ($p = .001$) than an embezzlement of $500, and all of the five most corrupt actions in table 11.1 involve at least moderate sums of money. Similarly, cases in which the tangible stakes are small are clustered toward the bottom of the table (a possible exception being the "city job" which a councilman gives to a supporter, or to a son). Also, as expected in hypothesis 2.b., direct forms of "taking" are judged as more corrupt than indirect forms. This holds true, not just in cases of clear-cut theft (embezzlement, for example), but also in more subtle ways. The cafe owner who gives free food to the police is spending more, even in the course of a few days, than the motorist who offers $20 in order to "beat a ticket"; but the motorist is proposing a direct *quid pro quo,* and his action is seen as more corrupt. Likewise, cash-only payments for services such as babysitting defraud the government of significant tax revenues, but the connection between one person's cash dealings and the wider "underground economy" is indirect.

3. *Actions of public officials will be judged more harshly than those of private citizens.* This hypothesis receives strong support. The mean judgment for actions initiated by public role holders was significantly higher than that for privately-initiated actions, as noted earlier. A private citizen's concealing remodeling work from the tax assessors is clearly illegal, and can involve at least moderate sums of money in avoided taxes. But this action was seen as much less corrupt than a public official's falsely claiming to hold a degree in management, an action involving little or no money. Similarly, petty "office crime" by a state employee—making long-distance calls—was seen as more corrupt than "an employee calling in sick and going to a ball game," even though the value of a missed day's labor may well be greater than that of a few telephone calls. The telephone calls, on the other hand, may be seen as a more direct form of "taking."

4.a. *Mitigating motives and circumstances will reduce the severity of judgments.* Table 11.1 shows strong support for this hypothesis: the judgment of a person's "bouncing" a check, for example, is significantly relaxed when it is added that he or she did so in order to buy clothing for children. An official's taking a cut of a contract was seen as slightly less corrupt ($p= .000$) if he gives the money to his political party instead of keeping it for himself, and as much less corrupt if he uses the money to pay his sick child's hospital bills.

While these results are not necessarily surprising, they do point to clear divergence between formal and social conceptions of corruption. In a court of law, the central issue would be whether or not the official took the money, not what he did with it. Indeed, the "hospital bills" item draws upon an actual case in which a highway official in a southern state took kickbacks in order to pay such expenses, and still went to prison, convicted of a felony under federal law. People may judge officials and other prominent, socially distant figures according to more demanding standards than they apply to others seen to be like themselves. But they may also be willing to relax those standards significantly if motives can be attributed that make the officials seem "more like us."

It may be useful to recall here Chibnall and Saunders' conclusions about the ways elites and citizens differ in their judgments of corruptness. Consider the much larger mitigation effect in the "hospital bills" situation than in the case in which the cut is given to a political party. In western Pennsylvania, the transfer of such funds to one's party has frequently been represented as a mitigating consideration, or even as the basis for a plea of innocence, by state and local officials charged in kickback cases. This argument is not accepted by all officials, but the frequency with which it has been offered suggests that it is construed as a genuinely mitigating factor among at least a segment of the elite stratum. For the public, however, it is a much less valid rationalization than the "hospital bills" motive, which falls closer to the realm of private equivocations discussed by Henry. When the excuse offered is understandable within this day-to-day context, people seem more willing to relax their judgments.

These differences may help make sense of another interesting comparison in table 11.1—the relatively harsh judgment applied when a council member gives a city job to a political supporter as compared to when he gives it to his son. My expectation was that the latter would be judged more corrupt; it qualifies as nepotism, and would be an illegal practice under many circumstances. But the respondents saw the rewarding of a supporter as significantly more corrupt (p=.000). Perhaps they perceived this reward as a *quid-pro-quo* "payoff," even though this is not as clearly a violation of formal rules. In western Pennsylvania, at least, many jobs—particularly those in youth programs—are exempt from civil service requirements, but are still covered by nepotism laws. Here again the motives attributed to an official who gives a job to his son are familiar and acceptable in everyday life, while those involved in rewarding one's political backers are not.

5. *Judgments of rule-breaking behavior will vary with the nature of the perpetrator and that of the victim.* Smigel suggests that such factors as the size of the "victim" organization affect popular judgments of acts of theft.[16] While not all possible variations on this notion were put to a test in the survey, table 11.1 shows support for hypotheses 5a, 5b, and 5c. They suggested that:

5(a) when a prominent person takes from a large organization, judgments should be relatively harsh;

5(b) when a prominent person or organization takes from ordinary citizens, judgments should also be harsh; and

5(c) when ordinary citizens take from a large organization, judgments should be more lenient.

Prominent persons' thefts from large organizations, such as embezzlement and cuts from contracts, are the four "most corrupt" actions in table 11.1. Similarly, a large organization's taking from a little person—a supermarket's raising prices on the days welfare checks come out—receives strong condemnation. The "ordinary person" in such a case is the welfare recipient, or possibly the taxpayer; either way, this action—again drawing upon actual events—was judged as seriously corrupt.

When the ordinary citizen takes from large organizations, reactions appear to be quite different. A homeowner who conceals remodeling work, an employee who calls in sick and goes to a ball game, a person who pays the trash collectors to take away items they are supposed to ignore, and a babysitter who asks for payment in cash are all "taking" from large organizations. One might argue that the cafe owner who offers the police free meals is trying to "buy" extra protection, but evidence suggests that this does not actually materialize. But if cafe owners *think* they get extra protection, or that they would get less if they did not treat the police, they too could be regarded as "taking." The material stakes of most such actions are of course small compared to embezzlements from the public purse. But some—unreported remodeling, for example—involve at least moderate sums of money and indirectly increase the tax bills of others. Still, actions in which an ordinary person gets back at a large organization receive some of the most lenient judgments in table 11.1— a result consistent with Smigel's findings.[17]

Not only are the situations familiar ones, open to the full range of private rationalizations already discussed; the "victims" are large, socially distant, and perceived as powerful and as possibly exploiting ordinary people. The types of "taking" involved, and the connections between the actions and their wider social costs, are indirect. Indeed, it is not altogether unlikely that the notion of large organizations' "taking" from ordinary citizens includes such routine actions as taxation in the public sector and price increases in the private, in addition to actual rule-breaking. The condemnation of that sort of "taking," together with tolerance of the "little guy's" getting back at large organizations, may then reflect strong feelings of inequality and alienation.

Table 11.2
Respondents' Mean Judgments of Twenty Behavior Examples, Broken Down by Social Class Grouping

Social Class Grouping:

	Low	Low-Middle	Middle	Upper-Middle	Upper
Mean	1.850	1.879	1.857	1.768	1.912
Std. Dev.	.707	.523	.437	.373	.502
N	7	51	75	42	32

Range of Judgments: 0 ("Not at all corrupt") to 3 ("Extremely corrupt")

Grand Mean = 1.853
Std. Dev. .466
Analysis of Variance: $F = .5174$ $p = .7230$
Test of Linearity: $F = .0212$ $p = .8844$
F (deviation) $= .6828$ $p = .5635$

Social Class and Perceptions of Corruption

So far, we have discussed some of the distinctions people employ in judging the corruptness of others' actions. But given the importance of everyday experience as a source of their criteria of judgment, we would expect different segments of the population to see things in different ways. And in our sample of respondents, perceptions of right and wrong do indeed vary with social class.

For the analysis which follows, I excluded all respondents who had withheld judgment on any of the twenty examples of behavior. This list-wise deletion reduced the sample from 241 to 207 cases, but it allowed a more thorough statistical analysis, and yielded comparisons based on a common population. In any event, the cases deleted in this manner did not come disproportionately from any class-status group. I then divided the sample into rough social class categories by summing each respondent's scores on ordinal measures of occupational status and educational attainment, and then dividing the resulting distribution into groups representing about one fifth *of the range of scores.* This procedure produced five class-status groups, labeled "low" (7 respondents), "lower-middle" (51), "middle" (75), "upper-middle" (42), and "upper" (32). It is important to remember that these terms refer to segments of the distribution of class attributes, and are not necessarily the identifications which our respondents might volunteer themselves. Still, this rough measure is based on two important components of the general concept of social class—occupation and educational attainment—and should yield valid comparisons among class-status groups.

If there are class differences in perceptions of corruption, however, they do not emerge in terms of overall severity of judgments. Table 11.2 presents respondents' mean judgments across all twenty examples of behavior—ranging from 0 ("not at all corrupt") to 3 ("extremely corrupt")—broken down by class-status group. No consistent relationship between class and the severity of judgment emerges in table 11.2. Indeed, none of the intergroup differences come close to being statistically significant. Very similar results appeared when behavior examples were grouped into categories of public—and private-sector actions.

As noted earlier, when people judge corruptness, they employ standards and categories of their own devising. Many factors which influence these judgments—everyday experience, complex rationalizations, and attributions of motives—should vary significantly across class lines. Thus, the most important class-related differences might well be qualitative, not quantitative: while people in various social strata may not differ greatly in the strength of their reactions to a whole range of rule-breaking actions, they might well perceive, and react most strongly to, different kinds of wrongdoing. To examine this possibility, I employed a factor analysis of respondents' judgments of the twenty examples of behavior (table 11.3). The analysis yielded five factors, four of which are worthy of discussion. These rotated factors can be thought of as categories of wrongdoing inferred from the respondents' judgments. While naming factors is in some ways as much an art as a science, I have labeled factors 1 through 4 as "personal taking," "official theft," "misrepresentation," and "favoritism," respectively. Some caution is in order in discussing the results, since a list of only twenty examples of rule-breaking behavior might omit types of wrongdoing important to our respondents. Still, these factors allow us to begin to discuss the categories of wrongdoing people perceive in the world around them.

The strength of the "personal taking" factor is particularly interesting in light of our emphasis upon everyday situations, problems, and rules. It seems that these considerations figure most strongly in popular judgments of corruptness. Most people, after all, will be much more familiar with the kinds of situations posed by these items than they are with questions of official conduct and wrongdoing. The "official theft" factor, while less important statistically than factor 1, represents another major category of judgments, a finding consistent with our earlier suggestion that popular conceptions of corruption will include the kinds of behavior specified by formal definitions. It is interesting to note that while factors 1 and 2 do reflect an apparent distinction between public—and private-sector wrongdoing, the personal taking factor also includes a public-sector case-that of a state employee's personal telephone calls.

The "misrepresentation" and "favoritism" factors are considerably less important in statistical terms, but are interesting for the kinds of behavior

Table 11.3
Factor Analysis of Judgments of the Twenty Behavior Examples

Varimax Rotation (only first four factors presented)

	Factor 1 "personal taking"	Factor 2 "official theft"	Factor 3 "misrepresentation"	Factor 4 "favoritism"
Officer asks driver for $20	.278	.174	.396	−.093
Official falsely claims management degree	.014	−.127	*.687*	.247
Offer trash collectors $20	*.695*	−.165	.199	.206
Councilman gives city job to son	.249	−.182	.156	*.689*
Conceals remodeling from assessor	*.748*	−.088	.030	.075
Long-distance calls on office phone	*.648*	.237	.127	.189
Purchasing agent accepts gifts	*.546*	.117	.141	.164
Treasurer embezzles $10,000	−.047	.156	.031	−.093
Free food for police	.106	.236	−.005	*.650*
Official keeps 5 percent cut for self	.182	*.629*	−.194	.151
Employee calls in sick, goes to game	*.580*	.196	.341	.232
Treasurer embezzles $500	−.069	*.623*	.183	.074
Person bounces a check	.446	.095	*.556*	.258
Official takes cut, gives to party	.022	*.709*	.113	.128
Bouncing check for kids' clothes	.398	.243	*.589*	.084
Higher prices on welfare days	.158	.173	.206	.376
Councilman gives job to political supporter	.248	.168	.193	*.665*
Babysitter asks for cash	*.731*	.134	.108	.069
Official takes cut, pays hospital bills	.179	*.650*	.355	−.128
Driver offers officer $20	.314	.378	*.565*	.042
EIGENVALUES	5.623	2.028	1.341	1.172
Percent of variance	28.12	10.14	6.71	5.86
Cumulative percent of variance	28.12	38.26	44.96	50.82

they encompass. Both point to perceived types of wrongdoing separate from personal taking or official theft; neither category is clearly public or private in nature. In both public and private life, people encounter situations in which they face temptations to misrepresent themselves or to cover up their actions (factor 3). The "favoritism" factor is interesting in light of our earlier comments on perceptions of corruption and inequality. Giving and getting unfair advantages, apparently, is another kind of wrongdoing which people perceive in both public and private life.

The relative strength of these factors lends support to our contention that in judging the behavior of others, people will frequently fall back upon everyday situations. This seems all the more likely to be true when the behavior in question does not fit other categories of wrongdoing. Perhaps these factors help us understand why, during the Watergate episode, many people were much more upset by Richard Nixon's tax evasion and use of public funds to renovate his own home, than by the much more serious (but less easily understood) kinds of official wrongdoing that came to light.

It still seems likely, however, that various kinds of wrongdoing will matter much more to some people than to others, as suggested above. Therefore, factor scores for each of the four categories of wrongdoing were broken down by social class; the results are presented in table 11.4.

All four of our factors represent important categories of perceived wrongdoing. But as table 11.4 shows, some of them vary considerably in their importance to different social classes, while others do not. Cases of official theft, for example, are much more the concern of middle—to upper-status respondents than of lower-status groups. The former scored significantly higher on the survey's six-item political information scale, which may mean that they have a more complete grasp of what constitutes wrongdoing in public settings, and are more familiar with the public misconduct that does come to light. They also ranked higher on an "input political efficacy" item;[18] perhaps higher-status individuals see official misconduct as a threat to the orderly operation of governments which would otherwise be responsive to their needs.

Class variations in scores for "personal taking," by contrast, are rather weak. This may be taken to mean that the rules and expectations governing personal conduct are shared across class lines to a greater extent than are conceptions of public ethics. The same might also be the case with the "misrepresentation" category. It is interesting to note, however, that both "personal taking" and "misrepresentation" received their strongest condemnations at the extremes of the class continuum. Perhaps lower-status individuals are the most frequently victimized by personal taking and misrepresentation, and upper-status groups have the most to lose to such practices. But the weak statistical significance of the breakdowns, and the exceedingly small size of the lowest-status group, mean that significant relationships between class

Table 11.4
Factor Scores Broken Down by Social Class Groupings

"Personal Taking"

Class Groupings:	Low (7)	Low-Middle (51)	Middle (75)	Upper Middle (42)	Upper (32)
Mean	.551	.115	−.207	−031	.162
Std. Dev.	1.248	.943	1.007	.894	1.187

Analysis of Variance: F = 1.6699 p = .1583
Test of Linearity: F(lin) = .0697 p = .7920
F(dev) = 2.2034   p = .0889

"Official Theft"

Class Groupings:	Low	Low-Middle	Middle	Upper Middle	Upper
Mean	−.148	−.401	.173	−.024	.198
Std. Dev.	.940	1.298	.812	.973	.715

Analysis of Variance: F = 3.0899 p = .0169
Test of Linearity: F(lin) = 5.2562 p = .0229
F(dev) = 2.3678   p = .0719

"Misrepresentation"

Class Groupings:	Low	Low-Middle	Middle	Upper Middle	Upper
Mean	.360	.023	−.035	−.130	.054
Std. Dev.	1.069	.925	1.182	1.182	.805

Analysis of Variance: F = .4501 p = .7722
Test of Linearity: F(lin) = .2446 p = .6214
F(dev) = .5186   p = .6699

"Favoritism"

Class Groupings:	Low	Low-Middle	Middle	Upper Middle	Upper
Mean	−.406	.210	.150	−.292	−.227
Std. Dev.	1.010	.900	1.062	.972	1.039

Analysis of Variance: F = 2.5763 p = .0388
Test of Linearity: F(lin) = 4.1691 p = .0425
F(dev) = 2.0454   p = .1087

distinctions and reactions to the above categories of misconduct cannot be asserted at this time.

The most interesting class-related contrasts emerge in the breakdown of "favoritism" factor scores. Setting aside the very small low-status group, we see a strong tendency for lower-middle and middle-status persons to resent cases of favoritism, and for upper-middle and upper-status respondents to be tolerant of them. This is especially striking for the "upper" status group, whose judgments of all three other categories of wrongdoing were stronger than the group mean. Higher-status individuals are probably more accustomed to expect and receive special privileges than are others. But there is more at stake than this, for here we see the intersection between notions of corruption and perceptions of inequality which Tocqueville pointed out 150 years ago. It may well be that what lower—and middle-status people regard as illegitimate favors and advantages are seen by higher-status groups as merely the fruits of merit and expertise. For lower-middle and middle-class persons, favoritism could certainly be seen as a threat to one's hopes of advancing through hard work, or as an explanation for the failure of such hopes in the past. Moreover, lower-status individuals are less likely to occupy roles in which they can give sizeable favors to others, while higher-status persons may have done so, or may at least regard the giving and withholding of favors as part of the routine authority of managers and decision-makers— people with whom they may have much in common. The legitimacy of special favors and privileges, it seems, has much to do with whether one views them from above or below.

Right and Wrong in American Politics

While public perceptions must be an important aspect of any analysis of corruption as a political issue, it would be most difficult to build those perceptions into basic definitions. Table 11.1 does show that many actions which are corrupt by formal definitions are also recognized as such by the public. But social perceptions of corruption are most intriguing and politically significant in the broad middle range of table 11.1, where they diverge from formal definitions. This part of the spectrum of judgments is the turf upon which issues of right and wrong in politics are contested. And here, gradations of judgment are fine, and levels of consensus are comparatively low. Definitions or typologies based on these judgments are likely to be unacceptably "soft" at their boundaries, or they will contain an unmanageable number of categories based on unstable distinctions.[19]

A better approach is to use a formal analytical definition to identify corruption, to posit social conceptions of corruption as an important factor affecting political response (or non-response) to corruption, and then to examine the divergence between the two outlooks. This strategy, rather than attempting somehow to merge two fundamentally contrasting conceptions of corruption, preserves the differences between them, and focuses our attention upon those contrasts as interesting political questions in their own right. Instead of using public opinion to decide whether or not patronage practices in a given system, for example, should be studied as corruption, why not ask the much more interesting political question as to why corrupt practices elicit, or fail to elicit, particular political responses—or, why citizens might perceive massive corruption in a government which, from an analytical perspective, seems to have little of it? Corruption and scandal, after all, are different things; we may find one without the other.[20]

This sort of analysis will be complex, involving many other factors beyond public opinion. But it can turn a difficulty into an advantage: the subtleties and contradictions of public judgment become not a problem to be somehow overcome in the construction of typologies, but rather indicators of important stresses and linkages between state and society, mass and elite.

Notes

1. Richard Hofstadter, *The Age of Reform* (New York: Vintage, 1955); see also William J. Crotty, *Political Reform and the American Experiment* (New York: Crowell, 1977).
2. Gunnar Myrdal, "Corruption: Its Causes and Effects," in G. Myrdal, *Asian Drama: An Enquiry into the Poverty of Nations,* vol.2 (New York: Twentieth Century, 1968). pp. 937–58.
3. Michael Johnston, *Political Corruption and Public Policy in America* (Monterey, Calif.: Brooks-Cole, 1982), ch. 1; James C. Scott, *Comparative Political Corruption* (Englewood Cliffs, N.J.: Prentice-Hall, 1972), pp. 3–9; Arnold J. Heidenheimer, "The Context of Analysis," in A. J. Heidenheimer, ed., *Political Corruption: Readings in Comparative Analysis* (New Brunswick, N.J.: Transaction Books, reprinted 1978), pp. 3–28.
4. Johnston, *Political Corruption,* ch. 2.
5. Arnold A. Rogow and Harold D. Lasswell, *Power, Corruption, and Rectitude* (Englewood Cliffs, N.J.: Prentice-Hall, 1963).
6. Alexis de Tocqueville, *Democracy in America,* vol.1 (New York: Vintage, 1945), pp. 234–35.
7. S. Chibnall and P. Saunders, "Worlds Apart: Notes on the Social Reality of Corruption," *British Journal of Sociology,* 28 (June 1977): 138–54.
8. Peter L. Berger and Thomas P. Luckmann, *The Social Construction of Reality: A Treatise in the Sociology of Knowledge* (Garden City, N.Y.: Doubleday, 1967).
9. Stuart Henry, *The Hidden Economy: The Context and Control of Borderline Crime* (London: Martin Robertson, 1978).
10. Ibid., pp.48–52.
11. Ibid., pp 52–60.
12. Donald R. Cressey, *Other People's Money* (New York: Free Press, 1953); Erwin O. Smigel, "Public Attitudes Toward 'Chiseling' with Reference to Unemployment Compensation," in Erwin O. Smigel and H. Laurence Ross, eds., *Crimes Against Bureaucracy* (New York: Van Nostrand Reinhold, 1970), pp. 29–45; Donald M. Horning, "Blue-Collar Theft: Conceptions of Property, Attitudes To-

ward Pilfering, and Work Group Norms in a Modern Industrial Plant," in Smigel and Ross., eds., *Crimes Against Bureaucracy,* pp. 46–64; Jason Ditton, *Part-Time Crime: An Ethnography of Fiddling and Pilferage* (London: Macmillan, 1977); Gerald Mars, *Cheats at Work: An Anthropology of Workplace Crime* (London: George Allen and Unwin, 1982).

13. Erwin O. Smigel, "Public Attitudes Toward Stealing as Related to the Size of the Victim Organization," in Smigel and Ross, eds., *Crimes Against Bureaucracy,* p.7.

14. Ibid.

15. One objection to this format might be that corruption, as a formal concept, refers to actions affecting public roles and resources, while these items invite respondents to label essentially private actions as corrupt. But the distinction between public and private is not precise, as noted above; and the ways in which people apply the label "corruption" to a variety of actions, both in and out of the public sphere, is part of the process of judgment at issue here. In any event, those who do apply a public-private distinction were given the opportunity to label actions by private individuals as "not at all corrupt."

16. Smigel, "Public Attitudes Toward Stealing," passim.

17. Smigel, "Public Attitudes Toward Stealing."

18. "Input political efficacy" refers to one dimension of the general concept of political efficacy—the belief that one can effectively make one's views and values an "input" into decision-making processes. See, for an application of this concept, David Lowery and Lee Sigelman, "Understanding the Tax Revolt: Eight Explanations," *American Political Science Review* 75 (December 1981): 963–74. The "input efficacy" item used in that study as well as this one, was: "Sometimes politics and government seem so complicated that a person like me can't really understand what's going on" (disagreement: high efficacy). Source: Stephen C. Craig, "Measuring Political Efficacy," unpublished manuscript, University of Florida, 1980, as cited in Lowery and Sigelman.

19. Michael Johnston, "Right and Wrong in American Politics," paper prepared for the annual meeting of the American Political Science Association, Chicago, September 1983.

20. Graeme C. Moodie, "On Political Scandals and Corruption," *Government and Opposition* 15 (1980): 208–22.

Part IV

POLITICAL DEVELOPMENT

Introduction to Part IV

One of the principal themes of this volume is that political corruption is best understood *in comparative context* of the histories, the cultures, the politics, and the particular societies in which it occurs. Such a perspective permits analysis of the ramifications, effects, and consequences of corruption, and of its origins, spread, and growth. This perspective also permits an examination of the relationship between corruption and the complex of changes usually associated with sociopolitical development. The questions that can arise from that examination not only identify possible critical relationships between corruption and development, but often suggest whole research agendas: What role did corruption play in the political development of the British and American democracies? How has it affected the development of the relatively new, "Third World" polities? Is political corruption a home-grown (endogenous) or imported (exogenous) phenomenon?

Clearly, both in England and in the United States, various forms of corruption affected political development, more often to some general benefit, although not all the authors excerpted here would agree to that conclusion. In Britain, for example, corruption may have eased the transition from royal absolutism to parliamentary rule by helping to secure the political cooperation of the aristocracy during and after the shift. On the other hand, after the eighteenth century, once the focus of corruption had shifted to the electoral arena, corrupt practices undoubtedly retarded, if not prevented, the appearance of the social and economic reforms that had been expected to go hand in hand with the growth of the franchise. In the United States, high electoral competition and mass suffrage gave rise to the political machine, which often grew into massive vehicles for illicit patronage networks and corrupt practices. At their best, however, the political machines provided goods, services, employment, and economic opportunity for masses of people often immigrants-still at the political and economic margins of the American system. In time, as their clients moved into the American mainstream, the machines outlived their usefulness, although the patterns of corruption they engendered often outlived the machines themselves.

If a negative relationship between systematic patronagebased corruption and political development and modernization seems plausible in some traditional societies, the experience of other new states complicates the issue. One such state, Israel, started out in 1948 with relatively little public corruption; however, as it became increasingly socially heterogeneous (with the arrival of large numbers of Oriental Jews beginning in the 1950s), the old socialist developmental ethos began to weaken, party machines began to make their appearance, and various forms of corruption came to be increasingly condoned. Corruption may well have helped the post-1950 immigrants to enter the national system more rapidly and productively, but the cost to the country-heightened political conflict, mounting political cynicism, decreased support for government-may have been too high.

Political Development and Corruption Incidence

In this section, the reader is presented with analyses that show how, when political institutions changed toward the democratic model, the perception and incidence of corruption changed as differing social groups were allowed to participate in the political process. The panorama extends from the sixteenth to the twentieth centuries, focusing on three countries with differing patterns of settlement and citizenship extension—Britain, the United States, and Israel. The comparisons build up various historical and developmental models which attempt to encompass the forces that changed and shaped the party, bureaucratic, and institutional structures within these three countries.

In Israel, the country examined by Simcha Werner, there were also differences between the old voters who had been pioneers in Palestine under the British mandate, and the newer immigrants who entered in particularly large numbers from North Africa and Asia in the 1950s. Lacking democratic traditions and located near the bottom of the social ladder, the newer Oriental immigrants were more dependent upon the party political machines, thus engendering networks of political clientelism. Generally negative attitudes toward bureaucracy engendered toleration and cover-ups for increasing corruption. Some of the ideological factors that had inhibited corruption earlier, parallel to the way they had come to operate in Britain, weakened in the 1970s which led to more pervasive corruption. Werner holds that the condoning of white corruption can encourage more insidious kinds of corruption and allow corruption to become institutionalized as the political system matures.

The American setting is analyzed comparatively by James C. Scott in the next chapter, to contrast the situations under which mass suffrage and high degrees of electoral competition engender political machines. Party machines, as they first developed in American cities around the time corruption was phasing out in Britain, are characterized by their use of particular material rewards as the cement holding together the followers of incumbent leaders. Scott argues that ma—chines develop more during certain phases of development in modernizing and democratizing countries, but that the timing and duration of such phases may vary widely. He distinguishes the factors involved, such as fragmentation of political power, social disorganization, and poverty.

In the final selection, Eva Etzioni-Halevy reexamines the theoretical constructs used in the preceding attempts to explain the rise and decline of corrupt practices in all three countries. Etzioni-Halevy avoids a developmental perspective, but rather examines how various factors adduced to explain corruption do not seem to have led to very consistent cross-national explanatory patterns. Immigration, poverty, education, and other variables are shown not to be consistently correlated with levels of corruption in Britain, America, and Israel at the same or similar periods. From a democratic elitist perspective, she argues that the single most important factor for the control of corruption in twentieth century mass democracies is the insulation of the bureaucracy so as to make its resources unavailable for party-political exploitation.

12

The Development of
Political Corruption in Israel

Simcha B. Werner

The developmental and structural-functional schools in political science of
the 1960s gave birth to the revisionist approach to political corruption. The
revisionists departed from the traditional school of political thought, which
regarded political corruption as an important factor in social decay, and instead classified it as a "functional dysfunction."

Cost-benefit analysis is central to the revisionist approach, and four functional propositions relevant to this discussion have been identified:[1]

1. *Economic Market Propositions.* Corruption brings with it a wider range
   of economic choices by encouraging foreign investment and strengthening the private *vis-a-vis* the public sector. It is, therefore, a means of
   bypassing cumbersome, genuinely hampering, governmental economic
   regulations.[2]
2. *The Integrative Function.* Corruption allows citizens access to public
   officials and thereby fosters the integration of immigrant or parochial
   groups.[3]
3. *Institutionalization Initiative.* Either corruption encourages institutionalization and party-building,[4] or an honest merit-oriented and incorruptible bureaucracy hampers the rise of political leadership.[5]

Source: Simcha B. Werner, "The Development of Political Corruption: A Case Study
of Israel," *Political Studies,* 31 (1983), pp. 620–39. By permission of author and
publisher.

4. *Administrative Advocacy.* Corruption brings flexibility and humanity to rigid bureaucracies.[6] It may also serve to increase the calibre of public servants because corruption brings with it opportunities for supplemental income which may counterbalance incentives within the non-governmental job market.[7]

The revisionists accepted as axiomatic that corruption is by now restricted to non-western nations undergoing political modernization and development. The corollary of the axiom was that "corruption as it strengthens parties and political institutionalization. . . undermines the conditions of its own existence', and, 'once the process of political modernization is completed, corruption inevitably will wither away."[8]

In the 1970s, research in political science indicated that the phenomenon of corruption was endemic globally. These studies shattered the functionalists' claims about the benefits of corruption to the developing countries, and about the alleged "built-in" self-destruct mechanism of corruption. Instead, it was argued, corruption is an instrument of under-development.[9] In the fully developed countries of the West, corruption not only manifests dysfunctional aspects, but also permeates a variety of social institutions; it becomes systemic. Thus, this research has led to a post-functional approach to the study of political corruption.[10]

At present, however, this new literature is an inconsistent corpus of descriptive studies. New definitions as well as a methodology for comparative analysis were not developed, nor was a theory of corruption. As a result, various dimensions of corruption are still unexplored. One such problem is the lifecycle of corruption. If corruption is not doomed to self-destruct with the completion of the maturation process, then what are the dynamic societal forces that allow it to prevail? If corruption thrives even in developed democratic countries, which proclaim ethical principles and presumably demonstrate rather high levels of political institutionalization, bureaucratization, and civil law and order, then what permits corruption to continue?

Thus, the next stage in the study of political corruption must be to determine what effect, if any, political development and modernization, as well as other societal factors, which are not necessarily developmental in nature, have upon the development of the phenomenon. By such effort, it may be possible to develop a theory which will explain the actual dynamics whereby old norms are transformed and new norms of corruption evolve, and identify what kinds of norms these will be.

It is obviously impossible for a single study to focus upon all aspects corruption on a global basis. A more prudent course is to concentrate upon the life-cycle of corruption in a country now achieving the final stages of political modernization. Such a country would possess sufficient political institutionalization to evidence corruption while retaining many of the norms of the premodern stage.

Israel provides an excellent example for this study, for it is a country achieving modernization. Moreover, modern Israel history exemplifies relevant political processes. Over the short span of fifty years, political and organizational changes have rapidly occurred as the early Jewish settlers of Palestine—Israel's immediate historical antecedent—have coped first with Ottoman corruption, then British imperial politics and finally their own national government. For these reasons, then, Israel is the focus of this study of the life-cycle of corruption.

Embryonic Corruption: The Period of Foreign Rule

Perhaps the most important characteristic of Ottoman government in Palestine from the middle of the nineteenth century to its final demise in 1917 was the unbridgeable gap between the formal/external outlook of the central administration and its informal/internal practices of the *satraps*. As often as the Turkish sultans initiated reform, local officials prevented its implementation. Not even the Young Turks Revolution of 1908, which succeeded in effecting numerous reforms within Turkey itself, eradicated bureaucratic corruption in the territories.

The Turkish system of government was a "proprietary state."[11] This view of office combined with systemic nepotism and the form of Levantine extortion known as *baksheesh* constituted a way of life. Ottoman Palestine thus bore a distinct resemblance to historical Europe, where capitalism involved "the granting by the state of privileged opportunities for profit."[12] Unprofitable activities were left to indigenous religious and charity organizations, which gradually assumed responsibilities usually reserved for official government by supplying a variety of services to their constituents. Such "limited" government was further limited by the utilization of two unique systems of self-government, namely: the *Millet* and the *Mukhtars*.

Since the middle of the nineteenth century, some non-Moslem entities in the empire were recognized by the Turkish government as a *Millet*. (While in its original Arabic it means a "religious community," in Turkish it usually denotes a "nation.") Such communities were granted considerable autonomy in internal religious and socio-cultural matters. Jews were organized along the lines of the *Millet*, and gradually they extended the principles of religious and cultural autonomy far beyond Turkish intentions. Toward the end of Ottoman rule in Palestine, the Jewish community operated an intensified and diversified set of institutions that delivered a variety of religious, social, cultural, welfare and technical services. In 1909, Jewish Peace Tribunals *(Mishpat Shalom Ivri)* were created in response to the inefficiency and corruption of Turkish courts.

Contact between the Arab Palestinian villagers and the central government was maintained by a "conveniently undefined and indefinite"[13] network of

Mukhtars, native elders who represented their rural communities before Ottoman officials.

The combination of the *Millet* system of self-government with that of the *Mukhtars,* not only helped to lessen an already lessened government, but also reduced contact between the official Ottoman authorities and their constituents. The major contacts with the corrupt Turkish officials were left to the representatives of the *Millet* communities and the *Mukhtars.* While a small *baksheesh* was a daily routine for low rank officials, the more black types of bribery were "reserved" for the respected representatives of the communities. Nepotism and the buying of officials and offices were exclusively reserved for the *effendis,* members of a dominant Arab upper class, who, being the landlords, possessed both the economic means and the political influence to use the proprietary state to achieve their own ends.

For the early Zionist leaders, confrontation with the corrupt and autocratic Turkish officialdom was neither unexpected nor new. Many of these leaders spent their formative years under similarly corrupt tsarist Russian and East European regimes where pogroms, social deprivation and prejudice produced hostile conditions of survival that led to circumventing the law. But, in Palestine, their moral dilemma became more acute, for Palestine was, in their eyes, to become again their homeland and was to be turned into a "laboratory of Utopian social experiments."[14]

The bulk of the Zionist new immigrants came to Palestine in pursuit of social equality and idealistic values. They were an elite group: "Instead of the fleshpots of America, they chose the desert . . . Instead of individual escape, they chose the collective ideal . . . Instead of middle-class careers, they chose to become peasants and manual workers."[15] Toward the end of the Ottoman domination of Palestine, the Jewish community became a diverse assortment of various groups (Ashkenazi and Sephardic Jews, Zionist new immigrants and non-Zionists who lived for generations in holy Jewish cities like Jerusalem, Hebron, Tiberia, and Sefat) who, with few exceptions, subsisted on philanthropy. Such an assortment was made homogeneous only by poverty. Thus, idealistic values combined with poverty denied both the wish and the means to corrupt.

In terms of political development, Jewish political parties entered their embryonic stage only when Britain was given the mandate over Palestine in 1922 and mass immigration of Jews began. Party machines were then quickly established to absorb the newcomers. The conditions which would allow patron-client relations to develop were then, for the first time, created in Palestine.

Political Institutionalization, Integration, and Civil Order during the British Mandate

The British governments of Palestine (first military and then civil) were quick to introduce a western model of bureaucracy based on structural hierarchy, formal and impersonal relationships with its clients, merit-oriented personnel administration and an intensive code of laws and regulations, which forbade and punished acts of administrative corruption. Simultaneously, Britain imposed a strong central government in Palestine. Because the Arab Palestinians were slow to develop political institutions at the national level, and because local government was their political stronghold, it is not surprising that Arab Palestinian officials were critical of such centralization policies. They accused the British Mandatory Government of "robbing" the municipalities of many of their prerogatives, of the "abrogation" of municipal powers and of "crippling" their sources of revenue.[16]

The case of the Jewish sector was markedly different. While semiautonomous Jewish organizations were allowed to develop at the local level under the *Millet* system, it was not until Britain was given the League of Nations mandate over Palestine that semi-autonomous Jewish national organizations were encouraged. This was due both to the avowed purpose of the mandate to secure the establishment of a Jewish national home, and to the subsequent increase in Jewish immigration. This led to the evolution of a national administration, the Jewish Agency, deriving its legal authority from Article 4 of the mandate. The Jewish agency gradually assumed increasing responsibilities, often replacing the official British administration in promoting social and economic modernization of the Jewish sector. But the demand for increasing national self-government did not proceed uncriticized:

> The demand for autonomy in every matter carries us too far. It separates us from the life of the state. . . . Thus we proceed to establish institutions which should in reality, be maintained by the government and which we ourselves shall never be able to support, institutions which exist not on the basis of healthy economics of governmental income but on philanthropy. The income of the government, in which our share is very large . . . is being spent for the benefit of the rest of the population . . . The government becomes accustomed to view us as a strange child which needs not to be taken care of.[17]

Political institutionalization assumed a three-tiered structure. An Elected Assembly was constituted by universal suffrage and convened for special purposes; a National Council Plenum served as the framework for a permanent parliament; and a National Council Executive took responsibility for implementing the decisions of the elected bodies.[18]

Until the mid-1930s, none of these developmental activities required corruption as a functional catalyst. This was due in large part to the unique Palestinian Jewish social values and the relatively egalitarian structure of the

Jewish community. The Zionist immigrants who continued to arrive during the 1920s and until the mid-1930s were driven by idealistic impulses and were, for the most part, highly educated. A common idea among them was *"avodah shechora"*—hard and dirty labor. Waging a social revolution, teachers, lawyers and physicians paved roads, drained malarial swamps and performed all the functions necessary to rebuild their homeland. Such national aspirations, idealism and egalitarian values inhibited materialistic demands and paved the way for the social and political integration of the Yishuv (the Hebrew term for the pre-independence Jewish community in Palestine). Several other factors further fostered integration, rendering corruption unnecessary as an integrative mechanism:[19]

1. The need for effective representation *vis-à-vis* the mandate government;
2. The need for national institutions to control the dissemination of resources, capital and personnel;
3. The recognition of the need to compromise in order to maintain intact the strength of the whole;
4. The concentration of Jews in cities, which weakened the urban-rural rivalry common to developing countries; and,
5. The existence of well-organized substructures *(kibbutzim* and *moshavim;* types of collective settlements) which generated social innovations, and served as a source for elite recruitment and political mobilization.

Thus, the revisionist premise that corruption fosters political development and aids the integration of disaffected and potentially excluded parochial groups or immigrants was not evident in the Yishuv Jewish polity in the same way it perhaps was in other developing countries.

Advocates of the functionality of corrupt bureaucracy have argued in parallel that an honest, merit-oriented and incorruptible bureaucracy cripples economic development,[20] and hampers the growth of a party system and political leadership of a developing nation.[21] Braibanti[22] suggests that, if Pakistan had not inherited an honest, efficient, and incorruptible British civil service, there might have been a better opportunity for the growth of a political party system. In contrast to other developing countries, the case of Israel is again markedly different for two reasons. First, the evolution of a Jewish polity and Bureaucracy took place parallel to, and external from, the British government and bureaucracy, so that functional political growth occurred independently of the dominant British bureaucracy, corrupt or not. Secondly, unlike the British central bureaucracy, the Jewish administrative body evolved on a non-Weberian basis. It did not endeavour to emulate the parallel and external British bureaucracy, which stressed formal regulations and rigid hierarchical structures. The Jewish bureaucracy "coped." It was open and willing to yield to the demands of its clientele. Jewish institutions stressed *"kol Yisrael chaverim"*—all Israelis are friends. In the long run, this spirit gave rise to that brand of Israel borderline corruption known as *"protekzia,"* upon which this study will elaborate in a moment.

The rise of the Nazis prompted a new wave of Jewish immigration to Palestine. Between 1932 and 1939, about 225,000 new immigrants arrived, most of them from Poland and Germany "to give the final stamp of Western character to the new Yishuv of Palestine."[23] Many of them (particularly the German Jews) possessed both financial means and professional expertise which quickly helped to create the nucleus of a private enterprise sector and "laid the foundation for the economic take-off of the Jewish community in Palestine."[24] In the long run, capitalism planted the very first seeds of social polarization and economic inequality which serve as a major cause of corruption.[25]

The new waves of immigrants of the 1930s and the 1940s fostered political institutionalization through party machines. Immigrants made few demands upon central government; rather, they came to rely upon the machines:

> In the pre-state period, an immigrant's first stop upon arrival would often be his local party branch headquarters. He lived in a party-affiliated . . . block of flats. He found employment through the party labor exchange. His children were educated in party-controlled schools. He read the party newspaper. When sick, he lay in a party-dominated hospital, and recuperated in a party convalescent home. He played football on the party soccer team.[26]

As party-client relations intensified on a personal level, so members of the evolving capitalist class came to resort to these machines for influence and subcontracting. But, until 1948, political clientelism still remained embryonic, for the machinery of a national government was not yet available. It was still vested in the hands of the British who, during the 1930s, first implicitly and then explicitly abandoned their support of the Jewish homeland. The effects of such a shift of imperial policies upon security, civil order, and law obedience in Palestine were, apparently, insurmountable.

In his study of the breakdown of public security in Ireland and Palestine, Tom Browden[27] has shown how Arab riots against Jews in 1936 were the immediate cause of a breakdown in civil order. British partisanship in support of the Arabs was displayed even by British judges. This partisanship had severe repercussions on both government and security. On the one hand, Arab *Fellahin* (mass peasants) who were active in brigand bands against the Jews or the mandate interpreted British officials' behavior as a "sympathy with their cause and tactics."[28] On the other hand, British police "had been demoralized by conflicting loyalties."[29] The Arab section of the police had disintegrated almost completely and had become little more than an easy source of supply of rifles and ammunition for the rebels. Circumvention of the law in the name of the national interest also became increasingly flagrant within the Jewish sector as a response to British behavior:

> Although the Jews in Palestine lived in a state of physical insecurity, their self-defense organization was never legalized. . . . Similarly, the rescue of Jews from European massacre was made an illegal act. Once again the Jews could only protect their lives and save some of their kin by circumventing the law. British rule, instead of being a school of democracy, became a school of conspiracy.[30]

It is important to note that this patriotic circumvention of the law did not present a moral dilemma to the Yishuv, because British law and policies came to be regarded as being both alien and arbitrarily imposed.

In sum, under the Turkish and later under the British, corruption did not play a significant role in the development of the Jewish polity. Rather, as has been demonstrated, the unique characteristics of self-government, idealistic values and socioeconomic homogeneity limited corruption. But the changing conditions of the 1930s produced the seeds of political clientelism, *protekzia* and patriotic corruption that survived the transition from Palestine to Israel.

The Development of Corruption: The Period Between 1948 and 1967

Between Independence and the Six Day War, Israel underwent a massive process of modernization and integration. These produced favorable conditions for the development of corruption.

Political Integration, Clientelism, and Protekzia

After the establishment of the state of Israel, new waves of Jewish immigrants altered the more homogeneous Western character of the pre-state Jewish society. Between 1948 and 1962, over half of the 1,100,000 new immigrants to Israel came from Asian and African countries. These Oriental Jews had high birthrates, high levels of illiteracy, unskilled professions and strong kinship ties. It was not unusual for them to continue to perceive themselves, not as citizens, but as subjects, recognizing and not necessarily endorsing a higher authority.[31] They did not have a democratic tradition but, instead, one which stressed Middle East bargaining and *baksheesh*.[32]

The announced goal of the state was to convert mass immigration into mass democratization through fostering social, cultural and economic integration. However, the political potential of the new immigrants was quickly discovered by all political parties. Lacking democratic traditions and bureaucratic socialization, and saddled with poor economic standing, poor housing and poor employment conditions, these Oriental immigrants were more susceptible to and more dependent upon the political machines than were the European immigrants. Networks of political clientelism, often bordering on political corruption, thrived between political parties and the immigrants. New immigrant votes became a commodity, transferred to the highest political bidder.

Ben-Dor[33] observed, however, that the patronization of these immigrants did not necessarily lead to their integration within the Israel polity. Access to the centers of influence was monopolized by exclusive small groups, whose members had the means to corrupt and be corrupt. This selectivity increased the alienation of the new immigrants.

Protekzia, which originated in the Yishuv and expanded during the 1950s, became accessible to these immigrants as part of the process of assimilation.

Protekzia has been defined as the "management of influence,"[34] a "political tool for bypassing bureaucracy";[35] and the management of informal contacts and exchange of favors to bypass bureaucratic procedures.[36] "In colloquial Hebrew, the concept has been narrowed to exclude all reference to graft, bribery or exchange of money—thus including only the exchange of non-monetary favors and activation of non-normative objectives."[37]

Studies of the socialization of *protekzia* have produced somewhat contradictory results. Danet found in the late 1960s that Jews of North African origin, where the system has been traditionally functional, now attach more negative than positive values to *protekzia*. However, while European Jews still disparage the practice, they nevertheless continue to follow it. A later study done by Nachmias and Rosenblum[38] showed that bureaucratic socialization in Israel is gradually giving rise to the attribution of negative values to *protekzia*. Socializing the Israelis against *protekzia* is slow, not only because of the prevalence of the system and its utility, but also because agents of socialization, such as parents, teachers and leaders, cannot teach values which they themselves have not incorporated. Also, the more society becomes materialistic, the more incentives there are to abuse political and bureaucratic trusts, and the greater the fear that the boundaries of the favors will change.

Administrative Regulation versus Informal Practices

The immediate needs of the newly established state—surviving the War of Independence, the subsequent reorganization of the Israeli Defense Force, the economic recession and rationing, and the massive waves of new immigration in the early 1950s—all precluded a rational transition from quasi-national organization to national government.

It was not until 1950, two years after the establishment of the state, that the Israel Civil Service Commission was inaugurated under the auspices of the prime minister's office. Three years later, jurisdiction was transferred to the powerful finance ministry. The civil service was immediately confronted by personnel and ideological problems. Although screening procedures were established, a manpower shortage made it necessary to admit into the bureaucracy some workers who had been tainted by corruption while working in the pre-state Jewish Agency administration or in the British civil administration.

During the first few years, various informal practices from the prestate Jewish institutions had penetrated into the political parties, into local government and, to a lesser degree, into the newly established Israeli civil service. The pre-state Jewish institutions not only used to "cover up" corrupt behavior, but also assumed responsibility for trying, sentencing and punishing the perpetrators, through internal courts regulated informally.[39] This informal system of justice differed from the Soviet and Chinese systems of community justice. In the Communist countries, social pressure was used to rehabilitate the offender. In the Israel model, the offense itself was secondary to the maintenance of organizational prestige. Often, the cover up was a result of yielding to pressures from powerful labour unions.

Idealistic corruption also led to leniency toward pecuniary corruption. Levi Eshkol, the late prime minister of Israel, when questioned about a corrupt official, replied with a quotation from Deuteronomy (25:4): "Thou shalt not muzzle the ox when he treadeth out the corn." Indeed, in Israel, when bureaucratic regulation was introduced, it had only an external resemblance to western standards. Internally, structures and behavior remained informal. It was accepted that Israelis were difficult to govern.

The general disregard of the Israelis for administrative laws, together with a generally negative attitude (although gradually changing for the better) toward state bureaucracy and bureaucratic procedures, are perhaps the key reasons for the poor enforcement of administrative regulations and procedures. For an eastern European Jewish immigrant, a bureaucrat is a *Tchinovnik* (a civil servant under tsarist regime): "He must be corrupt. He must be hostile. He is the enemy of the people."[40] Similar attitudes developed among Jewish refugees from the autocratic regimes of Asia and North Africa. Survival in such hostile environments necessitated circumvention of the law. This attitude found its counterpart in the belief that certain ideas are superior to law. The attitude was reinforced by Jewish experience that respect for any law was mitigated by weak enforcement mechanisms. Survival and philosophy toward state and law gave rise to the Israeli concept of *"le'histader"*—to take care of yourself:

> *(Le'histader)* is the Israeli password through the maze of authority, the thicket of law, the confines of impersonal regulations. Regulations are 'objective' and thus theoretically just; but the needs of the individual, his private concepts of right and wrong, are superior. The average Israeli recognizes few regulations of universal applicability. In his dealings with the authorities he invariably demands, firmly and loudly, exceptional treatment.[41]

Lack of Consistent Control

Although it is common to attribute to Israeli government machinery a high level of centralization, in practice the public enterprise sector, and also to some degree the local government system, are often free from consistent external control, resulting not only in administrative and economic inefficiencies, but also in cases of irregularities and corruption.

During the 1950s and 1960s, the government enterprise system was rapidly expanded to cope with ambitious economic projects, and the ministry of finance adopted the policy of seeking greater economic efficiency by allowing government corporations a greater degree of commercial and administrative freedom. Soon, these companies acquired sufficient power to be relatively independent of government control. The state comptroller had only limited ability to subject administrative inefficiencies to public and political scrutiny or to impose their correction. Because the state comptroller's office was chronically short of manpower, each state company was subject to controls only once every five years, on average. This gradually contributed to excesses of power in state companies, which after 1967 had been quite often abused for private gains. As a result, a long overdue State Companies Act was passed in 1975 designed to increase the accountability of state-owned-enterprises.

Similarly, in the local government, irregularities and corruption grew, primarily during the aftermath of the Six Day War. A number of reasons contributed to the gradual deterioration of morality and bureaucratic order in the local government machinery of Israel. Amongst these were the weakness of the state comptroller; political and bureaucratic opposition to the introduction of an internal city comptroller; and the one-party dominance of municipalities, which often retarded the formulation and exercise of adequate political and control mechanisms.

Thus a lack of consistent control is a key reason why the two networks of public enterprise and local government gradually became more vulnerable to the scandals of irregularities and corruption which erupted in the late 1960s and the 1970s.

Deepening of Social Inequality

The influx of Oriental Jews into Israel during the 1950s caused significant changes in the social stratification of the country. Using the Lorenz Index,[42] social inequality in Israel increased from 0.220 in 1950 (as compared, for example, with 0.320 in the United States) to 0.330 in 1959 and to 0.360 in 1967. In 1953, a sample of 450 families living in Jerusalem in a new neighborhood, comprising a heterogeneous population of immigrants, showed that 56 percent of the North Africans and 68 percent of the Iraqis belonged to the lower class as compared with 26 percent of East European immigrants and 18 percent of other European countries. Other contributing factors to the increase of social inequality were non-progressive taxation on products which weakened the effect of progressive taxes; the existence of a special system of fringe benefits available only to white-collar employees and which (until 1975) were not officially included in taxed income; and economic recession and high unemployment during the years 1966 and 1967. Thus Israel has followed the pattern suggested by contemporary research in that socioeconomic or political inequalities have stimulated the development of corruption. Inhibiting Factors on Corruption: Idealism, Egalitarianism, and National Insecurity

While the previous analysis has pointed to various factors that have helped to create murky political and administrative ethics, idealism, egalitarian philosophy and national insecurity have served as safeguards. The spirit of the early Zionists, drawn from Biblical thought, from the modern Hebrew renaissance and from contemporary East European socialism,[43] blossomed in the years following the War of Independence. Massive efforts at nation building, economic scarcity and rationing during the early 1950s, and a hostile political environment all contributed to a national spirit of idealism, of working for the benefit of all and of denying the material and physical pleasures of life.

The civil service was to become a vanguard of such idealistic notions. In 1964, a government commission (Horowitz Commission) had recommended the creation of a "uniform wage structure" in the civil service, proclaiming the principle of "equal pay for equal work." But changes in the wage structure were soon thwarted by powerful and restless unions that opposed the idea of wage uniformity. They argued that professional uniqueness requires unique compensation structures. Egalitarian values became a myth of the past, and workers waged a war against the artificial imposition of such values. In order to satisfy employee demands, the Israel government gradually formulated policies to bypass the rigid and egalitarian wage system. Improvements (*hatavot*) were introduced to increase the income of professional civil servants. The basic wage structure remained intact. People who never owned a car were provided with vehicle expenses, and office workers received hazardous duty allowances. Unskilled workers were given funds for "professional literature." The government, anxious to avoid bureaucratic unrest, chose to circumvent its own wage structures rather than adapt them to a more materialistic society.

While these changes originated in official policy, civil servants themselves began to emulate them. What apparently began prior to the Six Day War was a white, petty type of administrative corruption, that was rationalized, condoned and allowed to prevail. A few examples will suffice.

One example that borders on corruption is the artificial padding of overtime work. This system prevails primarily in local government, where high officials approve excessive overtime hours for devoted workers, or for workers with large families. The padding of the actual number of overtime hours now characterizes the entire Israeli public sector wage system.

Also, individual civil servants abuse their authority and increase income by padding various reports concerning their expenses (meals, travel allowances and accommodation expenses). The gaps between position and remuneration are also often narrowed by the petty abuse of privileges, by luxurious dinners, presents, vacations, all paid for by contractors seeking "clean bypasses" to influence over official decision-making.

Another example of white corruption that originated in the 1960s and prevails in Israel is petty bribery. The most common illustration of this is the custom of "bottles basket," where civil servants, at all administrative levels, receive a present of a basket of bottles from their clients. The giver sees it as a means of establishing favour or receiving preferential treatment. Today, because of the prevalence of this type of bribery, even the courts have found themselves in an embarrassing position. Although they are aware of the negative side they have difficulty in passing judgment upon such a widely condoned custom. The Israeli Civil Service Commission, which has again and again emphasized that these "presents" are forbidden by law, has found itself quite helpless in weeding out this practice.

A brief theoretical analysis of the dynamics of the dimensions of corruption now seems both timely and necessary.

Dimensions of Corruption: The Dynamics of White Corruption

In 1970, Heidenheimer[44] introduced a litmus test by which identification of corruption becomes possible. Corrupt behavior can be judged to be black, gray, or white, depending upon the perception by both the public and public officials. Agreement between the two groups that a specific "bad" action would be either condemned and punished, or condoned and unsanctioned, led to the classification of either black or white corruption, respectively, whereas areas of disagreement were classified as gray corruption. Heidenheimer argued that gray corruption is the most destructive to a democratic political system because the public and its representatives are either ambivalent towards corrupt behavior, or unconcerned with its restrictions.

Peters and Welch[45] next categorized a corrupt act according to its four components: the donor, the recipient, the favor and the payoff. Corruption will be perceived as limited when the recipient, if he/she is a public official, acts as a private citizen; when a constituent pays a public official as opposed to the official "putting his hand in the till"; when the favor to be performed is a routine of the job, or benefits the public as opposed to a private interest, or serves a constituent rather than a nonconstituent; and when the payoff is small, long range, general (such as an unspecified, future electoral consideration), or in the form of support rather than money.

These two classification systems of the dimensions of corruption are useful, but they are also too general and static, failing to elucidate the mechanism(s) by which corrupt acts change in intensity.

The salient characteristic of white corruption is its being a petty borderline type, which neither the public nor public officials regard as being punishable. Often it does not clearly and totally violate the law. While every codex of law will define corruption, it also "carries the seeds of its own neutralization"[46] because it does not account for extenuating circumstances.

More than any other type of crime, petty corruption involves a "denial of injury"[47] in that it asserts the pettiness of the act. Within an organization, potential "whistle-blowers" usually remain silent, not because they are intimidated, but because they feel their action would be quixotic. As petty corruption becomes the norm for individuals, the organization itself begins to rationalize and neutralize it.

Because of this rationalization of white corruption, and because of the system's failure to determine when corruption becomes destructive, the formulation and enforcement of control strategies are severely limited. Left unchecked, white corruption becomes a growth industry. When a corrupt act is regarded as being innocuous, that act is removed from previous definitions of corruption. The acceptance of white corruption as being "legitimate" will, in turn, tend to spill over to perceptions of other types of corruption. The gray and black shades become progressively lighter, and a momentum is established.

This premise will now be illustrated by the case of Israel after the Six Day War. As will be shown, the rationalization and trivialization of white corruption, coupled with socioeconomic changes that began to crystallize after the Six Day War, combined to allow corruption to mature.

Maturation of Corruption: 1967 to the Present

After the Six Day War of 1967, the euphoria of victory lifted national self-confidence and induced individuals to "turn their attention to personal goals that had long been postponed."[48] The period between 1968 and the Yom Kippur War of 1973 was one of full employment and unprecedented prosperity. It was also a period of boom years for Israeli contractors who capitalized from the vast government expenditures on military build-up and civil settlements in the Sinai, West Bank and the Golan Heights. In the short run, full employment and a somewhat artificial economic boom produced some positive results. The Lorentz inequality coefficient temporarily went down from 0.377 in 1968 to 0.298 in 1972. In the long run, materialism grew. The elders complained about the decline of idealism; past values of *halutziut* (a Biblical term which means "to vanguard") and *hitnadvut* (altruistic voluntarism) faded out and were quickly replaced by materialism and self-serving values.

Between 1967 and 1973, white corruption continued, along with some cases of major scandals in the state enterprises network. In 1969 black corruption in the form of embezzlement and fraud was found in *Netivei Neft,* the government-controlled, oil-producing company in Sinai. The scandal provoked public criticism, which reached its peaks when the then-powerful minister of justice first attempted to nullify public demands for a judicial investigation, and later when the huge legal fees he awarded to the attorney assisting the work of the inquiry were made known. Public outcry made the minister hand in his resignation, "an action unprecedented among Israeli politicians."[49] In 1972, bribery was discovered in the Amidar Housing Company, which is responsible for the distribution of apartments. This case clearly demonstrated how "*protekzia* without remuneration may degenerate into contacts between a briber and bribee . . . and that preferential treatment in return for money or another form of bribe had become a common phenomenon in Israel."[50]

The Yom Kippur War of 1973 itself seemed to be but the harbinger of bad times. National security was again questioned, immigration to Israel decreased while emigration increased, economic problems began to rage, and inflation soared to unprecedented levels. Israeli society became more consumer-oriented and the gap between desire and the means of its fulfilment increased. More white and even black corruption became a means of bridging the gap. Incentives for administrative corruption were particularly enhanced in Israel due to increasing gaps between salary and status, salary and rank, and salary and inflation.

Robert Price[51] introduces the salary-status gap in his study of Ghana's bureaucracy. Price argued that venality in Ghana closes the gap between the strong societal pressure on public officials to possess external symbols of status (as did their colonial predecessors), and the meager salaries they receive. Although Israelis still expect their public officials to adhere to a traditional Jewish norm of modest behavior, a double standard is being created as the society itself is becoming more materialistic. Indeed, as will be shown, various scandals of the 1970s involving white-collar crime indicate that some adherence to modest behavior is observed domestically, but not when officials go overseas on public business and the predilection for luxury is not socially inhibited.

The salary and rank gap derives from the formation of an Israeli civil service based on an idealistic sense of mission and egalitarianism. Basic salary differentiation between the various administrative ranks is slight. This, and the increasing salary-inflation gap (the inflation rate [in the early 1980s] . . . surpasse[d] 100 per cent per annum) increase the needs of public officials to look for means of supplementing income. One such means is "moonlighting" which now prevails to such an extent in the Israeli public sector as to constitute a whole system by itself. Another means is petty corruption as well as the willingness to take the risks involved in black corruption. As Israelis continue to expect their public officials to be content with a meager salary, while they themselves become more materialistic, the double standard that is created tends to erode even further the morality of civil servants.

In the 1970s, unprecedented white-collar crime and corruption ran rampant. Some examples will suffice:

1. In the summer of 1974, the general manager of the Israel-British Bank (IBB) was arrested for investigation for "huge discrepancies"[52] in bank records that eventually led to the collapse of the IBB. The losses, estimated to be over $40 million, had to be covered by the central Bank of Israel. Later, in September 1977, Menachem Begin, the newly elected prime minister, became the center of controversy when he recommended a pardon for the manager of the defunct IBB. The manager, serving a prison term, had been the financial backer of the ultranationalist movement, which is ideologically close to Likud. On the grounds of severe sickness, Begin stressed forgiveness.[53]

2. In April 1975, a major new scandal erupted involving charges of bribery, price-fixing, falsifying bids and orders, and embezzlement by government high officials and defense contractors. The scandal raised questions about the extent of dubious practices that were prevalent between the 1967 and 1973 wars, boom years for defense contractors.[54]

3. Also in April 1975, the then general manager of Israel Corporation (a government-supported development corporation) was indicted and later on 9 May 1975, pleaded guilty to 14 counts of larceny, bribery, fraud and corruption involving estimated losses of over $100 million. A vast proportion of the embezzled money was illegally transferred out of the country to the International Credit Bank of Geneva.[55]

4. In October 1976, the Israel political system was shaken by the arrest of the head of the huge Trade Union Sick Fund. The man was also then a nominee of the ruling Labor party for governor of the Bank of Israel. Approximately half a year later, after the charges had been made, the man admitted that real estate kickbacks had gone both to the Labor party's 1973 election campaign and to his own pocket.[56]

5. In April 1977, former Prime Minister Yitzhak Rabin was found to have violated Israel foreign currency regulations.[57] The resultant scandal forced Rabin to step out of the Labor government and resign as a Labor party candidate. These scandals played a significant role in the defeat of the Labor party during the next election of 1977.[58]

Scandals and black corruption continued under the Likud government during the years 1980 and 1981. Court actions were lenient but public obloquy was intense.

In September 1979, the French government sought extradition of Samuel Flatto-Sharon, Israeli member of parliament who previously, as a French citizen, was allegedly involved in embezzling $60 million in fraudulent real estate deals during the 1960s and 1970s.[59] In the 1977 election, he formed his one-man political party, but later in 1981 was accused of bribing voters, sentenced to imprisonment and suspended from parliament.

In September 1980, the then minister of religious affairs of the National Religious party was summoned for police questioning concerning alleged kickbacks, bribery and corruption in the ministry of religious affairs. In May 1981, a court in Jerusalem acquitted him of charges of accepting kickbacks, but denounced his moral standards in dispensing grants from his ministry.[60] The trial evoked conflicts between the minister and the National Religious party. Subsequently, he established a new Sephardic (Oriental) list, which won three seats in the June 1981 election. In November 1981, as the new minister of immigrant absorption, he stood trial again on charges of theft, fraud and violation of public trust whilst he was serving as Ramle mayor from 1973 to 1977.[61] Later, in early 1982, he was found guilty. While the court was lenient (imposing a fine and a suspended sentence), public outrage led to his resignation as a minister.

These selected cases of corruption not only support the argument about the maturation of corruption in contemporary Israel, but also point to the role of leadership in shaping societal attitudes toward law and order. Leaders, by definition, are the paradigms of the body politic, and by their corrupt behavior they set an example which tends to erode the moral base of law and provides an opportunity for their followers to emulate and rationalize corrupt behavior. In Israel where, due to past developments, public regard for law and order still cannot be taken for granted, the corrupt behavior of leaders is particularly dangerous. Also, as exemplified by Levi Eshkol and Menachem Begin, the failure of leaders to condemn corruption serves to increase the spread of corruption.

Another deleterious aspect of leadership behavior can be observed in the Israeli machinery of local government, namely, local-patriotic corruption. If central government regulation stifles local productivity, then, Israelis reason, these regulations can be circumvented for the good of the locality. Mayors will use their personal influence to build an important'' city project even if, for example, the license or budget is not yet approved by the responsible, but cumbersome, central agencies.[62] In February 1982, the head of a local authority, who was also a member of the Israel parliament, made the following statement which evoked enormous public criticism: "I give bonuses to my employees whom I find performing a good job. I do it under the table. It is perhaps illegal, but that does not concern me."[63]

Patriotic corruption is not new to Israelis: it was committed by Jewish officials during the end of the British mandate, but then it was concealed. It has now resurfaced in Israel's local government and is committed more and more openly. It creates a fear that, if left unchecked, it will become a *modus operandi*.

Reacting to increasing pressures for higher wage compensation, the government itself continued to circumvent its own wage structures. Labor unrest in the air ports administration led to numerous strikes that paralyzed Israel's international air communication. Afraid that yielding to the pressure for better salaries would lead to new demands from other unions in the civil service, the Labor government decided in 1976 to act by abusing the concept of the 'public corporation'. It was 'logical' to incorporate the air ports administration and, by doing so, to exclude both management personnel and the wage structures of the newly born Air Ports Authority from the umbrella of the civil service laws and regulation. This blunt policy was heavily criticized by the public. More significantly, it created a craze for incorporation: other professional unions (for example, workers of the Income-Tax Administration) sought incorporation of their relevant departmental agency.

Since 1977, when the Likud came to power, inflation has grown. The government continues to adopt policies designed to prevent the standard of living from falling. The historical peace treaty with Egypt has given the Israelis a new feeling of national security. Materialism has increased, whilst the idealistic values of the past have continued to fade. Artificial salary 'improvements' introduced by the Labor government have been conveniently adopted by the Likud government. The Israelis' disregard of law and order has not changed for the better, and the corrupt behavior of officials of high caliber sets a bad example for the common Israeli.

Nevertheless, the Likud government strives at changing some of the conditions that have allowed civil order to deteriorate. It began by launching an attack against organized crime. It has striven to tame powerful labor unions and to coordinate local government and state enterprises. Indeed, it seeks to become a central government in practice as well as on paper. On the other hand, it is getting more and more involved (after the June 1981 election) in personnel and contract political patronage, as well as in diverting accessible public funds to the religious parties that have the balancing power in the coalition. Because of other priorities, or perhaps because of a fear that the elimination of practices now bordering on white corruption may produce administrative chaos, these practices are left intact.

Furthermore, because of the failure of the system to determine when white corruption becomes destructive, and because of the acceptance of white corruption as being "legitimate," other types of gray and black shades of corruption become progressively lighter and a further momentum is established. This self-perpetuating nature of white corruption, in addition to the other factors discussed above allow corruption in Israel to mature along with the maturation of the political system.

Conclusion

This study of Israel has demonstrated that political and bureaucratic corruption are not necessarily associated with political modernization. Neither is corruption doomed to destruction as a political system matures. Corruption alters its character in response to changing socioeconomic, cultural and political factors. As these factors affect corruption, so does corruption affect them. Significantly, because corruption is in equilibrium, the concept of entropy is not applicable. Simply put, corruption may be controlled through alterations of its character but, most importantly, not destroyed. Corruption carries a dynamic mechanism that allows it to spill over and perpetuate itself. Such a corruptive mechanism is primarily evident in white corruption which is trivialized, condoned, rationalized, and which leads to a general sense of impunity, encouraging more insidious types of corruption.

In the pre-state period in Israel, corruption originated as a necessity. But after independence, corruption manifested dysfunctional aspects. It did not foster the integration of new immigrants and did not assist in economic development. White-collar crime of the post Yom-Kippur War manifested economic dysfunctionality almost entirely. Institutionalization of white bureaucratic corruption not only created an environment in which more serious types of corruption developed, but also blocked the process of bureaucratization. Also, political institutionalization was not necessarily affected by corruption, and corruption of the type of patron-client relations can thrive parallel or external to the level of political institutionalization.[64]

In terms of policy implication, the case of Israel has demonstrated that certain factors can inhibit corruption while political development is still enhanced, or can allow corruption to flourish while bureaucratic performance declines. When these factors are identified, it will be possible to begin to develop a multi-faceted effort to control corruption.

Notes

1. The classification is adopted from S. Werner, "New Directions in the Study of Administrative Corruption," *Public Administration Review,* 43:2 (March-April 1983), 146–54.
2. H.D. Bayley, "The Effects of Corruption in a Developing Nation," *Western Political Quarterly,* 19 (1966), 719–32; N.H. Leff, "Economic Development Through Bureaucratic Corruption," *American Behavioral Scientist,* 8 (1964), 10–12.

3. Bayley, "The Effects of Corruption in a Developing Nation"; J. Scott, *Comparative Political Corruption* (Englewood Cliff, NJ: Prentice-Hall, 1972).
4. J.V. Abueva, "The Contribution of Nepotism, Spoils, and Graft to Political Development," *East-West Center Review*, 3 (1966), 45–54; S. P. Huntington, *Political Order in Changing Societies* (New Haven, Conn.: Yale University Press, 1968); R. K. Merton, "Some Functions of the Political Machine," in R. K. Merton, *Social Theory and Social Structure* (New York: Free Press, 1957), 72–82.
5. R. Braibanti, "Public Bureaucracy and Judiciary in Pakistan," in J. LaPalombara (ed.), *Bureaucracy and Political Development* (Princeton: Princeton University Press, 1963); W. F. Riggs, "Bureaucrats and Political Development: A Paradoxical View," in J. LaPalombara (ed.), *Bureaucracy and Political Development.*
6. J. Nye, "Corruption and Political Development: A Cost Benefit Analysis," *American Political Science Review*, 61 (1967), 417–27.
7. Bayley, "The Effects of Corruption in a Developing Nation."
8. S. Varma, "Corruption and Political Development in India," *Political Science Review*, 13 (1974), 167.
9. D. Gould, *Bureaucratic Corruption and Underdevelopment in the Third World* (New York: Pergamon Press, 1980).
10. *On political dysfunctionalities* see: G. Benson, *Political Corruption in America* (Lexington: Lexington Books, 1978); S. Dasgupta, "Corruption," *Seminar*, 185 (1975), 194–300; J. Dobel, "The Corruption of a State," *The American Political Science Review*, 72 (1978), 958–73; T. Lowi, "The Intelligent Person's Guide to Political Corruption," *Public Affairs*, 82 (1981), 1–6; S. Mamoru and H. Auerbach, "Political Corruption and Social Structure in Japan," *Asian Survey*, 17 (1977), 556–64; N. Marican, "Combating Corruption: The Malaysian Experience," *Asian Survey*, 19 (1979), 597–610; T. Smith, "Corruption, Tradition and Change," *Indonesia*, 71 (1974), 21–40; S. Varma, *Corruption and Political Development in India;* J. Waterbury, "Endemic and Planned Corruption in a Monarchical Regime," *World Politics*, 25 (1973), 533–55.
On economic dysfunctionality see: G. Amick, *The American Way of Government* (Princeton, NJ: The Center for the Analysis of Public Issues, 1976); M. Goodman, "Does Political Corruption Really Help Economic Development: Yucatan, Mexico," *Polity*, 7 (1974), 143–62; F. McHenry, "Food Bungle in Bangladesh," *Foreign Policy*, 27(1977), 72–88; S. Rose-Ackerman, *Corruption: A Study in Political Economy* (New York: Academic Press, 1978); R. Tilman, "The Philippines Under Martial Law," *Current History*, 71 (1976), 201–25; H. Warren, "Banks and Banking in Paraguay," *Inter-American Economic Affairs*, 32 (1978), 39–55.
On bureaucratic dysfunctionalities see: G. Caiden and N. Caiden, "Administrative Corruption," *Public Administration Review*, 33 (1977), 301–8; P. Drucker, "What is Business Ethics," *The Public Interest* (1981), 18–36; O. Dwivedi, "Bureaucratic Corruption in Developing Countries," *Asian Survey*, 7 (1967), 245–53; J. Gardiner and T. Lyman, *Decisions for Sale: Corruption and Reform in Land-Use and Building Regulation* (New York: Praeger, 1978); L. Hager, "Bureaucratic Corruption in India: Legal Control of Maladministration," *Comparative Political Studies*, 6 (1973), 179–219; L. Sherman, *Scandal and Reform: Controlling Police Corruption* (Berkeley: University of California Press, 1978); N. Singhi, "Bureaucratic Corruption," *Administrative Change*, 2 (1977), 34–47.
11. Scott, *Comparative Political Corruption*, p. 77.
12. Scott, *Comparative Political Corruption*, p. 52.
13. Bentwich, *England and Palestine*, p. 245.
14. A. Koestler, *Promise and Fulfilment* (London: Macmillan, 1949), p. 240.

15. Koestler, *Promise and Fulfilment,* pp. 244–5.
16. Omar Bey Salih Al-Barghuthi, "Local Self-Government—Past and Present," *The Annals of the American Academy of Political and Social Science,* 164 (1932), p. 37.
17. D. Ismojik, *Bustna'i (Tel-Aviv Weekly),* 15, 22 and 29 May 1929. Quoted in Burstein, *Self-Government of the Jews in Palestine Since 1900,* pp. 281–2.
18. D. Horowitz and H. Lissak, *Origins of the Israeli Polity: Palestine Under the Mandate* (Chicago: University of Chicago Press, 1978).
19. D. Horowitz and M. Lissak, *Origins of the Israeli Polity,* p. 41.
20. Lapalombara, *Bureaucracy and Political Development.*
21. Riggs, "Bureaucrats and Political Development: A Paradoxical view."
22. Braibanti, *Public Bureaucracy and Judiciary in Pakistan.*
23. R. Patai, *Israel Between East and West: A Study in Human Relations* (Philadelphia: The Jewish Publication Society of America, 1953), p. 66.
24. Horowitz and Lissak, *Origins of the Israeli Polity,* p. 5.
25. J. Dobel, "The Corruption of a State."
26. Amos Elon, *The Israelis: Founders and Sons* (New York: Holt, Rinehart & Winston, 1971), p. 293.
27. T. Browden, *The Breakdown of Public Security: The Case of Ireland 1916–1921 and Palestine 1936–1939* (London: Sage, 1977).
28. T. Browden, *The Breakdown of Public Security.*
29. T. Browden, *The Breakdown of Public Security,* p. 233.
30. A. Koestler, *Promise and Fulfilment,* p. 296.
31. D. Elazar, "Israel's Compound Polity," in H.R. Penniman (ed.), *Israel at the Polls: The Knesset Elections of 1977* (Washington, DC: American Enterprise Institute for Public Policy Research, 1979), pp. 28–33.
32. G. Caiden, *Israel's Administrative Culture* (Berkeley: University of California, 1970).
33. G. Ben-Dor, "Schitut, Misud Ve'itpatchut Politit," *Rivon Le'Mechkar Chevarati,* 5 (1973), 5–2l Hebrew.
34. D. Elazar, "Israel's Compound Polity," p.15.
35. D. Nachmian and D. Rosenblum, *Bureaucratic Culture: Citizens and Administrators in Israel* (London: Croom Helm Ltd., 1975), p. 95.
36. G. Caiden, *Israel's Administrative Culture,* p.60.   1'
37. Danet and H. Hartman, "On Protekzia: Orientations Toward the Use of Personal Influence in Israeli Bureaucracy," *Journal of Comparative Administration,* 3 (1972), 407.
38. D. Nachmias and D. Rosenblum, *Bureaucratic Culture: Citizens and Administrators in Israel.*
39. Y. Reuveni, *Ha'Minhal Ha'ziburi Be 'Israel* (Ramat-Gan: Massada, 1972). Hebrew.
40. A Statement of a Jewish witness before the *Palestine Royal Commission Report* (London; HMSO, 1937), p.119. The page number refers to the 1946 reprint.
41. Elon, *The Israelis: Founders and Sons,* pp. 300–1.
42. On the Lorenz Index, absolute equality is indicated by a value of zero, and absolute inequality is indicated by a value of one.
43. *Palestine: A study of Jewish, Arab, and British Policies* (New Haven: Yale University Press, published for ESCO Foundation in Palestine, Inc., 1947), p. 349
44. A Heidenheimer (ed.), *Political Corruption: Readings in Comparative Analysis* (New York: Holt, 1970).
45. J. Peters and S. Welch, "Political Corruption in America. A Search for Definition

and Theory: Or, if Political Corruption is in the Mainstream of American Politics, Why is it not in the Mainstream of American Political Research?," *The American Political Science Review,* 72 (1978), 974–84.

46. D. Matza, *Delinquency and Drift* (New York: John Wiley, 1964), p. 60.
47. G. Skyes and D. Matza, "Technique of Neutralization: A Theory of Delinquency," *American Sociological Review,* 22 (1957), 664–70.
48. H. Greenberg and S. Nadler, *Poverty in Israel: Economic Realities and the Promise of Social Justice* (New York: Praeger, 1977), p.3.
49. Y. Elizur and E. Salpeter, *Who Rules Israel* (New York: Harper & Row, 1973), p. 86.
50. Y. Elizur and E. Salpeter, *Who Rules Israel,* p. 24.
51. R. Price, *Society and Bureaucracy in Contemporary Ghana* (Berkeley: University of California, 1975).
52. *New York Times,* 25 July 1974, 49: 7.
53. *New York Times,* 10 September 1977, 3:1.
54. *New York Times,* 15 April 1975, 3:1.
55. On the affair, see: *New York Times,* 9 April 1975, 12: 2; 10 April 1975, 41: 7; 14 April 1975, 1: 4; 8 May 1975, 5:1; 10 May 1975, 8:1; 22 May 1975,4:6.
56. On the affair, see: *New York Times,* 20 October 1976, 10: 3; 14 December 1976, 6:3; 15 February 1975, 1:1; 14 February 1975, 1:1.
57. *New York Times,* 21 March 1977, 1: 4; 8 April 1977, 1: 6.
58. See M. Aronoff, "The Decline of the Israeli Labor Party: Causes and Significance," in H. R. Penniman (ed.), *Israel at the Polls* (Washington, D.C.: American Enterprise Institute, 1979), pp. 115–145.
59. *New York Times,* 9 September 1979, III, 3:1.
60. *New York Times,* 26 May 1981, 5:1.
61. *New York Times,* 9 August 1981; 2: 1; 23 November 1981, 6:1.
62. On the mayor of Haifa see, *Ha'aretz,* 1 March 1982, 3; On the mayor of Tel-Aviv see, *Ha'aretz,* 10 October 1982, 8.
63. *Ha'aretz,* 2 February 1982, 9. Hebrew.
64. See Ben-Dor, "Schitut, Misud Ve'itpatchut Politit."

13

Corruption, Machine Politics and Political Change

James C. Scott

Despite formal obstacles, there is one political form that has not only been able to respond to particularistic interests but has thrived on them—the urban "machine," a form that flourished in the United States around the turn of the century. Although now virtually extinct, the machine once managed to fashion a cacophony of concrete, parochial demands in immigrant-choked cities into a system of rule that was at once reasonably effective and legitimate.

The purpose of this study is to outline the contours and dynamics of the "machine model" in comparative perspective and attempt to show that the social context that fostered "machine politics" in the United States is more or less present in many of the new states. This is done by first sketching the general character of "machine politics," then by suggesting a developmental model to account for the machine, and finally by analyzing the decline of the machine in the United States.

The Machine

To abstract the basic characteristics of a political machine obviously does some violence to the great variety of entrepreneurial talent that was devoted to creating this form. Nevertheless, as all but a few beleaguered machines have succumbed to the forces of "reform government" analysis has replaced accusation and the central features of most machines are reasonably clear.[1]

Source: James C. Scott, "Corruption, Machine Politics, and Social Change," *American Political Science Review,* 63:4 (1969), pp. 42–59. By permission of publisher.

It will be recognized at the outset that the machine form can occur only in certain political settings. At a minimum, the setting of the machine requires:

1. The selection of political leaders through elections
2. Mass (usually universal) adult suffrage
3. A relatively high degree of electoral competition over time-usually between parties, but occasionally within a dominant party

These conditions reflect the fact that since machine politics represents a distinctive way of mobilizing voters, it arises only in systems where getting out the vote is essential to gaining control of the government. While these conditions are necessary for machine-style politics, they are by no means sufficient, as we shall see later.

Always applied to a political party in power, the term *machine* connotes the reliable and repetitive control it exercises within its jurisdiction. What is distinctive about the machine, however, is not so much its control as the nature of the organizational cement that makes such control feasible. The machine is not the disciplined, ideological party held together by class ties and common programs that arose in continental Europe. Neither is it typically a charismatic party, depending on a belief in the almost superhuman qualities of its leader to ensure internal cohesion. Rather, it is a nonideological organization interested less in political principle than in securing and holding office for its leaders and distributing income to those who run it and work for it.[2] It relies on what it accomplishes in a concrete way for its supporters, not on what it stands for. A machine may, in fact, be likened to a business in which all members are stockholders and where dividends are paid in accordance with what has been invested.[3]

"Patronage, "spoils," and "corruption" are inevitably associated with the urban machine as it evolved in the United States. As these terms indicate, the machine dealt almost exclusively *in particularistic, material rewards* to maintain and extend its control over its personnel. Although pork-barrel legislation provided inducements for ethnic groups as a whole, the machine did most of its favors for individuals and families. The very nature of these rewards and favors naturally meant that the machine became *specialized in organizing and allocating influence at the enforcement stage.* The corruption it fostered was not random greed but was finely organized and articulated to maximize its electoral support.

Thus the machine is best characterized by the nature of the cement that binds leaders and followers. Ties based on charisma, coercion, or ideology were occasionally minor chords of machine orchestration; the "boss" might take on some heroic proportions: he might use hired toughs or the police now and again to discourage opposition; and a populist ideological aura might accompany his acts. For the machine such bonds were definitely subsidiary to the concrete, particularistic rewards that represented its stable means of political coordination. It is the predominance of these reward networks-the special quality of the ties between leaders and followers-that distinguishes the machine party from the nonmachine party.

Given its principal concern for retaining office, the machine was a *responsive, informal context* within which *bargaining* based on reciprocity relationships was facilitated. Leaders of the machine were rarely in a position to dictate: those who supported them did so on the basis of value received or anticipated. For the most part the machine accepted its electoral clients as they were and responded to their needs in a manner that would elicit their support. The pragmatic, opportunistic orientation of the machine thus made it a flexible institution that could accommodate new groups and leaders in highly dynamic situations.

In the United States, the rapid influx of new populations for whom family and ethnicity were the central identifications, when coupled with the award of important monopoly privileges (traction, electric power, and so forth) and the public payroll, provided the ideal soil for the emergence of party machines. Developing nations can be viewed as offering a social context with many of the same nutrients. New governments had in many cases only recently acquired control over the disposal of lucrative posts and privileges, and they faced electorates that included many poor, newly urbanized peasants with particularistic loyalties who could easily be swayed by concrete material incentives. The point each writer makes is not only that the machine is a suitable and relatively democratic political form that can manage such a complex environment, but that the social context typical of most new nations tends to encourage the growth of machinelike qualities in ruling parties. For America, Burnham has summarized the argument now being applied to less-developed nations:

> If the social context in which a two-party system operates is extensively fragmented along regional ethnic and other lines, its major components will tend to be overwhelmingly concerned with coalition building and internal conflict management. The need to unite for electoral [broad coalition building] purposes presupposes a corresponding need to generate consensus at whatever level consensus can be found.[4]

Given this sort of social context, so the reasoning goes, the price of effective political cooperation-at least in the short run-involves meeting narrow, particularistic demands, often through the patronage, favors, and corruption that are the hallmarks of machine politics. But why are other forms of association not feasible? What specific changes in the social context promote or undermine different styles of political collaboration? Unless the model is placed in a developmental perspective and considerably sharpened from its presently intriguing but impressionistic form, its explanatory value will remain limited.

Social Context of Political Ties

The schema presented in table 13.1 focuses on changes over time in the nature of loyalty ties that form the basis of political parties. It is tailored to a bargaining-particularly, electoral-context and is less applicable where force or threats of force are the basis of cooperation. Nothing is intended to be rigidly deterministic about the movement from phase A to phase B to phase C. The phases are, however, largely based on the empirical experience of the United States, England, and the new nations.

Although the phases have been separated for the purpose of conceptual clarity, they are likely to overlap considerably in the empirical experience of any nation. It is thus a question of which loyalty pattern is most common and which less common. Within new nations all three patterns typically coexist: rural villagers may remain deferential to their traditional leaders; the recent urban migrants may behave more as free agents seeking jobs or cash for their votes; and a small group of professionals, trade union leaders, and intellectuals may perhaps be preoccupied with ideological or class concerns. Even fully industrialized nations may contain recalcitrant, and usually isolated pockets where deference patterns have not yielded to more opportunistic modes of political expression.[5]

Prior to fuller treatment below, a brief word is in order about the process of change implied by table 13.1. Movement from phase A to phase B involves the shaking loose of traditional deference patterns, which can occur in a variety of ways. For the United States, large-scale immigration by basically peasant populations was often the occasion for this change, while for less developed nations the economic changes introduced by colonial regimes and rapid migration from village to city has provided the catalyst. The social disorganization that resulted was often exacerbated by ethnic, linguistic, or even caste fragmentation, but similar patterns have arisen in Thailand and the Philippines—for example, amid comparatively homogeneous populations. Elections themselves have, of course, played a central role in this transformation because they placed a new political resource of some significance at the disposal of even the most humble citizens.

Movement from phase B to phase C would appear to depend on the process of industrialization as new economic arrangements take hold and provide new focuses of identification and loyalty. As the case of the United States illustrates, however, the presence of sharp ethnic and sectional cleavage—the latter reinforced by constitutional arrangements—may considerably dilute the strength of these new bonds.

The duration of phase B, when the social context is most hospitable to machine-style politics, may vary widely. When the social disorganization accompanying urbanization and economic change is particularly severe and of long duration, when it is compounded by deep cultural differences, and

Table 13.1

PHASE A[1]	Political ties are determined largely by traditional patterns of deference (vertical ties) to established authorities. Material, particularistic inducements to cooperation play a minor role except among a limited number of local power holders.[2]
PHASE B	Deference patterns have weakened considerably in a period of rapid socioeconomic change. Vertical ties can only be maintained through a relationship of greater reciprocity.[3] Competition among leaders for support, coupled with the predominance of narrow, parochial loyalties, will encourage the widespread use of concrete, short-run, material inducements to secure cooperation. The greater the competitive electoral pressures, the wider the distribution of inducements is likely to be. Influence at enforcement stage is common.
PHASE C	New loyalties have emerged in the process of economic growth that increasingly stress horizontal (functional) class or occupational ties. The nature of inducements for political support are accordingly likely to stress policy concerns or ideology. Influence at the legislative stage becomes more appropriate to the nature of the new political loyalties.

1. The broad lines of this schema were suggested by an analysis of the use of money in elections contained in Arnold Heidenheimer. "Comparative Party Finance: Notes on Practices and Toward a Theory," pp. 790–811 in Richard Rose and Arnold Heidenheimer, eds., *Comparative Studies in Political Finance: A Symposium, Journal of Politics,* 25:4 (November 1963), especially pp. 808–809. Changes in the nature of political ties influence greatly the degree to which monetary incentives are successful in electoral campaigns, and I have thus borrowed from that analysis for the broader purpose of this study.
2. Traditional ties often allow some scope for bargaining and reciprocity: the ability of clients to flee to another jurisdiction and the economic and military need for a leader to attract and keep a sizable clientele provided subordinates with some leverage. The distinctions made here in the degree of reciprocity are relative, not absolute. See, for example, Herbert P. Phillips, *The Peasant Personality,* Berkeley, Calif. University of California Press, 1965, p.89, or George M. Foster, "The Dyadic Contract in Tzintzunzan, II: Patron Client Relationships," *American Anthropologist,* 65 (1963), pp. 1280–1294.
3. What appears to happen in the transitional situation is that the client is less ''locked-in'' to a single patron and the need for political support forces patrons to compete with one another to create larger clienteles. For a brilliant analysis of this pattern in Philippine politics see Carl H. Landé, *Leaders, Factions, and Parties-The Structure of Philippine Politics.* Monograph No. 6. New Haven. Conn.: Yale University-Southeast Asia Studies, 1965, throughout.

when competitive elections with a universal suffrage are introduced early, the pressures toward machine politics will be vastly greater than when demographic change is gradual and less severe, when it occurs with a minimum of cultural cleavage, and when the electorate is restricted. The historical circumstances of both the United States and most new nations have been, in this sense, quite conducive to the development of machine politics as opposed to, say, the Western European experience.

Inducements and the Nature of Loyalty

Political parties must generally offer inducements of one kind or another to potential supporters. The pressures to enlist adherents is obviously greatest when the party faces a competitive electoral struggle, but in the absence of battles for votes merely the desire to establish a broad following among the populace will create analogous pressures.

The sort of incentives most likely to "move" people is contingent, as the phase model clearly implies, on the kinds of loyalty ties that are most salient to the potential client. In the short run, at least, parties that need supporters are more apt to respond to the incentives that motivate their clientele than to transform the nature of those incentives. Elaborating on this relationship between loyalty bonds (independent variable) and party inducements (dependent variable), table 13.2 suggests the actual empirical patterns that are likely to occur.

Parties in the real world commonly confront all four patterns of loyalty simultaneously and fashion a mix of inducements that corresponds to the mix of loyalties.[6] Inducements, moreover, are not unifunctional; public works usually carry with them a host of jobs and contracts that can be distributed along more particularistic lines while patronage can be wielded in such a way as to actually favor an entire community or ethnic group.

With these qualifications in mind, it is suggested that, given pressure to gain support, a party will emphasize those inducements that are appropriate to the loyalty patterns among its clientele. Material inducements are as characteristic of occupational or class loyalties as they are of local or family loyalties; what is different is simply the scope and nature of the group being "bribed" by the party, not the fact of "bribery." In the case of occupational and class loyalties, the inducements can be offered as general legislation (and rationalized by ideology, too), whereas inducements at the individual or family level must often be supplied illegally ("corruptly") at the enforcement stage.[7] The classical machine faces a social context in which community and family orientations are most decisive. Responding to its environment, the machine is thus likely to become consummately skilled in both the political distribution of public works through pork-barrel legislation and in the dispensation of jobs and favors through more informal channels.

Table 13.2

Nature of Loyalties	Inducement
Ties of traditional deference or of charisma	Mostly symbolic, nonmaterial inducements
Community or locality orientation (also ethnic concentration)	Indivisible rewards; public works, schools, "pork-barrel" Communal inducements
Individual family, or small-group orientation	Material rewards; patronage, favors, cash payments, "corruption" Individual inducements
Occupational or class orientation	Policy commitments at tax law, subsidy programs, and soon "general legislation" Sectoral inducements

Historically, the expansion of the suffrage, together with the rupture of traditional economic and status arrangements, has signaled the rise of particularistic, material inducements. In Robert Walcott's masterful portrait of electoral politics in eighteenth-century England, this transition is vividly depicted in the contrast between the shire constituencies, where traditional landholders still commanded the allegiance of a small electorate, and the larger urban constituencies, where elections

> were notoriously venal and turbulent. Wealthy beer-barons with hireling armies of draymen battled for the representation of Southwark; while the mass of Westminster electors were marshalled out, with considerable efficiency, to vote for candidates set up by the court.[8]

Southwark and Westminster, at the time Walcott describes them, were the exception rather than the rule, and English parliamentary politics revolved around coalitions of clique leaders, each of whom was generally accepted as the "natural" representative of his constituency. The transition, however, was under way.

Changes in modal patterns of loyalty help account for not only the development of machine politics but for its decline as well. In addition to other factors (discussed later), the growth of political ties in which family bonds were less important than before and in which occupational and/or class considerations played a more prominent role undercut the very foundation of the machines.[9] The specific inducements that the machine was organized to supply worked their "magic" on an increasingly smaller proportion of party workers and supporters. Instead, as businessmen and laborers each came to appreciate their broader, more long-run interest as a sector of society, they increasingly required general legislation that met their interests in return for political support. Here and there a social context tailored to the machine style remained; but the machine either reconciled itself to the new loyalties— becoming less and less a machine in the process—or was the electoral victim of social change. Parties still continued to offer palpable inducements to voters, but the new inducements were more typically embodied in general legislation whereas previously they had been particularistic and often outside the law. As Banfield and Wilson summarize the transition,

> If in the old days specific material inducements were illegally given as bribes to favored individuals, now much bigger ones are legally given to a different class of favored individuals, and, in addition, general inducements are proffered in packages to every large group in the electorate and to tiny but intensely moved minorities as well.[10]

Ecology of Machine Coordination

The distinctive style of political coordination embodied in the machine has historically occurred in settings where, in addition to rapid social change and a competitive electoral system, (a) political power was fragmented, (b) ethnic cleavage, social disorganization or both were widespread, and (c) most of the population was poor. Drawn mostly from studies of urban machines in the United States, these features of the environment seem applicable to a large degree to the many underdeveloped nations in which political parties have begun to resemble machines.

Fragmentation of Power

In accounting for corruption and machine politics in Chicago, Merriam lays particular stress on the multiplicity of urban authorities and jurisdictions that existed within the city. He describes eight main "governments," each with different powers, which created so many jealously guarded centers of power that a mayor faced a host of potential veto groups, any one of which could paralyze him.[11] He could secure cooperation with these authorities only by striking informal bargains—often involving patronage, contracts, franchises—and thus putting together the necessary power piece by piece.

Power was fragmented in yet another sense. Party candidates did not face one electorate but several: each ethnic group had its own special interests and demands, and a successful campaign depended on assembling a temporary coalition on the basis of inducements suited to each group. The decentralization of power created by such a heterogeneous environment meant that the "boss's" control was forever tenuous, His temporary authority rested on his continuing capacity to keep rewards flowing at the acceptable rate.

New York in the era of Boss Tweed strikingly resembles Merriam's picture of Chicago. In spite of the prodigious manipulations attributed to him, Tweed was not especially powerful and had little control over party branches that could nominate their own candidates for many posts. What he did manage to do, however, was to create, for a time, a centralized, finely articulated coalition. Carefully assessing the nature of Tweed's feat, Seymour Mandelbaum declares,

> There was only one way New York could be "bossed" in the 1860s. The lines of communication were too narrow, the patterns of deference too weak to support freely acknowledged and stable leadership. Only a universal payment of benefits-a giant payoff-could pull the city together in a common effort. The only treasury big enough to support coordination was the public till.[12] . . .

Social Fragmentation and Disorganization

The immigrants who constituted the bulk of the clientele of the American urban machine came largely from the ranks of the European peasantry. They "required the most extensive acculturation simply to come to terms with urban-industrial existence as such, much less to enter the party system as relatively independent actors."[13] If the fragmentation of power made it advantageous for the politician to offer special inducements for support, the situation of the immigrant made him eager to respond to blandishments that corresponded with his most immediate needs. Machine inducements are thus particularly compelling among disoriented new arrivals, who value greatly the quick helping hand extended to them by the party.

The dependence of machine parties on a clientele that is both unfamiliar with the contours of the political system and economically on the defensive is underscored by the character of the small pockets where vestiges of once-powerful machines still exist. One such example is the Dawson machine (really a submachine) in Chicago. This machine rests squarely on favors and patronage among the Negro population, most of which has come to Chicago from the rural south within the last generation. Deprived of even this steadily diminishing social base, the machine has elsewhere withered as the populations it assisted became acculturated and could afford the luxury of wider loyalties and more long-range political goals.

It is no coincidence, then, that machines flourished during the period of most rapid urban growth in the United States, when the sense of community was especially weak, and when social fragmentation made particularistic ties virtually the only feasible means of cooperation. The machine bound its clientele to it by virtue of the employment, legal services, economic relief, and other services it supplied for them. "For the lower strata, in return for their votes, it provided a considerable measure of primitive welfare functions, personalized help for individuals caught up in the toils of the law, and political socialization."[14]

Poverty

Perhaps the most fundamental quality shared by the mass clientele of machines is poverty. Machines characteristically rely on the suffrage of the poor and, naturally, prosper best when the poor are many and the middle-class few. In America, Banfield and Wilson emphasized that "Almost without exception, the lower the average income and the fewer the average years of schooling in a ward, the more dependable the ward's allegiance to the machine."[15]

Poverty shortens a man's time horizon and maximizes the effectiveness of short-run material inducements. Quite rationally he is willing to accept a job, cash, or simply the promise of assistance when he needs it, in return for his vote and that of his family. Attachments to policy goals or to an ideology implies something of a future orientation as well as wide loyalties, while poverty discounts future gains and focuses unavoidably on the here and now.

The attitudes associated with poverty that facilitate machine-style politics are not just confined to a few urban centers in less-developed nations, but typify portions of the rural population as well.[16] In such circumstances, the jobs, money, and other favors at the disposal of the government represent compelling inducements. Deployed to best advantage, these incentives are formidable weapons in building coalitions or electioneering or both. The ease with which votes are bought-individually in many urban areas and in blocs where village or ethnic cohesion is sufficient to secure collaboration-during elections in the new nations is a measure of the power of narrow material rewards in the social context of poverty.[17]

Notes

1. Some of the more successful efforts at careful description and analysis include: V.O. Key, Jr., *The Techniques of Political Graft in the United States.* Chicago, Ill.: University of Chicago Libraries, 1936; Seymour J. Mandelbaum, *Boss Tweed's New York,* New York: Wiley, 1965; Edward C. Banfield and James Q. Wilson, *City Politics.* Cambridge, Mass.: Harvard University Press, 1965.
2. Banfield and Wilson, p.116.
3. This analogy was made by former Liberal party president José Avelino of the Philippines in the *Manila Chronicle,* Jan. 18, 1949. Quoted in Virginia Baterina, "A Study of Money in Elections in the Philippines," *Philippine Social Sciences and Humanities Review,* 20:1 (March 1955), pp. 39–86.
4. Walter Dean Burnham, "Party Systems and the Political Process," pp. 277–307, in William Nisbet Chambers and Walter Dean Burnham, eds., *The American Party Systems: Stages of Political Development,* New York: Oxford, 1967, p. 287. Fragment in brackets mine.
5. In this context, party labels are deceptive. The existence of parties proclaiming an ideology or class position are often found in rural areas where the labels have been appropriated in toto in a continuation of traditional feuds between powerful families and their respective clienteles. The key is the nature of loyalty patterns,

not the name of the organization. See Carlo Levi, *Christ Stopped at Eboli.* New York: Pocket Books, 1965.

6. The importance of one or another pattern can, in addition, be amplified or diminished by structural characteristics of the political system; in the U.S. federalism and local candidate selection tend to amplify geographical ties. See Theodore J. Lowi, "Party, Policy, and Constitution in America," pp. 238–276 in Chambers and Burnham.

7. Political systems vary significantly in the extent to which favors and patronage can be carried out within the law. In the United States, for example, the traditional use of postmasterships, ambassadorial posts, and a number of state jobs exempt from normal civil service requirements provides a pool of party spoils denied most Indian, Malaysian, or Nigerian politicians.

8. Robert Walcott, Jr., *English Politics in the Early Eighteenth Century.* Cambridge, Mass.: Harvard University Press, 1956, p. 13. The coincidence between the patterns Walcott describes and contemporary Philippine politics is discussed by Carl Landé, pp. 101–107.

9. Family loyalties are always of significance but in the typical machine case narrow family ties become a central factor in the evaluation of government action. Occupational, much less broad civic, sentiments play a marginal or even negligible role. Most immigrants to the United States, for example, at first "took for granted that the political life of the individual would arise out of family needs . . . " Richard Hofstadter, *The Age of Reform,* New York: Vintage Books, 1955, p. 9.

10. Banfield and Wilson, p. 340.

11. Charles Edward Merriam, *Chicago: A More Intimate View of Urban Politics,* New York: Crowell-Collier-Macmillan, 1929, pp. 68, 90. Merriam's analysis is especially valuable as he was simultaneously political scientist and politician throughout the period he describes.

12. Seymour J. Mandelbaum, p. 58. See also, Edward J. Flynn. *You're the Boss.* New York: Viking, 1947, p.21, for a twentieth-century account of New York City politics in which a similar argument is made.

13. Burnham, p. 286.

14. Burnham, p. 286. Merriam calls the precinct worker "something of a social worker not recognized by the profession," p. 173.

15. Banfield and Wilson, p. 118

16. For a more extended discussion of these attitudes and their origin, see James C. Scott, *Ideology in Malaysia.* New Haven, Conn.: Yale University Press, 1968, chap. 6.

17. Wurfel (p. 763), for example, claims that from l0 to 20 percent of Filipino voters *regularly* sell their votes.

14

Exchanging Material Benefits for Political Support: A Comparative Analysis

Eva Etzioni-Halevy

This chapter presents a comparative study of Britain, the United States, and Israel, focusing on the exchange of private material benefits for political support. Such practices have been dealt with by various scholars under the heading of "machine politics" or "clientelism." Each of these terms, however, has a slightly narrower connotation than the practices discussed here, hence my preference for the above term.

Framework for the Analysis

The comparison is presented in a democratic elitist framework, a well established but recently neglected perspective in the social sciences. Democracy, more than any other regime, restrains elites in the exercise of power by certain "rules of the game." by an institutionalized, constantly recurring threat of replacement and by confronting them in an institutionalized manner with the countervailing power of other elites. However, the effectiveness of these mechanisms varies from one democracy to another. Elites are the ones who chiefly safeguard the rules of democracy (see Dye and Zeigler, 1975). Nonetheless, by the same token they are also the ones who, under certain circumstances, augment their power by obviating or corrupting these rules and thereby the democratic procedures. Thus, when political corruption is at work in a democracy, elites are the ones who *make* it work.

233

The democratic perspective attempts to integrate elements of elite theory with elements of the pluralist theory of democracy. In this it follows in the footsteps of Mosca (1939), Schumpeter (1966), Keller (1963) and Aron (1968, 1978). Its basic contention is that there is no inconsistency between democracy and elitism: elites are as necessary for democracy as they are for all other political regimes. But the manner in which elites acquire power and exercise it is of the first order of importance.

Furthermore, there is a direct relationship between the various democratic restraints on elite power: when the power of the political elite is effectively countervailed by the power of other elites, its ability to contravene the "rules of the game" and thereby to engage in the corruption of democratic processes is commensurately restricted.

Conditions for Political Corruption and Its Decline

The corruption of the democratic process dealt with here is that of material inducement in return for political support. Such inducements, in turn, may be ordered on a continuum from the collective to the individual. On the collective level this device concerns the creation of overall policies—especially economic policies (e.g., tax cuts)—in accordance with the perceived wishes of the electorate. On the intermediate level it concerns the molding of policies in line with the demands of interest groups, communities, or constituencies. On the individual level it entails benefits to various institutions, firms, small groups, or to families and individuals in return for political support.

Such an exchange may take the form of outright bribing of voters. It may also take more subtle forms such as providing jobs, housing, services, preferential treatment by authorities, contracts, licenses, subsidies and the like, well in advance of election day, on the assumption that beneficiaries will feel an obligation or find it in their interest to support the donors at the polls, to give them general political or financial support, or even to become active on their behalf.

While the use of material benefits by political elites is considered legitimate on the collective level, it is considered increasingly illegitimate as one moves down to the individual level, where it usually contravenes accepted rules of the democratic process and falls under the headings of "political corruption." It is this practice (or malpractice) that is the concern of the present analysis. While the use of material benefits takes place at all times, in all societies at the collective and intermediary levels, present-day societies differ significantly in the extent to which this practice is prevalent on the individual level.

Several theories have been advanced to explain these differences. There are Marxist theories, which endeavor to explain these practices on the basis of ruling class interests and hegemony. There are also what may be called populist theories, which explain the practice on the basis of certain traits of the rank-and-file public, such as large numbers of immigrants not steeped in the political culture of democracy, wide-spread poverty, or low levels of education. The thesis presented here is that while these may be contributing factors in the development or decline of political corruption in each country, they are of little use in a comparative analysis, and cannot explain the differences between the various countries in this respect.

Rather, it will be shown that these differences can best be explained through the relationships between the political elite and the bureaucratic elite, and the elite-political culture that governs them. In particular, it will be shown that where the elite political culture is such that it enables the party-politically elected elite to be intermeshed with the appointed bureaucratic elite or to dominate it, the exchange of tangible benefits for political support flourishes and at times greatly biases the democratic process. Conversely, where the "rules of the game" are such that the bureaucratic elite has had to be separated from the political elite and has gained power independent of that of politicians, this type of political corruption has declined and proper democratic procedures have come into force. To substantiate this thesis, the relevant political experiences in Britain, the United States, and Israel will be briefly characterized and explained.

Factors in an Explanatory Schema

To recapitulate the analysis presented in the preceding selections: In Britain the handing out of material inducements on an individual basis had declined by the turn of the nineteenth century, and since then has not been in existence on any significant scale. In the United States and Israel, on the other hand, the practice has remained prevalent. Although in both countries a certain decline in political machines has recently set in, machine-type political practices are still in evidence.

How can the similarities and the differences among the countries be explained? On the face of it, the legal reforms, especially in Britain, go a long way towards explaining the elimination of corrupt electoral practices. But what needs explanation is why these legal reforms came about in the first place. Also, initially in Britain, and later on in the United States, legal reforms were less than effective because they were circumvented or not properly enforced. Hence, what counts is not so much the stringency of the laws, but rather the effectiveness of their enforcement. This once more raises the question of why such laws should be more effectively enforced in one country, or at one time—rather than another—so that other explanations must be looked for. One such explanation offered is the Marxist one.

The Marxist Conception: Ruling-Class Hegemony

From the Marxist conception it would follow that political manipulation through material inducements would be most likely to prevail where the economically dominant class (the ruling class in Marxist terms) has the clearest leverage over the political system and most clearly dominates the other classes. Thus Graziano (1977) and O'Connell (1980) have suggested that the practice develops and persists where there has been an incomplete development of the capitalist economy and where, therefore, the hegemony of the capitalist class over the working class prevents the latter from organizing and developing class consciousness. In such cases, it is argued, material inducements represent one method whereby the process of class formation on part of the labor force can be resisted.

This theory was originally applied to Ireland and southern Italy and may well be appropriate for these areas. But it does not explain the cases at hand. In eighteenth- and nineteenth-century Britain, the ruling classes (the aristocracy and later the bourgeoisie as well) had a virtual monopoly over political power. With the development of democratic procedures, this monopoly was maintained (among other things) through the introduction of material inducements into the political process. The further perpetuation of such inducements could thus have served the interests of the ruling classes in maintaining their monopoly. Yet Britain was the first country to largely relinquish the practice, thereby helping to pave the way for the working class's political organization and its participation in the political process.

The United States stands out among Western democracies in its lack of a large-scale labor party. This absence could be taken to indicate underdevelopment of working-class consciousness, and in line with Marxist reasoning could conceivably be used to explain the extraordinary development and tenacious persistence of machine politics in that country. However, a working-class consciousness (as indicated by the large-scale organization of labor) has not been more evident in this country in recent years than it was in previous years; yet the political machine has suffered a partial decline, even though it has by no means disappeared.

To clinch the argument, it must be pointed out that in Israel (both before and after independence) the capitalist class has been relatively weak and subdued. On the other hand, the working class has been highly organized, and its leaders have had a virtual monopoly over political power for almost a half a century. Yet throughout this period, material inducements in politics have flourished. Indeed, it has been the labor movement's leadership that has been most prominent in the perpetuation of this practice (though ably assisted by its coalition partners). When the right-wing Likud (a conglomeration of right-wing parties, literally: cohesion) came to power, and under the present widely based government, coalition parties are merely perpetuating (less adeptly) a tradition that was established and nurtured under Labor parties. In general, then, the strength and hegemony of the capitalist class and the lack of working-class consciousness and organization have little to do with material inducements in the electoral process.

The Populist Conception: Characteristics of the Rank and File

According to Scott (1973), machine (i.e., material) inducements in the electoral process may be explained by disorganization (the presence among the public of large numbers of immigrants as yet disoriented in the new society and not yet steeped in the political culture of democracy) and by poverty. These factors may serve to explain some of the developments in some of the countries studied, but neither can serve to explain the differences among them.

Immigration. The diminution of immigration to the United States after the World War I may explain the partial decline of the party machine from the 1940s and onward. Also, the large-scale immigration to Israel in the Yishuv era and in the 1950s may explain the flourishing of material inducements at these times. The decline in immigration later on may likewise possibly serve to explain whatever decline in machine-type corruption took place in Israel in recent years.

On the other hand again, as Johnston (1982) explains, many American cities with large numbers of immigrants have never been dominated by machine politics or shook off that dominance a long time ago. Conversely, there have been "Yankee machines" with little immigrant support. Examples are Platt's statewide machine in Newark and Brayton's machine in Rhode Island. Also, in some states like Indiana, where there are small numbers of foreign voters, machine politics have continued to flourish.

Immigration has even less explanatory power when the various countries are compared with one another. In the nineteenth century, for instance, the United States was a country of immigration, and Britain was not. Yet bribery of voters flourished in Britain and matched or surpassed this practice in the United States. It is true that large proportions of the nineteenth-century immigrants to America came from the United Kingdom. Coming from a similar culture, they did not face serious disorientation in the new society. Even so, how can Britain's especially prominent "achievements" in electoral corruption be explained?

A twentieth-century comparison casts similar doubts on the thesis. Britain, no less than the United States and Israel, has had an influx of immigrants in recent years. Yet in Britain, corruption of the type described here is no longer in existence on a significant scale (and certainly has not enjoyed a revival in recent years as a result of immigration), whereas in the United States and Israel the practice still persists.

Poverty. If immigration cannot account for differences among the countries, can poverty (among immigrants or other inhabitants)? The period in which material inducements were gradually eliminated from the political scene in Britain (the second half of the nineteenth century) was also the time in which a significant rise in the standard of living occurred. Real wages rose markedly in the last forty years of the nineteenth century, and this was supplemented by improvements in housing, education, health, and the like. Developments in that country then, would seem to confirm the poverty thesis.

This is not so when a cross-Atlantic comparison is made. In America, as in Britain, the late nineteenth century was a period of rapidly growing real incomes and of improvements in the living environment (Bagwell and Mingay, 1970). There is no reason to believe that the rise in real income and standard of living was greater in Britain than in the United States. Yet Britain far overtook the United States in the elimination of political corruption. On the contemporary scene, it seems the population's general level of affluence (or lack thereof) cannot explain the difference among the countries either. As comparisons of gross national product (GNP) generally show, of the countries dealt with here, the United States is the first in affluence but by no means first in the elimination of electoral corruption.

Perhaps, however, it is not a country's general level of poverty vs. affluence, but rather *pockets* of poverty which account for the exchange of benefits for political support. This contention seems plausible because the recipients of some of these benefits have frequently been the poorer elements in society. Thus, if pockets of poverty are eliminated or contracted, some parts of the public become less vulnerable to certain petty bribes and small-scale favors by politicians. But, again, the pockets-of-poverty theory has little value in explaining intercountry differences.

In the United States, for instance, despite the rise in the standard of living towards the end of the nineteenth century and the beginning of the twentieth century, there remained a mass of poverty and unemployment among the indigenous population. However, the situation in Britain was not greatly different. Despite the general improvement in living conditions towards the end of the nineteenth century, almost one-third of the population in industrial cities was comprised of poverty-stricken slum dwellers who existed at a bare subsistence level (Bagwell and Mingay, 1970).

In the United States there have been pockets of poverty in recent years as well: the proportion of persons living below the poverty line declined from 22.4 percent in 1959 to 12.6 percent in 1970, but has risen to 15.2 percent in 1983 *(Statistical Abstract of the United States,* 1985, Table 758. p. 454). In Israel the Prime Minister's Committee on Children and Youth in Distress reported that from 1968 to 1971 about 11 percent of the urban population (which accounts for about 90 percent of the population) lived in poverty. Since then the situation has worsened, as real wages suffered a cutback of some 20 to 30 percent in the wake of the recent economic crisis. By the same token there has been poverty in recent years in Britain as well. In 1979 7.45 percent of Britons were receiving support from the Supplementary Benefits Commission, and were thus living below the government's own estimate of the poverty line. In 1983 the proportion of the poor by this criterion had grown to 13.44 percent *(Great Britain Annual Abstract of Statistics,* 1985, Table 3.25, p.60). According to some observers, to this must be added an estimated 4 percent of the population who were eligible for benefits but did not claim them.

It is exceedingly difficult to compare levels of poverty and sizes of populations living in poverty from one country to another, as standards used to demarcate the poverty line vary from country to country. Still, the impression is that the proportions of the population living in poverty are no smaller in Britain than they are in the United States and Israel. Certainly pockets of poverty in Britain have been sufficiently large to have warranted the handing out of petty inducements by party machines, had there been such machines in existence. In their absence, or almost total absence, poverty could not bring them into existence.

Moreover, as Johnston (1982) shows, while political machines in America have usually done well in poor districts, this was only half of the story. Machines have also been successful with wealthy business people who have obtained contracts, licenses, franchises, and weak enforcement of regulatory laws in return for political and financial support to parties and candidates. More recently, the New York City corruption scandals have supplied new evidence of this form of exchange.

There is no reason why the advantages or favors from politicians should appeal only to the poor. Their appeal includes all those who want to do business with government, as well as those whose activities are subject to government regulation-indeed, all those affected by government decisions. Thus "help" shades into "pull". The need for "pull," moreover, increases in proportion to the size of one's dealings with government. And, the ability to use pull increases with the amount of knowledge of the workings of government (in other words, "you've got to know the ropes to pull the strings").

Education. In close conjunction with poverty, low levels of education have also been considered as explaining the exchange of benefits for votes (Sorauf, 1960). In fact, it has been reported that in nineteenth-century Britain, voters open to this type of manipulation were frequently (although not exclusively) at a low level of education. In America, too, the people most vulnerable to certain types of machine politics were the less educated (frequently, immigrants, and poor in the bargain).

In Israel, on the other hand, the situation is more complicated. While many of the immigrants of the 1950s, of whom a great proportion came from Middle Eastern countries, were indeed poorly educated, the situation was different from the pre-state era, when large proportions of immigrants belonged to the intelligentsia. Yet the highly educated immigrants (and old-timers) did not hesitate to accept material benefits from political organizations and to pledge their allegiance to these organizations in return.

Moreover, there seems to be no relationship between the countries' rating on level of education and their rating on electoral corruption. The British system of education has been characterized as an elitist system and the Israeli system fits this title as well: in these countries, changes toward greater equalization are slow and gradual. The American educational system, on the other hand, has been much more mass oriented, and the great majority of American youngsters attain at least a high school diploma.

It may be argued that the American high school diploma cannot be compared with its British counterpart. But it is significant that a far greater percentage of American youngsters (as compared with British ones, for instance) benefit from education up to a higher age. This difference is certainly not reflected in differences in the countries' political corruption through material inducements.

Immigration, poverty, and level of education of the rank-and-file public, therefore, do not explain differences among the countries in political corruption. Perhaps this is so because members of the rank-and-file public can make use of the practice (and it certainly helps if they are willing to do so), but they cannot initiate it. Hence the major explanation of political corruption involving material inducements is sought not in the character of the public that is the object of manipulation, but in the character of those who seek to dominate the public through such manipulation, and in the structures of domination they have devised—in other words, in the conceptions and structure of the elites. But if so, what features of the elites account for the practice, its resilience, or its decline?

Elite Culture and Structure: The Politicization of the Bureaucracy

A theory proposed by Heidenheimer (1970) involves the development of the elites' structure and power: according to this theory, electoral corruption and specifically the offering of material inducements arose where electoral assemblies, political parties, or other political instruments of mass mobilization were powerful prior to the development of a centralized, powerful, bureaucratized civil service. Conversely, it was curbed where fully developed bureaucracies antedate political parties. His theory may help explain why political corruption of this kind developed in both Britain and the United States, which fitted the first pattern. But it cannot help explain why it declined and has been largely eradicated in Britain but declined only in part and is still prevalent in the United States.

The present argument is that what counts on the contemporary scene is the independent power of the bureaucracy—not vis-à-vis the public, but vis-à-vis the party-political structures (or the polity) or, in other words, the independent power of the bureaucratic elite as against that of the political elite. Where the bureaucratic elite is intermeshed with the political elite or dominated by it to the extent that the interests of top politicians dictate the activities of top bureaucrats in the performance of their duties, the handing out of individual material inducements in the political process is likely to flourish. Conversely, where the bureaucratic elite can countervail the power of the political elite, where the actions of top bureaucrats are dictated by criteria other than those of the interests of top politicians, then the handing out of material inducements in return for political support is likely to decline or be absent.

In this context, two major types of public administration have been distinguished: a politically neutral one and a politically involved one. In the first, the selection, appointment, and advancement of personnel take place without political intervention and are made largely by objective criteria in an open competitive system. Bureaucratic activities are not guided overwhelmingly by party-political criteria. In the second type there is involvement of politicians in senior appointments, and a significant proportion of officials are appointed and promoted by party-political criteria. Since they owe allegiance to their party-political appointers and depend on them for advancement, such officials frequently engage in activities that promote those appointers and their party's interests. As a result, the administration's actions are shaped to a much greater extent by party-political considerations.

It is now generally agreed that no government bureaucracy is totally nonpolitical as the very formulation of policy—in which the bureaucracy is necessarily involved—has political and frequently party-political connotations. Nonetheless, not all bureaucracies are permeated by party politics to the same extent. Where the bureaucracy is strongly infiltrated by political appointments and political considerations, political corruption flourishes and biases the democratic process. Only a bureaucracy that is relatively independent politically can safeguard fully fledged democratic procedures.

This thesis fits the cases at hand. At one time (before the second half of the nineteenth century in Britain and America and before the establishment of the state in Israel) politicians and party politics had a grip on the bureaucracies in all three countries. During the same time-spans all three were pervaded by electoral corruption through material inducements. Subsequently, politicization declined at a different pace and to a different extent in the three countries. Political corruption through material inducements followed parallel trends.

In Britain the decline of the bureaucracy's politicization came earlier and was more extensive than in the other two countries. Recently some commentators have seen evidence of politicization in the top Thatcher appointments and promotions (Wass, 1985). Still, these concerns pertain only to a minute number of top appointments, and there has been no basic change in the character of the British bureaucracy in recent years. As Rose (1981) indicates, British higher civil servants are political in the sense of being involved in conflicts concerning policy. Their advice on these matters cannot be neutral and necessarily has political implications. But these civil servants are not party-political except in the sense that they serve the government of the day rather than the opposition.

By contrast, in the other two countries, the politicization of the bureaucracy was maintained much longer and when it declined, it did so only partially (the United States) or to a small extent (Israel). In the United States civil service reforms led to a situation where only a relatively small top layer of officials in the federal administration can be political appointees. There is a consensus among observers that President Reagan makes as many political patronage appointments as he can to positions not insulated by public service rules, and that he does so to a greater extent than recent presidents. According to Goldenberg (1984) the number of such appointments stood at 709 in 1983– still only less than one tenth of one percent of total direct federal employment.

However, according to Goldenberg, political appointees now have greater leverage over career civil servants than was the case before. Career civil servants now can be more easily relocated even against their will. In 1983 there were 1,100 such relocations. Only a small proportion of these were forced relocations. But career officials quickly realized that forced moves were possible. This has made them more politically compliant. Those who have not taken the hint have had close political supervision imposed on them.

Moreover, on the municipal level politicization of the bureaucracy has remained much more pervasive. Thus in Chicago in the 1970s, despite civil service reforms. there were still some 20,000 patronage positions available to the city government (Guterbock, 1980). In New York City, too, some departments are still packed with political appointments, especially the transportation department which has been the major focus of recent corruption scandals.

In Israel, as in the other two countries, there have been attempts at political reforms. But their practical results have not been far reaching. As Werner (chapter 12 in this volume) correctly perceived the situation, despite these reforms, "internally, structures and behavior remained informal." The fact that in recent years the bureaucracy has still been beset by political partisanship is illustrated by the fact that before the 1981 election the Ministry of Religious Affairs was reported to have been the site of hectic electoral activity in favor of two religious parties. Only in February 1986 did new regulations prohibiting political activity on the premises of government offices come into force, and it is not clear as yet what their effectiveness will be. Moreover, after the 1981 election political appointments continued to be rampant. At that time the Ministry of Absorption passed control from Likud to Tami, a small religious party. Subsequently there have been reports of Tami systematically ridding the ministry of all previously introduced Likud personnel. Even more recently my own research on the Israel Broadcasting Authority (a semi-independent but rather typical Israeli bureaucracy) has shown that party-political appointments reach down to the level of heads of units (Etzioni-Halevy, forthcoming). By the account of key informants, the situation is not much different in government departments proper.

It can be seen, then, that in Britain, where the penetration of politicians and party-politics declined earliest and most thoroughly, political corruption through material benefits has done likewise. In the United States, political intrusion into the federal bureaucracy has also declined, although by recent testimony it has increased to some extent under the Reagan administration. Concomitantly, no political machines with a clear implication on federal politics are visible today although indictments for corruption have been more prevalent under the Reagan administration than under recent administrations. On the municipal level political patronage appointments have remained much more widespread and so has machine-type political corruption. Finally, in Israel both party-political intrusion into the bureaucracy and political corruption have declined only to a small extent and both remain clearly visible on the political scene.

Politicization of the bureaucracy may explain the use of material inducements in return for political support in several ways. Firstly, such inducements include patronage appointments in the government bureaucracy itself. To the extent that these appointments are used as rewards or inducements for political support, politicization of the bureaucracy and political corruption coincide. However, as a rule, bureaucratic appointments are only a fraction of the material inducements political organizations or politicians have at their disposal.

Secondly, the introduction of political appointees into the government bureaucracy and its consequent cannibalization by the political ruling elite, make it possible to use that bureaucracy for the handing out of a wide array of additional rewards by political criteria. Since the government bureaucracy is usually in charge of massive resources, the material inducements that may be handed out in this manner are massive as well.

Some observers have seen it as self-evident that where a bureaucracy is party-politicized, it will make its resources available for political contests on a party-political basis. Hence, they argue, the above thesis needs no elaboration or empirical support. However, Marxist and populist theorists endeavored to account for this corruption through factors other than the politicization

of the bureaucracy, namely through class interests and rank-and-file characteristics. Hence, the importance of showing that it is, in fact, the politicization
of the bureaucracy (rather than other factors) that accounts for the practice.

Moreover, some observers who see the tie between political patronage in
the bureaucracy and electoral corruption as self-explanatory have, in fact,
posited a causal relationship between the two that is widely open to criticism.
Thus Scott (1973) conceives of political patronage as an important tool in the
hands of the political machine. Rather than viewing it as an outgrowth of the
politicization of the bureaucracy, he sees it as an outgrowth of party-politics.
These, in turn, he considers to be decisively influenced by conditions of
poverty and disorganization among the public (see above). Hence, the causal
chain, according to Scott, leads from the traits of the rank-and-file to the
machine and from that to patronage. A similar causal chain has been posited
by Sorauf (1960), who argues that the political involvement of the bureaucracy is the outgrowth of large-scale immigration and poverty.

However, in actual fact, the causal chain is the reverse of that posited by
these observers. Thus in Britain, since the initial development of its administration, there has been no clear distinction between political personnel and the
civil service, between political activities and administrative tasks. This was,
initially, the most striking feature of the British administration, and it continued well into he nineteenth century (Parris, I 969).

In America the penetration of party politics into the administration was in
place in the late 1 820s arid 1830s, although it developed further and reached
new heights at the turn of the twentieth century. As Ostrogorski (1902, vol. 2)
shows, the evolving parties' political machines' activists pressed heavily on
the government to perpetuate this politicization and employ it in their favor.
They would not have been able to do so had not the practice been institutionalized early in the system's development. Also, the politicization of the bureaucracy preceded the mass immigration from non—English-speaking countries, of immigrants not socialized to the culture of democracy, as well as
poverty, which supposedly explain this administrative pattern. Hence, it would
he more plausible to regard this pattern as the outgrowth of a tradition that
had its roots in the pre-reform British system, some elements of which were
institutionalized in America (Huntington, 1968).

In Israel the politicization of the bureaucracy had its roots in the prestate
Yishuv era, when administrative and political roles and structures intermeshed
to such an extent as to be practically indistinguishable (Shapiro, 1975). This,
in turn, has been explained by the absence of a commonly-accepted state
framework. The British government adopted a policy of minimum interference in the Yishuv society, and the Jewish community was run by its own
internal political authorities. Although this set of institutions, the Yishuv's
political center, enjoyed a fair degree of autonomy, it had, in the phrasing of
Horowitz and Lissak (1971), "authority without sovereignty." Lacking the

ultimate force of sanctions available to a sovereign state the national institution had to base their authority on the recognition of the various existent political bodies (parties and labor organizations). To elicit their cooperation the national institutions were obliged to cede several functions and large-scale resources to them, thereby turning them into political-administrative subcenters. It was largely this situation that gave rise to the fusion of politics and administration. Thus, as successive waves of immigrants arrived, they were confronted with existing, well-established political-administrative institutions that used the large-scale resources at their disposal to facilitate the immigrants' absorption, thereby gaining their political support.

It is thus clear that the causal chain is not as posited by the above observers. Indeed, since all three countries concerned had politically infused bureaucracies at the outset, yet their patterns of immigration varied widely, it is clear that the causal chain cannot proceed from immigration through machine politics to bureaucratic politicization. It would be more plausible to argue that such politicization was part and parcel of a tradition of fused, undifferentiated sociopolitical structures that marked the premodern and the initial stages of the modern era. This was clearly so in Britain and in America (which had initially imported the traditional British patterns). In prestate Israel the leaders who shaped the evolving sociopolitical patterns had immigrated mainly from Russia and Eastern Europe at the beginning of the century. From there they transplanted notions of pervasive political control on all facets of social life, and the fusion of political and administrative structures that these notions implied (Shapiro, 1975). These notions then helped them cope with the situation of authority without sovereignty, as previously described. There was, then, in all three countries, a clear causal chain leading from the traditions of government in general to the politicization of the bureaucracy and thence to political corruption through material inducements.

What still requires explanation are the differences among the countries in the decline of party-politicization of the bureaucracy. The explanation here proposed is in terms of the evolving elite political culture and the concomitantly changing power structures. In Britain the evolving notions of proper political-democratic and administrative procedures served to curb the power of the political elite while favoring the development of a politically independent, administrative elite. The gradual development of such codes of propriety restrained the political elite from encroaching on the administrative elite and separated its stronghold, the bureaucracy, from party-politics (cf. Sisson, 1971, p. 451). It occurred in the framework of a similar separation of other government institutions (e.g., the judiciary, the crown) from party-politics (Huntington, 1968). It was paralleled by the development of rules of proper administration, at least partly under the influence of Benthamite ideas (Parris. 1960), calling for a public service ethos of professionalism, and strict controls on rewards and benefits—to eliminate corruption (Hume, 1981; Rosen, 1983;

Rosenblum, 1978). Once independent public officials had been appointed, they played a leading role in legislation furthering the development of their own power (Parris. 1960).

In the United States and Israel no such clear notions of propriety restraining the power of the political elites developed, and the democratic-administrative "rules of the game" have remained ambiguous. Even where depoliticization of the bureaucracy was called for by formal rules and regulations, these precepts were only belatedly and partially followed in practice. In conjunction with this, the administrative elites never became independent enough to countervail the power and interests of politicians and corruption through tangible benefits in return for political support was not eliminated.

Contemporary support for this explanation comes from the fact that corruption resulting in political benefits is closely related to other types of corruption, resulting in private benefits. Where the elites' notions of propriety have not been explicit and stringent enough to eliminate the one, they have not been clear and strong enough to eliminate the other. Thus, as Schwartz (1979) observed in another context: "If one must falsify for the good of the cause, then why not add a little more for one's self."

Conclusion

Political corruption through material benefits in return for political support depends not on class characteristics and interests, nor on the characteristics and political culture of the rank-and-file public, but on the elite political culture and power structures dominated by the elites. Its presence depends upon political and bureaucratic elites and power structures being intermeshed, upon politicians and party-politics intruding into the bureaucracy, upon the consequent availability of bureaucratic resources for party-political purposes, and upon an elite political culture that treats such deployment of bureaucratic resources as (at least unofficially) acceptable. Conversely, elimination of this sort of political corruption and the development of (in this sense) proper democratic procedures hinges upon a certain change in the political-bureaucratic rules of the game, upon the bureaucratic elites countervailing the power of political elites, upon bureaucratic structures gaining independence from the intrusion of politicians and party politics, and upon the consequent withdrawal of bureaucratic resources from the party-political contest.

Paradoxically, then, only where the power of a democratically elected political elite has been restrained and counterbalanced by the power of a nonelected bureaucratic elite, have proper democratic procedures been put into place. In other words, restraint of the power of the elected political elite by a nonelected bureaucratic elite is a prerequisite for a properly functioning democracy. Not surprisingly, the independent power of a non-elected elite is also a source of problems for democracy. However, such analyses are beyond the scope of the present study (see Etzioni-Halevy, 1985).

References

ARON, R.
 1968   *Progress and Disillusion.* London, Pall Mall Press.
 1978   *Politics and History* (trans. M. Bernheim-Conant). New York, Free Press.

BAGWELL, P.S. AND MINGAY, G.E.
 1970   *Britain and America 1850–1939.* London, Routledge & Kegan Paul.

DYE, T.R., AND ZEIGLER, L.H.
 1975   *The Irony* of *Democracy* (3rd edn). North Scituate, Mass., Duxbury Press.

ETZIONI-HALEVY, E.
 1985   *Bureaucracy and Democracy.* Revised, paperback edition. London, Routledge
        & Kegan Paul. forthcoming *National Broadcasting Under Siege.* London,
        Macmillan.

GOLDENBERG. E.N.
 1984   "The Permanent Government in an Era of Retrenchment and Redirection,"
        in L.S. Salamon and M.S. Lund (eds). *The Reagan Presidency and the
        Governing of America.* Washington DC, The Urban Institute Press.

GRAZIANO, L.
 1977   "Patron-client Relationship in Southern Italy," in L.G. Schmidt. C. Lande,
        and J. Scott, (eds). *Friends, Followers, and Factions,* Berkeley, University
        of California Press, pp.360–78.

GREAT BRITAIN CENTRAL STATISTICAL OFFICE
 1985   *Annual Abstract of Statistics 1985.* London, Government Statistical Service.

GUTERBOCK, T.M.
 1980   *Machine Politics in Transition.* Chicago, University of Chicago Press.

HEIDENHEIMER, A.J. (ED.)
 1970   *Political Corruption.* New York, Holt, Rinehart & Winston.

HOROWITZ, D. AND LISSAK, M.
 1971   "Authority without Sovereignty," in M. Lissak and E. Gutman (eds), *Political Institutions and Processes in Israel.* Jerusalem, Akademon.

HUME,L.J.
 1981   *Bentham and Bureaucracy.* New York and London. Cambridge University
        Press.

HUNTINGTON, S.P.
 1968   *Political Order in Changing Societies.* New Haven, Ct., Yale University
        Press.

JOHNSTON. M.
 1979   "Patrons and Clients, Jobs and Machines," *American Political Science Review,* 73 (June) pp.385–98.
 1982   *Political Corruption and Public Policy in America.* Monterey, Cal., Brooks/
        Cole Publishing Co.

KELLER, S.
 1963   *Beyond the Ruling Class,* New York, Random House.

MOSCA, G.
 1939   *The Ruling Class.* (tr. H. D. Kahn). New York, McGraw Hill.

O'CONNELL, D.
 1980   "Clientelism and Political Culture in Ireland." (unpublished).

OSTROGORSKI, M.
1902   *Democracy and the Organization of Political Parties.* New York, Macmillan (in 2 volumes).
PARRIS, H.
1960   "The Nineteenth Century Revolution of Government," *The Historical Journal,* 3, 17–37.
1969   *Constitutional Bureaucracy.* London, Allen & Unwin.
ROSE, R.
1981   "The Political Status of Higher Civil Servants in Britain." paper No.92, Centre for the Study of Public Policy, University of Strathclyde, Glasgow.
ROSEN, F
1983   *Jeremy Bentham and the Modern State,* Oxford, Clarendon University Press.
ROSENBLUM, N.L.
1978   *Bentham's Theory of the Modern State.* Cambridge, Mass., Harvard University Press.
SCHUMPETER, J.
1966   *Capitalism, Socialism and Democracy.* London, Unwin University Books.
SCHWARTZ, A.C.
1979   "Corruption and Political Development in the USSR," *Comparative Politics, 11* (July) 431–32.
SCOTT, J.C.
1973   *Comparative Political Corruption.* Englewood Cliffs, N.J., Prentice Hall.
SHAPIRO, Y.
1975   *The Organization of Power.* Tel-Aviv, Am Oved (Hebrew).
1977   *Democracy in Israel.* Ramat Gan, Massada (Hebrew).
SHARKANSKY, I.
1986   "Distinguishing 'Corruption' from 'Flexibility' in the Israeli Public Sector." Paper prepared for delivery at the 1986 Annual Meeting of the American Political Science Association, Washington.
SISSON, C.H.
1971   "The Politician as Intruder," in R.A. Chapman and A. Dunsire (eds), *Style in Administration.* London, Allen & Unwin.
SORAUF, F.J.
1960   "The Silent Revolution in Patronage." *Public Administration Review,* 20, 28–34.
WASS. D.
1985   "The Civil Service at the Crossroads," *Political Quarterly.* 56 (July-September), 227–41.

Part V

MODERNIZATION AND CORRUPTION

Introduction to Part V

If the decade of the 1990s constituted an era for reconceptualizing world politics after the decline of communism, it also posed problems about how to capture revised ways of describing global developments. As between the decay of many dominant economic models, and the pervasive penetration of internet structures, it has proved difficult for the designers of global strategies, to capture the appropriate and compelling concepts and terminologies. Things were not so difficult back when modernization was still a useful concept. "Modernization," then, meant becoming like the countries of the capitalist West or socialist East.

Samuel Huntington, in the first selection offers the thesis that when modernizing countries buy rapid social modernization at the price of the decay of political institutions, corruption and violence become alternative means of making demands upon the system. While violence poses the greater and more direct threat to the system, corruption may simultaneously satisfy demands in ways that violence cannot. "Those who corrupt a country's police officers," argues the author, "are more likely to identify with the system than those who seize its police stations." In this sense, then, corruption can fulfill a useful function as a lesser among evils common in developing countries.

Gunnar Myrdal, unlike Huntington , finds little to praise in corruption. In chapter 16, drawn from his study into the causes of poverty in Asia, he asserts that the levels of public corruption in most Asian countries have risen rather than declined after the accession to independence. He attributes the growth of general cynicism to the unwillingness of post-independence governments to raise the issue lest in so doing they stimulate it further, thus strengthening socio-cultural patterns that encourage corrupt practices. The net effect, Myrdal argues, is to hinder rather than encourage the processes of modernization.

Joseph Nye, by contrast, identifies several important contingencies bearing upon the consequences of corruption. Development, for Nye, is not one problem, but many; thus the effects of corruption will depend upon a nation's developmental situation and particular range of tasks it confronts. Cases of corruption differ as well; with the level at which they occur, the kinds of stakes or inducements involved, and the seriousness of the deviation from stated norms and procedures. Nye develops how different constellation of this matrix affect the outcome of cost-benefit calculation.

Government capacity and the strength of national integration must a are among the which are considered as determining outcomes In most instances, Nye concludes, the costs of corruption will still exceed any benefits, but in some cases the reverse is true. Then certain constellations can on balance have positive effects, for instance on economic growth. Nye's categories and contingencies help to understand when such cases can be expected to occur. It is somewhat surprising that not more of the recent attempts at comparative analysis have attempted to use his schema.

15

Modernization and Corruption

Samuel P. Huntington

Corruption is behavior of public officials which deviates from accepted norms in order to serve private ends. Corruption obviously exists in all societies, but it is also obviously more common in some societies than in others and more common at some times in the evolution of a society than at other times. Impressionistic evidence suggests that its extent correlates reasonably well with rapid social and economic modernization. Political life in eighteenth-century America and in twentieth-century America, it would appear, was less corrupt than in nineteenth-century America. So also political life in seventeenth-century Britain and in late nineteenth-century Britain was, it would appear, less corrupt than it was in eighteenth-century Britain. Is it merely coincidence that this high point of corruption in English and American public life coincided with the impact of the industrial revolution, the development of new sources of wealth and power, and the appearance of new classes making new demands on government? In both periods political institutions suffered strain and some measure of decay. Corruption is, of course, one measure of the absence of effective political institutionalization. Public officials lack autonomy and coherence, and subordinate their institutional roles to exogenous demands. Corruption may be more prevalent in some cultures than in others but in most cultures it seems to be most prevalent during the most intense phases of modernization. The differences in the level of corruption which may exist between the modernized and politically developed societies

Source: Samuel P. Huntington, "Modernization and Corruption," *Political Order in Changing Societies*, New Haven, Conn.: Yale University Press, 1968, pp.59–71. By permission of the publisher. Copyright @ 1968 by Yale University.

of the Atlantic world and those of Latin America, Africa, and Asia in large part reflect their differences in political modernization and political development. When the leaders of military juntas and revolutionary movements condemn the "corruption" in their societies, they are, in effect, condemning the backwardness of their societies.

Why does modernization breed corruption? Three connections stand out. First, modernization involves a change in the basic values of the society. In particular it means the gradual acceptance by groups within the society of universalistic and achievement-based norms, the emergence of loyalties and identifications of individuals and groups with the nation-state, and the spread of the assumption that citizens have equal rights against the state and equal obligations to the state. These norms usually, of course, are first accepted by students, military officers, and others who have been exposed to them abroad. Such groups then begin to judge their own society by these new and alien norms. Behavior which was acceptable and legitimate according to traditional norms becomes unacceptable and corrupt when viewed through modern eyes. Corruption in a modernizing society is thus in part not so much the result of the deviance of behavior from accepted norms as it is the deviance of norms from the established patterns of behavior. New standards and criteria of what is right and wrong lead to a condemnation of at least some traditional behavior patterns as corrupt. "What Britons saw as corrupt and Hausa as oppressive," one scholar has noted of northern Nigeria, "Fulani might regard as both necessary and traditional."[1] The calling into question of old standards, moreover, tends to undermine the legitimacy of all standards. The conflict between modern and traditional norms opens opportunities for individuals to act in ways justified by neither.

Corruption requires some recognition of the difference between public role and private interest. If the culture of the society does not distinguish between the king's role as a private person and the king's role as king, it is impossible to accuse the king of corruption in the use of public monies. The distinction between the private purse and public expenditures only gradually evolved in Western Europe at the beginning of the modern period. Some notion of this distinction, however, is necessary to reach any conclusion as to whether the actions of the king are proper or corrupt. Similarly, according to traditional codes in many societies, an official had the responsibility and obligation to provide rewards and employment to members of his family. No distinction existed between obligation to the state and obligation to the family. Only when such a distinction becomes accepted by dominant groups within the society does it become possible to define such behavior as nepotism and hence corruption. Indeed, the introduction of achievement standards may stimulate greater family identification and more felt need to protect family interests against the threat posed by alien ways. Corruption is thus a product of the distinction between public welfare and private interest which comes with modernization.

Modernization also contributes to corruption by creating new sources of wealth and power, the relation of which to politics is undefined by the dominant traditional norms of the society and on which the modern norms are not yet accepted by the dominant groups within the society. Corruption in this sense is a direct product of the rise of new groups with new resources and the efforts of these groups to make themselves effective within the political sphere. Corruption may be the means of assimilating new groups into the political system by irregular means because the system has been unable to adapt sufficiently fast to provide legitimate and acceptable means for this purpose. In Africa, corruption threw "a bridge between those who hold political power and those who control wealth, enabling the two classes, markedly apart during the initial stages of African nationalist governments, to assimilate each other."[2] The new millionaires buy themselves seats in the Senate or the House of Lords and thereby become participants in the political system rather than alienated opponents of it, which might have been the case if this opportunity to corrupt the system were denied them. So also recently enfranchised masses or recently arrived immigrants use their new power of the ballot to buy themselves jobs and favors from the local political machine. There is thus the corruption of the poor and the corruption of the rich. The one trades political power for money, the other money for political power. But in both cases something public (a vote or an office or decision) is sold for private gain.

Modernization, thirdly, encourages corruption by the changes it produces on the output side of the political system. Modernization, particularly among the later modernizing countries, involves the expansion of governmental authority and the multiplication of the activities subjected to governmental regulation. In Northern Nigeria, "oppression and corruption tended to increase among the Hausa with political centralization and the increase of governmental tasks." All laws, as McMullan has pointed out, put some group at a disadvantage, and this group consequently becomes a potential source of corruption.[3] The multiplication of laws thus multiplies the possibilities of corruption. The extent to which this possibility is realized in practice depends in large part upon the extent to which the laws have the general support of the population, the ease with which the law can be broken without detection, and the profit to be made by breaking it. Laws affecting trade, customs, taxes plus those regulating popular and profitable activities such as gambling, prostitution, and liquor, consequently become major incentives to corruption. Hence in a society where corruption is widespread the passage of strict laws against corruption serves only to multiply the opportunities for corruption.

The initial adherence to modern values by a group in a transitional country often takes an extreme form. The ideals of honesty, probity, universalism, and merit often become so overriding that individuals and groups come to condemn as corrupt in their own society practices which are accepted as normal and even legitimate in more modern societies. The initial exposure to modernism tends to give rise to unreasonable puritanical standards even as it did among the Puritans themselves. This escalation in values leads to a denial and rejection of the bargaining and compromise essential to politics and promotes the identification of politics with corruption. To the modernizing zealot a politician's promise to build irrigation ditches for farmers in a village if he is elected seems to be just as corrupt as an offer to pay each villager for his vote before the election. Modernizing elites are nationalistic and stress the overriding preeminence of the general welfare of society as a whole. Hence in a country like Brazil, "efforts by private interests to influence public policy are considered, as in Rousseau, *inherently* 'corrupt.' By the same token government action which is fashioned in deference to particular claims and pressures from society is considered 'demagogy.'"[4] In a society like Brazil the modernizing elements condemn as corrupt ambassadorial appointments to reward friends or to appease critics and the establishment of government projects in return for interest group support. In the extreme case the antagonism to corruption may take the form of the intense fanatical puritanism characteristic of most revolutionary and some military regimes in at least their early phases. Paradoxically, this fanatical anticorruption mentality has ultimate effects similar to those of corruption itself. Both challenge the autonomy of politics: one substituting private goals for public ones and the other replacing political values with technical ones. The escalation of standards in a modernizing society and the concomitant devaluation and rejection of politics represent the victory of the values of modernity over the needs of society.

Reducing corruption in a society thus often involves both a scaling down of the norms thought appropriate for the behavior of public officials and at the same time changes in the general behavior of such officials in the direction of those norms. The result is a greater congruence between prevalent norms and prevalent behavior at the price of some inconsistency in both. Some behavior comes to be accepted as a normal part of the process of politics, as "honest" rather than "dishonest graft," while other, similar behavior comes to be generally condemned and generally avoided. Both England and the United States went through this process: at one point the former accepted the sale of peerages but not of ambassadorships, while the latter accepted the sale of ambassadorships but not of judgeships. "The result in the U.S.A.," as one observer has noted, "is a patchwork: the scope of political patronage has been greatly reduced and the cash bribery of higher public servants largely eliminated. At the same time, large areas of public life have so far remained more or less immune to reform, and practices that in one sphere would be regarded as corrupt are almost taken for granted in another."[5] The development within a society of the ability to make this discrimination is a sign of its movement from modernization to modernity.

The functions, as well as the causes, of corruption are similar to those of violence. Both are encouraged by modernization; both are symptomatic of the weakness of political institutions; both are characteristic of what we shall subsequently call praetorian societies; both are means by which individuals and groups relate themselves to the political system and, indeed, participate in the system in ways which violate the mores of the system. Hence the society which has a high capacity for corruption also has a high capacity for violence. In some measure, one form of deviant behavior may substitute for the other, but, more often different social forces simultaneously exploit their differing capacities for each. The prevalence of violence, however, does pose a greater threat to the functioning of the system than the prevalence of corruption. In the absence of agreement on public purposes, corruption substitutes agreement on private goals, while violence substitutes conflict over public or private ends. Both corruption and violence are illegitimate means of making demands upon the system, but corruption is also an illegitimate means of satisfying those demands. Violence is more often a symbolic gesture of protest which goes unrequited and is not designed to be requited. It is a symptom of more extreme alienation. He who corrupts a system's police officers is more likely to identify with the system than he who storms the system's police stations.

Like machine politics or clientelistic politics in general, corruption provides immediate, specific, and concrete benefits to groups which might otherwise be thoroughly alienated from society. Corruption may thus be functional to the maintenance of a political system in the same way that reform is. Corruption itself may be a substitute for reform and both corruption and reform may be substitutes for revolution. Corruption serves to reduce group pressures for policy changes, just as reform serves to reduce class pressures for structural changes. In Brazil, for instance, governmental loans to trade association leaders have caused them to give up "their associations' broader claims. Such betrayals have been an important factor in reducing class and trade association pressure upon the government."[6]

The degree of corruption which modernization produces in a society is, of course, a function of the nature of the traditional society as well as of the nature of the modernizing process. The presence of several competing value systems or cultures in a traditional society will, in itself, encourage corruption in that society. Given a relatively homogeneous culture, however, the amount of corruption likely to develop during modernization would appear to be inversely related to the degree of social stratification in the traditional society. A highly articulated class or caste structure means a highly developed system of norms regulating behavior between individuals of different status.

These norms are enforced both by the individual's socialization into his own group and by the expectations and potential sanctions of other groups. In such a society failure to follow the relevant norms in intergroup relations may lead to intense personal disorganization and unhappiness.

Corruption, consequently, should be less extensive in the modernization of feudal societies than it is in the modernization of centralized bureaucratic societies. It should have been less in Japan than in China and it should have been less in Hindu cultures than in Islamic ones. Impressionistic evidence suggests that these may well be the case. For Western societies, one comparative analysis shows that Australia and Great Britain have "fairly high levels of class voting" compared to the United States and Canada. Political corruption, however, appears to have been more extensive in the latter two countries than in the former, with Quebec perhaps being the most corrupt area in any of the four countries. Consequently, "the more class-polarized countries also seem to have less political corruption."[7] Similarly, in the "mulatto" countries (Panama, Cuba, Venezuela, Brazil, Dominican Republic. and Haiti) of Latin America, "there appears to be greater social equality and much less rigidity in the social structure" than in the Indian (Mexico, Ecuador, Guatemala, Peru, Bolivia) or *mestizo* (Chile, Colombia, El Salvador, Honduras, Nicaragua, Paraguay) countries. Correspondingly, however, the relative "absence of an entrenched upper class means also the relative absence of a governing class ethic, with its sense of noblesse oblige" and hence "there seems little doubt that it is countries in this socio-racial category in which political graft reaches its most flagrant heights. Perez Jimenez in Venezuela, Batista in Cuba, and Trujillo in the Dominican Republic all came from non-upper-class backgrounds and all became multimillionaires in office. So also, "Brazil and Panama are notorious for more 'democratic,' more widely-distributed, graft-taking."[8] The prevalence of corruption in the African states may well be related to the general absence of rigid class divisions. "The rapid mobility from poverty to wealth and from one occupation to another," one observer has noted of Africa, "has prevented the development of class phenomena, that is, of hereditary status or class consciousness."[9] The same mobility, however, multiplies the opportunities for and the attractions of corruption. Similarly, the Philippines and Thailand, both of which have had reasonably fluid and open societies with relatively high degrees of social mobility, have been characterized by frequent reports of widespread political corruption.

In most forms corruption involves an exchange of political action for economic wealth. The particular forms that will be prevalent in a society depend upon the ease of access to one as against the other. In a society with multiple opportunities for the accumulation of wealth and few positions of political power, the dominant pattern will be the use of the former to achieve the latter. In the United States, wealth has more commonly been a road to political influence than political office has been a road to wealth. The rules against using public office to obtain private profit are much stricter and more generally obeyed than those against using private wealth to obtain public office. That striking and yet common phenomenon of American politics, the cabinet minister or presidential assistant who feels forced to quit office *in order* to provide for his family, would be viewed with amazement and incredulity in most parts of the world. In modernizing countries, the reverse situation is usually the case. The opportunities for the accumulation of wealth through private activity are limited by traditional norms, the monopoly of economic roles by ethnic minorities, or the domination of the economy by foreign companies and investors. In such a society, politics becomes the road to wealth, and those enterprising ambitions and talents which cannot find what they want in business may yet do so in politics. It is, in many modernizing countries, easier for an able and ambitious young man to become a cabinet minister by way of politics than to become a millionaire by way of business. Consequently, contrary to American practice, modernizing countries may accept as normal widespread use of public office to obtain private wealth while at the same time taking a stricter view of the use of private wealth to obtain public office. Corruption, like violence, results when the absence of mobility opportunities outside politics, combined with weak and inflexible political institutions, channels energies into politically deviant behavior.

The prevalence of foreign business in a country in particular tends to promote corruption both because the foreigners have less scruples in violating the norms of the society and because their control of important avenues to economic wellbeing forces potential native entrepreneurs to attempt to make their fortunes through politics. Taylor's description of the Philippines undoubtedly has widespread application among modernizing countries: "Politics is a major industry for the Filipinos: it is a way of life. Politics is the main route to power, which, in turn, is the main route to wealth....More money can be made in a shorter time with the aid of political influence than by any other means."[10] The use of political office as a way to wealth implies a subordination of political values and institutions to economic ones. The principal purpose of politics becomes not the achievement of public goals but the promotion of individual interests.

In all societies the *scale* of corruption (i.e., the average value of the private goods and public services involved in a corrupt exchange) increases as one goes up the bureaucratic hierarchy or potential ladder. The *incidence* of corruption (i.e., the frequency with which a given population group engages in corrupt acts) on a given level in the political or bureaucratic structure, however, may vary significantly from one society to another. In most political systems, the incidence of corruption is high at the lower levels of bureaucratic and political authority. In some societies, the incidence of corruption seems to remain constant or to increase as one goes up the political hierarchy.

In terms of frequency as well as scale, national legislators are more corrupt than local officials; high level bureaucrats are more corrupt than low level ones; cabinet ministers are the most corrupt of all; and the president or top leader the most corrupt among them. In such societies the top leader—the Nkrumah, Sarit, San Martín, Pérez Jiménez, Trujillo—may make off with tens if not hundreds of millions of dollars. In such a system corruption tends to accentuate already existing inequalities. Those who gain access to the most political power also have the more frequent opportunities to gain access to the most wealth. Such a pattern of top-heavy corruption means a very low level of political institutionalization, since the top political institutions in the society which should be most independent of outside influences are in fact most susceptible to such influences. This pattern of corruption is not necessarily incompatible with political stability so long as the avenues of upward mobility through the political machine or the bureaucracy remain open. If, however, the younger generation of politicians sees itself indefinitely excluded from sharing in the gains of the older leaders, or if the colonels in the army see little hope of promotion and the chance to share in the opportunities open only to generals, the system becomes liable to violent overthrow. In such a society both political corruption and political stability depend upon vertical mobility.

The expectation of more corruption at the top is reversed in other societies. In these societies the incidence of corrupt behavior increases as one goes down the political or bureaucratic hierarchy. Low-level bureaucratic officials are more likely to be corrupt than high-level ones; state and local officials are more likely to be corrupt than national ones; the top national leadership and the national cabinet are comparatively free from corruption, while the town council and local offices are deeply involved in it. Scale and incidence of corruption are inversely related. This pattern would seem to be generally true for highly modern societies, such as the United States, and also for at least some modernizing societies, such as India. It is also probably the dominant pattern in communist states. The crucial factor in this type of society is the existence of fairly strong national political institutions which socialize rising political leaders into a code of values stressing the public responsibilities of the political leadership. National political institutions are reasonably autonomous and differentiated, while lower-level and local political individuals and organizations are more closely involved with other social forces and groups. This pattern of corruption may directly enhance the stability of the political system. The top leaders of the society remain true to the stated norms of the political culture and accept political power and moral virtue as substitutes for economic gain. Low-level officials, in turn, are compensated for their lack of political standing by their greater opportunity to engage in corruption. Their envy of the power of their leaders is tempered by the solace of their own petty graft.

Just as the corruption produced by the expansion of political participation helps to integrate new groups into the political system, so also the corruption produced by the expansion of governmental regulation may help stimulate economic development. Corruption may be one way of surmounting traditional laws or bureaucratic regulations which hamper economic expansion. In the United States during the 1870s and 1880s corruption of state legislatures and city councils by railroad, utility, and industrial corporations undoubtedly speeded the growth of the American economy. "Many economic activities would be paralyzed," Weiner observes of India, "were it not for the flexibility which *bakshish* contributes to the complex, rigid, administrative system."[11] In somewhat similar fashion, during the Kubitschek era in Brazil a high rate of economic development apparently corresponded with a high rate of parliamentary corruption, as industrializing entrepreneurs bought protection and assistance from conservative rural legislators. It has even been suggested that one result of governmental efforts to reduce corruption in societies such as Egypt is to produce additional obstacles to economic development. In terms of economic growth, the only thing worse than a society with a rigid, overcentralized, dishonest bureaucracy is one with a rigid, overcentralized, honest bureaucracy. A society which is relatively uncorrupt—a traditional society for instance where traditional norms are still powerful—may find a certain amount of corruption a welcome lubricant easing the path to modernization. A developed traditional society may be improved—or at least modernized—by a little corruption; a society in which corruption is already pervasive, however, is unlikely to be improved by more corruption.

Corruption naturally tends to weaken or to perpetuate the weakness of the government bureaucracy. In this respect, it is incompatible with political development. At times, however, some forms of corruption can contribute to political development by helping to strengthen political parties. "The corruption of one government," Harrington said, "is the generation of another."[12] Similarly, the corruption of one governmental organ may help the institutionalization of another. In most modernizing countries, the bureaucracy is overdeveloped in comparison with the institutions responsible for aggregating interests and handling the input side of the political system. Insofar as the governmental bureaucracy is corrupted in the interests of the political parties, political development may be helped rather than hindered. Party patronage is only a mild form of corruption, if indeed it deserves to be called that at all. For an official to award a public office in return for a payment to the official is clearly to place private interest over public interest. For an official to award a public office in return for a contribution of work or money to a party organization is to subordinate one public interest to another, more needy, public interest.

Historically strong party organizations have been built either by revolution from below or by patronage from above. The nineteenth-century experience of England and the United States is one long lesson in the use of public funds and public office to build party organization. The repetition of this pattern in the modernizing countries of today has contributed directly to the building of some of the most effective political parties and most stable political systems. In the later modernizing countries the sources of private wealth are too few and too small to make a major contribution to party building. Just as government in these countries has to play a more important role in economic development than it did in England and the United States, so also it must play a more important role in political development. In the 1920s and the 1930s, Ataturk used the resources of the Turkish government to foster the development of the Republican Peoples Party. After its creation in 1929 the Mexican Revolutionary Party similarly benefited from governmental corruption and patronage. The formation of the Democratic Republican Party in Korea in the early 1960s was directly helped by the use of governmental monies and governmental personnel. In Israel and India, governmental patronage has been a major source of strength for Mapai and Congress. The corruption in West Africa derived in part from the needs of the political parties. Of course, in the most obvious and blatant case of all, communist parties, once they acquire power, directly subordinate governmental bureaucracies and governmental resources to their own purposes.

The rationale for corrupting the bureaucracy on behalf of the parties does not derive simply from a preference for one organization as against another. Corruption is, as we have seen, a product of modernization and particularly of the expansion of political consciousness and political participation. The reduction of corruption in the long run requires the organization and structuring of that participation. Political parties are the principal institution of modern politics which can perform this function. Corruption thrives on disorganization, the absence of stable relationships among groups and of recognized patterns of authority. The development of political organizations which exercise effective authority and which give rise to organized group interests—the "machine," the "organization," the "party"—transcending those of individual and social groups reduces the opportunity for corruption. Corruption varies inversely with political organization, and to the extent that corruption builds parties, it undermines the conditions of its own existence.

Corruption is most prevalent in states which lack effective political parties, in societies where the interests of the individual, the family, the clique, or the clan predominate. In a modernizing polity the weaker and less accepted the political parties, the greater the likelihood of corruption. In countries like Thailand and Iran where parties have had a semi-legality at best, corruption on behalf of individual and family interests has been widespread. In the Philippines where political parties are notoriously weak, corruption has again been widely prevalent. In Brazil, also, the weakness of political parties has been reflected in a "clientelistic" pattern of politics in which corruption has been a major factor.[13] In contrast, it would seem that the incidence of corruption in those countries where governmental resources have been diverted or "corrupted" for party-building is on the whole less than it is where parties have remained weak. The historical experience of the West also reflects this pattern. The parties which at first are the leeches on the bureaucracy in the end become the bark protecting it from more destructive locusts of clique and family. Partisanship and corruption, as Henry Jones Ford argued, "are really antagonistic principles. Partisanship tends to establish a connection based upon an avowed public obligation, while corruption consults private and individual interests which secrete themselves from view and avoid accountability of any kind. The weakness of party organization is the opportunity of corruption."[14]

Notes

1. M.G. Smith, "Historical and Cultural Conditions of Political Corruption Among the Hausa," *Comparative Studies in Society and History,* 6 (Jan. 1964), 194.
2. M. McMullan, "A Theory of Corruption." *The Sociological Review,* 9 (July 1961), 196.
3. Smith, p.194: McMullan, pp. 190–91.
4. Nathaniel Leff, "Economic Development Through Bureaucratic Corruption," *American Behavioral Scientist,* 8 (Nov. 1964), 132; italics in original.
5. Colin Leys, "What Is the Problem About Corruption?" *Journal of Modern African Studies,* 3(1965), 230.
6. Leff, p.137.
7. Robert R. Alford, *Party and Society* (Skokie, Ill.: Rand McNally, 1963), p. 298.
8. Needler, *Political Development in Latin America,* chap. 6, pp. 15–16.
9. Peter C. Lloyd, "The Development of Political Parties in Western Nigeria," *American Political Science Review,* 49 (Sept. 1955), 695.
10. George E. Taylor, *The Philippines and the United States: Problems of Partnership* (New York: Praeger. 1964), p.157.
11. Myron Weiner, *The Politics of Scarcity* (Chicago: University of Chicago Press, 1962), p. 253. See in general Joseph S. Nye, "Corruption and Political Development: A Cost-Benefit Analysis," *American Political Science Review,* 61 (June 1967), 417–27.
12. James Harrington, quoted in George Sabine, *A History of Political Theory* (rev. ed. New York: Holt, Rinehart & Winston, 1950), p.501.
13. See Leff, pp. 10–12.
14. Henry Jones Ford, *The Rise and Growth of American Politics* (New York: Macmillan, 1898), pp. 322–23.

16

Corruption as a Hindrance to Modernization in South Asia

Gunnar Myrdal

The term "corruption" will be used in this chapter in its widest sense, to include not only all forms of "improper or selfish exercise of power and influence attached to a public office or to the special position one occupies in public life" but also the activity of the bribers.[1]

The significance of corruption in Asia is highlighted by the fact that wherever a political regime has crumbled—in Pakistan and Burma, for instance, and, outside South Asia, in China—a major and often decisive cause has been the prevalence of official misconduct among politicians and administrators, and the concomitant spread of unlawful practices among businessmen and the general public. The problem is therefore of vital concern to the governments in the region. Generally speaking, the habitual practice of bribery and dishonesty tends to pave the way for an authoritarian regime, whose disclosures of corrupt practices in the preceding government and whose punitive action against offenders provide a basis for its initial acceptance by the articulate strata of the population. The Communists maintain that corruption is bred by capitalism, and with considerable justification they pride themselves on its eradication under a Communist regime.[3] The elimination of corrupt practices has also been advanced as the main justification for military takeovers. Should the new regime be unsuccessful in its attempts to eradicate corruption, its failure will prepare the ground for a new putsch of some sort. Thus it is

Source: Gunnar Myrdal, ''Corruption-Its Causes and Effects,'' *Asian Drama: An Enquiry into the Poverty of Nations,* Vol. II. New York: Twentieth Century, 1968. pp. 937~51. By permission of the publisher

obvious that *the extent of corruption has a direct bearing on the stability of South Asian governments.*

A Taboo in Research on South Asia

Although corruption is very much an issue in the public debate in all South Asian countries, as we shall demonstrate. . . [later], it is almost taboo as a research topic and is rarely mentioned in scholarly discussions of the problems of government and planning. With regard to research conducted by Americans, the explanation might seem, at first glance, to lie in the fact that public life in the United States, particularly at the state and city levels, is still not as free of corruption as in Great Britain, Holland, or Scandinavia. But this explanation does not take us far, as social scientists in the United States, particularly in an earlier generation, never shied away from exposing corruption in public administration, politics, and business, nor were their inquiries censored. Moreover, scholars from the Western European countries mentioned have shown no greater interest than Americans in studying corruption in South Asia. Neither does the fact that Western enterprises are in league with corrupt elements in South Asia on a large scale explain the disinterest of Western scholars in the problem of South Asian corruption, for business has not been that influential in guiding research; many studies with conclusions unfavorable to Western business interests have in fact been made. For reasons we shall set forth later, the lack of investigation cannot be attributed, either, to the difficulty of finding an empirical basis for research on corruption.

Instead, the explanation lies in the general bias that we have characterized as diplomacy in research. Embarrassing questions are avoided by ignoring the problems of attitudes and institutions, except for occasional qualifications and reservations—which are not based on even the most rudimentary research and do not, of course, alter the basic approach. South Asian social scientists are particularly inclined to take this easy road, whether they are conservatives or radicals. The taboo on research on corruption is, indeed, one of the most flagrant examples of this general bias. It is rationalized, when challenged, by certain sweeping assertions: that there is corruption in all countries (this notion, eagerly advanced by students indigenous to the region, neglects the relative prevalence of corruption in South Asia and its specific effects in that social setting); that corruption is natural in South Asian countries because of deeply ingrained institutions and attitudes carried over from colonial and pre-colonial times (this primarily Western contention should, of course, provide an approach to research and a set of hypotheses, not an excuse for ignoring the problem); that corruption is needed to oil the intricate machinery of business and politics in South Asian countries and is, perhaps, not a liability given the conditions prevailing there (again, this mainly Western hypothesis about the functioning of the economic and social system should underline rather than obviate the need for research): that there is not as much corruption as is implied by the public outcry in the South Asian countries (this claim needs to be substantiated, and if it is true. the causes and effects of that outcry should be investigated). These excuses, irrelevant and transparently thin as they are, are more often expressed in conversation than in print. That the taboo on any discussion of corruption in South Asia is basically to be explained in terms of a certain condescension on the part of Westerners was pointed out in the Prologue [not reprinted here].

In our study we have not attempted to carry out the necessary research on corruption in South Asia, or even a small part of it: we had neither the time nor the facilities for an empirical investigation on this scale. The main purpose of this chapter is thus to explain why the taboo should be broken. In the course of the discussion we venture to sketch a theory of corruption in South Asia by offering some reasonable, though quite tentative, questions to be explored and hypotheses to be tested.

The "Folklore" of Corruption and the Anti-Corruption Campaigns

The problem of corruption, though not a subject of research, is, as we have said, very much on the minds of articulate South Asians. The newspapers devote much of their space and the political assemblies much of their time to the matter: conversation, when it is free and relaxed, frequently turns to political scandals. Periodically, anti-corruption campaigns are waged: laws are passed; vigilance agencies set up; special police establishments assigned to investigate reports of misconduct; sometimes officials, mostly in the lower brackets, are prosecuted and punished and occasionally a minister is forced to resign. Occasionally committees are appointed to deal more generally with the problem of counteracting corruption,[5] following the practice established in colonial times, particularly by the British. In India and Ceylon especially, but also in other South Asian countries, the authorities have, from the start of the independence era, tried to prevent corruption, and these efforts have, on the whole, been increasing. Yet the articulate in all these countries believe that corruption is rampant and that it is growing, particularly among higher officials and politicians, including legislators and ministers. The ostentatious efforts to prevent corruption and the assertions that the corrupt are being dealt with as they deserve only seem to spread cynicism, especially as to how far all this touches the "higher-ups."

Two things, then, are in evidence: (1) what may be called the "folklore of corruption, i.e., people's beliefs about corruption and the emotions attached to those beliefs, as disclosed in the public debate and in gossip; and (2) public policy measures that may be loosely labeled "anti-corruption campaigns," i.e., legislative, administrative, and judicial institutions set up to enforce the integrity of public officials at all levels. Both are reactions to the fact of corruption, and they are related to each other in circular causation. A study of these phenomena cannot, of course, provide an exhaustive and entirely accurate picture of the extent of corruption existing in a country—the number involved, the positions they hold, and what they are doing. But it is nevertheless true that *the folklore of corruption embodies important social facts worth intensive research in their own right.* The beliefs about corruption and the related emotions are easily observed and analyzed, and this folklore has a crucial bearing on how people conduct their private lives and how they view their government's efforts to consolidate the nation and to direct and spur development. The anti-corruption campaigns are also important social facts, having their effects, and they are just as easy, or even easier, to record and analyze.

A related question worth study is the extent to which the folklore of corruption reflects, at bottom, a weak sense of loyalty to organized society. Is there, in other words, a general asociality that leads people to think that anybody in a position of power is likely to exploit it in the interest of himself, his family, or other social groups to which he has a feeling of loyalty? If so, people's beliefs about the corruptibility of politicians and administrators would be in part a reflection of what they would like to do, given the means.

If corruption is taken for granted, resentment amounts essentially to envy of those who have opportunities for private gain by dishonest dealings. Viewed from another angle, these beliefs about corruptibility, especially the belief that known offenders can continue their corrupt practices with little risk of punishment, are apt to reinforce the conviction that this type of cynical asocial behavior is widely practiced. The folklore of corruption then becomes in itself damaging, for it can give an exaggerated impression of the prevalence of corruption, especially among officials at high levels. It is certain that fear of bolstering that impression influenced Nehru consistently to resist demands for bolder and more systematic efforts to cleanse his government and administration of corruption. "Merely shouting from the house-tops that everybody is corrupt creates an atmosphere of corruption," he said. "People feel they live in a climate of corruption and they get corrupted themselves. The man in the street says to himself: '*well, if everybody seems corrupt, why shouldn't I be corrupt?*' That is the climate sought to be created which must be discouraged."

The first task of research on corruption is thus to establish the ingredients of the folklore of corruption and the anticorruption campaigns. These phenomena are on the surface of social reality in South Asia and therefore lend themselves to systematic observation. The data, and the process of collecting them, should give clues for the further investigation of the facts of actual corruption. Analysis of the interplay of folklore, action, and fact and of the relationship of all three to the wider problems of national consolidation, stability of government, and effectiveness of development efforts must necessarily take one into murkier depths of social reality.

The Facts of Corruption

With public debate quite open and gossip flourishing, the facts in individual cases of wrongdoing should not be too difficult to ascertain. The true research task is, however, to establish the general nature and extent of corruption in a country, its incursion upon various levels and branches of political and economic life, and any trends that are discernible. In this section we shall make a start on this task, but our contribution should not be considered as more than a very preliminary sorting out of problems for research. What is said is based on extensive reading or parliamentary records, committee reports, newspapers, and other publications dealing with the subject, and even more, on conversations with knowledgeable persons in the region, including Western businessmen, as well as on personal observation. The fact that in the United States corruption has for generations been intensively and fruitfully researched should counter the notion that nothing can be learned about this phenomenon.

Concerning first the general level of corruption, it is unquestionably much higher than in the Western developed countries (even including the United States) or in the Communist countries. It serves no practical purpose, and certainly no scientific interest, to pretend that this is not so. This judgment will gain support when in the next section we turn to the causes of corruption; they are clearly much stronger in South Asia than in the other groups of countries mentioned. The relative extent of corruption in the South Asian countries is difficult to assess. There is more open discussion of corruption in the Philippines, where, in the American tradition, the press is particularly free and outspoken than in, say, Pakistan, Burma, and Thailand under their *present* regimes. In India, where a moralistic attitude is especially apparent, greater concern is expressed than in Ceylon, for instance. Whether the amount of public discussion reflects the real prevalence of corruption is doubtful. On the basis of scanty evidence, India may, on balance, be judged to have somewhat less corruption than any other country in South Asia. Nevertheless, a commonly expressed opinion in India is that "administrative corruption, in its various forms, is all around us all the time and that it is rising." The findings of the Santhanam Committee as to the prevalence of corruption in different branches and levels of responsibility will be reported below, in the text and in footnotes.

If a comparison is made with *conditions* in the colonial era, the usual view of both South Asian and Western observers is that corruption is more prevalent now than before independence and that, in particular, it has recently gained ground in the higher echelons of officials and politicians. This view, too, will gain support from our subsequent discussion of the causes of corruption. We know on the authority of J. S. Furnivall, moreover, that the Netherlands Indies was practically free of corruption in colonial times, unlike Burma where corruption was rampant except at very highest level; but in present-day Indonesia corruption seems to be at least as much a fact of life as in any other South Asian country.[10] In the Philippines corrupt practices at all levels of business and administration were common in colonial times, but it is generally assumed that they have increased substantially since then.[11]

There is said to have been much petty corruption in British India on the lower level where indigenous or Anglo-Indian officials were almost exclusively employed, though in most instances Europeans were served promptly and without having to pay a bribe. On the other hand, it is commonly asserted—not only by British observers—that the Indian Civil Service was largely incorrupt. Not all Indian intellectuals agree; some maintain that in later years, and especially during the Second World War, corruption tended to spread even to this select group, including British officials.[12] In the princely states corruption was often unchecked and infested the courts of the maharajahs and the higher echelons of administration. What has been said about British India holds broadly true even for Ceylon. The French administration in Indo-China was probably never as clean as its British counterpart in India and Ceylon, but it is generally acknowledged that corruption has increased very rapidly in the successor states.[13] Thailand was always corrupt in its peculiar fashion and is thought to have become more so of late.

There seems to be rather general agreement that in recent years corruption in South Asia has been increasing. The Santhanam Committee Report speaks of "the growth of corruption" and of the need to arrest "the deterioration in the standards of public life," the assumption that the recent trend of corruption in India is upwards is implicit in the whole report. In Pakistan and Burma the military takeovers in the late 1950s undoubtedly brought major purges in their wake, but many observers—both Westerners and nationals in these countries—are found who believe there has been a resurgence of corruption, particularly in Pakistan, though the bribes have to be bigger because of greater risks.

Statements such as these should be tested by research that could either confirm or refute them; even if broadly confirmed they need to be made much more specific. As for the different branches of administration in the South Asian governments, it is generally assumed that the public works departments and government purchasing agencies in all of the countries are particularly corrupt,[14] as are also the agencies running the railways, the offices issuing import and other licenses, and those responsible for the assessment and collection of taxes and customs duties.[15] More generally it is asserted that whenever discretionary power is given to officials, there will tend to be corruption. Corruption has spread to the courts of justice, and even to the universities.[17]

The spread of corruption among minor officials is understood to be consequent on a deterioration of the morals of some of the politicians and higher officials. Both as cause and effect, corruption has its counterpart in undesirable practices among the general public. The business world has been particularly active in promoting corrupt practices among politicians and administrators, even if it be granted that it is difficult or impossible to carry on business without resort to such practices when corruption is widespread. As the Santhanam Committee Report points out:

> Corruption can exist only if there is someone willing to corrupt and capable of corrupting. We regret to say that both willingness and capacity to corrupt is found in a large measure in the industrial and commercial classes. The ranks of these classes have been swelled by the speculators and adventurers of the war period. To these, corruption is not only an easy method to secure large unearned profits but also the necessary means to enable them to be in a position to pursue their vocations or retain their position among their own competitors....

Possession of large amounts of unaccounted money by various persons including those belonging to the industrial and commercial classes is a major impediment in the purification of public life. If anti-corruption activities are to be successful, it must be recognized that it is as important to fight these unscrupulous agencies of corruption as to eliminate corruption in the public services. In fact they go together.[19]

Our comments concerning the importance of corruption in various branches of the economy are necessarily cast in vague, qualitative terms, as are the judgments expressed in the Santhanam Committee Report, from which we have quoted so extensively. One important question on which the report of that Indian committee is silent is the role played by Western business interests competing for markets in South Asian countries or embarking on direct investments in industrial enterprises there, either independently or in joint ventures with indigenous firms or with governments. Western business representatives never touch on this matter publicly, but, as the writer can testify, in private conversation they are frank to admit that it is necessary to bribe high officials and politicians in order to get a business deal through and to bribe officials both high and low in order to run their businesses without too many obstacles. They are quite explicit about their own experiences and those of other firms. These bribes, they say, constitute a not inconsiderable part of their total costs of doing business in South Asian countries. Although hardly any foreign company can make it an absolute rule to abstain from giving bribes, it is apparent that there is a vast difference in regard to the willingness to bribe, not only between companies but also between nationalities. Among the Western nations, French, American, and, especially, West German companies are usually said to have the least inhibitions about bribing their way through. Japanese firms are said to be even more willing to pay up. On the other hand, the writer has never heard it alleged that bribes are offered or paid by the commercial agencies of Communist countries. These widely held opinions are part of the social setting in South Asia, as are all the elements that make up the folklore of corruption; to what extent they mirror actual business practices should be established by the research we recommend.

There is one specific difficulty facing researchers in their attempts to establish the facts about the taking and seeking of bribes, particularly on the part of higher officials and politicians. Bribes are seldom given directly: usually they go to a middleman, whether an indigenous businessman or an official at a lower level. In particular, a Western firm, operating in a South Asian country, often finds it convenient—and less objectionable—to give a negotiated lump sum to a more or less professional briber, an "agent," who then undertakes to pay off all those whose cooperation is necessary for the smooth conduct of production and business. More generally, when a business transaction is to be settled, an official somewhere down the line of authority will often inform the Western businessman that a minister or a higher official expects a certain sum of money. Even an indigenous businessman is occasionally placed in such an indirect relationship to the bribe-seeker. As the whole affair is secret, there is often no way of knowing whether the middleman is keeping the money for himself. Indeed, he may be using the weight of an innocent person's name to sweeten the deal and increase his take. This is, of course, one of the ways in which the folklore of corruption may exaggerate the extent of corruption at the higher levels.

In research designed to establish the facts of corruption, the role of Western business interests in the spread of corruption could be investigated best by Western researchers since they would in most cases have easier access to the confidence of the bribers, while the nationals in the several countries would probably meet fewer inhibitions and obstacles in carrying out the more general study of the spread of corruption in South Asia. But more important than such a division of labor is the researchers' seriousness of intent and their willingness to cooperate with one another.

The Causes

The folklore of corruption, the political, administrative, and judicial reverberations of these beliefs and emotions in the anti-corruption campaigns, the actual prevalence of corruption in the several countries at different times, and the present trends—all these social facts must be explained in causal terms by relating them to other conditions in South Asia.

When we observe that corruption is more prevalent in South Asia than in the developed Western countries, we are implying a difference in mores as to where, how, and when to make a personal gain. While it is, on the one hand, exceedingly difficult in South Asia to introduce profit motives and market behavior into the sector of social life where they operate in the West—that is, the economic sphere—it is, on the other hand, difficult to eliminate motivations of private gain from the sector where they have been suppressed in the West—the sphere of public responsibility and power. In South Asia those vested with official authority and power very often exploit their position in order to make a gain for themselves, their family, or social group. This is so whether that position is the high one of a minister, a member of the legislature, or a superior official, whose consent or cooperation is needed to obtain a license or settle a business deal, or the humble position of a petty clerk who can delay or prevent the presentation of an application, the use of a railroad car, or the prompt opening of the gates over the tracks. Certain behavioral reactions generally held to be outside profit considerations in the West are commonly for sale in South Asia; they have a "market," though certainly not a perfect one in the Western sense of the term.

The two differences are complementary and, to an extent, explain each other. Indeed, they are both remnants of the pre-capitalist, traditional society. Where, as often in South Asia, there is no market for services and goods or only an imperfect and fragmented one, and where economic behavior is not governed by rational calculations of costs and returns—and this is true not only in subsistence farming and crafts but to a degree also in the organized sector—"connections" must fill the gap. These "connections" range all the way from the absolute dependence of attached labor in agriculture and the peasants' relations with moneylenders and landlords, which are determined by custom and power, to the special considerations that lead to nepotism even in big business. In such a setting a bribe to a person holding a public position is not clearly differentiated from the "gifts," tributes, and other burdens sanctioned in traditional, pre-capitalist society or the special obligations attached to a favor given at any social level.

In pre-colonial times officials had to collect their remuneration themselves, usually without much regulation or control from above. As Furnivall points out in speaking about Burma:

> The officials drew no fixed salary. Some were paid by allotment of the revenue of a particular district, but for the most part their emoluments were derived from a commission on revenue collected, or from fees paid by the parties to a case. One great source of revenue was from local tolls on the transport or sale of goods.

A situation then became established that one Westerner viewed as follows:

> In nearly all Asian countries there has always been a tradition of corruption. Public office meant perquisites. Officials were not well paid and had to make ends meet. The well-timed bribe—which was often almost a conventional fee—was the emollient which made the wheels of administration turn more efficiently.

Even where the colonial powers in later years were able to establish a higher civil service, which was honest, well paid, and manned by both colonial and indigenous personnel—as the British, in particular, succeeded in doing—they still found it difficult to enforce rigid standards at the lower levels of administration.[23]

Traditionally, the South Asian countries were "plural societies," in the meaning given to the term by Furnivall, and under colonial rule became increasingly so. In the present context this implies above all a fragmentation of loyalties and, in particular, little loyalty to the community as a whole, whether on the local or the national level. Such wider loyalty, backed by firm rules and punitive measures, is the necessary foundation for the modern Western and Communist mores by which certain behavior reactions are kept apart from considerations of personal benefit. In South Asia the stronger loyalty to less inclusive groups—family, caste, ethnic, religious, or linguistic "community" (in the South Asian sense), and class—invites the special type of corruption we call nepotism and tends in general to encourage moral laxity. The prevalence of corruption is, moreover, one aspect of the ''soft state,'' to which we have often referred, it generally implies a low level of social discipline.

When explaining the presence of corruption in South Asia, this legacy from traditional society must be taken into account, mainly as part of social statics. But to explain the increase in corruption that is commonly assumed to have taken place in recent times, we must view the social system in dynamic terms. Many of the changes that have occurred have afforded greater incentives as well as greater opportunities for corruption. The winning of independence and the transition from colonial status to self-government were preceded and accompanied by profound disturbances. In all South Asian countries the goal of development was accepted, while the attainment of that goal was made more difficult by the accelerated growth of population, the deterioration of the trading position, and other trends. Independence greatly increased the role of the politicians. At the same time the repatriation, following independence, of a large number of officials from the metropolitan countries left South Asia few competent administrators with the stricter Western mores. This scarcity was much greater and more damaging in Indonesia, Burma, and even Pakistan than in the Philippines, India, and Ceylon.

...[T]he extensive—and generally increasing—resort to discretionary controls is apt to breed corruption;[26] the spread of corruption, in turn, gives corrupt politicians and dishonest officials a strong vested interest in retaining and increasing controls of this type. Another contributing factor has undoubtedly been the low real wages of officials, especially those at the lower and middle levels.[27] There is also, quite generally, a circular causation with cumulative effects working within the system of corruption itself. As we have indicated, it acts with special force as people become aware of the spread of corruption and feel that effective measures are not taken to punish the culprits, particularly those who are highly placed. Among the sophisticated the situation may become rationalized in the idea that corruption, like inflation, is an unavoidable appendage of development. The effect of this is to spread cynicism and to lower resistance to the giving or taking of bribes.

Notes

1. See India, Government of Ministry of Home Affairs, *Report of the Committee on Prevention of Corruption.* New Delhi, 1964, p.5; see pp.11ff. This committee is usually referred to as the Santhanam committee, after its chairman; we shall cite its report as the Santhanam committee report hereafter.
2. A few years before the military *putsch* of 1958 in Pakistan. Tibor Mende reported that: "Probably no other symptom of Pakistani public life has contributed more to the demoralization of the 'common man' than corruption." Illicit practices had reached such proportions that "their effect is likely to wipe out whatever benefits new economic projects might have secured for him." Some measures were taken by the government in response to "widespread demand for action" and "a few minor officials" were dismissed, but "they were the small culprits." (Tibor Mende, *South-East Asia between Two Worlds,* Turnstile Press, London, 1955, p. 227.)
3. "In the disorders in China since 1911 the scale of corruption had increased in a monstrous way, and reform was very much needed. The surprising achievement of the communists was to be able to induce among their party members, who were after all thoroughly Chinese, a militant and puritanical hatred of the old system. Here was one of the outstanding instances of ideas and institutions being able to change people's character. The communist party set out to hunt the corrupt; it disciplined its own members savagely if it caught them; it developed a steady pressure against corruption in all the administration—incidentally attaching charges of corruption to all of whom it disapproved upon other grounds." (Guy Wint, *Spotlight on Asia,* Penguin Books, Middlesex, 1955, p. 91.)
   The present writer's observations confirm the view that what has impressed the South Asian intellectuals most about China's communist revolution has been the establishment of a strong, disciplined state, one that is scrupulously honest by South Asian standards.
4. In India the number of vigilance cases reviewed is steadily increasing. See Santhanam committee report, Section 3, pp. 14 ff. Although the report places the statistics under the heading "extent of corruption," it makes clear (p. 14 *et passim*) that the statistics themselves do not indicate the actual amount of corruption in various branches of administration, or its recent trend.
5. The Santhanam committee report is the latest and the most ambitious South Asian study of corruption. The committee gives certain general judgments about the prevalence of corruption in India to which we shall refer below, but directs its main attention to establishing in considerable detail the various possibilities for corruption afforded by established administrative procedures in India, particularly in the central government, and to working out a system of reforms that would decrease corruption.
6. In the study of race relations it is the beliefs about race and the institutional and attitudinal systems of segregation and discrimination related to those beliefs that are important, not racial differences as such (see Gunnar Myrdal, *An American Dilemma,* Harper & Row, New York, 1944, p. 110 and throughout). Something

similar is true about corruption, though not to the same extent, as undoubtedly the corruption practices are important, independent of what is believed about them or done to combat them.

7. R.K. Karanjia, *The Mind of Mr. Nehru,* George Allen & Unwin Ltd., London, 1960, p.61.
   The Santhanam committee report states: "It was represented to us that corruption has increased to such an extent that people have started losing faith in the integrity of public administration. We heard from all sides that corruption has, in recent years, spread even to those levels of administration from which it was conspicuously absent in the past. We wish we could confidently and without reservation assert that at the political level, ministers, legislators, party officials were free from this malady. The general impressions are unfair and exaggerated. But the very fact that such impressions are there causes damage to the social fabric" (pp. 12, 13). ''The general belief about failure of integrity amongst ministers is as damaging as actual failure" (p. 101).

8. *The Economic Weekly,* December 21, 1963, Vol. XV, No.51, p. 2061.

9. J. S. Furnivall, *Colonial Policy and Practice: A Comparative Study Of Burma and Netherlands India,* Cambridge University Press, London, 1957, p. 269 and throughout.

10. In fact, a decade ago an Indonesian statesman, Mohammad Hatta, wrote:
   "Corruption runs riot through our society; corruption has also infected a great many of our government departments....Workers and government employees, whose wages and salaries are no longer adequate for their daily needs, are being exploited by enterprising adventurers who want to get rich quickly....This is why all businessmen who remain faithful to economic morality are constantly being pushed backward. Bribery and graft have become increasingly common, to the detriment of our community and our country. Each year the government loses hundreds of millions of rupiahs in duties and taxes which remain unpaid as a result of fraud and smuggling, both illegal and 'legal.' " (Mohammad Hatta, *The Co-operative Movement in Indonesia,* Cornell University Press, Ithaca, 1957, pp. 84–85.)
   The situation has certainly not improved since this was written.

11. An American congressional study group reported: "Those members of the study mission who had visited the Philippines previously on one or more occasions were startled and shocked to find an increase in lawlessness and of government corruption that was more than hinted at.'' *(Report of the Special Study Mission to Asia, Western Pacific, Middle East, Southern Europe and North Africa,* GPO, Washington, 1960, p.22.)

12. This view is also expressed, obliquely, by the Santhanam committee:
   Till about the beginning of the Second World War corruption was prevalent in considerable measure amongst revenue, police excise and public works department officials particularly of the lower grades and the higher ranks were comparatively free from this evil. The smaller compass of state activities, the 'great depression' and lack of fluid resources set limits to the opportunities and capacity to corrupt or be corrupted. The immense war efforts during 1939 to 1945 which involved an annual expenditure of hundreds of crores of rupees over all kinds of war supplies and contracts created unprecedented opportunities for acquisition of wealth by doubtful means. The wartime controls and scarcities provided ample opportunities for bribery, corruption, favoritism, etc. The then government subordinated all other considerations to that of making the war effort a success. Propriety of means was no consideration if it impeded the war effort. It would not be far

wrong to say that the high watermark of corruption was reached in India as perhaps in other countries also, during the period of the Second World War (pp. 6–7).

Any implication that corruption was more widespread among higher officials during the Second World War than now is probably groundless, however, and is gainsaid by the committee in other passages; see below.

13. About developments in North Vietnam we have no specific information; that communist regimes ordinarily stamp out corruption was pointed out before.

14. For India the Santhanam committee report states: 'We were told by a large number of witnesses, that in all contracts of construction, purchases, sales, and other regular business on behalf of the government, a regular percentage is paid by the parties to the transaction, and this is shared in agreed proportions among the various officials concerned. We were told that in the constructions of the public works department, seven to eleven percent was usually paid in this manner and this was shared by persons of the rank of executive engineer and below down to the ministry, and occasionally even the superintending engineer might have a share" (p. 18).

"During the Second Plan period the total expenditure on construction and purchases was of the order of Rs. 2800 crores....If it is assumed that even 5 percent...is accounted for by such corrupt practices, the total loss to the excheqer is about Rs. 140 crores" (p. 18).

15. On these the Santhanam committee report observes: "In the railways, besides the above [constructions and purchases], similar practice in connection with allotment of wagons and hooking of parcels particularly perishables, is said to be in vogue" (p. 10).

"We were told that corruption and lack of integrity are rampant in transactions relating to obtaining or quota certificates, essentiality certificates, licenses and their utilization" (p. 254).

"It is common knowledge that some portion of the tax avoided *or* evaded is shared by many including the assessing officers." (p. 19) This practice has wider effects: "Tax so evaded and avoided is kept as unaccounted money and one of the many uses to which it is put is for corrupting public servants" (p. 271).

16. Says the Santhanam committee report: "Where there is power and discretion, there is always the possibility of abuse, more so when the power and discretion have to be exercised in the context of scarcity and controls and pressure to spend public money" (p. 9).

17. The same report notes:

"Though we did not make any direct inquiries, we were informed by responsible persons including vigilance and special police establishment officers that corruption exists in the lower ranks of the judiciary all over India and in some places it has spread to the higher ranks also. We were deeply distressed at this information" (p. 108).

"It is a matter of great regret that in some universities, conditions are far from satisfactory for the admission of students, recruitment of lecturers and professors and the general management of university funds" (p. 109).

18. In India, according to the report on which we have been drawing, "There is a widespread impression that failure of integrity is not uncommon among ministers and that some ministers who have held office during the last 16 years have enriched themselves illegitimately, obtained good jobs for their sons and relations through nepotism, and have reaped other advantages inconsistent with any notion of purity in public life....We are convinced that ensuring absolute integrity on the

part of ministers at the center and the states is an indispensable condition for the establishment of a tradition of purity in public services" (pp. 101-102).
19. Santhanam committee report, pp. 11–12.
20. Of a somewhat different character is the corruption connected with grants and aid offered by western governments. That a considerable amount of the American aid to countries like Laos, South Vietnam, and even the Philippines has been dissipated in large-scale corruption is common knowledge and, in the frank American tradition, has been reported in congressional inquiries and in the press. The writer has not heard similar allegations in relation to foreign aid given India or Pakistan. Apparently the World Bank, the International Monetary Fund, and, more generally, the intergovernmental agencies within the United Nations family have on the whole been able to avoid playing into the hands of the corrupt, except that when aid is rendered in the form of commodities—as, for instance, powdered milk given by UNICEF—part of the deliveries tend to appear on the market instead of reaching their intended destinations. The World Bank, in particular, has increasingly exerted its authority to see that its loans are used to preserve fair competition among suppliers
21. *Colonial Policy and Practice,* pp. 14–15. Cf.. the Santhanam committee report's characterization of "primitive and medieval societies": "So long as the officials were loyal to the existing regime and did not resort to oppression and forcible expropriation, they were free to do as they liked. If through tactful methods, they amassed wealth for themselves or advanced their other material interests they were praised rather than censured. Often offices were hereditary and perquisites which would today amount to bribery were con-growth of the currently accepted standards of integrity" (p. 6).
22. Guy Wint. *Spotlight on Asia.* p.91.
23. A remarkable exception to the general rule was the Netherlands Indies. The lack of corruption there was commented on above. It resulted from cultivating incorruptibility in the higher brackets of civil service and from leaving the old village organization as undisturbed as possible. Furnivall, after stating that corruption was practically unknown in Java, explains:
> The absence of judicial corruption can easily be understood. Petty cases are settled by arbitration either out of court, or before a bench of notables with a senior and well-paid official as chairman; or they go before a civil servant or judicial officer with long service and on high pay. Moreover, the penalties imposed are so trivial that it is cheaper to be punished than to bribe a policeman or magistrate to escape punishment. Serious matters go before a bench containing at least three high judicial officers as well as laymen of good standing. It would be difficult and dangerous to bribe the whole bench. In civil cases the decision purports to follow customary law, and the people can know whether it is right; the court must justify itself to popular opinion and not to higher judicial authority. In these circumstances there is little scope for bribery. *(Colonial Policy and Practice,* p. 269.)
24. The conditions referred to so far in this section are reflected in the South Asian quest for a higher level of "morals" in business and public affairs—an improved "social climate" in which behavior patterns are judged in terms of the modernization ideals.
> "In the long run, the fight against corruption will succeed only to the extent to which a favorable social climate is created. When such a climate is created and corruption becomes abhorrent to the minds of the public and the public servants and social controls become effective, other administrative, disciplinary and puni-

tive measures may become unimportant and may be relaxed and reduced to a minimum. However, change in social outlook and traditions is necessarily slow and the more immediate measures cannot be neglected in its favour." (Santhanam committee report, p. 101.)

25. The dynamic factors hinted at in this paragraph are touched on in several places in the Santhanam committee report; see, in particular, pp. 8ff.

26. The Santhanam committee report in various contexts makes this point; see footnote 2, p. 945 above. "There is scope for harassment, malpractices and corruption in the exercise of discretionary powers" (p. 45). "It is necessary to take into account the root causes of which the most important is the wide discretionary power which has to be exercised by the executive in carrying on the complicated work of modern administration" (p. 209).

27. "We have found that low-paid government servants are entrusted with. matters like gradation of commodities, inspection of mines, supervision of implementation of labour laws and awards, various kinds of licensing, passing of goods at customs etc. While the general increase in the salaries of government servants is a matter to be decided in the light of national economy and the tax paying capacity of the people, it may be worthwhile in the country's interest to examine whether the categories of officials who have to exercise considerable discretion in matters relating to taxation, issue of valuable permits and licenses, or otherwise deal with matters which require [a] high degree of integrity, should not be given special attention regarding status and emoluments." (Santhanam committee report. p. 46.)

28. "Complaints against the highly placed in public life were not dealt with in the manner that they should have been dealt with if public confidence had to be maintained. Weakness in this respect created cynicism and the growth of the belief that while governments were against corruption they were not against corrupt individuals, if such individuals had the requisite amount of power, influence and protection." (Santhanam committee report, p. 8.).

29. "A society that goes in for a purposively initiated process of a fast rate of change has to pay a social price, the price being higher where the pace of change excludes the possibility of leisurely adjustment which is possible only in societies where change is gradual." (Santhanam committee report.)

17

Corruption and Political Development: A Cost-Benefit Analysis

J.S. Nye

The Study of Corruption in Less Developed Countries

Corruption, some say, is endemic in all governments.[1] Yet it has received remarkably little attention from students of government. Not only is the study of corruption prone to moralism, but it involves one of those aspects of government in which the interests of the politician and the political scientist are likely to conflict. It would probably be rather difficult to obtain (by honest means) a visa to a developing country which is to be the subject of a corruption study.

One of the first charges leveled at the previous regime by the leaders of the coup in the less developed country is "corruption." And generally the charge is accurate. One type of reaction to this among observers is highly moralistic and tends to see corruption as evil. "Throughout the fabric of public life in newly independent States," we are told in a recent work on the subject, "runs the scarlet thread of bribery and corruption. . . . " which is like a weed suffocating better plants. Another description of new states informs us that "corruption and nepotism rot good intentions and retard progressive policies."[2]

Others have reacted against this moralistic approach and warn us that we must. beware of basing our beliefs about the cause of coups on post-coup

Source: J.S. Nye, "Corruption and Political Development: A Cost-Benefit Analysis." *American Political Science Review*, LXI, 2 (June 1967), 417–27. By permission of the author and the publisher, The American Political Science Association.

rationalizations, and also of judging the social consequences of an act from the motives of the individuals performing it.[3] Under some circumstances Mandeville is right that private vice can cause public benefit. Corruption has probably been, on balance, a positive factor in both Russian and American economic development. At least two very important aspects of British and American political development—the establishment of the cabinet system in the eighteenth century and the national integration of millions of immigrants in the nineteenth century—were based in part on corruption. As for corruption and stability, an anthropologist has suggested that periodic scandals can sometimes "lead to the affirmation of general principles about how the country should be run, as if there were not posed impossible reconciliations of different interests. These inquiries may not alter what actually happens, but they affirm an ideal condition of unity and justice."[4] However, the "revisionists" who echo Mandeville's aphorism often underestimate tastes for moralism—concern for worthiness of causes as well as utilitarian consequences of behavior. There is always the danger for a corrupt system that someone will question what it profits to gain the world at the price of a soul. The purpose of this paper is less to settle the difference between "moralists" and "revisionists" about the general effect of corruption on development (although a tentative conclusion is presented) than to suggest a means to make the debate more fruitful. After discussing the problem in the usual general terms of possibility, we shall turn to more specific hypotheses about probability.

This chapter is concerned with the *effects* of corruption, but a word should be said about causes to dispel any impression that corruption is a uniquely Afro-Asian-Latin American problem. I assume no European or American monopoly of morals. After all, Lord Bryce saw corruption as a major American flaw and noted its outbreak in "virulent form" in the new states in Europe.[5] Yet behavior that will be considered corrupt is likely to be more prominent in less developed countries because of a variety of conditions involved in their underdevelopment-great inequality in distribution of wealth; political office as the primary means of gaining access to wealth; conflict between changing moral codes; the weakness of social and governmental enforcement mechanisms; and the absence of a strong sense of national community.[6] The weakness of the legitimacy of governmental institutions is also a contributing factor, though to attribute this entirely to the prevalence of a cash nexus or the divergence of moral codes under previous colonial governments or to the mere newness of the states concerned may be inadequate in light of the experience with corruption of older, non-colonial less developed states such as Thailand or Liberia. Regardless of causes, however, the conditions of less developed countries are such that corruption is likely to have different effects than in more developed countries.

Most researchers on developing areas gather some information on corruption, and this paper will suggest hypotheses about the costs and benefits of corruption for development that may lure some of this information into the open. However, in view of the fact that generalizations about corruption and development tend to be disguised descriptions of a particular area in which the generalizer has done field work, I will state at the outset that generalizations in this paper are unevenly based on field work in East Africa and Central America and on secondary sources for other areas.

Definitions pose a problem. Indeed, if we define political development as "rational, modern, honest government," then it cannot coexist with corruption in the same time period; and if corruption is endemic in government, a politically developed society cannot exist. "Political development" is not an entirely satisfactory term since it has an evaluative as well as a descriptive content. At least in the cases of economic development, there is general agreement on the units and scale by which to measure (growth of per capita income). In politics, however, there is agreement neither on the units nor on a single scale to measure development.[7] Emphasis on some scales rather than others tends to reflect an author's interests.

In this author's view, the term "political development" is best used to refer to the recurring problem of relating governmental structures and processes to social change. It seems useful to use one term to refer to the type of change which seems to be occurring in our age ("modernization") and another to refer to capacity of political structures and processes to cope with social change, to the extent it exists, in any period.[8] We generally assume that this means structures and processes which are regarded as legitimate by relevant sectors of the population and effective in producing outputs desired by relevant sectors of the population. I assume that legitimacy and effectiveness are linked in the "long run" but can compensate for each other in the "short run."[9] What constitutes a relevant sector of the population will vary with the period and with social changes within a period. In the modern period we tend to assume that at least a veneer of broad participation is essential for establishing or maintaining legitimacy. In other words, in the current period, political development and political modernization may come close to involving the same things.

In this paper, political development (or decay) will mean growth (or decline) in the capacity of a society's governmental structures and processes to maintain their legitimacy over time (i.e., presumably in the face of social change). This allows us to see development as a moving equilibrium and avoid some of the limitations of equating development and modernization. Of course, this definition does not solve all the concept's problems. Unless we treat development entirely ex post facto, there will still be differences over evaluation (legitimate in whose eyes?) and measurement (national integration. administrative capacity, institutionalization?) as well as what constitutes a "long" and "short" run. Thus we will find that forms of corruption which have been beneficial effects on economic development may be detrimental for political development; or may promote one form of political development (i.e., defined one way or measured along one scale) but be detrimental to another. We shall have to continue to beware of variations in what we mean by political development. (Alternatively, those who reject the term "political development" can still read the chapter as relating corruption to three problems of change discussed below.)

The definition of corruption also poses serious problems. Broadly defined as perversion or a change from good to bad, it covers a wide range of behavior from venality to ideological erosion. For instance, we might describe the revolutionary student who returns from Paris to a former French African country and accepts a (perfectly legal) overpaid civil service post as "corrupted." But used this broadly the term is more relevant to moral evaluation than political analysis. I will use a narrower definition which can be made operational. Corruption is behavior which deviates from the formal duties of a public role because of private-regarding (personal, close family, private clique) pecuniary or status gains; or violates rules against the exercise of certain types of private-regarding influence.[10] This includes such behavior as bribery (use of a reward to pervert the judgment of a person in a position of trust); nepotism (bestowal of patronage by reason of ascriptive relationship rather than merit); and misappropriation (illegal appropriation of public resources for private-regarding uses). This definition does not include much behavior that might nonetheless be regarded as offensive to moral standards. It also excludes any consideration of whether the behavior is in the public interest, since building the study of the effects of the behavior into the definition makes analysis of the relationship between corruption and development difficult. Similarly, it avoids the question of whether non-Western societies regard the behavior as corrupt, preferring to treat that also as a separate variable. To build such relativism into the definition is to make specific behavior which can be compared between countries hard to identify. Moreover, in most less developed countries, there are two standards regarding such behavior, one indigenous and one more or less Western, and the formal duties and rules concerning most public roles tend to be expressed in terms of the latter.[11] In short, while this definition of corruption is not entirely satisfactory in terms of inclusiveness of behavior and the handling of relativity of standards it has the merit of denoting specific behavior generally called corrupt by Western standards (which are at least partly relevant in most developing countries) and thus allowing us to ask what effects this specific behavior has under different conditions.

Possible Benefits and Costs

Discussion of the relation of corruption to development tends to be phrased in general terms. Usually the argument between moralists and revisionists tends to be about the possibility that corruption (type unspecified) *can* be beneficial for development. Leaving aside questions of probability, one can argue that corruption can be beneficial to political development, as here defined, by contributing to the solution of three major problems involved: economic development, national integration, and governmental capacity.

Economic Development

If corruption helps promote economic development which is generally necessary to maintain a capacity to preserve legitimacy in the face of social change, then (by definition) it is beneficial for political development.

There seem to be at least three major ways in which some kinds of corruption might promote economic development.

Capital Formation. Where private capital is scarce and government lacks a capacity to tax a surplus out of peasants or workers openly, corruption may be an important source of capital formation. There seems to be little question about the effectiveness of this form of taxation—Trujillo reputedly accumulated $500 million and Nkrumah and relatives probably more than $10 million.[12] The real question is whether the accumulated capital is then put to uses which promote economic development or winds up in Swiss banks.

Cutting Red Tape. In many new countries the association of profit with imperialism has led to a systematic bias against the market mechanism. Given inadequate administrative resources in most new states, it can be argued that corruption helps to mitigate the consequences of ideologically determined economic devices which may not be wholly appropriate for the countries concerned.[13] Even where the quality of bureaucrats is high, as in India, some observers believe that "too much checking on corruption can delay development. Trying to run a development economy with triple checking is impossible."[14] Corruption on the part of factory managers in the Soviet Union is sometimes credited with providing a flexibility that makes central planning more effective.

Entrepreneurship and Incentives. If Schumpeter is correct that the entrepreneur is a vital factor in economic growth and if there is an ideological bias against private incentives in a country, then corruption may provide one of the major means by which a developing country can make use of this factor. This becomes even more true if, as is often the case, the personal characteristics associated with entrepreneurship have a higher incidence among minority groups. Corruption may provide the means of overcoming discrimination against members of a minority group, and allow the entrepreneur from a minority to gain access to the political decisions necessary for him to provide his skills. In East Africa, for instance, corruption may be prolonging the effective life of an important economic asset—the Asian minority entrepreneur—beyond what political conditions would otherwise allow.

National Integration

It seems fair to assume that a society's political structures will be better able to cope with change and preserve their legitimacy if the members share a sense of community. Indeed, integration is sometimes used as one of the main scales for measuring political development.

Elite Integration. Corruption may help overcome divisions in a ruling elite that might otherwise result in destructive conflict. One observer believes that it helped bridge the gap between the groups based on power and those based on wealth that appeared in the early nationalist period in West Africa and allowed the groups to "assimilate each other." Certainly in Central America, corruption has been a major factor in the succession mechanism by integrating the leaders of the new coup into the existing upper class. Whether this is beneficial for political development or not is another question involving particular circumstances, different evaluation of the importance of continuity, and the question of the relevant period for measurement.

Integration of Non-Elites. Corruption may help to ease the transition from traditional life to modern. It can be argued that the man who has lived under "ascriptive, particularistic and diffuse" conditions cares far less about the rational impartiality of the government and its laws than he does about its awesomeness and seeming inhumanity. The vast gap between literate official and illiterate peasant which is often characteristic of the countryside may be bridged if the peasant approaches the official bearing traditional gifts or their (marginally corrupt) money equivalent. For the new urban resident, a political machine based on corruption may provide a comprehensible point at which to relate to government by other than purely ethnic or tribal means. In McMullan's words, a degree of low-level corruption can "soften relations of officials and people" or in Shils' words it "humanizes government and makes it less awesome."[15]

However, what is integrative for one group may be disintegrative for another. The "traditional" or "transitional" man may care far more that he has a means to get *his* son out of jail than that the system as a whole be incorruptible, but for "modern" groups such as students and middle classes (who have profited from achievement and universalism) the absence of honesty may destroy the legitimacy of the system. Finally, it is worth noting again Gluckman's statement that the scandals associated with corruption can sometimes have the effect of strengthening a value system as a whole.

Governmental Capacity

The capacity of the political structures of many new states to cope with change is frequently limited by the weakness of their new institutions and (often despite apparent centralization) the fragmentation of power in a country. Moreover, there is little "elasticity of power"—i.e., power does not expand or contract easily with a change of man or situation.[16]

To use a somewhat simplified scheme of motivations, one could say that the leaders in such a country have to rely (in various combinations) on ideal, coercive or material incentives to aggregate enough power to govern. Legal material incentives may have to be augmented by corrupt ones. Those who place great faith in ideal incentives (such as Wraith and Simpkins) see the use of corrupt material incentives as destructive ("these countries depend considerably on enthusiasm and on youthful pride of achievement . . .)[17] of governmental capacity. With a lower evaluation of the role of ideal incentives, however, corrupt material incentives may become a functional equivalent for violence. In Mexico, for instance, Needler has described the important role which corruption played in the transition from the violent phases of the revolution to its institutionalized form.[18] At the local level, Greenstone notes that while patronage and corruption was one factor contributing to an initial decline in governmental capacity in East Africa, corrupt material incentives may provide the glue for reassembling sufficient power to govern.[19]

Governmental capacity can be increased by the creation of supporting institutions such as political parties. Financing political parties tends to be a problem in developed as well as less developed countries, but it is a particular problem in poor countries. Broad-based mass financing is difficult to maintain after independence.[20] In some cases the major alternatives to corrupt proceeds as a means of party finance are party decay or reliance on outside funds. Needless to say, not all such investments are successful. The nearly $12 million diverted from Nigeria's Western Region Marketing Board into Action Group coffers from 1959–1962 (and probably equivalent amounts in other regions)[21] seem to have been wasted in terms of institution-building; but on the other hand, investment in India's Congress party or Mexico's *Partido Revolucionario Institucional* has been more profitable for political development.

Those who dispute the possible benefits of corruption could argue that it involves countervailing costs that interfere with the solution of each of the three problems. They could argue that corruption is economically wasteful, politically destabilizing, and destructive of governmental capacity.

Waste of Resources

Although corruption may help promote economic development, it can also hinder it or direct it in socially less desirable directions.

Capital Outflow. As we mentioned above, capital accumulated by corruption that winds up in Swiss banks is a net loss for the developing country. These costs can be considerable. For instance, one source estimates that from 1954–1959, four Latin American dictators (Peron, Perez, Jimenez, and Batista) removed a total of $1.15 billion from their countries.[22] It is no wonder that another source believes that economic development in some Latin American countries has been "checked" by corruption.[23]

Investment Distortions. Investment may be channeled into sectors such as construction not because of economic profitability, but because they are more susceptible to hiding corrupt fees through cost-plus contracts and use of suppliers' credits. This was the case, for instance, in Venezuela under Perez Jimenez and in Ghana under Nkrumah.

Waste of Skills. "If the top political elite of a country consumes its time and energy in trying to get rich by corrupt means, it is not likely that the development plans will be fulfilled."[24] Moreover, the costs in terms of time and energy spent attempting to set some limits to corruption can also be expensive. For instance, in Burma, U Nu's creation of a Bureau of Special Investigation to check corruption actually reduced administrative efficiency.[25]

Aid Foregone. Another possible wastage, the opportunity costs of aid foregone or withdrawn by outside donors because of disgust with corruption in a developing country could be a serious cost in the sense that developing countries are highly dependent upon external sources of capital. Thus far, however, there has not been a marked correlation between honesty of governments and their per capita receipt of aid. If corruption is a consideration with donors (presumably it weighs more heavily with multilateral institutions), it is not yet a primary one.

Instability

By destroying the legitimacy of political structures in the eyes of those who have power to do something about the situation, corruption can contribute to instability and possible national disintegration. But it is not clear that instability is always inimical to political development.

Social Revolution. An argument can be made that a full social revolution (whatever its short-run costs) can speed the development of new political structures better able to preserve their legitimacy in the face of social change. Thus, in this view if corruption led to social revolution, this might be a beneficial effect for political development. But it is not clear that corruption of the old regime is a primary cause of social revolution. Such revolutions are comparatively rare and often depend heavily on catalytic events (such as external wars).

Military Takeovers. If corruption causes a loss of legitimacy in the eyes of those with guns, it may be a direct cause of instability and the disintegration of existing political institutions. But the consequences for political development are again ambiguous. Much depends on differing evaluations of the ability of military regimes (which tend to comprise people and procedures oriented toward modernity) to maintain legitimacy in a democratic age either by self-transformation into political regimes or by being willing and able to foster new political institutions to which power can be returned. To the extent that this tends to be difficult, then if corruption leads to military takeover, it has hindered political development.[26]

The degree to which corruption is itself a major cause of military takeovers is, however, open to some question. Despite its prominence in post-coup rationalizations, one might suspect that it is only a secondary cause in most cases. Perhaps more significant is military leaders' total distaste for the messiness of politics—whether honest or not—and a tendency to blame civilian politicians for failures to meet overly optimistic popular aspirations which would be impossible of fulfillment even by a government of angels.[27] Indeed, to the extent that corruption contributes to governmental effectiveness in meeting these aspirations, it may enhance stability.

Crozier sees "revulsion against civilian incompetence and corruption" as a major cause of coups in several Asian countries including Burma, but he also states that the main cause of Ne Win's return to power was the Shan demand for a federal rather than unitary state.[28] Similarly, corruption is sometimes blamed for the first coup in Nigeria, but the post-electoral crisis in the Western region and the fear of permanent Northern domination was probably a more important and direct cause. In Ghana, corruption may have played a more important role in causing the coup, but not so much because of revulsion at dishonesty, as the fact that corruption had reached an extent where it contributed to an economic situation in which real wages had fallen. Nonetheless, its impact in relation to other factors should not be overestimated.[29]

Upsetting Ethnic Balances. Corruption can sometimes exacerbate problems of national integration in developing countries. If a corrupt leader must be fired, it may upset ethnic arithmetic as happened in both Kenya and Zambia in 1966. Of course this can be manipulated as a deliberate political weapon. In Western Nigeria in 1959, an anti-corruption officer was appointed but his jurisdiction was subject to approval by the cabinet, which meant that no case could be investigated "unless the party leader decided that a man needed to be challenged."[30] But as a weapon, charging corruption is a risky device. Efforts by southern politicians in Uganda to use it in 1966 precipitated a pre-emptive coup by the northern prime minister in alliance with the predominantly northern army.

Reduction of Governmental Capacity

While it may not be the sole or major cause, corruption can contribute to the loss of governmental capacity in developing countries.

Reduction of Administrative Capacity. Corruption may alienate modern-oriented civil servants (a scarce resource) and cause them to leave a country or withdraw or reduce their efforts. In addition to the obvious costs, this may involve considerable opportunity costs in the form of restriction of government programs because of fears that a new program (for instance, administration of new taxes) might be ineffective in practice. While this is a real cost, it is worth noting that efficient bureaucracy is not always a necessary condition for economic or political development (at least in the early stages), and in some eases can even hinder it.[31]

Loss of Legitimacy. It is often alleged that corruption squanders the most important asset a new country has—the legitimacy of its government. This is a serious cost but it must be analyzed in terms of groups. As we have seen, what may enhance legitimacy for the student or civil servant may not enhance it for the tradition-oriented man. It is interesting, for instance, that there is some evidence that in Tanganyika petty corruption at low levels seems to have increased during the year following the replacement of an "illegitimate" colonial regime by a "legitimate" nationalist one.[32] Loss of legitimacy as a cost must be coupled with assessment of the power or importance of the group in whose eyes legitimacy is lost. If they are young army officers, it can be important indeed.

Probabilities

Thus far I have been discussing *possible* benefits and costs. I have established that under some circumstances corruption can have beneficial effects on at least three major development problems. I have evaluated the importance of a number of frequently alleged countervailing costs. It remains to offer hypotheses about the *probabilities* of benefits outweighing costs. In general terms, such probabilities will vary with at least three conditions: (1) a tolerant culture and dominant groups; (2) a degree of security on the part of the members of the elite being corrupted; (3) the existence of societal and institutional checks and restraints on corrupt behavior.

1. Attitudes toward corruption vary greatly. In certain West African countries, observers have reported little widespread sense of indignation about corruption.[33] The Philippines, with its American colonial heritage of corruption, and appreciation of the politics of compromise, seems able to tolerate a higher level of corruption than formerly Dutch Indonesia. According to Higgins, the Indonesian attitude to corruption (which began on a large scale only in 1954) is that it is sinful. He attributes the civil war of 1958 to corruption and argues that in the Philippines, "anomalies" are taken more for granted.[34] Not only is the general level of tolerance of corruption relevant, variations of attitude within a country can be as important (or more so) than differences between countries. Very often, traditional sectors of the populace are likely to be more tolerant of corruption than some of the modern sectors (students, army, civil service). Thus the hypothesis must take into account not only the tolerant nature of the culture, but also the relative power of groups

representing more and less tolerant subcultures in a country. In Nigeria, tolerance was by many accounts considerable among the population at large, but not among the young army officers who overthrew the old regime.

2. Another condition which increases the probability that the benefits of corruption will outweigh the costs is a degree of security (and perception thereof) by the members of the elites indulging in coup practices. Too great insecurity means that any capital formed by corruption will tend to be exported rather than invested at home. In Nicaragua, for instance, it is argued that the sense of security of the Somoza family encouraged them in internal investments in economic projects and the strengthening of their political party, which led to impressive economic growth and diminished direct reliance on the army. In contrast are the numerous cases of capital outflow mentioned above. One might add that this sense of security, including the whole capitalist ethic, which is rare in less developed countries today, makes comparison with capital formation by the "robber barons" of the American nineteenth century of dubious relevance to less developed countries today.

3. It is probable that for the benefits of corruption to outweigh the costs depends on its being limited in various ways, much as the beneficial effects of inflation for economic growth tends to depend on limits. These limits depend upon the existence of societal or institutional restraints on corruption. These can be external to the leaders, e.g., the existence of an independent press, and honest elections; or internalized conceptions of public interest by a ruling group such as Leys argues that eighteenth century English aristocrats held.[35] In Mandeville's words, "Vice is beneficial found when it's by Justice lopt and bound."[36]

Given the characteristics of less developed countries, one can see that the general probability of the presence of one or more of these conditions (and thus of benefits outweighing costs) is not high. But to conclude merely that the moralists are more right than wrong (though for the wrong reasons) is insufficient because the whole issue remains unsatisfactory if left in these general terms. Though corruption may not prove beneficial for resolution of development problems in general, it may prove to be the only means to solution of a particular problem. If a country has some overriding problem, some "obstacle to development"—for instance, if capital can be formed by no other means, or ethnic hatred threatens all legal activities aimed at its alleviation—then it is possible that corruption is beneficial for development despite the high costs and risks involved. While there are dangers in identifying "obstacles to development,"[37] and while the corruption that is beneficial to the solution of one problem may be detrimental to another, we need to get away from general statements which are difficult to test and which provide us with no means of ordering the vast number of variables involved. We are more likely to advance this argument if we distinguish the roles of different types of corruption in relation to different types of development problems.

The matrix in table 17.1 relates three types of corruption to three types of development problems, first assuming favorable and then assuming unfavorable conditions described above. Favorable conditions (F) means a tolerant culture or dominance of more tolerant groups, relative security of the elite corrupted, and societal/institutional checks. Unfavorable conditions (U) means intolerant culture or groups, insecure elite, and few societal/institutional checks. The development problems are those discussed above: economic development, national integration, and governmental capacity. The scores are a priori judgments that the costs of a particular type of corruption are likely to outweigh the benefits for a particular development problem or subproblem. They represent a series of tentative hypotheses to be clarified or refuted by data. Under economic development, the specific sub-problems discussed are whether capital accumulation is promoted (benefit) without capital flight (cost): whether cutting bureaucratic red tape (benefit) outweighs distortion of rational criteria (cost); whether the attraction of unused scarce skills such as entrepreneurship (benefit) is greater than the wastage of scarce skills of, say, politicians and civil servants (cost).

Under the problem of national integration are the sub-problems of whether a particular type of corruption tends to make the elite more cohesive (benefit) or seriously splits them (cost); and whether it tends to humanize government and make national identification easier for the non-elites (benefit) or alienates them (cost). Under the problem of governmental capacity are the sub-problems of whether the additional power aggregated by corruption (benefit) outweighs possible damage to administrative efficiency (cost); and whether it enhances (benefit) or seriously weakens the governmental legitimacy (cost).

Level of Beneficiary

Shils argues that "freedom from corruption at the highest levels is a necessity for the maintenance of public respect of Government . . . " whereas a modicum of corruption at lower levels is probably not too injurious.[38] On the other hand, McMullan reports that West Africans show little sense of indignation about often fantastic stories of corruption by leaders, and impressions from Mexico indicate that petty corruption most saps morale.[39] In India, Bayley notes that "although corruption at the top attracts the most attention in public forums, and involves the largest amount of money in separate transactions, corruption at the very bottom levels is the more apparent and obvious and in total amounts of money involved may very well rival corruption at the top."[40]

The matrix in the exhibit suggests that under unfavorable conditions neither type of corruption is likely to be beneficial in general, although top level corruption may enhance governmental power more than it weakens administrative efficiency. It also suggests that under favorable conditions, top level

Table 17.1
Corruption Cost-Benefit Matrix

DEVELOPMENT PROBLEMS

Types of Corruption	Political Conditions	1. Economic development			2. National integration		3. Governmental capacity		General Probability that Costs Outweigh Benefits
		a. capital	b. bureaucracy	c. skills (Outweigh)	d. elite	e. non-elite	f. effectiveness	g. legitimacy	
1. Level									
top	F	low	uncertain	uncertain/low	low	uncertain	low	low	low/uncertain
bottom	F	high	uncertain	uncertain/high	uncertain	low	high	low	high
top	U	high	high	uncertain/low	high	high	low	high	high
bottom	U	high	uncertain	uncertain/high	little relevance	high	high	high	high
2. Inducements									
modern	F	low	uncertain	uncertain/low low	low	low	low/uncertain	uncertain	low/uncertain
traditional	F	high/uncertain	uncertain	high	high	uncertain	high	uncertain	high
modern	U	high	uncertain	uncertain/low	high	high	low/uncertain	high	high
traditional	U	high/uncertain	uncertain	high	high	uncertain	high	high	high
3. Deviation									
extensive	F	uncertain	high	uncertain	uncertain	low	uncertain/low	uncertain/high	high
marginal	F	uncertain	low	uncertain/low	low	low	low	low	low
extensive	U	uncertain	high	uncertain	high	high	uncertain	high	high
marginal	U	uncertain	low	uncertain/low	high	high	low	high	high

NOTES:

F   favorable political conditions (cultural tolerance, elite security, checks)
U   unfavorable political conditions
High   high probability that costs exceed benefits
Low   low probability that costs exceed benefits
Uncertain   little relationship or ambiguous relationship

corruption may be beneficial but bottom level corruption probably is not (except for non-elite integration). If these judgments are accurate, it suggests that countries with favorable conditions, like India, which have considerable bottom level corruption but pride themselves on the relative honesty of the higher levels may be falling between two stools.
The rationale of the scoring is as follows.

(A) Capital. Bottom level corruption with smaller size of each inducement will probably increase consumption more than capital formation. While top level corruption may represent the latter, whether it is invested productively rather than sent overseas depends on favorable political conditions.

(B) Bureaucracy. Other factors seem more important in determining whether expediting is more important than distortion; except that those with the power of the top levels will probably distort investment criteria considerably in conditions of uncertainty—witness the alleged selling of investment licenses under a previous government in Guatemala.

(C) Skills. Whether top level corruption permits the use of more skills than it wastes depends upon their supply. Where they exist, as with Asians in East Africa or "Turcos" in Honduras, it is probably beneficial. Corruption of those at lower levels of power may be more likely to waste energies than to be important in permission of use of new skills simply because their power is limited.

(D) Elite Integration. It is difficult to see a clear relation between bottom level corruption and elite integration. At the higher levels under unfavorable conditions, e.g., a powerful intolerant part of the elite such as students or army, corruption would probably have a more divisive than cohesive effect. Under favorable conditions it might be more cohesive.

(E) Non-elite Integration. Under unfavorable conditions it seems likely that both types of corruption would tend to alienate more than enhance identification, whereas under favorable conditions corruption by the lower levels that the populace deals with most frequently might have the humanizing effect mentioned above, and alienation would be slight in the tolerant culture. Top level corruption might have the same effect though the connection is less clear because of the lesser degree of direct contact.

(F) Effectiveness. Bottom level corruption is more likely to disperse rather than aggregate power by making governmental machinery less responsive than otherwise might be the case; whereas at top levels the ability to change the behavior of important power holders by corrupt inducements is likely to outweigh the loss of efficiency, even under unfavorable conditions.

(G) Legitimacy. Whether corruption enhances or reduces governmental legitimacy depends more on unfavorable conditions than on level of corruption. Much depends on another factor, visibility of corrupt behavior, which does not always have a clear relationship to level of corruption.

Inducements

Another distinction which can be made between types of corruption is the nature of the inducement used, for instance the extent to which they reflect the values of the traditional society or the values of the modern sector. A traditional inducement such as status in one's clan or tribe may be more tolerable to those who share the ascriptive affinity, but others outside the ascriptive relationship would prefer the use of money which would give them equality of access to the corruptee. Weiner writes of India that "from a political point of view, equal opportunity to corrupt is often more important than the amount of corruption, and therefore . . . an increase in *bakshish* is in the long run less serious than an increase in corruption by ascriptive criteria."[41]

As scored here, our matrix suggests that under favorable political conditions (e.g., India?) Weiner's hypothesis is probably correct but would not be correct under unfavorable conditions.

(A) Capital. Modern inducements (i.e., money) probably lead to capital formation (at top levels) which may be invested under favorable conditions or be sent abroad under unfavorable conditions. Traditional inducements (kin status) do not promote capital formation (and may even interfere with it) but probably have little effect on capital flight.

(B) Bureaucracy. What edge modern inducements may have in expediting procedure may be offset by distortion of criteria, so the relation between type of inducement and this problem is scored as uncertain.

(C) Skills. Assuming the existence of untapped skills (as above), modern inducements increase the access to power while traditional ones decrease it.

(D) Elite Integration. Under favorable conditions modern inducements are unlikely to divide elites more than make them cohere, but traditional inducements tend to preserve and emphasize ethnic divisions in the elites. Under unfavorable conditions, both types of inducements tend to be divisive.

(E) Non-elite Integration. Whether modern inducements promote identification or alienation varies with political conditions in the expected way, but the effect of traditional inducements is more ambiguous and probably varies from positive to negative according to the prevalence of traditional as against modern values in the particular country in question.

(F) Effectiveness. Modern inducements probably give the government greater range to aggregate more sources of power than traditional inducements do. The probabilities will vary not only with political conditions but also by the opportunity costs-whether there is an efficient administrative machine to be damaged or not.

(G) Legitimacy. Under favorable conditions whether traditional or modern inducements will decrease legitimacy more than they enhance it remains uncertain because it will vary with the (above-mentioned) degree of existence of modern and traditional values in a society. Under unfavorable conditions, both will likely have higher costs than benefits.

Deviation

We can also distinguish types of corruption by whether the corrupt behavior involves extensive deviation from the formal duties of a public role or marginal deviation. This is not the same thing as a scale of corrupt inducements, since the size of the inducements may bear little relation to the degree of deviation. For instance, it is alleged that in one Central American country under an insecure recent regime, a business could get the government to reverse a decision for as little as $2,000, whereas in a neighboring country the mere expediting of a decision cost $50,000. Such a distinction between types of corruption by extent of deviation is not uncommon among practitioners who use terms like "speed-up money" or "honest graft" in their rationalizations.[42]

(A) Capital. It is difficult to see that the extensiveness of the deviation (except insofar as it affects the scale of inducement) has much to do with the probabilities of capital formation or flight.

(B) Bureaucracy. On the other hand, marginal deviations (by definition) are unlikely to involve high costs in distortion of criteria and even under unfavorable conditions may help expedite matters. Extensive deviations are likely to have high costs in terms of rational criteria regardless of conditions.

(C) Skills. It is not clear that extensive deviations call forth more unused skills than they waste administrative skills; nor is the matter completely clear with marginal deviations, though the costs of administrative skills wasted may be lower because the tasks are simpler.

(D) Elite Integration. Under unfavorable conditions, the effects of corruption on elite cohesiveness are likely to be negative regardless of the extent of deviations, though they might be less negative for marginal deviations. Under favorable conditions, marginal deviations are likely to have low costs, but the effect of extensive deviations will be uncertain, varying with other factors such as existing cohesiveness of the elite and the nature of the extensive deviations.

(E) Non-elite Integration. Under unfavorable conditions, corruption is likely to have more alienative than identification effects regardless of the nature of the deviations. Under favorable conditions, marginal deviation will not have high costs in terms of alienation, and extensive deviation may have special appeal to those who are seeking human and "reversible" government more than impartial or "rational" government.

(F) Effectiveness. It is difficult to see that extensive deviations alone would increase governmental power more than weaken administrative efficiency, but with marginal deviation, the extent of the latter would be sufficiently small that the benefits would probably outweigh the costs.

(G) Legitimacy. Under unfavorable conditions either type of corruption would be more likely to weaken than to enhance legitimacy, but under favorable conditions the lesser challenge to rationality might make marginal corruption less detrimental than extensive—though this would depend on the proportion and dominance of groups in society placing emphasis on modern values.

Conclusion

The scoring of the matrix suggests that we can refine the general statements about corruption and political development to read "it is probable that the costs of corruption in less developed countries will exceed its benefits except for top level corruption involving modern inducements and marginal deviations and except for situations where corruption provides the only solution to an important obstacle to development." As our matrix shows, corruption can provide the solution to several of the more limited problems of development. Whether this is beneficial to development as a whole depends on how important the problems are and what alternatives exist. It is also interesting to note that while the three conditions we have identified seem to be necessary for corruption to be beneficial in general terms, they are not necessary for it to be beneficial in the solution of a number of particular problems.

At this point, however, not enough information is at hand to justify great confidence in the exact conclusions reached here. More important is the suggestion of the use of this or a similar matrix to advance the discussion of the relationship between corruption and development. The matrix can be expanded or elaborated in a number of ways if the data seem to justify it. Additional development problems can be added, as can additional types of corruption (e.g., by scale, visibility, income effects, and so forth). The above categories can be made more precise by adding possibilities; for instance intermediate as well as top and bottom levels of corruption, or distinctions between politicians and civil servants at top, bottom, and intermediate levels.

Despite the problems of systematic field research on corruption in developing countries mentioned above, there is probably much more data on corruption and development gleaned during field work on other topics than we realize. What we need to advance the study of the problem is to refute and replace *specific* a priori hypotheses with propositions based on such data rather than with the generalities of the moralists. Corruption in developing countries is too important a phenomenon to be left to moralists.

Notes

1. C. J. Friedrich, *Man and His Government* (New York, 1963), p. 167. See also "Political Pathology," *The Political Quarterly.* 37 (January-March 1966), 70–85.
2. Ronald Wraith and Edgar Simpkins, *Corruption in Developing Countries* (London, 1963), pp. 11, 12. K.T. Young, Jr., "New Politics in New States," *Foreign Affairs,* 39 (April 1961), at p.498.
3. See, for example: Nathaniel Leff, "Economic Development Through Bureaucratic Corruption," *The American Behavioral Scientist,* 8 (November, 1964), 8–14; David H. Bayley, "The Effects of Corruption in a Developing Nation," *The Western Political Quarterly,* 19 (December 1966),719–32; J. J. Van Klaveren in a "Comment" in *Comparative Studies in Society and History, 6* (January 1964), at p. 195, even argues that "recent experience in the so-called underdeveloped countries has most vividly brought home the fact that corruption is not a mass of incoherent phenomena, but a political system, capable of being steered with tolerable precision by those in power."
4. Max Gluckman, *Custom and Conflict in Africa* (Oxford, 1955), p.135.
5. James Bryce, *Modern Democracies* (New York, 1921), Vol. II, p. 509.
6. Colin Leys, "What is the Problem About Corruption?" *Journal of Modern African Studies,* 3, 2 (1965), 224–25; Ralph Braibanti, "Reflections on Bureaucratic Corruption," *Public Administration,* 40 (Winter 1962), 365–71.
7. Nor, by the nature of the subject, is there likely to be, in Pye's words, "no single scale can be used for measuring political development": Lucian Pye (ed.), *Communications and Political Development* (Princeton, 1963). See also Lucian Pye, "The Concept of Political Development," *The Annals,* 358 (March 1965), 1–19; Samuel Huntington, "Political Development and Political Decay," *World Politics,* 17 (April 1965), 386–430; Robert Packenham, "Political Development Doctrines in the American Foreign Aid Program," *World Politics,* 18 (January 1966), 194–235.
8. See Huntington, 389.
9. S. M. Lipset, *Political Man* (New York, 1959), 72–75.
10. The second part of the definition is taken from Edward C. Banfield, *Political Influence* (New York: Free Press, 1961), p. 315.
11. See, for example: M.G. Smith, "Historical and Cultural Conditions of Political Corruption Among the Hausa," *Comparative Studies in Society and History, 6* (January 1964), at p.194; Lloyd Fallers, "The Predicament of the Modern African Chief: An Instance from Uganda," *American Anthropologist,* 57 (1955), 290–305. I agree with Bayley on this point: 720–22.
12. A. Terry Rambo, "The Dominican Republic," in Martin Needler (ed.), *Political Systems of Latin America* (Princeton, 1964), p. 172; New York Times, March 5, 1966. Ayeh Kumi's quoted statement has almost certainly greatly underestimated his own assets.

13. On the economic problems of "African socialism." see Elliot Berg, "Socialism and Economic Development in Tropical Africa," *Quarterly Journal of Economics,* 78 (November 1964), 549–73

14. Barbara Ward, addressing the Harvard Center for International Affairs, Cambridge, Mass., March 3, 1966.

15. M. McMullan, "A Theory of Corruption," *The Sociological Review* (Keele), 9 (July 1961), at p. 196; Edward Shils, *Political Development in the New States* (The Hague, 1962), p. 385.

16. See Herbert Werlin, "The Nairobi City Council: A Study in Comparative Local Government," *Comparative Studies in Society and History,* 7 (January 1966), at p.185.

17. Wraith and Simpkins, p.172.

18. Martin Needler, "The Political Development of Mexico," *American Political Science Review,* 55 (June 1961), at pp. 310–11.

19. J. David Greenstone, "Corruption and Self Interest in Kampala and Nairobi," *Comparative Studies in Society and History,* 7 (January 1966), 199–210.

20. See J.S. Nye, "The Impact of Independence on Two African Nationalist Parties," in J. Butler and A. Castagno (eds.), *Boston University Papers on Africa* (New York, 1967), 224–45.

21. Richard L. Sklar, "Contradictions in the Nigerian Political System," *Journal of Modern African Studies,* 3, 2 (1965), at p.206.

22. Edwin Lieuwen, *Arms and Politics in Latin America* (New York, 1960), p.149

23. F. Benham and H.A. Holley, *A Short Introduction to the Economy of Latin America* (London, 1960), p.10.

24. Leys, at p. 229.

25. Brian Crozier, The Morning After: A Study of Independence (London, 1963), p.82.

26. In Pye's words, the military "can contribute to only a limited part of national development," *Aspects of Political Development* (Boston, 1966), p.187

27. "Have no fear," General Mobutu told the Congo people, "My government is not composed of politicians." Mobutu alleged that political corruption cost the Congo $43 million: *East Africa and Rhodesia,* January 13, 1966; *Africa Report,* January 1966, 23.

28. Crozier, pp. 62, 74.

29. For two interpretations, see Martin Kilson, "Behind Nigeria's Revolts"; Immanuel Wallerstein, "Autopsy of Nkrumah's Ghana," New *Leader,* January 31, 9–12; March 14, 1966, 3–5.

30. Henry Bretton, *Power and Stability in Nigeria* (New York, 1962), p.79.

31. Bert Hoselitz, "Levels of Economic Performance and Bureaucratic Structures," in Joseph LaPalombara (ed.), *Bureaucracy and Political Development* (Princeton, 1963), 193–95. See also Nathaniel Leff, 8–14.

32. See *Tanganyika Standard,* May 15, 1963.

33. McMullan, p. 195.

34. Benjamin Higgins, *Economic Development* (New York, 1959), p. 62.

35. Leys, p. 227. See also Eric McKitrick, "The Study of Corruption," *Political Science Quarterly,* 72 (December 1957), 502–15, for limits on corruption in urban America.

36. Bernard Mandeville, *The Fable of the Bees,* Vol. I (Oxford: Clarendon Press, by F. B. Kaye, 1924), p. 37.

37. See Albert O. Hirschman, "Obstacles to Development: A Classification and a

Quasi-Vanishing Act," *Economic Development and Cultural Change,* 13 (July 1965), 385–93.
38. Shils, p.385.
39. McMullan, p. 195; Oscar Lewis, *The Children of Sanchez* (New York, 1961).
40. Bayley, p. 724.
41. Myron Weiner, *The Politics of Scarcity* (Chicago: University of Chicago Press, 1962), p. 236.
42. Cf. William Riordan, *Plunkitt of Tammany Hall* (New York, 1948), p. 4.

Part VI

CORRUPTION AND ECONOMIC GROWTH

Introduction to Part VI

The resurgence of interest in corruption over the past decade has been driven, in large part, by economic development issues. Globalization of the economy, the accompanying intensification of economic competition, the growing realization in developing nations that international investment and not autarky offered the best hope for development, changing attitudes in international lending and aid organizations, and widely divergent economic growth rates in high-corruption regions of the world combined to put the corruption back on the international policy agenda. The new research was facilitated by the emergence of a large number of comparative corruption indices, offering individually (or collectively, via the Transparency International Corruption Perception Index, which combines the results of over a dozen other indices) intriguing comparisons of how corrupt various countries are perceived to be.

Such indices have their problems too (see the selection by Johnston in chapter 44), but the overall picture emerging from the new research was consistent both with recent trends in economic theory and with the general impressions of those familiar with international development. Indeed, it has framed what amounts to a new consensus: corruption is now regarded as delaying, distorting, and diverting economic growth, and as the functional equivalent of a heavy tax on foreign direct investment. As a consequence, it helps keep poor countries poor.

Not surprisingly, however, these connections are complex. Affluent countries have corruption too—sometimes, quite a lot of it. Poor countries share a number of interlinked development problems, of which corruption is just one; deeper difficulties might well encourage corruption and help keep it entrenched. But poor and high-corruption countries also differ in many ways, so that any country's problems—or, successes at reform—reflect a range of mediating social and political factors. Low-corruption countries tend (with some notable exceptions, such as Singapore) to be established democracies; so, how might political factors enter into the corruption/development connection? What do macro-level statistics tell us about the kinds of cases discussed by Leys, for example, (chapter 4) and by Leff in chapter 18, in which corruption might seem to be unimportant, or even broadly beneficial?

The selections in part 6 offer a useful introduction to the past decade's research on corruption and development. Nathaniel Leff offers a classic statement of a point of view that was widely held at one time, and has occasioned considerable debate—that is, that corruption facilitates economic development by (among other things) breaking through bureaucratic bottlenecks, serving as an informal price system, making rigid official development policies more flexible and humane, and by putting public resources and favorable decisions up for bids, channels them to people and groups able to use them efficiently. Those who blame underdevelopment upon corruption, or seek to control it, need to consider what the realistic alternatives are, and the development purposes that will have to be addressed by other means once it has been reduced.

Pranab Bardhan argues that while beneficial consequences of particular corrupt transactions cannot be ruled out, overall the economic effects are negative. Corruption, he reminds us, is an effect, as well as a cause, of economic events; deeper social forces shape both. Some of these are political and institutional; others have to do with the flow of information in both licit and illicit transactions; and still others have to do with the structure and control of corruption itself, which may be centralized or decentralized, coordinated or opportunistic. The extent and nature of the problem thus varies considerably from one country to the next—indeed, particularly so *among* developing countries—with past experience and present expectations strongly affecting future trends. Indeed, there may be multiple developmental equilibria, with interlinked problems inhibiting development and encouraging corrupt networks in poor countries, while elsewhere growth—and the political and institutional factors that support it—help keep corruption under control over the long run.

Paolo Mauro provides solid empirical evidence to support this view. Mauro, like many other economists, puts corruption in the context of *rent-seeking*. A "rent," broadly speaking, is "a payment for the services of a material asset for a specified period of time" (*International Encyclopedia of the Social Sciences,* 1968, vol. 13, p. 454); rent-seeking is "the use [of] resources both for productive purposes and to gain an advantage in dividing up the benefits of economic activity" (Rose-Ackerman, 1999: 2; see also Bhagwati, 1974; Krueger, 1974). The latter idea, which dates back at least as far as Ricardo, may apply to legitimate or illegitimate rents; looked at this way, the resources put to work in corruption may be official power and discretion, private wealth, friendship or kinship, or many others. Payments for specific official services would fall under this definition, and Mauro shows how these resemble a variety of other interventions into market processes, and distort growth, whether the transaction is originated by the official or by a private client. Using corruption indices for over a hundred countries over several years, Mauro shows that corruption does major harm to growth. The connections are both direct—via the disruption of markets—and indirect: scarce public resources are diverted away from education, a long-term investment in the human side of development, toward big-ticket expenditures where sizable rents can more readily be extracted.

But if we are to be sure that such macro-level comparisons really do reflect the economic effects of corruption, we also need to understand how it works in specific situations. Susan Rose-Ackerman begins her analysis at the micro level and works outwards to broader effects. This approach is revealing: claims of economic benefits from corruption often rest upon accounts of particular transactions—often, hypothetical—in isolation, but a detailed look at longer-term implications leads to strongly negative conclusions. Bribes may turn the bureaucratic wheels for one person or firm, but they also send a message to underpaid bureaucrats that they can augment their salaries by creating new requirements and delays—by collusion, if necessary. Corruption adds costs to transactions, rewards inefficiency while penalizing efficiency, and diverts human as well as economic resources away from productive activity into rent-seeking. Where corruption is extensive, investors insist on short-term profits, and keep their assets as mobile as possible, rather than planning for long-term returns. Serious corruption weakens economic and political institutions, makes for unfair and ineffective policies, and can thus delegitimate political regimes, reducing political predictability and harming development.

In the face of the recent research it is very difficult now to make a persuasive argument for economic benefits from corruption. But questions remain: apart from the need for better and more nuanced measures, we need to look more closely at differing patterns of corruption in developing countries, and at their effects upon various constituencies and governmental functions. So-called "petty corruption" needs to be reexamined in light of the new evidence that economic effects become most apparent in the broader context and over the long run. And much of the past decade's research remains open to the criticism of equating corruption as a general concept with bribery as a specific technique—indeed, of treating high-level bribery and corruption more or less as synonyms. In that connection, Bardhan's cautionary arguments about variations in corrupt processes under different social and institutional circumstances, Mauro's findings regarding indirect as well as direct effects, and Rose-Ackerman's argument that we must consider the extended consequences of corruption, may point the way toward a more complete account of the economic implications of corruption.

References

Bhagwati, Jadish N. 1974. *Illegal Transactions in International Trade.* Amsterdam: North Holland-Elsevier.

Krueger, Anne O. 1974. "The Political Economy of a Rent-Seeking Society." *American Economic Review* 64, pp. 291–303.

"Rent," *International Encyclopedia of the Social Sciences*, vol. 13, pp. 454 ff. New York: Macmillan/Free Press, 1968.

Rose-Ackerman, Susan. 1999. *Corruption and Government: Causes, Consequences, and Reform*. Cambridge and New York: Cambridge University Press.

18

Economic Development Through Bureaucratic Corruption[1]

Nathaniel H. Leff

The bureaucratic corruption of many underdeveloped countries has been widely condemned both by domestic and foreign observers. Apart from the criticism based on moral grounds and the technocratic impatience with inefficiency, corruption is usually assumed to have important prejudicial effects on the economic growth of these societies.[2]

Corruption is an extralegal institution used by individuals or groups to gain influence over the actions of the bureaucracy. As such, the existence of corruption *per se* indicates only that these groups participate in the decision making process to a greater extent than would otherwise be the case. This provides information about the effective—as opposed to the formal—political system, but in itself, tells us nothing about the content and development effects of the policies so determined. These depend on the specific orientation and interests of the groups which have gained political access. As we shall see, in the context of many underdeveloped countries, this point can be crucial. For example, if business groups are otherwise at a disadvantage in articulating their interests to the government, and if these groups are more likely to promote growth than is the government, then their enhanced participation in policy formulation can help development.

Furthermore, our discussion is limited to corruption of a particular type: namely, the practice of buying favors from the bureaucrats responsible for

Source: Nathaniel H. Leff, "Economic Development through Bureaucratic Corruption," *American Behavioral Scientist*, 8:3 (November 1964), pp. 8–14. By permission of the publisher, Sage Publications, Inc.

formulating and administering the government's economic policies. Typical examples are bribery to obtain foreign exchange, import, export, investment or production licenses, or to avoid paying taxes. Such bribes are in the nature of a tax levied on economic activity. These payments have not been legitimized by the correct political process, they are appropriated by the bureaucrat rather than the state, and they involve the subversion of the government's economic policies-hence the stigma that attaches to them. The question for us to decide is whether the net effects caused by such payments and policy redirection are likely to favor or hinder economic development.

We should also distinguish between bureaucratic corruption and bureaucratic inefficiency. Corruption refers to extralegal influence on policy formulation or implementation. Inefficiency, on the other hand, has to do with the success or failure, or the economy of means used by the bureaucracy in attaining given goals, whether those of its political directors, or those of the grafters. Empirically, inefficiency and corruption may appear together, and may blend into each other. Both as a policy problem and for analytical purposes, however, it is important to distinguish between two essentially different things.

Who Condemns Corruption?

Before proceeding to our analysis of the economic effects of bureaucratic corruption, it may be useful to make a brief detour. Any discussion of corruption must contend with the fact that the institution is almost universally condemned. Insofar as this criticism is based on moralizing—explicit or latent—self-interest, or ideology, it can be a formidable obstacle to rational analysis. Consequently, in order to gain a degree of perspective on the subject, I would like to consider the sources of the widespread prejudice against corruption. Identifying the specific sources of bias, and breaking down generalized censure to its component parts should help us to evaluate each argument on its own merits. For this purpose, let us consider the origins of the critical attitude held by such groups as foreign observers, government officials, and entrepreneurs, and by intellectuals, politicians, and businessmen in the underdeveloped countries themselves.

Foreigners living in the underdeveloped countries have been persistent critics of corruption. First, they have resented the payments of graft to which they are often subjected in the normal course of their business. Secondly, they have condemned corruption on moral grounds, and criticized it as both a cause and a characteristic of the backwardness of these countries.

A more sophisticated, and recent version of this argument derives from the new interest in promoting economic development. As economists and observers of economic development have grown aware of the enormous obstacles to spontaneous growth, they have come to assign an increasingly important role to the governments of the under-developed countries.

First, there has been an emphasis on the need for entrepreneurs, coupled with the fear that the underdeveloped countries may lack indigenous sources of entrepreneurship. Secondly, recent economic theory stressed the importance of indivisibilities, externalities, and other structural features that may prevent an underdeveloped economy from breaking out of a low-income equilibrium trap. In addition, there was the realization that the flow of private capital and technical skills was insufficient for promoting large-scale growth. With the ensuing flow of inter-governmental transfers, came the need for the governments of the underdeveloped countries to assume responsibility for the resources they were receiving.

Because of these reasons and political pressures, the governments of the underdeveloped countries have come to occupy a very prominent place in most visions of economic development. In a sense, economists have collected their problems, placed them in a box labeled "public policy," and turned them over to the governments of the underdeveloped countries.

In order for the governmental policies to be effective, however, the bureaucracies must actually implement them. Hence it becomes crucial that officials not be influenced, through graft, to deviate from their appointed tasks. The logic of this argument goes as follows: development-bureaucracy-efficiency-probity. This chain of reasoning is central to the whole critique of corruption, and we shall examine it carefully in the next section. Before going further, however, let us note a few important points about this argument.

First, it confuses bureaucratic inefficiency and bureaucratic redirection through dishonesty and graft. Secondly, transferring these problems to the governments and bureaucracies is hardly enough to solve them, for these institutions may not be at all likely to promote growth. Rather than leading the development process, the governments and bureaucracies may be lagging sectors. Finally, the argument implies that because the bureaucracy is so strategic an institution, an attack on bureaucratic corruption deserves high policy priority, offering relatively cheap and easy gains.

Foreign aid missions seem to have been particularly prone to draw such conclusions, for understandable reasons. The bureaucracy's performance will determine the success or failure of many other projects. Moreover, in contrast with some of the other problems facing foreign development specialists, reform of the civil service may seem a relatively straightforward matter. Furthermore, whereas in other development efforts foreign specialists may feel hampered by the lack of well-tested doctrine and procedures, in restructuring the bureaucracy, they can rely on the expertise of public administration and management science. Therefore, it is not surprising that so much foreign development attention and activity have been directed toward the reform of the bureaucracies of underdeveloped countries.

In the underdeveloped countries themselves, much of the condemnation of graft has also come from interest in economic development, and from the apparent cogency of the development-bureaucracy-efficiency-probity logic. Here, moreover, the special ideological perspectives and interests of powerful and articulate groups have reinforced the criticism. Let us consider the specific perspectives that intellectuals, politicians, and businessmen in the underdeveloped countries possess.

The attitudes of intellectuals and of politicians toward corruption overlap to a certain degree. As members of the same rising elite, they condemn corruption because of the idealistic streak which often pervades radicals and reformers. Contemporary intellectuals in underdeveloped countries often emulate the Jacobins in their seeking after virtue. Moreover, as Shils has pointed out,[3] they frequently attribute sacral value to the governmental sphere: hence their hostility to the venality that would corrupt it. More generally, they may see graft as an integral part of the political culture and system of the *ancien régime* which they want to destroy.

Furthermore, they also have a direct interest in discrediting and eliminating corruption because of its functional effects. In most underdeveloped countries, interest groups are weak, and political parties rarely permit the participation of elements outside the contending cliques. Consequently, graft may be the only institution allowing other interests to achieve articulation and representation in the political process. Therefore, if the ruling elite is to maintain its exclusive control of the bureaucracy, it must cut off or control this channel of influence.[4] Such considerations apply especially when the politically disadvantaged group consists of an ethnic minority or of foreign entrepreneurs over whom the elite would like to maintain its dominance.

Entrepreneurs in underdeveloped countries have also condemned bureaucratic corruption. This is understandable, for they must pay the bribes. Moreover, because of certain economic characteristics of graft, the discontent that it arouses probably goes far beyond the cost of the bribe alone.

It is important to realize that most of the objects of corruption are available only in fixed and limited supply. For example, at any point in time, there is only a given amount of foreign exchange or a given number of investment licenses to be allocated. Consequently, when the number of favors is small relative to the number of aspirants, entrepreneurs must bid against each other in what amounts to a clandestine and imperfect auction. With competition forcing prices up, the favors will tend to be allocated to those who can pay the highest prices. In the long run, the favors will go to the most efficient producers, for they will be able to make the highest bids which are compatible with remaining in the industry.

Marginal firms, on the other hand, will face severe pressures. Either they accept subnormal profits, or they must make the effort to increase efficiency, so as to muster the resources necessary to bid successfully. If they drop out of the contest, they are placed in a weakened position vis-à-vis the other firms, which are now even more intra-marginal because of the advantages given by the bureaucratic favor.

This sort of situation, where the efficient are able to outdo the inefficient, is not generally appreciated by businessmen. It is likely to be the less popular in underdeveloped countries where—in deference to the prevalence of inefficiency, and to local ideas of equity—the more usual practice is to tax efficient producers in order to subsidize the inefficient. Moreover, as we have seen, corruption may introduce an element of competition into what is otherwise a comfortably monopolistic industry.

Furthermore, in their bidding for bureaucratic favors, businessmen may have to give up a substantial part of the profits from the favor. The economic value of the favor is equal to the return expected from the favored position it makes possible. This value constitutes the upper limit to the bids made by entrepreneurs. The actual amount paid is indeterminate, and depends on the relative bargaining skills of the bureaucrats and the businessmen. The competitive bidding between businessmen, however, may force the price to approach the upper limit. In such a case, the bureaucrat captures the lion's share of the profits expected from the favor. Competitive selling by different bureaucrats may strengthen the bargaining position of the businessmen, but in general they are probably forced to pay out a relatively large portion of their expected gains. Hence, it is not surprising that they dislike an institution which deprives them of the fruits of their enterprise.[5]

The foregoing discussion suggests that many of the negative attitudes toward corruption are based upon special viewpoints and interests. We should also realize that the background material available on the subject is both scanty and one-sided. Those who engage in corruption maintain secrecy about their operations, so that the little data available comes from declared opponents of the institution. Moreover, those who profit from corruption may themselves have no idea of the socially beneficial effects of their activities.

The widespread condemnation of corruption has come to constitute a serious obstacle to any reexamination of the subject. Indeed, the criticism has become something of a ritual and symbol-laden preamble accompanying policy discussion and statements in the underdeveloped countries. As such, it is cherished for the modicum of consensus it provides to otherwise antagonistic groups.

Positive Effects of Corruption

The critique of bureaucratic corruption often seems to have in mind a picture in which the government and civil service of underdeveloped countries are working intelligently and actively to promote economic development, only to be thwarted by the efforts of grafters. Once the validity of this interpretation is disputed, the effects of corruption must also be reevaluated. This is the case if the government consists of a traditional elite which is indifferent if not hostile to development, or of a revolutionary group of intellectuals and politicians, who are primarily interested in other goals. At the same time, the propensity for investment and economic innovation may be higher outside the government than within it.

Indifference and Hostility of Government

In the first instance, the government and bureaucracy may simply be indifferent to the desires of entrepreneurs wanting to initiate or carry on economic activities. Such a situation is quite likely in the absence of effective popular pressure for economic development, or in the absence of effective participation of business interests in the policymaking process. This is especially the case when entrepreneurs are marginal groups or aliens. More generally, when the government does not attribute much value to economic pursuits or innovation, it may well be reluctant to move actively in the support of economic activity.

Even more important, the bureaucracy may be hostile to entrepreneurs, for it dislikes the emergence of a competing center of power. This is especially the case in colonial economies, where a large domestic middle class has not emerged to challenge traditional power-holders.

Governments Have Other Priorities

The foregoing relates to societies where although lip-service may be paid to the importance of economic development, the government and bureaucracy are oriented primarily to maintaining the status quo. It is also relevant in countries where a successful revolution against the *ancien régime* has occurred. There, the government may be proceeding dynamically, but not toward the promotion of economic development. Other goals, such as an increase in the military power available to the elite, or expansion of its control over society, may be justified in terms of economic development, however "ultimate." At the same time, the immediate effect of such policies is to impede growth.

Typically the bureaucracy plays an extensive interventionist role in the economy, and its consent or support is a sine qua non for the conduct of most economic enterprise. In such a situation, graft can have beneficial effects. First, it can induce the government to take a more favorable view of activities that would further economic growth. The policies or freedom sought by the entrepreneurs would help development, while those they subvert are keyed to other goals. Secondly, graft can provide the direct incentive necessary to mobilize the bureaucracy for more energetic action on behalf of the entrepreneurs. This is all the more important because of the necessity for bureaucratic help in so many areas—e.g., licenses, credit, and foreign exchange allocation—in order to get anything done.

Corruption Reduces Uncertainty and Increases Investment

Corruption can also help economic development by making possible a higher rate of investment than would otherwise be the case.

The investment decision always takes place in the midst of risk and uncertainty. As Aubrey has pointed out,[6] however, these difficulties are very much compounded in the economic and political environment of underdeveloped countries. The basic estimates of future demand and supply conditions are harder because of the lack of data and of the sharp shifts that can occur during a period of economic change. The dangers of misjudging the market are all the more serious because of the lower elasticities of substitution at low income levels.

Aside from the problems of making such economic estimates, the potential investor also faces a major political unknown—the behavior of the government. The possible dangers arising from the government's extensive role in the economy are increased because of the failure of representative government to put an effective check on arbitrary action. The personalist and irrational style of decision-making, and the frequent changes in government personnel and policies add to the risks. Consequently, if entrepreneurs are to make investments, they must have some assurance that the future will not bring harmful intervention in their affairs. We can see an illustration of these difficulties in the fact that in periods of political uncertainty and crisis, investment shrinks, and economic stagnation occurs. By enabling entrepreneurs to control and render predictable this important influence on their environment, corruption can increase the rate of investment.

Corruption and Innovation

The would-be innovator in an underdeveloped society must contend with serious opposition from existing economic interests. Unable to compete economically with the new processes or products, they will usually turn to the government for protection of their investments and future returns. If the bureaucracy supports innovation and refuses to intervene, the innovation can establish itself in the economy. In the more usual case, however, existing economic interests can depend on their long-standing associations with bureaucratic and political compadres for protection.

In this situation, graft may enable an economic innovator to introduce his innovations before he has had time to establish himself politically.[7] Economic innovators in underdeveloped countries have often supported oppositional political cliques or parties. Corruption is another, less radical way of adjusting to the same pressures of goals.

Corruption, Competition, and Efficiency

As we have seen in the previous section, bureaucratic corruption also brings an element of competition, with its attendant pressure for efficiency, to an underdeveloped economy. Since the licenses and favors available to the bureaucrats are in limited supply, they are allocated by competitive bidding among entrepreneurs. Because payment of the highest bribes is one of the principal criteria for allocation, the ability to muster revenue, either from reserves or from current operations, is put at a premium. In the long run, both of these sources are heavily dependent on efficiency in production. Hence, a tendency toward competition and efficiency is introduced into the system.

Such a pressure is all the more important in underdeveloped countries, where competition is usually absent from many sectors of the economy. In the product market, a high degree of monopoly often prevails. International competition is usually kept out by quotas, tariffs, and overvalued exchange rates. In the factor market, frictions and imperfections are common. Consequently, we can appreciate the value of introducing an element of competition, if only through the backdoor.

Corruption as a Hedge against Bad Policy

Corruption also performs the valuable function of a "hedge" and a safeguard against the full losses of bad economic policy. Even when the government of an underdeveloped country is proceeding actively and intelligently to promote growth, there is no assurance that its policies are well conceived to attain its goals. In effect, it may be taking a vigorous step in the wrong direction. Corruption can reduce the losses from such mistakes, for while the government is implementing one policy, the entrepreneurs, with their sabotage, are implementing another. Like all insurance, this involves a cost—if the government's policy is correct. On the other hand, like all insurance, it is sometimes very welcome.

An underdeveloped country often stands in special need of such a safeguard. First, even when policy goals are clearly specified, competent counsel may well be divided as to the best means of achieving them. For example, the experts may differ among themselves on such basic issues as export promotion vs. import substitution, or other intersectoral priorities. Consequently, if the government has erred in its decision, the course made possible by corruption may well be the better one, supported by a dissenting segment of expert opinion. Moreover, the pervasive effects of government policy in an etatistic economy compound the effects of poor decisions, and increase the advantages of having some kind of safeguard against the potential consequences of a serious policy mistake. Corruption provides the insurance that if the government decides to steam full-speed in the wrong direction, all will not be lost.

Some illustrations may help clarify this point. For example, the agricultural producers whose graft sabotaged Peron's economic policies were later thanked for having maintained Argentina's capacity to import. Another example shows in more detail how this process can operate. An important element in the recent Latin American inflations has been the stagnation of food production, and the rise in food prices. In both Chile and Brazil, the governments reacted by freezing food prices, and ordering the bureaucracy to enforce these controls. In Chile, the bureaucracy acted loyally to maintain price controls, and food supplies were relatively stagnant. Inflation rose faster, supported in part by the failure of food production to increase. In Brazil, however, the bureaucracy's ineffectiveness sabotaged the enforcement of price controls, and prices received by producers were allowed to rise. Responding to this price rise, food production also increased somewhat, partially limiting the course of the inflation.[8]

In this case, we see the success of entrepreneurs and corrupted officials in producing a more effective policy than the government. Moreover, subsequent economic analysis justified this "decision" by emphasizing the price elasticity of agricultural supply, and the consequent need to allow the terms of trade to turn in favor of rural producers.

These points are perhaps strengthened when viewed with some historical perspective. As John Nef has remarked, the honesty and efficiency of the French bureaucracy were in great measure responsible for the stifling of economic innovation and progress during the eighteenth century.[9] By way of contrast, the laxity of the British administration permitted the subversion of Colbertism, and allowed new economic processes and activities to flourish.

Alleged Negative Effects of Corruption

Most of the arguments concerning the negative effects of corruption are based on the assumption that development can best proceed through the policies of an uncorrupted government and bureaucracy. As noted in the previous section, this assumes that the government really wants economic development, and that its policies would favor growth more than the activities of an unregulated private sector. Actually, the economic policies of the governments of many underdeveloped countries may be predicated on priorities other than global economic development. Even in countries where there has been a successful revolution against the colonial *ancien régime,* policy may aim primarily at advancing the economic interests of the ruling clique or of the political group on which it bases its dominance. Although the economic policies of some countries may be foolish or catastrophic from the viewpoint of development, they may be well conceived for implementing these other goals.[2 10]

Impeding Taxation

One version of this argument focuses on taxation. Specifically, it asserts that bureaucratic corruption may hamper development by preventing the government from obtaining the tax revenues necessary for developmental policies.

This argument probably attributes to the government an unrealistically high propensity to spend for development purposes. Economic development usually has a less compelling priority among the elites of these societies than among the westerners who observe them. Even if the dominant groups are aware and sensitive to the situation of the lower classes, they may be reluctant to bear the costs of development. Hence, the actual level of taxes collected, and their allocation in the budget may represent the decision of the ruling group as to how hard they want to press forward with economic development. In these circumstances, it is misleading to criticize the bureaucracy for the effects of its ineffective tax collection on economic growth. Of the revenues they might have collected, only a part would have gone for development rather than for the many forms of nondevelopmental expenditure. Moreover, when the entrepreneurs' propensity to invest is higher than the government's, the money saved from the tax collector may be a gain rather than a loss for development.

Usefulness of Government Spending

Furthermore, there is no reason to assume that the government has a high *marginal* propensity to spend for developmental purposes, based on a high income elasticity of demand for development. Without changes in the factors determining the average allocational propensities, increases in governmental revenue may well go for more lavish satisfaction of the same appetites. For example, as budgetary receipts rise, the military may be supplied with jet aircraft rather than with less expensive weapons.

Cynicism

Another argument has emphasized the social effects of corruption as an impediment to development. For example, it has been claimed that immorality and self-seeking of bureaucratic corruption may cause widespread cynicism and social disunity, and thus reduce the willingness to make sacrifices for the society's economic development.

This argument can be criticized on several points.

First, insofar as the disillusion is engendered among the *lower* social orders, the effects on development may not be as important as assumed. Because of economic and social conditions, these people are probably being squeezed as much as is possible, so that with all good will, they could not sacrifice any more.

Secondly, if the cynicism caused by bureaucratic corruption leads to increased self-seeking in the rest of the society, this may not be a completely bad thing for economic development. Many of the wealth-creating activities which make up economic growth depend on such atomistic egoism for their stimulus. Consequently, if cynicism acts as a solvent on traditional inhibitions, and increased self-seeking leads to new ambitions, economic development may be furthered.

Moreover, this argument also exaggerates the extent to which economic growth depends on a popular rallying-around rather than on many individual selfish activities. The implicit picture seems to be that of an "all-together" social effort, perhaps under etatistic direction. Once stated explicitly, such a model appears more like a fantasy of intellectuals rather than an accurate guide to how economic development takes place.

More generally, we should recognize that there are very good reasons for the incivism and unwillingness to make sacrifices that are often characteristic of underdeveloped societies. Mutual distrust and hostility usually have much deeper roots in cultural gaps, inequitable income distribution, and long experience of mistreatment. Rapid change, dislocating existing institutions and values, also disrupts social solidarity. In such circumstances, reduced bureaucratic corruption would make only a marginal contribution to improved public morale.

Corruption as a Policy System

The foregoing analysis and perspective may also be helpful in dealing with bureaucratic corruption as a policy problem.

First, we should be clear as to the nature of "the problem" that policy is attempting to solve. As we have seen, much of the criticism of corruption derives from the political, economic, and ideological interests of particular groups. Presumably the elimination of corruption is a problem only insofar as we share their specific concerns.

Aside from these special interests, however, let us consider corruption from the point of view of its effects on economic development. As we have seen, under certain conditions, the consequences of corruption for development are not as serious as is usually assumed. At the same time, it may have important positive effects that are often overlooked. Consequently, to the extent that reality approaches the conditions of our model, corruption of the type discussed in this paper may not be a problem at all. This will depend on specific conditions, and will vary between countries and between sectors.

When the conditions of our model do not obtain, however, corruption will be an important barrier to development. To the extent that corruption exists as a policy problem, it is probably wise to accept it as a particularly intractable part of an underdeveloped country. On a superficial level, we should recognize that corruption creates its own political and economic interests that will resist efforts at its eradication. More important, corruption is deeply rooted in the psychological and social structure of the countries where it exists. On the psycho-cultural plane, corruption will persist until universalistic norms predominate over particularistic attitudes. Socially, the elimination of corruption probably requires the emergence of new centers of power outside the bureaucracy, and the development of competitive politics. Such changes will come, if at all, only as the result of a long period of economic and social development.

Bureaucracy the Lagging Sector

Two conclusions emerge from this discussion. First, we should realize how illusory is the expectation that bureaucratic policy can intervene as a deus ex machina to overcome the other barriers to economic growth. In many underdeveloped countries, the bureaucracy may be a lagging rather than a leading sector. Secondly, it should be clear that direct policy efforts against such deeply rooted psychological and social conditions cannot hope for much short-term success. As Braibanti concludes,[11] powerful investigatory commissions may have a limited success, but one should expect the problem to be improved "more by time than by effort."

Despite the pessimistic prospects for the usual direct-action policies against corruption, certain possibilities do exist for dealing with it indirectly. The problem is perhaps best conceptualized in terms of the need to economize in the use of a particularly scarce and important resource—honest and capable administrators. Indeed, for several reasons, this shortage may be more serious than others more often cited, e.g., the lack of capital. Because of political reasons, this input into the development process cannot be imported on a large scale. Furthermore as we have noted, available domestic supplies cannot be expected to increase for a long time in most underdeveloped countries. Finally, this input is all the more crucial because of its importance for the successful deployment of other resources. If we view corruption as a problem in the allocation of scarce administrative resources, two solutions are immediately suggested.

Two Techniques

First, the available resources should be concentrated in areas where their productivity in promoting development would be greatest. Such budgeting of administrators would avoid dispersion of honest and able personnel, and make them available only for tasks of the highest priority.

A second way of economizing in the use of this scarce resource would be the use of alternative production techniques to achieve the same development results. In our context, this would mean employing measures to achieve the goals of policy without reliance on direct administration and bureaucratic regulation of the economy.

In many cases, the desired effects could be achieved either by market forces, or by indirect measures creating the necessary incentives or disincentives—i.e., with much less direct government intervention, and the consequent need to rely on the bureaucracy. For example, a government which wants to keep down the domestic price level can either institute a cumbersome system of price regulation, or it can permit a measure of competition from imports. Similarly, a straightforward currency devaluation can have many of the beneficial effects achieved by an administration-intensive regime of differential exchange rates. Admittedly, such policies may have some undesired consequences and side-effects that ideally would be avoided by more sophisticated government management of the economy. The point is, however, that when policy alternatives are evaluated, it would be better to take explicit account of how bureaucratic corruption will affect the direct management policies contemplated. This would lead to a more realistic choice between the means which can accomplish similar goals. Perhaps the best procedure would be to select a mixture of direct and of indirect management policies, taking account of the bureaucratic resources available.

By way of contrast, the more usual practice is to choose the policies that would be best *if* the whole bureaucracy were dependable, and then to deplore its corruption, and condemn it for the failure of the policies chosen. Following the procedure suggested here, however, governments would accept corruption as an aspect of their societies, and try to optimize policy-making within this framework.

Finally, we should note that preoccupation with corruption can itself become an impediment to development. This occurs if the focus on corruption diverts attention from other political and economic deficiencies in the society, and from the measures that can be taken despite corruption. To avoid the losses from such misdirection, re-thinking of the sort suggested here may be helpful.

Notes

1. I am grateful to Richard Eckaus, John Plank, Lucien Pye, and Myron Weiner for their comments on an earlier draft of this paper. They bear no responsibility for the remaining deficiencies.
2. But see V.O. Key, *The Techniques of Political Graft in the United States,* privately printed, 1936. Robert K. Merton, *Social Theory and Social Structure,* New York, 1959, pp. 19–85. Harold Lasswell, "Bribery," in *The Encyclopedia of the Social Sciences,* vol. 2, New York, 1930. Cf. especially, F.W. Riggs, "Bureaucrats and Political Development: A Paradoxical View," paper prepared for the Social Science Research Council Committee on Comparative Politics Conference, January 29–February 2, 1962.
3. Edward Shils, "Political Development in the New States," *Comparative Studies in Society and History,* 1960, p. 279.
4. Cf. Riggs, pp. 28–30.
5. These processes are nicely brought out in Alexandre Kafka, "The Brazilian Exchange Auction." *The Review of Economics and Statistics,* October 1956.
6. H.C. Aubrey, "Investment Decisions in Underdeveloped Countries" in *Capital Formation and Economic Growth,* National Bureau of Economic Research. Princeton, 1955, pp. 404–15. Also cf. the finding of Y. Sayigh *(Entrepreneurs of Lebanon,* Cambridge, Mass. 1962, p.117) that political conditions constituted the greatest unknown facing the entrepreneurs surveyed.
7. Cf. Lasswell, p. 671.
8. I am indebted to an eminent expert in Latin American economic development for this observation.
9. *Industry and Government in France and England: 1540–1640.* Cf. also, J.J. Spengler, "The State and Economic Growth-Summary and Interpretations," p. 368, in H. Aitken, ed., *The State and Economic Growth,* N.Y. 1959.
10. Cf. Frank Golay, "Commercial Policy and Economic Nationalism," *Quarterly Journal of Economics,* 1958, and B. Glassburner, "Economic Policy-Making in Indonesia, 1950–1957," *Economic Development and Cultural Change,* January 1962.
11. Ralph Braibanti, "Reflections on Bureaucratic Corruption," *Public Administration,* Winter 1962, p. 370, and p. 372.

19

Corruption and Development: A Review of Issues

Pranab Bardhan

I. Introduction

Corruption is an ancient problem. In a treatise on public administration dating back to the fourth century B.C. in India, Kautiliya writes in his *Arthasastra:*

> Just as it is impossible not to taste the honey (or the poison) that finds itself at the tip of the tongue, so it is impossible for a government servant not to eat up, at least, a bit of the king's revenue. Just as fish moving under water cannot possibly be found out either as drinking or not drinking water, so government servants employed in the government work cannot be found out (while) taking money (for themselves). (R. P. Kangle 1972, p.91)

In a passage of characteristically remarkable precision Kautiliya states that there are "forty ways of embezzlement" and then goes on to enumerate these ways.

> While corruption in one form or another has always been with us, it has had variegated incidence in different times at different places, with varying degrees of damaging consequences. While the tenacity with which it tends to persist in some cases easily leads to despair and resignation on the part of those who are concerned about it, there can be and have been ways in which a whole range of policy measures make a significant dent. In this paper, we start with a discussion of some

Source: Journal of Economic Literature, vol. XXXV (September 1997) pp. 1320–1334.

of the alternative denotations of the problem of corruption; we then consider the ways in which the damaging consequences of corruption operate in the economy while not ignoring its possible redeeming features in some cases; [and] we pursue the question of why corruption is perceptibly so different in different societies . . .

In common usage the word "corruption" is used to mean different things in different contexts. Even if we choose to confine ourselves only to the economic context, staying away, for example, from related issues of political corruption (i.e., where the ill-gotten gains are primarily in terms of political power), there are alternative denotations of economic corruption. In a majority of cases such corruption ordinarily refers to the use of public office for private gains, where an official (the agent) entrusted with carrying out a task by the public (the principal) engages in some sort of malfeasance for private enrichment which is difficult to monitor for the principal. There are, of course, many everyday cases of other kinds of corruption some of which may take place entirely in the private sector. For example, a private seller sometimes rations the supply of a scarce good (instead of using the price mechanism to clear the market), and we use various ways of bribing him or an agent to jump the queue (paying a higher price to a "scalper" for a sold-out theater show or a game, tipping a "bouncer" for entry into a crowded nightclub, using "connections," i.e., some form of long-run gift exchange, to get a job, and so on).

Sometimes one invokes legality and almost interchangeably uses the word "corrupt" and "illicit" in describing a transaction. But just as clearly not all illegal transactions are corrupt, nor are all instances of corruption or bribery illegal[1] (as when you tip the maitre d' to get a better table at a restaurant than other customers, or in the much more important cases of gift-giving by lobbyists to politicians, campaign contributions to Political Action Committees, or post-retirement jobs in private firms to bureaucrats of agencies meant to regulate them). Similarly, one should keep a distinction between "immoral" and corrupt transactions. When you pay a blackmailer, you may consider him immoral, but you are paying to stop him from revealing some information which may be unpleasant for you but which may be neither illegal nor corrupt. On the other hand, one can think of instances of corruption and bribery which some people may not regard as immoral (particularly those for whom end justifies means), as when you bribe a policeman not to torture a suspect. Having referred to these alternative meanings of even economic corruption, let me state that in this paper I shall mostly confine myself to the application of this term to imply the use of public office for private gain or the agency problem referred to in the preceding paragraph.

Even with this common use of the term among economists, there are many ambiguities. Does striving for private gain include policies that are primarily oriented to increasing the chances for remaining in office? The distinction between political and economic corruption can get blurred here. Then there are problems in common comparative use of the term in the obvious absence of any publicly available objective measures. A particular African country may be in some sense more corrupt than a particular East Asian country, even though the actual amount of bribe money exchanging hands may be much larger in the latter; this may be simply because rampant corruption may have choked off large parts of economic transactions in the former. Then there are cases where the bribe per unit of transaction (and the consequent inefficiency) may be higher (in the case of decentralized corruption, as we shall note later) than in situations of centralized ("one-stop shopping") corruption where the inefficiency may be less, even though the total amount of bribe paid may be larger.

II. Effects on Efficiency

There is a strand in the corruption literature, contributed both by economists and non-economists, suggesting that, in the context of pervasive and cumbersome regulations in developing countries, corruption may actually improve efficiency and help growth. Economists have shown that, in the second-best world when there are pre-existing policy induced distortions, additional distortions in the form of black-marketeering, smuggling, etc., may actually improve welfare even when some resources have to be spent in such activities. The argument for efficiency-improving corruption is a simple extension of this idea. As Nathaniel H. Leff (1964, p.11) puts it simply: "if the government has erred in its decision, the course made possible by corruption may well be the better one." As non-economists usually point out, corruption is the much-needed grease for the squeaking wheels of a rigid administration. Samuel P. Huntington (1968, p. 386) states it bluntly: "In terms of economic growth, the only thing worse than a society with a rigid, over-centralized, dishonest bureaucracy is one with a rigid, over-centralized, honest bureaucracy."

Even without pre-existing distortions, one may look upon corruption as part of a Coasean bargaining process in which a bureaucrat (who is in the illicit business of selling property rights to a public resource in the form of issuing permits and licenses) and the private agent (the prospective buyer) may negotiate their way to an efficient outcome. If in a bribery game there is competitive bidding by private firms for a government procurement contract, and the corrupt official awards the contract to the highest bidder in bribes, then allocation efficiency is maintained, as only the lowest-cost firm can afford the largest bribe. (This, of course, assumes that other goals of the program are not violated: this bidding procedure is clearly not acceptable in the case of University admissions, for example.) That the producer surplus lines the pocket of the bureaucrat and does not go to the public treasury (as would have happened in an open auction for the contract) does not seemingly affect the allocation efficiency.

This argument, however, is more complex when a briber does not have full information about the cost levels and therefore the bribing capacity of his competitors, and when he has to take into account strategic considerations in making any particular offer of a bribe. But the situation can be modeled as an n-person symmetric game with incomplete information on the part of each player and one can draw upon the theory of sealed-bid auctions. In such a context Paul J. Beck and Michael W. Maher (1986) and Donald H. D. Lien (1986) have shown that under the assumptions of the model, the lowest-cost firm is always the winner of the contract, and thus bribery can reproduce the efficiency consequences of competitive bidding procedures under imperfect information. Inefficiency may, of course, result if the official is influenced by considerations other than just the size of the bribe (for example, favoritism for a particular client or nepotism); or when the briber can get away with supplying a low-quality good at a high-quality price, and the official lets in unqualified applicants with a high willingness to pay; or when bribery is used to limit the competition (as in the case of bribing the police or tax inspectors to harass rival firms).[2]

Another efficiency argument in favor of corruption is to look upon it as "speed money" (for which there are distinct terms in different countries, like *lagay* in the Philippines), which reduces delay in moving files in administrative offices and in getting ahead in slow-moving queues for public services. Queuing models which have received some attention in the theoretical literature allow the possibility for the corrupt bureaucrat to practice price discrimination among clients with different time preference. In an interesting equilibrium queuing model with some special assumptions Francis T. Lui (1985) derives bribing functions where the size of the bribe (decided by the briber, not the server of the queue) is linked to the opportunity costs of time for the individual client and shows that the bribing strategies will form a Nash equilibrium of this noncooperative game that will minimize the waiting costs associated with the queue, thereby reducing the inefficiency in public administration. (The model can also be useful in designing schedules of incentive payments in the pay structure of civil servants.)

One does not have to take a moralistic position on corruption to see that some of these arguments above in favor of the efficiency effects of corruption are fraught with general problems, even though in individual instances some redeeming features of corruption may be present. For example, in the second-best case made above, it is usually presumed that a given set of distortions are mitigated or circumvented by the effects of corruption; but quite often these distortions and corruption are caused or at least preserved or aggravated by the same common factors. The distortions are not exogenous to the system and are instead often part of the built-in corrupt practices of a patron-client political system. As we have indicated above, bidding procedures in such a system may still end up in allocational inefficiency.

As for speed money, Gunnar Myrdal (1968), citing the 1964 Santhanam Committee on the Prevention of Corruption appointed by the Government of India, has argued that corrupt officials may, instead of speeding up, actually cause administrative delays in order to attract more bribes.[3] (I am told that in Russia there is a clear terminological distinction between *mzdoimstvo*, taking a remuneration to do what you are supposed to do anyway, and *likhoimstvo*, taking a remuneration for what you are not supposed to do.) Lui's equilibrium queuing model is meant to question the validity of Myrdal's hypothesis at the theoretical level. But, as Jens C. Andvig (1991) points out, from the point of view of imperfect information and strategic considerations queues as allocation mechanisms are more complex and many-sided than has been recognized in the literature, and different ways of organizing the queue may give rise to different outcomes on the average waiting time. In Lui's otherwise very interesting model, for example, both sides in the corrupt transaction are honest in the sense that they stick to a deal, that no new bribe offers are made by the waiting clients after the new entrants have arrived, that there is no moral hazard about the reliability of the sale by the server of a priority in the queue, and so on. The model's results may not be robust to these kinds of considerations.

This also suggests the problem with looking upon bribes simply as side payments in a Coasean bargaining process between officials or politicians and firms (even apart from the agency problem that the bribee is not representing the interests of the principal, the public). Of course, the briber and the bribee may fail to agree on the appropriate size of the bribe on account of bargaining in a situation of asymmetric information and also, there are collective action problems when several firms have to get together to bribe a single politician or bureaucrat. But more important than these is the fact, emphasized by Maxim Boycko, Shleifer, and Robert Vishny (1995), that corruption contracts are not enforceable in courts and there is many a slip between the bribing transaction and the actual delivery of the good or the service involved. The control rights on the latter are often arbitrary and uncertain, leaving a lot of leeway for the bribee to renege on his understanding with the briber, or to come back and demand another bribe. (It used to be said of General Noriega of Panama in his heyday that he could not be *bought,* he could only be *rented.*) Of course, the bribee may have to worry about his reputation in the long run about keeping promises (but many corrupt politicians have too short a time horizon), or sometimes the briber can hire hoodlums to discipline the bribee (but the transaction costs for such ways of enforcement can be high).

A. Centralization of Bribery

Sometimes the bribee cannot deliver not because he wants to cheat, but because there is a multiple veto power system in operation, which makes centralized collection of bribes in exchange of guaranteed favors very difficult. One high official in New Delhi is reported to have told a friend : "if you want me to move a file faster, I am not sure if I can help you; but if you want me to stop a file I can do it immediately." This ability to "stop a file" at multiple points (a system often installed to keep corrupt officials in check) may result in increasing the inefficiency as well as the rate of bribes. In general centralized corruption has less adverse consequences for efficiency than decentralized bribe-taking, because in the former case the bribee will internalize some of the distortionary effects of corruption (assuming similar powers at all levels to determine the overall rents in the system).

Shleifer and Vishny (1993) illustrate this point with an elementary model comparing a case of independent monopolists (where different public agencies provide complementary government goods or services independently) with that of a joint monopolist agency providing the same goods or services. Suppose a customer needs two permits or two complementary inputs from two different agencies in the former case. Each agency as an independent monopolist will take the other agency's sales as given and so the bureaucrat in charge of it will set the bribe-inclusive price in such a way that marginal revenue is equal to the marginal cost, the bribe per unit of sale being the difference between the price and the monopolist's marginal cost (i.e., the official price of the good supplied). The joint monopolist, on the other hand, takes into account the effect of an extra unit sold on the sales of the complementary good and thus on the revenue from bribes from the other source as well, so that in equilibrium the marginal revenue in the supply of each good is less than the marginal cost. Thus the per unit bribe is higher and the supply of each good lower in the independent monopolist case than in the case of collusion. Of course, the aggregate revenue from bribes is larger in the latter case, but the customer gets a larger supply of both inputs. The problem is made much worse when complementarity can be artificially created (just when you think you have bribed two agencies to get the required two permits, another independent monopolist comes along and tells you that you need a third permit from him to get your business in place) and corruption opportunities stimulate the entry of permit-dispensers armed with new regulations. Free entry in this game allows the officials to "overfish" in the "commons" or the rental havens.

Shleifer and Vishny would explain the increase in the inefficiency flowing from corruption in post-Communist Russia in comparison with Communist Russia in these terms. Formerly, the Communist Party used to centralize the collection of bribes and effectively monitored (sometimes with the help of the

KGB) deviations from agreed-upon patterns of corruption. Now different ministries, agencies, and levels of local government all set their own bribes independently in a decentralized attempt to maximize their own revenue. It is usually suggested that the regulatory state is at the root of the inefficiency due to corruption spawned by the regulations; the above analysis suggests that a weak central government with its inability to stop the setting up of independent corruption rackets (a kind of economic warlordism) makes the problem of inefficiency particularly acute. This may be relevant in a comparison of corruption in, say, Indonesia with that in India. . . . in the perception of foreign businessmen the two countries are about equally corrupt; and yet the economic performance by most accounts has been much better in Indonesia. Could it be that Indonesian corruption is more centralized (controlled largely by the first family and the top military leadership in cahoots with the ethnic Chinese-run conglomerates) and thus somewhat more predictable, whereas in India it is a more fragmented, often anarchic, system of bribery?

Centralization of the political machine also makes it possible to have a system approximating "lump-sum" corruption, without distorting too many decisions at the margin. It has been suggested, for example, that corruption in countries like South Korea may have been more in the form of lump-sum contributions by the major business leaders to the president's campaign slush fund, without taxing economic activity at the margin. The important question here is how the ruler can credibly promise to keep the contributions lump-sum, and not come back again for individual quid pro quo deals at the margin. This ability to credibly commit is a feature of "strong" states that very few developing countries have.

The idea of the differential efficiency effects of centralized versus decentralized corruption is akin to Olson's (1993) idea of smaller distortionary effects of the tax impositions of the state as a "stationary bandit" (having thus an "encompassing interest" in the domain over which its rent-exacting power is exercised) as opposed to those of the "roving bandit." One may, however, point out that even centralized corruption is more distortionary than taxation (not to speak of the extra burden of taxes that public revenue losses from corruption may necessitate). This is because of the need to keep corruption secret, as Shleifer and Vishny (1993) point out. Efforts to avoid detection and punishment cause corruption to be more distortionary than taxation. Because different activities have different chances of detection for bribes, there will be some substitution effect following from corruption by which corrupt officials will try to induce investment and transactions in the direction of lower-detection activities (or contractors who are less likely to squeal, even though they may be less efficient). Bureaucrats in poor countries may, for example, opt for imports of complex technology or goods (where detecting improper valuation or overinvoicing is more difficult) in preference to more standardized, but possibly more appropriate, technology or goods. For similar reasons, allocating government funds in a few large defense contracts may look more attractive to the officials involved than spending the money in building numerous small rural health clinics. To preserve the secrecy of deals, a small elite group may also try to raise entry barriers for outsiders, which in many situations has the effect of discouraging the flow of new ideas and innovations. Secret payments, particularly by foreign companies, also tend to be accumulated and spent not inside the country but abroad.

B. Bribes Relative to Rents

Before we leave the subject of costs of corruption, it may be useful to comment on the magnitude of bribes in relation to that of the rent they are supposed to procure for the briber. The early literature on rent-seeking, as in Anne O. Krueger (1974), assumed a process of competitive bidding by the rent-seekers which resulted in a complete dissipation of the rent. Since then there have been models of barriers to entry in the rent-seeking sector (including models of dynamic games of moves and counter-moves of the contending rent-seekers) and of the various transaction costs and risks that the rent-seekers have to face. But what is still astonishing is the extremely small size of the usual bribe compared to the rent collected (Gordon Tullock, 1980, had pointed this out quite early, and the phenomenon is sometimes referred to in the public choice literature as the "Tullock paradox"). The anecdotes are endless. Tullock (1990) cites the case of the New York Congressman Mario Biaggi, who manipulated the federal government to save from bankruptcy an enormous Brooklyn dockyard, for which he received three Florida vacations worth $3,000. Spiro Agnew had to resign from the Vice Presidency of the Nixon Administration for continuing to take bribes of an incredibly trifling amount from an arrangement made earlier in his political career. Most such anecdotes are from democratic polities. On the other hand, there are anecdotes of corrupt income running to billions of dollars for authoritarian rulers in much poorer countries, like Mobutu sese Seko in Zaire or Ferdinand Marcos in the Philippines. This may point to a particular coordination problem in bribe collection in democratic polities that Eric Rasmusen and Mark Ramseyer (1994) have tried to model.

They use a coordination game among wealth-maximizing legislators to show that, if the latter cannot coordinate their actions, they may supply private-interest statutes for bribes even less than the costs they incur. Only when they can enforce agreements with one another, solving a prisoner's dilemma problem, will they come close to collecting the full benefits of the statutes they pass. Rasmusen and Ramsayer (1994) have a simple example to illustrate the difference between a democratic and an autocratic government in this context. Suppose that private-interest statute S14 would provide a benefit of 14 for a lobbyist and would cost an autocratic government 50 because of, say, an increased probability of public discontent or even rebellion. The autocrat will supply this statute only if offered at least 50, which the lobbyist will be unwilling to offer, so S14 will not pass. Suppose that a second statute, S80, would cost the autocrat 50 but benefit the lobbyist by 80; the autocrat will supply this statute for a bribe anywhere between 50 and 80.

Now take a democracy where five legislators vote on statutes S14 and S80. For each statute, each legislator loses 5 by voting "yes" when the others vote "no," but 10 if the statute passes. The government thus loses (again in terms of public discontent) a total of 50 if a statute passes, exactly the same cost as in the case of the autocratic government. Take first the statute S14. If each legislator thinks that the others will vote "no," then all voting "no" will be the equilibrium. The lobbyist could overcome these expectations by offering a bribe of 5 to three legislators, but that is too costly for him for a statute worth 14. But if each legislator thinks the others will vote "yes," then each may as well vote "yes" for an infinitesimally small bribe, because he will lose 10, no matter how he votes (so that his marginal cost of voting "yes" is 0). Thus a democratic government may sell a private-interest statute at below cost when the autocratic government would not. Consider now the statute S80. Here too there is an equilibrium in which the statute passes in the democratic legislature with an infinitesimally small bribe, when the autocrat would do it only for a large bribe.

It is often said that autocratic rulers are more corrupt than democratic ones because the former do not have to worry about re-election. (This is not quite true as elections have become very expensive, and to dispense favors in exchange for campaign contributions is a major source of corruption in democratic regimes.) In the example above, the cost of corruption is deliberately kept the same for both autocratic and democratic governments, and yet the equilibrium bribe amount is larger under the former. The essential problem is due to an externality that each democratic legislator's vote potentially imposes on every other legislator, when they cannot coordinate their votes to demand a bribe which compensates them for that externality. In some actual democratic polities, of course, such coordination problems are reduced by committee systems, disciplined factions and party political machines.[4] It is reported that in the past few decades Japan's Liberal Democratic Party (particularly its so-called Policy Affairs Research Council, where important policies were made and payoffs were coordinated behind closed doors) has been quite successful in centralizing bribery and raking off billions of dollars' worth in the process.

III. The Growth Process

Corruption has its adverse effects not just on static efficiency but also on investment and growth. A payment of bribes to get an investment license clearly reduces the incentive to invest (even apart from affecting the composition of investment, in view of the considerations of secrecy and uncertainty alluded to in the previous section). One might add that in the taxation system of many countries, negative profits (losses) can be deducted from taxable investment income, but there is no corresponding loss offset in the case of bribes, so that the latter are particularly harmful for risk-taking in the context of innovation.

Similarly, when public resources meant for building productivity-enhancing infrastructure are diverted for politicians' private consumption (cement for public roads or dams used for luxury homes) growth rates obviously will be affected adversely. Another growth effect follows from the fact that higher bribes imply declining profitability on productive investments relative to rent-seeking investments, thus tending to crowd out the former. As Kevin Murphy, Shleifer, and Vishny (1993) point out, there are many reasons why there are increasing returns to rent-seeking, so that an increase in rent-seeking lowers the cost of further rent-seeking relative to that of productive investment. In general when there is slow growth the returns to entrepreneurship (particularly in production of new goods) fall relative to those to rent-seeking, and the ensuing increase in the pace of rent-seeking activities further slows down growth. Besides, innovators are particularly at the mercy of corrupt public officials, because new producers need government-supplied goods like permits and licenses more than established producers. In any case, as Romer (1994) has suggested, corruption as a tax on *ex post* profits may in general stifle entry of new goods or technology which require an initial fixed cost investment.

Some of these growth effects have been statistically corroborated from cross-country data. On the basis of corruption rankings data assembled from the Business International correspondents[5] in 70 countries in the early 1980s. . . . Paolo Mauro (1995) finds a significant negative association between the corruption index and the investment rate or the rate of growth (even after controlling for some other determinants of the latter, and correcting for a possible endogeneity bias in the data). A one-standard-deviation improvement in the corruption index is estimated to be associated with an increase in the investment rate by about 3 percent of GDP. The negative relation seems to hold even in subsamples of countries where bureaucratic regulations are reported to be cumbersome, indicating that corruption as a way of by-passing these regulations may not have been very beneficial.

Historians, of course, point to many cases when a great deal of corruption in dispensing licenses, or loans, or mining and land concessions has been associated with (and may have even helped in) the emergence of an entrepreneurial class. In European history the latter class grew out of the sales of monopoly rights, tax farms, and other forms of privileged access to public resources. In the U.S. "gilded age" of [the] 1860s and 1870s widespread corruption of state legislatures and city governments by business interests and those seeking franchises for public utilities is reported to have helped rather than hindered economic growth.[6] More generally, corruption may have historically played some role in undermining the sway of collective passions that used to fuel internecine group warfare. As Ronald Wraith and Edgar Simpkins (1963, p. 60) say of English history: "For two hundred and fifty years before 1688, Englishmen had been killing each other to obtain power. . . . The settlements of 1660 and 1688 inaugurated the Age of Reason, and substituted a system of patronage, bribery, and corruption for the previous method of bloodletting." In this century, the highly corrupt system institutionalized in the PRI enabled Mexico to transcend the decade of bloodletting that followed the Revolution. Without denying the positive role that corruption may have played in history in some situations, in many developing countries today, however, corruption is perceived to be so pervasive and endemic that it is unlikely to have good net effects, on grounds that we have discussed earlier in this section and because corruption tends to feed on itself (as we shall discuss in the next section) and it is impossible to confine corruption to areas, if any, of relative beneficial effects.

What about the effects of the growth process on the extent of corruption? Although the requisite time-series evidence in terms of hard data is absent, circumstantial evidence suggests that over the last 100 years or so corruption has generally declined with economic growth in most rich countries (and in some developing countries, like Singapore, it is reported to have declined quite fast in recent decades). While the historical relationship between economic growth and corruption is thus likely to have been negative in general, it is possible to envisage some non-linearities in this relationship: in particular, in some countries with the process of modernization and growth corruption may have got worse for some time before getting better. What kind of forces work toward possibly increasing corruption at the earlier stages of economic growth? As the economy expands and becomes more complex, public officials see more opportunities for making money from their decisions, which now go beyond simple functions like maintaining law and order and collecting land revenue. As the markets in many new products are "thin" for quite some time, this gives scope for those officials to milk the process of granting monopoly rights and franchises. In the process of transition from controlled to market economy in Eastern Europe, China, and Vietnam it has often been observed that there are some special factors increasing corruption even as income grows. For a considerable period of time the transition economy is on a dual-track system: a part of output is still under obligatory delivery at controlled prices, while the rest is allowed to be sold at market prices. This creates all kinds of new opportunities for corruption. The process of

privatization of state-owned enterprises in many countries has also given rise
to opportunities for public officials to get kickbacks from "crony capitalist"
buyers of those enterprises and contractors.

Yet, it is probably correct to say that the process of economic growth
ultimately generates enough forces to reduce corruption. Rewards to entrepreneurship and productive investment relative to rent-seeking investment
rise when there is sustained growth. A prospering economy can also afford to
pay its civil servants well, reducing their motivation for corruption. And to
the extent prosperity in the long run brings more demand, at least on the part
of the middle classes, for democratic reforms, the latter may install institutions that check corruption. Not merely is the coordination problem in bribe-
collection among legislators rendered more difficult under democracy, as we
have discussed at the end of the preceding section, but, more important,
democratic institutions build mechanisms of accountability and transparency
at different levels which make it difficult for the networks of corruption to be
sustained for long. A qualifier to this argument relates, as we have noted
before, to campaign finance in democratic elections which leads to influence
peddling on the part of politicians. Thus while rich democracies have been
quite successful in better *enforcement* of laws, they have been in some cases
less successful in reducing the influence of money on the process of *enactment* of those laws.

IV. Factors Behind Differential Incidence and Persistence

We now turn to the question of why the incidence of corruption is so
palpably different in different countries and the related question of why in
some cases corruption is so persistent. Liberal economists, of course, have an
easy answer to this: it is the regulatory state with its elaborate system of
permits and licenses that spawns corruption, and different countries with
different degrees of insertion of the regulatory state in the economy give rise
to varying amounts of corruption. This explanation is no doubt valid to a
large extent, but inadequate. It cannot, for example, explain why corruption,
in the judgment of many perceptive observers, may have increased in post-
Communist Russia or in China after the onset of the market reforms in recent
years ... [and] it cannot explain why corruption is supposed to be so much
more in Mexico than in, say, South Korea or Taiwan in the early 1980s
(when in the latter countries the state was not much less interventionist than
in Mexico).

Another common explanation of differential corruption, popular among
sociologists, is that social norms are very different in different countries.
What is regarded in one culture as corrupt may be considered a part of
routine transaction in another. (Visiting Westerners are often aghast that an
Asian or an African will sometimes not carry out his ordinary service without

baksheesh or tips; the latter, on the other hand, finds the high degree of monetization even in personal transactions in advanced capitalist countries somehow "corrupt.") But a more important issue is involved. It is widely recognized that in developing countries gift-exchange is a major social norm in business transactions, and allegiance to kinship-based or clan-based loyalties often takes precedence over public duties even for salaried public officials. Under such circumstances use of public resources to cater to particularistic loyalties become quite common and routinely expected. At the same time, it will be wrong to suggest that concern about public corruption is peculiarly Western. In most of the same developing countries, public opinion polls indicate that corruption is usually at the top of the list of problems cited by respondents. But there is a certain schizophrenia in this voicing of concern: the same people who are most vocal and genuinely worried about widespread corruption and fraud in the public arena do not hesitate at all in abusing public resources when it comes to helping out people belonging to their own kinship network. (It is a bit like the U.S. Congressmen who are usually livid about the rampant pork-barrel politics they see all around them but they will fiercely protect the "pork" they bring to their own constituency.) Edward C Banfield (1958) comments on the prevalence of what he calls "amoral familism" in the Mezzogiorno in Italy, but Robert Putnam (1993) observes in his study of comparative civicness in the regions of Italy that the amoral individuals in the less civic regions clamor most for sterner law enforcement. Mayfair Yang (1989) notes how people in China generally condemn the widespread use of *guanxi* (connections) in securing public resources, but at the same time admire the ingenuity of individual exploits among their acquaintances in its use.

A major problem with norm-based explanations is that they can very easily be near-tautological ("a country has more corruption because its norms are more favorable to corruption"). A more satisfactory explanation on these lines has to go into how otherwise similar countries (or regions in the same country like North and South in Italy) may settle with different social norms in equilibrium in, say, a repeated game framework, and how a country may sometimes shift from one equilibrium into another (as has happened in the case of today's developed countries in recent history with respect to corruption).

The idea of multiple equilibria in the incidence of corruption is salient in some of the recent economic theorists' explanations. The basic idea is that corruption represents an example of what are called frequency-dependent equilibria, and our expected gain from corruption depends crucially on the number of other people we expect to be corrupt. . . . The problem . . . is that the mechanisms through which the economy reaches one or the other equilibrium are not fully spelled out. There are now several theoretical models in the literature which try to do that rigorously. . . Olivier Cadot (1987) has a mode of corruption as a gamble, where every time an official asks for a bribe in a bilateral situation, there is a risk of being reported to and sacked by a superior officer. The optimal Nash strategy of a corrupt official is derived under alternative assumptions about the information structure. The comparative-static results show that a higher time discount rate, a lower degree of risk-aversion and a lower wage rate will induce him, under certain conditions, to be more corrupt. Then Cadot goes on to introduce corruption also at the level of the superior officer who can be bribed (beyond a certain threshold) to cover up lower-level corruption. The interaction of corruption at different hierarchical levels of administration leads to multiple equilibria (one with only petty corruption and the other with more pervasive corruption), as the probability of being sacked diminishes with the general level of corruption in the civil service, and corruption at each level feeds on the other. In the rent-seeking literature also it has been pointed out by Arye L. Hillman and Eliakim Katz (1987) that there are extra social costs when there is a hierarchical structure such that a lowly customs official is obliged to pay a part of his take of bribes to a superior. The usual presumption of that literature-which is, as we have seen, in any case questionable-that bribes used in contesting a rent do not entail a social cost because they are only transfers, is seriously vitiated when one takes into account multi-tiered rent-seeking, with the official positions to which the bribes accrue themselves contested with real resources.

Andvig and Karl O. Moene (1990) in their model assume, as in Cadot (1987), that the expected punishment for corruption when detected declines as more officials become corrupt, because it is cheaper to be discovered by a corrupt rather than a noncorrupt superior. There is a bell-shaped frequency distribution of officials with respect to their costs of supplying corrupt services. On the demand side the potential bribers' demand for corrupt services decreases as the bribe size increases and as the fraction of officials who are corrupt decreases (raising the search cost for a potential bribee). This model generates two stable stationary equilibria of the Nash type and highlights how the profitability of corruption is positively related to its frequency and how temporary shifts may lead to permanent changes in corruption.

Raaj Sah (1988) has a model of corruption with intertemporal behavioral externalities in the context of overlapping generations and a Bayesian learning process in belief formation. The bureaucrats and citizens both start off with a subjective probability distribution which tells them how likely it is that the agent they will meet in a transaction is corrupt. Corrupt (noncorrupt) agents would prefer meeting agents on the other side of the transaction who are similarly corrupt (noncorrupt). For each corrupt agent they meet, they will revise upwards their subjective probability estimates of meeting corrupt people, and are more likely to initiate a corrupt act in the next period. This is how beliefs about the nature of an economic environment one faces formed on the basis of one's past experience of dealing with that environment feed into the perpetuation of a culture of corruption. Again, there are multiple equilibria and two economies with an identical set of parameters can have significantly different levels of corruption; the particular steady state to which the economy settles is influenced by the history of the economy preceding the steady state.

Sah's model admits the possibility that sometimes there may be discrepancies between beliefs about corruption frequency and its actual incidence. Philip Oldenburg's (1987) account of the land consolidation program in villages in [Uttar Pradesh] in Northern India provides an interesting case study in this context. A land consolidation program involves a major reorganization of the mapping of the existing cultivation plots, their valuation and carving out of new plots in a village, and thus provides a lot of scope for corruption for the petty officials in charge. But Oldenburg's field investigations found very little evidence of actual *official* corruption. Complaints of corruption usually came from farmers who had not got precisely what they wanted, and did not understand the process fully, and so assumed that other farmers who in their perception did better must have bribed to get their way. Bribes were often paid to a middleman, who pocketed the money while telling the villagers that it was primarily meant to bribe the Assistant Consolidation Officer. (He even made a show of paying a visit to the Officer.) There may actually be more corruption in other cases, but Oldenburg makes a valid point that the middlemen in general have a vested interest in spreading (dis)information that "nothing gets done without bribing the Officials," and when everybody believes that, it may even have the effect of inducing an official to indulge in corruption, as he is assumed to be corrupt anyway. This is a familiar self-fulfilling equilibrium of corruption.[7] (The middleman's role in corruption is similar to what Diego Gambetta (1988, p. 173) observes in his study of the Italian Mafia: "the mafioso himself has an interest in *regulated injections of distrust* into the market to increase the demand for the product he sells-that is, protection.")

In an overlapping generations framework with dynamic complementarity between past and future reputation Jean Tirole (1996) has argued that the persistence of corruption in a society may be explained partly by the bad collective reputation of previous generations: younger generations may inherit the reputation of their elders with the consequence that they may have no incentive to be honest themselves. This means, if for some temporary reasons (say, due to a war or some other disruption in the economic system) corruption in an economy increases, it has lasting effects: collective reputation once shattered is difficult to rebuild. Similarly, a one-shot reduction in corruption (through, say, an anti-corruption campaign) may have no lasting effect: it may take a minimum number of periods without corruption to return to a path leading to the low-corruption steady state.

We have discussed in this section the reasons for the persistence of corruption that have to do with frequency-dependent equilibria or intertemporal externalities. Let us end it by referring to a simpler reason for persistence in the case of some types of corruption. There are many cases where corruption is mutually beneficial between the official and his client, so neither the briber nor the bribee has an incentive to report or protest, for example, when a customs officer lets contraband through, or a tax auditor purposely overlooks a case of tax evasion, and so on. Shleifer and Vishny (1993) call it corruption with theft (a better name may be collusive corruption), to distinguish it from cases where the official does not hide the transaction in which the client pays the requisite price, fee, or fine to the government, but only charges something extra for himself, what Shleifer and Vishny call corruption without theft. The former type is more insidious, difficult to detect and therefore more persistent. One should add that this type also includes many cases of official relaxation of quality control standards, in inspection of safety in construction of buildings and bridges or in supplies of food and drugs, in pollution control, etc. . . .

References

Adams, Gordon. *The iron triangle: The politics of defense contracting.* New Brunswick: Transaction Books, 1981.

Andvig, Jens Christopher. "The Economics of Corruption: A Survey," *Studi Economici,* 1991, 43, pp. 57–94.

Andvig, J. C,. and Moene, Karl Ove. "How Corruption May Corrupt," *J. Econ. Behav. Organ.*, Jan.1990, *13*(1), pp. 63–76.

Banerjee, Abhijit. "A Theory of Misgovernance." Working Paper. MIT Economics Dept., 1994.

Banfield, Edward C. *The moral basis of a backward society.* New York: Free Press, 1958.

Beck, Paul J. and Maher, Michael W. "A Comparison of Bribery and Bidding in Thin Markets," *Econ. Letters,* 1986, *20*, pp. 1-5.

Boycko, Maxim; Shleifer, Andrei; and Vishny, Robert. *Privatizing Russia.* Cambridge, MA: MIT Press, 1995.

Cadot, Olivier. "Corruption as a Gamble," *J. Public Econ.*, July 1987, *33*(2), pp. 223–44.

Gambetta, Diego. "Mafia: The Price of Distrust," in *Trust making and breaking cooperative relations.* Ed.: Diego Gambetta. Oxford: Blackwell, 1988, pp. 158–75.

Hillman, Arye L. and Katz, Eliakim, "Hierarchical Structure and the Social Costs of Bribes and Transfers," *J. Public Econ.*, Nov. 1987, *34*(2), pp. 129–42.

Huntington, Samuel P. *Political order in changing societies.* New Haven: Yale U. Press, 1968.

Kangle, R. P. *The Kautiliya Arthasastra, Part II.* Bombay: U. of Bombay, 1972.

Krueger, Anne O. "The Political Economy of the Rent-Seeking Society," *Amer. Econ. Rev.*, June 1974, *64*(3), pp. 291–303.

Leff, Nathaniel H. "Economic Development through Bureaucratic Corruption." *The American Behavioral Scientist*, Nov. 1964, *8*(2), pp. 8–14.

Lien, Donald H. D. "A Note on Competitive Bribery Games," *Econ. Letters*, 1986, *22*, pp. 337–41.

Lui, Francis T. "An Equilibrium Queuing Model of Bribery," *J. Polit. Econ.*, Aug. 1985, *93*(4), pp. 760–81.

Mauro, Paolo. "Corruption and Growth," *Quart. J. Econ.*. Aug.1995, *110*(93), pp. 681–712.

Murphy, Kevin M.; Shleifer, Andrei; and Vishny, Robert W. "Why Is Rent-Seeking So Costly to Growth?" *Amer. Econ. Rev.*, May 1993, *83*(2), pp. 409–14.

Myrdal, Gunnar. *Asian drama.* Vol. II. New York: Random House, 1968.

Oldenburg, Philip. "Middlemen in Third-World Corruption," *World Politics*, 1987, *39*, pp. 508–35.

Olson, Mancur. "Dictatorship, Democracy, and Development," *Amer. Polit. Sci. Rev.*, Sept. 1993, *87*(3), pp. 567–75.

Putnam, Robert D. *Making democracy work: Civic traditions in modern Italy.* Princeton: Princeton U. Press, 1993.

Rasmusen, Eric and Ramseyer, J. Mark. "Cheap Bribes and the Corruption Ban: A Coordination Game among Rational Legislators," *Public Choice*, Mar. 1994, *78*(3–4), pp. 305–27.

Romer, Paul. "New Goods, Old Theory, and the Welfare Costs of Trade Restrictions," *J. Develop. Econ.*, Feb.1994, *43*(1), pp. 5–38.

Rose-Ackerman, Susan. *Corruption: A study in political economy.* New York: Academic Press, 1978.

———. "When is Corruption Harmful?" Working Paper. The World Bank, 1996.

Sah, Raaj Kumar. "Persistence and Pervasiveness of Corruption: New Perspectives." Yale Economic Growth Center Discussion Paper: 560, 48, Aug.1988.

Shleifer, Aandrei and Vishny, Robert W. "Corruption," *Quart. J. Econ.*, Aug. 1993, *108*(3), pp. 599–617.

Theobald, Robin. *Corruption. development, and underdevelopment.* Durham, NC: Duke U. Press, 1990.

Tirole, Jean. "A Theory of Collective Reputations," *Rev. Econ. Stud.*, Jan. 1996, *63*(1), pp. 1–22.

Tullock, Gordon. "Rent-Seeking as a Negative-Sum Game," in *Toward a theory of the rent-seeking society.* Eds.: James M. Buchanan, Robert D. Tollison, and Gordon Tullock. College Station: Texas A&M U. Press, 1980, pp.16–36.

———. "The Costs of Special Privilege," in *Perspectives on positive political economy.* Eds.: James E. Alt and Kenneth A. Shepsle. Cambridge and New York: Cambridge U. Press, 1990, pp. 195–211.

Wraith, Ronald E. and Simkins, Edgar. *Corruption in developing countries.* London: Allen and Unwin, 1963.

Yang, Mayfair Mei-Hui. "The Gift Economy and State Power in China," *Comparative Studies in Society and History,* Jan.1989, *31*(1), pp. 25–54.

Notes

I am grateful for useful comments on earlier drafts from Jean-Claude Berthelemy, Andrew Goudie, Mancur Olson, Dani Rodrik, Susan Rose-Ackerman, and Andrei Shleifer. The first draft of the paper was written for and presented at a meeting of the OECD Development Center, Paris.

1. As Gordon Adams (1981, p. 177) notes, the U.S. Department of Defense directive 55007 allows gratuities when they are a part of a "customary exchange of social amenities between personal friends and relatives when motivated by such relationships and extended on a personal basis."

2. For an account of many such harmful effects of corruption, see Rose-Ackerman (1996).
3. Abhijit Banerjee (1994) examines situations where bureaucrats create red tape and use it to screen clients of different types.
4. Rose-Ackerman (1978) has noted that well-organized legislators may he able to extort larger amounts than disorganized legislators.
5. One problem with this data set is that it is based on the perception of foreign businessmen whose experience of corruption may be different from what domestic businessmen face in a country. The former may have less insider knowledge about the intricacies of the indigenous bureaucracy and even less patience with its slow processes. So they may end up paying much bigger bribes than what the latter settle for at the end of long negotiations and endless cups of coffee in familiar terrain. This discrepancy may vary from country to country and thus bias the results of statistical analysis on the basis of this data set.
6. See Robin Theobald (1990) for a discussion.
7. Myrdal (1968, pp. 408–09) quotes Prime Minister Nehru: "Merely shouting from the housetops that everybody is corrupt creates an atmosphere of corruption. People feel they live in a climate of corruption and they get corrupted themselves."

20

The Effects of Corruption on
Growth and Public Expenditure

Paolo Mauro[1]

I. Introduction

The study of the causes and consequences of corruption has a long history in economics, dating back at least to the seminal contributions to the rent-seeking literature by Bhagwati (1982), Krueger (1974), Rose-Ackerman (1978), Tullock (1967) and others. However, related empirical work has been rather limited, partly because the degree of efficiency of government institutions cannot easily be quantified. Corruption in particular is a difficult phenomenon to measure, owing to its very nature.

Renewed interest in the topic has recently led a number of researchers to attempt to quantify the extent to which corruption permeates economic interactions by using indices sold by private rating agencies. These indices are typically based on the replies to standardized questionnaires by consultants located in a variety of countries, and therefore have the obvious drawback of being subjective. Nevertheless, the correlation between indices produced by different rating agencies is very high, suggesting that there seems to be a certain consensus among observers on the ranking of countries according to their degree of corruption.. . .

At the same time, the consultants who produce these indices may sometimes be influenced in their judgment by the economic performance of the countries that they monitor. Thus, when using such indices to analyze the relationship between corruption and economic variables, it is important to be extremely cautious before interpreting correlations in a causal sense. . . . An additional drawback of the indicators of corruption that are currently available is that they do not distinguish among the various types of corruption, such as, for example, high-level versus low-level corruption,[2] or well-organized versus poorly-organized corruption.[3] In spite of these limitations, the indices provide a wealth of information that has enabled researchers to obtain a number of interesting results.

This paper has two main goals. The first one is to list a number of possible causes and consequences of corruption, with emphasis on those links that have been, or at least in principle could be, investigated through the use of cross-country regression analysis. In doing so, it provides a synthetic review of recent studies that make use of cross-country regressions on corruption. While data limitations imply that the empirical work is subject to a number of difficulties, these studies provide tentative evidence that corruption may have considerable, adverse effects on economic performance, suggesting that it is important for policy makers to pay attention to this phenomenon. More interestingly, the identification of possible causes of corruption may suggest a number of ways in which attempts could be made to curb it. While in some cases the distinction between causes and consequences is rather blurred, there are cases in which the importance of the direction of causality should not be overstated in the process of drawing possible policy conclusions.. . .

The second goal of this paper is to present further results on the effects of corruption on investment and economic growth by using a larger data set to expand the analysis of Mauro (1995), and to present new evidence on the relationship between corruption and the composition of government expenditure. Even though the results need to be interpreted with caution, corruption is found to lower investment and economic growth, and to alter the composition of government expenditure, specifically by reducing the share of spending on education . . . .

II. Causes and Consequences of Corruption—A Synthetic Survey

A. Causes of Corruption

In the original literature on rent-seeking, the existence of rents (typically, governmentinduced ones) constitutes the ultimate source of rent-seeking behavior. Building upon these theoretical contributions, recent empirical studies analyze the possible causes of corruption by regressing indices of corruption on potential explanatory variables.

A number of possible causes of corruption are related to the extent of government intervention in the economy, and—more generally—to variables (such as the level of import tariffs or civil service wages) that are determined by government policy. When pervasive regulations exist and government officials have an excessive degree of discretion in applying them, private parties may be willing to pay bribes to government officials in order to obtain any rents that the regulations may generate. Identification of such policy-induced sources of corruption is obviously helpful in bringing it under control. The following are some of the sources of corruption that have been identified in the literature.

- The original rent-seeking literature emphasizes trade restrictions as the prime example of government-induced sources of rents (Krueger, 1974). For example, in the presence of quantitative restrictions on imports of a certain good, the necessary import licenses are very valuable and importers may be willing to bribe the relevant official in order to obtain them. More generally, protection of home industries from international competition generates rents that local entrepreneurs may be willing to pay for, in the form of bribes. Ades and Di Tella (1994) find that a higher degree of openness of the economy (measured on the basis of the sum of imports and exports as a share of GDP) is significantly associated with lower corruption.
- Government subsidies (including tax expenditures) can constitute sources of rents, as argued by Clements, Hugounenq and Schwartz (1995). Ades and Di Tella (1995) explain corruption as a function of industrial policy, showing that subsidies to manufacturing as a proportion of GDP are related to corruption indices.
- Price controls . . . are also a potential source of rents, and of the ensuing rent-seeking behavior. For example, entrepreneurs may be willing to bribe government officials to maintain the provision of inputs at below-market prices.
- Similarly, multiple exchange rate practices and foreign exchange allocation schemes . . . lead to rents. For example, supposing that, in a given country, state-owned commercial banks conduct rationing of foreign exchange by allocating it according to the priorities established by each bank manager, then entrepreneurs may be willing to pay bribes in order to obtain the necessary foreign exchange to purchase their imported inputs.
- Low wages in the civil service relative to private sector wages or per capita GDP are also a potential source of (low-level) corruption, following efficiency-wage mechanisms (Kraay and Van Rijckeghem, 1995, and Haque and Sahay, 1996). When civil service pay is too low, civil servants may be obliged to use their positions to collect bribes as a way of making ends meet, and in any case their expected cost of being caught and fired is correspondingly low. It might be useful to take such considerations into account when faced with difficult tradeoffs on

whether an excessive civil service wage bill should be lowered through cutting salaries or through reducing the number of staff. . . .

At the same time, there are a number of other sources of rents that are not due to government policy. In their presence, policy makers need to be alert to the fact that rentseeking behavior may be more likely to arise. Furthermore, attempts to evaluate the effects of certain aspects of government policy on corruption need to take these other factors into account. The following are some of these additional causes of corruption.

* Natural-resource endowments constitute a textbook example of sources of rents, since they can typically be sold at a price that far exceeds their cost of extraction. Sachs and Warner (1995) argue that resource-rich economies may be more likely to be subject to extreme rent-seeking behavior than resource-poor economies are . . .
* Finally, sociological factors may contribute to creating an environment in which the availability of rents is more likely to result in rent-seeking behavior. Shleifer and Vishny (1993) suggest that countries where the population consists of several different ethnic groups are more likely to be characterized by a less organizedand therefore more deleterioustype of corruption. This hypothesis is used in Mauro (1995), where it is found that an index of ethnolinguistic fractionalization is correlated with corruption. Tanzi (1994) argues that public officials are more likely to do favors to their relatives in societies where family ties are strong.

B. Consequences of Corruption

Corruption has a number of adverse consequences that economists and policy makers are concerned about. In particular, recent empirical evidence seems to suggest that corruption lowers economic growth. There is a wide range of channels through which this may happen.
* In the presence of corruption, entrepreneurs are aware that a portion of the proceeds from their investments may be claimed by corrupt officials. Payment of bribes is often required up front if the necessary permits are to be issued. Therefore, corruption may be interpreted to act as a tax—though of a particularly pernicious nature, given the need for secrecy and the uncertainty that come with it—which correspondingly reduces incentives to invest. Mauro (1995) provides tentative empirical evidence that corruption lowers investment and economic growth. The magnitudes of these effects are considerable: a one standard-deviation improvement in corruption indices drawn from Business International (BI) causes investment to rise by 5 percent of GDP and the annual per capita GDP growth rate to rise by half a percentage point. The evidence

seems to suggest that a large portion of the effects on economic growth takes place through the effects on investment. Using indices from the *International Country Risk Guide* (ICRG), Keefer and Knack (1994) obtain broadly similar results and, in their estimates, institutional variables have a significant direct effect on growth in addition to the indirect effect through investment.[4] . . .

- Murphy, Shleifer and Vishny (1991) argue that in situations where rent-seeking provides more lucrative opportunities than productive work does, the allocation of talent will be worse: the more talented and highly educated individuals will be more likely to engage in rent-seeking than in productive work, with adverse consequences on their country's growth rate.

- The possibility that corruption might reduce the effectiveness of aid flows, through the diversion of funds, is of particular relevance to developing countries. The vast literature on aid flows has addressed the question of whether the fungibility of aid resources may imply that aid flows ultimately finance unproductive public expenditures. Perhaps as a result of this ongoing debate, many donor countries have focused increasingly on issues of good governance, and in some cases where governance is judged to be very poor, some donors have scaled back their assistance . . .

- Corruption may also bring about loss of tax revenue when it takes the form of tax evasion or the improper use of discretionary tax exemptions. Strictly speaking, these phenomena fall under the definition of corruption only when there is a counterpart payment to the tax official responsible.

- By affecting tax collection or the level of public expenditure, corruption may lead to adverse budgetary consequences. Alternatively, in the case where it takes the form of the improper use of directed lending at below-market interest rates by public sector financial institutions, corruption may result in an undesirable monetary stance.

- The allocation of public procurement contracts through a corrupt system may lead to lower quality of public infrastructure and services. For example, corrupt bureaucrats could allow the use of cheap materials in the construction of buildings or bridges that would subsequently collapse.

- Finally, corruption may affect the composition of government expenditure, a possibility that the empirical section of this paper focuses on. Corrupt government officials may be more likely to choose to undertake types of government expenditure that allow them to collect bribes and to maintain them secret. Shleifer and Vishny (1993) suggest that large projects on specialized items—whose exact value is difficult to monitor—lead to more lucrative opportunities for corruption. More generally, opportunities for levying bribes may be expected to be more abundant on items produced by firms operating in oligopolistic markets, where rents are available. A priori, one might expect that it is easier to collect substantial bribes on large infrastructure projects or high-technology defense equipment than on textbooks and teachers' salaries. For example, Hines (1995) argues that international trade in military aircraft is particularly susceptible to corruption. In other areas, such as health, the picture is less clear-cut: opportunities to collect bribes may be abundant in the case of hospital buildings and state-of-the-art medical equipment, but may be more limited in the case of doctors' and nurses' salaries. Previous empirical work on the potential links between corruption and the composition of government expenditure is extremely limited. Among the few contributions, Rauch (1993) analyzes both the determinants and the effects of government expenditure composition by using a data set on U.S. cities. He finds that the wave of municipal reform that took place during the Progressive Era increased the share of total municipal expenditure allocated to road and sewer investment, which in turn increased the growth in city manufacturing employment . . .

III. Empirical Results

A. Description of the Data

This paper uses the (simple) indices of corruption drawn from two private firms:

(1) *Political Risk Services, Inc.*, which publishes the *International Country Risk Guide*, used and described in detail by Keefer and Knack (1995). The index used in this paper, which was compiled by the IRIS Center (University of Maryland), is the 1982-1995 average and is available for over a hundred countries.

(2) *Business International* (now incorporated into *The Economist Intelligence Unit*), for which the full data set used in this paper is provided, together with a more complete description, in Mauro (1995). The index is the 1980–83 average and is available for 67 countries.

Both indices are on a scale from 0 (most corrupt) to 10 (least corrupt), with similar distributions. The corruption index used in this paper's empirical analysis is the simple average of the two above indices, when both are available.[5] The two indices are very strongly correlated (r=0.81). At the same time, it may be argued that the process of averaging helps reduce the errors in each individual index. There are 106 observations in the Barro (1991) sample for which the overall corruption index is available. The sample statistics are as follows: mean = 5.85, standard deviation = 2.38, minimum = 0.59, maximum = 10 . . .

B. The Effects of Corruption on Investment and Economic Growth

. . . [T]his section provide[s] further evidence that corruption may affect investment and economic growth. A univariate regression of the 1960–85 average investment rate on the corruption index shows that the association between these variables is significant at the conventional levels (table 20.1a, column 1). This is also the case for a univariate regression of the 1960–85 average annual per capita GDP growth on the corruption index (table 20.1b, column 1). The magnitude of the effects is considerable: a one-standard-deviation (2.38) improvement in the corruption index is associated with over a 4 percentage point increase in its investment rate and over a 1/2 percentage point increase in the annual growth rate of per capita GDP. This means that if a given country were to improve its corruption "grade" from a "6 out of 10" to an "8 out of 10", then its investment/GDP ratio would rise by almost 4 percentage points and its annual per capita GDP growth would rise by almost half a percentage point.

The estimated coefficients become even larger when two-stage least squares techniques, with the index of ethnolinguistic fractionalization as an instrument, are used to address possible endogeneity bias (table 20.1a, column 2, and table 20.1b, column 2). The relationships continue to be significant even in multivariate regressions that take into account the effects of other standard

Table 20.1a
The Effects of Corruption on Investment (as a ratio to GDP, 1960–85 average)

Independent Variable	(1)	(2)	(3)	(4)
Constant	0.0780	-0.0025	0.1226	0.0543
	(4.19)	(-0.05)	(3.66)	(0.47)
Corruption index	0.0187	0.0320	0.0095	0.0281
	(7.03)	(3.93)	(2.09)	(0.99)
Per capita GDP in 1960			-0.0062	-0.0213
			(-0.91)	(-0.96)
Secondary education in 1960			0.1749	0.1241
			(2.95)	(1.21)
Population growth			-0.8226	-1.0160
			(-0.82)	(-1.05)
Estimation method	OLS	2SLS	OLS	2SLS
R^2	0.32	(*)	0.44	(*)

Table 20.1b
The Effects of Corruption on GDP Growth (per capita, 1960–85 average)

Independent Variable	(1)	(2)	(3)	(4)	(5)
Constant	0.0035	-0.0284	0.0012	-0.0404	-0.0012
	(0.85)	(-2.12)	(1.50)	(-0.81)	(-0.16)
Corruption index	0.0029	0.0081	0.0038	0.0175	0.0028
	(4.74)	(3.61)	(2.95)	(1.40)	(2.01)
Per capita GDP in 1960			-0.0075	-0.0182	-0.0069
			(-4.49)	(-1.79)	(-4.78)
Secondary education in 1960			0.0401	0.0034	0.0217
			(3.09)	(0.09)	(1.82)
Population growth			-0.4124	-0.5192	-0.3255
			(-1.83)	(-1.29)	(-1.81)
Investment					0.1056
					(3.09)
Estimation method	OLS	2SLS	OLS	2SLS	OLS
R^2	0.14	(*)	0.31	(*)	0.42

Data sources: Barro (1991), Business International, and Political Risk Services/IRIS.

There are 94 observations. The *corruption* index is the simple average of the indices produced by Political Risk Services (compiled by IRIS, for 1982–95) and Business International (for 1980–83). One standard deviation of the *corruption* index equals 2.38. A *high* value of the *corruption* index means that the country has *good* institutions in that respect. White-corrected *t*-statistics are reported in parentheses. *N* is the number of observations. 2SLS indicates that the index of ethnolinguistic fractionalization from Taylor and Hudson (1972) was used as an instrument. (*) The R^2 is not an appropriate measure of goodness of fit with 2SLS.

determinants of investment and growth (table 20.1a, column 3 and table 20.1b, column 3). Also in this case, the magnitude of the coefficients rises when instrumental variables are used for the corruption index (table 20.1a, column 4 and table 20.1b, column 4). Finally, when the investment rate is added to the list of independent variables in the growth regression, the coefficient on the corruption index falls by two thirds (table 20.1b, column 5, compared to table 20.1a, column 3), though it remains just significant at the 5 percent level. This result implies that a large portion of the effects of corruption on economic growth takes place through investment, though it leaves open the possibility that some of the effects take place directly, rather than through the investment rate . . .

C. The Effects of Corruption on the Composition of Government Expenditure

This section analyzes the potential effects of corruption on the composition of government expenditure, a previously unexplored issue at least in the context of cross-country work. It asks whether corrupt politicians choose to spend more on those components of public expenditure on which it is easier to levy bribes. The Appendix derives a generalization of the Barro (1990) model that shows that if corruption acted simply as though it were a tax on income, then the amount and composition of government expenditure would be independent of corruption. As a consequence, it seems reasonable to interpret any empirical relationships between corruption indices and particular components of government spending as tentative evidence that the way in which corrupt bureaucrats obtain revenue is not simply as a proportion of total income, but rather, that bribes can be more efficiently collected on some government expenditure components than on others.

The question whether corruption affects the composition of government expenditure is an interesting one to consider because, even though the empirical literature has so far yielded mixed results on the effects of government expenditure and, in particular, its composition, on economic growth, most economists seem to think that the level and type of spending undertaken by governments do matter for economic performance. For example, even though cross-country regression work has not conclusively shown a relationship between government spending on education and economic growth, it has gathered fairly robust evidence that school enrollment rates (Levine and Renelt, 1992) and educational attainment (Barro, 1992) play a considerable role in determining economic growth.

Perhaps part of the reason why it has proved difficult to find significant and robust effects of the composition of government expenditure on economic growth is that the quality of the available data may be relatively low, both because it is difficult to ensure that all countries apply the same criteria in allocating projects among the various categories of government expenditure and because each public expenditure component presumably contains both productive and unproductive projects. The relatively noisy quality of the expenditure data implies that the nature of this study must necessarily be exploratory, and that a priori it is not very likely that significant relationships can be found. In spite of such data limitations, this section presents new, tentative evidence that corrupt governments may display predatory behavior in choosing the composition of government expenditure. Specifically, government spending on education seems to be negatively affected by corruption.

Table 20.2 analyzes the relationship between each component of public expenditure (as a ratio to GDP) reported in the Barro (1991) data set, and the corruption index. Government spending on education as a ratio to GDP is

Table 20.2
Corruption and the Composition of Government Expenditure

Dependent Variable (average 1970-85, in percent of GDP)	Constant	*Corruption* Index	Per capita GDP (1980)	R^2	N
Government Expenditure on Education	0.028 (7.48)	0.0023 (3.97)		0.13	103
Government Consumption Expenditure	0.213 (11.85)	-0.0047 (-1.70)		0.03	106
Government Consumption Expenditure excluding education and defense	0.146 (10.69)	-0.0070 (-3.35)		0.10	93
Government Expenditure on Defense	0.032 (3.64)	0.0004 (0.28)		0.00	93
Government Transfer Payments	-0.039 (-2.22)	0.0208 (7.22)		0.45	73
Social Insurance and Welfare Payments	-0.044 (-4.41)	0.0156 (7.94)		0.48	75
Government Expenditure on Education	0.029 (6.85)	0.0020 (2.20)	0.0003 (0.43)	0.13	103
Government Consumption Expenditure	0.189 (10.20)	0.0052 (1.46)	-0.0094 (-4.88)	0.16	106
Government Consumption Expenditure excluding education and defense	0.116 (7.79)	0.0049 (1.41)	-0.011 (-4.54)	0.25	93
Government Expenditure on Defense	0.030 (2.25)	0.0009 (0.25)	-0.0004 (-0.17)	0.00	93
Government Transfer Payments	0.013 (0.78)	0.0001 (0.03)	0.018 (5.60)	0.64	73
Social Insurance and Welfare Payments	-0.015 (-1.70)	0.0041 (1.64)	0.010 (4.47)	0.59	75

Data sources: Barro (1991), Business International, and Political Risk Services/IRIS.

The *corruption* index is the simple average of the indices produced by Political Risk Services (compiled by IRIS, for 1982-95) and Business International (for 1980-83). One standard deviation of the *corruption* index equals 2.38. A *high* value of the *corruption* index means that the country has *good* institutions in that respect. White-corrected *t*-statistics are reported in parentheses. N is the number of observations.

negatively and significantly correlated with corruption. The magnitude of the coefficient is considerable: a one-standard-deviation improvement in the corruption index is associated with an increase in government spending on education by around half a percent of GDP. Taken at face value, this result implies that if a given country were to improve its "grade" on corruption from—say—a "6 out of 10" to a "8 out of 10", on average its government would increase its spending on education by about half a percent of GDP. Figure 1 shows that this result is not just driven by a small group of countries.

Other components of government expenditure (though interestingly, not total government consumption expenditure) are also significantly associated with the corruption index at the conventional levels, most notably in the case of transfer payments, and social insurance and welfare payments. However, it is important to take into account the well-known empirical observation that government expenditure as a ratio to GDP tends to rise as a country becomes richer—a relationship known as Wagner's law. When the level of per capita income in 1980 is used as an additional explanatory variable, education turns out to be the only component of public spending whose association with the corruption index remains significant at the 95 percent level. The magnitude of the coefficient remains broadly the same as in the univariate regression. . . .

Overall, it seems that there is suggestive, though by no means conclusive, evidence that corruption is negatively associated with government expenditure on education and possibly on health. Even though there are indications that the direction of the causal link may be at least in part from corruption to the composition of spending, the issue of the direction of causality remains somewhat unresolved. At the same time, the extent to which potential policy conclusions depend on the direction of causality should not be overstated.

IV. The Direction of Causality: Is It Relevant for Policy?

While [our] review of the literature has presented the variables that might be related to corruption as though they could unambiguously be categorized as either causes or consequences of it, the direction of causality is rather blurred in some cases. For example, it is not clear whether the existence of regulations may lead bureaucrats to ask for bribes to help entrepreneurs circumvent them, or whether corrupt bureaucrats may be more likely to create regulations. The same is true for the empirical relationship that this paper focuses on: just as the existence of corruption may cause a less-than-optimal composition of government expenditure, it may be the case that high government spending on items where monitoring is difficult causes opportunities for corruption. The empirical section of this paper has made some attempts to identify the correct direction of the causal links, but the issue of causality has not been fully resolved, and perhaps it is unlikely to be even with further research, since causality may well operate in both directions.

In general, the direction of causality has important implications for policy prescriptions, but in some cases policy conclusions are not entirely dependent on it. With reference to the specific case of the composition of government spending, it seems that the observed *correlation* between corruption and the composition of government expenditure may constitute sufficient grounds to consider whether it might be desirable to encourage governments to allocate a larger proportion of their spending to those items that are less susceptible to corruption, subject to the following qualifications.

If it is a less-than-optimal composition of government spending causes corruption by creating opportunities for it, then encouraging governments to improve the composition of their spending might be an effective way of reducing corruption. If, on the other hand, corruption causes a less-than-optimal composition of government expenditure, then corrupt governments would attempt to circumvent steps designed to encourage them to spend proportionately more on items that are less susceptible to corruption. In fact, corrupt governments could substitute publicly-unproductive but privately-lucrative projects for publicly-productive but privately-not-lucrative ones *within* a given expenditure category and still be able to show that—say—their share of spending on education has risen. In this second case, would encouraging governments to improve the composition of their spending be an effective way of curbing corruption? The answer hinges on whether, as a practical matter, it is possible to specify the composition of government expenditure in such a way as to make it difficult for corrupt officials to find scope for raising bribes while still appearing to adopt a more desirable composition of government spending.

V. Concluding Remarks

This paper has analyzed a number of causes and consequences of corruption. It has provided a synthetic review of recent studies that estimate empirically some of these links, but several others remain on the agenda for future research. In addition, even though . . . the results must be interpreted with caution, it has presented further evidence that corruption may have considerable, adverse effects economic growth, largely by reducing private investment, but perhaps also through a variety of other channels, which may include a worsening in the composition of public expenditure. More specifically, this paper has presented new, tentative evidence of a negative and significant relationship between corruption and government expenditure on education, which is a reason for concern, since previous literature has shown that educational attainment is an important determinant of economic growth. A possible interpretation of the observed correlation between corruption and government expenditure composition is that corrupt governments find it easier to collect bribes on some expenditure items than on others. While a potential

policy implication might be that it would be desirable to encourage governments to improve the composition of their expenditure, an important issue is
whether, as a practical matter, that composition can be specified in such a
way that corrupt officials would not be able to substitute publicly unproductive but privately lucrative projects *within* the various expenditure categories.

References

Ades, Alberto, and Di Tella, Rafael, 1994, "Competition and Corruption." Institute of
    Economics and Statistics Discussion Papers 169. University of Oxford.
————, 1995, "National Champions and Corruption: Some Unpleasant Competitive-
    ness Arithmetic." University of Oxford. Photocopy.
Barro, Robert, 1992, "Human Capital and Economic Growth." In *Policies for Long-
    Run Economic Growth*. Federal Reserve Bank of Kansas City: 199–216.
————, 1990, "Government Spending in a Simple Model of Endogenous Growth."
    Journal of Political Economy, 98, no. 5, part 2, S103–S125.
Bhagwati, Jagdish, 1982, "Directly Unproductive, Profit-Seeking (DUP) Activities."
    Journal of Political Economy, 90, no. 5.
Clements, Benedict, Réjane Hugounenq, and Gerd Schwartz, 1995, "Government Sub-
    sidies: Concepts, International Trends and Reform Options". IMF Working Pa-
    pers 95/91. Washington, DC: International Monetary Fund.
Easterly, William, 1990, "Endogenous Growth in Developing Countries with
    GovernmentInduced Distortions." In Vittorio Corbo, Stanley Fischer and Steve
    Webb, *Policies to Restore Growth*. Washington DC: The World Bank.
Haque, Nadeem Ul, and Ratna Sahay, 1996, "Do Government Wage Cuts Close
    Budget Deficits?" IMF Working Papers 96/19. Washington, DC: International
    Monetary Fund.
Hines, James, 1995, "Forbidden Payment: Foreign Bribery and American Business."
    NBER Working Papers 5266. Cambridge, MA: National Bureau of Economic
    Research.
Keefer, Philip, and Stephen Knack, 1995, "Institutions and Economic Performance:
    Cross-Country Tests Using Alternative Institutional Measures." *Economics and
    Politics*.
Kraay, Aart, and Van Rijckeghem, Caroline, 1995, "Employment and Wages in the
    Public Sector—A Cross-Country Study." IMF Working Papers 95/70. Washing-
    ton, DC: International Monetary Fund.
Krueger, Anne, 1974, "The Political Economy of the Rent-Seeking Society." *Ameri-
    can Economic Review* 64, no. 3 (June): 291–303.
Levine, Ross and David Renelt, 1992, "A Sensitivity Analysis of Cross-Country Growth
    Regressions." *American Economic Review* 82, no. 4 (September): 942–963.
Loayza, Norman, 1996, "The Economics of the Informal Sector: A Simple Model and
    Some Empirical Evidence from Latin America." The World Bank. Photocopy.
Mauro, Paolo, 1995, "Corruption and Growth." *Quarterly Journal of Economics* CX,
    no. 3 (August): 681–712.
Murphy, Kevin, Andrei Shleifer and Robert Vishny, 1991, "Allocation of Talent:
    Implications for Growth." *Quarterly Journal of Economics*, 106.
Rauch, James, 1995, "Bureaucracy, Infrastructure and Economic Growth: Evidence
    from U.S. Cities During the Progressive Era." *American Economic Review* 85, no.
    4 (September): 968-979.

Rose-Ackerman, Susan, 1978, *Corruption: A Study in Political Economy*, New York, NY: Academic Press.
Sachs, Jeffrey, and Warner, Andrew, 1995, "Natural Resource Abundance and Economic Growth." NBER Working Papers 5398. Cambridge, MA: National Bureau of Economic Research.
Shleifer, Andrei, and Robert Vishny, 1993, "Corruption." *Quarterly Journal of Economics* CIX: 599–617.
Tanzi, Vito, 1994, "Corruption, Governmental Activities and Markets." IMF Working Papers 94/99. Washington, DC: International Monetary Fund.
Taylor, Charles L. and Michael C. Hudson, 1972, *World Handbook of Political and Social Indicators*. Ann Arbor, MI: ICPSR.
Tullock, Gordon, 1967, "The Welfare Costs of Tariffs, Monopolies and Theft." *Western Economic Journal* 5.

Notes

1. Helpful conversations with Andrei Shleifer and Vito Tanzi are gratefully acknowledged. The views expressed here are strictly personal. The author does not necessarily agree with the subjective indices relating to any given country.
2. An example of the former might be the decision by top ministers to purchase an expensive aircraft fighter in order to be able to obtain large bribes, while an example of the latter could be the request for a petty bribe by a public official in order to speed up the issue of a driver's license.
3. Under poorly organized corruption, the required amount and appropriate recipient of a bribe are not clear, and payment does not guarantee that the favor will be actually obtained. The uncertainty that characterizes poorly organized corruption systems makes them even more deleterious (Shleifer and Vishny, 1993).
4. One way in which the growth rate may be affected even for a given investment rate is through changes in the allocation of resources among sectors (Easterly, 1990), and perhaps—more specifically—between the formal and informal sectors (Loayza, 1996).
5. The ICRG index covers all the 106 countries in the sample, while the BI index covers only 67 countries.

21

When is Corruption Harmful?

Susan Rose-Ackerman

Under what conditions is corruption especially harmful and when is it less costly? To consider this question we need to define corruption, to place it in a particular context, and to establish an evaluative standard. By corruption I mean an illegal payment to a public agent to obtain a benefit that may or may not be deserved in the absence of payoffs (Klitgaard 1988, Rose-Ackerman 1978, 1996). The context can range from a low level official accepting a bribe to overlook a traffic ticket or reduce a customs fee to a country's ruler accepting many millions of dollars to favor a particular international firm. . . . I will be considering five types of evaluative standards and will show that even when corruption promotes short-term efficiency in private markets and in bureaucracies, a broader, more long term perspective casts doubt on the normative force of these results. The standards are as follows:

1. Short term efficiency in private markets, holding government policies constant. (When public benefits are scare, do payoffs allocate them to those who value them the most?)
2. Efficient bureaucratic behavior. (Does toleration of corruption improve the efficiency of bureaucrats?)
3. Efficiency and economic growth when the role of the state and the

Source: Susan Rose-Ackerman, Background paper for the World Bank's 1997 World Development Report, *The State in a Changing World*. (New York: Oxford University Press). These arguments and cases are developed in greater detail in Susan Rose-Ackerman, *Corruption and Government*. (Cambridge: Cambridge University Press, 1999).

organization of markets can change over time. (Do payoffs generate incentives to change the rules to create future corrupt incentives, or will payoffs fall as growth proceeds? Does corruption encourage people to spend time in rent seeking instead of productive activity, or is corruption a means for entrepreneurial people to get around rigid rules and undertake growth enhancing projects? Does corruption contribute to capital flight or does it facilitate the influx of foreign investment?)

4. Equity. (Do payoffs create inequities in the distribution of income and wealth, or do they help overcome existing inequities? Under what conditions does corruption have only equity and no efficiency implications?)

5. Political legitimacy. (Does corruption undermine state institutions, or does it help a state to maintain legitimacy so long as political leaders share the wealth?)

. . . I show that, although corruption can be efficient under some quite restrictive assumptions, it is inefficient in many contexts and may also be unfair and undermine state legitimacy. These harmful effects suggest reasons why the macrolevel research shows an adverse effect of growth.

Empirical Regularities

Development economists have long recognized that government policies and institutions matter to growth. For example, according to Howard Pack (1988, p. 343) the pattern of export and import substitution depends on the policy environment. Only 50 percent of the variation in manufacturing value added to total value added is explained by income per capita and population. High levels of protection are frequently associated with substantial rents earned by domestic producers, and successful growth appears to require the state to find a way to mute the opposition of these groups (Pack 1988, p. 349; Olson 1982). Inefficient public enterprises and uneconomic regional development policies depress domestic productivity (Pack 1988, p. 351. p. 353). Industrial licensing schemes may be designed to maintain rents and dampen market discipline (Pack 1988, p. 358) . . . The central issue for research is then whether corrupt payoffs are a way around inefficient rules or a source of inefficiency on their own. Are they an explanation for some of the evident distortions obvious to an observer of government policies or are they an efficient response to these distortions?

. . . Research on corruption and on the quality of government institutions has been made possible by the existence of data sets prepared by proprietary firms that provide information to companies trying to decide where to invest. Although the methodology behind these data series is not always transparent, they are generally based on the opinions of people knowledgeable about the countries in question such as investors, scholars, bankers, financial analysts, etc. The use of such data by scholars is justified by the claim that they have withstood a market test, but the proprietary nature of the information does mean that it not as well documented or as replicable as most social scientists would like. Nevertheless, it is the best macrolevel data we have at present.

Statistical studies using these data series indicate that strong legal and governmental institutions and low levels of corruption have beneficial effects on economic growth and other economic variables. Other work provides evidence that more competitive economies have less corruption because they have fewer economic rents available for capture by corrupt agents.

Paolo Mauro (1995; see also chapter 20 in this volume) using a corruption index from the early eighties demonstrates that high levels of corruption are associated with lower levels of investment as a share of GDP. . . In a recent paper Mauro combines the Business International data with an index for 1982–1995 derived from the International Country Risk Guide prepared by Political Risk Services, Inc. (Mauro 1996). Statistical tests can then be run for a group of 106 countries.[1] The results are similar. In the 1996 study, a one standard deviation (2.4) improvement in the corruption index is associated with over a 4 percentage point increase in the investment rate and over a half a percentage point increase in the annual growth rate of per capita GDP.

Because the corruption indices are highly correlated with other measures of bureaucratic efficiency, such as the level of red tape and the quality of the judiciary, however, Mauro was unable to measure the marginal effect of any one of these measures holding the others constant. The data are, however, consistent with the claim that the level of red tape is a function of the prevalence of corruption, not something that is reduced by the payment of bribes. Corruption is a symptom of other underlying problems rather than an independent variable. . .[2] The results suggest that corruption's main impact on growth is through its impact on the level of investment, not on the composition of the physical investment portfolio. However, Mauro also demonstrates that highly corrupt countries tend to under invest in human capital by spending less on education (Mauro 1996).

A complementary study by Stephen Knack and Phillip Keefer (1996) uses the International Country Risk Guide index as well as one compiled by Business Environmental Risk Intelligence. The authors' primary focus is on the importance of strong property rights regimes in facilitating investment and growth, but as part of this effort they examine the importance of government institutions including the measure of corruption included in the ICRG data. Like Mauro, they discovered that the corruption index was so highly correlated with other measures of government quality that it could not legitimately be used alone. Instead, they averaged it in with expropriation risk, rule of law, risk of contract repudiation by the government, and the quality of the bureaucracy. The study examined rates of economic growth for 97 countries over the period 1974 to 1989. The authors show that indices of the quality of government institutions do at least as well as in explaining investment and growth as measures of political freedoms, civil liberties, and the frequency of political violence. An improvement of one standard deviation in the ICRG index leads to an increase in growth rates that would make Honduras equivalent to Costa Rica or Argentina equivalent to Italy. . . .

Finally, Alberto Ades and Rafael Di Tella (1994), using the Business International corruption index from early eighties supplemented by additional information from the early nineties, ask how the competitiveness of the economy affects a country's corruption ranking.[3] They argue that more competitive countries should be less corrupt. Lacking a direct measure of competitiveness, they use various proxies and obtain results consistent with their theory.[4] Their competitiveness measures include some under control of the state and some, such as distance from world markets, that are not.

These studies suggest that countries that have poorly functioning government institutions tend to be relatively corrupt, and that payoffs are seldom an adequate compensation for other governmental failures. The results indicate that corruption is harmful to economic growth, but the magnitude of the effect is unclear. Furthermore, because corruption is tied to other features of government structure, reducing corruption without a more fundamental change in the behavior of public institutions is unlikely to be successful. Why then have some analysts argued that corruption can be an efficient response to government failures? . . .

Theoretical Models of Corruption's Impact

The most sanguine view of the impact of corruption arises in models where payoffs allocate scarce public services and where bribes provide incentives to civil servants. I begin with these cases of low level corruption and then consider the more controversial case of high level or "grand" corruption in the awarding of contracts, concessions, and privatized firms. One consequence of "grand" corruption may be the export of bribes to off shore accounts. Thus I next ask whether this flow of funds is damaging to a country's efforts to encourage investment at home. Finally, I analyze the political consequences of bribes that permit those who pay to avoid compliance with burdensome and costly laws.

Payments that Equate Supply and Demand

The simplest case occurs when the briber is qualified for the benefit he seeks but is required by the official to pay for it. Suppose the service is scarce so that the number of people qualified to obtain the service exceeds the supply. If the corrupt market operates efficiently, the service will be provided to the applicants with the highest willingness to pay. If there is no price discrimination, the "market clearing" bribe will be equivalent to the price in an efficient market. The state could have legally sold the service with the same result except for the distribution of the revenue. Bribes increase the incomes of civil servants. Legal payments go into the government's treasury. But even that difference may be illusory. If the labor market is competitive, the government can reduce the pay of civil servants to below private sector wages because of the payoffs available to public officials (Besley and McLaren 1993, Flatters and MacLeod 1995). At least for marginal employees, public and private sector earnings must be equal. In short, if competitive conditions exist both in the corrupt market and in the labor market, corruption is as efficient as the direct, legal sale of a scarce publicly provided service. The winners, relative to an honest nonmarket system, are those willing to pay the most in bribes; the losers are those willing to pay in other forms such as time spent in a queue or persistence in petitioning officials.

Consider, however, the ways in which this simple case can be modified to generate inefficient results. First, the goals of a program may be undermined if the services are provided only to those with the highest willingness to pay. Thus the sale of import and export licenses or restaurant licenses would be efficient, but the allocation of subsidized housing or university admissions by price would undermine the programs' distributive goals even if those admitted are nominally "qualified" under the law. Introducing goals other than efficiency in a situation where demand exceeds supply, implies that bureaucratic discretion exists. Discretion may be exercised through bribery, but this method of allocation is costly given the program's goals. One's response should be to rethink the way the "worthy" are selected, not condone bribery. If, for example, an honest system is characterized by costly queues, the public agency needs to redesign the way it reviews applications or set clearer and tougher standards of worthiness to reduce the gap between supply and demand.

Second, consider cases where allocation to those with the highest willingness to pay is acceptable. Then one must ask whether corrupt markets are likely to differ much from open competitive ones. There are several reasons to suppose that they will not work as efficiently as legal markets (Bardhan 1995, p. 8; Cartier-Bresson 1995, Gambetta 1993, Rose-Ackerman 1978). The illegality of bribery induces participants to spend resources keeping the transaction secret. This in turn means that information about bribe-prices will not be well publicized. Prices may be relatively sticky because of the difficulty of communicating market information. Some potential participants may refuse to enter the market because of moral scruples and fear of punishment, and public officials may themselves limit their dealing to insiders and trusted friends and relations to avoid disclosure. For all these reason, a corrupt system may be not only less competitive but also more uncertain than a legal market. The bribe-price paid may vary widely . . . (Rose-Ackerman and Stone 1996), and those who obtain the service corruptly will have no recourse if the official does not live up to his side of the bargain. Of course, all of these costs will be less serious the more acceptable payoffs are to the society at large, that is, the lower the fear of disclosure and the broader the level of participation.

If the official must allocate a *fixed* number of licenses each year or grant a contract with well-specified terms, then bribery is essentially redistributive unless the problems raised in the previous paragraph prevail. However, in practice, many officials can exercise monopoly power by determining the quantity of services provided. They may be the only person with authority to issue a permit, overlook a violation of the law, grant a contract (Findlay 1989, Klitgaard 1988, Rose-Ackerman 1978, Shleifer and Vishney 1993). The official, like a private monopolist, may seek to set supply below the officially sanctioned level to increase the economic rents available for division between himself and the bribe payers. Conversely, under other conditions the corrupt official might seek to provide an increased supply of the service if the government has set the supply below the monopoly level.

Instead of assuming that the service is scarce, suppose that it is an entitlement that is meant to be available to all who meet certain qualifications. It is a service like a passport or a driver's license or a benefit like old age pensions in the United States. Bribery is clearly not an efficient way to allocate the benefit even to the qualified, but one might wonder whether it would even occur at all in the absence of scarcity. In fact, it can only occur when officials have sufficient monopoly power to create scarcity either by delaying approvals or withholding them unless paid bribes (Paul 1995). Officials with monopoly power will set the level of supply to maximize their profits (Dey 1989, Shleifer and Vishney 1992, 1993). These attempts to create scarcity can successfully generate bribes if applicants have no alternative source of the service and no effective means of appeal. The willingness to pay of qualified applicants will be lower if they have other options and if denunciations are not very costly in time and money (Alam 1995, Cadot 1987). Thus in assessing both the likelihood and the impact of corruption, the behavioral options of firms and officials play a critical role. The greater the discretion available to officials and the fewer the options open to private firms and individuals, the higher the costs of a system that condones corruption even when all those who obtain the service are, in fact qualified. The costs take the form of the transactions costs introduced by the officials' efforts to create corrupt demands (Bardhan 1995, p. 5; Klitgaard 1988).

Finally, why should officials only provide services to those who are qualified? Instead, bribes are frequently paid to permit unqualified people and firms to obtain a benefit. Corrupt officials can be expected, not only to allocate a scarce benefit to the qualified, but also to provide the benefit to high bribers who do not qualify. Similarly, even those who are qualified for the benefit may seek unauthorized gains or try to avoid costs. Shleifer and Vishney (1993, p. 601) call this case "corruption with theft" since their archetypal example is a firm that bribes to be excused from paying customs duties, but the range of examples is broader than those in which the government loses revenue. It also includes those in which a qualifications process is undermined or a regulation violated. Clearly, the unqualified may often be those with the highest willingness to pay since they have no legal way to obtain the service.

In cases where corruption's only efficiency cost stems from its illegality, the payments should be legalized. Surveys of private individuals and firms in Pakistan and India indicate that even quite poor people would be willing to make legal payments for improved service (Paul 1995, Stone and Rose-Ackerman 1996). Toleration of corruption is problematic because it is difficult to limit bribery to the cases where payments are efficient and not perceived as unfair. If legalization is indicated, should the payments should go to the public officials as bonuses or to the government treasury? The answer depends both upon whether bonuses will induce officials to perform better and upon whether such bonuses will be more effective if paid by clients or if paid by the state agency on the basis of performance reviews. If incentive payments simply induce officials to act like monopoly rent seekers, legalizing payments is not efficient.

Bribes as Incentive Payments for Bureaucrats

The strongest case for the efficiency of bribery, focuses not on the role of bribes in allocating public services to private citizens, but on the way bribery of low level officials can solve the agency/principal problem faced by top officials. Bribes may give an incentive to low level officials to do their job effectively. But in what situations is toleration indicated? In the cases discussed above, even when corruption served an allocative function, it was a second best response. A legal sale would be superior. Such is generally the case here as well, although some research suggests why the first best solution will often be infeasible.

The most careful analyses of the possibly desirable incentive properties of bribes have been provided by Lui (1985) and Flatters and MacLeod (1995). Lui (1985) argues that payoffs to those who manage queues can be efficient. The payments will give the officials incentives both to favor those with a high opportunity cost of time and to work quickly. Lui concludes that his model of corruption in queuing can be used to design a legal auctioning procedure. The effectiveness of a legal procedure, however, will depend upon whether the server "owns" the payments so that he has an incentive to speed up service. Lui's paper can be read as an argument for legal reimbursement schemes that reward civil servants for high levels of effort. It is consistent with reform proposals that establish dual tracks—expensive fast tracks for those who value speed and a slower track for the rest. Under such a system a portion of the "speed" payments would be used to reward officials for good performance (Paul 1995, p. 163). In the design of such systems, however, it is important to avoid giving bureaucrats monopoly power that they can use to extract increased levels of rents (Rose-Ackerman 1978, pp. 85–108). The availability of either bribes or performance pay can, if the system is not carefully organized, simply give officials an incentive to create onerous background conditions that they then take payments to correct.

Flatters and MacLeod (1995) argue that in developing countries the corruption of tax collectors can be efficient so long as the government can impose a binding overall revenue constraint. In their model the Minister sets a revenue target, a nominal tax liability schedule, and the wage rate of the Tax Collector. Corruption is tolerated so long as the Collector turns in an amount equal to the revenue target. The larger the difference between nominal tax liabilities and the revenue target, the higher is corruption. The higher the level of bribe payments, the lower the official wage. When the Minister is free to set any wage he wishes and the Collector's effort is a constant, corruption is harmless, but unnecessary. Thus if any of the factors discussed above limits the efficiency of corruption, it will be undesirable.

Flatters and MacLeod, however, go on to point out that many countries are not free to pay tax collectors more than other civil servants. Other strategies such as increased monitoring or tax law simplification may not be feasible. In such cases, corruption is a substitute for incentive-based civil service reform. Furthermore, if the Collector must spend time and effort determining tax liabilities, tolerance of corruption is one way to give him an incentive to carry out this task. The Collector is given an incentive to perform well by being able to claim a share of the nominal tax liabilities.[5] The model, however, requires the Minister to set the parameters of the system so the Collector has no incentive simply to abscond with the tax collections. Even if garden variety corruption is tolerated, excessive greed must be punished severely. According to Flatters and MacLeod, this pattern describes the situation in many developing countries where corruption of tax authorities in endemic, but major scandals occasionally erupt.

Although their model does seem to capture some elements of reality, their prescription that routine corruption of tax collectors be tolerated has several problematic aspects. First, toleration of corruption in an important agency, such as tax collection, may encourage its spread to other areas where Flatters and MacLeod's arguments do not hold. Second, the authors assume that with some effort the Collector can "discover" the tax liability of a citizen or firm. Instead, he might "create" that tax liability as a bribe extraction device. If firms' and individuals' vulnerability to corrupt demands varies, the result could be an arbitrary and unfair pattern of payments. The sum of taxes and bribes might vary across taxpayers in a way that reflects the Collector's leverage, not the underlying tax rules. If firms differ in their propensity and willingness to bribe and if the tax breaks given in return for the payoffs are not publicized, the result can be a system based on special favors given to some firms but not others. The overall legitimacy of the government may suffer. At the very least the disadvantaged taxpayers will feel unfairly treated.

In general, Flatters and MacLeod have ignored the way a corrupt bureaucracy of the sort they discuss can contribute to an uncertain business climate. Firms pay bribes to obtain certainty, in this case about their tax liabilities, but the certainty may be illusory since corrupt deals cannot be enforced. The short-term equilibrium impact of bribes may be to enhance efficiency in tax collection or business regulation. Businesses pay to regularize the environment in which they operate and reduce tax and regulatory burdens. However, difficulties arise when one looks at the issue systemically. Payments made to increase certainty for individual firms result in a wide variance in conditions across firms. Potential entrants, unsure how they will fare, will view the economic environment as risky and unpredictable. . . . Ingrained corruption can also hold back state reform. Firms that have benefited from payoffs will resist efforts to increase the clarity of rules and laws. They and their allies within the state apparatus will oppose reform efforts designed to make the economy more open and competitive.

In short, bribes can sometimes be characterized as incentive payments to public officials that substitute for legal reforms in the civil service system. Although they do operate in that way in some cases, a policy of active tolerance . . . is likely to be destructive of the prospects for long term reform and will make it difficult to create a state viewed as legitimate by its citizens. Payoffs that are widely viewed as acceptable should be legalized, but not all "incentive pay" schemes will actually improve bureaucratic efficiency.

Payments to Obtain Major Contracts, Concessions, and Privatized Firms

Corrupt payments to win contracts, concessions, and privatizing companies are generally the preserve of large businesses and high level officials. Although sometimes low level clerks are bribed to reveal information, and some smaller businesses bribe to get routine supply contracts, the important cases represent a substantial expenditure of funds and can have a major impact on the government budget and the country's growth prospects. These deals are by definition the preserve of top officials and frequently involve multinational corporations operating alone or in consortia with local partners.

Is there anything distinctive about such deals other than their size? At one level they appear analogous to cases in which government disburses a scarce benefit, only this time the value of the benefit is valued in many million, not a few thousand dollars. Under competitive conditions the high briber will be the most efficient firm, and the winner will behave efficiently *ex post* irrespective of whether or not it used a bribe to obtain the benefit. The same caveats about bribes paid to obtain benefits or avoid costs apply here although the efficiency goal seems less problematic in this context, and the benefit obtained is not itself illegal. Nevertheless, systemic corruption can introduce inefficiencies that reduce competitiveness. It may limit the number of bidders, favor those with inside connections over the most efficient candidates, limit the information available to participants, and introduce added transactions costs. But does the scale of the corrupt deal and involvement of high level officials change anything?

One essential difference is the likelihood that rulers are effectively insulated from prosecution. They will thus be less restrained in their corrupt demands than lower level officials who may be subject to more external and internal constraints. This circumstance may imply that high level corrupt officials can obtain a higher share of the rents available than lower level ones. Since deals involving major contracts, concessions and privatizations can each have a noticeable impact on the government budget and the country's overall prosperity, the size and incidence of the payoffs is especially relevant. Furthermore, although those who obtain licenses and tax breaks through bribery are rarely thought to behave inefficiently once the benefit is obtained, the contrary argument is often made for the kind of major deals considered here. Thus we need to consider this question explicitly. . . .

To isolate these distinct issues consider a logging concession obtained corruptly by a company over the higher bids of competitors. Suppose, to begin, that the corruption "market" is efficient so that it operates just like an idealized competitive bidding process. Then we can distinguish between, on the one hand, the locus of corrupt payments and their impact on government and, on the other, the possible inefficient operation of the concessionaire.

Suppose that as a result of corruption, the government obtains less than fair market value for the resources under its control. If corruption does not restrict entry and if the official cannot affect the size of the concession, however, the high briber is the firm that values the benefit the most. It is the most efficient firm that would offer the highest price in a fair bidding procedure. The losses are the dead weight losses of the extra taxes that must be collected and the foregone benefits of public programs not undertaken. Honest officials receive distorted information about the value of the concession and may in the future support fewer of them. A similar analysis applies to corrupt contracts and privatization projects. The most efficient firm will be selected under competitive bribery, but the benefits to the government are reduced. In the contracting case, for example, part of the cost of the bribe may be hidden in the value of the contract reducing the support of honest officials for future contracts.

With a monopoly official and a competitive corruption "market" allocating a fixed benefit, the official will extract all the rents. The benefit to the firm will be exactly what it would obtain in a comparable auction (Beck and Maher 1986). The bribe is a transfer from the government to the public official. Suppose, instead, that the market is an oligopolistic one and that the most efficient firm would earn economic rents if it bid just enough to beat its closest competitor. Then a bargaining range exists. If no one has any scruples, the most efficient firm will still win the bid, but it may be able to retain some economic rents for itself. Now the comparison with an honest system is more complex since one cannot be sure exactly what would have transpired in an honest auction. The firm's profits will be lower than in a honest system under some types of auction mechanisms. For example, if an English auction is used, the winning bid is just above the reservation price of the second most efficient firm. With corruption, the official will try to extract some of the winner's surplus, as well as some of the gains that would have flowed to the government. If the losing bidder can plausibly threaten to challenge the outcome, the entire bribe may need to come out of the firm's profits with no loss to the government.

A third case is possible in which the sum of the bribe and the concession payment is *less* than the expected payment in a fair auction. This could occur if the official is constrained by a fear of exposure and if the probability of this happening is a function of the size of the bribe he receives. Then even an official with no scruples will be deterred from extracting all of the firm's rents. If deterrence is strong enough, the presumption that the winning firm is the most efficient competitor must be abandoned. Instead, bidders that are least likely to reveal the corrupt deal will be favored (cf. Lien 1990b).

In general, the bribe will be extracted partly from returns that would otherwise flow to government and partly from the profits of the winning firm. However, in some cases a corrupt deal may be more lucrative for firms than an honest deal in spite of the monopoly power of the rulers. From a development point of view, the greater the loss to the government, the more serious the problem, especially in countries that have few alternative sources of revenue. Even when the bribes are mostly extracted from firm profits, however, there may be a longer term impact depending upon whether corruption increases or decreases firms' profits. The same analysis can be carried out for privatization projects and, in reverse, for contracts.

Now consider a firm that has obtained a secure long-term timber concession at a bargain price even when the bribe is added in. If it operates in the international market, its subsequent actions should depend upon the market for timber. The fact that is has underpaid for the concession should not affect its production decisions. It still seeks to maximize profits, and the concession payment is a sunk cost. The cost of corruption is felt by the public fisc, but no inefficiency has been introduced into the international timber market. Even if the total payment is above that expected in an honest system, there should be no impact.

The claim of no impact on firm behavior is an important result, but it is too simple to reflect reality. The operative terms are *secure* and *long term*. A corrupt system is not just one in which individuals in key positions can benefit at the expense of the state and ordinary citizens. Rather, the corrupt nature of the deal introduces uncertainties into the economic environment that can have additional effects on the way private firms do business. Difficulties may arise even if the most efficient firm wins. The corrupt nature of the deal may give the firm a short run orientation. There are two reasons for this. First, the concessionaire (or contractor or purchaser of a privatized firm) may fear that those in power are vulnerable to overthrow because of their corruption. A new regime may not honor the old one's commitments. Second, even if the current regime remains in power, the winner may fear the imposition of arbitrary rules and financial demands once investments are sunk. It may be concerned that competitors will be permitted to enter the market or even worry that its contract will be voided for reasons of politics or greed.[6] Having paid a bribe in the past, the firm is vulnerable to extortionary demands by those who can document the illegal payments. For these reasons, the corrupt firm with a timber contract may cut down trees more quickly than it would in less corrupt countries. It may also be reluctant to invest in immovable capital that would be difficult to take out of the country should conditions change. In the electric power area, the most dramatic examples of this are the floating power stations put in place in several developing countries to make exit easy and relatively inexpensive. . . .

Furthermore, it is unlikely that corruption will be limited to a one time payment to top officials to cement the deal. Instead, the winner may be a firm more willing than others to engage in ongoing corrupt relationships up and down the hierarchy to protect its interests. For example, if the timber concession includes a royalty per log that is calibrated by the type of timber, the firm may pay inspectors to misgrade the logs. It may also pay to cut down more trees than the concession permits. Under a construction contract, the high briber may anticipate bribing building inspectors to approve work that does not meet the nation's safety standards (Park 1995). In fact, the expectation of a long-term ongoing relationship may be part of the appeal of signing with a corrupt firm in the first place. Alternatively, the corrupt firm may itself hold back some promised bribes as a way to guarantee performance by the country's officials. Thus a firm might sign a contract to deliver cement to a road-building agency but only pay bribes as payments are received from the public authority. Frequently, such arrangements take the nominal form of consulting contracts with payments tied to the receipt of funds under the contract.

Even when the exploitation of a country's natural resources is carried out efficiently by the corrupt firm that wins the bid, the struggle for rents can have a destructive impact on the economic and political system. Talented people may concentrate their effort on rent seeking rather than on productive activities. This can occur on both sides of the corrupt transaction. Thus potential entrepreneurs may decide to abandon the private sector and become public officials charged with allocating rents. In a democracy, people may seek political office, not to fulfill some idea of public service, but to extract as many rents for themselves and their supporters as possible (Diamond 1993, 1995). Similarly, private business people may concentrate on the struggle for publicly provided benefits, be they mineral concessions or aid contracts, rather than on establishing productive enterprises. Considerable evidence suggests that a strong natural resource base may be a hindrance to economic development (Gelb 1988, Sachs and Warner 1994). The reason for this outcome is presumably the incentive to substitute rent seeking for productive activity. Each individual sees that most effective way to seek wealth is to try to take it from someone else or from the state rather than to produce an increment (Krueger 1974).

Capital Flight

Some argue that the kind of high level or "grand" corruption discussed above will contribute to capital flight. Those who accept bribes seek to hide them from public view and to assure their prosperity even if ousted from office. A little thought, however, will show that this result is not obvious. . . .

If capital markets are efficient and if the corrupt country imposes no constraints on the export and import of capital, the funds deposited in "financial paradises" by corrupt rulers will have no impact. International investors will respond to opportunities in the country in question and act to take up the slack. No country will suffer a "shortage" of capital. Of course, if corruption implies a risky environment and a predatory state, those conditions will discourage investment, but there is no additional problem introduced by the export of bribes. Furthermore, to the extent that bribes are simply paid out of the profits of multinational firms, there is only a transfer from a bank in an OECD country to a numbered account somewhere else. The funds would not have entered the country in any case. Of course, such an extreme assumption about the incidence of bribes is unlikely to hold, but even if some portion of the bribe is reflected in a higher contract price or a lower privatization contract price, the basic result follows. There may be substantial transactions costs involved in keeping the transaction secret, but there are no other efficiency costs.

But this view of capital markets is surely utopian for much of the developed world. Knowledge of local conditions is likely to be a key aspect of investment choices. Although international investors can, of course, buy such local knowledge, this may be an imperfect substitute for actually having that knowledge oneself. Furthermore, bribe receipts, being illegal, have a comparative advantage in providing capital to illegal businesses worldwide. This reduces the cost of capital to such industries and fuels their growth relative to legal business ventures. Thus corruption on a grand scale by a country's rulers will often limit the supply of capital available within the country and aid illegal businesses both within the country and internationally. One way to reduce the impact of corruption is to encourage a free market in capital and to help countries disseminate information globally about investment opportunities. Efforts to crack down on money laundering will be useful as a way to increase the costs of organized crime and to make corruption more risky. Such law enforcement activities are, however, unlikely to be a very effective way to increase investment in capital poor countries. A highly corrupt country is likely to be one where business operates in an uncertain and arbitrary environment. Such an environment encourages local elites to invest abroad and discourages foreign direct investment. The export of bribe receipts, themselves, although it may have a marginal impact on the supply of capital is unlikely to be of first order importance compared with efforts to reduce the benefits of rent seeking.

Payments to Avoid Inefficient Rules and Burdensome Taxes

Suppose a state has many inefficient regulations and levies burdensome taxes on business. Given the existing inefficient legal framework, payoffs to avoid regulations and taxes increase efficiency.[7] Even if the corrupt "market" has some of the problems outlined above, the result may still be superior on efficiency grounds to compliance with the law. This defense of payoffs is commonly espoused by foreign investors in the developing world and appears in discussions of investment in eastern Europe and the former Soviet Union as well. It is a pragmatic justification that grows out of frustration with the existing legal order. The case is important because it attempts to justify corruption carried out to obtain benefits to which one is *not* legally entitled. Bribers are better off than they would be in an honest system in which they had to comply with the law.[8]

This argument raises the question of whether individuals and firms are obligated to obey only laws that they judge to be efficient and just. Clearly, in the developed world individuals and firms are not entitled to decide on their own what laws to respect. Industry's response to environmental and health and safety rules that it finds burdensome is not generally to bribe U. S. officials or enlist the help of criminals to evade the law. Of course, both do happen with some frequency, but the scandals seldom involve firms with national reputations. Instead, such firms work to change the laws in Congress, make legal campaign contributions, lobby public agencies, and bring lawsuits that challenge laws and regulations. One can complain about the importance of wealth and large corporations in American political life, but, at least, well-documented lobbying activities and campaign contributions are superior to secret bribes in maintaining democratic institutions.

Some of the same firms that engage in legal political activities at home feel less constraint about violating laws in developing and transitional economies. Since the United States outlaws bribes paid abroad to obtain business, American companies face a domestic legal constraint.[9] But the perceived importance of that constraint suggests that multinationals do not generally feel an obligation to obey the law in the developing countries where they operate. However, it is not just multinationals that behave in this way. Domestic companies often operate in the same fashion.

There are two difficulties with widespread tolerance of such corruption. First, one cannot rely on investors only to pay bribes to avoid *inefficient* rules and taxes. They will, instead, want to reduce the impact of *all* state-imposed burdens, justified or not. Under redistributive programs, both individuals and firms will seek to use to bribery to obtain benefits to which they are not entitled. Of course, one can construct models in which the laws on the books are all payoffs to politically powerful groups with no public legitimacy (Brennan and Buchanan 1980, Stigler 1971, Oxford Analytica 1996). Then avoiding the burdens imposed by such laws seems a worthy goal. Unless one is a strong libertarian who believes that all state action is illegitimate, however, such a criterion is not readily operationalizable. Should firms or individuals be able to defend against a charge of corruption with a showing that the law was unjust or inefficient? This would put a policy analytic burden on the law enforcement system that it is ill-equipped to handle in practice and that it is illegitimate to impose on them in theory.

Second, it seems strange indeed to tolerate business firms' judgments that a well-placed payoff is justified because it increases their profits. Such an attitude can do serious harm in nations struggling to build a viable state. These states need to develop public choice mechanisms that translate popular demands into law, that provide a credible commitment to the enforcement of these laws, and that provide legal recourse to those who think they have been wronged. If, instead, investors and ordinary citizens make individualized judgments about which laws are legitimate, the attempt to create state institutions will founder. Bribery will determine not only which laws are enforced, but also what laws are enacted.[10] All states, even those that have most successfully curbed the power of special interests, enact inefficient laws, but no state could operate effectively if individuals could take the law into their own hands and justify doing so by reference to cost-benefit criteria.

The discussion thus suggests that corruption may be more tolerable, not when it increases the efficiency of individual deals, but when it is carried out in clearly illegitimate regimes that can make no claim to popular support.

Then even bribes to avoid taxes seem less harmful than in other contexts since the fewer resources available to the state, the less powerful it is. However, costs do remain. Those who benefit from making payoffs will be a strong constituency against reform because they will fear the loss of their special advantages (Pack 1988, pp. 340, 349; Olson 1982). Furthermore, when a reform regime does take power, its efforts will be made more difficult if corruption has become systemic. One of the regime's first tasks must be to change the behavior of corrupt officials, firms, and individuals. Tolerating individual efforts to circumvent even burdensome laws is not consistent with state legitimacy. . . .

Corruption cannot be expected to wither away just because a reform government has taken power or because economic growth is vigorous. So long as officials with monopoly power have discretionary authority, corrupt incentives will remain and can be especially harmful for fragile new states. Reformers will have to take concrete action, not just assume that entrenched habits will change with a change in top personnel. Those who benefited from the corrupt regime must not be permitted to hold back change.

Similarly, strong economic growth is not a cure. A growing pie may just imply that there are more rents to divide (Diamond 1993, 1995; Gelb 1988, pp. 134–144, Sachs and Warner 1994). Corruption may be more tolerable if the pie is growing since everyone can receive some benefits, but for that very reason it may be more likely to spread. An economic downturn will then leave the regime in power vulnerable to overthrow since it can no longer satisfy all those who have shared in the spoils (Chhibber 1996).

The link between corruption and growth depends on what benefits are received in return for payoffs. If corruption is associated with the facilitation of illegal businesses, such as the drug trade, then growth based on the success of other types of investment may indeed reduce the appeal of illegal businesses with a corresponding reduction in payoffs. If, instead, corruption is a commonplace activity of legal businesses, prosperity will simply fuel corruption unless the rules and regulations that generate rents are modified or more honestly enforced. If organized crime has become intertwined with legitimate businesses through the provision of protection services and payoffs to the police, the growth of legal businesses may simply increase the profits of the illegal ones thus ultimately discouraging outside investors with a choice of where to locate (Gambetta 1993, Handelman 1995, Shelley 1994, Varese 1994).

The cross-country empirical studies that show a negative relationship between corruption and weak public institutions, on the one hand, and growth, on the other, thus receive broad support from a more fine-grained consideration of the operation of corrupt public programs and activities. Corruption can further short term efficiency in a subset of quite specific cases, but neither theory or evidence suggests that it is a spur to economic growth.

Stable states that operate under the rule of law have a development advantage according to a number of studies. Thus since corruption undermines this commitment, it undermines state legitimacy and in the process harms the prospects for growth.

References

Ades, A., and Di Tella, R. "Competition and Corruption," draft, June 13, 1994.

Alam, M. S., "A Theory of Limits on Corruption and Some Applications," *Kyklos* 48: 419–435 (1995).

Bardhan, Pranab, "The Economics of Corruption in Less Developed Countries: A Review of Issues," draft, University of California, Berkeley, November 1995.

Beck, Paul J., and Michael W. Maher, "Competition, Regulation and Bribery," *Managerial and Decision Economics*, 10: 1–12 (1989).

Besley, Timothy, and John McLaren, "Taxes and Bribery: The Role of Wage Incentives," *Economic Journal* 103: 119–141 (1993).

Brennan, Geoffrey, and James Buchanan, *The Power to Tax*, New York: Cambridge University Press, 1980.

Cadot, O., "Corruption as a Gamble," *Journal of Public Economics*, 33:223–244 (1987).

Cartier-Bresson, J. "L'Economie de la Corruption," in D. Della Porta and Y. Mény, eds., *Démocratie et Corruption en Europe*. Paris: La Découverte, 1995, pp.149–164.

Chhibber Pradeep K., "State Policy, Rent Seeking, and the Electoral Success of a Religious Party in Algeria," *Journal of Politics* 58:126–148 (1996).

Dey, Harendra Kanti, "The Genesis and Spread of Economic Corruption: A Microtheoretical Interpretation," *World Development* 17: 503–511 (1989).

Diamond, Larry, "Nigeria's Perennial Struggle Against Corruption: Prospects for the Third Republic." *Corruption and Reform* 7:215–25 (1993).

Diamond, Larry, "Nigeria: The Uncivic Society and the Descent into Praetorianism," in Larry Diamond, Juan Linz, and Seymour Maritn Lipset, eds., *Politics in Developing Countries: Comparing Experiences with Democracy*, 2d edition, Boulder CO: Lynne Rienner Publishing, 1995, pp. 417–491.

Findlay, Ronald, *Is the New Political Economy Relevant to Developing Countries?*, Policy, Planning, and Research Working Paper 292, Country Economics Department, World Bank, Washington DC, 1989.

Flatters, Frank, and W. Bentley MacLeod, "Administrative Corruption and Taxation," *International Tax and Public Finance*, 2:397–417 (1995).

Gambetta, Diego, *The Sicilian Mafia*, Cambridge MA: Harvard University Press, 1993.

Gelb, Alan, and associates, *Oil Windfalls: Blessing or Curse?* Published for the World Bank by Oxford University Press, 1988.

Handelman, Stephen, *Comrade Criminal*, New Haven CT: Yale University Press, 1995.

Keefer, Philip, and Stephen Knack, "Institutions and Economic Performance: Cross-Country Tests Using Alternative Institutional Measures," *Economics and Politics*, forthcoming 1996.

Klitgaard, Robert, *Controlling Corruption*, Berkeley CA: University of California Press, 1988.

Krueger, Anne O., "The Political Economy of a Rent-Seeking Society, *American Economic Review* 64:291–303 (1974).

Lien, Da-Hsiang Donald, "Corruption and Allocation Efficiency," *Journal of Development Economics* 33: 153–164 (1990b).

Lui, Francis.T., "An Equilibrium Queuing Model of Bribery," *Journal of Political Economy*, 93:760–781 (1985).

Mauro, Paolo, "Corruption and Growth." *Quarterly Journal of Economics*, 109:681–712 (1995).

Mauro, Paolo, "The Effects of Corruption on Growth, Investment, and Government Expenditure: A Cross-Country Analysis" in Fred Bergsten and Kimberly Elliott, eds., *Corruption in the World Economy*, Washington DC: Institute for International Economics, forthcoming 1996.

Olson, Mancur, *The Rise and Decline of Nations*, New Haven: Yale University Press, 1982.

Oxford Analytica, "Bribery Benefits," June 5, 1996.

Pack, Howard, "Industrialization and Growth," in H. Chenery and T. N. Srinivasan, eds., *Handbook of Development Economics,* Volume I, Elsevier Science Publishers B. V., 1988, pp. 333–377.

Park, B.-S. "Political Corruption in Non-Western Democracies: The Case of South-Korea Party Politics," draft, Kim Dae-Jung Peace Foundation, Seoul, Korea, 1995.

Paul, Sam, "Evaluating Public Services: A Case Study on Bangalore, India," *New Directions for Evaluation*, American Evaluation Association, No. 67, Fall 1995.

Przeworski, Adam, and Fernando Limongi, "Political Regimes and Economic Growth," *Journal of Economic Perspectives* 7:51–69 (1993).

Rasmusen, Eric, and Mark Ramseyer, "Cheap Bribes and the Corruption Ban: A Coordination Game Among Rational Legislators," *Public Choice*, 78:305–327 (1994).

Rose-Ackerman, Susan, *Corruption: A Study in Political Economy*. NY: Academic Press, 1978.

Rose-Ackerman, Susan, "The Political Economy of Corruption," in Fred Bergsten and Kimberly Elliott, eds., *Corruption in the World Economy*, Washington DC: Institute for International Economics, forthcoming 1996.

Rose-Ackerman, Susan, and Andrew Stone, "The Costs of Corruption for Private Business: Evidence from World Bank Surveys," draft, May 1996.

Sachs, Jeffrey D., and Andrew M. Warner, "Natural Resources and Economic Growth," unpublished paper, Harvard University, August 1994

Shelley, Louise, "Post-Soviet Organized Crime," *Demokratizatsiya* 2: 341–358 (1994).

Shleifer, A., and Vishney, R. "Corruption." *Quarterly Journal of Economics* 108:599–617 (1993).

Shleifer, A., and Vishney, R. 1992. "Pervasive Shortages under Socialism," *Rand Journal of Economics* 23:237–246.

Stigler, George, "The Theory of Regulation," *Bell Journal of Economics and Management Science* 2: 3–21 (1971)

Varese, Federico, "Is Sicily the Future of Russia? Private Protection and the Rise of the Russian Mafia," *Archives of European Sociology* 35:224–258 (1994).

Notes

1. The two indices are very highly correlated (r=0.81). When both are available, Mauro averaged them together. Otherwise he used the value of the single available index.

2. An overall index of the riskiness of investing in a country based on eleven factors

from the Business international index (one of which is the corruption index) was associated with both lower investment rates and lower growth rates (Mauro 1995).

3. The second index they used is from the *World Competitiveness Report* published by the EMF Foundation in Geneva, It covers only 32 countries and excludes Africa, eastern Europe except Hungary, and Latin America except Mexico and Brazil.

4. Their proxies are the share of merchandise imports in GDP, the distance of the country from world markets, an index of labor power, and the strength of antitrust laws. They also include as controls measures of economic prosperity, educational levels, and political rights. As Ades and Di Tella themselves recognize, these measures all have weaknesses. The share of imports ought to take the size of the economy into account. The United States has a relatively small import share but is quite competitive because of the size of the internal market. Import share has a quite different meaning in China compared to Mali. In addition, the proxies ignore the competitiveness of export markets and the nature of the government contracting process.

5. The authors mention the possibility of legal bounty systems for tax collectors. In Grenada they report that tax collectors receive a 10 percent commission on collections. The Commissioner of Inland Revenue in Zambia has proposed that his office's budget be met out of a 10 percent commission on all income tax revenues but this scheme has not been implemented (Flatters and MacLeod 1995, p. 408).

6. For example, in Malaysia firms involved in the privatization of both electricity and telecoms have complained that the government has subsequently admitted numerous additional competitors with strong political links. See Kieran Cooke, "Malaysian Privatisation Loses Allure," *Financial Times*, October 13, 1995.

7. See Oxford Analytica (1996). The note states that: "If assumptions that some state bureaucracies are inefficient are made, and that the degree of regulation or taxation that they impose is excessive, three possible benefit of corruption emerge." The benefits are as follows. Bribes can speed up processing for profitable projects by permitting them to get to the head of the queue [see Lui 1985]. Bribes can overcome excessive regulation, and bribes can reduce tax payments. The authors conclude that, given the costs of prevention, corruption "may offer a 'second best' alternative [to more fundamental reforms]."

8. The case is analogous to Shleifer and Vishney's corruption "with theft" (1993, p. 602).

9. The act is the Foreign Corrupt Practices Act, 15 U.S.C. §§ 78m(b) & (d)(1) & (g)-(h), 78dd-1, 78dd-2, 78ff (a) & (c) (1988 & Supp. IV 1992). For a review of the case law see Pendergast (1995).

10. Bribes paid to obtain the enactment of favorable laws by a democratic legislature are a particularly good example of the often large gap between the size of the bribe paid and the impact of corruption on society. If legislators cannot coordinate their actions, they may be inexpensive to bribe since no one lawmaker has much bargaining power (Rose-Ackerman, 1978). Rasmusen and Ramseyer (1994) develop an interesting model of this case.

Part VII

ENDEMIC CORRUPTION AND AFRICAN UNDERDEVELOPMENT

Introduction to Part VII

Sub-Saharan Africa has the reputation of being the most corrupt area of the world. This assessment has never been really empirically substantiated. At first glance, corruption in China or in Indonesia reaches levels of the same magnitude as Africa. The fact remains that in Africa, corruption is both systemic and generalized in all spheres of social, economic, political and administrative life, and the amount of the sums involved, in absolute terms, and in relation to economic activity, is extremely high. Its effects, economically and politically are devastating. It is no longer possible to suggest that corruption in Africa is tonic, even if some functional political effects may be stressed. Corruption is held responsible in large part for the failure of development, and the truth is that the very word development looks like a «myth» when the extent and the nature of corruption is considered. This is why, after having ignored the problem for decades, the World Bank and the IMF, have recently declared war on corruption and concentrated their efforts particularly on the African continent. It remains to be seen whether this situation is reversible or not. Is it possible to get rid of a "culture of corruption"? We are facing rather a vicious circle, where underdevelopment breeds corruption, and corruption breeds underdevelopment. The following chapters deal with the phenomenon of corruption from different perspectives: economic and political, case studies and comparative studies between African countries and between the African continent and East Asia, and the efforts toward the institutionalization of "good governance".

Jean-François Médard's article bases his study of corruption in Africa on the specific nature of the African state which can be qualified as a neo-patrimonial state. It is characterized by the privatization of the public sphere, where power is personalized at every level, and political and economic ressources, wealth and political power, are exchangeable. This however is a generalization; it does not mean that all the African states are the same. There are differences in the level of corruption between the different African states and between historical periods. Even an exception exists with Bostwana which cannot be labelled as a neo-patrimonial state. This neo-patrimonial state relies on the extensive use of different kinds of corrupt practice involving both social exchange corruption (nepotism, friendship, patronage and clientelism, ethnicity), transactive economic corruption, misappropriation and extortion. In some African countries, neo-patrimonialism was compatible with some degree of economic growth and political stability. There existed a patrimonial mode of socio-political regulation based on a systematic use of patronage. In the eighties, Africa entered a period of deep economic crisis which generated a fiscal crisis of the state. Redistribution was no longer possible and this undermined political stability. The crisis became generalized and multidimensional. In most cases, the economic and administrative remedies imposed by the international organizations, such as the structural adjustment plans, privatization and decentralization, made the situation worse. Instead of undermining the opportunities of corruption as was expected, they had the perverse effect of increasing corruption. The introduction of political pluralism has produced other opportunities of corruption, with more transparency, but not more accountability. In large parts of the continent, warlordism is developing in connexion with globalization and international criminal operations. Corruption has become only one dimension of a more general process of criminalization of politics and this has caused the collapse of the state. In other countries, systematic anti corruption reforms have been introduced with mixed results.

The general impression, suggested by Tom Lodge's article on political corruption in South Africa, is that it is quite extended, and even on the rise. The study of the South African case is of special interest because of the singularity of the political and economic trajectory of this country within Sub-Saharan Africa. The South African economy was the most developed in Africa, and political office was not the only path to wealth. The state apparatus was autonomous and effective. Thus South Africa, since it not shared the same structural constraints as the other parts of Africa, seemed to have been relatively immune from corruption. However, in spite of this, corruption appeared to flourish in pre-democratic South Africa, and this corruption was largely rooted in the apartheid system. It was mostly the misuse of secret money for covert operations which left room for official venality and supplied most of the opportunity for private gain. In addition, though, the central government departments have had a history of routinized corruption as in the case of the departments of Health or of Development Aid. This refer to elite and grand corruption in departments especially concerned with political and strategic goals of government. In addition, several homeland governments have been particularly affected by grand corruption of a patrimonial kind. Many cases of routine petty corruption have been uncovered in homelands as elsewhere. Among white South Africans, corruption was exceptional rather than normal. In post-apartheid South Africa, there are good reasons to expect a continuation of corruption. In addition, the changes and reforms that have taken place had some negative effects on good governance. They are the unintended consequence of measures of affirmative action aiming at upgrading and empowering the former victims of apartheid. Large numbers of senior officials have been replaced by fresh recruits to senior managerial levels, as political appointees. This has eroded professional ethics already weakened by demoralization. Government policies favoring black business empowerment as well as of the movement of members of the ANC toward the corporate sector has blurred the boundaries between the public and private sector. On the other hand, the new government's public commitment to an ethic of transparency stimulates the publication of corruption stories by the newspapers. Tom Lodge then proceeds to give examples of corruption at both provincial and central levels. At the central level, it does not appear to be so prevalent, and it is concentrated in particular departments, such as the Department of Health, Social Welfare, Safety and Security and Justice. The case of the police is extremely serious. The parastatal sector is also involved. It does not seem to have become entrenched at the levels of policy making to the point of having an effect on public expenditures. In conclusion, it appears that, in addition to old types of corruption, there are new sources for corrupt behavior, but ANC's conservative fiscal policies represents an important limit to patronage. South Africa is still in a category of its own.

The Uganda case presented by Sahr John Kpundeh introduces us to the most systematic attempt to fight corruption observed so far in Africa. This case is even more relevant if we keep in mind the fact that pre-Museveni Uganda could be considered as a collapsed state characterized by pervasive corruption (*magendo*), predation and violence. The new institutional framework for good governance is very comprehensive. It includes a Ministry of Ethics and Integrity; an Inspector General of Government; a Public Service Reform aiming at making Civil Service, smaller better paid and more efficient, a Leadership Code of Conduct and a Director of Public Prosecutions. In addition, other government reforms were initiated to help reduce the scope and incidences of corruption. The role of the press and the role of the President completes the picture. It is too early for a definitive assessment of the reforms which need time and continuity. A major challenge is the difficulty of operationizing the strategy. Progress has been made in some areas, but a lot more work remains to be done. One side effect of this comprehensive strategy is the lack of coordination among various anti-corruption agencies. Laws and regulations grant overlapping authority which lead to duplication of efforts and dissipation of resources. Civil society and the private sector are weakly included in the coalition against corruption. Civil society is weak and not empowered to question corrupt practices. The reform agencies have been allocated inadequate resources in qualified personnel and funding. The real challenge is sustainability.

Alice Sindzingre's article constitutes the first attempt to compare corruption in Africa and East Asia. Such a comparison helps to illustrate the specific nature of corruption in Africa. She starts from the widely shared observation, that corruption seems as widespread in Asia as in Africa, but that it does not have the same effects on development. In Africa, in spite of the amount of aid, local and foreign investments are very limited because of the political and economic incertitude, the lack of guarantees of propriety rights and of the security of investments. By contrast, Asian countries have attracted a huge amount of foreign and local investments. The question then, is to understand the reasons why corruption has not prevented growth in Asia as in Africa. Her hypothesis is that it is the context more than corruption per se which is relevant. According to Alice Sindzingre, corruption is not deeper or more largely spread in Africa, but the political, economic and institutional contexts generate a different relation to time. She starts by dismissing the explanatory value of the type of political regime and of political history. She also dismisses the culturalist type of explanation. For her, the most important dimension is the relation between the State and the private actors. In opposition to Asia, African states are not developmental states. Historically, they have been characterized by illegitimacy, instability, and a weak credibility. In addition, Alice Sindzingre compares the Asian diaspora and the African networks. The former are connected to the international markets and active at the same time in the local markets. This not the case of African networks. She suggests that the situation of poverty in Africa and the lack of social protection is specific to Africa in the sense that the logics of social, economic and political survival are at the basis of the rationality of corruption. This behavior is rational in the context of the Hobbesian war of everybody against everybody. The total impunity of the political elites encourage petty corruption, while the idea of the state, and of public good is not internalized. The "communitarism" encourages parasitism, and the so-called African solidarity is limited by segmentarity. The last dimension is the insertion of Africa within the international order. More and more African states find a comparative advantage in the fictitious character of the state and the porosity of their boundaries. This mode of insertion is intensified by the economic marginalization of Africa and its increasing dependency on international aid.

22

Corruption in the Neo-Patrimonial States of Sub-Saharan Africa

Jean-François Médard[1]

Corruption, long ignored by international organizations, is now one of their major preoccupations: it is considered largely responsible for the failure of development in Africa. To evaluate the extent of the phenomenon, we cannot simply say that it is an important factor. We must distinguish the levels of corruption, its extent and its cost. In Africa, corruption is both systemic and generalized: systemic, in the sense that it is the rule rather than the exception, generalized, because it is not just limited to certain sectors, but extended to the point that it covers the whole of the political, judicial, administrative sectors. Its price is very high in both absolute and relative terms, and this has serious economic consequences. We may even speak of a "culture of corruption" (Le Vine, 1975). Facing corruption of such a nature, the current economic models are ineffective. They are not adapted, because corruption does not correspond to economic rationality only, but also to political and social rationality. In addition, the notion of a rent seeking State is too limited as it implies that the State is rent seeking by essence: this does not allow for the difference between a Scandinavian state and an African state. It is better to say that it is the elite rather than the State that are rent seeking (Sindzingre, 1997).

This is why we prefer to approach the question globally from the Weberian ideal type of patrimonial domination. It is concerned with a type of traditional domination which is characterized by the confusion of the public and private domains, even though, objectively, there is political differentiation, since the chief commands people who are not his relatives. The king is the owner of his kingdom; there is no distinction between his personal property and public property; he governs with the support of his clients and patrimonial servants. The characteristics of patrimonialism are the personalization of power at the top as well as at all levels of authority, and the direct interchangeability of economic and political resources, that is wealth and power. Max Weber provides for a sub-type of patrimonialism, the "sultanism," to cover a patrimonial situation, where the arbitrary power of the chief does not function within a traditional framework. This is the case that is found in contemporary Africa. However, we prefer to use the expression of "neo-patrimonialism" in opposition to "traditional patrimonialism" (Eisenstadt, 1973). We are concerned with a mixed type rather than an ideal type (Médard, 1991). Where as in Europe, patrimonialism preceded bureaucratization, in Africa, the contradictory processes of bureaucratization and patrimonialization developed together (Médard, 1996). We can oppose the patrimonialized bureaucracy of African States to the bureaucratic patrimonialism of European absolute monarchies.

Strictly speaking, in the case of traditional patrimonialism we cannot use the term corruption, since the distinction between public and private is not clearly formulated and there is a confusion between the public and the private domains. In the contemporary neo-patrimonial context, where the public and private sectors are formally differentiated, and where this objective differentiation is accompanied at varying degrees by a subjective awareness of it, we can speak of corruption, when this distinction is not respected, in spite of the contradictions between traditional and modern cultural norms. For practical reasons, in our use here of the term corruption, we refer both to the subjective confusion of the public and private domains and to the disrespect of the distinction when it is formulated.

This conception has two implications. The first one is that we cannot limit corruption to corrupt exchange, as is notably the case in the economic definitions of corruption. It is necessary to extend the notion of corruption to practices which, like embezzlement, do not respect the distinction between the public and private sectors, but do not imply exchanges. This is particularly important in the African context where direct predation plays a larger role than in our countries. Furthermore, the concept of market corruption is insufficient, and must be completed by the notions of "corruption networks" (Cartier-Bresson, 1995), "parochial corruption" (Scott, 1969) or "social exchange corruption" (Padioleau, 1975), and extortion (Alatas, 1990). The second implication is that this formulation responds to the never-ending debate over the cultural relativism of the concept of corruption. A positive meaning, related to objective distinction between public and private sectors, and a normative and subjective meaning can be given. The first corresponds to corruption in a large sense as we have characterized it, the second, to corruption in a restrictive meaning which refers precisely to legal and/or moral norms.

To appreciate the changes in corruption in Africa over the past fifteen years, we will begin with the model of the neo-patrimonial state and the specific nature of corruption, which we qualify as (neo)patrimonial, in order to examine the effects of the generalization of the crisis in Africa in the eighties and nineties, and of the proposed remedies, to corruption.

Neo-Patrimonial Corruption in Africa

We will briefly recall the causes, nature, forms and consequences of corruption in Africa (Williams, 1987; Médard, 1986).

The Causes of (Neo)Patrimonial Corruption

We will not repeat in detail the causes of the patrimonialization of the State. We think that only an historical approach can explain how this corruption became institutionalized. However, once corruption is both systemic and generalized, it is self-maintained by a circular causal relationship.

On a political level, the post-colonial State, heir of the colonial State, could only benefit from a very precarious legitimacy. The new elite in power were in a structurally insecure political situation (Sindzingre, 1997): combining corruption with clientelism, with recourse to violence, constituted the most adapted modes of government for political survival. Power was personal more than institutional, which explains the contradiction between the short-term consolidation of personal power and the institutionalization of the State in the long run (Médard, 1990).

On the economic level, lacking a national bourgeoisie, economic accumulation came necessarily, directly and indirectly, through the State. The economy and politics became inextricably entangled. Such a situation took root in the historical extraversion of the continent (Bayart, 1989). This resulted in a rent seeking State based on a rent economy. In turn, the rent seeking elite connected themselves to the rent seeking State, turning the State monopoly to their personal benefit and to the benefit of their family, friends and clients.

We consider the culturalist explanation of neo-patrimonialism referring to an intemporal "African culture" as a pseudo-explanation (Sindzingre, 1994). First of all, traditional African culture should not be confused with contemporary African culture. Secondly, culture itself has to be explained, it is not primordial nor can be considered as a given, but it is constructed as the result of a historical process. However, if nothing or little can be explained by culture, nothing can be understood without it. We cannot make abstractions of the cultural representations accumulated in the course of history. The attitudes to the family, to the invisible world, the extreme personalization of social relationships, play a decisive role in the African context. Finally, the "culture of corruption," also a product of history, engenders specific representations which refer to the universal logics of survival, more than something specifically African: anomie, cynicism, resignation do not necessarily imply the approval of corruption, in reference or not, to so-called "African" values. It is not because one is resigned to corruption, because integrated in the system, and it has become normal, that one considers it good. It has simply become a necessity for survival. One then adjusts one's values to one's behavior.

The Nature of (Neo) Patrimonial Corruption

To say that corruption is all together systemic, generalized and that its price is high, enables us to distinguish it from the corruption observable in most industrial societies. In Africa, corruption encompasses both the government administration and the political levels, grand and petty corruption, corruption for survival and corruption for enrichment. The entire state apparatus is affected (Médard, 1991). The sums involved, whether in bribes or embezzlement, are considerable compared to the public expenses and economic transactions. Without underestimating the seriousness of the problem of corruption in our countries, the difference of degree transforms the nature of the phenomenon. While in Western countries, corruption threatens the bases of the democratic system, in Africa, it is the foundations of the State and of the economic system that are shaken.

The techniques of corruption are varied (Gould, 1980). They cannot be reduced to bribery alone, that is too restricted a legal and economic meaning of corruption, based on a contract of corruption, a mere market exchange. Corruption is not a simple transaction, but often pertains to extortion purely and simply: just think of all the road blocks where policemen or soldiers ransom the road users. Although market corruption is systematically used, it must not be confused with traditional gift giving practices, as it often is (Ekpo, 1979). Social exchange corruption (Padioleau, 1975) holds an important role in the forms of nepotism, "tribalism," clientelism and friendship ties. In addition, the articulation between social exchange corruption and market corruption presents itself differently. In Western countries, social exchange corruption is more to help economic exchange corruption, while in Africa, economic corruption is more to help social exchange corruption: family and ethnic pressures are much stronger, because of the importance of family ties. In general, social relationships are more personalized. These social pressures do not only bring about a generalization of nepotism, but also lead to economic corruption in order to fulfill social obligations of redistribution. In our countries, social exchange corruption is more a corollary of economic corruption. It is instrumentalized by economic corruption, because clandestine economic transactions must be regulated by recourse to corruption networks.

These corruption networks rely on trust, that only social exchange can create and foster (Cartier-Bresson, 1995).

Because of Africa's economic extroversion, the political-administrative grand corruption is in priority linked to international exchanges which are structures according to a type of clientelist logic: it is the case in Franco-African relationships (Glaser, Smith, 1993–1997; Verschave, 1998; Verschave, Boisgallais, 1994; Médard, 1996, 1997). In the West, corruption is mainly linked to political financing. Personal corruption of elected representatives constitutes a kind of prolongation of political financing. It remains a secondary means of economic accumulation within the society. Corruption is above all a privileged way of the business world to influence the political circles. In Africa, because of straddling (Bayart, 1989), the differentiation between the business world and the political spheres is less clear. Politicians are businessmen and business men are politicians (Médard, 1992, Fauré, Médard, 1994). However, it is to their interest, politically speaking, to redistribute part of the stolen money to keep their political clientele. In the sixties, the transition from multiparty systems to one party systems deprived the voters of the possibility of cashing in on their votes. But even without competitive elections, the leaders needed to keep their clientele. Electoral clientelism reappeared in the semi-competitive systems such as Kenya (Barkan, Okumu, 1978), and then in the pluralistic systems. It takes a pluralistic political system to develop fully. The mechanics of patronage and therefore stability are at the heart of a leader's political stability. The art of governing is not only the art of extracting resources, but also of redistribution: it is the only way of legitimizing power, in the absence of ideological legitimacy. In this way, corruption fits into the logic of the accumulation of political-economical goods, within the framework of survival strategies where the economy and politics are closely articulated. It is at the heart of the economic, social and political stratification process and the formation of social classes.

In comparison to other underdeveloped or developing countries, the differences are less noticeable. Everyone seems to admit that corruption in Asia is also systemic, generalized and costly. The difference is not so much of a quantitative nature, although there has never been a precise empirical comparison on the subject. What seems determinant is the relationship between corruption and the social, economic and political context. A working hypothesis could be formulated in this way: the decisive variable would be the degree of differentiation between the political environment and the economic environment, as well as the balance of power both opposing and uniting them at the same time. The question is to know whether the economic world dominates politics, or the politics dominate economics, or whether there is a certain balance of power and a degree of autonomy between them; or in other words, if it is the offer or the demand that predominates (Cartier-Bresson,

1997). To simplify to the extreme, one might say that in Africa, politics dominate the economy, to the extent that private economy lacks autonomy to develop. In Asia, the differentiation between the political and the economic worlds is more developed. In contrast to Africa, the business world has strength and influence, but the government has conserved a degree of autonomy which allows it to eventually impose its policy (Evans, 1989, 1994). According to Peter Evans, what distinguishes a developing state from a predatory state is that the public and private sectors dispose of a relative autonomy in relationship to each other, while keeping a close relationship. That is to say, there exists a strong differentiation between the political and economic spheres, combined with strong ties. But we cannot content ourselves with generalizations at the regional level, because within each region there are important differences between countries.

The Differences between African Countries

Even if the similarity to the patrimonial ideal type allows us to refer to neo-patrimonial corruption or to qualify the post-colonial State as neo-patrimonial, it is only an approximation. Even before the crisis, many differences in degree or of nature could be observed between the countries and regions of Africa. Most of the States of Southern Africa did not deserve the qualification of neo-patrimonial. This is the case of South Africa, of Zimbabwe (Darbon, 1991), of Malawi (L'Hoiry, 1991) and Botswana (Charlton, 1990, Good, 1994, Médard, to be published). One could add the socialist state of Mozambique. Conversely, other States were so close to the ideal type of the patrimonial sultanic State, that to use the prefix "neo" seems superfluous. The record was held by Zaïre under Mobutu (Gould, 1980) and Nigeria (Diamond, 1994; Tignor, 1993; Osoba, 1996). We could also add the Central African Republic(or "empire") under Bokassa (Bigo, 1988), Uganda under Amin Dada, or Equatorial Guinea under Macias Ngema. In this country, the President had stored all the bank notes of his country in his house in his village. To a journalist who asked him why, he answered: "I am the chief of my people, everything belongs to me." The majority of African States which we label as neo-patrimonial, lies between these two extremes. They are not completely patrimonialized, in the sense that patrimonial logics are articulated to bureaucratic logics. But at the two extremities, the difference in degree becomes a difference in nature.

With the systematic use of public commissions of inquiry, grand corruption is better known to the public in anglophone countries like Ghana (Le Vine, 1980), Sierra Leone (Kpunde, 1994) of Nigeria than in francophone countries. But the influence of the nationality of the former colonizer on corruption has been rather limited. Even if the British administrative legacy was "cleaner" than the French one, it did not last, and the former British colonies have become as patrimonialized as the French ones. One can, however, notice that there was often in anglophone Africa, a relatively independent press, judiciary system and Parliament. It may have contributed, if not to limiting corruption, at least to making it known to the public. In addition, academic corruption was more limited in former British colonies.

On the whole, one gets the impression that corruption in leading African countries like Ivory Coast, Kenya or Cameroon, was not completely generalized. Systemic administrative corruption was not as strong in Ivory Coast (Crook, 1989) or Kenya as in Cameroon where it was quite extensive. This had direct consequences on the level of administrative efficiency which was higher in the first two countries. Systemic grand political corruption was extremely high in the three countries. But President Ahmadou Ahidjo in Cameroon was less corrupted than Felix Houphouët-Boigny in Ivory Coast, who managed the "Caistab" as his own private fund. In Kenya, Jomo Kenyatta was considered as a "land grabber." But Ahmadou Ahidjo, who had direct control on the oil rent, left important financial reserves, which did not last very long after his departure. Not all the presidents were personally corrupt, even if their entourage was corrupt most of the time. The personal integrity of Julius Nyerere and of his entourage has never been in doubt, and corruption was rather limited when he was ruling the country.

The nature of the political regime, pluralist or authoritarian, civilian or military, did not have clear-cut consequences on corruption. The military, regularly, in order to justify their coups, denounce the corruption of their civilian predecessors, and without any delay, fall into the same trap. There has been an exception with the "redemptory" military regimes such as Rawling's and Sankara's. Socialist ideology had some effect on corruption in a certain number of cases, such as Mozambique and Ethiopia, but not in cases like Benin and Congo-Brazzaville. Socialist ideology may have played a certain role at the beginning of the regime, but by contributing to the slowing of economic growth and ruining the economy, it opened the path to the generalization of survival corruption. As to the elite, it encouraged the formation of a *nomenklatura*.

To conclude this quick overview, let us mention a few cases where administrative corruption was very low. In Malawi, under Banda (L'Hoiry, 1991), there was curiously very little corruption. Banda, relied on a single party, the efficiency of which in controlling the population, could have made the socialist countries jealous. It succeeded in disciplining the administration as well as the country. One might think that if the State in Malawi looked rather legal-rational at the bottom, at the top, it was patrimonial. In Burundi, Rwanda and Haute Volta, corruption was limited, and the administrative offices were rather efficient. Perhaps, these former traditional kingdoms had succeeded with time, in creating a habit of submission to public authority.

The Ambivalence of the Consequences of Corruption: The Patrimonial Mode of Political Regulation

The harmful effects of patrimonialism in Africa have been largely ignored during one quarter of a century. They are now publicly recognized. Politically, it is at the same time, the cause, the symptom and the consequence of the failure in the institutionalization of the State. Economically, corruption is considered as the main reason for the failure of development. Everybody agrees now, that with this kind of State, development is a myth. But at that level of corruption, causes and consequences interact and become entangled. Beyond this general acknowledgement, in order to evaluate more precisely the consequences of patrimonialism, we must oppose two contrasting situations. A few neo-patrimonial States, in spite of their manifest dysfunctions, have experienced for a long period, a relative political stability, combined with a rather high rate of growth. This has only been possible because the political leaders have been able to implement a mode of socio-political regulation (Fauré, Médard, 1982) which can be qualified as a patrimonial mode of regulation. This supposed a controlled use of corruption, respecting a tolerable rate of redistribution in proportion to extraction, and a politically rational particularistic mode of redistribution through patronage, allowing for a middle-term reproduction of the regime. At the other extreme, one could observe purely kleptocrat and predatory States, where in addition, violence was rampant and unchecked. This kind of political system, oriented in priority towards the short-term political survival of its leaders, sacrificed the middle and long term consolidation and institutionalization of the State.

A certain number of African countries enjoyed a fair degree of political stability, in spite of their structural fragility. Their leaders, often the founding fathers, died while still in power, and their successor came to power legally. They thus succeeded in constructing a political order, creating the conditions, if not of real development, at least of steady economic growth. Ivory Coast, Senegal, Kenya, Gabon and Cameroon, before the economic crisis, were among them. In spite of the inequality of distribution, everybody took, or could hope to take, advantage of the fruits of growth. Part of the surplus was redistributed according to the particularistic logic of political patronage, under the cover of the politicization of the administration, combined with the penetration of the political system by the civil servants. Patronage was used as a kind of cement to hold the ruling class in formation together, according to Bayart's scenario of "assimilation of elites" (Bayart, 1989). The direct beneficiaries of the presidential favor, under community pressures, and/or by political calculation, felt themselves under the obligation to redistribute in turn, to their relatives and friends. In spite of the fact that this redistribution was basically unequal, this inequality was bearable in periods of growth, because those who did not enjoy it, could hope that their turn would come.

Political stability has thus been based on favoritism, combined with a rational use of physical constraint. Clientelism helped economize the use of force. Economic accumulation to the benefit of the ruling class was practiced both legally and illegally. Legally, through the extraction of the peasant surplus through the stabilizing funds of the peasants income. Illegally, by means of embezzlement, bribes and frauds in public markets. This clientelist redistribution, that is the exchange of public goods for political support, does not respect the distinction between the public and private domains and constitutes a kind of social exchange corruption. As long as economic growth was sustained, redistribution, if it was well managed, was an efficient means of political control of the elite and of the people. As long as the people expected to enjoy personal benefits from corruption, they did not worry about the perverse secondary effects of corruption. This mode of regulation supposed a "reasonable" level of predation, that is a level that did not cause the source of the rent to dry up. This corresponds to the case, already documented, where systemic corruption is regulated and controlled through "stabilizing codes" (Cartier-Bresson, 1997). In spite of the fact that the administrations and the parastatals were a source of waste and functioned very badly, they were functioning enough to allow the continuation of growth. In addition, in francophone Africa, the power was stabilized because of the special ties these countries kept with their former colonial master, according to a neo-colonialist model of international clientelism (Médard, 1996, 1997). This helped to obtain a diversified assistance, a part of which was used to run the country thanks to civilian and military technical assistants. The remaining, directly or indirectly, contributed to the private economic accumulation of the leaders, together with their political and military protection (Verschave, Boisgallais, 1994).

Between these two extremes, other African countries, lacking an adequate political regulation, or deprived of sufficient resources, turned to unstable military dictatorships. Some of them, because of mineral wealth, managed to be stabilized for a while (Niger, Togo, Guinea, Congo-Brazzaville, and Benin through Nigeria). A few of these countries could use their mineral rent to finance a socialist experiment. Joining the socialist club contributed to their political stabilization. It was based more on techniques of political control, with the assistance of communist countries, than on sound economic policies or politics of redistribution. The economic policies which were chosen for ideological reasons prevented any development of agriculture.

At the other extreme, appeared a few "sultanic" regimes, like, Zaïre of Mobutu, Uganda of Amin Dada and Obote, Central African Republic of Bokassa, or Equatorial Guinea of Macias Ngema. These "states" were uniquely oriented toward plunder and predation and relied above all on violence. They prefigured political situations which, with the generalization of the economic crisis, have become common. It corresponds to a borderline case of patrimonialism, where the privatization of the public domain destroys the basis of patrimonialism itself. Patrimonialism, devouring itself, leads to what has been qualified as the "criminalization of politics" (Bayars, Ellis, Hibou, 1997).

The African Crisis and the Evolution of Corruption

During the eighties and the nineties, the economic crisis develops and becomes permanent. Africa enters the era of structural adjustment. The Structural Adjustment Plans are, on the whole, ineffective. They worsen the social situation which had already been undermined by the economic crisis, without bringing any serious remedy to the economic situation. At the beginning of the eighties, with a certain time lag, countries which had enjoyed an appreciable sustained growth until then, were struck by the crisis, because of the fall of the prices of raw materials (coffee, cocoa, oil...). They are unable to face the situation. The State does not function anymore. The rulers lose their means of political regulation and suffer an erosion of their political support. All the economic indicators turn to red: budget deficit, balance of payments, unemployment, foreign disinvestment...Africa enters the path of economic marginalization. Its share in the world trade becomes negligible. Brought about by the economic crisis and encouraged by the fall of the Soviet Empire and the end of the Cold War, a political crisis bursts out and destabililizes the authoritarian regimes. The result of democratic transitions is weakened and the new multiparty regimes find themselves in a difficult situation. The economic and political crisis linked together, has a multiplying effect, contributing to the increase of corruption.

If reality was conform to theory, economic liberalization and democratization should have encouraged a regression of corruption in Africa. This has not been the case, and the dominant impression is quite the opposite, that corruption has increased and extended. In the worse case, one notices a real "criminalization of politics" of which corruption is one dimension.

A General Increase of Corruption

Not only do we lack precise data, but it is also difficult to untangle, analytically, the respective effects of the economic crisis, of structural adjustment, of democratic transitions, and of the recent anti-corruption attempts. It is not clear whether the observed effects are the results of the economic and political reforms, or of the incapacity to implement them. However, there is a convergence of evaluations to suggest an increase of corruption.

Let us take the example of Cameroon. This country, under the presidency of Ahmadou Ahidjo (1960–1982), was an excellent illustration of both the very negative effects of neo-patrimonial corruption, and of the efficiency of a neo-patrimonial mode of political regulation, in the context of a very authoritarian regime (Médard, 1978). The level and the extent of corruption which could be observed in the seventies could raise strong doubts about the reality of its economic development in spite of a reasonable rate of growth. However, because of the political ability of Ahidjo, Cameroon enjoyed a real political stability. At the end of the seventies, at the time when Ivory Coast was encountering economic problems, Cameroon's rate of growth increased, boosted by the exploitation of oil. When the rest of Africa was falling into the economic crisis, Cameroon's economic situation still looked quite sound. But when Biya succeeded Ahidjo as president, there was a change for the worst. In 1986, the economy failed brutally. A political crisis followed, which aggravated the economic crisis. An unsuccessful democratic transition worsened the economic situation. The structural adjustment plans were largely circumvented, and if applied, resulted in increasing the suffering of the population, without contributing to economic recovery. The wages of the civil servants were drastically reduced (close to 70 percent), which had, through redistribution, a repercussion on the income of the population as a whole. After the devaluation in 1994, the population was in a state of shock, and the political situation prevented the economy of taking advantage of it. The struggle for life became exacerbated. Ethnicity was instrumentalized and politicized by the political leaders to a point that put the country on the brink of civil war. Predation by the elite in power intensified. The economic and political situation had never been so difficult, and corruption had never reached such levels and extent. In spite of a largely cosmetic multipartyism, there was no return to the point of departure. A certain degree of freedom of the press has been instituted, and an independent press struggles for survival (Médard, 1996). Thanks to the press, we are better informed about the corruption at the top, than at the time of Ahidjo. We have learned for instance, that the second bank of the country, the Société Camerounaise de Banque, had become bankrupt because of the presidential couple. The problem, though, is to sort out the truth in the middle of such a profusion of news about corruption. In 1998, Transparency International ranked Cameroon as the worldwide champion of corruption. However, more recently a sort of political and economical stabilization was noticeable. An identical portrait of the situation in Kenya could be painted: acceleration of predation by the elite in power (Goldenberg scandal), exacerbation of ethnicity for political survival, failure of the democratic transition and facade multipartyism, division of opposition, but also the role of the independent press, and important political mobilizations (Kibwana, et al, 1996); Bigsten, Moene, 1996; Finance 1995).

    Apparently, Ivory Coast is coming out better, economically and politically, even if the situation is far from being bright. It has been able to benefit from the devaluation, and economic growth is back to a moderate rate. The ethnic tension has been well controlled by Houphouët-Boigny, but with the democratic transition, a North-South cleavage has developed with ethno-regional and religious connotations. However, the politicization of ethnicity did not go as far as in Kenya and Cameroon. The level of conflict did not go too far. The democratic transition led to a facade multipartyism, and the transition has been more controlled. But corruption has generalized within the administration into sectors which were previously relatively free of it. The experience of privatization has been exemplary: the public utilities of water and electricity have been privatized and offered to Bouygues public works company, without any tendering. The good personal relations Bouygues entertained with Houphouët were sufficient. (Glaser, Smith, 1993).

Privatizations have opened in Africa an additional opportunity for corruption, without any guarantee that the expected positive effects will ensue. When the parastatals have not been sold to foreign interests, as in Soviet Union, it is the "nomenklatura," the only one with the necessary capital, which has been able to buy them. One can also be skeptical about the effects of decentralization on corruption: there is no reason to believe that the local elite behave in a different way than the central authorities. In addition, to decentralize the administration without decentralizing the financial resources does not look like a practical solution. In the same token, to substitute the non-governmental organizations for the State may have just the effect of restructuring the networks of rent extraction.

Democratization, including the countries where it had some success, did not have the expected effects on corruption (Harsh 1993; Beck 1995), it even seems to have increased it. It is impossible, however, to know to what extent democratization contributed to this result. Because of the relative freedom of the press, corruption is better publicized and it contributes to the impression that it has increased. Corruption at the top was hidden more effectively before. What is certain, is that corruption in a context of economic crisis is not as well tolerated. If democracy was more effective, it would introduce more transparency and better controls on corruption. This failure corresponds to the failure of democratization, but also to the fact that democracy offers new opportunities for corruption. The newly elected leaders are under the same pressures as the former ones. In addition, they need to finance their election, which will necessarily involve corruption. As in Western countries when elections were first introduced, electoral corruption became unavoidable. It is therefore not surprising, that so many scandals have erupted. In Zambia, the new rulers have been compromised in a number of scandals. The same thing has happened in Malawi, where corruption is a serious problem now (Africa confidential, 1995). In Benin, the nepotism of Soglo, the newly elected president, and of his family contributed to his defeat and his replacement by the former dictator Kerekou.

In Southern Africa, which was less touched by corruption than the rest of Africa, the same increase of corruption is noticed. In Mozambique, grand politico-administrative corruption has broken out. In Zimbabwe, Mugabe's regime is in the process of patrimonialization, and this contributes to its delegitimation: the scandals of the new airport, of the market of telecommunications, of the veterans fund...Its pernicious effects are not yet visible at the level of the administration whose efficiency is still striking in comparison to the northern regions. But corruption threatens to become generalized because of the absence of the determination at the top to stop it. In South Africa, corruption is also on the agenda (Lodge, 1998). Even in Botswana, which was and still is the most democratic, the best-managed and the least corrupt country in Africa, scandals have appeared in the beginning of the nineties (Good, 1994). These scandals reveal that corruption has become systemic in certain sectors, like the public markets, and the building industries, access to housing and real estate. But corruption is still far behind the rest of Africa, and the government has demonstrated a capacity to react to the problem, which may be related in this case to the democratic process. In an increasing number of countries, there is even a mutation of corruption in the sense that corruption has become only one dimension of a larger problem of the criminalization of politics, which constitutes the "supreme stage of patrimonialism."

The Criminalization of Politics

The expression of "criminalization of politics" proposed by Bayart et al, in spite of, or because of its lack of precision, is convenient because of its strong power of suggestion. The rulers of a certain number of neo-patrimonial States, in their desperate search for survival, rely mostly on violence and criminality, to stay in power, without worrying about the middle term conditions of the reproduction of their domination. They grab all the available opportunities for predation, mostly those offered by access to the informal transnational markets and networks (Reno, 1996). Recourse to violence has become the main instrument for predation and accumulation. The "big men" become a combination of warlords and gangsters. The States, or what is left of them, exist only because their international sovereignty is recognized by international law and the United Nations. They become smugglers, "narcostates," like Nigeria or Equatorial Guinea (Observatoire Géopolitique de la Drogue), money forgering States, like Zaïre, "gemmocracies" like Sierra Leone (Missier, Vallée, 1997). At this stage, it is not only corruption that is globalized, systemic and generalized, it is criminality itself in connection to international crime.

This new type of State corresponds precisely to the "sultanic state" of Max Weber. The privatization of power and the privatization of violence are interconnected. This is why, another way of describing this political situation, is to talk of "privatization of the State" (Hibou, 1999). We have seen that it is not a new phenomenon in Africa. What is new, though, is the tendency towards its geographic extension. It is also, through globalization, more strongly connected to international crime networks. Many States, which would have been qualified before as neo-patrimonial States are criminalized, completely or in part. Completely criminalized are Somalia, Angola, Sierra Leone, Liberia, Equatorial Guinea...Partly criminalized are, Nigeria, Cameroon, Kenya....This gives the impression of an irresistible process of criminalization. This impression may be exaggerated, and we should be careful not to see the criminalization of politics everywhere. This evolution corresponds to the strategies of political and economic survival of the political leaders in an internal context of generalized economic and political crisis, and in an international environment characterized paradoxically, by economic and political marginalization on one side, and globalization on the other. This situation offers new opportunities of a criminal nature, at a time when legitimate opportunities are declining.

This mutation of the neo-patrimonial State illustrates the in-built contradictions of neo-patrimonialism. The privatization of the public domain, when pushed to its limits, makes the public sector and the State itself vanish. The political survival of rulers is less and less based on the control of formal institutions, but is rooted in the national and international informal networks. This leads to the following paradox: the neo-patrimonial State, which was, in a way, a kind of State, is dismantled by its own rulers in their obsessional search for survival. The cases of Uganda before Museveni, or Sierra Leone as it is described by Reno, or the Zaïre of Mobutu are perfect illustrations.

Amin Dada's and Obote's Uganda foreshadowed the present situation. Amin Dada had ruined the economy of the country by expelling the Asians to share their spoils with his clients. Obote who replaced him, installed an even more sanguinary, although less publicized, dictatorship. It was the reign of "magendo" (Prunier, 1983). Under this expression was much more than corruption, but all the forms of economic criminality and also, all the techniques of survival and resourcefulness, including the legitimate ones. At the forefront, the smuggling of coffee, frauds in currencies, black market, extortion and plundering by the army which was living off the country. There was no drug dealing at that time. Apart from the help Obote was able to extract from international organizations ($800 millions), the main and traditional resource was coffee. The army directly controlled the parastatal which had the monopoly of the commercialization of coffee. The head of the army was the head of the parastatal. The army or company trucks were indistinctly transporting the ammunition and the coffee bags. This led to a fall of the production on the part of the peasants who tried to smuggle the coffee out of the country. The smuggling was organized with the complicity of the military and civilian leaders....The classic type of corruption could not exist any more since the civil servants had nothing to sell. They kept their positions, however, even if the monthly salary of a university professor, for instance, covered only the basic cost of life of one day. At least, he could keep his house and a piece of land where he could cultivate bananas or raise a cow. The material basis of accumulation was still based on agriculture, however.

With the case of Sierra Leone, the material basis is mineral, and lighter, if we may say so, since it is diamonds (Misser, Vallee, 1997). William Reno has shown how the political and military leaders in the end completely privatized the economic basis of their power, by becoming an integral part of the informal diamond smuggling network. It is what he calls the "Shadow State" (Reno 1995). It is a return to the age of mercenaries, when violence itself is privatized through the services of private security firms, as the South-African Executive Outcome. These companies take in charge the security of the mineral companies, and are economically interested in their exploitation. This is done with the benediction of the international creditors, since it is the only way they have to get repaid (Reno, 1997).

The evolution of Mobutu's Zaïre is another extraordinary example. Mobutu has demonstrated, since the apogee of his power in the times of "authenticity," and of "mobutism" (1974), an exceptional capacity for survival in a context of shrinking economic resources, caused by the fall of the price of copper, and of his catastrophic mode of economic and political management. With the end of the Cold War, he lost the international protection that he had been able to benefit from. The territorial State was replaced by an "Archipelago State" (Pourtier, 1995), exclusively limited to the control of the key points of access to fungible resources such as diamonds and gems. At the end he even used currency forgery.

When a State reaches this degree of informality (Chabal and Daloz, 1998), any thought of fighting corruption is surrealistic.

The Reactions against Corruption

Reactions against corruption have developed at both international and African levels. It is only recently that the international organization have put corruption on their agenda (Médard, to be published). They have evolved progressively. In 1983, the Elliot Berg report raised the question of the responsibility of the African State for the failure of development. Then the "good governance" approach was developed. It implied structural reforms of a political nature and not only economic and administrative reforms. The institution of a minimum state, a State of Law, and a democratic state were supposed to bring in accountability and transparency, which are by also the basis of the prevention of corruption. Finally, in September 1996, the president of the World Bank declared war on corruption. All the international organizations have been associated in this movement against corruption, from the OCDE (Goudie 1996) to the UN (Charlick 1992). All this led to an anticorruption strategy, with the National Integrity System (Lambeth et al. 1997).

There is no doubt that the African continent was considered as the first target of this movement, particularly as far as the World Bank and the FMI were concerned. In Africa, denunciation of corruption has always been a tradition (Olivier de Sardan 1996), but with the crisis it became a general complaint. Until recently, the measures against corruption had been indecisive or based exclusively on political opportunity. Later, under the pressure and the help of the outside world a more systematic anti-corruption action has been implemented.

The Denunciation of Corruption

For a long time, there was a kind of passive acceptance of corruption, at least when the economic situation was favorable. As it had became a real way of life, its advantages seemed to override its inconvenience. It is, however, simplistic to pretend that the "African" ignores what corruption means. (Decraene, 1984). One has to be more explicit and cannot talk about the "African" or corruption in general. It is not only, as it is frequently said, that there is a contradiction between traditional and modern norms. There is no doubt about the influence of kinship relations on corruption in Africa. Peter Ekeh thus opposed what he calls the "civic public" to the "primordial public" (Ekeh 1975). But it corresponds more often to a conflict between practical norms and ethical norms corresponding to a double normative structure, both instrumental and symbolic (Becquart-Leclerc, 1984). In some extreme cases we could talk of anomie. Once corruption becomes the rule, and non corruption the exception, the practice transforms itself into a norm. Against the relativists, Alatas insisted, quite correctly, that Westerners did not have the monopoly of the conscience of corruption (Alatas, 1990). Even before the generalization of the economic crisis, corruption was an object of scandal, as is demonstrated by the many commissions of inquiry on corruption in anglophone Africa (Ghana, Sierra-Leone, Nigeria...). If corruption did not have any meaning for Africans, there would be no reason for the military after a coup to expose the corruption of their predecessors in order to justify their taking over.

With the generalization of the economic crisis, corruption becomes literally unbearable for the mass of the population, even if they have to practice it in order to survive. Its fundamentally inegalitarian effects become visible and are resented as intolerable. Clientelism, which made inequality and arbitrariness acceptable, no longer functions and becomes deeply unbalanced. The number of the recipients of favors diminishes in proportion to the non-beneficiaries, and they lose hope of having their turn. In cleverly managing the stock of patronage and of prebends, it was possible to divide and rule. In this sense, the particularist mode of clientelistic redistribution is much more economical than the universalist mode of the welfare state redistribution, and it permits in addition, to control the subjects more closely. But, with resources declining, there is less for redistribution. In the surrounding shortage, the life of luxury led by the "big men" which until then was shared in a symbolic manner, becomes a source of scandal. The demand increases as offer shrinks leading, with the stimulation and the manipulation of the leaders, to a politicization and exacerbation of ethnicity. Formerly the leader, in order to cement and consolidate his personal alliance of power, was able to co-opt his opponents, and to regroup around himself a large ethno-regional coalition. The politicization of ethnicity, while helping to strengthen the ranks, leads to a zero sum conflict.

It is, therefore, not surprising that the theme of corruption was at the heart of the popular mobilizations everywhere during democratic transitions, as the national conferences and the independent press show. The democratic demands and the fight against corruption were, as in Tien An Men, closely connected. The political authorities, in their effort to get around the pressure of international organizations through structural adjustment, have been able to transfer the necessary sacrifices to the mass of the population, including part of the rising middle class, in order to spare themselves of the cost of reforms. They even accelerated predation at the time when the economic situation was becoming catastrophic. The structural adjustment plans, the privatizations, deregulation, in brief, economic liberalization, which was supposed to be the remedy to the crisis, put the newly created pluralist political systems in an impossible situation. It was the favorable aim for mobilization against corruption.

The Fight against Corruption

Controlling corruption is not a new idea in Africa, the legislation has always been there, but impunity has been the rule. When sanctions were taken, it was not to fight corruption, but to get rid of someone for political reasons, or, in response to a scandal, and some kind of reaction was necessary. In any case the culprits were not forced to pay back what they had stolen. Occasionally, after military coups, action, and even violent action, was taken against the corrupt, as in Ghana or Liberia.

It was with the apparition of the "redemptory regimes" of Rawlings in Ghana, and of Sankara in Burkina Faso, that corruption became the target of a systematic policy, with apparently some success, since observers, at least for Burkina, agree that there is less corruption in these countries than elsewhere. In Ghana, Rawlings succeeded with the help of international organizations, but following his own agenda, to strengthen the economic, administrative and political situation (Chavaneux, 1997). Corruption is still a huge problem, but has diminished in comparison to the former regimes. The country is relatively well managed, and economic growth is back. We are far from the "kalabule" years of Acheampong (Le Vine, 1980). Sankara, when he took power, wanted to break symbolically with the past, in changing significantly the name of his country, Haute Volta, to Burkina Faso, that is the "country of honest people." He set up "popular" courts and organized public trials against former "big men" accused of corruption, and led a vigorous campaign against corruption. He himself, ostensibly, chose to live a very unaffected life. This made him very popular with the African youth. In fact, his country was not then very corrupt in comparison to its neighbors. Since his assassination and replacement by Compraore, corruption has increased, but is still relatively moderate. The Administration is less corrupt than elsewhere and fairly well managed.

In Botswana, following the scandals at the beginning of the nineties, important political leaders (the vice-president and the general secretary of the dominant party), were forced to resign. Parliament voted an anti-corruption law, which has created an anti-corruption unit, on the same model as in Hong Kong. It has started to function, but it is criticized for looking for the "small fry" more than for the "big fish." This is the main problem facing the countries engaged in the control of corruption, because of the capacity, everywhere, of the ruling class to protect itself. It is the same problem in Uganda.

According to a recent report of the World Bank, the most encouraging case is Uganda, where the persevering action of Museveni to rebuilt a political order has had some result. Since he conquered power in 1986, he started an experiment in reconstructing, economically and politically, a country which was in a desperate situation, after the dictatorships of Amin Dada and Obote (Banegas, 1996). He has not yet succeeded in pacifying the northern part of the country, but the economic and political situation have greatly improved. Museveni refused multipartyism without rejecting pluralism. More recently, the situation has been compromised by the international situation and the question of the security of the borders. With the help of the World Bank, Uganda has launched an anti-corruption program, inspired by the "National Integrity Systems of the World Bank (Langseth et al., 1997 b). Among the specific measures which have been taken, should be mentioned: the creation of an anti-corruption organization, the General Inspectorate of Government; a drastic reduction of the public sector; the adoption of an accountability system within the public service; an increase in the wages of the public servants and the promotion of a code of ethics. But nothing is really solved, even if some progress has been noticed. Here again, the main problem is to challenge the corruption of the "big fish." Museveni needs to keep his coalition in power. The case of Uganda should be watched carefully, since it is the very rare case of a country which has succeeded in overcoming the criminalization of politics: Uganda is no longer a "sultanic" state.

Tanzania also started a "National Integrity system," with still limited results (Langseth, et al., 1997 b). Recently, a report from a presidential commission of inquiry was published, and for the first time the President took serious measures against very "big fish." In many African countries, the fight against corruption is on the political agenda, under the pressure and with the help of the international organizations. It is the case in Benin, South Africa, etc. Local branches of Transparency International are created, as in Zimbabwe, where pressure from inside can lead to international support. The great problem, however, is that in many countries, we are facing a comedy of action against corruption, as it was for structural adjustment and democracy, in order to gain the favors of the external world. The case of Cameroon is exemplary: The President named a new Prime Minister with the special task of leading the war against corruption. When he took, naively, his job seriously, he was fired....

In conclusion, we may make four remarks. The first one is the increasing seriousness of the problem of corruption in Africa: if economic growth can accommodate even with, systemic and generalized corruption, provided it is auto-regulated, economic development, is incompatible with patrimonialism. The second observation is that the fight against corruption is impossible in the context of systemic and generalized corruption, a fortiori with criminalization of politics. The first condition for the effectiveness of the fight against corruption, is that it must have real internal support, a leadership which is seriously dedicated to the problem and on collective action. This supposes a radical transformation of society, the elite, and the social, economic and political system which is not likely to happen. The problem is that corruption is not only a cause, it is also a symptom. This change, even if it can be encouraged, cannot be generated from outside. This does not seem to leave much space for change but, the third remark, is that the evolution toward the worse is not always and everywhere inescapable. There is no fatality nor determinism. To accept a determinist approach leads to a self-fulfilling prophecy. Even if the constraints are strong, one cannot neglect the role of the actors. The last observation is that corruption does not only undermine the State and development, it is in itself the negation of democracy, it is "the reverse of the Rights of Man" (Borghi and Meyer-Bish, 1995). It is not a coincidence if pluralism, transparency and accountability constitute the foundations of democracy and at the same time the principles of action for an anti-corruption strategy. The problem is, that if the democratic mechanisms are the best weapons against corruption, corruption is one of the main threats to democracy.

Bibliography

Adediji, O. (1991), "Role of Government in Bureaucratic Corruption: the Case of Politicization of the Civil Service," *The Quarterly Journal of Administration*, vol.XXV, n°2, January, p. 208–217.
Africa Confidential (1995), vol. 36, n°25, 15/12 (Malawi).

African Rights (1996), *Kenya's shadow justice*, London, "a rotten system, corruption in the court," ch. 5.

Agere, S. (1992), "The Promotion of Good Ethical Standards and Behaviour in Public Services in Africa: the Case for Zimbabwe," *Africanus*, vol. 22, nos 1&2.

Alatas, S. H. (1990), "Corruption: its Nature, Causes and Functions," Aldershot, Avebury.

Anyang'nyongo (1997), "Divestiture, a flop due to corruption," *Nation*, Sunday 7 September 1997.

Banegas, R. (1996), "Ouganda: la construction d'un ordre politique, Karthala, *L'Afrique politique*.

Bayart, J.-F. (1989), *l'Etat en Afrique, la politique du ventre*, Paris, Fayard.

Bayart, J.-F., Ellis, S. and Hibou, B. (1997), *La criminalisation de l'Etat en Afrique*, Bruxelles, Editions Complexe, 1997.

Beck, L. (1995), "Patrimonial Democrats: Incremental Reform and the Obstacles to Consolidating Democracy in Senegal," conference paper for the APSA conference, Chicago, 31 August-3 September.

Becquart-Leclercq, J. (1984), "Paradoxes de la corruption politique," *Pouvoirs*, n°31, p.19–36, Paris, PUF.

Bigo, D. (1988), *Pouvoir et obéissance en Centrafrique*, Paris, Karthala.

Bigsten, A. and Moene, K.O. (1996), "Growth and Rent Dissipation: the Case of Kenya," *Journal of African Economies*, vol 5, n°2, p.177–98, June.

Borghi, M. and Meyer-Bisch, P. (1995), ed. *La corruption, l'envers des droits de l'homme*, Fribourg, Editions Universitaires.

Cartier-Bresson, J. (1995), "Les réseaux de corruption et la stratégie des trois S: Sleep-Silence-Smile," in Borghi, M. and Meyer-Bisch, P. eds. *La Corruption, l'envers des droits de l'homme*, Editions Universitaires de Fribourg, p. 81–106.

Cartier-Bresson, J. (1997), "Quelques propositions pour une analyse de la corruption en Europe de l'Est," in "La corruption," *Revue Internationale de Politique Comparée*, vol. 4, n°2, septembre.

Chabal, P. and Daloz, J.-P. *Africa works: disorder as political intrument,* Oxford, James Currey, Bloomington, Indiana University Press, 1998.

Charlick, R. ed. (1992/3a), "Limiting Administrative Corruption in the Democratizing States of Africa," proceedings of a conference held in Washington D.C. September 11, 1992, *Corruption and Reform*, Special issue, 7, 3.

Charlick, R. (1992/3b), "Corruption in Political Transition: a Governance Perspective," p.177, in Charlick R. ed.

Charlick, R. (1992/3c), "Combatting Corruption in an era of Political Liberalization, Implications for Donors Agencies," p. 283, in Charlick, R., ed. op. cit.

Charlton, R. (1990), "Exploring the Byways of African Political Corruption: Botswana and Deviant Case Analysis," *Corruption and Reform*, vol.5, n°1, 1990.

Chavanieux, C. (1997), "Ghana, une révolution de bon sens, Economie politique d'un ajustement structurel," Paris, Karthala.

Coussy, J. (1991), "Economie et politiques du développement, p.205–228, in Coulon, C. and Martin, D. dir. *Les Afriques politiques*, Paris, Karthala.

Crook, R. (1989), "Patrimonialism, Administrative Effectiveness and Economic Development in Ivory Coast," *African Affairs*, p. 205–228.

Decraene, P. (1984) "La corruption en Afrique noire, *Pouvoirs,* n°31, Paris PUF.

Diamond, L. (1994), "Corruption: Nigeria's Perennial Struggle, *Journal of democracy,"* vol. 2, n°4, fall.

Darbon, D. (1991), "Zimbabwe: contruire la maison de pierre," in Medard, J.-F. dir. *Etats d'Afrique Noire*, op. cit. p. 305–322.

Ekeh, P. (1975), "Colonialism and the two Publics in Africa: a Theoretical Statement, *Comparative Studies in Society and History*, n°17.

Ellis, S. (1996), "Africa and International Corruption: the Strange Case of South Africa and Seychelles," *African Affairs*, 95, p.165–196.

Ellis, S. and MacGaffey, J. (1997), "Le commerce international informel en Afrique sub-saharienne, Quelques problèmes méthodologiques et conceptuels," *Cahiers d'Etudes Africaines*, XXXVII, 1, 145, p.11–38.

Eisenstadt, S. (1973), *Traditional Patrimonialism and Modern Neo-Patrimonialism*, London, Sage.

Ekpo, M. (1979), "Gift-giving practices and bureaucratic corruption in Nigeria," in Epko, M. ed. *Bureaucratic Corruption in Sub-Saharan Africa*, Washington, Praeger.

Evans, P. (1994), *Embedded Autonomy, States and Industrial Transformation*, Princeton University Press.

Evans, P. (1989), "Predatory, Developmental and other Apparatus: a Comparative Political Economy Perspective in the Third World states," *Sociological forum*, vol.4, n°4, 1989.

Faure, Y. and Medard, J.-F. (1994), "L'Etat-Business et les politiciens-entrepreneurs " in Ellis, S. and Faure, Y. *Les entrepreneurs en Afrique*, Paris, Karthala.

Faure, Y. and Medard, J-F, eds. (1982), *Etat et bourgeoisie en Côte d'Ivoire*, Paris Karthala.

Finance (Nairobi) (1995), special issue *Corruption, the Kenyan Cancer*, January 15.

Glaser, A. (1993), "Afrique: la roue de la fortune," *Histoires de développement*, n°24.

Glaser, A. and Smith, S. eds. (1992)(1997), *Ces Messieurs Afrique*, Paris, Calmann Levy, tome 1 and 2.

Gould, D. (1980), *Bureaucratic Corruption and Underdevelopment in the Third World: the Case of Zaïre*, Pergamon Press, (appendice A, p.123–149).

Greenstone, D. (1965/6), "Corruption and Self Interest in Kampala and Nairobi," *Comparative studies in History and Society*, 8, p.199–210.

Good, K. (1994), "Corruption and mis-Management in Botswana: a best case example?," *The Journal of Modern African Studies* 32, 3, p. 499–521.

Goudie, A.W. and Stasavage, D. (1996), *A Framework for the Analysis of Corruption*, Paris, OCDE Development Center, October.

Harsch, E. (1993), "Accumulators and Democrats: Challenging State Corruption in Africa," *The Journal of Modern African Studies*, 31, I, p. 31–48.

Heilbrunn, J. (1997), "Corruption, Democracy and Reform in Africa, Institutionalizing Horizontal Accountability: how Democracies can Fight Corruption and the Abuse of Power," Third Vienna Dialogue on democracy, 26–29 June.

Hibou, B. ed. "L'Etat en voie de privatisation," *Politique Africaine*, n°73, 1999.

IRIS (no date), *Governance and the economy in Africa, tools for analysis and reform of corruption*, IRIS, University of Maryland at College Perk.

Johnston, M. "Entrenched Corruption and long term Anti-Corruption Opportunities," IDS workshop on corruption and development, May 7, 1997.

Johnston, M. "Micro and Micro Possibilities for Reforms," p.189 et suiv. in Charlick R. ed., 1992/3.

Kpundeh, S. J. (1994), "Limiting Administrative Corruption in Sierra Leone," *The Journal of Modern African Studies*, 32, 1, p.131–157.

Kpundeh, S. J. (1994), *Politics and corruption in Africa, a case study of Sierra Leone*, Lanham, University of America Press.

Kibwana, K.; Wanjala S.; Oketh-Owitti, eds. (1996), *The anatomy of corruption in Kenya, legal, political and socio-economic perspectives*, Nairobi, Clarion, Claripress limited.

400   Political Corruption

Langseth, P.; Stapenhust, R.; Pope, J. (1997a), *National Integrity System Country Studies* (Uganda and Tanzania), Washington, the Economic Development Institute of the World Bank.
Langseth, P.; Stapenhust, R.; Pope, J. (1997b), *The role of National Integrity System in fighting corruption,* Washington, the Economic Development Institute of the World Bank, 1997.
Le Vine, Victor (1975), *Political corruption: the Ghana case,* Stanford, Hoover Institution press.
Le Vine, Victor (1992/3), "Administrative Corruption and Democratization in Africa: Aspects of the Theoretic Agenda," in Charlick R., ed. op. cit. 1992/3.
Lodge, T., "Corruption in South Africa," *African Affairs,* June 1998.
L'Hoiry (1991), "L'Etat au Malawi: l'Afrique disciplinée," in Medard J-F dir. p. 291–304.
Mbaku, J. (1994), "Bureaucratic Corruption and Policy Reform in Africa," *The Journal of Social, Political and Economic Studies*, vol.19, number 2, Summer.
Mbembe, A. (1992), "Afrique des comptoirs ou Afrique du développement," *Le Monde Diplomatique,* janvier.
Médard, J.-F., (1976) "Le rapport de clientèle," *Revue française de science politique,* 31, p.103–131, février.
Médard, J.-F. (1977), "L'Etat sous-développé au Cameroun, Pedone, *L'Année africaine.*
Médard, J.-F. (1986), "Public corruption in Africa: a comparative perspective," *Corruption and Reform*, vol. 1, n°2, p.115–131.
Médard, J.-F. (1990), "L'Etat patrimonialisé," *Politique africaine*, n°39, p. 25–36, Septembre.
Médard, J.-F. (1991), L'Etat néo-patrimonial en Afrique noire, in J-F Médard dir. *Etats d'Afrique Noire*, Paris, Karthala, p.323–354.
Médard, J.-F. "Le "big man" en Afrique," *L'Année Sociologique*, n°42, p.1991.
Médard, J.-F. (1996 a), Etat, démocratie et développement: l'expérience camerounaise, in Mappa, S. *Développer par la démocratie,* p.355–390.
Médard, J.-F. (1996 b), "Patrimonialism, Neo-Patrimonialism and the Study of the African Post-Colonial State in sub-Saharian Africa," in Markussen, H. ed. *Improved Natural Resource Management—the Role of Formal Organization and Informal Networks and Institutions*, Occasional paper n°17, International Development Studies, Roskilde University, p.193–206.
Médard, J.-F. (to be published), "Corruption et non corruption au Botswana: la normalisation d'un cas déviant ?," in Compagnon, D. and Mokopakgosi, B. dir. *Le Botswana contemporain*, Paris Karthala-IFRA.
Médard, J.-F. (To be published), "La Banque Mondiale, l'Afrique et la corruption."
Médard, J.-F. (1997), "L'Afrique et la corruption internationale: une approche comparative," *Revue Internationale de politique comparée*, vol 4, n°3, Septembre.
Mescheriakov (1987), "L'ordre patrimonial: essai d'interprétation du fonctionnement de l'administration d'Afrique francophone sub-saharienne," p. 323–351, *Revue française d'administration publique*, 42, avril-juin.
Misser, R. and Vallee, O.(1997), *Les gemmocraties, l'économie politique du diamant africain*, Desclée de Brouwer.
Owona, M. (1986), "L'Etat et les milieux d'affaires au Cameroun (1986–1996), autoritarisme, ajustement au marché et démocratie," *Polis*, n°2, vol.2.
Owona, M. (1997), *La sociogenèse de l'ordre politique au Cameroun entre autoritarisme et démocratie (1978–1996),* Thèse, Bordeaux, Université Montesquieu Bordeaux IV, Septembre.
Observatoire Géopolitique de la Drogue, (OGD), *La Dépêche Internationale des Drogues*, Paris.

Olowu, D. (1992/3), "Roots and Remedies of Governmental Corruption in Africa," p.227 et suiv. in Charlick R., ed., op. cit. 1992:3.

Osoba, S. O. (1996), "Corruption in Nigeria: Historical Perspectives," *Review of African Political Economy*, n°69: p. 371–386.

Ouma, S. (1991), "Corruption in Public Policy and its Impact on Development: the Case of Uganda since 1979," *Public administration and Development*, vol.11, p. 473–490.

Padioleau, G. (1975), "De la corruption dans les oligarchies pluralistes, *Revue française de sociologie*, vol.XVI, n°1, janvier-mars 1975, p. 33–58.

Pean, P. (1983), *Affaires Africaines* , Paris Fayard.

Pean, P. (1988), *L'argent noir* Paris, Fayard.

Pourtier, R. (1995), "L'Etat archipel, *Hérodote, *p. 65 et suiv. 2ième et 3ième trim, Paris.

Prunier, G. (1983), "le Magendo," *Politique africaine*, 9, Mars, p. 53–62.

Government of Tanzania (1996), Presidential Commission of Inquiry Against Corruption, executive summary, *Commission report on the state of corruption in the country*, December 1996.

Quantin, P. (1994), "Corruption et résistance à la démocratie au Congo," *Afrique politique* 1994.

Reno, W. (1995), *Corruption and State Politics in Sierra Leone*, Cambridge, Cambridge University Press.

Reno, W. (1997), "African Weak States and Commercial Alliances," *African Affairs*, 96, p.165–185.

Riley S. (1992/3), "Post-Independence and Anti-Corruption Strategies and the Contemporary Effects of Democratization," p. 249 et suiv. in Charlick R. ed. op. cit.

Rosenberg, A. (1992/3), "Corruption as a Policy Issue," p.173 et suiv. in Charlick R. ed. op. cit.

Sardan, de J.-P. O. (1996), "L'économie morale de la corruption en Afrique," *Politique africaine*, 63, p. 97–116, Octobre.

Scott, J. S. (1969), "The analysis of corruption in developing countries," *The Journal of Modern African Studies*, 2, 31, p. 315–341, June.

Sindzingre, A. (1997), "Corruptions africaines: éléments d'analyse comparative avec l'Asie de l'Est," *Revue Internationale de Politique Comparée*, septembre.

Sindzingre, A. (1994), *Etat, développement et rationalité en Afrique: contribution à une analyse de la corruption*, Bordeaux, CEAN, Travaux et documents, n°43.

Smith, M.G. (1963/4), "Historical and cultural conditions of political corruption among the Hausa," *Comparative Studies in History and Society*, 6, p.164–198.

Theobald, R. (1994), "Lancing the African Swollen State: will it alleviate the Problem of Corruption?," *The Journal of Modern African Studies*, 1994, p.701–706.

Thobald, R. (1990), *Corruption, Development and Underdevelopment*, Durham, NC, Duke University Press, 1990.

Tignor, P. (1993), "Political Corruption in Nigeria before Independence," *The Journal of Modern African Studies*, 31, 2, p.175–202.

Toye, J. (1996), *Corruption, Ethics and Accountability in the African Public Sector: Challenges and Agenda for Action*, paper, I.D.S.

Verschave, F.X. and Boisallais, A.-S. (1994), *L'aide publique au développement*, Paris, Syros, ch. 4, Affairisme et corruption, p. 70–89.

Williams, R. (1987), *Political Corruption in Africa*, Aldershot, Hamphire, England, Avebury, Gower Publishing Group.

Note

1. This paper is a translation, with few modifications, of an article published in *Mondes en Développement,* 1998, tome 26, 102, pp. 55–67.

23

Political Corruption in South Africa: From Apartheid to Multiracial State

Tom Lodge

1. Introduction

Many South Africans think that political corruption is prevalent in their government. Moreover, since the accession of a democratically elected administration in 1994, the number of citizens who feel that most public officials are venal has increased. In 1995 a national survey conducted by IDASA found that 46 percent of its respondents though that most civil servants took bribes; by 1998 this proportion had increased to 55 percent.[1] South Africa's foreign reputation for good governance has also deteriorated: its grading in the Transparency International perception index fell from 7.35 in 1985 to 5.0 in 1999, the 34th position in 85 countries surveyed. These perceptions have probably been stimulated by the proliferation of press reportage on corruption as well as debates between national politicians. They are, of course, unreliable indicators of the scope or seriousness of administrative venality. A survey by Statistics South Africa, though, suggested that more than four percent of the adult population had encountered corrupt officials between 1993 and 1997.[2] Whether perceptions that government is corrupt are derived from experience or rumour, such opinions can be very influential and in themselves they encourage corrupt transactions between officials and citizens. The issue of public corruption in South Africa merits much more serious consideration than it has received hitherto.

In reviewing the South African evidence[3] this paper will attempt to answer several questions. Is the present South African political environment peculiarly susceptible to corruption? Were previous South African administrations especially corrupt? What forms has political corruption assumed since 1994 and how serious has been its incidence? Does modern South African corruption mainly represent habits inherited from the past, or is it a manifestation of new kinds of behaviour, or is it a consequence of institutional change, a by-product of political transition? Finally, is corruption in South Africa a singular product of very unusual circumstances?

A widely cited definition of political corruption is the "unsanctioned or unscheduled use of public resources for private ends."[4] Political corruption can be described as "a method of exploitation by which a constituent part of the public order sphere is exploited as if it were part of the market sphere."[5] Broader definitions of public corruption also embrace electoral fraud as well as the rewarding by political parties of specific constituencies in return for electoral support ("transactive corruption"). It is constituted by transactions or exchanges of public resources and benefits between actors some or all of whom are officials or public representatives. It must involve acts which are intentionally dishonest.

Most writers on corruption distinguish between degrees of severity of corruption. Different administrations may be characterised by routine, petty bureaucratic corruption (for example, the habitual extortion of bribes by minor officials) and grand corruption (the large scale misuse of public resources by senior civil servants and politicians) or by both simultaneously.[6] Corruption becomes systemic when corrupt activity begins to appear at all levels within a political system and when it becomes repetitious, constituting a parallel set of procedures to those which properly constitute the formal functions of the bureaucracy. Routine and open petty corruption usually signifies a systemic condition of corruption; secretive grand corruption may exist despite the absence of more pervasive bureaucratic misbehaviour. In administrations in which corruption assumes systemic and epidemic forms the scale of misappropriation substantially reduces public expenditure on development and services. Certain authorities have argued that corruption may have beneficial developmental effects, especially in those cases in which formal bureaucratic controls obstruct entrepreneurial growth,[7] but such instances usually involve the grandiose corruption of senior officials in exchange for subverting tender procedures rather than routine petty venality which is generally agreed to be developmentally harmful.

Political corruption is often perceived to be especially characteristic of government in developing countries.[8] Samuel Huntington has argued that its presence "correlates with rapid social and economic modernisation."[9] There are several reasons for believing this. In countries in which large scale centralised bureaucratic administrations are fairly recent and imposed by outsiders there may exist a "wide divergence between the aims, attitudes and methods of the government and those of the societies in which they operate".[10] In such contexts patrimonial values which arise from the persistence in social relationships of kinship, clanship and clientship"[11] may infuse bureaucracy from below. Modernisation can enlarge government very swiftly, widening its scope of intervention and regulation well beyond the capacity and supply of properly trained personnel[12] and the accompanying expansion of functions and services "multiplies opportunities for corruption".[13] Obviously this situation is accentuated if experienced officials are replaced with junior functionaries or with bureaucratic neophytes as often happens in rapidly implemented programmes of indigenisation following independence. The pressure to recruit civil servants *en masse* may be particularly intense following extensive political mobilisation and the construction of huge armies of political party employees during the decolonisation period. Cases of extreme corruption often coincide with situations in which the state derives the majority of its revenues from external sources of easily controlled enclaves within the national economy: African states' dependence upon customs receipts, foreign aid, and state controlled monopolies in such commodities as oil or diamonds, exploited under very restrictive conditions, are all cases in point. Each of these represent weak imperatives for domestic fiscal accountability and facilitate elite venality. In developing countries the state is usually the major force within the modern economy and in general conditions of economic scarcity and low levels of social stratification political and bureaucratic power brings unprecedented opportunities for control over material resources; in such circumstances, political office becomes the main route to personal wealth.[14] Accordingly, relatively low levels of official corruption in, for example, Botswana, are attributable to the existence of an indigenous ruling class which acquired its wealth before it became ascendant in national politics.[15] Similarly, the more widespread corruption in communist countries in comparison to liberal democracies is explained by the difficulty in the former of maintaining moral and conceptual distinctions between private and public property and individual and collective interests.[16] Recently, though, a succession of political scandals in well established industrial democracies have helped to shift the focus of corruption studies away from the developing world. Three political developments which have simultaneously affected both mature industrial democracies and poor third world countries are believed to have promoted corrupt government: the decentralisation of administration and with it the delegation of financial authority; the introduction of market values into public administration; and the growing costs of political competition in party systems in which political organisations increasingly depend upon external sources of finance.[17]

As well these historical or contextual causes of corruption, a series of features associated with particular kinds of polities help to encourage the proliferation of political corruption. These include: bureaucratic secrecy and the absence of mutual surveillance procedures by government agencies; protracted rule by one political party or an aging one-party dominant system;

administrative inefficiency and complicated hierarchical decision-making procedures which create lengthy delays; and extensive patterns of political appointment in the civil service.

2. South African Susceptibility

Do these generalisations which arise from comparative studies suggest that post Apartheid South Africa may be particularly susceptible to political corruption? Ostensibly, South Africa may not seem to share the structural predisposition towards corruption which many authorities believe makes the condition endemic in other African countries. South Africa is not a typical "developing country" nor is its current experience of socio-economic and political change easily encapsulated by notions of modernisation. Compared to many former colonial territories the state plays a minor, albeit an important, role in the economy and it by no means provides the main path for economic accumulation. South African relative immunity from corruption is also suggested by those studies which contend that a particular historical sequence of state development in which modernisation of the state, the development of welfare functions and the extension of the franchise occur consecutively and are separated by quite lengthy periods tends to produce less corrupt administrations than states in which these developments occur simultaneously.[18] Arguably, state formation during a long period of white political monopolies made it more difficult than elsewhere in African for the state to be influenced by the persistence of old pre-industrial cultures of tribute. Finally the South African state has for a long time depended for a major sources of its revenues on various forms of personal taxation—even within the restricted democracy of white minority politics this helped to limit the scope of official misbehaviour.

3. The Historical Legacy

Despite these apparent structural constraints, corruption appeared to flourish in pre-democratic South African public administration. Of course, it is arguable that a bureaucracy which was deliberately used as an instrument to foster the social and economic fortunes of one ethnically defined group had at least a form of transactive corruption built into its functioning from the inception of National Party rule. Deborah Posel, for example, has documented how the Native Affairs Department in the 1950s "made a concerted effort to fill as many administrative posts as possible with National Party supporters" while in the 1960s Broederbond infiltration of agricultural cooperatives and the Land Bank ensured that political considerations would predominate in credit allocation.[19] However these forms of patronage and favouritism were mainly geared to the strategic goals of Afrikaner nationalism and they did not, at least at their inception, involve personal gain and individualised relationships.[20] As late as the mid 1970s, J. N. Cloete, director of the South African Institute for Public administration, could maintain that the controls in the civil service were so stringent that bureaucrats had "little opportunity to use patronage and the conferment of financial benefits for the achievement of improper objectives."[21] This seems to be confirmed by Auditor-General's reports for the 1950s and early 1960s—the number of financial irregularities documented reached a comparatively modest 252 in 1967, and were mainly concentrated in the post office, as well, as to much lesser extents in justice, defence and police. There is plenty of evidence, though, to suggest that by the 1980s, political corruption within the terms of the definition used in this paper, was quite common in certain government departments as well as in homeland administrations. The 1978 Information Department scandal featured senior officials using public funds to pay for holidays for their families, tax free supplementary allowances, and properties registered in their own names, as well as the R13 million loaned to Mr Louis Luyt to start up a newspaper, most of which was subsequently invested on one of Luyt's companies.

The Information scandal arose from the misuse of secret money and might have been exceptional on those grounds but the Department's closure did not end the practice of secret financial grants to government agencies. In the 1980s these were to expand considerably within Defence expenditure. By 1994, for example, parliament was ready to transfer a total of R3.7 billion to the Department of Defence's secret account. Within the loose accounting employed in the funding of arms procurement and front companies there was plenty of room for official venality. A suggestive case was the trial of David Komansky, a Johannesburg commodities broker, charged in 1990 with the illegal export of R29 million, money he said he had been given by the Department of Defence's Civil Cooperation Bureau to establish an arms buying company in Britain. Ten years later, evidence submitted in the trial of Dr Wouter Basson, former head of the Defence Force's secret chemical weapons programme, indicated that Basson misappropriated R10 million which he had received in 1993 to buy equipment. Covert operations inside South Africa undertaken by the military supplied plenty of opportunities for private gain. For example, between 1985 and 1990, R10 million was paid over to five front companies established by the Eastern Cape Command. The companies were intended to organise youth camps and leadership training as well as propaganda activities against the ANC and the PAC. All their equipment became the private property of those in charge of their management. Whether these bodies actually undertook all the activities for which they were paid is rather questionable. It is extremely unlikely, for instance, that the Eagles Youth Clubs really assembled a following to match their claim of 600,000 active supporters in the Orange Free State.

Even outside the mysterious world of covert operations, though, central government departments seem to have had a history of routinised corruption. For example, in September 1994 a deputy director in the Department of Health official was suspended for the second time as a consequence of his acceptance of a consultancy with a company which supplied foods to prisons: the Van der Watt Commission confirmed that after the award of the contract in 1989, the official, nutrition specialist Dr. Johan Kotze, had received nearly R400,000 in various deposits into his bank account from the company. The allegations had originally come to light in 1991 but Kotze was reinstated when an initial investigation failed to unearth definitive proof. A correctional services Lieutenant General was also found to have received gifts from the company after helping Kotze to arrange the contract. The Commission also discovered evidence of systematic efforts to conceal the irregularities, suggesting a conspiracy embracing several more senior officials over a three year period.

Kotze's cupidity might have represented an exceptional lapse in the administrative domain to which he belonged but the case of the Department of Development Aid, the successor to the Native Affairs Department, suggests a pattern of very generalised misbehaviour. A 1991 inquiry discovered "dishonesty and abuse (to be) rife," concluding that the "majority of officials . . . have developed a syndrome of lack of enthusiasm to the extent sometimes of apathy." Specific irregularities included fictitious tenders and the subsequent award of contracts to spouses, the receipt of gifts by officials in return for contracts, and payments to firms for imaginary work and materials: over the years several hundreds of millions of rands was lost through various forms of nepotism and fraud in a department which administered about 11 percent of the government's budget.[22] Nor was abuse in this sphere confined to the final years of apartheid: other official inquiries suggest that land transfers administered by the South African Development Trust (a body under the authority of the Department of Native affairs and its successors) had for decades been managed dishonestly and incompetently.

All these examples refer to elite or grand corruption, involving dishonest practices by senior officials resulting in large scale misappropriation. Those departments which were especially concerned with political/strategic goals of government—information, defence, and homeland development seem to have been particularly affected by high level corruption. In addition, several homeland governments, both "independent" and "self governing" supplied documentation of political corruption on a major scale. In Kwandebele, the Parsons Commission discovered a R1 million "kickback" to officials from contractors for building work never undertaken and cabinet ministers appropriated discounts from the government's purchases of luxury cars. One member of the Kwandebele Tender Board, J. Morgan, managed to secure a contract in 1991 for his own firm, Professional Project Services, to supervise the erection of 164 classrooms; several were built in the wrong villages and many not at all, even so PPS received cheques for R105,000 in excess of the original agreement. Meanwhile Mr. Morgan's brother in law was the beneficiary of another agreement, in which his company, Hata Butle homes undertook to supply 200 pre-fabricated toilets, despite an original resolution by the Board to award the contract to a firm which supplied a lower estimate. No record could be found of the toilets reaching their supposed destination.

In Lebowa, the De Meyer report described misdoings in the Chief Minister's Department as well as the Departments of Water, Law and Order, Transport, Water Affairs and Education. Lebowa's chief minister, Nelson Ramodike, a former traffic policeman, attracted a major share of De Meyer's criticisms. At the time of the report's appearance there were fresh press allegations. In addition to the two illegal liquor licences uncovered by De Meyer, Ramodike was alleged to be running a string of state funded businesses through various brothers and cousins as well as maintaining a personal fleet of three top of the range Mercedes. Ramodike was unabashed by De Meyer's revelations. Announcing the dismissal of two members of his cabinet named in the report he said: "The public should praise and thank me for having been brave enough to expose the mismanagement of funds in Lebowa's government services before I was elected as head of the territory." Meanwhile, 200 officials within the Lebowa Department of Justice received a 100 percent pay increase in April 1993, and in October 1992 the Lebowa Tender Board, already under fire from De Meyer, was prevailed upon despite objections from three of its members, to accede to the purchase of R15 million worth of cleaning chemicals, enough for seven years' supply to the government.

To be sure, these occurrences in the final years of these administrations may have represented behaviour motivated by the realisation among officials that their powers and privileges were shortly to be curtailed, but there are other reports dating from earlier periods which suggest that graft was entrenched and routine in the highest echelons of homeland administrations through much of their history.

What about routine petty corruption before 1994? Its incidence probably varied in accordance with the degree of rightlessness of the people seeking benefits or services from officials. In the Transkei in 1975 more than R600,000 was stolen by civil servants from pensioners and an official observed "that there were frequently shortages at points where money passes from hand to hand between officials and the public." Within the Ministry of Justice, which included the payment of pensions and disability grants within its functions, at least ten percent of its employees were known in 1971 to have accepted bribes.[23] In the Ciskei, the Quail Commission in 1978 "heard evidence that pension payments were sometimes refused for reasons the pensioners concerned could not understand, such as that 'no more money is available'".[24] In Kwa Zulu, legislative assembly debates in 1978 attested to the widespread incidence of bribery within the civil service. Research conducted by Paulus Zulu in the early 1980s suggested that indunas and chiefs routinely extorted payments for site permits, work seeker permits, pensions and disability grants.[25] Nor was everyday extortion confined to homeland administrations: in Cape Town, for example, in the late 1980s, Bantu Administration Board officials sold residence permits to inhabitants of Crossroads; as one of Josette Cole's informants told her, "They always did this at the Nyanga and Langa offices. It wasn't something new to us."[26] On the East Rand, in 1959, Brandel-Syrier found that African clerks in the administrative offices of the township in which she conducted fieldwork charged a fixed "under the counter" fee for advice, referrals and appointments.[27] In the 1970s, black policemen were commonly believed to refrain from charging pass offenders in exchange for bribes.[28]

Pre-1994 police corruption is especially difficult to estimate; SAP Commissioners reports list dismissals for misconduct but these would have embraced a wider range of miscreants than simply officers charged with corruption. Auditor-General's annual reports ceased to detail "defalcations and irregularities" in 1967, significantly after the 1966 figures reported 58 such incidences with respect to the police, an unprecedentedly high figure and following a steady increase in police fraud in previous years.[29] It is true, though, that the repeal of pass laws and racially restrictive liquor legislation in the 1980s ended the two most common opportunities for police bribery and extortion.

The practice of extortion, though, was not endemic in all the lower echelons of the South African bureaucracy, rather, before 1994 it tended to be concentrated in those areas in which officials encountered people who were particularly rightless and defenceless. Amongst white South Africans experience of corruption would have been exceptional rather than normal, and concentrated in municipal rather than national state agencies (municipal traffic officers being notoriously susceptible to bribes). Other forms of corruption, though, may have been more widespread in the bureaucracy of "white" South Africa. Audits of the provincial administrations for 1992/1993 uncovered frauds to a total of R399,000 in the Cape Province (as well as the removal from Groot Schuur hospital of R1 million worth of bed linen) and the fraudulent issue of vouchers to the value of R64.2 million in the Transvaal.

As this quite selective review of the evidence suggests, administrative corruption was almost systemic in certain government departments for at least two decades before the end of minority rule. In certain respects, the Apartheid state must have been structurally susceptible to such behaviour by its officials. Obviously the denial of any democratic sanctions to most of its subjects substantially reduced its accountability. The more powerless people were the more officials abused their position. The increasing secrecy of its undertakings especially from the 1960s enhanced the arbitrary discretion enjoyed by bureaucrats. The proliferation of autonomous homeland governments widened the scope of the administrative transactions which may have been influenced by pre-industrial social values, that is the "obligations of mutual support, imperatives of reciprocity, and importance of gift exchange" which for certain observers constitute the "key ingredients" in Africa's "modernity."[30] A less contentious explanations for the extent of corruption during this period refers to another aspect of the state's expansion. Bureaucratic inflation in which the civil service establishment quadrupled in size during the Apartheid era was achieved through a process of politically motivated and ethnically exclusive recruitment. As the number of unskilled and underqualified clerical-level entrants increased so did the exodus of competent managers, just as the tasks of public administration were becoming increasingly complicated. In particular, oversight functions of government became very difficult to maintain; by 1961 staff shortages in the Auditor-General's office were held to be "critical." The public service's pay scales deteriorated as its professionalism declined; by 1973 civil service demoralisation had reached the point that a "state of rebellion" characterised labour relations in several government departments.[31] There can be no question that the erosion of capacity caused by this expansion facilitated and encouraged rent-seeking well decades before apartheid's end appeared inevitable of its administrators.

4. The Incidence and Location of Political Corruption in Post-Apartheid South Africa

Given this heritage, it would be surprising if there was no significant political corruption in contemporary democratic South Africa. Authoritarian and secretive governments are especially susceptible to bureaucratic venality and, as we have seen during the last decades of apartheid South Africa's administration was no exception to this generalization. Given that much of the administration is still run by the same people, it would be reasonable to expect the continuation of a certain amount of corruption. Has democratisation weakened or strengthened corrupt predispositions in South African. What have been the consequences of changes and reforms?

The formation of nine regional governments was accompanied by a delegation downwards of certain areas of budgetary authority and this may have interfered with previous controls though the dissolution of homelands in which administrative corruption was sometimes endemic may have compensated for this. On the other hand, the incorporation into regional administrations of homeland civil services may merely have transferred the bureaucratic location of corrupt behaviour and made regional governments vulnerable to the patrimonial politics which affected certain homeland administrations. Though the overall number of civil servants has not altered significantly in certain departments and regional governments large numbers of senior officials have been replaced and many of the fresh recruits to senior managerial levels have been political appointments. This, together with the demoralisation and fears about job insecurity amongst officials employed by the pre-1994 administration may have helped to erode already weak professional ethics. These in any case have been under attack with the adoption of new management policies which are highly critical of "authoritarian, centralised, and rule bound" operations and seek to replace them with an organisational culture "with a new emphasis on communicating, consulting, supporting, motivating and directing" and directed towards "the satisfaction of needs, both of the public and of staff."[32] Though the White Paper on public service transformation stresses accountability and anti corruption measures the new policies require a new range of managerial skills and quite different control systems. Meanwhile the government is undertaking a range of new activities, extending welfare and development services and establishing a set of new statutory bodies to safeguard constitutional rights. All these present new challenges for financial regulation. Government policies which favour black business empowerment as well as the movement of members of the ANC leadership into the corporate sector may have also helped to promote a culture in which "public behaviour is less prized than private, (and) producing results comes to matter more than observing standards, monetary values more than ethical and symbolic values."[33] On the other hand, the new government's public commitment to an ethic of transparency and the institution of the office of the Public Protector as well as the appointment of a number of official inquiries into corruption has helped to stimulate a fresh willingness among newspaper editors to publish corruption stories (which especially in the case of homeland venality used to be virtually ignored). Moreover, partly as a consequence of affirmative action policies, government tendering has become more fiercely contested and more subject to public commentary. In short, a democratic constitution and the demise of racially and ethnically separated administrations has considerably expanded the area of government open to scrutiny and inspection though bureaucratic reform and new social entitlements may also have created fresh opportunities for dishonest officials. This needs to be kept in mind when considering the proliferation of reports of corruption since 1994. The following overview of new South African corruption begins with references to its incidence in provincial governments, where it appears to be most concentrated, before considering political corruption in central government.

Seven of the nine regional governments had to absorb homeland administrations into their bureaucracies. The least corrupt regional administrations seem to be the two which have not incorporated former homelands, Gauteng and the Western Cape. Gauteng, the province accommodating Johannesburg and Pretoria and the country's main industrial region, achieved an early reputation for the probity and efficiency of its administration. Premier Tokyo

Sexwale's boast in early 1997 that his government could claim "three corruption free years" was an overstatement, though. Between 1994 and 1997, Gauteng's record was marred by the widespread sale of matriculation examination papers, huge amounts of thefts by officials in Johannesburg pension offices, sometimes to the scale of R2 million a month, as well as frequent bribery to jump the pension queues, fraud to the tune of R1 million in the Housing and Land Affairs Department (which might help to explain the large discrepancy between the number of subsidies handed out and the number of low cost homes which are under construction), accusations of nepotism in the appointment of school principals, and the defrauding of R800,000 from the department of education by senior bureaucrats. Gauteng's leaders could not plead that they have had to absorb corrupt homelands—there were none within the region's boundaries. Moreover, by 1996 half the senior administrative posts had been filled by new people. Therefore, much of this corruption cannot be explained by references to the apartheid heritage. In the province's most notorious corruption scandal, the MEC for Safety and Security, Jessie Duarte, lost her portfolio in 1998 during the course of an official investigation into her use of public money to pay for a friend to accompany on a working visit to Portugal. She was also found to have been driving a government vehicle without a driving license. More alarming than Duarte's own misbehaviour were the efforts of her subordinates (who included an improperly appointed former fraudster) to engineer a cover-up.

Compared to their colleagues in other provinces, though, Gauteng's officials appeared exceptionally virtuous. Mpumalanga's experience is illustrative of the difficulties arising from the incorporation of dishonest homeland administrations into the new regions. For the first five years of its history, Mpumalanga's administration was characterised by extreme forms of graft amongst political notables. Just before the 1994 elections, Kngwane politicians and civil servants took advantage of the final measures instituted by the homeland parliament to buy their official vehicles for bargain prices: beneficiaries of the scheme included the speaker of the new regional legislature, the MEC for Environmental Affairs, an ANC MP, Professor Ripinga, and Mrs Yvonne Phosa, wife of the new premier. The Kngwane government also divested itself of several publicly owned farms, selling them to political incumbents for prices equal to the transfer costs. Shortly after the accession of the new regional authority, R1.3 million from the low cost housing budget was used by the region's MEC's to renovate their state houses. An additional home improvement, this time involving the construction of a guard-house at the deputy speaker's residence, led to the overpayment of R208,000 to a local building firm in 1996. The MEC for Environmental Affairs, David Mkhwanazi, was discovered in late 1996 to have filed false expense claims for an official visit to Disneyworld. Mkhwanazi, whose political career began in the Kngwane homeland government, survived this revelation but was dismissed in 1998 after accusations of appointing family members to senior positions in his department. The MEC for Safety and Security, Steve Mabona, lost his post in 1997 after an official inquiry found him to have colluded with officials in his traffic department to issue illegal driving licenses, including one to the Deputy Speaker of the House of Assembly. Earlier, Mabona had been the Minister of Police in the KwaNdebele government and was identified by the Parsons Commission as the recipient of an illegal government loan. Three years later in January 2000, one of the testing stations investigated during the inquiry was found to be issuing 1,400 fraudulent licenses a month, still under the same managers who had run the station when it was controlled by the KwaNdebele government. Another former homeland government employee was at the centre of the province's most serious scandal. Ex-Kngwane parks director and head of the Provincial Parks Board, Alan Gray, not content with the R34,000 salary he received every month, hired out to the Board the services of two businesses he owned. Gray was eventually removed from his position after it was discovered that he had obtained loans to the Board in return for illegal "promissory notes." These loan agreements also led to the suspension in 1998 of Finance MEC, Jacques Modipane, who had counter-signed the notes. During the Parks Board investigation it emerged that Gray had attempted to secure political protection through contributions to the provincial ANC's 1999 elections fund. More damaging to the government, he had also authorised R1 million expenditure on improvements to the premier Mathews Phosa's home. Another political embarrassment for the ANC in 1998 concerned the deputy speaker of the Mpumalanga legislative assembly, Cynthia Maropeng, who connived with officials to divert nearly R1 million from a parlimentary constituency grant into personal bank accounts. Maropeng was provincial secretary of the ANC's Women's League.

In 1997, the provincial housing department was the centre of a major financial scandal as a consequence of the award of a huge R190 million contract without regular tendering procedures; the extent to which corruption may have featured in this undertaking was never established but the fact that one member of the provincial housing board, Job Mthombeni, was also a director of the company, Motheo Construction, which won the contract, was suggestive. The firm's chief executive, Thandi Ddlovu was an old associate of the national Minister of Housing; they became friends in exile. The housing scheme included provision for a profit margin in excess of 15 percent, about three times what was normal in the industry. The Housing Board was reconstituted after an official inquiry but one year later two more officials, a husband and wife, were sacked after awarding housing contracts to their own company.

Completing this survey of cupidity among Mpumalanga's officials, audits identified in 1996 amounts ranging from R4.1million to R30 million as missing and unaccounted for from the primary school feedings scheme. Between

1994 and 1999 the scheme supplied rich pickings nation-wide for minor officials, school administrators and small contractors in most of the provinces, though losses seem to have been largest in Mpumalanga; only in the Western Cape where black business empowerment principles were ignored and it was handed over to an experienced NGO, the Peninsula School Feeding Scheme, has it functioned with complete honesty. Altogether the total sum siphoned off provincial feeding schemes may have reached R140 million by 1998.

Between 1994 and 1999, eleven Members of (Regional) Executive Councils were identified in the press as being implicated in corrupt practices: that is about ten percent of the total number of regional "ministers." If this was the proportion of corruption embodied in regional political leadership, its prevalence among senior managers and junior officials was probably even wider. Nine of the MEC's accused of corruption lost their posts two in the Free State and two in the North West, two in the Northern Province, one in Gauteng and two in Mpumalanga; in the case of the Free State, though, despite the findings of a investigative commission which confirmed the accusations against one of the sacked MEC's, the premier, Patrick Lekota, was removed from his office and "redeployed" because of his willingness to publicise the culpability of his colleagues.

Political corruption does not appear to be so prevalent in central government: here it is concentrated in particular departments. For the ruling party the most politically troublesome corruption scandal emerged from the events which unfolded after the commissioning of an anti-AIDS musical by the Department of Health. Though the Public Protector's investigation of the "Sarafina" affair did not indicate that officials sought personal gain through neglecting regular tendering procedures, it did encounter the kind of heavy handed efforts to prevent disclosures which cause corruption. The Sarafina saga opened with the award of a R14 million contract to impresario Mbongeni Ngema to mount a musical to promote aids education. The budget drew upon a European Union donation, and included provisions for two luxury buses, R300,000 director's fees, and office facilities totalling R1.4 million. The allocation for the production exceeded the Health Department's expenditure for provincial Aids education. Director General Olive Shisana in the month following the outcry over the Sarafina contract ordered her subordinates to sign an oath of secrecy to stop "sensitive information which can cause the department and eventually the state embarrassment from falling into the wrong hands." The misuse of European Union money to fund the Sarafina aids musical was partly a consequence of officials not realising that donor money was subject to the normal rules, though it may also have been an effect of ministerial impatience with established bureaucratic procedures. In parliament, the ANC whip changed the order of the debate to ensure that the Minister would not be present while the ANC chair of the portfolio committee dismissed opposition calls for an inquiry as "spurious and politically motivated."[34] Later, ANC members in the National Assembly passed a vote of confidence in the Health Minister. The ANC publicity department issued a statement, commending the Minister for ensuring that "the resources of our country are used in a cost effective manner in the fight against Aids." In 1998 the minister dismissed her director-general, apparently because Shisana refused to accept full responsibility for the affair. Subsequently to the Sarafina scandal, a further report appeared of health department officials awarding a contract despite Tender Board refusal of two applications for approval.

The real citadels of official self-enrichment during the Mandela administration, though, were to be found in three central government ministries: Social Welfare, Safety and Security, and Justice. In the case of Welfare, the problems are mainly attributable to the legacy of pre-1994 era. The Department inherited 14 separate bureaucracies, many of them very venal and extremely incompetent. There was no centralised record of 2.8 million entitlements to pension payments and many of the supposed recipients were dead. As noted in the Department's 1996 white paper: "The fragmentation of government has led to gross inefficiencies . . . any loopholes were created which could be exploited by officials and the public."[35] It was reckoned that about ten percent of the Department's budget was lost to official fraud. Reform was slow, partly because of the complexity of the task, but also perhaps that the first Minister of Welfare, Abe Williams, was himself a major culprit in a pension fraud scandal which affected the old pension department of the apartheid era (Coloured) House of Representatives. Williams was forced to resign after an investigation by the Western Cape MEC for Health and Social services suggested that he had accepted a bribe from a company contracted to distribute pension funds and which had been allowed access to the interest accumulated from banking the unpaid pensions. Under a new minister, Geraldine Fraser-Moleketi, a clean-up campaign gained additional impetus: by the end of 1997, 94,000 illegal beneficiaries of various grants had been discovered in the Northern Province alone. In this province syndicates within the administration would charge people R400 to enable them to receive disability grants. The small sum extorted for each grant is indicative of just how widespread and routine this practice had become.

The police rivalled the pension administrators in their predisposition towards corruption. In 1995–1996, 8,000 police in Gauteng alone were reported to have committed crimes of one kind or another. In Johannesburg, according to the divisional police chief interviewed in 1996, four police a week were suspended for corruption and 1,076 policemen nationally were under investigation for corruption, an increase from 89 investigations in 1995, 56 in 1994 and 32 in 1993. In 1996, again merely in Gauteng, R5 million worth of cars were stolen, most likely by policemen from the car pounds in which the police keep the cars which have already been stolen. Ten million rands were allocated at the beginning of 1997 to build new police proof maximum security car forts to prevent further thefts of this kind. In Rustenberg, a station commander was discovered in 1995 to be running a car theft syndicate in complicity with professional criminals. Since then there has been an epidemic of reports of collusion between police and vehicle theft syndicates with police supplying registration papers for stolen cars; police are also believed to be involved in contract killings and prostitution rackets. In 1995 2,000 policemen defrauded their medical aid scheme of R60 million. A major bribery scandal implicated police at Johannesburg's container port. In February 1997 five members of the Benoni flying squad were arrested on bribery charges. Police were discovered to have extorted thousands of rands from people they illegally arrested during 1996 and held in cells in the Sandton area, mainly on suspicion of illegal immigration. According to the SAP Anti-Corruption Unit, police corruption was believed to have increased by 8 percent in 1995; about half the 800 allegations investigated by the unit were located in Gauteng. Among the officers charged with corruption was Charlie Landman, head of the elite Brixton Murder and Robbery Squad. Lax disciplinary regulations continue to obstruct efforts to reduce corruption in the police service: it is still the case in 2000 that officers can only be dismissed after conviction for a crime in which a prison sentence is mandatory. Odds are against such convictions happening: policemen regularly conspire with employees of the Department of Justice to massively expand the scope of public corruption through assisting magistrates and prosecutors in the wholesale theft and deliberate loss of dockets in return for bribes from charged criminals. This practice is especially widespread in the Western Cape and in Gauteng but it exists everywhere: several thousand cases each year do not reach court, causing wastage and loss of millions of rands. It may reflect historically entrenched habits but a recent wave of resignations by prosecutors and threats of strike action suggest that the present demoralisation of the prosecution service caused by poor pay and affirmative action may have encouraged the spread of court venality.

5. A Crisis in Public Administration?

Does the extent of corruption in central and regional government represent a problem of crisis level proportions? In 1997 Deloitte and Touche spokesmen suggested that the overall cost of public sector fraud and mismanagement could easily exceed R10 billion, which would make it comparable in scale to the extent of abuse in countries considered to be endemically corrupt. A calculation from the National Party suggests that the cost of maladministration between 1994 and 1998 may have reached R16.3 billion while fraud and theft from provincial and national governments absorbed another R18.7 billion.[36] It is certainly systemic in certain provincial departments—its appearance at both high and lowly levels and its evident repetition confirm this and it seems to be routinised in many police stations. So far, there is little evidence of corruption amongst National Assembly members or amongst national cabinet members, or amongst senior officials in national state departments. At seven percent of public expenditure its real proportional cost could be much higher because only a small proportion of the government's budget is invested in capital or developmental projects. On the other hand, in the South Africa's new democracy corruption does not seem to have so entrenched at policy-making or senior managerial levels that it effects the emphases in public expenditure. Analysis of the developmental effects of corruption suggest that corrupt administration tend to spend less on social services and more on capital investment; in other words, public spending "is diverted to those areas where gains from corruption are greatest or where discretion is widest."[37] General trends in South African public expenditure have been in the opposite direction as any comparative examination of defence and education expenditure would indicate. However, corruption amongst more junior officials is certainly one factor which helps to explain why increased resource allocation to schools in poor communities has failed to improve their performance.

While it would be difficult to find any evidence in South Africa to support a case for corruption having beneficial developmental effects it might be argued that its prevalence represents the lesser of two evils, the cost of a relatively peaceful political transition to democracy. Samuel Huntington has noted that "both corruption and violence are illegitimate means of making demands upon the system, but corruption is also an illegitimate means of satisfying those demands . . . he who corrupts a system's police officers is more likely to identify with the system than he who storms the systems police stations."[38] The implication here is that a venal administration may in certain contexts be preferable to an honest one. Certainly, during apartheid, official susceptibility to bribery helped to soften the impact of the pass laws. Corruption's more benign effects in pre-1994 South Africa also include the diversion of secret defence funding from lethal official projects into comparatively harmless private peccadilloes. In a more subtle vein, the extent of corruption among apartheid's bureaucrats may have helped to reconcile them to political change, especially when their jobs were guaranteed in the news dispensation. As the Pickard Commission suggested in 1991, there were very few officials who retained genuine commitment to regime goals, instead "self preservation and self protection against criticism have become matters of primary importance even to the detriment of the very cause itself".[39] At least for a time, it would have been expedient for Mandela's new government to tolerate a certain level of corruption among such people rather than having to encounter their active hostility. The limits to any such expediency become rather evident, though, when the involvement of officials and policemen with criminal syndicates reaches such an extent that the government's ability to enforce laws is as widely questioned as it is in modern South Africa.[40]

6. Is Political Corruption Primarily an Inheritance from the Old Regime?

It is difficult to know for certain whether the present levels of corruption represent a substantial expansion of public dishonesty: corruption was very extensive in the old regime and some of the conditions which allowed it to flourish have disappeared: homeland administrations have been incorporated and all government activities are now subject to well publicised audits and the extension of the franchise should in theory make government more accountable. The Department of Defence no longer receives secret funding for arms procurement and political subversion. Old habits die hard, though, amongst many of the administrative cadres who have been absorbed from the old homeland governments into the new provincial bureaucracies. Within central government much of the post-1994 corruption has occurred in bureaucratic spheres already notoriously venal: social welfare and police would be two instances. The efforts to reorganize the Social Welfare Department and establish a unified record system has had some success in checking the misappropriation of pensions. Continuing reports of abuse in the police might fairly be perceived as the lingering effects of the old system.

However there are many new sources of stimulation for corrupt behaviour. These include non-meritocratic processes of bureaucratic recruitment and promotion inherent in certain kinds of "affirmative action," tendering principles which favour small businesses (and which require much more efficient administration if they are to be handled honestly), increasing shortages of skilled manpower in the public service especially in its financial control systems, a range of new sources of public finance, including foreign-derived development aid, and an ambitious expansion of the kinds and quantity of citizen entitlements to public resources. Inexperienced ministers and new public managers are often ignorant of tendering procedures: as the spokesmen for one of the Northern Province's MEC's conceded: "We have never ruled before. We never even knew what a tender board was before we came to power." Apparent favouritism in public tendering in certain contexts might be very difficult to avoid given the small sizes and the overlapping character of the black political and business elites, as well as the frequent and rapid movement of prominent personalities between them. Government determination to use the privatisation of parastatal companies or the contracting-out of government programmes as opportunities for black business empowerment helps to accentuate the dangers of cronyism. The Motheo Housing Company's contract in Mpumalanga is illustrative of this.

New types of corruption which cannot be attributed to habits instilled during the previous administration include the nepotism arising from political solidarity: at a workshop in January 1997 participants "agreed that comradeship was becoming more of an issue in their studies. Senior black officials . . . felt duty bound to appoint comrades who fought with them in the struggle for democracy, regardless of their skills or qualifications." The promotion of teachers in Gauteng or the award of a contract by director general of the Education Department to an old AZAPO associate might be cases in point. Not all the self serving behaviour by provincial MEC's be explained by reference to the predisposition of old homeland politicians who have remained in high office: most of the MEC's concerned had strong "struggle" credentials before their appointments to ANC governments. In these cases, the rapid social mobility from situations of material hardship which modernisation theorists suggest as a prime cause of political corruption may help their behaviour. In any case, even ANC veterans may not be unaffected by patrimonial cultures of tribute. Jackson Mthembu, MEC for Transport in Mpumalanga, was contemptuous of any critics who expressed reservations about his department's purchase of 10 BMW 528's for his fellow executive members. They were racists, he said, and moreover: "I am a leader in my community and therefore have a certain status—you can't therefore be saying that I should drive a 1600 vehicle."

Culturally-based explanations of corruption which suggest that in Africa "formal rules of conduct which characterise the modern state" fail "to supersede the informal compacts derived from ethnic, factional, or nepotistic ties of solidarity" may seem very apposite in modern Mpumalanga.[41] One should be careful not to overstate their salience, though. What may appear to be an increased incidence of abuse in these domains is probably a consequence of more stringent controls and more open disclosure. And at least one provincial government, the Eastern Cape, in 1996 introduced financial restrictions which have reduced the budgetary authority of its officials and made false claims and dishonest tendering much more difficult.

Another rather impressive example of institutional resilience has been the government's determination to "downsize" the bureaucracy from 1.2 million to 900,000 over three years. In fact in 1996 only 15,000 jobs were cut but given the demands from the ANC's trade union allies to expand public sector this represented a considerable commitment to austerity. The two million applications for the 11,000 affirmative action posts advertised by the public service commission were evidence of the extent of social pressure on political leadership to create jobs; significantly, only 2,000 of these posts could be filled with appropriately qualified people and the remainder were kept vacant. The ANC's fiscal conservatism in this respect represents an important limit to the deployment of patronage by office holders and suggests that the official political realm operates through rather more complicated dynamics than the "politics of the belly" attributed to African politics by its detractors.

Democracy and the consequent extension party politics can themselves serve as incentives for particular kinds of corruption. To date, electoral politics and representative institutions do not seem particularly susceptible to corruption, public perceptions notwithstanding. Fresh sources of stimulation may develop, though. In a newly competitive political environment, political parties are increasingly dependent upon private sector finance. The ANC which in 1994 accepted a secret R500,000 campaign donation from Sol Kerzner, the hotel and casino chain proprietor facing bribery charges and subsequently denied it has since adopted the practice of taking fees for private appearances at business functions by cabinet ministers. At the time of the dispute over the Kerzner donation, the ANC's deputy secretary general, Cheryl Carolus, told reporters that the organisation "would not disclose donations because donors were entitled to privacy." Newly "empowered" black businessmen have become a major source or organizational finance: at the ANC's fiftieth conference in Mafeking in 1997, the party's treasurer reported that iot was now possible to solicit from such people R2 million donations rather than the R250,000 they had customarily been asked for in the past. In return for this generosity, outgoing treasurer Makhenkesi Stofile told his audience, "We opted for the role of facilitators for black business in the country." The Inkatha Freedom Party accepted donations from illegal casino operators while the Kwa-Zulu Natal government began preparing legislation regulate the gambling industry. These kinds of actions are at the very least conducive to transactive forms of political corruption.

As noted at the beginning of this essay, many people think that there has been an increase in corruption: even Nelson Mandela's Minister of Justice, Dullah Omar, admitted that there had been a growth in administrative corruption since 1994, though he qualified this assertion by acknowledging that its "seeds . . . were sown long before we came into the government." The evidence surveyed here suggests that old habits and predispositions may well sustain plenty of the existing administrative corruption, for one of the consequences of a "pacted" transition to democracy has been that much of the *ancien régime* remains in place. Corruption is also the consequence of change, though. As the theoretical literature surveyed at the beginning of the paper suggests, the simultaneous democratisation and restructuring of the South African state makes it very vulnerable to corruption, as has the absorption into its cadres and governors of a new political class with recent experience of severe poverty. New public obligations and expanded social entitlements strain the state's capacity and render obsolete its regulatory systems. Corruption caused by these conditions may be transient, an effect of stress and demoralisation. Six years since South Africa's democratisation, perceptions of corruption as a function of political transition remain just about persuasive but they will not for much longer.

7. Is South Africa Unique?

Finally, is political corruption in South Africa an unusual phenomenon, a consequence of very distinctive circumstances?

In an African context, South Africa is unusual for the depth and experience of its administrative and political institutions and the degree of separation between them. It is probably the case that the state depends rather less in South Africa then in many African countries on "particularistic and personalised social structures" to serve as "brokers" in its transactions with society.[42] Though the case studies from Mpumalanga cited in this essay are certainly a reflection of soft administration embedded in localised patrimonial networks, such situations do not represent the totality of South African corruption. Much of it is located in central government within institutions which for decades have functioned with considerable social autonomy. Corruption in central government departments such as social welfare or even safety and security (policing) are probably more amenable to bureaucratic reform than regional administrations inherited from homelands in which distinctions between public and private domains were often very blurred.

Why then, has corruption not been addressed by a new democratic administration more effectively? There are, in fact, an impressive range of institutions which have been established to check corruption. These include a Public Protector's Office, a roving investigative body, the Heath Commission, an Office of Serious Offences and several dedicated units within different government departments including the police. One difficulty confronting these bodies has been the reluctance of authority to enforce sufficiently punitive sanctions. The virtual immunity of corrupt police officers referred to above is a case in point. The amnesties and guarantees which were preconditions for South Africa's democratisation help to explain this reluctance to punish venal officials, and again, they make South Africa's condition quite distinctive. Another way in which governments can discourage corruption is by reducing the scope of their economic responsibilities, through liberalisation, privatisation and deregulation. When such strategies are combined with efforts to create new entrepreneurial elites, though, the process of liberalisation can engender corruption rather than inhibiting it, particularly if there already exist intimate social ties between politicians and the targeted beneficiaries of empowerment programmes. In South Africa it is often quite difficult to distinguish political favouritism from social affirmation. Finally, while the state attempts to disengage from its participation in the productive economy it is assuming new kinds of social responsibilities as the entitlements of citizens increase, a consequence of democratisation. South Africa's historically retarded conversion to social democracy places its current experience with corruption in a category of its own; no other comparably liberal administrations confront such high popular expectations and such tough institutional challenges.

Notes

1. Robert Mattes and Cherrel Africa, *Corruption—The Attitudinal Component: Tracking Public perceptions of Official Corruption in South Africa, 1995–1998*, IDASA, Cape Town, 1999, p 2.
2. F. M. Orkin, *Victims of Crime Survey*, Statistics South Africa, Pretoria, 1998, p. 17.
3. Indications of the sources for much of the information in this paper have been omitted: the illustrative examples have been collected from the press, from the Public Protectors reports, and the findings of various investigative commissions. For comprehensive references see an earlier version of this paper in *African Affairs*, 97, 1998. pp. 157–187.
4. Victor Levine, *Political Corruption: The Ghana Case*, Stanford University Press, 1975.
5. Jacob van Klaveren, "The Concept of Corruption" in Arnold Heidenheimer (ed.), *Op cit*, p. 38.
6. Robert Theobold, "Lancing the swollen African state: will it alleviate the problem of corruption?," *Journal of Modern African Studies*, 1994, 32, 4, pp. 701–706.
7. See Nathanial Leff, "Economic development through corruption" in Heidenheimer, *op cit*, J. S. Nye, "Corruption and political development: a cost benefit analysis," *American Political Science Review*, Vol. 56, 1967, and M. Beenstock, "Corruption and development," *World Development*, 7 1 1979.
8. Bekker, J. C., "Nepotism, corruption and discrimination: A predicament for a post apartheid South African public service," *Politikon*, 18 2 1991.
9. Samuel Huntington, "Modernisation and corruption" in Heidenheimer (ed.), *op cit.*, p. 490,
10. M. McMullen, "A Theory of Corruption," *Sociological Review*, 1961, p. 184.
11. Theobold, *op cit.*
12. See, for example: Paul Wellings, "Making a fast buck: capital leakage and public accounts in Lesotho," *African Affairs*, 82, 329, October 1983.
13. Gillespie, K., and Okruhlik, G., "The political dimensions of corruption cleanups: a framework for analysis," *Comparative Politics*, 1991, 24, 1, p.78.
14. Jean-Francois Bayart, *The State in Africa: the Politics of the Belly*, Longman, London, 1993.
15. Kenneth Good, "Interpreting the exceptionality of Botswana," *Journal of Modern African Studies*, 30 1 1992. p. 72.
16. Leslie Holmes, *The End of Communist Power*, Polity Press, Cambridge, 1993.
17. Donatella Della Porta and Yves Meny (eds.), *Democracy and Corruption In Europe*, Pinter, London, 1997.
18. Andrew Adonis, "The UK: Civic virtue put to the test," Donnatella Della Porta and Yves Meny (eds.), *op cit.*
19. Deborah Posel, *The Making of Apartheid*, 1948–1961, Oxford University Press, Cape Town, 1997, pp. 117 and 243–244.
20. Annette Seegers, "Toward an understanding of the Afrikanerisation of the South African state," *Africa*, 63 (4), 1993.
21. J N Cloete, "The Bureaucracy" in Anthony de Crespigny and Robert Schrire, *The Government and Politics of South Africa*, Juta, Cape Town, 1978, p. 74.
22. Republic of South Africa, *Commission of Inquiry into Development Aid*, Pretoria, RP 73/1992.
23. Roger Southall, *South Africa's Transkei, The Political Economy of an Independent Bantustan*, Heinemann, London, 1982, p. 179.

24. *The Report of the Ciskei Commission*, Conference Associates, Pretoria, 1980, p. 33.

25. Gerhard Mare and Georgina Hamilton, *An Appetite for Power: Buthelezi's Inkatha and the Politics of "Loyal Resistance,"* Ravan, Johannesburg, 1987, p. 91.

26. Josette Cole, *Crossroads: The Politics of Reform and Repression*, 1976–1986, Ravan, Johannesburg, 1987, p. 63.

27. Mia Brandel Syrier, *Reeftown Elite*, Routledge and Kegan Paul, 1971, p. 33.

28. Philip Frankel, "The Politics of Police Control," *Comparative Politics*, 12, 4, 1980, p. 487.

29. Republic of South Africa, *Report of the Controller and the Auditor-General for the financial year, 1966–1967*, Pretoria, RP 60, 1967.

30. Patrick Chabal and J P Daloz, *Africa Works: Disorders as Political Instrument*, London, 1999, p. 101.

31. Deborah Posel, "Whiteness and Power in the South African Civil Service: Paradoxes of the Apartheid State," *Journal of Southern African Studies*, 25, 1, 1999, pp. 105–114.

32. *Government Gazette*, 15 May 1995, "Draft White Paper on the Transformation of the Public Service," pp. 7 and 15.

33. Yves Meny, "France, the end of the republican ethic," in Donatella Della Porta and Yves Meny, *op. cit.*, p. 18.

34. "It was obvious to all observers who attended the meeting that ANC MP's had been primed to refrain from asking anything that resembled a probing question" (Patrick Bulger, "Parliamentary Review," *The Star*, 4 March, 1996).

35. Republic of South Africa, *Government Gazette*, vol. 368, no. 16943, 2 February, 1996.

36. Shaun Vorster, *Corruption Barometer*, 1994–1998, National Party, Cape Town, 1998, p. 13.

37. Donatella della Porta and Alberto Vannucci, "The 'Perverse Effects' of Political Corruption" in *Political Studies*, 45, 3, 1997, pp. 518. See also Paulo Mauro, "Corruption: causes, consequences, and agenda for future research," *Finance and Development*, 35 1 March 1998, p. 12.

38. Samuel P. Huntington, *Political Order in Changing Societies*, Yale University Press, 1968, p. 64.

39. Constanze Bauer, "Public sector corruption and its control in South Africa," Kempe Ronald Hope and Bornwell Chikulo (ed.), *Corruption and Development in Africa*, Macmillan, London, 1999, p.220.

40. For the operation of criminal organisations within police and security agencies see: Chiara Carter, "Scambuster unit busted," *Mail and Guardian*, 2 October 1998; Justin Arenstein, "Spies caught in R180m scam," *Mail and Guardian*, 2 October 1998; Paul Kirk, "How SA's spies smuggled dope," *Star*, 2 May 1998.

41. Patrick Chabal and J. P. Daloz, *op cit*, p. 101.

42. Paul Heywood, "Political Corruption: Problems and Perspectives," *Political Studies*, 45 3 1997, p. 428.1

24

The Institutional Framework for Corruption Control in Uganda

Sahr John Kpundeh

Uganda's turbulent history resulted from, among other things, a break-down of ethical systems and values in society. During this period petty and grand corruption spread systematically throughout government. A small group of elites held most of the political power. The country was plagued with weak institutions, an almost non-existent rule of law, symptomatic low social trust and consensus, excessive use of patronage and nepotism, lack of accountability and low public sector salaries. When the National Resistance Movement (NRM) took power in 1986, it inherited a country traumatized by civil war and state terror. Uganda had been reduced to poverty through lawlessness, corruption and mismanagement. The civil service once hailed as one of the best in sub-Saharan Africa for its performance and motivation and a well-paid and fully equipped work force had become inefficient, demoralized and unresponsive.

Unlike a majority of African governments, the NRM demonstrated political will and commitment to curb corruption. Soon after taking power, President Museveni made it clear he viewed corruption as one of the evils he inherited and a key obstacle to economic progress. He often spoke of the seriousness of the issue, describing it as a threat to Uganda's stability and the democratization process. The NRM government's 1986 ten-point program included the following commitment:

> Africa, being a continent that is never in shortage of problems, has also the prob-
> lem of corruption particularly bribery and misuse of office to serve personal inter-
> ests. Corruption is indeed a problem that ranks with the problems of structural

425

distortions. . . . Therefore, to enable the tackling of our backwardness, corruption must be eliminated once and for all. (Museveni, Y.K., 1997)

Strategy for Change

To address the corruption problem, the NRM government developed a strategy that had at its core a number of institutions and passed laws designed to establish good governance and curb malfeasance. An integral part of the strategy was to establish an independent, impartial and efficient public office. Several institutions continue to play a role in the fight against corruption. They include the following: the Ministry of Ethics and Integrity; the Inspector General of Government; the Auditor General; the Director of Public Prosecution; the Public Accounts Committee of Parliament; and a number of special tribunals. The most recent is the Judicial Commission of Inquiry into corruption in the Uganda Police Force. Over the years, laws have been enacted to fight corruption, which include the Penal Code Act of Uganda Chapter X; the Prevention of Corruption Act No. 8 of 1970; and more recently, the Leadership Code Act of Uganda.

Despite the work of institutions and changes in the law, little progress has been made. For example, according to the 1999 Transparency International Corruption Perception Index, Uganda ranked eleventh as the most corrupt country in the world. In a 1998 service delivery and integrity survey[1] conducted by the Inspectorate of Government and CIET International, the data revealed that abuses were common in primary education, health, police and the local, judicial and tax administrations. A review of the institutions and components of the government's strategy may be useful to begin to understand why its efforts have failed.

The Ministry of Ethics and Integrity

In July 1998, a new Ministry was created—the Ministry of Ethics and Integrity. A Minister of State was appointed by the President to head the office with the mandate to propose new laws or reform existing ones to address corrupt government practices and monitor adherence to ethics and integrity regulations. The Minister established a Directorate of Ethics and Integrity (DEI) to "spearhead and coordinate Government efforts to fight corruption by minimizing the opportunities and making it a *high risk* activity" (Matembe, M, 2000). Through this Directorate, the government has designed an action plan to fight corruption. The plan's focus is:

- effective coordination of government efforts;
- follow through on high-profile cases;
- implement procurement reform;

- amend and implement the Leadership Code, which requires leaders to annually declare their assets;
- establish a fast-track judicial mechanism to expedite cases of abuse;
- support capacity building for the anti-corruption agencies; and
- mobilize the public on corruption and unethical conduct issues.

The Inspector General of Government

The Inspector General of Government (IGG) was established in 1986 to protect and promote human rights and the rule of law. It was designated to lead the fight against corruption and foster the elimination of the abuse of the public office and promote fair, efficient government and good governance. Initially, the IGG was directly responsible to the President of Uganda. However, since 1995 it has been required to answer only to Parliament. This change in Uganda's constitution in 1995 insulated the IGG from undue interference. Chapter 13, Article 225 of the Constitution recognized and strengthened the central role of the IGG. Specifically, it states the functions of the IGG are to:

- promote and foster strict adherence to the rule of law and principles of natural justice in administration;
- eliminate and foster the elimination of corruption and abuse of authority in public office;
- investigate any act, omission, or recommendation by any public authority regulated by this article despite whether the complainant has personally suffered any injustice;
- stimulate public awareness about constitutional values and the activities of the IGG;
- establish local and regional branches; and,
- submit to Parliament, at least once every six months, a performance report.

Article 227 of the Constitution grants the Inspectorate autonomy to perform its functions and requires that this office is responsible only to Parliament. Article 230 gives the Inspectorate the power to investigate, issue arrest warrants, and prosecute cases of corruption and abuse of authority or public office. This article also gives the IGG power to make orders or directions as are necessary in the course of its duties or as a consequence of its findings.

Public Service Reform

The Public Service Review and Reorganization Commission (PSRRC) was established to make specific recommendations to reorganize all public offices, procedures and systems. The new vision required that by the year 2000, Uganda's civil service would be smaller, better paid, more efficient and effective than it was in 1986. Fair, simple, consistent rules and procedures would be implemented to foster discipline while promoting personal initiative. Levels of corruption would be reduced, backed by an effective police and prosecutorial staff. Clear organizational goals would be implemented, workers made fully responsible and accountable for their assigned duties, and individuals encouraged to commit to clearly identified objectives.

Introducing a Leadership Code of Conduct

The government called for a new culture of leadership for both elected and appointed officials in the public sector. The Ugandan Constitution is based on the notion that the country's future prospects depend, to a very great extent, on the quality and honesty of its leaders. Based on constitutional principles, the government utilized a broad concept to determine what constitutes "leadership." Officials decided that role modeling is critical to establishing leadership guidelines. Along with an honest, impartial and non-discriminatory administration, public sector officials should be sensitive to marginalized groups; develop leadership instruction; adhere to democratic principles; respect the rule of law; undergo periodic testing; carefully follow rules of transparency and accountability; and cultivate a "sense of shame." A code of conduct for those occupying leadership positions was first proposed in 1992. Its provisions were debated in the Constituent Assembly and finalized when the Constitution was passed in 1995.

The proposed Leadership Code Statute detailed the expected and prohibited forms of conduct for government leaders. For example, it required them to make annual disclosures of income, assets and liabilities to the IGG. This disclosure also covered his or her "nominees" (defined as anyone who controls or manages businesses or other activities in which the leader is principal beneficiary). Activities which were forbidden included requesting or accepting gifts or benefits in exchange for the exercise of official duties; failure to seek prior approval from the Leadership Code Committee to contract with the government or with certain kinds of foreign businesses; abuse of government property; and misuse of confidential official information.

The proposed Code prohibited the misappropriation of public funds; the use of an official's position to obtain property; the use of official time for private business; conduct prejudicial to official status; the evasion of taxes or other financial obligations; furthering the interests of a foreign government contrary to Uganda's interests; acts prejudicial to citizens' rights; and activities designed to undermine the government's integrity. It prevented senior leaders from holding shares, proprietary interests or office in foreign business organizations, or from operating as commissioned agents. In addition to establishing a minimum standard of behavior, the proposed Code delineated penalties for offenders.

The Role of the Director of Public Prosecutions

The Penal Code was revised in 1987 to address specific punishments for corruption offenses. Since the 1960s, Ugandan law has given police and prosecutors the power to deal with malfeasance. For example, the Prevention of Corruption Act 8 of 1970 specifically authorizes a special section within the Directorate of Public Prosecutions (DPP) to handle corruption and fraud-related cases and has preventive, investigative and prosecutorial functions. Other relevant pieces of legislation include the 1987 IGG Statute, the 1964 Police Act, the 1964 Public Finance Act, the Leadership Code, Statute No. 8 of 1964 and the Evidence Act.

The Auditor General

The Auditor General (AG) was given the authority to examine "all" rather than "some" government accounts. The frequency of audits of government operations was increased. The new constitution allowed the AG to identify poor accounting practices and ensure that revenue is spent wisely and prudently. Government departments and agencies were required to submit their accounts to Parliament for scrutiny and publication.

The Public Accounts Committee

After several decades of inactivity the Public Accounts Committee (PAC) of Parliament was reactivated to investigate the misuse of public funds. The tasks of the PAC are to review the Auditor General's reports and inquire into any improprieties.

Other Government Reforms

Public sector reform, in particular civil service reform, is likely to have the most direct impact on corruption. However, changes in economic, constitutional and military areas of government were initiated to help reduce the scope and incidences of corruption.

The Role of the Press

The press is considered critical in the fight against malfeasance. The government encouraged the development of a free press as a part of the country's movement towards greater freedom and democracy.

The Role of the President

President Museveni of Uganda assumed a large role in the fight against corruption. He missed few opportunities to "drive the anti-corruption message home." For example, while opening the new international facilities at Entebbe Airport in 1994, he rebuked the corrupt practices of customs and immigration officials—a speech that attracted extensive media coverage. More recently, he referred to personnel at the Uganda Revenue Authority (URA) as "a den of thieves" and called for reform in management practices. As a result of the President's statement, the URA is currently being reviewed to assess the level of malfeasance within the agency and to offer remedies and improve its image.

Assessment of Reforms

A major challenge in any reform effort is the difficulty of operationalizing the strategy. Several factors such as political will, available resources, committed reformers, collective action and coalition building among stakeholders play significant roles in the success of such efforts. In the case of Uganda, progress has been made in some areas, but a lot more work remains to be done.

The Department of Ethics and Integrity

This department was strategically placed within the President's office and its political direction channeled through a Cabinet Minister, enabling it to articulate corruption issues at the highest levels of government and Parliament. Since its establishment, its coordinating role has garnered it a highly visible position in the government's overall action plan. The Ministry of Ethics describes the Government's Action Plan as a dual-pronged approach of "Reactive and Preventive" measures. The reactive approach provides "curative" initiatives to deal with corruption where it has taken place. This requires coordinated activities with the Criminal Investigations Division (CID), Inspectorate of Government (IGG), Department of Public Prosecutions (DPP), the Auditor General, Parliament's Public Accounts Committee (PAC), and the Judiciary. The preventive approach provides preventive measures against corruption and helps build an integrity system and culture that specifies the framework for Public sector ethics (Matembe, M, 2000).

The Inspector General of Government

With strong constitutional backing, the IGG has uncovered several cases illustrating the many faces of fiscal mismanagement and has demanded severe punishment for offenders. A number of officials have been dismissed or suspended from their positions because of their involvement in corruption. Some political leaders have also been relieved of their duties following investigations by the IGG and ensuing public pressure.

The Inspectorate of Government has embarked on an extensive expansion programme. Since 1998, it has opened five regional offices to take services closer to the people and adopted a new strategy that focuses more on grassroots awareness raising. For example, as of February 2000, twenty-one district integrity workshops have been held with the purpose of "removing the mentality and ignorance that encourages corrupt government officials to con the public." (Tumwesigye, J, 1999) Radio programmes in English and local dialects are also efforts to heighten awareness. Radio Uganda produces the *"Inspector Programme."* Radio Capital plays spots on corruption. Top Radio broadcasts discussion programmes on corruption and Radio Paidha and Radio West produce programmes on corruption in local dialects (ibid.).

Despite these gains, the work of the Inspectorate is impeded by a number of constraints, including insufficient funding, inadequate staffing and a shortage of vehicles, computers, photocopiers and investigative equipment such as video cameras and recorders. Although government increased the budget and staffing levels of the Inspectorate for the 1999/2000 fiscal year, they still remain under-facilitated. Five regional offices are inadequately staffed and improperly trained. According to the Inspector General, most officers are young graduates with no training in investigation and prosecution (Tumwesigye, J, 2000).

Public Service Reform

The government has given high priority to public service reform, concentrating government around its core functions, decentralizing service delivery to district administration, removing "ghost workers," "right-sizing" the work force and improving pay.[2] Government has made impressive progress in these areas in recent years with support from the World Bank, UNDP, and bilateral donors (World Bank, 1998).

In 1997, the government, with continuing donor support, launched a new phase of civil service reform entitled Public Service 2002—a five year plan "to develop a public service which delivers timely, high quality, and appropriate services, at minimal cost to the nation, supports national development and facilitates growth of a wealth-creating private sector." The thrust of the program is to improve performance through the introduction of Results-Oriented Management (ROM) at the ministerial and district levels, creation of executive agencies, improvements in budgeting and financial management systems, linking pay to performance and improving service delivery standards and training (ibid.).

One challenging issue remains—creating an adequate and progressively fair pay structure. At the lower levels, pay is still below a "living wage." At the middle and upper levels, it is sufficient for family survival, but well below market comparators. However, the government is crippled in its efforts to substantially improve wages by severe budgetary constraints. Inadequate pay prevents the recruitment, retention and motivation of a professional, well-motivated staff equipped to play effectively the regulatory and service delivery roles designed in the Constitution and elaborated in Public Service 2002. Present salaries lock public service employees into unproductive patterns of behavior and offset efforts to improve discipline, promote ethical conduct and adhere to conflict-of-interest guidelines. When workers do not have sufficient income, they engage in fraud and bribery or fail to report such incidents. The government is not fulfilling the contract that sustains a well-functioning bureaucracy—adequate pay in return for hard work and professional integrity. Consequently, it is difficult for the State to hold civil servants accountable for performance. The government is forced to condone the multiple ways in which public servants participate in aberrant behavior, which is their adjustment for insufficient remuneration (ibid.).

Information and Communication Strategies

The public, civil servants and the donor community have been regularly notified of reform developments. The media, both print and broadcast, describe the government's progress toward implementing its action plan. Direct, accurate, and timely news stories are intended to help achieve transparency and encourage continued progress.

Introducing a Leadership Code of Conduct

A Leadership Code of Conduct was passed in 1992. It attempts to ensure a minimum standard for leaders' conduct and requires them to declare their assets. The law establishes a five-member committee to enforce the Code. Although the activity most commonly associated with this law is the declaration of wealth, it contains other provisions that are important to promote integrity. They are conflict of interest, gifts to leaders, abuse of government property, misuse of official information, nepotism and harassment of subordinate staff. The government is currently trying to extend the number of public officials who must declare their assets.

In addition to a section based on the proposed leadership statute, the Constitution adopted in 1995 includes another provision that promotes greater integrity within public service. It directs Parliament to establish a National Council of State to review the backgrounds and qualifications of individuals seeking, or being considered for, political office or senior positions in government. If this law is enforced, any candidate with a questionable background, where there is suspicion of dishonesty or corruption, will be disqualified during the screening stage.

The Role of the Director of Public Prosecutions

Uganda's former Director of Public Prosecutions, Alfred P. W. Nasaba, observed that while the legal framework is generally adequate, the laws of evidence, particularly the accomplice rule, have hampered prosecutors. This rule states that the testimony of an accomplice must be corroborated with independent evidence before seeking a conviction. Mr. Nasaba comments: "In cases of corruption, both the giver and recipient are accomplices. If corrupt people are to be convicted, this rule should be changed to allow an accomplice to give credible evidence against corrupt officials or persons" (Nasaba, A, 1995).

It is vital that only those officials above reproach are responsible for malfeasance cases. Investigators, prosecutors and judges, especially those dealing with these types of offenses, must have the highest integrity. Too often, this has not been the case. Moreover, if evidentiary standards are changed, the impact of testimony by interested parties or co-conspirators has to be controlled.

The Auditor General

The Auditor General's annual reports to Parliament have regularly exposed corruption and inefficiencies. In 1992, for example, he discovered approximately $4 million in missing funds. To aid the work of the AG, the Inspectorate system has been reinstated after many years of neglect. Audits are conducted regularly to ascertain whether funds are utilized for their intended purposes.

The Public Accounts Committee

The Public Accounts Committee (PAC) has been vigorous in demanding proper accounting procedures in ministries and government agencies. Many senior officials have been prosecuted and dismissed for improper use of expenditures. Parliament has exposed corruption among senior officials forcing the censure and resignation of some government ministers. To ensure its continued success, the PAC has been decentralized, resulting in several district accounts committees. This has strengthened the auditing function at all levels of government and society. Consequently, it is becoming increasingly difficult for aberrant behavior to go unnoticed.

Other Government Reforms

Economic Reforms and Liberalization

A series of macroeconomic modifications have gradually eradicated numerous distortions that encourage malfeasance. Changes include eliminating monopolies, encouraging competition between the private sector and the State to trade basic commodities, and abolishing quota systems and importation rights on certain products. Export monopolies in traditional commodities (coffee, cotton) have ended, procedures have been simplified, and new regulations encourage investment in export-oriented activities.

The privatization of parastatals has reduced the State's total control over the economy. Other measures, which have expanded the economy are the removal of price controls, both direct and indirect on major, locally manufactured products; an end to the monopoly of exported foodstuffs; the elimination of the Coffee Marketing Board; and the deregulation of foreign exchange markets. As a result, confidence in the Ugandan shilling has returned and funds held abroad are now flowing back into the country. The government has sought to "de-personalize" the delivery of services. Customers should not have to contact a particular official for information. Procedures and penalties are now easily obtained through posters, notices or other information bulletins.

Changes in the Military

Military spending was reduced from 35 percent of GNP in 1990 to 16 percent in 1994 through demobilization and other measures. Under a plan approved by the NRA Council in May 1992, the government decreased the military establishment over a three-year period by 40 percent to 50,000 personnel, a savings of $14m per year. (Langseth, 1995) This reduction has diminished the role of the military and freed funds to be better utilized in other areas.

Decentralization

Decentralization is important in the fight against corruption because public sector decision making in Uganda has been largely secret, through highly centralized institutions with little accountability. The government has embarked on a major program to decentralize the administration and the delivery of many public services.

The success of this effort depends on a process of institution building, now under way at regional levels; improved communication between civil servants and local authorities; and increased interaction between public and local institutions to ensure that needs and priorities are coordinated. Although some progress has been made, many difficulties remain. Physical facilities are inadequate in many regional districts and managerial and technical skills are deficient. But more important, it is difficult to manage the devolution of power while the central government is undergoing radical change. The success of decentralization will depend on the ability of district-level structures to deliver services responsively and accountably to their designated populations. Channels of communication are widening; citizens are encouraged to participate in District Resistance Council meetings; and regular consultations are scheduled between local councilors, civil servants, and non-governmental organizations (NGOs). Whether these measures will succeed is yet to be determined.

The Role of the Press

Government-controlled media have been moderately free to expose public office abuses and frequently file stories on the fight against corruption. The newspaper, *Uganda Confidential,* has been especially diligent in its reports. However, the media has not realized its full potential. Because a free press is a new phenomenon, professional journalists lack proper training in unbiased, investigative techniques. There are cases where professionalism has been sabotaged as underpaid reporters and editors succumb to bribery. For example, management at *New Vision* newspaper fired one of its photographers for submitting an obsolete picture while purporting its newsworthiness for a recent story. Another journalist with a local daily was implicated earlier this year in a bribery scandal. Several reports were even accused of being slanderous (Ogoso-Opolot, Erich, 2000).

Nevertheless, the media has on many occasions published well-researched stories, which expose corruption and are instrumental in subsequent legal action. The media has raised the public's awareness. Radio, television, and newspaper exposés have created a heightened sense of accountability among public officials. Unfortunately, most of the stories are not investigative—due mainly to factors such as lack of adequate resources to conduct investigations, lack of laws that guarantee access to information, problems of ownership of the media, and poorly skilled journalists. Legal impediments play a major role in constraining Ugandan journalists. For example, although Article 41 of the 1995 Constitution guarantees freedom of access to information, Parliament has still not enacted legislation that delineates the rights, responsibilities and penalties for enforcement. Public officials take advantage of this limitation in the law, hiding information that should be public under the guise of "confidential or classified." In contrast, this same Parliament nearly three years ago passed laws requiring journalists to register and obtain government licenses, and meet the minimum qualification of a university degree in mass communication. Additionally, it installed a Media Council to supervise the activities of journalists (ibid.).

Another constraint is media ownership. In Uganda, the media is primarily government owned. Before 1986, it was the sole owner of the media, which it used for propaganda purposes. It is unlikely that well-investigated corruption stories that implicate senior government officials or popular politicians will appear in government-controlled media.

Lessons Learned from Uganda

Coordination Among Anti-Corruption Agencies

Uganda has demonstrated the value of involving multiple agencies in corruption reform. However, it has also highlighted the inherent problems associated with a lack of coordination among various agencies. There is concern about the dissipation of resources due to duplicate efforts. For example, the case of the valley dams involving the Ministry of Agriculture, Animal Industry and Fisheries has been a subject of investigation by Parliament, the Inspectorate of Government, the Police and the Auditor General. The Uganda Commercial Bank and Uganda National Social Security Fund are also being investigated by several government agencies. The experiences above have clearly illustrated the need for coordination by anti-corruption institutions. Steps are now being taken to address the problem through regular anti-corruption institution meetings coordinated by the Minister of Ethics and Integrity where common issues and suspect agencies are discussed. In one of the meetings, it was agreed that agencies should inform each other about corruption cases under investigation and all reform agencies should keep lines of communication open (Tumwesigye, 2000).

Relationships among Institutions: Streamlining the Law

Anti-corruption institutions face similar problems as laws and regulations grant overlapping authority and investigative privileges or insufficient authority. For example, powers given to the IGG under Article 230 cut across a wide spectrum of laws and jurisdictions which can cause functional contradictions within the government's legal machinery. Similar and/or related powers already belong to other institutions such as the police, the DPP, the Auditor General, Parliament and the judiciary. (Byakagaba, S. 1999) Article 227 of the Constitution states the IGG is autonomous. However, this office still needs the consent of the DPP to charge and prosecute abuse of office and corruption cases. Some argue that Article 230 should take precedence over

227, but perhaps it is more efficient if the Penal Code and the Prevention of Corruption Act are amended to include the IGG's powers, which secures its independence and coherence of law (ibid.).

Collective action and Coalition Building

Given the mutual suspicion that exists between the country's anti-corruption agencies and civil society, it is unclear whether reform groups genuinely attempt to involve civil society and the private sector in anti-corruption activities. Coalition building between civil society and the government continues to be one of the foci in future reform strategies. Relying solely on the law and government institutions is inadequate. In Uganda, while a coalition is growing among the anti-corruption agencies, there is little inclusion of civil society and the private sector. The need for collective action assumes various stakeholders have a role to play in minimizing aberrant behavior. Historically, anti-corruption programmes in African countries and elsewhere have had little input from civil society. However, successful reform programmes in Hong Kong, Singapore and to some extent Botswana have included all stakeholders, especially civil society.

The Inspectorate of Government has conducted awareness raising campaigns. However, members of civil society harbor some mistrust and suspicion as government did not include them in the design and implementation of the overall programme. Consequently, collective action and a coalition among the various stakeholders could help to reduce or remove some of that suspicion. The mechanisms for achieving accountability are manifold and are probably more effective when reinforced within various branches of government and between government and civil society.

The Role of Civil Society

It is clear that there is a role for civil society in the reform movement. However, experience indicates that civil society is weak and not empowered to question corrupt practices. To be effective, it must be strengthened. Increased publicity could raise awareness about the levels of corruption and its negative impact on people's lives as well as informs civil society of the country's institutional framework, which has a mandate to fight corruption. For example, of all the households that were interviewed in the corruption perception survey, only thirty-two percent were aware of the Inspectorate of Government and only half actually understood its function. Arguably, the data demonstrate that people's inability to identify these institutions' anti-corruption efforts highlights the weaknesses in the government's publicity campaigns. Community based non-government organizations, religious organizations, pressure groups, activists movements, and interest groups have made contributions to successful anti-corruption efforts elsewhere. Government agencies increase their effectiveness when they involve civil society as active members in the coalition against corruption, specifically in the implementation of reforms.

Adequate Resources

Successful anti-corruption efforts in many areas of the world have illustrated that adequate resources to support the work of reform agencies are directly correlated with success. Insufficient funding and inadequately trained personnel, for example, impede the work of the Inspectorate; and despite increases in the 1999/2000 budget, funds remain insufficient. It is important to note that anti-corruption agencies are more likely to succeed when material conditions and incentive structures favor professionalism and quality in the performance of public officials.

Sustained Political Will

There must be political will. No legislative or administrative changes can ever be effective unless there is political will and commitment at all levels of government. In the case of Uganda, it is important to encourage existing political will and maintain the momentum of current reform initiatives. The challenge is sustainability. The current drive is extremely fragile, as reform initiatives are not participative and do not include the full range of political actors and civil society.

Donor Coordination

Donor activity is prevalent in supporting the various indigenous reform institutions, which makes the case for more effective donor coordination to avoid duplication and competition. The government's current action plan that includes donor support will be more useful if it correlates donor activities with stated priorities and goals. A detailed inventory of anti-corruption support provided by various donors may be a productive place to begin.

Conclusion

Corruption is an insidious, invasive disease that can infect all levels of government and society. It becomes an integral part of the body politic through a complex set of circumstances that are the result of the actions of domestic and international actors as well as individual and group behavior. While it is a complex set of circumstances that create the breeding ground for corruption, an equally complex set of occurrences, policies and actions are necessary to bring about its end. Anti-corruption institutions, laws, political will and commitment must all come together not only to institute a reform strategy but also develop a paradigm to sustain the carefully orchestrated efforts for change. Without the participation and efforts of every level of government, the private sector, the public and civil society, even the most strategically planned efforts will fail. However, it is the success of these reform movements that will determine the future not only of Uganda but countries around the world that must strive to eliminate the ravages of corruption from their societies.

Bibliography

Buterra, R. "Effective Institutions can Play a Role in the Fight Against Corruption: The Role of Parliament and other Institutions" Paper presented at a workshop on "The Challenge of Building Coalitions in the Fight Against Corruption in Africa" in Durban, South Africa, October 16–18, 1999.

Byakagaba, S . "The IGG and the Law" *The Inspectorate Magazine,* vol.1, Issue No. 2, December, 1999.

Langseth, P. and Mugaju, J.(eds.) *Post-Conflict Uganda: Towards an Effective Civil Service* Fountain Publishers, Uganda, 1996.

———, Katorobo, Brett, and Munene (eds.) *Uganda: Landmarks in Rebuilding a Nation* Fountain Publishers, Uganda 1995.

———, and Simpkins, F (eds.) *Integrity Workshop in Uganda: Final Workshop Proceedings,* Economic Development Institute, 1996.

Matembe, M. "Ethics and Integrity for Public Officials" Paper presented at a seminar on Government Integrity at the International Law Institute in Uganda, February 7 –18, 2000.

———, "Working Together to Fight Corruption: State, Society, and the Private Sector in Partnership" Paper presented at a workshop on "The Challenge of Building Coalitions in the Fight Against Corruption in Africa" in Durban, South Africa, October 16–18, 1999.

Museveni, Y.K. *Sowing the Mustard Seed: The Struggle for Freedom and Democracy in Uganda* Macmillan Press, 1997.

Nasaba, A.P.W. "The Role of the DPP and Police in Crime Prevention" in *Integrity Workshop in Uganda: Final Workshop Proceedings,* edited by Langseth and Simpkins, Economic Development Institute, 1996.

Ogoso-Opolot, E. "The Role of the Media in Controlling Corruption" Paper presented at a workshop on "The Challenge of Building Coalitions in the Fight Against Corruption in Africa" in Durban, South Africa, October 16–18, 1999.

Rukare, D. "Legal Inadequacy Against Corruption" *The Inspectorate Magazine,* vol.1, Issue No. 2, December, 1999.

Ruzindana, Langseth and Gakwandi (eds.) *Fighting Corruption in Uganda: The Process of Building a National Integrity System* Fountain Publishers, Uganda, 1998.

Tumwesigye, J, "The Activities of the Inspectorate of Government" Paper presented at a seminar on Government Integrity at the International Law Institute in Uganda, February 7 –18, 2000.

———, "The Significance of Building Coalitions in the Fight Against Corruption" Paper presented at a workshop on "The Challenge of Building Coalitions in the Fight Against Corruption in Africa" in Durban, South Africa, October 16–18, 1999.

————, "Inspectorate of Government Registers Achievements" *The Inspectorate Magazine,* vol.1, Issue No. 2, December, 1999.

Wangusa, M. "A Worrying Diagnosis: Revelations of the Survey" *The Inspectorate Magazine,* vol.1, Issue No. 2, December, 1999.

World Bank,. *Recommendations for Strengthening the Anti-Corruption Program in Uganda* (PRSD Anti-Corruption Series, No.1, 1998).

Notes

1. See for example, *Uganda National Integrity Survey, 1998.* Some of the major findings include: 70 percent of households reported their perception of corruption in public service was very high; four out of ten (40 percent) consumers had paid a bribe to service workers; the payment of bribes was perceived to be more prevalent in the police (63 percent of households), the judiciary (50 percent of households), primary schools (49 percent of parents pay extra for tuition), the local administration (39 percent of households), and in health services (28 percent of households). More than half of the interviewed households thought the problem of corruption had increased; only 19 percent thought the situation had improved.
2. Total public service numbers have been reduced from 320,000 in 1993 to 164,000 in early 1998.

25

A Comparative Analysis of African and East Asian Corruption

Alice Sindzingre

Introduction[1]

Contemporary afropessimism is often based on the image of Africa as a place of out-and-out corruption of both governments and societal institutions. After decades of reticence on this theme, the "aid fatigue" of donors reflects dominant Western opinion. Corruption is now recognized in the aid donors' literature as a key element in the efficacy of their strategy, with the flow of public aid continuing to drop in real terms.[2] . . . But corruption also appears to be equally endemic in some countries in East Asia, if not more so considering the sheer financial scale and "modernity" of illegal practices in this area. Even after 1997 and the financial crisis, perceptions of corruption are high for certain countries, such as Indonesia. Proof of the reality of corruption are the regular politico-financial scandals—e.g., in Japan, Thailand, and Indonesia. Many Asian countries were at levels of economic development comparable with Africa at the time of its decolonization,[3] but have nonetheless realized high growth rates and attracted considerable foreign investment.[4] The interesting fact is that this growth—which was not accompanied by unequal distribution and benefitted the emerging middle classes[5]—was not hindered by corruption. Thailand long exhibited a political system based on the open purchase of votes by local "bosses." Indonesian nepotism, where the former President's family and entourage obtained control of the country's largest private enterprises, has operated on a much larger scale than analogous African phenomena.[6] The spectacular growth of China after its opening up[7] is another case in point. The impact of corruption on foreign direct

441

investment is no different in Asia relative to other countries, other things being equal, but the negative effects of corruption have been counterbalanced by faster growth.[8] Furthermore, in the vast literature about the causes of the Asian crisis, "crony capitalism" and the weakness of financial institutions and regulatory systems are considered to have emerged only because of international factors—above all, the sudden lack of confidence on the part of investors and the instability of very high volumes of international capital flows.[9] In itself, corruption is not incompatible with development, and does not explain the economic situation in Africa. Africa is not the world champion in corruption. Development may very well be accompanied by an increase in corruption, and the causal relationship between the two does not constitute an explanation of the process.

The question thus becomes why corruption has not been deleterious to Asian growth compared to the poor performance of Africa. We might also question the solidity and reality of economic development. In Asia a dependent, "ersatz" capitalism[10] has been described as dividing entrepreneurial dynamics up among politically connected rent-seekers and speculators, where magnates of the Chinese diaspora have carried out primitive accumulation and diversified into numerous economic sectors.[11] In this view favoritism is the basis of business in Indonesia, and business is supported everywhere—with the notable exception of Singapore—by foreign investment and networks of the Chinese diaspora who tend to prefer rapid gain.[12] In addition, the notion that sub-Saharan Africa will sink into prolonged stagnation has its detractors.[13] One must thus examine both the context and nature of corrupt phenomena in the two regions.

We will not dwell on all the various definitions of corruption, nor on the differences among fraud, bribery, embezzlement, and influence peddling, between personal gain and gain benefiting a group, or whether or not the notion should be limited to the activities of public agents.[14] One concise definition . . . is that of Shleifer and Vishny:[15] "the sale by government officials of government property for personal gain." This may also apply to private corruption, even if the latter is dealt with much less in the literature on developing countries.[16] We will focus on the reasons corruption takes the form it does in sub-Saharan Africa, contrasting it with East Asia.

"Petty" and "large scale" corruption must be distinguished from one another.[17] They may certainly be situated along a continuum, as Reno has shown in Sierra Leone:[18] the history of internal corruption cannot be dissociated from the country's external economic relationships. In the African context—of "community pressure," the scarcity of resources and the instability of value, patrimony, status, and social position—it is difficult, from a theoretical point of view, to separate a government minister's search for personal gain from that of the common man. Meanwhile, large scale corruption has mainly to do with international criminality,[19] which is globalized and shares common "rules" of trans-state illegality. "Petty corruption" applies to the totality of daily transactions and does not fall under the same category. When this kind of corruption is aggregated, however, it can be devastating in its consequences.

First, I present the principal theoretical and explanatory elements relating to corruption in the literature on the political economy of developing countries, and an overview of current research on the subject. Then, a number of salient empirical factors will be singled out to allow a comparison between sub-Saharan Africa and East Asia. The goal is to understand African corruption as more visible but less efficient from an economic point of view—as well as from the standpoint of corruption itself—compared to corruption in East Asia, which is perhaps even more extensive but has not prevented an economic "miracle" from taking place.[20]

Theoretical Evolution

The literature on corruption in developing countries is vast. A smaller body of literature based on economic perspectives has evolved in its analysis of the effects of corruption on growth and development. Corruption has often been conceived . . . within a principal-agent framework—the relationship of "agency," or delegation—or within game theory.[21] The "principal," or upper level of government, expresses its preferences and awaits results from an agent, *e.g.* a civil servant, whom it instructs to produce such results. Controlling these agents has a cost, and the agents enjoy a certain margin of manoeuvre. A private third party who stands to benefit from the action of this agent by obtaining a good produced by government may pay the agent (in monetary form or otherwise) in order to influence him. The payment will not be retransmitted to the principal, thus defining the corrupt act (without any reference to the public interest or the interest of the principal).[22] This line of analysis focuses on the mechanisms, arbitrations, incentives, and sanctions that lead an agent to be honest or not.

It has been argued that corruption can be efficient and have beneficial effects by lessening transaction costs induced by excessive bureaucratic regulation or by helping solidify fragile political systems.[23] Some assert that corruption may even encourage economic growth by accelerating transactions and reducing bureaucratic delays, and by inducing the state employee to work harder.[24] The specious character of these functionalist conceptualizations has long been revealed. The line of causality is reversed: it is because distortions created by the state exist[25] that behavior aimed at reducing them contributes to the general well-being. From an epistemological point of view, the assigning of an effect to a given cause has never justified this effect. It would be better to examine the cause, i.e., the disfunctional state (even if one cannot confidently qualify certain collapsed systems as "states") and to grasp the implicit logic in these distortions. The understandable reactions to distortions do not imply an improvement of wellbeing. Reactive, generalized, petty corruption cannot be justified by state corruption, and only perpetuates a vicious circle in which each fuels the other. Corruption never constitutes a "second best" solution: it is difficult to limit corruption to those situations where it appears economically desirable, and there is no reason that it should not spread to the totality of governmental institutions.[26]

The concept of the state as rent-seeker[27] applies where states are held responsible for distortions to which private agents rationally adapt through bribes, fraud, tax evasion, or operating in the informal economy. This is a recurrent argument in studies on the informal sector or cross-border African trade, where one reads of "real" prices or the expression of freer market forces, and of corrupt behavior primarily conceived as reactive in nature.[28] The influence of this concept—which blurs causalities—has been notable. In the early 1980s the "structural adjustment" reforms recommended by the Bretton Woods institutions to deal with the crises of African states were based on liberal notions of an intrusive state as the main culprit,[29] and entailed a contraction of public spending, the shedding of personnel, and freezing of wages in the state administration.

Economic research has clearly evolved since then, taking into account the context of the political economy of reform, the role of governments and interest groups, and the existence of a logic of predation. Crises have been attributed more to elites and less to the state as an institution, and to the capacity of these elites to implement discretionary policies and complex regulations to their own benefit. In the latter case, the excess of bureaucratic rules is seen as voluntary, designed to create a climate in which extortionate behavior prevails. The OECD, World Bank, IMF, and the EU, beginning in the mid-1990s, established new conditionalities for their programs, predicating aid on reforms that are "internalized" by state administrations and procedures that are more "transparent."[30] The development analysts speak of "good governance," and of reforming the" capacities" of local administrations. . . . Meanwhile, critical research is increasing. Political science work on Africa has long described the varying modalities of African governments and how they function: states that are predatory, too strong or too weak, "suspended," irresponsible, post-colonial kleptocracies supported by foreign interests owing to their natural resource wealth, or as fictions by aid agencies.[31] The political economy literature on East Asian countries is likewise reevaluating their successes in contexts propitious to corruption.[32]

The Costs of Corruption for Development

Within economics, it has been increasingly demonstrated that corruption can be deleterious for growth. It is impossible to know the precise cost, for corruption ranges from petty racketeering to major commissions on international contracts.[33] Baumol has argued—contrary to the economists mentioned above—that even entrepreneurship is not always productive; it may even have a destructive character for economies in which parasitic activities are well compensated.[34] Schleifer and Vishny advance two models of corrupt systems: one where payments are organized, centralized, and fixed, guaranteeing certain property rights (the kind in former communist regimes); the other decentralized, where any number of bureaucrats may independently demand payments, and where the acquisition of goods is never reliably guaranteed. Having emerged in post-Soviet Russia, and in post-reform China to a lesser degree,[35] the latter system is chronic in sub-Saharan Africa. There, bribe amounts can increase infinitely while production plummets, underscoring the link between corruption and poverty. Decentralization may not have beneficial effects in such contexts, and may even be dangerous.[36]

The African recession of the 1980s induced this multiplication of new entrants into the corruption market in certain countries, apart from merchant and administrative networks that organize corruption and cooperate to maintain the payer-payee system, such as for customs agents in Cameroon. This has led to a drying up of rents, as private agents cease unprofitable activities.[37] Despite the difficulty in adding up the cost, they represent a very high levy on existing wealth and wreak havoc on the economy.[38] Such a system either returns to the prior equilibrium of rent or results in the situation of "collapsed" states, where the aggregation of individual calculations contribute to a general impoverishment without anyone wanting to be the first to renounce it (which is rational). The secrecy involved in corruption also makes it a distorting factor in regard to taxation—to which economists often compare it—inducing a preference for goods and activities where bribes are less detectable (e.g., certain imports, or maintaining enterprises in the public sector as sources of rent).[39] Private firms, innovative enterprises, and above all small businesses, whether or not they pay the "informal tax", are severely penalized through additional costs, barriers to entry, or exclusion from the market.[40]

Mauro demonstrates the inverse relationship between corruption, on the one hand, and investment and growth on the other.[41] These costs are reinforced by governmental spending more conducive to corruption (e.g., neglecting education and health, and favoring capital intensive projects and opportunities for hidden payments).[42] Countries clearly diverge within each region: for example, Singapore, Hong Kong, and Botswana, where corruption is low, versus the Philippines (with its well-documented "crony capitalism"), Thailand, China, and most African states—be they formerly British or French colonies—suggesting complex determinants not attributable to colonial legacies.

Elements of Causality in Africa and contrasts with East Asia

Corruption, with its wide variations between countries, is not more serious or widespread in sub-Saharan Africa than in Asia. It responds to contents, rationalities, and political, economic, and institutional contexts generating different time frames. These have complemented productive economic processes in Asia much more than in Africa.

The Weak Heuristic Capacity of Two Dimensions: Political History and Cultural Values

The type of political regime is not a convincing determinant for corruption.[43] Types of political regimes are in no way linked to a given level of economic development.[44] The transition from an authoritarian state toward a more democratic one may be accompanied by increased corruption: decentralized decision-making coupled with weak institutions may lower entry costs that had limited the ability to impose bribes, thus leading to more corruption. Authoritarian regimes such as Singapore exhibit low levels of corruption,[45] in contrast to others that seem similar. Some are endowed with anti-corruption agencies, such as Malaysia, an example of an" enlightened" regime that has embarked on modernization but asserts the specificity of Asian political cultures.[46] In Indonesia, by contrast, corruption is endemic. In Nigeria, civilian regimes have been as permeable to corruption as military ones.[47] The case of the former communist regimes is well-known: as with African countries after independence, the old corrupt machines simply disintegrated.[48] Exploring possible "pathologies" in the process—which is not a priori inscribed in existing institutions—Andreski assigns considerable weight to the colonial heritage at the moment of decolonization.[49] Young also sees colonization as an essential factor.[50] One reason is the type of economy it put in place, based on natural resources, minerals, cash crops, hydrocarbons, and various other sources of rent.[51] These are models African countries have not been able to break free from. Second, colonial rulers created successor regimes to protect their interests, and these were often illegitimate. This was notably the case in central Africa, and contributed to political factionalization, the politicization of bureaucracies, and the impoverishment of institutions and the educational system. The colonial style is, however, not a sufficient determinant, as the Anglophone countries are not less corrupt than others. Also, Thailand was never colonized but has a serious problem with corruption.

Ethnic fragmentation is noted by economists as weakening local resistance to divisions sown by the colonial power. Mauro, and Easterly and Levine have shown correlations between weak growth in sub-Saharan Africa and ethnic heterogeneity, instability, and factionalized executives.[52] By contrast,

Botswana's economic success and relatively low level of corruption are often attributed to its ethnic homogeneity.[53] The argument for homogeneity is inconclusive, however, as an ethnic group may be segmented into antagonistic sub-groups. Homogeneous countries do not necessarily exhibit better performances in the area of corruption.[54] Likewise, the longevity of dictators who methodically led their countries to ruin renders useless the argument that . . . stability is desirable in and of itself. On the contrary, a predatory ruler wishing to remain in power can encourage disorganization and corruption in order to prevent the formation of a strong opposition.[55] Thailand too has had a propensity to coup d'etats but at the same time has experienced economic growth. More pertinent is the quality and will of leaders and their administrations: a deeper analysis of Botswana shows that the relevant determinant is less ethnicity than the ways authorities manage ethnic segmentation.[56] The unequal status of different ethnic groups within countries, notably diaspora minorities (e.g., Indians, Chinese, Lebanese) also renders ethnic fragmentation a superficial variable.

Culture—or its "moral economy" variant, the "ethic of subsistence"—is a facile explanatory trap utilized excessively by political scientists and economists. Following Scott, whose notion of a moral communitarian solidarity came in for criticism—notably from Popkin,[57] who argued for an opportunistic rationality—many economists[58] advance a cultural relativist argument. According to this, some acts are not perceived as corrupt by certain social groups, but rather as a part of "traditional culture" and community redistribution. But these groups may be segmented on multiple levels, and ties, rights, and obligations depend strictly on situations and statuses within groups. Secondly, a "culture" of embezzlement cannot explain corruption in China any more than it does in Africa. Corruption is unknown in the peasant societies of sub-Saharan Africa and incompatible with their modes of regulation. In these societies, the act of theft can upset fragile and conflict-ridden social systems, and is thus subject to quick and severe sanction. Likewise, villagers disapprove of visible inequality and personal enrichment, which are precisely what occurred under the colonial and post-colonial state. . . More relevant are heterogeneous, contextual rationalities, and the existence of recognized and defined individual and collective private property rights in the "traditional" sphere of society. This is in contrast with the absence of recognition of state property rights, which brings one back to the state's history and legitimacy.[59]

The Nature and Credibility of the State

The most important dimension is that of the state and its relationship with private agents. A series of features are to be taken into account: (i) the nature of the state, its "developmental" character, its credibility and legitimacy; its economic history and values, and the capacity of a government to think ahead, which determines the expectations of agents, their investment decisions, and their choice of certain types of goods: consumption, insuring the security of property and productive assets, the latter with a short-term horizon or betting on the long term (e.g., industry); (ii) the nature and rules of social organization; (iii) and the relationship between these two levels.

The much analyzed" developmental" character of East Asian states has been emphasized by Wade in the case of Taiwan, and by Amsden for South Korea.[60] These states embarked on "developmental" polices in the 1960s, in contrast to their African counterparts. Evans counterposes them to African "predatory" states (epitomized by ex-Zaire), through their "benevolent" authoritarianism and "encapsulated" technocrats and bureaucracies, who are able to take economic decisions that are heavily influenced by politics but not disconnected from medium-term economic constraints. Taking up the distinction between "subordinate" and "autonomous" states—the latter based on clearly defined rules and sanctions—Rodrik reminds us that no state is born autonomous but instead becomes so.[61] Economic policies—e.g., import substitution, public investment, protectionism—were similar at the outset, but those in Asia were more flexible, were intended to gradually disappear, and above all never lost sight of the imperative of profitability. South Korea, with its corrupt, clientelistic ties between the state and large enterprises (*chaebols*), had followed the same policies as African states in the early-mid 1960s: the state as champion of the "big push," public enterprises, and industrial take-off. It was able to revise this strategy despite the existence of a public sector heavily supported by massive state intervention and networks of *chaebol* heads embedded in the power apparatus. These long-term, future-oriented projects were indeed justified, as they culminated in an upgrading of accountability and were accompanied by the growth of a middle class. The latter was not promoted in Africa, given the mistrust of its leaders and hostility of state administrations toward their private sectors. In East Asia, enterprises receiving aid from the state were obliged to submit regular reports on their performance, even if they were linked to their governments through corruption. The long-term view that there was no interest in aiding inefficient enterprises . . . is one factor differentiating the time frame of governement in East Asia from that in African states.

Throughout their short history, the states of Africa, unlike those in East Asia, have been characterized by illegitimacy,[62] unstable leadership, and weak credibility. The few leaders[63] who sent out strong signals that they intended to change the rules and combat routine illegality encountered great difficulty in reversing expectations rooted in decades of colonial and post-colonial state construction. These leaders were overtaken by the weakness of institutions and often by the fatigue that comes with being in power a long time: the "developmental" dimension of authoritarianism was relegated to secondary status. The illusions maintained by economic prosperity and massive public investment were shattered after the slump in commodities prices in the mid-eighties.

Over the long run African societies have been characterized by instability of the value of assets and money, which Berry has shown to be the basis of individual strategies of protection against uncertainty.[64] Local elites are implementing rational strategies, with modern contents, in regard to their new endowments, i.e., shifting assets to the ex-colonial power or to other safe havens. Strategies for safeguarding assets once took the form of investments in stable assets in real estate. The flight of capital abroad, which is very high in Africa compared to East Asia, is an essential diffentiating factor. For African agents, moving capital abroad is entirely rational given domestic instability and the need to protect their patrimony. In Southeast Asia, wealth is reinvested locally or regionally. This is likewise the case for the *Nanyang* Chinese diaspora, whose horizon encompasses the "southern ocean" and not just China.[65] Much of the foreign investment in China comes from overseas Chinese: informal ties and norms give an intertemporal dimension to corruption and shape its impact on investment.[66]

Political and institutional credibility does not boil down only to formal institutions but also to the perceptions of leaders and mechanisms of social coordination. It affects foreign and domestic decisions on savings and investment. Because few want to invest in sub-Saharan Africa, the return on such investments has to be high: since African governments and their economic policies have so little credibility, this can only occur at the price of safeguarding "extractive niches," of monopolies acquired with bribes, short-term deals, and national and international clientele networks controlled by the local regime. The private sectors in illegitimate states are dangerous, by their very nature, due to their possibilities for accumulation independent of the political leadership; the mistrust of the state toward private operators thus continues, in Anglophone as well as Francophone countries, in capitalist as well as ex-Marxist ones, or those which have had a succession of coups.[67] Asian leaderships, by contrast, have been aware that they can benefit by the prosperity of their private firms, with corruption being a means to reinforce this.

The State and the Private Sector: Asian Networks vs.
African Loose Relationships

Why such contrasts? All this suggests another difference between sub-Saharan Africa and East Asia: the interface of entrepreneurs and the state, and the nature of social structures outside of the state. African countries inherited fragmented structures—occupational, political, ethnic—and narrowly-based markets (labor and goods) rarely enlarged by multinational connections and diasporas, with the exception of the Lebanese and Indians. The Chinese diaspora is both foreign and indigenous in the eyes of Southeast Asian states, a minority with its typical behaviour, and simultaneously assimilationist and oriented toward China and Chinese elsewhere. It has been the object of reciprocal, well-understood interests on both sides because of the utility of its longstanding position as merchants, courtiers, and tax collectors.[68] The authorities could control them politically through their dependent status and periodically threaten them, as in Indonesia. The diasporas, in return, could guarantee their prosperity through close proximity to the authorities, which involved a sharing of the wealth with the latter.

The role of diasporas necessitates a precise definition of the notion of networks. Large-scale networks are rare in Sub-Saharan Africa, where the term is mistakenly used to refer to heterogenous relations and extensions. In Sub-Saharan Africa—apart from Indian and Lebanese diasporas, and international mafia groups—"networks" are indigenously-based, limited by the boundaries of circumscribed groups (through kinship, religion, occupation) and locally fragmented. There are no networks in the Asian sense and the term is too heavily used in the literature. With the exception of some large diasporic ethnic groups like the Hausa in West Africa, autochtonous networks remain for the most part at micro-organisational scales, aiming at preventing individual risk, activated by opportunities like cross-border price differentials, largely absent from industrial and financial activity, focused on profits from trade, and/or confined to particular regions. Relations of mutual obligation based on membership of ethnic groups—groups which are themselves segmented and decentralized, imposing few common norms and values—fluctuate depending on access to resources, particularly those of the State. These relations often form paired links which are not necessarily transitive—yet this transitivity, *i.e.* shared norms and expected behaviour, is the condition for the existence of a network (as opposed to occasional transactions and gains). Asian diasporas, by contrast, tend to operate along a whole chain of economic activities and complementary sectors. They are both connected to international markets and active in local ones.[69] The extension of corruption, its organization, the use and investment of its proceeds, and its links with public resources, power and legality, thus differ between the two regions. Corruption in Sub-Saharan Africa does not feed economic networks and tends to be used for purposes of local or foreign consumption, for secure investment in property, or for political purposes, benefiting restricted groups that gravitate around officials who possess a capacity for making money for services rendered.

The economic scale on which diasporas operate and their utilitarian, profit-oriented relationship with local rulers and bureaucrats—resulting from the diasporas' political vulnerability—is linked to corruption in East Asia. The Chinese diaspora dominates the financial and industrial sectors in Indonesia, Malaysia, Thailand, and South-East Asia out of proportion to its demographic weight, and has played an important role in the region's economic "miracle."[70]

Corruption was not a problem here. The relevant factor is the state's support of entrepreneurial activity, in contrast to sub-Saharan Africa.[71] In Asia, corruption is limited by the economic rules of "developmental" states and by the norms of networks (e. g. relative to reputation within them). This is not the case of some predatory states in sub-Saharan Africa.

The consequences are clear. In Southeast Asia the local and international connection, along with the efficacy of common rules, allows for the functioning of internal networks, with this "internal" space operating on a global scale. Even though African networks may be extensive, their international penetration and economic weight remains dependent and circumscribed; this is in contrast with Asian counterparts seeking to dominate the commercial, industrial, and financial sectors.[72] Private operators in Asia did not need to move capital abroad while East Asia was booming, as their credit relationships are coextensive with the globalization of the diaspora. Nor did they feel compelled to siphon off resources from the state, as they were in an economic alliance with it. The prevailing interest is more in a certain equilibrium, in maintaining and reproducing the resource in order to insure future flows. These strategies, which occur on a scale well beyond micro-transactions, are supported by efficient mechanisms of intra-group cooperation, even when dispersed over several countries, as well as by relationships of reputation and trust linked to well-defined kinship ties.[73] These are sometimes found in sub-Saharan Africa, designated by the cliche of communitarianism, but despite surface resemblances are different and operate in differing contexts. In sub-Saharan Africa rights and obligations are segmentary, and solidarities are confined to circumscribed and potentially agonistic groups of kinsfolk, in-laws, or generations.[74] For corruption as any other activity, "free riding" is always possible and coordination can be weak. Asian networks, based on different notions of kinship and collective action, use reinforcing relationships that are more transitive: notably a common reference via household structures and rituals over the place of origin of their emigration stream. Above all, the internal rules and contracts of dispersed groups are based on trust and confidence—guarantees for other members of saving, credit, and sanctions. As Greif has shown in the case of medieval guilds, these mechanisms of reputation allow the maintenance of coalitions in exchange relationships.[75] Yet again, African redistributions and savings groups (*tontines*) may evoke similarities. In sub-Saharan Africa they make it possible to provide social protection to non-productive individuals; in Asia, on the other hand, group strategies are focused on the labor market and making sure each group member engages in profitable activity, however modest. In addition, these institutions in sub-Saharan Africa, unlike Asia, do not involve international markets and individuals of all statuses—some rich, others less so—but rather are based on local markets, with everyone affected by the same constraints and shortages.

The important point is the relation to time, which involves the relationship to value. The expectations of agents in Asia are over the medium-term, due to the stability of the environment. This does not necessarily refer to formal political stability but rather to the stability of relationships between private operators and political interests. Stability is assured for the local diaspora by both its international ties and alliances with the domestic political leadership. Thailand has witnessed repeated *coups*, but the alliance of the bourgeoisie and the armed forces is stable,[76] in contrast with numerous African countries where each *coup* results in a new stratum of clientelized private entrepreneurs. These anticipations are exemplified by China after its opening, with operators in the Chinese diaspora ignoring Western doubts about the Chinese regime as they knew their interests there would be socially guaranteed over the long run.[77] The same was true with Taiwan, a political enemy of China but major investor there. The determining variable is a long temporal horizon (Asia) versus a short one (Africa). In sub-Saharan Africa this involves both men in power—well aware of their political fragility, and siphoning off as much as possible as quickly as possible—and common people confronted with misery and the arbitrary behaviour of authorities.

The Vicious Circle of Poverty and Differences in the Rules Regarding Social Protection

Poor individuals in sub-Saharan Africa make microeconomic calculations reflecting the rationalities underlying petty corruption. Time frames are so short that survival is the sole referent, which may be social, economic, or political, which leaves politicians with little time to deal with development. Even the "ethic within corruption"—mentioned above in relation to organized, centralized systems—is no longer valid. Economic survival is not only about mere survival but more about a desperate quest for money and its signs. Rational calculation should, in principle, lead people to remain in the workforce and safeguard their reputations, as, for example, drivers and chauffeurs with safe vehicles, or customs agents who don't discourage travellers through exorbitant tolls and customs duties. These trade-offs are "irrational" from the point of view of a long-term time frame and of collective action. They are rational, however, in a Hobbesian "war of all against all", of decentralized individual maximizing, where no authority exists to guarantee rights or social protection and where the horizon configured by poverty is one of living from day to day.

The absence of sanctions for predatory behavior by political *parvenus* and bureaucrats encourages imitation by those further down the scale, the depreciation by the authorities of professionally conscientious individuals (which is a reminder that simply increasing salaries is not a sufficient solution), and redundant administrative posts, devoid of content and motivation, inducing state employees to act in arbitrary, authoritarian ways. Traditional reciprocities are perverted by money debts, and peasant "altruism" by indifference toward the consequences of one's acts outside of microsolidarities. Misery, everywhere a larger phenomenon than poverty, engenders behavior linked to the absence of an internalization of the state, of public service, or public goods, as well as to the absence of allegiances going beyond local beliefs. This misery is also linked to a "communitarianism" quite different from Asian networks; conceived as a provider of social protection, it materially supports its members who do not work but is not wholeheartedly accepted by those who contribute the funds. They do nothing to render their charges more productive, unlike Chinese extended kinship networks for which this is a priority. "Traditional" social protection, or "social safety nets," are one feature differentiating the two zones. The supposed community solidarity in Africa stops at the outer limits of segmentarity and according to whether or not individuals are members of networks, individuals outside them being irrelevant. The lack of state welfare schemes forces individuals into a perpetual quest for resources to protect themselves in case of adversity, which always looms on the horizon. In Africa, the prevailing microeconomic calculation is *community* investment without a guarantee of return (donations in time and in money, as soon as a good position renders them possible). In Asia, the microeconomic calculations take the form of *collective* investment, which is as constraining as it is inciting for petty corruption, which a group can do on one of its members within firms. One finds collective investment in sub-Saharan Africa, but only as a rational calculation by poor peasant families deep in debt and hoping that one of their offspring will be able to support them in the future—once again in the context of patrimonies that are not secure and in unstable political and economic conditions existing even before colonialism.

Asian networks follow different rules, also seen in other large diasporas such as the Hausa in West Africa, based on honor—giving one's word and not needing to put things in writing—credit, and social sanctions. He who absconds with the safe puts himself outside the meta-stability of organized levies and implicit contracts sealed by reputation (exchange, bureaucratic transactions, public tenders, etc.). These internal rules are necessary in order to perpetuate the dispersed, transnational, diasporic structure. "Losing face," for example—a primordial notion in Asia—is punished by denying access to claims and debts circuits, not being allowed to be married within the community, not to be eligible for credit, and therefore to be banished, sometimes for generations. Such sanctions are effective precisely because a network is diasporic, or international. If they were local, the sanctions would be inconsequential, as free riding and exit options would exist.

Conclusion

This article attempts to define the rules and sanctions through which individual rationalities are aggregated in order to configure economic and political contexts in which the criteria are stability and the temporal horizon. These have a retroactive effect on individual rationalities. In an unstable world, status depends more on the ability to mobilize dependents than capital, and underlies acts of petty and large-scale corruption (with politics caught up in this process). African networks emerge as a response to instability, as do the rights and obligations associated with them. One looks to acquire the largest number of them in proportion to the level of economic precariousness; this may generate economic behavior that appears irrational, unprofitable, but that aims to keep options open. They entail costs that may lead the state employee to impose a levy on "external" financial flows—including those of state origin—since public goods are tainted with illegitimacy or with the distance of the political regimes. Corrupt behavior tends to be mimetic, for it both discourages legal transactions and deprecates those who respect laws and formal procedures.

Asian diaspora networks have similar rules but are different, as they are both transnational *and* nationally-based across Southeast Asia. Individual rationality favors long term consequences in economic transactions: the corrupt act must leave part of the resource for the future, as the prosperity of operators (Chinese or not) depends on that of the country and on stable, common interests with local political elites. Similarly, the product of levies is territorialized locally and partly reinvested inside the country. In contrast, African agents invest their capital abroad, particularly in the ex-colonial powers. The contexts that specify the forms, and make predatory behavior rational, are misery, short-term horizons, and the absence of shared rules, or of a meta-rule: the state.

The economic environment—depressed in Africa since the 1970s, promising in Asia even after the financial crisis—remains the cause and consequence of disparities between the two regions. Corruption is, however, not linked to poverty at a macroeconomic level. It has its effects at the level of microeconomic rationality and calculations, of what agents consider rational in an environment whose historical repetitions have solidified and routinized individual, political, and economic expectations. Corruption is more devastating—and induces vicious circles more often—in poor countries. Analogous to the "poverty trap," which was theorized in regard to development in the 1950s, is a "corruption trap" that has an implacable rationality and coherence, articulating economic and political contexts and their representation by individuals.

Notes

1. The author wishes to thank Arun Kapil for his translation, Yann Barbe for his help with documentation and many enlightening discussions, and Jean-François Medard for his most helpful comments on this article. All errors are the responsibility of the author alone.
2. DAC (Development Assistance Committee), *Development Cooperation, Report 1996*, OECD, Paris, 1997, p. 63.
3. Mogenet, Luc and Jean-Christophe Simon, Côte d'Ivoire et Thaïlande, *Afrique Contemporaine*, n°176, October-December 1995, pp. 18–28, or, in the same issue, Collange, Gérald, Deux pays pétroliers : l'Indonésie et le Nigeria.
4. The net flow of capital toward Asia (direct foreign and portfolio investment), which has steadily increased since 1990, represented more than half ($104 billion) of that received by the ensemble of developing countries in 1995. International Monetary Fund, *International Capital Markets*, International Monetary Fund, Washington D. C., 1996; IMF, *World Economic Outlook*, bi-annual reports. According to the OECD DAC report for 1996 (p. 63), Asia took in 70 percent of the increase of private capital in 1990–95 period, whereas in Sub-Saharan Africa the private inflow, already weak, fell by two-thirds in real terms.
5. World Bank, *The East Asian Miracle*, The World Bank, Washington D. C., 1993, p. 29 sq.
6. Sidel, John T., Siam and its Twin? Democratization and Bossism in Contemporary Thaïland and the Philippines, *IDS Bulletin*, vol. 27, n°2, april 1996, pp. 56–63. Hewison, Kevin, La formation de la classe capitaliste thaïlandaise et son mouvement de recomposition dans les années quatre-vingts, *Tiers-Monde*, t. 31, n°124, October-December 1990, pp. 763–788; Van Roy, Edward, On the Theory of Corruption, *Economic Development and Cultural Change*, vol. 19, n°1, October 1970, pp. 86–110; Robison, Richard, Industrialization and the Economic and Political Development of Capital: The Case of Indonesia, in Ruth McVey ed., *Southeast Asian Capitalists*, Cornell University Press, Ithaca, 1992; Robison, Richard, Etats autoritaires, classes possédantes et politique des nouveaux pays industriels : le cas de l'Indonésie, *Tiers-Monde*, t. 31, n°124, Octobre-December 1990, pp. 853–876.
7. Lee, Peter Nan-Shong, Bureaucratic Corruption During the Deng Xiaoping Era, *Corruption and Reform*, vol. 5, n°1, 1990, pp. 29–47; Rocca, Jean-Louis, Pouvoir et corruption en Chine Populaire, *Perspectives Chinoises*, n°11–12, January-February 1993, pp. 20–30; White, Gordon, Corruption and Market Reform in China, *IDS Bulletin*, vol. 27, n°2, April 1996, pp. 40–47.
8. Wei, Shang-Jin, *How Taxing is Corruption on International Investors?*, NBER Working Paper n°6030, Cambridge MA, 1997, and Campos, J. Edgardo, Donald Lien, and Sanjay Pradhan, The Impact of Corruption on Investment : Predictability Matters, *World Development*, vol. 27, n°6, pp. 1059–1067, 1999.
9. World Bank, *East Asia : The Road to Recovery*, the World Bank, Washington D. C., 1998.
10. Yoshihara, Kunio, *The Rise of Ersatz Capitalism in South-East Asia*, Oxford University Press, Singapore, 1988.
11. Paix, Catherine and Michèle Petit, Itinéraires et stratégies d'une bourgeoisie : le cas de Singapour, *Strates*, n°1, Université Paris I, 1986, pp. 49–119.
12. Clad, James, *Behind the Myth: Business, Money, and Power in Southeast Asia*, Unwin Hyman, London, 1989; Bello, Walden and Stephanie Rosenfield, *Dragons*

in Distress, Penguin Books, London (1st ed. 1990); Krugman, Paul, The Myth of Asia's Miracle, *Foreign Affairs*, November-December, pp. 62–78; Young, Alwyn, The Tyranny of Numbers: Confronting the Statistical Realities of the East Asian Growth Experience, *Quarterly Journal of Economics*, vol. CX, n°3, August 1995, pp. 641–680.

13. Sachs, Jeffrey, Growth in Africa: It Can be Done, *The Economist*, June 26, 1996, pp. 23–25.

14. Sindzingre, Alice, *Etat, développement et rationalité en Afrique : contribution à une analyse de la corruption*, Centre d'Etude d'Afrique Noire, Bordeaux, Travaux et documents n°43, 1994; Heidenheimer, Arnold J., Michael Johnston, and Victor Le Vine, eds., *Political Corruption: A Handbook*, Transaction Publishers, New Brunswick and Oxford, 1989; Theobald, Robin, *Corruption, Development and Underdevelopment*, Macmillan, Basingtoke, 1990; Klitgaard, Robert, *Controlling Corruption*, University of California Press, 1988; Williams, Robert, *Political Corruption in Africa*, Gower, Aldershot, 1987.

15. Shliefer, Andrei and Robert W. Vishny, Corruption, *Quarterly Journal of Economics*, vol.CVIII, n°3, august 1993, pp. 599–618.

16. Wade, Robert, The Market for Public Office: Why India is Not Better at Development, *World Development*, vol. 13, n°4, 1985, pp. 467–497.

17. Medard, Jean-François, Public Corruption in Africa: A Comparative Perspective, *Corruption and Reform*, vol. 1, 1986, pp. 115–131.

18. Reno, William, *Corruption and State Politics in Sierra Leone*, Cambridge University Press, Cambridge, 1995.

19. Naylor, Robert T., *Hot Money and the Politics of Debt*, Unwin Hyman, London, 1987; Ellis, Stephen, Africa and International Corruption: the Strange Case of South Africa and Seychelles, *African Affairs*, vol. 95, n°379, April 1996, pp. 165–196.

20. World Bank, *The East Asian Miracle*, op. cit.

21. Klitgaard, op.cit.; Rose-Ackerman, Susan, *Corruption: A Study in Political Economy*, Academic Press, New York, 1978; Banfield, Edward C., Corruption as a Feature of Governmental Organization, *Journal of Law and Economics*, vol. 18, n°3, December 1975, pp. 587–606; Daubrée, Cécile, *Marchés parallèles et équilibres économiques: expériences africaines*, L'Harmattan, Paris, 1995; Basu, Kaushik, Sudipto Bhattacharya, and Ajit Mishra, Notes on Bribery and the Control of Corruption, *Journal of Public Economics*, vol. 48, 1992, pp. 349–359, or Lui, F. T., A Dynamic Model of Corruption Deterrence, *Journal of Public Economics*, vol. 31, 1986, pp. 1

22. Goudie, Andrew W. and David Stasavage, *Corruption: the Issues*, OECD, Paris, Development Centre, 1997, Technical Paper n°122.

22. Rose-Ackerman, op. cit., p. 6–7.

23. Nye, Joseph S., Corruption and Political Development: A Cost-Benefit Analysis, *American Political Science Review*, vol. 61, June 1967, pp. 417–428; Bayley, David H., The Effects of Corruption in a Developing Nation, *Western Political Quarterly*, vol. XIX, n°4, December 1966, pp. 719–732; Beenstock, Michael, Corruption and Development, *World Development*, vol. 7, n°1, 1979, pp. 15–24.

24. Huntington, Samuel P., Modernization and Corruption, in *Political Order in Changing Societies*, Yale University Press, New Haven, 1968; Leff, Nathaniel H., Economic Development through Bureaucratic Corruption, *American Behavioral Scientist*, vol. 8, n°3, 1964, pp. 8–14.

25. Mauro, Paolo, *Why Worry About Corruption?*, International Monetary Fund, Washington D. C., Economic Issues n°6, 1997.

26. Rose-Ackerman, op. cit., p.8; Gould, David J., *Bureaucratic Corruption and Underdevelopment in the Third World: the Case of Zaïre*, Pergamon Press, New York, 1980.

27. Krueger, Anne O., The Political Economy of the Rent-Seeking Society, *American Economic Review*, vol. 64, n°3, 1974, pp. 291–303; Tollison, R. D., Rent-Seeking: A Survey, *Kyklos*, vol. 35, n°4, 1982, pp. 575–602.

28. De Soto, Hernando, *The Other Path: The Invisible Revolution in the Third World*, Harper and Row, New York, 1989; McGaffey, Janet, *Entrepreneurs and Parasites: The Struggle for Indigenous Capitalism in Zaïre*, Cambridge University Press, Cambridge, 1987; McGaffey, Janet et al., *The Real Economy of Zaïre: The Contribution of Smuggling and Other Unofficial Activities To National Wealth*, University of Pennsylvania Press, Philadelphia; and James Currey, 1991, on the positive aspects of Zaire's "second economy." Critical views appear in Lautier, Bruno, Claude de Miras, and Alain Morice, *L'Etat et l'informel*, L'Harmattan, Paris, 1991, and in Reno, op.cit., chap. 1.

29. World Bank, *Accelerated Development in Sub-Saharan Africa*, the World Bank, Washington D. C., 1981.

30. Recommendations of the 1996 DAC Report, p. 116 (french version), following the 1994 recommendations against bribes in international transactions. For the World Bank, see the projects for anti-corruption programmes announced by its President at the Spring 1997 meetings, or Shihata, Ibrahim, *The Role of the World Bank in Combatting Corruption*, mimeo, The World Bank, Washington D. C., September 1996; for the Fund, Tanzi, Vito, Corruption: Arm's-length Relationships and Markets, in Gianluca Fiorentini and Sam Peltzman eds., *The Economics of Organised Crime*, CEPR and Cambridge University Press, Cambridge, 1995; for the EU, FRISCH Dieter, art. cit.; for USAID, USAID's bulletins, e. g. Rhodes, Jill, Seeking the Causes of and Cures for Corruption, *African Voices* (USAID), vol. 5, n°1, 1996, pp. 1 and 7, and IRIS, *Governance and the Economy in Africa: Tools for Analysis and Reform of Corruption*, College Park, University of Maryland, Center for Institutional Reform and the Informal Sector, 1996; and the emergence of NGOs such as Transparency International, which are used by donors to promote better "governance" in aid-receiving countries.

31. Evans, Peter, The State as a Problem and Solution: Predation, Embedded Autonomy, and Structural Change, in Stephen Haggard and Robert R. Kaufman eds., *The Politics of Economic Adjustment*, Princeton University Press, Princeton, 1992; Hyden, Goran, *No Shortcuts To Progress: African Development in Management Perspective*, University of California Press, Berkeley, 1983; Andreski, Stanislav, *The African Predicament: Study in the Pathology of Modernisation*, Michael Joseph, London, 1968; Jackson, Robert H. and Carl G. Rosberg, Why African Weak States Persist: the Empirical and the Juridical in Statehood, *World Politics*, vol. 35, n°1, October 1982, pp. 1–24, and Reno, op. cit.

32. Deyo, Frederick C. ed., *The Political Economy of New Asian Industrialism*, Cornell University Press, Ithaca, 1987.

33. The international laundering of illegal activity is estimated at 2 percent of world GDP—between $300 and $500 billion, which is only an average and for which no information on the breakdown by continent exists. Tanzi, Vito, *Money Laundering and the International Financial System*, International Monetary Fund, Washington D. C., 1996, working paper WP/96/55, and Quirk, Peter J., *Macroeconomic Implications of Money Laundering*, International Monetary Fund, Washington D. C., 1996, working paper WP/96/66.

34. Baumol, William, Entrepreneurship : Productive, Unproductive, and Destructive, *Journal of Political Economy*, vol. 98, n°5, 1990.
35. Sands, Barbara, Market Clearing by Corruption: the Political Economy of China's Recent Economic Reforms, *Journal of Institutional and Theoretical Economics*, vol. 145, n°1, 1989, pp. 116–126.
36. Prud'homme, Rémy, The Dangers of Decentralization, *World Bank Research Observer*, vol. 10, n°2, August 1995, pp. 201–220, see pp. 211–212, and McLure, Charles E., Comment on Prud'homme, same issue, pp. 221–226.
37. Herrera, Javier, *Vers un rééquilibrage du commerce transfrontalier entre le Cameroun et le Nigeria*, Orstom-Dial, Paris, working paper 07–T, 1995, on Cameroun, and *Les échanges transfrontaliers entre le Cameroun et le Nigeria depuis la dévaluation*, Dial, Paris, March 1997, pp. 85sq.
38. A voyage from Côte d'Ivoire to Niger involves "informal" levies representing three-fourths of "administrative expenses", *Marchés Tropicaux et Méditerranéens*, Une évaluation de la crise des transports en Afrique sub-saharienne, n°2612, 1er Décembre 1995, pp. 2629–2631. IRIS, op. cit. p. 74, in Benin cites the case of 25 roadblocks over 753 km that are manned by state agents. The bribes which they demand represent 87 percent of the total cost.
39. Schliefer and Vishny, art. cit., p. 611 sq. Alam, M. S., Some Economic Costs of Corruption in LDCs, *Journal of Development Studies*, vol. 27, n°1, October 1990, pp. 89–97.
40. Murphy, Kevin M., Andrei Schliefer and Robert W. Vishny, Why is Rent-Seeking So Costly To Growth?, *American Economic Review*, vol. 83, n°2, may 1993, pp. 409–414. Susan Rose-Ackerman and Andrew Stone, *The Costs of Corruption for Private Business: Evidence from World Bank Surveys*, draft, The World Bank, Washington D. C., 1996.
41. Mauro Paolo, Corruption and Growth, *Quarterly Journal of Economics*, vol.CX, n°3, august 1995, pp. 681–712.
42. Mauro, Paolo, *The Effects of Corruption on Growth, Investment, and Government Expenditures*, International Monetary Fund, Washington D. C., 1996, Working Paper 96/98.
43. Ben-Dor Gabriel, Corruption, Institutionalization, and Political Development: The Revisionist Theses Revisited, *Comparative Political Studies*, vol. 7, n°1, April 1974, pp. 63–83; Harsch, Ernest, Accumulators and Democrats: Challenging State Corruption in Africa, *Journal of Modern African Studies*, vol. 31, n°1, 1993, pp. 31–48.
44. Bratton, Michael and Nicolas Van de Walle, *Democratic Experiments in Africa: Regime Transitions in Comparative Perspective*, Cambridge University Press, New York, 1997.
45. Margolin, Jean-Louis, *Singapour 1959–1987: genèse d'un nouveau pays industriel*, L'Harmattan, Paris, 1988.
46. Camroux, David, *Le tournant vers l'est de la Malaisie*, presentation at the Meeting "Vers une réinvention de l'Asie?", Centre d'Etudes et de Recherches Internationales, Paris, 8–9 June 1995.
47. Forrest, Tom, *Politics and Economic Development in Nigeria*, Westview Press, Boulder, 1993.
48. Schliefer and Vishny, art. cit, p. 610; Ekpo, Monday ed., *Bureaucratic Corruption in Sub-Saharan Africa: Towards a Search of Causes and Consequences*, University Press of America, Washington D. C., 1979.
49. Andreski Stanislav, *The African Predicament*, Michael Joseph, London, 1968.

50. Young, Crawford, *The African Colonial State in Comparative Perspective*, Yale University Press, New Haven, 1994.
51. Mauro, 1997, op. cit. , p. 5.
52. Easterly, William and Ross Levine, Africa's Growth Tragedy: Policies and Ethnic Divisions, *Quarterly Journal of Economics*, vol. 112, pp. 1203–1250, 1997.
53. Good, Kenneth, Corruption and Mismanagement in Botswana: A Best Case Example?, *Journal of Development Studies*, vol. 32, n°3, 1994, pp. 499–521; Maipose, Gervase S., Gloria M. Somolakae and Timothy A. Johnston, *Aid Effectiveness in Botswana*, Overseas Development Council, Washington D. C., 1996. Samatar, Abdi Ismail and Sophie Oldfield, Class and Effective State Institutions: The Botswana Meat Commission, *Journal of Modern African Studies*, vol. 33, n°4, 1995, pp. 651–668.
54. This is for instance the case in Senegal.
55. Robinson, James A., *When is a State Predatory?*, mimeo, University of Southern California, Los Angeles, 1996.
56. Medard, Jean-François, *Corruption et non corruption au Botswana: la normalisation d'un cas déviant?*, 1997.
57. Scott, James, *The Moral Economy of the Peasant: Rebellion and Subsistence in South-East Asia*, Yale University Press, New Haven and London, 1976; Popkin, Samuel L., *The Rational Peasant: The Political Economy of Rural Society in Vietnam*, University of California Press, Berkeley and Los Angeles, 1979; Plateau, Jean-Philippe, Traditional Systems of Social Security and Hunger Insurance: Past Achievements and Modern Challenges, in Ehtisham Ahmad, Jean Drèze, John Hills and Amartya Sen eds., *Social Security in Developing Countries*, Clarendon Press, Oxford, 1991; and Fafchamps, Marcel, Solidarity Networks in Preindustrial Societies: Rational Peasants with a Moral Economy, *Economic Development and Cultural Change*, vol. 41, n°1, October 1992, pp. 147–174.
58. Tanzi, art. cit., insists on the relativism of norms governing exchange between parents, friends, and neighbours.
59. Rocca, Jean-Louis, La corruption et la communauté : contre une analyse culturaliste de l'économie chinoise, *Tiers-Monde*, t.37, n°147, 1996, pp. 689–702; Sindzingre Alice, The Use and Abuse of the Notion of "Culture" in Development Studies of Sub-Saharan Africa, in Michel Griffon ed., *Economie institutionnelle et agriculture*, Proceedings of the 13th seminar of rural economics, CIRAD, Montpellier, 1992.
60. Evans, art. cit.; Wade, Robert, *Governing the Market: Economic Theory and the Role of Government in East Asian Industrialization*, Princeton University Press, Princeton, 1990; Amsden, Alice, *Asia's Next Giant: South Korea and Late Industrialization*, Oxford University Press, New York, 1989; Moon, Chung-In and Rashemi Prasad, Beyond the Developmental State: Networks, Politics and Institutions, *Governance*, vol. 7, n°4, October 1994, pp. 360–386.
61. Rodrik, Dani, Political Economy and Development Policy, *European Economic Review*, vol. 36, 1992, p. 335.
62. Englebert, Pierre, *Institutional Legitimation and Economic Performance: Statehood, Stagnation and Growth in Sub-saharan Africa*, mimeo, African Studies Association, San Francisco, November 23–26, 1996.
63. For example T. Sankara in Burkina Faso, J. J. Rawlings in Ghana.
64. Berry, Sara, *No Condition is Permanent: The Social Dynamics of Agrarian Change in Sub-Saharan Africa*, The University of Wisconsin Press, Madison, 1993.
65. Wang, Gungwu, A Short History of Nanyang Chinese, in *Community and Nation: China, Southeast Asia and Australia*, Allen and Unwin, Sydney, 1981.

Vandermeersch, Léon, *Le nouveau monde sinisé*, Presses Universitaires de France, Paris, 1986.

66. Wei, Shang-Jin, art. cit.

67. Austen, Ralph, *African Economic History*, James Currey and Heinemann, London and Portsmouth, 1987.

68. Redding, S. Gordon, *The Spirit of Chinese Capitalism*, De Gruyter, Berlin, 1993; Brown, Rajeswary Ampalavanar, *Capital and Entrepreneurship in Southeast Asia*, St Martin's Press, New York, 1994, Salmon, Claudine, Les marchands chinois en Asie du sud-est, in Denys Lombard and Jean Aubin eds., *Marchands et hommes d'affaires asiatiques dans l'Océan Indien et la Mer de Chine, 13è-20è siècle*, Editions de l'EHESS, Paris, 1988; Suryadinata, Leo ed., *The Ethnic Chinese in the ASEAN States: Bibliographical Essays*, Institute of Southeast Asian Studies, Singapore, 1989, Lim, Linda Y. C. and L. A. Peter Gosling, eds., *The Chinese in Southeast Asia*, Maruzen Asia, Singapore, 1983.

69. Malaize, Vincent and Sindzingre Alice, Politique économique, secteur privé et réseaux en Asie du sud-est et en Afrique de l'Ouest, *Revue Tiers-Monde*, t. XXXIX, n°155, juillet-septembre 1998, pp. 647–672; Sindzingre Alice, Réseaux, organisations et marchés : exemples du Bénin, *Autrepart (Cahiers des Sciences Humaines)*, n°6, 1998, pp. 73–90.

70 For example, and depending on the period, 4 percent of the Indonesian population own 70–75 percent of the nation's privately-held assets; in Thailand, 8–10 percent of the population own 90 percent of assets in the commercial and manufacturing sector, and half the capital of banks. *Economist*, The Overseas Chinese, July 18th, 1992.

71. Kinoshita, Toshihiko, How to Facilitate Private Investment in Africa Based on the Experiences in East Asia, in Claire Liuksila ed., *External Assistance and Policies for Growth in Africa*, International Monetary Fund, Ministry of Finance of Japan, Washington D. C., 1995, p. 10.

72. Redding, op. cit.

73. Granovetter, Mark, The Economic Sociology of Firms and Entrepreneurs, in Alejandro Portes ed., *The Economic Sociology of Immigration: Essays on Networks, Ethnicity, and Entrepreneurship*, Russell Sage Foundation, New York, pp. 142sq.

74. Fafchamps, art. cit., p. 151.

75. Greif, Avner, Reputation and Coalitions in Medieval Trade: Evidence on the Maghribi Traders, *Journal of Economic History*, vol. XLIX, n°4, December 1989, pp. 857–882; Granovetter, Mark, Economic Institutions as Social Constructions: A Framework for Analysis, in André Orléan org., *L'Economie des conventions*, colloque, CREA, Paris, 1991; Tsai, Maw-Kuey, *Les Chinois au Sud-Vietnam*, Mémoire de la section de Géographie, Bibliothèque Nationale, Paris, 1968.

76. Bernard, Mitchell, States, Social Forces, and Regions in Historical Time: Toward a Critical Political Economy of Eastern Asia, *Third World Quarterly*, vol. 17, n°4, 1996, pp. 649–665; Sindzingre Alice, *Industrie, ajustement et "entrepreneurship" en Côte d'Ivoire et au Ghana*, Leipzig University, Leipzig, papers on Africa n°2, 1996

77. Bouteiller Eric and Michel Fouquin, *Le développement économique de l'Asie Orientale*, La Découverte, Paris, 1995.

Part VIII

THE ASIAN EXCEPTION?
CORRUPTION AS A LESSER HANDICAP

Introduction to Part VIII

The Asian economic crisis that began in Thailand during 1997 focused considerable public attention upon corruption problems that had long been the focus of scholarly debate. It was not that there had been any doubt about the scope of corruption in the region: Japan, Korea, Thailand, Indonesia, and India, among others, all had well-known cases. And it was not that reforms had yet to be tried: indeed, two of the best-known success stories were those of Hong Kong and Singapore. Rather, Asia seemed to contradict what we thought we knew about corruption and economic development elsewhere: over a thirty-year period extensive corruption and rapid growth had coexisted—and in some instances, had seemed to reinforce each other—in nation after nation across the region. In Africa, by contrast, levels of economic development had been broadly similar to those in much of Asia at the time most countries became independent, and yet corruption had been an economic blight. Was there something special about corruption or development in Asia, or was it the long-term relationship between the two that we did not understand?

When the crisis came, it seemed to show that Asia was not so exceptional after all. Extensive corruption lay behind the currency manipulations in Thailand that triggered the economic meltdown. In Korea, Indonesia, and Malaysia, official collusion among businessmen, lenders, and politicians—at times, integrated along family lines and involving military figures too—had built outwardly prosperous business networks on a foundation of shaky loans and currencies, poorly enforced development policies, and licenses and concessions that had been bought and sold at the highest levels. Corruption was not the only cause of the crisis, but it had certainly left the region's economies unbalanced, poorly institutionalized, and vulnerable. Singapore, with its long record of success in controlling corruption, suffered relatively little economic damage. The consensus was that recovery would be a long time in coming, and that before it occurred Asian countries would have to bring corruption firmly under control.

But by the year 2000 things were becoming less clear-cut once again. While Indonesia's economic and political difficulties continued to worsen, many of the region's other major economies were on the upswing. Some notable anti-corruption initiatives—including a new "anti-corruption constitution" in Thailand—were underway, but such reforms were uneven across the region, and even where they were in progress it seemed too soon, and too unrealistic, to credit them with the economic recovery. At the analytical level too, questions were numerous; corruption had played a role in the crisis, but what had that role been? Had the collapse shown that corruption in Asia was essentially the same as everywhere else? Or had its costs been overstated? Had those costs been real all along, but *deferred*, until tight-knit corrupt networks had become so inflexible that they could not adapt to international economic pressures? Or would the Asian economies have grown even faster, and in more balanced ways, had corruption been keep under control?

The answers to such questions, if they ever become known, will take some time to discern. But the selections in this chapter illuminate the variations in forms and practices of corruption, and the contrasts among countries and sub-regions, that make Asia's corruption-and-development story so complex and important.

Mushtaq Khan places patron-client networks in the broader context of development policy, and shows that what is often treated almost as a generic process—clientelism—in fact varies significantly in scope, structure, and implications among several Asian countries. Economic development decisions, whether made by the state, by private institutions, or by (licit or illicit) combinations between them, confer major privileges upon a few people that are not available to all. These privileges and assets are a source of considerable power, both economic and political, in poor and developing societies. Khan shows how they have been used to build patronage networks reflecting contrasting historical factors and elite alignments. "Modernization theory" once suggested that development affected both broad social structures and individual outlooks, but told us little about the connections between those levels. Like Susan Rose-Ackerman, in her discussion of the economic effects of corrupt transactions (chapter 21), Khan places specific transactions and relationships within a broader context, and helps us understand both their developmental effects and the ways such processes differ from one country to the next.

Khan argues, in effect, that to understand corruption and development in Asia one needs to understand the ways privileges are conferred and used. Paul Hutchcroft pursues a similar theme, adding a subtle analysis of various patterns of rent-seeking to the mix. The emphasis is upon variations in practices and effects, as revealed through the study of seven aspects: the ways comparable acts of corruption produce different "takes"; the ways advantages are allocated; what becomes of proceeds; effects upon market processes, and upon state capacity to foster development; how corruption affects the institutionalization of both the state agencies and the political parties; and factors that may help reduce the developmental effects of corruption. Hutchcroft argues that the literatures on rent-seeking, clientelism, and corruption do not by themselves sufficiently address all of these issues, but that the three concepts are, collectively, crucial to understanding the problems and prospects of developing nations.

Corruption problems vary among the nations of Asia, and so do approaches to reform. Reform successes in Singapore and Hong Kong contrast with the pervasive, disruptive corruption of Indonesia—and with its chaotic aftermath. In other cases, such as the Philippines, the record has been mixed at best, and in still others, like Malaysia, the degree of real commitment behind highly-publicized anti-corruption agencies and campaigns is open to considerable doubt. Jon S. T. Quah's comparison of anti-corruption efforts in five Asian societies—Singapore, Hong Kong, the Philippines, Mongolia, and India— shows that these differing degrees of success correspond to differing reform strategies, and that they also point to six specific lessons for those who would undertake reform. Political support at the highest level, the independence of anti-corruption agencies and the honesty of their staffs, and the consistent implementation of broad-based, well-integrated strategies, are among the critical variables. Careful attention must be paid to civil service salaries; if a society can maintain them at high levels it must do so, but if it cannot there are other actions to be taken in the interim. Public attitudes are also critical: if corruption is seen as the norm, and as a high-reward/low-risk activity, reformers will make little headway. Changing such attitudes is a long-term task, and requires extensive cooperation among the government, the civil service, the news media, and society.

In some ways Asia seems less distinctive now—both in its corruption and in its growth—than we may have thought it to be just a few years ago. But both its rapid—if strikingly uneven—recovery from the 1997 economic meltdown, and what we still do not know about the role corruption might play in both, make a careful consideration of the region imperative. Contrasts among Asian societies make it unlikely that any single set of answers will be found, either for the analytical issues or for the question of best practices against corruption. The independent-commission model of reform, for example, has worked best in two city-states; can it work in larger and much more diverse societies such as Indonesia? Can democratic initiatives based upon anti-corruption reform in Thailand survive major scandals, when and if they occur? And do the lessons learned anywhere else apply to China's immense society, increasingly fragmented bureaucracy, and rapidly changing economy (see chapter 31 by Hao and Johnston)? As noted above, important questions about the sources and effects of corruption in Asia remain to be answered. The selections in this chapter, however, offer analytical tools and comparisons that will be valuable in coming to grips with these issues.

26

Patron-Client Networks and the Economic Effects of Corruption in Asia

Mushtaq H. Khan[1]

Corruption has been associated with very different economic effects across Asian countries. In some North East Asian countries such as South Korea, widespread corruption has accompanied decades of very high growth. In others, such as the South Asian countries of the Indian subcontinent, corruption has been associated with relatively low growth. In a third group of countries in South East Asia, high levels of corruption have been associated with moderately high long-run growth rates. These differences could be the result of differences in underlying rates of growth. On the other hand they could also be the result of corruption having *differential* effects across countries (while their underlying growth rates can, of course, vary as well). Economic theory has identified a number of factors that could explain differences in the economic effects of corruption. However economic explanations have given little attention to differences in the political power of the groups competing for resources allocated by the state. This chapter argues that the distribution of political power is revealed in differences in the structure of patron-client networks across countries and these can be important for explaining the differential effects of corruption. The bargaining power of patrons and clients can explain differences in the rights and resources that they exchange (often in corrupt transactions). This in turn can contribute to our understanding of the differential effects of corruption. We will examine the patron-client networks linking states and competing groups of clients in the Indian subcontinent, Malaysia, Thailand, and South Korea, and investigate

Source: European Journal of Development Research 10:1 (June 1998).

the ways in which the structure of these networks can determine the economic effects associated with corruption in those countries . . .

Southeast Asian countries present a number of interesting variants that in different ways resulted in more dynamic economies than in South Asia despite the presence of large intermediate classes and more complex patterns of patron-client exchanges than in South Korea. Malaysia inherited a large class of individuals whose demands could potentially have resulted in patron-client exchanges of the Indian variety. However, in Malaysia the clear ethnic division between intermediate classes who were largely Malay and a capitalist class that was initially largely Chinese paradoxically allowed the construction of a structure of patron-client exchanges that allowed fairly rapid growth. Instead of many decentralized patron-client exchanges between many different patrons and groups of clients, the ethnic redistribution adopted by the New Economic Policy in the seventies allowed a centralized sharing of rents in Malaysia. This served to prevent structural sclerosis from developing along Indian lines.

Thailand provides yet another Southeast Asian variant. Here Chinese capitalists were well-integrated into local political elites and an ethnic-based patronage politics along Malaysian lines did not emerge. Instead, the relatively well-developed capitalist class took over patronage networks themselves. They became the patrons "buying off" the demands of potential clients from amongst the aspiring intermediate classes and using this political power to bargain for resource allocation to their particular faction. The role of capitalists in Thai politics is apparent in the exceptionally large number of capitalists (by developing country standards) involved in Thai electoral politics. Here we have yet another structure of patron-client exchanges that allowed a relatively decentralized type of capitalism to thrive. These explorations suggest how the location of corrupt transactions within specific structures of patron-client exchanges can help to make sense of differential economic performance.

It may be utopian to believe that the transition to capitalism can be entirely just. Yet unless the transition process is widely perceived to be just, it is difficult for it to be organized in a legally regulated way in an open polity. External pressure to tackle corruption may help development only if such pressure contributes to the legitimization of the processes through which capitalism is being created. On the other hand, it is very likely that anti-corruption strategies may sometimes make the problem of organizing internal political stability more difficult during processes of capitalist transition that could in turn prolong instability and the perpetuation of underdevelopment. The issue of corruption thus brings to the fore the limits of attempts to establish high standards of justice in the transition to capitalism in the absence of any global political commitment to equitably share the costs of structural change.

1. Corruption in Developing Countries.

It is not very useful to quibble over formal definitions of corruption. Most usually corruption is defined as the violation of the formal rules governing the allocation of public resources by officials in response to offers of financial gain or political support (Nye 1967, Khan 1996b). However it is defined, corruption appears to be endemic in developing countries and indeed there are systematic reasons why this should be the case. Accumulation and the allocation of public resources in developing countries very frequently involve changes in established property rights and institutions or the creation of entirely new ones. To put it simply, the state is allocating rights and resources at a time when a new capitalist class is emerging. Given the long-run and even inter-generational consequences of these allocations, there are huge incentives to dispute, contest, and attempt to change all such allocations.

For these processes *not* to involve corruption, the allocation and creation of these new rights would have to follow strict rules so that particular individuals could not change these allocations by bribing. The problem is that any such rules would themselves have to be publicly set up. Given the post-colonial political settlement in most developing countries, it is unlikely that explicit rules that aim to create new capitalist classes could be set up in such a way as to enjoy widespread legitimacy. If we recognize that what is happening in developing countries is the creation of new classes by the allocation and stabilization of new rights, it is easy to appreciate the substantial difficulties in following a transparent and accountable route to the construction of capitalism even if developing country leaders had always been minded to follow such a route.

Suppose we were to try to construct a set of transparent and legitimate rules through which capitalist property rights were to be created. On the one hand, the *supply* of the resources through which the emergence of the new class is being encouraged is severely limited in developing countries. This is a manifestation of underdevelopment and poverty. On the other hand, there is likely to be a very great *demand* for access to these resources so that particular individuals can join this emerging class. Anti-colonial struggles mobilized large multi-class populist alliances in many developing countries and post-colonial states could not explicitly formulate rules of allocation which appeared to leave any of these groups out of the contest. Constitutions and laws enshrined principles of allocation that were egalitarian and fair at a time when underlying resource constraints made following such principles extremely difficult. The large gap between demand and supply has often meant that the actual allocation of property rights often failed the principles of allocation that the law set out. Very great incentives were created for corruption. This was as true for the allocation of land, credit or licenses to emerging industrialists as for the allocation of irrigation water or credit to emerging capitalist farmers.

The contest over public resources is particularly severe because the early beneficiaries of these contests are winners in a game of class evolution that is likely to have consequences for generations to come. In many cases, the individuals who succeed in establishing themselves at this critical stage only do so as a result of a great deal of good fortune, political connections, some initial wealth or corruption. None of these characteristics can legitimize the large differences in income and wealth that subsequently emerge. Given the inherent unfairness involved in these processes it has been relatively easy to organize opposition to these characteristics of the development processes in most developing countries. Opposition has typically been organized by members of emerging middle class groups who have been left behind in the development process and is therefore more intense in societies where these groups are better organized and entrenched.

Paradoxically, the opposition of these groups has often resulted in a second set of structural pressures generating high levels of corruption in developing countries. The opposition of organized groups has often had to be bought off by payoffs from existing elites or directly from the state to the most troublesome or vociferous opponents in an attempt to "purchase" support or legitimacy. This type of corruption is more overtly political in motivation as opposed to the corruption that results from the excess demand for publicly allocated resources and rights. Here the state allocates resources to those with the greatest ability to create political problems rather than to those who have the greatest ability to pay (see Khan 1996a for a discussion of the significance of the distinction). Political corruption too results in surreptitious transfers because (in most cases) payoffs to opponents in proportion to their ability to make trouble could not by its nature be publicly recorded in the budget . . .

Clearly we need to have an analytical framework which allows corruption to have different effects in different countries. If indeed corruption has a uniform effect (whether good or bad) everywhere, this should be the conclusion reached at the end of a process of evaluation and analysis rather than a presumption made at the outset. If on the other hand, corruption can have variable effects, identifying these differences could be of great policy importance. Even if all corruption is equally undesirable on moral grounds, the differences between them in terms of their *economic* effects may inform the direction of policy and institutional attention. Two sets of observations constitute the starting point of our enquiry: (1) the association of corruption with poor performance in the South Asian countries and (2) the comparatively much better performance of East and Southeast Asian countries despite the prevalence of substantial corruption there.

Informal journalistic evidence suggests that corruption has been wide-

Table 26.1
Corruption and Economic Performance

Country	Corruption Index 1980–83	GDP Growth Rates 1970–80	1980–92
Malaysia	6.0	7.9	5.9
South Korea	5.7	9.6	9.4
India	5.25	3.4	5.2
Pakistan	4.0	4.9	6.1
Bangladesh	4.0	2.3	4.2
Thailand	1.5	7.1	8.2

Note: A Corruption Index of 10 indicates "No Corruption", an Index of 0 indicates "Maximum Corruption"
Sources: Mauro, 1995; World Development Report, 1994.

spread in virtually all developing countries. This view is corroborated by the subjective responses of foreigners who have done business in these countries. These responses are summarized in the *Business International* corruption index that is reported in table 26.1 for our sample of countries for the period 1980–83. Table 26.1 shows that for this group of countries, the extent of corruption correlates very poorly with economic performance. The differences between subjective corruption indices ranging from 6 to 4 are not necessarily significant but the table does suggest that over the relevant period, very corrupt Thailand did not perform significantly worse than apparently less corrupt South Korea and probably better than less corrupt and more resource-rich Malaysia. As a group, these countries combined good performance with high levels of corruption. The South Asian countries fit more closely with the perception that corruption is associated with poor performance. But even here, more corrupt Pakistan appears to have performed somewhat better than less corrupt India . . .

2. Some Determinants of the Effects of Corruption.

The overall economic effect of corruption can be broken down into two components. The first is the economic effect of the bribe. The resources transferred in the bribe itself often result in a reduction in social value and are therefore an economic cost for society. In theory, however, bribes could be pure transfers that simply redistribute wealth but keep total wealth unchanged. In this rare case the bribe itself may be costless for society. In the more usual case, bribes from industrialists or other social actors to state officials represent a social cost of variable magnitude as social wealth is reduced to a greater or lesser extent. This is typically the case if the bribe-giver would otherwise have invested the bribe in production whereas the transfer to the official typically results in consumption with possible value-reduction for the

Figure 26.1
The Two Economic Effects of Corruption

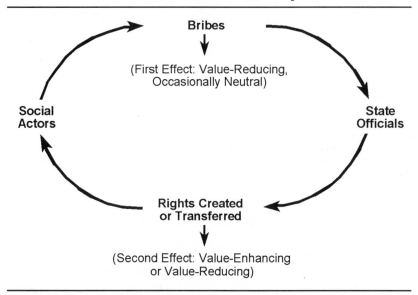

economy over time. This is the first effect of corruption, that is, the effect of the flow of resources from social actors to state officials shown by the higher arrow in figure 26.1.

The second effect of corruption is the economic consequence of the new rights or reallocations of rights brought about by state officials as the quid pro quo of the bribes they have received. This is the effect of the rights created or transferred by state officials in response to the bribe shown by the lower arrow in figure 26.1. This part of the analysis is much more complicated as it is not always the case that the changes brought about as a result of or in association with corruption are always value reducing for society (Leff's argument was a simple version of the value-enhancing possibility). There is also a problem of choosing the benchmark quite carefully (the structure and allocation of rights which would have existed *in the absence* of corruption) to judge this effect correctly (Khan 1996b). Clearly figure 26.1 is a simplification of the possibly complex flows of bribes and payoffs from social actors to state officials on the one hand and flows of rights, subsidies and allocations of public resources from officials to social actors on the other. We examine some of these complexities in greater detail later.

The overall effect of corruption is the joint effect of the direct implications of the bribe and the effect of the rights created or transferred as a result. Differential effects across countries can be due to differences in either or both of these effects (Khan 2000). In some cases corruption may be damaging mainly because the bribes are large or may have particularly damaging effects on the economy because of lost opportunities for investors or the use made of the bribes by recipients. In other cases the significant negative effect of corruption may be due to the types of rights created, who they are created for and the terms under which they are created. The patron-client networks which we will concentrate on in this chapter have implications for the effects of corruption particularly because of their role in determining the second effect, that is, in determining the types of rights which are created or transferred through corrupt transactions.

Patron-client networks describe a set of transactions that may overlap with and yet are analytically distinct from corruption. Patron-client relationships are repeated relationships of exchange between specific patrons and their clients. A number of features distinguish patron-client exchanges from other types of exchange. First, such exchanges are usually personalized. They involve an identifiable patron and an identifiable set of clients. Entry and exit is considerably less free compared to normal market transactions. Secondly, the exchange is between two distinct *types* of agents, distinguished by status, power or other characteristics (Schmidt et al. 1977 in particular Landé: xiii-xxxvii). Typically the superior member is the patron and the inferior member the client. Clearly a wide range of exchanges in developing countries between state officials and privileged groups of clients can be described in these terms. Nevertheless, the power or status of the patron can vary across a broad range and these differences may be important for understanding the types of exchanges taking place within different patron-client networks (Khan 1996a,b). It is this insight which makes patron-client networks interesting for the study of corruption. The type of network can give us critical additional information about the types of rights being transacted and the terms on which these transactions take place. Some characteristics of patrons and clients that are likely to influence the economic implications of the transactions are easily dealt with by economists; others are less simple to model.

1. Objectives and Ideologies

Economists normally assume that actors in state and society will want to maximize value for themselves. At the very least, they will want to maximize value for someone. In fact both state officials and social actors may be motivated by ends that are primarily non-economic such as race or ethnicity. To the extent that transactions between patrons and clients reflect such non-economic goals, economic value may obviously not be maximized (North 1981, 1995).

The objectives of state officials and social actors determine their goals while their ideologies (shared assumptions about how the world works) influence the ways in which they attempt to achieve them. Exchanges within patron-client networks can only be value-maximizing if the partners to the exchange want to achieve value maximization for themselves or at least for others. It is not necessary that they be totally motivated by value maximization as long as a substantial part of decision-making is motivated by it. If transactions are value-maximizing for individuals they may also, under certain conditions, be value-maximizing for society. On the other hand, transactions which are not even value-maximizing for the transactors are very unlikely to be value-maximizing for society. Apart from being motivated (to a large extent at least) by economic value-maximization, it is also necessary that the participants have ideologies which enable them to learn rapidly so that they do not hold on to beliefs about causes and effects which do not stand up to repeated experience. North (1995) has recently stressed the importance of ideologies and learning processes in explaining differences in performance across countries. Ideologies could therefore have some role to play in explaining why both corrupt and non-corrupt transactions within patron-client networks may differ across countries. While ideologies and learning processes may be important it is likely that their importance has been exaggerated in some recent work (Khan 1995: 79–85).

2. Numbers of Clients

The numbers of potential clients of each type can affect their success in organizing collective action in bargaining with patrons. If small groups with specific interests are more successful in organizing collective action, they may bribe or lobby more effectively than bigger groups and indeed the rest of society (Olson 1965, 1982). This could result in rights being created to favor small groups even when they are value-reducing for society as a whole. However, small numbers are only part of the story. In most developing countries, resources have to be directed to and rights created for small numbers of emerging "capitalists." But in fact their expected advantage in lobbying or bribing due to their small numbers is often over-ridden by the bargaining power of other groups such as the urban middle classes or rich peasants whose power is often based on their *large* numbers. Thus while numbers are important, their effect on bargaining power is more complicated than is suggested by the simplest interpretations of Olson's model.

3. The Homogeneity of Clients

This too may determine the chances of successful collective action by different groups of clients. More important, the homogeneity or otherwise of particular groups may determine the relative transaction costs facing state officials or political patrons in collecting bribes from that group. If some clients are relatively easy to transact with (say because they are of the same ethnic group as the patrons), the latter may prefer to deal with them even if others may notionally have been willing to pay more. Thus for instance the relative homogeneity of small groups demanding value-reducing rights may be successful while less homogenous larger groups demanding value-enhancing rights may fail. The relative transaction costs of dealing with different groups of clients may be relevant for explaining some outcomes of patron-client exchanges in developing countries (Khan 2000).

4. The Institutions through which Patrons and Clients Interact

These include in particular the institutions of the state through which patrons and clients negotiate and carry out exchanges. Institutions can influence both the "demand" for new rights (the flow of bribes to state officials) as well as influencing the "supply" of rights (the flows of rights from patrons to those offering bribes). On the demand side, institutions may allow or prevent particular groups of clients to compete for new rights or resources. They also describe the rules of the game that define how clients who bribe can expect their chances of winning to change as a result. These institutional features determine the magnitude of the bribes offered by particular groups of clients demanding particular rights or re-allocations of rights (Mueller 1989: 229–235). On the supply side, the degree of fragmentation of institutions may determine how easy it is for different patrons to coordinate their transactions. A failure to coordinate may sometimes result in lower-valued rights being created even though patrons might collectively have extracted bigger bribes by collectively creating higher valued rights (Rose-Ackerman 1978, Shleifer & Vishny 1993) . . .

5. The Relative Political Power of Patrons and Clients

The potential role of relative political power in determining the types of rights transacted between patrons and clients has not been adequately recognized in the literature. The relative political power of clients determines the *type* of payoff they can offer to the patron. If clients are politically weak, the patron is likely to extract the maximum *economic* payoff from the client in the form of a bribe commensurate with the right being created or transferred. At the other extreme, if the patron is politically weak, the client may instead be offering political support rather than an economic payoff. The payoff to the patron in this case is not just the value of the bribe paid to state officials and politicians but also the political support (or absence of political opposition) which is often also offered (Khan 1996a, 1996b). We argue that a critical factor determining differences in the rights that are transacted between patrons and clients in different settings is the relative power of competing groups of clients and their patrons in the state.

One reason why political power has received little attention from economists is that it is relatively difficult to define. Steven Lukes distinguished between power defined as a *collective capacity* that he called power$_1$ and power defined as an *asymmetric relationship* between individuals or groups that he called power$_2$ (Lukes 1978: 636). The first type of power is relevant when we want to discuss power as a transformative capacity. However, for our purposes, the relevant notion of power is power$_2$ in Lukes' terminology. Power$_2$ determines whether clients are able to bargain a more or less attractive deal with their patrons. Udehn (1996: 150) suggests an even narrower version of power$_2$ that he calls power$_3$ that he defines as the capacity of some actors to reward and/or punish other actors. Power$_3$ and its determinants may be most relevant for looking at differential bargaining outcomes within patron-client networks. The determinants of power$_3$ determine the extent to which clients are able to inflict political costs on patrons if they are ignored. The greater the power of clients in terms of the second and third definitions, the more likely is it that patrons will be offering powerful groups of clients rights in exchange for political support rather than economic payoffs.

Differences in the power of specific groups of clients across countries may then be important for understanding differences in the bargains they are able to strike with their patrons. It may determine whether patrons are primarily motivated by economic or political considerations when negotiating with clients. When clients lack political power in the form of power$_3$, patrons can focus on economic considerations alone. Other things being equal (the factors discussed earlier), a patron allocating a right will prefer to allocate or create rights for clients who add the most value. This is because these clients will in principle be able to offer the biggest bribes. In contrast when clients have the power to disrupt or otherwise impose political costs on patrons, purely economic considerations are not enough. We have elsewhere described the costs that clients can threaten to impose as *transition costs* (Khan 1995: 81–83). To avoid these costs, rights may be created for or allocated to clients on the basis of their relative power to disrupt . . .

3. Corruption and Power in Patron-Client Networks.

Exchanges within patron-client networks are in reality much more complex than the neat bilateral exchanges shown in figure 26.1. While some of these complexities may be usefully abstracted from, others are critically important for picking up economically relevant differences in a comparative analysis. In particular, the position of different types of clients and actors within the state and their bargaining relationships need to be identified even if in a highly simplified way in different contexts. Nevertheless, the basic format of the implicit exchanges outlined in figure 26.1 can still be used to keep track of what is going on in transactions involving several groups of patrons and clients.

In what follows, we identify what we think are several key features of exchanges within patron-client networks in several Asian countries. The characteristics identified are based on the work of political scientists and political economists and refer to exchanges which may be described as typical of those countries without suggesting that these are the only types of patron-client exchanges occurring. We then identify why these patterns may be relevant for understanding the economic performance of these countries, and therefore the economic consequences of the associated corruptions.

1. South Asia

Despite important differences between India, Pakistan and Bangladesh there are substantial similarities in the predominant types of corruption observed in these three populous South Asian countries. The basic patterns of subcontinental corruption were described by Wade in his classic studies of corruption in the irrigation bureaucracy of a South Indian state (Wade 1984, 1985, 1989). The distinguishing characteristic of corruption in the Indian subcontinent is the close intermeshing of economic and political calculations in exchanges between patrons and clients at different levels.

A number of factors have contributed to the evolution of complex networks of interlinked exchanges in the Indian subcontinent. The factor that is probably the single most important one for the exchanges that concern us is the political importance of intermediate classes in the Indian social structure. Important groups of clients in the Indian subcontinent have been drawn from these intermediate or "middle" classes. Often the professional members of these groups have been recognized as equal members of the dominant class coalition in India, along with capitalists and landlords (Bardhan 1984). However, for our purposes it is useful to distinguish between the capitalist members of the dominant coalition and the much larger non-capitalist section that consists of emerging middle class groups, the educated sections of the population, both employed and unemployed and others who use political power to get access to resources. The importance of these non-capitalist intermediate classes in the subcontinental political space far outweighs their numbers that in any case would run into many millions.

The relevant power of this latter group is very largely the third type of power discussed earlier. It is a power that is based fundamentally on their organizational and political ability to disrupt and challenge the legitimacy of patrons who fail to deliver (Khan 1989). This is reflected in a state tradition of rapid and ongoing accommodation and incorporation of emerging intermediate groups even while fairly ruthless suppression appears to be taking place.

One of the most important mechanisms of incorporation is the transfer of surpluses to these classes through patron-client exchanges, some of which are perfectly legal (such as subsidies) while others are corrupt and involve illegal transfers of resources or the transfer of resources which were illegally generated.

Both Pakistan and India and subsequently Bangladesh inherited the effects of a deep-rooted anti-colonial political mobilization that empowered their emerging "middle classes." They inherited a tradition of political activity on the basis of a wide variety of emotive symbols including language, caste and religion and these patterns of mobilization were widely accepted as legitimate in the post-colonial society. Politics based on these symbols has not enriched the vast majority of the populations of these countries but *has* enabled successive layers of emerging middle class groups to get access to public resources on the basis of their ability to organize much more numerous groups below them. Those amongst the intermediate classes who happened to be in power found it necessary to organize transfers to the most vociferous of the excluded groups in ongoing processes of accommodation and incorporation.

What is important is that a large part of the transfer (whether legal or illegal) from patrons to intermediate classes of clients has been based on the political bargaining power of these pyramidally organized groups of clients. These transfers in turn have had to be financed and patrons had to find the resources for such transfers either in general taxation or through exchanges with other groups of clients. The inadequacy of general fiscal resources is an important part of the reason why we observe a complex intermeshing of political and economic exchanges in patron-client networks in the Indian subcontinent. Political elites have often found the resources with which they "finance" their political survival in their economic exchanges with other groups of clients, in particular the slowly emerging class of industrial capitalists. This is an important factor explaining the dense structure of interlinked economic and political exchanges that Wade identified but did not adequately explain. Political "corruption" led to economic corruption as each group of politicians organized their own networks of resource collection and distribution.

The interlocked networks based around each political faction in turn have had important implications for the rights which are created or allocated to capitalists and which in turn have implications for long-run performance. Capitalists too are rational political actors and in a context where no political actor or bureaucrat is able to operate without satisfying their constituencies, it has been relatively easy for capitalists to ensure that they too were funding powerful constituencies so that their interest in leading the easy life could not be challenged. As a result, the politicians and bureaucrats who have organized their political survival through such localized arrangements are often unable to change the structure or allocation of rights to capitalists even when

Figure 26.2
Patron-Client Networks in the Indian Subcontinent

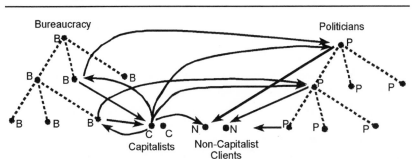

this would raise value. The difficulty of *changing* the structure of rights because of such interlinked patron-client exchanges thus serves to block structural change and productivity growth when growth requires the creation of new rights or the re-allocation or alteration of existing rights.

Figure 26.2 shows the potential complexity of the flows of resources between patrons and clients in the political context typical of most South Asian countries. Bureaucrats and politicians constitute two parallel hierarchies and at each level bureaucrats or politicians may be patrons for lower level colleagues or for groups elsewhere in society. For simplicity figure 26.2 only distinguishes between two social groups, the capitalist and non-capitalist clients of the state, the latter being the intermediate classes discussed earlier. The most successful non-capitalist clients often become political leaders or even capitalists over time. The most distinctive feature of these patron-client exchanges is the transfers going from politicians at different levels to different groups of non-capitalist clients. The quid pro quo from these clients to the state is not shown in figure 26.2 because it is typically not an economic payoff but rather a "payoff" in the form of political quiescence or support.

The resources for the economic payoffs to the intermediate classes come from the rest of society in the form of taxes or transfers from other groups of clients. If we look at the nodes representing the "capitalist" clients of the state, we see a number of transfers going the other way, this time from these clients to patrons in the bureaucracy and in the political structure. Emerging capitalists are willing to make these transfers to politicians and bureaucrats because they too are often receiving subsidies, allocations of valuable property rights or at the very least the protection of their property rights. Emerging capitalists in both India and Pakistan have received large subsidies and were allocated scarce resources such as land, credit and foreign exchange on a preferential basis. This was justified by the claim that these were transfers that would induce industrialization or agricultural growth that in turn was perceived by the respective states as essential for the survival of the economy and of their country's sovereignty. The kickbacks from industrialists have in turn been an important source of finance for the political survival strategies of subcontinental politicians.

While the networks of corruption and political payoffs in India have often been commented on, the economic implications of these complex networks have not been analysed. An important consequence was that allocations of rights and subsidies which were to create a new capitalist class rapidly got embroiled in the networks of transfers which maintained political stability. As a result, any particular allocation proved very difficult to change once it had become established as change provoked opposition from many different quarters. Economic allocations to particular capitalists were soon difficult to separate from the political payoffs to the non-capitalist clients who had been accommodated through interlocking transfers. The eventual result was the emergence of persistent subsidies for poorly performing industries and sectors that were difficult to change in response to performance failures or changes in technology and markets.

This result was common to both India and Pakistan in the sixties and beyond despite the institutional and policy differences between Nehru's Five Year Plans and Ayub's authoritarian industrial policy. Declining economic performance combined with a sustained growth in political demands from emerging middle classes led to dramatic political crises in the Indian subcontinent. These twin features characterized the dismemberment of Pakistan in 1971, ethnic violence in post-1971 Pakistan, deep-seated political instability in Bangladesh and the growth of centrifugal political forces in India as linguistic and regional forces gathered strength in the seventies and eighties.

2. South Korea

The revelations of corruption in South Korea which have begun to emerge in the nineties suggests that corruption in North East Asia has probably been as extensive in terms of the relative magnitudes of the transfers as it has been in South Asia. On the other hand, the pattern of resource flows appears to be both different and simpler. This seems to have been particularly the case in the early days of industrial policy in the sixties (Kim 1994: 59–70, Kong 1996). There is evidence, however, that political power has become more dispersed over the eighties resulting in more complex patterns of transfers (Khan 2000). The broad features of the South Korean case suggest a much higher degree of concentration of political power that allowed the political executive to extract rents from beneficiaries of new rights without having to make political side-payments to non-capitalist clients to anything like the extent that we observe in South Asia.

Figure 26.3 is a simplified picture of resource flows within patron-client networks in South Korea. Given the lesser importance of non-capitalist cli-

Figure 26.3
Patron-Client Networks in South Korea

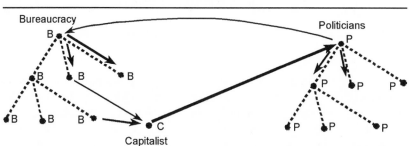

ents of the state in this case, we simplify by excluding non-capitalist clients from the figure. This outline is consistent with Amsden's (1989) account of the flows associated with industrial policy in South Korea and is in its main features corroborated by a number of subsequent observers (Kim & Ma 1997). The main features of the state-society transfers taking place were first the transfer of large subsidies from the state to emerging capitalists. These are shown by the arrows from different sets of patrons in the bureaucratic apparatus to specific clients in the industrial sector. We now also know that there were in exchange substantial kickbacks from these favored industrial groups to the political leadership as rents from the growing industrial sector were redistributed to the political leadership and through this route to bureaucrats as well (Kong 1996). . . . [P]art of these rents were later distributed in a relatively orderly fashion down the higher levels of the political and bureaucratic hierarchies.

The centralized rent collection and distribution of industrial rents by the peak political leaders created powerful incentives to allocate and create rights in ways that maximized these rents over time. Rents are maximized *over time* if growth is maximized. This is simply saying that the economic ability of investors to pay bribes is proportional to the productivity of the investor. Recalling the factors considered in Section 2, in the absence of a short time horizon or other constraints on allocation, even politicians or officials who are merely concerned with maximizing bribes over time will allocate rights or subsidies in such a way as to maximize growth. This involves making sure that the most productive entrepreneurs are favored and the less productive ones are weeded out. The top politician in the South Korean state was able to operate in this way because the political bargaining power of unrelated individuals to bargain for payoffs was virtually absent during a critical phase of the country's development when key property rights were being established and developmental resources were being allocated for rapid industrialization (*Woo-Cumings 1997*). The absence of a powerful intermediate class which could demand payoffs from the state at this critical stage of industrialization can in turn be traced to Korea's social history and the nature of the Japanese colonial impact which prevented these classes from developing or consolidating (Kohli 1994).

3. Malaysia

Unlike South Korea and Taiwan with their fairly exceptional social structures formed under the Japanese colonial impact (Kohli 1994), the South East Asian countries were closer to the South Asian pattern. Although less powerful and entrenched than in the Indian sub-continent, emergent middle classes in these countries possessed a greater ability to organize political opposition and thereby demand political payoffs compared to their North Asian counterparts. The political and institutional responses in these South East Asian countries show a wide range of variation in terms of the patterns of political side-payments organized to maintain political viability. Malaysia and Thailand provide two interesting contrasts to the South Asian case. In both these countries political payoffs and corruption were very important but did not prevent rapid accumulation and growth.

Malaysia inherited an ethnic problem that could have spelt disaster. In the sixties it possessed an enterprising capitalist sector based on small-scale trade and production but this sector was dominated by ethnic Chinese capitalists. An emerging Malay middle class was increasingly willing to use its political muscle to organize the Malay majority to get a larger share of the pie for itself. Luckily for Malaysia, the co-incidence of ethnic identities with class ones to some extent helped the organization of political payoffs in a centralized way. The orderly solution to the legitimation problem emerged as an unintended consequence of the 1969 riots and the adoption of the New Eco-

Figure 26.4
Patron-Client Networks in Malaysia

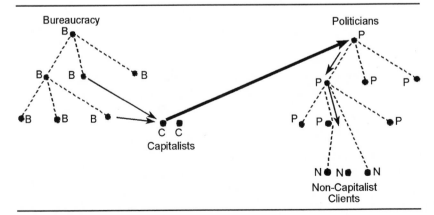

nomic Policy. The political bargain between patrons in the state and politically powerful claimants for resources was resolved through centralizing the demands of the emerging Malay middle classes in an ethnically aligned political system. This allowed the state to organize political transfers centrally without constructing decentralized and interlocked exchanges between competing groups of political factions, their intermediate group clients and particular subsets of capitalists. The de-linking of political payoffs from economic corruption allowed in turn a greater degree of rationality in the allocation of subsidies and the protection of capitalist property rights than was possible in the Indian subcontinent (Khan 2000; Jomo & Gomez 2000).

The characteristic features of the economic flows between patrons and clients in post-1969 Malaysia are shown in figure 26.4. The most important transfers are shown in the arrow from the (largely) Chinese capitalists to the political leadership of the Malay party UMNO that dominated the political system. These transfers included both taxes and illegal extractions. The rents extracted were then centrally distributed through the political apparatus to the non-capitalist clients of UMNO shown by the arrows cascading down the political apparatus to non-capitalist clients. In return domestic capitalists received protection and increasingly, assistance for moving into high technology industries through the provision of good infrastructure and the negotiation of backward linkages between the state and the multinationals operating in Malaysia. These quid pro quo payoffs to Malaysia's capitalists were typically not large explicit subsidies (as in South Korea) but they were nevertheless of economic significance and are shown in figure 26.4 by the arrows from the bureaucracy to capitalists. The distinctiveness of this system compared to the South Asian system was that rent extraction from the Chinese capitalists was centralized and initially at least, direct links between particular capitalists and political factions in the Indian manner did not exist. This has changed to some extent over time as the Malaysian economy has grown and with it the political power of competing Malay factions within UMNO. But the picture sketched above is reasonably accurate for the late sixties and early seventies when Malaysia began its economic takeoff.

One feature that distinguishes Malaysia from the South Asian countries and partly explains why Malaysia's clientelist politics was able to coexist with a more dynamic and competitive capitalist sector is that country's vast resource wealth. This allowed the distribution of political payoffs to the emerging Malay middle class on a big enough scale to keep them satisfied. It is doubtful whether the small productive sector in any of the post-colonial South Asian countries could have transferred rents to the state for centralized distribution on a scale which would have satisfied all the demands being made. On the other hand, the bi-polar ethnic dimension of the conflict in Malaysia helped rather than hindered the construction of an efficient solution to the clientelist problem. It allowed the construction of a fairly explicit and centralized "tax" system that taxed capitalists for the benefit of emerging intermediate groups. The language of ethnic deprivation allowed a high proportion of these exactions to be legitimized and therefore organized through centralized and legal party and state structures without secret deals and personalized bargains. This is consistent with the observation that Malaysia is the least corrupt of the group of countries shown in Table 1 according to subjective corruption indices. A non-ethnic and purely welfarist argument for transfers would not have been equivalent because it would have required that the bulk of the transfers went to the poorest groups in Malaysia and not necessarily to the leading factions of the intermediate classes who had the greatest political power. Given this problem facing a purely welfarist argument, it is difficult to imagine an equivalent ideology in India which could have served to justify a similar centralized transfer from capitalists to the leaders of India's contesting and diverse intermediate groups.

The accommodation of the Malay intermediate classes through the centralized collection and distribution of rents prevented the build-up of dense localized networks of exchanges between patrons and clients along the Indian pattern. This in turn allowed the structure of rights and subsidies allocated by the state to remain relatively fluid and allowed structural change without insuperable resistance being offered by large collections of localized intermediate groups. This fluidity has undoubtedly decreased somewhat over time as factions of intermediate groups within UMNO have become more powerful over time and have established decentralized alliances with large Chinese capitalist groups (Jomo & Gomez 2000). Secondly, by satisfying the Malay intermediate classes through rent transfers from Malaysian Chinese capitalists and by deploying natural resource rents, the Malaysian state could offer multinationals locating in the country a credible level of security for property rights and profits which was untypical by developing country standards. This too proved to be of great importance in encouraging relatively high-technology firms to locate in Malaysia in the seventies and late eighties and engage in backward linkages with Malaysian firms.

4. Thailand

In contrast to Malaysia, the Chinese capitalists of Thailand were much more ethnically integrated with the Thai middle class. The Malaysian pattern of patron-client exchanges that separated political from economic exchanges along ethnic lines could not therefore emerge in Thailand. Thailand was also different from all the countries discussed so far in not having experienced direct colonial occupation and rule. The absence of anti-colonial mobilizations explains why the political leadership of its emerging intermediate classes appears to have been weaker compared to the Indian subcontinent or even Malaysia. On the other hand, its intermediate classes were not as atomized as

Figure 26.5
Patron-Client Networks in Thailand

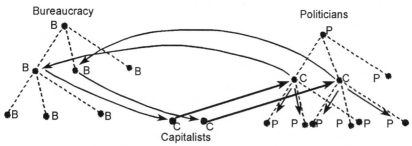

they were in South Korea that was subjected to Japanese colonial strategies. Unlike South Korea where Japanese land reform displaced rural power blocs, Thailand had powerful networks of rural politicians who had to be accommodated at a much earlier stage of development. Thus despite its differences with India, it is quite possible that decentralized networks of patronage may have developed in Thailand to meet the political demands of powerful and largely rural clients. Instead, over the last twenty years Thailand seems to have witnessed a gradual taking over of localized political networks by local capitalists.

The key arrows in figure 26.5 are the ones showing transfers from capitalists to political factions which allowed many Thai capitalists (almost uniquely in the Asian development context) to take over and run their own political factions. Thailand has the highest number of businessmen in parliament in the region (Sidel 1996). The most important feature distinguishing the Thai political system has been the ability and willingness of its capitalists to buy their own political factions. Control over their own factions has not only given Thai capitalists places in parliament. It has also given them the political power to directly gain access to favored subsidies and the allocation of rights, for instance in the form of franchises and licenses (Rock 2000, Doner & Ramsay 2000). Uniquely perhaps in Asia, the political power of Thai capitalists frequently places them in the position of patrons within their own patron-client networks. While Thai capitalists like their counterparts in the other Asian countries have had to make transfers to the political system as part of the maintenance cost of their property rights, their payoffs were managed by the "private" political networks which they controlled.

The Thai pattern of patron-client exchanges (both legal and illegal) has also had identifiable and important effects in Thailand. The fact that Thai capitalists have been directly involved in the protection of their property rights meant that resources were not centrally controlled or allocated by the state to quite the same extent as in the other countries. As a result Thai capitalism has been based on the acquisition of relatively small-scale technology with property rights over these assets being protected in a decentralized way by this type of political corruption and patron-client exchanges.

The number of capitalists going into the political fray in Thailand has also been large, a result of a long history of accumulation by small-scale immigrant Chinese traders many of whom became extremely wealthy over a long period of time. This has ensured vigorous political competition between capitalists for the spoils of power that has prevented the political system from being monopolized by any particular capitalist faction. Instead there has been vigorous competition for entry into markets through political competition between competing factions in the parliament and the bureaucracy. Though the political costs of this competition have been high in the form of rampant corruption and political instability, the long-run economic performance of Thailand has been better than that of its South Asian neighbors. If political stability does not collapse entirely, long run economic growth may eventually make it possible to attenuate the worst effects of Thai political corruption through constitutional and political reforms.

Conclusions

The proposition discussed in this paper has been that the existence and effects of corruption cannot be properly studied outside the context of capitalist accumulation and the political contests that it faces from other emerging classes in the surrounding social milieu. Economists have typically examined the economic incentives promoting corruption while leaving to political scientists the task of analysing its political roots. This paper argues that the forms of economic corruption and their effects are closely tied to the forms of political corruption. This approach raises fundamental dilemmas for policy approaches to corruption. The public face of corruption is clearly unacceptable and in the long run it may destroy the limited legitimacy of some developing country states. On the other hand, the visible face of corruption is often an integral part of processes of accumulation and social compromise that are no less ugly in themselves . . .

Drawing the line between "acceptable" types of accumulation in early capitalism and "unacceptable" types is never going to be easy. The more interesting question is to distinguish between situations where corruption has impoverishing effects from those where corruption allows rapid growth. We have argued that there are good reasons why corruption in South Korea may not have been that damaging for growth. While there may be other reasons for South Korea's performance as well, our argument suggest that we do not need to rely entirely on these compensating factors to explain why this economy performed well despite the presence of substantial corruption. In fact a fair amount of corruption was involved during the transitional phases of all countries. The real issue is why the transition process is blocked in some developing countries as in South Asia. Here we have argued that the *patterns* of corruption may be integrally implicated which are in turn determined by the distribution of power between the state, capitalists and intermediate classes. The economic (as opposed to moral) problem is not corruption *per se* but the political structures that generate growth-retarding corruption. This analysis suggests that anti-corruption strategies that are concerned with the possible effects of corruption on development have to explicitly identify the underlying political problems . . .

Bibliography

Amsden, A. 1989. *Asia's Next Giant: South Korea and Late Industrialization*. Oxford: Oxford University Press.

Bardhan, P. 1984. *The Political Economy of Development in India*. Oxford: Basil Blackwell.

Doner, R.F. & Ramsay, A. 2000. "Rent-seeking and Economic Development in Thailand," in Khan, M.H. & Jomo, K.S. (eds.) *Rents, Rent-Seeking and Economic Development*. Cambridge: Cambridge University Press.

Jomo, K.S. & Gomez, E.T. 2000. "The Malaysian Dilemma," in Khan, M.H. & Jomo, K.S. (eds.) *Rents, Rent-Seeking and Economic Development*. Cambridge: Cambridge University Press.

Khan, M.H. 1989. *Clientelism, Corruption and Capitalist Development*. Unpublished PhD dissertation University of Cambridge, forthcoming Oxford: Oxford University Press.

Khan, M.H. 1995. "State Failure in Weak States: A Critique of New Institutionalist Explanations," in J. Hunter, J. Harriss and C. Lewis (eds.) *The New Institutional Economics and Third World Development*. London: Routledge.

Khan, M.H. 1996a. "A Typology of Corrupt Transactions in Developing Countries," *IDS Bulletin* 27 (2).

Khan, M.H. 1996b. "The Efficiency Implications of Corruption," *Journal of International Development* 8 (5).

Khan, M.H. 2000. "Rent-Seeking as Process" in Khan, M.H. & Jomo, K.S. (eds.) *Rents, Rent-Seeking and Economic Development*. Cambridge: Cambridge University Press.

Kim, H-K. & Ma, J. 1997. "The Role of Government in Acquiring Technological Capability: The Case of the Petrochemical Industry in East Asia," in Aoki, M., Kim, H-K and Okuno-Fujiwara, M. (eds.) *The Role of Government in East Asian Economic Development: Comparative Institutional Analysis*. Oxford: Clarendon Press.

Kim, J.K. 1994. *Bureaucratic Corruption: The Case of Korea*. Seoul: Cho Myung Press.

Kohli, A. 1994. "Where Do High Growth Political Economies Come From? The Japanese Lineage of Korea's 'Developmental State,'" in *World Development* 22 (9).

Kong, T.Y. 1996. "Corruption and its Institutional Foundation," *IDS Bulletin* 27 (2).

Lukes, S. 1978. "Power and Authority," in Bottomore, T. & Nisbet, R. (eds.) *A History of Sociological Analysis*. London: Heinemann.

Mauro, P. 1995. "Corruption and Growth," *Quarterly Journal of Economics* 110 (3).

Mueller, D. C. 1989. *Public Choice II: A Revised Edition of Public Choice.* Cambridge: Cambridge University Press.

North, D. C. 1981. *Structure and Change in Economic History.* New York: Norton & Co.

North, D. 1995. "The New Institutional Economics and Development," in J. Hunter, J. Harriss and C. Lewis (eds.) *The New Institutional Economics and Third World Development.* London: Routledge.

Nye, J. S. 1967. "Corruption and Political Development: A Cost-Benefit Analysis," *American Political Science Review* 61 (2).

Olson, M. 1965. *The Logic of Collective Action.* Cambridge Massachusetts: Harvard University Press.

Olson, M. 1982. *The Rise and Decline of Nations.* London: Yale University Press.

Rock, M.T. 2000. "Thailand's Old Bureaucratic Polity and its New Semi-Democracy," in Khan, M.H. and Jomo, K.S. (eds.) *Rents, Rent-Seeking and Economic Development.* Cambridge: Cambridge University Press.

Rose-Ackerman, S. 1978. *Corruption: A Study in Political Economy.* New York: Academic Press.

Schmidt, S.W., Guasti, L., Landé, C. H. & Scott, J. C. (eds.) 1977. *Friends, Followers, and Factions.* Berkeley: University of California Press.

Sidel, J. T. 1996. "Siam and its Twin? Democratization and Bossism in Contemporary Thailand and the Philippines," *IDS Bulletin* 27 (2).

Shleifer, A. and Vishny, R. W. 1993. "Corruption," *Quarterly Journal of Economics,* Vol 108 No 3.

Udehn, L. 1996. *The Limits of Public Choice: A Sociological Critique of the Economic Theory of Politics.* London: Routledge.

Wade, R. 1984. "The System of Administrative and Political Corruption: Canal Irrigation in South India," *Journal of Development Studies* 18 (3).

Wade, R. 1985. "The Market for Public Office: Why the Indian State is not Better at Development," *World Development* 13 (4).

Wade, R. 1989. "Politics and Graft: Recruitment, Appointment, and Promotions to Public Office in India," in Ward, P.M. (ed.) *Corruption, Development and Inequality: Soft Touch or Hard Graft?* London: Routledge.

Woo-Cumings, M. 1997. "The Political Economy of Growth in East Asia: A Perspective on the State, Market and Ideology," in Aoki, M., Kim, H-K and Okuno-Fujiwara, M. (eds.) *The Role of Government in East Asian Economic Development: Comparative Institutional Analysis.* Oxford: Clarendon Press.

World Development Report 1994. *Infrastructure for Development.* Oxford: Oxford University Press for the World Bank.

Note

1. I am grateful to Mark Robinson for his comments as well as to the participants at the IDS Workshop on Corruption and Development.

27

The Politics of Privilege:
Rents and Corruption in Asia

Paul D. Hutchcroft

Introduction

"I am me," explains Singaporean Senior Minister Lee Kuan Yew in response to criticism that he derived substantial personal advantage from a recent deal involving luxury condominiums. "It's not a level playing field."[1] To be sure, some element of particularistic privilege is found in all political systems—most clearly in those where corruption and rent havens predominate, but even in meritocracies such as that built up by Lee himself during his three decades as Prime Minister. While no "playing field" is entirely level, however, it is equally obvious that landscapes of special advantage vary enormously in shape from one political economy to another: some varieties of unevenness may actually promote economic growth, while other types of rough terrain seem to pose enormous barriers to sustained development.

This paper takes initial steps toward building a framework able to explain why a range of related phenomena—variously described as rent-seeking, corruption, and clientelism—may be relatively more compatible or relatively more obstructive to the process of Third World development. In doing so, I will highlight how contrasting political settings spawn very different patterns of seeking—and dispensing—particularistic advantage. Moreover, I will seek to demonstrate that the process of creating such a broad framework benefits from an eclectic approach; specifically, it is valuable to draw insights from three literatures, with distinct lineages, that overlap but all too rarely interact: those relating to rents, corruption, and clientelism.

The first section of this paper discusses the utility of drawing on the three major paradigms, and the relative advantages and disadvantages of each in building a broad comparative framework. Second, I propose a preliminary framework for assessing the varying impact of major phenomena described by the literature on rents, corruption, and clientelism, focusing attention on seven elements not fully captured in any one of the paradigms. Together, they examine the variability of the "take" among comparable acts of corruption, the processes by which advantages are allocated, the way in which gains obtained are invested, the manner in which corruption affects the operation of markets, the impact of corruption on a state's capacity to execute a range of essential developmental tasks, the role that corruption may play in promoting or impeding the institutionalization of both state agencies and political parties, and the relative presence of factors able to mitigate or counterbalance the prevalence of corruption. The conclusion summarizes key lessons, and proposes paths that may be fruitful in further comparative research.

Surveying the Paradigms: Rents, Corruption, and Clientelism

The quest for and allocation of particularistic advantage has long been the subject of academic investigation, but the language and concepts employed in this process of inquiry have varied across time and across disciplines. Each of the major paradigms—rents, corruption, and clientelism—offers important insights to political economists, yet all would be enhanced by a more concerted effort at cross-fertilization. The following is a preliminary attempt to encourage useful hybrids.

The most recent addition to the theoretical repertoire is, of course, the literature on rents that has emerged from economics. The strength of this body of thought is its attention to market processes, and it is not surprising that rent theorists have achieved prominence in an era in which markets are widely praised and governments routinely reviled. Rents are, by definition, created when the state restricts the operations of the market. The processes of rationing foreign exchange, curbing free trade, and licensing some aspect of economic activity—to give just a few examples—serve to create "rent havens" that can be captured by some combination of well-placed businesspersons and bureaucrats. The fight for privilege, known as rent-seeking, encourages "directly unproductive profit-seeking" activities—sometimes legal (e.g., lobbying) and sometimes not (e.g., bribery). Overall, the focus is on "the rent-seeking *society*"; analysis of the specific types of *state* structures in which this behavior most thrives is commonly thwarted by distrust of states in general. Because rent-seeking is said to be "directly related to the scope and range of governmental activity in the economy, and to the relative size of the public sector," the solution (as paraphrased by Peter Evans) is self-evident: "the state's sphere should be reduced to the minimum, and bureaucratic control should be replaced by market mechanisms wherever possible."[2]

Indeed, a major problem with the rent-seeking literature is its often strong ideological bias. The majority of theorists

> are obsessed with demonstrating the negative impact of government on the economy. They view competitive markets as the most socially efficient means to produce goods and services. . . . [and] do not treat the effects of government intervention as variable, sometimes reducing and sometimes stimulating social waste.[3]

This bias is best refuted by Peter Evans, who points out that many bureaucracies do indeed possess the capacity to restrain rent-seeking tendencies and promote collective effort among individual officeholders; "strict adherence to a neo-utilitarian logic," he asserts, "makes the existence of a collective actor difficult to explain and the nightwatchman state [favored by neo-utilitarians] a theoretical impossibility." His analysis of the role of states in economic transformation, moreover, highlights major problems with the assumption that competitive markets "are sufficient to the kind of structural transformation that lies at the heart of development."[4]

Ideological bias aside, there are at least four other major deficiencies with much of the rent-seeking literature. First, even if a bureaucracy is pared down to a minimalist role, it is likely to retain ultimate responsibility for such basic tasks as building infrastructure and providing law and order. As long as bureaucrats continue to be tasked with supplying these goods, there remain "rent havens." In settings where (to quote Weber) individual bureaucrats can easily "squirm out of the [bureaucratic] apparatus," the provision of public goods may bring significant opportunities for private profit. Even in a minimalist state, for example, motor vehicle licensing authorities will potentially be able to extract an extra unofficial sum for a scarce resource, and police may be able to transform their public power into lucrative kidnap-for-ransom schemes. Privatization by no means resolves the dilemma: the process of bidding and negotiating with private companies seeking to build and maintain a road, for example, can provide enormous rent havens easily tapped by those with the most favorable political connections. Because rent theorists have little to say about such post-market-shrinking problems, the solution necessarily shifts away from market remedies and toward the realm of politics and public administration.

Second, the literature on rents generally neglects vitally important political elements of government-business relations. As Jomo and Gomez explain, there are major problems with the presumption that rents will be allocated solely according to market processes—and a "certain irony" that

> the very people who assume that markets have been distorted with the creation of rents also seem to assume the existence of perfectly competitive markets for rent capture involving a fully competitive process. Rent-seeking may, in fact, not be very competitive—due to the clandestine, illegal, closed, exclusive or protected nature of rent capture processes—thus limiting rent-seeking activity and keeping down rent-seeking costs.[5]

The allocation is likely to be based not only on the market but also on a range of non-market considerations, including ethnic, regional, party, and old-school ties. Politics, not the market, provides the best clues to these processes.

Third, and closely related, is the problem of determining the degree to which rents will be primarily captured by those in the state or those outside the state. This likely brings in even larger structural considerations, based on analysis of the historical development of state-society relations. Within Southeast Asia, I argue elsewhere, the "'bureaucratic' capitalism" associated with the former bureaucratic polity of Thailand, for example, needs to be differentiated from the "booty capitalism" spawned by the oligarchic patrimonial state found in the Philippines. In the first type of rent capitalism, the major beneficiaries of largesse are found in the state; in the latter, major beneficiaries have an independent economic base outside the state.[6]

Fourth, rent theorists rarely make a clear distinction between whether those who compete for advantage are seeking generalizable policy benefits (as when a exporters' association lobbies for reduced tariffs) or particularistic privileges (as when a family conglomerate bribes customs officials for lower duties on a specific importation, or lobbies congresspersons for the construction of a particular road). Taken together—whether lobbying or bribery, general or particularistic—all are seen as examples of unproductive rent-seeking activities.[7] For a purely market-based standpoint, it is no problem to aggregate such activities into one category; from the standpoint of political economy, however, there are certain disadvantages. Because such distinctions are largely reflective of the degree of institutionalization and differentiation of business interests, they are indeed important to those investigating larger questions of political power and future possibilities of political economic transformation. Moreover, because the relative incidence of bribery versus lobbying has an impact on the character of bureaucratic agencies, such distinctions are important to those analyzing state capacity to promote developmental goals.

As useful as rent theory can be to understanding the allocation of particularistic advantage, its limitations suggest the need to search elsewhere for additional insights. Studies of corruption may have had their heyday in the era of modernization theory, but it is a mistake to suggest that corruption is merely a "primitive" way of conceptualizing rent-seeking.[8] It is a distinct paradigm that, over the course of many years, has yielded many important lessons for contemporary analysis. Indeed, it is worthwhile inquiring into why the concept of corruption is often given only cursory scholarly attention—and sometimes eschewed in favor of other conceptual approaches. Because corruption is nearly omnipresent, some analysts seem inclined to treat it as an invariable element of the political economic woodwork; in other words, they are content to note that it exists almost everywhere without inquiring into how it varies in character and impact from one setting to another. Others, quite likely, have shunned the concept because it is more difficult to compile reliable empirical data on the often-shadowy world of corruption (based, quite inconveniently, on the "what is") than it is to construct abstract models of how rent havens are created in the absence of perfect markets (based on the far less troublesome investigation of "what is not").[9] "Primitive" (i.e., early postwar) language, conceptual complexity, and dilemmas of data-gathering, however, are no excuses for throwing the baby out with the bath water.

Corruption focuses attention on the public sector and on the distinction between official and private activity. Nye's oft-cited definition is a useful starting point: "Corruption is behavior which deviates from the formal duties of a public role because of private-regarding (personal, close family, private clique) pecuniary or status gains; or violates rules against the exercise of certain types of private-regarding influence."[10] With this as a starting point, one is able to go beyond the central concern of rent theorists (how states may distort markets) and move into other important terrain as well (e.g., how markets may distort states).

Theorists of corruption, as a group, cannot be accused of any strong ideological bias; on the contrary, one finds enormous variance in how to approach the issue. In the early days of modernization theory, corruption was commonly condemned on moralistic grounds but rarely accompanied by much careful analysis of its precise consequences (not to mention its causes, mechanics, or remedies). Later "revisionist" approaches of the late 1960s found that corruption could, at least occasionally and sometimes systematically, have a beneficial impact on a range of important goals: "nation-building," economic development, administrative capacity, and democratization. Subsequent literature continues the on-going evaluation of costs and benefits.[11]

Such attention to larger context is at once both a strength and a weakness of this body of literature. On the one hand, it is essential to view corruption as an element of broader political interactions, and understand that the prevalence of bribery may have both benefits as well as costs. On the other hand, in the course of achieving breadth there is sometimes a lack of specificity as to which goals are being included in the cost-benefit analysis. Modernization theory's tendency to conflate distinct goals and presume that "all good things go together" spills over into the Great Corruption Debate, as rival camps are at times over-eager to declare corrupt behavior either an overall good or an overall bad. Many scholars who have contributed to this literature, however, are quite explicit as to how costs and benefits need to be evaluated in terms of specific goals.[12]

At the risk of simplifying what is indeed a very large body of work spanning a wide time period—from the earliest distinctions between private and public domains until present—there are at least four other advantages to building on previous studies of corruption. First, as noted above, the very definition of corruption focuses attention on the character of state agencies, specifically the degree to which any given system reflects a clear distinction between a public and a private sphere. The work of Max Weber not only highlights how polities vary enormously in the degree to which such a distinction is recognized, but also how corruption can have a different impact from one setting to another. Unfortunately, the potential for carrying forth Weber's nuanced comparative analysis of the interaction of politics, bureaucratic structures, and economies has been hampered in recent decades by disciplinary overspecialization: economists tend to treat all states as the same, political scientists rarely devote much attention to bureaucratic structures, and public administration specialists all too often ignore the larger political and structural contexts in which their subject agencies are situated.[13]

Second, the corruption literature almost universally recognizes that corruption can be expressed both according to non-market and market factors. Scott explains that

> [a]s ideal types, "parochial" (nonmarket) corruption is a situation where only ties of kinship, affection, caste, and so forth determine access to the favors of power-holders, whereas "market" corruption signifies an impersonal process in which influence is accorded those who can "pay" the most, regardless of who they are. The real world, of course, rarely ever contains such pure cases. The proportion of market to parochial corruption, and hence the pattern of beneficiaries, varies widely among underdeveloped nations.

Modes of payment, he further explains, can be in cash or in kind; in electoral settings, they may of course include delivery of a bloc of votes.

Third, the best of the literature on corruption insists that the concept can only be properly analyzed "within a broader analysis of a regime's political dynamics." Scott's own analysis leads him to suggest that its impact may be at times be expected to have a counter-hegemonic influence by promoting the entry of new forces, but its more "normal effect . . . is to cement together a conservative coalition and hold back or cancel out the effects of growing collective demands." Waterbury concludes that "endemic and planned corruption" in Morocco "serves only one 'positive' function—that of the survival of the regime. Resources are absorbed in patronage and are drained away from rational productive investment."[14] Whether or not other theorists agree with such conclusions, the very tendency to focus on how issues of politics and political power are played out among major social forces can be seen as welcome relief in an era in which the realm of macropolitics is often no longer the premier consideration of political economy.

A final advantage of employing the term "corruption" is that it re-connects academics with real politics and real political discourse. There has probably never been a major political demonstration against rent-seeking, but popular disgust over corruption—the violation of norms based on a distinction between what is public and what is private—has in countless cases nurtured reform movements, provoked riots, and contributed to the downfall of regimes. As long as corruption scandals dominate the headlines of many national newspapers, it seems a worthy objective for academics to continue to investigate such phenomena.

Further political nuance comes from a third major paradigm, clientelism, which is above all a study of relationships of power. Persons of higher social status (patrons) are linked to those of lower social status (clients) in personal ties of reciprocity that can vary in content and purpose across time. Patron-client ties may or may not be corrupt, but (as John Waterbury explains) "when a patron occupies a public position or extracts favors from those in public positions, patronage and corruption overlap."[15] Conversely, purely market corruption has no element of clientelism: it is a one-time transaction lacking in affective ties. Although concrete empirical evidence may be elusive, it is probable that—contrary to the expectations of many economists—purely market corruption is far less common than other variants of corruption. Power and social relationships regularly interact with everyday market relations; in all likelihood, markets of a corrupt nature—involving the complex interplay of private and public spheres—are even more heavily infused with such ties. Integration of the clientelist paradigm into an analysis of the search for particularistic advantage encourages analysts to go beyond both the excessive attention to market transactions often found in economics and the legalistic-formalistic approaches commonly found in the field of public administration.

Along with the other two paradigms, however, clientelist literature generally gives insufficient attention to the role of coercion in the search for particularistic advantage. Since coercion plays a major role in certain forms of corrupt behavior (especially in extortion and in the delivery of a bloc of votes), it is important to supplement all three paradigms with careful consideration of the often prominent role of violence. Scott tends to treat corruption and violence as alternative expressions of political influence (the former "a more peaceful route to influence" than the latter), but in practice the two often reinforce each other in quite effective ways.[16] A New York mafioso, for example, may threaten an uncooperative city official with the proverbial "swim with concrete overshoes" in the East River, or a Philippine influential may utilize state resources (the local police, or temporarily released and heavily armed prison convicts) to strike out at his or her political enemies.

Together, the three paradigms encourage careful analysis of the search for and dispensing of particularistic privilege. Rent literature focuses attention on what happens when state actions distort markets, corruption literature examines how public roles and private influences conflict within state agencies, and clientelism encourages clearer analysis of the relationships of power that permeate states, societies, and markets. The next task is to draw on these eclectic sources and begin to build a larger framework in which to analyze more effectively the very diverse impacts of the allocation of particularistic advantage.

Building an Eclectic Theoretical Framework

In varying settings, it was asserted at the outset, the range of related phenomena variously described as rent-seeking, corruption, and clientelism may be relatively more compatible or relatively more obstructive to the process of development. This paper does not aim to provide a generalizable framework able to explain when, where, why, and how the impact may be more or less positive, nor does it seek to provide a comprehensive new typology of the range of phenomena encompassed by these complementary paradigms. Rather, the purpose is to propose a series of initial questions that may build on previous insights—from eclectic sources—and contribute toward the longer term goal of building such a framework and such a typology. In other words, it is a preliminary treatment intended to promote discussion and further refinement of ideas.

There are seven sets of questions, I shall propose, that are useful in beginning to assess the differential impact of rents, corruption, and clientelism. It is important to emphasize that the focus here is *the impact of corruption on economic development*; separate assessments of the impact of corruption would be necessary if other goals (e.g., harmonious inter-ethnic relations, democracy, or political stability) are to be considered. Distinct analysis would also be required if one is investigating the causes or mechanics of corruption, or optimal strategies to curb the phenomenon.

1. Is corruption relatively more variable or calculable?

A key factor in understanding the diverging impact of corruption and bribery on capitalist growth, Weber suggests, is the variability of the phenomena: they have the "least serious effect" when calculable, and become most onerous when fees are "highly variable" and "settled from case to case with every individual official." Indeed, if bribery is a calculable element of a business firm's environment, its impact is no different than a tax; to the extent that a firm must devote major effort to negotiating each bribe, on the other hand, there is a high degree of unpredictability in the amount of time and resources to be expended. Overall, Weber expected that advanced forms of capitalism relied upon "the rational, predictable functioning of the legal and administrative agencies."[17] If correct, a major obstacle to the development of more sophisticated forms of capitalist accumulation is not corruption *per se*, but highly variable corruption.

What sort of polities are most likely to spawn highly variable types of corruption? Analysis of this question begins with Rudolph and Rudolph's important distinction between authority (the formal roles conferred upon individuals in their official capacities) and power (when incumbents pursue "values, interests, and goals of their own choosing that conflict with those of the administrative structure"). Few would disagree with Scott's observation, over two decades ago, that "[n]ominally modern institutions such as bureaucracies and political parties in Southeast Asia are often thoroughly penetrated by informal patron-client networks that undermine the formal structure of authority."[18] For present purposes, it is worthwhile building on previous scholarship and examining further two key aspects of the interaction of power and authority within bureaucracies and parties. First, what are the relative strengths of informal and formal power? Clearly, the formal structures of authority are stronger in some national settings than others; within any national administrative apparatus, as well, some agencies exhibit clearer lines of formal authority than others. By definition, the stronger the formal authority relative to informal networks the less prevalent will be the incidence of corruption.

Second, it is important to examine the process by which the power and authority interact: do patron-client networks tend to coincide with formal lines of authority, or do they constitute a competing source of orders and inducements? Higher degrees of coincidence, I propose, are likely to yield more predictable forms of corruption; conversely, the greater the degree of divergence between power and authority, the more variable is the form of corruption that is likely to emerge.[19] In the former (pre-1980s) Thai bureaucratic polity, for example, formal bureaucratic authority was well developed and informal networks of power and formal status overlapped to a large degree; in such a system, businesspersons were likely to have a good sense of whom to approach and what to expect from one transaction to another.[20] In the Philippines, by contrast, lines of formal authority are weaker and the disjuncture between authority and power is often quite pronounced. In this loosely structured system, where patrons are as often found outside formal structures of authority as within them, there is likely less regularization of corruption from one case to another. As Rose-Ackerman describes her category "disorganized" bureaucracy,

> the official chain of command is unclear and constantly shifting and the decision-making criteria are similarly arbitrary and unknown. . . . While corrupt bureaucrats may be willing to accept bribes, applicants cannot be sure that officials have the power to perform their side of the bargain. Chaotic legal procedures increase the *demand* for more certain illegal ones, but if the disorganization of government is far advanced, no bureaucrats may be able to *supply* the requisite certainty even when offered a monetary incentive."[21]

To the extent that this description resembles any given country, businesspersons (especially those without favorable access to the political machinery) will often find it very difficult to predict the cost, frequency, or results of their bribery of state officials. The basic "rules of the game" will be far more arbitrary, and corruption will have a more obstructive impact on the process of capitalist growth.

2. To what extent are rents "dissipated" in the course of their allocation? In other words, to what extent (if at all) are resources wasted in processes that determine who obtains particularistic advantage?

Analysis of corruption and rents has focused considerable attention on the process by which particularistic privileges are allocated, but has unfortunately achieved little consensus as to the impact of these processes on development. Key elements of inquiry, as we shall see, involve the extent to which allocation is competitive and the degree to which it generates efficiency.

Many economists—ever faithful to market processes—begin with the presumption that bureaucrats will allocate scarce resources such as licenses and other favors via "competitive bidding among entrepreneurs." Leff argues that within such a system "favors will go to the most efficient producers, for they will be able to make the highest bids which are compatible with remaining in the industry." A decade later, Krueger developed a model which also tends to presume that that bidding will be competitive—but came to the opposite conclusion about efficiency. Competition for rents diverts resources toward such unproductive activities as lobbying and bribery, and in the end generates welfare costs for society as a whole.[22]

As discussed above, however, it is quite problematic to suppose that the allocation of privilege will be decided according to market processes. The recognition that rents can be allocated according to either market or non-market processes has led some neoclassical economists to propose—with further irony—that limits on competition might actually yield higher levels of efficiency. As paraphrased by Mendoza, these economists have argued that since less competition over the allocation of rents is considered less wasteful, "the least wasteful situation is one where an absolute dictator who will brook no complaint will dispense rents as he sees fit." Campos argues that the costs of directly unproductive profit-seeking (DUP) activities will "likely be smaller in an environment in which only a limited elite can acquire rents."[23]

Jomo and Gomez suggest, similarly, that "the existence of rents, in itself, does not necessarily result in rent-seeking behavior." Because "certain political groups, individuals, or institutions usually have much more influence on or even hegemony over the state," some will likely do better than others in the process of securing advantage. Knowing that there is indeed "uneven access to opportunities for rent capture," many parties will not even bother to enter the market. It is thus useful to make an analytical distinction between two broad forms of allocation: "rent-seeking" and "rent deployment." Rents are sometimes obtained by persons or groups that actively seek out the advantage, and in other cases deployed from above to persons or groups who exert relatively little effort. To the extent that rents are deployed rather than sought after, there may in fact be far fewer wasted resources in the process of rent allocation than is commonly presumed.[24]

Just as Scott suggests that there are likely few cases of pure "market" or pure "non-market" corruption, so also are there likely few cases of pure "competitive rent-seeking" or pure "rent deployment." A given claimant, for example, might have close affective ties to those who allocate privileges, and still have to expend considerable effort and resources to ensure that a) the allocator does not forget to take care of what that claimant thinks is his/her due; and b) this claimant's needs are taken care of before other claimants whose affective ties with the allocator are equally close. In short, both market versus non-market corruption as well as rent-seeking versus rent deployment are best conceived of as continua, across which one finds varying combinations of the two "pure" types.

Overall, we can expect that the centralization of authority and/or power within a political economy will encourage a greater degree of rent deployment and a lesser degree of rent seeking. Rent deployment, in turn, seems likely to promote relatively less dissipation than rent-seeking and thus have the potential for more positive (or less detrimental) outcomes from the standpoint of development. Despite the considerable attention that these issues have received in the rents literature, however, it is quite likely that other elements of analysis may prove far more important in assessing developmental outcomes.

3. Once gains from corruption and rents are obtained, how are they invested?

Whereas the previous question focuses attention of the processes by which rents are allocated, this question focuses attention on the purpose to which rents—once obtained—are employed. It has long been recognized not only that one of the "benefits" of corruption may be to promote rapid capital accumulation, but also that one must inquire as to whether the capital itself is invested in productive ways.[25] At one end of the continuum, an entrepreneur invests his or her gains in a high-value-added industry that creates a great many positive externalities to the rest of the economy; at the other end of the continuum, advantages are hustled out of the country and into Swiss banks and Manhattan real estate.

There is no reason to expect that rents sought after in competitive environments will necessarily result in more productive investment than those that have been deployed. On the other hand, in the event that rents are deployed there is no reason to expect that either deployers—or those who obtain rents via deployment—are necessarily going to be interested in promoting productive investment. As asserted above, one must look at the larger context in which rents are allocated. I propose that there are at least three key variables to examine in assessing the productivity of privileges obtained: (1) what are the motivations of those who allocate and obtain privileges?; (2) presuming that rents are allocated in order to promote developmental goals, what is the capacity of the state to enforce or promote productivity criteria?; and (3) how secure is the environment in which a given entrepreneur is operating?

The motivations of those who obtain privileges through competitive rent-seeking are likely impossible to evaluate with any precision: some will be inclined to productive investment and some will not. In the case of deployment, however, one is by definition evaluating a systematic effort toward a clear objective. The nature of the objective, however, may have little to do with the promotion of explicit developmental outcomes—and may just as likely be oriented toward clearly political objectives. Such goals may in fact be relatively harmless—or actually promote—developmental objectives, as when privilege is extended to a particular region or ethnic group. In other cases, political goals may have a very harmful impact on the process of economic development, as when a highly unproductive businessperson is given a trading monopoly and extraordinary access to state credit in exchange for building political support for the regime in an important bailiwick. If the deployer is highly dependent on such local powerbrokers for political survival, it is particularly unlikely that developmental goals will figure prominently in the bargain.

Second, when rents are in fact allocated with clear developmental goals, what is the capacity of the state to enforce or promote such goals? In an optimal "rent-seeking" scenario, those who obtain privilege through competitive bidding must invest them in productive enterprise. In an optimal "deployment" scenario, those who give out the rents are not only very skilled in choosing the right entrepreneurs but also quite capable of enforcing strict performance guidelines from those they have provided a particular benefit. Entrepreneurs favored by South Korea's Park Chung Hee, for example, were granted enormous privilege but at the same time forced to meet performance criteria (commonly in the form of export targets). In many cases, however, those who obtain advantages will be able to pursue their own goals—which may or may not be oriented toward productive investment.

The clearest analysis, here again, requires careful examination of the broader configuration of authority and power within which rent allocation takes place. Privilege may be extended to collective interests (a particular region, ethnic group, political party, or military faction) or to far more particular interests (family members, fraternity brothers, golfing partners, etc.). It is necessary to examine the relationship of rent allocators to each of these types of interests. Moreover, one must note that while in some settings major beneficiaries will be found within the state (commonly top bureaucrats and military officers), elsewhere major beneficiaries have an independent economic base outside the state. Overall, analysis of the ability of allocators to enforce and promote performance criteria requires that one examine such basic issues as the distribution of political power, the character of bureaucratic agencies, and the institutionalization and differentiation of business interests. Questions of enforcement cannot be understood without careful attention to the larger realms of power and authority.

Third, rent recipients operating in a very insecure environment may have little incentive to adopt a long-run strategy in the country where their advantage was obtained; capital flight, rather than productive investment of capital, will likely predominate.[26] To the extent that corruption and cronyism undercut the legitimacy of a regime, of course, they may at the same time undermine the overall stability in which rents are invested.

4. What is the impact of corruption and clientelism on levels of competition and the overall functioning of the market?

This question moves analysis from issues of investor productivity to those of market performance: does rent allocation, corruption, and clientelism tend to promote or discourage competition among firms? Doner and Ramsay contrast "competitive clientelism" (in which competition among political elites keeps barriers to entry low and thus fosters business competition) with "monopoly cronyism" or "monopoly clientelism" (in which entrepreneurs can use their access to the state machinery to enforce higher entry barriers and reduce competition).[27] Quite clearly the former can be expected to promote more favorable conditions for capitalist development, particularly where the state lacks the regulatory capacity to ensure efficient performance from cartelized and monopolized sectors.

Second, and closely related, is the need to examine whether corrupt acts provide an end-run around policies that obstruct markets, or whether the acts themselves obstruct the efficient functioning of competitive markets. The first case is perhaps best illustrated by West African cocoa farmers evading laws that require them to sell their produce to state marketing boards, and smuggling their produce to markets in neighboring countries.[28] The second occurs when an anti-trust lawsuit is squelched through bribery of key officials.

5. What is the impact of corruption on the capacity of state agencies to undertake important developmental roles?

States have important tasks to achieve in promoting development. Even advocates of a relatively minimalist role for the state, such as the World Bank, assert that

> governments need to do more in those areas where markets alone cannot be relied upon. Above all, this means investing in education, health, nutrition, family planning, and poverty alleviation; building social, physical, administrative, regulatory, and legal infrastructure of better quality; mobilizing resources to finance public

expenditures; and providing a stable macroeconomic foundation, without which little can be achieved.

To the extent that corruption inhibits the achievement of these vital foundations of laissez-faire capitalism, opportunities for sustained growth will be impaired. If one expects that promotion of late, late industrialization requires an even more extensive role for the state, quite clearly, it will be necessary to build up an even greater degree of capacity throughout the bureaucratic apparatus. For present purposes, however, it is possible to confine our attention to the impact of corruption on the basic political foundations of capitalist growth.

Some argue that corruption promotes development by promoting administrative responsiveness. "Many economic activities would be paralyzed," wrote Myron Weiner of Indian politics in 1962, "were it not for the flexibility which *bakshish* contributes to the complex, rigid, administrative system." Huntington concurs: "In terms of economic growth, the only thing worse than a society with a rigid, overcentralized, dishonest bureaucracy is one with a rigid, overcentralized, honest bureaucracy."[29] Others introduce the distinction between "speed payments" (involving "bribes that *expedite* a decision without changing it") and "distortive payments" (which "change the decision and contravene formal government policy").[30]

From the standpoint of an individual businessperson or citizen, corruption does indeed grease the wheels of a bureaucracy; to be sure, "honest bureaucracies" can be infuriatingly inflexible to those with a justifiable need to bend the rules, and "dishonest bureaucracies" highly responsive to those who have the means and/or connections to do so. From a macro perspective, however, it is important to consider the impact of even seemingly innocuous "speed" payments on the likelihood of a bureaucratic agency to deliver the services it was set up to deliver. Such payments can encourage systematic delays, precisely because slowing things down brings such handsome financial rewards to those in a strategic position within the bureaucracy. Corruption may in some cases be a valuable "lubricant" to individual claimants, but one must not neglect the degree to which such incentives build more bureaucratic "toll posts," and in the end exacerbate delays in the system as a whole.[31]

Moreover, one must assess the longer-term impact of corruption on administrative capacity to perform essential developmental tasks. Theobald asserts that

> widespread venality, far from drawing together the different departments and areas of the public service, provokes fragmentation, dissension, inter- and intra-departmental rivalry. . . . the low levels of morale and paranoia which are typically associated with an acutely unstable work situation . . . will have very marked consequences for job performance. . . . [A prevalence of] nepotism, political patronage and bribery. . . . [means] there is little incentive for functionaries to work efficiently or honestly.

While not denying that corruption may have some "positive consequences," Theobald asserts that "it is virtually impossible to confine corruption to those areas where its effects are deemed to be beneficial." Even Huntington, who sees many positive benefits to corruption, acknowledges that it "naturally tends to weaken or to perpetuate the weakness of the government bureaucracy."[32]

Aside from questions of flexibility and capacity one must consider the impact of corruption on government budgets. How much of an expenditure intended to promote certain developmental goals actually ends up being utilized for such purpose, and how much gets leaked to promote private gain? On the revenue side, as well, corruption may reduce the proportion of a given tax that actually ends up in public coffers; taxpayers can bribe the right officials to informally bargain down their tax burden or obtain a formal exemption. Either way, funds are diverted from public to private ends. Leff argues that "there is no reason to assume that the government has a high *marginal* propensity to spend for developmental purposes"; moreover, "when the entrepreneurs' propensity to invest is higher than the government's, the money saved from the tax collector may be a gain rather than a loss for development."[33] This begs the question, however, of whether the private hands that dip into the till will be investing their resources in the provision of public goods essential to the promotion of development. In many cases, even the most basic political foundations of economic development are severely disrupted by corruption: such tasks, for example, as law enforcement, fire protection, and the construction and maintenance of infrastructure. While entrepreneurs may invest some resources in provisioning themselves with these goods (private security guards, fire brigades, and roads), it will be rare for private investors to charitably provide public goods when governments fail to do so. As the World Bank explains, governments must do what markets alone fail to do.

A key question, then, is how much corruption actually reduces public expenditure on developmental goals (whether it be an irrigation project, a road, or a rural health clinic). Wade has provided an exceptionally detailed empirical portrait of how corruption in a South Indian system of canal irrigation impedes developmental goals. Irrigation engineers are able to raise "vast amounts of illicit revenue" in the construction of irrigation works and in deciding how water is allocated; in the process, the "economic well-being of local communities" is often poorly served.[34] Overall, one can expect that five percent diversion of resources from public purpose to private hands is relatively harmless compared to ten percent, and ten percent far less damaging than 25 percent and above.

Within any given country, some elements of the political machinery are likely to divert more resources than others: the actual incidence of corruption may vary, for example, depending on whether one is examining the upper level or the lower levels of a bureaucracy, Agency A or Agency B.[35] Huntington asserts that "most political systems" exhibit a high *incidence* of corruption "at the lower levels of bureaucratic and political authority," and that as one moves to higher levels the frequency of corruption may—depending on the country—remain constant, increase, or decrease. In all cases, however, "the *scale* of corruption (i.e. the average value of the private goods and services involved in a corrupt exchange) increases as one goes up the bureaucratic hierarchy or political ladder."[36] Broad judgments as to whether upper—or lower-level corruption will tend to be more damaging to developmental prospects are difficult to make: bribes at the lower level involve less money per transaction, but may well prove more disruptive to the functioning of the overall legal and administrative order. One can presume, however, that corruption will have the most debilitating impact when it is pervasive throughout a system, not only obstructing the provision of basic services through petty corruption at the lower levels but also resulting in large-scale graft at the top.

From one agency to another, as well, there are commonly great variations in the prevalence of corruption and rent-seeking. "Unable to transform the bureaucracy as a whole," Evans explains of Brazil, "political leaders try to create 'pockets of efficiency'" in which universalistic norms governed recruitment and an "ethic of public service" nurtured a "clear esprit de corps." Doner and Ramsay similarly call Thailand a "bifurcated state . . . divided between politically well insulated macroeconomic agencies [including the Ministry of Finance and the Bank of Thailand] and highly politicized line agencies."[37]

Moreover, the character—and hence impact—of corruption can vary according to whether or not democratic institutions are present. While some systems exhibit a clearer demarcation of administrative agencies and parliamentary bodies than others, in general one can say that the presence of representative institutions and electoral competition opens up the system to the influence of a wider array of actors: party leaders, politicians, and at least some element of a broader public. Moreover, electoral systems offer

> noncorrupt channels for influence that simply do not exist in autocratic systems. For a businessman to give money to a civil servant is generally illegal, whereas the same amount given to a politician's campaign fund may 'buy' just as much influence over government decisions but is quite proper. . . . The over-all level of corruption (legally defined) is not necessarily lower in party systems, but the party system generally does legitimize certain patterns of influence that could only occur corruptly in a military/bureaucratic system.[38]

Finally, democratic institutions can in some cases provide new incentives for corruption. In his study of India, Wade concludes that "it is likely that elective institutions have amplified the pressures towards corruption and made it more systematic. . . . because of the spiralling cost of fighting elections and nursing a constituency between elections." The relationship between democratic institutions and corruption, however, depends on a broad range of political dynamics: at the same time it enables more persons to seek a place at the trough, it can also provide greater influence to those trying to topple the trough.

Despite the analytical utility of locating where resources may be diverted from developmental goals, it is important to recognize how the various parts generally fit together as one single system of corruption. Wade criticizes those who "treat 'administrative' and 'political,' 'high' and 'low' level corruption as distinct and unconnected forms," demonstrating that they are often "systematically interconnected." Theobald, similarly, treats "administrative and political corruption as dimensions of the same phenomenon, as different sides of the same coin."[39]

6. Does corruption tend to promote or inhibit the institutionalization of state agencies? What is the impact of corruption on the institutionalization of political parties?

In addition to examining the impact of corruption on the capacity of states to perform important developmental tasks, it is also valuable to consider whether certain types of corruption may promote the institutionalization of bureaucracies and militaries. Returning to the discussion above of the relationship between formal lines of authority and informal networks of power, I propose that a higher degree of convergence between power and authority may occasionally promote state institutionalization. In the late 1950s, for example, then-Colonel Suharto was transferred from his post as regional commander for Central Java because of involvement in a "smuggling scheme ostensibly to raise funds for the 'welfare' of his troops." While personal gain was clearly a major factor, Indonesian generals engaging in such economic activities were also motivated to "maintain the functioning of their units and the loyalty of their troops." State appropriations were insufficient to provision adequately the rank-and-file soldiers, and it was wise for patron-generals to share part of the gains from corrupt activities with a clientele located within the state apparatus.[40] Anderson makes a similar point in his analysis of the "morphology of corruption" in postindependence Indonesia:

> In most cases the corruption is not chiefly for the immediate personal advantage of the official assigned to supervise a particular sector of the economy (though such an official is rarely in straitened circumstances). The corruption is typically used to finance a whole sub-sector of the administrative apparatus. That is to say there is a system of parallel financing of favored sectors of the bureaucracy through the invisible flow of corruption running alongside the formal salary-structure. The flow, channeled down through an informal pyramid of patron-client clusters on a typical patrimonial model, serves to reinforce the cohesion of such clusters. . . . Thus

in many sectors, corruption has become an essential element in the stability of bureaucratic organization.

The second consideration is the impact of corruption on the institutionalization of political parties. This question draws on Huntington, who connects the achievement of more institutionalized parties with the demise of corruption itself:

> For an official to award a public office in return for payment to the official is clearly to place private interest over public interest. For an official to award a public office in return for a contribution of work or money to a party organization is to subordinate one public interest to another, more needy, public interest. . . . Corruption thrives on disorganization, the absence of stable relationships among groups and of recognized patterns of authority. . . . [It] varies inversely with political organization, and *to the extent that corruption builds parties, it undermines the conditions of its own existence.* . . . the incidence of corruption in those countries where governmental resources have been diverted or 'corrupted' for party-building is on the whole less than it is where parties have remained weak.

Historically, he continues, political parties of the West which were initially "leeches on the bureaucracy in the end become the bark protecting it from more destructive locusts of clique and family."[41]

As Huntington suggests, however, one should not presume that the mere contribution of money to a political party will necessarily strengthen the party itself. Just like bureaucracies, political parties combine formal lines of authority with informal networks of power. In some cases, grants of money obtained via corruption will promote the institutionalization of the party, but in other cases parties themselves are so riven along the lines of cliques, factions, and personalities that new resources are unlikely to have that result. Corruption can indeed contribute to the important goal of party-building, but weak parties may endure even when they are major beneficiaries of corruption. It is important to take Huntington's observations a step further, and ask why "corruption builds parties" in some settings but not others.

7. To what extent is corruption's impact on economic development counterbalanced by other "growth-promoting economic and political factors"? Does a political system generate an internal "sense of limits" able to mitigate the extent of corruption?

In assessing the impact of corruption on economic performance, it is commonly argued that other factors may insulate economies—at least temporarily—from its possibly detrimental effects. In some settings, as MacIntyre summarizes the argument, it seems that "clientelism . . . has been sufficiently counterbalanced by other growth-promoting economic and political factors that have enabled strong economic growth to continue in the face of rampant rent-seeking, or served to rectify the situation when the cumulative effect of rent-seeking activities threatened to endanger the economy." Among these factors may be large endowments of natural resources, sizable quantities of foreign aid, strong investor confidence, and the presence of nascent "market-oriented reform coalitions." The basic notion of considering countervailing factors is valid, but as MacIntyre demonstrates this line of inquiry tends to raise as many questions as it answers. Indeed, a simple comparison of how Indonesia and Nigeria utilized their petroleum resources and developed investor confidence during the "oil boom" years returns analysis quite quickly to the question of how some political economies are better equipped than others in insulating themselves from the impact of "rampant rent-seeking."

A far more fundamental "mitigating factor" is the extent to which political system may be compelled to provide its own internal limits, however modest, to the prevalence of corruption. The presence of external threat is often a key factor in encouraging "a sense of limits," explains Scott, and "an elite which enjoys a measure of cohesion and security can develop a sense of its collective, long-run interest." In many cases, however, "limits are virtually absent."[42] To the extent that corrupt practices become culturally embedded over the course of decades or even generations, it will likely be all the more difficult to promote a stronger sense that "enough is enough."

Conclusion

For many decades, scholars have inquired into the impact of corruption, clientelism, and rents on the process of economic growth in the developing world. This paper has attempted to draw very broadly on some of the lessons developed in the course of past inquiry, and contribute toward a framework that can help us to understand better why a range of related phenemona may be relatively more compatible or obstructive to developmental goals. The content of the framework presented here is tentative, but in the process of construction I hope to have demonstrated the utility of an eclectic approach, able to extract valuable insights not only from recent contributions to the topic but also from those made in decades past.

Moreover, I hope to have highlighted how "the politics of privilege" may vary in both character and impact from one Third World setting to another. Applying the framework above to a range of polities—each with its own particular landscape of special advantage—will likely yield very different conclusions about the impact of rents, corruption, and clientelism on developmental outcomes.[43] Admittedly, the model proposed above lacks parsimony; but so, for that matter, have many previous attempts at explaining these issues.[44] Perhaps a narrower or more abstract approach could produce greater simplicity—not to mention more scientific precision; but in all likelihood, some important aspects of (not surprisingly, complex and diverse) reality would be discarded in the process. For all the efforts that have gone into this line of inquiry in the past, it remains the case that corruption, "a phenomenon which affects administration, politics, business, education, health and a host of other crucial areas of social life . . . has been so little studied."[45]

Future comparative research is necessary to prioritize the elements of analysis more clearly, and pursue major issues in greater detail. To the extent possible, it would be useful to develop measures of the variability of corruption, the dissipation of resources in the process of allocating particularistic advantage, and the diversion of budgetary resources from developmental purposes. It is also worthwhile to review the presence or absence of performance criteria across various sectors, and seek to understand more clearly the political processes by which barriers to competition are imposed and maintained. Finally, more research is needed to understand the interconnections of various forms of corruption as found throughout the entire political system, and the structural conditions that may promote (but by no means guarantee) a stronger "sense of limits." As inquiry continues, it is sure to be hobbled by many of the same obstacles that have long plagued the study of corruption. Research can only benefit, however, by drawing freely from the various literatures that have sought to answer, in the past, many of the same questions we are seeking to answer today.

Notes

Thanks to Don Emmerson, Jomo K.S., Mushtaq Khan, Andrew MacIntyre, Amado Mendoza, Jr., T.J. Pempel, Ansil Ramsay, Temario Rivera, and Joel Rocamora— as well as to participants in both a panel of the Association of Asian Studies annual meetings, 11–14 April 1996, Honolulu, Hawaii and the "Rents and Development in Southeast Asia" workshop, 27–28 August 1996, Kuala Lumpur, Malaysia—for offering comments that contributed to this article. All errors, of course, are mine alone.

1. *New York Times*, June 5, 1996. Lee was responding to a report that he and his son, Deputy Prime Minister Lee Hsien Loong, accepted discounts of more than $700,000 in a "soft sale" of condominiums conducted before bids were opened to the public.

2. James M. Buchanan, "Rent Seeking and Profit Seeking," in *Toward A Theory of the Rent-Seeking Society*, ed. James M. Buchanan, Robert D. Tollison and Gordon Tullock (College Station, Texas: Texas A & M Press, 1980), p. 9; Peter Evans, *Embedded Autonomy: States and Industrial Transformation* (Princeton: Princeton University Press, 1995), p. 24.

3. Margaret Levi, *Of Rule and Revenue* (Berkeley and Los Angeles: University of California Press, 1988), p. 24.

4. Evans, *Embedded Autonomy*, p. 25. Fortunately, as Evans demonstrates, use of a rents framework does not require that one adopt the anti-statist perspective of a neo-utilitarian.

5. Max Weber, *Economy and Society* (Berkeley and Los Angeles: University of California Press, 1978), p. 987; Jomo K.S. and Edmund Terence Gomez, "Rents, Rent Seeking and Rent Deployment in Malaysia" (Kuala Lumpur: unpublished ms., 1995), p. 3.

6. Paul D. Hutchcroft, *Booty Capitalism: The Politics of Banking in the Philippines* (Ithaca: Cornell University Press, 1998).

7. See, for example, Anne O. Krueger, "The Political Economy of the Rent-Seeking Society," *The American Economic Review* 64, 3: 291–303.

8. Evans, *Embedded Autonomy*, p. 24.

9. As one scholar noted thirty years ago, "[e]stimates of the extent of corruption practices in underdeveloped countries are, expectedly, very imprecise. Rumor abounds, facts are scarce." David H. Bayley, "The Effects of Corruption in a Developing Nation," in Political Corruption: A Handbook, ed. Arnold J. Heidenheimer, Michael Johnston, and Victor T. LeVine (New Brunswick: Transaction Publishers, 1989 [1966], pp. 935-52, at 939.

10. J.S. Nye, "Corruption and Political Development: A Cost-Benefit Analysis," in Heidenheimer et al., *Political Corruption* 1989 [1967], pp. 963–83, at 966). Alternative definitions are based on notions of the public interest and public opinion, but by far the most widely accepted definitions are based on legal norms. See the discussions of James C. Scott, *Comparative Political Corruption* (Englewood Cliffs, N.J.: Prentice-Hall, 1972), pp. 3–5; and Robin Theobald, *Corruption, Development and Underdevelopment* (Durham: Duke University Press, 1990), pp. 1–18.

11. In 1965, Leys noted that "the question of corruption in the contemporary world has so far been taken up almost solely by moralists. . . . Emotionally and intellectually, this seems to be in a direct line of descent from the viewpoint of those missionaries who were dedicated to the suppression of native dancing. The subject seems to deserve a more systematic and openminded approach." Colin Leys, "What is the Problem About Corruption?," in Heidenheimer et al., *Political Corruption*, 1989 [1965], pp. 51–66, at 52–53. The term "revisionist" is derived from Cariño, who argues the need to combine analysis with moral judgements. "Compare," she writes, "the outrage of American scholars against Nixon's indiscretions and their near-approval of more blatantly corrupt regimes in countries where they have worked." Ledivina V. Cariño, "Tonic or Toxic: The Effects of Graft and Corruption," in Cariño, *Bureaucratic Corruption in Asia: Causes, Consequences and Controls* (Quezon City: College of Public Administration, University of the Philippines, 1986), pp. 163–94, at 168. Among those who perceive at least occasional benefits to corruption are Nye, "Corruption and Political Development," and Scott, *Comparative Political Corruption*; more systematic benefits are asserted in the work of Samuel P. Huntington, *Political Order in Changing Societies* (New Haven: Yale University Press, 1968) and Nathaniel H. Leff, "Economic Development Through Bureaucratic Corruption," in this volume pgs. 305-322. For additional analysis of costs and benefits, see Theobald, *Corruption*.

12. See, for example, Nye, "Corruption and Political Development"; John Waterbury, "Endemic and Planned Corruption in a Monarchical Regime," *World Politics* 25, 4 (July 1973): 533–55; and Theobald, *Corruption*.

13. See Fred Riggs' analysis of how "the gulf between the study of politics and administration . . . became institutionalized" both in developed and in developing countries. Fred W. Riggs, "The Interdependence of Politics and Administration," *Philippine Journal of Public Administration* 31, 4 (October 1987): 418–38, at 429.

14. Scott, *Comparative Political Corruption*, pp. 88–89, 6, and viii-ix; Waterbury, "Endemic and Planned Corruption," p. 555.

15. James C. Scott, "Patron-Client Politics and Political Change in Southeast Asia," *American Political Science Review* 66, no. 1 (1972): 91–113; Waterbury, "Endemic and Planned Corruption," p. 537.

16. See John Thayer Sidel, "Coercion, Capital, and the Post-Colonial State: Bossism

in the Postwar Philippines," Ph.D., Cornell University, 1995, pp. 11–12; Scott, *Comparative Political Corruption*, pp. 34–35.

17. Weber, *Economy and Society*, pp. 240, 1095.

18. Lloyd I. Rudolph and Susanne Hoeber Rudolph, "Authority and Power in Bureaucratic and Patrimonial Administration: A Revisionist Interpretation of Weber on Bureaucracy," *World Politics* 31, 2 (January 1979): 195–227, at 198; Scott, "Patron-Client Politics," p. 92.

19. Scott concurs that more predictable corruption is "less likely to seriously retard economic growth." Not only is the price more certain, but there is also greater "probability of receiving the paid-for 'decision.'" This type of corruption is more likely when: (a) "The political and bureaucratic elites are strong *and* cohesive" and (b) "Corruption has become 'regularized'—even institutionalized after a fashion—by long practice." *Comparative Political Corruption*, pp. 90–91. These insights, I will seek to demonstrate, are strengthened by analysis of the relationship between power and authority.

20. John L.S. Girling, *Thailand: Society and Politics* (Ithaca: Cornell University Press, 1981), pp. 37–38, 42. Anderson, similarly, speaks of the frequent standardization of "cuts and commissions" in post-independence Indonesia. Benedict R. O'G. Anderson, "The Idea of Power in Javanese Culture," in Claire Holt, ed., Culture and Politics in Indonesia (Ithaca: Cornell University Press, 1972), pp. 1–69, at 49.

21. Susan Rose-Ackerman, "Which Bureaucracies are Less Corruptible?," in Heidenheimer et al., *Political Corruption* 1989 [1978], pp. 803–25, at 805, 816. Legal procedures, in fact, may be intentionally obscured in order to heighten the demand for illegal services. In such a system, moreover, those with specialized powers to interpret often opaque rules (i.e., lawyers) will likely play a prominent role.

22. Leff, "Economic Development," pp. 396–7, 393; Krueger, "The Political Economy of the Rent-Seeking Society," pp. 292, 195.

23. A. M. Mendoza Jr., "Notes for a Second Look at Rent-Seeking, Profit-Making, and Economic Change in the Philippines," (Quezon City, unpublished manuscript, 1995), p. 13; Jose Edgardo L. Campos, "The 'Political Economy of the Rent-Seeking Society' Revisited: Cronyism, Political Instability, and Development (Washington, D.C.: unpublished manuscript, 1992), p. 15. See also Krueger, "Rent-Seeking Society," p. 301 and Emmanuel S. de Dios, "Parcellised Capital and Underdevelopment: A Reinterpretation of the Specific-Factors Model," *Philippine Review of Economics and Business* 30 (June 1993): 141–55, at 154. Other neo-classical economists, notes Mendoza in his review of the literature, acknowledge that rent-seeking is not always competitive yet nonetheless "assert that a more competitive situation will reduce wastes associated with rent-seeking" (p. 13).

24. Jomo and Gomez, "Rents," pp. 3–4. Jomo and Gomez do not provide a definition for their passing reference to the term "rent deployment" (in their title as well as on pp. 21 and 22). I may be employing the term in a somewhat different sense than they originally intended, but I have taken the liberty to retain the term because it best suggests a systematic, purposive allocation of rents. The basic distinction between two types of rent allocation, however, derives from their discussion.

25. I am indebted to Jomo and Gomez for highlighting the important distinction between these two processes ("Rents," p. 5). On corruption and capital accumulation, see Nye, "Corruption and Political Development," p. 967.

26. Indeed, one could argue that an entrepreneur who benefits from a deployed rent (and is thus probably close to the regime in power) is likely more secure than an

entrepreneur who has won out in a process of competitive rent-seeking. If the regime as a whole is in danger of collapsing, however, neither category of entrepreneur is likely to have much sense of security.

27. Richard F. Doner and Ansil Ramsay, "An Institutional Explanation of Thai Economic Success," a paper presented at the annual meetings of the Association for Asian Studies, Washington, D.C., April 6–9, 1995, pp. 3–4. See also Richard F. Doner and Ansil Ramsay, "Competitive Clientelism and Economic Governance The Case of Thailand," in Sylvia Maxfield and Ben Ross Schneider, eds., Business and the State in Developing Countries (Ithaca: Cornell University Press, 1997), pp. 237–276, at 248; and Scott, *Comparative Political Corruption*, p. 91.
28. Robert H. Bates, *Markets and States in Tropical Africa: The Political Basis of Agricultural Policies* (Berkeley and Los Angeles: University of California Press, 1981).
29. World Bank, *World Development Report 1991* (Oxford: Oxford University Press, 1991), p. 9; Huntington, *Political Order*, p. 69.
30. Scott, *Comparative Political Corruption*, p. 67. Fegan offers a broadly similar distinction between "facilitative corruption" (in which the law is bent to the mutual benefit of both a bribing businessperson and a bribed bureaucrat, and neither has reason to complain to a third party) and "obstructive corruption" (in which legitimate applications are blocked until a bribe is paid, and the businessperson is likely to complain to a third party). The former is "probably a necessary lubricant to capitalist development," while the latter is an impediment. Brian Fegan, "Contributions From Sir Arthur Conan Doyle and Mick Inder to a Theory of Bureacratisation and Corruption in Southeast Asia," (Sydney: unpublished ms., 1994), pp. 4–5.
31. Syed Hussein Alatas, *The Sociology of Corruption: The Nature, Function, Causes, and Prevention of Corruption* (Singapore: Times Books International, 1980), pp. 31–35.
32. Theobald, *Corruption*, p. 128, 131; Huntington, *Political Order*, p. 69.
33. Leff, "Economic Development," p. 399.
34. Robert Wade, "The System of Administrative and Political Corruption: Canal Irrigation in South India," *The Journal of Development Studies* 18, 3 (April 1982): 287–328, at 287–88.
35. Insights can also be drawn from comparisons of the incidence (and impact) of corruption at the national level versus the regional level, or Region A versus Region B. The more decentralized a polity, the more important such analysis would be.
36. Huntington, *Political Order*, p. 67, emphasis in original.
37. Evans, *Embedded Autonomy*, p. 61; Doner and Ramsay, "Thai Economic Success," pp. 2–3. The relatively more efficient agencies may be more insulated from clientelistic pressures, but one should not presume that formal authority completely displaces informal networks of power. As Rudolph and Rudolph argue in their "revisionist interpretation" of Weber's work on bureaucracy, effective administration depends not only on rational-legal authority but also on the persistence of patrimonial features able to "[mitigate] conflict and [promote] organizational loyalty, discipline, and efficiency." "Authority and Power," p. 196. Evans argues that informal networks within developmentalist states "reinforce the binding character of participation in the formal organizational structure rather than undercutting it in the way that informal networks based on kinship or parochial geographic loyalties would." *Embedded Autonomy*, p. 59.
38. Scott, *Comparative Political Corruption*, p. 94. I prefer the term "electoral sys-

tem" to "party system," since (as discussed below) well-institutionalized parties may or may not play an important role within a system centered around competitive elections.

39. Wade, "Administrative and Political Corruption," pp. 318–19, 288; Theobald, *Corruption*, p. 18. See also Riggs, "Interdependence."

40. Harold Crouch, *The Army and Politics in Indonesia* (Ithaca: Cornell University Press, 1988), pp. 40, 38. Overall, this period is of course known as one in which corruption in Indonesia lacked any real limits. Scott, *Comparative Political Corruption*, pp. 80–84. To the extent that institutionalization was taking place, it was seemingly almost entirely within a military that—after 1965—came to "backbone" the rest of the bureaucracy. Donald K. Emmerson, "The Bureaucracy in Political Context: Weakness in Strength," in Political Power and Communications in Indonesia, ed. Karl D. Jackson and Lucian W. Pye (Berkeley and Los Angeles: University of California Press, 1978), pp. 82–136; see also Crouch, *Army and Politics* and Benedict Anderson, "Old State, New Society: Indonesia's New Order in Comparative Historical Perspective," *Journal of Asian Studies* 42 (May 1983): 477–496.

41. Anderson, "The Idea of Power," p. 49; Huntington, *Political Order*, pp. 70–71, emphasis added.

42. Andrew MacIntyre, Clientelism and Economic Growth: The Politics of Economic Policymaking in Indonesia," a paper presented at the annual meetings of the Association for Asian Studies, Washington, D.C., April 6–9, 1995, pp. 10–16; Scott, *Comparative Political Corruption*, pp. 79–80.

43. In Paul D. Hutchcroft, "Obstructive Corruption: The Politics of Privilege in the Philippines," in Rent Seeking and Development in Asia, ed. Jomo K.S. and Mushtaq Khan (Cambridge: Cambridge University Press, forthcoming 2000), I apply the various elements of this framework to the Philippines, a notoriously skewed, irregular political economic landscape long the playfield of both established oligarchs and favored cronies. The country's particular configuration of political power, I conclude, has nurtured types of rent-seeking, corruption, and clientelistic ties that have proven generally obstructive to sustained economic development.

44. See, for example, Nye, "Corruption and Political Development"; Scott, *Comparative Political Development*, pp. 90–91; and Theobald, *Corruption*, pp. 107–32.

45. Wade, "Administrative and Political Corruption," p. 288.

28

Responses to Corruption in
Asian Societies

Jon S.T. Quah

Introduction

Corruption is no longer a sensitive issue or taboo subject for research,[1] judging from the frequent reporting on corruption scandals round the world and the increasing amount of research on corruption in many countries.[2] According to Robert Leiken, a survey of the *Economist,* the *Financial Times,* and the *New York Times* showed that articles dealing with official corruption "quadrupled between 1984 and 1995."[3] Similarly, the *Far Eastern Economic Review* reported that corruption was the biggest story in 1996 as a great deal of "newsprint and television time was devoted to reports and discussions on corruption in government."[4]

Corruption is a serious problem in many Asian countries according to the annual surveys conducted by the Hong Kong-based Political and Economic Risk Consultancy Ltd. (PERC) and the Berlin-based Transparency International (TI) in recent years. In 1996, PERC ranked Singapore as the third least corrupt country in the world and the least corrupt of the 12 Asian countries in the study. During the same year, Singapore's seventh ranking on TI's Corruption Perception Index (CPI) made it the least corrupt of the 13 Asian countries in the 54–nation study, with Pakistan (ranked 53rd) as the most corrupt Asian country.[5] Even though Singapore's ranking on the 1997 CPI dropped to ninth position, it is still the least corrupt of the 13 Asian countries in the 52–nation survey, with Pakistan (ranked 48th) retaining its position as the most corrupt Asian country.[6] In the 1998 CPI, Singapore's seventh ranking confirms its status as the least corrupt of the 13 Asian countries among the 85

Table 28.1
Average Ranking of 12 Asian Countries on Transparency International's
Corruption Perception Index, 1996–1998

Country	Ranking (from least to most corrupt)
Singapore	1
Hong Kong	2
Japan	3
Malaysia	4
Taiwan	5
South Korea	6
Thailand	7
Philippines	8
China	9
India	10
Indonesia	11
Pakistan	12

Source: See footnotes 6–8.

countries surveyed, while Indonesia (ranked 80th) replaced Pakistan (ranked joint 71st) as the most corrupt country in Asia.[7] Table 28.1 below shows the average ranking of 12 Asian countries on the CPI from 1996–1998.

If corruption is defined as "the misuse of public power, office or authority for private benefit–through bribery, extortion, influence peddling, nepotism, fraud, speed money or embezzlement,"[8] why is corruption a fact of life in Singapore and Hong Kong on the one hand, and a way of life in Indonesia and Pakistan on the other hand?[9] How do we explain the different levels of corruption in Asian countries?

As the extent of corruption depends on the nature of its causes, and on the degree of effectiveness of the anti-corruption measures introduced by governments, those that diagnose correctly the causes of corruption and take appropriate measures to minimize, if not eliminate them will be more effective than those governments which do not observe this logic of corruption control. Countries like Singapore and Hong Kong which follow this logic of corruption control are more successful in combating corruption than Indonesia and Pakistan which do not.

Causes of Corruption

Under what conditions does corruption thrive? What are the factors which induce individuals to commit corrupt acts? Conversely, what prevents or discourages individuals from becoming corrupt? An individual is likely to commit a corrupt act if he or she (1) is paid a low salary; (2) is provided with the opportunities for corruption; and (3) perceives corruption to be a low risk, high reward activity. In other words, corruption thrives when the individuals concerned receive meager salaries, have ample opportunities to be corrupt, and are unlikely to be caught and not severely punished even if they are caught.

In his comparative study of the control of bureaucratic corruption in Hong Kong, India and Indonesia, Leslie Palmier has identified the above factors as important causes of corruption: *opportunities* (which depended on the extent of involvement of civil servants in the administration or control of lucrative activities), *salaries* and *policing* (i.e., the probability of detection and punishment). Palmier contends that bureaucratic corruption seems to depend not on any one of the [three] factors identified, but rather on the *balance* between them. At one extreme, *with few opportunities, good salaries, and effective policing, corruption will be minimal;* at the other, *with many opportunities, poor salaries, and weak policing, it will be considerable.*[10]

Thus, an effective anti-corruption strategy should reduce or remove the opportunities for corruption, raise the salaries of civil servants and political leaders, and ensure a high degree of policing.

Low Salaries

Palmier has identified low salaries as an important factor contributing to corruption. "If the official is not to be tempted into corruption and disaffection, clearly there is an obligation on the government to provide or at least allow such benefits as will ensure his loyalty; one might call it an implicit contract." He concluded that "adequate pay" was "an essential ingredient in reform."[11] In the same vein, Mauro has argued that "when civil service pay is too low, civil servants may be obliged to use their positions to collect bribes as a way of making ends meet, particularly when the expected cost of being caught is low."[12]

In Indonesia, corruption was a serious problem during the Dutch colonial period as the salaries of the Dutch East India Company's personnel were inadequate. Day observed that these personnel "were underpaid and exposed to every temptation that was offered by the combination of a weak native organization, extraordinary opportunities in trade, and an almost complete absence of checks from home or in Java."[13] Corruption became endemic during Sukarno's rule because his "disastrously inflationary budgets eroded civil service salaries to the point where people simply could not live on them and where financial accountability virtually collapsed because of administrative deterioration."[14]

In South Korea, Meredith Woo-Cummings has recommended that civil service salaries, which constitute only 70 percent of private sector wages, should be raised to reduce corruption.[15] Similarly, Jun and Voon have suggested that it is unrealistic to expect South Korean civil servants "to show dedication without providing adequate remuneration and changing the administrative culture."[16] In Thailand, Kasem Suwanagul found that the low salaries of civil servants during the post-war period contributed to more bureaucratic corruption as their low salaries were insufficient to meet inflation and below those offered in the private sector.[17]

Corruption was introduced into the Philippines during the Spanish colonial period, when civil servants were poorly paid and had many opportunities for corruption.[18] On the other hand, the bureaucracy was less corrupt during the American colonial period as "the bureaucrats received higher salaries and corrupt officials were promptly prosecuted."[19] Finally, in his analysis of the consequences of low salaries on the Philippine Civil Service's prestige, Padilla found that civil servants supplemented their low wages by vending within the office, holding a second job, teaching part-time, practising their profession after office hours, engaging in research and consultancy projects, and resorting to petty corrupt practices.[20]

The most important factor responsible for police corruption in Singapore during the colonial period was the low salaries in the Singapore Police Force (SPF), especially in the lower ranks. This was also blamed for the SPF's inefficiency and its inability to recruit suitably qualified personnel.[21] The *Straits Times* noted: "It is at once evident that the native constables and the European police of the Inspector class are so underpaid that scandals are unavoidable."[22]

In short, "if bureaucrats are paid a high enough wage, even a small chance of losing their jobs would discourage them from being corrupt." On the other hand, if the real salary of civil servants decreases drastically, "even the most rigidly honest bureaucrats will be tempted to go beyond the law to preserve their standard of living."[23]

Ample Opportunities for Corruption

According to Gould and Amaro-Reyes, "the expanding role of government in development has placed the bureaucracy in a monopolistic position and has enhanced the opportunities for administrative discretion. Excessive regulations together with this increased bureaucratic discretion provide opportunities and incentives for corruption in that regulations governing access to goods and services can be exploited by civil servants in extracting 'rents' from groups vying for access to such goods and services."[24] For example, in Hong Kong, "the necessity for the government to regulate, control and prohibit certain activities" provided "ample opportunity for the corrupt in the areas of construction, import and export, health, hygiene, safety, prostitution, gambling, drugs, markets and stalls, immigration and emigration."[25]

In Indonesia, Donald P. Warwick referred to the distinction made by civil servants between "wet" and "dry" agencies:

"wet" agencies . . . are generous with honoraria, allowances, service on committees, boards, and development projects, and, recently, opportunities for foreign training. They are departments that deal in money, planning, banking, or public enterprises. "Dry" agencies are those doing traditional administrative work. Perceptions of unfairness about benefits not only reduce staff morale, but lead to the feeling that illegal compensation is a fair way to even out staff benefits across agencies.[26]

"Wet" agencies like the police, customs, immigration and internal revenue will provide more opportunities for corruption than "dry" agencies like research and administrative departments which do not interact with the public.

The Knapp Commission found that three factors determined the opportunities for corrupt behavior among policemen in New York City. First, the branch of the department to which an officer is assigned is important: plainclothesmen will have more and different opportunities than uniformed officers. Second, the area to which an officer is assigned not only influences the opportunities for corrupt behavior but also the major sources of corruption payments. For example, in New York City, some precincts in Harlem provide more opportunities for corruption than Central Park. Finally, the officer's assignment determines the amount and type of graft available: an officer in a patrol car will have more opportunities to be corrupt than his counterpart on guard duty.[27]

The Corruption Prevention Department (CPD) of Hong Kong's Independent Commission Against Corruption (ICAC) identified four "more pernicious and prevalent" factors which provided opportunities for corruption. The first factor is delay, which "provides both the opportunity to extort a bribe and the incentive to offer one, and is also an inevitable consequence of bureaucratic processes." Second, insufficient publicity "leads the public to believe that individual public servants have the authority to decide whether a particular law shall be enforced or who shall benefit from a public service, so creating a situation ripe for exploitation." The third factor providing opportunities for corruption is excessive discretion, which often results from "a well-intended delegation of authority in order to expedite business." The fourth and most important factor was the lack of supervision or accountability especially of junior officers who operate away from an office. As supervisors are usually preoccupied with other administrative duties which require their presence in their comfortable offices, they are reluctant to visit their junior officers in the field and resort to supervision through correspondence. To minimize the lack of supervision or accountability of junior officers, the CPD recommended that "all supervisory officers should spend sufficient time with their staff and in the field, to gain their own insight into the problems within their area of responsibility and conditions on the ground."[28]

Low Risk of Detection and Punishment

The probability of detection and punishment of corrupt offences varies in the different Asian countries. Corruption thrives in those Asian countries where the public perceives it to be a "low risk, high reward" activity as corrupt offenders are unlikely to be detected and punished. In contrast, corruption is not a serious problem in those Asian countries where corruption is perceived as a "high risk, low reward" activity as those involved in corrupt behavior are likely to be caught and severely punished.

An important cause of the pervasive corruption in the Soviet Union before its collapse was the lack of fear of punishment among the corrupt officials. According to Syed Hussein Alatas:

> Cases of high-level corruption are rarely truly punished. The regime has always been permissive towards its ruling elite. Corruption has developed to the extent that offices can be bought, as newspaper accounts reveal. Involvement of the highest leadership in turn causes permissiveness towards corruption. This is the greatest cause of its perpetuation.[29]

Similarly, even though bribery exceeding 100,000 yuan (US$12,000) is a capital offence in the People's Republic of China (PRC), the death penalty has not been imposed on some senior party officials found guilty of accepting bribes exceeding this amount. For example, in 1998 the former Beijing party chief, Chen Xitong, became the highest-ranking Chinese Communist Party member to be jailed for corruption when he was sentenced to 16 years for graft of 555,000 yuan and dereliction of duty. Indeed, Chen's sentence is lenient as more junior party cadres have been given life imprisonment or the death penalty for corruption involving smaller sums.[30] Senior party officials in the PRC can "short-circuit corruption investigations by appealing to their protectors in the party hierarchy."[31]

In Bangladesh, corruption is a dominant component of its bureaucratic culture and has been institutionalized in the public service during the last 25 years. Mohammad Mohabbat Khan explains the high level of corruption in Bangladesh thus:

> First, bureaucrats involved in corrupt practices in most cases do not lose their jobs. Very rarely they are dismissed from service on charges pertaining to corruption. Still rarely they are sent to prison for misusing public funds. They have never been compelled to return to the state their ill-gotten wealth. Second, the law-enforcing officials including police personnel are extremely corrupt. They are happy to share the booty with other corrupt bureaucrats. Third, the people have a tendency not only to tolerate corruption but to show respect to those bureaucrats who made fortune through dubious means. . . . Fourth, it is easier for a citizen to get quick service because he has already "paid" the bureaucrat rather than wait for his turn.[32]

For corruption to be seen as a "high risk, low reward" activity, the government must publicize corrupt behaviour among civil servants and politicians, and their punishment according to the law if they are found guilty. In this connection, Palmier stresses the crucial role of the communications media, as corruption "thrives in secrecy, and withers in the light."[33] Negative publicity can serve as an effective deterrent; indeed, according to Singapore's former prime minister, Lee Kuan Yew, "The strongest deterrent is in a public opinion which censures and condemns corrupt persons, in other words, in attitudes which make corruption so unacceptable that the stigma of corruption cannot be washed away by serving a prison sentence."[34] Conversely, those governments which "shackle the media" as in the case of Indonesia under Suharto or India during the Emergency of the 1970s, "are in effect encouraging the corrupt."[35]

Anti-Corruption Measures in Asian Countries

What are the anti-corruption measures employed by the governments in Asian countries? C.V. Narasimhan, a former Director of the Central Bureau of Investigation (CBI) in India, there are three types of anti-corruption measures: preventive, punitive and promotional. Preventive measures refer to those electoral and administrative reforms concerned with making all government transactions "more transparent and accountable to the people." Punitive measures include the "laws, rules and the mechanism for effective investigation, court trial, departmental disciplinary action and other means to deter the corrupt functionaries." Finally, promotional measures focus on the "encouragement of value-based politics, inculcation of moral and ethical principles among the younger generation in schools and colleges and the build-up of a kind of social ostracisation of corrupt people by the society."[36]

While preventive and promotional measures are also important, our analysis will focus on those punitive measures employed by the governments in Hong Kong, India, Mongolia, Philippines and Singapore to curb corruption as these measures are designed to reduce the opportunities for corruption as well as increase the risk of detecting and punishing corrupt behavior. These five countries exhibit three patterns in controlling corruption.

Pattern 1: Anti-corruption Legislation with No Independent Agency

Mongolia follows the first pattern as it has anti-corruption legislation like the Law on Anti-Corruption (LAC) enacted in April 1996 and provisions restricting bribery in the Criminal Code, but it does not have an independent anti-corruption agency (ACA). Instead, the task of controlling corruption in Mongolia is shared between the police, the General Prosecutor's Office, and the courts.[37]

Apart from identifying the six categories of civil servants under its jurisdiction, the LAC requires all public officials in Mongolia to declare their incomes and assets and those of their families within 30 days of assuming their positions and thereafter to submit annual declarations during February 1–15 of each year. Those fail to do so will be fined between 5,000 and 25,000 togrogs (US$5.90 to US$29.40). Furthermore, higher officials who fail to monitor the declarations must pay fines of between 20,000 to 30,000 togrogs (US$23.50 to US$35.30). The penalty for failing to declare gifts or foreign bank accounts is higher—between 30,000 to 40,000 togrogs (US$35.30 to US$47.05) in fines. Finally, officials found guilty of corruption will be discharged or displaced according to the procedure provided in the law.

Articles 195–197 of the Criminal Code focus on bribery. Article 195 states that an official who receives bribes directly or through a mediator can be suspended from his position or sentenced to six years of imprisonment without suspension of power. The penalty is increased to suspension from his position and imprisonment of between 10 to 25 years if the official is a repeat offender, a senior civil servant, if he accepts a large bribe, or if bribery is committed by an organized group. Article 196 punishes bribe-givers with imprisonment of up to four years or performing public work for 18 months. Recalcitrant bribe-givers can be jailed from three to ten years. Finally, Article 197 stipulates that those who mediate in bribe-taking and giving will be punished by imprisonment of up to four years or performing 18 months of public work.

Reports of crime, including corruption offences, are received by the Criminal Police Department (CPD), which investigates these reports and refers them to the Investigation Department (ID) for the next stage of the investigation, which can last from two to 26 months. If there is evidence to verify these complaints, cases are handed over to the General Prosecutor's Office (GPO), which supervises "inquiries by the police in both criminal and civil cases" and represents "the state in both civil and criminal proceedings."[38] From the GPO, the cases are processed by the *aimag* courts and the Capital City Court (for serious crimes where the amount exceeds 10 million togrogs or US$22,000) and the Supreme Court (for those cases outside the jurisdiction of other courts and appeals from decisions of the *aimag* courts and the Capital City Court).[39]

Pattern 2: Anti-Corruption Legislation with Several Agencies

The second pattern of combating corruption combines anti-corruption legislation with several agencies, as is the case in India and the Philippines. In India, the Prevention of Corruption Act (POCA) is implemented by the Central Bureau of Investigation (CBI), the Central Vigilance Commission (CVC), the anti-corruption bureaus and vigilance commissions at the state level. Similarly, in the Philippines, the anti-graft laws and policies are supplemented by the *Sandiganbayan* (special anti-corruption court), the Ombudsman, and the Presidential Commission Against Graft and Corruption (PCAGC), the latest presidential anti-graft agency created by President Ramos in 1994.

Anti-corruption measures in India. The fight against corruption in India began in 1941, when the colonial government created the Delhi Special Police Establishment (DSPE) to "investigate cases of bribery and corruption in transactions" involving the War and Supply Departments. In 1943, the government issued Ordinance XXII which empowered the DSPE's officers to investigate corruption cases involving central government departments in India. This Ordinance lapsed on September 30, 1946 and was replaced by the DSPE Act, 1946, which transferred control of the DSPE to the Home Department (now known as the Ministry of Home Affairs).[40]

In March 1947, the POCA became law. In 1949, the government formed a Committee chaired by Baksi Tek Chand to review, *inter alia*, the operation of the POCA, 1947 and to assess the DSPE's effectiveness in combating corruption. In 1952, the Chand Committee recommended that the DSPE's activities should be expanded. Accordingly, an Enforcement Wing was added in 1953 to handle offences involving violation of import and export regulations at Bombay, Calcutta and Madras. In 1955, an Administrative Vigilance Division (AVD) was formed within the Ministry of Home Affairs (MHA) to coordinate anti-corruption measures within the central government.

In June 1962, a Committee on the Prevention of Corruption was appointed and chaired by K. Santhanam. Its purpose was "to review the existing instruments for checking corruption in the Central Services" and to provide advice on the "practical steps that should be taken to make anti-corruption measures more effective." The Santhanam Report had far-reaching consequences as it first recommended the formation of a CVC, which has the power to "investigate any complaint or suspicion of improper behaviour" against a civil servant. Secondly, a Chief Vigilance Officer (CVO) was appointed in each ministry or department. Finally, the Santhanam Report recommended the amendment of the POCA of 1947 to provide that "the possession by a public servant of assets disproportionate to income, and for which a satisfactory explanation could not be made, was itself criminal misconduct."

In April 1963, the government established the CBI by incorporating the DSPE as one of its six divisions *viz.*, the Investigation and Anti-Corruption Division. As the CBI's role is to investigate crimes handled by the DSPE, the DSPE Act, 1946 remains in force and provides the legal sanction and authority for investigations by the CBI, which does not have any statutory basis itself. Thus, the MHA, through its AVD assumed control of the CBI's work and provided for its budget. The CBI and AVD were transferred from the MHA to the new Department of Personnel, Cabinet Secretariat in 1970.

The CBI derives its investigating powers from the DSPE Act, 1946, section 5 of which empowers the CBI to investigate the notified offences in any state, with the consent of the government of that state. According to Narasimhan, the CBI did not encounter any difficulty within the states during the post-independent period when the Congress Party was in power in the states and centre. However, the situation changed when different political parties assumed power in the states because some state governments withdrew the consent given by their predecessors "whenever they felt that an investigation taken up by the CBI was politically embarrassing or uncomfortable for them." In short, the CBI's status as an investigating agency in a state is "unstable and dependent" on that state government's mercy.[41]

The states have their own anti-corruption bureaus (ACBs) for dealing with vigilance and anti-corruption work, but these derive their powers from the Police Act as they are regular police units. If there is public pressure for an inquiry into the misconduct of a minister, the central or state government will form a Commission of Inquiry. It will present its report on the facts ascertained during the inquiry to the government concerned, which will refer the matter to the CBI or state ACB for investigation if a person is to be prosecuted. However, the investigation process and the ensuing trial are time-consuming and do not result in quick or severe punishment. Indeed, no CBI case involving ministers has resulted in a firm court conviction during the last 40 years.

The CVC was established in 1964 to perform four functions: (1) investigate any transaction in which a public servant is alleged to act for an improper purpose; (2) examine (a) any complaint that a public servant had exercised his powers for improper or corrupt purposes; and (b) any complaint of corruption, misconduct, lack of integrity or other malpractices by a public servant, including members of the All India Services; (3) request reports from ministries, departments and public enterprises to enable it to check and supervise their vigilance and anti-corruption work; and (4) request the CBI to investigate a case, or to entrust the complaint, information or case for inquiry to the CBI or the ministry, department or public enterprise concerned. It is headed by a Commissioner, who is appointed by the President for six years. The CVOs in ministries and departments are appointed in consultation with the Commissioner, who assesses their performance. The CVC submits an annual report on its activities to the MHA.

Apart from receiving complaints from individuals, the CVC collects and collates data on corruption and malpractices from such sources as press reports, parliamentary speeches, audit objections, reports of parliamentary committees, and CBI reports.[42] The Commissioner advises the departments on the action to be taken on CBI reports on gazetted officers. He also reviews the preventive work of the CVOs and Vigilance Officers in different departments and provides them with the necessary directions.[43]

Anti-corruption measures in the Philippines. The Philippines is the Asian country with the most number of anti-corruption measures. More specifically, it has relied on seven laws and 13 anti-graft agencies since its battle against corruption began in the 1950s. The first anti-corruption law was the Forfeiture Law of 1955, which authorized "the state to forfeit in its favor any property found to have been unlawfully acquired by any public officer or employer."[44] This law was ineffective, as there were no convictions even four years after its passage. The Republic Act (R.A.) 3019, entitled the Anti-graft and Corrupt Practices Act, was the second law and it was passed in April 1960.[45] R.A. 3019 identified eleven types of corrupt acts, and required public officials to file every two years a detailed and sworn statement of their assets and liabilities. The third anti-corruption law–R.A. 6028–which provided for the formation of the Office of the Citizens' Counsellor, was passed in August 1969, but was not implemented.

The other laws were the four Presidential Decrees (P.D.) issued by President Marcos after the establishment of martial law in September 1972. P.D. No. 6 identified 29 administrative offences and empowered heads of departments to dismiss guilty officials immediately. This resulted in the sacking of nearly 8,000 officials. Two months later, P.D. No. 46 prevented public officials from receiving and private individuals from giving gifts on any occasion including Christmas. Finally, P.D. No. 677, and P.D. No. 749, are amendments to R.A. 3019, requiring all government employees to declare their assets and liabilities every year, instead of every other year; and providing immunity from prosecution for those willing to testify against public officials or citizens accused of corruption.[46]

The many anti-graft agencies in the Philippines reflect frequent changes in political leadership as such agencies are either created or abolished by the President. Between May 1950 and January 1966, five anti-corruption agencies were formed and dissolved, as there were five changes in political leadership during that period. Similarly, President Marcos created another five anti-graft agencies during his two decades in power because the first three agencies were ineffective and lasted between eight months and two years.[47] Indeed, according to Varela, "graft and corruption reached its all time high during the martial law regime under Marcos" as corruption "had permeated almost all aspects of bureaucratic life and institutions which saw the start of the systematic plunder of the country."[48]

In July 1979, President Marcos created the *Sandiganbayan* (Special Anti-Graft Court) and the *Tanodbayan* (Ombudsman) by issuing P.D. No. 1606 and P.D. No. 1630 respectively. Section 4 of P.D. No.1606 gives the *Sandiganbayan* jurisdiction over violations of R.A. No. 3019 (the Anti-Graft and Corrupt Practices Act) and R.A. No. 1379; and crimes committed by public officers and employees. Section 10 of P.D. No. 1630 describes the various powers of the *Tanodbayan*, who "may file and prosecute civil and administrative cases involving graft and corrupt practices and such other offenses committed by public officers and employees."[49]

When President Corazon Aquino assumed office in February 1986, "there was high expectation that the end of the culture of graft and corruption was near."[50] She formed the Presidential Commission on Good Government (PCGG) to identify and retrieve the money stolen by the Marcos family and their cronies. Unfortunately, Aquino's "avowed anti-graft and corruption" stance was viewed with cynicism by the public as two of her Cabinet members and her relatives (referred to derisively as "rela-thieves") were accused of corruption. The PCGG was also a target for charges of corruption, favoritism and incompetence, and by June 1988, five of its agents faced graft charges and 13 more were under investigation. In May 1987, Aquino created the Presidential Committee on Public Ethics and Accountability (PCPEA) to respond to increasing public criticism, but it PCPEA lacked staff and funds. Aquino's "honesty has not been matched by the political will to punish the corrupt."[51]

The *Tanodbayan* or Office of the Ombudsman was "reborn" in 1988 during Aquino's term of office. However, according to Balgos, "during the first seven years after its rebirth in 1988, the Office of the Ombudsman failed to attract much public scrutiny, the limelight hogged by the more high-profile Sandiganbayan." However, instead of "inspiring confidence in the judicial system," the Ombudsman has elicited "only disappointment–if not contempt–among many of those seeking redress for the wrong done them by public officials." Indeed, the Ombudsman has a notorious reputation for taking a long time in processing the complaints received by it.[52] A more serious weakness was the quota system introduced by Conrado Vasquez, who was appointed as Ombudsman in 1988. This system encouraged inefficiency as investigators "finished the easier cases first to fulfill their quota" and left the more complex ones "untouched for months, or even years." Consequently, by December 1994, the Ombudsman had accumulated a backlog of 14,652 cases, or 65% of its total workload. Indeed, in August 1997, the Ombudsman had pending cases dating back to 1979. It should be noted that the *Sandiganbayan* has an even poorer record, completing only 13% of its total caseload in 1996.

In 1994, President Ramos appointed Eufemio Domingo to head the Presidential Commission against Graft and Corruption (PCGC). Three years later, Domingo concluded that "the system is not working. We are not making it work." According to him:

> We have all the laws, rules and regulations and especially institutions not only to curb, but to eliminate, corruption. The problem is that these laws, rules and regulations are not being faithfully implemented. . . . I am afraid that many people are accepting (corruption) as another part of our way of life. Big-time grafters are lionized in society. They are invited to all sorts of social events, elected and re-

elected to government offices. It is considered an honor–in fact a social distinction–to have them as guests in family and community affairs.[53]

Pattern 3: Anti-Corruption Legislation with an Independent Agency

The third and most effective pattern of fighting corruption is the combination of comprehensive anti-corruption legislation impartially implemented by
an independent anti-corruption agency. Singapore and Hong Kong employ
this combination to curb corruption, and are perceived to be the two least
corrupt countries in Asia.

Anti-corruption measures in Singapore. Corruption was a way of life in
Singapore during the colonial period as it was perceived by the public as a
low risk, high reward activity. Corrupt officials were seldom caught, and
even if they were they were not severely punished. Singapore's fight against
corruption began in 1871 with the enactment of the Penal Code of the Straits
Settlements. However, nothing was done until December 1937, when the first
anti-corruption law was introduced with the enactment of the Prevention of
Corruption Ordinance (POCO).[54]

The Japanese Occupation (February 1942–August 1945) aggravated the
problem as civil servants could not make ends meet on their low salaries
because of the rampant inflation. Conditions deteriorated during the postwar
period: low salaries and inflation increased the need for civil servants to be
corrupt on the one hand, while poor supervision by their superior officers
provided them with many opportunities for corrupt behavior with minimal
risk of being caught, on the other.[55] Thus, it was not surprising that the
Commissioner of Police, J.P. Pennefather-Evans, reported in 1950 that graft
was rife in many government departments. This assessment was confirmed
by the Chief of the Anti-Corruption Branch (ACB) of the Criminal Investigation Department (CID), which was responsible for dealing with corruption.

The ACB was ineffective because it was inadequately staffed with only 17
members and had to compete with other sections of the CID for limited
manpower and resources. Its Achilles heel was its inability to deal impartially
with the police. A team appointed to investigate the theft of S$400,000 of
opium in October 1951 found that there was widespread police corruption
and that not all senior officers involved in protection rackets were prosecuted
and some had even escaped punishment because of insufficient evidence. The
opium hijacking case highlighted the ACB's ineffectiveness in fighting corruption and made the British colonial government realize the importance and
value of establishing an independent anti-corruption agency that was autonomous of the police. Consequently, the ACB was dissolved and replaced by an
independent agency known as the Corrupt Practices Investigation Bureau
(CPIB) in 1952.[56]

When the People's Action Party (PAP) government assumed office in

June 1959, corruption was rampant in Singapore and perceived by many to be a low risk, high reward activity. Accordingly, the immediate task was to minimize corruption and change public perceptions. PAP leaders initiated a comprehensive anti-corruption strategy in 1960 by enacting the Prevention of Corruption Act (POCA) and strengthening the CPIB. This new strategy is based on the following logic of corruption: as corruption is caused by both the incentives and opportunities to be corrupt, "attempts to eradicate corruption must be designed to minimize or remove the conditions of both the incentives and opportunities that make individual corrupt behavior irresistible."[57]

Singapore was a poor country then as its Gross National Product (GNP) per capita in 1960 was S$1,330 or US$443.[58] The government could not afford to raise the salaries of civil servants; it was left with the alternative of strengthening the existing anti-corruption legislation to reduce opportunities and increase penalties for corrupt behavior. The POCA of 1960 had five features to remove the POCO's deficiencies and to empower the CPIB in performing its duties. First, the POCA's scope was increased as it had 32 sections (now, 37) compared to the POCO's 12. Second, corruption was clearly defined in section 2, which also identified for the first time the CPIB and its Director. Third, the penalty for corruption was increased to five years' imprisonment and/or a fine of S$10,000[59] to enhance the POCA's deterrent effect (section 5). Fourth, a person found guilty of accepting an illegal gratification had to pay the amount he had taken as a bribe in addition to any other punishment imposed by a court (section 13).

The fifth and most significant feature of the POCA was that it gave the CPIB more powers and a new lease of life. Section 15 provided CPIB officers with powers of arrest and search of arrested persons. Section 17 empowered the Public Prosecutor to authorize the CPIB's Director and his senior staff to investigate "any bank account, share account or purchase account" of any one suspected of having committed an offence against the POCA. Section 18 enabled the CPIB officers to inspect a civil servant's banker's book and those of his wife, child or agent, if necessary. To enhance the POCA's effectiveness, the PAP government has amended the POCA whenever necessary or introduced new legislation to deal with unanticipated problems.[60]

The CPIB is the anti-corruption agency responsible for enforcing the POCA's provisions. It has grown by nine times from eight officers in 1960 to its current establishment of 71 officers, comprising 49 investigators and 22 clerical and support staff. Its functions are threefold: (1) to receive and investigate complaints concerning corruption in the public and private sectors; (2) to investigate malpractice and misconduct by public officers; and (3) to examine the practices and procedures in the public service to minimize opportunities for corrupt practices.[61] The CPIB is much smaller than Hong Kong's ICAC; it does not need a large staff even though it has a heavy workload, as its location within the Prime Minister's Office (PMO) and its legal powers enable it to obtain the required cooperation from both public and private organizations.

Anti-corruption measures in Hong Kong. When the British acquired Hong Kong in 1841, corruption was already a way of life as its Chinese population was "accustomed to a system where most of an official's income depended on what he was able to extort from the public." Indeed, corruption "prospered at all levels of government" and the police were the most corrupt public agency.[62] The fight against corruption began in 1898, when the first local law against corruption, the Misdemeanours Punishment Ordinance (MPO) was enacted. However, nothing was done for the next five decades until 1948, when the Prevention of Corruption Ordinance (POCO) was introduced.

The POCO's scope was broader than the MPO as the conduct made punishable by the former was extended to include legislators and employees of public agencies and private firms. Second, corruption was defined in a more comprehensive and elaborate way in the POCO as a distinction was made between corruption in office involving public officials and corrupt transactions with agents, which included civil servants and private sector employees.[63] Thirdly, the POCO increased the maximum penalty for corruption to five years' imprisonment, a fine of HK$10,000 and a "possible forfeiture of the bribe to be paid to the public body or to the agent's principal."

As was the case in Singapore, an ACB was formed in Hong Kong in 1948 as a special unit within the CID of the Royal Hong Kong Police Force (RHKPF) to handle corruption cases. The ACB was separated from the CID in 1952, but it kept its title and remained within the RHKPF.[64] In 1968, the ACB reviewed the POCO and recommended a scrutiny of the anti-corruption legislation of Singapore and Ceylon (now Sri Lanka). Accordingly, a study team visited the two countries during 1968 to examine how their anti-corruption laws worked in practice. The study team was impressed with the independence of the anti-corruption agencies in these countries and attributed Singapore's success in minimizing corruption to the CPIB's independence from the police. The knowledge gained from the study tour contributed to the enactment of the Prevention of Bribery Ordinance (POBO) on May 15, 1971.

The introduction of the POBO in May 1971 led to the upgrading of the ACB into an Anti-Corruption Office (ACO). The escape of a corruption suspect, Chief Superintendent P.F. Godber, to England in 1973 angered the public and undermined the ACO's credibility. The government responded by appointing a Commission of Inquiry chaired by Sir Alastair Blair-Kerr to investigate the circumstances which enabled Godber to leave Hong Kong and to evaluate the POBO's effectiveness. In his second report, Sir Alastair dealt with the issue of whether the anti-corruption agency should be independent of the RHKPF by stating that the arguments for keeping the ACO within the RHKPF are "largely organizational" and the arguments for removing it are "largely political and psychological." The Governor, Sir Murray MacLehose, accepted Sir Alastair's advice of considering public opinion and decided (for political and psychological reasons) to establish a new anti-corruption agency independent of the RHKPF.

Accordingly, on February 15, 1974, the ICAC was formed with the enactment of the ICAC Ordinance and was entrusted with the tasks: to root out corruption and to restore public confidence in the Government. It is independent in terms of structure, personnel, finance and power. Before the handover of Hong Kong to China in July 1997, the ICAC was directly responsible to the Governor, and its Commissioner reported directly to the former and had easy access to him. Since July 1997, the ICAC has reported directly to the Chief Executive of Hong Kong Special Administrative Region.

Conclusion: Lessons to be Learnt

Of the three patterns exhibited by these countries, the third pattern of anti-corruption legislation with an independent agency is the most effective as Singapore and Hong Kong have been more successful than the other three countries in minimizing corruption. Since low salaries, ample opportunities for corruption, and low risk of detection and punishment are the major causes of corrupt behavior, an effective anti-corruption strategy must reduce opportunities for corruption, increase the risk of detection and punishment, and improve salaries only when the country concerned can afford to do so.

Six lessons can be learnt from the experiences of the five Asian countries discussed above.

Lesson 1: Commitment of the Political Leadership is Crucial

The political leaders must be sincerely committed to the elimination of corruption. They must show exemplary conduct and adopt a modest life-style and should not be involved in corrupt practices themselves. Anyone found guilty of corruption must be punished, regardless of his position or status in society. If the "big fish" (rich and famous) are protected from prosecution for corruption, and only the "small fry" (ordinary people) are caught, the anti-corruption agency lacks credibility and will fail. For example, in China and Vietnam, corruption is a capital offence but only junior officials have been executed, while senior officials are imprisoned or not even punished.

Lesson 2: Comprehensive Strategy is More Effective

It is futile to combat corruption incrementally: comprehensive anti-corruption measures are needed to minimize corrupt behavior among civil servants and the population. More specifically, the anti-corruption legislation must close loopholes, and must be periodically reviewed to introduce relevant amendments whenever required. Singapore's POCA was amended several times to enhance its effectiveness.

Lesson 3: The Anti-Corruption Agency Must Itself be Incorruptible

This seems obvious because if the members of the anti-corruption agency are corrupt themselves, it will be ineffective in curbing corruption. To ensure the integrity of its staff, the agency must be controlled or supervised by a political leader who is himself honest and incorrupt. The agency must also be staffed by honest and competent personnel. Any member found guilty of corruption must be punished and dismissed from the civil service.

Lesson 4: The Anti-Corruption Agency Must be Removed from Police Control

The anti-corruption agency must be removed from the police as soon as possible as its location within the police prevents its from functioning effectively, especially when the police forces are corrupt. This can be seen in the case of Singapore and Hong Kong, which became more effective in fighting corruption after the ACB and ACO were removed from the police forces. In Mongolia and India, the fight against corruption has been made more difficult and less effective before of the police's involvement in anti-corruption activities.

Lesson 5: Reduce Opportunities for Corruption in Vulnerable Agencies

It is necessary to reduce or minimize the opportunities for corruption, especially in those government departments vulnerable to corrupt activities, such as customs, immigration, internal revenue, and police. These agencies should review their procedures periodically in order to reduce the opportunities for corruption. Both the CPIB in Singapore and the ICAC in Hong Kong conduct studies and provide corruption prevention advice to public and private agencies. Those civil servants found guilty of corruption should be promptly and severely punished to act as a deterrent for others bent on such behavior.

Lesson 6: Reduce Corruption by Raising Salaries if Country Can Afford to do so

Finally, it is important to reduce the incentive for corruption among public officials by ensuring that their salaries and fringe benefits are competitive with the private sector. Other things being equal, a civil servant or political leader will be more vulnerable to corruption if his salary is low, or not commensurate with his position and responsibilities. However, governments might not be able to raise salaries substantially unless there is economic growth and adequate financial resources.

Notes

1. Gunnar Myrdal, *Asian Drama: An Inquiry into the Poverty of Nations*, Vol. II (New York: Twentieth Century Fund, 1968), pp. 938–939.
2. See for examples: Arnold J. Heidenheimer, Michael Johnston and Victor T. LeVine (eds.), *Political Corruption: A Handbook* (New Brunswick: Transaction Publishers, 1989); Michael Levi and David Nelken (eds.), *The Corruption of Politics and the Politics of Corruption* (Oxford: Blackwell Publishers, 1996); Walter Little and Eduardo Posada-Carbo (eds.), *Political Corruption in Europe and Latin America* (Basingstoke: Macmillan Press, 1996); Kimberly Ann Elliott (ed.), *Corruption and the Global Economy* (Washington, D.C.: Institute for International Economics, 1997); Paul Heywood (ed.), *Political Corruption* (Oxford: Blackwell Publishers, 1997); and Mark Robinson (ed.), *Corruption and Development* (London: Frank Cass Publishers, 1998).
3. Robert S. Leiken, "Controlling the Global Corruption Epidemic," *Foreign Policy*, No. 105 (Winter 1996–97), p. 58.
4. Aparisim Ghosh, et al. "Corruption: Reform's Dark Side," *Far Eastern Economic Review*, March 20, 1997, p. 18.
5. *The Fight Against Corruption: Is the Tide Now Turning? Transparency International Report 1997* (Berlin: Transparency International, 1997), p. 65.
6. *Combating Corruption: Are lasting solutions emerging? Transparency International Report 1998* (Berlin: Transparency International, 1998), p. 195.
7. See "The Corruption Perception Index" at *http://www.transparency.de/documents/cpi/index.htm* for the 1998 CPI.
8. *Fighting Corruption to Improve Governance* (New York: United Nations Development Programme, 1999), p. 7.
9. This distinction was introduced by Gerald E. Caiden in his article, "Public Maladministration and Bureaucratic Corruption," *Hong Kong Journal of Public Administration*, Vol. 3, No. 1 (June 1981), pp. 58–62.
10. Leslie Palmier, *The Control of Bureaucratic Corruption: Case Studies in Asia* (New Delhi: Allied Publishers, 1985), pp. 271–272, emphasis added.
11. Ibid., pp. 2, 6.
12. Paulo Mauro, *Why Worry about Corruption?* (Washington, D.C.: International Monetary Fund, 1997), p. 5.
13. Clive Day, *The Dutch in Java* (London: 1966), pp. 100–103.
14. J.A.C. Mackie, "The Commission of Four Report on Corruption," *Bulletin of Indonesian Economic Studies*, Vol. 6, No. 3 (1970), pp. 87–88.
15. Meredith Woo-Cummings, "Developmental Bureaucracy in Comparative Perspective: The Evolution of the Korean Civil Service," in Hyung-Ki Kim, *et al.*, *The Japanese Civil Service and Economic Development: Catalysts of Change* (Oxford: Clarendon Press, 1995), pp. 455–456.
16. Jong S. Jun and Jae Poong Yoon, "Korean Public Administration at a Crossroads: Culture, Development and Change," in Ahmed S. Huque et al. (eds.), *Public Administration in the NICs: Challenges and Accomplishments* (Basingstoke: Macmillan Press, 1996), p. 107.
17. Kasem Suwanagul, "The Civil Service of Thailand," (Ph.D. dissertation, New York University, 1962), pp. 79–80.

18. Onofre D. Corpuz, *The Bureaucracy in the Philippines* (Quezon City: Institute of Public Administration, University of the Philippines, 1957), p. 129.
19. Jon S.T. Quah, "Bureaucratic Corruption in the ASEAN Countries: A Comparative Analysis of Their Anti-Corruption Strategies," *Journal of Southeast Asian Studies*, Vol. 13, No. 1 (March 1983), p. 159.
20. Perfecto L. Padilla, "Low Salary Grades, Income-Augmentation Schemes and the Merit Principle," in Proserpina Domingo Tapales and Nestor N. Pilar (eds.), *Public Administration by the Year 2000: Looking Back into Future* (Quezon City: College of Public Administration, University of the Philippines, 1995), pp. 195–202, and 206.
21. Jon S.T. Quah, "Police Corruption in Singapore: An Analysis of its Forms, Extent and Causes," *Singapore Police Journal*, Vol. 10, No. 1 (January 1979), p. 28.
22. *Straits Times*, October 4, 1887, quoted in ibid., p. 29.
23. Abhijit Banerjee, "Can Anything Be Done About Corruption?" in M.G. Quibria and J. Malcolm Dowling (eds.), *Current Issues in Economic Development: An Asian Perspective* (Hong Kong: Oxford University Press for the Asian Development Bank, 1996), p. 110.
24. David J. Gould and Jose A. Amaro-Reyes, *The Effects of Corruption on Administrative Performance: Illustrations from Developing Countries* (Washington, D.C.: World Bank Staff Working Papers No. 580, 1983), p. 17.
25. Bertrand de Speville, *Hong Kong: Policy Initiatives Against Corruption* (Paris: Organisation for Economic Co-operation and Development, 1997), p. 14.
26. Donald P. Warwick, "The Effectiveness of the Indonesian Civil Service," *Southeast Asian Journal of Social Science*, Vol. 15, No. 2 (1987), p. 43.
27. *The Knapp Commission Report on Police Corruption* (New York: George Braziller, 1972), pp. 67–68.
28. Palmier, *The Control of Bureaucratic Corruption*, pp. 179–181.
29. Syed Hussein Alatas, *Corruption: Its Nature, Causes and Functions* (Kuala Lumpur: S. Abdul Majeed, 1991), p. 121.
30. *Straits Times*, August 1, 1998, p. 14.
31. Hilton Root, "Corruption in China: Has it Become Systemic?" *Asian Survey*, Vol. 36, No. 8 (August 1996), p. 752.
32. Mohammad Mohabbat Khan, *Administrative Reforms in Bangladesh* (New Delhi: South Asian Publishers, 1998), pp. 35, 36.
33. Palmier, *The Control of Bureaucratic Corruption*, p. 279.
34. *Straits Times*, January 27, 1987, p. 11, quoted in Jon S.T. Quah, "Corruption in Asia with special reference to Singapore: Patterns and Consequences," *Asian Journal of Public Administration*, Vol. 10, No. 1 (June 1988), p. 93.
35. Palmier, *The Control of Bureaucratic Corruption*, p. 279.
36. C.V. Narasimhan, "Prevention of Corruption: Towards Effective Enforcement," in S. Guhan and Samuel Paul (eds.), *Corruption in India: Agenda for Action* (New Delhi: Vision Books, 1997), pp. 251–252.
37. The following discussion of Mongolia's anti-corruption strategy is based on Jon S.T. Quah, "Combating Corruption in Mongolia: Problems and Prospects," (Paper presented at the Public Administration and Development Jubilee Conference at St. Anne's College, Oxford University 12–14 April, 1999), pp. 19–22.
38. Stephanie McPhail, *Developing Mongolia's Legal Framework: A Needs Analysis* (Manila: Asian Development Bank, 1995), pp. 49–50.
39. Ibid., p. 38.
40. The following discussion of anti-corruption initiatives in India is based on Palmier, *The Control of Bureaucratic Corruption*, pp. 13–32.

532   **Political Corruption**

41. The following discussion is based on Narasimhan, "Prevention of Corruption," pp. 255–265.
42. Palmier, *The Control of Bureaucratic Corruption*, p. 52.
43. Narasimhan, "Prevention of Corruption," p. 266.
44. Ma. Concepcion P. Alfiler, "Administrative Measures against Bureaucratic Corruption: The Philippine Experience," *Philippine Journal of Public Administration*, Vol. 23, Nos. 3 & 4 (July-October 1979), pp. 324–325.
45. Gabriel U. Iglesias, "The Passage of the Anti-Graft Law," in Raul P. De Guzman (ed.), *Patterns in Decision-Making: Case Studies in Philippine Public Administration* (Manila: College of Public Administration, University of the Philippines, 1963), pp. 17–68.
46. Alfiler, "Administrative Measures against Bureaucratic Corruption," pp. 326–327.
47. Quah, "Bureaucratic Corruption in the ASEAN Countries," pp. 168–169.
48. Amelia Varela, "Different Faces of Filipino Administrative Culture," in Proserpina Domingo Tapales and Nestor N. Pilar (eds.), *Public Administration by the Year 2000: Looking Back into the Future* (Quezon City: College of Public Administration, University of the Philippines, 1995), p. 174.
49. "The *Sandiganbayan* and *Tanodbayan* Decrees," *Philippine Journal of Public Administration*, Vol. 23, Nos. 3 & 4 (July-October 1979), pp. 387–388, 402.
50. Varela, "Different Faces of Filipino Administrative Culture," p. 174.
51. David G. Timberman, *A Changeless Land: Continuity and Charge in Philippine Politics* (Singapore: Institute of Southeast Asian Studies, 1991), pp. 233–234; quotation from p. 235.
52. This discussion is based on Cecile C.A. Balgos, "Ombudsman," in Sheila S. Coronel (ed.), *Pork and Other Perks: Corruption and Governance in the Philippines* (Metro Manila: Philippine Center for Investigative Journalism, 1998), pp. 247, 248, 250–251.
53. Ibid., pp. 267–268.
54. Jon S.T. Quah, "Controlling Corruption in City-States: A Comparative Study of Hong Kong and Singapore," *Crime, Law and Social Change*, Vol. 22 (1995), p. 393.
55. Quah, "Bureaucratic Corruption in the ASEAN Countries," pp. 161–162.
56. Quah, "Controlling Corruption in City-States," pp. 393–394.
57. Jon S.T. Quah, "Singapore's Experience in Curbing Corruption," in Arnold J. Heidenheimer, Michael Johnston and Victor T. LeVine (eds.), *Political Corruption: A Handbook* (New Brunswick: Transaction Publishers, 1989), p. 842.
58. Republic of Singapore, *Economic Survey of Singapore 1985* (Singapore: Ministry of Trade and Industry, 1986), p. ix.
59. The fine was increased by 10 times to S$100,000 in 1989. See ibid., p. 4.
60. For details of these amendments, see Quah, "Controlling Corruption in City-States," pp. 395–396.
61. *The Corrupt Practices Investigation Bureau* (Singapore: CPIB, 1990), p. 2.
62. Palmier, *The Control of Bureaucratic Corruption*, p. 123.
63. This discussion is based on Hsin-Chi Kuan, "Anti-Corruption Legislation in Hong Kong–A History," in Rance P.L. Lee (ed.), *Corruption and Its Control in Hong Kong* (Hong Kong: The Chinese University Press, 1981), pp. 20–24.
64. H.J. Lethbridge, *Hard Graft in Hong Kong: Scandal, Corruption, the ICAC* (Hong Kong: Oxford University Press, 1985), p. 87.

Part IX

REACTIONS TO CORRUPTION IN AUTHORITARIAN REGIMES

Introduction to Part IX

How do the forms of political corruption prevalent in autocratic regimes differ from those that are found in systems with competing political parties and elites? In this chapter, corruption experiences in a number of large countries are examined for periods during which they were governed as single-party dictatorships. Two articles analyze corruption phenomena in settings where territorially large states are governed by centralized Communist parties, the Soviet Union in the late 1970s and the People's Republic of China during more recent years, which saw a transition to a more market oriented economy while one-party-rule was kept in place. The comparative analyses of corruption experiences is undertaken for countries that underwent a more complete transition in both their economies and their political systems, such as in post-communist countries of Central and Eastern Europe. The workings of corruption in a system where private property and a relatively free market was retained after political dictatorship had been installed is looked at in the fourth article dealing with Nazi Germany.

Since policy making influence is foreclosed to all ordinary citizens in these systems, their efforts to bend the rules are directed towards influencing the output side of politics, that is the administration. DiFranceisco and Gitelman base their study of corruption in the Soviet Union on interviews with over 1,000 Soviet emigrés in the 1970s, providing insights into the attitudinal and behavioral aspects of elements in the Soviet political culture which nurtured and encouraged widespread corruption. The authors' findings suggest that the dominant social ethos was one of private self-interest. Experiences seem to have dictated a preference for informal access to and influence on individual bureaucrats and a general disdain for formal and legalistic procedures and norms. Thus, *blat* (bribes and other kinds of side payments) and *proteksiia* (personal cultivation and use of influential people) were considered normal ways of extracting preferences, favors, or even ordinary services from the official system. This covert participation is seen as an indicator for a syncretic political culture, adapting traditional clientelistic and pre-revolutionary modes of citizen-state relationship to institutions that strained to keep a democratic appearance on the surface while methods to ameliorate a centralized tsarist regime were carried over to the Communist one.

535

Such ritualistic participation has now all but vanished since the demise of Communism in Eastern Europe, but the means of covert participation seem to have been retained if not strengthened in the post-communist systems described by William L. Miller and his co-authors in the second selection. They aim at discerning varying patterns of low-level bureaucratic corruption ordinary citizens face on a daily basis in the Czech Republic, Slovakia, Bulgaria, and the Ukraine during the 1990s. The latter share most of the historical experiences of what has been described for Russia, which the authors suggest as one reason why corruption is still a much greater problem in the Ukraine than in the Czech Republic,— the "least" corrupt of the four countries, with Slovakia ranking second and Bulgaria third. The authors arrive at these results through a series of focus group discussions, in-depth interviews, public opinion surveys in the respective countries and a fruitful mix of qualitative and quantitative analyses of their empirical data. Thus it is only the Czechs feeling that their new post-communist political and economic system is less corrupt than the old communist one, whereas the analysis for the Ukraine and Bulgaria suggests that the behavior of officials under the post-communist regime is much worse. The four countries furthered the transformation process with varying intensity and continuation of old elites. They argue that the opportunities for corruption had been greatly increased by privatization, economic chaos, and a dismantled value system. Thus *blat* (contacts/influence) survived mainly in the upper *nomenklatura* that turned into quasi-criminal networks, and bribes superseded *blat* in the lower bureaucratic level as a crude method of income generation and rent-seeking. This is also reflected by the methods citizens would use to obtain a bureaucratic decision. In the Ukraine 42 percent suggested using a bribe, while only 26 percent of Czechs would follow that strategy.

Opportunities for corruption amid a crumbling value system are examined by Yufan Hao and Michael Johnston for the People's Republic of China, and diagnosed as subject to ills similar to those of the transition countries in Central and Eastern Europe. This applied especially since decentralization and reforms of the planned economy in the late 1980s and early 1990s, which not only legitimized private wealth but also brought into being many markets that are exploited by both businessmen and bureaucrats alike. Here as there corruption seems to benefit the well-connected and newly rich and *guanxi* (networks of personal connections), like *blat* in the Ukraine, serves the elites while ordinary citizens have to resort to techniques of crude bribery. As Hao and Johnston point out in chapter 31, China has experienced a shift of underlying motives and venues of corruption, which they see as having changed from a power oriented "game" of the political elite into a profit oriented means of wide spread rent-seeking even for low level bureaucrats. Both the scope and scale of public corruption seems to have increased, leading also to strong public reactions as is seen in the student demonstration in Tiananmen

Square in 1989 where corruption was also a prominent issue. The 1990s also witnessed the strengthening of the legal infrastructure and the rule of law as a counter measure to keep rampant corruption in check, thus acknowledging corruption as a structural problem. This represents a shift away from the mass campaigns the Chinese government conducted in periodic bouts of cleansing all kinds of social wrongs since the 1950s, pillorying and publicly punishing individual offenders as a deterrent for the masses.

A technique also widely practiced by other authoritarian regimes the use of show trials and violent cleansing raids. Whether used as pretexts for the government to rid itself of political competitors outside or within the dictatorial system, to legitimize their seizing of power, or to fight "genuine" corruption, these were part of the whole gamut of anti-corruption rhetoric and practices Angermund describes for Nazi Germany. Even building a whole system of support and loyalties among intra-party factions and rival party chiefs through corruption or the tolerance thereof seems to have been a means to retain absolute power of the Nazi leadership, thus forming a structural and propping element of the Nazi regime itself. Though many features shown in the other dictatorial systems did not have the time to fully mature, given the much briefer period of rule one half of which was under war-time conditions, they were present as well.

29

Soviet Political Culture and Modes
of Covert Influence

Wayne DiFranceisco and Zvi Gitelman

. . . if Soviet political relationships are as we shall describe them, then conventional notions of Soviet political culture need to be revised. Neither the "parochial-subject-participant" trichotomy developed by Almond and Verba (1963), nor the idea of a "subject-participatory" (Barghoorn, 1972. p. 25) political culture, where structures are designed for participation but the operative culture seems to treat the citizen as a subject, apply accurately to the Soviet case. This is not a subject political culture marginally affected by participatory institutions because there is a meaningful form of participation, but it takes place either outside the nominally participatory institutions, or within those institutions but in nonprescribed ways. But because this participation is limited to affecting political outputs that concern the individual directly, it would be misleading to equate the Soviet kind of political culture with those that are conventionally thought of as largely participant. Moreover, the Russian-Soviet case (like others, especially in the Third World) demonstrates that there is no ineluctable progression from parochial to subject to participant political cultures. The Soviet system, like many others, is syncretic, adapting traditional clientelist modes to what appear to be institutions for democratic participation.

One might expect a radical revolutionary regime not to adapt but to eliminate completely traditional political modes. But as Jowitt (1974) points out,

Source: Wayne DiFranceisco and Zvi Gitelman, "Soviet Political Culture and 'Covert Participation' in Policy Implementation," *American Political Science Review,* 78, 3 (1984), 603–21. By permission of the authors and publisher.

Marxist-Leninist elites are induced by their ideology to select a set of system-building institutions which, ironically, reinforce traditional values and orientations toward politics. Jowitt cites three of these structural components of communist system building and their ramifications for political beliefs at the mass level. The first component, the "dictatorship of the proletariat," with its stress on discipline, coercion, and party control of both public and private sectors of the society, preserves much of the essence of traditional authority relationships—a bifurcation of society into the elite and a mistrusted populace. The second element involves the Leninist-Stalinist "commanding-heights" formula for development and a phenomenon that Jowitt (p. 1175) labels "revolutionary laissez-faire." Under this rubric, the emphasis is on rapid economic progress and mobilization such that the regime focuses on a rather limited set of priority areas, leaving vast segments of the society untransformed. "In return for performance in priority sectors. . . members of society are 'allowed' to manipulate non-priority sectors for their private benefit." This lack of development in nonpriority sectors allows, as we shall see in the Soviet case, for the perpetuation of traditional clientelistic orientations toward officials, i.e., the use of *blat* (pull) or *sviazy* (connections) or even bribery. It is this pattern of interactions with public officials and institutions that we label covert participation.

A third component of Leninist system-building regimes is the elites' production mentality. The leadership believes that political culture change will inevitably follow transformation in social and economic spheres, which in practice means that the party tends to deemphasize cultural issues except where its primary goals of socioeconomic development are affected. Of course, the Soviet Union has long passed the system-building stage, and its intensive and extensive efforts at political socialization have narrowed the gap between political structures and political culture. (Even among our sample of emigres described below, 47 percent acknowledge that they read agitation-propaganda material in the USSR, at least some of the time.)

Our observations on the nature of political participation and its implications for Soviet culture are based on Soviet writings and on our interviews with recent Soviet emigres. These observations lead us to conclude that the way Soviet people relate to the political administrative system is to go through the motions of participation in the nominally democratic process of making decisions, but to put far more serious effort into trying to influence the way decisions are implemented. Thus the view of Soviet political culture as subject or subject-participant is misleading. Soviet political culture is neither a democratic nor a subject one, but an amalgam of traditional, pre-revolutionary modes of citizen-state relations and a superstructure of participatory institutions that superficially resemble those of Western democracies in many respects.

Sample and Method

A group of 1,161 ex-Soviet citizens who left the USSR from 1977 through 1980 were interviewed during 1980–1981 in Israel (n = 590), the Federal Republic of Germany *(n =* 100) and the United States (n = 471). The sample was drawn as a quota, nonprobability sample, in line with hypotheses that led to a certain distribution of age, sex, education, nationality, and republic of residence. On some variables, such as age and sex, the proportions in the sample approximate those in the Soviet adult population rather closely. On the other hand, nearly half the respondents have had higher education (approximately 40 percent of all Soviet immigrants to Israel and the United States have come with higher education), 38 percent had secondary education, and only 15 percent had grade school education or less. Seventy-seven percent, or 889 people, had been registered as Jews on their internal Soviet passports, 129 as Russians, 98 as Germans, 18 as Ukrainians, and 27 as other nationalities.

Men and women are quite evenly distributed in age and regional categories, but men dominate blue collar and women white collar occupations, despite very similar educational levels. (Among the sample, 48 percent of the men and 46 percent of the women have higher education.) Educational levels are highest among those from the RSFSR, and, from the ethnic groups, among the Russians; 69 percent of the former and 72 percent of the latter have some higher education. The lowest educational levels are found among people from Central Asia (only 18 percent have higher education) and from Moldavia (23 percent). These people were interviewed in Russian or Georgian by native speakers. There were remarkably few refusals to be interviewed, although the average interview lasted between two and three hours. In addition to the standard questionnaire administered to the entire group, nearly 60 in-depth interviews were conducted with people who had been employees of the Soviet government agencies we inquired about, or who seemed to have unusually extensive knowledge about how citizens and government agencies operated in their respective republics.

The Problem of Bias

It cannot be claimed that the results obtained from any emigre sample are generalizable to the population in the Soviet Union, because not only are the emigres demographically different from the population as a whole, but presumably their attitudes and assessments are different as well. Having chosen to leave the USSR, it is reasonable to assume that they were less pleased with the system than those who stayed behind. While accepting the inadmissibility of generalizing easily from the emigre to the original population, the assumption of emigre bias can be exaggerated. . . . Lacking any reliable data on the

Table 29.1
Best Way to Influence a Government Decision *(n* = 1,161)

Connections	Letters	Group	Party	Protest Demonstration	None	NR
35.5	4.5	9.9	5.9	3.4	25.8	15.2

Text of question: If a group of Soviet people were trying to influence some government decision, which way would be most effective?

Soviet population's attitude toward the system, it cannot be assumed that the attitudes of the emigres are significantly more hostile, and in our sample, at least, we see that alienation from the political system was by no means the primary motivation for leaving it. Moreover, as in other emigre studies our respondents demonstrated considerable support for many Soviet institutions and practices. One can also assume that whatever biases may be present in the sample as a whole, they are distributed fairly uniformly across population subgroups. Therefore, we anticipate that any differences observed across the subgroup strata are similar to those characterizing the same groups within the Soviet population. . . .

In any case, even alienated citizens have no choice but to participate in many ways. They are not able to avoid some of the ritualistic forms of participation, such as voting, attending meetings, joining trade unions and, usually, the Komsomol. Because the state controls so many basic necessities, they must resort to official agencies, if only for the satisfaction of their private needs. The crucial question for us then becomes not whether they participate, but how they do so, and in this there seems no prima facie reason for thinking that they differ substantially from those who did not leave the country. . . .

The data presented in table 29.1 further illustrate the unique aspects of Soviet political activity and hint at the widespread persistence of clientelism in the political culture. Table 29.1 lists the responses of the emigres to a question about "the best way to influence a Soviet government decision." Despite the inclusion of the word "group" in the question, fewer than 10 percent mentioned forming an interest group as a viable option. The combined frequencies for officially sanctioned methods of interest articulation— "writing letters to officials" and "exerting influence through the Party"— account for only 10.4 percent of the respondents. The modal response is "personal or family connections *(sviazy)*," at 35.5 percent. It seems likely that these individuals interpreted the phrase, "government decision," in terms of its implementation or output aspects—for example, the disposition of an individual case—and not in the much broader sense of policymaking, a conversion function, for which *sviazy* would be inappropriate. These findings fit the proposition stated above, that the Soviet citizen tends to avoid or denigrate cooperative activity and formal channels of interest articulation. Where he does participate he orients himself toward a specific individual or agency in an informal, and often covert, manner.

Politics on the Output Side

Thus far we have discussed two types of participation: ritualistic participation and citizen-initiated contacts with people who hold positions in policymaking institutions. In neither case is there much expectation of input into policymaking, but in the second there is some hope that action will be taken to benefit the individual, just as in the United States a congressman is asked to render constituency service without trying to influence legislation. Soviet citizens are more oriented toward the administrative side of the system. They are "subject competent," but not in the way described by Almond and Verba, that is, trying to get legally prescribed, proper treatment. According to Almond and Verba (1963, p. 162), the competent subject obeys the law, does not help shape it, and "if he is competent, he knows the law, knows what he must do, and what is due him." In the Soviet system, however, the "competent subject" is not content to demand fair play and the universal application of the law, for he does not expect that of the system. Rather he takes matters into his own hands when he is convinced that the routine workings of the system will not automatically confer upon him the benefits he desires. He does this by approaching those who implement policy, not those who make it, and by following traditional ways of handling administrators, adapted to the modern Soviet political system. "Thus a premium is placed on informal adaptive mechanisms . . . that allow for some stability and certainty in response to what is often perceived as an arbitrary and threatening regime." These mechanisms "obstruct the development of a political culture based on overt, public, and cooperative relationships. Instead they reinforce the traditional community and regime political cultures with their stress on covert, personalized, hierarchical relationships involving complicity rather than public agreements" (Jowitt, 1974, p.1183). It may well be that the Soviet development process has actually reinforced clientelistic cultural patterns. By raising society's overall level of education to facilitate modernization, by focusing on heavy industry to the detriment of the individual's standard of living, and by failing to develop meaningful citizen participation and emotional attachment to the policymaking process, the communist leadership has created a large number of "socialist entrepreneurs" who are highly capable of and heavily predisposed toward working nonpriority public sectors for their own benefit. Our data suggest that Soviet citizens are open to entering into informal or even illegal interactions with officials. For example, we find that three-quarters of our respondents believe that at least half of the Soviet officials "derive material benefit from citizens who approach them for help," and

60 percent believe that a bribe could persuade a policeman to overlook a minor traffic violation. Bribery is not a last resort or an activity limited to society's marginal elements, but seems to be accepted by a large number of people as a common way of handling difficult situations. We posed an open-ended question to our respondents: "If a government official clearly lied to you or refused to give what you had coming to you, what would be the best way of making him tell the truth or giving you what was due you?" The modal response was to "offer him a gift," with 46 percent of the total sample mentioning this, and only 31 percent—the next largest group—suggesting an appeal to the official's superior. A second open question was, "What is the main precondition for success in life in the USSR?" Two responses were coded, with 42 percent and 64 percent mentioning it either first or second. Clearly, informal, and even illegal, means are those that immediately suggest themselves to Soviet people who have to interact with the state bureaucracy.

Working the Output Side

How Soviet citizens attempt to influence actively the implementation of policy seems to vary according to two factors: their own education and the particular agency involved. Regional differences are not as great as might be supposed. Sex and age are not important in differentiating styles of confronting and dealing with the bureaucracy. The influence of education is seen in responses to the question, "Which type of government official would you prefer—the one who treats everyone equally regardless of circumstances or the one who treats each case individually, taking account of its special characteristics?"

The preference of the most educated people for a case-by-case differentiation is striking. As an engineer from Kharkov expressed it, "Taking each case on its own merits means that the opportunity to use *blat* (pull) or *znakomstvo* (connections) is present, and that's the only way to survive in the USSR. In the United States, on the other hand, I prefer that state employees treat everyone the same." In the country of immigration, in other words, the engineer felt disadvantaged vis-à-vis the rest of the population and no longer had confidence in his ability to swing things his way in bureaucratic encounters. But in the Soviet Union educated people may think their education gives them status greater than that conferred on the bureaucrat by his position. It also gives them *savoir faire,* which they can use to their advantage. Less-educated people have no such illusions. They defer to the status conferred on the official by his position, making no judgments about the person. The more educated look at the individual and figure they can handle him because they are better educated; the less educated look at the position and are not prepared to challenge it.

However, this does not mean that they will meekly accept whatever fate, speaking through the bureaucrat, will ordain. Many people, irrespective of their educational background, try to influence the implementation of policy and the decisions of administrators, although the more educated are more likely to take an activist posture even in rigid bureaucracies such as the armed forces.

But the tactics of the more and less educated differ. Less-educated people are more inclined to bribery, whereas more-educated ones will use personal connections to extract what they want from a bureaucracy. Obviously, the highly educated are more likely to know people in high places, how to get to them, and how to approach them. This tactical difference has probably been the pattern in Russia and elsewhere for centuries; the best that the peasant could do to gain the favor of the all-mighty official was to bring him a chicken or some moonshine, whereas the educated and the wealthy were more likely to mix socially with the official and, probably, his superiors.

It is also quite clear that different agencies evoke different kinds of behavior on the part of the clients, probably not because of differences in the structure and personnel of the agencies so much as differences in the availability and nature of the services they provide, and in the importance they have been assigned by the regime.

In this study we found three categories of administrative agencies. The first category includes bureaucracies toward which citizen initiative is either unnecessary, because the agency will most likely produce the desired output without special efforts by the client, or it is useless, because the agency will not be responsive to such efforts. The great majority of respondents who had personal experience with pension agencies (*gorsobes*, *raisobes*) did not find it necessary to undertake any extraordinary initiatives in order to receive their pensions (although some "improved" their pensions by various means). Asked what a person should do if he did not receive a pension to which he was entitled, more than half the respondents said that a letter to a higher authority should suffice. Another 20 percent recommended that the person simply wait patiently, for he would surely get the pension. There was also widespread agreement that in the armed forces it would be useless to try to change one's assignment and to get around orders.

Table 29.2
Bureaucratic Style Preferred by Education (*n* = 1,113)

	Grade School %	Secondary %	Higher %
Equal treatment	21.9	14.8	5.9
Sometimes equal, sometimes differentiated	30.9	24.7	17.4
Differentiated	36.5	55.7	73.8
Don't know, no answer	10.7	4.8	3.0

Housing falls into a second category. Although some accept the routine workings of the official housing agencies, others try to influence those workings by illegal means, and still others choose to ignore the official agencies and opt for private, legal solutions to their housing problems.

The third category of agency includes admissions committees in higher educational institutions, hiring departments of enterprises, and *raspredelenie* commissions, whose job it is to assign higher education graduates to their first post. In these institutions, it is widely felt, the routine workings of the system were highly unlikely to produce the desired result without a special "push" by the citizen which might involve semilegal or illegal measures. Thus, two-thirds of the respondents suggested bribery or using connections (*sviazy*) to avoid an undesirable job assignment, and three-quarters suggested the same tactics for gaining admission to a university or institute of higher education.

We arrived at this categorization partially on the basis of a battery of five open-ended questions consisting of hypothetical situations that asked what a (third) person could do in response to a negative decision by each of five[1] Soviet institutions. Paraphrased versions of these questions are listed below.

Soviet Army. How could a Soviet Army officer in 1980, stationed in a good staff position in Leningrad, avoid being transferred to a unit headed for Afghanistan?

Pensions. What should a person do if he is entitled to a pension, has not received it, and is told by officials to "be patient"?

Table 29.3
Actions Suggested by Respondents (%) (*n* = 1,161)

	Bribery	Connections[a]	Legal or Semi-Legal	Other	Nothing/ Passive[b]
Soviet army	2.9	11.1	10.2[c]	3.6	72.2
Raspredelenie	19.6	37.6	10.5[d]	11.6	20.6
University admissions committee	29.4	32.7	13.8[e]	3.5	20.6
Housing authority (*zhilotdel*)	18.4	14.1	39.5[f]	5.3	22.7

a   includes both *protektsiia* (patronage) and *sviazy* (connections).
b   Those who responded that one could do nothing, or who could not think of anything to do.
c   "Threaten to resign from the army" or "plead illness or family problems."
d   "Marry someone with the right of residence in one's home town" or "find a medical excuse."
e   "Appeal to the committee," "apply to a different school," or "engage a private tutor."
f   "Enter a cooperative," "exchange apartments with someone," or "buy a private apartment."

Raspredelenie (assignment commission). What should a person do if he is assigned to work in a remote area after graduating from an institution of higher education?

University Admissions Committee. What should a woman do who wants to get her mediocre son into the mathematics department of a university?

Zhilotdel (local housing authority). What should a person do to get a better apartment, if the one he has is, by legal standards, large enough?

We observed that few respondents felt it advisable to resort to manipulative tactics in dealing with the army, but a large proportion suggested covert measures in dealing with job assignments, university admissions, and housing. Moreover, approximately 80 percent of the respondents were in the "active" range of the three variables, suggesting that regime control of these sectors is relatively lax and more willing to tolerate flexibility in them. (As we shall see, there are legal alternatives for those who fail to obtain satisfactory housing, which explains the relatively low proportion of responses in the covert range regarding housing.)

The final portion of our data analysis illustrates the combined impact of structure and education on the preferred strategy of the respondents. The findings in table 29.4 follow fairly closely from our predictions. First, the higher one's education, the greater his or her sense of competence and resulting activity vis-à-vis Soviet allocative structures. This can be discerned from a glance at the column headed "passive": in every administrative setting there is a uniform decline in passivity with increasing levels of education. However, the results clearly indicate that the more powerful and strategically located is the institution, the less is the perceived opportunity to influence that institution by any means, regardless of one's social status. This is indicated by the contrast between the frequencies for the military and those for the other bureaucratic agencies.

There is ample evidence to confirm our hypothesis that the modern Soviet system has tended to reinforce traditional clientelistic orientations toward the structures of government. Soviet citizens defer to the status or power of an official and his agency as much for pragmatic as for normative reasons. Where a bureaucratic encounter can be exploited for private gain, the "competent" Soviet citizen, particularly if he or she is highly skilled and educated, will attempt to do so. There appears to be less confidence in legal rules and procedures as a means of extracting services from the state, as demonstrated by the fact that for every institution in table 29.4 except the housing authority, to which legal alternatives exist, the proportions of respondents suggesting covert tactics (bribes and connections) are higher than any other type of approach. It should be also pointed out that all of the legal avenues suggested in regard to housing were private (enter a cooperative or exchange apartments) rather than public solutions.

The data also confirm that, although covert forms of participation appeal

Table 28.4
Actions suggested by Respondents, by Education (%) (n = 1,161)

	Bribery	Connections	Legal/ Semi-Legal	Other	Nothing/ Passive
Soviet army					
Primary or less	2.2	6.7	5.1	2.2	83.7
Secondary	3.7	8.2	8.2	3.9	76.0
Some college	2.2	14.9	13.4	3.9	65.3
Raspredelenie					
Primary or less	22.5	18.5	8.4	6.2	44.4
Secondary	22.1	37.7	9.6	8.2	22.4
Some college	16.7	43.9	11.9	16.1	11.4
College admissions					
Primary or less	34.8	15.7	6.2	4.5	38.8
Secondary	32.2	33.6	11.0	3.2	20.1
Some college	25.3	37.6	18.5	3.5	15.0
Housing agency					
Primary or less	19.7	9.6	34.3	7.3	29.2
Secondary	18.5	11.6	41.6	5.9	22.4
Some college	18.0	17.6	39.6	4.0	20.7

to all social classes in the Soviet Union, different educational groups have different preferences for strategies of influence. Bribery is (of necessity) the chosen method of the less educated, whereas *blat* is the favored instrument of the intelligentsia. In fact, for every institution, the college-educated typically outdistanced the low-status respondents in all spheres of specified activity *except bribery.* This finding confirms our hypothesis about the higher level of skills and resources available to upper-status individuals and their more expansive repertoires of tactics for pulling the right strings in their dealings with the bureaucracy.

One must exercise caution in interpreting these data, since some of the hypothetical stories we presented to the respondents more often than not involve a character who is trying to get something to which he or she is not legally entitled in the first place. One could argue that, as such, they almost force the respondents to suggest illicit and unethical activities. On the other hand, the high rate of passive responses toward the military, in contrast to the willingness of the emigres to recommend covert and manipulative tactics with respect to the other institutions, supports the decision to utilize these variables in the analysis. Furthermore, in a total of 4,644 responses to the four questions, there was not a single instance in which a former Soviet suggested that the character in the situation attempt individually or in a group to effect a change in the policy or procedure, thus corroborating the previous evidence that Soviet citizens concede that policymaking itself is a foregone conclusion. They are inclined instead to concentrate their efforts at political influence in the appropriate output sectors.

We turn now to the actual tactics used by citizens to extract their desiderata from the institutions, and observe how the nature of the institution influences the ways in which citizens will approach it. The agencies we investigated included those dealing with housing, employment, pensions, admission to higher education, the police and armed forces. Soviet sources provide ample evidence that the pension agencies are plagued by poorly trained personnel and inefficient procedures, and yet we find that our respondents evaluate the agency and its personnel favorably, and that the great majority see no need to resort to any special tactics in order to receive their pensions. The apparent paradox is explained by the fact that almost all who are entitled to pensions receive them, whereas the housing problem is perhaps the most difficult one in the daily life of the Soviet citizen. Even though the USSR has been building 2.2 million housing units annually since 1957, in the mid-1970s the average per-capita living space in urban areas was only 8 square meters (10 in Moscow). An estimated 30 percent of urban households still shared apartments, and it is not uncommon for people to wait as long as 10 years to get an apartment (Morton, 1980, pp 235–236). Even getting on the list is a problem, as only those with less than nine square meters of living space (a minimum standard set in the 1920s) are eligible. Twenty percent of our respondents had been on a waiting list for an apartment.

The scramble to obtain housing is fairly general, and not a few short stories, feuilletons, and even novels have been written on the subject. Small wonder that the most imaginative tactics are devised to obtain even the most modest apartments. An informant who worked in two housing administrations in Moscow in the late 1940s and 1950s, when housing was especially short, notes that bribery to obtain an apartment was so widespread that "people did not ask each other 'did you give' but only 'how much.'" Party officials, those with "responsible posts," those who had other favors to trade or simply had relatives and friends working in the housing administration were advantaged in the struggle for a dwelling. Although the situation has improved markedly in recent decades, nearly two-thirds of our respondents report that they tried to advance their position on the waiting list, either through appealing to a higher Soviet organ or, less frequently, using illegal tactics. The intervention of one's supervisor at work is often sought. Of those who went through the appeal process ($n = 129$), just over half reported that the appeal was successful and they obtained the apartment. Those who do not appeal successfully use other tactics and enter what Morton (1980) calls the "subsidiary housing market" (private rentals, cooperatives, exchanges of apartments and private houses). Exchanging apartments is the remedy most often prescribed by our respondents for those who have been unsuccessful in getting one from the official lists, but bribery is the second best. The official list is quite "flexible," as Soviet sources explain. "Too often the decisive factor is not the waiting list," *Pravda* commented, "but a sudden telephone call [after which] they give the flats to the families of football players and the whole queue is pushed back." Even to purchase a cooperative apartment involves waiting lists.

A Bukharan Jewish woman from Tashkent whom we interviewed grew up in an eight-room private house with her own room. After marriage, she applied for a co-op because all her mother's children and grandchildren were registered as living in the big house, making it look like crowded conditions, The Uzbek clerk could not read Russian well and asked her to fill out the application for the co-op and then have it typed. "When I brought the typed version I put a bottle of vodka on the desk. He didn't take money, only vodka. Uzbeks don't take money. They are very humane people. He took vodka because, as an Uzbek, he is not allowed to drink. He can't go into a store to buy vodka because the clerks are Uzbeks and it would be embarrassing. So they get vodka from us, the 'foreigners.'"

Getting a pension rarely involves this much chicanery, although the press reports numerous instances of bureaucratic snafus connected with pensions, and there are occasional reports of pension officials making money from "dead souls" in the Gogolian tradition *(Trud,* 1980). But some pensioners also monkey with the system, especially since many pensions are very low. (We have reports from Central Asia of pensions as low as 24 rubles a month, and many instances in the European USSR of pensions of approximately 60 rubles, the latter being roughly one-third the average urban wage in the 1970s.) A bookkeeper from a small town in Moldavia explained that since pensions are based on average salary in the last years of employment, "sometimes to help out a worker who was going on pension the administration would promote him to a vacancy with a higher pay scale, even if he was not qualified for the job." Bonuses and overtime pay would be calculated into the figures for average salary in order to inflate the pension. All of this, she claimed, was assumed to be legal.

Getting into an institution of higher education is a far more complicated matter, especially for Jews, in the periods from 1945 to 1958 and from 1971 to the present. Although some respondents indicate that *blat* rather than bribery is used to gain entrance to higher education, two former members of admissions committees recall the widespread use of bribery, and one woman from the Ukraine frankly said that she was admitted only because her mother paid a 3,000 ruble bribe. Another person who was on the admissions committee of a polytechnic in Leningrad reports that in his institute the bribes ran about 500 rubles, but were into the thousands for the pediatric faculty and the First Medical Institute in Leningrad. But other forms of chicanery are more prevalent. A Georgian Jew tells how he paid 100 rubles in Kulashi to have his nationality changed from Jew to Georgian so that he would be admitted to the pediatric institute in Leningrad. This trick having worked, he returned as a pediatrician to Kulashi. But when he went to change his nationality back to

Jew—"everyone knew me there and it was silly to be registered as a Georgian"—"the boys" demanded 200 rubles, for, they explained, because the Jews were getting out of the country, it was now worth more to be a Jew! Our Leningrad informant, who was himself helped in getting into the school of his choice because he was a basketball player, tells us that athletes and residents of Leningrad were favored for admission, as were children of faculty. Admissions committee members in Leningrad got written instructions not to admit anyone to the journalism faculty without recommendations from the party *raikom.* Certain specialties even in the philological faculty were explicitly closed to Jews. In such cases, bribery, connections, and other tactics will not work, except very rarely, and people learn quickly to give upon these institutions.

The other side of this is an "affirmative-action" program designed to increase the number of natives in the republic's higher educational institutions. Two Soviet authors assert that "It is understood that in socialist societies objectively there can be no discrimination against any national group. Soviet educational practice knows no such examples." At the same time, they say that, "It must be assumed that the more the proportion of a nationality in higher education corresponds to its proportion in the population as a whole, the more the system of higher education lives up to the democratic ideal of equal educational opportunity for all people irrespective of nationality." To achieve this one can permit . . . conditional influence of a variable such as the nationality of an individual" on admissions decisions (Prikhodko & Pan, 1974, pp. 70, 61). Indeed, informants from two cities in Moldavia reported independently that in the 1970s they were told quite openly not to bother applying to Kishinev Polytechnical Institute because that was being reserved for ethnic Moldavians. Central Asian respondents portray admissions officials desperately trying to fill ethnic quotas. One woman draws a perhaps exaggerated picture of Uzbek officials scouring the countryside for young Uzbek women who could be persuaded to attend a pedagogical institute training music teachers for elementary schools. Other informants report that in the Ukraine and Moldavia, at least, rural students were favored for admission to institutes and were eagerly recruited, and this is confirmed as policy by official sources.

For those departments and schools that are realistic possibilities for Jews, the way in is not always a direct one. A common practice is to hire a tutor for the applicant, not so much to prepare the applicant as to prepare the way with the admissions committee. Often, the tutor is a member of the faculty, and he will see to it that his student gets in, sometimes by turning over some of his fees to his colleagues (reported in Moscow, Kharkov, Leningrad). One operator told parents: "I'll get your child into the institute for 1,000 rubles. Give me 300 now and the rest only if he gets in." The advance would be used to bribe clerks to put the child's name on the list of those admitted, bypassing the admissions committee, and then the rest was pocketed by the fixer. One admissions committee member admitted frankly that he gave higher admission grades to students who had been tutored by his friends.

If citizens and members of admissions committees fool with the system, so, of course, does the party. A woman who taught in several pedagogical institutes reports that at the final meeting of the admissions committee a representative of the party *raikom* and another of the *obshchestvennost* (usually someone working with the party) would come and express their opinions freely. They would insure that certain ethnic distributions were achieved and that certain individuals were admitted or turned down. In Kharkov, it is claimed, there are three lists of applicants: those who must be admitted, those who must not be, and the rest. In the Kharkovite's experience, the party did not directly participate in the admissions process, but did so indirectly by approving members of admissions committees, making up the above-mentioned lists, and providing written guidelines for admission policies.

The Soviet press does not hide the fact that the struggle for admission to higher education is a fierce one, and that all kinds of means are employed in it. "Every summer when the school-graduates boom starts and the doors of *vuzy* (higher educational institutions) are blocked by lines of applicants, ripples of that wave sweep over editorial staffs as well. Parents and grandparents of school graduates call up and come in person (the person who failed the exams never comes). With great inspiration they tell what profound knowledge their child has, how diligent he was, how well he replied to each question, but the perfidy of the examiner was beyond all expectations." The writer notes, however, that "the majority of complaints are quite just" (Loginova, 1980, p.11).

The intelligentsia is especially anxious to have its children gain higher education. In Azerbaijan none other than the first secretary of the republic Party organization, now a member of the All-Union Politburo, Gaidar Aliev (1981, p.10), complained that in the law faculty of the local university, "We discovered that the overwhelming majority of the students are children of militia, procurators, judges, law professors and employees of Party and state organs. . . . We were concerned with the threat of nepotism and 'heredity' within the administrative organs." He complained also about the fashion of the 1960s, when senior officials "arranged" to receive higher degrees, commenting sardonically on a popular saying that, "A scholar you might not be, but *a kandidat* you surely must become."

If one gets into the institute or university and then graduates. a *raspredelenie* commission will normally assign the graduate his or her first job. Very often this is an undesirable position in an even less desirable location. For example, it is common practice to assign teachers or physicians, many of whom are single women, to rural areas in Siberia and Central Asia. To avoid such assignments, some will simply take a job outside their field, others arrange fictitious marriages with spouses who have residence permits in desirable locations, and many will appeal the decision and try to get a "free diploma," that is, one without a specific job assignment, leaving them to their own devices. In only one instance were we told of a bribe being used (in the West Ukraine) to get a good assignment. Several informants report being assigned to jobs in Central Asia, only to find upon arrival that there was no need for them, that the local institutions had not requested them, and the local authorities were not eager to have non-natives take jobs there. Despite the inconvenience, such *contretemps* were welcomed because they freed the person from the assignment. In 1979 nearly 30 percent of assigned jobs were not taken *(Uchitel'skaia gazeta,* 1980, p.2), and in some rural areas the proportion of those who did not show up to their assignments was higher.[6] Of course, some graduates try to use *blat,* to try and pull strings with the job assignment commission, and this is reported to work fairly well. The other use of *blat* is to get some big boss to request the graduate specifically as an employee of his institution.

The Use of *Blat* and *Protektsiia*

Since *blat* and *protektsiia* are so commonly used, they are frequently commented on by the Soviet press. One detailed analysis raised both principled and pragmatic objections to *protektsiia.* It is said to be objectionable because it violates the socialist principle of "from each according to his capabilities, to each according to his work." On the practical level, *protektsiia* is said to reward the incompetent, discourage hard work and initiative, allow people to make buying and selling favors their profession, and promote calculations of self-interest "incompatible with communist morality." The resort to *protektsiia* arises, it is suggested, because social norms are not well defined and because of the "underdevelopment of certain branches of our economy." The law is said to be too vague for curbing the use of *protektsiia.* Unlike bribery, using *protektsiia* is not generally considered a crime except if "substantial harm is done to state or public interests, or to the rights of individuals" (Kiselev, 1981, p. 152).[7]

As this argument implicitly acknowledges, the use of *protektsiia*—and in some areas and under certain circumstances, even of bribery—is socially acceptable and not discouraged by law or custom. It is in line with age-old traditions in many areas of the USSR. A Georgian author shows how traditional birthdays, weddings, mourning rituals, the departure of young men to the army, and even funerals are occasions for trading influence and subtle forms of bribery (Dzhafarli, 1978, p.72; see also Verbitskii, 1981, p.2), Soviet authors decry "survivals of the past" which are said to contradict "socialist morality and way of life." Some Western observers see not just survivals but a Soviet failure to resocialize the population to Marxist-Leninist norms. One student of Soviet political culture asserts that "'New Soviet man,' in short, does not yet exist: Soviet citizens remain overwhelmingly the product of their historical experience rather than of Marxist-Leninist ideological training" (White, 1979b, p.49) This is an exaggeration—there has been successful resocialization in many areas of life—but it is true that prerevolutionary styles and practices survive in certain spheres, even among third and fourth generation Soviet citizens. The relationship between the government official and the citizen closely resembles pre-communist forms in the USSR and other socialist countries. Jowitt's (1974. p. 1176) argument that traditional attitudes and behavior patterns survive the communist revolution—and are even reinforced by it—is borne out by our investigation.

The prevalence of *blat* should not be attributed to some mystical staying power of pre-revolutionary political culture. Rather, it is supported by present-day structural factors which are themselves continuations of tsarist practices. The highly centralized and hierarchical administrative structure of tsarist days has been continued and reinforced by its heirs, so the kind of tactics used to ameliorate the harshness of tsarist administration are well suited to the present day as well. In the light of weak rational-legal authority and of interest groups in both historical periods, the average citizen is without influence over policymaking and has little legal protection against administrative arbitrariness or even the mindless application of what is construed as the law. He is left to devise individual strategies and tactics which will not change the making of the law, but will, he hopes, turn its implementation (or non-application) in his favor. Each person, then, is reduced to being a special pleader, and not with those who make the rules but with those who are charged with applying and enforcing them.

Conclusion

. . . Our findings repeatedly suggest that the dominant social ethos of Soviet citizens vis-à-vis their government is one of private self-interest. Furthermore, they display clear preference for informal access to and influence on bureaucratic officials and a general disdain for formal and legalistic procedures and norms. This observation leads us to think of the Soviet political culture (or at least the dominant subculture) as covert-participant. The covert-participant individual is oriented toward system outputs, but he exhibits few of the deferential, passive attributes of the classic subject. Rather, he participates in (or more precisely, attempts to manipulate) the implementation process in whichever institutions he can, utilizing a varied repertoire of assertive, creative, and illegal methods to secure his private welfare from the extensive Soviet public sector. Our research also indicates that covert orientations are to be found in every stratum in the USSR, but that different educational groups prefer different manipulative strategies, and these variations are probably rooted in both tradition and in the structure of the confrontation between citizens and the state. In a critique of *The Civic Culture,* a distinguished Polish social scientist who has considerable firsthand experience with the workings of his country's political system notes that "Some social groups feel . . . that their chances of performing effectively within the system are minimal or nil; in this case political apathy may be interpreted in terms of the critical evaluation of the existing system rather than in terms of the psychological characteristics of inactive citizens" (Wiatr, 1980, pp. 116–117). He suggests that Almond and Verba err in their "tendency to explain discrepancies between normative standards of democracy and political reality in terms of psychological deficiencies rather than structural conditions within the system." Though Wiatr makes these points with regard to Western democracies, they seem equally applicable to the Soviet Union and other socialist countries. Rational political behavior in the USSR should involve pro forma participation in the system's rituals, occasional contacting of approved agencies in approved ways in order to influence policy implementation in individual cases, and more frequent transactions with officials charged with policy implementation for the same purpose. Ritualistic participation is rational, not because it influences policy, but because it protects one against charges of nonconformity and antisocial attitudes, and for some it may provide emotional satisfaction. For others, however, the effect is to emphasize the gap between rhetoric and reality and to reinforce political cynicism.[8] Despite the Khrushchevian rhetoric of the "state of the whole people" succeeding the "dictatorship of the proletariat," only the formal franchise has been broadened in the last decades. The Soviet citizen participates politically in several ways, but, except for a small elite, his (and especially her) ability to influence policy decisions, even indirectly, is practically nil. The citizen does have some ability to influence the implementation of policy. But this can be done only on an ad hoc and ad hominem basis, so that no systemic effects and changes are felt. Despite the expansion of opportunities for formal participation and the grudging increase in opportunities for expressing opinions, the Soviet system remains fundamentally directed from above. As Verba and Nie (1972, p. 113) comment in their analysis of political participation in America:

> Particularized contacts can be effective for the individual contactor but they are inadequate as a guide to more general social policy . . . The ability of the citizen to make himself heard . . . by contacting the officials . . . represents an important aspect of citizen control. Though such contacts may be important in filling the policy gaps and in adjusting policy to the individual, effective citizen control over governmental policy would be limited indeed if citizens related to their government only as isolated individuals concerned with their narrow parochial problems. The larger political questions would remain outside popular control. Therefore, though electoral mechanisms remain crude, they are the most effective for these purposes.

For the foreseeable future the "larger political questions" will remain the domain of the *verkhushka.* Our respondents appear to be much more interested in private benefits than in democratic institutions. We infer from our analysis of respondents' evaluations of Soviet bureaucracies and their dissatisfaction with its operations, that much of the Soviet population would probably be more interested in increasing levels of performance by the present system than in fundamental systemic change. Until such time as either of these comes about, the citizen is left to grapple as best he can with those small questions of daily life that he and those who administer the system must solve together.

Notes

1. Since the question concerning attitudes toward pension agencies was asked only of those who had actually received a Soviet pension, the data could not be incorporated into Exhibit 29.3. However, the responses fell within the predicted range. For example, more than 72 percent of those who answered advised patience or writing a letter of appeal.

2. See, for example, Azarova (1979). She notes that more than two-thirds of district and city social security inspectors in the Russian republic have neither higher nor secondary specialized education. She strongly criticizes red tape, "illegal acts of employees," and the appeals process, whereby citizens are supposed to get a hearing on the size of their pensions. She goes so far as to imply quite clearly that the administration of pensions in the USSR is inferior to that in other socialist countries, citing specific examples.

    Other articles along these lines are Tarasova (1976) and Tosunian (1981). The latter describes some of the pension officials: "Often the nature of the bureaucrat does not depend on his appearance. For some, rudeness and caddishness are the way they treat all visitors. Others are polite, well-mannered, speak softly to everyone, but they are nevertheless capable of confusing the simplest cases. Many experienced employees are well versed in the nuances of their job, but they use their knowledge, however strange it may sound, not to benefit but to harm their clients."

3. Examples include Plekhanov, "Order na kvartiru," *Literaturnaia gazeta,* July 25, 1979, p.12; Ia. Ianovskii, "O sudebnoi praktike po grazhdansko-pravovym sporam mezhdu grazhdanami zhilishchnostroitel'nymi kooperativami," *Sovetskoe gosudarstvo i pravo* No. 1, 1967; "Fiancees with Dowries," *Pravda,* January 20, 1979. translated in *Current Digest of the Soviet Press* 31,3 (February 14, 1979); "Discussing an Urgent Problem: An Apartment for the Newlyweds." *Sovietskaia Rossia* February 14, 1979, translated in *CDSP* 31,8 (March 21, 1979). A well-known novel on the subject is by the recently emigrated Vladimir Voinovich, *The Ivankiad* (New York: Farrar, Straus and Giroux, 1977).

4. Cited in Morton (1980, p. 250).

5. Corruption is involved in admissions even to military schools. *Krasnaia zvezda* reports a case where a general got his relatives admitted despite their poor grades and admits this is not an isolated case. "When applications to the military school are being considered the admissions committee is besieged with phone calls. . . . There are really two competitions for admission: the regular competition and the competition of relatives" (Filatov, 1980, p.2).

6. In Orel province in 1979 only 179 of 323 graduates of agricultural institutes showed up to their assigned jobs, some " 'signed in' only to vanish immediately

afterward. . . . In all fairness it must be said that not all farm managers create proper conditions under which young specialists can work. . . . In other cases, they simply 'forget' to provide them with apartments . . . leave them on their own to solve all the problems of everyday life." See Troyan (1980).

7. See the frank article by the first secretary of the Georgian writers' union, Tengiz Buachidze (1975, p. 12).

8. Unger's (1981, p. 122) interviews with 46 former Soviet political activists of the party and Komsomol lead him to conclude that "they did not believe their own participation to be effective. . . . The combination of compulsion and formalism which characterizes participation in the Komsomol and party arenas clearly provides no scope at all for the development of a sense of efficacy. Indeed, one may well hypothesize that it has the opposite effect, that the induction of the individual into the 'spectacle' of Komsomol and party activities produces not a sense of efficacy but of inefficacy, not subjective competence but subjective incompetence."

References

Aliev, G. Interview, *Literaturnaia gazeta,* November 18, 1981, p 10.

Almond, G.A. The intellectual history of the civic culture concept. In G.A. Almond & S. Verba (eds.), *The civic culture revisited.* Boston: Little, Brown, 1980, 1–36.

Almond, G.A., and Verba, S. *The civic culture.* Princeton, N.J.: Princeton University Press. 1963,

Azarova, E. O zashchite pensionnykh prav grazhdan. *Sovetskoe gosudarstvo i pravo,* 1979, 2, 44–49.

Barghoorn, F.C. *Politics in the USSR* (2nd ed.). Boston: Little, Brown, 1972.

Bennett, W.L. "Culture, communication, and political control." Presented at the annual meeting of the American Political Science Association, Washington, D.C., August 18,1980.

Bialer, S. *Stalin's successors.* New York: Cambridge University Press, 1980.

Brown., A., and Gray, J. (eds.), *Political culture and political change in Communist states* (2nd ed.). New York: Holmes and Meier, 1979.

Buachidze, T. Protektsiia. *Literaturnaia gazeta,* January 8, 1975, p. 12.

Connor, W.D., & Gitelman, Z. (eds.), *Public opinion in European socialist systems.* New York: Praeger. 1977

Dzhafarli, T.M. Izuchenie obshchestvennogo mneniia-neobkhodimoe uslovie priniatiia pravil'nykh reshenii. *Sotsiologicheskie issledovanie,* 1978, 1, 69–75.

Falkenheim. V. Political participation in China. *Problems of Communism,* 1978, 27, 18–32.

Filatov, V. Plemianniki: k chemu privodit protektsiia pri prieme v voennoe uchilishche. *Krasnaia zvezda,* November 12, 1980, p. 2.

Friedgut, T.H. *Political participation in the USSR.* Princeton, N.J.: Princeton University Press, 1979

Gitelman. Z. Becoming Israelis: political resocialization of Soviet and American immigrants. New York, Praeger, 1982.

Gray. J. Conclusion. In A. Brown and J. Gray (eds.), *Political culture and political change in Communist states* (2nd ed.). New York: Holmes and Meier, 1979, 251–72.

Hasenfeld, Y. Client-organization relations: a systems perspective. In R. Sarri and Y. Hasenfeld (eds.). *The management of human services.* New York: Columbia University Press. 1978, 184–206.

Hasenfeld, Y., and Steinmetz, D. Client-official encounters in social service agencies. In C. Goodsell (ed.). *The public encounter: delivering human services in the 1980s.* Bloomington: Indiana University Press, 1981, 83–101.

Hough, J. Political participation in the Soviet Union. *Soviet Studies,* 1976, *28,* 3–20.

Hough, J., and Fainsod, M. *How the Soviet Union is governed.* Cambridge, Mass.: Harvard University Press, 1979

Inkeles, A., and Bauer, R. *The Soviet citizen.* Cambridge, Mass.: Harvard University Press, 1961.

Jowitt, K. An organizational approach to the study of political culture in Marxist-Leninist systems. *American Political Science Review,* 1974, *68,* 1171–91.

Katz, E., and Danet, B. *Bureaucracy and the public.* New York: Basic Books, 1973.

Kiselev, V. P. O povyshenii deistvennosti prava v bor'be s protektsionizmom. *Sotsiologicheskie Issledovanie,* 1981, *1,* 151–54.

Loginova. N. Chervi kozyri. *Literaturnaia gazeta,* January 23, 1980.

Morton, H. Who gets what, when and how? Housing in the Soviet Union. *Soviet Studies,* 1980, *32,* 235–59.

Odom, W. A dissenting view on the group approach to Soviet politics. *World Politics,* 1976, *28,* 542–67.

Odom, W. *The Soviet volunteers.* Princeton, N.J.: Princeton University Press, 1973.

Oliver, J. Citizen demands and the Soviet political system. *American Political Science Review,* 1969, *62,* 465–75.

Prikhodko, D.N., and Pan, V.V. *Obrazovanie i sotsial'nyi status lichnosti: tendentsii internatsional-izatsii i dukhovnaia kultura.* Tomsk: izdatel'stvo Tomskogo Universiteta, 1974.

Sadowski, C. The fragile link: citizen voluntary association and polity in People's Poland. Unpublished doctoral dissertation. Department of Sociology, The University of Michigan, 1979.

Schulz. D., and Adams, J. *Political participation in communist systems.* New York: Pergamon Press, 1981.

Sharlet, R. Concept formation in political science and communist studies: conceptualizing political participation, *Canadian Slavic Studies,* 1967, *1,* 640–49.

Skilling, H. D., and Griffiths, F. *Interest groups in Soviet politics.* Princeton, N.J.: Princeton University Press, 1971.

Tarasova, V.A. Okhrana subiektivnykh prav grazhdanin v oblasti pensionnogo obespecheniia. *Sovetskoe gosudarstvo i pravo,* 1976, *8,* 133–36.

Tosunian, I. Vot dozhivem do pensii. *Literaturnaia gazeta,* September 30, 1981.

Troyan, S. They never arrived for their assigned jobs. *Izvestiia,* June 11, 1980, 3. Translated in *Current Digest of the Soviet Press.* July 9, 1980, *32,* 16–17.

Trud, October 16, 1980, p. 4.

Uchitel'skaia gazeta, January 15, 1980, p. 2.

Unger, A. Political participation in the USSR: YCL and CPSU. *Soviet Studies,* 1981, *33,* 107–24.

Verba, S., and Nie, N. *Participation in America.* New York: Harper and Row, 1972.

Verbitsky, A. Vziatki, vziatki, vziatki. *Novoe Russkoe slovo,* August 4, 1981, p.2.

White, S. *Political culture and Soviet politics.* New York: St. Martin's Press, 1979.

White, S. The USSR: patterns of autocracy and industrialism. In A. Brown and J. Gray (eds.), *Political culture and political change in Communist states* (2nd ed.). New York: Holmes and Meier, 1979, pp. 25–65.

Wiatr, J. The civic culture from a Marxist-sociological perspective. In G. A. Almond and S. Verba (eds.), *The civic culture revisited.* Boston: Little, Brown, 1980, pp.103–23.

30

Bribery and Other Ways of Coping With Officialdom in Post-Communist Eastern Europe

*William L. Miller, Åse B. Grødeland and
Tatyana Y. Koshechkina[1]*

Introduction

Good governance is not just a matter of high politics.[2] Free elections should do more than offer an often confused or misleading choice of programmes and leadership: they should affect the general political culture, set the tone of democratic government, legitimate voters individually as well as collectively, turn officials and bureaucrats into "civil servants" and encourage government to respect individual citizens as well as the collective decision of the whole electorate.[3] In their analysis of democratic culture, Almond and Verba[4] drew attention to the importance of what they called "citizen competence" and "subject competence," both of which, they claimed, were required for a healthy functioning democracy.[5] In terms of perceptions, Almond and Verba distinguished between *citizen competence* (% who say they can do something about an unjust law on both the national and local level) and *subject competence* (% who expect serious consideration both in a government office and from the police).

Communist regimes were traditionally depicted as bureaucratic, in Laski's sense of that word rather than Weber's: "a system of government . . . so completely in the hands of officials that their power jeopardises the liberties of ordinary citizens."[6] Citizens could expect neither serious consideration nor fair treatment without some means of "interesting" the official in their case.

Dependence upon the use of bribes and contacts was notorious. Like the Tsarist regime before it, parodied so well by Gogol in *The Government Inspector*, the Soviet regime could reasonably be described as an "autocracy tempered by corruption" if nothing worse. A majority of respondents in DiFranceisco and Gitelman's survey of émigrés from the old USSR regime suggested bribery or connections could be used to change an unwelcome work assignment or to get a dull child into a good university department[7]; and surveys of those still living in the USSR tended to corroborate these findings.[8] Yet it was never quite clear whether the use of bribes and contacts reflected a lack of "subject competence" and the ability of officials to dominate citizens, or an excess of "subject competence" and the ability of citizens to manipulate officials. In this connection, DiFranceisco and Gitelman found that university graduates were only a little less likely than others to suggest bribery but far more likely than others to suggest using connections; and, moreover, they found graduates were overwhelmingly *in favour* of a system of unequal treatment—which they could manipulate to their advantage.[9] Even after the transition to democracy at the top such aspects of the political culture may be resistant to change.[10]

Or they may have changed for the worse. Since 1989 there have been several changes in the institutional and social context which might be expected to impact upon the behaviour of postcommunist officials—an uneven mix of reform and chaos. Of the countries in our study only the former Czechoslovakia has implemented a far reaching purge of officials from the old regime,[11] and any improvements there have been offset by the loss of more competent officials to better paid jobs in the growing private sector. So the issue is essentially one of "new thinking," the location of officials within a new more democratic structure, a new working environment and new relationships, rather than "new people."

Local government reforms have been characterised as a move "from democratic centralism to local democracy"[12] which should have encouraged more respect for citizens. But privatisation and restitution have encouraged more self-interested action by citizens and officials alike. They were designed in principle to widen consumer choice and provide fair treatment for the formerly persecuted, but they also provided enormous opportunities for officials to enrich themselves.[13] Privatisation or restitution is usually "a lengthy and tedious bureaucratic process, complete with audits and appraisals that generate legal quagmires"[14]; so that "it is often only a (substantial) bribe or an offer to share the property that can speed up the procedure."[15] Farmers operate in "a climate dominated by clientelism and distrust for public institutions" and "the dependence of the private sector on selected individuals in the collective and state farm system" for access to equipment and supplies.[16]

Finally, there is the impact of a general climate of economic and moral chaos. The transition to democracy has been accompanied by a collapse both of the old communist economic system, and of belief in the old communist value system.[17] Verheijen and Dimitrova point to "the general deterioration of values" and the "moral wasteland" in postcommunist countries as a prime cause of increasing corruption amongst officials.[18] The end of communism brought unemployment (often well disguised[19]), poverty, a sharp decline in health and welfare services, a rise in nationalist tensions, and a general climate of aggressive, often desperate, individualism and communalism, all of which are likely to affect the relationship between citizens and officials adversely. Economic dislocation made many entrepreneurs and senior officials conspicuously—and not always legitimately—rich, while putting the incomes of junior officials under severe pressure. So while democratisation in itself should have encouraged junior officials to behave better, the moral chaos and economic pressures of the transition may have encouraged them to behave worse.[20] How these contending influences are balanced is an empirical question.

In her study of the use of "blat" (contacts and influence) in Soviet and post-Soviet Russia, Alena Ledeneva suggests that the transition from communism to a market economy had two effects upon the use of contacts and bribery in the FSU: *first*, the predominant use of "blat" shifted from the everyday life of ordinary citizens up to the networks of former nomenklatura now turning themselves into quasi-criminal businessmen, from the mass to the elite—which takes it out of the range of our research; but *second*, in the everyday life of citizens—which is what concerns us here—crude monetary bribes increasingly supplemented or even replaced the subtle and sometimes civilising use of contacts.[21] Our focus group discussions lend some support to both those conclusions.

ECE and the FSU

Our previous surveys of public opinion and democracy in five countries of the FSU/ECE showed relatively modest differences between the FSU and ECE on Almond and Verba's first aspect of democracy: citizens in the FSU were only 10 percent less likely than in ECE to agree that regular elections had at least some effect in making politicians do what ordinary people want, for example.[22] But there were much larger differences on "subject competence." We used a slight variant of Almond and Verba's original questions: "Suppose there were some problems you had to take to a government office—for example, a problem about tax or housing. Do you think you would be treated fairly by the officials in that office?" We found citizens in the FSU were 39 percent less likely than those in ECE to expect fair treatment without recourse to bribes or contacts[23]; and Members of Parliament in the FSU 59 percent less than those in ECE.[24] Ukraine and the Czech Republic were at the extremes: citizens in Ukraine were 49 percent less likely to expect fair treatment without recourse to bribes or contacts than those in the Czech Republic; and Ukrainian MPs 58 percent less than Czech MPs.

Expectations of fair treatment correlated with trust in "the government" but those who "completely distrusted" the Czech or Slovak governments nonetheless expected fairer treatment from officials than those who "completely trusted" the governments in Russia or Ukraine. Similarly those who described themselves as "opponents" of the government in Slovakia or the Czech Republic were much more likely to expect fair treatment from officials than those who described themselves as "supporters" of the government in Russia or Ukraine. So expectations of fair treatment by officials reflected more than general political satisfaction or dissatisfaction.

Methodology

To investigate the interaction between postcommunist officials and citizens in more depth we have chosen the countries that differed most in our previous surveys, Ukraine and the Czech Republic. We have added Slovakia and Bulgaria, because they are close geographically and culturally to the Czech Republic and Ukraine respectively, without being quite the same in either case.

Our full study involves four phases—focus group discussions, followed by one-to-one in-depth interviews, then large-scale surveys of public-opinion and of junior officials.[25] The focus-group discussions were designed to see whether people were willing to discuss such a sensitive topic openly and, if so, how they did so—in their own words and with a minimum of prompting. The corresponding in-depth interviews were designed to see whether they said different things in the context of a semi-public group discussion or a more private and confidential one-to-one discussion. Since these are small-sample techniques, large scale public opinion surveys are necessary both to provide representative findings for each country and to permit detailed analysis of patterns within countries, while interviews with officials will provide a "right of reply."

We completed 26 focus group discussions, each approximately two hours long, in the second half of 1996. Since no more than 187 people participated in our focus group discussions, and there were never more than 55 focus group participants in any one country, we cannot be sure that they are fully representative of the countries in question. Moreover, only those who had had some recent personal contact with officials were invited to participate. Nonetheless the design (see Appendix for details) ensures that the discussion groups in each country ranged from capital cities down to villages, that they ranged widely across the regions of each country, and that they were inclusive of ethnic Ukrainian and Russian areas in Ukraine, as well as concentrations of small ethnic minorities in Ukraine, Bulgaria and Slovakia. Although we cannot assume that they were strictly representative of the entire population in each country, it would be equally wrong to assume that they were wildly unrepresentative, and insofar as strict representativeness is critical our large scale follow up surveys provide the necessary check.

The focus group discussions were video-recorded and computer-readable transcripts produced in both the original language and English. There is a popular but fundamentally misconceived dictum that "qualitative data should not be subjected to quantitative analysis." Findings based upon the limited numbers of participants in focus groups may be unrepresentative of the country as a whole. Alas, that is equally true, whether the findings are expressed in words or in numbers. Analysis of focus group material is usually based on the reviewer's impressions supported by selected quotations. Unfortunately that compounds the problem of representativeness rather than solving it, because the selected quotations may not even be representative of the discussions. Quantitative analysis is entirely valid and appropriate *as a precise description of the discussions*; it is the assertion that the discussions are necessarily representative of the country as a whole that is not valid—irrespective of whether the description of the discussions is expressed in words or numbers. To provide an accurate description of what people actually said in the discussions we shall use numbers as well as sufficient representative quotations. The QSR:NUD•IST package provided a convenient method of selecting those quotations as well as quantifying them.[26]

But what are we to quantify? We have chosen the "text-unit" as our unit of analysis, defined as the contribution made by one person at one point in the discussion, starting when that person starts speaking and ending when the next person intervenes. Such text-units could be as short as a word or as long as a paragraph, though typically they extend to about two lines of text. We read through the transcripts, indexing each text-unit according to various classification schemes reflecting, for example, whether the text-unit referred to generalised hearsay and gossip or something more personal, whether it mentioned arguing with an official or bribing them, whether the purpose was to obtain fair treatment or favourable treatment, and so on. This allows us to calculate how much *of the actual discussion* fell into various categories and combinations of categories. It is important to note that all percentages in our focus group analysis are percentages of text-units, not percentages of participants. They tell us about the discussion itself, rather than about the participants.

It is also important to note one essential difference between text-units in focus group discussions and the answers given in a typical opinion survey: a single text-unit can answer several questions, or give several answers to the same question: for example, "I have heard that some people give large bribes, but I have never given anything more than a box of chocolates as a token of appreciation" would be classified as both "general hearsay" and a "personal statement," because it talks about both. This need for "double indexing" means that the percentages of text-units in different categories usually sum to a little over 100 percent. Similarly it would be classified as referring to "large bribes" and mere "tokens"; and in a statistical analysis it would count, misleadingly, as referring to both a "personal statement" and "large bribes." In practice, however, such pathologies do not cause major problems for our analysis, since most—though not all—text-units do, in fact, make a single integrated point.

We drew up a detailed schedule of suggested questions which was translated into the local languages and used by moderators to guide the focus group discussions. It had five sections, raising increasingly personal and sensitive questions about:

(i) attitudes towards the transition—both to democracy and to a market economy

(ii) general expectations—how officials would "typically" treat citizens, and how citizens would typically respond

(iii) projective situations—what participants "would do" in certain specific scenarios

(iv) personal experience—what had actually happened to participants, their close friends or their relatives

(v) past and future—how things had changed since the fall of communism, their expectations for the future, their proposals for reform.

Moderators retained the flexibility to adjust to the flow of the discussion, however. Participants might spontaneously raise the "scenario" situations, or respond with tales of personal experiences when they had only been asked about "typical" situations, for example, making later sections of the schedule largely redundant. Variations in the sequence of discussion topics have no effect upon our analysis, since we index all comments according to their content, not the point in the discussion where they occurred.

Perspectives on the Transition

While there was wide support for the transition from communism, there was also wide criticism of the way the transition had been handled: "it is a good thing but I think it should not be the way it has started in this country" (Ky-B 1)[27]; "they broke everything apart and haven't built anything" (Se 1). In Bulgaria especially, there was a degree of economic pessimism that bordered on despair: "democracy is something very nice, but we misinterpreted it. . . . instead of achieving . . . we kept destroying" (Te 4); "a country this beautiful and nice . . . it has all been ruined." (Stral 1).

There was also a perception, especially in Ukraine, that the transition was itself the final criminal act of the communist regime and its officials. That perception was bound to encourage, or at the least excuse, corrupt behaviour by ordinary citizens in their dealings with the state. "It's clear that [the transition] is being effected with the old Soviet methods—the same special shares, special distributions, and special privileges everywhere" (Se 4); "those in power are the same, but [our] life has become 100 times worse" (Vo 1).

Elected deputies were widely seen as being in politics for their own personal advantage: "power is necessary for money" (Ky-B 6); "we've got nothing to buy a piece of bread with, and the comrades travel to Atlanta, can afford cruises" (Kh 3); "shielding yourself with the help of deputies' immunity is necessary when your pocket is full" (Vo 1).

Indexing text-units by whether they suggested the behaviour of officials under the postcommunist regime was now better or worse than under communism indicated an improvement in the Czech Republic, even if only by the narrow margin of 8 percent, but a turn for the worse elsewhere—by a margin of 20 percent in Slovakia, 32 percent in Bulgaria and 37 percent in Ukraine.

Strategies for Dealing with Officials

How can citizens deal with officials? What coping strategies can they use when faced with unfair, or simply unacceptable, treatment? Participants in our discussions mentioned a range of possibilities.

Acceptance: "I clearly understood from the very beginning that it would not do any good . . . I came there, turned round, and went home" (Striy 4); "Circumstances made me give up, because if somebody else were in my position . . . it's no wonder why there are structures of force, racket, batons." (Ya 4).

Persistence: "drop in there every week and when they see me at the door they say to themselves 'Oh God, she's here again, let's give it to her and get rid of her.'" (Pra-B 6).

Table 30.1
Perceptions of postcommunist changes in official behaviour

| | Text-units about changes which mention officials | | | |
	Czech Rep	Slovakia	Bulgaria	Ukraine
	%	%	%	%
Better now	31	10	15	8
Neutral	46	60	38	48
Worse now	23	30	47	45
Diff: better - worse	+8	-20	-32	-37
(Total N)	(64)	(30)	(34)	(183)

Note: Percentages are percentages of relevant 'text-units' in the focus group discussions, not of participants. The total number of relevant text-units on which percentages are based is shown in brackets at the foot of each column.

Argue/threaten: "I succeeded in persuading them—maybe they were in good moods, it was just after lunch." (Do 5); "I phoned the KGB and asked 'who are you trying to catch? . . . we're not in Moscow, we're in Ukraine, on our own land!'" (Se 6); "I had to throw a hysterical fit—then they gave it to me" (Kh 2).

Appeal: "Go higher" (Hr 6); "up the ladder" (Ho 2); to "her superior" (Br-B 7); "the MP Boncho Rashkov" (Te 1); "the village soviet" (Ni 1); "the Region executive office" (Vo 1); "the Mayor" (Pra-A 7); "the Minister" (Ol 3); or even "the Supreme Council" (Ky-A 6); but "it was easier, when there was the first secretary of the party city committee . . . now there's no power like that." (Kh 3).

Bribery: Bribery could vary from a "present" of box of chocolates or a packet of coffee to money: and "money as a rule is not 'coupons' [Ukrainian temporary currency]" (Ky-B 4); "people give dollars" (Sh 4). "Now, anywhere you go, they can even tell you how much, whom to give, and for what sort of matters." (Ho 1); "they'd better have a price list." (Sh 5); "maybe you wanted to, maybe you didn't want to, but they took it from you—they tell you a specific sum," (Kh 6); "if a bureaucrat has even a slight chance to make something on you, he will do everything in order to get it from you." (Ky-A 4).

Contacts: Although contacts could be useful on their own, they were often a necessary precondition for successful bribery: "I know roughly the price, plus the friend in the appropriate position." (So-B 2); "I had the best entrance exam results, but they only admitted people according to their contacts . . . my mum . . . knew someone there who knew the Dean. Money was even involved." (NZ 8). And even contacts might require payment in the new market economy: "of course, acquaintances wouldn't do anything for you without money either." (Se 6).

Other strategies: There were a very few references to forming a protest group, or going to court. More frequently participants mentioned knowledge based strategies, from checking up on the law to "knowing the ropes." Finally there was a miscellaneous set of other strategies, mainly concerned with personal appearance and behaviour, and frequently described by participants as using "psychology"—politeness, a pleasant smile: "It depends on sex-appeal or on psychology, yes just that, how to talk the policeman round" (KH 7); or a style of dress that was neither so slovenly as to fuel the official's arrogance nor so stylish as to excite the official's jealousy: "when I got dressed up and was wearing something better than the women [officials] there, everything went wrong." (Pra-A 3).

Bribery was the most frequently mentioned strategy in all countries—in 26 percent of relevant text-units in the Czech Republic, 36 percent in Slovakia, 35 percent in Bulgaria and 42 percent in Ukraine. It was also the most frequently denied. But other strategies were also mentioned frequently—including contacts, argument (especially in the Czech and Slovak Republics), and appeal to higher authority (especially in Ukraine). Bulgarians were the most likely to mention passive if frustrated acceptance.

Strategies for Objectives

Indexing text-units on dealing with officials according to whether the citizen appeared to be seeking an entitlement or a favour showed that the Czech discussions focused more on seeking favours than on fair treatment—by a margin of 10 percent. But everywhere else discussions focused more on the minimum objective of obtaining fair rather than favourable treatment—and by even larger margins of between 25 and 31 percent.

Strategies were clearly related to objectives. In all countries, acceptance, persistence, argument and appeal were mentioned much more frequently in connection with attempts to get *fair* treatment than to get favours. Conversely, bribes and contacts were mentioned much more frequently in connection with attempts to get *favourable* treatment. "Do you mean you need to pay only when you are doing something illegal?" asked the moderator in the Sholomia discussion; "I think when everything is legal people pay less" came the response. (Sh 2). Even in Ukraine, where bribes were mentioned in 28 percent of text-units concerned with obtaining rights, they were mentioned in far more, in 73 percent of text-units concerned with obtaining favours. This is a point of some importance. Citizens can reasonably complain when they are

Table 30.2
Coping strategies by objective

Objective:	Czech Rep Rights	Favour ↓ %	Slovakia Rights	Favour ↓ %	Bulgaria Rights	Favour ↓ %	Ukraine Rights	Favour ↓ %
	%	%	%	%	%	%	%	%
NOW :								
Accept	25	12	26	7	28	12	25	3
Persist	13	2	9	3	8	2	7	2
Argue	20	11	16	8	7	8	6	1
Appeal	7	4	10	3	12	1	17	2
Bribe	18	42	22	55	30	60	28	73
Contact	11	15	5	25	15	37	8	21
Knowledge	3	3	11	0	12	2	4	0
'Psychology' etc.	5	8	6	4	4	6	2	1
Court	0	1	1	1	2	0	4	0
DENY:								
Bribe	4	10	8	7	7	3	3	5
(Total N)	(151)	(196)	(205)	(100)	(252)	(125)	(512)	(195)
Net assertion of bribery (% now - % deny)	14	32	14	48	23	57	25	68

Note: Percentages are percentages of relevant 'text-units' in the focus group discussions, not of participants. The total number of relevant text-units on which percentages are based is shown in brackets at the foot of each column.

forced to take extraordinary measures to obtain their rights, but they cannot reasonably complain when they use bribery to obtain special favours. Complain they may still do, but their complaints lack moral force and they know it. There is no need to take such complaints too seriously—unless, of course, the whole system is so perverse that what are favours within that system would be rights anywhere else.

General Gossip versus Specific Personal Experience

To what extent do complaints about officials reflect general gossip and to what extent do they reflect real personal experience? We indexed all text-units according to whether they were about: (i) general hearsay or gossip about how people typically behaved; (ii) what people might do in various hypothetical scenarios; (iii) the experience of friends and acquaintances; and (iv) more personal experience.

As the discussion moved from general gossip through hypothetical scenarios to personal statements the nature of the discussion changed sharply. First, the balance between seeking rights and favours changed: personal statements focused much more on rights, and much less on seeking favours, than did general gossip. In parallel with this, references to different coping strategies also changed: bribes were always mentioned much less in personal statements than in general gossip, and they were usually denied rather more. The use of contacts was also mentioned less in personal statements than in gossip,

Table 30.3
Coping stategies by talk style

		Czech Rep		Slovakia		Bulgaria		Ukraine	
	Talk style:	Gossip	Experience	Gossip	Experience	Gossip	Experience	Gossip	Experience
		%	%	%	%	%	%	%	%
NOW :									
	Accept	10	18	14	19	21	31	16	18
	Persist	3	7	6	7	4	9	4	8
	Argue	5	17	8	16	7	9	4	7
	Appeal	3	4	4	6	4	9	8	17
	Bribe	36	16	47	29	42	27	46	33
	Contact	20	16	10	10	23	17	12	10
	Knowledge	7	7	6	7	9	9	4	5
	'Psychology' etc.	11	8	4	7	6	5	2	4
DENY:									
	Bribe	7	13	9	15	3	9	5	4
	(Total N)	(277)	(275)	(192)	(215)	(235)	(236)	(612)	(314)
	Net assertion of bribery (% now - % deny)	29	3	38	14	39	18	41	29

Note: Percentages are percentages of relevant 'text-units' in the focus group discussions, not of participants. The total number of relevant text-units on which percentages are based is shown in brackets at the foot of each column.

though the margin was not so large as with bribes. Conversely, passive acceptance was mentioned more in personal statements than in gossip, especially in Bulgaria; but, much more important, so were other more active strategies like persistence, argument and appeal. Overall therefore, there is a striking contrast between the repertoire of coping strategies discussed in general gossip and that reported in personal experience.

Personal Experience of Bribery

Since assertions of bribery always fell as the conversation moved from general gossip to specific personal statements, and denials usually increased, the *net difference* between assertions and denials of bribery fell sharply. The fall was particularly sharp in the Czech Republic. When people were talking in general terms, net assertions of bribery were about as frequent in Slovakia and Bulgaria as in Ukraine—and only around ten percent less in the Czech Republic. But when people began to talk about their personal experiences or intentions, net assertions of bribery occurred only half as often in Slovakia and Bulgaria as in Ukraine, and sank almost to zero in the Czech Republic. Particularly in the Czech Republic, but also in Slovakia, a number of text-units actually combined a general assertion that bribery existed with a specific personal denial: "I would not try it, but I know people who have done it" (Hr 2); "not from our own experience, rather from what I hear" (Ol 4); "everybody waits for something to be slipped into his or her pocket, a bribe. . . . [but] I would never bribe anybody, I would not know how. . . . am I really supposed to add to their salaries if I want something settled?" (Prv 6).

In Slovakia, references to bribery were more frequent than in the Czech Republic. Some were, in the donor's eyes at least, not a bribe but "just a little token" (Prv 2). From the standpoint of the official however, even "tokens" might add up: "My cousin cannot praise it enough, being a customs officer. He says: "Yesterday I brought home slippers for the whole family. I get so many chickens that I don't know where to put them—I need a second fridge." These are tokens for customs clearance." (Zv 5). Slovaks also listed monetary bribes quite explicitly, especially bribes to the traffic police and the health services: "Sometimes [the police] give you a penalty without a receipt— sometimes this satisfies both parties—this has already happened to me." (Br-B 9). Bribery to get medical attention was mentioned particularly frequently: "special deliveries, paid-for, fast, painless, and naturally the attitude of nurses to those patients was different" (Zv 1); "When my wife went to the maternity ward, the obstetrician said 3,000 crowns for treatment and 1,000 for the delivery. I felt it would be better, that he would take care of her . . . I felt life was at stake" (Br-B 4). But other Slovak officials were also mentioned: "The housing office—we could have had a flat but only if we had given 30,000 crowns—that is 30,000 crowns to the officials there . . . my husband had started a business . . . he had to give something to the officials there in order that we could get a flat." (Zv 1).

On balance Bulgaria was somewhat similar to Slovakia, though some of the stories of extortion were more horrific even if no more frequent. Most references to the Bulgarian police involved real or imaginary traffic offences: "I had enclosed in my passport 1,000 levs . . . He took 200 levs . . . and recommended for me a brush-up course of driving." (So-A 5). One particularly attractive and smartly dressed young woman claimed she had never paid a fine or a monetary bribe to the police: " . . . so far I haven't paid a single penalty. When they stop me I start deviating their attention . . . 'Let's go and have a cup of coffee.' . . . I might call the coffee 'friendly.'" (Ya 5)—to which an older woman in the group added wryly: "Your youth is your advantage. If they stopped me, even if I offered them whisky, they wouldn't be lenient to me." (Ya 6). But there was one more serious allegation against the police. A gypsy woman reported: "My daughter was raped a year ago, at the age of 17. Three months ago she was taken away [again] . . . the bar girl told me "Your daughter cried her head off" . . . [I] went to the police department, beside myself, and they said 'Maybe she wanted a man and that's why they took her.' But if I provided 2,000 lev for petrol they would go looking for her . . . I did not have the money so I went on my own.'" (Stral 5).

Health care was the other main focus of allegations about bribery: "The fee of the midwife was 15,000 levs, whereas the fee of the doctor was 30,000 levs." (Ya 6); "In my room I saw it—doctors took money from those in the beds next to mine." (Ku 5); "Some time ago my father had to be placed in a hospital. We had to offer a bribe. . . . it was a question of 30,000 levs—a year and a half ago that was quite a sum . . . I don't know where this sum of 30,000 levs sank, but two hours later a doctor came and my father was placed in the hospital." (So-B 8).

Bribery was not restricted to police and health workers: "I know the price is 300 dollars, but I haven't given any mark without examining the student. So I've become the "black sheep" among my fellow lecturers and they"ve become nasty to me." (So-B 5). "[My friend's] son . . . is serving at a distance of 15 klms from Sofiya . . . every two or three days he comes home—but that has its price, too." (So-B 3). Even MPs were involved: "In accordance with the Law of Restitution, friends of mine . . . are entitled to the real-estate [but the Municipality would not hand it over] . . . so they decided to contact their MP. The MP found the guts and told them how much it would cost them for the favour . . . 10 percent of the cost of the real-estate." (Ya 4).

Sometimes, especially in small villages, Bulgarians reported: "People know each other. Bribes are not expected." (Te 1). Some could not afford the bribe: "When I was in hospital, a guy whose father had to undergo an operation was told he had to give 20,000 levs. He said he could afford only 10,000 levs . . . and two days later his father died." (Te 5); "I knew the price of my case in the hospital . . . plus the friend in the appropriate position . . . but I cannot afford it." (So-B 2). More surprisingly, there were some tales of Bulgarian officials refusing to accept bribes. That even surprised and slightly disconcerted those who had offered them: "I underwent two operations at Medical Academy in Plovdiv. I was ready to pay, but the doctor I ran into turned down my money offer. . . . Upon leaving I hinted about money, but he felt pained. Then he accepted, most unwillingly, a bottle of grape-brandy as a token of gratitude. . . . .Now I am not sure what's going on there." (Ya 4).

Every group discussion in Ukraine, apart from the Crimean Tatars, produced specific personal statements about the use of bribery. Sometimes it clearly was for a favour: "there was another instructor who had a tariff: a bottle of vodka for [an undeserved pass in] the mid-term test" (Kh 1). Sometimes it was at least partly out of gratitude and relief: "I had an operation last year, a professor did it . . . we all knew, the patients talked about it, that he only took things after the operation." (Ky-A 1). But on many occasions it clearly was simply a case of extortion: "they put you in a situation that you have to." (Ho 6); "the surgeon said that she [the patient] was to give so much to the surgeon, so much to the neuropathologist, so much to the anaesthetist, and so much to the assistant. He directly said how much." (Ho 4); "there they say loud and clear, how much for what." (Kh 3); "I needed an operation . . . it [would, they said] cost fifty dollars. Okay . . . when I go in, she looked at me, all very pleasantly, then says "it'll cost a hundred dollars.'..it's already gone up!" (Ky-A 2).

Extortion was not limited to heath care: "until I gave a bribe he did not receive me . . . I gave him 20 dollars and he signed it." (Striy 2); "yes, to have a position at school I have to give up my salary . . . for this whole year, if not longer, I will be earning money for them [those who appointed her]." (Striy 5); "I faced it myself in the notary's office . . . if you haven't brought anything you will probably sit there for three days minimum if not three weeks . . . I have been there five or six days. Until you buy something and bring it there, you are given no attention and no service." (Vo 5); "she says 'give me 500 thousand so that I make a labour card for you.'..and I never heard that you must pay for a labour card." (Vo 2). And they paid frequently: "for this half-year, two times." (Ky-B 1); "family for the last half-year of time, five times probably, not less." (Ky-B 3) "I also had to do it frequently." (Ky-B 4).

What is to be Done?

Some of our findings might encourage complacency. From the perspective of the citizen, it appears that the situation is not as bad as it at first appears. While allegations about the need to use bribery or contacts in dealing with officials are widespread, they need to be treated with some scepticism. Such allegations are at least twice as frequent in general gossip as in reports of specific personal experience; and bribery is associated more with citizens' attempts to get favourable treatment than with their attempts to get fair treatment. To some extent therefore, they have only themselves to blame. Indeed some recognise this: "we've taught them this; we ourselves are guilty; we take them things . . . the first and the second bring something, and the third can't not bring something." (Kh 3). But this confession of guilt is atypical. Rightly or wrongly, most people blame officials for extorting bribes; they interpret the present situation as a problem; and they propose solutions. Very few comments suggested that it was impossible to change the relationship between citizens and officials—the percentage ranged from zero in the Czech Republic to only 6 percent in Ukraine.

A *better quality of official* was a popular suggestion: between 24 and 32 percent of relevant text-units in each country mentioned it. That was almost, but not quite, as vacuous as it sounds. Comments about better officials were often tautologous: "Pleasant people should work there—a private businessman would not hire a waitress or a shop assistant who would turn her back on a customer." (Br-B 2). In Ukraine especially there were calls to "change [officials"] psychology" (Ho 1); for "more responsible [officials]" (Ho 6); "conscience" (Ho 3), "competence" (Kh 6), "understanding" (Vo 3), "culture" (Ky-B 5), and—the ultimate in tautologies—"honesty" (Striy 3 and 4).

But other comments about better quality officials suggested better systems of selection, more qualified entrants, and more in-service training—including training in customer relations as well as in more technical matters. Selection could be improved: less "so-called nepotism" (So-B 1). Czechs and Slovaks especially, but others also, emphasised qualifications and training: "higher qualifications [are needed]" (Pra-B 1); "better training" (Br-B 5); "there's little professionalism. . . . they are poor souls, typing with just one finger—do not take this literally . . . I sometimes feel they must have studied at a special university for mentally handicapped students." (Pra-A 7). And a course in customer relations might help: "[officials] should be aware that those coming to them, or their 'customers,' are not experts in filling out forms." (Hr 3).

In the Czech Republic, 46 percent of text-units—far more than anywhere else—mentioned a need to improve *administrative efficiency and organisation*—which reflected the burden of the Czech participants' complaints: that they found the bureaucracy tedious and unhelpful rather than corrupt, forcing them to waste too much time on filling out forms, going to offices, and standing in queues. So they proposed a better administrative structure, less bureaucracy, better located offices, or simply longer office opening hours: "[individual departments] are unable to communicate between themselves" (KH 7); "fewer useless forms" (KH 5); "and above all fewer bureaucrats" (KH 4); and "longer opening hours" (Pra-B 4). Slovaks made similar but less frequent suggestions for administrative reform: "less bureaucracy, more flexibility" (NZ 3, with noises of agreement from NZ 1 and NZ

2); "premises—people cram in there and the clerk gets irritable . . . slightly more human conditions would do." (Br-B 2). They wanted more information: "at all these offices where most people have to go, there should be one person whose sole responsibility it is to provide information." (Zv 4); and a "one-stop shop" such as they had enjoyed under communism: "formerly everything was in one place [at "National Committees"], it was a well-established system and . . . people there knew their jobs" (Br-A 2). There were also a few similar suggestions in Bulgaria and Ukraine: "There should be everywhere computers." (Ya 5); "they should tell you everything you need to bring the first time." (Ky-A 6); "it's not everywhere [i.e., in every country] you need such a quantity of certificates." (Ky-A 2).

Conversely, discussion groups outside the Czech Republic put more emphasis on other reforms, reflecting the different nature of their complaints which were more about extortion and rather less about mere time-wasting— *more pay for officials* to make extortion less necessary, *stricter control* to make extortion more dangerous, or some combination of the two.

More pay was a popular suggestion in Slovakia: "insufficient salaries, that's the cause of all that bribing." (Br-B 8). Sometimes there was special pleading however: "because they are not actually rewarded in any way, they don't care. . . . the system of doctors' remuneration should be quite different in my opinion . . . . my husband is a doctor." (Prv 8). Sometimes the idea was qualified: "I think salaries should be raised in health care and in education. . . . [though] not to all of them without any discrimination." (Zv 9). Or even resisted: "but even if they got more money, they would behave in the same way." (Br-A 6).

Table 30.4
What is to be done?

	Czech Rep %	Slovakia %	Bulgaria %	Ukraine %
Improve personal qualities of staff	29	32	24	31
Better administrative organisation	46	18	15	9
More pay	7	18	14	13
More control	4	20	22	16
Better legal framework	21	15	15	29
More demanding citizens	0	3	17	4
Impossible to change	0	4	2	6
More funding	0	0	7	0
(Total N)	(72)	(99)	(152)	(271)

Note: Percentages are percentages of revelant "text units" in the focus group discussion, not of participants. The total number of revelant text-units on which percentages are based is shown in brackets at the foot of each column.

Similarly in Bulgaria: "perhaps they are underpaid" (So-A 4); "if the inspectors within this system were well-paid, they wouldn't give way to tipping of 500 levs or 5,000 levs—they wouldn't be tempted so easily." (So-A 1). But again the suggestion for more pay was sometimes linked to performance: "I think people should be paid according to their performance . . . . for an operation made our doctors get small change, and when a plumber screws in a bolt in his house, he asks for money, worth ten operations." (So-B 4). And occasionally resisted: "I don't think the explanation lies only in the low salaries. Salaries will be raised, and they will become corrupt again. . . . there are no moral values." (So-A 6).

Ukrainians too, sympathised with underpaid officials: "he has to live; he doesn't earn enough money, that's why he takes bribes." (Ni 3); "if they receive appropriate payment, they will work professionally in their positions and will not take bribes." (Sh 4).

Stricter control was seldom mentioned in the Czech Republic but quite frequently elsewhere. Slovaks complained that "it's worse now than under the rule of communism . . . you could lodge even an anonymous complaint and now there's no one to complain to. . . . now they are not afraid of anything." (Do 4). One Slovak wanted: "really harsh conditions, strict sanctions . . . we would have to start from the top and proceed downwards." (Prv 6). In Bulgaria participants complained: "there used to be some order . . . " (Ya 2); "Now the situation is very bad—perhaps because we have no one to take our complaints to for injustices." (Ya 1); "There should be control." (So-A 3).

Ukrainians also emphasized the need for control, even fear: "it is necessary that he simply be afraid that he can lose his place" (Ky-B 3); "there should be power in the country" (Kh 4); "there was discipline—everybody was afraid of the party" (Striy 3); "we are missing discipline . . . there is no fear now" (Striy 1). Against the great preponderance of such sentiments, there were only a couple of atypical remarks expressing reservations: "control can be strengthened, but that's not the way out." (Ky-A 4); "the innocent suffer." (Ni 1).

Sticks and Carrots. Sympathetic attitudes towards officials' salaries were accompanied and often combined with less sympathetic suggestions. Pay rises could be combined with stricter control or a cut in the number of officials: "If it were up to me they should be controlled." (Stral 2); "Nothing terrible would happen if the official apparatus were cut back by two thirds." (Ky-A 4) "And raise the salaries of the ones who are left." (Ky-A 5) But one pessimist dismissed both ideas: "I disagree on the score of salaries. . . . appetite grows in the course of eating, [and] sanctions won't do—they will be carried out by people who might perhaps have the same weaknesses." (So-B 8).

At first sight, the frequency of proposals for a *better legal framework* appear to provide a point of similarity between the Czech Republic and

Ukraine. But what did they mean by a better legal framework? In the Czech Republic, simpler and more stable laws: "a simpler, easily understandable law" (Ol 4). In Bulgaria too, there were also references to simplifying the laws: "Legislation should be simplified and made clear to the people." (So-A 7); "Laws should be clear. At the moment I have the feeling we are ruled by decrees and regulations." (So-A 1). But in Bulgaria there was also a plea for laws to replace anarchy, to fill a vacuum, and thereby exert control over officials: "There are no laws, they say. When will these laws be passed?" (Stral 6). And there was some emphasis on simply enforcing obedience to the law: "In a West-European country, corruption is controlled . . . the penalty is serious . . . We all have to work towards creating a normal state, a law-abiding state." (So-A 6).

Suggestions for improved legislation were also voiced in Ukraine: "[we have] no developed legislation" (Ky-A 4). But two thirds of the references to the law in Ukraine did not focus on this need for clearer, simpler and better publicised laws. One third consisted of complaints from Crimean Tatars that the laws of Ukraine were biased against them: "discrimination against nationality" (Se 4 and 5). More typically however, the remaining third of Ukrainian suggestions for legal reform concerned enforcement rather than clarification: "there should be organs that would make sure this law was followed." (Kh 4).

Bulgarians in particular placed some responsibility on *citizens themselves*: "There's a rule—the more you are informed, the less corrupt the official" (So-A 7); "When I know my legal rights . . . I can defend them and I can demand." (Ya 4). This is of course, just another perspective on the need for more information about citizens' rights which was mentioned in other countries, but now with the onus placed upon citizens to inform themselves.

Inevitably the solutions proposed by ordinary citizens in our focus group discussions are less complex and sophisticated than those prescribed by public administration specialists[28] and they differ considerably in the details but both highlight the importance of a mix of encouragement, control and public information.

Discussion

No doubt our focus group participants held something back. We do not suppose that they revealed all. But it is remarkable how much they were willing to say in front of the video-cameras at our focus groups. Partly that reflected the expertise of our focus group moderators, all of whom had extensive experience in leading group discussions. But it also reflected the openness of the participants themselves. Most did not seem over-inhibited by the long years of life under communism. On the contrary they seemed to revel in their new freedom to criticise the state.

Of course the opposite danger is that people will tell extravagant but untruthful stories to impress their fellow participants or to please the investigators. We did find a sharp difference between allegations made in general terms and those based on more personal experience. In the Czech Republic general gossip about widespread corruption simply did not correspond to more personal accounts of experience and behaviour. But by contrast, the discrepancy between general allegations and personal experience was less elsewhere, and much less in Ukraine. We think it unlikely that this reflected greater reticence, more fear, or less openness in the Czech Republic than elsewhere. And that has important implications: the difference between Czech and Ukrainian experience of interacting with officials was actually greater than was implied by more superficial questions about the general climate of corruption. A climate of exaggerated suspicion and criticism in the Czech Republic, influenced no doubt by press reports of high-level corruption, actually obscured the extent of the difference between Czech and Ukrainian citizens' own, immediate and direct personal experience.

We found evidence of a gradation in official corruption from the Czech Republic through Slovakia and Bulgaria to Ukraine. In terms of how citizens dealt with officials, there were clear differences between the Czech Republic and Slovakia—both, to varying degrees, "Catholic" and both former Hapsburg territories; and on our data "Catholic" west Ukraine was actually more inclined to bribe officials than "Orthodox" east Ukraine. That contradicts any notion that we should simplistically divide the world into Catholic, Orthodox and Muslim cultures—or, more locally, into former Hapsburg, Romanov, and Ottoman cultures.[29] While we do not suggest that long established culture and history have no continuing impact other factors may be still more important. Differences in the interactions between citizens and officials in the different postcommunist countries may reflect more recent differences in the way these states have actually treated their citizens—the half century of direct experience of Soviet bureaucracy that applied equally to east and west Ukraine for example. They may also reflect variations in contemporary postcommunist circumstances: economic collapse in Bulgaria and dislocation in Ukraine but better living standards in the Czech Republic; and a greater discontinuity both of personnel and ethos in the administration of the Czech Republic, contrasting with more continuity elsewhere. Indeed, insofar as any one of our postcommunist countries stands out very much from the others in terms of the behaviour of its officials, it is the Czech Republic.

It is worth drawing attention, once again, to the infrequency of suggestions that it was impossible to improve the relationship between citizens and officials. And also worth recalling the widespread allegation that, except in the Czech Republic, the behaviour of officials had changed for the worse since the fall of the communist system. Both those findings imply movement and change, whether for better or for worse; so both contradict the thesis that the relationship between citizens and officials is determined by an unchanging and unchangeable culture. Ironically, recent changes for the worse show that change is possible and therefore hold out the possibility of change, perhaps for the better, in the future.

Does low level corruption matter? To ordinary citizens going about their daily business it does. That is the level of corruption which makes the most immediate and most visible difference to their lives. In his study of rampant corruption in the British colony of Hong Kong, Wing Lo found wide support for repressive measures against corrupt, usually junior, civil servants though much less for similar action against corrupt millionaire businessmen because "the public do not always feel as threatened by corrupt businessmen as they do by corrupt public servants . . . public sector corruption is often related to extortion and solicitation of bribes by civil servants . . . [which is] far more annoying and disturbing to the daily lives of people."[30] We found that same public resentment of "extortion and solicitation" in our group discussions.

Corruption may have helped to lubricate the creaky old machinery of communism. Huntington, amongst others, once argued that "corruption may thus be functional to the maintenance of a political system in the same way that reform is . . . and both corruption and reform may be substitutes for revolution."[31] By improving both the economic efficiency and the human rights record of a dictatorship, public sector corruption nay well be functional to the maintenance of such a regime. But public sector corruption degrades both the economic efficiency and the civil rights record of a free market democracy, and contributes to its instability. Democracy is founded on the principle of political equality, and public sector corruption is founded on the principle that the state will treat its citizens arbitrarily and unequally. In a democracy, political equality offsets inequalities of wealth and power; but public sector corruption reinforces those inequalities. That is why Almond and Verba defined a well-functioning democracy not only in terms of citizen influence over high policy, but also in terms of fair and equal treatment by junior state officials.

Moreover, low level corruption is not divorced from high level corruption. A corrupt example at the top is likely to encourage corruption at the bottom. Conversely, however, it is unlikely that a junior official trained by experience in bribery and extortion will suddenly give it all up when he or she gets promoted. Wider horizons simply present new opportunities. So-called "zero-tolerance policing" is now fashionable in Britain and America. It is based upon the assumption that a permissive attitude to low level crime not only degrades the living environment and life style of ordinary citizens but also encourages low level criminals to graduate to higher level crime. The analogy with corruption is close.

What is clear from our focus group discussions is that citizens in Bulgaria and Ukraine do not regard official corruption any more kindly than in the Czech Republic; they do *not* regard it as a curse in the Czech Republic but a blessing in Bulgaria or Ukraine. It may be a necessity for the individual citizen perhaps, but an unwelcome one: extortion, not a facility. And that also has implications for the possibility of reform. There is no dispute anywhere about the direction of "improvement," no deep cultural attachment to corruption as a systemic virtue in postcommunist circumstances as it arguably may have been under communism; and no shortage of sensible suggestions for reform that take account of the specific circumstances and contemporary problems in each country. The concrete reality of variations in official behaviour disguises more uniform aspirations amongst the citizens of different countries.

Notes

1. This research was funded by the Overseas Development Administration under award number R6445 to William L. Miller and Tatyana Koshechkina and by the ESRC under award number R222474 to William L. Miller and Åse Berit Grødeland.
2. Indeed, Seweryn Bialer *Stalin"s Successors: Leadership, Stability and Change in the Soviet Union* (Cambridge: Cambridge University Press, 1980), pp. 166–7, claims that "low politics" constituted "the very substance of the Soviet system of political participation." As the euphoria associated with the "high politics" of 1989–91 subsides the continuing importance of "low politics" becomes more evident.
3. See Martin Harrop and William L. Miller *Elections and Voters: a Comparative Introduction* (London: Macmillan, 1987) Chapter 9.
4. Gabriel A. Almond and Sidney Verba *The Civic Culture: Political Attitudes and Democracy in Five Nations* (Princeton University Press, 1963; reprinted by Sage, 1989) especially Chapter 7: "Citizen Competence and Subject Competence."
5. Wayne DiFranceisco and Zvi Gitelman "Soviet Political Culture and Covert Participation in Policy Implementation," *American Political Science Review*, (1984) vol. 78 pt. 3 pp.603–21. They discuss citizen participation in the old Soviet Union in precisely these terms.
6. Quoted by Ferrel Heady "Bureaucracies" in Mary Hawkesworth and Maurice Kogan *Encyclopedia of Government and Politics* (London: Routledge, 1992) p.305.
7. DiFranceisco and Gitelman (1984) p. 613.
8. A. Sogomonov and A. Tolstykh. "O nashikh zabotakh" *Kommunist* (1989) no. 9. p.75. They put "the wide-spread use of pull" in third place on the list of "most pressing problems facing our country today," and in first place if combined with "dependence on officials in solving housing questions" which probably reflected the use of bribes or influence to get better state flats.
9. DiFranceisco and Gitelman (1984), p. 612–614.
10. For the cultural legacy of the FSU see Stephen White *Political Culture and Soviet Politics* (London: Macmillan, 1979) Chapters 2 and 5 especially.
11. The former Czechoslovakia passed a law to purge up to 140,000 alleged communist "informers"—see Keith Grime and Vic Duke "A Czech on privatisation," *Regional Studies*, (1993) vol. 27, no. 8, pp. 751–57 at p. 754; and Jirina Siklora "Lustration or the Czech way of screening" *East European Constitutional Review* (1996) vol. 5, no. 1, pp. 57–62 who notes at p. 58 that President Havel opposed

the purge law on the grounds that it presumed guilt rather than innocence. However this law was not adopted by the new Slovak Republic when Czechoslovakia split up in 1992. See Quentin Reed "Transition, dysfunctionality and change in the Czech and Slovak Republics" *Crime, Law and Social Change* (1995) vol. 22, no. 4, pp 323–337 at p. 334.

12. See Andrew Coulson (ed.) *Local Government in Eastern Europe: Establishing Democracy at the Grassroots* (London: Edward Elgar, 1995) especially Chpt 1: "From Democratic Centralism to Local Democracy" by Andrew Coulson.

13. See for example, Jeffrey Levine "Excuse me . . . I've no machinery, no money and no market; how do I farm?," *Demokratizatsiya*, (1995) vol. 3, no. 1, p. 99; or Quentin Reed (1995) p. 326; or Lubomir Faltan and Richard A. Dodder "Privatising the housing sector: the case of Slovakia," *Public Administration and Development*, (1995) vol. 15, no. 4, pp. 391–96 at p. 394.

14. Faltan and Dodder (1995) p. 394.

15. Vladimir Benacek, Alena Zemplinerova "Problems and Environment of Small Businesses in the Czech Republic," *Small Business Economics* (1995) vol.7, no. 6, pp.437–50 at p. 442.

16. Alessandro Bonanno, Andrei Kuznetsov, Simon Geletta and Mary Hendrickson "To farm or not to farm: rural dilemma in Russia and Ukraine," *Rural Sociology* (1993) vol. 58, no. 3, pp. 404–23 at p. 419.

17. In 1993, 31 percent in ECE and 56 percent in the FSU told us they had "believed in communist ideals" at some time, though only 20 percent in ECE and a mere 18 percent in the FSU did so "now." See W. L. Miller, S. White and P. Heywood *Values and Political Change in Postcommunist Europe* (London: Macmillan, 1998) Chapter 4.

18. Tony Verheijen and Antoaneta Dimitrova "Private interests and public administration: the Central and East European experience" *International Review of Administrative Sciences* (1996) vol. 62, no.2, pp. 197–218 at p. 212.

19. Volodymyr Zviglyanich "Ukraine's labour policy: underemployment" *The Jamestown Foundation Prism. A Bi-weekly on the Post-Soviet States*, vol. 2, no. 10, part 3, 17 May 1996, pp. 1–6.

20. See for example, Steve Kettle "Of money and morality (in the Czech Republic)" *Transition* (formerly *RFE/RL Report*) 15th March 1995; James Meek "Scourge of corruption fends off Ukraine''s hostile elite" *The Guardian* 15th August 1995. Boskholov claims that there has been a growth in the use of bribery in Russia over the last few years. In 1993 4,500 cases of bribery in government (an increase of 34.8% compared to 1992) involving some 1,500 officials were revealed; 42.7 of these cases involved officials working in ministries, committees and other structures in the provinces. Bribery was also wide-spread in the legal administration, accounting for 25.8% of the cases revealed (Sergei Boskholov "Organized Crime and Corruption in Russia" *Demokratizatsiya* (1995) vol. 3, no. 3, pp. 271–72). Although Russia differs significantly from the Czech Republic, it differs less from Slovakia, Bulgaria, and especially Ukraine. So we might expect the situation to be somewhat similar in these countries.

21. Alena V. Ledeneva *An Economy of Favours: Informal Exchanges and Networking in Russia* (Cambridge: Cambridge University Press, 1998) Chapter 6.

22. See Miller, White and Heywood (1998) Chapter 9.

23. Ibid. Chapter 5.

24. Ibid. Chapter 10.

25. Other focus group findings are available in: William L. Miller, Tatyana Y. Koshechkina and Åse B. Grødeland "How citizens cope with postcommunist

580   Political Corruption

officials: evidence from focus group discussions in Ukraine and the Czech Republic." *Political Studies*, (Special Issue 1997) vol. 45, no. 3, pp. 597–625, and Åse
B. Grødeland, Tatyana Y. Koshechkina and William L. Miller "Alternative strategies for coping with officials in different postcommunist regimes: the worm's eye
view." *Public Administration and Development*, (1997) vol. 17, no. 5, pp. 511–
528. Findings from our in-depth interviews are presented in Åse B. Grødeland,
Tatyana Y. Koshechkina and William L. Miller " 'Foolish to give and yet more
foolish not to take': in-depth interviews with postcommunist citizens on their
everyday use of bribes and contacts." *Europe-Asia Studies*, (1998) vol. 50, no. 4,
pp. 649–675. Findings from the survey of the public are published in William L.
Miller, Åse B. Grødeland and Tatyana Y. Koshechkina "Are the people victims or
accomplices? The use of presents and bribes to influence officials in Eastern
Europe." *Crime, Law and Social Change,* (1998 forthcoming) vol. 28, no. 4.
26. For a recent review of this methodology see Eben Weitzman *Computer Programs
for Qualitative Data Analysis* (London: Sage, 1995).
27. The code in brackets indicates that this is a quotation from respondent 1 in focus-
group B in Kyiv. See the Appendix for details.
28. Tony Verheijen and Antoaneta Dimitrova. "Corruption and unethical behaviour of
civil and public servants: causes and possible solutions," *NISPAcee 5ᵗʰ Annual
Conference*, Tallin, April 1997.
29. Samuel P. Huntington. "The clash of civilisations" *Foreign Affairs* (1993) vol. 72,
no. 3, pp. 22–49; more crudely stated in Samuel P. Huntington. "The West v the
rest" *The Guardian* 23 November 1996, p.23.
30. T. Wing Lo, *Corruption and Politics in Hong Kong and China* (Buckingham,
Open University Press, 1993) at pp. 148–9.
31. Samuel P. Huntington, "Modernization and Corruption," in Arnold J. Heidenheimer
(ed.), *Political Corruption* (New Brunswick NJ, Transaction Books, 1970), pp.
492–500 at p. 495.

Appendix
Design of the Focus Group StudyNotes:

	Ukraine		Bulgaria	Former Czechoslovakia	
	East	West		Slovakia	Czech Rep
Capital city (higher educ)	Kyiv-A		*Sofya-A	*Bratislava-A	Praha-B
Capital city (lower educ)	Kyiv-B		*Sofya-B	*Bratislava-B	Praha-A
Medium town	*Khartsysk	*Striy	*Yambol	Zvolen	*Hradec Kralove
Small town	Volnovakha	*Horodok	*Straldja	Presov	*Kutna Hora
Village	Nikolayevka	*Sholomia	*Tenevo	Dolny Kubin	*Olesnice
Ethnic Minority	Sevastopol (Tatars)		*Kurdjali (Turks)	*Nove Zamky (Hungarians)	——
Total participants in Focus Groups	55		45	49	38

Notes

1. Focus groups were organised by USM (Ukrainian Surveys and Market Research) of Kyiv, CSD (Center for the Study of Democracy) of Sofia, and OPW (Opinion Window Market Research and Analysis) of Praha—covering both the Czech and Slovak Republics.
2. All 26 FG discussions were video-taped. Computer readable vernacular and English-language transcripts were made from these tapes. In addition, simultaneous translation was provided by Marichka Padalko in Ukraine, Mitra Myanova in Bulgaria, Zuzana Vrastiakova in Slovakia, and Klara Flemrova in the Czech Republic during the 16 FGs marked with an asterisk which were all attended by the authors.
3. FGs in East Ukraine were located in the Donetsk region, those in West Ukraine in the Lviv region, all chaired by Alexander Fedorishin, using the language chosen by the participants—Russian in Kyiv, Sevastopol and East Ukraine, Ukrainian in West Ukraine. FGs in Bulgaria were chaired by Andrej Nonchev (except for the one in Straldja which was chaired by Elena Lazarova), all in Bulgarian. FGs in Slovakia were chaired by Patrik Minar in Slovak (except for the one in Nove Zamky which was chaired by Ladislav Koppl speaking in Czech while participants responded in Slovak). FGs in the Czech Republic were chaired by Ladislav Koppl using Czech.
4. Underlining indicates the short form of town names used to identify respondents in the text. Thus, for example, (Ky-B 1) in the text indicates a quotation from the first participant in the focus group Kyiv-B.

31

Corruption and the Future of Economic Reform in China

Yufan Hao and Michael Johnston

Introduction

Corruption has become a major phenomenon in the People's Republic of China.[1] While its economy experiences spectacular growth under market-oriented reforms, embezzlement, bribery, extortion, favoritism, and smuggling have increased in frequency and variety, and have spread into every corner of society. Many bureaucrats accept bribes and speculate in raw materials and finished products. Officials supervising economic, administrative, and legal functions through both party and state agencies often solicit money and favors for their services. Even reporters, lawyers, teachers, and doctors can be caught up in the epidemic. Indeed, many see corruption as undermining the Communist Party's political legitimacy, weakening social stability, and harming the country's economic future. In this chapter we survey trends, causes, and consequences of corruption over the generation since market-oriented reforms were launched in 1978. We argue that in both economic and—perhaps more surprising—political terms, corruption confronts China with both serious challenges and unexpected opportunities.

The Outlines of the Problem

Corruption is virtually impossible to measure with precision. Often it is a clandestine activity lacking individual victims or other witnesses who might make reports: those who know about corruption generally wish to keep it secret.[2] Estimates are all the more difficult in China because official figures

583

are unreliable, and because market reforms—which are changing official powers and interpersonal dealings in fundamental ways—have left rules and roles very much in flux. However, in 1998 alone Party discipline inspection committees punished 158,000 officials, of whom 5357 were at the county or department level, 410 at the prefecture level, and 12 at the provincial or ministerial level.[3] The scale of corrupt transactions has also expanded: in early 1980s, bribes and embezzlements usually ranged from several hundred to several thousand yuan. Now it is common to find cases involving millions, or even billions, as we shall see.

Above and beyond statistics on cases, there is the political significance of corruption. Corruption was one of the main grievances of the 1989 Democracy Movement. Deng Xiaoping himself once stated that "We must face up to the serious nature of corruption within the party. Things have become so serious and pernicious that they are not only disturbing and undermining the party's central tasks, but also are threatening party leadership. If we do not gear up to fight corruption and eradicate it, the party will probably lose people's support and its foundation deteriorate and go under. This is entirely possible."[4] Party chief Jiang Zemin went further: "We cannot underestimate the seriousness and harm of corruption, which is like a virus invading the body of the party and state. It will bury our party, our people's regime, and socialist modernization if we do not attack it seriously and [if we] allow it to spread unchecked."[5] Indeed, we believe that corruption has brought China and its reform process to a crossroads. The proliferation and increasing strength of interests unleashed by market-oriented policies, contributing to both the growth of corruption and demands for reform, pose fundamental questions of governance, legitimacy, and values.

The varieties of corruption have proliferated too, along with the words and ideas used to describe them. In the late 1970s "corruption," in Chinese political terminology, had three meanings: *tanwu*, *shouhui* and *tequan*. *Tanwu* (malpractice) involved state officials who misappropriated public property by embezzlement, theft or swindling. *Shouhui* meant using official positions to extort or to accept bribes. *Tequan* (privileges) covered widespread privilege-seeking activities by officials, including "back-door" practices. Since the early 1990s, however, "corruption" has more often meant *fubai*—decay and putrefaction. The sheer breadth of this concept can be seen in the range of activities cited in the Chinese press, between June 1993 and September 1998, as "corrupt": economic offenses violating law or financial and economic disciplines; embezzlement, bribery, breaches of law and discipline by law enforcement officers; indiscriminate collection of fees, resale profiteering and speculation, blackmail, black market currency exchanges, swindling, extortion, establishing illegal businesses, smuggling; abuse of governmental authority, misappropriation or waste of public funds; producing or selling counterfeit or defective goods; tax evasion, making false reports for refunds; excessive housing, using public funds for extravagant banquets, overseas travels, and gift-giving; illegal price increases, indiscriminate issuance of bonuses, ticket scalping, nepotism and favoritism; speculation in stock and real estate with public funds, work units' "small treasuries" (*xiao jinku*); gambling, visiting prostitutes, "decadent behavior," usury, outright piracy, insider trading in the new security and futures markets, imposing fines and financial levies at random, deceiving superiors or subordinates, vocational misconduct—and so on.[6] As this list suggests, the distinctions between public and private dealings, and between bribers and bribees, that help define corruption in many western settings are not easily applied in China. Many participants hold both public and private roles—or roles that do not fit neatly into either sphere—and operate in economic gray areas. It is often difficult to say where corruption ends and market reform begins.

But corruption, and *responses* to it, may also be moving China away from a traditional authoritarian society ruled by man and toward a more rational society ruled by law. Economic reforms have unleashed powerful forces in a nation that was so dominated by the Party-state that basic boundaries and distinctions defining the limits of market and official power, and of public and private interest, were weak or non-existent.[7] At one level, this has made both for more corruption and for confusion about the meanings of the term. At another, it has produced a demand for changes to institutionalize the new system. Two and a half millennia of Chinese tradition, the changing outlooks of the leadership, and the sheer difficulty of describing—much less reforming—the largest society on earth make it a gross exaggeration to say that these trends are building democracy. Nonetheless, the issue of defining and enforcing workable rules is squarely on the agenda. While China is a long way from attaining rule *of* law, in important respects rule *by* law may be beginning to limit the extent of rule by man.[8]

Behind the Surge of Corruption

Why has corruption become so rampant? We see five mutually reinforcing causes: (1) systemic and structural problems; (2) increased opportunities and incentives for corruption brought forth by market-oriented reforms; (3) a crisis of values; (4) deficient legal and supervisory mechanisms; and (5) cultural factors.

Systemic and Structural Problems

China's hierarchical Leninist State, as well as economic reforms, both contribute to corruption. The state system had two salient features prior to 1978. First, there was a highly centralized power structure in which the party and state intertwined at all levels. This Party-state controlled all, reaching from the center outward and downward to all neighborhoods and villages. People were organized into work units of all sizes (factories, agricultural production teams, schools, hospitals, and banks)—all-inclusive political, economic, and social entities giving officials personal discretion over the necessities of everyday life.[9] The resulting patron-client networks reinforced state hegemony in almost every aspect of life, and provided opportunities for local officials to pursue their own personal and institutional interests. Second, after the land redistribution and conversion of private into public property of the 1950s, the state replaced decentralized markets with hierarchical control over all significant economic activities, command-style planning, and public ownership of nearly all significant economic organizations. Bureaucrats set prices and distributed resources, determined what to plant or manufacture, and decided what would be shipped where and when. Enterprises were little more than appendages of the bureaucracies that administered them.

These two features made China's system hierarchical, political, and inefficient, and generated distinctive kinds of corruption. In capitalist economies market processes guide resource distribution, and government's role is primarily to maintain fair play. In China before 1978, by contrast, individual preferences were supplanted by centralized planning. The major determinant of resource allocation was bureaucratic influence bought with time and/or money, a situation that well-placed bureaucrats found easy to exploit. Yet, corruption in Mao's era was contained, both in scope and meaning, by a strict communist value system and political movements, orchestrated from above, against corruption and bureaucratism. Periodic rectification campaigns and the *xiafang* movement (sending cadres down to lower levels to remold bureaucrats' attitudes) afforded the center considerable control over local officials' behavior.

2. Increased Opportunities and Incentives for Corruption Brought by Reform

In 1978 the leadership began to abandon Mao's radical policy. Aware of the serious bureaucratic rigidities, inefficiency, and irrationalities embedded in the system, Deng Xiaoping sought decentralization, partial reliance upon market forces, and a limited private economy. These three reforms all affected bureaucrats' behavior.

Decentralization. The decentralization launched at the Third Party Plenum in December, 1978, began in some ministries and industries but spread gradually throughout the country. Decisionmaking was delegated to regions, major cities, and even to individual industrial enterprises. The goal was to promote autonomy in enterprise management, and to make enterprises "legal persons with certain rights and duties."[10] Thus, enterprises were given power over the production, pricing, and distribution of above-quota or nonplanned output, and over the hiring, promotion, remuneration and dismissal of their workers. By 1987 this "managers' responsibility system" had been introduced to most large state-owned enterprises, and the party had withdrawn from daily administration of factories. Enterprises were allowed to keep 39 percent of total profits, a threefold increase over 1979. Smaller state enterprises and many collectively owned firms were subcontracted out to their managers or other bidders, who ran them virtually as private businesses.

The new system was meant to create incentives to efficiency, but produced mixed results. Many managers used their newfound discretion in dubious ways. Some participated in speculation or illegal trade, buying materials or products at low state prices and reselling them on black markets.[11] Others increased their own salaries, spent public funds for excessive housing and extravagant banquets, or engaged in tax evasion and smuggling. Rare commodities were hoarded for resale at a profit. Permits to import foreign goods could yield fortunes from black market currency exchanges. In Hainan in 1985, for example, 89,000 cars, 2.9 million color televisions and over 250,000 videotape recorders were imported under a duty-free policy for goods to be used locally, and then resold on the mainland for large profits.[12] Other opportunities arose because decentralization was incomplete. Some control over finance, tax revenues, foreign trade, investment, raw materials and capital construction was devolved to lower-level bureaucracies, leaving the center more dependent on local cadres to implement its policies but not reducing people's dependence on immediate bureaucratic superiors.[13] For example, in 1984 the central government decentralized control over state enterprises' after-tax profits to encourage efficiency while increasing state revenue. But enterprises took advantage of the changes to evade taxes. In 1985, the Ministry of Finance reported that more than 50 percent of all state-and collectively-owned enterprises and individual businesses were cheating on their taxes.[14] The situation became even worse as decentralization continued. Qingdao City studied a sample of 100 enterprises and found out that 95 of them had committed tax evasion in 1989.[15] The public procuratorate revealed that more than 80 percent of all enterprises cheated on state taxes in 1992, contributing to a huge state deficit.[16]

Decentralization in the financial system also led to corruption. In the past, enterprises received their capital through allocations from their ministries. Now various specialized banks supply significant capital in the form of loans of state funds. The booming collective and private enterprises rely heavily on these banks for credit, and even the state-owned enterprises have become customers. While instructed to make loans purely on the economic merits, bankers are always subject to pressures from local officials. For example, one Wang Zhiqiang, the manager of Zhoukou District Pharmacy Factory, gave 6,000 yuan as a bribe to Cui Donghua, the Deputy County chief in charge of agriculture. Cui then instructed the county branch of the Agricultural Bank to give Wang an interest-free "loan" of 400,000 yuan that was never paid back.[17] Local bankers also proved unable to discipline investment or to force prompt repayments, making banks the targets of economic criminals both inside and outside of the financial system. Wan Xiaoting, the manager of Fenjiang branch (Feshan City branch) of the China Bank, violated financial regulations by lending out 5.1 billion yuan illegally, for which he received large kickbacks.[18] In Liaoning Province, Cong Songbo obtained 47 loans totaling about 79 million yuan by bribing a dozen officials of Beijing banks. The case was only exposed when he was murdered by his partner.[19]

Price reforms. Proposals give market forces a greater role in pricing commodities were implemented in the early 1980s. State-owned factories were allowed to produce for the market as long as they fulfilled state quotas, and to purchase raw materials through the market rather than remaining dependent on central allocation. The number of industrial products sold at fixed prices was reduced from 356 to 30, and the number of agricultural products from 113 to 25. In theory, this dual-track system reserved state-listed prices for materials and products distributed or produced under the plan, and market prices for transactions not subject to state control. But goods produced above (or off) the plan quickly began to sell at two to three times the planned prices, and enterprises and governmental organs thus found it profitable to engage in speculation. Jiangxi Provincial Bureau of Commerce officials, for example, purchased 250 tons of fertilizer at the state price and resold it on the market for twice as much.[20] Officials and bureaucrats often engaged in such speculation without even seeing the goods in question. In Nanjing, 1,000 tons of steel were purchased and resold among 83 companies and working units a total of 223 times over several months, with the price rising from 1,663 to 4,650 yuan per ton.[21]

Private Economy. Meanwhile, government encouraged the collective and privately-owned sectors to compete with state enterprises in production and services. Since the early 1980s, private shops, family-run restaurants and individual vendors have sprung up all over China's cities: in 1979, 140,000 small private enterprises were operating in cities. The total increased to 3.4 million in 1987, and to 15.3 million by the end of 1992.[22] By the end of 1993, more than 53% of the national output was reportedly produced by the non-state sector.[23] This development has produced dramatic changes, not only offering superior service and more convenience for urban residents but also legitimating private wealth and creating a rich new class. The ostentatious lifestyles of private businesspeople have made them the target of both admiration and envy, and triggered an entrepreneurial fever, with people from all walks of life "jumping into the business sea."

Many such companies were formed by officials or their relatives, who were in a position to distribute state goods at market prices, issue production and foreign trade licenses, obtain bank loans, and otherwise use their offices and connections to do business in a kind of gray area neither wholly public nor private.[24] Some simply created "briefcase companies" for speculation, while others engaged in actual trade. *China Daily* revealed that 250,000 of the 360,000 new companies established by 1987 were involved in dual-price speculation.[25] In Yunan Province, 6,234 companies were involved in such speculation in 1986; some 1,830 had their licenses suspended in an anti-corruption campaign.[26]

Decentralization and price decontrol did not curb the growth of bureaucratic power and prerogatives, nor did it fundamentally change the hierarchical nature of the system. It did, however, shift discretion to middle and local levels, where bureaucrats could determine who would receive contracts and when. Indeed, reform yielded two conflicting trends: one was bureaucratic resistance to market reforms as threats to their roles as planners and supervisors. But at the same time, bureaucrats were the ultimate beneficiaries of reform, since they had information and administrative power that could be exploited to enrich themselves. Official profiteering (*guandao*) became a major problem, taking on various forms such as moonlighting in enterprises, engaging in stock dealing, taking gifts, and giving and accepting bribes to allow both legal and illegal operations to take place. In 1992, the Party Central Committee issued Document No. 5, encouraging institutions to run various economic entities to "make a profit" (*chuangshou*) and legalizing official speculation and power-backed business for two years.[27] After that directive, hundreds of thousands of officials "jumped into the business sea."

Thus, while the plan no longer sharply constrained decision-makers enough official power remained to prevent the market from working in an effective fashion. Increasingly, officials and managers operated in a no-man's-land between plan and market, their dealings following the logic of neither. China arguably got the worst of both worlds, lacking the dynamics of the market and the discipline of the plan. After a generation of reform, China has a substantially dismantled planned economy and uncoordinated, imperfect markets for various goods. The dual-price system, semi-private companies, and increased administrative power at local levels have created a situation ripe for speculative corruption.

3. A Crisis of Values

Post-Mao China is also passing through a crisis of values. Reform-minded leaders encourage a new spirit of entrepreneurship, urging people "to get rich and to get rich fast."[28] This is a clear reversal of Mao's view that a society cannot and need not sacrifice the socialist goal of equality for short-term economic development. Deng, however, believed that egalitarianism encourages laziness, inefficiency, and ultimately pauperism. The Party's encouragement of entrepreneurship happened at a time of widespread disillusionment among Chinese people, a natural reaction to the tragedy of the Cultural Revolution. Many, especially among the young, lost confidence in communist ideals, turning instead to money as an outlet for emptiness and frustration, or as a symbol of status and success. This "moral vacuum" blurred the boundaries between legitimate and illegitimate behavior, and led to "an increasing sense of normlessness."[29] Party leaders appealed to a sense of "socialist spiritual civilization" and "lofty ideals," but with little effect.

The thirst for money was partly due to inflation caused by rapid growth. Inflation at times reached 30 percent annually in major cities in the 1980s. Although the incomes of most citizens increased during these years, they trailed both prices and expectations. Each social group seemed to feel that its own gains were less than those of others. The failure of official salaries to keep up led bureaucrats to rely on bribes to protect or increase their incomes. Indeed, where middle-level officials made the equivalent of about $50 a month, while a waitress in a joint-venture hotel could earn triple that figure, officials became all the more likely to use their power, the chops they could put on a piece of paper, and their ability to grant contracts and access to markets and materials, to make money.

With this mind-set of materialism, doing anything has a price. One visitor asked for directions in Canton and was told, "Sure I'll tell you—if you pay me."[30] Bribes and "gratitude" are so widespread that the situation resembles an auction of state resources and official services. As one foreign businessman observed:

> to get a small contract, say $20,000, I figure it's a couple dinners out and bowling. For a $250,000 contract, it's a "familiarization' trip for the official to the States. A contract of a million and above? Then we're talking about helping get a visa for the guy's son.[31]

Cadres' aspirations to luxury magnify demand for other privileges. Housing shortages in urban areas persist while many officials occupy more rooms than they need or are entitled to have. Many acquire extra apartments for their children and even baby grandchildren. Housing reform programs allowed some officials to buy high-quality homes at extremely low prices. One County chief in Heilongjiang Province, while occupying several houses, bought another apartment at 2,800 yuan and sold it immediately for 17,000 yuan.[32] Since 1990, discipline inspection committees at various levels have investigated such practices, evacuating nearly 180,000 units of government-owned housing and collecting 650 million yuan in refunds and fines.[33] In 1998, about 1.46 million residential telephones were installed, and about 792,000 mobile telephone purchased, with public money in violation of regulations.[34]

Pre-reform China had suffered from inefficiencies, mismanagement, embezzlement and fraud, but the current "normlessness" leads people to seek profits by any means available. The Chinese hospital system, for example, used to be quite inefficient, with patients waiting in long lines and doctors and nurses chatting. But hospital reforms tied doctors' wages to the number of patients treated and the amounts of medicine prescribed. Not surprisingly, some medical staff now rush patients through clinics and prescribe more drugs than necessary. Patients have little incentive to protest the latter practice, since most medical expenses are taken care of by their work units. But petty bribes are still required to ensure decent treatment: according to one study, 43 percent of hospital patients speed up their admission by giving "red packets."[35]

In this money-first atmosphere, bureaucrats and officials have new opportunities (and fewer disincentives) to put their influence up for hire. State land can be bought very cheaply in exchange for large bribes; loans that need never be repaid are available to those willing to share the proceeds with the bankers.[36] Huang Shengou, manager of the Real Estate Development Company affiliated to the State Land Bureau of Qingyuan City, Guangdong Province, was charged with selling land at a cheap price after accepting more than 1 million yuan in bribes.[37] Meng Qingping, the Vice-Governor of Hubei, traded power for women and money at will. When one of his mistresses was arrested for smuggling cars, he instructed the local authority to release her with only a fine as punishment.[38] While leading officials cash in on their power, middle-level functionaries solicit bribes for routine duties. Many enterprises report that department personnel are rude and arrogant; if they are not "gratified," they make it difficult to gain access to raw materials and markets. The Mayor of Shanghai recently made a public call for a serious fight against this trend. "At present, the masses have reacted strongly to the phenomenon [of] 'no service without money, and poor service with little money,'" said Mr Wu Bangguo. "This practice is still spreading and is very likely to penetrate all trades and professions."[39]

4. Insufficient Supervisory and Legal Systems.

China's hybrid system lacks clear ethical, legal and commercial codes to regulate market activities. Markets need credible legal systems to define relationships among private parties, and between them and the state. Yet China, after four decades of command economics under one-party rule, and a much longer tradition of skepticism about extensive legal codes, was unprepared in this respect. There are four aspects of this problem: (1) there is little systematic supervision of bureaucrats or of their deviant behavior; (2) irrational policies exacerbate the situation; (3) the legal system is weak and widely disregarded; and (4) penalties are insufficient and ineffectively applied.

First, while China's bureaucracy is gigantic, its internal checking systems have never been fully developed. In fact, much corruption is facilitated by inconsistent procedures and deficient supervision. Ji Tongen, the former chief of the organization department of the Hubei Provincial Communist Youth League Committee, embezzled 56,072 yuan (including 38,056 yuan in membership fees) over a five-and-a-half year period by exploiting irregular accounting procedures with forged receipts.[40] After being caught, Ji blamed institutional rules that invited his venality. Zhang Liangjie, a tax collector in Shandou district, Guandong Province, embezzled 70,000 yuan between 1985 and 1988 by underreporting his collections; checking procedures were almost non-existent.[41] Similar problems are found in the banking system: Zhang Zhenpu, an accountant in a local branch of the Inner Mongolian Construction Bank, embezzled 33,500 yuan between 1981 and 1987, during which time he had been awarded the titles of "Model Worker" and "A Good Communist" several times. He claimed that loopholes in the system and the fact he always operated alone tempted him to commit these embezzlements.[42]

Irrational policy also fosters wrongdoing. Much corruption involves tax officers because there has been no unified tax system and local officials have extensive discretionary power. Huang Jinxin, director of a taxation office of Chongming County (Shanghai City), accepted 6,000 yuan from two companies in exchange for reducing their taxes and helping them secure interest-free loans. Zhao Hongxiang, deputy director of the Zhenbao taxation office, accepted 4,200 yuan from three enterprises for reducing their tax payments.[43] Bribery of local tax officials is seen by many entrepreneurs as just another way to keep expenses down. Ge Yali, director of the Anshan Bicycle Factory, admitted that although his factory earned $20 million profit in 1993, it would pay little or no tax because of deals with tax officers.[44]

Third, inadequate monitoring mechanisms are part of the backwardness of China's overall legal development. In the 1960s and 1970s law was seen as an instrument of state and party policy to be directly controlled by the party leadership. The lack of an independent judiciary further politicized the legal system. Party policies constrained the laws, rather than the other way around; abuses of law were frequent, and it was dangerous for ordinary people to accuse anyone in power of illegalities. The resulting lack of respect for, and ignorance of, the law long impeded the development of an effective legal system in the new China. They also contributed to corruption. Some judicial and law enforcement officials resort to blackmail, ask for and accept bribes, practice graft, and bend the law for the benefit of their relatives and friends.[45] Police bureaus in some areas have reportedly charged "fees" for providing protection.[46] Some police officers in prisons or educate-through-labor schools (*laodong jiaoyang*) extort money from prisoners or their families. Others take advantage of criminals who want to shorten their sentences or be released on parole, to see non-prison doctors or to request time off, often obtaining private services in exchange.[47] In 1993, 10.4 percent of the 4,128 lawsuits filed with the discipline inspection departments in Henan Province dealt with violations by law enforcement officers. Hong Yonglin, former public security bureau director in Huizhou City, Guangdong Province, was involved in smuggling 100 cars, through which he made more than 1 million yuan, and in extorting large sums from 30 people approved to migrate to Hong Kong. For these offenses he was executed.[48] In Jiangxi and Anhui in 1992, a total of 600 unqualified officers were ordered to leave public security agencies, and over 100 were sacked and sent to reform-through-labor camps. In 1998, courts at various level took actions against 2,512 judges and other court personnel who had acted in violation of law, and procuratorates at various levels filed cases against 1,557 procuratorate personnel who had violated the law.[49]

The PRC's traditional anti-corruption method was the Maoist mass campaign. Since corruption was perceived as individual wrongdoing rather than as an institutional or systemic problem, people were mobilized in periodic rectification campaigns to report wrongdoing and criticize decadent thoughts and behavior. Corruption was attributed to feudalistic influences, bourgeois money-worship and out-and-out egoism; corrupt officials were punished in public to shame other "lawbreakers" and to educate the masses. The "Three-Antis" (corruption, waste, and bureaucracy) and "Five-Antis" movements (bribery, tax evasion, theft of state property, cheating on government contracts and stealing economic information) in the early 1950s, and the "Four Cleans" Campaign (investigating how cadres determined workpoints, kept accounts, distributed supplies, and handled warehouses and granaries) in the early 1960s were examples. Deviance control was combined with ideological and political education, and with thought reform. Since corruption mainly took the form of perks and privileges in Mao's time, the political approach was relatively effective. But despite the changes since 1978, the current leadership still resorted to ad hoc campaigns, as for example the anti-corruption campaigns during 1982–83, 1988–1989, and again in 1991–93. However, there is little evidence that corruption has abated since.

Another problem has been the deficiency of investigations by the Chinese press. The press, like the legal system, has been an instrument of state policy since 1949. Its main purpose has been to pass information from the center to the masses and to propagate Party goals and values, not to be a forum for news and contending opinions. Corruption is reported in the press, but only after the offenders are convicted and punished.

Finally, ineffective penalties also contribute to corruption. Corrupt officials may be punished both by law and also by the loss of their reputations; but because of the scope of corruption and of the bureaucracy itself, the probability of being caught is low. This is particularly true for those with high-level connections. Even if the odds of being caught were close to certainty, punishments have generally been lenient, except at the peak of anti-corruption campaigns when the central leaders want to kill a monkey to frighten the chicken. In 1952, the embezzlement of 10,000 yuan could bring capital punishment. In 1993, however, only those taking over 1 million yuan would face life sentences. For most, the penalty would simply be expulsion from the party or removal from the office.[50] Moreover, expected gains from corruption far exceed likely penalties: a mid-level functionary might make 36,000 yuan in ten years' time, while even a modest corrupt transaction might bring in 100,000 yuan.

5. Cultural Dimensions

Chinese traditions may also add to the current corruption. Chinese society has traditionally been based not on a legalisms, but on Confucian ideals and face-to-face relationships of loyalty, favor, and friendship. It was in these personal exchanges that the individual sought and found security, not in any legal code. Chinese prefer to do things through people they know, and chains of connections play an important role in daily life. Some such connections are vertical, between people of greater and lesser status, as well as horizontal. Therefore it is important to cultivate all manner of personal ties (*guanxi*). *Guanxi* can be built on a basis of common birthplace, common schools, colleagues, or comrades-in-arms, to name a few examples. Even without such associations, *guanxi* can be cultivated by acquaintances and confirmed by a banquet, gift-giving, or an expectation of favors.[51]

But *guanxi* and favors also breed corruption. Clientelism has become a major feature in economic transactions and in day-to-day life. Almost every household uses connections to meet basic needs. In order to run even a legal business or obtain basic services, networks have to be "gratified." People use connections to get a telephone installed, buy a train ticket, find a hospital bed, have surgery scheduled, find a school place, obtain a passport, and even to get a marriage certificate. *Guanxi* has also been widely practiced by work units, both before and after the economic reforms. In order to ensure supplies, promote sales, and maintain long-term contractual relationships, some work units give gifts and favorable terms of trade to others. Enterprises also maintain *guanxi* with their immediate administrative superiors to cultivate good will: managers give "gifts" and banquets to officials whose help might be needed in future. The case of Wei Mingsheng is typical: after his promotion to Deputy Director of the Economic Commission of Shanxi Province, he and his wife attended more than 60 farewell banquets, hosted by 75 work units, within 51 days.[52] Reports of extravagant banqueting (*dachi dahe*) are common in the Chinese press; it occurs in almost all institutions and work units, including those in poorer areas. In 1986, it was estimated that public funds spent on eating and drinking totaled 13 billion yuan; the figure jumped to 25 billion in 1988. One work unit spent 365,000 yuan to organize 219 banquets in one year.[53] Although these practices are a form of embezzlement, they are directly linked to the imperatives of *guanxi* in contemporary China.

Practices such as buying official positions and making appointments by favoritism are also motivated by kinship and patron-client ties; benefactors promote their *protégées* in exchange for their allegiance and loyalty—or money. This allows leading Party officials and bureaucrats to form power bases and *guanxi* networks for personal and economic gain. Such trends have only been intensified by the growth of markets: as bureaucrats gradually lose strategic advantages, some try to catch the last boat of prosperity by selling services to supplement fixed salaries.

Some Assessments

Post-reform corruption is notable not only for its scope, but also for its complex patterns and consequences. In this section, we return to the three kinds of corruption noted at the outset—1) abusing power purely for personal benefits; 2) deviating from "normal" duties for the benefit of one's institution or work unit; and 3) abuse of power for *both* reasons. We consider what they might tell us about the implications of the problem for China's future.

New Patterns of Corruption

Corruption in China has not only significantly increased; it has also taken on at least four new, distinctively post-reform, features. First, the pre-reform corruption was power-oriented—that is, aimed at obtaining or protecting political and bureaucratic advantage—and dominated by officials. Outsiders did buy political and administrative favors, but the main focus was *tanwu, shouhui* and *tequan* among insiders. The growth of markets and the weakening of norms in post-reform China, however, has spurred the growth of profit-oriented economic corruption, often in the group-oriented and mixed individual/ group forms. Li Jizhou, the Vice Minister of the Public Security, was recently involved in smuggling more than 1000 vehicles valued at more than 100 million yuan.[54] Yu Fei, the former vice chairman of the standing committee of the Guangdong provincial People's Congress, abused his power to obtain land for his children.[55] With many autonomous private businesses emerging, exchanges of power and money between business people and office holders—who, as noted above, can be difficult to distinguish from each other— has become more frequent than before, with the initiative increasingly coming from those offering bribes.

Secondly, corruption before 1979 was concentrated in upper levels of the hierarchy—often, among senior officials and their relatives. Administrative decentralization has changed this, however: high-ranking officials and their offspring still embezzle large sums of public funds, often by engaging in trade, but corruption has increased among those bureaucrats in the middle and lower hierarchy who control services and goods. Many middle-level officials commercialize their administrative power, rendering services only when they are "gratified"; some justify such behavior as the sorts of exchanges at equal value practiced in a market economy. Thus, functionaries exploit household registration, passport issuance, and vehicle licensing to extort money,[56] and some customs officials deliberately damage the goods of those who refuse to pay bribes.

Third, post-reform corruption has spread beyond the bureaucracy into every corner of society. Some reporters on Chinese major newspapers will only write about certain working units or persons after they are "gratified."[57] Bookstores threatened not to sell textbooks to nearby schools unless school authorities ordered students to buy thirty other "supplementary books." Authorities in some schools force pupils to buy magazines and newspapers that they market, and some even require their pupils to use certain brands of toothpaste and school bags that they sell in their "moonlighting" jobs.[58] When trains are crowded, railway officials have "rented out" cargo space to enterprises at high prices, and speculated on train tickets. A campaign against corruption in the railway ministry led to the closure of 1,200 companies that speculated on the price of tickets.[59] Members of the military even sold their vehicle license plates to local enterprises, allowing purchasers to avoid vehicle inspections, road tolls, and other impediments.[60]

Fourth, pre-reform corruption mostly financed private consumption. Now, while new millionaires do spend money at night clubs, a growing sector of corruption—profiteering in the production process—diverts funds into investment, producing (if only as a byproduct) the sorts of group-oriented economic benefits noted at the outset. One Canton bureaucrat used embezzled funds to open three shops and a restaurant.[61] A manager of a branch of the China Agricultural Bank in Beijing diverted 1.2 million yuan of public money, intended for the procurement of peasants' grain, into an automobile business.[62] The former chief of Shenzhen Housing Administration Bureau misappropriated several million yuan and obtained an "insider" loan of 5 million yuan to develop his personal real estate project.[63]

Public Attitudes Toward Corruption

Most Chinese resent corruption but feel helpless to do anything about it. Official corruption was a prominent reason for the student demonstrations in Tiananmen Square in 1989 and, according to many, is the issue most likely to activate another eruption of widespread public disaffection. Corruption for personal benefit is universally resented: such actions plunder public funds and impair the functions of the state. Most people would punish this sort of corruption on principle, particularly when offspring of high officials are involved. Ordinary citizens are also unhappy about middle-and lower-level officials who extort "fees" to perform their duties. But they are also pessimistic about the prospects for bringing corruption under control: according to a survey of 90,000 people, conducted by the CCP Discipline Investigation

Committee, 66.98 percent were unsatisfied with the results of the 1992 anti-corruption campaign. Only 15 percent said they were satisfied with current anti-corruption policies.[64] In all, our first category of corruption undermines reform, discredits the state, and foments social discontent, as well as hurting the public.

However, some practices in the second and third categories are seen as only quasi-corruption because the beneficiaries are numerous and because economic reform has changed or blurred the rules. Managers now may distribute bonuses to reward good workers; while this has made workers more dependent on their employers, it has also produced pressure upon managers to issue bonuses. Regional leaders, in turn, are expected to invigorate local economies to prove their leadership, even if by illicit means. Shangdong Province reportedly engaged in organized smuggling to promote its regional economy. The governor was under investigation for a time because of his approval of the large-scale smuggling of Hyundai automobiles from South Korea.[65] In June 1999, the biggest smuggling case in the history of the PRC was revealed in Zhanjiang City, Guangdong province; six officials, including the head of Zhanjiang customs and the director of investigations, were executed. The case involved more than 6 billion yuan tax evasion.[66] The public may also be developing greater tolerance of some kinds of "questionable" behavior, especially when *guanxi* is involved. Petty bribery is becoming more acceptable to many Chinese, especially the young: if someone bribes you, it just means you have something to offer. According to the *Workers' Daily*, "[B]ribery is becoming a normal social phenomenon. The popular saying nowadays is, `bribe before any favor is asked; small bribe for small favor, big bribe for big favor; everyone has to give bribes, and every one has a reason to accept bribes.'"[67]

Thus there is popular outrage over some forms of corruption in a political setting offering few legitimate outlets for it. This discontent coexists with a limited tolerance for other varieties of corrupt conduct in a system in which it is often unclear just what is corruption and what is reform.

Economic Incentives

The second and third categories of corruption aid some kinds of economic activity. Bribery can help break rigid bureaucratic monopolies and controls.[68] One enterprise planned to produce a special commodity needing 43 chops on a production permit; it took six months just to have three chops done. The manager then paid 20,000 yuan to a middleman; within one month the factory got the rest of the seals it needed.[69] While private companies formed by officials and their relatives profited from the dual price system, corruption does help some producers and consumers obtain resources and services, and can create an informal—if disjointed and often unreliable—price system.

From another perspective, it is a way for a new class of entrepreneurs to challenge the rigid party-state system. The argument here is emphatically *not* that corruption is somehow a good thing in itself, nor that it is in some sense functional for broad-based economic development. It contributes to growing economic inequalities in cities, and between the cities and the countryside, and to the extent that it facilitates growth it may drive the economy in directions that conflict with official goals and/or broader social expectations. While it has obvious benefits for those who participate—otherwise it would not occur—its broader effects upon the system may be to subsidize inefficiency and to create further incentives for official abuses and delays. We do suggest, however, that comparing corrupt practices *to their perceived alternatives*— not to idealized markets, but rather to the current hybrid system with its bureaucratic "squeeze points" and weak legal system—helps us understand why corruption is so widespread and tenacious. For many, it is a way to survive and succeed in a time of rapid transformation.

Indeed, as the growth in types 2 and 3 would imply, corruption can be difficult to distinguish from market reforms. Corruption violates rules; but in China, rules are ambiguous. Law is overshadowed by ideology and political power. Partial market reforms have left public-private distinctions unclear, and notions of service or merit confused. In 1985 a professor of electrical engineering in Laioning Province, who had helped an enterprise solve a technical problem, was arrested for accepting a fee from the factory. In the same year, another engineer who provided similar assistance in Guangdong Province was given an economic reward.[70] Is such moonlighting a legitimate professional activity or an illegal solicitation? Matters are further blurred when activities are not purely for personal gain, but for the interests of an enterprise or a local community. As Heidenheimer points out, the more complex the network of social interaction and the more complicated and diverse the ways that tangible benefits can be exchanged, the less likely it is that particular actions can clearly be labeled corrupt.[71]

Institutionalization

Samuel Huntington believes that corruption is one symptom of the absence of effective political institutionalization.[72] Anti-corruption efforts, therefore, must focus on institutionalization, among many other issues. Both rulers and ruled acknowledge the need for such action; corruption is one of the most corrosive challenges to state authority, and mass resentment, especially as regards our first category of corruption, is palpable. The Beijing leadership for many years manipulated the issue by making corrupt individuals, rather than the system itself, the target of public reaction. But during the 1990s more consideration was given to legal strategies, and to administrative and institutional reforms. Ironically, corruption—or more specifically, sustained action against it—may contribute to the rise of a new legalistic culture. The 1990s witnessed a legislative explosion in China. Several categories of legislation are now aimed at regulating the market economy, and other varieties—criminal law, law of criminal procedure, and laws governing administrative processes—are directly relevant as well. It is estimated that National People's Congress has passed 333 laws—on average, 16 pieces a year— and the State Council has enacted more than 800 administrative regulations (or about 40 per year). Legislative bodies in provinces and municipalities have also enacted more than 6000 laws and regulations concerning local matters.[73] Since 1988, the People's Congress has passed a series of laws dealing with bribery, speculation, profiteering, and abuse of power,[74] and judicial organs have stepped up the processing of corruption allegations. Over 215,000 graft and bribery cases were investigated by supervisory agencies nationwide in 1992, a figure that rose to 430,000 by 1998. Moreover, there has been real, if limited, progress in the area of civil liberties. The New York-based Lawyers Committee for Human Rights has found meaningful improvement in China's legal development—in the areas of pretrial detention, the right to counsel, presumptions of innocence, and the conduct of trials. The U.S. State Department's 1998 annual report on human rights acknowledged that the Chinese "government launched new efforts to reform the legal system and widely disseminated information about new legislation. It also initiated a highly publicized campaign to 'rectify' endemic problems such as corruption and abuse of power on the part of judges, prosecutors and police."[75]

Beijing also passed a State compensation law in December 1995 intended to enable citizens and organizations to demand and receive compensation from the state whenever their legal rights or interests are violated. Although there is strong resistance from bureaucrats, this can be viewed as an advance of both Chinese legality and the role of the individual; for thousands of years, governments in China had been immune to such claims. Since the implementation of the law, people's courts have settled 870 cases of which 364 resulted in compensation by the state. During the same period, procuratorial organs handled 762 cases involving criminal compensation requests, with the final ruling in 179 cases requiring compensation by the state.[76] Similarly, the government has recently allowed and even encouraged press coverage of police brutality.[77]

This shift from the old mass mobilization approach, based on the infallibility of the party, toward legal and institutional mechanisms requires increasing number of legal staff. In 1995, China had about 50,000 lawyers and 4,100 law agencies representing 140,000 enterprises and institutions. By the end of 1997, the number had reached 100,200 in about 8500 law firms representing

more than 210,000 enterprises and institutions. However, many Chinese lawyers are ill-prepared to work independently and barely one-fifth have earned
law degrees. China may need to train 150,000 lawyers as a step toward
meeting the increasing need.[78] In May 1996, the Chinese "lawyers law" was
passed by the NPC. It changed the definition of "lawyer" from "state legal
worker" in the previous regulation (1981) to what is now called "legal personnel who provide legal service to society," from state cadres who receive
governmental salaries to self-employed people who set up business on their
own and are responsible for their own profit and losses. This represents
progress in China's legal development, since the separation of legal personnel
from the state administration is a prerequisite in creating an independent
judicial system.

Conclusion

China's corruption is linked both to its heritage of party-state dominance
and to its new mixed economy. The economic system remains irrational, both
despite and because of reform, creating enormous opportunities legitimate
and otherwise. Communist values have given way to materialism and cynicism, hampering efforts to address corruption, while the legal system is unable to handle the new problems. Leading officials plunder assets, while the
new mixed class of entrepreneurial and bureaucratic elites enrich themselves;
such trends are producing major redistribution of wealth.

Corruption has brought China to a crossroads. In some ways, it is both
cause and effect of progress, in the form of the partial shift from Party-state
dominance toward a market economy, and—perhaps—the first tentative steps
away from a totalitarian regime as growth and reform strengthen groups in
society. Official responses to corruption may be molding a new institutionalization, aiding the transition from ideological and collective to legalistic and
individualistic norms. Such reforms, and the growing political grievances that
necessitate them, may in time more clearly delineate the limits of the state
and society, politics and markets, and may restrain bureaucratic interventions
into day-to-day affairs. Corruption also weakens opposition to continued reform by disrupting the still-considerable remnants of the old bureaucratic
order, and by creating both incentives to economic change and the need for
new values and institutions to contain those changes.

But there are worries too. First, corruption primarily benefits the well-
connected and newly rich, widening income inequalities among people and
regions. If, as is likely, such income disparities continue to grow, the resulting discontent could threaten the political order. Second—and related—corruption has already weakened the state's capacity to rule. The functional role
of the state—to "penetrate society, regulate social relationships, extract resources, and appropriate and use resources in determined ways"[79]—is being

called into question. Indeed, corruption is seen by some intellectuals as leading China toward a kind of "anarchy . . . a paradise for those who have money and power."[80] These forces for change might be viewed as positive consequence of reform, but if it is becoming more difficult to govern China from Beijing *and* there is no clear alternative to Party-state dominance, there are reasons for concern.

Corruption might help move China toward the rule of law, or at least toward "rule *by* law"[81] —or it could wipe out the remarkable economic accomplishments of the past generation. All depends upon whether the government has the capacity and the will to confront the *political* aspects of the corruption crisis. Much of the public is outraged about some forms of corruption, but lacks legitimate channels through which to express those grievances (and, since 1989, knows well the risks of doing so). Other forms of corruption are more widely tolerated, but this both reflects and intensifies the current crisis of values. The result is that it will be very difficult to address the corruption problem in ways that are effective *and* legitimate.

Given the tenacity of China's regime, and the resilience of its people, it is risky to predict the outcomes of this dilemma. It seems that the post-Deng leaders may continue both the current policy of market-oriented economic reform and opening China to the world and their efforts to sustain political control by the Party. Politics may remain authoritarian, with the CCP still in power; but a market economy will continue to develop, and to be further integrated into world economic system. Such events will only intensify the impasse, and continue to challenge the political authority of the Party. Economic reforms may have brought China to a crossroads, but what happens next is a profoundly political question.

Notes

1. For a useful early assessment, see Alan P. L. Liu, "The Politics of Corruption in the People's Republic of China," *American Political Science Review* 77 (1983), pp. 602-623.
2. Michael Johnston, Political Corruption and Public Policy in America. (Monterey, CA: Brooks-Cole, 1982), Ch. 1-2.
3. Renmin Ribao, March 1, 1999, p. 4.
4. Foreign Broadcast Information Service (hereafter, "FBIS"): *China* September 9, 1993, p. 30.
5. *FBIS: China* September 9, 1993, p. 30.
6. *Renmin Ribao,* June 28, 1993, p. 3, November 12, 1993, p. 2; also see *FBIS: China*, November 12, 1993, pp. 43-46, *Renmin Ribao,* September 11, 1998, p.2.
7. Johnston and Hao, "China's Surge of Corruption," *Journal of Democracy* 6:4 (October, 1995), pp. 80-94.
8. Yufan Hao "From Rule of Man to Rule of Law: An Unintended Consequence of Corruption in China in the 1990s," *Journal of Contemporary China*, 1999, 8(22), pp. 405-423; see also James Feinerman, *The Limits of the Rule of Law in China*, Seattle: University of Washington Press, 2000.

9. Barrett L. McCormick, *Political Reform in Post-Mao China* (University of California Press, 1990).
10. See "Selected Works of Deng Xiaoping," *Renmin Ribao*, November 13, 1993, p. 3.
11. Marc Blecher, "Sounds of Silence and Distant Thunder: The Crisis of Economic and Political Administration," in *China in the Nineties*, David S. G. Goodman and Gerald Segal (eds.) (Oxford: Clarendon Press, 1991), p. 41.
12. *New York Times*, November 12, 1985, Sec IV., p 12.
13. Ting Gong, *The Politics of Corruption in Contemporary China: An Analysis of Policy Outcomes* (Westport, CT: Praeger, 1994).
14. *Beijing Review* 32 (August 12, 1985), p. 8.
15. Su Ya & Jia Lusheng, *Who is Responsible for China* (Guangzhou: Huacheng Press, 1990), p. 264.
16. *World Journal*, October 15, 1993, p. A15.
17. *Renmin Ribao*, October 17, 1993, p. 2.
18. *World Journal*, October 22, 1993, p. a18.
19. Beijing People's Procuratorate (ed.), *The Judge of History*, (Beijing Law Press, 1992), pp. 1-58.
20. Li Yunxia, *China Corruptor (zhonghua zhuchong): The Report on the Breaching of Law by Officials at Various Levels* (Beijing: Chinese Legal Press, 1991), p. 126.
21. *Renmin Ribao*, July 21, 1989, p. 2.
22. Thomas B. Gold, "Urban Private Business and China's Reform," in R. Baum (ed.), *Reform and Reaction in Post-Mao China* (New York: Routledge, 1991); *Beijing Review*, February 15-21, 1993, p. 4.
23. Figures are from China Statistical Bureau, see New York Times, June 25, 1995, pp.A1 and A7.
24. Dorothy J. Solinger, "Urban Entrepreneurs and the State: The Merger of
25. *China Daily,* July 28, 1988, p. 3.
26. *Chinese Youth Daily,* August 14, 1989, p. 2.
27. This policy was revoked in December 1993.
28. *Select Works of Deng Xiaoping* (Beijing: People's Press, 1983), pp. 313–333.
29. A. Nathan, *China's Crisis: Dilemmas of Reform and Prospects for Democracy* (New York: Columbia University Press, 1990), p. 108 and *passim*.
30. *Wall Street Journal,* December 10, 1993, p. R1.
31. Ibid., p. R1.
32. *Renmin Ribao,* May 29, 1989, p. 2.
33. *FBIS: China,* September 1, 1993, pp. 16-17.
34. *FBIS China,* Jan. 15, 1999.
35. *World Journal,* October 18, 1993, p. A17.
36. *Renmin Ribao,* October 17, 1993, p. 2.
37. *World Journal,* November 23, 1993, p. A.19.
38. *FBIS: China,* Feb. 11, 1999.
39. *FBIS: China*, September 28, 1993, p. 47.
40. Li Yunxia, *op. cit.*, p. 5.
41. *Dang Feng* (Party Style) 4 (1989).
42. *Fazhi Ribao*, May 2, 1989, p.2.
43. *FBIS: China*, November 23, 1993, p. 58.
44. *New York Times*, December 2, 1993, p. A4.
45. *Renmin Ribao*, Nov. 1, 1993, p. 1.

46. *Jingji Ribao*, December 17, 1986, p. 2.
47. *Beijing Review*, August 9-15, 1993, p. 4.
48. *World Journal*, October 29, 1993, p. a19.
49. *FBIS: China*, Feb. 8, 1999.
50. Between 1988 and 1993 Party Discipline Inspection Commissions at various levels investigated over 870,000 party discipline violations; 730,000 guilty party members were disciplined and 150,000 expelled from the party. For a non-party member, the punishment might be a jail sentence, but party membership was a buffer, reducing some penalties.
51. Mayfair Mei-hui Yang, *Gifts, Favors, and Banquets: The Art of Social Relationships in China* (Ithaca: Cornell University Press, 1994), Ch. 2, 3, and 5.
52. Li Yunxia, *op. cit.*, p. 34.
53. *Zhenli De Zhuiqiu (Seeking Truth)*, p. 26.
54. *FBIS: China*, June 10, 1999.
55. *FBIS: China*, Feb. 1, 1999.
56. *Fazhi Ribao*, June 17, 1993, p. 1.
57. Interviews (by Hao) with twelve journalists in Beijing and Nanjing in the Spring of 1993. Most said they accept money before using a story in the paper; some share this income with editors.
58. *Guangmin Ribao*, May 24, 1993, p. 1.
59. *Renmin Ribao*, September 23, 1993, p. 2.
60. June Teufel Dryer, "The People's Army: Serving Whose Interests?" *Current History* 5 (September, 1994), 268.
61. *Guangdong Daily*, April 14, 1991, p. 2.
62. *Renmin Ribao*, June 28, 1993, p. 2.
63. He was executed in Shenzhen on October 28, 1993. *Renmin Ribao*, October 30, 1993, p. 1.
64. *World Journal*, October 30, 1994, p. A14.
65. *World Journal*, September 20, 1993, p. A16.
66. Beijing Review, June 21, 1999, p.8.
67. *Workers' Daily*, May 12, 1989, p. 2.
68. James T. Myers, "China: Modernization and 'Unhealthy Tendencies'" *Comparative Politics* 21 (January 1989); a classic argument is Colin Leys, "What Is the Problem about Corruption?" *Journal of Modern African Studies* 3:2 (1965), pp. 215-230.
69. Su Ya and Jia Lusheng, *White Cat and Black Cat* (Guangzhou: Huacheng Press, 1993), p. 180.
70. *Ibid.*, p. 76.
71. Arnold J. Heidenheimer, "Perspectives on the Perception of Corruption," in A. J. Heidenheimer, M. Johnston, and V.T. LeVine, *Political Corruption: A Handbook* (New Brunswick, N.J.: Transaction Publishers, 1989), pp. 149-163.
72. Samuel Huntington, *Political Order in Changing Societies* (New Haven: Yale University Press, 1968), p. 59.
73. "China: 20 Years of Legal Development," in *Quishi*, December 1998, pp. 12-13.
74. *Zhenli De Zhuiqiu (Seeking Truth)*, March 1992, p. 29.
75. 1998 Human Rights Report, http://www.state.gov.
76. "China: 20 Years of Legal Development," *Quishi*, December, 1998.
77. New York Times, March 8, 1999, p. A1
78. China: 20 years of Legal development, *Quishi* (December 1998), p. 12.
79. Joel Migdal, *Strong Societies and Weak States: State-Society Relations and State*

Capabilities in the Third World (Princeton, NJ: Princeton University Press, 1988), p. 4.
80. Interviews, by Hao, 1993.
81. Hao, "From Rule of Man to Rule of Law," *loc. cit.;* Feinerman, *op. cit.*

32

Corruption under German National Socialism

Ralph Angermund

I

Historical research holds many answers to the question of how National Socialist rule worked and how it was legitimized before the people. The range of views is as multifaceted and often contradictory as are the various aspects of the history of National Socialism itself. Very simply speaking, one finds stronger or weaker emphasis, depending on the subject matter and the author's outlook, being placed on elements such as violence and terror on the one hand or temptation and assent on the other hand. The Nazi regime is then either characterized as a dictatorship under Hitler's firm rule or as an internally divided polycratic mesh with competing power centers in the party, the SS, and the state, or it is viewed as a kind of mixture of these two notions in one way or another.

However, all of these views have in common that they have up to now turned a blind eye to one element of this rule, namely, corruption; despite the fact that especially the presence of corruption or its intensity can be an important indicator for the inner constitution and mechanisms of state rule.

The large lacunae and the fact that there has been no comprehensive analysis of corruption in the Nazi regime yet[1] is all the more astonishing as important historical sources of the regime such as the situation reports of the security service of the SS (SD)[2] or the files of the administration and the judiciary contain ample indications for corruption being a subject that both the governing and the governed between 1933 and 1945 were concerned with intensively. Consequently, during the first couple of years after the collapse of the Nazi dictatorship its corruptive phenomena were widely discussed, for example with regard to Hermann Göring's connections to various industrial and trade companies in the region of Hamburg. However, the topic virtually disappeared at the times when the German "economic miracle" set in.

As German research on contemporary history looks more closely at corruption within the Nazi regime it faces hitherto unfamiliar problems and difficulties of historical corruption research in general. Besides the limited conclusions that can be drawn from the sources about the intensity and the extent of corruption, one is also confronted with methodological problems, especially which corruption concept to apply and how to verify what can be found in the opinion, morale and situation reports of the so called "Third Reich," which, for the most part, take on the form of general observations and allusions.

A first glance at the files and documents of the "Third Reich" shows rather that the corruption concept appears in very distinct contexts and with different connotations. In the court files and those of the administration corruption generally equals bribery or embezzlement in accordance with the crimes provided for in the German penal code. Here corruption is essentially synonymous to violating legal criminal norms as well as duties of office for private regarding ends.

The reports drawn up by the justice department,[3] the SD, and by the Social Democratic underground (Reports on Germany of the Social Democratic Party—SOPADE)[4] about the opinions and morale in the "Third Reich" adopt main elements of this conceptualization. What makes the definition and any subsequent analysis difficult is the fact that these reports aimed for a comprehensive rendering of the general opinions and moods of the people and therefore broadened the concept to what was perceived and labeled as corrupt by the general public. This includes in particular the lesser and greater official and moral transgressions of the rulers, the privileges and perquisites of office and many other things that were viewed as portents of the decline of law and order in Nazi Germany.

This comes close to Nye's corruption definition on the one hand and to the public opinion based definition of corruption on the other hand, but much remains indistinct still. Of course, this problem could be solved by a deductive definition of corruption *ex ante*—and many studies proceed thus to obtain a clear framework for analysis, yet this would narrow the approach to this relatively new field of research. Furthermore, one should consider what Carl J. Friedrich observed, namely that despite accusations of corruption having been raised at all times "the phenomenon had not at all been the same throughout time."[5] In case there are any time specific features to the corruption concept, they would most likely remain undetected in the sources if one were only to apply definitions developed by modern corruption research.

The historian is therefore well advised to collect observations in a tentative and searching process from which to analyze what symptoms can be ascertained and how they fit the different explanatory models of Nazi rule. He should chart the field and otherwise heed Theodor Adorno's example, who in similar cases took it that the method follows from the work.

II

"Still, up to now every regime, whether dictatorship or democracy, has entered the stage with the sonorous claim: now the old pigsty will be mucked out. Then a transfer of accounts took place, that is, the old cronies were replaced by new ones, and they were often more numerous than their predecessors." This remark dates from 1929 when it appeared in the *Weltbühne*, the periodical of Carl von Ossietzky. It was made in reference to the "Sklarek-scandal," the discovery of large scale bribery in the city administration of Berlin through which the Jewish brothers Sklarek obtained the monopoly for the work uniforms of the city's civil servants and employees.[6]

It is debatable whether the *Weltbühne* was an authority in matters of corruption and democratic theory; as an historical source it is interesting in any case. Its deep sigh about the "Sklarek-scandal" was not least an expression of the bitter experience that the opponents of the Weimar Republic increasingly succeeded in decrying the democratic "system" with the help of an intensive propaganda campaign about actual and putative corruption incidents. Since 1919 the nationalist right wing had regularly put onto the political agenda the assertion that Marxism—meaning particularly the Social Democrats—had permeated the administration and the courts through "party-book civil servants," who had unscrupulously feathered their nests at the expense of the German people.

Despite the fact that the relationship between the imperial army and German industry during World War I was apparently to a large extend characterized by bribery,[7] corruption was taken by the "antidemocratic thinking" (Kurt Sontheimer) of the Germans in the Weimar Republic first and foremost as a typical phenomenon of the "rule of parties" and parliamentarianism. Against the backdrop of severe economic difficulties and in face of a press that after 1919 was continually revealing new transgressions of politicians and the business community more openly and ruthlessly then ever before, the memory of many was transfigured and the apparent differences between the monarchy and the new "Jewish Republic," as the Weimar Republic was called by the national right, became all the more obvious.

For the most part Marxism, democracy, coalition, compromises, and corruption was all the same to them: Only by abolishing democracy and through a strong, unselfish leadership personality was "political purity" to be attained again.

The party decrying most vociferously the corruption of the "system" was the NSDAP (the National Socialists). In contrast to other parties they could present themselves as a young, unspent force, which was beyond any suspicion due to its absence from government and involvement in the state apparatus. In the opinion of those who witnessed the times the rise of the Nazis had commenced with the "Sklarek-scandal" and the subsequent elections in Berlin, at which the National Socialists gained representation in the city council for the first time, and capturing 13 seats at once. Of course, historical election research is unable to quantify how much the corruption propaganda contributed to this success. To the Nazis themselves, however, the connection seemed very much plausible. At any rate, they tried to utilize the corruption topic propagandistically still after January 30, 1933, the day of their power seizing.

III

In the spring of 1933 special anti-corruption police sections had been created and placed directly under the Prussian minister of justice, Hans Kerrl. They were supposed to take up "with greatest rigor what was pulled into daylight by the disappointed German people." About eight months after the "seizure of power" far more than 1,500 corruption cases were pending in Prussia alone.

In a certain way the anti-corruption sections formed the political site of the "fight against crime," the National Socialist's efforts to achieve a "clean" society. By an intensive fight against crime as well as through the destruction of *"Volksschädlinge"* (people's pest) and *"erbkranke Elemente"* (people considered sick by heredity) everything "impure" and "un-German" was to be eradicated.

The "fight against crime" belongs, without doubt, to the most lasting successes of Nazi propaganda, in part because the regime implemented in many cases only that what the people longed for after the crises of the 1920s (and which in parts had been prepared to the minute detail by the administration of the Weimar republic). Even long after the destruction of the Third Reich the Nazis enjoyed a reputation for having gotten things "cleaned up." In the face of old elites being taken over seamlessly by the new system and the general yearning for "positive" things, this view was encouraged by the fact that one fought shy of questions about the actual conditions in the state and society of the Nazi era. It was soon forgotten that Leo Menne labeled the Nazi regime an Augean stable (Kölner Zeitschrift für Soziologie, 1948/49) and that the members of the resistance, too, decidedly denounced the unrestrained spreading of corruption in the regime. One was more inclined to believe Theodor Eschenburg, who still thought in 1956 that "thanks to the good tradition of the civil service" corruption had always been comparatively rare in Germany.

Of course, Menne was right. There was a blatant difference between aim and reality of the anti-corruption propaganda. Despite its swaggering declarations, the Nazi regime was unable to get the upper hand of the corruption problem on the contrary. Instead, the Prussian corruption departments were dissolved again already in early September 1933. This was officially justified with the argument that there had been no further need for a special fight against corruption after the demise of "Marxism," which is what the Nazi propaganda called not only the Communists but also any democratic party and the whole democratic "system" itself. In the interest of "reconstruction" a "calming down of the people" had to set in according to the Nazis. Yet, in fact the interest in the fight against corruption waned because it developed into a double-edged sword for the new potentates after a short while already.

The most important reason for that were those approximately 700,000 "old campaigners" of the NSDAP, its followers in the 1920s. In their majority they were young, often déclassé, agitated men in a wild revolutionary mood, who sensed that they could finally make up for the deprivations suffered in the Weimar period. The party tried to give them this opportunity in order to integrate them and keep them calm. They were provided with jobs in the party organizations, which experienced a rampant, cancer-like growth, or in the state's administration or had been referred with preferential treatment to other jobs. Here, the *Gauleiters* (heads of Nazi administrative districts), who usually had been "old campaigners" themselves, played a prominent role. They presumed to impose their wishes even onto the justice ministry of the Reich when nominating judges and prosecutors as was the case for *Gauleiter* Fritz Sauckel in Thuringia.[8] In Hamburg, the smallest *Gau* of the Reich, the penetration of the administration by Nazi sources seems to have been particularly pronounced, leading practically to the creation of a parallel administration by the party. In 1934/35 more than 10,000 "old campaigners" had been granted new jobs especially with city owned businesses, though most of them were in no way sufficiently qualified for these posts.[9]

Nonetheless, the craving for spoils of the "old campaigners" as well as of many "*Mittläufer*" (followers) was almost insatiable. What Theodor Geiger had said about the driving forces of National Socialism in 1932 was very much confirmed: "Not an economic-materialistic mentality has been surmounted here, it is rather that economic materialisms are scarcely and thinly disguised up to now."[10] The public was provoked by the audacious behavior of the new office holders and it called into question the authority of the National Socialist government. In addition, the Nazi leadership faced a further problem: when the *Gauleiters* and subordinate party officials were presuming to decide the personnel questions for the upper echelons of the civil service—what authority, then, would remain with Rudolf Hess, the deputy of the Führer, and the Reich's agencies like the Nazi federation of civil servants or the Nazi federation of justice protectors (*NS-Rechtswahrerbund*)?

They saw themselves forced to get at least a moderate grip on the interests within the "movement." To this end it was first necessary to tame those at the grass roots and to strengthen the authority of the government. Hence the Prussian minister president, Hermann Göring, gave orders in July 1933 to have the "old campaigners" feel the power of the state. All crimes by members of the SA (Storm Troopers) and the NSDAP committed after the seizure of power were to be prosecuted "most relentlessly and severely."[11]

The ensuing court trials clamped down on the vainglory of many a local party boss, yet they had a surely unwanted side effect on public opinion—these trials unambiguously presented to the public how shamelessly many party members and followers had exploited their new positions in the shortest time possible. It is telling that most of these trials dealt with embezzlement and misappropriation. In most cases the sums involved amounted to several thousand Reichsmark—which was quite a fortune at that time. In individual cases the damages to the "common good" were much greater especially where virtual networks of corruption had been uncovered. For example in Berlin the entire new leadership of the municipal health insurance company stood trial— 26 directors and employees in managerial positions had "rechannelled" insurance fees on a grand scale to buy themselves plots of land.[12] The damage ran into the millions.

IV

Mostly the courts sentenced the perpetrators in those cases to several years' imprisonment and at times even to imprisonment in penitentiaries. The leadership of party and state was normally left unchallenged—which is in all likelihood not to be assessed as a peculiarity of the Nazi regime alone. It was, of course, not subject to investigations that Hermann Göring had his "official flat" refurbished into a palace embellished by a film hall and a "home organ" that included some 2,000 pipes, neither was it prosecuted that he was in addition "palm greased" by various firms—at least since 1936 when he practically gained dictatorial authority over the country's industry as plenipotentiary of the four year plans.[13] At lower levels also legal proceedings against Nazi functionaries went nowhere because the *Gauleiters* protected their followers or openly threatened to have the judge beaten.[14] The fact that the *Gauleiters* had more often than not a sizable criminal record themselves dating from their "fighting times" surely played an important role together with their disappointment about the "system" actually gaining penal authority over the party. In the end, in 1933/34 only the most conspicuous excesses of the state's rapid usurpation by the NSDAP were fought down. A truly sweeping and principled fight against corruption could not have been in the interest of the Nazi regime.

The NSDAP was a "movement," which was held together by the will of the Führer, yet it was internally split into rival factions whose loyalty Hitler secured through promises and rewards,[15] and the party's stability was guaranteed, in turn, by the same principle. Exercising and stabilizing political power in the "Third Reich" were intimately related to profit-seeking and self-interest. Typically, the elite of the Nazi regime were exploiting the state on all levels in a manner not unlike the practices in some "kleptocracies." The state had been divided among Hitler's rivaling chiefs and it had been used consistently as a "rent-seeking-system."

To this end the principles of a civil service of experts and specialists was pushed aside wherever possible to provide posts for "party comrades." Government and party offices were mixed together as, for example, through the involvement of the NSDAP in material and personnel decisions on the local level, which was secured by law in 1935. Beyond that, central governmental tasks like overseeing the road infrastructure and the administration of state works were passed on to newly created departments and special agencies. Their area of responsibility was as often left unclear as the question remained unanswered of who was to control them politically and budgetwise. Generally these controls did not exist—which made it all the easier for them to pocket the bribes of firms and industrial companies who were wooing for public procurement contracts.

Typically, then, the Nazi officials were not concerned at all with creating a "lean" administration. The special agencies of competing party leaders were rather prone to "rank growth" (Dieter Rebentisch), prone to creating new departments and posts all the time, which further increased the "anarchy of remits" in the Third Reich.

V

Despite a guided press and intensive propaganda the Nazi regime could not completely paper over the gulf between its noble claims and its shabby political reality. The insolent manner in which Nazi functionaries often feathered their nests was off putting to the *Volksgenossen* (supposed community of German people) and increasingly frustrated the many rank and file party members who had not managed to cut off a piece of the cake for themselves after 1933. Some of those "party comrades" who had come off badly showed to be deeply disappointed. For example, an "old campaigner" from Saxony wrote in May 1935: "Earlier we had fought against anti-social actions, corruption and high salaries, and for a clean and free Germany; but now the opposite of what we wanted has happened. If we called the leaders of the system bigwigs back then, today the "bigwigtocracy" is three times bigger than before."[16]

Waste and corruption regularly put a strain on public opinion in the "Third Reich," however, Germans seem to have attached greater importance to the very ambiguous and unstable "successes" of the regime in its economic and foreign policies, at least during the 1930s. In addition, for a long time they tended to compensate the misdemeanors and insolence of subordinate Nazi officials through an almost unshakable belief in the Führer. As Ian Kershaw has demonstrated, they thought Hitler would remedy all cases of misgovernment as soon as he had only heard of them.

Paradoxically, many saw these hopes confirmed by a most brutal act of governmental crime in the summer of 1934, namely the killing of Ernst Röhm and other members of the SA (Storm Troops, the Nazi party's thugs) leadership. Large sections of society accepted eagerly the claim of the Nazi propaganda that the Führer had dealt this blow against the SA—which was extremely unpopular because of its numerous excesses and provocative behavior—in order to eradicate once and for all the causes for treason, corruption, and immorality within the "movement."[17]

However, in reality Hitler showed little inclination to intervene even when his chiefs exhibited their splendor and luxury right before his very eyes. For one reason, despite his conspicuous modesty, the Führer had quickly emerged as one of the richest men in Germany, among other things, because he gained twice as author and board member of the Eher publishing house on the success of his book "Mein Kampf," which had been made compulsory reading for all Germans.

On the other hand, Hitler was probably very much conscious of the fact that taking decisive measures against corruption and mismanagement would have weakened the loyalty of the party and state leadership. After all, it would have meant cutting the assumed authority of the party and its leaders rigorously as well as subjecting the party to being controlled by budgetary rules. It is revealing that exactly the opposite happened. The head of the Reich's audit division, Friedrich Saemisch, had initially been led to believe after personal conversations with Hitler that there would be a strict control of all state finances in the Third Reich. But soon he—as well as finance minister Schwerin von Krosik—had to learn otherwise and the Nazi ministers showed little regard for such profane things as budgetary rules.

During the budgetary consultations in 1934 Hitler himself made it unmistakably clear to Schwerin von Krosik that he was not willing to have himself or his followers being fettered in any way. When Goebbels demanded all of a sudden 25 million Reichsmark for theaters and Schwerin von Krosik objected that there had been no budget for it, Hitler intervened and commenced describing his gigantic plans for the rebuilding of Berlin. At the end he exclaimed to his finance minister: "You will have to get used to much bigger things than 25 million for theaters with me."[18]

In 1938 the audit division of the Reich was made directly answerable to Hitler himself and its task should no longer be to control but rather to "advice" ministries. At that time an effective budgetary control would have been already impossible because the delegation of tasks to the special agencies had often been given only by verbal order of the Führer, so that one could not check their usefulness or necessity on the basis of written decrees or suchlike. The administration of finances in the Nazi regime increasingly took on features of a bond economy where traditional rules of budgetary planning were suspended for the most part. It was standard operating procedure to directly transfer and cover funds from one department to another as well as creating off-record accounts, and slush funds or taking it upon themselves to decide what to do with funds not used up. Against the backdrop of financial irresponsibility according to the motto "money is of no importance" (Rainer Weinert) Hitler created the "structural basis" for corruption—which did not prevent him at all from viewing corruption mainly as a problem of "Western plutocracies."

VI

Corruption in the Third Reich was not only an important element in securing the grip on power but it was also an essential concomitant feature of the crimes against the Jews. Corruption and abuse of public office played a major role during the '30s and especially in "Aryanizing" Jewish property and the roughly 100,000 Jewish businesses that existed in Germany.[19] Thus "party comrades" but also "respectable" entrepreneurs utilized the help of town clerks' offices and public health departments to attain the property of "Aryanization objects" for the cheapest rate possible. If a Jew rejected the takeover of his business the aforementioned departments or the Gestapo would accuse him of misdemeanors or crimes. The then ensuing and unavoidable "protective custody" usually led to the desired conditions for sale.

Through another, even more perfidious, variation on this scheme they could make the Jewish businessmen pay for the "Aryanization" themselves: "Party comrades" offered their services against remuneration to take care of the problems for those Jews having run into difficulties with subordinate agencies. As soon as confidence grew stronger, higher departments intervened and obtained a shorter "protective custody" term out of which the "councilor" "rescued" the Jew by getting him out on bail with the latter's own money. At this occasion he presented himself as an uninterested mediator for selling or transferring the Jew's property rights. This practice was so prevalent that in July 1935 the Gestapo felt compelled to ascertain that "the party program of fighting Jews is being exploited by certain circles . . . through an unseemly use of their party and official position."[20]

VII

With the outbreak of war and when the opportunities of attaining much greater fortunes arose in the wake of the conquests and the progressing "final solution," the Reich's security head office (RSHA) had much more reason to be concerned about National Socialist "propriety." While art treasures were being piled up across Europe for the personal collections of the Führer, Göring, or Rosenberg, the lower ranks of party chiefs and SS directly took the belongings of the Holocaust victims without much ado. As Rudolf Höss, the commander of Auschwitz, wrote, within the concentration camps and ghettos arose "huge and unstoppable problems through the Jews' valuables." Firing squads and SS sentries but also members of various agencies stole and misappropriated money, gold, watches, jewelry, cloths and everything that one could sell with a profit. Even high ranking Nazi officials like Hans Frank, general governor of Poland, did not exercise restrain. Not without reason did he soon gain the questionable reputation as being the "chief corruptionist."[21] He provided himself with furs, luxury goods and suchlike in great quantities from the warehouses of the Warsaw ghetto or bought them from Jews for half the price they were actually worth. Correspondingly, Mrs. Frank had fruits, vegetables and other rare foodstuff shipped back into the Reich with truck convoys and fright trains and though they came from a government estate she sold them for her own profit.

At times the corrupt tendencies of the Nazi thugs had also positive effects: some of them were bribed by inmates of concentration camps and for money offered them some advantages or even the opportunity to flee.[22] Thus corruption also contributed to cut little holes into the Nazi net of terror.

The way in which the SS reacted to these phenomena reveals the remarkable and difficult to grasp hypocrisy of the Third Reich. According to Heinrich Himmler's infamous speech in Posen 1943, the SS-man had to be absolutely "honest, decent, loyal and comradely." This meant: the killing of the "subhuman" was a duty, but it had to be done in a "clean" way. Any form of corruption in the process was a severe breach of the code of honor.

Therefore the RSHA tried to take counter measures against the looming deterioration of discipline and morale, on the one hand by making appeals to the SS-men's honesty and "decency" and on the other hand through help of the "Reich's head office for the fight against corruption"[23] or the SS and police courts and special "corruption officers." The "corruption officers" investigated cases of embezzlement, theft and suchlike and also incidents of all too conspicuous sadism against camp prisoners.

However, their successes were modest, even though the investigations against Karl Koch, commander in Buchenwald, led to him being sentenced to death. One was able to prove that he had a witness for the prosecution, an SS-*Hauptscharführer* (high ranking SS officer), poisoned. Yet, in many other cases investigations went nowhere, for the SS leaders were able to obstruct the work of the "corruption officers" massively. One was extremely unscrupulous when it came to cover over traces—camp prisoners who would have been able to give evidence for embezzlement and misappropriation had been killed without further ado before the "corruption officers" would arrive.[24]

Reports about these occurrences apparently did not reach the Reich. Nevertheless, there also the corruption topic gained in importance after 1939. The Nazi potentates had tried to preclude this danger. Since they were of the opinion that the defeat of 1918 was due to the breakdown of the "homefront" and caused by an unrestrained war-profiteering, they had passed a whole set of martial laws, which were supposed to nip any form of "subversion" and "sloppiness" in the bud. Among those were several laws against "war-profiteers" and black-marketeers of foods. Even home slaughtering was prohibited and sanctioned with severe punishments. It lay within the remit of the special courts to sentence the offenders of these laws. These courts could pass in many cases a death sentence and could do so as well under special circumstances even if the relevant martial law did not really stipulate this punishment.

In spite of this, soon after the war started Germans tried to obtain rationed foodstuff and other things by utilizing "connections" or through presents for civil servants. As the war dragged on and the worse the supply situation became, the more it was feared at the security service of the SS (SD) that "war morale" and law consciousness would deteriorate. This was not without good reason, for the number of sentences that had been passed by the special courts on offenses against the "war economy rules" were continually increasing, namely from 743 in the year 1940 to 3053 in the year 1941. Despite draconian punishments—in 1943 alone 236 death sentences were passed on grounds of crimes against the "rules of the war economy"[25]—the number of prison term convictions ran already at 10,361 for the first half of the year 1943.[26] In the cities, where food supply was particularly precarious, even the majority of all sentences passed by the special courts in 1943/44 were apparently related to cases of crimes against the laws of the war economy. Among those accused were—according to the president of the provincial high court of Munich—a growing number of employees and civil servants of the nutrition departments who had embezzled food-ration cards.[27] The courts of the capital Berlin, where the ministries and the most important agencies were located, were confronted with a growing number of bribery cases "that were related almost exclusively to the procurement system of the German army".[28]

What was even more perturbing to the SD was the observation that the "lack of posture" of "higher ranking personages" increasingly manifested itself in "notions of mistrust against the leadership."[29] One major reason for this was that Nazi officials "stashed away" rationed foodstuff in great quantities. In this regard people were very touchy and showed themselves to be deeply disappointed when another "party chief" was again treated mildly by the courts and the expected harsh punishment failed to materialize. Then people doubted openly and bluntly whether the Third Reich was still able to establish "justice."

The leadership of the Nazi regime recognized the danger posed by this and tried to confront it—even though with varying commitment and determination. Thus in March 1942 and May 1943 the head of the Chancellery, Lammers, issued a decree of the Führer to the upper echelons of the party, the state, and the army to demand of them a "conduct suitable to the war situation."[30] The immediate occasion for this had been a special case of foodstuff black-marketeering, which the Berlin courts and police were dealing with in 1942/43. If this case had become public it would indeed have had a greatly adverse effect on public opinion, for among the regular customers of that black-marketeer, who had dealt mainly with luxury goods, had also been the minister of the interior, Frick, employment minister Hierl, education minister Rust, as well as such high ranking military officers as Brauchitsch and Raeder.

The Führer decrees were rather general and had not been made public. This upset especially propaganda minister Goebbels, who viewed the behavior of his "party comrades" as outright "war sabotaging," not least because in face of it he was deeply concerned about the success of his propaganda efforts to weld together the German people and to ask everything of them for "total war."

Goebbels found an ally in justice minister Thierack. Both struggled to appease the rage about the "crony economy" (Bonzenwirtschaft) by running a press campaign documenting the rigorous court actions taken against "party favorites." In addition they addressed the people via radio in March and July 1944 to assure them of a "merciless fight against all phenomena of corruption." And indeed, even if it was the quasi customary right of the "party chiefs" to feather their nests at the expense of the "common people," those who overdid it may have run a high risk. Thus the leader of the party district office in Lübeck, the mayor of Altenahr as well as the brother of Rober Ley, leader of the German work front, had all been sentenced to death and executed on grounds of embezzlement and black-marketeering on a grand scale.[31]

The administration, too, strained to keep a tighter rein. Himmler, minister of the interior, emphatically denounced the practice of "employing relatives in the same department . . . and at the same location in cities of less than 300,000 inhabitants,"[32] and Heinrich Müller, the new head of the Reich's audit division, focused on shutting the gateways for corruption in public procurement. In March of 1945 Müller presented an extensive set of measures to fight corruption in the public administration. He wanted to penalize cases of corruption among civil servants through the death penalty more often.[33]

VIII

Even through these measures the principle causes for corruption in the "Third Reich" could hardly have been eliminated, for corruption had been a structural and propping element of the Nazi regime, its politics, and its polycratic structures. As mentioned earlier, since 1945 Germans have quickly suppressed this trait of the Nazi reign as well. For instance, the "office for fighting mismanagement and corruption," which after 1945 fought against the detrimental effects of the Nazi war economy in the British occupied area, was dissolved in 1948 shortly after the new currency, the Deutsche Mark, had been introduced. For now there was a new economic order and hence a reasonable hope that everything would run smoothly and orderly again. Incidentally, part of the staff of that department went to work for the North Rhine-Westphalian office responsible for defending the constitution (*Verfassungsschutz*, one of the domestic intelligence services), only to more or less stand and watch the new rise of many old Nazis.

Had this been different, then the discussion about corruption in Germany might have another background, namely the experience that corruption is by no means a new phenomenon in German history and that it has been first and foremost a problem of dictatorship, not of democracy.

The observations a historian can make on the basis of the presently accessible sources on the history of corruption in Nazi Germany—and considering that the files of industrial and other companies have not yet been analyzed under this aspect—permit at least the following assertions and urge certain questions.

- An intensive anti-corruption propaganda facilitated the Nazis' rise to power as well as the discrediting and elimination of their democratic opponents. Doing so the Nazi propaganda could build on a strongly developed element of the political culture in Germany at the time, namely, that any kind of political negotiating and compromise, in short the whole democratic process of will-formation and decision making as such, was seen as essentially corrupt, which in turn determined the "antidemocratic thinking" of many Germans at the time.
- Corruption had as well a stabilizing and integrating function for the Nazi regime insofar as bribery, patronage, nepotism and similar means served to heal the wounds inflicted upon the small and big "party comrades" during the times when they fought for power, to satisfy the desires of the party elite, and to strengthen the loyalty towards the regime and the Führer, the subleaders, and their organizations respectively. Invoking Theodor Geiger once again: self-enrichment was apparently an essential driving force of the "Third Reich."
- It appears that one can speak of universal corruption, i.e. the enmeshing of the whole state apparatus and a majority of the elite in corruption, as well as of a mix between individual and organizational corruption according to the definition of Montias and Rose-Ackerman.[34]
- In addition, the destabilizing effects of corruption became apparent in the "opinion and mood" of the people despite a public forced into line. This was especially true after the defeat of the German army in Stalingrad. From that point on the Nazi regime could no longer dole out gains and hopes of future prosperity, but for most it held out only

scarcity and utter need. It is striking that corruption was mainly viewed as a problem of "justice" and equal treatment of the *"Volksgenossen"* (members of the supposed community of German people) especially in regard to problems of necessary food supply.

This should not be brushed aside as less important low-level corruption, for one would run the risk of underestimating the significance of these phenomena for the sense of justice and loyalty of the German people towards the regime. Typically enough, the SD (security service of the SS) greatly stressed the "opinion"-political importance of black-marketeering of foodstuff and luxury items many members of the Nazi elite had been involved in virtually as a matter of course.

- This poses the question whether in societies where the public is forced into line and depoliticized the destabilizing effects of corruption unfold mainly on the low-level. In regard to the history of the Soviet Union it has been discussed at times whether corruption and especially corruption in the supply system of rare foodstuff, cars, luxury articles etc. had been one decisive factor in the demise of "state socialism."[35] Though corruption was apparently an essential cause for the crises in "opinion and mood" of the people in the Nazi regime, one should not exaggerate and overestimate this argument—the military collapse was too sudden for a destabilizing effect of the corrupt practices to develop fully.
- It would also be more fruitful to take up different considerations that have been put forward in studies on Soviet rule in the '70s and '80s.[36] Thus it would be interesting to further analyze whether corruption and anti-corruption measures were in the end also an expression and a means of power struggles within the clique of the Nazi leadership and of a persistently smoldering rivalry between the state and the party. At least for Goebbels and Thierack it was conspicuous that they were zeroing in on certain *Gauleiters* and their followers with draconian measures, but they also focused on high-handed functionaries on the lowest level, the *Kreisleiter* (local leaders).

Only further research can help answer some of these questions. For a general assessment of the significance of corruption in the Nazi state one question is of particular importance and still difficult to answer given the political and economic lay of the country: how intensively and to what extent were the relationships of German industry and business to the Nazi potentates determined by corruption?

Translated by Holger Moroff

Notes

1. See Bajohr, Frank: Nationalsozialismus und Korruption, in: *Mittelweg*, (36) 1998, p. 57–77, including a brief review of the research literature. Bajohr points out that especially the political models for analyzing corruption in less developed countries, focusing on the political and societal functions of corruption, can not be applied to Nazi Germany. It would, according to Bajohr, not explain the tragic role corruption played in the Holocaust.

2. A brief explanation: The SD had —to use the words of its head for domestic intelligence, Otto Ohlendorf —among other things the task to supply the Nazi leadership with information about "public and mass opinion" and to provide a substitute for opinion surveys by spying and surveillance. Boberach, heinz (ed.): *Meldungen aus dem Reich. Die geheimen Lageberichte des Sicherheitsdienstes der SS*, 17 volumes, Herrsching, 1984.

3. For a general information on this source see Michelberger, Hans: *Berichte aus der Justiz des Dritten Reiches*, Pfaffenweiler, 1989.

4. *Deutschland-Berichte der Sozialdemokratischen Partei Deutschlnads (SOPADE)*, 7 year's issues, Salzhausen-Frankfurt, 1980.

5. Friedrich, Carl J.: "The Pathology of Politics: Violence, Betrayal, Corruption, Secrecy and Propaganda", New York, 1972, quoted in Erhard Blankenburg: "Der Aufstand der kleinen Richter gegen die Korruption der großen Politik" in: *Kritische Justiz*, 1999, p. 355–356.

6. *Weltbühne*, (1929) 43, quoted in Cordula Ludwig, *Korruption und National-sozialismus in Berlin 1924–1934*, Frankfurt 1998.

7. The research literature says little about the relationship between industry and army during World War I, even though it played an important role in the debates of parliament in the first years of the Weimar Republic. As a reaction to corruption agitation of the right wing German National Peoples Party (DNV) against Matthias Erzberger, the German parliamentarian who signed the cease fire in Compiegne and who was falsely accused of tax evasion, the parliamentary faction of the SPD demanded that 85 million Mark of "surplus gains" through war contracts of Daimler were to be transferred back into state coffers. They also uncovered the case of the right wing member of parliament and factory owner, van den Kerkholl. He had evidently obtained army contracts between 1916 and 1918 through the payment of grease money. And he could only escape final conviction by destroying his books that had already been in a sealed safe. (no author) *Die deutschnationalen Drachentöter der Korruption. Der erbrochene Geldschrank.* Berlin 1921.

8. Angermund, Ralph: *Deutsche Richterschaft 1919–1945*, Frankfurt 1990, p. 68.

9. Bajohr, Frank, Joachim Szondrynski eds.: *Hamburg in der NS-Zeit*, Hamburg 1995; for cases of "embezzlement" see Hamburg ministry of justice ed.: *"Von Gewohnheitsverbrechern, Volksschädlingen und Asozialen"*, Hamburg 1995, p. 56.

10. Quoted in: Schmidt, Christoph, Zu den Motiven "alter Kämpfer" in der NSDAP, in: Peukert, Detlev and Jürgen Reulecke eds. *Die Reihen fast geschlossen*, Wuppertal 1981, p. 21–44, here p. 44.

11. *Justizministerblatt für die preußische Gesetzgebung und Rechtspflege*, (1933), p. 235.

12. Sopade, 2 (1935), p. 495.

13. Sopade, 2 (1935), pp. 102.; Bajohr, op. cit., p. 70.

14. Angermund, op. cit., pp. 75.

15. Uebeschär, Gerd R., Winfried Vogel: *Dienen und Verdienen. Hitlers Geschenke an seine Eliten*, Frankfurt 1999.
16. Sopade, 2 (1935), p. 599.
17. Kershaw, Ian: *The "Hitler-Myth". Image and Reality in the Third Reich*, Oxford 1987.
18. Weinert, Werner: *"Sie Sauberkeit der Verwaltung". Der Rechnungshof des Deutschen Reiches 1938–1946*, Opladen 1993, pp. 20, quote p. 24.
19. Barkai, Avraham: *Vom Boykott zur "Entjudung". Der wirtschaftliche Existenzkampf der Juden im Dritten Reich 1933–1943*, Frankfurt 1988, pp. 80.
20. Quoted in: Pätzold, Kurt ed.: *Verfolgung —Vertreibung —Vernichtung. Dokumente des faschistischen Antisemitismus 1933 bis 1942*, Leipzig 1984, 2nd edition, p. 98.
21. Hilger, Raul: *Die Vernichtung der europäischen Juden*, Frankfurt 1990, p. 259.
22. Höß, Rudolf: *Kommandant in Auschwitz. Autobiographische Aufzeichnungen*, München 1981, 8th edition, pp. 168, Wolfgang Sofsky: *Die Ordnung des Terrors. Das Konzentrationslager*, Frankfurt 1993.
23. Bajohr, op. cit., p. 65.
24. Hilberg, op. cit., pp. 969.
25. *Die Strafrechtspflege im fünften Kriegsjahr*, Bundesarchiv R 22/4692.
26. Reichsamt für Statistik: *Die Entwicklung der Kriminalität im Deutschen Reich vom Kriegsmeginn bis Mitte 1943*, Bundesarchiv R22/1160.
27. *Lagebericht des Oberlandesgerichtspräsidenten von München vom 3.8.1943.* Bundesarchiv R 22/2958.
28. "Lagerbericht des Generalstaatsanwalts bei dem Kammergericht vom 30. Januar 1941", quoted in: Schimmler, Bernd: *"Stimmung der Bevölkerung und politische Lage". Die Lageberichte der Berliner Justiz 1940–1945*, Berlin 1986, p. 52, see also p. 57 and p. 83.
29. Boberach, Heinz ed.: *Meldungen aus dem Reich. Die geheimen Lageberichte des SD*, Herrsching 1984, vol. 15, pp. 6065, vol. 17, pp. 6711.
30. Reuth, Ralf Georg (ed.): *Joseph Goebbels Tagebücher*, vol. 5 1943–1945, Munich 1992, p. 1914. See also Lothar Gruchmann: *Korruption im Dritten Reich. Zur "Lebensmittelversorgung" der NS-Führerschaft*, in: VfZ, 42(1994), p. 571–594.
31. Bundesarchiv R 43/1159b, 1544a; R 22/3374 (3.12.1941)
32. Mommsen, Hans: *Ein Erlaß Himmlers zur Bekämpfung der Korruption in der inneren Verwaltung*, in: VfZ, 16 (1968).
33. Weinert, op. cit., pp. 144.
34. As an overview about different approaches to analysing the Communist systems in the '70s and '80s see Herberer, Thomas: *Korruption in China. Analyse eines politieschen, ökonomischen und sozialen Problems*, Opladen 1991, pp. 25.
35. See von Beyme, Klaus: *Systemwechsel in Osteuropa*, Frankfurt 1994, pp. 67.
36. See Herberer, op.cit., pp. 15.

Part X

CORRUPTION IN THE LEVELS OF AMERICAN GOVERNMENT

Introduction to Part X

The particular venality and virtues of American politics make that country a challenging case for comparative analysis. They are the results of the values animating the American political culture, of governing institutions, and of patterns of participation—that is, an emphasis upon private action and interests and a liberal style of institutionalizing both. But these forces have not defined the American corruption story once and for all. Indeed, as the selections in this chapter make clear, important tensions and changes continue today.

Moralists on the Make

More than many others, Americans see the stakes of politics in moralistic terms, and expect its processes and institutions to embody major values. Arriving in the New World, rid of many of the hereditary claims and historical conflicts that shaped concepts of office, and the uses of power, in the Old, and seeking to govern a nation both fragmented and ambitious, Americans tried to have things all ways at once—to be moralistic and to exercise individual liberty, to be both equal and free. Madison captured this challenge in *The Federalist*, number 51:

> If men were angels, no government would be necessary. If angels were to govern men, neither external nor internal controls on government would be necessary. In framing a government which is to be administered by men over men, the great difficulty lies in this: you must first enable the government to control the governed; and in the next place oblige it to control itself.

Americans are *moralists* in many ways: they feel entitled, even obliged, to judge others in both public and private life. Most believe governments should not only be effective, but should also be just and *good,* though they disagree over what that means. They are skeptical of those who govern, and do not accept *raison d'etat* as a justification for policy. But surprisingly, they remain comparatively free from political cynicism. Indeed, Americans may not be cynical enough: scandals over official behavior that would draw little notice elsewhere create cycles of political Puritanism, distorting politics and policy making for years after (Woodward, 1999).

At the same time Americans are *individualists*, jealous of personal liberties and property; most see markets as both efficient and just. Self-interest is celebrated not only as the engine that moves society forward, but also as a safeguard against official abuses:

> [T]he great security against a gradual concentration of the several powers in the same department consists in giving to those who administer each department the necessary constitutional means and personal motives to resist encroachments of the others . . . Ambition must be made to counteract ambition. The interest of the man must be connected with the constitutional rights of the place (*Federalist* 51, 1961 ed.: 322).

Scandal and Reform, American Style

Sooner or later, however, moralism and individualism end up in conflict (Eisenstadt, 1978). Not surprisingly, corruption, scandal and reform are perennial features of American politics, and they engage both fundamental values and a pragmatic taste for institutional tinkering. The current debate over campaign finance is only partly about corruption; it also raises questions of equality, free speech, and the nature of a good democracy. Previous attempts to institutionalize these values via legislation have proven unsatisfying, but the general response has been to demand new institutional changes rather than to reconsider the nature of equality, or the role of wealth, in a democracy. Not only the formal rules, but also the unwritten codes and boundaries, of politics are continually redrawn. Whatever one thinks of the principal actions and antagonists in the Clinton saga, for example, it is clear that public-private boundaries have been moved, and the moral expectations accompanying public office have been changed. The rules of reform changed too: the most important long-run consequence of the scandal may well be the non-renewal of the portions of the Ethics in Government Act of 1978 providing for the appointment of Independent Counsels.

The selections in part 10 draw out some of the major forces driving corruption and reform in the United States, and explore parallels and contrasts with other democracies. Frank Anechiarico and Jim Jacobs examine the history and legacy of what they term the "Anti-Corruption Project" in New York City—a city marked not only by legendary cases of corruption, but also by some of the most extensive reform efforts in the country. Anti-corruption crusades have culminated in a "panoptic vision" of reform, institutionalizing an all-encompassing system of monitoring and supervision that penetrates all aspects of local government. But the results are not encouraging: these measures often raise the cost and lower the efficiency of government, stifle initiative and innovation, and drive able people away from public service. So strong is the consensus behind such reforms that it is difficult to conceive of alternatives; but in both the United States and the Netherlands other approaches—relying at times upon the initiative of officials themselves, in ways Madison might applaud—show promising results.

Generalizations about "American" corruption are risky, however, because of the size and diversity of the society. Comparisons among states and regions are particularly useful for examining the deeper forces shaping trends in corruption. Thomas Schlesinger and Kenneth J. Meier use Justice Department data on corruption *prosecutions*—not the same thing as corruption itself, but a useful proxy variable for a range of factors influencing corruption issues—to make such comparisons. Their findings not only reveal the importance of historical patterns, but also show the effects of the states' differing capacities for administration, monitoring, and reform. Characteristics of the states as civil societies—cosmopolitan versus traditional values, and the extent of their "social capital" (see, for a related discussion, Susan Pharr on Japan in chapter 48)—also help predict patterns of prosecutions. Perhaps the most provocative result is evidence that corruption prosecutions may be "targeted" along partisan lines under some circumstances.

Campaign finance reform—the leading corruption issue in American politics at the moment—poses both highly technical and deeply political issues. Much of the evolution of policy has taken place in the courts. Debates there have raised major questions about the nature of corruption, the boundaries of free speech, and distinctions between political speech and participation, on the one hand, and property on the other. Thomas Burke's analysis of the evolving jurisprudence on these issues not only reveals their complexity but shows how major values and political issues lie very near the surface of the legal and technical debate. The Supreme Court's reasoning about corruption has been tortured at times. Ultimately the issue comes down to conceptions of democracy, and of the sorts of activities that sustain or threaten it. Burke illuminates these complexities using concepts of representation, deliberation and community, in the process making it clear why a broadly satisfactory approach to campaign finance reform will be difficult to devise, and even more difficult to reconcile with important Constitutional principles.

How does America's ambivalence about private political influence and freedom of expression work out in practice, compared to other democracies? Holger Moroff offers an historical and comparative view, drawing upon German and American cases over the past generation. Both countries value equality and participatory politics—indeed, Germany's *Grundgesetz* (Basic Law) mandates extensive guarantees in that area, and the state backs them up with substantial subsidies—and both have liberal economies and political systems in which corporate influence, and the political uses of wealth, can be extensive and controversial. Indeed, early in the year 2000 Germany became embroiled in a serious scandal involving its center-right political party (the

CDU/CSU) and former Chancellor Helmut Kohl. Moroff's discussion of the "Keating Five" in the US, and the Flick affair in Germany, helps explain the roots and significance of the current episodes, and the implications of the two countries' differing approaches to reconciling political money with open politics. In both, legal provisions are under close examination, but ultimately the political arena is where new settlements between conflicting values and clashing interests may have to be worked out.

References

Eisenstadt, Abraham S. 1978. "Political Corruption in American History: Some Further Thoughts." Abraham S. Eisenstadt, Ari Hoogenboom and Hans L. Trefousse, eds. *Before Watergate: Problems of Corruption in American History.* Brooklyn, NY: Brooklyn College Press, 193–226.
Alexander Hamilton, James Madison, John Jay. 1961 ed. *The Federalist Papers.* New York: New American Library.
Woodward, Bob. 1999. *Shadow: Five Presidents and the Legacy of Watergate.* New York: Simon and Schuster.

33

Variations in Corruption among the American States*

Thomas Schlesinger and Kenneth J. Meier

In "I Seen My Opportunities and I Took 'Em: Political Corruption in the American States" (1992), we argued that federal prosecution of corrupt public officials was a good surrogate for the level of political corruption in the American states.[1] These prosecutions were unrelated to prosecutorial or judicial resources but were linked to theoretically important variables in four categories: historical and cultural, political, structural, and bureaucratic. For each of the four categories we developed a model containing several variables. The study found that among the historical/cultural factors, the traditional corruption of urban areas and the informed nature of the electorate affect the relative level of political corruption. In the political category, corruption declined when a political system had closely contested elections and high voter turnout. Despite a wealth of arguments that link government structure to corruption, the analysis failed to find any structural correlates of corruption except for the capacity to conduct computer-based audits. Finally, corruption was strongly associated with bureaucratic factors; both the size of the bureaucracy and potential bribery (gambling arrests) were positively correlated with corruption. Perhaps the most striking finding in that study was that after controls for all these factors, there was some evidence that prosecutions in the Reagan administration targeted both black public officials and Democratic officials and that black public officials were also targeted by the Carter administration.

Given the limited time frame of that original study (1977–1987), however, these findings could be unique to that period. This paper revisits the set of questions addressed in our earlier paper to determine if its findings are time-bound or still apply today. The analysis takes four parts. First, using current data and slightly revised measures, we re-create the four general models of political corruption (historical/cultural, political, structural, and bureaucratic) devised in our earlier paper (1992). Second, based on the results of the models, we attempt to re-create a single "best" model to explain the variation in political corruption. Third, using the variables of the "best" model as control variables, we again examine the question of targeting, that is, the use of targeted prosecutions to harass political opponents. We determine whether or not prosecutions of public officials are linked to party control or the number of black elected officials. Finally, we discuss the implications of our findings for the study of political corruption.

Measuring Corruption

In seeking to identify the causes of political corruption in America, one may study either the rise and fall of levels of corruption over time or the differing levels of corruption among the fifty states during one period in time. Data availability problems essentially dictate that we adopt the latter approach, aggregating all prosecutions for the period 1986–1995 for each of the fifty states.

In our earlier paper (1992, 136) we argued the best measure of political corruption was the number of prosecutions of public officials on corruption charges per 100 elected officials. The term "public officials" includes both elected and appointed officials but falls far short of the total number of government employees. We adopted this measure in lieu of a per capita measure used by Nice (1983) or simply the raw numbers used by Johnston (1983).

By standardizing the number of prosecutions of *public* officials by the number of *elected* officials, we do encounter one problem. Hawaii has a highly centralized government that elects very few of its public officials (160 compared to 1,120 in Rhode Island, the next smallest state). As a result, Hawaii has an exceptionally high number of prosecutions *per 100 elected officials*. To avoid this measurement problem, all analysis in this paper will be done on 49 states, excluding Hawaii. With or without Hawaii, the results of concern are essentially the same.

Table 33.1 shows the dependent variable used in this analysis and that of our earlier article (1992). Our measure is the number of prosecutions for 1986 through 1995, a ten-year period in contrast to the eleven-year period in the prior work. Thirty-nine of fifty states show an increase in the number of prosecutions, and overall prosecutions increase by 18 percent. Regionally, the

Table 33.1
Rate of Prosecutions of Public Officials

State	1982	1995
Alabama	5.00	2.94
Alaska	3.08	1.48
Arizona	1.33	2.98
Arkansas	0.50	0.59
California	2.38	4.88
Colorado	0.65	0.73
Connecticut	0.88	1.08
Delaware	1.10	1.30
Florida	3.55	9.78
Georgia	2.97	5.26
Idaho	0.36	0.56
Illinois	0.89	1.86
Indiana	0.93	1.34
Iowa	0.16	0.39
Kansas	0.30	0.32
Kentucky	1.27	1.77
Louisiana	2.84	4.93
Maine	0.27	0.64
Maryland	5.34	8.18
Massachusetts	1.05	1.28
Michigan	0.92	1.10
Minnesota	0.17	0.40
Missouri	0.44	1.01
Mississippi	2.33	3.92
Montana	0.46	0.73
Nebraska	0.20	0.21
Nevada	2.10	1.36
New Hampshire	0.32	0.13
New Jersey	1.48	1.52
New Mexico	2.29	1.77
New York	2.98	3.61
North Carolina	2.05	2.31
North Dakota	0.03	0.27
Ohio	1.23	2.23
Oklahoma	2.62	0.64
Oregon	0.27	0.33
Pennsylvania	1.47	1.40
Rhode Island	1.99	3.04
South Carolina	5.13	4.33
South Dakota	0.41	0.48
Tennessee	3.67	4.06
Texas	1.10	1.32
Utah	0.93	0.58
Vermont	0.03	0.10
Virginia	3.73	10.38
Washington	0.33	0.63
West Virginia	1.86	2.33
Wisconsin	0.44	0.41
Wyoming	0.18	0.77

South appears to have considerably higher levels of corruption while New England and the Midwest show lower levels. The greatest absolute increases in prosecutions between 1982 and 1995 also occurred in the South. The eleven states that showed decreased prosecutions follow no geographical pattern. Both the correlation between the two measures (.77) and an examination of the rankings show a reasonable amount of consistency over time.

The top half of table 33.2 shows the ten most corrupt states in the two time periods. Seven states appear on both lists–Maryland, South Carolina, Virginia, Tennessee, Florida, Georgia, and Louisiana; Alabama, Alaska and New York drop out of the top ten (but remain highly ranked) to be replaced by Mississippi, Rhode Island, and California. The least corrupt states show even greater consistency with eight of the states ranked in the top ten both time periods–Vermont, North Dakota, Iowa, Minnesota, Nebraska, Oregon, Kansas and New Hampshire. Wyoming and Maine drop from the top ten to be replaced by Wisconsin and South Dakota. The 1982 figures reveal considerable variation among the states with North Dakota and Vermont having the least corruption (.03) and Alabama having the most (5.00). The variation among states remains large in the later period. Vermont again enjoys the lowest level of corruption (.10) while Virginia, whose prosecutions more than

Table 33.2
States with the Highest and Lowest Prosecution Rates

Most Prosecutions Rank	1977–87 Rate		1986–95 Rate
1. Maryland	5.34	Virginia	10.38
2. South Carolina	5.13	Florida	9.78
3. Alabama	5.00	Maryland	8.18
4. Virginia	4.73	Georgia	5.26
5. Tennessee	3.67	Louisiana	4.93
6. Florida	3.55	California	4.88
7. Alaska	3.08	South Carolina	4.33
8. New York	2.98	Tennessee	4.06
9. Georgia	2.97	Mississippi	3.92
10. Louisiana	2.84	Rhode Island	3.04

Fewest Prosecutions	1977–87		1986–95
1. Vermont	.03	Vermont	.10
2. North Dakota	.03	New Hampshire	.13
3. Iowa	.16	Nebraska	.21
4. Minnesota	.17	North Dakota	.27
5. Wyoming	.18	Kansas	.32
6. Nebraska	.20	Oregon	.33
7. Oregon	.27	Iowa	.39
8. Maine	.27	Minnesota	.40
9. Kansas	.30	Wisconsin	.41
10. New Hampshire	.32	South Dakota	.48

doubled, has *100 times* that amount (10). The rankings have a great deal of face validity. States with reputations for corruption tend to have high scores, and states with reputations for clean government tend to have low scores.

Explanations of Political Corruption

Prior to analyzing the role of targeting in political corruption, we must first identify the set of forces that influence the level of corruption. To do this, we review the independent variables developed in our earlier article (1992) and re-create the four models of political corruption (with minor changes in some measures).

These models are all based on the notion that the decision to engage in corrupt activities is, in the end, a comparison of costs and benefits. That is, public officials act in a corrupt manner for a simple reason: they perceive that the potential benefits of corruption exceed the potential costs (Rose-Ackerman 1978). If the benefits of corruption minus the probability of being caught times the penalties for being caught is greater than the benefits of not being corrupt, then a rational individual will choose to be corrupt. Within this general benefit/cost approach, we will consider the four explanations of corruption we developed in our earlier article: historical/cultural, political, structural, and bureaucratic.

Historical/Cultural Explanations of Corruption

Historical/cultural explanations of political corruption proliferate in American politics. These explanations hold that corruption is the result of the weakness of individuals or a pattern of politics that has routinely accepted corruption. In other words, corruption exists because individuals perceive that there are benefits to corruption and that the costs are relatively low compared to the benefits.

We identified and sought to measure four different historical/cultural explanations of political corruption: urbanism, middle-class preferences, immigration, and criminal activities. Urban environments loosen the social controls of family and religion and at the same time concentrate government programs and resources. In these environments, political machines were established to benefit individuals who supported the machine, and corruption was used to compensate machine operators for their efforts. Although most American cities have been subjected to substantial structural change to eliminate corruption, cities still provide weaker social controls and greater opportunities for corruption. Our measure for the impact of an urban environment will be the percentage of state population living in urban areas.

While some aspects of political corruption may have worked in favor of the lower classes, the middle class is more likely to have opposed it. An

632   Political Corruption

indication of middle-class strength can be tapped by the educational levels of the population, in this case by the percentage of the population with a college degree. Although past studies have linked immigration to corruption (Werner 1983, 148; Nye 1967, 417; Wilson 1966, 30), these arguments clearly are not intended to apply to all immigrants. Within the context of political corruption, many perceive immigrants to mean the Irish or Italian immigrants who first challenged Yankee hegemony in the major cities. Since immigrants have few economic resources to lose, they might perceive that the costs of corruption are fairly low. Our measure for the impact of immigration will be the percentage of the population that identifies their ancestral group as Irish or Italian.[2]

Finally, Nice (1983, 509) argues that political corruption is merely the extension of private behavior in the public realm and that crime rates might be a good surrogate for tolerance of corruption. High crime rates, therefore, should indicate the inability of the political system to establish penalties high enough or certain enough to deter crime (including corruption). The historical/cultural explanation of corruption, therefore, suggests positive correlations between political corruption and urbanism, Irish/Italian ancestry, and crime rates, and a negative correlation with education.

Table 33.3 reports the unstandardized regression coefficients for the historical and cultural variables. As expected, the level of urban development and the crime rate are positively associated with the level of corruption: an increase in urbanization and an increase in the overall crime rate yield an increase in corruption prosecutions. On the other hand, an increase in college graduates is associated with a decline in the number of prosecutions. This suggests that an informed electorate is less tolerant of corruption and perhaps exerts political pressures in that direction. The Irish/Italian variable was insignificant. The overall fit of the model indicates that historical and cultural

Table 33.3
Historical and Cultural Impacts on Political Corruption

Variable	Slope	T-score
Percent College Grads	–2.15	–2.75*
Crime Rate	.0001	1.94*
Irish and Italian Immigration	.003	.25
Percent Urban	.009	2.15*

R-Square	=	.36
Adjusted R-Square	=	.31
F		6.31
Standard Error		.39
N		49

*p < .05 (one-tailed test)

factors affect prosecutions for political corruption, but much of the variation remains unexplained.

Political Explanations of Corruption

Perhaps the most political explanation of corruption is presented by Susan Rose-Ackerman (1978). Rose-Ackerman rejects the common economic prescription for combating corruption—decentralization and economic competition. She argues that politics can be used to combat corruption by increasing the probability that a corrupt individual will be punished. Focusing on elected officials, she states, "politicians may sell their votes on particular issues if they are either very confident of re-election or practically certain to be defeated" (Rose-Ackerman 1978, 213). Competitive elections, however, are not a sufficient condition for reducing corruption; an intelligent electorate is also required. She concludes: "Combining an informed and concerned electorate with a political process that regularly produces closely contested elections leads to a world in which corruption is limited by competition" (Rose-Ackerman 1978, 213).

The linkage between corruption and electoral defeat has received a fair amount of empirical research. Peters and Welch (1980) found that corruption reduced a candidate's vote by 6 to 11 percentage points in congressional elections. Other studies have also found an electoral impact to charges of corruption (see Rundquist, Strom, and Peters 1977; Ragsdale and Cook 1987; Krasno and Green 1988).

The most obvious indicator of competitive elections is party competition (see Bibby and Holbrook. 1996, 103–9), operationalized here as the competitiveness of state-level elections from 1989 to 1994. To tap into the electorate's interest in the political process, we use the relative turnout in House elections from 1989 to 1994 (Bibby and Holbrook 1996, 110). Johnston (1983) found that turnout was negatively related to corruption but found no relationship between party competition and corruption. In addition to turnout, the college graduates measure in the historical/cultural section might also indicate an involved, politically informed electorate (Campbell, Converse, Miller, and Stokes 1960; Verba and Nie 1972; Nie, Verba, and Petrocik 1976).

If contested elections contribute to less corruption, then another political structure that should be considered is the institutional power of the governor. More powerful governors should be able to centralize power and gain more control over the governmental mechanism; on the other hand, the greater the number of officials appointed by the governor, the less control exerted by competitive elections. We use the measure of the institutional power of the governor developed by Beyle (1996, 237).

Finally, political ideology could be linked to the tolerance of corruption. One argument might be that conservative electorates would be more tolerant of politicians who view politics as a means of maximizing political utility, thereby leading politicians to believe that the chance of being punished for corrupt practices is low. Alternatively, conservatives are generally supporters of law enforcement and are opposed to the waste of tax money. We used the Erikson, Wright, and McIver (1993, 16) measure of political ideology.[3] The political explanation of corruption, therefore, predicts that corruption is negatively related to voter turnout and party competition, and positively or negatively related to the institutional powers of the governor and the level of electorate's conservatism.

The analysis of political influences on corruption is presented in table 33.4. Political participation (voter turnout) is negatively related to political corruption, supporting Rose-Ackerman's theory that exposure to the threat of electoral retribution acts as a deterrent to potentially corrupt public officials. Given this relationship, the absence of a relationship between party competition and corruption seems odd. Perhaps the Ranney measure better captures party control than electoral competition, yet an alternate measure of electoral competition (Bibby and Holbrook 1996, 108) also proved insignificant. In addition, neither the institutional powers of the governor nor political conservatism appeared to be related to the amount of public corruption. Among the various possible political explanations for corruption, it appears that only a concerned and active electorate has an effect.

Structural Explanations of Corruption

Within American politics, the primary perceived deterrent to corruption has been the advocacy of structural reforms. Variation in governmental structures is perceived to be an influence on corruption. Wilson (1966, 35) argues that American political systems, because they are fragmented, allow individu-

Table 33.4
Political Forces and Political Corruption

Variable	Slope	T-score
Voter Turnout	–.042	–6.86*
Party Competition	.000	.00
Powers of the Governor	.027	.20
Political Conservatism	–.005	.38

R-Square	=	**.54**
Adjusted R-Square	=	**.49**
F		**12.66**
Standard Error		**.34**
N		**49**

*p < .05 (one-tailed test)

als to exploit politics for their gain. Fragmented political systems make public officials less visible and thus reduce the perceived probability that corrupt actions will be discovered. Walsh (1978) and Henriques (1986) claim that the fragmentation of political authority resulting from the proliferation of single purpose special districts (e.g., water districts, public corporations) is a stimulus to corruption. Such districts are obscured from public view yet control substantial public funds, thus providing good opportunities for corruption (Henriques 1986). Furthermore, the number of special districts have proliferated in recent years. While the number of governmental units has declined almost 25 percent from 1950 to 1995, the number of special districts has increased almost 300 percent during the same period.

The political reform movements of the early twentieth century explicitly stressed structural reforms with city managers, nonpartisan elections, at-large elections, etc. Populist reforms at the state level such as direct election of senators, initiative, referendum, and recall also provide structural changes for voter actions. In their study of corruption, Berg, Hahn, and Schmidhauser (1976, 23) suggest that direct democracy methods such as these can do a great deal to limit corruption by increasing political action. In contemporary government, campaign contributions are perceived as a source of corruption; advocacy groups such as Common Cause support laws that require greater campaign finance reporting.

To deal with this broad array of problems, an elaborate series of structural reforms have been adopted to either increase the risk or the penalties for getting caught. Generally, these reforms seek to increase centralized control, visibility of action, regulation, and popular control. We have devised the following measures to capture these four aspects of reform. Two variables capture the degree of centralization/decentralization in a state; the first measures centralization as the percentage of state and local employees who are employed by the state government and the second (actually a measure of decentralization) is the number of special districts as a percent of all governmental units. Special districts, as noted earlier, are perceived as especially amenable to corruption.

Increasing the visibility of public officials can be achieved through greater use of audit controls. We use audit capacity as a surrogate for the use of audit controls and measure it as the computer facilities available to the state legislature (Council of State Governments, 1992–3, table 3.30). As a measure of efforts to control the corrupting influences of campaign contributions, we have devised an index based on the degree to which campaign donations are regulated (Council of State Governments, 1992–3, table 5.11). Finally, as a measure of populist direct democracy reforms, we use a dummy variable to indicate the presence of the initiative process in a state. Structural explanations of corruption, in short, predict that political corruption will be nega-

Table 33.5
Political Reform and Political Corruption

Variable	Slope	T-score
Computer Audit Capabilities	.003	1.47
Campaign Finance Restrictions	−.037	−1.25
State Centralization	−.015	−1.53
Percent Special Districts	.005	1.41
Presence of Initiative	−.285	−2.16*

R-Square	=	.20
Adjusted R-Square	=	.11
F		2.15
Standard Error		.45
N		49

*p < .05 (one-tailed test)

tively related to centralization, computers, campaign finance restrictions, and the presence of the initiative, and positively related to special districts.

Table 33.5 presents the evidence for structural effects on political corruption. Only the presence of the initiative is associated with federal prosecutions of public officials. The remaining variables are not statistically significant although campaign finance restrictions, state centralization, and percent special districts are all are in the direction predicted and would be significant at the .10 level. The findings do provide some support for the notion that the structure of government affects the level of corruption, and thus by altering the structure of government, that we may reduce public corruption.

Bureaucratic Opportunity Explanations of Corruption

According to Wilson (1966, 31) "men steal when there is a lot of money lying around loose and no one is watching." In other words, all public servants are susceptible to corruption, and what increases corruption is the opportunity for it (an increase in perceived benefits.) As the size of government increases, the potential reward of corruption should also increase (Johnston 1986, 27). Corruption exists because public service offers individuals a way to become rich that is not available to private citizens (Nye 1967, 418; Nas et al. 1986, 109; Huntington 1968). This logic suggests that corruption should increase as the size of government increases and more opportunities for corruption are thus presented. One measure of the level of opportunity for corrupt activity is the size of the state budget. The ratio of budgets to employees should indicate, in Wilson's terms, the relative amount of money lying around.

Other than increasing opportunities, the size of the bureaucracy may be related to corruption for another reason. Corruption can be used to overcome bureaucratic inertia and make bureaucracies respond to demands for change (Nas et al. 1986, 109; Werner 1983, 148; Klitgaard 1988, 37). Bureaucracy is viewed by many as an obstacle to change, and corruption is perceived as positive since it can be used to motivate the bureaucracy to act in support of some public good. We use the number of government employees per one thousand population as a direct measure of size and bureaucracy.

Another bureaucratic hypothesis is related to what can be called the income inequality or the poverty argument (see Huntington 1968, 66; Nye 1967, 418). Because government service provides opportunities for corruption, governments need to reduce the temptation on the part of its employees through the use of positive incentives. If civil servants are paid fairly well, government attracts better qualified individuals and the lure of corrupt practices may be lessened. Higher pay could also be associated with a more professional bureaucracy, which Heidenheimer (1990, 579) feels is more difficult to bribe. The mean salary of public employees should indicate the relative temptation of inducements to corruption.

Each of these hypotheses concerning bureaucracy and political corruption recognizes that increasing the perceived benefits of corruption will produce greater corruption. Another possibility is that bureaucracies may act in such a manner as to increase the temptations of corruption. Law enforcement associated with organized crime is perceived as a potentially corrupt area of public administration. Greater enforcement in such areas as gambling, drugs, and prostitution will likely increase the need for "police protection" and thus generate more bribe attempts (Johnston 1986, 25). In addition, those states where organized crime has a powerful presence are likely to have greater levels of corruption. We use two indicators to capture the relationship between public officials and crime. First, the number of gambling arrests, standardized by population, reflects police involvement in criminal areas likely to involve bribe attempts. Second, the number of criminal investigations involving organized crime, standardized by population, is a measure of the penetration of organized crime in a given state.

According to the results in table 33.6, the bureaucratic opportunity arguments are significant only in the area of crime; the number of gambling arrests and organized crime investigations are both positively related to levels of public corruption. Corruption, however, is not responsive to total government employment, the salary levels of government employees, or expenditures per employee. The lack of relationships involving salary levels and expenditures per employee, however, may be due to the high level of collinearity. Coupled with the significance of the overall crime rate in the first model, this model suggests that by increasing the rewards for corrupt activity, criminal elements are able to alter the cost/benefit returns that normally constrain corrupt activity.

Table 33.6
Bureaucratic Opportunity and Political Corruption

Variable	Slope	T-score
Total Government Employment	−.00016	−.17
Budget Per Employee	−.000002	−.26
Mean Government Salary	.0002	.86
Gambling Arrests/Population	.0046	2.74*
Organized Crime Investigations/Population	.181	1.67*

R-Square	=	.24
Adjusted R-Square	=	.15
F		2.74
Standard Error		.43
N		49

*p < .05 (one-tailed test)

Controlling for Other Factors

In the foregoing analysis, we created four models employing 18 different variables, seven significant, to determine which factors affected the level of public corruption. Data searching processes, such as this one, run the risk of over fitting a model to a sample. Furthermore, our analysis is necessarily incomplete until the seven significant variables are combined into a single model. Only after creating this single "best" model and controlling for these factors can we begin to investigate the second topic of concern here, the incidence of partisan or racial targeting.

When we combined those seven variables to create a single best model, it was marked by a relatively high degree of collinearity making the individual coefficients unstable. To produce a model with the same relative forces without these problems, we took the seven significant variables (plus proportion of special districts) of the preceding models and factor analyzed them.[4] This analysis produced four new variables that identify the underlying factors that explain the variation among the seven original variables without the collinearity problems. These four underlying factors were retained as control variables for the targeting analysis: a *cosmopolitan* factor with loadings for college graduates, crime rates, and urbanism; a *traditionalist* factor with *negative* loadings for turnout and direct democracy measures; an *absence of social capital* factor with a positive loading for organized crime and negative loadings for turnout and education, and an *opportunities* factor with loadings for special districts and gambling arrests. The opportunities factor, however, resulted primarily from the uniqueness of Hawaii, and; when Hawaii is omitted from the models, it ceased to be statistically significant.

Table 33.7 presents the regression results when the level of corruption is

Table 33.7
Determinants of Corruption Prosecutions

Factor	Slope	T-score
Cosmopolitanism	.2458	5.50*
Traditionalist	.2058	4.47*
Low Social Capital	.1588	3.37*
Opportunities	.0696	.90
Intercept	.0991	2.18

R-Square	=	**.60**
Adjusted R-Square	=	**.57**
F		**16.61**
Standard Error		**.43**
N		**49**
*p < .05 (one-tailed test)		

predicted by these four factors. Together they explain about 60 percent of the variance in corruption levels, not as high as the 78 percent that we found in 1992, but with many fewer variables (the F-tests are approximately equal). Prosecutions are higher in states that are cosmopolitan, traditionalist, and lacking in social capital. The opportunities factor is unrelated to prosecutions.

Targeting

The preceding discussion of historical, political, structural, and bureaucratic sources of corruption assumes that various factors result in increased levels of corruption. Certain factors, however, might simply result in increased levels of *prosecution* for the *same* absolute levels of corruption. In particular, politics might motivate some prosecutions for racial or partisan reasons (Heidenheimer 1990, 583–584).

The best way to measure either racial or partisan targeting would be to analyze the number of minority public officials prosecuted or the number of politicians from the other political party. The Department of Justice, however, does not release this data and has responded to Freedom of Information Act requests with the statement that the data do not exist.[5] The result is that attempts to deal with the targeting issue have to do so in an indirect manner. Essentially the argument is this. If racial targeting exists, then states with higher numbers of black public officials will have higher prosecution rates all other things being equal. Similarly, if partisan targeting exists, then Republican administrations should generate more prosecutions in states with more Democratic office holders, and Democratic administrations should prosecute more officials in states with more Republican office holders.

To distinguish the impact of Democratic and Republican administrations, we split the dependent variable into two periods. We included the prosecutions that occurred from 1986 to 1992 in the Republican administration dependent variable and those that occurred from 1993 to 1995 in the Democratic variable.

To measure black public officials, we take the number of black elected officials reported by the Joint Center for Political Studies and divide it by the total number of elected officials in the state. The partisan targeting measure is more elaborate. For a Republican administration (1986–1992) states were given one point for a Democratic governor, and a half point for each legislative chamber controlled by the Democrats. For a Democratic administration (1993–5) the same process was used to code Republican dominance of state government.

These two variables were then added to our base model; the regressions are reported in table 33.8. The results are weaker and less consistent than those that we had found for the earlier time period. For Republican administrations, states with more black elected officials and with Democratic control have a higher rate of prosecutions, but the relationships are not strong and only significant at the .1 level with a one-tailed test. In the Democratic Clinton administration there was no relationship between racial and partisan variables and the level of prosecutions. The lower level of variation explained in the Democratic model is probably because only three years of data were available and thus idiosyncratic aspects of individual years did not have time to wash out.

The weak findings in table 33.8 suggest that the level of targeting is not as strong as it was in the period 1977–87 when both parties appeared to target black public officials and the Reagan administration appeared to target Demo-

Table 33.8
Partisan and Racial Targeting

Independent Variable	Republican Administrations		Democratic Administrations	
	Slope	T-score	Slope	T-score
Racial Targeting	.0284	1.35	.0034	.09
Partisan Targeting	.0208	1.29	−.0325	−.83
Cosmopolitan	.2201	4.53*	.1950	2.15*
Traditional	.0970	1.25	.3221	2.22*
Non Social Capital	.1329	2.40*	.1319	1.28
Opportunities	.0540	.66	.0011	.01
Intercept	−.3115	−2.29	−.3646	−1.90
R-Square	.59		.37	
Adjusted R-Square	.53		.28	
F	10.10		4.12	
Standard Error	.33		.62	
N	49		49	

*$p < .05$ (one-tailed test)

Table 33.9
Partisan and Racial Targeting: Another View

Independent Variable	Republican Administrations		Democratic Administrations	
	Slope	T-score	Slope	T-score
Racial Targeting	.0131	.83	−.0060	−.15
Partisan Targeting	.0243	2.05*	−.0319	−.82
Prosecutions 1980s	.6597	6.06*	.4038	1.48
Cosmopolitan	.0400	.86	.0854	.74
Traditional	−.0166	−.28	.2547	1.69*
Non Social Capital	.0193	.43	.0642	.58
Opportunities	−.0042	−.07	−.0329	−.20
Intercept	−.2806	−.86	−.3316	−1.74
R-Square	.78		.40	
Adjusted R-Square	.75		.30	
F	21.24		3.94	
Standard Error	.24		.61	
N	49		49	

*$p < .05$ (one-tailed test)

crats. Another way to look at the targeting issue is in contrast to past prosecution levels. For targeting to occur, it would mean that one administration's prosecutions should be different from that of earlier ones. One way to incorporate the behavior of prior administrations is to simply include the prosecution rate for the earlier time period in the model. This is done in table 33.9.

Table 33.9 shows the same results for the Clinton administration. The level of explained variation remains small indicating that the factors under consideration do not account for the pattern of prosecutions very well. Both the racial and the partisan targeting variable are negative and statistically indistinguishable from zero.[6]

The results for the Republican administrations are somewhat different. Explained variation is significantly higher in Republican years. While racial targeting does not appear to be present, partisan targeting does. The coefficient still remains relatively small however, so that the extent of targeting cannot be large.

Conclusion

This study reexamined whether or not federal prosecution of corruption public officials is linked to race or partisanship. Overall the study found less evidence of targeting than we did from 1977–87. No evidence of targeting was found in the Clinton administration; and a modest level of partisan targeting appeared in the later years of the Reagan-Bush administration. Comparing the two studies, it appears that targeting has declined over time.

The declining use of the prosecutorial resources of the federal government to target black or opposition public officials is consistent with two other trends. First, the idea of targeting has become quite visible; the NAACP among others was highly critical of the Reagan administration in this regard. If the process receives more public scrutiny, the ability to target is likely to drop. Second, there are fewer one party dominant states now than in an earlier time period as Republicans have made strong inroads into the South. Our crude measure of partisan targeting works best when a single party dominates the electoral process in the state. As states become more competitive and divided government becomes more common, this measure will not reflect any partisan targeting that does occur in these states.

This study has several implications for the broader study of political corruption. First, although the extent of targeting appeared to decline, this should not be taken to imply that targeting *per se* is not possible. The decision to prosecute an individual or to include one in a government sting operation is highly discretionary. Whenever discretion exists, so does the possibility that the discretion will be used for political purposes.

Second, the level of prosecutions in the United States is a reasonably good surrogate for the level of official corruption in the state. It is by no means a perfect measure but it does correlate with theoretically relevant variables as a good measure of political corruption should. Refinements of this measure should be pursued, but it serves as a good starting point for assessing corruption.

Third, the analysis finds that corruption is associated with the costs of benefits of corrupt behavior. This theoretical and empirical linkage suggests that reforms targeted at reducing the level of corruption are possible. Among the most promising reforms are those that increase turnout or add other democratic processes to the political system. The "motor voter" effort in the United States to permit voter registration where driver's licenses are obtained, as a result, might have some future impact in this regard. The strong negative relationship to an educated electorate also implies that policy reforms in education could have positive second order consequences for political corruption.

Finally, this study indicates that government can generate its own inducements to corruption. Some government policies create situations where efforts to corrupt public officials are more likely. Gambling enforcement was the illustration used, but other types of discretionary law enforcement such as that targeted at prostitution, drugs, and smuggling are also likely to increase the benefits of corruption simply because of the massive flows of illicit money.

References

Berg, Larry L., Harlan Hahn, and John R. Schmidhauser. 1976. *Corruption in the American Political System*. Morristown, NJ: General Learning Press.

Beyle, Thad. 1996. "Governors." 1996. In *Politics in the American States*. 6th ed., ed. Virginia Gray, Herbert Jacob. Washington D.C.: CQ Press.

Bibby, John, and Thomas Holbrook. "Parties and Elections." 1996. In *Politics in the American States*. 6th ed., ed. Virginia Gray, Herbert Jacob. Washington D.C.: CQ Press.

Campbell, Angus, Philip Converse, Warren Miller, and Donald Stokes. 1960. *The American Voter*. Chicago: University of Chicago Press.

Council of State Governments. *The Book of the States*. Lexington: Author.

Erikson, Robert S., Gerald C. Wright, and John P. McIver. 1993. *Statehouse Democracy*. New York: Cambridge University Press.

Heidenheimer, Arnold J. 1970. *Political Corruption: Readings in Comparative Analysis*. New York: Holt, Rinehart and Winston.

Heidenheimer, Arnold J. 1990. "Problems of Comparing American Political Corruption." In *Political Corruption: Readings in Comparative Analysis,* ed. Arnold J. Heidenheimer, Michael Johnston, and Victor T. LeVine. New Brunswick, NJ: Transaction Publisherss.

Heidenheimer, Arnold J., Michael Johnston, and Victor T. LeVine. 1990. *Political Corruption: Readings in Comparative Analysis,* ed. New Brunswick, NJ: Transaction Publisherss.

Henriques, Diana B. 1986. *The Machinery of Greed*. Lexington, MA: Lexington Books.

Holbrook-Provow, Thomas M., and Steven C. Poe. 1987. "Measuring State Political Ideology." *American Politics Quarterly* 15:399–416.

Huntington, Samuel. 1968. *Political Order in Changing Societies*. New Haven: Yale University Press.

Johnston, Michael. 1983. "Corruption and Political Culture in America: An Empirical Perspective." *Publius* 13:19–39.

Johnston, Michael. 1986. "Systematic Origins of Fraud, Waste, and Abuse." In *Fraud, Waste, and Abuse in Government*, ed. Jerome B. McInney and Michael Johnston. Philadelphia: ISHI Publications.

Klitgaard, Robert. 1988. *Controlling Corruption*. Berkeley: University of California Press.

Krasno, Jonathan S. and Donald P. Green. 1988. "Preempting Quality Challengers in House Elections." *Journal of Politics* 50:920–36.

Meier, Kenneth J., and Thomas M. Holbrook. "I Seen My Opportunities and I Took 'Em." *Journal of Politics* 54:135–155.

Nas, Tevfik F., Albert C. Price, and Charles T. Weber. 1986. " A Policy-Oriented Theory of Corruption." *American Political Science Review* 80:107–19.

Nice, David C. 1983. "Political Corruption in the American States." *American Politics Quarterly* 11:507–11.

Nie, Norman H., Sidney Verba, and John Petrocik. 1976. *The Changing American Voter*. Cambridge, MA: Harvard University Press.

Nye, J.S. 1967. "Corruption and Political Development: A Cost-Benefit Analysis." *American Political Science Review*: 61:417–27.

Peters, John G. and Susan Welch. 1980. "The Effects of Charges of Political Corruption on Voting Behavior in Congressional Elections." *American Political Science Review* 74:697–708.

Ragsdale, Lyn and Timothy E. Cook. 1987. "Representatives' Actions and Challengers' Reactions." *American Journal of Political Science* 31:45–81.

Rose-Ackerman, Susan. 1978. *Corruption: A Study in Political Economy*. New York: Academic Press.

Rundquist, Barry W., Gerald S. Strom, and John G. Peters. 1977. "Corrupt Politicians and Their Electoral Support. *American Political Science Review* 71: 954–63.

U.S. Department of Justice. 1995. *Report to Congress on the Activities and Operations of the Public Integrity Section for 1995*. Washington, DC: Author.

Verba, Sidney, and Norman H. Nie. 1972. *Participation in America*. New York: Harper and Row.

Walsh, Annmarie. 1978. *The Public's Business*. Cambridge: MIT Press.

Werner, Simcha B. 1983. "New Directions in the Study of Administrative Corruption." *Public Administration Review*: 43:146–54.

Wilson, James Q. 1966. "Corruption: The Shame of the States." *The Public Interest* 1:28–38.

Witt, Elder. 1989. "Is Government Full of Crooks, or Are We Just Better at Finding Them?" *Governing* 2:33–38.

Notes

* All data and documentation necessary to replicate this analysis is available from the authors.

1. Thomas Holbrook, a co-author of the original article, was unable to take part in this revised version.

2. We should reiterate that we find the immigration hypothesis both silly and xenophobic. The idea that certain types of immigrants are likely to be more corrupt than others is without empirical foundation as far as we can tell.

3. The Erikson, Wright, McIver measure excludes Alaska and Hawaii. In order to include these states, public opinion conservativism was estimated using the roll-call liberalism of the state's congressional delegation (Holbrook-Provow and Poe 1987).

4. The results of the factor analysis are available from the authors.

5. We are skeptical that these data do not exist. A prosecution is an activity that takes place in an open court on the record. As a result there are no confidentiality concerns. While the federal court data system does not report information on the race of the defendant, the Federal Bureau of Investigation does maintain this information on arrests.

6. Three explanations exist for this general lack of pattern. The first is that the Clinton prosecutions are not targeted in any sense, that is, they are generated by factors other than the variables linked to corruption or the targeting factors. Whether this is good or bad depends on what those factors are. The second explanation is that the intent might be to target but the Clinton Justice Department is simply not very good at it. Finally, the Clinton administration was particularly slow about replacing Republican appointees and thus its efforts might be muted.

34

Corruption Concepts and Federal Campaign Finance Law

Thomas Burke

In *Buckley vs. Valeo*, the Supreme Court put the concept of corruption at the center of American campaign finance law. The Court held that only society's interest in preventing "corruption and the appearance of corruption" outweighed the limits on First Amendment rights created by restrictions on campaign contributions and expenditures. Other goals, such as equalizing the influence of citizens over elections, limiting the influence of money in electoral politics, or creating more competitive elections, were rejected as insufficiently compelling to justify regulating political speech.[1] The Court's focus on corruption has been reiterated in a series of cases following *Buckley* which have decided whether local laws and various provisions of the Federal Election Campaign Act violate the First Amendment.[2] Barring a major shift in this area of law, corruption is the criterion by which the constitutionality of further reforms in American campaign finance regulation will be measured.

The Supreme Court's emphasis on "corruption and the appearance of corruption" has stimulated criticism on several fronts. From the left, the Court is criticized for not giving credence to other interests in campaign finance regulation.[3] From the right comes the criticism that the Court has been inconsistent in its application of the corruption standard.[4] Others find the problem in the term "corruption" itself. Frank Sorauf argues that while the phrase "has a ring that most Americans will like . . . its apparent clarity is deceptive and its origin is at best clouded."[5] Yet whatever its flaws, politicians, activists, judges and even picky academics are constantly drawn to employing the concept of corruption in their claims about the American campaign finance system. I

645

hope in this chapter to give some sense of both the possibilities and the limits of understanding campaign finance as an issue of corruption. The first part of the chapter briefly considers the concept of corruption and the ways in which academic commentators have explored it. The second part analyzes how "corruption" has been employed in a series of Supreme Court cases beginning with *Buckley*. Finally the third part defends what I call the "monetary influence" standard of corruption as the most appropriate one to use in controversies over campaign finance. This defense turns out to be a rather complex enterprise; it requires a turn back to the foundations of representative democracy. Any adequate standard of corruption in campaign finance, I argue, must be grounded in a convincing theory of representation.

I. The Concept of Corruption

Even the dictionary definitions of corruption suggest that it is a tricky term. The *Oxford English Dictionary* gives nine basic definitions of corruption, but there is an element common to all: a notion that something pure, or natural, or ordered has decayed or become degraded. Corruption was used in medieval times to denote physical processes such as infection or decomposition.[6] When corruption is proclaimed in political life it presumes some ideal state. Corruption is thus a loaded term: you can't call something corrupt without an implicit reference to some ideal. So for example, at the core of what Arnold Heidenheimer has termed the "public office" approach to corruption is the ideal of disinterested public service, the commonly held view that an officeholder shouldn't trade public good for private gain.[7] Similarly the classical sense of corruption as involving luxuriousness and indolence implies an ideal of asceticism and civic virtue.[8] The Aristotlean conception of corruption as self-interested factionalism depends on an ideal of a polity united in dedication to the common good.[9] The more recent notion of corruption in liberal polities as a loss of vigor presumes an ideal of energetic political competition.[10]

How to decide among these ideals—and their corresponding standards of corruption? James Scott divides attempts into three approaches: legal norms, public opinion and the public interest.[11] A legal norms approach focuses on the laws and formal rules of a given society in determining what is corrupt and what is not.[12] While such an approach may be useful in comparative research, it seems unlikely that it can help us in a discussion of a legal controversy.[13] After all, we can't very well refer to the rules of our society when the issue is what those rules should be.

The public opinion approach is similarly problematic. It may seem sensible to define what is corrupt by finding out what most people in a given society consider corrupt, but on most of the interesting questions public opinion is likely to be ambiguous. As Scott points out, there is no clear, non-arbitrary way to decide what level of social consensus is necessary before we declare a given act corrupt.[14] Should a mere majority be sufficient, or should unanimity be required? Should the opinions of the more educated, those better informed, or those more interested in politics, be given more weight? Public opinion will always be an unsteady guide except in the easy cases.

Finally there is the public interest approach, which involves defining some ideal against which corrupt conduct can be measured. This approach merely gauges what is corrupt in terms of an even more contested concept, the "public interest." Political scientists, the group that has thought the most about the concept of corruption, have had trouble even agreeing that there is some such thing as the public interest, much less defining what that interest involves.[15] Thus all three approaches have serious problems.

Fortunately, for the purposes of this chapter I need not pretend that there is some unifying, global criterion of corruption, one that can resolve all ethical issues in politics. Rather, my task is to give some sense to the term as it is used in the discussion of campaign finance law. Yet even in this more limited realm it is hard to see where we are to draw our standards from.

II. Corruption and the Campaign Finance Cases

Buckley and its progeny are complex, confusing cases. Thus it is no surprise that commentators and judges have differed in their interpretation of the Court's treatment of "corruption." Lillian BeVier, writing in 1985, concludes that under the Court's rulings the "only activity that may become the target of corruption-preventing legislation is that of securing or attempting to secure 'political quid pro quos from current and potential officeholders.'"[16] By this criterion, only pre-arranged deals—trades of votes for money—qualify legally as corrupt. Paul Edwards further develops the quid pro quo standard of corruption and claims that, in a later campaign finance case, *Austin v. Michigan Chamber of Commerce*, the Court made a "dramatic change" in its approach by veering away from this limited definition of corruption to a much broader one, influenced perhaps by Rawlsian liberalism.[17] Frank Sorauf, by contrast, finds hints even in the earlier cases that the Court's concerns went beyond pure quid pro quos.[18]

In its most recent campaign finance case, *Nixon v. Shrink Missouri Government PAC*, the Supreme Court itself divided on the proper standard of corruption. Shrink Missouri Government, an organization which made campaign contributions to candidates in state elections, challenged limits to those contributions as not falling within the corruption rationale for regulation advanced in *Buckley*. This challenge led the justices to argue with each other over what kinds of conduct had been considered corrupt in *Buckley* and succeeding cases. The majority, led by Justice Souter, insists that in these cases the Court "recognized a concern not confined to bribery of public officials, but extending to the broader threat from politicians too compliant with the wishes of large contributors." Justice Thomas, in his dissent, claims that in *Buckley* "the Court repeatedly used the word 'corruption' in the narrow quid pro quo sense". Thomas contends that the *Nixon* majority "separates 'corruption' from its quid pro quo roots and gives it a new, far-reaching (and speech-suppressing) definition . . . "[19] Thus debate over "corruption" continues to be a central aspect of campaign finance jurisprudence.

Justice Thomas to the contrary, the Court has clearly gone beyond a quid pro quo standard of corruption well before *Nixon*. In the series of cases beginning with *Buckley* and ending with *Nixon*, three distinct standards of corruption are advanced, though at several points the Court blurs them. I label them quid pro quo, monetary influence, and distortion.

The quid pro quo standard is simply that it is corrupt for an officeholder to take money in exchange for some action. The money may be a bribe for personal use or a campaign contribution. The deal is explicit, with both sides acknowledging that a trade is being made.

The monetary influence standard is broader. Here the root idea is that it is corrupt for officeholders to perform their public duties with monetary considerations in mind. The influence of money is corrupting under this standard even if no explicit deal is made.

The third standard of corruption is distortion. The ideal behind this standard is that the decisions of officeholders should closely reflect the views of the public. Campaign contributions are corrupting to the extent that they do not reflect the balance of public opinion and thus distort policymaking through their influence on elections.

The three standards of corruption—quid pro quo, monetary influence and distortion—have been jumbled together in the corpus of campaign finance law.

Quid Pro Quo Versus Monetary Influence

In *Buckley* the Court struck down limitations on the amounts candidates could spend on their campaigns, yet it upheld restrictions on contributions to candidates. Contributions, the Court said, were less speech-like than expenditures and thus deserved lesser protection. But contributions are also more regulatable because they, unlike expenditures, can be a source of corruption. While the Court at first emphasizes the danger of quid pro quos in discussing the problem of corruption,[20] it also notes that the state's interest goes beyond mere bribery: "But laws making criminal the giving and taking of bribes deal with only the most blatant and specific attempts of those with money to influence governmental action."[21] This pattern is repeated in succeeding cases. The Court mentions the quid pro quo standard, but also suggests that corruption goes beyond pre-arranged trading of votes for contributions. Here the Court is hinting at the monetary influence standard.

In *National Bank of Boston v. Bellotti*, the Court struck down a Massachusetts law forbidding corporations and banks from spending money in referenda campaigns.[22] The Court followed *Buckley* in reasoning that while the First Amendment interest in such independent expenditures is high, there is no threat of corruption because in referenda elections there is no candidate to corrupt. In a footnote the majority opinion distinguished the Massachusetts law from the longstanding Federal Corrupt Practices Act, which bars corporate spending in candidate elections:

> The overriding concern behind the enactment of statutes such as the Federal Corrupt Practices Act was the problem of corruption of elected representatives through the creation of political debts. The importance of the governmental interest in preventing this occurrence has never been doubted.[23]

Here again the Court seems to go beyond the concern about quid pro quo vote-trading, this time to characterize corruption as "the creation of political debts." Four years later, in *FEC v. National to Right Work Committee*, the Court again discussed the need to insure that corporate "war chests" not be used to create "political debts."[24]

For the most part in these early cases the Court does little to explain its notion of corruption, and we are left to read between the lines. But in the 1984 case of *FEC v. National Conservative Political Action Committee*, the majority opinion by Justice Rehnquist offers a definition:

> Corruption is a subversion of the political process. Elected officials are influenced to act contrary to their obligations of office by the prospect of financial gain to themselves or infusions of money into their campaigns. The hallmark of corruption is the financial quid pro quo: dollars for political favors.[25]

Here a much wider standard of corruption appears with a restatement of the familiar quid pro quo as a "hallmark." Rehnquist says that elected officials violate their public trust when they are influenced by the "prospect of financial gain to themselves or infusions of money into their campaigns." If Rehnquist had wanted to limit the corruption interest to quid pro quos, he could simply have said so. Instead he calls quid pro quo vote-trading the "hallmark" of political corruption. Again in this passage the Court seems to be acknowledging the second standard, the monetary influence standard of corruption.

Rehnquist is more clear in another passage, when he relies on *Buckley* in distinguishing the regulation of expenditures from regulations governing contributions. Rehnquist concludes that expenditures made independently by a political action committee to support a particular candidate pose little danger of corruption. Here he emphasizes that "the absence of prearrangement and coordination undermines the value of the expenditure to the candidate, and thereby alleviates the danger that expenditures will be given as a quid pro quo for improper commitments from a candidate."[26] Overall, then, in *NCPAC* the Court seems to be moving towards the more narrow quid pro quo standard.

Distortion

That movement is reversed in the 1986 case *FEC v. Massachusetts Citizens for Life, Inc.*[27] Justice Brennan, writing for the majority, held that a state law restricting independent expenditures for candidate elections was overbroad as applied to the appellee, a non-profit corporation. Brennan argued that advocacy groups such as MCFLI should be distinguished from profit-seeking corporations, who pose a real danger of distorting the political process through their accretion of wealth. Citing several earlier corporate cases, Brennan said the precedents reflected concern "about the potential for unfair deployment of wealth for political purposes." Non-profit corporations "do not pose that danger of corruption."[28] This is the only point in the opinion in where Brennan clarifies, even by implication, just what he means by corruption. Brennan's main argument is that corporate political spending poses a threat to the "political marketplace" because the "resources in the treasury of a business corporation . . . are not an indication of popular support for the corporation's political ideas."[29] Here Brennan embraces the distortion standard.

Austin v. Michigan Chamber of Commerce, decided in 1990, amplifies this theme and links it more clearly to the concept of corruption. *Austin* concerned an independent expenditure made by the Chamber of Commerce to promote a candidate for the U.S. House. In *Buckley* the Court had concluded that such independent expenditures posed a relatively small risk of corruption since candidates were far less likely to feel a debt to independent spenders than contributors. In upholding a law barring such independent expenditures, the Court could merely have taken issue with this assessment and declared that independent expenditures also create political debts.[30] Instead, Justice Marshall's opinion defines a new concept of corruption, borrowed partly from Brennan's opinion in *MCFLI*:

> Regardless of whether [the] danger of "financial quid pro quo" corruption . . . may be sufficient to justify a restriction on independent expenditures, Michigan's regulation aims at a different type of corruption in the political arena: the corrosive and distorting effects of immense aggregations of wealth that are accumulated with the help of the corporate form and that have little or no correlation to the public's support for the corporation's political ideas.[31]

Here corruption is no longer tied to the conduct of the officeholder, but instead concerns the power of the corporate spender in the political marketplace. Although some of Marshall's argument was anticipated in *MCFLI*, the *Austin* opinion represents the flowering of the distortion conception of corruption.

In a typically bombastic dissent Justice Scalia castigated the majority's "New Corruption":

> Under this mode of analysis, virtually anything the Court deems politically undesirable can be turned into political corruption—by simply describing its effects as politically "corrosive," which is close enough to "corruptive" to qualify . . . The Court's opinion ultimately rests upon that proposition whose violation constitutes the New Corruption: expenditures must "reflect actual public support for the political ideas espoused." This illiberal free-speech principle of "one man, one minute" was proposed and soundly rejected in *Buckley*.[32]

In *Buckley* the Court had rejected an equalization goal for campaign finance law, concluding that "the concept that government may restrict the speech of some elements of our society in order to enhance the relative voice of others is wholly foreign to the First Amendment".[33] Scalia charged that the majority had simply resurrected the equalization theory in a new guise—the New Corruption.

Scalia's fear that the distortion standard would become a central aspect of campaign finance jurisprudence has not, however, been realized. in its most recent campaign finance decision, *Nixon v. Shrink*, the Court has instead reinvigorated both the "monetary influence" standard of corruption and the "appearance of corruption" prong of *Buckley*. The *Nixon* opinion emphasizes *Buckley*'s concern that large contributors can "influence governmental action," and that the resulting perception that "large donors call the tune" might "jeopardize the willingness of voters to take part in democratic governance."[34] No mention is made of distortion, or indeed of *Austin* itself. *Nixon* seems to limit *Austin* and the distortion standard to cases involving corporate contributions.

Evaluating the Standards

Both *Austin* and *Nixon* illustrate the difficulties in developing standards for corruption. *Austin*'s distortion standard of corruption has broad implications. As noted above, to use the term "corruption" one must have some underlying notion of an ideal state. Marshall's opinion suggests that in his ideal state expenditures are calibrated to actual public support. A deviation from this constitutes corruption and may be regulated. Because just about any private financing scheme is likely to have "distortions"—to not reflect underlying public support—Marshall's principle would justify very strong regulatory measures.[35] Indeed it is difficult to square Marshall's principle with any system of private financing for political campaigns.

Marshall's opinion reflects the broad concerns of many about the connection between wealth and power, politics and markets, in a capitalist, democratic society. Indeed, many would argue that this is the main problem in campaign finance, far outstripping any concerns we might have about the intentions and actions of individual legislators. This broader concern has not, outside of Marshall's opinion in *Austin*, received much attention from the Court.[36] But even those who might be attracted to Marshall's ideal, or think that corporations can constitutionally be kept from throwing their monetary weight around, may shrink from describing this as a problem of corruption. "Corruption" can be used to describe any movement away from an ideal; this is the sense in which illness is a corruption of the body. But in politics "corruption" has a more specific connotation, that an officeholder has been led by private inducements away from the ideal of disinterested public service. As Justice Scalia charges, the majority opinion in *Austin* takes advantage of this connotation by conflating the relatively uncontroversial ideal of disinterested public service with the far more problematic ideal of "undistorted" campaign finance. The rhetoric of corruption is used to champion an ideal so sweeping that, if taken literally, would condemn any imaginable private campaign finance system—and perhaps even *public* financing systems in which the funding is not carefully calibrated to public support.

But while *Austin*'s standard of corruption is too broad, the quid pro quo standard is too narrow, as the Court has recognized from time to time. Indeed, as Justice Thomas has argued, if only pure vote-trading is considered corrupt, it is difficult to see how the Court could uphold the constitutionality of any limits on contributions.[37]

The quid pro quo conception focuses on pre-arrangement as the truly corrupting aspect of vote-trading. Under this standard, it does not matter whether public officials are influenced in their stands on public policy by contributions so long as there is no formal deal made. But deals—trades of votes for money—were outlawed long before the advent of campaign finance regulation. As Daniel Lowenstein has pointed out, many courts have held that campaign contributions can be bribes, and bribery convictions based on campaign contributions have been upheld in many jurisdictions.[38] Traditionally in First Amendment law, regulations which impair free speech must be judged "narrowly tailored" to achieving a "compelling state interest" to be considered constitutional. If there is a less restrictive way to achieve the same interest, the regulation is struck down. This creates a puzzle: if governments can only regulate quid pro quos, why should they be allowed to go beyond simple bribery laws? Why regulate so much legitimate "speech" in an effort to stop bribery when you can instead simply outlaw bribery? As Justice Thomas has argued, contribution limits are only distantly related to the goal of stopping quid pro quo vote-trading, and certainly would never meet the Court's "narrowly tailored" test.

The truth is that the contribution limits the Court upheld in *Buckley* were aimed at far more than quid pro quo corruption. The *Buckley* Court recognized this when it concluded that "laws making criminal the giving and taking of bribes deal with only the most blatant and specific attempts of those with money to influence governmental action."[39] Instead the Court sees the problem as one of "political debts," that officials are "influenced to contrary to their obligations of office by the prospect of . . . infusions of money into their campaign."[40] The problem recognized here is one of generalized financial influence on legislators, not pure vote-trading.

Indeed, it is not clear why a quid pro quo is any more corrupting than a contribution which influences a public official more indirectly. In bribery law it makes sense to require that there be evidence that the official explicitly agreed to trade a vote for a contribution. Otherwise, we will never know for sure if she was influenced by the money; there will always be doubt about whether the gift was taken innocently.[41] But the object of bribery laws is not the deal itself; the deal is just evidence that influence has taken place. The reason we make bribery illegal is that we don't want officials to be affected by monetary considerations, not that we have a particular animus against deal-making. Even in bribery, then, the ultimate interest is not quid pro quo corruption, but the corruptive influence of money. Campaign finance laws can address this problem by creating a contribution system that limits the influence of money. Thus it makes no sense to say that the contribution limits are aimed only at quid pro quo corruption.

In *Nixon* a majority of the Court recognized this. But oftentimes the Court's campaign finance decisions lapse back into quid pro quo language, perhaps because the justices realize the open-endedness of considering general financial influence a problem. If the ideal is a system in which public officials are not influenced by campaign contributions, how broadly should campaign finance laws be allowed to sweep? One can imagine at the least that more extensive campaign regulation could be upheld under this standard. The Court might, for example, uphold a law regulating independent expenditures in candidate elections, or take a deferential view towards a ban on "soft money"— unregulated contributions to parties. (The soft money ban was the centerpiece of the much-publicized McCain-Feingold bill.)

Nonetheless, the Court in its more thoughtful moments has employed the monetary interest standard. When the prospect or the receipt of campaign money influences the behavior of public officials, they are corrupted, whether or not a deal has been made. Although the goal of stopping this kind of corruption must be weighed against First Amendment interests, the Court has upheld contribution limits on this basis.

III. Does Money Corrupt?

I have argued that the Court is on firmest ground when it adopts the "monetary influence" standard of corruption. But what is it about monetary influence—or, for that matter, quid pro quo trading—that is so corrupting? On what basis can we say that public officials who are influenced by contributions are corrupt?[42] Because the Court does not develop its own account of what makes an action corrupt, we must go beyond the campaign finance cases to answer these questions.

Daniel Lowenstein argues that the "payment of money to bias the judgment or sway the loyalty of persons holding positions of public trust is a practice whose condemnation is deeply rooted in our most ancient heritage."[43] Lowenstein believes that there is a strong cultural norm in our society that public officials not be influenced by money, either in the form of gifts or campaign contributions. As evidence, Lowenstein cites the writings of various scholars on the subject and the law of bribery, which in many jurisdictions makes quid pro quo campaign contributions illegal.[44] Thus Lowenstein appeals to the public opinion and legal norms approaches in defining financial influence as corruption. As noted above,[45] these are problematic appeals. Lowenstein has no polling data to show that the vast majority of Americans agree with his norm, but even if he did we might still contend that Americans are simply misguided in believing that financial influence is corrupting. Martin Shapiro argues that Lowenstein, by operating as a "cultural anthropologist," may be able to discover a societal norm, but such a norm cannot be the basis of constitutional law: "There is a cultural norm of racism in our society. Does the existence of such a norm give constitutional legitimacy to racist statutes?"[46] Shapiro maintains that Lowenstein cannot define what is corrupt merely by reference to social norms or legal principles. Even the fact that bribery statutes often cover campaign contributions traded for political favors is not determinative. Only a theoretical argument can answer the question. Everything else is question-begging.

Thus any serious thinking about corruption must move us back to first principles, to fundamental beliefs about government. The debate over the place of corruption in campaign finance ultimately turns on the theoretical foundations of representative democracy. In several recent articles, Dennis Thompson has grounded his approach to legislative ethics in a theory of representation which stresses deliberation. The debate between Thompson and Bruce Cain, another expert on campaign finance, illustrates the deep roots of the controversy over corruption.

Representation and Deliberation

Thompson advances a seemingly simple idea: in a functioning democracy, representatives must deliberate about the public good. Private interests have a legitimate place in a democracy as long as they subject themselves to "the rigors of the democratic process." To get their way, private interests must convincingly articulate public purposes.[47]

Private interests which attempt to bypass this deliberative process are "agents of corruption."[48] They tempt representatives to ignore public purposes and to pay attention to influences "that are clearly irrelevant to any process of deliberation."[49] What influences are clearly irrelevant? Thompson gives as his primary example personal gain. Personal gain tends to take time and attention away from what should be the job of the legislator and can overwhelm the "unsteady inclination to pursue the public good."[50] Thus bribes, for example, corrupt the deliberative process.

Campaign contributions, Thompson says, are different from bribes because they are a necessary part of the political process. Moreover, Thompson says we should admire those who, within limits, pursue political gain, including campaign contributions.[51] But campaign contributions corrupt deliberative democracy when they influence representatives to change their stands or refocus their energies.[52] Thus Thompson accepts what I have called the "monetary influence" standard of corruption. For him, campaign contributions aimed at influencing elections are vital to the democratic process, but those aimed at influencing the representatives' decisions corrupt the process. Thompson shows how a deliberative theory of representation leads to a "monetary influence" standard of corruption.

In his article "Moralism and Realism in Campaign Finance," however, Bruce Cain rejects both deliberative theory and the monetary interest standard. Cain argues that deliberative theory is "excessively restrictive and very naive," and that it is out of step with the philosophical foundations of American government.[53] Further, Cain suggests that Thompson's approach relies on Edmund Burke's trustee concept of representation, which, Cain claims, is not widely accepted.

Instead Cain offers his own "procedural fairness" vision of democracy, drawn from the pluralist tradition in political science. He groups under this label theorists such as Joseph Schumpeter, Anthony Downs, Robert Dahl and James Madison (or at least, Dahl's rendition of Madison). What these otherwise disparate theorists share, according to Cain, is an approach to politics that is nondeliberative. Each treats democracy as a matter of preference aggregation, and each expects representatives to act as delegates in order to be elected. For proceduralists, Cain seems to conclude, the notion of corruption in campaign finance is simply meaningless. If, after all, politics is simply a matter of counting preferences, campaign contributions can be seen as a kind of vote, a way to signal the direction (and intensity) of one's desires. Money is then just another currency in the counting process, one which advantages some groups and disadvantages others. The only real issue in campaign finance, according to Cain, is how to count fairly, and opinions about this will naturally differ depending on which groups one favors.[54]

The conflict between Thompson and Cain is so fundamental that it is difficult to arbitrate. Perhaps the best place to start with Cain's contention that deliberative theory is a "nontraditional conception of American democracy."[55] This is a surprising claim, for as Thompson argues, deliberation was at the center of the Framers' conception of representative government.[56] The *Federalist Papers*, for example, justify many aspects of the Constitution—separation of powers, bicameralism, methods of election, size of legislative bodies—in terms of their effect on the deliberative process. The aim was to replace the excess of passion and "local spirit" that had overtaken state legislators with a concern for "the permanent and aggregate interests of the community," or as the *Federalist Papers* variously puts it, "the good of the whole," "the public weal," "great and national objects," "the great and aggregate interests," the "common interest," the "common good of the society," and the "comprehensive interests of [the] country."[57] Indeed, Madison's famous defense of an extended republic in *Federalist #10* was built on deliberative theory. He argued that such a republic was more likely than other systems of government

> to refine and enlarge the public views by passing them through the medium of a chosen body of citizens, whose wisdom may best discern the true interest of their country and whose patriotism and love of justice will be less likely to sacrifice it to temporary or partial considerations.[58]

Madison was, of course, a subtle thinker who understood the complex interplay of interests and deliberation, so one is likely to oversimplify his views by selective quotation. Yet the deliberative aspects of his thought cannot be denied. Over the past three decades, scholars in law, history and political science have demonstrated the profound influence of republican theory, with its emphasis on deliberation about the public good, on the thought of the Framers, particularly Madison. The historian Gordon Wood concludes that Madison and the Federalists believed in a government that rose above factional interests:

> They still clung to the republican ideal of an autonomous public authority that was different from the many private interests of the society. . . Nor did they see public policy or the common interest of the national government emerging naturally from the give-and-take of these clashing private interests. . . Far, then, from the new national government being a mere integrator and harmonizer of the different special interests in the society, it would become a "disinterested and dispassionate umpire in disputes between different passions and interest in the State."[59]

The Framers, in sum, embraced deliberative theory.

The elitism of the Framers, who envisioned rule by a virtuous gentry, soon fell out of favor.[60] But their concern for deliberation has lived on. A long list of studies highlights the continuing importance of deliberation in American democratic theory and practice.[61] This attention to deliberation is hardly limited to theorists. Political scientists have confirmed the central role of deliberation in American government in their study of legislatures, courts, bureaucracies and the presidency. In his book on deliberative theory and practice Joseph Bessette cites 33 such studies.[62]

A few examples should suffice. Cass Sunstein argues, based on a review of the fundamentals of constitutional jurisprudence, that we live in a "republic of reasons." Courts, he says, will strike down laws based only on "naked preferences," the mere assertion of private power. To act constitutionally, legislators must provide a public-regarding rationale for their policies. It is through the process of deliberation that these rationales are articulated and judged.[63] Martha Derthick and Paul Quirk trace the influence of ideas and deliberation on regulatory reform of the telecommunications, trucking and airline industries in *The Politics of Deregulation*.[64] Richard F. Fenno finds that making "good public policy" through careful study of issues is the dominant goal of representatives who seek a position on the Education and Labor and Foreign Affairs committees.[65] As Joseph Bessette has suggested, when political scientists actually examine the process of policymaking they find plenty of deliberation going on.[66]

Deliberative theory is untraditional only among some political scientists who, beginning with Robert Dahl, have downplayed the republican and deliberative aspects of American government. The tradition from which Cain works starts not with Jefferson, Hamilton, or Madison, but rather Arthur Bentley, David Truman and Dahl.[67] The vision of American democracy as preference aggregation is widespread among political scientists and public choice theorists, but outside of these narrow realms it is hard to say how well it resonates. Whatever popular opinion would hold, though, Cain clearly underestimates the centrality of deliberative theory in American political thought and practice.

Cain's argument that Thompson relies on a trustee theory of representation, however, points to a more troubling issue. In fact Thompson attempts to distinguish his approach from the trustee conception. He points out that the views of the constituency and the views of the representative about what is in the public interest are likely on many issues to coincide. Where they do conflict, however, Thompson says that representatives may voice their constituents' views in order to give them a hearing in the deliberative process. As long as the process itself is deliberative, as long as it focuses on the merits of the issue, it does not matter whether the individual representative is delegate or trustee.[68] And this suggests an important difference between trustee/delegate theories of representation and deliberative theory: where the trustee/delegate dichotomy focuses on the level of the individual representative, the deliberative theory leads us to look at what is happening to the institution as a whole.

Yet this refinement creates another difficulty, one that Thompson does not address. If in a deliberative democracy representatives can in some circumstances act as delegates for their constituents, why can they not also act as delegates for their contributors?[69] I think the answer is that Thompson allows for only a narrow exception to the basic rule that representatives must deliberate. In giving voice to the views of their constituents, representatives can on some occasions move deliberation forward. But if a significant number of representatives are acting *solely* as delegates, ignoring not only the arguments of others but even their own views, deliberative democracy is imperiled. This corruption of the deliberative process is much more likely when representatives fall under the sway of their contributors. Contributor-influenced representatives are unlikely to be candid about the motivation for their actions; the last thing they want is an open examination of the quality of their reasons and their process of deliberation. Thus where contributor-influenced representatives predominate, legislative deliberation becomes a sham. By contrast, constituent-influenced legislators can acknowledge the pressures on them and, where their own views conflict with those of the constituents, can even deliberate publicly about how the two can be reconciled.[70] Constituent influence can itself become a matter for deliberation in a way that contributor influence never can. Hence contributor influence is much more likely than constituent influence to have a pernicious effect on deliberative democracy.

Deliberative theory, then, provides a grounding for the monetary influence standard of corruption. If politics is nothing more than a market, and politicians nothing more than retailers, than there is no need for deliberation, and no necessary problem with bribery through the campaign finance process. That is the vision behind Cain's procedural theory. But if representation involves deliberation about the public good, then contributions that influence representatives are a corruption of the democratic process.

Deliberative theory is well-grounded in American political philosophy and practice. It is an attractive, approachable ideal. Its appeal explains why, despite criticisms like those voiced by Cain, academic, legal and popular debate about campaign finance continues to revolve around notions of corruption.

IV. Alternative Standards of Corruption

I have argued that the concept of corruption can be applied to one of the major problems in campaign finance, the influence that contributors get over the actions of representatives. The monetary influence standard of corruption has been invoked in several Supreme Court cases, but the Court has drifted in its treatment of corruption.

At some points the Court has characterized the problem as one of distortion of public opinion. At other times the Court has portrayed the issue as a matter of vote trading, of quid pro quos. Both of these characterizations are problematic. *Austin*'s proclamation that the political system is corrupted when campaign contributions don't mirror public opinion is unpersuasive, because "corruption" is not a synonym for "inequality." Yet when, as in Justice Thomas's recent campaign finance opinions, corruption is reduced to a concern about quid pro quos, it fails to provide a rationale for any campaign finance law beyond prohibitions on bribery.

All standards of corruption rest on some notion of what constitutes an ideal political community. The ideal behind the quid pro quo standard seems to arise out of what Arnold Heidenheimer has called the "public office" approach to corruption. Here the ideal of a healthy political community is one in which representatives do not make deals in which they exchange public policy for some private gain.[71] This ideal seems uncontroversial, but, standing by itself, it is also thin, individualized, and, as I have argued, unconvincing as a rationale for campaign finance regulation. It is unconvincing because absent some broader notion of an ideal political community it is not at all clear why deal-making is corrupt. Even to understand what is wrong with campaign contribution bribery we need a thicker, more institutionally focused ideal.

Deliberative theory provides such an ideal. It turns our attention beyond the behavior of individuals to the functioning of representative institutions, and so provides a richer account of a good political community, in which officeholders come together to deliberate over the public good.

Deliberation is just one among many ideals of political community available to the Court in its campaign finance jurisprudence. In *Nixon*, for example, the Court has at last begun to take seriously the idea that a healthy political community is one in which citizens trust their representatives, and thus has given weight to the "appearance of corruption" prong of *Buckley*, as many commentators have urged. Another ideal, thus far unrecognized by the Court, is that of robust, competitive elections. The Court could approve of campaign finance regulations that move the electoral system closer to this ideal. These approaches to corruption have the virtue of being grounded not in judgments about individual transgressions, but in larger institutional visions. In this they would hearken back to the classical conception of corruption as a "disease of the body politic."[72]

There is, however, a danger in adopting more expansive standards of corruption in the context of campaign finance law. The difficulty is that they can move too far beyond the contemporary connotation of "corruption," which clearly does involve some notion of a private use of public office. This is the point Scalia makes in his dissent from *Austin*, when he argues that the Court has conflated "corruption" with concerns about inequality. Inequality in campaign finance may be troubling to some American citizens, he suggests, but would they really consider this an issue of corruption? Scalia's argument rests on what has been called the "public opinion" approach to corruption, in which what counts as corrupt depends on what public opinion considers corrupt. Used as an unqualified guide to creating standards of corruption, the public opinion approach is problematic, because on most hard questions public opinion is ambiguous. Nonetheless, as Scalia's dissent suggests, we should be wary of standards of corruption that have little connection to popular understandings.

The Court has, I believe, been most persuasive when it has seen "corruption" in campaign finance as an issue of monetary influence. This is a standard roughly in line with public opinion, and yet it can be grounded in one of America's founding ideals, of vigorous deliberation in representative institutions. Thus the monetary influence standard is compatible with both the "public opinion" and "public interest" approaches to corruption.

Of course, the monetary influence standard does not by itself determine the constitutionality of any particular regulatory scheme. After all, people may balance the goal of preventing corruption and the First Amendment interests at stake differently even though they recognize the legitimacy of both claims. Moreover, there is no easy way to separate contributions whose main effect is to influence legislators and so corrupt democratic deliberation from those which promote deliberation by giving candidates for office the chance to make their views known. Contributions have mixed effects, just as contributors have mixed motives. Still, by thinking more carefully about corruption the Court can build a campaign finance law that is more coherent, more convincing, and more faithful to the highest ideals of American democracy.

Notes

1. Buckley v. Valeo 424 U.S. 1 (1975) at 25–27.
2. *First National Bank of Boston v. Bellotti* 435 U.S. 765 (1978); *Citizens Against Rent Control v. Berkeley* 454 U.S. 290 (1980); *California Medical Association v. Federal Elections Commission* 453 U.S. 182 (1982); *Federal Elections Commission v. National Right to Work Committee* 459 U.S. 197 (1982); *Federal Elections Commission v. National Conservative Political Action Committee* 470 U.S. 480 (1985); *Massachusetts Citizens For Life* 479 U.S. 238 (1986); *Austin v. Michigan Chamber of Commerce* 494 U.S. 652 (1990); *Colorado Republican Campaign Committee v. Federal Elections Commission* 116 S.Ct. 2309 (1996); *Nixon v. Shrink Missouri Government PAC* (120 S.Ct. 897 (2000).
3. Skelley Wright, "Money and the Pollution of Politics: Is the First Amendment an Obstacle to Political Equality?" Columbia Law Review 82:609 (1982).
4. See Antonin Scalia's dissent in *Austin*, 479 U.S. 679 (1990).
5. Frank J. Sorauf, "Caught in a Political Thicket: The Supreme Court and Campaign Finance" Constitutional Commentary 3:97 (1986).
6. The Oxford English Dictionary, 2nd ed., v.3 (Oxford: Clarendon Press, 1989), 972–4.
7. "Terms, Concept, and Definitions," in Arnold Heidenheimer, Michael Johnston and Victor T. LeVine, eds., *Political Corruption: A Handbook*, 2nd ed., (New Brunswick, NJ: Transaction, 1990), 8.

8. For a discussion of the many conceptions of corruption in European history, see Carl Friedrich, "Corruption Concepts in Historical Perspective," in *Political Corruption: A Handbook*, 15–24. See also Hannah Arendt's discussion of how the leaders of the American Revolution and the leaders of the French Revolution saw corruption in French society. Arendt, *On Revolution* (New York: Viking, 1963) 61–63, 100–103.

9. J. Peter Euben, "Corruption," in Terence Ball, James Farr and Russell Hanson, eds., *Political Innovation and Conceptual Change* (Cambridge: Cambridge University Press, 1989), 220–245.

10. Dennis Thompson, "Mediated Corruption: The Case of the Keating Five, American Political Science Review (1993) 87:2:369.

11. See James C. Scott, Comparative Political Corruption (New Jersey: Prentice Hall, 1972) 3–5.

12. This is the approach taken, for example, by Joseph Nye, who defines corruption as "behavior which deviates from the formal duties of a public role because of private-regarding (personal, close family, private clique) pecuniary or status gains; or violates rules against the exercise of certain types of private-regarding influence." Although Nye's study was based mainly on the developing world, he used what he called a "Western" standard of corruption. Joseph S. Nye, "Corruption and Political Development: A Cost-Benefit Analysis" in Heidenheimer et. al., *Political Corruption*, 966.

13. This is a point Dan Lowenstein makes in his article "Political Bribery and the Intermediate Theory of Politics," UCLA Law Review (1985) 32:784. Lowenstein discusses the problem of defining corruption at 798–804.

14. James Scott, *Comparative Political Corruption*, 4.

15. Frank Sorauf reviewed this debate in "The Public Interest Reconsidered," Journal of Politics (1957) 19:616–639. Sorauf criticizes the term as "subjective and imprecise" and calls various definitions of it "illogical" (633). Sorauf argues that outcomes of public policymaking cannot be judged by a public interest standard. Nevertheless, Sorauf says there is a public interest in the *process* by which policies are created. Thus Sorauf identifies the public interest with the "process of group accommodation" (638). This leaves some ground for pluralists like Sorauf to use a public interest concept in evaluating campaign finance procedures. Robert Dahl similarly finds the "common good" in "practices, arrangements, institutions, and processes that . . . promote the well-being of ourselves and others . . . " (Dahl, *Democracy and Its Critics* (New Haven, Conn.: Yale University Press, 1989), 307. Like Sorauf, Dahl's discussion of practices that promote the common good suggests that Dahl could employ a public interest concept in evaluating issues of campaign finance.

16. Lillian BeVier, "Money & Politics: A Perspective on the First Amendment and Campaign Finance Reform," California Law Review 73:1045 (1985) at 1082. BeVier is quoting from *Buckley* 424 U.S. at 26.

17. Paul S. Edwards, "Defining Political Corruption: The Supreme Court's Role," The BYU Journal of Public Law 10:1 (1996) at 3.

18. "But while the quid pro quo is the nub of the matter, it is perhaps not the totality of it." Sorauf, "Caught in the Constitutional Thicket," 103.

19. *Nixon v. Shrink*, 120 S.Ct. 897 .

20. "To the extent that large contributions are given to secure a political quid pro quo from current and potential office holders, the integrity of our system of representative democracy is undermined." *Buckley*, 424 U.S. 1 at 27.

21. Ibid., 27.

22. 435 U.S. 765 (1978).
23. 435 U.S. 788 n.26 (1978).
24. FEC v. NRWC 459 U.S. 197 (1982).
25. FEC v. NCPAC 470 U.S. 497 (1984).
26. 470 U.S. 498.
27. 479 U.S. 238.
28. 479 U.S. 259.
29. 479 U.S. 258.
30. This is what Justice Stevens, who wrote a concurring opinion, would do, at least for corporate contributions. See *Austin* 494 U.S. 652 at 678.
31. *Austin* 494 U.S. 659–60.
32. 424 U.S. 48–49.
33. 424 U.S. 48–49.
34. *Nixon v. Shrink* 120 S.Ct , quoting from *Buckley v. Valeo*, 424 U.S. 28.
35. It is important to remember that Marshall limits his principle to "the unique legal and economic characteristics of corporations." See *Austin* 494 U.S. 652 at 660.
36. For an influential analysis from this perspective, see Charles E. Lindbloom, *Politics and Markets: The World's Political-Economic Systems*, (New York: Basic Books, 1970), 170–200.
37. *Colorado Republican Campaign Committee v. FEC* 116 S.Ct. 2317.
38. Such convictions have become far more common recently; see Daniel H. Lowenstein, "When Is a Campaign Contribution a Bribe?" Midwest Political Science Association, Chicago, Illinois, April 1996. This article updates Lowenstein's earlier article on bribery law, Lowenstein, "Political Bribery and the Intermediate Theory of Politics," *UCLA Law Review* 32:784 (1985). For a general review of bribery and campaign finance law, see Lowenstein, *Election Law: Cases and Materials* (Durham, N.C.: Carolina Academic Press), 1996.
39. 424 U.S. 47.
40. Supra notes 18, 19 and 20.
41. Even in bribery law it is not absolutely clear that a public official must agree to a quid pro quo to be convicted. See Lowenstein, "When is a Campaign Contribution a Bribe?"
42. A related question is whether campaign contributions actually do influence representatives. Political scientists have produced a welter a studies on this question but are only beginning to answer it. Most of the research focuses on the effects of contributions on legislators' floor votes, with very little work on other important aspects of the legislator's activities—for example committee activity (including votes), meetings with constituents, and interactions with federal regulatory agencies. Some recent studies include Stephen G. Bronars and John R. Lott, Jr., "Do Campaign Donations Alter How a Politician Votes?" Journal of Law and Economics (1997) 15:317; and Jeffrey Milyo and Timothy Groseclose, "The Electoral Effects of Incumbent Wealth," Journal of Law and Economics, forthcoming. For a listing of further studies, see Thomas F. Burke, "The Concept of Corruption in Campaign Finance Law," Constitutional Commentary (1997) 14:139 fn. 45.
43. Lowenstein, "On Campaign Finance Reform: The Root of All Evil is Deeply Rooted," Hofstra Law Review 18:301 (1989) at 302.
44. Lowenstein, "On Campaign Finance Reform," 301.
45. See pages above.
46. Martin Shapiro, "Corruption, Freedom and Equality," Hofstra Law Review 18:385 (1989) at 386.
47. Thompson, *Ethics in Congress: From Individual to Institutional Corruption* (Wash-

ington DC: The Brookings Institution, 1995), 28. The only alternative is logrolling, but recent research suggests that logrolling is both more difficult and more rare than is commonly supposed. Keith Krehbiel, *Information and Legislative Organization* (Ann Arbor, University of Michigan Press, 1991).

48. Thompson, *Ethics in Congress*, 28.
49. Thompson, *Ethics in Congress*, 20. Thompson calls this the independence principle. In his earlier writings Thompson calls it the principle of autonomy; see Thompson, *Political Ethics and Public Office* (Cambridge: Harvard University Press, 1987). The argument is also outlined in Thompson, "Mediated Corruption."
50. Thompson, *Ethics in Congress*, 21.
51. Ibid., 66.
52. Ibid., 117.
53. Bruce Cain, "Moralism and Realism in Campaign Finance Reform," (University of Chicago Legal Forum 1995:111 at 120.
54. Cain argues that "By littering the intellectual landscape with irrelevant issues, moral/idealists obstruct the path to a full, open discussion of the public's views about the proper distribution of power and influence." Cain, 112.
55. Cain, 120.
56. Thompson, *Ethics in Congress*, 19.
57. This point is made by Joseph Bessette in *The Mild Voice of Reason: Deliberative Democracy and American National Government* (Chicago: University of Chicago Press, 1994), quoting from the Federalist Papers, 27.
58. *Federalist Papers #10* (New York: Mentor, 1961), 83. Of course Madison was not so naive as to believe that representatives would always deliberate in the public interest, but he thought this ideal would be more closely approached in an extended republic, where factions would have a difficult time gaining control over the government.
59. Wood, *The Radicalism of the American Revolution* (New York: Vintage Books, 1993), 252, quoting from a letter by Madison to Edmund Randolph, April 8, 1787, in the *Papers of Madison*, IX, 384, 370.
60. Wood documents this process in *The Radicalism of the American Revolution*, 255–305.
61. Selznick, "Defining democracy up," *The Public Interest* (1995) 119:106. There is a huge literature on deliberative democracy in political theory. For some examples see James Fishkin, *Democracy and Deliberation: New Directions for Democratic Reform* (New Haven: Yale University Press, 1991); Joshua Cohen, "Deliberation and Democratic Legitimacy," in Alan Hamlin and Philip Pettit, eds., *The Good Polity: Normative Analysis of the State* (Oxford: Basil Blackwell, 1989); John W. Kingdon, "Politicians, Self-Interest, and Ideas, in *Reconsidering the Democratic Public*, eds. George E. Marcus and Russell L. Hanson (University Park, Penn.: Pennsylvania State University Press, 1993); Amy Gutmann, "The Disharmony of Democracy," in *Democratic Community: Nomos XXXV*, John W. Chapman and Ian Shapiro, eds. (New York: New York University Press, 1993), 126–160; and David Miller, "Deliberative Democracy and Social Choice," *Political Studies* (1992) 60:54–67.
62. Bessette, *The Mild Voice of Reason*, footnotes on 251–2.
63. See Sunstein, *The Partial Constitution*, 17–39.
64. Martha Derthick and Paul Quirk, *The Politics of Deregulation* (Washington DC: The Brookings Institution, 1985).
65. Fenno, *Congressmen in Committees* (Boston: Little, Brown and Company, 1991). Fenno's classic work on representation in practice is *Home Style: House Members*

in Their Districts (New York: Harper Collins, 1978). For an updating of this book see Jonathan Bernstein, Adrienne Jamieson and Christine Trost, eds., *Campaigning for Congress: Politicians at Home and in Washington* (Berkeley, Cal.: Institute of Governmental Studies Press, 1995)

66. Bessette, *Mild Voice of Reason*, 67–99.
67. The most influential books in this tradition are Robert A. Dahl, *A Preface To Democratic Theory* (Chicago: University of Chicago Press, 1956); David B. Truman, *The Governmental Process*, 2nd ed. (Berkeley: Institute of Governmental Studies Press, reprinted 1993); and Arthur F. Bentley, *The Process of Government* (Chicago: University of Chicago Press, 1908).
68. Thompson is somewhat elusive on this point:
    [T]he ideal legislator in a representative system does not pursue the public interest exclusively (whatever it may be). Such a legislator also has an ethical obligation to constituents that must be weighed against the obligation to a broader public. To find the balance between these obligations, even to decide whether they conflict, the legislator must consider the particular political circumstances at the time . . . Ethical obligations of these kinds are contingent on what is going on in the legislative process as a whole and may differ for different members and vary over time for all members." (*Ethics in Congress*, 70–71)
    Elsewhere Thompson says that the deliberative principle "is consistent with conceptions of representation ranging from delegate to trustee." The principle requires only that representatives defend their views on public policy "in a public forum—and at the risk of political defeat." (*Ethics in Congress*, 114)
    Similarly:
    [R]eelection or party loyalty could also count as principled reasons, when they are consistent with . . . legislative deliberation." (*Political Ethics and Public Office*, 113)
    Thompson does not specify how far this goes. At some point, presumably, the forces of constituency pressure, reelection anxiety, or party loyalty overwhelm the process of deliberation.
    As these passages indicate, Thompson, like many other political theorists, is quite critical of the delegate/trustee dichotomy. See for example Thompson, "Representatives in the Welfare State," in *Democracy and the Welfare State* (Princeton, New Jersey: Princeton University Press, 1995), 132–136.
69. This is the crux of David Strauss's argument against the deliberative approach to the concept of corruption. See Strauss, "What is the Goal of Campaign Finance Reform?" University of Chicago Legal Forum 1995:141–161.
70. This is a point that Lowenstein makes; see "Campaign Contributions and Corruption," 191.
71. Heidenheimer, 8.
72. Friedrich, 21.

35

Corruption Control in New York
and Its Discontents

Frank Anechiarico and James B. Jacobs

Introduction

What we call the anticorruption project—the development of laws, institutions and regulations to ensure honest government—began as an attempt to rescue government from the venality of machine politics.[1] The irony is that as the project became more powerful it undermined its own foundation. Step-by-step, the image of American public administrators has been transformed from the Progressive ideal of independent expert-professionals, deferred to because of their training and dedication, into low-status functionaries, controlled like probationers.

The role and status of the public service should remain in focus as reformers consider additional anticorruption reforms. The parallel effort to reinvent government using models adapted from corporate practice cannot succeed if it neglects either the problem of corruption itself or the costs of the current scheme of controls.[2] Integrity and control are irreducible elements of administrative design, but they have been implemented by the anticorruption project in both narrow and ineffective ways. Reestablishing integrity, control, and effectiveness in the public service will require reform of the premises and practices of the anticorruption project.

The Anticorruption Project in Action

In the early 1990s, the New York City Comptroller, subsequent to an audit of the Department of Buildings, discovered that a few inspectors would occasionally cut an hour or two off the workday by returning home directly from their last assignment. In order to prevent a form of official corruption called "theft of time," the Department responded by requiring all inspectors to return to borough headquarters at the end of the day. While no one knows how much corruption has been prevented by the policy, there was an almost immediate 30 percent productivity loss due to the time spent checking in at the end of the day.

The Department of Buildings is perhaps the most heavily investigated, audited, prosecuted and reformed public agency in New York City. It is also, with the possible exception of the New York Police Department (NYPD), the most scandal-plagued. The list of investigations and arrests in the Department of Buildings since 1940 includes twenty incidents significant enough to warrant condemnation in the press. In spite of the outcry and imposition of controls following each incident, another would surface within two or three years. Even though intensive efforts at prevention, detection, and control were made by municipal, state and federal officials, the Department of Buildings remained chronically corrupt.

While the cycle is longer, much the same point can be made about the NYPD. The revelations by Detective Frank Serpico that lead to the Knapp Commission investigation in the 1970s, and the reaction to the brutality and theft by informal patrol "crews" that led to the Mollen Commission in the 1990s, have had more dramatic and symbolic effect than real impact on behavior at the precinct level.[3] Shortly after the Mollen Commission hearings, there were reports that precinct protection and patronage of brothels in Manhattan—practices of long standing—continued, despite a century of corruption controls.[4]

Even where controls have been most extensive, corruption continues. Indeed, the accretion of controls and their increased intrusiveness have made it more difficult for agencies to serve the public. The sharp drop in inspector productivity resulting from an anticorruption rule is one example of a widespread phenomenon characterizing New York and other large governments in the United States.

New York City is important to the study of the anticorruption project because of the variety and pervasiveness of both corrupt behavior and control efforts. Virtually all forms of misconduct can be found in the annals of New York municipal agencies, from Boss Tweed's gigantic New York County Courthouse swindle in the 1870s to conflicts of interest in the regulation of cable television in the 1990s.[5] Likewise, all of the institutions, regulations and administrative procedures used for corruption control in the United States were either developed, or have been adopted, in New York City.

The Evolution of the Anticorruption Project

An Expanding Definition

Whether defined in terms of criminal law categories or ethical standards, the concept of corruption has expanded over the twentieth century to embrace more, and more varied, types of conduct. Tammany Hall politicians bragged about their ability of use government to help themselves and their friends financially; indeed, they ridiculed the Progressives who demanded high standards of integrity. In those days, some practices now regarded as corrupt were considered legitimate; yesterday's "honest graft" is today's illegal conflict of interest. The New York City Department of Investigation's definition of corruption, since the 1970s, has included the "subversion of fairness, of distributive and common justice, and of equal opportunity." Under this definition, even acknowledged error leading to waste would be corrupt.

Most states have expanded the concept of bribery to cover gifts and payments to public officials (so-called antigratuity statutes) whether or not there was an intent to corrupt or a provable *quid pro quo*. Politicians have been indicted for using their employees to provide personal services or work on their campaigns. Officeholders have been convicted for using campaign funds for personal use. Former public employees have been branded corrupt for engaging in lobbying and other private business after they left office. Low-level employees have been dismissed for petty thefts, and even for doing personal business during work hours. Conflict-of-interest laws and financial disclosure requirements have proliferated. Today, it is considered corrupt just to be in a decision-making role that *could be* affected financially by the decision, regardless of the decision actually rendered. Officials face disciplinary action if their conduct creates the "appearance of impropriety."[6]

This escalation of official morality is linked to wider cultural shifts—the war on drugs, the rise of the religious right, and diminished confidence in public officials.[7] Watergate triggered waves of denunciation of "politics as usual" and demands to close the gap between what Reisman calls the "mythical" and "operating" systems of government.[8] Congress responded by passing the Ethics in Government Act of 1978,[9] intended not only to "deter and punish exploitation of positions of public trust, but also to foster public confidence in the integrity of government employees."[10] Among other things, the Act established the Office of Government Ethics (OGE), which was given the task of developing and enforcing rules of ethical conduct for federal employees.[11] The 1978 Act stimulated a great deal of parallel anticorruption activity by state and local governments.

Just as the criminal law and law enforcement have expanded and intensified over the course of the century, the anticorruption project encompasses more aspects of official conduct. New offices, practices, and laws have been added—some borrowed directly from law enforcement, and others invented as corruption-specific remedies. Furthermore, there has been slow but steady penetration of government by the law-enforcement establishment itself. At times, fiscal crises and competition for scarce resources have slowed the creation and maintenance of anticorruption mechanisms. However, a lack of resources does not limit the proliferation of new laws and rules. It is always possible, and even politically advantageous, to throw law at a problem. By doing so, politicians can make a symbolic statement without spending much public money. Agency reorganization in the wake of scandal has many of the same advantages.

Visions of Corruption Control

The Anti-Patronage Vision (1870–1900)

The movement to end the spoils system[12] and create an American civil service began in earnest during Reconstruction, and should be understood as the second phase of a powerful moral movement beginning with the Abolitionists.[13] Senator Carl Schurz's reflections on the moral impetus of civil service reform make this point:

> The question whether the Departments at Washington are managed well or badly, is, in proportion to the whole problem, an insignificant question after all. Neither does the question whether our civil service is as efficient as it ought to be, cover the whole ground. The most important point to my mind is, how can we remove that element of demoralization which the now prevailing mode of distributing office has introduced into the body politic.[14]

According to Schurz, "demoralization," the moral debasing of character by patronage, made changing the nature of leadership in American government a moral necessity. Creating a civil service would "make active politics once more attractive to men of self-respect and high patriotic aspirations."[15]

Julius Bing, another proponent of civil service reform, saw the campaign as a clear moral imperative:

> At present, there is no organization save that of corruption; no system save that of chaos; no test of integrity save that of partisanship; no test of qualification save that of intrigue. . . we have to deal with a wide-spread evil, which defrauds the country in the collection of taxes on a scale so gigantic that the commissioners of revenue, collectors, assessors, and Treasury officers—at least those of them who are honest—bow their heads in shame and despair. We have to deal with an evil that is manifest here and there and everywhere.[16]

The desire to reform personnel administration powered one of the most significant movements in the history of American government. The belief that a professional civil service will assure the integrity and competence of public employees has not diminished since that time; indeed, the Anti-Patronage vision has become accepted political wisdom and constitutional dogma.[17]

The Progressive Vision (1900–1930)

Progressives believed that the key to rooting out corruption was complete reform of the political system, not just personnel policy. Corruption control was a precondition to government efficiency and democratic accountability. By studying European administration, scholars like Woodrow Wilson came to believe in the possibility of public administration independent of party politics, the root cause of corruption. "The object of administrative study is to rescue executive methods from the confusion and costliness of empirical experiment and set them upon foundations laid deep in stable principle."[18] The great and small questions of human governance would be answered by wedding American democracy's moral superiority to European administration's scientific superiority. The result would be honest, democratic, and scientifically sound administration.[19]

Wilson proposed integrity as the first principle of public administration. Similarly, Frank Goodnow argued that politics had debased administration and limited its utility. His solution was to separate politics from administration and to centralize government so that procedures and rules might be standardized.[20] These reforms, in his view, would make public administration responsive to the public interest rather than to party bosses.[21]

The Progressives aimed to establish an autonomous public sector by insulating administration from politics, and to staff government with nonpartisan experts. Experts themselves might be politically appointed, but their tenure was to outlast the appointing authority's term of office, and they were not to be removed without cause. The staffs of agencies like the Interstate Commerce Commission would be selected from the top scorers on civil service exams. Even sitting for the exam would require credentials and perhaps prior experience relevant to a specific job description. The Progressives' professionalization agenda was never fully instituted; public administration, at least below the city-manager level, did not become professionalized like law and medicine. In the largest cities, like New York, reform was minimal. Each reform initiative in New York was followed by the Tammany Hall machine's return to power.[22]

The Scientific Management Vision (1930–1970)

Whether or not it was a result of the incomplete nature of Progressive reform, several decades of municipal civil service did not eliminate corruption. New waves of corruption scandals undermined the notion that professional administrators would be self-policing. The old reforms were supplanted, or at least supplemented, by a new approach that sought to control public behavior through scientific administration and organizational reform.

Though its goals were rooted in the Progressive period, the 1930s generation of scientific managers emphasized bureaucratic control over general political reforms. It considered the Progressive philosophy to be "outmoded and insufficient to meet the problems of an industrialized, urbanized world power."[23] Modern agencies were too large to be controlled by regulations. The mutual scrutiny that might evolve naturally to keep officials honest in smaller agencies could not work in post-New Deal bureaucracies employing hundreds of professionals vested with discretionary authority. Seeing themselves as engineers of corruption control and armed with theories of scientific management, they approached corruption as a problem in the structural design of organizations, rather than one of politics or morals.

Reformers embraced theories of scientific management, optimal "spans of control," perfection of hierarchy, and new auditing and accounting techniques.[24] They believed integrity would flow from sound organization. Their basic premise was that the correct deployment of administrative authority, coupled with comprehensive monitoring and evaluation, would prevent corruption or quickly bring it to light.

Leonard White expressed this scientific management vision as follows:

> Out of reform, moral in its motivation, came reorganization, technical and managerial in connotation. Expertness, once assured its place, could continue a steady drive for better standards from within rather than from without.[25]

> [We] note the further development of the technique of large-scale management, especially overhead direction, long-range planning, and the effective coordination of the parts of a constantly expanding machine. Here government may learn from the methods of great industrial organizations, where similar problems exist.[26]

Clearly, scientific management had goals beyond corruption control, including organizational efficiency and rationality. Nevertheless, it was shaped by the belief that integrity could be achieved through administrative control. As tasks became more complex in ever-larger bureaucracies, it became more difficult to guarantee integrity through such Progressive innovations as peer pressure, professional ethics, and voter accountability. Luther Gulick proposed an administrative strategy called "external control,"[27] which is investigative evaluation of government operations by specialized officials located in units external to operating agencies. Gulick pointed to the New York City Department of Investigation as the prototype of an external controller capable of providing the needed scrutiny. He saw no contradiction between corruption control and efficiency; indeed he saw external control as a necessary condition of efficient public administration.[28]

The Panoptic Vision (1970—Present)

Since the early 1970s a "panoptic vision" has become dominant. This vision assumes that officials will succumb to corrupt opportunities and advocates comprehensive surveillance, investigation and "target hardening" strategies. It is built on a hundred years of ideology, rules, institutions, legal techniques and reformist ideas. While the beefed-up law enforcement techniques that are a major component of the panoptic vision are a qualitative change from earlier efforts, they reinforce the goals articulated by the Progressives and expanded by later reformers. Like its predecessors, the panoptic vision has critical implications for government organization and public administration—if anything, even more significant ones because of its much broader definition of corruption and much greater authority given to corruption-control personnel and agencies.

This newest vision of corruption control recalls the panoptic ideal described by Jeremy Bentham and Michel Foucault.[29] Bentham's design for a prison in which all inmate activity would be observable from a louvered and unobservable central tower was used by Foucault as a metaphor for the aggressive gaze of the modern state; a gaze that translates knowledge into power. Panoptic reform transforms the Progressive mission and New Deal engineering into comprehensive controls based on surveillance, massive information collection, auditing and aggressive enforcement of an wide array of criminal and administrative sanctions. The pervasive gaze itself results in less need for coercion, as subjects internalize the demands of the controllers. Under the Panopticon, management and control merge. Each administrative routine has its place in the scheme of observation. The business of control becomes the everyday business of governing.

If the Progressives generated moral theory and scientific managers engineered control structures, contemporary corruption controllers emphasize law enforcement strategies and punitive sanctions.[30] The political, legal, and institutional legacies of past visions remain, but the panoptic vision is of public administration fraught with corruption vulnerability that can only be addressed by comprehensive administrative, organizational and law enforcement strategies. Wasting resources through incompetence, indifference, negligence, and nonfeasance came under the corruption umbrella as legislation established a federal Inspector General system to focus on "fraud, waste and abuse." Command and control mechanisms of all types were strengthened; public managers were scrutinized with respect to their compliance with stringent ethics laws and financial controls. New technologies, institutions, and routines emphasize intensive scrutiny of public employees. While these techniques are clearly successors to external control and other earlier approaches, taken together they are *different in kind* from earlier methods. Perhaps more important, they create a self-conscious interest group within government.

Instead of theorists like Woodrow Wilson, or administrative engineers like William Herlands, the central figures in the contemporary fight against corruption are prosecutors, inspectors general, corruption vulnerability experts, auditors and fraud specialists. Their anti-corruption project is extraordinarily ambitious, having radically expanded the definition of corruption to include appearance of conflict of interest, failure to disclose financial interests, misstatements on job applications, unauthorized use of government telephones, leaving work early, accepting favors and gifts, and entering into public contracts with morally tainted private companies. With each exposé, corruption-hunters lobby for greater resources and a broader definition of their mission.[31] The inevitable result is that more corruption is uncovered. Thus, the panoptic vision feeds on corruption scandals, and generates initiatives that have increasingly profound impacts on public administration.

According to the panoptic vision, corruption is no longer primarily attributable to incompetence, absenteeism, laziness, and partisan influence, but to inadequate rules, controls and deterrence. This vision de-emphasizes governmental accountability,[32] recruitment and training. It views public officials, politicians, managers, and rank and file personnel as seekers of corrupt opportunities, and government as generating those opportunities in abundance.[33] Corruption is to be expected, and all public employees are suspect. New York reform commissions in the late 1980s concluded that systemic strategies were necessary but insufficient;[34] the time had come to apply the criminal law model based upon surveillance, investigation, punishment and deterrence. The priorities of investigation and prosecution now determine the structure of authority and control in administrative agencies.

The kind of organizational reforms associated with the panoptic approach should not be confused with the political reforms demanded by the Progressives or with today's "reinventing government" movement. According to the panoptic vision, the purpose of administrative reform is to deter and prevent corruption via thorough and efficient surveillance. Public employees, under the panoptic gaze, are governed by a comprehensive system of administrative/criminal law, enforced by law enforcement agencies using a full array of investigative tools, including covert operations. This system is backed by threat and sanctions, including jail, fines, and job and pension forfeiture. The panoptic vision has led to the expansion of anti-corruption institutions and strategies, and to enhancement of the authority of anti-corruption units and personnel.

Contemporary Elements of the Anticorruption Project

Civil Service

A 1993 study of the New York City civil service found that reform had rendered city government ineffective and, ironically, subject to political manipulation—the worst of both worlds.[35] The study surveyed managers of all ranks in three agencies and found uniform negativism about the personnel system. Criticism centered on five major problems: hiring takes too long; testing does not assess relevant abilities; promotion is not controlled at the agency level and so deprives managers of a basic incentive; job descriptions are so technically and narrowly written that a minor internal transfer becomes a major bureaucratic issue; and discipline, punishment, and removal have been made all but impossible by civil service protections. Many of these same problems had been highlighted by a 1963 Brookings Institution study.[36]

In response to some of these problems, an office was created by Mayor Edward Koch in 1983 to recruit minorities and women for administrative positions in New York City government. This office, the Talent Bank, came under blistering attack in a New York State anti-corruption investigation because it accepted referrals from politicians.[37] The lack of "formal standards," in the view of investigators, tainted the employment of everyone hired through the Talent Bank. One long-serving administrator, whose name was included in the investigation and published by the *New York Times* simply because he had been referred to a Deputy Mayor by the Talent Bank, wrote a response to the *Times*: "By 1981 [when the Talent Bank forwarded his name], I had 12 years of public sector experience—federal, state, and city . . . I guess you have destroyed my credibility and that of others. Too bad for government, whose professionals and managers seem relentlessly and often inaccurately criticized by the news media, further discouraging talented people from entering its ranks and staying."[38] Although no legal violations were found, pressure from the media and the state commission forced the Talent Bank to close.

Conflicts of Interest and Financial Disclosure

To suggest that governmental ethics legislation may be understood in terms of symbolic politics is not to deny its impact on the real world. The 1989 New York City Charter includes a complex personnel code that has practical consequences for the lives of tens of thousands of New York City employees and for public administration.[39] If an account of such consequences were possible, it would probably show that these administrative consequences are more significant than the impact of the ethics laws on corruption.

Passage of the New York State ethics law in May 1991, which included significantly enhanced conflict of interest provisions, precipitated a rash of resignations among local officials all over the state. The New York State Association of Counties reported over one hundred resignations from county government positions, especially from county health boards, zoning and planning commissions, and community college boards.[40] But even if these laws do not deter people from seeking or accepting public office, public administration will suffer if ethics legislation negatively affects morale or if decision making becomes slower and more defensive.

Whistleblower Protection

The Federal Whistleblower Protection Act of 1989 strengthened the provisions of the 1978 Ethics in Government Act by making the Office of Special Counsel independent of the Merit Systems Protection Board (MSPB), and allowing whistleblowers to bypass the former and take complaints directly to the latter.[41] The 1989 Act also lowered the standard of proof necessary to make a case of protected whistleblowing: now, the employee need show that his or her disclosure of information was "a factor" (rather than the *predominant or motivating factor*) in a subsequent negative personnel action or inaction.

Similar laws are in place in half of the states and most large cities. The New York City Code gives authority to investigate allegations of whistleblower retaliation to the Department of Investigation. One agency's experience with whistleblower cases illustrates the kind of tensions this strategy can generate. G.P. (not the individual's real initials) accused coworkers of corruption around the same time that the agency attempted to fire him for poor work. Because G.P.'s corruption charge came first, the DOI investigated the situation and declared him a whistleblower. The agency's case against G.P. included a long list of complaints from citizens about arbitrary and abusive treatment. The agency also had considerable documentation of G.P.'s poor work record. Once the DOI became involved, the agency had to suspend its disciplinary action; it could neither remove nor transfer him while the investigation was pending. Because interview transcripts and other evidence are not available to the agency, the DOI's presumption of retaliation is difficult to rebut. In G.P.'s case it took the DOI *four years* to close the investigation and approve the termination. By this time, the agency head refused to act, fearing criticism. It took two more years, a change of leadership in the agency, and a full hearing by the Office of Administrative Trials and Hearings to finally remove G.P. In the meantime, productivity in G.P.'s unit plummeted and morale hit an all-time low.

The protection and encouragement of whistleblowers encourages all public employees to be investigators and activists in the anticorruption project. The whistleblower machinery itself is a good example of the entrenchment of external control mechanisms. This machinery is predicated on the belief that the public service cannot police itself. It assumes that anticorruption responsibility can only be effectively discharged by those who are independent of and have no stake in the target agency's reputation. However, such people are likely to have little information about the agency's operations and little interest in whether it achieves its goals.

Internal Investigation

The presence of Inspectors General and undercover field associates in various agencies has created a system in New York City government that some employees describe as "Big Brother" and "like the old Soviet Union." No one knows whether a city employee is actually working for the DOI, or whether an apparent member of the public is actually an undercover investigator conducting a sting or integrity test. A commissioner in the Koch Administration commented that the worst part of the job was the fear that the DOI would one day summon her for questioning about a matter that had escaped her attention. "It's like living with the sword of Damocles perpetually threatening to drop." At one point, she found herself using pay phones because DOI might be wiretapping. "It seems funny now, but at the time it was frightening." Another employee explained that "you cannot assume that innocence will protect you."

The DOI can require city employees "to answer questions concerning any matter related to the performance of his or her official duties."[42] One employee, K.R. (not real initials) was summoned to answer questions about charges that his agency was coercing women employees who were pregnant to have abortions if they wanted to keep their jobs. He disclaimed knowledge of any such policy and was told the matter was closed. But shortly thereafter, the agency commissioner gave K.R. five days to respond to DOI charges in a report he was not allowed to see. His response was rejected, and he was given three alternatives: termination, resignation, or demotion and a $10,000 fine. He chose the third option and hired a lawyer. His appeal was rejected. However, when the original complainants filed a multimillion-dollar suit against K.R., other agency officials, and the City itself, the City's corporation counsel was suddenly interested in establishing K.R.'s innocence. He was ultimately "cleared" and reimbursed for the fine, but not for legal fees of over $50,000 or for a year of torment. K.R. resigned and moved to another city.

The transformation of the DOI into a law enforcement agency has important implications for public administration. Agency heads constantly look over their shoulders trying to anticipate how their decisions will be perceived by DOI investigators and wondering which of their operations may be surreptitiously monitored.

State and Federal Prosecution

The biggest change in the law enforcement component of the anticorruption project is the aggressive role of federal agencies in investigating and prosecuting corruption by high-level state and local officials.[43] Since the mid-1970s, when the Department of Justice declared local corruption an enforcement priority, a number of governors, dozens of mayors, and hundreds of local officials have been indicted and convicted for official corruption in federal court.[44] The expansion of criminal law, especially regarding federal mail and wire fraud, has enabled the FBI to investigate, and the Department of Justice to prosecute, just about any significant local corruption. Federal officials may be more willing and able to prosecute local corruption than their state and local counterparts; they have more resources and are not as involved in local politics as local prosecutors,[45] but also may be unfamiliar with the local realities, and, as a result, must work with local law enforcement. Prosecutors are thus a greater presence in the daily lives of public administrators than they were a generation ago. Federal and large local prosecutors' offices are likely to have specialized public corruption units. Prosecutors now expect public administrators to share the high priority given to fighting corruption and racketeering.

Procurement Regulation

Willie Sutton robbed banks for the same reason procurement systems are vulnerable to corruption: "That's where the money is." In order to break the cycle of corruption in contracting, many governments have put special controls in place in addition to the usual lowest responsible bidder rule. New York City's Parking Violations Bureau scandal, which reached two borough presidents among many others in the Koch administration, led to the establishment of the Procurement Policy Board (PPB) by way of the 1989 Charter revision. Within a year, the PPB issued several hundred pages of regulations covering every aspect of contracting.[46]

The PPB rules are a good example of the way that contract regulation has changed around the country. The PPB procurement code requires each agency's chief contracting officer and chief administrator to determine whether a contractor or vendor is financially, operationally, and morally responsible.[47] The burden of proving responsibility falls on the contractor, who must demonstrate a satisfactory record of business activity and pass screening through a computerized data bank, the Vendor Information Exchange System (VENDEX). VENDEX includes background information on all principals in contracting firms, their tax returns, and whether they have run afoul of any other part of the anticorruption project.[48] Such practices are expanding: dozens of municipal and other public agencies are making independent judgments about contractors' honesty; a negative determination by one agency may eliminate opportunities to obtain city contracts because other agency heads will want to avoid criticism for doing business with "racketeers." A favorable finding, however, will not qualify a firm to do business with every other agency, because each is responsible for its own responsibility determination every time a contract is awarded.

The negative impact of competitive bidding, the principal anticorruption strategy in contracting, is hard to exaggerate. By removing the public official's discretion over choice of contractor, competitive bidding eliminates officials' ability to obtain superior goods and services, especially for construction projects. Under lowest responsible bidding rules, government does not choose its contractors; they choose themselves. Not surprisingly, the quality of goods and services suffers: contracts are awarded according to lowest cost, not according to performance record. Even a contractor who does a shoddy job must be awarded future contracts, if it is the lowest bidder, unless it is found nonresponsible. The result is a race to the bottom, which many companies refuse to join. The Feerick Commission found that many contracts advertised by the New York City Human Resources Administration attracted very few bidders.

> HRA was unable to attract more than two bids for a wide range of services. For instance, only two vendors stepped forward to bid on a $5.2 million contract to provide cooked meals for the homeless, although 30 companies had been invited to bid.[49]

The field is further limited by the near-obsession in New York City (and elsewhere) with avoiding contractors having even a tangential connection with racketeers. Examinations of family connections by the New York City Comptroller have eliminated contractors who are related to reputed racketeers by marriage. Even if policy makers determine to pay the high costs of screening and eliminating competent businesses in order to weaken organized crime, protect the city from potential fraud, and maintain "purity" in contractual relations, it is hardly clear that they will succeed. In New York City and many other construction market, contractors have no real option to refuse to deal with racketeers if they want to work.

An entire system of norms, rules, and procedures, not to mention a large bureaucracy, will be necessary to implement a fair and comprehensive system to assess the integrity of government contractors. Ironically, the higher the moral position the government takes, the greater the criticism to which it will be subjected when it becomes known—as it will inevitably—that a particular contract is being performed by a firm "associated" with this or that "gangster."[50] That kind of exaggerated ambition reinforces the cycle of scandal and reform.

Auditing

Auditors have become influential actors in American government because of their numerous mandates and responsibilities and because negative audits, particularly those charging or intimating corruption, have the potential to undermine or destroy administrators. Scandal-sensitive politicians and bureaucrats implement financial controls, pre-audits, and post-audits to protect themselves against the possibility of future charges that they ignored fraud and corruption.

Reformers have long advocated the use of financial control in order to achieve corruption-free government. They have understood implicitly what Bentham and Foucault understood explicitly, that conformity can be produced by surveillance, monitoring, and control of information. Toward that end they have constantly lobbied for more intensive and comprehensive financial controls, promising that such controls would contribute to governmental efficiency as well as honesty. The most powerful auditing agency in the United States, the General Accounting Office (GAO), has authority to review any agency or program in New York City government receiving federal funds. In the early 1990's it found that the administration of federal grants by the New York City Transit Authority and the Long Island Railroad lacked adequate controls to prevent "fraud, waste, and mismanagement." The result of a long investigation and critical report was to cede control over a portion of the local agencies' budgets to federal auditors.[51]

The expansion of financial controls contributes to a steady shift in power from executive and legislative officials to comptrollers and other auditing agencies. These information-gathering and monitoring agencies are becoming more important units of government. Their wide-ranging audits generate recommendations aimed at practically every aspect of agency organization, operation, and personnel policy. Because of the politics of corruption and reform, administrators ignore such recommendations at their peril. The auditing agencies have become key shapers of public administration.

Corruption Control and Bureaucratic Pathologies

It is no coincidence that the anticorruption project and public bureaucracy have developed in tandem. Bureaucracy was the model of public administration admired by Woodrow Wilson and other Progressives precisely because it promised to be an antidote to the spoils system.[52] To its admirers in the late 19th and early 20th centuries, bureaucracy offered the possibility of rationalized governance by apolitical specialists according to scientific principles, neutral rules, and fair procedures, the very antithesis of corruption.

Corruption was not supposed to occur within a properly functioning bureaucracy. Indeed, it was viewed as a blight on the purity of bureaucracy. Therefore, the occurrence of a scandal meant that bureaucracy was not yet functioning properly and needed repair. Thus, what we call the anticorruption project is a necessary component of the vision that attempts to bring actual bureaucracy closer to the ideal. But in fact the anticorruption project supports some of the worst aspects of modern, public organization. A summary list would include:

- Decision-Making Delay: Anticorruption contract regulations including the lowest responsible bidder rule and the State requirement that large projects rely on separate, smaller contracts, draw out attempts to initiate and complete public works both large and small.
- Defensive Management: We heard from several agency heads that, because of the quicksand of ethics rules and audits surrounding them, it was, as one of them put it, "better to look honest than to get anything done." The bold leadership that characterizes local government at its best is blunted by the extent of corruption control in most large governments in the United States.
- Goal Displacement: Several agencies we studied were undergoing two or three audits from different agencies at the same time. Responding to these audits becomes an vital part of an agency's work and shapes its routine and mission, to the detriment of serving the public.
- Poor Morale: The number and intensity of internal investigations in most large American governments (one per 150 municipal personnel in the late 1980s in New York City) puts public employees in the role of probationers. While investigations are opened with considerable public fanfare, those that do not produce indictments are seldom officially closed, nor are the unindicted, who may be named as targets in press conferences, ever formally exonerated.
- Barriers to Intergovernmental Cooperation: State and local laws barring the fact or even appearance of conflicts of interest have made it very difficult for public agencies to cooperate with non-governmental organizations parallel to their mission. Creative coalitions based on personal contacts and trust between public and private agencies are risky and often discouraged.
- A Combination of Overcentralization and Inadequate Managerial Authority: The distrust of middle management has drawn policy making authority toward the top in large governments. Those public officials closest to citizens and with the most complete knowledge of a given service area have less and less authority under anticorruption rules.

Toward a New Theory of Public Service Conduct

The failure of the anticorruption project indicates several possible remedies at increasing levels of intensity and depth. Changes should improve upon current corruption controls while imposing fewer costs on public administration.

A first-level remedy would involve fine-tuning the anticorruption project as it stands. The first step would be a careful assessment of the costs imposed by the corruption control agency in question. A second step would be measurement of corrupt activity and corruption vulnerability in the purview of the control agency. While vulnerability assessment is now done by corruption control agencies, it should be shifted to an agency with a more general mission. An administrative office in the legislative branch similar to the Congressional Budget Office or the Congressional Office of Technology Assessment would survey managers and line personnel to gather perceptions and experiences regarding actual and potential corruption. These would be matched against the corruption vulnerability audits done by agencies like the Department of Investigation in New York City and by comptroller's offices around the country. These two measures—costs of control and extent of threat—will allow elected officials to reassess the extent and size of the anticorruption project in their jurisdiction. A number of other changes can be made by adjusting audit routines to prevent disruption of agency work, revising conflict-of-interest rules to allow government employees to engage in non-related civic activity beyond their official duties (this would require relaxing the "appearance of conflicts" standard, a change some would consider more than fine-tuning), and requiring that employees being interviewed by internal investigators be given notice of their status as inquiry targets, and of the conclusion of an inquiry that finds no evidence against them.

Mid-level remedies would require more fundamental consideration of institutions and rules to eliminate disincentives to good public service. Examples would be a move toward long-term, negotiated contract relationships in place of the lowest responsible bidder system, or a reconsideration of basic civil service rules. The accretion of rules in the heat of scandal has built a system that is too well insulated from criticism and redesign. Recognizing that corruption control has systemic effects on governance is a beginning. For example, the interaction of procurement rules and auditing requirements makes it virtually impossible for government managers to influence the quality of a good or service purchased by his or her agency for the public. Auditors resolve any ambiguity in the lowest, responsible bidder procedures against managerial discretion. Deviation from anticorruption regimens can ruin a manager's career. Likewise, conflict of interest rules, which might be considered guidelines to be kept in mind alongside other professional ethics, have a more ominous tone when they are enforced by inspectors general with broad investigatory authority.

A third level remedy recognizes the basic political and theoretical problems caused by contemporary corruption control. As it has grown over more than 100 years, the anticorruption project has lost any discernible connection to the Progressive reform theories and administrative science premises behind its establishment. The panoptic perspective is articulated with surprising frankness by some corruption controllers, but it has not been widely debated as a foundation for government integrity. It should be. If panoptic control and its attendant costs are to be adopted as the administrative culture of American government, the public should be better informed about it. If it is not adopted or if its influence on service provision is called into question, a new perspective on the role and function of the public service will be needed.

It is logical that corruption control should lead us to rethink public service, since it is the reaction to corruption that has shaped it until now. The idea that American administrative culture should be a culture of control should be examined for the damage that it has done, not only to government efficiency, but to the democratic nature of public administration. At the most general level, the anticorruption project has created a barrier between citizens and public service providers, reduced government responsiveness, and increased public distrust and cynicism about public institutions. In order to reconnect government with the public and ensure integrity, the citizens must be integrated more thoroughly into the everyday business of public administration. This turns Progressive theory on its head by embracing public involvement and scrutiny as the only real way to ensure integrity and responsiveness. Progressive efforts to break the close connection between citizens and politicians in the political machine resulted in a century of changes that removed the last speck of public accountability.

An administrative culture based on civic involvement would also challenge a long-established culture of expert professionalism in both the public and private sectors. The Progressives designed modern public administration at the same time that the professions were emerging as powerful, social forces in American life. The independence and non-partisanship of engineers, physicians, lawyers, and accountants was the core of Progressive administration. However, in a few jurisdictions around the country, like Santa Rosa, California, administrative professionals have reformed classic Progressive council-manager systems to include close, formal relationships with neighborhood groups and citizen governing boards. In those cases, both citizens and public officials report that public goods and services are provided more efficiently and effectively than before reforms were in place. The shifts are not without frustration. Agency managers, as one Santa Rosa commissioner put it, "must now be politicians, not just engineers." Decisions often take longer as many official actions from zoning revision to the planning of a new park require an elaborate series of meetings, neighborhood by neighborhood. But several officials report that their skills as "facilitators, rather than bureaucrats" make their jobs more enjoyable as the burden of decision-making is dispersed through collaboration. [53]

The long evolution and deep entrenchment of the anti-corruption project have made the *status quo* seem unalterable. In order to evaluate alternative directions for public administration, comparative study of official ethics is necessary. A good example is the way the Netherlands has dealt with official corruption, reflecting an administrative culture based on broad civic engagement. In the mid-1990s, the Dutch Audit Court (AR) conducted a two-year investigation of the Director of the Netherlands State Lottery, whom it suspected of having an equity interest in companies doing business with his office. The AR requires a special executive decree to audit the finances of any individual. Once the decree was obtained, the AR's findings forced the Director from office. Subsequently, the entire national lottery board resigned. Instead of responding with rules and laws constraining the behavior of lottery and other officials, the Dutch government impaneled an interagency working group on public employee ethics. Its mission was to determine the extent of vulnerability to corruption in various parts of the government and to recommend new rules and other institutional reforms. In addition, in 1995 a cabinet group on crime control chaired by the Justice Minister established a foundation on Crime Control and Professional Ethics focusing on corruption control. The foundation is a public-private consortium including labor and business leaders as well as government officials and citizen reform advocates.

This comparison is instructive. The circumspect administrative culture of the Netherlands proceeds with an understanding of the complexity of reform and the pitfalls of expedient solutions. As one Dutch scholar put it, "Instead of waging crime-fighting wars, the sense of integrity should be strengthened. Of more fundamental importance, therefore, is action to improve the professional ethics of trade and industry as well as the public sector."[54]

A serious discussion of the costs of the anticorruption project may start by fine-tuning certain rules and institutions, but will sooner or later raise the larger issue of the mission and design of the public service and the nature of administrative culture. Such a debate will return to the foundational question of American public administration, one that has been confounded by the accretion of corruption controls: what form of public service will guarantee integrity while providing efficient, effective service to the people?

Notes

1. The research reported here was published in different form in Frank Anechiarico and James B. Jacobs, *The Pursuit of Absolute Integrity: How Corruption Control Makes Government Ineffective* (Chicago: University of Chicago Press, 1996) and in Frank Anechiarico, "Administrative Culture and Civil Society: A Comparative Perspective," *Administration and Society* 30 (March 1998): 13–34.
2. David Osborne and Ted Gaebler, *Reinventing Government: How the Entrepreneurial Spirit Is Transforming the Public Sector from Schoolhouse to Statehouse, City Hall to the Pentagon* (Reading, Mass.: Addison-Wesley, 1992).
3. Commission to Investigate Alleged Police Corruption and the City's Anti-Corruption Procedures (Knapp Commission), *Commission Report* (26 December 1972); Commission to Investigate Allegation of Police Corruption and the Anti-Corruption Procedures of the Police Department (Mollen Commission) *Commission Report* (7 July 1994).
4. Clifford Krauss, "Hunting Rogues: Police Corruption Signals Abound," *New York Times*, 6 February 1995, p. B1.

5. S.J. Mandelbaum, Boss Tweed's New York (New York: Wiley, 1965); Todd S. Purdum, "When Life Itself is a Conflict of Interest," *New York Times*, 22 April 1990, p. E8.
6. Peter W. Morgan, "The Appearance of Propriety: Ethics Reform and the Blifil Paradox," *Stanford Law Review* 44 (Feb. 1992): 593.
7. Morgan, "The Appearance of Propriety," 593, 595; Abraham Eisenstadt, "Political Corruption in American History," in Arnold J. Heidenheimer, Michael Johnston, and Victor LeVine, eds., *Political Corruption: A Handbook* (New Brunswick, N.J.: Transaction Publishers, 1993), 567.
8. Michael Reisman, *Folded Lies: Bribery Crusades and Reforms* (New York: Free Press, 1979): chapter 1.
9. Public Law 95–521, 92 Stat. 1824 (1978) (codified at 2 *United States Code* §§ 701–709 and other scattered sections of the *United States Code*).
10. For analysis of the *Ethics in Government Act of 1978*, see "Developments in the Law—Public Employment," *Harvard Law Review* 97 (May 1984): 1669–76.
11. 5 *United States Code* § 402 (app. 1988).
12. The statement from which the system gets it name, "To the victors belong the spoils," is credited to Senator William Marcy around 1850: Ari Hoogenboom, *Outlawing the Spoils: A History of the Civil Service Reform Movement, 1865–1883* (Urbana, Ill.: University of Illinois Press, 1961), p.6.
13. William E. Nelson, *The Roots of American Bureaucracy: 1830–1900* (Cambridge, Mass.: Harvard University Press, 1982), p.121.
14. Quoted in Nelson, *op. cit.*, p.121; cf. speech of Carl Schurz before the Senate, January 27, 1871, in Frederick Bancroft, ed., *Speeches, Correspondence, and Political Papers of Carl Schurz* (New York: G.P. Putnam, 1913), vol.3, p.123.
15. Carl Schurz, "Editorial," H*arper's Weekly* XXXVII, July 1, 1893, p. 614; quoted in David H. Rosenbloom, "The Inherent Politicality of Public Personnel Policy," in David H. Rosenbloom, ed. *Public Personnel Policy: The Politics of Civil Service* (Port Washington, NY: Associated Faculty Press, 1985), p. 7.
16. Quoted in Hoogenboom, *op. cit.*, p.1; cf. Julius Bing, "Our Civil Service," *Putnam Magazine,* New Series, II, No. 8 (August, 1868), pp. 233, 236.
17. In 1975, in *Elrod* v. *Burns*, 427 US 347 (1975), and in 1990, in *Rutan* v. *Republican Party of Illinois*, 497 US 62 (1990) the Court held unconstitutional (on First Amendment grounds) hiring, firing, transfer, promotion or recall based on partisan affiliation for all but a few, top administrative jobs.
18. Arthur S. Link, ed., *The Papers of Woodrow Wilson* (Princeton, N.J.: Princeton University Press, 1966). p. 370.
19. Nelson, *op. cit.* , p.121.
20. Frank J. Goodnow, *Politics and Administration* (New York: Russell and Russell, 1900).
21. Goodnow, *Politics and Administration*, p.129:
   "As soon, however, as the administration became somewhat centralized, this control of the political parties became unnecessary, except to the highest officers, since these could control more fully the actions of their subordinates, and being themselves subject to party control, might bring about the necessary harmony in the governmental system."
22. Arthur Cerillo, "The Impact of Reform Ideology: Early Twentieth Century Municipal Government in New York City," in *The Age of Reform: New Perspectives on the Progressive Era*, edited by Michael H. Eisner and Eugene M. Tobin (Port Washington, N.Y.: Kennikat Press, 1977); Charles Garrett, *The LaGuardia Years: Machine and Reform Politics in New York City* (New Brunswick, N.J.: Rutgers University Press, 1961).

23. Ronald L. Feinman, *Twilight of Progressivism: The Western Republican Senators and the New Deal* (Baltimore: Johns Hopkins University Press, 1981), p.208.

24. One study of the post-Progressive period found that "[t]he promising development of public administration as a profession during the Progressive era has dissipated . . . The post-Progressive era was an age in which concern for the practical use and application of administrative techniques extended beyond any theoretical or normative standard for application. . . Attention turned to more narrow technical problems rather than broader concerns." J.A. Stever, *The End of Public Administration: Problems of the Profession in the Post-Progressive Era* (Dobbs Ferry, N.Y.: Transnational, 1988), p. 66.

25. Leonard White, *Introduction to the Study of Public Administration*, 3rd ed. (New York: Macmillan, 1948), p. 16.

26. Leonard White, *Introduction to the Study of Public Administration*, 2nd ed. (New York: Macmillan, 1942), p.597.

27. Luther Gulick, "Foreword," in Harold Seidman, *Investigating Municipal Administration: A Study of the New York City Department of Investigation* (New York: Columbia University Institute of Public Administration, 1941), pp.vii-xi.

28. Gulick found support in Woodrow Wilson's famous essay on "The Study of Administration": "All sovereigns are suspicious of their servants. . . How is suspicion to be allayed by knowledge? Trust is strength in all relations of life and, as it is the office of the constitutional reformer to create conditions of trustfulness, so it is the office of the administrative organizer to fit administration with conditions of clear-cut responsibility which will insure trustworthiness." Quoted in Gulick, "Foreword," in Harold Seidman, *Investigating Municipal Administration: A Study of the New York City Department of Investigation*, p.vii.

29. In *Discipline and Punish*, Foucault argued that the panopticon's architecture and operation were paradigmatic of a 19th century vision of a disciplinary society in which surveillance, monitoring, and control would make undetected deviance impossible. Michel Foucault, *Discipline and Punish: The Birth of the Prison* (New York: Vintage, 1979)), p.204. However, the first Panopticon, built by Jeremy Bentham's brother, was not a prison, but a Russian factory. Scohana Zuboff, *In the Age of the Smart Machine* (New York: Basic Books, 1988), pp. 320–322.

30. A history of the New York City Department of Investigation concluded that "the defense of democracy and the struggle for a decent life begins and continues with the fight against corruption." See: Richard S. Winslow and David W. Burke, *Rogues, Rascals, and Heroes: A History of the New York City Department of Investigation* (New York: New York City Department of Investigation, 1992), p. 87.

31. Thompson argues that, in light of the scandal surrounding the Keating Five, the definition of corruption should be expanded to include "mediated corruption" which "links the acts of individual officials to effects on the democratic process." (p.369). Dennis F. Thompson, "Mediated Corruption: The Case of the Keating Five," *American Political Science Review*, vol.87, no.2 (June, 1993), pp. 369–381.

32. *The Federalist* argued that a plethora of rules was useless at best and possibly dangerous to liberty. On federalist theory and urban government, see Robert L. Bish and Vincent Ostrom, *Understanding Urban Government* (Washington, D.C.: American Enterprise Institute, 1973).

33. Gary T. Marx, "When the Guards Guard Themselves: Undercover Tactics Turned Inward," *Policing and Society*, 2, pp. 151–172 (1992).

34. Bruce Green and John D. Feerick, *Government Ethics Reform for the 1990s: The*

Collected Reports of the New York State Commission on Government Integrity (New York: Fordam University Press, 1991) and New York State Organized Crime Task Force, *Corruption and Racketeering in the New York City Construction Industry* (New York: New York University Press, 1991).

35. Steven Cohen and William B. Eimicke, eds., *New York City Solutions II: Transforming the Public Personnel System* (New York: Columbia University Program in Politics and Public Policy, February, 1993).

36. David T. Stanley, *Professional Personnel for the City of New York* (Washington, D.C.: The Brookings Institution, 1963).

37. New York State Commission on Government Integrity, "Playing Ball with City Hall: A Case Study of Political Patronage in New York City," in New York State Commission on Government Integrity, *Government Ethics Reform for the 1990s* (New York: Fordham University Press, 1991), 498–99.

38. Letter to the Editor, Brooke Trent, *New York Times*, 10 February 1989, p. A34.

39. New York City Charter §2604(b) (1989).

40. Kevin Sack, "New York Ethics Law Leads Local Officials to Quit Posts," New York Times, 18 May 1991, p. 26: "The [New York State ethics] law has generated a backlash across the state in which an effort to stop corruption is threatening to stop government instead. Officials in some municipalities fear that the resignations will paralyze local government by making it difficult to convene quorums of zoning boards, community college boards and development agencies."

41. Public Law 101–12, 103 *Stat.* 16, §2(a) (10 April 1989).

42. Winslow and Burke, *op. cit.*

43. 18 *United States Code* §§1341 and 1343 (1988 and Supp. IV 1992).

44. One the most important, precedent-setting cases was *U.S. v. Margiotta*, 688 F.2d 108 (2d Cir. 1982), involving the conviction of the Republican boss of Nassau County.

45. Arthur Maass, "Public Prosecution," *The Public Interest* 89 (Fall 1987): 107–27.

46. Procurement Policy Board Rules, 1 August 1990.

47. Procurement Policy Board Rule 521.

48. New York City Mayor's Office of Contracts, "VENDEX: Policies and Procedures Manual," (March 1990), 30.

49. New York State Commission on Government Integrity, "A Ship Without a Captain: The Contracting Process in New York City," in *Government Ethics Reform for the 1990s* (New York: Fordham University Press, 1991), 471.

50. In the winter of 1994 the media blasted Mayor Rudolph Guiliani for inefficient snow removal. The problem was not that the city was overcharged when it awarded these emergency contracts, but that eleven of the companies hired had "checkered pasts, ranging from suspected mob ties to criminal conviction." Kevin Flynn, "Plow Now Anyhow, Buried City Hired Tainted Contractors," *Newsday*, 28 February 1994, p. 7.

51. U.S. General Accounting Office, "Report to Selected Members of Congress: Mass Transit Grants, Noncompliance, and Misspent Funds by Two Grantees in UMTA's New York Region" (January 1992).

52. Henry Jacoby, *The Bureaucratization of the World* (Berkeley: University of California Press, 1973); Ralph Humel, *The Bureaucratic Experience* (New York: St. Martin's Press, 1987); David Nachmias and David H. Rosenbloom, *Bureaucratic Government USA* (New York: St. Martin's Press, 1980); Victor A. Thompson, *Bureaucracy and the Modern World* (Morristown, N.J.: General Learning Press, 1976); Philip B. Heymann, *The Politics of Public Management* (New Haven, Conn.: Yale University Press, 1987); Herbert Kaufman, *Red Tape: Its Origins, Uses, and Abuses* (Washington, D.C.: The Brookings Institution, 1977).

53. The civic involvement model also conflicts with proposals of administrative discretion made by the "reinventing government" movement. That movement is based on a model of the citizen as consumer of public goods, and on competition between public managers and private contractors to provide public goods and services. Missing from this picture is public integrity. With neither the apparatus of the anticorruption project (tossed out with the rest of public bureaucracy), nor civic engagement, the vagaries of market competition—an ineffective corruption deterrent in the private sector—is all that remains to check self-dealing. For those functions less amenable to competitive bidding, like zoning and planning, not even that unreliable check would be available. Osborne, *Reinventing Government* and Donald F. Kettl, *Reinventing Government? Appraising the National Performance Review* (Washington, D.C.: Center for Public Management, Brookings Institution, 1994).

54. Petrus van Duyne, "Organized Crime, Corruption, and Power," Conference on Corruption in Contemporary Politics, European Studies Research Institute, University of Salford, Manchester, England, November 14–16, 1996, p. 30.

36

American and German Fund Raising Fiascoes and their Aftermath

Holger Moroff

In the mid 1980s somewhat analogous scandals in the United States and Germany brought leading politicians close to indictments and criminal proceedings for bribery and corruption. Some fifteen years later a political rerun of the two national party finance dramas came to be staged. This led to the type casting of Helmut Kohl in Germany as an unrepentant violator of German party finance rules he himself helped put in place, while one of the chief actors in the U.S., Senator John McCain, became known as a convert on the road to Damascus and the White House, sounding the virtues of campaign finance reform from his bandwagon. The two politicians had been implicated in earlier fund raising fiascoes, which triggered extensive debates about political finance and corruption in both national arenas. Thus at the turn of the millennium the German Christian Democrats (CDU) experienced their worst crisis after revelations of secret accounts of its former leader Kohl, while in the U.S. the Republicans became deeply split over these issues.

The original ethical contests, partly setting the stage for the subsequent ones, are the main focus of this study, which looks at complex patterns of alleged political corruption that took place in the two countries independently of each other. One is the German Flick case of the early 1980s and the other one is the "Keating Five" case in the U.S., unfolding in the late 1980s. Both can be viewed as cases of *institutional corruption*[1] in the sense that they were either so pervasive that all established parties were involved as in Germany, or the actions of individual senators were rather indicative of general patterns of supposedly corrupt practices in Congress.

The first part gives a brief account of the two cases in question and identifies parallels and differences of the actual occurrences, that is to say, the exchange processes of political goods for monetary goods. The purpose of the money involved and the ways of channeling it are the main themes of establishing and recapitulating the facts of both cases. Subsequently, these facts are related to three areas of the respective political systems. First, why did the incidents take place in the *political arena* they did and what influence did the *party systems* have? Second, how can these cases be interpreted in a *constituency responsiveness* model? Finally, what is the history of their repercussions on political finance attitudes and practices in both settings, exemplified by the recasting of former Chancellor Helmut Kohl and presidential hopeful Senator John McCain?

Despite the many aspects of political corruption the basic definitional denominator applied here is derived form J.S. Nye's definition of corruption as "behavior which deviates from the formal duties of a public role because of private-regarding pecuniary or status gains; or violates rules against the

Table 36.1
Relevant Systemic Differences between the United States and Germany

	USA	Germany
Systems of government	Presidential	parliamentary
Chief executive	popularly elected	elected by parliament
Compatibility of executive office and membership in legislature	non-compatible	compatible and usual
Bureaucratic resources of legislature (staff)	own (shadow) bureaucracy 16,000 staff members	no equivalent (1200 staff) apparatus, relies on ministerial bureaucracies
Executive posts filled by politicians with prior legislative career	only sometimes	almost always
Constituency	single member districts (Senate 2 member district)	1/2 proportional representation, 1/2 single member district
Constituency responsiveness of representatives	through individual reps in their home districts	through parties
Political finance	candidate centered (private, except for Presidential elections)	party centered (about 1/2 public)

exercise of certain types of private-regarding influence."[2] Some case-relevant differences of the two political systems have to be kept in mind while reviewing and assessing their more particular details. The table below provides a succinct though by no means comprehensive overview of these differences.

The Flick Case

The Flick case[3] is usually looked at from two angles. The first and broader perspective is that of Flick's role in party finance in general and his political influence over the parties his industrial concern supported. The second and narrower one deals with the specific issue of political bribery.

From 1969 up to 1980 Flick donated a total of 26 million Deutschmarks to all four parties represented in the Bundestag, out of which 15 million went to the Christian Democratic Union (CDU) and the Bavarian Christian Social Union (CSU), 6.5 million to the Free Democrats (FDP), and 4.5 million to the Social Democrats (SPD).[4] These donations had neither been declared to the federal revenue service nor were they accounted for in any party records, which clearly violated the laws on party finance at that time. Some of the money was destined for a particular wing of a party[5] or even earmarked for individual politicians. Especially within the ranks of the FDP and the CDU one could speak of hand-picked politicians, who were singled out by Flick and his political manager in Bonn, von Brauchitsch. Thus Helmut Kohl as leader of the CDU opposition received 565,000 DM directly as cash in brown envelopes between 1974 and 1980, some of which was given on his behalf to commendable party members Kohl wanted to promote. In light of developments in late 1999 and Kohl's own admissions this general practice was never discontinued even throughout his sixteen years as Chancellor. Such offerings could also entice and soften the surrender of power as was the case with CDU chairman Rainer Barzel whose resigning in favor of Kohl was facilitated by a consultantship with a law office associated with the Flick concern, which paid Barzel about 1.7 million DM. Beyond that, it has been shown that Flick's and others'[6] funding of the right wing of the FDP helped precipitate the change of coalition partners from the SPD to the CDU in 1982.

The other side of the Flick affair concerns a case of direct bribery for purely financial and not political gain, which puts it onto a more particularistic plane. In 1975/76 Flick sold his share in Daimler-Benz stocks, which brought him a total revenue gain of almost two billion Deutschmarks. Any such profits had to be taxed, unless the economics ministry in consultation with the finance ministry agreed that the reinvestment of the money serves the national interest and can thus be tax exempt. In this way Flick could avoid paying some 800 DM million in sales taxes. The tax waivers were granted in three installments over the period from 1976 to 1981.

Beyond such an unprecedented scale some of the tax waivers could hardly be justified and one decision had to be reversed in 1983 under the pressure of the investigation with the ministry admitting it had made a mistake.[7]

How were the FDP, SPD, and CDU brought to acquiescence? The FDP was in great financial difficulties during the early 1970s and accrued a debt of more than 10.5 million DM with one Swiss bank alone. During that time the leader of the FDP, Hans-Dietrich Genscher, and the economics minister of the years 1975–76, Friderichs, sought in informal consultations with banks and large businesses massive financial support. Von Brauchitsch donated on behalf of Flick three million DM to the FDP. Over the whole five year period during which the three tax waivers had been granted Friderichs received 315,000 DM directly from him. Similarly, donations were made directly to Graf Lambsdorff once he took over the economics ministry from Friderichs, thus a payment of 40,000 DM was made out to him in early 1980 and an additional 40,000 to the finance minister Hans Matthöfer (SPD). Von Brauchitsch notes also reveal the actions undertaken by leading FDP politicians in Flick's favor and the difficulties they encountered with "independent" civil servants in the ministries. Genscher, for instance, mentioned that he had a handle to influence a tax expert in the finance ministry, who was unfortunately also "a puritanical justice fanatic."[8]

As for the acquiescence of the CDU opposition similar methods were used. To preclude any resistance from the ranks of the CDU von Brauchitsch contacted the party leader, Kohl, and noted down that "Kohl suggests he will make sure that the left wing of the party won't emotionalize the tax issue negatively . . ."[9] During that time period Kohl received direct donations of 150,000 DM.

The final verdicts of the ensuing court case were announced on 16 February 1987. There were three defendants in the trial: Eberhard von Brauchitsch, the general manager for Flick and his holding company, Otto Graf Lambsdorff, and Hans Friderichs, both former economics ministers and FDP party treasurers. They were accused of bribery and tax evasion. The first charge was dropped for lack of evidence, but all three were convicted of tax evasion.[10]

Helmut Kohl maintained that all cash donations given to him before personally had been turned over to the party treasury. This version saved him before the investigating committee and in the public opinion. The treasury's plenipotentiary who confirmed this version at the time, now admits to having lied about it in order to save Kohl's chancellorship. In fact, it appears, Kohl disposed of these funds freely ("Der Spiegel, Oct. 2nd, 2000, p.22")

The parliamentary investigation committee, after interviewing virtually all leading politicians with indeterminate results, could not make out a case of individual bribery either, and reached essentially the same conclusion as the court did with the exception of a dissenting opinion by Otto Schily (the Greens) where he renders it as a clear case of political corruption:

By means of donations the Flick corporation has systematically gained spheres of influence, so that it must be stated that political corruption on a large scale is involved, regardless of whether the punishable act of bribery or corruptibility has been realized in one case or another. By means of the conspiratorial money distributed by the Flick corporation, the benefiting parties gained a remarkable financial advantage compared to their political competitors. The fact that these donations were concealed from the public is a massive intervention into the process of the formation of political opinion.[11]

The "Keating Five" Case

Charles Keating was the owner of a California thrift institution, Lincoln Savings & Loan, and was being investigated in the mid-1980s by the Federal Home Loan Bank Board.[12] At the same time Keating substantially supported the election campaigns of several politicians, among them five U.S. senators, who, in turn, rendered considerable "constituency" service to him by pressuring administrators of a federal agency, namely two successive chairmen of the Federal Home Loan Bank Board, Edwin Gray and Danny Wall. The most serious charges revolved around two meetings in April 1987 where the senators pressured Gray to make concessions that would help Keating save his ailing savings and loan. This delayed action against him and thus accounts of depositors could be further depleted. The subsequent failure of Lincoln cost the American taxpayer $2.6 billion alone. Together with a whole stack of other thrift failures it was the costliest bailout in American history.

As in the Flick case, many activities can be distinguished, ranging from broad interest group lobbying to seeking very particular favors for only one's own company. The overall support for ideologically like-minded politicians and broad issues was in accord with a whole branch of industry, like Keating's efforts to make direct investments of savings and loan companies legal; on the other end of the spectrum are his attempts to influence the way his firm was examined and how he tried to expedite and obtain administrative clearance for the sale of his savings and loan company when it hovered on the verge of bankruptcy. The often invoked degrees of darkness or blackness of various forms of political corruption[13] are also reflected in the gamut of Keating's requests. This mix of legitimate pressure group activity and highly particularized "constituent service" is in good part responsible for definitional pitfalls of political corruption in a legislative context.

The five senators who provided substantial support for Keating with members of the Federal Home Loan Bank Board were the Democratic senators Dennis DeConcini (Arizona), Alan Cranston (California), John Glenn (Ohio), Donald Riegel (Michigan), and the Republican senator John McCain (Arizona). Keating's links to these senators date back to the time before he acquired the California savings and loan company, Lincoln, in 1984.

)

Most of Keating's contributions did not go directly to the senators' campaign accounts. As the Senate Committee notes:

> [M]ore than 80 percent of the funds at issue were not funds raised by candidates of Senate or House campaigns under the Federal Election Campaign Act. Rather, such funds were undisclosed, unregulated, funds raised for private organizations with political activities, political "soft money" and a non-federal political action committee.[14]

No outright illegal contributions were ever made, as in the Flick case, and the mode of finance was also a different one. Whereas all the money Flick donated was his own, Keating collected and bundled contributions and thus fulfilled a broker function, laying claim to the thus bundled money and giving substantial sums himself as well.

In the 1980s Charles Keating, his associates and friends contributed $85,000 to Senator DeConcini, $242,200 to Senator Glenn, and $78,250 to Senator Riegel.

Senator McCain received from Keating $56,000 for his two House campaigns in 1982 and 1984 and $56,000 for his Senate race in 1986. Their families had vacationed together at Keating's home on Cat's Key in the Bahamas from 1984 through 1986, underpinning a personal friendship. The senator had also used Keating's corporate plane multiple times, paying $13,433 for his travels only after the scandal had broken.

Senator Cranston received over all $1.4 million out of which $250,000 were solicited by Cranston as soon as Danny Wall was named Gray's successor as the new Chairman of the Federal Home Loan Bank Board, whose views were more favorable towards the S&L industry as a whole.[15] And another $250,000 were given by Keating to USA Votes and Forum. This payment was discussed during a meeting in which Cranston promised to arrange for a get-together between Keating and Wall. After that meeting took place in January 1988 Keating handed him personally $500,000 in contributions for two voter registration groups affiliated with Senator Cranston. All this resembles a "mutual aid society" in which active soliciting of senators is matched by an unreluctant willingness to pay by Keating. There seems to have been no pressure or duress on either side.[16]

The most spectacular "show of force" took place at a meeting between the senators and Bank Board Chairman Gray on April 2nd, 1987. Gray testified that he was told to bring no aides, and the senators inquired why the investigation of Lincoln and their "friend" Keating was taking so long.[17] In this context it is important to recognize the considerable regulatory powers enjoyed by the Senate's Security and Exchange Commission. Gray was dependent on them not only in a renomination process but also for budget appropriations, ironically urgently needed to take over troubled S&Ls. Given these dependency structures, it is not surprising that Gray said he felt intimidated by this show of force.

Nevertheless no evidence of direct linkage between contributions and political actions could be established, despite written evidence of linking the two. All senators were found by the Senate Ethics Committee to have acted on Keating's behalf as a constituent and could have acted likewise solely on the basis of the case's merits. It was the *appearance of impropriety* that led it to rebuke all for "poor judgment" and reprimand Senator Cranston for mixing fundraising so blatantly with "constituency service." Here it is important to note how the Senate Ethics Committee defines a constituent:

> As a resident of Arizona, Mr. Keating was a constituent of Senators DeConcini and McCain. Moreover, Mr. Keating's company, American Continental Corporation [ACC] (parent company of Lincoln), employed approximately 2,000 Arizona residents and was the largest home builder in the state. Senator Cranston had an interest as a member of the Banking Committee and because Lincoln employed hundreds, and held deposits of thousands, of people in California. Senator Riegel also had an interest as a member of the Banking Committee. In addition, ACC [Keating's company] had invested approximately 37 million dollars in a downtown Detroit hotel and had plans to pursue another significant Detroit development project. Finally, with respect to Senator Glenn, Mr.Keating was an Ohio native and ACC was an Ohio chartered corporation.[18]

It is plain that only McCain and DeConcini could claim Keating as a constituent in the traditional sense as a member of the electorate in an official's district. To put forward such a broad definition, as the Ethics Committee does, lacks clear distinctions. For it does not only encompass a separate economic constituency but could also comprise financial constituencies, ideological and religious constituencies, "old boys" constituencies, party and media constituencies, and so forth.

However, as a defense strategy the claim of constituency service is of utmost importance in the U.S. setting, for it provides a handle to justify particularized and personalized interventions by legislators on behalf of their geographically confined electorate. Attempts to go beyond this clearly delimited group and to construe one kind of constituent relationship or other were made by all the five of "Keating's Senators." Whereas the concept of constituent does not travel well to Germany's parliamentary system with its proportional representation, here a constituency is often seen as the section of the electorate voting for a particular party. Also, it has never been explicitly evoked by the implicated politicians as a legitimate reason for intervening on Flick's behalf.

Parallels and Differences, Variations on Similar Themes

At the core of both cases lies the exchange of monetary goods for political ones. On the monetary side of the transactions both took place in the realm of political finance. Though some of the money involved was given directly to individual politicians, this money was, as far as the evidence goes, used for political purposes and no private gain such as personal enrichment of politicians seems to have played a major role, not at least because of the general affluence of the politicians involved, which stood in clear contrast to the financially strained party political institutions they led.

An obvious difference in this area is that Keating's contributions were all legal, whereas a substantial part of Flick's donations evaded the tax authorities as well as reporting requirements and were thus illegal. Likewise, Flick's payments were cached and part of a collusive scheme where only the benefiting politicians knew about the source and amounts of money. In contrast, Keating's methods were not clandestine at all: one could trace amounts and destinations of his contributions, even though 80 percent of his contributions were so called "soft money," given to affiliated organizations and non-federal PACs without any reporting obligations. On the other hand, the origin was not quite so clear. Keating was a "bundler" of donations, though contributing substantial sums through his own corporations as well. His importance and influence depended on how successfully he could raise money and support for "his" politicians. Sorauf notes that Keating apparently brokered contributions of friends, family, employees, and associates for senators or their personal PACs:

> The relationship is three-sided with advantages for all, but with greater advantages for the mediating broker. [. . .] Charles Keating's much-chronicled brokering on behalf of the savings-and-loan industry provides an illustration. The broker in such cases is again the big gainer; even though his cash contributions may be no greater than that of his fellow contributors, the candidate's gratitude, and whatever flows from it, is disproportionally his. [. . .] The brokers' interests are those of the contributor writ large, and their many brokerings make themselves into an influential elite that some have called the new fat cats of American campaign finance.[19]

The broker's and thus Keating's special role in political finance is difficult to relate to Flick's ways. The absence of such a highly developed PAC infrastructure in Germany precludes this indirect mode of support and influence. Also, the high profile and publicity of the American fund raising events contrasts sharply with the low profile finance activities in the German setting.

Even if one took the position that political money constitutes a private gain since it is used to secure an income-providing public office, one would have difficulties viewing money contributed to a party or partisan voter registration groups as personal gain of the politician on whose request or through whose channels the money was funneled. A further similarity consists in the fact that neither Keating nor Flick were obtrusive in their financial offerings. Both had been approached by politicians who actively solicited their contributions.

*Electoral Affinities: How Coincidental are Financial and
Personal Relations?*

Active seeking of contributions combined with overburdening financial
strains characterize both groups of politicians. But while the business community was the "natural," that is ideological, constituent of the FDP, this can
not be said of the American liberal Democrats. They might be described as
ideologically remote from the businesses that supported them, but practically
close, reflecting the possibility of differing voting and financial or lobbying
constituencies. However, if the set of political convictions is far removed
from those of the "constituent" and his cause, then politicians face a much
greater credibility problem. Thus the direct donations of Flick to the SPD
treasurer Naumann were deemed less permissible by the CDU-led Bundestag
investigative committee than those to Helmut Kohl on grounds of the much
longer history of support and ideological like like-mindedness with the latter.
Likewise, Republican Senator McCain was perceived as less culpable than
the other four Democratic senators.

It is also a common feature that both cases involved particular policy areas
which can be described as the sphere of industry and finance, whose natural
constituents are those heavily involved in either business or banking activities
like Flick and Keating respectively. Certain policy and administrative areas
are more corruption-prone than others due to the enhanced opportunities for
immediate financial gains or losses associated with political decisions in
these policy fields.

Both contributors were lobbyists in a sense that they sought to influence
policy decisions, for the most part legislation. This form of influence seeking
will be called input influence according to the stage of impact and as opposed
to output influence that targets the administrative process of law implementation and regulation. Allegations of corruption did not arise with regard to
their input oriented lobbying activities. Only where they tried to influence
policy implementation at the executive level were questions and eyebrows
raised. Still, these are cases of political and not bureaucratic corruption, even
though they ultimately aimed at the bureaucracies. In the German Flick case
the corrupt activities were directly executive-centered from the beginning,
whereas Keating tried to exert pressure on the administration indirectly via
the influence of senators.

An immediate reaction to the Flick affair were two unsuccessful attempts
at granting a general amnesty to all implicated politicians and businessmen.
Public outrage, a disapproving press, The Greens, and many backbenchers of
the established parties forestalled theses attempts. Supposedly "impractical"
and overly rigid laws were blamed for the parties' "misconduct" and in 1984
the party law was changed, making financial contributions to parties largely
tax deductible, thus legitimizing former illegal practices and favoring large

donations. This policy response was also condoned by the constitutional court (BVG) and judged permissible in 1989, exculpating earlier practices in this way. This position was partly reversed in a 1992 decision that abolished tax deductibility of contributions and lowered their limits. This reflects the court's half-century long swaying and mediating between two principles, namely that of guaranteeing an equal voice of citizens in the political process and that of *Staatsferne* (parties' distance from the state), prohibiting parties from becoming state dependent entities through public financing of more than 50 percent of their expenses. Whereas in the U.S. such a debate has been precluded by the Supreme Court's *Buckley v. Valeo* decision, conceptualizing and protecting campaign contributions as free speech, though permitting donation limits where "corruption" could threaten the political process. However, the Keating Five scandal led to entrenching the "appearance standard" as an indicator of impropriety, which the Senate Ethics Committee invoked for their reprimands and sanctions.

A further similarity is that all implicated politicians continued their careers, Lambsdorff even becoming FDP party chairman, Friderichs CEO of the third largest German bank, Genscher continuing as foreign minister for another decade, and Helmut Kohl going on to become Chancellor not least

Table 36.2
Parallels and Differences

Parallels	Differences Flick versus Keating
events take place in the realm of political finance on the one hand and in the sphere of economic policy on the other	illegal vs. legal financial contributions
money used for political purposes and partly given to politicians directly	party vs. candidate focus
active solicitation of contributions	"bundler" vs. single donor
long established personal relationships with multiple transactions before corrupt actions	directly executive-centered vs. indirect influence via legislators
great financial needs of involved politicians and parties	verdicts of tax evasion vs. reprimands for appearance of impropriety
business community as main financial constituent	low-profile sponsoring vs. high-profile fund raising
low consciousness of wrong doing on all parts	constituency service as vindication vs. blaming too rigid legal provisions
all continued their careers	"adjusting" party finance law to actual practices vs. establishing "appearance standard"

because he intended to protect the more vulnerably exposed FDP ministers from further prosecution. None of the five U.S. senators resigned over the affair, though the Western liberal Democrats turned into lame ducks, while the only Republican, McCain, survived the affair relatively untarnished, being in the best position to claim constituency service as vindication. Later on he could utilize it as a formative experience for his 2000 Presidential campaign against the influence of special interests in national politics.

The following table presents a brief overview of the cases' parallels and differences as a summary of the above discussion.

Embedding Interpretations in the Political Contexts

The Political Arenas

It has been shown that the two corruption cases aimed at manipulating essentially administrative decisions. Why did Keating and Flick not just try to influence, if not to bribe, the bureaucrats and regulators in charge of their cases? Considering that the only main obstacles lay within the respective bureaucracies, this would have been a more direct, faster, and probably cost-efficient way. However, one might object that a tax exemption amounting to nearly one billion Deutschmarks, as in the Flick case, was a minister's decision to make in any event, but ministerial approval would have been possible, if only the leading civil servants had assessed the deal as tax exemptable according to law. This was true even more so for Keating, since his requests lay entirely within the discretion of the responsible regulatory agency, the Home Loan Bank Board.

A direct one-time bribe would have borne out the prevalent theories of corruption in advanced industrial societies, which hold that the complexity of such societies requires pervasive bureaucratization and formalized economic and political interactions leading to impersonal exchange processes. Secondly, it would also confirm what has been known about lobbyists' ways of pressuring, which are mostly rendered as "bottom up" strategies: to go through the prescribed channels and stages of the responsible authorities until resistance is met, then the "top down" strategy is pursued, from the political superior down to the administrative level of blockage.[20] But this was not the way Keating or Flick chose to operate.

It may very well be that the outcome of their attempts to influence would have been the same if they had bribed the right bureaucrats. However, direct bribing also involves a direct corrupt intent, whereas exerting influence through politicians could always be rationalized as legitimate interest representation, which it was in both cases. Furthermore, in both countries the statutes on bureaucratic bribery are much more stringent and straightforward than those on legislative corruption.[21] As for Germany, it had not even had a law against bribery of members of parliament until 1995 and even that covers only crude cases of vote selling. Also, the politicians in question were long time lobbying targets of the two businessmen, a circumstance indicating that it is a small step from legitimately influencing the formation of policies on the legislative input level to the illegitimate and corrupt manipulation of the executive output or implementation level.

Three conditions facilitate and invite taking the political rather than the bureaucratic road to influence. First, it is almost impossible to prove corrupt intent. Second, the lack of "legal infrastructure" governing the field of political decision making (this lack is not least due to contesting theories of democracy and representation); and lastly, the vaguely defined boundaries of political finance and lobbyism, make for a preferred use of the political rather than the bureaucratic venue of corruption.

Legislative and executive interaction differs considerably between the American and German systems of government and the same political channels have varying meanderings. The parliamentary system of the Federal Republic provides for a direct link between the legislative and executive bodies in form of personal union. Thus making redundant any subtle detours of seeking influence with the administration through members of parliament, and arriving at the desired goal by contact with the top executive and party leadership. Another, more German, peculiarity is the extent to which consensus government is practiced through an "integrated" opposition. It finds its expression especially in a cooperative parliamentarism, with only 10 per cent of the legislation passing without the "opposition's" approval.[22] From the perspective of influencing legislative and to a lesser extent also executive processes a broader, all encompassing strategy must be pursued. These circumstances are reflected in the hedged bets and general "cultivation of the political landscape" practiced by Flick.

Turning to the American scene of legislative-executive relations a trend towards legislative dominance can be discerned since the mid-1970s, which explains in part the mediating position key legislators play when it comes to the accommodation of special interests. Against this backdrop of possibly shifting balances of power, variously in favor of the executive, the legislative, or the judiciary, much like a pendulum swinging in a three dimensional circular way, one has to view recent developments in the composition and number of power centers.

A further commonality between the two governmental systems are the great leverage politicians have on members of their respective bureaucracies. Either through extensive nomination, confirmation and budget appropriation rights politicians can influence the top layer of the administration as in the United States, or one finds that mainly party-book bureaucrats gain access to the highest administrative posts as in Germany. This additional device of political "micromanagement" was applied in both corruption cases considered here, drawing attention to the respective party systems and hierarchies to which I turn next.

Power of Parties and in Parties

In the introduction it was already mentioned that candidate-centered campaigns are typical of the American scene. Since the introduction of open primaries, state and regional branches of the two parties lost much of their nominating control and it reinforced the two main parties' tendencies of being campaign platforms for any candidate who happens to win the primaries. Thus the two big American parties are much more open and permeable than their German counterparts.

Loose national and organizational structures also affect the capability of parties to mount effective election campaigns. In this sense, each candidate for federal office is his or her own campaign manager and boss of his or her geographically limited party organization. All this leads to a structural decentralization. A contested direct primary ordinarily requires an ad hoc candidate organization, and once up and running such organizations tend to be carried over into subsequent general election campaigns.

In Germany, on the other hand, nominations are an intra-party affair, strongly influenced by the leadership of that party. What is more, electoral arrangements and the parliamentary system call for close party union as a precondition for successful campaigns. Though local and state (Länder) politics are the most common pools of recruitment for the national party leadership, there exists a top-down party structure, providing for congruence on all levels. Politicians move up through adaptation and loyal party support and can not expect to gain any advantage from an independent anti-Berlin attitude (analogous to the often invoked anti-Washington attitude). In contrast to the United States, a steeper hierarchy, greater centralization, and party oligarchy-centeredness instead of candidate-centeredness prevail. The necessity of a permanent party organization and coordination is also given by the incessant campaigns in the 16 federal states. One of the leading positions concerning the large party administration is that of party treasurer, procuring money for the party bureaucracy, its permanent administrative staff, and for election campaigns on all levels and for all candidates on the party ticket.

While the procurement of political money is institutionalized within the German parties through the office of treasurer, each American candidate has to round up sufficient funds him or herself. But even within the relatively flat American party hierarchies positions of leadership exist and carry certain responsibilities, among them also a party wide financial procurement responsibility, though not as far reaching as that of German party treasurers. Thus it is not unusual for members of Congress, particularly those who are or aspire to be party leaders or presidential candidates, to have their own PACs and affiliated non-profit organizations promote their efforts by raising money for other candidates and party organizations. Here also, as demonstrated for the political system, parallels between the American and German party systems can at least be drawn along the intra-party flow of money and power.

Despite public finance provided for German parties since the late 1960s it could not quench their thirst for money. Corporate and labor donations were sought with the same intensity as before the introduction of public finance. A second variable is the existence of donation limits. During the 1970s limits on tax exempted contributions as well as reporting requirements existed in Germany but were laxly enforced and easily circumvented as the Flick methods and the number of indicted corporations using similar channels show. Though once these illegal practices were prosecuted everyone was vulnerable. On the other hand, it is important not to overemphasize these illegal donations; they were still only a fraction of what conveyer organizations and business associations such as the *Staatsbürgerliche Vereinigung Köln, 1954 e.V.* contributed during that period.[23] In the end, virtually all 204 million Deutschmarks channeled through this association between 1969 and 1980 were illegal also, since most of the money was given in order to be transferred to and earmarked for individual politicians within a given party. Though abolished in 1982, some, if not all, of the remaining funds of the *Staatsbürgerliche Vereinigung* seemed to have found their way into secret accounts of the CDU in Switzerland. Thus, in December 1999 the CDU in the state of Hesse admitted that they alone had a secret Swiss bank account of more than 20 million DM. In earlier times, earmarking and direct business contributions bypassing the associations was not welcomed or condoned; only after the introduction of public party finance in 1968 were these more particularistic strategies pursued. It is detrimental to party unity and intra-party loyalty if individual politicians are singled out for special financial support by external associations and businesses, which thus undermine what little intra-party democracy there might exist. Which was one reason why backbenchers withdrew their support for amnesty in 1982. This effect is of no relevance in the American setting where independence of party is rather an asset than a liability for a candidate's success.

In contrast, U.S. law provides for ways to bypass its stipulated and comparatively much lower limits on campaign contributions. The system intends to promote a large number of small donors instead of a few big ones, but, it is also conducive to intricate networks of PACs pooling their limited contributions and channeling them into the election accounts of a particular politician, or to big business owners pressuring employees to donate a certain sum for which they will be reimbursed unofficially on their paycheck. One effect of these pooling, bundling, and channeling techniques is the emergence of professional fund-raisers and brokers like Mr. Keating. Given the absence of such a closely knit PAC infrastructure in Germany one could certainly relate the activities of the *Staatsbürgerliche Vereinigung* to the practice by American businesses that are financing an individual politician's PAC or "campaigning" for him or her through parallel issue ads.

Constituency Responsiveness: A Theoretical View

To help conceptualize the corruption cases in question it is important to put them into theoretical perspective. Depending on one's theory of democratic representation a member of Congress or the Bundestag could either be viewed as a trustee or delegate, which can be further broken down into trustee or delegate of an election district, of the whole country, or of the socioeconomic strata from which most votes are drawn, or, finally, of a financial constituency of political financiers. There can be considerable overlap among the various "constituencies," and a politician's mode of representation seems to incorporate elements of both fiduciary and delegate behavior. The legislators mixing both styles of representation to fit political circumstances have been called *politicos* and about half of American congressmen and women and their German counterparts said that this was their style when questioned.[24] Thompson also speaks of mixed and multiple motives a legislator acts upon. They act "for the benefit of particular constituents, for the good of the whole district or state, for the good of the nation, and for their own interest in reelection or future political ambition."[25] One might read into Thompson's analysis a certain hierarchy of representation in the sense that the nation's good comes before the district's good, which, in turn, comes before the benefits of an individual constituent and so forth.

The following table shows an overview of the possible forms and components a representative's responsiveness can take on and how it might be viewed in a black, gray, and white gradation of potentially corrupt interactions. Demands placed on an elected deputy vary with the different *constituencies* to whose needs he or she must respond (with the financial constituency being considered least legitimate when attaching "strings" to their money, and thus running counter the democratic concept of equal opportunity in political participation). The mode of response, on the other hand, varies with the self-image of the representative. It depends on whether he or she sees him/herself acting as a *delegate*, taking up those demands and arguing for them in a lawyer's fashion; or whether the representative acts as a *trustee*, aggregating and weighing those demands with a view to a "common good." Such a purely fiduciary posture is as scarcely found as is its opposite; they serve as ideal types to spread out the analytical frame.

Ideally, the official stage of societal and interest group influence in a democracy should be the *input* level of policy debate and formulation, through which to participate in the deliberative process.[26] However, intervening with the bureaucracy on behalf of a constituent (of whatever nature) is as time

Table 36.3
Types of Political Responsiveness and Constituencies in Light of Different Modes of Representation and Stages of Intervention

Constituency	Delegate		Trustee	
	input	output	input	output
district	white	white	white	gray
party	white	white	white	gray
socioeconomic	white	white	white	white/gray
financial	gray	gray	gray/black	black
ideological	white	white	white	gray

honored as there has always existed a large discretionary latitude in implementing and administering legislative decisions. This *output* "manipulation" becomes even more prominent as one considers the rise of cooperative or informal administrative decision making in a decentralized system, moving away from a strictly hierarchical chain of command and compliance.[27] The following matrix categorizes politicians' intervention on behalf of five different constituencies at two different levels of government (input and output) and taking into consideration the two ideal types of representation (delegate and trustee). Depending on the combination of these variables and conditions, politicians' behavior is viewed in various shades of potential corruptness.

The column generally associated with undue influence is the last one concerning output or implementation oriented decisions in light of a trustee theory of democratic representation; these cases are almost always seen as corrupt when coupled with a fiduciary style of representation. It takes place in the natural realm of the executive bureaucracy, and when it takes on an additional high degree of particularization, that is decisions to the advantage of only a few or one individual, it is definitely considered corrupt. All other combinations can be rationalized in one way or another as legitimate forms of representation or constituency service. It is thus not surprising that the Keating and Flick incidents occurred in the field of the only truly black combination, the field where a financial constituent tries to influence administrative processes.

Scandalization efforts are fairly successful when the involved politicians are self-professed "purists," subscribing to a fiduciary mode of representation and politics at large. Then the "moral height of drop" is much greater. It is difficult to judge whether a representative acted as delegate or trustee in case of ideological overlap with the person on whose behalf he intervenes, which often involves a form of friendship where personal relations and interactions are concomitant features. As Loewenberg points out, "[m]any legislators are sufficiently similar to their constituents that they notice no difference between their own views and those of their constituents."[28] In turn, this subjective perception phenomenon makes it impossible to prove a corrupt intent if there is a chance that a politician could have acted the same way had there not been any financial inducement. It is the problem of establishing that an office holder, despite diverging views, engaged in behavior which was sought by one or a group of his financial constituency. This predicament lies at the heart of the "appearance standard" embraced not only by the Senate Ethics Committee but also by jurists, and even the German court couched its very lenient verdicts in similar terms, implying that there is no effective legal handle to such cases.[29]

How to Treat the Flawed Nexus?

At the height of the Keating Five controversy, former Senator William Proxmire proposed that members of Congress should refuse to accept campaign contributions from the special interests over which their committees have jurisdiction.[30] Proxmire stressed that under this "modest" reform proposal, congressmen could still accept contributions from persons or organizations who did not work in or for industries over which the member's committee assignment had given them special power—the "unique power to push legislation through Congress that will bring, for example, millions of dollars of benefits to banks, savings and loans, real estate firms, and housing developers."[31] Proxmire describes the congressional response to his proposal thus:

> The legislators said I was playing to the wild public prejudice that all Members of Congress are on the take. Was I serious? You better believe I was serious. Here is the heart of the problem: After serving 31 years in the Senate, every day of that time on the Senate Banking Committee, eight years as chairman, I am convinced good moral people serve on that committee.
> I am also convinced they are sincerely, honestly hypnotized by a system of thinly concealed bribery that not only buys their attention but frequently buys their vote. The special interests that make these contributions know exactly what they are doing. They know exactly what changes they want to make . . . Any Senators or House Members who believe they are getting this big money because the lobbyist admires their character or personality are kidding themselves.[32]

The strong reaction to Proxmire's proposal shows also how unrealistic it is to break the ties linking a policy community together and how impractical his suggestions are. One of those ties, campaign contributions, underpin commitment and indicate an identity of interest and financial constituencies as well as providing a means to participate in the input deliberations of the democratic process. His demand would also have had a serious impact on the lobbying "industry," which essentially would have been prohibited from contributing to those office holders they want to influence most. Secondly, the reaction Proxmire describes points to a sort of "perception trap" among the involved politicians, who think their judgment unimpaired by their financial proximity to the industry they regulate. This phenomenon is not unlike that encountered in the analysis of "functional" friendship relations, where the critics stress the instrumentality of that relationship and those involved point to the like-mindedness and personal responsibility in form of constituency service. Here the degree of informality, long term and personal relations play into the notion of what could be honestly perceived as friendship, or just cloaked up and rendered to the public or the prosecution as such an ideologically congenial community within which the flow of money is more coincidental and concomitant than formative, which was how both Flick and Keating painted the relationships with "their" politicians.

Thus it was all the more surprising that a decade later the once "ex-Keating" Senator McCain should take up the suggestions of his former colleague Proxmire, making the break up of the "iron triangle" between special interests, politicians, and bureaucrats the key slogan of his bid for the Republican presidential nomination in 2000. However, his Keating "incident" did not figure prominently in the campaign as an occasion for conversion, though when questioned about it he showed himself to be an active repentant and compared the ordeal he went through in the scandalization process to his prisoner of war experience in Vietnam. On the other hand it did not form a lasting bottleneck for him and his cause either, since he could claim constituency service as a vindication with greater success than any of his four colleagues. He used this defense again when charged in January 2000 with accepting political contributions from Microsoft, Bell South, US West and Viacom, all companies that were likely to have business before the very Senate Commerce Committee McCain chaired at the time.[33]

His campaign portrayed him as the knight-errant of American politics who bravely aimed his lance at special interests and the establishment at large, but his support for overhauling political finance dates back to 1996 when the McCain-Feingold bill was first introduced as a bipartisan effort to close loopholes involving soft money and issue-oriented television advertising expenditures. Although passing in the House it fell afoul of Republican-led filibusters in the Senate in four consecutive years, last in October 1999. This measure was much criticized by McCain's Republican colleagues with Phil Gramm commenting that "his views on campaign finance reform would make us the minority party for 25 years."[34] Also, many academics doubt that the McCain-Feingold bill could actually be administered by the Federal Election Commission or otherwise.[35]

This is exactly the opposite of what the German political scene represents at the turn of the century. Revelations of secret party financing schemes of the CDU, which closely resemble those of the Flick days and even date back to the early 1980s, suggest a seamless continuation of old habits despite all legal and perfunctory remedies that had been put in place as a reaction to the

Flick affair. It turns out that Helmut Kohl used extensive private slush funds filled by donations of so far unknown contributors to build up his own support structure within the CDU and undermining potential intra-party rivals. This served him in securing his twenty-five-year long party leadership. Amid all these revelations, triggered by an investigation into an arms trading deal that also seems to have involved secret contributions to the CDU, Kohl had to step down as honorary chairman of the party in December 1999 because he proved himself defiantly uncooperative in subsequent attempts at shedding light into the affair by his successor as party chairman, Wolfgang Schäuble, who sought to bring about a catharsis through "unrestrained disclosure." However, Schäuble himself did not survive this undertaking and was forced to resign as chairman and party whip by a rank and file revolt that could not endure seeing the statue of the former leader Kohl being dismantled and turned into a symbol for disregard of fundamental democratic principles.

Kohl and Schäuble came full circle from their first governmental endeavors in 1982, when Kohl delegated the task of bringing about a general amnesty for all politicians implicated in the finance affair to Schäuble. These attempts were only forestalled by public outrage and backbenchers withdrawing support, feeling that their own leadership had deceived and circumvented them as well as the rules of intra-party democracy. The second time Schäuble had to deal with such a scandal in early 2000, he chose disclosure over coverup and amnesty, also because an attempt at the latter would have been futile since only his own party seemed implicated. The factual parallels to the Flick affair are rather striking. In a general ambit of secret party funds and donations available only to certain politicians like Kohl the allegation of venal ministerial decisions also arose and led to the institution of a Bundestag investigation committee in December 1999. The only remarkable difference lies with the role of the press. The Flick affair was almost exclusively scandalized by one German weekly, *Der Spiegel*, and it was thus much easier for those politicians involved to brush all allegations aside as an isolated attempt of an insurgent paper agitating against the government and engaging in "character assassination" while the rest of the media kept their *raison d'état* posture. Two decades later all major national dailies took their stab at investigative journalism and joined in the scandalizing process, reducing the prospects for successful counter accusations and scandalization significantly.[36]

Looking at the aftermath of the Keating and the Flick affairs, at first glance it seems the Germans had got their act together in providing a new legal framework and developing a precise jurisdiction after the mid 1980s, thus precluding major debates on issues of corruption over the next decade. Even though in the U.S. the debate on "soft money," PACs and undue influence of special interests would not ebb in the 1990s, no attempt at providing a legal infrastructure was successful. This was one element in turning McCain into an "anti-establishment" hero, which would serve him quite well in his campaign for the presidential nomination, against Governor George W. Bush, who made extensive use of the flexible U.S. campaign finance provisions and outspent McCain handily while being flanked by parallel issue ads from his main Texan contributor. Despite the double victories of the party favorites in both camps, the two major parties' presidential nominees, Bush and Gore, could not ignore the topic McCain used in galvanizing a large number of independent voters.

The party maverick McCain who reacted with candor and frankness to "his" affair, even testifying as a chief witness against his former friend and contributor Keating in a subsequent criminal trial, forms a stark contrast to Kohl's survival strategy of cover up, counter scandalization and undeterred furtherance of his "arcane empire." While Kohl tried to stay on as honorary chairman of his party, McCain eventually ran against the Republican Party leadership, alienating many of his senatorial party colleagues of whom less than half a dozen endorsed him and his presidential aspirations.

The disregard for party finance laws enacted by the CDU itself came home to roost when in February 2000, Bundestag President Wolfgang Thierse imposed a DM 41 million fine on the party for violating donation reporting requirements. The *Land*-election in Hesse also became subject to judicial review one month later because of DM 1.5 million from secret Swiss accounts which had been used in the CDU's election campaign. It has yet to be confirmed whether the ministerial decisions had been venal, and whether the charge of the Geneva prosecutor that DM 100 million was paid in commissions by the French oil concern Elf Aquitaine in relation to a refinery privatization in the early 1990s would be substantiated. If so, the belief of the former EU commissioner Karel Van Miert would be confirmed that high level corruption and bribery was involved in this deal.[36]

Although viewed as the worst crisis in the CDU's history, it seemed to spare the party the fate of its Italian sister party, which fell apart after its vast corruption networks had been uncovered. Even though the scale of the CDU's corruption scandal might have reached "Italian dimensions," it appears that it lacked a comparable scope, for only some top leaders seem to have been involved and kept the system in place while it did not constitute such a pervasive trait on all levels as was true for the Italian Christian Democrats. Even so, this time Kohl's reaction was not repentance but a forward strategy of publicly collecting donations in order to make good the financial damage he inflicted upon his party without naming the original contributors, and thus placing his "word of honor" above the German constitution. By admitting to having accepted DM 2.1 million in secret contributions since 1993 he made the party liable for a DM 6.3 million fine, an amount he had already rounded up in new and legal donations by March 2000, thus suggesting the affair to be finished while at the same time hoping to avoid a criminal investigation into the nebulous charge of acting in bad faith to the detriment of the CDU by reimbursing the fines levied upon it.

One set of outcomes of the two national developments of the year 2000 were rather similar. Where McCain forced the debate about special interests, lobbying, and ultimately corruption onto the presidential campaign agenda in the U.S., the sheer force of events surrounding the secret finance history of the CDU during its sixteen years of governmental power under Kohl propelled these issues onto the German political agenda even more strongly. But another set of intermediate party outcomes were strikingly different. In Germany, a large cohort of party leaders who had served with and under Kohl suffered from his disgrace thus leading to a wholesale replacement of the national party leadership. This was exemplified by the selection as CDU party chairperson of Angela Merkel, who had led the campaign to disavow Kohl and then became both the first woman and the first politician from an East German Land to become head of a major German party. In the United States by contrast, the inability of Senator McCain to displace Governor Bush led to a confirmation of the Republican Party establishment.

The fact that the American party finance debate gained so much momentum in the U.S. without a trigger as a major corruption scandal might be rooted in even more profoundly historical soil than merely in the contemporary party system that happens to lend itself to insurgent anti-establishment campaigns.

Comparing the elite political cultures of the two countries, one postwar German inheritance was a theme of perpetual mistrust of "the people" by the "state-propping," state building, and state sustaining class, who often claimed a higher cause—the stability of Germany itself—which then might have justified "lower means."

The German *leitmotiv* of the elites mistrusting "the people," while "the people" seem to harbor less suspicion in return, is projected upside-down in the American setting. The general mistrust of (big) government is a pervasive and a deeply rooted phenomenon of American political culture which can be traced back to its constitutional debates that focused on questions of how to avoid the abuse of power. Many of *The Federalist Papers* are dedicated to the question of how to protect the people from an arbitrary government, and not how to protect the government from an erratic and arbitrary people. Hence awareness of potential corruption is greater, and builds on a more than two-century-old theme in American political discourse

Notes

1. This view of institutional corruption differs from Thompson's (1995) definition in so far as he takes institutional corruption as undermining the democratic process, whereas it is argued here that it might very well be an outgrowth of a certain

theory and practice of the democratic process itself. Especially when the central tenets of a pluralistic theory of interest representation through delegates are applied. (See also Burke's discussion of Thompson and Cain in this book)

2. Nye in Heidenheimer et al. (1989), p. 966.
3. This review draws mainly on the renderings of the Flick case by Landfried (1994), and Noack (1985). For a concise English review see Glees (1987), von Alemann in Heidenheimer et al. (1989), or Blankenburg et al.: In Heidenheimer et al. (1989). A detailed account is given by the Bundestag committee's documentation: cf. Deutscher Bundestag, Drucksache 10/5079.
4. For the exact amounts per year and party see Landfried (1994), p.205.
5. Landfried (1994), p.151.
6. Investigations for illegal party donations were also conducted into Bosch, Commerzbank, Deutsche Bank, Dresdner Bank, Henkel, Karstadt, Kaufhof, Melitta, Mercedes, Otto-Versand, Porsche, and Siemens. This underpins the assertion that Flick's donation practices were by no means exceptional.
7. For the details of the deal see Landfried (1994), p. 190–192.
8. Landgericht Bonn, 27 F 7/83, sentence from 2/16/1987, p. 159.
9. Bundestag-Drucksache 10/5079 from 2.21.1986, p. 41: quoted in Landfried (1994), p. 195.
10. *Frankfurter Allgemeine Zeitung*, Feb. 17th, 1987.
11. Deutscher Bundestag, *Abweichender Bericht des Abgeordneten Schily zum Bericht des 1. Untersuchungsausschusses*, Drucksache 10/5079, supplement 1, p. 19.
12. The following account of events draws mainly on the report of the Select Committee on Ethics of the United States Senate: *The Investigation of Senator Alan Cranston*, S.Rep. No. 223, 102d Cong., 1st Sess. (1991) [hereafter KEATING REPORT].
13. See Heidenheimer's white, gray, and black corruption model (1989), p. 161. Thompson (1993) also talks about a chiaroscuro and degrees of darkness, p. 369.
14. Keating Report, p.16.
15. In a note to Cranston by his campaign finance chief it reads: " [The Bank Board Chairman's] views are good news to Keating. You should ask Keating for $250,000." See Keating Report, supra note 19, p. 22.
16. *The Washington Post*, Dec 5, 1990, A 23.
17. Thompson (1995), p. 39.
18. Keating Report, p. 14.
19. Sorauf (1992), p. 126. He likens these new brokers to "old time" party treasurers who fulfilled essentially the same functions.
20. Smith (1995), and *Die Zeit*, July 30, 1996, pp. 3-4.
21. Eser (1997), pp. 660.
22. von Beyme (1993), p. 184.
23. Ibid., p.135.
24. Davidson (1969), p. 117.
25. Thompson (1993), p. 375.
26. Habermas (1998), pp. 383.
27. Benz (1992), p. 34
28. Loewenberg (1979), p. 180.
29. Morgan (1992), pp. 593–600.
30. Proxmire: "Take the Pledge: No More Special Interest Money" in: *Roll Call* , Sept. 17th, 1990, p. 5
31. Ibid., at 5.
32. Ibid.

33. *The New York Times*, Jan. 7th, 2000, A16.
34. Quoted in *The Economist*, Feb. 19th, 2000, p.49.
35. see Brent Thompson, "A Flawed Institution Should Not Expand" in: Anthony Corrado et al. (1997), *Campaign Finance Reform: A Sourcebook.*
36. Recent books written by some main figures in the Flick affair like von Brauchitsch (1999) and Schäuble (2000) as well as those journalists who helped uncover the latest Kohl affair have provided further impetus for the debate. Von Brauchitsch dubs the party finance affair and calls it the "protection money affair", thus conceptualizing his role as one who saved industrial interests against a "business hostile" political class that was encroaching on the free economic sphere and had disregard for the free market principle.

The journalists of Süddeutsche Zeitung who helped uncover the recent Kohl party finance affair, Hans Leyendecker et al. (2000), contextualize this as a seamless continuation of the conservative daily Frankfurter Allgemeine Zeitung, Günther Nonnenmacher ed. (2000), a CDU member of the Bundestag, scolds Kohl for his October, 2000 reunification speech, implied that his breach of the constitution, by not naming his financial supporters and thus placing his "word of honor" above the constitution, was a minor misdemeanor compared to the SPD's "betrayal" of the sublime goal of reunification.

References

Beyme, Klaus von. (1993). *Die politische Klasse im Parteienstaat.* Frankfurt a.M.
Benz, Arthur and Wolfgang Seibel (eds). (1992). *Zwischen Kooperation und Korruption: Abweichendes Verhalten in der Verwaltung.* Baden-Baden.
Corrado, Anthony et al. (1997). *Campaign Finance Reform: A Sourcebook.* Washington D.C.
Davidson, Roger. (1969). *The Role of Congressmen.* New York.
Ebbinghausen, Rolf et al. (1996). *Die Kosten der Parteiedemokratie–Studien und Materialien zu liner Bilanz staatlicher Parteien-finanzierung in der BRD.*
Eser, Albin and Michael Überhofen (eds). (1997). *Korruptionsbekämpfung durch Strafrecht: ein rechtsvergleichendes Gutachten zu den Bestechungsdelikten.* Freiburg i.Br.
Glees, Anthony. (1987). "The Flick affair: a hint of corruption in the Bonn Republic" in: *Corruption and Reform* 2: 111–126.
Habermas, Jürgen. (1998). *Faktizität und Geltung: Beiträge zur Diskurstheorie des Rechts und des demokratischen Rechtsstaats.* Frankfurt a.M.
Heidenheimer, Arnold J., Michael Johnston and Victor T. LeVine (eds). (1989). *Political Corruption: A Handbook.* New Brunswick.
Landfried, Chritine. (1994). *Parteienfinanzen und politische Macht—Eine vergleichende Studie zur Bundesrepublik Deutschland, zu Italien und den USA.* Baden-Baden.
Leyendecker; Hans et al. (2000). *Helmut Kohl, die Macht und das Geld.* Göttingen.
Loewenberg, Gerhard and Samuel C.Patterson. (1979). *Comparing Legislatures.* Boston, Toronto.
Morgan, Peter W. (1992). "The Appearance of Propriety: Ethics Reform and the Blifil Paradoxes" in: *Stanford Law Review* 44: 593–621.
Noack, Paul. (1985). *Korruption—die andere Seite der Macht.* München.
Nonnenmacher, Günther ed. (2000). *Gespendete Macht. Parteiendemokratie in der Krise.* Berlin
Pflüger, Friedbert. (2000). *Ehrenwort-Das System Kohl und der Neubeginn.* Berlin.

Schäuble, Wolfgang. (2000). *Mitten im Leben.* München.

Smith, Richard A. (1995). "Interest Group Influence in the U.S. Congress" in: *Legislative Studies Quarterly* 20(1): 89–139.

Sorauf, Frank J. (1992). *Inside Campaign Finance, Myths and Realities.* New Haven.

Thompson, Dennis F. (1995). *Ethics in Congress: From Individual to Institutional Corruption.* Washington D.C.

Thompson, Dennis F. (1993). "Mediated Corruption: The case of the Keating five" in: *American Political Science Review* 87(2): 369–381.

Part XI

POLITICAL PARTIES
AND CORRUPTION

Introduction to Part XI

Political parties pose a special dilemma. They are on the one hand the political structures that are most frequently linked to perceived patterns of political corruption. Yet they are also the components of political systems whose relationship to corruption phenomena academic analysts find most difficult to generalize about in a consistent and refutable manner.

The factors underlying this dilemma are on the one hand conceptual in manner, and on the other, institutional and contextual in nature. These are some of the problems.

Some basic ingredients of corruption phenomena, such as the exchange of public goods for private advantage, are in many ways also the essence of what keeps parties in business. Votes are partly won by symbolic issues related to civic projects, but frequently also by how public expenditures can be directed to the material advantage of target groups of voters and/or potential donors to party campaign funds.

Parties require funding for upkeep and campaigns, and there are pervasive problems about whether and how corrupt tendencies are embedded in party donations and campaign fund-raising. Is a proven quid pro quo an absolute prerequisite for linking donations to corruption? Or may indirect economic benefits also be considered grounds for scrutinizing evidence of "corruption or the appearance of corruption"? The German and American constitutional courts have weighed decisions in this arena somewhat differently, partly due to the way particular rights were anchored in their constitutions. The German constitution recognized parties explicitly, and requires equality of policy outcomes, in ways that are not found in American jurisprudence. Hence decisions on the acceptability of limits on political donations and campaign expenditures have differed, which in turn has affected whether particular types of payments to party and politicians might be suspected of being scrutinized as potential cases of corruption.

Our analysis of party involvement in corruption commences with an article on Italy, in good part because this is the country whose longest lasting post-war head of government was buried abroad as a convicted criminal. This fate came about not because regime enemies came to power, but rather as the result of relations which revealed that the organizations of the leading government parties were largely dependent on pervasive kickbacks and collusion through which most parts of the Italian private and public sectors found that these occult means of exchange were a necessary part of daily operations.

Dellaporta and Vannucci demonstrate that resort to these techniques was not so much an abuse linked to the growth of mass parties as a reflection of the domination of all levels of government by networks of party officials that in effect levied the equivalent of informal tax or insurance payments. Sometimes the parties were allocated projects for monopolistic exploitation, as in the case of the Liberal party in Naples; at other times the side payments from huge project like the Milan subway had to be divided through negotiation among the party treasurers of several parties.

The consequences of Italian money political corruption scandals of the 1990s led to a more critical examination of pervasive practices of questionable exchanges involving parties in quite a few other European countries. The uncovering of exploitative connections involving parties was pursued with vigor also in France and Spain. A comparison of the developments in these three national settings constitutes the basis of the comparative article by Pujas and Rhodes. They ask why corruption also developed in the less entrenched Spanish party system, where public subsidies to political parties had been expanded even more generously. They go on to uncover evidence as to whether the extent of corruption linked to public work contracts and public sector management found in Italy could also be substantiated for the other two countries.

They do find a smaller array of corrupt practices in France due partly to a lower level of "colonization" of state institutions by the parties, and to the bulwark constituted by the professional ethos of career civil servants. Deconcentration of political power away from the central national agencies became popular in all three countries, but they varied in how the relaxation of central controls led to increased administrative corruption.

Somewhat surprising distinctions become apparent when comparison focuses on how specific kinds of parties were found to be involved in corruption revelations. It was not surprising that a party which had been continuously in power for many decades, like the Italian Christian Democrats, was deeply incriminated. More surprising was the way in which some parties of the center left, like the Socialist parties in all three countries, were hurt by the corruption revelations which surfaced as a consequence of prosecutorial investigations in the 1990s.

Comparison of party-corruption relationships is extended in the article by Heidenheimer to both a larger number of countries and to a longer time frame. He asks how writers on parties at the opening of the twentieth century saw such relationships manifested in Europe and America, and traces bow these were altered. Attention is focused on the changing scope and nature of party finance patterns, and how regulation by legislatures and courts affected how the interface between corruption and party financing developed differently in several European and Asian countries. He seeks the reasons why the place of the United States, as the country with the worst record in the anchoring of party finance in corruption, came to be usurped by the 1990s by certain countries in the old continents – particularly Italy and India – as countries where high party and campaign expenditures went hand in hand with high incidence of corruption throughout the political system.

The focus on Italy is thus continued from the preceding articles, but other countries are also highlighted in complementary contexts. Thus the German and British cases are examined with reference to the question of whether the introduction of large-scale public financing of parties affected comparative corruption rankings. Also scrutinized is whether systems with differently prevalent party system types—such as cartel or mass parties—are more visibly vulnerable to higher prevalence of political corruption.

If weak or stalemated party systems are linked to corruption, can healthier, competitive ones help control it? Michael Johnston considers this question at a macro level, using statistical evidence to consider patterns across eighty countries. Governments that stand to lose power because of corruption would seem to have a strong incentive to keep it within limits, while opposition parties could make good governance a cornerstone of their own electoral appeals. But in practice the connections are not so clear: the *quality* of competition and the depth of its institutionalization matter a great deal. There are many democracies—Japan and Italy, to name two prominent examples— where competition has tended to take place within parties rather than between them, or where groups of parties collude to share power. Factions and coalition partners that are never really wholly in, and never altogether out of power, are less likely to be punished politically for corruption, and have fewer incentives to move strongly against it. Indeed, corruption may be what holds the coalition together. In other countries, such as the United States, parties are apparently competitive at the national level, but not in the local districts where campaigns are organized and (in large part) funded—again, reducing any corruption-restraining properties of political competition. The data suggest that the benefits of competition are most apparent where democracies have been institutionalized for a long time, and where competition is balanced and election results are decisive. But given the limitations of aggregate data—and particularly, of corruption measures—these results must be treated with considerable caution. For now, they help frame and refine important questions for further work on corruption and party systems.

37

Corrupt Exchanges and the Implosion of the Italian Party System

Donatella della Porta and Alberto Vannucci

When Bettino Craxi, leader of the Italian Socialist Party (PSI) since 1976 and prime minister of the longest-lived government in Italy's post-war history (between 1983 and 1987), rose to speak in the Chamber of Deputies on 3rd July 1992 he was a political leader in grave difficulties. To understand why it is necessary to take a short step back in time, to February 17th 1992. In Milan Mario Chiesa, Socialist president of a municipal old people's home, the Pio Albergo Trivulzio, was arrested while accepting a small bribe. Thirty-five days later Chiesa began to collaborate with the magistrates, setting off a chain of confessions which resulted in indictments against a great many businessmen, bureaucrats, and politicians, all of them closely associated with the country's ruling political elite. Although most of the political parties were implicated in the scandal, Craxi's Socialist Party was from the outset the hardest hit. In the summer of 1992, as the party's Milanese exponents fell one by one, the investigation approached the national leadership.

Craxi was still an influential figure when he took the floor of the Chamber on July 3rd. His speech, to all intents and purposes an act of self-incrimination (the magistrates later called it an "extra-judicial confession of the offences [he had] committed"), sketched out a political line of defence which he would stick to firmly throughout the following months and years. In more general terms his attempt to play down the significance of the scandal with the generic declaration that "everybody knew" what was going on came to sound like an indictment of the functioning of the democratic system itself.

"The political parties," Craxi claimed, "have been the body and soul of our democratic structures. . . . Unfortunately, it is often difficult to identify, pre-

717

vent and remove areas of infection in the life of parties. . . . Thus, under the cover of irregular funding to the parties cases of corruption and extortion have flourished and become intertwined. . . . What needs to said, and which in any case everyone knows, is that the greater part of political funding is irregular or illegal. The parties and those who rely on a party machine (large, medium, or small); on newspapers, propaganda, promotional, and associational activities . . . have had, or have, recourse to irregular or illegal additional resources. If the greater part of this is to be considered criminal pure and simple then the greater part of the political system is a criminal system. I do not believe there is anybody in this hall who has had responsibility for a large organisation who can stand up and deny what I have just said. Sooner or later the facts would make a liar of him" (TNM, 87–8).

The "*mani pulite*" investigations continued and Craxi was backed into an ever tighter corner until, on 12th January the following year, the decisive blow—in the shape of a first, richly documented request to Parliament for authorisation to proceed against him—was struck. The testimony of numerous businessmen and members of his party confirmed the former premier's personal involvement in the administration of corruption. The party treasurer "presented him with the 'budget' for illegal funding from business" and "obtained his approval for it." Craxi in person urged party members holding office in the public administration "not to sit there keeping the seat warm, making it clear that they were expected to procure votes and funds for the party from the exercise of their functions." He reminded one entrepreneur that "'you had to put two billion on the table to get into the game', 'getting in' referring to the possibility of being considered for public contracts." Craxi also gathered information on corrupt activities of opponents within his own party so that he "could keep them in line" (CD, n. 166, 13/1/1993, 48; CD, n. 210, 5/3/1993, 8 and 14). Forced to resign as Socialist Party secretary on February 11th 1993, and violently contested on every public appearance, Craxi took refuge in his Tunisian villa, in Hammamet, a few months later. He continued to reside there with an international warrant for his arrest and prison sentences hanging over his head until his death in January 2000. His daughter scornfully rejected an offer from the Italian government to allow him to be buried in Italy.

In its development, the "clean hands" investigation brought about the most serious political crisis in the history of the Italian Republic, quickly extending to the uppermost levels of political and economic system. In a matter of months, the magistracy had opened a breach on a scene of corruption and political illegality without precedent in the history of the Western democracies, involving the entire political class of the country and broad sectors of its business community. The investigation reached the highest levels of the public administration and affected most areas of the state's activity. More than 500 former parliamentarians were implicated, many former ministers, five former premiers, thousands of local administrators and public functionaries, the army, the customs service (responsible for investigating financial crimes in general), the main publicly-owned companies and even sectors of the magistracy itself. The equilibrium that had long characterised Italian politics was swept away. After forty-five years of uninterrupted government the country's largest single party, the DC, was eclipsed along with its leaders, accompanied by the other parties of the ruling coalition, the PSI included. An idea of the sheer size of the investigation can be gleaned from the statistics for corruption and extortion accusations: between 1984 and 1991 the average ran at 252 cases a year involving 365 individuals; between 1992 and 1995 it increased to 1,095 cases involving 2,085 individuals. In the last of these years 1,065 accusations were made involving 2,731 persons. The Public Prosecutor of Milan has, between 1992 and October 1996, produced 2,319 demands for formal charge related to corruption crimes (Procura di Milano, 1996).

On the bases of those investigations, we shall discuss a main issue for the analysis of political corruption: the role of political parties. In the first part, we describe the changing role of the political parties in situation of systemic corruption, focusing in particular on the distortion in the institutional policy making which corruption brings about. In the second part, we analyze the supply of political protection which can be "produced" and exchanged by political parties through corrupt transactions. In the third part, we look at the development of "consociational" agreements between different political par-ties—mutual pacts of reciprocal protection against scandals. In the conclud-ing part, we compare our results with the information available on other countries, focusing especially on the central question of the cost of politics in contemporary democracies. In particular, we would emphasize that previous interpretations have concentrated prevalently on the "visible" side of the party, neglecting what has taken place in the "hidden" party structure.

1. Traditional Party Functions and Corruption

Political corruption, as a means by which money influences politics (Key 1936), depends upon the characteristics of the principal actor in the political system: the party. Samuel Huntington, in particular, has linked the develop-ment of corruption to party weakness during phases of growing political participation. Corruption spreads in those specific paths to modernisation in which popular participation in political decision-making is not immediately accompanied by a strengthening of those institutions which should filter and direct collective demands: "the weaker and less accepted the political parties, the greater the likelihood of corruption" (Huntington 1968, 71). Apparently in contradiction to this hypothesis is the widespread belief that corruption is favoured by the ubiquity and omnipotence of the parties, powerful and well-organised political machines capable of controlling civil society and the mar-

ket. In Italy, *partitocrazia*, a concept derived from the political science literature, has been taken up in the press and in political debate to stigmatise the
ills of the "First Republic." Participation in covert transactions transforms the
ways in which the parties fulfill their traditional tasks, acting on their three
main functions: the selection of personnel, the integration of the citizenry,
and the formation of public policies.

As far as the *selection of political personnel* is concerned, in a functioning
democracy politicians must be capable of elaborating general programs, convincing citizens of their benefits and putting them into practice. The rewards
will be public: appreciation, power, and prestige should count for more than
material advantage. With the development of political corruption, however,
the characteristics of the political class are transformed, as the parties begin
to select those individuals most proficient in the organisation of illegal financing. In a public structure where information circulates concerning the
gains which can be made in certain positions from bribery it is to be expected
that given agents will try to influence the internal decision-making process in
order to occupy these positions, spending both their own resources and, where
possible, those of the organization. In other words, the institutional mechanisms for selecting political and bureaucratic personnel are altered in favour
of individuals with fewer scruples and who are willing to "invest" in creating
influence: "Thus many more teams will be formed to capture control of
Government, and each team will employ more factors of production in its
political activities—more, that is, than if there were no corruption revenue
expected from being the government" (Johnson 1975, 54). In this way political corruption leads to the proliferation of actors who do not properly belong
either to the state or to the market and therefore "violate" the rules of functioning of both. The party selects business politicians, who use administrative
positions for private, material aims (della Porta 1992; Pizzorno 1992, 27).

A second function of political parties is the legitimation of the political
system through the *integration of citizens*. In a democracy, the parties are the
principal actors in the structuring of the vote, creating electoral identifications
which are frequently maintained over generations. The structuring of the vote
takes place by the definition of programmes which are then proposed to the
electorate. The search for the highest number of votes should lead the various
parties to represent the opinions and interests of particular groups of citizens.
The diffusion of corruption would seem, however, to transform the structure
of electoral preferences: rather than the vote of identification or opinion, the
cliental use of the vote as an object of exchange prevails—vote in exchange
for favours. Political corruption produces, in fact, a value system oriented to
the fulfillment of individual objectives through interaction based on extrinsic
or instrumental benefits at the same time as it discourages "ideological" types
of relations based on intrinsic or expressive benefits. We can say, therefore,
that political corruption, by encouraging the diffusion of a structure of prefer-

ences oriented to individual mobilisation, erodes the effective capacity of the parties to integrate, select and mediate citizens' interests. In Italy the use of corrupt practices has reduced the capacity of the parties to mobilise ideological resources and distribute participatory incentives. While political analyses, including those on the Italian case, have normally underlined the negative consequences of the excessive use of ideological incentives by political parties, the recent investigations by the magistracy lead to an emphasis on the risks attached to the opposite condition: the excessive availability of material incentives.

A third function of political parties in a democracy is *the formation of public policy*: in a functioning democracy the parties have the job of defining the direction of public policy and controlling its implementation. Concentrating on the organisation of corruption the parties have privileged instead those decisions most "productive" in terms of *tangenti*; the tendency is to spend most in those sectors where controls are weakest. Political mediation is the filter through which interests are articulated and aggregated, and its task, as Pizzorno has pointed out, is "to identify and interpret the needs and desires of the population; select and generalize those which can be expressed in political terms; propose, justify and criticize policies and measures to achieve these ends or, when necessary, to explain why they cannot be satisfied" (Pizzorno 1992, 22). When political corruption is systemic, the parties' discretional management of public spending often becomes an objective *in itself*. The aim of administrators is to attract as large a quantity of resources as possible to the areas where they have power in order to pocket a fee for mediation in the form of a bribe and/or gain support as a result of the effects of public investment on employment (treated as a sphere for clientelistic exchange). Public spending is therefore diverted to those sectors where gains from corruption are greatest and in which the discretional nature of the procedures reduces the risks involved. In general, little attention is paid to whether the needs of the collectivity are served by these works or services. Public demand may remain unsatisfied in this context if the politicians involved do not find the amount offered by way of bribes sufficient.

2. Political Parties and Political Protection

On some occasions entrepreneurs or other private actors engage in bribery not to obtain a specific advantage but rather a more general political protection of their rights, either within corrupt exchange or in everyday relationships with the state. A firm "twinning" with a centre of power generally hopes to obtain protection in its dealings with public institutions, discourage competition and protect itself from the dangers of being cheated in corrupt exchanges. According to the ex-President of the INADEL, Nevol Querci, hidden exchange sometimes takes place on a one-off basis (with immediate payment) while in other cases protection is based on a long-term "contract": "All acquisitions were from entrepreneurs for whom the party had given me the go-ahead. In some cases the entrepreneur paid directly to the national secretariats of the parties, and afterwards I would be given the green light. In others, they paid the money directly to me" (TNM, 76). Political guarantors, as the national secretariats of the parties, have the power to prevent or settle disputes arising with regard to both legal and illegal activities: bribes unpaid, services promised but not performed, the non-fulfillment of contracts or inadequate protection of rights through state inefficiency (Vannucci 1997). Those acquiring protection reduce the uncertainty involved in future transactions and contacts with the state, counting on the fact that someone will intervene on their behalf should any problems arise. Such uncertainty is extremely high in both the illegal market of corruption and in relations with a state sector characterised by inefficiency and/or a lack of transparency in decision making.

If the actors of corruption realize that their relationship has a wider expected duration, with a sufficient frequency of contacts, *ties of greater density* may be profitable between certain political actors and their "clients." A number of entrepreneurs—specialised in satisfying public-sector demand—have then shown an interest in establishing (only thinly disguised) *long-lasting relations* with centres of political power, particularly with political parties. In their turn, the latter press for a long-term contractual relationship whose object is a wide-range protection of the firm in its dealings with the public administration. In this sense, "the party system in Italy was not a *participation* system anymore, having become a *protection* system. Joining a party was not aimed at participation to public activity, but at being favoured, backed up, *protected* in one's own private activity. A good politician, especially at the local level, was mainly a good protection supplier" (Pizzorno 1996, 269).

Numerous corrupting firms were in fact distinguished by a *party label*. In return for the informal use of this "trademark"—which ensured a stable and prolonged influence on public decision-making—party enterprises provided stable finance for that particular centre of power. With these political ties firms can plan future investment and activities with greater certainty, without having to overcome "political" obstacles. The Milanese cashier of the Socialist Party, Sergio Radaelli, recounted that he had been approached by an entrepreneur who was looking for protection: "He gave me a white envelope filled with money. . . . He simply said: 'I have good relationship with the party, but I am not able to meet the mayor'" (TM, 59).

The *personal* component which characterizes many illegal relations becomes less important in such cases: a collector for bribes (the administrative secretary, or someone else trusted by the party leadership) is secretly selected within the party and firms then deal with them, regardless of the individual delegated at any particular moment. Bribes paid to the cashier of the party for this more general guarantee rather than a specific service are, to all intents and purposes, a "tax" paid to political protectors, either at a fixed rate or in proportion to profits. Augusto Rezzonico, a member of the DC, recalls: "Many entrepreneurs came with money asking to be introduced within institutional organs . . . The Right Hon. Citaristi [party administrative secretary] was the person who managed relations between the enterprises and public bodies in order to establish a privileged channel of access to public contracts" (*Panorama*, 6/12/1992, 47).

The sums of money paid by "contributors," then, become a kind of "insurance policy" taken out against the difficulties and obstacles which may arise for those maintaining periodic relations with public bodies—a "contract" to be taken up only where required: to unblock a particular dossier, silence an over-zealous inspector or speed up a given operation.

Illegal by definition, there can be no legal recourse for settling disputes within the market of corruption. The risk of being "sold a lemon" in such a situation can become extremely high, also because the transaction is generally non-simultaneous in nature and one party must rely on the word of the other. Having secured their payoff politicians might fail to deliver what they promised; an entrepreneur, having won the contract, may forget to pay the bribe promised. Fear of being "sold a lemon" may result in otherwise profitable transactions being passed up and a demand for protection will arise. By handing a *third party* the power to sanction agreements and intervene to discipline the market both corrupted and corrupters protect themselves from any improper behaviour by the other party. Where this demand meets someone both willing and able to satisfy it, a portion of the money from the market of corruption will go to this external guarantor who, being a sort of "judge," has the power to resolve disputes and inflict sanctions. In such cases the bribe split into two parts, each having a distinct destinations and paying for a distinct service. Correspondingly, such market is organized into two levels: in the first specific benefits are exchanged with bribes; in the second, the Milanese magistrates remarked:

> Those who demanded (or received at least) these sums retained only a part, and that not always. More often they were also forwarded to other more powerful politicians who, regardless of whether they held public office, were or would be guarantor on those directly responsible for success in the tender and in the management of the contract, because of their influence over those who did. (CD, n. 266, 13/4/1993, 2)

In other cases, bribes were paid to political parties in order to guarantee *protection from other corrupt agents*. Even a extortionists' gang has an interest in maintaining exclusive control over their victims, preventing that others take advantage of them: "Protection is primarily against the one who offers it, but it has to include protection against rival taxing authority" (Schelling 1984, 185). A similar process occurs in the market of corruption: more powerful politicians protect their "clients" against demands for bribes from others because in doing so they can collect a greater amount with lower risk. Thus, in a context of widespread corruption *one* subject may be paid simply in order to avoid paying many and paying continually. The entrepreneur Angelo Simontacchi claimed, for example, that "paying at the level of the national secretariat allowed [him] to refuse the demands of individual local politicians" (*Il Giornale*, 14/1/1993, 4). When the *public* and *impartial* protection offered by the state's laws is uncertain or ineffective, the *private* and *selective* protection offered by a given centre of power may appear more convenient and effectual. The growth of the public sphere has multiplied the occasions where citizens or businessmen have an interest in asserting their right to certain public services or resources, or in entering contractual relationships with the state. Lack of confidence in the efficiency and impartiality of official procedures may then give rise to a demand for political protection. By paying bribes to those with long-term influence over the exercise of public power corrupters hope to prevent contention with the state or to resolve such contention in their favour.

3. Party Connivance: Corruption and Consociation

The distribution of public power frequently means that it is impossible for a single agent to offer the service demanded by a corrupter. When corruption is practised by a number of politicians in collaboration, centralised power management and a consensual division of the proceeds become necessary; power-sharing brings the risk of contention, reciprocal denunciations and judicial investigation if disagreements arise (Harendra 1989, 507). As long as those involved are all subject to a single centre of power (a party secretariat to whom all owe their election or nomination, for example) disagreements can be recomposed at that level. However, many decisions involve individuals from different parties, party currents or factions, who are not therefore subject to a single authority having the power to smooth over subterranean antagonisms and conflict. In such cases open conflict may well lead to disastrous consequences for all. If the likelihood of success in what are extremely contentious questions is outweighed by the likely costs of failure then the various power centres involved in corruption may seek an understanding based on a) a consensual and jointly managed division of the proceeds of corruption, b) a long-term division of public power into spheres of influence, this division being cemented by mutual silence over their corruption.

In concrete terms such agreements are sometimes based on a fixed distribution of public contracts among firms based on the colour of their political protection (or to consortia whose composition reflects the relative weight of

the various power centres) or on distributing payoffs according to the electoral strength of the parties involved (TRIB, 81). In others the agreement
takes place in an earlier phase and regards the powers employed in attracting
bribes rather than the proceeds. The management board of the ENEL, for
example, was composed of eight directors appointed by the political parties.
According to one "each director was responsible for procuring his own party
money. A tacit understanding was reached: each looked after their own back
yard and stayed out of the others' business" (*Panorama* 14/2/1993, 46). The
apportioning of offices among the various political parties therefore gave
each political actor control over certain, defined areas of public activity, areas
which were negotiated or arranged at a higher level. The former DC regional
councillor Luigi Martinelli reconstructed the tacit division made in Lombardy
between the regional secretaries of the DC and PSI, Gianstefano Frigerio and
Sergio Moroni:

> I remember that Moroni got particularly annoyed about the Mozzate refuse dis-
> posal site. I told him, as Frigerio instructed, that there was no use getting angry
> because the regional DC was in credit with the PSI for the period in which [he] had
> been regional transport assessor . . . [and] had not given anything from that to the
> DC. On this subject Moroni told me that he would happily have spoken to Frigerio
> about it . . . but that the DC, in turn, had given nothing from low-cost municipal
> housing. He likewise said that, in virtue of the last question, everything cancelled
> out. (CD, 27 July 1992, n. 66, 7)

In this particular case, the balance arrived at was the result of an unspoken
agreement. Other agreements, however, were more explicit. Luigi Manco, a
former communal assessor in Naples, confessed: "In what I can confirm was
the division of major public works among the parties, the construction of car
parks was considered a sphere of influence of the Liberal Party." When a
subsequent round of payoffs was due "De Lorenzo was not satisfied [with the
100 million]: he insisted that the Liberals should get a larger share because
they controlled the assessorship with the greatest input as far as car parks
were concerned" (CD, n. 386, 28 May 1993, 3 and 4).

There are also, of course, incentives for politicians to defect from such
agreements: if backed by the leader of the faction to which he belongs, for
example, a politician may try to hang on to the bribes he has collected
personally. The situations which can bring on a crisis are numerous: the
extension of corruption to new areas, the emergence of "rampant" and unscrupulous politicians demanding a bigger share for themselves, a hiatus
between changes in the balance of forces brought about by elections and their
recognition in the criteria for sharing out the proceeds of corruption. Any
temporary attenuation in the flow of public resources, moreover, heightens
internal conflict by placing established privileges into question. In the absence of a "court of higher instance" with the power of maintaining discipline, the tenacity (or fragility) of the equilibrium depends on a number of

factors—such as the frequency with which exchange takes place, and the easy detection of defection and the severity of punishment: "Enforcement of joint profit maximization in bribe collection is closely related to the problem of enforcing collusion in oligolopy" (Shleifer and Vishny 1993, 609). During the construction of Milan's underground, for example, "the question of public contracts created tensions—the DC exactor, Maurizio Prada, claimed—because the work could not be portioned out in such a way as to keep everybody happy . . . A race to find the 'best political sponsorship' therefore took place through the intervention of the national secretariats, certainly that of the DC and, as far as I am concerned, that of the PSI as well" (*La Repubblica*, 12/2/1993, 10). In fact, where one enormous business transaction is concerned there is a strong risk that the successful company will recompense only its own political protectors and ignore the others. The absence of an agreement among the politicians encourages competition between entrepreneurs to secure the most effective political guarantees. When the opportunities for corruption are recurrent, on the other hand, it is more likely that the proceeds will be peaceably shared out among the politicians involved.

The emergence of spontaneous forms of cooperation is also favoured by the prospect that the same political actors will stay in power over a prolonged period of time (Axelrod 1984). In the case being discussed, forms of coordination and communication did in fact develop between the various political actors thus allowing rapid counter-measures to be taken when disagreements or defections threatened. According to Vincenzo D'Urso (CD, n. 210, 5/3/1993, 10):

> the Rt. Hon. Balzamo [administrative secretary of the PSI] and Rt. Hon. Citaristi, administrative secretary of the DC, met frequently to define the best strategies for obtaining contributions from firms together . . . I understand that lately Citaristi and Balzamo were working on a common strategy for obtaining contributions from enterprises operating the 'high speed [train]' business and those who would operate in the 'light urban railway' business.

Insofar as there is full understanding between the various power centres, their action can be compared to that of a unitary organisation, a sort of 'super-party' coordinating the actions of corrupt administrators independent of their party affiliation. Giovanni Cavalli told the Milanese magistrates:

> Senator Severino Citaristi instructed him to keep an eye on what was happening in the environmental sector in order to ensure that a satisfactory equilibrium was maintained between companies 'friendly' to the DC and companies 'friendly' to the PSI and also in order to guarantee that there was a satisfactory division of the money coming from companies operating in the sector between the two parties. He proceeded by saying that he carried out this job in collaboration with Bartolomeo De Toma of the PSI. (CD, 5 March 1993, n. 210, 8)

In this way highly resistant, horizontal alliances form in certain areas or particular illegal transactions: "In Pescara—the entrepreneur Sergio Pelagatti claimed—what amounts to a business committee has operated since 1986 and still operates, cutting across party lines. It has decision-making power over all the activities of the commune and province . . . regardless of who is mayor or provincial president. Nothing happened, and nothing happens, without it being decided or approved by that committee" (CD, n. 330, 6 May 1993, 7).

In this situation, shared adhesion to the rules on payment minimises the danger of mishaps or contestation, facilitating reciprocal control and the avoidance of controversy. It is not by chance that the criteria for dividing bribery money between the different political parties or party factions were often regulated on a customary and agreed percentage basis. In the SEA of Milan, for example, considered a socialist fiefdom, the party took half, the DC 35 percent, the Italian republican party (PRI) 10 percent and the Social-democrats 5 percent (TNM, 46). According to the Socialist ex-board member of the National Electricity Board (Ente nazionale per l'energia elettrica, ENEL), Valerio Bitetto, management of tenders was shared with the DC, each party taking half of a bribe which varied, according to the type of work, from 2 to 3 percent. In this way occasions for conflict between corrupt politicians are reduced because it is easier to verify that the sum expected is that actually handed over. A Codelfa employee specialising in speeding up the firm's requests for payment to different public bodies thus states: "Asked to specify the method of establishing the amount to be paid, I should make clear that all the firms who dealt with those buyers operated in the same way. There wasn't, therefore, a system for knowing how much it was opportune to pay: *there was a recognized custom*" (VICM, 4, emphasis added).

The cashiers of the various parties co-ordinate the task of collection among themselves, reducing the amount of energy any one party needs to invest in occult exchange. The "municipal cashiers" in particular operated with each other in a coordinated way, taking it in turn to demand and collect bribes for all the parties and thereafter redistributing them according to precise (but unwritten) rules (della Porta 1993). Within the transversal structures which existed for the collection and distribution of illegal funds, the various party representatives even alternated in fulfilling the functions of cashier and redistributor. In complete consociational agreement, the "cashiers" of one party would occasionally carry out their activities in the headquarters of another or would meet together in order to redistribute the proceeds of bribery. Thus the figure of the "collective cashier" emerged. The "national cashiers" also met in order "to work out in agreement between themselves the best strategies for obtaining contributions from enterprises, even where this is in violation of the law on political financing" (CD, n. 210, 5/3/1993, 10).

In the Italian party system, the concentration of single parties on gathering illegal income has favoured the search for reciprocal connivance. On at least one point the fierce clandestine battles over the division of these funds was accompanied by a secret, non-belligerence treaty: the non-denunciation of the system of corruption. In a democratic system, political competition—in particular between the governmental party and the opposition—should in fact help deter "bad behavior" by politicians in power, limiting the willingness of public agents to indulge in illegal activities. The competition between different parties and individuals aspiring to govern (in order to fulfil the targets defined by contending programs) should help those who are most honest or more willing to denounce the illegal actions of others. Defeated parties and politicians should have a definite interest in exposing the misappropriation of resources on the part of those in government. In this way, citizens can acquire the necessary information to inflict electoral retribution on parties indulging in illegal business at their expense.

The dynamics of the Italian political system, however, have powerfully limited this possibility. For over forty years, the absence of turn over in the national government of the country has represented the principal "anomaly" of Italian democracy (among others, Pasquino 1985 and 1991). The very low expectation of change in the short term has made the discovery and denunciation of corruption more difficult. The strong ideological identifications of the electorate, moreover, have largely circumscribed its mobility, rendering voting behavior impervious to political scandals. The main opposition party, PCI, was strong enough to challenge the majority effectively, but not to take on direct responsibility for government. On the government side, the absence of turnover weakened the capacity for planning, favoring instead the immediate interest in dividing up and occupying public offices for clientelist ends [*lottizzazione*]. In the management of the public and semi-public agencies and in the enterprises with public capital, members of those very parties that had nominated their protégés inside the administrative bodies were in charge of the institutional controls. As one of them explained, "In practice and beyond the bureaucratic procedures that were legally established, the names listed [for the nomination in the administrative body of the MM] were those chosen by the party secretaries, that is by those who are the final receivers of the bribes" (TM, 36). Consociational agreements extended to those bodies who had to control the functioning of the public administration.

The opposition's strength could however not be ignored in either general or distributive political decisions precisely because of the weakness of the government coalitions and the fractionating of the parties. Continuous negotiation was necessary to avoid the danger of paralysis through obstructionism and head-on conflict. At the same time, the opposition (with no immediate prospect of winning power) found a way of "governing" from its minority position. Sharp verbal and public dissension was accompanied, in reality, by a practice of under-the-table negotiations and deals. This related in the first place to legislative activity but, from a certain moment, included also the division of minor government posts. A tenacious "consociational" equilibrium was thus created: formally opposed political forces became part of a hidden network of relationships. In most cases, the opposition exchanged a silence on corruption for political influences, while the various parties of the governmental area actively shared bribes, developing therefore a connivance relating to their respective illicit activities. According to the actual results of the investigations, in a few cases—such as the ENEL—the opposition also participated in the distribution of the bribes. The consociational agreements eliminated, even inside the elective organs, the normal controls between the majority and the opposition.

> While in the *visible* political arena, in which various political groups seek to gain votes by distinguishing between themselves (Pizzorno 1993), the corruption creates social costs by inducing an excessive expenditure of resources on political and electoral competition, in the *secret* political arena (including the market for corruption) there is a tendency towards inter-party collusion. The Italian party system can be likened to an oligopoly in which the consumer-citizen paid a rather high "price" for collusion between the parties as exemplified by the level of public intervention, designed to ensure large parasitic incomes for the political class. The major political parties demonstrate an underlying homogeneity in this regard, notwithstanding the different objectives they *declared* to pursue through control of the state. Agreeing on this fundamental point, political conflict was prevalently about image, as between firms who collude in maintaining high prices but at the same time spare nothing in advertising in order to win a larger share of the market. (della Porta and Vannucci 1994, chap. XI)

4. Political Parties, the Costs of Politics, and Corruption:
Comparative Remarks

Gathering the threads of what has been said so far, we can return to the initial question: does corruption favour strong or weak political parties?

4.1. Partitocracies?

The Italian (corrupt) party system has often been described as a *partitocrazia*. The first element for defining *partitocrazia* is the presence of mass political parties, tightly controlled by their leadership. According to Gianfranco Pasquino, *partitocrazia* is "the social and political presence and diffusion of mass parties. . . . Rather than party government, [*partitocrazia*] means their domination of, or ambition to dominate, the political system" (1990, 774). In fact, in the years immediately after the Second World War the term *partitocrazia* was used in Italy to indicate—and attack—the growing power of the mass parties compared with the older parties of individual representation. Similar terms were used in other countries to refer to the same phenomenon. In particular, the large number of functionaries and professional politicians necessary for the functioning of mass parties has been considered as a main cause of an increase in the costs of politics, and therefore an incentive to corruption. The *partitocrazia* has been linked to high political costs: "Political costs were always high in Italy, in part because of the length of political campaigns and the importance, until recent years, of competition between party list for preference vote—a practice that not only increased the ferocity and expense of campaigns but also encourages personalized and often corrupt forms of campaigning and party organization" (Rhodes 1996, 10). Similarly, the low costs of electoral campaigns in Great Britain have been quoted to explain low level of corruption in that country (Adonis 1997).

Is political corruption favoured by the presence of a centralized, mass party? As we have seen in our research, systemic political corruption had in Italy centrifugal effects on the political parties. The mass parties which had emerged with the formation of the Italian Republic after the Second World War—either of an ideological or a clientelistic nature—gradually transformed themselves. A hidden structure emerged in the organization of corrupt exchanges, becoming more and more influential in determining party decisions. Moreover, the concurrence on the corrupt market was reflected in internal fights between party fractions, temporarily aggregated around business interests. When the scandals exploded in the nineties, the structure of the parties did not correspond to a model of *partitocrazia*. As Pizzorno noted:

> The term *partitocrazia* is not suitable for such a system. The very term "party" is a term of open political discourse. . . . Certainly it is too indistinct a term for the language of analysis. There are not many acts easily imputable to a party as such. The term *partitocrazia* comes from a period in which the parties acted as collective subjects, guided by powerful leaderships responsible, if not to the membership as such, at least to elite circles composed of members. The leadership could answer for their members, parliamentary groups and mass associations before other actors within the political system, represented for their part by other parties. Decisions regarding the selection of political personnel were taken by the party leaderships according to largely pre-established rules. (1993, 304–5)

Political corruption does not seem therefore to be the effects of ideological mass parties; instead, it seems to grow with the transformation of the political parties into "cartel parties," with fluid ideology and small grass-roots presence. Unable to mobilize a stable constituency, with no membership available for paying for the party expenses, and a political class who, lacking ideological motivation, sees enrichment as the only selective incentives to politics, these political parties would be more and more available to corrupt practices. "Political entrepreneurs face serious financial problems. Not only are there no party members to voluntarily help with their campaigns, there are no party members paying their dues either. The party has to buy in services, but has no income, or projected income, with which to do it" (Hopkins 1996, 15). Together with the fall of membership financing, an increase in the costs of campaigning has been observed.

4.2. Party Power and Corruption

The Italian case can also help in considering another definition of *partitocrazia* as the degeneration of a specific form of regulation of social conflict, counterpoised to neo-corporatist (organisation of strong interests), pluralist (strong civil society) and policy network (strong technocracy) formulations: that is to say, *party government*. The Italian system has been defined as a government by the parties, with the parties in a position to control pressure groups (counting only through a client or kin relation to the parties themselves), the technocrats (*"lottizzati,"* ie., appointed in proportion to party strength), and civil society (social movements too being aligned around party actors). The power of the parties, therefore, is seen as having characterized both society and institutions. As Pasquino has observed:

> The party presence in Italian society, in the centres of decision-making, has been permitted by the expansion of the public sector, by the existence of municipal enterprises, by the number of positions subject to political nomination . . . As regards the institutions, at the risk of furnishing too rudimentary an explanation, it is opportune to remember: firstly, that recruitment to administrative and political posts is largely the monopoly of the parties; secondly, that in the formal centres of decision-making the presence of personnel of party extraction is not only dominant but frequently absolute. (1987, 60)

In our research, we saw in fact that an overreaching presence of the political parties have been often stigmatized. However, as Alessandro Pizzorno (1971) argued many years ago, the "strength" or "weakness" of parties can be differently evaluated depending on whether one considers the power of reinforcing delegation, procuring advantages for the representatives (the party apparatuses, in other words), or that of transmitting the demands of the represented.

The use of corrupt practices would seem to be negatively correlated with the second kind of party power, *reducing parties' ability to elaborate long-term programmes, mobilise ideological resources, distribute participatory incentives and gain the support of an electorate of opinion.* As revealed in the Italian case, by concentrating on the organisation of corruption the political parties privilege those decisions most productive in terms of bribes rather than those which might generate the greatest support among the electorate. In addition, corruption, by its very nature, leads to the dominance of hidden over visible politics, small-group logic over the search for wider participation. As in the case of the American political machine, "the party organization did not play an important role in developing alternative courses of municipal governmental action. Indeed, since machine politicians drew their resources from the routine operation of government, they did not concern themselves with policy formulation" (Wolfinger 1973, 104). The diffusion of corruption has been related to the weakness of political parties in such different context as Latin America—for instance, the fragmentation in Colombia, with 628 electoral lists in the 1994 elections (Zuluaga Nieto 1996; Njaim, 1996)—as well as in France (Ruggiero 1996b). In the long term, the evident squandering of resources connected to maladministration impedes corrupt politicians from attracting an electorate of opinion by presenting themselves as the bearers of prosperity and progress. The pragmatism of under-the-counter deals substitutes for ideological appeals.

Political corruption interacted with *the parties' power to reinforce delegation*. With the alibi of the "political" nature of administrative decisions, the parties have invaded the managing boards of public bodies, using their power in ways not always directed to the collective welfare and not always lawful. More or less official mechanisms of political control over the nomination of certain public-sector bureaucrats have led to the *partitizzazione* of the public administration, producing feuds which the parties and their representatives have used for patronage and corruption. The influence of the parties in areas beyond the public administration—from banks to newspapers—has led to the an occupation of civil society, further lowering the defences against corruption and mismanagement. The political parties have occupied civil society not in order to realize long-term political programs but to facilitate the extraction of a parasitic rent. As we observed, the parties acquired an important function as organizers of political corruption. First of all, they diffused in the political system values that justified corruption as the "normal" way of doing politics. White collar crime has been explained with reference to work-related subcultures: "These work-related subcultures tend to isolate their members from the mainstream of social life and its construction of reality. . . . Because of this isolation, work-related subcultures are often able to maintain a definition of certain criminal activities as acceptable or even required behavior, when they are clearly condemned by society as a whole" (Coleman, 1987, 422–23). In the case of corruption, political parties facilitate corruption reducing the moral barrier against illegal actions:

> Political party membership, and the experience of political life in general, also has secondary socializing effects which become constitutive of a person's identity and therefore of their moral principles. Someone belonging to a political association can receive recognition for: technical or cultural abilities; loyalty, or conformism, in ideological commitment; loyalty to a particular leader; astuteness, aggressivity or lack of scruples in "taking out" adversaries; capacity for forming links with the wider society and bringing in money for party funds or other kinds of contribution; or, naturally, some combination of these qualities. The "moral quality" of associated life will vary according to the prevailing criteria for recognition. The more an individual's activity and relations are restricted to the concerns of party life the more the identifications on which identity is modelled will reflect its "moral quality," and on this will depend the moral cost of corruption. The more corruption is diffuse the more political parties themselves function as agencies for socialization in illegality, reducing the moral cost paid by their members for participation in corrupt practices. (Pizzorno 1992, 47)

In systems of extensive corruption the parties not only socialize into illicit practices, reducing the moral costs of corruption, they also secure a kind of continuity to the game of corruption through its diffusion in every geographical area, in the various public bodies and in the different sectors of the public administration: whoever respects the unlawful agreements can continue to do business with the public administration; anyone who opts out on a given occasion will be permanently excluded from the market for public works. Controlling the nominations to public bodies, the parties can generalise the *kickback*, transforming corruption from an exception into an established practice with accepted norms, at the same time guaranteeing the continuity of the system over time despite changes in the political personnel of the public administration. The parties assume, that is to say, the *function of guarantors of the illegal bargain*, participating in those operations demanding a "certification of trust: in other words, the promises of others, requiring to be guaranteed in some way, are used to obtain a benefit" (Pizzorno 1992, 31). Moreover, reaching an agreement between them, majority and opposition reduce the material risks connected with identifying suitable parties and negotiating the bribes.

Italy is of course not the only case in which political parties seemed particularly involved in the organization of corruption. In France, for instance, various associations, often financed by the state, have developed with links to the political parties, allowing them to collect money and escape, at the same time, the rules for the public accounts. These associations provide salaries to members of the party they are related with, finance in various ways their campaigns, and pay for party activities (Becquart-Leclerc 1993, 9–10; Mény 1992). One of the scandals which pushed the Socialists out of power was related with the disclosure of the activities of Urba, a *bureau d'études* that collected illegal party financing for the Socialist Party, distributing them, in the word of its director, "according to the principle 40–30–30 (40 percent for the functioning of Urba, 30 percent for the national headquarters of the party, 30 percent for the local elected politicians)" (in *Le Monde*, 3/3/1995). Collecting bribes by local entrepreneurs (hidden as compensations for services which had not been provided), Urba paid the salary to functionaries of the central headquarters of the party, as well as various expenses for political campaigning at the local or the central level (ibid.).

Moreover, not only in Italy a collusion between governmental and opposition parties seems to be a common practice as far as corruption is concerned. An extreme case is Japan, where the silence of the opposition seems to have been bought through relevant sums of money paid from the conservatives to their adversaries—sometimes behind the screen of a fake *mah-jong* game between politicians of the government and the opposition (Bouissou 1997: 140–2). In general, cartel parties, characterized already by collusion with a massive use of public financing, manifest they reciprocal solidarity when scandals related with party financing emerge. In the French context Becquart-Leclercq (1989, 205) observed within the network of corruption a shared adherence to operational modes of implicit codes which include "the conspiracy of silence: it operates particularly between leaders of various political parties, despite their sometimes bitter and violent conflicts; to survive, all must respect the rules of the game and maintain silence about the rules themselves." In Germany, resiliance to scandals was connected to

> the organizational oligopoly on which parties could build. The stability of this system rests, above all, on a strong interparty consensus about the basic rules of the game (including the legal/illegal ways of party financing), and on the commonly shared interest of the 'established' parties to retain their de facto monopoly of public decision-making and to guard it against outside forces. This common interest has in good part suspended the functioning of the checks and balances and the institutional mechanisms of control usually associated, at least in theory, with competitive party systems, replacing them with conventional patterns of tacit agreement and mutual privilege enhancement. (Blankenburg, Staudhammer, Steinert 1989, 922)

If corruption has transformed the foundations of power within the parties and their functions, it can be added that the influence of the parties in the operation of networks of corruption varies considerably from one geographical area to another. As the ex-mayor of Reggio Calabria, Agatino Licandro, observed:

> The difference between *kickbacks* in the North and South is that [in the North] there is a centralised structure. A collection point controlled and run in a unitary fashion. The party collects the money and then divides it among the factions, after retaining what is required for the party itself. Here [in the South], on the other hand, it is exactly the reverse. If whoever collects is the head of the party at that moment, that's where the money finishes up. But it's a subterfuge. In reality, the party means one's own faction or corresponds to immediate group interests. It is not a small difference. The mechanism provokes tensions and dramatises the whole of political life. Worse than that, everything else—alliances, decisions—is subordinated to bribery and money. (Licandro and Varano 1993, 122–23)

In certain regions of Southern Italy in particular, organised crime partly substitutes for the political parties in the function of certifying trust between those involved in occult exchange and consequently receives a part of the bribes.

This observation leads to our final remark. If it is true that the parties function as guarantors of illegal exchange, they are not alone in doing so. Alongside them, in fact, are ranged a series of aggregations—some of them formal, others not—all of which have in common a low level of visibility. Political corruption, being occult exchange, subtracts power from visible sites. The arenas of decision-making therefore shifted from visible to hidden politics, where the parties are not necessarily the dominant actors. Weakened by the spread of corruption, the parties become supporting actors, behind the scenes of the crypto-government in which the real decisions concerning the public sphere were taken.

Sources

TNM *Tangentopoli. Le carte che scottano* (from p. 65 to p. 86 Excerpt from the "Richiesta di autorizzazione a procedere nei confronti dell'on. Bettino Craxi," 12/1/1993), supplement to "Panorama," February 1993.

TM A. Carlucci, *Tangentomani*, Baldini & Castoldi, 1992. (this and the preceding book are published reports of evidence of interrogations).

SDM Senate of the Republic, doc. IV n.13, "Domanda di autorizzazione a procedere," 12/6/1992.

VICM Public Prosecutor at the Court of Milan, Report of evidence of the interrogation with Mura Giovanni in JP n.5805/85.

CPDT Parliamentary Committee of Inquiry in the reconstruction after the earthquake in Basilicata and Campania on November 1980, Final report approved on January 27, 1991, Vol. I, Tomo I.

CD Chamber of Deputies, "Domanda di autorizzazione a procedere in giudizio," doc.IV.

CC State Auditors' Department: Report to the Parliament for the years 1987–1992

Bibliography

Adonis, A. (1997), *The UK: Civic Virtues Put to the Test*, in D. della Porta and Y. Mény (eds.), *Democracy and Corruption in Europe*, London, Pinter, pp. 103–117.

Becquart-Leclercq, J. (1989), *Paradoxes of Political Corruption: A French View*, in A.J. Heidenheimer, M. Johnston and V.T. LeVine (eds.), *Political Corruption,* New Brunswick and Oxford, Transaction Publishers, pp. 191–210.

Becquart-Leclercq, J. (1993), *Corruption politique: la recherche des victimes*, Paper presented at the Joint Sessions of the European Consortium for Political research, Leide, April.

Bettin, G. and Magnier, A. (1991), *Chi governa la citt^*, Padova, Cedam.

Blankenburg E., Staudhammer R. and Steinert H. (1989), *Political Scandals and Corruption Issues in West Germany*, in A.J. Heidenheimer, M. Johnston and V.T. LeVine (eds.), *Political Corruption,* New Brunswick and Oxford, Transaction Publishers, pp. 913–931

Bouissou, J.M. (1997), *Gifts, Networks and Clienteles: Corruption in Japan as a Redistributive System*, in D. della Porta and Y. Mény (eds.), *Democracy and Corruption in Europe*, London, Pinter, pp. 132–147.

Buchanan, J.M. (1980), *Rent Seeking and Profit Seeking*, in Buchanan J.M., Tollison R.D., Tullock G. (eds.), *Toward a Theory of the Rent Seeking Society*, A&M University Press.

Buchanan, J.M., Tollison R.D., Tullock G. (eds.) (1980), *Toward a Theory of the Rent Seeking Society*, A&M University Press.

Coleman, J.W. (1987), *Toward an Integrated Theory of White Collar Crime*, in "American Journal of Sociology," 93, 406–439.

Cotta, M. and P. Isernia (eds.) (1996), *Il gigante dai piedi d'argilla*, Bologna, Il Mulino.

della Porta, D. (1993), *Milano: Capitale immorale*, in G. Pasquino and S. Hellman (eds.), *Politica in Italia*, Bologna, Il Mulino.

della Porta, D. and Vannucci, A. (1994), *Corruzione politica e amministrazione pubblica*. Risorse, attori, meccanismi, Bologna, Il Mulino.

Di Palma, G. (1978), *Sopravvivere senza governare. I partiti nel parlamento italiano*, Il Mulino, Bologna.

Fleisher D. (1997), *Political corruption in Brasil*, in "Crime, Law and Social Change," 25, pp. 297–321.

Frognier, A.P. (1986), *Corruption and Consociational Democracy: First Thoughts on the Belgian Case*, in "Corruption and Reform," 1, pp. 143–8.

Harendra, K. D. (1989), *The Genesis and Spread of Economic Corruption: A Microtheoretic Interpretation*, in "World Development," 17, pp. 503–511.

Heywood, P. (1997), *From Dictatorship to Democracy: the Changing Forms of Corruption in Spain*, in D. della Porta and Y. Mény (eds.) (1996), *Democracy and Corruption in Europe*, London, Pinter, pp. 65–84.

Holzner, B. (1972), *Reality Construction in Society*, Cambridge MA., Schenkman.

Hopkins, J. (1996), *Political Entrepreneurs and Political Corruption: The Party as Business Firm*, Paper presented at the International Conference on Corruption in Contemporary Politics, University of Salford, November.

Huntington, S.P. (1968), *Political Order in Changing Society*, New Haven, Yale University Press.

Jiménez Sanchez, F. (1996*), Possibilities and Limits of Political Scandals as a Form of Social Control*, in *Revista Espanola de Investigaciones Sociologicas*, English edition, pp. 49–76.

Johnson, O.E.G. (1975), *An Economic Analysis of Corrupt Government with Special Application to LDC's*, Kyklos, 28, pp. 47–61.

Katz, R.S. (1986), *Party Government: A Rationalistic Conception*, in F.G. Castles and R. Wildenmann (eds.), *Visions and Reality of Party Government*, Berlin, De Gruyter, pp. 31–71.

Key, V.O. (1936), *The Technique of Political Graft in the United States*, Chicago, University of Chicago Press.

Licandro, A. and Varano, A. (1993), *La città dolente. Confessioni di un sindaco corrotto*, Torino, Einaudi.

Loïma, A. (1993), *Les emb ches de la transition en Russia: corruption et pratiques mafiouses*, in *Le Courrier des pays de l'Est*, 381, pp. 20–36.

Macdougall, T. (1988), *The Lockheed Scandal and the High Cost of Politics in Japan*, in A.S. Markovits and M. Silverstein (eds.), *The Politics of Scandal*, New York, Holmes and Meyer, pp. 193–229.

Magone, J.M. (1996), *Political Corruption and Sustainable Democracy in Small Countries: The Portuguese Case in Comparative European Perspective*, Paper presented at the International Conference on Corruption in Contemporary Politics, University of Salford, November.

Mauro, P. (1996), *The Effects of Corruption on Growth, Investment, and Government Expenditure*, IMF Working Paper, WP/96/98.

Mény, Y (1992), *La Corruption de la République*, Paris, Fayard.

Nelken, D. (1996), *A Legal Revolution? The Judges and Tangentopoli*, in S. Gundle and S. Parker (eds.), *The New Italian Republic: From the Fall of Communism to the Rise of Berlusconi*, London, Routledge.

Njaim, H. (1996), *Clientelismo, mercado y Liderazgo partidista en America Latina*, in "Nueva Sociedad," 145, pp. 138–147.

Pasquino, G. (1985), *Partiti, societá civile e istituzioni*, in G. Pasquino (ed.), *Il sistema politico italiano*, Bari-Roma, Laterza.

Pasquino, G. (1987), *Regolatori sregolati: partiti e governo dei partiti*, in P. Lange and M. Regini (eds.), *Stato e regolazione sociale. Nuove prospettive sul caso italiano*, Bologna, Il Mulino, pp. 53–81.

Pasquino, G. (1990), *Partitocrazia*, in N. Bobbio, N. Matteucci and G. Pasquino (eds.), *Dizionario di politica*, Torino, Utet, pp. 774–777.

Pasquino, G. (1991), *La repubblica dei cittadini ombra*, Milano, Garzanti.

Pelinka, A. (1988), *Austria: The Withering of Consociational Democracy*, in A.S. Markovits and M. Silverstein (eds.), *The Politics of Scandal*, New York, Holmes and Mayer, pp. 166–189.

Pizzorno, A. (1971), *I due poteri dei partiti*, in "Politica del diritto," 2, pp. 197–209.

Pizzorno, A. (1992), *La corruzione nel sistema politico*, in D. della Porta *Lo scambio occulto*, Bologna, Il Mulino.

Pizzorno, A. (1993), *Le radici della politica assoluta*, Milano, Feltrinelli.

Pizzorno, A. (1996), *Vecchio e nuovo nella transizione italiana*, in N. Negri and L. Sciolla (eds.), *Il paese dei paradossi*, Roma, La Nuova Italia Scientifica, pp. 253–285.

Procura di Milano (1996), *Prospetto riepilogativo di "mani pulite,"* updated to October 10.

Pujas, V. (1996), *Political Scandals: The Illegal Financing of Political Parties in France, Spain and Italy*, Paper presented at the International Conference on Corruption in Contemporary Politics, University of Salford, November.

Rhodes, M. (1996), *Financing Party Politics in Italy: A Case of Systemic Corruption*, Paper presented at the International Conference on Corruption in Contemporary Politics, University of Salford, November.

Roth, R. (1989), *Eine korrupte Republik? Konturen politischer Korruption in der Bundesrepublik*, in R. Ebbighausen and S. Neckel (eds.), *Anatomie des politischen Skandals*, Frankfurt am Main, Suhrkamp, pp. 201–233.

Rothacher, A. (1996), *Structural Corruption in a Gift Culture*, Paper presented at the International Conference on Corruption in Contemporary Politics, University of Salford, November.

Rowley, C. K., Tollison R.D. and Tullock G (eds.). (1987), *The Political Economy of Rent Seeking*, Huwer.

Ruggiero, V. (1996), "France: Corruption as Resentment," in *Journal of Law and Society*, XXIII, pp. 113–131.

Sartori, G. (1982), *Teoria dei partiti e caso italiano*, Milano, Sogarco.

Schelling, T. (1984), *What is the Business of Organized Crime?*, in T. Schelling, *Choice and Consequence*, Cambridge, Mass, Harvard University Press.

Scheuch, E.K., and U. Scheuch, (1992), *Cliquen, Klügel und Karrieren*, Hamburg, Rowohlt Taschenbuch.

Seibel, W. (1997), Corruption in the Federal Republic of Germany Before and in the Wake of Reunification, in D. della Porta and Y. Mény (eds.), *Democracy and Corruption in Europe*, London, Pinter, pp. 85–102.

Shleifer A. and R.W. Vishny (1993), *Corruption*, in "The Quarterly Journal of Economics, pp. 599–617.

Vannucci, A. (1997), *Il mercato della corruzione*, Milano, Societá Aperta.

Wolfinger, R.E., 1973, *The Politics of Progress*, Englewood Cliffs, Prentice Hall.

Zuluaga Nieto, J. (1996), *Cuando la corrupcion invade el tejido social*, in "Nueva sociedad," 145, 148–159.

38

Party Finance and Political Scandal: Comparing Italy, Spain, and France

Véronique Pujas and Martin Rhodes

Introduction

Scandals connected to the illegal financing of political parties have prolif-erated throughout Latin Europe in recent years. Although the Italian *tangentopoli* (bribe-city) prosecutions provide the most dramatic case, scan-dals have also damaged the reputation, credibility and legitimacy of the po-litical class in Spain and France. This phenomenon raises three sets of ques-tions. First there is the specific issue of party finance and its connection with corruption. Second, there are general issues concerning the nature of scandal and the perception of illegality: for while far from new, illicit funding has only recently been the subject of public disapproval, media investigation and judicial prosecution. Third, exploring the connection between party finance and political corruption raises questions about the nature of democracy in the Latin countries. Is the Italian case simply the most acute example of a wider spread Latin European phenomenon; are the political cultures of the region predisposed towards "illicit governance"; is there a "southern syndrome" that separates these countries from their northern neighbours?

This article explores these issues via three case studies. The Italian case reveals the most extensive and systemic use of corrupt practice and the most effective wielding of "scandal" as a political weapon by opposition forces. The inclusion of Spain and France, where parallel, if less calamitous develop-ments, have occurred, allows for comparative reflections on our two key hypotheses. First, we argue that the emergence and expansion of corrupt forms of political finance are linked to particular "political opportunity structures" rather than a "cultural" predisposition towards corruption. The Italian case has much in common with other countries of the region, in terms both of the practice of corrupt finance and its origins in weakly institutionalized party systems, interlocking élites and inadequate regulations for political party funding. Second, we suggest that the appearance of scandal and of scandalized public opinion—after many years in which corruption was considered routine and unremarkable—has been driven by the "competitive mobilization" of actors in the judiciary, politics, and the media. In section one we consider the existence of a "southern syndrome" and introduce the concept of "political opportunity structure." Coined by Herbert Kitschelt for the analysis of protest movements, it proves useful for explaining national variations in the intensity and methods of corruption.[1] Section two analyses the specific contribution made to corruption opportunity structures by party finance regulation. Section three considers why long acknowledged—although illicit—forms of political finance have only recently become "scandalous" as a result of the "competitive mobilization" of élites.

A Cultural Syndrome? Corruption and Party
Finance in Southern Europe

Changing Perceptions of Corruption

Our two hypotheses—that there is indeed a southern "pattern" of political opportunity for corruption, and that the mobilization of opinion against it has been the result, in large part, of élite competition—require some initial justification.

First, we need to acknowledge the politically and socially contingent nature of illegality and corruption. What is "illegal" or "corrupt" in some societies may be considered acceptable in others. What the British would see as nepotism or shameless patronage might be considered fair or even a moral duty elsewhere. It is the *perception* of the practice that makes it corrupt and scandalous. Societies that modernize and democratize tend to move, albeit unevenly, through different phases of perception.[2] For this reason, any definition of corruption can only be fluid. An act tolerated during a given period in a particular society may not be in another, since the values of that society will have changed. Practices accepted in a period of prosperity may not be in a context of growing inequality or poverty or increasingly sclerotic public services.[3] The corrupt behaviour of political élites known to only a limited number of citizens (who may be actively complicit or not) can become scandalous when revealed to a wider public. As for legality, or rather the illegality of certain acts such as the illegal financing of political parties, it is insufficient simply to think in terms of the legitimacy of such practices. "Intolerable" practices, which have not been defined as illegal in law, can remain unsanctioned even when citizens consider them to be scandalous. Likewise, numerous conditions (which we will elaborate below) must be present to create a scandal, even when a practice is illegal in law but, for one reason or another, remains hidden from, or tolerated by public opinion and the media.[4]

In this light, the recent corruption scandals in Italy, France, and Spain do not reveal that these societies have suddenly become corrupt (although corrupt practice certainly proliferated in the 1980s). Rather, the accepted and routine has become unacceptable and illicit. The process by which this occurs is not automatic or politically innocent. Key social actors have been instrumental in changing societal perceptions—and not always for altruistic reasons.[5] Corruption scandals are intrinsic to a process of ethical and democratic transition and are often the outcome of a clash between élites.

Second, we need to define the nature of this transition. Is it primarily one of cultural transformation or institutional change? In fact, the two are inseparable. In most categorizations of countries by degrees of corruption, a distinction tends to be drawn between the northern Protestant countries (e.g., Britain and Scandinavia) and the Latin Catholic countries, with others ranged between.[6] This division is usually accounted for in terms of political culture or national character: Spanish *"amiguismo,"*[7] *"l'arrangement à la française"* or *"l'arrangiarsi"* of the Italians. But do these social practices alert us to a specific southern mentality or culture or to differences in socio-political development and organization? Institutional settings breed certain types of relationship and social practice. For example, the notion of "conflict of interest" as an antidote to corruption is much stronger in northern Protestant than in Latin and Catholic countries. This can be attributed to different "political cultures" and levels of "trust," as in the work of Putnam and Fukuyama.[8] But attempts to locate the origins of "civicness" in the Italian case have foundered on the fact that those regions defined as "civic" (the centre and north) have been hit equally hard by corruption revelations as those traditionally considered "amoral" (the south). It is important that both "culture" and "trust" are defined historically and institutionally. Why is it, for example, that multiple office holding, patron-client relations across the public-private divide and informal channels for exercising political influence have been more accepted in southern than in northern Europe? We suggest that developmental factors and the "structure of political opportunity" provide a major part of the answer.

Democratic Development and Political Opportunity Structures

Explaining the causes of corruption is a complex task. A useful alternative to "culture-based" explanations is to explore the *political opportunity structures* of different societies and their historical origins. Depending on the way political and administrative power is structured, it will be more or less obscure or transparent, open or closed, sensitive or indifferent to pressure. Since it is likely that the agents will seek to manipulate rules or exploit resources for private gain whatever the regime or organization, systems will differ mainly in their capacity for preventing such behaviour. It is this, in essence, that defines the local or national "culture" of corruption.

Developmental factors are important in shaping these structures and can be examined in four major areas: relations between parties and the state; the ineffectiveness of political checks and balances; the rules and norms regulating financial and economic behaviour; and the nature of party finance regulation.

The relationship between parties and the state. All three countries in this study have built their democracies on interlocking spheres of influence. While absorbing anti-democratic elements within new political structures, this has frequently also encouraged conflicts of interest and corruption. A clear contrast can be drawn between Britain and the countries of southern Europe. In Britain, the civil service has long had a reputation for integrity and patron-client relations have been rare (even if recent years have seen a decline in public standards). Unlike most continental countries, Britain consolidated its parties and party system well before it institutionalized bureaucracies. This meant that the political penetration of bureaucratic structures was declining in Britain as it was increasing in Italy and France. While the state in Italy and Spain has taken on the appearance of modernity, its late development alongside the emergence of parties meant that it was founded on particularistic, personalized social structures.[9] Authoritarian rule did not eliminate these practices but institutionalized them: the Francoist state saw the proliferation of networks of personal influence, involving large numbers of badly paid bureaucrats and the expansion of black market practices (*estraperlo*).[10] In some cases, democratic reform has compounded the problem. For while the strengthening of British democracy in the nineteenth century required closed borders between parties and bureaucracy,[11] many continental countries saw party penetration of bureaucracies and judiciaries as an essential check against anti-democratic forces.

In Italy and Spain, the patron-client relations that had always substituted for rational, administrative interaction were transposed into new institutional structures. As Sapelli has argued, it is precisely this collusion between clientelism, a lack of "sense of state" and the ubiquity of clannish parties, which creates the weakness of southern politics.[12] But there are important differences among the southern countries in this respect. In Italy, parties have shared power through the *lottizzazione* spoils system and dominated a weak executive, eventually destroying any notion of "the public interest" in the process. In both Spain and France, by contrast, parties of government have been able to *use* a strong executive to dominate the administration by political placements.[13] Nevertheless, in all three cases, the outcome has been a confusion of powers. Recent administrative reforms have exacerbated this problem. The devolution of government in Italy and Spain has created greater opportunities for corruption, while in France—where, unique to these countries, there has long been a strong sense of *"service public"*—the dominance of the local notable has always facilitated such behaviour.

The ineffectiveness of political checks and balances. Italy's "consociative democracy" has long seen a remarkable degree of cross-party consensus, not just in coalition governments, but between government and opposition.[14] Although *consociativismo* cannot be reduced to clientelism or *lottizzazione*, the key to the post-war settlement was the use of state resources for building consensus under DC (Christian Democrat) hegemony. In turn, corruption and the emulation of DC empire building became the most effective means of challenging that hegemony, as demonstrated by the ascendancy of Bettino Craxi and his Socialist Party from the mid-1970s.[15] Elsewhere in Latin Europe, the pursuit of political hegemony has been less virulent. But checks and balances on power have nonetheless been weak, including the absence of strong judiciaries and an independent press. In Spain, the weakness of political parties has been compounded by a political apathy bred from cynicism and a long period of repression.[16] In order to protect a difficult democratic equilibrium when democracy was restored, a *modus vivendi* was achieved whereby parties quietly shadowed—rather than challenged—the executive.[17] In France, the weakness of checks and balances has long been evident. On the one hand parliament is quite ineffective: it lacks opportunities to act and the President of the Republic holds most executive power. On the other, local power in the hands of notables has spawned complex clientelistic networks, reinforced by devolution in the 1980s. The resulting state of collusion has facilitated corruption and hindered its disclosure.

The regulation of financial and economic behaviour. Only in the 1980s were modern fiscal and financial systems introduced in Spain and Greece or consolidated in Italy. Untill then (and even now), tax evasion was considered normal practice, insider trading legal, stock market activity based on privileged information, and shareholders poorly protected—if at all—by legal regulation. Before new rules and norms could be consolidated in Spain, the country experienced a sudden spurt of growth that, together with increasing state intervention,[18] created an ethos of easy enrichment (*cultura del pelotazo*). The financial deregulation which stimulated the speculative use of *"dinero negro"* was, of course, part of a much wider process of change, affecting all of southern Europe, including the neo-liberal devaluation of the state and public service and the traditional values underpinning them. On the one hand, EU integration has produced a clash of regulatory cultures and an imposition of certain "Protestant" norms and values on the South. But financial market deregulation and the retreat of the state—as well as the proliferation of EU funds through complex and poorly monitored channels—have provided new opportunities for the expansion of corruption and fraud. Italian corruption could not have been so extensive without facilitating banking practices, financial transactions and offshore operations.[19]

The problematic regulation of party finances. It is worth noting that problems of party finance and its regulation have increased in all countries in recent years, assuming a particular, rather than unique, character in Italy, France and Spain. There are numerous interrelated explanations for these problems, including:

- The growing bureaucratization of party organizations, linked to the emergence of "cartel parties."[20] State funding for parties has not only strengthened their oligarchic tendencies but also their capacity to resist new challenges, given that state funding is often tied to prior party performance or position;[21]
- The increasing costs of campaign expenditure, driven in part by the new and expanded role of the media. Television has enhanced the conditions that allow, or compel, parties to make universal appeals to voters, rather than communicate through and to their core supporters;[22]
- A change in the nature of political competition. Greater use of the media helps create new rules of party competition, based on leadership-focused contests, which weakens the traditional character of parties and increases the cost of politics;
- The decline of traditional means of party finance (e.g., membership dues, voluntary donations, fund-raising events, lotteries) as well as in contributions from business and labour (as politics becomes less ideologically driven), has led parties to seek alternative, and often illegal, sources of funds.

Within this general context of change, Italy, France, and Spain share a number of characteristics. Firstly, apart from the communist parties of Italy and France, parties in these countries have always been weakly organized or riven by factions. The southern socialist parties so prominent in recent corruption scandals—Felipe Gonzalez's PSOE and Bettino Craxi's PSI—have been élite organizations with little in the way of militant base or mass membership. Secondly, as argued above, the proximity of parties and state has been close and this has been critical in shaping systems—both formal and informal—of party finance:

- In Italy, the extensive colonization by parties of the state, alongside links in the south with criminal organizations, produced "transactive" as well as "extortive" corruption (the former is an arrangement of mutual benefit, while the latter involves coercion);[23]
- In Spain, constitutional recognition and public financing of parties was

considered a means of guaranteeing democracy. But in the absence of widespread and active public support for parties, this has made the latter almost wholly dependent on the state;

- In France, the interpenetration of élites, ministerial *cabinets* and the public sector has led to less exploitation of the state than in Italy, and less dependence on it than in Spain. But weak parties and poor funding regulation have encouraged illegality.

Finally, in all three cases, not only has party finance regulation emerged relatively late, but there has been an enormous gap between the constitutional recognition of parties as guarantors of pluralism, and the provision of the adequate and transparent public funding essential for that role.

Party Finance Regulation and Corruption Opportunity Structures

Italy: A Case of "Systemic Corruption"[24]

Party finance in Italy was totally unregulated until 1974. Until the mid-1970s, the multiple channels of party finance of the pre-Fascist period remained in use. These included membership subscriptions, contributions from private organizations (including "kickbacks" or bribes on contracts and supplies), the diversion of public money into party accounts, "black" (i.e., unofficial and illegal) contracts and interest on the accounts of public agencies, income from party economic activities and donations from "flanking organizations" (e.g., trade unions) or from abroad.[25] As occurred in Spain some thirty years later, the Italian transition to democracy in the late 1940s and early 1950s simply transposed old practices into new political structures. Clearly, an extensive, unregulated system of this type provides ample opportunities for dubious—although not necessarily illegal—funding.

Many of these were revealed and investigated in the 1960s, amid calls for tighter regulation. But it was not until the 1973 oil scandal (the discovery that *Unione Petrolifera*—the association of oil derivatives producers—was influencing energy policy by funding all government parties) that politicians acknowledged the need for new rules. Law No. 195 of 2 May 1974 established a system of public subventions for parties receiving more than 2 percent of the valid votes in general elections. It also outlawed contributions to parties from public sector companies and required the declaration of contributions from private sources in publicized party balance sheets (individuals contributing more than L1 million were to be named). Sanctions were introduced against those who contributed and received funds illegally and parties which violated the rules on the annual publication of accounts. But given the nature of the "political culture"—a blocked democratic process, dedicated to excluding the large Italian Communist Party (PCI) from power, and extensive interpenetration between parties, public agencies and corporations—the 1974 law had perverse effects. Arguably, these contributed to the corruption and—in the 1980s—degeneration of the main Italian parties.

The 1974 law emerged at the intersection of the "visible" and "invisible" states and introduced new elements into Italy's complex corruption opportunity structure. Its regulatory flaws were many and mutually compounding. Strict and cumbersome regulations made *legal* contributions very difficult— encouraging, in effect, a level of illegality that could not be checked. It was impossible to verify the income received or its source, for the legislation failed to ensure that parties revealed their total revenues[26] or to standardize spending categories. Each party could therefore interpret the requirements of the law and itemize spending in different ways. Moreover, the authorities were unable or unwilling to impose the sanctions made available by law. There were actually fewer corruption prosecutions after the law was introduced than before.[27]

During the twenty years between the 1974 law and the abolition of public funding via referendum in 1993, the *stato dei partiti* (party-state) was strengthened by two major developments. While the expansion of the welfare state (and a consequent extension of party and party faction influence over central and local government) expanded the corruption opportunity structure, the accession of Bettino Craxi to the leadership of the Italian Socialist Party (PSI) created the conditions for its further exploitation. Craxi's vigorous challenge to DC hegemony produced a more intense and virulent form of party competition and collusion, in both the visible/legal and invisible/illicit realms of power. These developments deepened the divide between the party-state and civil society. Having lost the capacity to transmit group or class demands, the increasingly fragmented parties built their success on articulating particular interests. And in order to consolidate these particularistic links, party fractions (*correnti*) extended their colonization of the state.

In this context, a new type of actor, the "business politician", emerged, organizing the transfer and distribution of *tangenti* (bribes and kickbacks) and becoming the privileged intermediary of *scambio occulto*.[28] Whenever major public works were contracted, entrepreneurs paid pre-established percentages of the project's value—bribes then split among the parties. The prevalence of such practices led to the rise of professional mediators in the market for illicit finance at the expense of traditional party functionaries.[29] The ascent of these figures went hand in hand with the degradation of party sections and the exclusion of party activists from influence. The most extreme example of degeneration was Craxi's Socialist Party. At the same time, relations between the parties were transformed. Behind their surface political struggles lay an increasingly important transversal structure of collusion. Henceforth, the real conflicts were within the parties themselves, triggering an inflationary dynamic in the *mercato occulto*.[30] The higher the cost of political activity, the more incentive to raise funds from *tangenti*; the more funds raised from *tangenti*, the more could be spent on electoral and factional competition.[31]

But this system developed destructive internal contradictions: the erosion of the notion of "public interest" by such activities led to a general loss of legitimacy and the rise of anti-system forces.[32] The collapse of the major parties in the wake of the *tangentopoli* scandals was accompanied by a citizenship revolt. In April 1993, Italians voted by referendum to abolish public funding for political parties and to inject a strong dose of majoritarianism into the electoral system. The massive vote against state funding of parties, the collapse of the traditional parties in local elections and the accompanying haemorrhage of membership created a completely new context for legislation. As a result, the new law (Law no. 515, 10 December 1993) departed completely from the twenty-year tradition of party finance and introduced a system based primarily on the reimbursement of campaign spending to candidates, rather than subsidies to parties. It also regulated access to the media, controlled the use of opinion polls close to the election, limited funding and spending, created a new system for monitoring the parties, and backed the new rules with tough sanctions.[33]

The introduction of monitoring and tough sanctions helped modify party behaviour in the 1994 and 1996 general elections: in 1995, large fines were levied on major parties of both the left and right for exceeding spending limits and failing to reveal the source of funds. But the bankruptcy of most parties that followed the collapse of the covert funding system produced a new problem: finding adequate legal funds to finance their activities. An interim solution introduced in January 1997—allowing tax payers to channel 4 in every 1,000 lire of their tax payments to a fund for the parties—completely failed: in the first six months of its operation, only 0.5 percent of tax payers agreed to participate! After much debate, a new law was approved by the Parliament (but not fully by the Senate) at the end of April 1999. Parties are now reimbursed 4,000 lire for each voter they attract – directly contradicting the result of the 1993 referendum. Meanwhile, the Italian Parliament has failed to pass into law any of the 10 draft laws proposed by the Chamber of Deputies Anti-Corruption Commission in 1997.

Spain: Corruption and "Cartel" Parties

Italy undoubtedly represents an extreme case. For neither in Spain nor France have the scandals of the 1980s and 1990s revealed an equivalent degradation of public life or such extensive exploitation of the state's resources for private or party political ends. Nonetheless, there are clear parallels.

We should begin, however, by pointing to the differences. The Spanish case is unusual because of the late emergence of democracy and because it was the first country to adopt the public financing of parties *before* the emergence of a party system. After the dictatorship, political parties were seen as the guarantors of pluralism. So the law of 1977 provided state subsidies to political parties for their campaign expenses in local, regional and national elections and further funds for ordinary activities. Contributions from the public administration and from abroad were prohibited. This system was intended to help newly formed and very weak parties with scant economic resources to develop. But to receive these subsidies, parties had to obtain at least one parliamentary seat; and finance is linked only to votes obtained in the electoral districts where the party achieves parliamentary representation, and not for all the votes it obtains nationally. As a result, the Spanish system is one of the most discriminatory towards extra-parliamentary parties. The first obvious consequence of the law has been the marginalization of new or smaller parties. Since three percent of the vote is needed to get a seat in the congress of deputies, it is very hard for a party to reach the point where it can benefit from subsidies.

As in Italy, the Spanish case also reveals the perverse results of incomplete or ill-planned regulation. In 1977, Spain was a country with a high level of economic development and a complex degree of social stratification. But the majority of voters were only weakly integrated into active political life, and party income from membership was amongst the lowest in Europe. On the other hand, while the amount of public subsidies is substantial, it has proven insufficient to cover the rising costs of campaigns. So as elsewhere, parties—in particular the Socialists—developed alternative funding techniques. As in France, the Spanish Socialists failed to benefit from the sources of finance (from business) enjoyed by more conservative parties, or, as in Italy, from controlling vast areas of the public sector. This partly explains their heavier involvement in new and illicit forms of finance. Other factors explaining PSOE corruption include the duration of its hold on the state, the "monocratic" leadership of Felipe Gonzalez (which bears considerable similarity to Craxi's dominance of the PSI) and the continuation of many illicit practices from the Franco years.

Public funding, therefore, did not prevent extensive corruption. Its real effect was to integrate Spanish parties—and especially the Socialists—more closely into the state and distance them from civil society. Again, the parallels with Craxi's Italian Socialist Party are clear. In Spain, the system of party finance seems to have been more important even than in Italy in strengthening the oligarchic tendencies already present in party organization. The proportion of public funds going to the coffers of Spanish political parties is probably the highest in Europe: 100 percent for the PSOE and 90 percent for the Partido Popular (Popular Party). Meanwhile, funding from membership dues is the lowest: less than 1 percent for the PSOE and 1.5 percent for the

Partido Popular. Antonio Torres del Moral concludes that Spanish parties are completely dependent on government control—more the embodiment of "raison d'état" than independent representatives of public opinion.[34] The role of the media also seems to have been more important in Spain. Expenditure by Spanish political parties in election campaigns is higher than in most European countries and the cost of electoral campaigns for the large Spanish parties increased especially between 1977 and 1982 when spending grew by around 200 percent.[35] These expenses were driven in part by the central role played by the media in Spanish election campaigns. Spain, after all, was the first country in the western world to build its party and electoral system after the advent of television, making the impact of the media on party leadership image, campaigns and political competition more important than elsewhere.[36]

Regardless of differences in the causes of corruption, both the Spanish and Italian Socialist parties developed what Sapelli has called "a specific form of southern European *caciquismo"*—i.e., a party-leader based clientelism, linking an amoral élite with "other actors of a widespread illegality."[37] The Filesa affair, uncovered in early 1993, revealed that two elected PSOE representatives ran a front company that paid party bills by charging businesses and banks for fictitious consultancy work. Other revelations showed how a Portuguese company, Rio Cocon SL, and the German Siemens had both paid large kickbacks to the PSOE or firms run by its officials.[38] This type of operation was facilitated immensely by the PSOE's monopoly of state power. As Elorza explains, this monopoly was linked to two other sources of corrupt activity: the decline of ideology and emergence of new relations between leftist political élites and business and the legacy of Francoist administrative corruption, fuelled by the 1980s expansion of public finances. Thus, while the system of state funding may have encouraged corrupt practices, the real problem, as in Italy, was its reinforcement of an existing opportunity structure. For this reason, recent reform proposals—which seek to limit campaign expenditure, restrict increases in public funding, prohibit anonymous contributions and make party accounts transparent and accessible—also emphasize the need for a legal regulation and guarantee of internal party democracy.[39] A new system of party finance will only work well if party democracy is revitalized.

France: A Case of Political Hypocrisy

The French case contrasts with both Italy and Spain, in that public finance for parties was not available until relatively recently. Indeed, until the 1988 law on party finance, not only was direct public funding unavailable but donations were prohibited. As a result, French parties raised money increasingly through illegal methods.[40] In refusing to confront the issue of party funding, France provides the clearest case of political hypocrisy. For while decrying illegality in public, in practice the political parties developed multiple techniques of illegal financing. They were eventually forced to regulate only by revelations of scandal and the hostility of public opinion. Thus France before 1988 bears some similarities to Italy before 1974, in that it was assumed that neither party finance regulation nor public funding were necessary. However, the historical reasons for this state of affairs were quite different, even if the corruption opportunity structure bears many similarities.

Thus, while the issue of party funding seemed not to feature in Italy's constitutional settlement, when the Fifth Republic was founded some ten years later, De Gaulle's negative view of political parties discouraged the elaboration of funding regulation. As a result, parties were subject to the restrictions on funding contained in the 1901 law on associations. As a case *par excellence* of perverse—and in this case indirect—regulation, this law hindered the legal raising of funds by prohibiting parties from accepting donations and gifts from individuals as well as from legal and neutral entities such as endowments. Except for the Communist Party, which had a sizeable income from membership dues—in addition to "fraternal funding" from Eastern Europe and the USSR—most parties were unable to finance themselves in this way. Since the parties did not receive any direct payments from the Treasury either, they were more or less forced into illegality.

One of the few subsidies granted by the Treasury before 1988 was awarded to presidential candidates receiving more than 5 percent of the votes in the first ballot. But the intention was to ensure equal opportunity amongst the individual candidates rather than support for their parties. For elections to parliament, certain campaign expenditures were also refunded by the state. "Quasi-legal" methods of party finance were also important. For example, Article 6 of the 1901 law that prohibited the acceptance of donations was circumvented in various ways. There was often a resort to cash donations that was tolerated by government officials. Firms associated with the parties often paid campaign expenses arising from opinion polls or printing costs. One of the most important funding methods—also used in Spain, to fight ETA terrorism for example—were the "secret funds" made available to the party of government every year. These could be used to finance plans that were not to be made public on the grounds of "raison d'état."[41]

Given these regulatory circumstances, it is not hard to understand why illegal practices proliferated or why French parties have been embroiled in financial scandal. Local level politicians and officials have been particularly susceptible. In 1987, several scandals were revealed in the newspapers: the "affaire Luchaire," "Carrefour du Développement," and the "Urba" case in Marseilles in which, similarly to the Spanish Filesa affair, a Socialist Party fund was uncovered which was fed by exchanging political favours for "donations." These cases pointed to the need for legislation and candidates for the presidential elections had to take a position on the issue. The crisis peaked when, under pressure from President Mitterrand, who perceived that "something had to be done," Prime Minister Michel Rocard and Minister of the Interior Pierre Joxe prepared a law on party funding. Unfortunately, one article of the project was the amnesty for parliamentarians linked to political finance "affairs." Cases of personal enrichment and infractions qualified as corruption were excluded. Thus, the law was morally questionable and its timing bad: the public saw it only as a means of absolving corrupt politicians.

Nevertheless, reforms since the late 1980s have imposed a strong regulatory system, setting campaign spending limits, preventing political campaigning on television apart from that organized by the state, limiting private and corporate contributions and introducing strict rules of disclosure on income and spending.[42] While these rules will not prevent abuses, they are a step in the right direction. The objectives of the 1988 law on the "transparency of finance in political life" are suggested by its title.[43] Article 1 required that presidential candidates disclose their financial circumstances prior to the election. Article 2 governed the public financing of the election campaigns of presidential candidates. Above and beyond the previous reimbursement of expenses, the candidates received a set sum reimbursement for campaign costs. In addition to private and public subsidies, candidates could finance their election campaign through private donations within a maximum fixed by the law. In order to encourage donations from private individuals and companies, contributions to candidates were provided with special tax privileges, amounting to an indirect form of public funding. A further source of income for candidates included the allocations guaranteed by the party: in 1988, Chirac received 40.3 percent of his campaign funding from the RPR, and Mitterrand received 37.3 percent from the PS, while candidates from smaller parties received less.[44] The legislation also aimed to limit campaign expenditure. Candidates receiving public finance were not only bound by expenditure limits but were also required to account for campaign costs. Finally, a candidate had to collect funds through a "society for the funding of the election" or by appointing a neutral person as an "authorized financial agent."[45] This regulation permitted, at least in theory, an easier control of their accounts.

Most of this legislation is still in place, but successive scandals made necessary further reform to defuse the increasing discontent and mistrust of public opinion. Further laws in the 1990s have sought to reduce campaign spending, make party financing more transparent and increase funding by the general public. The 1990 law limits electoral expenses and clarifies the financing of political activities. The 1993 law, which aimed to make funding more transparent, was more restrictive. Private donations were made legal and verifiable, even if it remains possible to finance a candidate secretly through donations to the party. In 1995, the 1990 law was strengthened by prohibiting the financing of parties and campaigns by private and public-sector companies. Among other minor innovations, the funds authorized for presidential campaigns were reduced by 30 percent and the income and wealth of members of the National Assembly has now to be declared to a special commission. All of these rules should contribute to reducing corruption and illicit funding.

*   *   *

There are clear contrasts as well as similarities among all three cases. In Italy, an inadequate and incomplete system of political funding compounded the covert forms of finance inherited from the pre-fascist period and expanded under the early years of DC rule and state colonization. In France, a more rational-legal state structure with less extensive party penetration saw, nonetheless, the emergence of illicit finance as the main source of party funding. To a large extent, it was the system of regulation—or rather the absence of one directly tailored to the needs of political parties in an era of increasing political costs—that provided the scope and necessity for dubious and illegitimate means. In Italy, by contrast, the regulations were simply subverted by pre-existing practice. Nevertheless, what the three countries share is a wider political opportunity structure conducive to corruption characterized by weak checks and balances—particularly in local government—alongside closely interlocking political, bureaucratic and economic élites. This opportunity structure allowed several modes of illicit financing to develop:

- A centralized form, organized nationally through fictitious enterprises (Urba in the case of the French Socialist Party, Filesa-Time Export for the Spanish Socialists) which accumulated and distributed kickbacks;[46]
- A more fragmented and complicated form of illegal financing, involving the accumulation of kickbacks and their transfer and laundering (e.g., into unnumbered Swiss bank accounts) by particular party entrepreneurs via various intermediary companies (alleged examples include Bettino Craxi and his immediate entourage in the Italian Socialist Party and Francois Léotard and his main collaborator, Renaud Donnedieu, in the *Parti Républicain Francais*);[47]
- And the Italian system of *lotizzazione* which occurred at a general level throughout the political system, with parties benefiting according to their electoral importance.

The mechanisms whereby a political opportunity structure is exploited therefore vary, both between and within countries, according to circumstances.

Political Scandals and Party Finance Reform

Why have long-established forms of political finance only been denounced on a wide scale since the late 1980s? As discussed above, part of the explanation lies in the recent expansion of the opportunity structure of corruption, including the growth of the public sector and the deregulation of finance. These changes coincided with a "cultural" shift, involving a transformation of the ethics of public service and the emergence of a "get rich" ethos amongst political and business élites. In the Italian case, the *tangentopoli* revelations were part of a series of events thrown up by a structural crisis with four dimensions: a crisis of the parties, a crisis of the political class, a crisis of institutions, and a crisis of the state. The structural problems of Spain and France were less acute and certainly less system threatening. However, in all three cases, a number of *conjunctural* factors were important in creating scandals, redefining acceptable practice and driving forward the "ethical" transition. It was the interaction of these factors—greater political competition, the role (supine or protagonistic) of the media and the intervention of prosecuting magistrates—that produced revelations of corruption, defined them as "scandalous," secured prosecution and helped generate public support for reform. At the core of these developments lay the competitive mobilization of actors with a new agenda.

In setting out the macro-variables that have contributed to the emergence of scandal, we do not wish to suggest that these are the only important factors. Micro-level mechanisms sustaining the process of corrupt exchange are critically important, as set out most instructively in the work of Della Porta and Vanucci on Italy.[48] Our point here is not to provide a complete picture of the mechanisms whereby, for example, individuals, as in the Italian case, began to testify against corrupt politicians. It is rather to stress the importance of understanding the interaction between actors with specific personal and professional interests in creating the context in which such anti-corruption mobilisation could be sustained.

Thus, it is clear that the denunciation of a corrupt person or practice requires not only that an act contravenes a country's penal code. For a denunciation to gain support within the judicial sphere depends on the definition of the law, the extent to which magistrates have the power and independence to pursue the case (high in Italy, much lower in France) and on the legal culture of the country concerned. Once taken up by magistrates, the case can produce a scandal only if the media choose to transform it into one by focusing on the public figures concerned and identify their behaviour with a wider set of practices, thereby mobilising public opinion. The media are thus a strategic site for breaking open what we can call "coalitions of silence." The transformation of judicial and political events into a scandal is by and large the result of media activity, which filters and communicates, but also simplifies, personalizes and sensationalizes information at high speed, a relatively new situation in countries like Spain and France following the liberalization of the media market. At the same time, the process of scandal production is also facilitated if various political actors decide to exploit corruption as a power resource in political competition.[49] In looking in greater detail at the importance of political competition, the media and the judiciary in this regard, we can begin to assess their relative importance in each country, without detracting from our thesis that it is their *interaction* that explains the explosion of political scandal in recent years.

The increase in the stakes of *political competition* has impelled certain groups to fan the flames of scandal and exploit it to their own advantage. Party competition has increased as much within the main political parties as between them. In Italy, the transformation of the Communist Party into the post-communist PDS (now DS – Democratic Left) removed the only justification for its exclusion from government by the DC and its allies. The dizzying rise of the regionalist, populist, anti-Southern and anti-corruption Lombard (later Northern) League seriously threatened the DC vote in the North and tore through the fabric of the old party system. That system was itself generating more and more internal contradictions as the emergence of a transversal structure of collusion transferred the most important conflicts to the level of internal party factions.[50] This kind of competition was accentuated in the early 1990s when resources in the political market place diminished, just as new competitors (the Northern League, *Forza Italia*) were becoming active. In Spain, the hegemony of the PSOE came under threat in the 1990s, eventually leading to the victory of the *Partido Popular* (PP) in 1996. Disillusion grew amongst Socialist supporters when the economic boom of the 1980s turned to recession, exacerbating competition both with the opposition PP and *within* the PSOE. This is why the Filesa case in Spain became such a landmark scandal in the runup to the 1993 elections. For the early 1990s had witnessed a struggle between two tendencies—the *Guerristas* (supporters of Alfonso Guerra, the party vice-secretary and deputy Prime Minister) and the *renovadores* ("renovators"): Guerra was forced to resign in 1991 over revelations that his brother Juan had used Socialist Party premises for dubious business practices. In France, micro-competition was most important, given relative stability in the bipolar party system. When in the Botton/Noir case, a shareholder of a chemical business denounced its director, Pierre Botton, for mismanagement, the real target, in fact, was his father-in-law, Michel Noir, the mayor of Lyon for whom he acted as campaign manager. Noir had left the RPR after a fight in 1990 to be more independent after trying to create a group of "renovators" in the party in the 1980s.

As for the *role of the media*, only in the Spanish case have they been arguably the *major* protagonist. In Italian broadcasting, private channels have been dominated by Silvio Berlusconi's *Fininvest* group (now *Mediaset*) while the main public channels were divided among the parties, with the DC and PSI controlling RAI 1 and RAI 2. In exchange for not obstructing the deal, the PCI/PDS was given RAI 3. Investigative reporting has little tradition in either television or the written press. The pursuit of corruption was therefore left to a new generation of magistrates whose investigative powers were strengthened in the struggle against terrorism and organized crime (see below). In Spain, by contrast, it seems that the role of political opposition is played increasingly by newspapers rather than parties. Nevertheless, the role of the media is difficult to evaluate because, although the Spanish appear to be more confident in their press, fewer of them actually read it than in either Italy or France. Political influence on the Spanish press is also important. Even *El Mundo*, the paper that has been most assiduous in exposing corruption and generating scandal, is suspected of being backed by obscure economic interests and sustaining right-wing parties, particularly the PP. In France, investigative journalism is being practised by more and more newspapers, but it is still not common or routine, perhaps because they have always been close to institutional communication. The management of TV channels is regularly subject to political deals and pressures. *Le Monde*, however, occupies a special place and its prominent investigative journalist, now chief editor, Edwy Plenel, has been important as an opinion leader in defining "affairs," such as Botton/Noir, as scandals.[51]

The third key factor is the *judiciary*. Its role is linked to judicial independence and this has been greater in consensual than majoritarian polities, partly explaining its relative weakness in Spain and France.[52] Nevertheless, the confidence of the general public in judicial institutions has increased in all three countries as their confidence in politicians has declined—an important, but highly problematic, transfer of legitimacy. This has been especially evident in Italy where judicial independence and ability of prosecuting magistrates to investigate the activities of politicians is constitutionally guaranteed. Judges are not political appointees, even if their political preferences are sometimes rather evident and closer to the centre-left. Their role was strengthened in the struggle against terrorism in the 1970s and the investigative powers of public prosecutors was reinforced by the 1989 Code of Criminal Procedure and by subsequent legislation following the high-profile murders of anti-Mafia judges Falcone and Borsellino. These extensive powers were used to considerable (and controversial) effect in the prosecution of political corruption in the early-to-mid-1990s. Indeed, *tangentopoli* could not have been uncovered without these powers—although in the last few years, the support of politicians and public opinion has begun to wane and the independence and virtual unaccountability of the public prosecutors called into question.[53] In Spain, by contrast, the judiciary has long been accused of collaborating with the executive, and the Socialist government tried to appoint party sympathizers to leading posts in the General Council of the Judiciary (*Consejo General del Poder Judicial*, CGPJ). Tensions were at their strongest in the mid-1980s when a law reduced the powers of the CGPJ and assigned the election of its members to parliament rather than the judicial corps. But, as in Italy, judges and investigative magistrates have become key figures in the process of struggle against political corruption. Moreover, although the judiciary is still often criticized for being slow in investigations, its role as upholder of the law and in pursuing corruption cases has steadily become more important.

The independent role of the magistracy is probably weakest in France, where political power remains quite influential. The *Gardes des Sceaux* (Ministers of Justice) from both the left and the right have provoked conflicts with the judiciary when they have tried to hush up "affairs" linked to their respective parties. Harsh debates between the judiciary and the executive are frequent. Among significant recent examples (1997) were the clash provoked by a letter from the Minister of Justice Jacques Toubon to his Swiss counterpart, in which he requested that diplomatic channels be used when French prosecuting judges needed information from their Swiss counterparts (in effect keeping investigations under the control of the Justice Minister), and the attempt to narrow the legal content of criminal prosecution, such as *"abus de biens sociaux"* (use of a public organization's resources for private ends). This latter measure was opposed by the magistrates and reopened the debate on their independence and the prosecution of politicians. An attempt to resolve these problems has been made by the *Commission Truche*, which advocated, among other measures, that the intervention of the Minister of Justice be proscribed in individual cases. But the fact that its report has been widely attacked for not advocating a removal of the magistracy from ministerial tutelage suggests that the debate is far from over.[54]

Broadly speaking, then, although these three factors have all played a role in the revelation and prosecution of illicit party funding, the disclosure of corruption as scandal has been more influenced by the judiciary in Italy, by the media in Spain and by the use of scandal in political competition in France. What is striking about all three cases is the way in which an expansion in illicit practice in the 1980s and 1990s was only checked by the mobilization of public opinion by actors whose powers are ill-defined and potentially subject to new limitations and constraints. The role of the judiciary in both Italy and Spain is notable in this regard. In the confusion of powers that tends to characterize the Latin democracies, the absence of an unambiguous recognition of the role of checks and balances on power will continue to hamper those forces dedicated to the fight against corruption.

Conclusions

This article began by arguing that the problem of political finance and widespread corruption in Latin European countries stems from particular developmental patterns and political opportunity structures. Despite the more dramatic nature and specific character of the Italian example, the problem of party finance derives from several common sources: the permanent institutional weakness of political parties in these democracies; the crisis of political funding, common to all democracies in the recent period, but which has taken a particular—and arguably more acute—form in Latin Europe; and the relatively late or inadequate systems of funding regulation put in place. Given the absence of adequate checks and balances in these systems and interlocking political, bureaucratic and economic élites, complex corruption opportunity structures have emerged. In these circumstances, the objectives of regulatory reform in political funding have frequently been subverted.

In recent years, the explosion of political scandals in these countries has been the symptom simultaneously of an "ethical transition" and the manipulation of revelations by particular interests. The resulting clash between politicians and public opinion—mediated and governed to a greater or lesser extent by the media and magistrates—has produced an ongoing struggle over the desirable extent of prosecution, the relationship between politics and the judiciary and the most appropriate mode of party finance. Nowhere in Latin Europe have these issues been fully resolved. Spain still awaits an effective set of reforms, despite numerous proposals for re-regulating party funding and revitalizing party democracy. In France and Italy, the independence of the judiciary and its proper role in pursuing and prosecuting corruption is still a subject of intense daily debate; and judges and politicians are likely to remain antagonists rather than collaborators. In France, a rather detailed and effective system of regulation has been put in place over the last few years, while in Italy, the direct funding of party organizations abolished in 1993 has been resurrected by the new 1999 law, even if public opinion remains largely hostile to state funding for parties as such as opposed to their legitimate electoral expenses.

This raises a more general question concerning the role of parties in democracy. While a pluralistic system of representation and mediation of interests is critical to the effective functioning of democracy, the key agents of that system—political parties—have been steadily losing legitimacy, a process actually accelerated in Italy and other Latin countries by the disclosure of scandals. One result has been widespread opposition to party funding and a transfer of support to other actors such as the judiciary—raising complex issues about judicial independence and accountability, as well as the legitimacy of the governing class. Yet while the experience of the southern European countries reveals the immense difficulties in installing an effective system of party funding, it also shows that regulation can be effective if well-designed, backed by effective sanctions and accompanied by a parallel diffusion of appropriate ethics and norms. Despite the prevalence of self-serving and materialist values in recent years, and their erosion of an often already weak support for ideals of public service, we have also witnessed in Italy, Spain and elsewhere a reaction against the degeneration of public life. There has also been a reassertion of democratic principles, underpinned by a new belief in the rule of law—thanks largely to the actions of judges and magistrates, and, albeit infrequent, a crusading, investigative press. The importance of renovated systems of party finance for this new or revitalized order should not be underestimated.

Notes

* This is a slightly modified version of an article which appeared in *West European Politics*, Vol. 22, No. 3, July 1999.
** Véronique Pujas is a lecturer at the Institut d'Etudes Politiques in Grenoble, France. Martin Rhodes is Professor of European Public Policy in the Department of Political and Social Science, European University Institute, Florence, Italy.
1. H. Kitschelt, 'Political Opportunity Structures and Political Protest', *British Journal of Political Science*, vol. 16, no. 1 (1986), pp. 57-85.
2. As characterized by Heidenheimer, these range from 'white corruption' (which is accepted and tolerated) through 'grey corruption' (which is accepted and/or repudiated in a sort of moral limbo) to 'black corruption', which is widely rejected. A. J. Heidenheimer, 'Perspectives on the Perception of Corruption', in A. J. Heidenheimer, M. Johnston and V. T. Levine (eds.), *Political Corruption: A Handbook* (New Brunswick N.J.: Transaction Publishers 1989).
3. As expressed by a Milanese judge from the Italian *Mani Pulite* Pool: "Yes, I could imagine a situation in which there was a certain level of corruption (in France and Spain) but in which schools, trains and social services also function . . . and I could say, OK, we have a corrupt political class but it is also effective, therefore the problem is less serious. In Italy, by contrast, the state has become less efficient as corruption has expanded. We have a country which is the world's fifth economic power but which has the public services of a third world country. It is the progressive widening of this 'gap' that has made the scandals explode". See V. Pujas, *Les scandales politiques en France, en Italie et en Espagne. Construction, usages et conflits de légitimité*, Ph. D. thesis, (Florence: European University Institute 1999) p. 99.
4. Ibid., p. 293ff.
5. See E. Lama de Espinosa, 'Corrupción política y ética económica', in J. Tusell, E. Lama de Espinosa and R. Pardo (eds.), *Entre dos siglos. Reflexiones sobre la democracia español* (Madrid: Alianza 1996), pp. 521-555.
6. See, for example, A. J. Heidenheimer, 'The Topography of European Scandals and Corruption', *International Social Science Journal*, no. 149 (1996), pp.
7. P. Heywood, 'Continuity and Change: Analysing Political Corruption in Modern Spain', in W. Little and E. Posada-Carbó, *Political Corruption in Europe and Latin America* (London: Macmillan 1996), p. 127.
8. R. D. Putnam, *Making Democracy Work: Civic Traditions in Modern Italy* (Princeton, N.J.: Princeton University Press 1993) and F. Fukuyama, *Trust: The Social Virtues and the Creation of Prosperity* (London: Hamish Hamilton 1995).
9. Heywood, 'Continuity and Change'.
10. *Ibid.*, p. 128ff and A. Elorza, 'Tradition et modernité: la corruption politique en Espagne', *Confluences Méditerrannée*, no. 15 (1995), pp. 83-92.
11. Heidenheimer, 'The Topography of European Scandals'.
12. G. Sapelli, *Southern Europe Since 1945: Tradition and Modernity in Portugal, Spain, Italy, Greece and Turkey* (London: Longman 1995), pp. 17-18.
13. On Spain, see R. Cotarelo (ed.), *Transición política y consolidación democrática en España* (Madrid: CIS 1992).

14. See M. Giuliani, 'Measures of Consensual Law-Making: Italian *Consociativismo*', *South European Society & Politics*, vol. 2, no. 1 (1997), pp. 67-97.

15. M. Rhodes, 'Financing Party Politics in Italy: A Case of Systemic Corruption', *West European Politics*, vol. 20, no. 1 (1997), pp. 54-80 (special issue on 'Crisis and Transition in Italian Politics', edited by Martin Bull and Martin Rhodes).

16. See P. Heywood, 'Sleaze in Spain', *Parliamentary Affairs* vol. 48, no. 4 (1994), p. 734.

17. See F. Jiménez-Sánchez, 'Posibilidades y limites del escandolo politico commo una forma de control social', *Rivista Española de Investigaciones Sociológicas*, no. 66 (1994), pp. 7-36.

18. Lama de Espinosa, 'Corrupción política y ética económica'.

19. See M. Magatti, *Corruzione politica e società italiana* (Bologna: Il Mulino 1996), pp. 20-21.

20. See R. S. Katz and P. Mair, 'Changing Models of Party Organization and Party Democracy: The Emergence of the Cartel Party', *Party Politics,* vol. 1, no. 1 (1995), pp. 5-28.

21. *Ibid.*, pp. 15-16.

22. See HERMES, *Communication et politique*, nos. 17-18 (Paris: CNRS Ed. 1995).

23. See S. H. Alatas, *Corruption: Its Nature, Causes and Functions* (Aldershot: Avebury 1990).

24. This section draws heavily on Rhodes, 'Financing Party Politics in Italy'.

25. G. F. Ciaurro, 'Public Financing of Parties in Italy', in H. E. Alexander (ed.). *Comparative Political Finance in the 1980s* (Cambridge: Cambridge University Press 1989), pp. 153-171

26. See A. M. Chiesi, 'I meccanismi di allocazione nello scambio corrotto', *Stato e Mercato*, no. 43 (1995), p. 153 and E. Auci, 'Verità e problemi dei bilanci dei partiti', *Il Mulino*, no. 253 (1978), pp. 65-73.

27. See F. Cazzola, *Della Corruzione: Fisiologia e patologia di un sistema politico* (Bologna: Il Mulino, 1988), p. 119, Table 4.

28. A. Pizzorno, 'Lo scambio occulto', *Stato e mercato*, no. 34 (1992), pp. 3-34.

29. See D. Della Porta and A. Vannucci, *Corruzione politica e amministrazione pubblica* (Bologna: Il Mulino, 1994), p. 429ff.

30. M. Andreoli, *Andavamo in Piazza Duomo: Nella testimonianza di Mario Chiesa* (Milano: Sperling & Kupfer, 1993).

31. *Ibid.*, p. 483.

32. See M. Magatti, 'La modernizzazione fallita della società italiana: Tra fiducia personale e fiducia istituzionale', *Quaderni di Sociologia*, vol. 38-39, no. 8 (1994-5), pp. 33-53.

33. For details see Rhodes, 'Financing Party Politics'.

34. A. Torres Del Moral, 'El estado español de partidos', *Revista del Centro de Estudios Constitucionales*, no. 8 (1991), pp. 99-145.

35. See P. del Castillo, 'Financing of Spanish Political Parties' in Alexander, *Comparative Political Finance*, pp. 172-199.

36. See G. Colomé and L. Lopez Nieto, 'The Selection of Party Leaders in Spain', *European Journal of Political Research*, vol. 24, no. 3 (1993), pp. 349-360.

37. G. Sapelli, *Cleptocrazia: 'il meccanismo unico' della corruzione tra economia e politica* (Milan: Feltrinelli 1994), p. 123.

38. For details, see Heywood, 'Continuity and Change' and Elorza, 'Tradition et modernité'.

39. See D. López Garrido, 'La financiación de los partidos políticos. Diez propuestas de reforma', in *La financiación de los partidos políticos. Debate celebrado en el*

Centro de Estudios Constitucional, Madrid, 23 de novembre 1993 (Madrid: CEC 1994).

40. On French corruption, see Y. Mény, *La corruption de la République* (Paris: Fayard 1992)

41. See Y.-M. Doublet, 'L'argent et l'élection presidentielle', *Pouvoirs*, no. 70 (1994), pp. 43-52.

42. T. Drysch, 'The New French System of Political Finance', in A. B. Gunlicks (ed.), *Campaign and Party Finance in North America and Western Europe* (Boulder, Co.: Westview Press 1993), pp. 155-177.

43. G. Carcassone, 'Du non-droit au droit', *Pouvoirs*, no. 70 (1994), pp. 7-17.

44. Drysch, 'The New French System of Political Finance'.

45. A. Urgin, 'Les recettes des candidats', *Pouvoirs*, no. 70 (1994), pp. 19-31.

46. J.W. Dereymez, 'Les socialistes français, les socialistes espagnols et la corruption (1980-1990)', *Revue Internationale de Politique Comparée*, vol.4, no. 2 (1997), pp. 297-332.

47. *Le Monde*, 27 August 1998.

48. Della Porta and Vannucci, *Corruzione politica e amministrazione pubblica*.

49. Pujas, *Les scandales politiques en France, en Italie et en Espagne*, chapter four.

50. Rhodes, 'Financing Party Politics in Italy', p. 71ff.

51. See V. Pujas, *Le scandale comme mobilisation: Etude de l'Affaire Botton*, Mémoire de DEA, Institut d'Études Politiques de Grenoble (1994).

52. See P. Pederzoli and C. Guarnieri, 'Italy: A Case of Judicial Democracy?', *International Social Science Journal*, no. 152 (1997), pp. 253-270.

53. See C. Guarnieri, 'The Judiciary in the Italian Political Crisis', *West European Politics*, vol. 20, no. 1 (1997), pp. 157-175 (special issue on 'Crisis and Transition in Italian Politics', edited by Martin Bull and Martin Rhodes) and Mary L. Volcansek, 'Justice as Spettacolo: The Magistrature in 1997', in L. Bardi and M. Rhodes (eds.), *Italian Politics: Mapping the Future* (Westview Press/Istituto Cattaneo 1998), pp. 133-148.

54. See L. Cohen-Tanguy, 'Le procureur, le juge et le journaliste', *Le Monde*, 22 July (1997).

39

Parties, Campaign Finance and Political Corruption: Tracing Long-Term Comparative Dynamics

Arnold J. Heidenheimer

At a time when much is made of time series data that encompass only a few years, it is well to try to understand how perceptions of corruption have varied in Europe and America since the initial appearance of modern mass parties. Hence we will probe changing patterns in the interface between party finance processes and the perception of corruption incidence among the United States, West European states, as well as Japan and other Asian countries. Seeking to identify and compare relationships between party finance processes and political corruption poses many problems, and the basic assumption underlying this paper is that one way of illuminating them is to utilize a very broad canvas.

* * *

If we start by asking what connection political science wisdom at the turn of the twentieth century perceived between political party finance and political corruption, and where the two phenomena were most closely linked, the answer is both Europeans and Americans perceived that corruption was most highly nurtured through the patronage based party machines in America. At that time writers like Robert Michels discerned the emergence of party machines also in the German Social Democratic party. But then, American tendencies toward disciplined party organizations became radically undermined by the Progressive movement and the wave of legislation that it initiated.

Around 1900 the American reform coalition mounted a frontal attack against parties and their corporate allies, and was able to stop the party-controlled flow of legislation. This occurred almost simultaneously with belated Civil Service reform, leading to the creation of the "bastard in the party state." Subsequently the initiation of political finance limits and publicity culminated a quarter century during which the American party system seemed about to be propelled into a trajectory following the British pattern, but then spun off into a quite different direction with the diminution of the power of party leaders through the imposition of party primaries, and the reliance on publicity as a control mechanism.

It would be fruitful to project what European party theorists like Moisei Ostrogorski and Max Weber might have prognosticated around 1910 about how party finance and political corruption would come to be linked. Ostrogorski preferred the British model in part because of its lower corruption levels. Max Weber acknowledged parties as vectors of the political system, but followed Ostrogorski's critique in lamenting the persistence of public office patronage within the lower levels of American administration (Senigaglia, 164, 179).

Weber's insistence on sharply distinguishing between the roles of politicians and bureaucrats might have led him to accept the relative expansion of campaign fund raising by both parties and individual party candidates. For him the dominant question was "How political leadership in and through parties was possible, when party organizations became more bureaucratic and elections more democratic" (Bendix, 438–9). He would probably have endorsed the imposition of limits to donations to parties and candidates because of the consideration that the regulation of monetary influence was necessary to prevent "corruption or the appearance of corruption." He supported strengthening the party organizations, but he also would have attacked the alternative varieties of intermixing of party political and bureaucratic careers and domains which later came to be associated in varying degree with the party-state development in countries like France, Germany, and Italy.

It was only after World War I, a century after America, that most European countries came to have fully developed mass parties based on male adult suffrage. By then earlier America Progressive legislation reducing the power of party hierarchies was followed by limitations on party finance practices, which in 1925 were adopted as the Corrupt Practices Act. Thus the corruption labels of the Progressive period remained in use in inter-war America, as an instrument for monitoring electoral practices.

Such was scarcely the case in the Continental European countries, where the banner of exposing politico-financial scandals was waved mainly by anti-democratic parties of the Right, as in the attacks on the Zentrum politician Matthias Erzberger in Weimar Germany. If today we find it scarcely possible to reconstruct objective indicators of corruption for this period it is in part because, from the democratic perspective, potentially corrupt behavior patterns came to be eclipsed by, or intertwined with, the widespread reliance on violence and intimidation in the struggle among mass parties of various types. Thus, jealousy of the safe jobs which some German sickness funds provided for loyal Social Democratic workers provided ample targets for the Nazi attacks on alleged "Marxist corruption" The special offices set up after the Nazi takeover to combat such doings were dissolved in short order after the trade unions were dissolved and the SPD declared illegal. They were not needed to publicize that the Nazi stalwarts appointed to some health insurance posts were found to have feathered their nests as much or more than their predecessors (Angermund, chapter 32).

With different accents the relative neglect of corruption as a major national political issue continued into the post-World War II period.[1] During the 1940s and 50s there was only limited American-European comparison or invidious contrasting to highlight just how funding of parties and candidates violated rules against the mixing of public and private interests. When observers wrote about the "Americanization" of some European party systems, or when Kirchheimer wrote about the displacement of mass by catch-all parties, they usually did not significantly employ corruption-related concepts in their analysis of the play of interest groups and parties. The spin-off pattern that would catapult campaign costs, and diminish reliance on dues income from party members, was largely yet to come. Interest-group fundraising became controversial in the 1950s, but Adenauer as CDU party chairman did not find it necessary to use cash distributions to maintain intra-party loyalties, in the way later taken by his successor, Helmut Kohl.

Although the American campaign legislation which introduced limits on campaign contributions and publicity requirements was characterized by "faulty conception and casual enforcement," it was held to set standards in contrast with which the objectives of British legislation "were modest" (Heard, EB, 1959, 549–50). The only other European corrupt practices legislation briefly mentioned by political scientists in the 1959 edition of the *Encyclopedia Britannica* was the French legislation of 1913/14 (Gosnell, ibid. 124) Later, under the Fourth and Fifth Republics, French politicians lagged behind Germany in the legal regulation of party finance practices, and it took many decades until this was rectified in the late 1980s.

It was during the 1960s that social scientists began to examine both party finance and political corruption phenomena on a less nation-bound and parochial basis. At the start of that decade the basis for internationally comparative research was established through the creation of a committee on Party Finance and Political Corruption of the International Political Science Association. But the numerous scholars who came to pursue research presented to meetings of that body continued in a tradition of distinguishing rather sharply between, in the main, socially acceptable ways of financing political parties, and patterns of political corruption. Papers and books analyzed topics under one of the two categories, not both. For several decades there were virtually no attempts to simultaneously examine linkages between party finance processes and explicitly recognized patterns of political corruption.

There remained strong differences in the prevailing national core notions of corruption, particularly as to how they should be related to legality or unlawfulness. By itself, legality provides an inadequate criterion for cross-national comparison. For party finance practices provide a generally striking example of, "What is illegal in one country may not be in another, leading to situations in which similar acts may be defined as corrupt or not according to where they take place?" (Heywood, 1997,7). Even within the same national legal tradition, there was considerable variation among jurisdictions and over time in what was meant by the terms "corrupt" or "corruptly." In the United States, many states followed a model penal code by dropping the term, but other state courts refused to follow this pattern (Noonan, 644, 799). The struggle between those who wanted to keep or remove the corruption label from party and campaign finance legislation went back and forth. In its 1971 electoral law reform act Congress dropped the term corruption from the title, but a few years later the Supreme Court, in *Buckley v. Valeo* (1976), reasserted its status as a key concept with regard to the regulation of campaign finance.

A Three-Country Comparison: Germany, Italy, Japan

For theoretical perspectives that would help generalize about the party finance/corruption problem, a promising set of countries are the trio of Germany, Italy, and Japan. All three countries have developed party systems with limited pre-1945 antecedents. Apart from their heritage of renewing democratic traditions under post-1945 occupation tutelage, the emergent political systems of these three countries subsequently had in common long periods of dominance by conservative parties, whose funding depended mainly on business financing. Their electoral systems encouraged varying degrees of factionalism, and these countries also exhibited considerable differences with regard to their party laws, tendencies toward effective inter-party competition, public financing of parties and campaign use of private media, and the monitoring role of public prosecutors and especially their constitutional courts.

These factors conditioned the degree to which party-financing activities within the three party systems led to the incidence of extensive political corruption cases. Corruption here is conceptualized under the "abuse of public office for private profit" definition, whether or not it is combined with partisan use of public office.[2] Building on the widely cited definition by Nye (chapter 17) we recognize that definitions can employ the abuse of public office for private gain in numerous ways, including the utilization of party power in quid pro quos for policies benefiting the interests of donors at the expense of voters and tax-payers. But how directly the connection is perceived may depend on judicial and public opinion judgments.

Significant for the developments in the three countries were whether nineteenth-century political development had created conditions for bureaucratic autonomy, or whether the post-1945 inheritors of party traditions build upon broad patterns of patronage. In Germany the Christian Democrats evolved within the former mold, whereas in Italy the Christian Democrats utilized control of the bureaucracy to continue operating a patronage-based systems functioning within and through their factions (Shefter, 443–5). During the occupation period, party politicians in national parliaments held decision-making power earlier in Japan, where large scale corruption scandals erupted at a time, as in 1946–7, when German politicians still held only limited power in *Land* governments. Election laws adopted in Japan and Italy permitted or even encouraged organized intra-party factions.

Concern of business leaders to prevent flagrant corruption from enflaming anti-capitalist sentiments led in all three national cases to the evolution of mechanisms through which political contributions were funneled through associational channels. But due to the early German implementation of both the parties law and an effective constitutional court, the subsequent German development was distinctive because of the immense amounts of litigation and legislative energies that came to be devoted to monitoring the boundary between legitimate party financing and illegitimate corrupt and political exchanges.[3]

Here constitutional-based jurisprudence was crucial. In contrast to Germany, Italy activated its constitutional court only in the 1960s and its 1974 Parties Law was never tested for constitutionality by its highest court. Japan did not even have a parties law until the 1990s whereas the German party law and related legislation were subject to intensive and repeated scrutiny by the Constitutional Court (BVG) from the 1950s to date. As West Germany became the European pacesetter in public party subsidies, the repercussions of alternative subsidy formulas on the equality of chances of both citizens and parties were examined by successive generations of judges with excruciating dexterity. Hordes of party law specialists became adroit in the ritualistic dance steps that came to constitute a republican substitute for the ballet performances that had once graced the Archducal palace in Karlsruhe. It was in the context of such a highly refined network of rule-making, rule-testing and rule-adaptation that the charges of high level corruption involved in the Flick scandal exploded in the 1980s. What the handling of this case showed about the prevalence and punishment of political corruption remained in sharp dispute.

Did the constitutional court in its 1989 decision, in effect increasing the permissible monetary limits of party donations, legalize activities which had been potentially criminal, and exculpate those politicians who had been re-garded as guilty of trading ministerial decisions for party donations? This complex panorama snapshot captures how the court set a moving stage in front of which German audiences were enabled to judge whether their leading party politicians had transgressed, according to intuitive perception the bound-aries delineating between the zones of white, gray, and black corruption.

When in the early 1960s public financing of parties was first discussed as an alternative to the reliance on associational funding from business, the President of the German Industrial Federation, Berg, angrily told a journalist that he would be quite happy if all parties were financed by the state, because "then we in industry can save a lot of money, for we could then go out and simply buy the number of deputies which we require" (Heidenheimer/Langdon). Twenty years later, the Flick case achieved notoriety because the donations came directly from the Flick firm to top party leaders and minis-ters, with plausible links to tax policy outcomes directly benefiting the firm. The transactions were potentially illegal, because ministers were subject to the same rules as the civil servants, and not just those of parliamentarians.

Writing much later, a sociologist judged that the financing pattern which Berg defended "allows the establishment of clientelistic relationships be-tween donors and politicians and lends itself to outright bribery" (Blankenburg 1989, PC, 115). But in 1985, all members of the BVG Senate which heard the Flick case, and all except one member the Bundestag committee which exam-ined the charges subsequently, agreed that the donations did not fall afoul of the legal rules relating to either the bribery or the corruption criterion. The only dissident was a Green Party committee member named Otto Schily (who later switched to the SPD and became Interior Minister in 1999) who in a dissenting opinion said it constituted a clear case of political corruption.[4]

When the Italian public was confronted in 1993 by the Milan revelations which triggered the *mani puliti* investigations, it had the benefit of much less prolonged tutoring in the legal conditionality of political exchange relation-ships. They had been alerted through the 1988 CENSIS study to widely prevalent administrative corruption of 136 trillion Lira a year (Landfried, 244). The contract kickbacks involved went partly to private pockets, but largely into party treasuries. The greater need for these was partly due to the fact that whereas public subsidies were covering an increasing share of Ger-man party expenditures, the equivalent ratio was decreasing in the Italian case[5] (Landfried, 116). Thus the illegal contributions from public and other companies were estimated to have totaled as much as the public subsidies, and later on, several times as much as these (Bardi/Morlino, 260).

Most unique in the Italian use of corruptly gained funds, in European comparison, was the way in which these were used to buy membership cards by the various party factions. Thus the subtlety of clientelistic networks was accompanied by the apparently crude purchase of intra-party power (Dellaporta and Vannucci, 118–9). By contrast, within the PSI *truppe cammellate* were mobilized by "falanges" of competing factions (Rhodes, 71). These ways were scarcely paralleled in the German or other north-European cases, where centralized party leadership generally was able to force factions to sublimate their conflicts. But the secret and illegal receipt of funds which the 1999 revelations showed Chancellor Kohl to have engaged in seemed to have been triggered in good part by his attempt as CDU leader to maintain the personal loyalty of groups of CDU local leaders. Kohl became a very different Chancellor and party leader from what Adenauer had been, in good part because "the legalistic web generated by the ceaseless rule amending process may have woven silken threads which have enervated Chancellors' aloof standing" (Heidenheimer, 1989, 225).

Where the locus of the German legal development differed was in that the growth of public party financing related to the debate about the legality of various practices, centered in a crucial way on the question of whether the funding practices, violated the "Equality principle" which guaranteed citizens equal voice in political decision-making. In the aftermath of the Flick case, the BVG was accused of weakening its equality stand by accepting higher donor limits. Subsequently it seems to have tried to correct this by the 1992 decision in which it required a lower donation limit and outlawed tax deductibility of corporate contributions,

Party Finance and Corruption Rankings

If one seeks to bring together data pertaining to comparisons of party finance practices and corruption incidence for all three countries over the four decades since the 1960s, one can start with a 1963 issue of the *Journal of Politics* which included articles on party finance in eight countries. In a summary article, "Notes On Practices and Towards a Theory," the best estimates of campaign-year party expenditures were translated into how much per-capita costs were equivalent to in terms of the hourly wage income of an industrial worker. The index numbers varied from a half-hour to more than twenty hours.

As our table 39.1 bears out, the rank order which the three countries held with regard to 1960 campaign expenditures correlated closely with their ranking on perceived corruption incidence in the 1990s. Italy, which was the highest in party expenditures in Western countries in 1960, was also the developed country with the highest corruption ranking in the 1990s.

One might go on to ask why Japan's campaign and corruption placements are higher than those of the U.S., but so much lower than those of Italy? It seems that we may partly attribute the lower U.S. ranking to the fact that whereas American party factions compete with each other, they do not do so in the general elections within the same electoral districts, as was the case in

Table 39.1
Party Campaign Expenditures and Corruption Incidence

Country	Party & Campaign Expenditure Index, early 1960s	Corruption Perception Index 1995–97
Australia	0.45	1.25
United Kingdom	0.64	1.59
Germany	0.95	1.79
United States	1.12	2.31
India	1.25	7.45
Japan	1.36	3.2
Italy	4.50	6.19
Philippines	16.00	6.95
Israel	20.50	2.12

Sources: A.J. Heidenheimer. 1963. "Comparative Party Finance: Notes on Practices and Toward a Theory," *The Journal of Politics*, **25: 790–811. Corruption Index from Transparency International. Indexes are averages of 1995, 1996 and 1997 reports, except for Israel (1996–7 only) and Philippines (1997 only). Index numbers subtracted from ten.**

the other two countries. In turn the Italian corruption perception index was probably higher than the Japanese because of the way in which sectors of the public administration were colonized by particular parties to a degree not apparent in Japan. If political ministers and their entourage were themselves involved in taking kickbacks for their party coffers, it was difficult for them to police bureaucratic subordinates who were accepting bribes for personal benefit. For, "where. . .the interests of top politicians dictate the activities of top bureaucrats in the performance of their duties, the handing out of individual material inducements in the political process is likely to flourish" (Etzioni-Halevy, 295).

The much greater vulnerability to corruption charges of Italian parties may be attributed to lesser efficacy of legal and institutional controls over practices by cartel parties. Lacking the kinds of built-in class- and religious-based moral monitoring found more efficacious in North Europe, Italians were unable to keep dominant clientelistic relations from infiltrating both the party and bureaucratic components (Dellaporta/Vannucci). The resultant partial fusion of the two sectors distinguished it from Japan, where larger parts of the national bureaucracy were long able to keep somewhat aloof from the contract kickbacks and similar corrupt practices, even though some were indiscrete in gift-taking practices.

Global Party Finance and Corruption Rankings

If one relates the above-cited sets of data graphically for the entire set of countries, one can estimate more easily why which contrasts between national patterns are more fruitful for comparison. Given that the other countries differ much more than our original trio, we find to our astonishment a pretty consistent relationship between the two quite different rankings, based on observations made thirty-five years apart. With two exceptions, those of India and Israel, the rank order of the countries on the two very different scales are similar and symmetrical.

Why would seven of the nine cases show such a strong linear fit, given that most of the corruption perception ratings relate to behavior of bureaucrats who are probably extracting bribes for their personal use, rather than passing funds on to parties?[6]

An initial thesis for how the relationship is demonstrated over time would postulate that the parties' need for money leads to institutionalized ways of favor trading, which encourages or condones corrupt exchanges even in arenas relatively remote from partisan campaign politics. Even though party finance may not rely predominantly on quid-pro quo contributions, the extent that some prevail may symbolize societal toleration of exploiting public offices for individual private benefit. Clearly party finance donations can provide access, but often they do more than that. How much more varies from case to case, but also among systems with varying modes and levels of campaign expenditures. Therefore, one should perhaps perceive high expenditure systems as adjusting the higher framework of opportunity costs and benefits. Hence, intended disincentives like publicity and public financing may have diminishing effects the higher the expenditure level.

Cartel Partisan Corruption

Ostrogorski might be delighted to hear that critics of the emergence of so called cartel parties declare themselves as continuing his wariness about the evolution from party government to "the party state." Ideological statements such as those alluding to an "invasion of the state by the parties" (Mair, Katz) seem to follow in his footsteps, and those of some earlier American Progressives. These recent hard-nosed European academic analyses seem to have emerged especially in the wake of the implosion of the Italian party system in the early 1990s.

But how well do other European parties in cartel party systems sustain a more generalized thesis? If the Scandinavian party systems are perceived as strong examples of cartel party systems, then their relative lack of corruption incidence would call the development of a causal thesis into question. In Scandinavia these are regulated and monitored by a tight network of both public and private organizations which bridge the public-private boundary. If "occultness" does not thrive in Malmö, it is largely because in Sweden pecuniary interests are made apparent in many ways. But recently Scandinavian parties are seen as having abandoned many mass party characteristics, and as having moved closer to the Swedish state and become almost "semi-state agencies" (Pierre and Widfeldt). In Denmark it is anticipated that they will shortly be financed entirely by the state, with resulting downgrading of intra-party channels (Bille, 156). Despite these tendencies, the countries run by these parties have come to be consistently identified as ranking lowest in Europe and the world in corruption perception.

Catchall Systems

It might be useful to ponder how theorists like Weber and Ostrogorski would have reconciled some year 2000 American roles with regard to corruption enhancement propensities. On the one hand, the enormous American effort aimed at the publicity of the regulation, subsidy and sanitation of party finance and campaign practices has scarcely grown more effective over time. Despite large bureaucracies monitoring the raising and spending of campaign funds by parties and candidates the achievement of a regulatory reputational equilibrium has remained well beyond grasp. As the *New York Times* bemoaned editorially in 1998, "It took nearly 75 years for the United States to enact laws protecting elections from the corrupting influence of campaign contributions. But it has taken only four years to eviscerate those reforms" (*NYT*, 10 October 1998). Hence, the vast scope of regulatory and enforcement efforts with regard to party finance failed to achieve a high ranking with regard to corruption enhancement propensities.

In the 1990s, the United States stayed well in the middle field of international ranking regarding domestic corruption, well below those of Britain and most European countries. With regard to international corruption it was pushing other OECD member to criminalize bribery of foreign officials by companies based in the advanced industrial countries. The key American goal in these negotiations was the inclusion of payments to political parties which would be criminalized if they entailed bribery. Some of its friends questioned whether the results of such endeavors could be expected to achieve higher benefit/cost ratios than those achieved on home territory.

An India-Israel Axis?

Should the three countries of India, Italy and Israel also be treated as a potential axis? The question is worth pondering. It may be that Israel is unique in having to be analyzed in exogenous terms that go beyond the characteristics of the national party systems. This uniqueness can be attributed partly to the predominance of the military, and the security for which only it could vouch, and would go far to explain why despite all its scandals, Israel never suffered the equivalent of a Bofors or Lockheed affair. Whereas the security concern was regionally focused, the related economic goal of becoming a center of technological innovation evolved within a global context. Thus the drive to make Israel second only to California as a center of advanced technical innovation put a much greater premium on the suppression of corruption tendencies in defense and other technology contracts.

To explain the outlier status of India and Israel, we can begin by noting that they became generally distinguished during most of the period since the 1960s by inclusion into their systems of many new ethnic groups, and their political parties. These were able to wrest national political supremacy from previously dominant parties which had earlier perpetuated more Western European political and bureaucratic models, but also tolerated increasing corruption.

By the 1990s, after two generations of achieving independence from British control, it is evident that the two countries excelled in setting different kinds of world records: Israel for party and campaign expenditures, and India for the reputation of having a most thoroughly corrupt democratic regime.

The record which Israel posted in the 1990s with regard to party and campaign expenditures is partly as a result of public subsidies which are the highest in the world, and three times those of Germany on a per-capita basis. Campaign expenditures reached a total of $20 per capita in the 1992 national elections. "While the influence of big money was severely limited in interparty competition, new avenues of corruption were opened in internal party primaries," (Hoffnung, 146) leading to per-capita party spending of $38, in the municipal elections of 1993.

Whereas corruption charges contributed to erosion of the Labor party's dominance in Israel in the 1970s, scandalization in India remained inhibited by the fact that even politically conscious Indians had "not yet fully grasped the corrupting influence of big money in the absence of adequate institutional safeguards" (Somjee, 70). Subsequently "the Neruvian State" itself "institutionalized corruption," as grace and favor from government leaders led to pervasive corruption at all levels of government. In the 1989 campaign, a poster showed Rajiv Ghandi as Pinocchio with a nose resembling a long Bofors gun (Singh, 213–218), an allusion to the huge bribe paid by the Swedish arms manufacturer to the Ghandi family.

Since the economic position of the poorer Israeli immigrants was considerably above that of the Indian masses, it was not claimed that, as in India, "the corruption of the poor and their leaders is a necessary strategy of their survival" (Singh 219). In Israel extensive courting of the newer electorates was largely made feasible by public party subsidies, and experiences there were linked to a renewed trend towards "catchall" parties, hence demonstrating that "cartel party formation can be arrested or even reversed" (Mendilow 270).

Corruption Enhancement Propensities

For the other seven countries the strongly positive correlation between campaign expenditures and corruption along the Australia –Philippines axis is the predominant pattern. Given the temporal lag of three decades between the two data sets, one can conclude, at a minimum, that the implication that campaign expenditure induced higher corruption incidence is fairly strong. But the way in which this came to play out varied greatly.

Australia and the Philippines

Looking at the two extreme national cases in the graph, one can explain the contrasts between Australia and the Philippines as polar examples of the intensity and efficacy of monitoring and prosecution of potential corrupt activity. The Philippines combine and magnify the corruption inducing tendencies of candidate-centered politics of the American and Latin types. Clientelistic politics predominate in appeals to a geo-politically heterogeneous electorate which has inhibited the formation of mass parties. Australia by contrast inherited the world's first electoral successful working-class mass party in a political culture where "mateship" ideology probably facilitated various forms of favoritism. Australian states have in recent decades implemented relatively massive anti-corruption control programs, like the New

Figure 39.1
Party Expenditures, c. 1960 and Corruption Incidence Perceptions, 1995-97

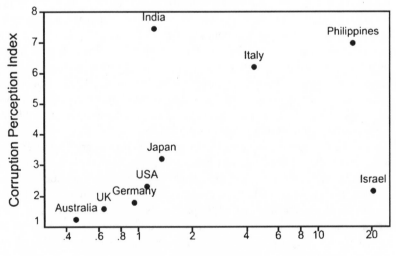

Log Party Expenditure Index

Table 39.2
Attempt to Model Party Finance – Corruption Linkages

Aquatic Model of Party Finance – Corruption Linkage	Specifics of Party Finance, Public Bureaucracy Meshing	Country and period most predominantly affected by	Party Finance Corruption Enhancement Propensity
Cascading across institutional borders	-Parties and Factions as guarantors of contracts assuring corrupt perpetual replay	Italy 1990s	High
Oozing of Supports In Bubble Polity	-Relaxation of Central Monitoring of bureaucracy -Localization of political campaigns	India	High
Targeted Camouflaged Seepage	-Soft money evades spending limits -Donations give appearance of enhanced access -Perceptions of influence purchase increases tolerance of corruption	US 1990s	Medium
Subterranean Channels	-Permit circumvention of support stream markers -Enhanced media markets outmatch public financing - Party leaders ignore publicity need	Germany 1980s	Medium
Boundary Maintenance Between Overt Channels	-Easy monitoring in long ensconced two party system -Barriers re: elected/appointed office career combinations	Britain	Low

South Wales Independent Commission Against Corruption, whose efficacy in mobilizing taboos against even marginal favor-giving by civil servants may have helped to produce the favorable Australian rating achieved in the corruption perception indexes.

As table 39.2 bears out, it is useful to utilize simplified hydraulic models to illustrate how various party systems differed in handling transmissions and spillovers between the party political and the bureaucratic arenas. Where national bureaucracies are effectively insulated from partisan influences, as in Britain, something akin to iron flood-gates can be seen to prevent spillovers from the party finance to the policy making bureaucrats in the executive agencies.

In theory the expansion of public campaign financing should have diminished the parties' financial requirements. This in turn should have reduced pressures for exploiting control of bureaucracies. But evidently some countries which broadened public financing, like Italy, came off worse in comparison with countries like Britain, where public financing has remained minimal. One way of explaining this counter-intuitive result is to regard the Italian factions and parties as guaranteeing the predominance of the "constituency of patronage" over the constituency of bureaucratic autonomy, thus ensuring the continuous replay of the corrupt exchange patterns established by what we can label the "Cascading" pattern of an aquatic model of party finance-corruption linkage.

Of the national cases that have been extensively examined, Germany is probably one where assessments came to vary most sharply over time. Low corruption levels attributed to West Germany in the 1960s later came to be challenged by subsequent analysts (see articles by Eschenburg and Alemann in the appendix listing of contents of previous editions). Thus an earlier academic observer like Theodore Eschenburg would have been astounded by a prediction that he would almost come to see the day when attributed levels of corruption would be higher in Germany than in the United States. Yet this is what occurred in the aftermath of German unification and the subsequent revelations about Helmut Kohl and the CDU, as the Transparency International rankings of September, 2000 demonstrated. But where Eschenburg might have been dismayed, a skeptical student of parties and bureaucracies like Max Weber might well have chortled.

American public agencies have been kept from becoming fiefs of particular party factions, so that the way that political money influences policy outcomes requires recourse to another kind of hydraulic model. We can label this a "targeted seepage" pattern, through which the superimposition of donation patterns between socio-economic interests and parties and candidates developed so-called "iron triangle" relationships to create patterns of reciprocal obligation. The conventional theorists of pluralist politics accept these relationships as necessary and unavoidable, with only occasional legislators like Proxmire and McCain attacking their legitimacy. Thus although the party machines bemoaned by men like Ostrogorski have been displaced by new technologies, the American polity remains a giant with clay feet, fighting corruption internationally, yet vulnerable to ridicule at home for failures to devise ways of legitimating the financing of just those competitive party instruments which have distinguished its way of welding capitalism and democracy.

Notes

1. To the extent that cross-national secret transfers of funds was one of the ways in which the pro-capitalist side aided European parties in the struggle against communism, it reduced the likelihood that their allied media in Europe or elsewhere highlighted illegal party finance practices as issues of political corruption.
2. See Heidenheimer, Johnston, LeVine, eds. *Political Corruption*: A Handbook, 1989: 4–6
3. A sketch of major developments: Indirect subventions/court 1954, ordered replaced 1958; Direct subsidies introduced 1959, declared invalid 1966; Election reimbursements 1967, coupled with the tight limits: 1989-1989 tax deductibility

limits raised to DM120,000; 1992 – invalidation of high deductible limits as well as of a equalizing formula. (Poguntke 192–193)

4. "By means of donations the Flick corporation has systematically gained spheres of influence, so that it must be stated that political corruption on a large scale is involved, regardless of whether the punishable act of bribery or corruptibility has been realized in one case or another. By means of the conspiratorial money distributed by the Flick Corporation, the benefiting parties gained a remarkable financial advantage compared to their political competitors."

5. German subsidies increased from about one-third to about 45% of party receipts over the 1974–87 period, while the Italian share decreased from 55–60% to the 40–45% range. (Landfried, 117)

References

Alexander, Herbert. ed. 1989. *Comparative Political Finance in the 1980s.* Cambridge: Cambridge University Press.

Arnim, Hans Herbert von. 1997. *Fetter Bauch Regiert nicht gern: Die politische Klasse: Selbstbezogen und Abgehoben.* Munich: Kindler,

Bardi, Luciano and Leonardo Morlino. 1994. "Italy": Tracing the Roots of the Great Transformation," in Katz and Mair, ed *How Parties Organize*, op cit. 242–278

Bendix, Reinhard. 1960. *Max Weber: An Intellectual Portrait.* London: Heinemann.

Bille, Lars. 1994 "Denmark: The Decline of the Membership Party?" in Katz and Mair, eds. 134–57.

Della Porta, Donatella and Yves Mény. 1997. "Conclusion: Democracy and Corruption Towards a Comparative Analysis," in *Democracy and Corruption in Europe.*

Della Porta, Donatella, and Alberto Vannucci. 1997. "The Perverse Effects of Political Corruption," in Heywood, ed., *Political Corruption*: 100–123.

Gunlicks, Arthur B., ed., 1993. *Campaign and Party Finance in North America and Western Europe.* Boulder, CO: Westview Press

Etzioni-Halevy, Eva. 2000 "Exchanging Material benefits for Political Support: A Comparative Analysis," in this volume

Heidenheimer, Arnold J. 1963 "Comparative Party Finance: Notes on Practices and Toward a Theory" *Journal of Politics*, (25:4) 790–810

Heidenheimer, Arnold J. 1989 "Adenauer's Legacies: Party Finance and the Decline of Chancellor Democracy." in Peter H. Merkl ed. *The Federal Republic of Germany at Forty.* New York: NYU Press, 213–227.

Heidenheimer, Arnold J. 1996 "The Topography of Corruption: Explorations in a Comparative Perspective," *International Social Science Journal (48:3), 337–347.*

Heidenheimer, Arnold J. amd Frank C. Langdon, 1968, *Business Associations and the Financing of Political Parties: Germany, Norway and Japan.* The Hague: Nijhoff.

Hofnung, Menachim.1996. "Political Finance in Israel," in M. Levi & D. Nelken, eds., *The Corruption of Politics and the Politics of Corruption*: 132–148. Cambridge: Blackwell.

Heywood, Paul. Ed. 1997. *Political Corruption.* Malden: Blackwell.

Johnston, Michael. 1997. "Public Officials, Private Interests, and Sustainable Democracy: When Politics and Corruption Meet," in Elliott, *Corruption and the Global Economy.* Washington: Institute for International Economics.

Katz, Richard S. and Robin Kolodny. 1994. "Parties in American Politics," in Katz and Mair, eds., *How Parties Organize* 29–50.

Katz, Richard S. and Peter Mair. 1995. "Changing Models of Party Organization and Party Democracy: The Emergence of the Cartel Party," *Party Politics*, 1: 5–28.

Katz, Richard S. and Peter Mair, ed. 1994. *How Parties Organize: Change and*

Adaptation in Party Organizations in Western Democracies. Thousand Oaks, CA: Sage Publications.

Landfried, Christine 1994 *Parteifinanzen und politische Macht.*, 2nd ed. Baden-Baden: Nomos.

Losche, Peter. 1993. "Problems of Party Finance and Campaign Financing in Germany and the United States – Some Comparative Reflections," in Arthur B. Gunlicks, ed., *Campaign and Party Finance in North America and Western Europe*: 219–233.

Mair, Peter. 1997. *Party System Change: Approaches and Interpretations.* Oxford: Clarendon Press.

Mendilow, Jonathan. 1996. "Public Party Funding and the Schemes of Mice and Men: The 1992 Elections in Israel," *Party Politics*, 2: 329–354.

Mény, Yves. 1992. *La Corruption De La Republique.* Fayard.

Noonan, John T. 1984. *Bribes.* New York: Macmillan.

Pierre, Jon and Anders Widfeldt. 1994 "Party Organization in Sweden: Colossuses with Feet of Clay or Flexible Pillars of Government?" in Katz and Mair, ed. *How Parties Organize* 332–56.

Poguntke, Thomas. 1994. "Parties in a Legalistic Culture: the Case of Germany," in Katz and Mair, eds. 185–215

Rhodes, Martin. 1997. "Financing Party Politics in Italy: A Case of Systemic Corruption," *West European Politics*, 20:1, 54–81

Senigaglia. Cristiana. 1995. "Analysen zur Entstehung der Massenparteien und zu Ihrem Einfluss auf das Parlament: Ostrogorski, Michels, Weber." *Parliaments, Estates and Representation* (15) 159–184.

Shefter, Martin, 1977 "Party and Patronage: Germany, England, and Italy" *Politics and Society* (7:4) 403–451

Singh, Gurhapal. 1997. "Understanding Political Corruption in Contemporary Indian Politics," Paul Heywood, ed, *Political Corruption*: 210–222.

Somjee, A.H. and G.G. (1963) "India," "Comparative Studies in Political Finance" *Journal of Politics* (25:4) 686–702

Widfeldt, Anders. 1999 *Linking Parties with People: Party Membership in Sweden 1960–1997.* Aldershot: Ashgate.

40

Party Systems, Competition, and Political Checks against Corruption

Michael Johnston

"Good politics is good government."
—Richard J. Daley, mayor of Chicago,
1955–1976

Introduction

The new generation of corruption research emerging in the 1990s has focused more on economic variables than upon the political. Economic trends are more easily quantified than political ones, and the theoretical case for economic effects of corruption can be made and tested in a variety of ways (see the chapters in part 6 for examples). Moreover, much of the renewed interest in corruption has been generated by international business groups and aid or lending organizations, which are understandably concerned with economic aspects of serious corruption. As a result, politics has been treated primarily in terms of institutions (often with useful results: see Knack and Keefer, 1995) or under the broad banner of "political will"—that is, determination on the part of top leadership to resist corruption and attack its causes. Few would dispute the need for such commitment, but even fewer have devoted extensive attention to the kinds of politics needed to sustain it.

This paper is a preliminary discussion of the ways good politics can help check corruption (see, more generally, Johnston, 1998, and Johnston, 1999). My focus is the relationship between political competition and levels of corruption; drawing upon aggregate statistics I will suggest that high-quality, well-institutionalized political competition can help reduce levels of corruption. The connection is not always straightforward: most low-corruption countries are democracies, and highly-corrupt countries tend to be undemocratic, but the exceptions are at least as interesting as the general pattern. Understanding both the potential, and the limitations, of competitive politics as an anti-corruption strategy can not only enhance our knowledge of the developmental implications of corruption; it may also point to opportunities for reform.

Corruption, Democracy, and Development: Multiple Patterns

> *"Happy families are all alike; every unhappy family is unhappy in its own way."*
> —Leo Tolstoi, *Anna Karenina*

Recent research, aided by a variety of quantitative measures of corruption of varying validity and reliability, has taken direct issue with an earlier tradition that pointed to positive as well as negative consequences of significant corruption (see, for example, Leff, 1964). Mauro (1997) presents evidence of marginal but significant reductions in economic growth as levels of corruption mount. Wei (1997) likens corruption to a tax on foreign direct investment. Rose-Ackerman points out that arguments about the efficiency benefits of corruption often rest upon individual transactions considered in isolation; when we consider broader effects, it becomes evident that corruption rewards inefficiency, short-circuits competition, and diverts resources and effort from productive activities into rent-seeking (Rose-Ackerman, 1996). Mauro (1997) and Rauch (1995) present at least tentative evidence that corruption channels resources away from human development toward rent-producing projects such as heavy construction. Kaufmann (1994; 1996) sees corruption as linked to large "informal sectors" of economies, poor tax collection, and long bureaucratic delays; far from greasing the wheels, corruption is associated with *more* inefficiency, as officials—sensing the opportunity to augment their often-insufficient salaries—contrive new delays and requirements. Meanwhile, investors in high-corruption states are likely to focus on short-term profits, and to keep their assets as mobile as possible (Keefer, 1996)—scarcely a recipe for sustained development. So-called "petty corruption" is a serious concern too: demands for payments in exchange for licenses, passage along roads, and basic services help keep poor people poor, and force many small enterprises into the informal sector—making it difficult for excluded groups to gain an economic toehold.

Political development is likely to be inhibited as well. Because corruption involves the informal use of scarce resources (money, access, expertise), it typically benefits the "haves" at the expense of the have-nots, and shifts policy processes out of the public, supposedly accountable, institutions into private networks of influence. Patronage networks may bring large numbers of people into the political process, but they do so on the terms and in the interests of the patron, not of the clients. Such machines control the poor and working class rather than empowering them, neutralizing their biggest asset—the strength of numbers—through the politicized use of divisible incentives (Johnston, 1979; Webman, 1973). Where corruption is entrenched civil society is usually weak; playing the role of political opposition may mean little more than cutting oneself out of the benefits, and competition can thus implode into a disorganized scramble for spoils (see, for ethnically divided societies, Easterly and Levine, 1996). When political change does threaten corrupt elites, hyper-corruption may result as those unsure of their hold on power take as much as they can, as quickly as they can take it (Scott, 1972: Ch. 5). Democracies do have corruption, of course. But they also benefit from an underlying consensus on the rules, from independent law enforcement bodies, news media, and political oppositions, and from the voters' ability to throw out the government without threatening the constitutional regime (Przeworski and Limongi, 1993).

For these reasons we might expect to find straightforward connections among corruption, poor economic development, and undemocratic politics. But while considerable evidence, both statistical and anecdotal, supports the broad outlines of this view, there are enough exceptions to suggest that we still have much to learn. East Asian countries, for example, coupled extensive corruption with very high levels of economic growth for many years, while African states suffered (see Sindzingre, chapter 25). The two most widely discussed anti-corruption success stories—Hong Kong and Singapore—both took place in city-states, and neither in a democracy. Democratization in places as diverse as Central Europe and the Philippines did not directly reduce corruption; if anything, those nations experienced a surge of scandal as established corrupt relationships gave way to a fragmented scramble for spoils, and as increasingly independent jurists and journalists mounted new investigations while political rivals moved to settle old scores. Italy in particular is a fascinating case: it is an established democracy with a strong economy but has a long tradition of corruption, and its scandals over the past decade have shaken the foundations of the political system.

The complexities of these patterns become more evident if we consider the following scatter plot (figure 40.1) comparing 83 countries on two variables. The vertical axis represents the United Nations Development Program's 1995 Human Development Index (HDI); the horizontal is the Transparency International Corruption Perceptions Index, "inverted" (by subtracting the TI scores from ten) so that higher values indicate higher levels of corruption. The HDI is a weighted composite of indicators not only of affluence, but also of quality-of-life factors such as education, literacy, and life expectancy. The TI scale—the most widely-employed of the many corruption scales to emerge in recent years—is a survey of surveys: a variety of corruption indices are pooled, averaged, and standardized. This scale is an approximate ranking at best (see Johnston, chapter 44).

High levels of corruption are indeed linked to developmental difficulties: the linear correlation between corruption scores and HDI is strongly negative ($r =-.6709$, one-tailed $p=.000$). There are no low-corruption, low development societies on the plot; moreover, there is a concentration of affluent democracies in the low-corruption, high-development area in the upper left. But beyond a "tipping point" of about 4 on the scale of ten (an arbitrary number to be sure) things are different. Here we find a wide scattering of countries with moderate-to-high levels of corruption—including many of the world's poorest and least democratic societies. The quadratic regression line suggests that as levels of corruption increase, HDI levels decrease more and more precipitously.

But there are also obvious complications. There is a cluster of successful, affluent democracies in the upper left, as noted: happy families happy in the same ways, with a variety of factors reinforcing to produce affluence, democracy and low corruption (Johnston, 1998). But Singapore—nobody's democracy—is also located in that quadrant; moreover, there are high-HDI countries at all levels of the TI scale. Further to the right, the most striking result is diversity: there are moderate- to high-corruption societies at many levels of HDI. Here, the unhappy families seem to be unhappy in their own ways, with some perhaps much less unhappy than others. Causation is complex as well: the void in the lower left might suggest that reducing corruption makes high levels of development nearly a certainty, but it seems much more likely that countries successful at development have the institutional and political capacity reduce or mitigate corruption in the process of addressing a broad range of challenges.

This last idea may bear more thought. It suggests that (a) serious corruption is embedded in a much broader set of interlinked development difficulties, and (b) the countries in the upper left have the capacity to address those difficulties comprehensively. In part this may be a function of affluence—economically successful societies are more likely to have strong civil societies, the resources to deal with a variety of problems, and an economy that offers people alternatives to being exploited by corrupt officials and their clients (see Alam, chapter 42). And indeed, real GDP per capita is the strongest single predictor of corruption scores for the countries in the plot above, with a simple correlation of-.85 ($p = .000$). But again Causation is complex: affluent societies may be better able to control corruption, but if the economic evidence discussed above is valid, those that can control corruption have a better shot at affluence. And what do we make of cases such as Italy, Greece, the Republic of Korea, or Argentina—democracies (some in various stages of

Figure 40.1

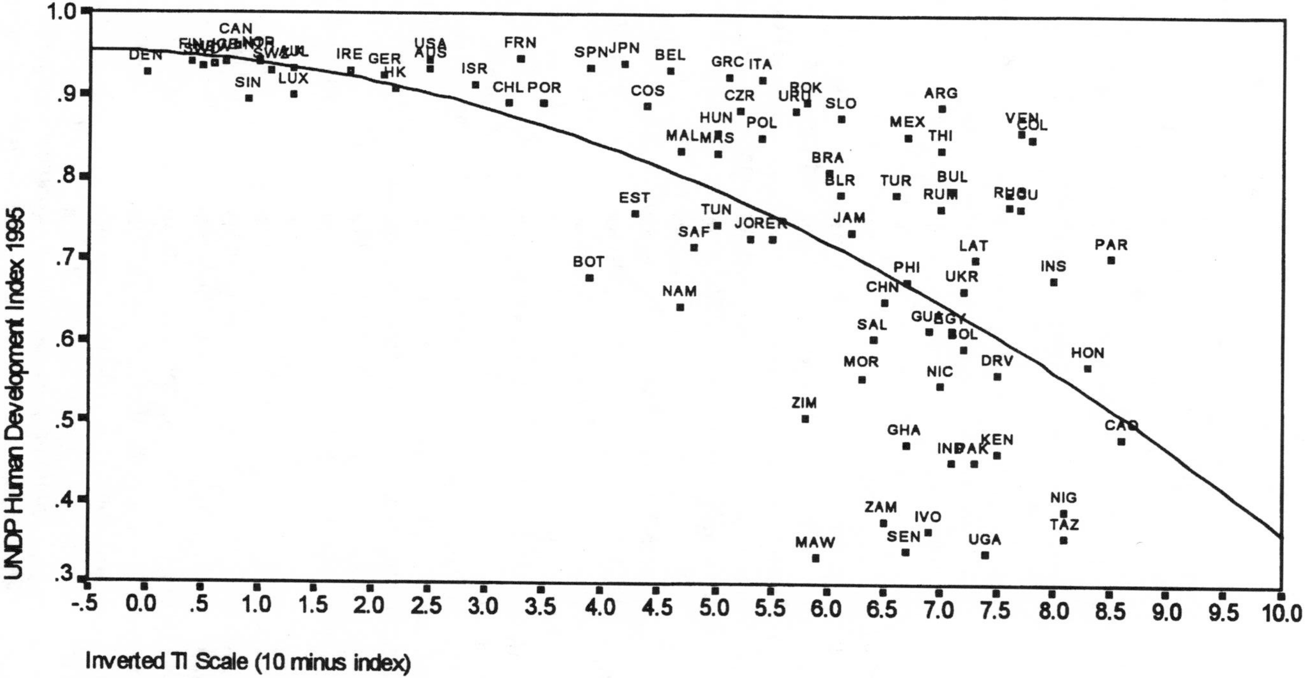

Inverted TI Scale (10 minus index)

1995 HDI: http://www.undp.org/hdro/98hdi1.htm

1998 TI Index: http://www.transparency.de/documents/cpi/index.html

consolidation) whose HDI levels are higher than their corruption scores would lead us to expect?

All of this is consistent with the notion that other factors—"governance," "state capacity," or political institutionalization—also influence the types and amounts of corruption a society experiences. In the following section I will take up just one aspect of that possible connection—the possible significance of political competition.

Participation, Institutions, and Balance

Many democracies are affluent societies with moderate to low corruption, while in some other countries undemocratic politics, poor economic development and serious corruption seem to perpetuate each other. But as the scatter plot shows, this pattern is far from universal, and market and democratic institutions do not guarantee success. Where democracy and growth do support each other, I suggest that such synergy is driven by open yet structured competition *within* the economic and political arenas, and sustained by institutionalized boundaries and paths of access *between* them. We would expect competition to enhance the vitality of markets and accountability in the political realm, and to weaken the ability of political and economic interests to dominate their own arenas or intrude unduly upon the other. Citizens who have economic and political alternatives are in a better position to resist corruption (Alam, 1995). But while competition must be vigorous, *it must also be of high quality*. That is, it must be fair and well-structured, engaging real interests and groups in society. Total laissez-faire in the economic realm is likely to enrich the few and impoverish the many. In politics, a free-for-all will likely produce a state of political insecurity in which politicians, unsure of their hold on power, enrich themselves as quickly as they can (Scott, 1972; Knack and Keefer, 1995). Significant power must be won and lost through the process: simply changing governments without altering the underlying distribution of (and channels of access to) power is unlikely to check corruption. A balance between active participation and sound institutions is thus essential.

The notion of high-quality competition is complicated, because the political and economic arenas are asymmetrical in significant ways. Democratic politics rests not only on open competition, but also on normative, and institutionalized, assumptions of equality, encapsulated by the notion of "one person, one vote." Self-interest may drive the process, but it is assumed that private interests will contend in well-regulated ways, and that in the end democratic processes will not only respond to them, but also *aggregate* them[1] into broadly-accepted public policies. Markets, by contrast, incorporate few presumptions of equality, either in process or outcome; such procedural rights and mechanisms of accountability as exist are grounded primarily in ownership, not citizenship. Gains are presumed to be private and separable, rather than aggregated and public. Competition, while open to new participants, is continuous and less structured than politics, with more uncertain outcomes; losers are routinely driven out of markets, and winners enjoy advantages, in ways that lack real political parallels. Political regimes hold power over a limited territory and population, while markets are increasingly global and can override official policies and political mandates.

If these asymmetries—which rest on normative foundations in many respects—did not exist, corruption would not be a problem: more or less anything, including official power, could be bought and sold under a common set of rules, and public office could be used like any other resource in the pursuit of private gain. But exist they do, and thus ordered relationships between the political and economic arenas are just as important as vigorous competition within them. There must be clear, and accepted, boundaries and distinctions between state and society; public and private roles and resources; personal and collective interests; and market, bureaucratic, and patrimonial modes of allocation (Johnston and Hao, 1995). In well-institutionalized systems there are realms where official power may not intrude, and there are things that may not be bought and sold. Where such boundaries exist, free interaction within each realm is more secure: it will be more difficult for economic interests to turn politics into an auction, and for officials to plunder the economy. But the two arenas cannot and should not be utterly separate: there must be legitimate access between them. Policies must respond to social and economic realities; self-interested behavior must be subject to the rule of law. Institutions must have some degree of *autonomy*: both political and economic decision makers need—within broad limits—to act authoritatively and in an uncompromised manner. But paths of access must also be open enough to link the political and economic arenas in regularized, legitimate ways. If they are not—as in contemporary China, where new market forces have few legitimate ways to influence the still-powerful (if increasingly fragmented) bureaucracy—they will be created corruptly.

Political Competition as a Check against Corruption

While there are many kinds of institutions providing legitimate linkages and maintaining sound boundaries in modern societies—bureaucracies, the news media, jurists and prosecutors are just a few—political parties are of particular importance. More than most other institutions, they are central to the aggregation function performed above; they both convey important preferences from society to government, and help earn legitimacy for and compliance with official policies. They are potentially important mechanisms of accountability and bureaucratic oversight, and managers of the electoral process. Serious corruption involves the contrivance or protection of various kinds of monopolies (Rose-Ackerman, 1978; Klitgaard, 1988); competitive politics is a way to guard against such monopolies, or to weaken them where they exist. Strong government parties can discipline both elected and appointed officials, while strong oppositions can check the government, offering an organizational vehicle and political alternatives for citizens seeking change.

Significant and institutionalized political competition creates opportunities for political forces to win *or lose* power through publicly visible processes. Well-institutionalized, competitive parties may thus develop an interest in credible action against corruption, both in the political arena and through independent judiciary and in investigative agencies. They can encourage, protect, and follow through on direct responses to corruption by citizens and civil society groups—building resistance to corruption in civil society, in place of the kinds of evasive or illicit responses common where citizens are vulnerable to exploitation and have little political recourse (Alam, 1995). Competition will be beneficial even if the major groups do not represent everyone in the country. England's seventeenth century parliaments, for example, played major roles in resisting the abuses of royal patronage both before and after the civil wars, even though they were strikingly unrepresentative by modern standards (Peck 1990).

We must distinguish here between competition and *insecurity*. The latter, as noted, can lead to voracious corruption when officials do not know how much longer their power will last (Knack and Keefer 1995; Scott 1972). Why should the threat of losing power through political competition be any different? The answer lies in the way in which it is lost and won, and in what happens next. Insecurity—the threat of a coup, for example—means that the identity and strength of one's opponents, and their timing and tactics, may be difficult to know or predict. Uncertain timing is of particular importance, as it creates an incentive to enrich oneself as quickly as possible. The issues and grievances involved are likely to be personal or factional, and thus resistant to negotiation or compromise as they are aimed at overall dominance. When power is lost, it is lost altogether and permanently: rather than remaining as an opposition group or coalition partner, the losers may be killed, imprisoned, or exiled. The contest, therefore, is not just for spoils, but for survival.

Political competition, on the other hand, involves known opponents, tactics, and timing. The broad outlines of competitors' strengths, appeals, and support are discernible, and competition, if well-institutionalized, takes place within agreed rules and social norms. Many of the main issues are addressable through routine policy, are open to compromise, and can be made matters of public commitment—facts that encourage accountability and active oversight of policy formation and implementation. While the winners obtain agreed-on powers for a limited period of time, the losers remain to fight another day—an incentive in itself to refrain from last-minute looting of the public purse. Political competition is quite different from political insecurity, and creates incentives to avoid, rather than to indulge in, corruption. But such competition is a matter of contending forces, not just institutional architecture: where opposition is weak, elected elites engage in entrenched corruption too. Doig (1984) cites examples such as County Durham in England to suggest that in many democracies, the most entrenched corrupt processes are often found in politically uncompetitive locales (but for contrary findings, see Schlesinger and Meier, chapter 33).

Competition, of course, can give rise to corruption problems of its own, as recent political finance scandals in many democracies demonstrate. Moreover, not just any kind of competition will do. It must be meaningful, but structured: one party presents no choice at all, but a swarm of small parties will not likely be able to govern, or indeed to have agendas much broader than the personal interests of their leaders. Indeed, winners would likely use their tenuous hold on power for self-enrichment, while other contenders might resort to corrupt activities in order to build a following. The organizational strength of parties is important too: where parties are internally divided along factional lines or cross-cut by other loyalties (ranging from ethnic divisions to ideological fights to the influences of localism in societies such as the United States), or where electoral systems encourage intra-party contention (as in most of the postwar era in Japan: see Susan Pharr, chapter 43), competition becomes less decisive. Splinter groups of losing parties may cut deals with the winners, while factions of the governing party may demand side-payments of their own in exchange for their "loyalty." The leverage of such factions will be increased where electoral laws or political realities tend to deliver small majorities. Party discipline may thus become a matter of distributing patronage, policy spoils, or outright bribes. Coalitions of parties too might lead to corrupt deal-cutting among leaders. Weak, divided parties will be less effective at bureaucratic oversight; indeed, factions or leaders within them may seek corrupt alliances with bureaucrats. The possible variations are numerous; the point is that the notion of political competition as a limit on corrupt activity presupposes a particular kind of competition: orderly, fair, decisive competition among a small-number of well-institutionalized parties with strong links to significant, lasting groups and interests in society. Where competition falls short of this ideal, it may not reduce corruption, but rather lead to more of it.

Party Systems and Corruption

The extent and quality of political competition in various countries are part of a growing concern over the vitality of democracy. Mair and Katz (1997: 108), for example, write of "a new type of party, the cartel party, characterized by the interpenetration of party and state, and by a pattern of inter-party collusion." While they are concerned with many issues besides corruption, we might well expect that "interpenetration" of parties—as aggregators and articulators of private interests—and the state would create, or protect, a range of potentially corrupt connections between wealth and power, and that such parties would do little to check each other's abuses. Colluding parties are never wholly in or out of power; there is little to gain, and potentially much to lose (both legitimate and illegitimate) by disrupting the linkages and deals that sustain the cartel. Elections may reshuffle personnel and bring about symbolic change, but corruption could remain deeply embedded in elite alliances and patterns of interaction.

In Italy in particular a kind of cartel situation seems to have helped shape and sustain corrupt dealings. Colazingari and Rose-Ackerman (1998) have described the situation succinctly, noting

> . . . the similarity between political and economic life in Italy. Large companies felt secure because of their privileged relationship to the state, and political parties were similarly secure with stable niches in the political structure. Italy's paternalistic state-protected industry and paradoxically the fragmentation and ideological polarization of the political system protected the ruling parties from turnover, making them unaccountable to the electorate. (Colazingari and Rose-Ackerman, 1998: 448)

Polarization led to stalemate in the form of a working consensus among major non-communist parties that the PCI was not to become a partner in government. The Christian Democrats, while never winning an outright majority, were "the only large party capable of forming a government coalition. As a result of its secure position, the DC did not need to be accountable to the voters. Forced to govern by coalition, it formed governments with different parties at different points in time and shared the benefits of political power with them" (Ibid., 449–450). Collusion even benefited the Communists: in Milan, for example, the major parties cut them in on the spoils as a way of maintaining the status quo (Ibid., 450). Governments came and went, but underlying the situation was a mutually profitable political cartel. Przeworski and Limongi (1993) are correct in pointing out that a strong point of democracy is citizens' ability to change the government without bringing down the fundamental political order, but changes of government that alter nothing other than personnel will do little to check corruption.

"Cartel parties" are not the only form of impaired competition to facilitate corruption. In Japan the party-list system of elections long encouraged candidates within major parties, such as the LDP, to compete with each other more than with opposing parties. Lacking distinctive policy positions, they often resorted to extravagant vote-buying or to factional deals with major business interests. In the United States, a loosely-disciplined party system is made more so by the preeminent role of state and local interests in many policy debates, and by a campaign-finance system that in effect turns candidates into free agents. Current laws restrict campaign contributions to unrealistically small amounts, making fundraising a full-time concern. Legislation is a disjointed process of logrolling and side payments—some, in the form of policy concessions, others in the form of campaign contributions, with some of the latter bankrolled by party leaders' personal Political Action Committees. Popular suspicions that roll-call votes are put up for sale to the highest bidder are misplaced, but the incentives for candidates officials to seek collective party mandates based on coherent policies are nonetheless weak.

The result of this intense individual scramble, ironically, is reduced party competition. Candidates build free-standing campaign organizations aimed mostly at protecting their own seat—often using the disclosure provisions of the law to demonstrate their fundraising prowess to erstwhile competitors. Cumulative incumbent advantages and favorable redistricting further reduce the chances for defeat. Thus, in the midst of the Clinton impeachment debate, the *New York Times* noted that

> In the insular world of the House of Representatives, few members really have to fear the other party. Districts are drawn for continuity, not contests. Among the Republicans re-elected last month, for example, only 10 won with 52 percent or less of the vote. Among the Democrats, only five. (*New York Times,* 13 December 1998, p. 45)

Some of the most significant conflicts over impeachment took place *within* the Republican party; there, a number of wavering moderates were brought into line by the threat of primary-election challenges supported—and funded— by their own party leaders' PACs.

Claims of reduced party competition might seem paradoxical in light of the deeply partisan impeachment debate, but I would suggest that the lack of real party competition *at the district level* left zealots largely unchecked by the threat of losing their seats. Meanwhile the stalemate between the two major parties nationally makes it tempting to substitute scandal for policy initiatives and genuine oversight. The state of political competition in the United States is not encouraging from the standpoint of building good government through good politics.

Preliminary Evidence

Do democracies with impaired political competition have more corruption, then? A very preliminary judgment can be made by comparing the TI Corruption Perceptions Index figures discussed earlier with an index of political competitiveness available in the Polity III database.[2] PARCOMP is an index ranging from 1–5, assessing the degree of organization and competitiveness of political participation outside the realm of the state. As such it is a useful

Figure 40.2

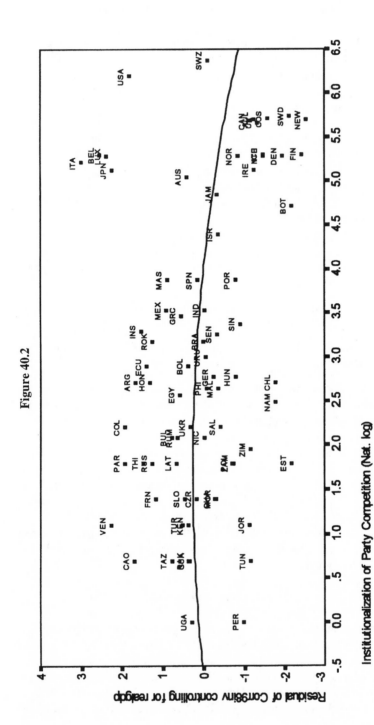

Institutionalization of Party Competition (Nat. log)

Party data from Polity III database:

http://www.colorado.edu/IBS/GAD/spacetime/data/Polity.html

approximation of the state of political competition (if not a nuanced verdict on the quality of that competition in any one country). The simple correlation between PARCOMP and the "inverted" TI index for our 83 countries is .61 (p = .000): extensive, organized competition tends to coincide with lower levels of corruption. But neither politics nor corruption develops in isolation; they reflect the broader state of society. Indeed, when PARCOMP is entered in a regression equation as an independent variable along with real GDP per capita—the strongest predictor of TI corruption scores—GDP becomes a strong negative predictor and PARCOMP is not statistically significant.

But that may not be the whole story. Any corruption-checking effects of sound party competition would seem to be long-term in nature, reflecting the cumulative impact of the logic and incentives of competition upon the choices of political and economic actors, and in some countries competition has been institutionalized much longer than in others. Second, the regression noted above estimates *linear* relationships among variables; it is possible that other patterns exist. As a result, I conducted another kind of analysis. First, I calculated a residual of the TI index, controlling for GDP per capita. This not only controls for the most likely confounding variable as we compare party systems; in addition, if party systems are important linking/boundary-maintaining institutions between wealth and power, variations in levels of affluence are likely to affect the kinds of economic pressures bearing upon the political system. Also, the Polity III database contains an estimate of how long a given "polity" (as opposed to a state or regime) has been in existence (as of 1994) in the form summarized by the data. This I used to estimate the institutionalization of competition, by multiplying the PARCOMP score (minus one, to reset completely uncompetitive systems to zero) by the number of years a given polity has been in place. Because early phases of institutionalization are likely to be critical—that is, more institutionalization of a party system should take place between years 5 and 10 than between years 105 and 110—I then calculated the natural logarithm of the resulting measure.

The result is the scatter plot appearing below (figure 40.1). On the Y axis are the values for the residual corruption score controlling for wealth: values above zero mean that a country had a higher corruption score than we would expect on the basis of wealth alone, while values less than zero correspond to less. On the X axis are the logged values of my rough index of institutionalization of competition (PARCOMP times years of duration of a given polity).

The data present some intriguing patterns that at least help frame important issues for more detailed research. For example, the largest scattering of data points shows that residuals are greatest—both positive and negative—where competitive party systems exist, but are least institutionalized. This does not in itself mean that absolute levels of corruption are high, but may suggest that where politics is uncompetitive and/or poorly institutionalized, many other factors affect levels of corruption. As institutionalization proceeds along the X axis, however, the points cluster closer to the value of zero—that is, closer to the corruption levels we would predict based upon a country's affluence. This suggests that to the extent that there is a link between affluence and lower levels of corruption (as indicated by the strongly negative simple correlation between GDP per capita and the corruption index, and by the clustering of affluent countries in the upper left of the HDI scatter plot), such synergy is better realized where party systems are competitive and well-institutionalized.

A further speculation—one that the data may suggest but cannot test— flows from the fact that *negative* as well as positive residuals tend to decrease as institutionalization increases. The data here are a snapshot, and not an account of how particular countries change over time; still, it is worth asking whether the rise and institutionalization of competitive politics reduces some kinds of corruption while increasing or facilitating others. Egregious political or economic abuses by top government officials, for example, might be checked by competitive politics, or at least the malefactors could be removed. But the rise of competitive politics might also contribute to corrupt activities and influence by donors to parties, certain kinds of vote fraud, and so forth. This remains conjectural for now, but is an interesting hypothesis.

I find two clusters of countries toward the right-hand side of the scatter plot of particular interest. In one, several established democracies—Italy, Japan, Belgium, Luxembourg (and possibly the U.S.?)—have higher levels of corruption than we would expect on the basis of affluence. In another larger group, thirteen countries—Norway, Iceland, Botswana, Denmark, Finland, Sweden, New Zealand, Canada, the United Kingdom, Ireland, Australia, the Netherlands, and Costa Rica—all have less corruption than their GDP-per-capita levels would predict. Neither cluster is wholly homogeneous, nor can we be certain without further analysis precisely what (if anything substantive) might account for their higher-and lower-than-expected corruption rankings. But several of the high- residual countries do have party systems characterized by impaired competition. The situations in Italy, Japan, and the United States were briefly outlined above; Belgium's complex ethnic divisions have been papered over for many years by settlements brokered among parties and elites rather than aggregated (or changed) at the ballot box. Luxembourg has been governed by essentially a constant grouping of parties, through carefully orchestrated coalitions, since the end of World War II (Dumont and DeWinter, 1999). In these countries parties are unlikely to win or lose power altogether; in many of them the competing factions are able to retain fragments of power, and to take part in the legislative process, though side-payments and compromises that further weaken the potentially corrective effects of competition. In the lower-residual cluster, by contrast, parties tend to be more tightly organized and to compete in elections that confer decisive results. Few of these countries exhibit any characteristics of a "cartel parties" syndrome.

Data give some preliminary support to this account. The POLCON dataset, assembled by Witold Henisz,[3] contains useful measures of the numbers of parties in various houses of parliament, party development, and the fragmentation of parliamentary bodies as measured by the distribution of seats among various numbers of parties (the dataset is described in detail in Henisz, 1999). These numbers suggest that the two clusters may be worth further study. Countries in the high-residual cluster had a score of .809 on a zero-to-one scale of party fragmentation in their lower houses (or .744 if the U.S. is included in this group) calculated in 1994, compared to a figure of .597 for the low-residual countries. In the lower houses of the high-residual group, an average of 9.5 parties held seats in 1994 (8.2 if the U.S. is included), while in the low-residual group the figure is 5.8 parties. The numbers of countries in each group are so small that tests of statistical significance would not be meaningful, and data such as these reduce complex political realities to single numbers. Still, these results support the notion that both quantity *and quality* of party competition matter in terms of checking corruption.

Two other differences between these clusters are worth noting. One has to do with the sizes of the societies involved in each. Daniel Kaufmann (1997), borrowing from epidemiology, has argued that smaller societies find it easier to control corruption than do larger ones. This might be so because of logistical as well as political factors, or because a durable national normative consensus might be less likely to be cross-cut by local and regional issues. The high-residual cluster is only partly consistent with this hypothesis: Italy and Japan are larger societies, as is the U.S., if we include it in this group, but Luxembourg and Belgium are not. All but one (the U.K.) of the low-residual countries are small, however. The second contrast reflects some of the developmental costs of corruption. The HDI data include a comparison of countries calculated by subtracting their rank on GDP per capita from their rank in terms of the non-GDP components of the scale (such as education, life expectancy, and so forth). A positive ranking indicates that a country ranks higher on the quality-of-life indicators than wealth alone would predict, and a negative ranking indicates that it falls lower. For the high-corruption cluster in the scatter plot this ranking averages -5.6 with the U.S. included in the group, and -6.7 with the U.S. excluded; for the low-corruption cluster the average is +6.9. Countries with serious corruption are apparently less effective at human development than their wealth would predict, while those with institutions and political processes capable of reducing corruption also seem capable of delivering a higher quality of life.

Conclusion

As already noted, these data and results do more to frame questions than to answer them. A range of other variables not yet included or controlled, and tricky problems of simultaneity among factors in political and economic development, further complicate matters. It will also be important to track these contrasts over time to ensure that they are sustained rather than ephemeral.

Still, these results justify further consideration of the connections among party systems, amounts and quality of political competition, and types and amounts of corruption. The significance of what we may learn should not be underestimated: while much is known about specific institutional reforms that can reduce corruption, and we have learned a great deal about some of the economic origins and consequences of the problem, we are only beginning to understand what makes reductions in corruption *sustainable*. As noted at the outset, much is written about "political will" as a factor in reform; what is much less well-understood are the ways such commitment can be encouraged and rewarded. This is a significant question historically, as well as for reform: many of today's low-corruption societies once had very serious corruption which declined as politics became more intense and broad-based (Johnston, 1993). What kinds of causal connections were involved, and can they be replicated in new democracies today?

It is one thing to identify such patterns in retrospect, and quite another to say where countries stand in such a process at any given time. Were Italy's scandals in the 1990s bad news—conclusive evidence of pervasive, entrenched corruption—or are they good news—evidence of gathering anti-corruption strength, and of the end of the old party cartel? Will changes in electoral laws in recent years, intended to produce more decisive election results and true alternation in power along party lines, help reduce corruption? A careful comparative analysis of the state and quality of party competition, based upon detailed case study and historical as well as contemporary evidence, will aid us in making those sorts of judgments.

Notes

1. I thank Dr. Salvador Valdés-Prieto, Centro Estudios Públicos in Santiago, Chile, for his comments on this point.
2. The data and documentation are available at http://www.colorado.edu/IBS/GAD/spacetime/data/Polity.html.
3. I gratefully acknowledge the help of Philip Keefer at the World Bank, who made these data available to me.

References

Alam, M. S. 1995. "A Theory of Limits on Corruption and Some Applications." *Kyklos* 48(3): 419–35.

Colazingari, Silvia, and Susan Rose-Ackerman. 1998. "Corruption in a Paternalistic Democracy: Lessons from Italy for Latin America." *Political Science Quarterly* 113:3 (Fall), pp. 447–470.

Doig, Alan. 1984. *Corruption and Misconduct in Contemporary British Politics*. Harmondsworth: Penguin.

Dumont, Patrick, and Lieven De Winter. 1999. "Luxembourg: Stable Coalitions in A Pivotal-Party System." unpublished manuscript.

Easterly, William, and Ross Levine. 1996. "Africa's Growth Tragedy: Policies and Ethnic Divisions." World Bank, Policy Research Department, Macroeconomics and Growth Division, Washington, D.C.

Henisz, Witold J. 1999. "The Institutional Environment for Economic Growth." University of Pennsylvania: unpublished manuscript.

Johnston, Michael. 1999. "Corruption and Democratic Consolidation." Presented at a Conference on "Democracy and Corruption," Shelby Cullom Davis Center for Historical Studies, Princeton University, March 12.

Johnston, Michael. 1998. "What Can Be Done About Entrenched Corruption?," pp. 149–180 in Boris Pleskovic (ed.), *Annual World Bank Conference on Development Economics 1997*. Washington, DC: The World Bank, 1998.

Johnston, Michael. 1993. "Political Corruption: Historical Conflict and the Rise of Standards." In Larry Diamond and Marc F. Plattner, eds. *The Global Resurgence of Democracy*. Baltimore: Johns Hopkins University Press.

Johnston, Michael. 1979. "Patrons and Clients, Jobs and Machines: A Case Study of the Uses of Patronage." *American Political Science Review* 73(2): 385–98.

Johnston, Michael, and Yufan Hao. 1995. "China's Surge of Corruption." *Journal of Democracy* 6(4): 80–94.

Kaufmann, Daniel. 1997. "Are We Being 'Good' or Smart in the Fight against Corruption?" Paper presented to the VIII International Anti-Corruption Conference, Lima, Peru (September).

Kaufmann, Daniel, and Aleksander Kaliberda. 1996. "Integrating the Unofficial Economy into the Dynamics of Post-Socialist Economies." In B. Kaminiski, ed. *Economic Transition in Russia and the New States of Eurasia*. Armonk, New York: M. E. Sharpe.

Kaufmann, Daniel. 1994. "Diminishing Returns to Administrative Controls and the Emergence of the Unofficial Economy: A Framework of Analysis and Applications to Ukraine." *Economic Policy* pp. 51–69.

Keefer, Philip. 1996. "Protection Against a Capricious State: French Investment and Spanish Railroads, 1845–1875." *Journal of Economic History* 56(1): 170–92.

Klitgaard, Robert. 1988. *Controlling Corruption*. Berkeley: University of California Press.

Knack, Stephen, and P. Keefer. 1995. "Institutions and Economic Performance: Cross-Country Tests Using Alternative Institutional Measures." *Economics and Politics* 7(3): 207–27.

Leff, N. 1964. "Economic Development through Bureaucratic Corruption." *American Behavioral Scientist* 8(3) (November), pp. 8–14.

Mair, Peter (with Richard S. Katz). 1997. "Party Organization, Party Democracy, and the Emergence of the Cartel Party." Ch. 5 (pp. 93–119) in Peter Mair, *Party System Change: Approaches and Interpretations*. Oxford: Clarendon Press.

Mauro, Paolo. 1997. "The Effects of Corruption on Growth, Investment, and Government Expenditure: A Cross-Country Analysis." In Kimberly A. Elliott, ed., *Corruption and the Global Economy*. Washington, D.C.: Institute for International Economics.

New York Times. 1998. "At the Brink, Waiting for the Undecided." 13 December, pp. 1, 45.

Peck, Linda L. 1990. *Court Patronage and Corruption in Early Stuart England*. Boston: Unwin Hyman.

Przeworski, Adam, and Fernando Limongi. 1993. "Political Regimes and Economic Growth." *Journal of Economic Literature* 7(3): 51–69.

Rauch, James. 1995. "Bureaucracy, Infrastructure, and Economic Growth: Evidence from US Cities During the Progressive Era." *American Economic Review* 85(4): 968–979.

Rose-Ackerman, Susan. 1996. "When is Corruption Harmful?" World Bank, Washington, D.C.

Rose-Ackerman, Susan. 1978. *Corruption: A Study in Political Economy.* New York: Academic Press.

Schlesinger, Thomas, and Kenneth J. Meier. 1999 (forthcoming). "Variations in Corruption among the American States."

Scott, James C. 1972. *Comparative Political Corruption.* Englewood Cliffs, New Jersey: Prentice-Hall.

Webman, Jerry A. 1973. "Political Institutions and Political Leadership: Black Politics in Philadelphia and Detroit." New Haven: Yale University, Department of Political Science.

Wei, Shang-Jin. 1997. "How Taxing is Corruption on International Investors?" Cambridge, MA: Harvard University, Kennedy School of Government, mimeo.

Part XII

CORRUPTION INHERITANCE: ENTRENCHED OR TRANSITIONAL

Introduction to Part XII

Whatever forms serious corruption may take, it its deeply embedded in the societies where it occurs. It reflects a variety of influences, some constant over the long term and others embodying major changes. Its scope and incidence are complicated issues: extremely corrupt societies encompass honest people and agencies, while in countries or regions where the problem is less pronounced there are still pockets of venality, and vulnerabilities to the future emergence of corrupt officials and activities. At one level, these complex cause-and-effect connections make it difficult to say how corruption affects a society, for as John Waterbury (1973: 534) has pointed out, we can only make educated guesses as to what might have developed without it. At a more fundamental level, it is important to remember that history matters.

This has never been more true than today. Globalization, the end of the cold war, and such new international policies as the OECD Anti-Bribery Treaty and the anti-corruption convention negotiated by the Organization of American States have all changed the political and economic context of corruption, and have arguably strengthened the forces arrayed against it. On the other side, a perception (accurate or otherwise) that corruption has spread may be a part of the malaise confronting many established democracies. A mix of traditional and transitional factors—or, looked at another way, constants and forces for change—shape not only the forms, but also the significance, of corruption in various societies.

Laurence Whitehead takes a very broad view of these kinds of dynamics in his discussion of Latin America. Both political and economic liberalization are transforming that region, though not necessarily in the same ways in all countries. The neo-liberal theories that have dominated international policy over the past decade suggest that while statist, interventionist policies foster extensive corruption, liberalization should make for less of it. But Whitehead points out major difficulties with that argument. As the theme of this chapter suggests, liberalization does not wipe the slate clean: continuing factors, as well as new policies, will shape the system that emerges. Liberalization encourages the growth of legitimate enterprises and social movements, but it may strengthen illicit ones (such as drug cartels) too, and while weakening the ability of the state to deal with them. Wholesale liberalization of politics and the economy may thus be only one aspect of a more complex reality marked by a mix of deregulation and re-regulation. High-level political corruption consists of a complex mix of practices; investors and aid partners from outside the region would do well, in Whitehead's view, to avoid a moralizing stance, and to maintain realistic expectations as to the pace of reform. Time will be needed, both to strengthen public institutions and to adapt societies to the brave new globalized world.

The ways people respond to corruption, in the context of the pressures and opportunities encountered in changing societies, will critically influence the types and extent of the problem. M. Shahid Alam suggests that the best way to understand these responses is to look at the actions of the *losers* in corruption. These he characterizes as *direct, evasive,* and *illicit* responses. The first involves confronting and opposing corruption, whether by political action or appeal to higher authorities. The second category encompasses a range of tactics to avoid it—by foregoing certain goods, taking a different road to market rather than pay informal "tolls" at police roadblocks, or relocating or going out of business. The third refers to using corruption of one's own, or violence, in response. Clearly the latter two responses are less promising as anti-corruption strategies, and help make it clear how corruption harms political and economic development. But choosing among them is not just a matter of will; these responses reflect the different types of stakes and opportunities involved in various sorts of activities and official functions. Like Whitehead, Alam reminds us that there are significant islands of integrity even in the most corrupt countries; the factors influencing both the types of corruption that occur, and the avenues of response open to the losers, help us understand both how both those islands, and significant corruption, persist and change.

Public responses to corruption are also the focus of Susan J. Pharr's article on Japan; and like Whitehead, she puts her findings in the context of longer-term trends. Her focus is the political malaise that many observers see in the world's established democracies (see, for example, Norris, 1999; Pharr and Putnam, 2000)—not a sudden collapse of democracy, but rather a long, slow deterioration of trust in democratic institutions and those who run them. Such a trend might have several causes, and Pharr examines two common hypotheses—that it is the failings of policy, particularly as regards economic wellbeing, or a decline in "social capital," that are draining the vitality from democracy. In Japan, however, neither of these views seems persuasive; whatever the economic difficulties of the past decade, Japanese citizens are vastly better off materially than they were just a generation or two ago. And social capital, as measured by the proliferation of organized activity—particularly that which strengthens ties among people, rather than integrating them into structures built from the top down—is actually richer than ever before. Much more convincing as an explanation are public perceptions and judgments of leaders' performance in office, and many of these have to do with corruption.

While it seems almost intuitive that corruption would undermine the trust essential to democracy, only rarely have analysts put that proposition to a real test. In Japan, Pharr's evidence bears it out, and indeed gives us reasons to be all the more concerned about corruption and the vitality of democracy. Like Whitehead and Alam, Pharr points to ways in which both long-term forces and popular responses shape the scope and significance of corruption, influencing political development (as well as economic, as suggested in part 6) in significant and worrisome ways.

References

Norris, Pippa (ed.). 1999. *Critical Citizens: Global Support for Democratic Government*. Oxford: Oxford University Press.

Pharr, Susan J. and Robert D. Putnam (eds.). 2000. *Disaffected Democracies: What's Troubling the Trilateral Countries?* Princeton: Princeton University Press.

Waterbury, John. 1973. "Endemic and Planned Corruption in a Monarchical Regime," *World Politics,* 25 (July), See also Appendix to this volume.

41

High Level Political Corruption in Latin America: A "Transitional" Phenomenon?

Laurence Whitehead

In principle high level political corruption[1] is to be expected under authoritarian rule, where those in power enjoy impunity and are sheltered from public criticism. By the same token a transition to democracy should lead to the emergence of a free press and independent media; the creation of competitive parties and counterbalanced institutions; and the subordination of all citizens (including the most powerful) to an impersonal constitution and the rule of law administered by an independent judiciary. All this can be expected, *pari passu*, to discourage high level political corruption by increasing the likelihood of exposure and punishment, and by reducing expectations that the perpetrators of such crimes will retain the freedom to reward their loyal followers, and to retaliate against those who stand against them.

This dichotomous political analysis (authoritarian rule favours high level corruption; democracy discourages it) has an exact counterpart in the realm of economic analysis. Here the argument is that a statist, interventionist, or "politicised" system of economic management favours high level political corruption by distorting the market, and so creating monopoly profits or rents that can be allocated discretionarily by public office-holders. Such cross-subsidies and rentier incomes are non-transparent, and therefore escape public inspection and control. By the same token, a transition to an open competitive market economy without politicised distortions can be expected, *pari passu*, to reduce the range of illicit and concealed profit opportunities available to the holders of political power; and to subject economic policy-marking to more effective public scrutiny and control, backed up by the force of an independent business community, which can be presumed to favour transparent institutional procedures and legal accountability for the use of public monies. This dichotomous economic analysis therefore postulates that interventionist policies favour high level corruption, whereas free markets discourage it.

Although these two hypotheses concerning the incidence of high level political corruption are parallel and overlapping, they are in principle distinct. Latin America certainly provides clear examples of authoritarian rule combined with market economics, (e.g., Pinochet's Chile) and also of interventionist economics combined with political democracy (most recently Caldera's Venezuela). The political diagnosis of corruption emphasises simple abuse of public office, whereas the economic diagnosis points towards a more complex, discriminating, and enterprise-related account of surplus misappropriation. The anti-corruption mechanisms postulated by political liberalism assume an empowered citizenry or electorate, whereas economic liberals rely more on an autonomous private sector pursuing its interests through the market. In practice nearly all of Latin America has recently experienced both types of liberalisation, usually proceeding more or less in tandem. Even Pinochet's Chile proceeded to a democratic transition after a decade or so of economic liberalisation, and even Caldera's Venezuela seems to have returned towards economic liberalization after its brief experiment with democratic interventionism. So although our two initial hypotheses are in principle distinct, most of the available Latin American evidence relates somewhat indistinctly to both. What follows, therefore, is a provisional review of the relationship between high level political corruption in Latin America, and the region's recent shift to political-cum-economic liberalisation (without much disaggregation of the two).

Although the two initial hypotheses are fairly clear and cogent, it is not a straightforward matter to relate them to the (no doubt highly incomplete) evidence presently available. Like most dichotomous analyses, the postulated contrasts are stylised and overstated. Yet in contrast to these neat theoretical constructs the evidence refers to a range of intermediate or partial regimes that may contain elements from both sides of the dichotomy, bound together in various combinations. In Brazil, for example, although military rule was unquestionably authoritarian, some elements of impersonal constitutionalism and a division of powers was always retained. Likewise, an "interventionist" style of economic policy-making was always operated in conjunction with a relatively strong and autonomous private sector, largely coordinated through the market. In Peru, over the same period, both authoritarian military rule and economic interventionism took much more drastic forms. Even *within* Brazil economic-cum-political liberalisation has affected the calculus of corruption very differently in for example the northeastern state of Alagoas, on the one hand, and in the federal capital of Brasilia on the other. (Local power structures and institutional practices vary widely across the huge subcontinent that is Brazil). Without further multiplying these examples it can be seen that all evidence concerning the scale and distribution of political corruption needs to be interpreted within a context that is too elaborate to be captured by the two initial dichotomies.

A second limitation of the two opening hypotheses is equally severe. They are exercises in "comparative statics." That is to say, they refer to a stable initial condition (authoritarian rule, interventionist economics) which can be contrasted with a stable alternative condition (democracy, a market economy). Such evidence as we have, however, refers to dynamic or unstable situations between these two poles ("transition"). However convincing may be the arguments from first principles linking a consolidated democracy and a secure market economy to the control of high level corruption, (and the evidence from Italy and elsewhere indicates that this is not in fact a straightforward link), it in no way follows that such malfeasance will diminish *before* those desired states are irreversibly entrenched. On the contrary, both theory and experience offer good grounds for anticipating that the transition may be associated with an increase in the frequency and intensity of illicit enrichment. On precautionary grounds those who had previously enjoyed impunity and immunity from public criticism can be expected to step up their acts of malfeasance when these defences begin to crumble during periods of regime breakdown and uncertainty over the stability of the rules of the game (either economic or political). During periods of transition the time horizons of many actors are foreshortened by uncertainties concerning their career prospects, and by fears of regression. Hence new actors too may have precautionary motives for seizing immediate opportunities of self-enrichment. Also, when new rules of the game are still fresh and untested, it is easy through inexperience or lack of clear guidance to commit acts that will be interpreted by competitors as corrupt. The main monitoring and control mechanisms postulated by the theorists of economic-cum-political liberalisation (a vigilant press, a well-organised private sector, a reliable justice system, an informed public opinion) cannot emerge overnight. If they *do* eventually become established this can only be after a protracted process of testing and learning. Until then the transition from an illiberal to a more liberal order may increase rather than diminish the opportunities and incentives for high level political corruption.

Since such reasoning from first principles about high level political corruption seems to generate inconclusive results, the obvious alternative is to appeal to the evidence, and to construct generalisations inductively. But unfortunately there are also serious impediments to empirical work in this area. Individual, sometimes spectacular, episodes of high level corruption may sometimes be well documented through investigative journalism, congressional hearings, and indeed judicial processes. But even in the most visible and well-documented of cases, large areas of unclarity typically remain.

For example . . . Brazil's first democratically elected civilian president in thirty years, Fernando Collor de Mello, was forced to resign after less than three years in office, as congressional enquiries uncovered the scale of his illicit fundraising activities. On some key questions of responsibility and illegality the public record seems incontrovertible. Yet, it was only through an improbable succession of accidents that so much came to light in this case. Even then, it remains uncertain how much other evidence was effectively suppressed, and at what point and by what mechanisms the spreading circle of complicities was limited. Subsequently, the very Congress which had championed the anticorruption case against an unpopular President was in turn exposed as riddled with comparable abuses. A close relative of the disgraced President remains on the Supreme Court bench to which he was nominated by the chief executive before the impeachment vote. In any case, the evidence uncovered in this case is mostly concerned with narrow issues of criminal liability. It does not address the broader questions of political strategy or economic motivation that would need to be uncovered in order to construct a broad gauge analysis of high level political corruption in the course of Brazil's liberalisation experience.

Objective and dispassionate data collection on the topic of political corruption is an inherently problematic enterprise.[2] The very term "corruption" denotes passion and subjectivity, and the charges and countercharges surrounding each case are infused with partisanship. This is hardly surprising when the stakes are so high for the powerful actors involved, and when the control mechanisms are so controversial and distrusted as they are in contemporary Latin America. In relation to almost every case it will be possible to find well-informed sources that will claim defamation and the planting of evidence, together with equally articulate exponents of the doctrine of the cover-up. The imperfections of Latin American mechanisms for the monitoring and control of public office-holders more or less ensure that for every convincingly proven case of high level corruption there must be multiple others which could not be conclusively documented.

Some observers will tend to conclude from this fact that most unproven allegations are also probably true, whereas others will argue that in such circumstances unfounded accusations of corruption constitute a virtually costless instrument of political warfare.

It is small wonder, then, that many political scientists and academic observers of liberalisation and transition tend to shrink away from this aspect, and to focus instead on other topics.

For my part, about twenty years ago, well before the latest cluster of transitions to democracy and economic liberalisation, I attempted a synoptic survey of the available evidence, concerning systematic and macro-economically significant corruption in twentieth century Latin America.[3] In contrast to an alternative literature concerned with low-level corruption, and inclined to rely on explanations based on various more or less "cultural" or traditional features of Latin American society, my chapter stressed hyper-presidentialism and executive impunity as the key explanatory variables, and it paraded a wide range of examples in which consciously designed strategies of illegal rent-seeking and extortion were orchestrated from the very top of the political system. The evidence assembled was approximate and impressionistic, but sufficient to suggest that this had been a rather recurrent pattern in the region's political economy; that the magnitudes involved were often highly significant in macro terms; that a top-down institutional analysis was warranted; and that rather than serving some functional purpose, such large scale presidential graft was potentially highly destabilising. During the Cold War it was tempting for some political scientists to implicitly condone such corruption, either on the grounds that the detached observer should eschew value judgements, or in the belief that corruption assisted economic growth and provided an alternative to communism. Since 1990 both these assumptions have been abandoned, and most political scientists are now normatively committed to honest markets and good government. But . . . economic-cum-political liberalisation can also be associated with high-level political corruption orchestrated from the presidential palace.

[It may well be] that new forms of corruption appeared and that corruption intensified, as Brazil and Argentina democratised. But . . . the evidence for such assertions is problematic. In order to judge just how "new," or how increased, was the corruption under President Collor, one would need comparable evidence concerning his predecessors (both military and civilian) and also concerning his successors. Perhaps the Collor scandals were an aberration. Perhaps, behind the repression and censorship of the military dictatorship even larger illicit fortunes were politically sanctioned?

Certainly after the 1964 coup great publicity was given to allegations concerning the corruption that had occurred during the final years of the preceding and discredited democratic regime. Yet some business observers commented in the late 1960s that the only real difference was that the pre-1964 Brazilian corruption had been chaotic and decentralised, whereas under military control it was methodical and concentrated at the top. In a similar vein, business informants in Argentina explained to me (anecdotally, of course) that in the 1980s, under the first democratic administration of President Alfonsin, it was difficult to know when a bribe was expected, which officials were or were not corrupt, or what the appropriate tariff might be. In the 1990s, under President Menem and the Peronists, by contrast, there was, according to these sources, no ambiguity or embarrassment, and the rates and procedures were clear-cut and predictable.

Finally, still at this anecdotal level, it was common in 1990/1 to hear American businessmen enthusing about the way the Salinas administration in Mexico had put an end to the extortion of foreign investors, and had installed a new cohort of well-educated, properly paid, public officials with good command of English and a commitment to transparency. The *Wall Street Journal* was so impressed that it put Carlos Salinas de Gortari on the board of its management company, Dow Jones. Such U.S. businessmen, and the Journal, were apparently among the last to awaken to the sorry truth revealed at the end of that administration. . .

Yet averting one's gaze is hardly an option for anyone seriously concerned with the task of examining how Latin America's economic-cum-political liberalisations are actually proceeding, and where they may be leading. Any list of the most prominent figureheads in Latin America's liberalisation drive would necessarily include ex-Presidents Collor and Perez (both impeached); ex-President Salinas (disgraced); and incumbent Presidents Fujimori and Menem (both surrounded by associates facing serious charges of dishonesty). Whatever one's judgement of each individual leader on this list, taken as a group their achievements and limitations can hardly be evaluated without considering the problems of malfeasance and inadequate accountability. Nor can subsequent tendencies to amend Latin America's constitutions in order to permit the re-election of incumbent chief executives be adequately assessed without regard to these issues. Nor can the stability and legitimacy of a wider range of liberalising reforms (including privatisation) be determined in isolation from the controversies that have arisen concerning alleged political corruption in these areas.

In global terms the most decisive consideration is the need to explain what it was that almost derailed the liberalisation process associated with the Salinas administration, and caused the resulting crisis of the Mexican regime, (and perhaps even of the NAFTA model) thereby casting a deep shadow across all similar experiments. At least within Mexico it is widely believed that discredit of the Salinas style of reform can be attributed in substantial measure to his administration's immersion in high level political corruption. In view of all this, serious empirically based work on economic-cum-political liberalisation cannot afford to disregard the subject.

One way of advancing the analysis, given the limitations of the available theory, and the inadequacies of the empirical data, would be to distinguish more precisely between various alternative patterns of behaviour that may all be subsumed under the rather vague rubric of "high level political corruption." The political rationale and institutional logic for, say, amassing hidden funds that can be used to influence election outcomes, should not be confused with that for, say, arms trafficking; or for, say, blocking judicial investigations into the narcotics industry; or for manipulating central bank assistance to insolvent privatised banks.

After all, each of these potential patterns of illicit behaviour stands in its own distinctive relation to economic-cum-political processes of liberalisation, and each may therefore be either curbed or facilitated by relatively specific public policy decisions. Admittedly, in practice, the scandals in Brazil, Mexico, Argentina and elsewhere indicate how easily one variety of high level political corruption runs into another; how readily electoral corruption can lead on to money laundering, then to complicity with *narco-traficantes*, and eventually to court-rigging, and perhaps even political assassination. But even if there may well be a corrosive logic to the dynamics of complicity and impunity which often over-runs the neat boundaries that analysts try to erect between one type of illicit practice and the next, it may still help to illuminate this murky sub-world if we separate out the various component elements, and examine them one by one.

Fund-raising for political parties, and to finance election campaigns, is a good place to start. Under authoritarian rule political parties were often supervised or even banned, and electoral contests were frequently manipulated by those in power. But even then, most countries held periodic elections and these were often rather expensive affairs. Typically the incumbent authorities would favour a particular party or slate of candidates, and would provide abundant resources to pay for the associated campaigning and publicity. Such resources would come in part from the public sector, and might include the secondment of public employees, deductions from employee payrolls to finance more or less compulsory party membership subscriptions, free advertising and unrestricted access to the (normally censored) media, the loan of official premises and vehicles, and so forth. Obviously approved parties could run very well-financed election campaigns, while opposition parties were generally denied official resources and were often starved even of private funds. Whereas private donors were officially encouraged and rewarded if they contributed to approved campaigns, they were liable to penalties if they supported opposition candidates. The ARENA party in Brazil, Mexico's PRI, and the Colorado Party of Paraguay all exemplified this authoritarian style of electioneering.

Following the transition to a more authentically competitive and genuinely multi-party electoral democracy new systems of party fund-raising and campaign financing would necessarily be required. But old reflexes and assumptions, and the vested interests created by the previous history, were not likely to disappear overnight. Nor was it usually a straightforward matter to agree on a new "level playing field" of rules governing political financing, let alone to establish the effective monitoring and reliable implementation of such rules, once they were adopted. When, for example, the Colorado party of Paraguay mounts a strong and well-financed election campaign under democratic auspices, it is hardly surprising if some sections of the electorate find it hard to believe that all its campaign contributions are now voluntary and above board, especially considering that many contributors and beneficiaries continue to be very same people who previously engaged in collusive and anti-democratic styles of electioneering.

In addition to the legacy of suspicion and distrust that may arise from pre-democratic experiences of party fund-raising, new sources of unease about election finances may arise during a democratization from the emerging post-transition incentive structure. As elections become more competitive the stakes rise for the rival contenders. Incumbents may fear that if they once lose office their chances of return will be severely impaired by the emergence of new options. Opposition politicians may also regard defeat in a competitive election as far more damaging to their reputations and prospects than previous defeats incurred against overwhelming odds. Thus early post-democratization elections may arouse both more hopes and more fears than conventional campaigns in stable balance-of-party contests. It may help to explain why allegations of high level corruption linked to campaign financing have proved a recurrent feature of democratization experiments in contemporary Latin America.

This . . . is not the place for an exhaustive survey of the evidence concerning party financing in democratic Latin America.[4] A few highlights must suffice, simply in order to indicate the magnitudes of the sums allegedly misappropriated for this purpose, and the widespread nature of the phenomenon. In accordance with my emphasis on "high level" corruption, and in consonance with the presidentialism that characterises most Latin American neo-democracies, the examples quoted referred to the national levels of party leadership. Regional and local party financing also deserves careful scrutiny however.

By the time he was impeached in December 1992, President Collor de Mello of Brazil had amassed secret funds, reportedly in excess of one billion dollars, through a systematic programme of commission-taking on public contracts organised by his financial henchman, P.C. Farias (the treasurer of his 1989 presidential campaign). Lacking a strong party of his own, or a solid base in Congress, the President nevertheless expected to build up a loyal political following and secure passage of his preferred legislation by making judicious payments from this slush fund. Brazilian election campaigns are now both frequent and costly, and party discipline is weak. One of the most plausible uses for these secret funds was to bankroll the election of candidates who would undertake to vote as the president required on key measures. Compare Venezuela. When he was forced from office in May 1993 President Carlos Andrés Pérez of Venezuela was no longer on good terms with the party he had headed since the 1970s. Acción Democrática was a well-funded mass social democratic party which had repeatedly mounted lavish, and often highly successful, election campaigns. Venezuela was accustomed to competitive elections, but not to transparent rules on party financing. The charge against Pérez was that he had diverted $17 million of secret government funds intended for security and defence into the black market, where they had been used to finance the president's political campaigns, thus freeing him from dependence of his party machine. Compare Mexico. In February 1993 the Mexican PRI's Secretary of Finance organised a private dinner, attended by President Salinas, at which the twenty-five prominent guests were "invited" to contribute $25 million to the funds of the ruling party, in order to cover its expenses in the forthcoming 1994 election campaign. Compare Colombia. In July 1995 the treasurer of the Colombian Liberal Party was arrested and admitted to receiving $6 million from the Cali drugs cartel as a contribution towards the second round campaign of Ernesto Samper, the party's standard-bearer who had secured the presidency after a close race in June 1994.

As these miscellaneous examples make clear, various elected Presidents of Latin America seem to require control over large sums of money of questionable provenance, in order to win elections and to reward loyal followers. Here we are not dealing with funds collected in small tranches from the rank and file of the ruling party. On the contrary, part of the object seems to be to free the head of state from undue dependence upon independent party structures. When individual donations are for sums in excess of a million dollars apiece it is difficult to believe that they express unrequited loyalty alone. Especially when the funds are secretly managed and are only provided to incumbents, a presumption of high level political corruption is difficult to avoid. What could wealthy donors hope to obtain in return for secretly financing the election or re-election of certain candidates or parties? All the four leaders reviewed above were identified with politics of economic liberalization and state reform in their respective countries. It is difficult to escape the inference that wealthy donors might hope to profit from inside information or privileged access regarding such liberalising reforms.

[S]tate-shrinking can provide opportunities for rent-seekers no less rewarding than those previously associated with state expansion. Although this type of corruption may be connected with election finances the two are not necessarily linked, and they should be kept analytically distinct—after all the range of possible countermeasures are quite different. So we now briefly review the theory and evidence relating high political corruption to programmes of economic liberalisation and "state shrinking." This discussion draws attention to an intervening variable—the "rule of law," or independence and effectiveness of the justice system—which goes far to explain why in some countries policies of state reform can be implemented without extremes of high level corruption, whereas in others this is much harder.

According to prevailing neo-liberal orthodoxies, corruption is inherently built into the incentive structure of state interventionism (which stimulates "rent-seeking") and becomes a marginal or inexpedient activity in a fully competitive market economy (based on "profit-seeking"). The conclusion therefore drawn is that the best antidote to corruption is to proceed at maximum speed with a strategy of wholesale economic liberalization and privatization. One line of cautious criticism has been to accept the basic premises of the argument (without necessarily endorsing its binary extremism), while arguing for a gradualist approach to reform, since too much haste could itself provide additional incentives and excuses for misappropriation. But true believers in neo-liberal doctrine have always tended to reject gradualism and prefer "shock treatment." On the corruption issue, they argued that even if rapid privatisation did create additional transient opportunities for corruption, the speedy adoption of free market disciplines would soon extinguish such incentives. Protracted methods of privatization would be worse, in that in the interim the "insiders" controlling the state assets would have time and motive to "loot" the enterprises in their care. This would both weaken state finances, and undermine the momentum needed to make privatization irreversible.

It is not easy to reconcile this theoretical position with the comparative and historical evidence on high level corruption available from Latin America. For example, comparing Costa Rica and Nicaragua, it would be hard to deny that the former had a long and effective record of broadly "social democratic" economic interventionism, while under the Somoza dictatorship the latter eschewed public ownership or welfare provision and allowed prices to be set by world markets.

Yet, in interventionist Costa Rica the incentives for high level political corruption were tempered by an independent and vigilant justice system, a free press, and a constitutional division of powers that normally held successive single term presidents to account for the performance of their public duties. In less interventionist Nicaragua, by contrast, the ruling dynasty amassed a fortune which, on the eve of the 1979 Revolution, was worth at least several hundred million dollars, and occupied the "commanding heights" of the republic's small economy. None of the constitutional checks and balances that worked so powerfully in neighbouring Costa Rica provided restraints on the rapacity of the Somoza family, which had retained effective political control for over forty years, either through presidential re-election or the nomination of place men, and which operated in a "sultanistic" manner—that is, without really recognising a distinction between public property and the private wealth of the rulers. Generalising from these two polar cases one can list a succession of Latin American regimes with small state sectors that practised high level corruption of the Nicaraguan type (from Battista's Cuba and Stroessner's Paraguay, onwards). There is also a significant cluster of social democratic or interventionist regimes with institutional defences against high level corruption of a Costa Rican calibre (in Chile and Uruguay most notably). Between these two clusters we can find a wide variety of hybrid cases, but in any case comparative analysis of high level corruption in pre-debt crisis Latin American history offers scant support for the simple binary opposition between rent-seeking interventionists and profit-seeking market postulated by neo-liberal theory.

In defence of the neo-liberal position it might be argued that pre-1990s history is irrelevant to the new structure of incentives and disciplines arising from a globalised market economy after the end of the Cold War. International markets and the standards of government demanded by foreign investors are now far more transparent than in the past . . . and at least in this new setting it can still be argued that the best way to curb high level political corruption is to privatise and liberalise as fast and as thoroughly as possible. Inevitably this argument will have to rest as much on deduction as on induction, at least until sufficient time has elapsed to confront the theory with conclusive evidence. But unless the theory is very compelling, this lack of historical confirmation or of corroborative pilot studies ought to incline practitioners and analysts towards gradualism and caution rather than root-and-branch constructivism. So just how compelling is the theory that urges "shock treatment" as a cure for corruption, and what provisional evidence can it invoke so far?

Neo-liberal reform characteristically requires concentration of discretionary power in the hands of a well-insulated team of economic technocrats, usually acting on authority delegated by a powerful president. This is true of most neo-liberal reform programmes, but it is especially true of those geared to wholesale and irreversible institutional change in the short run (i.e., "shock treatment" state reforms). The theory underlying such reforms is that since economic agents are generally self-regarding the rules of the economic game must be authoritatively redesigned from above, by those best equipped to understand the logic of alternative incentive structures. Discretionary executive power should be used to dismantle those institutions and rules of the game that encourage self-interested agents to engage in rent-seeking, and to create or reinforce those that favour profit-seeking. However, if it is assumed that all economic agents are self-regarding, how can one exempt the economic technocrats who are most committed to this theory from falling prey to the conduct they detect in others? And if institutions and rules of the game are to be evaluated according to the incentives for corruption they create, can the prescription that discretionary power should be concentrated in the hands of a well-insulated group within the most powerful branch of the state apparatus be exempted from that type of evaluation? In purely theoretical terms these seem troubling lacunae in the neo-liberal analysis.

The evidence available so far is inconclusive, but not entirely reassuring. Reference has already been made to the disputed allegations concerning Cavallo, Salinas and so forth. On the other hand it can be argued that the "Chicago Boys" in Chile broadly lived up to the promise of neoliberal theory, and a similar claim may be defensible concerning neo-liberal reformism in Bolivia (particularly since some of the key reformers were themselves already very wealthy as private mine-owners). On the empirical side the most disconcerting indicators relate to a succession of experiences of bank privatization. The Mexican case is extreme, [but] by no means unique. Over the past fifteen years the main banks have been successively nationalised, privatised, and most recently bailed out at great taxpayer expense. (The 1995 rescue effort is currently estimated to have cost around 12 percent of Mexico's annual GNP). In each case a small group of well-insulated technocrats, acting under the protection of an imperial presidency, have deployed discretionary power on a massive scale. It really does not seem very important whether private assets are being seized, or public assets are being sold off or state subsidies are being granted, or uncollectable debts are being written off. Whichever of these activities happen to be engaging the energies of Mexico's bank regulators at any specific moment, they are in any case allowed to act non-transparently, and without much in the way of effective legal or political accountability. Neo-liberal theory would predict that if this is the incentive structure then the agents in question will abuse these huge financial powers, and will act in such a way as to ensure that financial crises keep recurring, so that their privileges remain in place. Strategies of financial "shock treatment" have been justified on the grounds that the quickest route to a stable market economy is the strongest guarantee against future corruption. But it can just as plausibly be argued that reckless and indiscriminate bank privatizations ensure that the resulting privatised financial system will not be solid, and therefore that the neo-liberal "insiders" in charge of the process will also enjoy future opportunities for discretionary abuse of power, to sort out the consequences of their own imprudencies.

Similar issues arise with regard to one of the latest neo-liberal prescriptions: the need to entrench central bank "independence," following democratization and financial liberalization. The theory is that a legally and institutionally untouchable central bank can be mandated to protect the integrity of the currency, and to shield the financial system from the temptations to engage in monetary manipulation that afflict election-driven politicians. But the available evidence from neo-democracies in general, and from Latin America experiments with central bank independence in particular, suggests that if these huge powers of financial supervision are insulated from democratic accountability it is more than possible that those entrusted with them will succumb to other, more concealed, forms of societal influence. In the absence of effective public accountability, strong legal supervision, or a vigilant public opinion, independent central banks can themselves become an institutionally secure base for high level political corruption.[5]

Election financing and corruption arising from the discretionary implementation of liberalising economic reforms may be the two forms of high level political corruption most obviously associated with economic-cum-political liberalization projects, but they are not the only forms that require investigation here. More briefly, then, we need also to consider arms trafficking, money laundering, narcotics related corruption and finally abuse of the justice system. All of these take distinctive forms as a consequence of the contemporary liberalization trends in Latin America.

With the end of the Cold War and the shift to fiscal austerity and state shrinking the military and security establishments of the sub-hemisphere have lost much of their former *raison d' etre* and their political protection against budget and costs. This situation creates new pressures and incentives, as institutional protections weaken, and [as] the time horizons of defence ministers and senior military personnel are fore-shortened. Expensive weaponry may become surplus to requirements, or impossible to service and update. Yet in a liberalised and internationalised environment there are usually eager buyers for modern military equipment, especially if it can be delivered clandestinely.

In mid-1996 the Argentine Minister of Defence was forced to resign when it became apparent that his department had secretly supplied Ecuador with weapons used in its border dispute with Peru, notwithstanding Argentina's official status as guarantor of the cease-fire between these two sister republics. Whether the motive was simply personal enrichment, or included some intention to supplement the resources available to the military establishment, remains to be clarified, as do the broader political ramifications. Perhaps this was an unrepresentative incident, but it would be rash to assume that economic-cum-political liberalization necessarily diminishes the scope for this type of high level corruption, either in the short run, or still over the long run.

Another feature of a liberalised international environment is that it can increase the opportunities for money laundering. At any rate the IMF seems to accept that the twin forces of economic liberalization and technological innovation have between them boosted this activity to a (conservatively estimated) annual turnover of $300–$500 billion. According to Vito Tanzi, a senior economist at the Fund, the rapid growth of loosely regulated "emerging" financial markets, and the expansion of private financing operations conducted by companies technically headquartered in tax havens (notably located in the Caribbean), have both made it easier to invest large amounts of anonymous capital without raising suspicion. He also argues that such laundered funds tend to work against the goal of economic efficiency because their distribution is not driven so much by economic fundamentals (e.g., after-tax rates of return or real interest rates) but rather by differences in the degree of regulatory oversight in different markets, which accordingly attract these types of funds regardless of the associated inefficiency and misallocation of resources. Governments which are not greatly concerned about the provenance of the funds they receive thereby secure a margin of freedom to pursue wasteful economic policies of the kind that the IMF is always trying to curb.[6] Nothing in this analysis suggests that the growth of money laundering is a purely "transitional" phenomenon that can be relied on to go into reverse once liberalisation programmes have been completed. Only some form of "re-regulation," presumably with enhanced powers of intervention for the IMF or related international bodies, would be likely to promote such a reversal.

The question of de-regulation versus re-regulation is closely connected to the issues arising from the proliferation of international drug-related business, politics, and criminality. In Latin America the central issue concerns the cocaine trade, which has been primarily geared to supplying the huge U.S. domestic market for narcotics. Authoritarian military regimes, such as the García Meza dictatorship in Bolivia and the Noriega dictatorship in Panama, were initially the most visible culprits in this area of high level criminality. (Both these ex-Presidents are currently serving jail sentences for their drug-related crimes). But the economic-cum-political liberalization of the region has done nothing to reduce the scale of consumer demand for these illicit substances, and consequently has done nothing to curb the incentives for engaging this type of transaction, or indeed for providing political protection to the big players in the business. While on the one hand the financial community based in Washington has been strenuously promoting economic liberalization, and the OAS-based political community has stepped up international support for democratization in the Americas, elsewhere in Washington other agencies have more aggressive in trying to counter international drug-trafficking.

Thus, both de-regulation and certain forms of re-regulation are being promoted throughout Latin America at the same time. In a number of cases the result has been that a democratically elected head of state with a clear commitment to economic reform may be simultaneously subjected to equal and, in a certain sense, opposite forms of pressure from the international community. "Improve your human rights performance, but crush the drugs barons by any means necessary," for example. Or privatise and deregulate your banks, but vet them more intensively than ever before for illicit deposits. Allow more open and competitive elections, but stamp out all expression of narcotics-related interest in your political system—even from regions where the cultivation of cocaine provides the main source of livelihood for most small producers. Uphold the constitutional order, founded upon a commitment to national sovereignty, but accept external certification of your conduct concerning the most delicate questions of internal security and bow to foreign demands for extradition or for extra-territorial rights, whenever they serve the cause of narcotics control. Despite economic-cum-political liberalization a succession of Bolivian, Colombian, Mexican and Peruvian presidents have struggled with limited success to reconcile these competing and insistent external demands. It is far from clear that narcotics-related corruption and political de-legitimisation will prove a merely transitional phenomenon in such countries.

More generally, in much of Latin America, over long periods of time, substantial amounts of "high level political corruption" have coexisted with substantial "islands" of institutional integrity, and with rather extensive and durable areas of conventional and respectable profit-driven economic activity. Only in relatively exceptional cases has the first run out of control to the point of overwhelming the second. Equally, the neo-liberal theory that the expansion of the market economy will drive back and eventually eliminate large scale politicised misappropriation of resources can only invoke quite a limited range of supporting instances from this region. Comparative experience—including from the Anglo-Saxon democracies—suggests that where the progressive elimination of corruption *has* occurred, it has been an incremental process extending over various decades, requiring cumulative pressure from a variety of sources, usually internally driven, and by no means linear in character.[7] This chapter has reviewed a series of indications tending to cast doubt upon the view that in the near future the incidence of high level political corruption in Latin America will be drastically different from in the past . . .

The implications of this analysis for western policy-makers is that neither traditional complacency nor a new surge of righteousness is the appropriate reaction. To effectively combat such long-standing and deeply entrenched practices would require patience, vigilance, and discrimination. High level political corruption may be a scourge in many parts of Latin America, but it is not generally a terminal affliction. Over time, with persistence, and through co-operation with the extensive local professional and institutional groupings committed to the strengthening of the rule of law, it should be possible to make progress in promoting an ethos of public responsibility and accountability. But this will only be durable if it has solid domestic support. Flamboyant interventions from without can easily undercut the construction of such local coalitions, providing a nationalist cover for the reaction against them. This is especially the case when outside policy-makers are suspected of grand-standing for their own political advantage, and when short-term gestures are perceived as selective and unlikely to last. A dense network of interlocking formal and informal institutions enjoying external support but resting primarily on internal bases of legitimacy, would provide the most secure defence against the region's old habits of patrimonialism and abuse of power. In consequence, effective long run reforms to curb high level political corruption would need to be constructed in the interests of the home population, promoted in a spirit of self-respect, and guaranteed by institutions that are locally authentic. Where external support is provided it will work better if it is multilateral, durable, predictable and aimed at reinforcing well-established "islands of integrity" within the country concerned . . .

Although my focus has been on domestic Latin American institutions and practices we should never forget that in a liberalised and internationalised environment, corruption is unlikely to stay confined within narrow national boundaries. Drug-trafficking, for example, requires an external market, and some complicity by developed country banks, customs officials and law enforcement agencies. Arms-trafficking requires manufacturers and pushers outside Latin America as well as within the region. There have to be bribe *givers* as well as bribe *takers*, and both seek the security provided by international banking safe havens. It is not a cultural inevitability that Latin Americans must continue to live under governments characterised by high levels of impunity and power abuse, but neither can these patterns be eliminated from one day to the next by "just saying no." Underlying incentive structures would have to be refashioned, and anti-corruption monitoring reinforced. An ethos of public responsibility would have to be nurtured. Any progress on these fronts would take a considerable time, would vary with complex local conditions, and would require seriousness of purpose from a wide array of actors and institutions, both locally based and internationally. Such anti-corruption networks will only be durable, credible, and eventually successful, if they are willing to challenge entrenched interests and practices opposed to their agenda wherever they lurk—whether *within* Latin America or *outside* the region—whether condemned by international financial institutions or tacitly condoned by them. Reforms and adaptations are likely to be slow and uncertain. Before we lose patience with this, we all need to consider the hard cases. If *our* arms manufacturers need time and support to adjust to the disappearance of lucrative markets, than so do *their* coca growers. If we would not tolerate intrusive foreign monitoring of the projects of our own elected leaders, then we should not expect the citizens of other democracies to be that enthusiastic either.

Notes

1. This discussion is only concerned with "high level" and "political" corruption, and not with "societal" or economic corruption more generally. The distinction rests on the claim—abundantly supported by evidence from Latin America—that a substantial proportion of the resources that are illegally captured or misappropriated in these economies are handled by national level public office-holders. . . Given the executive dominance that characterises these political systems, presidents and their immediate associates are particularly prone to such activities, which should not be confused with lower-level forms of clientelism, or asymmetric exchange of favours.

2. Consider, for example, the problem of the time lags that may separate the commission of an offence from its public exposure. . . . [F]ollowing the military coup of 1964 one of the key conspirators used his privileged access to the authoritarian regime to build up a major Brazilian private bank, Unibanco. For twenty years under the shelter of impunity and immunity, this enterprise seemed to prosper. But with the return to democracy its advantages ceased. By 1986 it was effectively bankrupt. Yet, through the negligence or connivance of its regulators and the inexperience of new democratic actors it continued to take deposits and to roll over debts for a further ten years. It was not until February 1996 that the Central Bank uncovered the fraud (which by then had snowballed to around five billion U.S. dollars of unbacked liabilities, currently loaded onto the Brazilian taxpayer). Thus the scandal that broke in 1996 referred to offences committed perhaps decades earlier. But of course the political fallout accrued to the present democratic administration. No one can be sure how many other long-buried corruption scandals await exposure in other Latin American market-based neo-democracies.

3. "On Presidential Graft; The Latin American Evidence," in Arnold J. Heidenheimer, Michael Johnston and Victor T. LeVine (Editors). *Political Corruption: A Handbook* (Transaction Publishers, New Jersey, 1989).

4. See Eduardo Posada (ed)., *Party Finances in Europe and Latin America* (ILAS, London, 1997.

5. I have assembled some evidence on this in my "Models of Central Banking: How Much Convergence in Neo-Democracies?" (Paper presented at a conference on The Political Economy of Central Bank Independence, St Peter's College, Oxford, 21 September 1996).

6. Vito Tanzi, "Money Laundering and the International Financial System" IMF Working Paper, (Washington DC), May 1996.

7. On Britain, see "The Decline of Patronage" in H. Parris, *Constitutional Bureaucracy,* (London, 1969) and W. D. Rubinstein "The End of 'Old Corruption'" in *Past and Present,* (1983).

42

A Theory of Limits on Corruption and Some Applications

M.S. Alam[1]

Introduction

Why does corruption vary across government agencies within the same country and, frequently, across different functions within the same agency?[2]

Even in countries with a well-deserved reputation for widespread corruption, there is relatively little of it in their postal services or college admissions. Corruption may also vary across different functions in the same agency. Thus, post offices are almost completely free from corruption in the sale of stamps, but pilferage of letters and packages is more common. Similarly, there is little corruption in the servicing of deposits at state-owned banks, but a great deal more of it in their lending activities.

While an account of such differences might be offered in terms of differences in *potential* gains from corruption, this is obviously inadequate. For instance, the potential for illicit earnings in college admissions is considerably higher than in passport offices, yet corruption in passport offices is more common than in college admissions. A complete account of variations in corruption must be pursued in terms of differences in the *ability to realize* the potential gains from corruption; and this requires that we look at the countervailing actions (CA) which victims of corruption can take to resist their losses. An approach to corruption which turns on the concept of CA can explain both the details about corruption and identify the forces which account for variations in corruption across societies and over time.

Source: *Kyklos* 48:3 (1995), pp. 419–435. Reprinted by Permission

Although losses are at least as reliable a spur to action as gains, there has been little systematic analysis concerning whether, and how, actions taken by losers might work to resist and set limits on corruption.[3] Curiously, the literature on corruption has been silent about its victims. Instead, it looks at corruption primarily from the perspective of winners, emphasizing the different *inducements* and *pressures* they face for engaging in corruption. As a result, variations in levels of corruption across countries and over time are generally explained in terms of the potential for illicit gains created by government interventions, although differences in value-systems and social structures also enter the analyses.[4]

It is time to take the victims of corruption more seriously. Whenever corruption creates visible losses, its victims are likely to resist their losses by three broadly defined means: *evasive* CA which seek to reduce dependence on corrupt officials; *direct* CA which raise the costs to officials of engaging in corruption; and *illicit* CA which use corruption as a means of combating the losses from corruption. It is the primary task of this paper to work out the logic of these CA. The ability of losers to engage in CA depends on two types of factors. The first set of factors are *specific* to agencies and affect a society's capacity to engage in CA against corruption in those agencies. A second set of *global* factors affect the capacity of a society for engaging in CA, per se. Variations in global factors account for differences in levels of corruption across countries and over time.

Corruption and Countervailing Actions

The efficacy of CA in explaining variations in corruption across agencies will be examined vis-à-vis postal services, state-owned banks, passports, utility departments, irrigation, the police, college admissions, and a land-consolidation program; we also consider the possibility of CA against embezzlement in government. It may be noted that these examples are drawn from countries in South Asia.[5]

Postal Services. Corruption in this agency is relatively uncommon, although it is higher in some activities than others. It is quite rare in the sale of postage stamps; more common in the processing of mail when letters may be pilfered for their mint stamps; and valuable packages are almost certain to be stolen. The reasons for these variations can be explained in terms of CA.

We should not underrate the potential for illicit gains in the sale of postage stamps. Most users of stamps would be willing to pay a considerable premium rather than go without them. The inability of postal officials to appropriate these premia can be explained by the ease of CA. Users have access to many post offices, making evasive actions easy. It is relatively inexpensive to stock up on stamps, reducing dependence on corrupt post offices. Also, post offices are generally small, and hence quite vulnerable to clients they might anger by demanding bribes.[6]

Users can counter the pilferage of letters by having the stamps cancelled before they are mailed; they can substitute aerograms for envelopes; or, where this option exists, they can turn to post offices served by franking machines. On the other hand, there is little that users can do to prevent the pilferage of packages containing valuables.

Banking. While state-owned banks are notorious for corruption in their lending activities, there are few reports of corruption in the servicing of deposits. Corruption in lending is quite easily explained by its potential for large gains—with lending rates often below market-clearing levels—as well as the difficulty of mounting direct CA because kickbacks to bank officials are made in secrecy and cannot be substantiated in courts of law. Further, losers with high-yield uses for loans may prefer to respond with their own kickbacks, or turn to private banks or curb markets instead of engaging in direct CA.

The virtual absence of corruption in the servicing of deposits results from the strong CA available to depositors.[7] First, there generally exist several competing banks, each with multiple branches, ensuring that bank branches which impose illicit taxes on withdrawals will lose their deposits to other branches and banks. If such illicit taxes were to become pervasive, they would almost certainly persuade many depositors to shun the banks altogether, leading to a serious erosion of the formal banking system, a development which most governments would be at some pains to avoid.[8]

Passports. Passport officials create the potential for illicit gains by causing delays and uncertainty in the processing of applications. Anticipating these dilatory tactics, some applicants will circumvent them by applying for passports ahead of time. Failure to do so leaves little room for evasive actions. There are few offices which issue passports; often they are located only in the big towns or cities, and frequently applications may be filed only in the province of the applicant's permanent residence. Direct CA against corrupt officials are also often difficult. The applicants do not have access to officials; they can only communicate with clerks sitting behind well-protected counters. Further, since the one-time bribe is generally small compared to the anticipated gains, most applicants will be unwilling to risk further delays by engaging in direct CA.

Utility Connections. Utility departments extract bribes in the same way as passports: by building delays and uncertainty in the procedures for receiving connections. CA are difficult for several reasons: these departments are monopolies; applicants have access to only one outlet; the bribes are one-time and small relative to losses from delays; and there are many losers, making collective action difficult. However, there is generally less corruption in the servicing of utility connections such as water and gas, explainable in part by the difficulty of stopping the flow of these services selectively. Stopping services to an entire area—in order to collect bribes—is not without serious risks since field offices of these departments, located in the areas they service, would become vulnerable to attacks from the users.

Irrigation. This department's reputation for corruption is supported by Wade's (1982) case study of irrigation projects in an Indian state. He estimates that the rake-offs from investments in irrigation projects are at least as high as 25 percent of the total value of the project and sometimes as high as 50 percent.

The high levels of corruption in irrigation projects can be explained by the difficulties of CA. Contractors finance their kickbacks to irrigation officials by skimping on the quality and quantity of inputs used in the projects. Such skimping primarily reduces the life-span of the projects, and hence is not immediately discernible. Even when corruption is recognized to be the primary cause of the poor quality of projects, CA will be unlikely for two reasons. There are many users of an irrigation project, most of whom are small, often illiterate peasants, making it unlikely that they can organize for action. In any case, the affected peasants would prefer to lobby for quick repairs or replacements rather than organize CA against long-departed corrupt officials.

The Police. Corruption in the police is endemic. They enjoy wide powers which are used only infrequently to enforce the law; more often, they are used for extortion and to protect illegal activities. Why doesn't all this give rise to strong CA? Police corruption creates many victims, who seek legal protection, take their grievances to the press, and occasionally resort to attacks on police and police stations; but with little effect. The Government uses the police to implement strong-arm tactics against its opponents. Police corruption is, therefore, condoned as a cost of doing business with them.

College Admissions. Since professional degrees carry high—often very high—premiums over alternative academic programs, the relatively low levels of corruption in college admissions is surprising.[9] This anomaly can, however, be explained by the capacity of students to engage forcefully in direct CA.

Admission to professional colleges is based on average grades: colleges announce cut-off grades at which admission begins. Since student unions can generally obtain lists of students admitted, irregularities in admissions are easily discovered. Applicants who are crowded out by backdoor admissions are unlikely to take this lying down. They will organize, seek support of student unions, take the matter to the press, the minister of education, and perhaps to the streets. Such protests will almost certainly draw support from the entire student body who will see their own chances of admission being put at risk by corruption. Governments, anxious to avoid these protests, will generally be eager to limit backdoor admissions.

Land Consolidation Program. In a study of land consolidation in the Indian state of Uttar Pradesh, Oldenburg (1987) concluded that corruption had a marginal impact on the outcome of the program. This is contrary to what one might expect, given that the program was staffed by poorly paid officials who were expected to make vital decisions about land rights in villages with high levels of illiteracy and significant inequalities of power. How, then, was corruption kept to a minimum?

Three related factors have been identified by Oldenburg (1987, pp. 514–519) to account for this result: the openness of the procedures followed for land-consolidation, provisions for speedy appeals, and the high stakes which each farmer has in his land. Land consolidation exercises were carried out openly, in the villages rather than in government offices, and villagers were kept informed of how the decisions affected them. Peasants had direct access to consolidation officers, ensuring that the latter were "vulnerable to physical attack as they worked, exposed, in the villages; in several cases, officials are said to have been beaten or killed by enraged farmers."[10]

All this, however, gives rise to a further question. Why were administrative procedures in this program designed to minimize the incidence of corruption? Although Oldenburg (1987) treats the official procedures as data that do not need explaining, the reasons are fairly obvious. In a democracy, where peasants have the right to vote, the discontent caused by widespread corruption in land consolidation would almost certainly be used by a radical Opposition to undermine the ruling party.

Embezzlement. CA against embezzlement are difficult for two reasons: embezzlement is likely to remain invisible, and the losses it inflicts, although large, are collective.[11] Embezzlement can be checked only in countries that possess truly competitive partisan politics and a vigorous press. The scale of embezzlement one might expect in countries which lack vigorous democratic institutions is fully supported by *ex post* revelations regarding the fortunes of fallen heads of state.

In the long run, some indirect checks on large-scale embezzlement may come into play. Large and persistent drains on the treasury caused by embezzlement may invite corrective measures if they precipitate repeated economic crises which threaten the legitimacy of the government. Multinational corporations, international banks and multilateral development agencies may add to these pressures if they find their investments and loans placed in jeopardy by the government's corruption. Once mobilized, these institutions are capable of taking strong actions: they can pull out of the host country, refuse to make new loans, and threaten economic boycott in case of failure to service foreign debts. During the Cold War such actions were not encouraged because the host countries often provided valuable services in combating communism. The end of the Cold War has greatly altered the conditions. Aid donors and creditors are now demanding political reforms as a condition for economic assistance, and increasingly they are asking for improvements in governance.[12]

A Theory of Countervailing Actions

The preceding examples of CA demonstrate that we have grasped an important social mechanism which, driven as it is by self-interest, acts automatically to set limits upon corruption. Our next task is to develop a theory of CA: to examine the forms of CA, their causes, and effects on corruption.

Corruption can evoke CA only if it creates losses that are visible to its victims. Although losses from corruption can be moral as well as material, this paper will only examine the latter.[13] This is because we seek to explore the dynamics of corruption in societies that have yet to internalize the norms of public office and where, as a consequence, moral losses are not strong enough to restrain corruption.

Forms. It was pointed out earlier that CA may take three forms: evasive, direct and illicit. Some additional comments are offered here on each of these forms.

When faced with corrupt demands, losers may relocate (to escape extortion), seek out officials who are not corrupt, find substitutes or private alternatives to goods or services provided by corrupt officials, forego such goods and services altogether, or take actions which alter the nature of their dependence on corrupt officials.[14] All these *evasive* CA have the effect of reducing the potential and actual gains from corrupt activities. Some of them are comparable to Hirschman's (1970) exit option.

Losers may also seek to reduce their losses by deterrent actions which raise the costs of engaging in corrupt activities. A partial list of such *direct* CA includes (1) confronting corrupt officials with evidence of their corrupt activities; (2) taking complaints about corrupt officials to their superiors; (3) taking corrupt officials to court; (4) facilitating media reports about corrupt acts or officials; (5) use of violence, or its threat, against corrupt officials; (6) voting against elected officials who are corrupt or tolerate corruption; (7) picketing offices that engage in corruption; (8) organizing strikes, boycotts or shutdowns against corruption; (9) organizing campaigns or political parties to fight corruption; or (10) imposing sanctions against corrupt officials. These actions are comparable to Hirschman's (1970) voice option.

Illicit CA may take two forms. An individual may bribe officials to counter actual or anticipated losses from corruption. Alternatively, he may respond to actual or anticipated losses from corruption by using coercion against corrupt officials.

Factors Influencing CA. Attention may first be drawn to factors which determine the overall ability of losers to engage in CA. These *global* factors encompass (a) the state of human, political, and property rights; (b) an efficient and impartial judiciary; (c) media competition; (d) level and distribution of incomes; (e) level of education; (f) decentralization of government; (g) the state of communications technology; etc. These factors affect the ability to engage in CA *via* several channels. Most importantly, they determine the flow of information about corrupt activities and the range of instruments available for engaging in direct and evasive CA. But they also affect the ability of losers to evaluate information, to organize collective actions to resist their losses, and their bargaining powers in relation to gainers from corruption.

Decentralization has some interesting implications for CA. By creating multiple centers of authority, it amplifies the scope for evasive CA. Since it creates smaller units of government, it may also be expected to reduce the costs of information; not only does this reduce the cost of making trips to government offices, but it may also activate new informal flows of information about corrupt activities. Most important, matched against smaller units of government, the losers are likely to be more effective in their direct CA against corrupt officials.

There are several influences on CA which are likely to vary across corrupt activities: type of corruption, nature of losses from corruption, nature of transactions between officials and private agents, degree of access to corrupt officials, and characteristics of losers. The effects of these *specific* factors on incentives for engaging in CA will be examined briefly.

Losses from corruption are not always visible. Coercive corruption always creates visible losses, since coercion cannot be concealed from its direct victims. On the other hand, losses from collusive corruption, since they are borne by third parties, may not be visible to the losers. Losses from collusive corruption can be attributed to corruption only when corruption itself is visible.

Official transactions which occur in the open, or across the counter, are less amenable to corruption: buying stamps at the post office, or tickets at the railway station, or cashing a cheque at the bank belong in this category. Most government transactions, however, occur on a one-on-one basis, making it easier to make collusive deals in secrecy. Transactions at airports, ports, immigration offices, or border crossings, which occur in enclosed spaces, or under the cover of security arrangements, are likely to facilitate coercive forms of corruption.

The character of losses from corruption may also vary across corrupt activities. Losses from corruption are *direct* when they have a direct bearing on individual rights or entitlements; they are *derived* when they are inferred from knowledge of a collective loss. Direct losses are likely to cause a stronger sense of deprivation than comparable derived losses. Similarly, the incentive for CA will vary directly with the size of losses relative to the incomes of losers. Losses from corruption may reduce present incomes or additions to incomes. Even when they are quantitatively the same, the principle of diminishing marginal utility alone ensures that welfare reductions from the first loss will be larger than those from the latter.

Various characteristics of losers—their numbers, incomes, or educational levels—also have a bearing on CA. The relationship between the number of losers and CA is not a simple one. Large numbers worsen the free-rider problem; but once losers are organized, their power is likely to increase as their numbers grow.[15] Thus, societies with a dense network of associations—whether of producers, traders, importers, exporters, workers, retirees, consumers, and neighbors—will be more supportive of direct CA.

The ability to engage in direct CA will depend on the educational levels and incomes of losers. Education is likely to deepen the understanding of rights and the ability to use them to mount CA. At higher levels of incomes, losers can draw upon a greater abundance of resources with which to organize resistance; they may also be more willing to assume greater risks in their confrontation with corrupt bureaucracies. It may be noted that educational characteristics and incomes of losers may vary systematically across government agencies. Thus, peasants in developing countries who are often both illiterate and poor will be less likely to engage in direct CA than college students who are both literate and well off.

Effects of CA. This varies with the type of CA. Thus, the potential for evasive CA will tend to lower the "price" of *a* corrupt act—or the illicit revenue it generates—though the opposite may also occur, while the frequency of corrupt transactions may go up or down. This may be illustrated with the help of a case study which involves evasive CA in response to extortion. Let P be the official price of X (goods, services or permits) sold by a government agency, with a perfectly elastic official supply of X at price P: Q is the corresponding quantity sold. Let $P^*>P$ be the price ($Q^* < Q$ is the corresponding quantity), which maximizes the *total* rent from the illicit auction of X *in the absence of evasive CA.* Now, let X be available from private sources at a price equal to $(P+m) < P^*$, creating the potential for evasive CA. Officials may respond to this potential by lowering their price to a little below $P+m$ in order to undersell the private suppliers of X; this will increase the quantity of X sold on the illicit auction.

The effects of direct CA on the price and frequency of corrupt acts are unambiguous. An inventory of direct CA, presented earlier in this section, shows that they are capable of imposing a variety of material and psychic costs on corrupt officials, including inconvenience, social censure, risk of violent action by losers, punitive action from superiors, loss of jobs for elected officials, and loss of legitimacy for governments. An increase in these costs is likely to reduce corruption in at least four ways. First, even at unchanged levels of official anti-corruption activity, some corrupt officials will decide to reduce their corrupt activity. Second, where honest officials are in charge, they may respond to direct CA by intensifying anti-corruption activity. Third, a government may respond to threatened loss of legitimacy by increasing their visible anti-corruption activity. Finally, in the long run, the government may institute reforms to reduce the incentives for engaging in corruption or take actions to strengthen countervailing forces.

Most forms of direct CA may be undertaken singly or collectively. Which of them is likely to be more effective? Paradoxically, when corrupt officials are unable to engage in retaliatory actions against individuals engaging in direct CA, the sum of individual acts may often be more effective than collective action. To illustrate the point, a hundred independent court cases or complaints are likely to have a greater impact on corrupt officials than a single court case, or complaint, made by a single committee of a hundred losers. This paradox can be a boon in disguise. Failure to act collectively, because of free-rider problems, may well be an advantage where the same individuals are willing and able to act on their own.

Illicit CA aimed at *reversing* deviations from the rules of public office are likely to reduce—or eliminate—these deviations, whether actual or anticipated, while the "price" of corrupt acts may go up or down. This result will be illustrated by means of three case studies.

The first case is set in the context of rationing X (goods, services, utilities, permits, jobs, or college admissions). Some private agents use bribes to increase their shares of X, thus reducing the shares of other agents who, aware of these losses, may, in the next round of rationing, offer bribes to restore their shares of X. To the extent that they succeed, these illicit CA reduce—or eliminate—the deviations. Their effect on total illicit revenue, however, will be ambiguous. On the one hand, second-round bribes, by increasing competition for official decisions, will increase their price. But also, the second-round bribes pay for *restoring* official rules, and since this reduces risks of detection for officials, they may be willing to eliminate—or reduce—the deviations in return for bribes lower than the ones that created them,

The next case looks at losses from corruption that are transmitted *via* technological externalities. A paper mill bribes officials to dump prohibited effluents into a river. This hurts downstream fisheries that respond with bribes of their own, and succeed in reducing or stopping the illegal dumping. Since the second round of bribes has restored the enforcement of anti-pollution laws, the corrupt officials may be willing to accept lower bribes to reflect the reduced risks of detection they now face.

In some cases, illicit CA may *create* their own deviations in order to counter losses from corruption. This may be illustrated with a case that involves negative pecuniary externalities. Some firms in the garments industry use bribes to reduce their indirect taxes; this places their competitors at a disadvantage, some of whom, in turn, use bribes to have their taxes reduced. These tax-cuts, however, cannot go on indefinitely. At some point, the missing tax revenues will become unacceptable to the government, and provoke corrective action. To forestall this, tax officials are likely to place an upper bound on total tax-cuts traded for bribes.

Corruption across Countries and over Time

The explanation of why levels of corruption vary across countries can be framed directly in terms of varying combinations of global factors across these countries.

Variations in corruption across countries may be assessed at the level of particular agencies, or globally in terms of overall levels of corruption. It is the first type of comparison which is more easily undertaken. Provided that there are no important differences in the ways in which specific agencies are organized in the countries under comparison, thus ensuring uniformity in the influence of specific factors, variations in levels of agency-specific corruption may be regarded as representative of overall levels of corruption in those countries.

In the long run, the presence of democratic institutions, competitive mass media, decentralization in government, higher per capita incomes, a more equal distribution of income, urbanization and education, may be expected, as argued earlier, to work asymmetrically in favor of losers and, therefore, result in reduced levels of overall corruption. These linkages between global factors and levels of corruption can, in principle, be subjected to empirical testing. If data were available on a ranking of countries by levels of corruption in some key agencies, it would be quite easy to explore whether variations in corruption can be explained by some suitable set of global factors.

The effects of economic development on corruption can be analyzed in terms of how its correlates are likely to affect forces arrayed against and favoring corruption. A partial list of these correlates might include: (a) secular increases in wages, education and urbanization; (b) growth of mass media; (c) advances in transportation and communications technology; (d) improvements in managerial and accounting skills; (e) growth of capitalist classes, urban middle classes, and an urban labor force; and (f) upward pressures on government expenditure.

A little reflection will show that (a), (b) and (c) have the potential for increasing information flows as well as the range and effectiveness of direct CA. The spread of education increases access to information and may also lead to a growing sophistication in the understanding of individual rights and entitlements. Growth of mass media, when it is not a government monopoly, can lead to more penetrating coverage of corruption. Telephones and faxes open up additional channels of communications to officials. The proliferation of short-wave radios and dish antennae, by providing access to international news services, can dilute the state's control over sources of information.

Some of the correlates of development listed above have the potential for reducing the costs of engaging in collective forms of CA. Tendencies listed under (b), (c) and (e) can facilitate collective action by slowly putting in place associations which aggregate the interests of various business, professional and workers' groups. Collective action may also be advanced by the formation of cooperative movements, community organizations, human rights groups, and other non-governmental organizations engaged in welfare or development work. At some point, the common interests of various subsets of these groups may be aggregated at the state or national levels by political parties. The formation of community organizations, interest groups, and their aggregation into political parties will also weaken particularistic demands and their tendency to promote corruption.[16]

Finally, as the demand for physical and social infrastructure, social security, and regulatory activities increases with economic development, the resulting increases in public expenditure are likely to place the government under mounting pressures to reduce revenue losses from corruption—as an alternative to raising new taxes. The same pressures may also emerge from unexpected sources, such as wars or natural disasters. Over time, and in increments, these pressures are likely to result in the streamlining of revenue collection and public expenditures in order to reduce leakages from corruption.

An important qualification to the argument developed thus far must now be introduced. Direct CA depend crucially on respect for human, political and property rights. Where these rights are repressed, the tendency of economic development to strengthen CA may contribute to a perverse result, increasing the severity of repression in order to close off the new opportunities for CA.

Continuing and mounting repression, however, is not compatible with economic development in the long run. In a dynamic world economy, firms can remain competitive only if they have free access to international information flows, can draw upon an increasingly sophisticated physical and social infrastructure, and can expect quick adjustment of government policies to a changing global economy. An economy that is coupled with a corrupt and repressive government is unlikely to meet these demands. It must liberalize its political system, or increasingly find itself trapped with lagging technologies and outmoded industries.

It is also important to note that in the poorest countries where corruption is deeply entrenched, poverty is likely to be perpetuated because of systematic negative feedbacks from corruption. The point has often been made that corruption can improve efficiency of resource allocation by creating illicit markets to replace bureaucratic decisions.[17] A more careful assessment of this argument, however, reveals several flaws. First, corruption motivated by nepotism and politics does not simulate markets. Second, when corruption does create illicit markets they may not be efficient for three reasons: entry to these markets will be restricted in order to reduce risks of detection; honest but efficient producers may be pushed out by inefficient and dishonest producers; there will be waste of resources used in the cover-up of illicit activities. Thus, it seems more likely that corruption may undermine instead of improving static efficiency. More to the point, corruption is also likely to retard growth by reducing the quantity and quality of public investments in physical infrastructure, education, health, or soil conservation; by increasing uncertainty in the provision of publicly provided inputs, such as utilities, irrigation water, fertilizers, or seeds; by crowding out honest and efficient entrepreneurs; and, by undermining property rights, thus reducing the incentives for savings, innovations, investment and effort.[18] Clearly, where these negative feedbacks are severe, it is unlikely that a country will be able to pull itself out of poverty—or experience the therapeutic effects of sustained economic development on corruption.

Summary and Policy Implications

Starting from a simple premise, this paper has proposed a framework that is at once capable of explaining variations in levels of corruption across governments, their subunits, and over time.

The simple premise is that corruption nearly always creates losers who may take CA to reduce their losses. The incentives to engage in CA depend on two sets of factors, global and specific. Global factors, such as human, political and property rights, education, income levels and income distribution, have across-the-board effects on the ability to engage in CA; variations in levels of corruption across countries and over time can be explained, among other things, in terms of these factors. Specific factors, such as the type of corruption, number of losers, and the size of their losses, may vary across government agencies within the same country and, therefore, can explain different levels of corruption across these agencies.

This paper has argued that corruption is a contest between two parties: those who gain and others who lose from corruption. The outcome of this contest depends upon political, economic, legal and cultural institutions which determine the relative power of the two contestants. Since corruption is embedded in the matrix of society's institutions, any quick resolution to the problems of corruption may not be possible. The relative power of the two contestants in any country depends on the nature of its global factors— broadly, its system of rights—which are correlated to its level of economic development, but are also products of its history. Shifts in corruption generally result from shifts in the system of rights which determine the relative power of the two contestants. All this has several interesting implications.

First, corruption in any country is not likely to be altered by changes in government which do not result from changes in the relative power of the two contestants. The government is not a *deus ex machina:* it generally mirrors the relative social power of the two contestants. Frequent changes in government, which merely reflect shifting alliances amongst winners over distribution of the loot from corruption, may actually intensify corruption, as each new cohort of winners which rises to the top seeks to capture its share of the spoils.

Second, this theory suggests that a government which contains some forces that are opposed to corruption may, without directly challenging the winners, slowly be able to alter the balance of power in favor of the losers. These anti-corruption forces may be able to implement selective measures that increase the visibility of losses from corruption, lower the costs of engaging in evasive or direct CA, or reduce incentives for engaging in corruption. Where these anti-corruption forces are stronger, they may even direct their reforms to strategic nodes of law enforcement, such as the courts and police.

Third, this theory suggests that the balance of social power between winners and losers from corruption can be altered by actions taken by members of civil society. Through greater activism, greater use of existing channels of resistance and widening these channels by organizing sports clubs, libraries, local committees, charities, associations encompassing interest groups, or political parties, the balance of power can be altered, at least in some activities, in favor of the losers.

Notes

1. I am grateful to Professors John Adams, Alice Amsden, Jonathan Haughton, Mancur Olson, Salim Rashid and Paul Streeten for their comments on earlier versions of this paper.
2. This paper defines corruption to include all deviations from the rules of public office, even those that are forced upon officials by outside threats: see Schenk (1989) and Wade (1982) for discussions on coercion of public officials by private agents. This is broader than Nye's (1967) definition which only includes deviations motivated by private gain.
3. Wade (1982) and Oldenburg (1987) have examined the actions of losers in the context of two specific programs—irrigation and land consolidation—in India.
4. Theobald (1990, ch. 4), Alam (1989) and Caiden and Caiden (1977) have reviewed this literature. More recent additions to this literature include Murphy, Shleifer and Vishny (1993) and Shleifer and Vishny (1993).
5. The intensity of corruption in any government agency may be defined as the *ratio* of actual to maximum gains from corruption in any activity. Although not without problems, this definition has the advantage of being consistent with our theory of CA: the *ratio* depends on the power of losers relative to winners from corruption.

6. Since postal services are a basic amenity the authorities are under pressure to service this need by opening post offices in every locality.
7. Corruption in servicing of deposits is not unknown. During his visit to Vietnam in February 1993, my colleague, Professor Jonathan Haughton, found that depositors had to pay a bribe of 5–8% on withdrawals from banks during the Tet holiday, and 1–2% after the holiday.
8. Government with a capitalized G refers to the decision-making elites in the executive, military and legislative branches of government.
9. According to Lekha Rattanani (1993, p. 49), some staffers at Bombay University estimate that "at least 10 to 15 percent of the students who get junior college seats attached to schools and degree colleges (in Bombay) do so through money-backed backdoor admissions."
10. Oldenburg (1987, p. 519).
11. Embezzlement can take many forms: loans from state-owned banks; diversion of funds from the treasury; theft of funds intended for office supplies; maintaining ghost workers on payrolls; excess billing for development expenditures; etc.
12. Riley (1992, p. 542).
13. Some agents may feel a *moral* loss from corruption because it is a deviation *per se* from the norms of public office; all other losses from corruption are described as *material*.
14. A farmer who grows crops which depend on timely supply of water from irrigation officials and, therefore, has to submit to their corrupt demands, may respond by switching to crops whose productivity is less dependent on timely supply of water.
15. Olson (1965, pp. 9–16, 22–65).
16. Scott (1967).
17. The most comprehensive statement of this argument is found in Leff (1964).
18. Many of these points have been made in Alam (1989, 1991), Wade (1985) and Murphy, Shleifer and Vishny (1993).

References

Alam, M. S. (1989). Anatomy of Corruption: An Approach to the Political Economy of Underdevelopment, *The American Journal of Economics and Sociology.* 48: 441–456.
Alam, M. S. (1991). Some Economic Costs of Corruption in LDCs, *Journal of Development Studies.* 27: 89–97.
Caiden, Gerald E. and Naomi J. Caiden (1977). Administrative Corruption, *Public Administration Review.* 37: 301–309.
Hirschman, Albert (1970). *Exit, Voice and Loyalty: Responses to Decline in Firms, Organisations and States.* Cambridge (Mass.): Harvard University Press.
Leff, Nathaniel L. (1964). Economic Development through Bureaucratic Corruption, *American Behavioral Scientist.* 8.3 (November 1964): 8–14.
Murphy, Kevin M., Andrei Shleifer and Robert W. Vishny (1993). Why Is Rent-Seeking So Costly to Growth, *American Economic Review.* 83: 409–414.
Nye, Joseph S. (1967). Corruption and Political Development: A Cost-Benefit Analysis, *American Political Science Review.* 61: 417–427.
Oldenburg, Philip (1987). Middlemen in Third World Corruption: Implications for an Indian Case, *World Politics.* 39: 508–535.
Olson, Mancur (1965). *The Logic of Collective Action.* Cambridge *(Mass.)*: Harvard University Press.

Rattanani, Lekha (1993). Backdoor Admissions, *India Today.* September 15: 49.

Riley, Stephen P. (1992). Political Adjustment or Domestic Pressure: Democratic Politics and Political Choice in Africa, *Third World Quarterly.* 13: 539–551.

Schenk, Hans (1989). Corruption . . . What Corruption? Notes on Bribery and Urban Dependency in Urban India, in: Peter M. Ward (ed.), *Corruption, Development and Inequality.* London: Routledge.

Scott, James C. (1967). An Essay on the Political Functions of Corruption, *Asian Studies.* 5: 501–523.

Shleifer, Andrei and Robert Vishny (1993). Corruption, *Quarterly Journal of Economics.* 108: 599–617.

Theobald, Robin (1990). *Corruption, Development and Underdevelopment.* Durham (N. C.): Duke University Press.

Wade, Robert S. (1982). The System of Administrative and Political Corruption: Canal Irrigation in South India, *Journal of Development Studies.* 18: 287–328.

Wade, Robert S. (1985). The Market for Public Office: Why the Indian State Is Not Better at Development? *World Development.* 13: 467–497.

43

Public Trust and Corruption in Japan

Susan J. Pharr

Introduction

Citizen distrust of government is a troubling trend. From Washington to Milan, from Tokyo to Seoul, public disaffection is an everyday reality. Declining or low levels of confidence in government and the institutions of representative democracy is widespread among the advanced industrial countries (Pharr and Putnam 2000; Dalton 1997; Nye, Zelikow, and King 1997), and the problem of "critical citizens" extends to new democracies as well (Norris 1999).

In the litany of candidate causes, two explanations stand out. The first points to the policy performance of leaders, notably their handling of the economy, and holds that good times boost citizens' confidence in government while economic downturns erode it. The second explanation looks to society, arguing, in effect, that confidence in government springs from a vibrant civil society, and that confidence levels diminish when stores of social capital run low. Though more sophisticated formulations of this thesis posit a complex, indirect relationship between social capital and political trust (Pharr and Putnam 2000), much of the contemporary debate over social capital assumes that a direct relationship exists. This chapter tests both of these theories by examining the experience of Japan with comparisons to other East Asian countries, notably South Korea. Neither explanation, we hold, can account for trends in East Asia. Looking in depth at Japan's experience, we offer a far more compelling explanation—corruption as a source of public mistrust. For the past two decades, we show, misconduct (as reported in the press) by politicians and bureaucrats has been by far the single best predictor of citizen confidence in government. We explore the relevance of this finding for other countries, including South Korea.

Why do corruption and other forms of misconduct on the part of leaders have such dire consequences for public trust? Leadership, we hold, has two distinct dimensions: actual policy performance and "character," an amalgam of attributes that bear on conduct in office, independent of policies themselves. Both policy performance and character are obviously important, and indeed, severe misconduct by leaders can undermine policy performance, as numerous studies by the World Bank and other bodies on the effects of corruption on economic development attest. But in democracies, quite independent of their specific policy consequences, issues of character and conduct merit attention for their potential effects on the trust binding citizens to the leaders who represent them.

The "Declining Confidence" Thesis in the East Asian Context

Disaffection has distinctive features that vary by country. The United States and a number of other advanced industrial democracies have seen public trust plummet from more halcyon days in the 1950s and 1960s. In contrast, the pattern in Japan is one of persistently low levels of trust from the early postwar era to even lower confidence levels in the 1990s. The experience of losing rather than winning a war almost surely accounts for Japan's low postwar starting point. In place for more than a century, American political institutions, after all, had carried the country to victory and global preeminence; Japan's prewar political institutions, in contrast, had brought defeat and seeming economic ruin, and democratic institutions—imposed by the Allied Occupation (1945–52)—were new and untested.

Japan's situation at the outset of the postwar era, and the climate of citizen uncertainty and distrust it engendered, is obviously far closer to the postwar context elsewhere in East Asia than is American experience. Countries such as South Korea must contend with fledgling democratic institutions and the legacies of discredited regimes when attempting to build public trust (Rose, Shin, and Munro 1999,146). As John Kie Oh notes, of the major types of crisis—economic depression, rebellion, and war—that can confront a democratic nation, South Korea experienced all three after the Americans installed a democratic constitution (as in Japan). Basic guarantees were under siege from that period until the late 1980s (Oh 1999: 33). Recent research shows that confidence in governmental institutions is significantly lower in countries without well-established civil liberties (Norris 1999: 233). While systematic survey data are lacking for the initial postwar decades, these factors suggest why the enviroment in South Korea, as in Japan, posed obstacles to fostering public trust in political istitutions, and why the high confidence levels found in many Western countries in the early postwar years were lacking.

Nor did South Korea's democratic transistion after 1987 reverse an overall pattern of relatively low levels of public trust. Indeed, comparing World Value Survey results for the early 1990s with those for the early 1980s, using an "Institutional Confidence" scale that combines mean levels of confidence in parliament, the civil service, legal institutions, and the military, shows that confidence levels actually declined. Among seventeen countries, institutional confidence declined in all of them between 1980–83 and 1990–93, but while in Japan the trend was "only marginally downwards," South Korea, along with Finland and Argentina, experienced the sharpest drop of all (Norris 1999, 227–29).

For Japan, the basic pattern has been relatively low levels of confidence in government over the past forty years. According to the World Values Survey for 1990–91, Japan's level of citizen confidence in parliament (4.0) and the civil service (4.2) was well below the mean (4.5 for parliament and 4.6 for the civil service) among twenty-four countries. Indeed, when the scores for the two institutions are combined, Japan ranked in the bottom five nations, ahead of only Spain, Portugal, Italy, and Mexico. South Korea's combined score actually placed it above Japan (9.4 vs. 8.2). When it came to confidence in parliament (3.9), South Korea lagged Japan, but it led Japan (5.5) in confidence in the civil service (McAllister 1999, 192).

Low public trust levels persisted in Japan from the early postwar decades through the 1970s. Nor did the trend change appreciably in the 1980s, after the country attained the status of economic superpower. A majority of respondents reported dissatisfaction with politics in eighteen out of twenty-two Asahi Newspaper surveys conducted between 1978 and 1996; only in the mid 1980s and once again in 1991 did less than a majority report dissatisfaction. (Pharr 2000: 174-5)

Long periods of one-party rule have sometimes been associated with popular malaise, and Japan's conservative Liberal Democratic Party (LDP) was in power continuously from 1955 to 1993. Although one might thus have expected confidence in government to surge with the LDP's fall in 1993, that was not the case. Despite a major overhaul of the electoral system and other political reforms, citizen dissatisfaction with government soared to 65 percent at mid-decade.[1] Indeed, according to one survey conducted in December 1995, only 29 percent of respondents subscribed to the view that democracy was functioning well in Japan, while 61 percent disagreed (*Nihon Keizai Shimbun* 19 December, 1995, 1). Both for Japan and South Korea, then, public trust-never very high-declined in the 1990s, mirroring the broad trends discussed at the outset.

Is East Asian Democracy Different?

This pattern, of course, is subject to various interpretations. Looking at Japan, some observers might argue that disaffection is not deeply held. Thirty-eight years of one-party rule, the argument goes, established a pattern in which voters sounded off about the LDP, secure in the knowledge that it would remain in power. Voicing disapproval of the party and the political system with which it was synonymous may have been a reasonable way to check LDP excesses, but the practice makes survey evidence of distrust suspect. This logic is not compelling, however. If signals of dissatisfaction were deliberate voter strategies, then we would have expected to see satisfaction with politics rise after 1993, particularly in the wake of reforms that voters themselves had sought. But there has been no such upswing; indeed, dissatisfaction has grown.

Others might question whether expressions of disaffection in Japan, an Asian nation with a relatively short liberal democratic tradition, mean the same thing as they do in Western countries where democracy has deeper roots. A quarter of a century ago, *The Crisis of Democracy*, which focused on the United States, Western Europe, and Japan, saw Japan as something of an outlier: because Japanese citizens were somewhat less efficacious and active in their orientation toward politics than their counterparts elsewhere, its democracy was somewhat more fragile, the report implied (Crozier, Huntington, and Watanuki 1975). The so-called "revisionist" school, which first appeared in the late 1980s, also regards Japan as unique rather than Western and casts similar doubts on the state of Japanese democracy (Fallows 1994; van Wolferen 1989). Survey data fail to support this view, however, showing instead a steadily deepening acceptance of the values associated with democracy. In Japan, for example, a key index is whether people are prepared to defer to authority, as in the prewar era, or adopt a more participatory stance. Data collected over fifty years by the Clean Election League reveal that citizens have steadily moved away from a belief that leaving things to leaders is preferable; far more than in the past, they believe that they should be active—"debating among themselves" rather than passively accepting what leaders do. Similarly, following from top-down patterns of authority in prewar Japan, early postwar generations saw voting as a duty rather than a right. Younger people today, however, overwhelmingly view voting as a right: in the 25 to 29 year-old age group, for example, 57 percent of respondents in one study saw voting as a right, while only 35 percent called it a duty (Kabashima 1987). In this sense, Japanese democracy has matured, and any lag that may have existed has virtually disappeared.

Evidence from South Korea and Taiwan similarly casts doubt on the notion that East Asian democracy is somehow different. In South Korea, where free elections were introduced in 1987, there is much evidence of a deepening of democratic values. The 1997 New Korea Barometer showed that ideals of democracy now enjoy widespread support—stronger than that found in most Latin American countries (Rose, Shin, and Munro 1999, 157; Diamond 1999, 186). Among South Koreans, 81 percent said they would disapprove if parliament were suspended and political parties abolished, a figure that is somewhat higher than the average for seven countries in Central and Eastern Europe (Diamond 1999, 186). Since its democratization began in the mid-1980s, Taiwan too reveals a "generally steady increase" in the proportion of citizens "expressing prodemocratic sentiment and rejecting the paternalistic, collectivist, illiberal norms associated with the 'Asian values' perspective." For example, the proportion rejecting the idea that "elders should manage politics" almost doubled between 1985 (49 percent) and 1991 (81 percent) (Diamond 1999, 188).

Why citizen distrust persists in Japan and elsewhere in East Asia, despite major political reforms and evidence of a deepening in values associated with democracy, calls for an explanation.

Economic Policy Performance

No explanation for citizen disaffection with politics has greater currency among media pundits and political scientists alike than economic malaise. When times are good, the theory holds, citizens credit their leaders with wise economic policies. And deservedly or not, the public also holds leaders responsible for poor economic performance and registers dissatisfaction with government. Undergirding this popular interpretation is a wealth of research that establishes the existence of significant links between key economic variables and political behavior and attitudes. On the one hand are theories that link citizen opinions and behavior such as voting to "pocketbook" reasoning, that is, people's estimates of how government actions affect their personal finances; and on the other are theories that focus on "sociotropic" assessments, that is, citizen evaluations of how the economy is performing overall (Kinder 1981; Kinder and Kiewiet 1979, 1981; Meehl 1977).

On the face of it, economic explanations of citizen dissatisfaction make sense for Japan. Since 1992, the country has endured the longest recession in its postwar history, and other economic tensions date back well into the 1980s. At the level of individual lives, signs of a modest economic ratcheting-down can be detected long before the 1990s. Although more than 90 percent of Japanese have routinely classified themselves as "middle class" since 1970, according to surveys conducted by the Prime Minister's Office, the percentage of respondents who said they considered themselves "middle" as opposed to "lower" middle class began to fall during the "bubble era" of the late 1980s, as inflated values of land and stocks created a perceived gap between those who owned such assets and those who did not. Although these differences have been fairly small,[2] if people's relative sense of economic well-being affects how they judge their government and leaders, then even relatively minor shifts of this kind might matter.

Other evidence points in the opposite direction, however. Where one is coming from should affect assessments of one's current economic situation (Samuelson 1955, cited in Nye, Zelikow, and King 1997, 124). In the United States and many other democracies, for example, a golden era of past productivity casts a shadow over the present. But in Japan (as elsewhere in East Asia) real prosperity is recent, so historical comparisons look very different. Japanese respondents in a 1995 study were almost twice as likely as Americans (60 percent versus 35 percent) to compare their own situation favorably with that in which their parents grew up (International Gallup Poll, April 1995; "no opinion" responses excluded). Perhaps for similar reasons, the same survey found Japanese to be less pessimistic about the future than the people of any other advanced industrial country included in the survey except France. In Japan, any subjective sense of economic reverses might be offset by widely shared perceptions that things used to be much worse.

Against this background, we consider the fit between economic performance and citizens' satisfaction with politics and government. Most research on how economic variables affect political behavior and opinion focuses on election outcomes and the popularity of particular governments (the so-called vote-popularity, or VP, functions). According to Lewis-Beck, "all but a handful" of over one hundred studies of democracies conducted before the late 1980s found economic conditions "significantly related to electoral outcomes"; economic factors accounted for roughly one-third of the change in the vote for the government (Lewis-Beck 1988, 29; Nannestad and Paldam 1994, 237). Looking at the years 1960 to 1976, Inoguchi (1980, 147) found that economic conditions significantly affected public support for the government and the party in power in Japan. Do economic conditions matter, however, when it comes to more basic feelings about politics and the political system?

We looked at several major economic variables, unemployment, inflation, and income growth, along with several others, over the years 1978 to 1996 (see table 43.1).[3] We also included a political variable—strength of the Liberal Democratic party as measured by its number of seats in the Lower House of the Diet—to test the proposition that a strong LDP majority would be associated, whether positively or negatively, with trust. The economic variable most strongly associated with political satisfaction is per capita national income (with a correlation of .342), but the relationship is not in the expected direction: as per capita income increases, so does dissatisfaction. While the state of the economy may significantly affect electoral outcomes and the popularity of particular governments, the results suggest that it has relatively little bearing on more fundamental feelings about politics.

Recent work on Korea raises similar doubts about the power of economic explanations when it comes to more basic feelings about government and the political system. As one study showed, Koreans' judgments of economic conditions had little effect on whether they judged the current system to be democratic, or on their basic attitudes towards democracy; nor were people's

Table 43.1
LDP Strength, Economic Conditions, and Dissatisfaction with Politics in
Japan, 1978–96

	Correlationwith Dissatisfaction	Spearman's Rho	Pr > |T|
LDP strength	0.303	0.347	0.145
Income per capita	0.342	0.256	0.29
GDP	0.327	0.294	0.222
Income	0.231	0.194	0.427
Inflation	0.218	0.14	0.568
Unemployment	0.209	0.23	0.344

Notes: Political dissatisfaction: The percentage of respondents who answered "dissatisfied" in reply to the question, "In general, are you satisfied with politics today, or are you dissatisfied?" in surveys conducted by *Asahi Shimbun* at fairly regular intervals over the period in question.
LDP strength: Percentage of Lower House seats held by the Liberal Democratic Party.
Income per capita: Real national income (at factor prices) per capita; base year of 1990.
GDP: Real gross domestic product; base year of 1990. *Income*: Percent annual change in real gross domestic product; base year of 1990. *Inflation*: Percentage change in the consumer price index from the preceding year. *Unemployment*: Annual change in percentage of the workforce that was completely unemployed.
Sources:
Dissatisfaction and LDP data: *Asahi Shimbun* (morning edition), 1978–96.
National income data: Ministry of Finance, *Financial Statistics of Japan, 1997*. Data on price deflators used to calculate real national income come from the Prime Ministers' Office, *Japan Statistical Yearbook, 1998*.
Unemployment and inflation data: Bank of Japan, *Economic Statistics Annual*, selected years through 1995, and for 1996, from the Economic Planning Agency, *Pocket Statistical Indicators, 1998*.
GDP data: International Monetary Fund (IMF), *International Financial Statistics* [cd-rom], January 1998.

assessments of economic conditions significantly related in most cases to how they saw the gap between ideal and achieved democracy (Rose, Shin, and Munro 1999, 159–62).

Social Capital

Civic-ness, a wide variety of scholars, pundits, and politicians alike now say, is fundamental to social trust and attitudes of cooperation that in turn promote and sustain good government. Putnam (1995a) argues that in the United States, "social connections and civic engagement pervasively influence our public life" and that civic disengagement—a lack of social connectedness and involvement in associational life—may have dire adverse effects on society and politics. Whether social capital stores are depleting and, if so, whether this explains public distrust across the industrial democracies is a hotly contested issue (Newton 1997a; Hall 1997), and thus it is reasonable to take the inquiry to East Asia. What constitutes social capital is itself open to debate, but certainly the spectrum ranges from the quality and intensity of associational life—often, as measured by the number of interest groups—to the density of more informal social networks.

Linking "civic disengagement" in Japan to declining public trust is a relatively recent idea, but a focus on social networks and group associations there is not at all new. As it operates in the workplace and organizes leisure activities outside of it, social capital by other names has been at the heart of many analyses of the Japanese economic model. Indeed, Japan's "communitarian capitalism," the dense network of "wet" social relations within the firm that binds workers and brings them together after hours for baseball, golf, mahjong, or karaoke, has, along with other social network attributes, triggered a raft of Western management theories (Thurow 1993; Vogel 1987; Fukuyama 1995, 28). Social capital figured into many analyses of Japanese politics long before the term came into vogue. At least among conservative voters, a "social network model" best explains voting behavior in Japan, and both formal and informal groups operating around opinion leaders have been critical not only for mobilizing the vote, but also for shaping basic political attitudes (Flanagan et al. 1991, 85, 152–53; Richardson 1997; Richardson 1974). Indeed, research on Japan has tended to discount ideology and class as bases for voting behavior, instead assigning the greatest importance to the values and social networks that lie at the center of social capital research today.

The distinction often made between horizontal and vertical interest associations—the "good" and "bad cholesterol" of social capital, as it were—is also familiar in Japanese studies. Prewar Japan was rife with interest groups "organized by elites for elites" (Allinson and Sone 1993, 26), such as residential associations (*chokai,* or *chonaikai*). Tracing their origins to castle towns in the Tokugawa era, these were originally administered by landowners and house agents as omnibus religious, recreational, occupational, and residential units. In the twentieth century they became the basic unit of daily life for most people, organizing local festivals and carrying out a variety of grassroots activities; while they elected their leaders they were routinely used by the state as a means of administrative control and, later, mobilization for war (Hastings 1995, 70–79; Watanuki 1977). Such organizations are different from voluntary associations, which are modern, horizontally organized, and more participatory (McKean 1981). Even types of associations not seen as building social capital elsewhere are credited with fostering dense social networks in Japan. Political parties frequently offer a clubhouse environment, for example. Among the recreational and social activities provided to members of individual LDP politicians' support groups (*koenkai*) are "baseball games and marathon races for the youth division, chess tournaments and golf outings for the middle-aged, cooking classes for the housewives, volleyball for the women, kimono-wearing lessons, tea ceremony and flower-arranging classes, and on and on" (Abe, Shindo, and Kawato 1994, 179).

But trends in social capital have remarkably little explanatory power with regard to levels of confidence in Japan, for by almost any available measure, social capital has been on the rise. The number of interest groups in general, and of voluntary associations in particular, has soared: in 1960 there were 11.1 non-governmental, non-profit organizations per 100,000 people, a figure that rose to 18.4 in 1975, 27.7 in 1986, 29.2 in 1991, and 30.3 in 1996 (Tsujinaka, 1996, 1999). Interest groups proliferated in Japan over the first two decades of the postwar period (Muramatsu, Ito, and Tsujinaka 1986, 72–76). Since then, the most ambitious study to date concludes, Japan's interest groups have moved toward "greater participation and pluralization" (Tsujinaka 1999, table1; see also Tsujinaka 1996 and 1986).

In tracking factors eroding social capital in the United States, television viewing habits have been subject to scrutiny (Putnam 1996), and on the face of it, this explanation invites investigation for Japan. The average number of hours Japanese spend watching television easily surpasses even the U.S. level. While 53 percent of Americans watched two or more hours of television per day in 1995, the figure was 59 percent in Japan (Inglehart 1996). Nevertheless, such an explanation can hardly account for trends in satisfaction with government and politics in Japan: low levels of political trust *precede* the television era, and heavy television viewing has actually *declined*: whereas 34 percent of respondents watched more than three hours a day in 1976, that figure had dropped to 24 percent by 1996 (Inglehart 1996; Flanagan 1996, 281).

To give the social capital explanation its due, we examined cross-sectional data from the 1996 Japan Election and Democracy Study (JEDS). If associational life is related to confidence in politics and government, people embedded in dense social networks by means of multiple group memberships should have higher levels of political trust. But this is not the case: belonging to three or more groups of any kind or to several voluntary groups had no significant effect on one's level of political trust (Pharr 2000). Belonging to sports or hobby groups also made no significant difference. The only type of membership that was positively associated with satisfaction with politics was belonging to farmers' cooperatives, a type of "non-voluntary" association found in the rural stamping ground of Japan's conservative ruling Liberal Democratic Party. Perhaps it is no surprise that farmers, who constitute the core of the party's support, would be more satisfied than most with a political system dominated by that party. Indeed, the relationship between membership in farmers' groups and satisfaction with politics became statistically insignificant once we controlled for political ideology.

At the other end of the continuum, membership in a residential, consumer, citizens', or women's movement was inversely related to satisfaction levels. This, too, is not surprising: citizens who join social movements are likely less trusting of government and politics than are people with more conventional affiliations (Tarrow 2000; Hall 1997). It is nevertheless troubling that members of citizens' movements, which are widely interpreted as a bellwether of grassroots civic-ness in Japan, should be less satisfied with politics than members of other groups. Indeed, when we combine this finding with the fact that voluntary group membership was a better predictor of *dissatisfaction* than satisfaction with politics (even though it did not approach levels of statistical significance), then claims of a direct link between an individual's social capital and civic engagement on the one hand, and political confidence on the other, seem suspect.

Civic-ness, then, appears to have almost nothing to do with satisfaction with politics, at least in Japan. Furthermore, the data challenge even the "rainmaker" hypothesis which posits that the relationship between social capital and public trust is indirect, not direct. According to this thesis, like rain, the bad government produced by low social capital descends on all citizens—the social-capital-rich and social-capital-poor—alike (Putnam, Pharr, and Dalton, 2000). The logic of the "rainmaker" hypothesis would lead us to predict better government in Japan as a consequence of the rise of associational life and increasing social trust, which in turn should translate into higher levels of satisfaction with the quality of political life. But this has not occurred.

South Korea

How does Japan compare to other places in East Asia, notably South Korea? For the period before 1981, data are lacking, but since then patterns of interest group formation have varied widely (Tsujinaka, 1996, 1999). Business groups—in 1981 the most prominent type of association—have dropped dramatically in number, while citizens' and labor groups have multiplied, to the point that by 1996 they predominated in South Korea's associational life. If we are to believe the evidence presented by Tsujinaka, between 1981 and 1986, social capital, to the extent that it is measured by the number of interest associations, actually declined. However, if we focus on the overall period between 1981 and 1996, the pattern strikingly parallels that of Japan: a major percent increase in South Korean interest associations. In 1981 there were 4,962 such groups in South Korea, of which 3,576 were business groups; by 1996 the total had mounted to 13,078, of which only 1,230 were business organizations (Tsujinaka, 1996, 1999). Indeed, a 1987 upsurge in civil society—in a coalition including student and labor groups, writers, academics, professional association members, and members of religious groups of all persuasions, Buddhist, Protestant, and Catholic—is credited (as in the Philippines the previous year) with triggering the transition to democracy (Diamond 1999: 235–6). Furthermore, the dramatic increase occurred precisely when confidence in government and institutions suffered a downturn. For these reasons, then, the notion that social capital declines explain a downturn in citizen confidence in government is no more plausible in South Korea than in Japan.

The Problem is Political

Low levels of satisfaction with politics in Japan and South Korea reflect neither depleted social capital nor the government's recent or past misman-agement of the economy. A more compelling explanation targets politics.

In Japan, the first and most obvious possibility is that political satisfaction varies with the strength of the ruling party. Voters consistently returned the Liberal Democratic Party to power between 1955 and 1993, and once again after 1995. If party politicians are agents of voters, then it should follow that when an election results in a strong majority for the ruling party, a corre-spondingly large portion of voters should be satisfied with this outcome, and this in turn should translate into higher overall levels of political satisfaction. But the evidence provide little support for this hypothesis (see table 43.1). While LDP strength was in fact positively correlated with political satisfac-tion (or, as stated in table 43.1, it was inversely related to political dissatisfac-tion), the relationship was not strong enough to be statistically significant. We therefore turn to other political explanations.

Misconduct and Public Distrust

Although performance in managing the economy is a surprisingly poor predictor of satisfaction with leaders, leaders' performance still remains a logical place to look. As Inglehart (1997, 294–95) notes, it "seems inconceiv-able that governmental performance *would not* influence public evaluations" of the political system and government (italics in the original). Thus we step back to consider leaders' performance more broadly.

This approach is all the more compelling because of the close correlation in so many countries between low satisfaction with government and politics and negative evaluations of specific institutions of government, including the prime ministership, legislature, and bureaucracy (Putnam, Pharr, and Dalton 2000; Newton and Norris 2000). Over postwar decades marked by low levels of satisfaction with politics, distrust of politicians has been a regular feature of Japanese survey results. Although bureaucrats previously fared better, as overall levels of public distrust reached near-highs in the 1990s citizens re-ported little trust in them too. In a December 1995 survey, for example, 70 percent answered "no" when asked if they had confidence in legislators, and 65 percent distrusted central government bureaucrats (*Nihon Keizai Shimbun*

19 December, 1995, 1). In contrast to leaders at the national level, prefectural and local officials have enjoyed more trust, and this overall trend continues: the closer to the voter, the greater the trust (Clean Election League surveys). Trust in local leaders dropped precipitously in the 1990s, however. Only 12 percent of respondents in one survey judged local government to be "quite responsive" or "somewhat responsive" to people's opinions and wishes (*Nihon Keizai Shimbun* 19 December, 1995, 1).

Some would argue that negative evaluations of public officials reflect a more general increase in anti-authority attitudes resulting from broad socio-economic transformations (such as rising educational levels) in the advanced industrial democracies (Dalton 2000; Inglehart 1997). Such an explanation is not very applicable to Japan, however. Asked to rate the trustworthiness of various domestic institutions in 1995, Japanese reported far more favorable impressions of the courts (29 percent), police and prosecutors (42 percent), hospitals (35 percent), and newspapers (34 percent) than of the prime minister (3 percent), the legislature (6 percent), central government offices (4 percent), and local government offices (9 percent). The Japanese public, in other words, makes distinctions when awarding trust, as did citizens in the United States, England, Germany, and France responding to the same survey (Gallup-Yomiuri Poll, May 1995, reported in *Yomiuri Shimbun* 22 June, 1995), making it doubtful that generalized citizen cynicism accounts for persistently low or declining political trust.

Performance of public officials involves two dimensions: policy performance and "character." By the latter term we mean conduct, or deportment, with respect to handling the duties and privileges of public office. A great deal of research has focused on how leaders perform in policy roles and how this affects a whole range of public responses, from voting to issue support. But as we showed, policy performance even in the crucial economic area appears to explain little about basic levels of public confidence or satisfaction with politics in Japan or elsewhere. We argue that a perceived leadership deficit in the second performance dimension—character—is a far better predictor of citizens' level of satisfaction with government and politics, at least in Japan.

This thesis flies in the face of much political science literature, in which citizens' judgments of character and of misconduct cases have been regarded as less stable than their issue preferences (Page and Shapiro 1992). Despite the maelstrom of media furor and public debate that frequently greets corruption, the public reaction is thought to be epiphenomenal, in contrast to its views on policy issues. Some scholars treat corruption and other ethics scandals as socially constructed, implying that they have no real or lasting weight (Giglioli 1996, 381–93). Others claim, in the absence of any particular evidence, that low evaluations of politicians are a cause rather than an effect of official misconduct: negative judgments supposedly give license to officials' wrongdoing or, alternately and more cynically still, such wrongdoing should be taken as a given and comes to light only when citizens register low evaluations of leaders in general (Mortimore 1995, 579). Anthony King's call (1986, 173–222) for research that would link issues of official misconduct with larger characteristics of political systems was met with a deafening silence punctuated only rarely by serious investigations (Markovits and Silverstein 1988). And indeed, political science research grounded in economic theory, with its assumptions about self-interested, rent-seeking utility maximization, in effect treats corrupt government as normal and makes it hard to explain how the impulse to constrain corruption could arise (Miller 1992; Miller forthcoming; Bicchieri 1999). Although studies of individual cases go forward, and corruption itself, its causes and cures, attracts research, the deeper significance of character and misconduct issues in democracies goes largely unexplored.

The frequency with which politicians charged with major ethics violations are returned to office reinforces the assumption that character and ethical conduct are secondary to other dimensions of job performance (Peters and Welch 1980; Dolan, McKeown, and Carlson 1988). The view that leaders' misconduct is of little importance to the Japanese (and also Korea) public has been a persistent feature of research. Periodic corruption scandals have so flooded the political landscape that elections have even been named for them (e.g., the Lockheed Election of 1976, the 1983 Tanaka Verdict Election, the 1989 Recruit Election), leading to the conclusion that "structural corruption" prevails and is widely tolerated (Johnson 1986; MacDougall 1988; Reed 1994). Throughout the postwar era, the argument runs, citizens readily accepted corruption in exchange for pork barrel benefits and high growth (Ramseyer and Rosenbluth 1993). The high reelection rates of Diet members implicated in corruption scandals seemed to support such claims. Although Reed (1996, 5) shows that scandal-tainted Diet members routinely have incurred a significant vote penalty (an average of 15,000 votes in 1976, for example), the simple fact that they were frequently reelected was taken as sufficient evidence that citizens accepted a Faustian bargain with the LDP: high growth in exchange for tolerance of corruption. Indeed, thirty-eight years of uninterrupted rule by the LDP was taken as proof positive of citizen acceptance of character lapses.

But this perspective overlooks the many reasons why corruption and ethics scandals—whether socially constructed or not, and regardless of the forces that bring them to light—have to make a difference in the bond between the governed and those who govern them in the moral universe of democracies. After all, the basis for that bond involves a covenant between leaders and followers based on trust. Indeed, it is mainly in democracies that scandals over political ethics arise in the first place; elsewhere, they are generally suppressed. It is basic to democracy that there is continuing tension over the uses of political power, which is addressed—but never fully resolved—by sharply differentiating the public and private realms and relying on due process and public scrutiny to contain the secrecy and arbitrariness inevitably involved in the exercise of power (Markovits and Silverstein 1988, 5–6; Huntington 1981; Sandel 1996). Given this tension, the exercise of power is inherently suspect, and legitimate only when it occurs in public (Markovits and Silverstein 1988, 6). In countries with recent histories of massive abuses of authority, like Japan, Germany, and Italy with their legacies of fascism, and in South Korea, with its recent history of authoritarianism and repression, it is reasonable to believe that such suspicion is greater still.

Despite the suppositions of many political scientists, there is abundant evidence to support the claim that mass publics take misconduct charges seriously. Studying trends in American public opinion and policy preferences over a fifty-year period, Page and Shapiro found that official misconduct and corruption were among the very small number of triggering events for abrupt but enduring shifts in public opinion. Among other things, the Watergate revelations "led many people to conclude that campaign finances needed closer regulation . . . and that the presidency itself should be restrained"; similarly, corruption in labor unions "contributed to increased support for strict regulation of labor" (Page and Shapiro 1992, 337–38). Even in Japan public opinion surveys routinely show that citizens rate political ethics violations among the most important issues. In one national study, 20 percent ranked political ethics among the top problems facing Japan, and an additional 40 percent listed administrative reform, which to many people means downsizing bureaucracy and reducing its discretion as a response to recent cases of wrongdoing (Pharr 1998). Furthermore, there is substantial evidence that the quality of politics is of considerable importance to citizens: in a 1987 survey, when asked whether improving politics had any relation to their lives, 65 percent said that it did; only 15 percent saw no meaningful connection between the two (Yamamoto 1995, 93).

There is ample evidence that what people do, as well as what they say, is affected by their perceptions of how their leaders are behaving in office. The thesis that voter disapproval of scandal-tainted candidates can be measured only by whether they lose, or win by reduced margins, has been strongly challenged; the total movement of votes may be a far more accurate measure (Lodge, Steenburgen, and Blau 1995). By analyzing the results of three major Lower House elections in Japan in which corruption figured prominently, Reed calculated both the "scandal penalty" to incumbents and the vote gain to alternative new party candidates as a result of vote-switching, and he concluded that the 1993 defeat of the ruling LDP is best interpreted as a delayed response to corruption and the lack of significant political reform. Japanese voters routinely penalize incumbents implicated in ethical lapses by switching votes away from them when a new alternative candidate appears

(Reed 1996, 8–9). If misconduct can have these kinds of effects on citizen behavior, then it is reasonable to explore its effects on more basic orientations.

Corruption Reports

There are formidable obstacles to testing these hypotheses. Because the absolute amount of wrongdoing by public officials is unknowable, our assessments must be based on reported corruption. But reports of misconduct can increase for two alternative reasons. First, the actual amount of wrongdoing may have actually increased. Second, it is possible that more cases are simply being reported than in the past, either because the legal environment became more restrictive or because of increased media attention to misconduct cases.

For the purpose of investigating the relation between reported misconduct and citizen confidence, we take the position that which of these reasons applies is not really relevant. A given report of misconduct is a fact, a data point, in that it records a specific occurrence in which a public official is accused of wrongdoing. Obviously, it matters a great deal to democracy and the quality of political life whether misconduct is actually growing, or whether reports are increasing. The remedies for the former (e.g., increasing the penalties for wrongdoing, raising the salaries of public officials to reduce incentives to misbehave) are not the same as those for the latter (e.g., changing the nature and amount of media coverage). The issue here, however, is not what remedies are in order, but simply whether reports of misconduct have increased, and if so, whether this change affects citizens' satisfaction with politics.

To test for this relationship over recent decades in Japan, we first compiled an *Asahi* Corruption Report Database for the years 1948 through 1996. The database consists of all stories that appeared in *Asahi* Newspaper, one of Japan's four leading mass circulation dailies, on the subject of corruption, categorized as political, bureaucratic, subnational, and other. Selecting one newspaper might be a problem in some countries such as the United States, where almost all newspapers are local. In Japan, however, the major newspapers are national, and while there are modest ideological differences among them, a number of characteristics of the Japanese news media assure relative uniformity of coverage (Pharr and Krauss 1996). Stories that dealt with corruption occurring in other countries were excluded unless they involved Japanese nationals, in which case they were classified as "other." The resulting database consisted of over 15,000 corruption reports.

A number of features stand out. An obvious one is the importance of a single watershed case, the Lockheed scandal of 1976. Like Watergate in the United States, no scandal since has attracted comparable coverage.[4] But if the Lockheed case is in a league of its own in the number of corruption reports it generated, there has been a dramatic ratcheting-up since then in the average number of corruption reports per year. Thus, between 1948 and 1975, the annual number of misconduct reports exceeded 200 in only five years; following 1976, with over 1200 reports, for the years through 1996 the number of such reports exceeded 200 on *all but* five occasions. Furthermore, in the first half of the 1990s the average annual number of misconduct reports implicating bureaucrats increased by 27 percent over the annual average in the 1980s.

To determine whether misconduct reports influence satisfaction with politics and government in Japan, we conducted a time-series analysis for the years 1978 through 1996 and plotted the result (see figure 43.1). The result is quite striking. Not only do confidence levels closely track swings in the number of misconduct reports, causation is strongly implied by the fact that a spike in dissatisfaction follows closely on the heels of a spike in misconduct reports. The pattern is especially dramatic over the years 1988 and 1989. The Recruit scandal broke in 1988, sending the number of corruption stories soaring, and soon after, citizen dissatisfaction reached a record high.

Figure 43.1

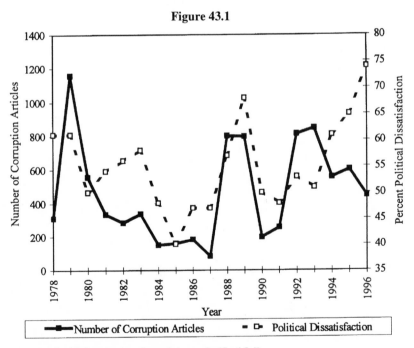

Notes: Political dissatisfaction: percentage of respondents answering "dissatisfied" when asked, "In general, are you satisfied with politics today, or are you dissatisfied?" See Table 1 for details.
Sources: Political dissatisfaction data: *Asahi Shimbun*, Tokyo Morning Edition, selected years.
Corruption reports: the annual number of stories on corruption in Japan reported in *Asahi Shimbun*. See Figure 1 for details.

Table 43.2
The Effect of Corruption Reports, LDP Strength, and Changes in Economic
Conditions on Political Dissatisfaction in Japan, 1978–96

	Coeffi-cient	Std. Error	T-Statistic	P>T
Number of corruption articles				
in *Asahi Shimbun*	0.017	0.007	2.23	0.050
Dissatisfaction, preceding year	0.524	0.336	1.56	0.149
GDP, annual change	-1.45	1.48	-0.986	0.369
Inflation	0.073	1.35	0.054	0.958
Unemployment	11.6	7.47	1.55	0.153
LDP Strength	0.767	0.581	1.32	0.216
Constant	-45.7	50.5	-0.905	0.387
Adjusted R-squared	0.46			
Number of observations	17			

Notes: **Cochrane-Orcutt regression correcting for serial auto-correlation.** *Political dissatisfaction*: **The percentage of respondents who answered "dissatisfied" to the question, "In general, are you satisfied with politics today, or are you dissatisfied?"** *GDP, annual change*: **annual percent change in real gross domestic product; base year of 1990.** *Unemployment*: **percentage of the workforce that was completely unemployed.** *Inflation*: **annual percentage change in the consumer price index; base year of 1995.** *LDP strength*: **percent of total seats in the Lower House held by the Liberal Democratic Party. Sources:** *Dissatisfaction data*: *Asahi Shimbun*, **Tokyo Morning Edition, selected years.** *Corruption reports*: *Asahi Shimbun.* *Unemployment and inflation data*: **Japan Management and Coordination Agency.** *GDP data*: **International Monetary Fund (IMF).**

To take into account other explanations for changes in levels of citizen confidence, we ran a Cochrane-Orcutt regression that included LDP strength and the most promising of the many economic variables we had tested earlier. The result offers exceedingly strong evidence of a positive relationship between reports of officials' misconduct and citizen dissatisfaction (see table 43.2). The tepid correlations for the "Big Three" economic variables of unemployment, inflation, and income growth (see table 43.1) pale beside the robust correlation (.58) between misconduct reports and citizens' dissatisfaction with politics. Misconduct reports are the only variable that rises to the level of statistical significance (p<.050).

Conclusion: Perspectives on East Asia

In explaining satisfaction or dissatisfaction with leaders and government, many observers claim that the state of the economy, above all else, shapes how citizens feel about their government and leaders. Meanwhile, an outpouring of scholarship in recent years posits that social capital holds the key for taking the measure of democracy and, by extension, for shaping public orientations toward political life. This chapter has demonstrated that at least for Japan, neither explanation has much relevance for understanding and interpreting changes in citizens' basic level of satisfaction with government and politics over the past two decades.

That economic conditions have limited explanatory power is supported not only by the results in this chapter, but by studies elsewhere. McAllister, for example, argues that "the political economy of confidence in democratic institutions is . . . strictly limited." The finding, he concludes, holds especially well for the established democracies, but less well in newer democracies where economic volatility is far greater, and where democratic institutions have less legitimacy and are more likely to be blamed in a downturn (McAllister 1999: 203). For South Korea and Taiwan, however, the case can be made that these potential effects have been offset by the broad consensus on economic growth across the political spectrum. Thus South Korea and Taiwan, Diamond argues, are more like the advanced industrial countries in that the "band of variation" in debate over macroeconomic policy, tax policy, wage increases, and the like is much narrower than in many new democracies in other regions, including Latin America and Central and Eastern Europe (Diamond 1999, 86). While there is evidence that the Asian financial crisis of 1997 may have had some adverse effects on citizen evaluations of South Korea's democratic institutions (Rose, Shin, and Munro 1999, 164), there is little to suggest that absent a crisis, leaders' economic performance is the best guide to public trust levels.

The finding that stores of social capital have little bearing on citizen satisfaction echoes conclusions reached in a variety of advanced industrial countries (Hall 1997; Newton 1997a). Low satisfaction with government—which fell lower still in the 1990s—has characterized decades over which Japan's stores of social capital have increased steadily by a wide variety of measures, and in South Korea, the downturn in institutional confidence at the start of an era when voluntary associations, including civil society groups, were soaring in number further challenges the claims for such a relationship.

Governmental performance, then, is the key to citizen confidence. But policy performance—at least in the all-important economic domain—explains little when it comes to public trust. We therefore shifted our focus to a second dimension of leaders' performance, which we call "character," their deportment in carrying out their duties on behalf of the citizens they serve. This chapter has provided a strong basis for the claim that reported corruption is a far more important cause of citizen distrust in leaders and political institutions than either economic or social capital deficits. Indeed, the chapter showed that at least for Japan, leaders' reported corruption was by far the single best predictor at any given point in time of confidence in government over two decades.

Is this result surprising? As noted earlier, previous research often has been dismissive of corruption as a major factor in dramatically. Alternately, research has seen the public as critical of corruption, but only cyclically: that is, it is claimed that the public normally tolerates it, but in the face of a major scandal rises up against it only to return to passive acceptance once the case disappears from the headlines. But for Japan, through both good economic times and downturns, the level of reported corruption consistently predicted public trust levels, and there was little evidence of a cyclical trend. It is true that the pronounced downturn in public satisfaction in government in Japan dates from 1988 and the Recruit scandal, which involved gifts of stock by an upstart service sector firm to a wide circle of Japan's leadership in exchange for mostly unspecified favors, but there is little evidence of a cyclical effect since then. Public concern over corruption, far from fading, appears to have been sustained over the past decade, creating an environment of greater public scrutiny of the conduct of leaders to which the Japanese media have been highly responsive, and leading to pressure for reform. Indeed, so great have been the public's demands for reform that the Liberal Democratic party, in power virtually continuously for 38 years, fell in 1993 when internal division over how to respond to reform pressures caused fractures within it. In South Korea, there is considerable evidence that a climate of fairly sustained public scrutiny of leaders prevailed there as well in the 1990s, also set in motion by major corruption cases.

A major issue, of course, is why corruption reports apparently matter so much to citizens. After all, leaders' policy performance has a far more direct effect on their lives than do many types of misconduct. Even in Japan, which has experienced a series of major corruption scandals implicating a significant number of politicians (if far fewer than in Italy's *Tangentopoli* scandal of 1992), most incidents have involved illegal campaign contributions; in other words, citizens experienced no direct harm. In order to explain why misconduct matters, four factors stand out. First, since democracy depends on the accountability of public officials to citizens, misconduct reports represent information that is relevant to everyone, not just a select few (unlike many public policies). Second, official misconduct violates the rules and procedures that are supposed to govern political life, giving rise to perceptions that the political system is basically unfair. Lind and Tyler found that procedural fairness generally mattered more to people than actual outcomes, suggesting why policy performance may trail officials' misconduct in shaping basic orientations toward the political system (Lind and Tyler 1988; Tyler 1990). Third, compared to many other kinds of information about what the government does, newspaper accounts of official misconduct are generally easy to understand, in part because they closely parallel ethical and moral dilemmas in everyday life or can easily be related to citizens' lives through media priming (Iyengar and Kinder 1987, 114–16). Fourth, because of the presumption of accountability in democracies and also because of the often-strong moral content of the charges themselves, misconduct reports are likely to trigger what cognitive psychologists call "hot cognitions," judgments that carry powerful emotions, facilitating the retention of such reports (Zajonc 1980). Across class, educational, and age lines, people tend to be remarkably aware of major corruption cases, often far more than about other domains of government or policy. For all these reasons, leaders' misconduct offers an important key for understanding declining citizen confidence in government.

Finally, there is the issue of how widely our findings hold. Though systematic comparative data are lacking, preliminary evidence for Italy, France, and Germany, and indeed for a wide range of industrial nations, reveals a striking (albeit rough) correlation between citizen confidence in government and perceived level of corruption (della Porta 2000). Apart from Japan, for much of Asia there is a strong basis for believing that corruption could spark distrust. After all, by the standards of many Asia nations, corruption in Japan has been on a modest scale. Even the Lockheed scandal of 1976, which generated more media coverage than any other postwar scandal, involved a bribe to Japan's prime minister of under $3 million. In a substantial number of Asian countries, the sheer scale and frequency of corruption, before and after the era of democratization, is vast in comparison. By the time of his death in 1963, for example, the Thai military dictator Sarit Thanarat had amassed a fortune that corrected for inflation equaled 26 percent of Thai government spending in 1990, and according to *Time* Magazine, the wealth of Indonesia's President Suharto came to $15 billion during an era when his salary was $36,000 per annum (*International Herald Tribune*, July 21, 1999). Major scandals over corruption on a massive scale have rocked governments and leaders in South Korea, Cambodia, and the Philippines as well. Furthermore, for many of these countries there is hard evidence of the seriousness citizens assign to corruption. Among South Koreans surveyed in 1990, for example, when asked about obstacles to democratization, "politicians' corruption" outranked all other replies (Cotton 1995).

Much attention has focused on the harmful social and economic effects of corruption, and major international institutions, from the World Bank to OECD, have taken steps in the 1990s designed to curb it. This study suggests yet another adverse and until recently, little-studied effect—its corrosive effects on the bonds that link citizens in democracies to their leaders and political institutions. In a post cold war world, democracy has emerged as the leading political system with no real rivals, but sustaining democracy requires, above all else, public trust. Taking steps to foster and maintain responsible leadership, political and bureaucratic, is thus a critical issue for the millennium.

Acknowledgments

The research upon which this chapter is based was funded by grants from the Social Science Research Council's Abe Fellowship Program, the National Science Foundation, and the POSCO Fellowship Program, East West Center. A somewhat different version of this chapter focusing on Japan in comparison with the United States and Western European nations (the Trilateral countries) appears in Susan J. Pharr and Robert D. Putnam, eds., *Disaffected Democracies: What's Troubling the Trilateral Countries?* Princeton: Princeton University Press, 2000. I would like to express warm appreciation to Robert Putnam, Russell Dalton, Bradley Richardson, Paul Beck, Ellis Krauss, Steve Reed, Anthony King, Samuel P. Huntington, Donatella della Porta, Yasunori Sone, Choong Nam Kim, Larry Diamond, and Doh C. Shin for their comments on earlier drafts, and to Emily Morris, Paul Talcott, Christian Brunelli, Christina Davis, Shigeo Hirano, and Emer O'Dwyer for their able research assistance.

Notes

1. The two-decade trend revealed in the Asahi Newspaper data is mirrored in NHK data as well as other data sources (Pharr 1997). Unfortunately, most surveys relevant to this inquiry have asked about "satisfaction" (*manzoku*) with politics rather than about "confidence" or "trust."
2. The percentage of people considering themselves middle-middle class fell from 60.6 percent in 1979 to 53.6 percent in 1992, while the percentage who considered themselves lower-middle class correspondingly rose from 22.2 percent to 26.2 percent (NHK 1995, 229–33).
3. The "Big Three" economic variables in VP work are widely agreed to be inflation, unemployment, and income growth (Fair 1978, 164; Lewis-Beck 1988, 29; Nannestad and Paldam 1994; Schneider and Frey 1988, 243). In many industrial countries unemployment typically trumps inflation or income growth in importance for electoral outcomes; in Japan, however, inflation and income growth have been found to matter more (Schneider and Frey 1988, 247).
4. According to preliminary work on a similar database for the United States that uses a Lexus-Nexus search of the *New York Times* for the years 1969–96, the nearest rival to Watergate (which resulted in 6,874 reports in 1973) was Whitewater (with 727 reports in 1994). The other leading conduct-in-office cases in the United States for this period (and the number of reports for each) were: Ellsberg Break-In/Pentagon Papers, 1971 (661); Abscam, 1980 (555); Wedtech, 1987 (409); Tongsun Park, 1977 (266); Vesco, 1973 (215); Keating, 1990 (117); House banking scandal, 1993 (113); FBI files ("Filegate"), 1996 (43); and the White House Travel Office, 1993 (42).

References

Abe, Hitoshi, Muneyuki Shindo, and Sadafumi Kawato. 1994. *The Government and Politics of Japan.* Trans. James W. White. Tokyo: University of Tokyo Press.

856 Political Corruption

Allinson, Gary D., and Yasunori Sone, (eds.). 1993. *Political Dynamics in Contemporary Japan.* Ithaca, NY: Cornell University Press.

Bicchieri, Cristina and Y. Fukui. 1999. "The Great Illusion: Ignorance, Informational Cascades and the Persistence of Unpopular Norms," *Business Ethics Quarterly,* 1, 1.

Cotton, James (ed.). 1995. *Politics and Policy in the New Korean State: From Roh Tae-woo to Kim Young-sam.* New York: St. Martin's Press.

Crozier, Michel, Samuel P. Huntington, and Joji Watanuki. 1975. *The Crisis of Democracy: Report on the Governability of Democracies to the Trilateral Commission.* New York: New York University Press.

Dalton, Russell J. 1997. "Citizens and Democracy: Political Support in Advanced Industrial Democracies." Presented at the John F. Kennedy School of Government Workshop on Confidence in Democratic Institutions: America in Comparative Perspective, Washington, DC.

Dalton, Russell J. 2000. "Value Change and Democracy." In *Disaffected Democracies: What's Troubling the Trilateral Countries?* ed. Susan J. Pharr and Robert D. Putnam. Princeton: Princeton University Press.

della Porta, Donatella. 2000. "Social Capital, Beliefs in Government, and Political Corruption." In *Disaffected Democracies: What's Troubling the Trilateral Countries?* ed. Susan J. Pharr and Robert D. Putnam. Princeton: Princeton University Press.

Diamond, Larry. 1999. *Developing Democracy towards Consolidation.* Baltimore: Johns Hopkins University Press.

Dolan, Kathleen, Bruce McKeown, and James M. Carlson. 1988. "Popular Conceptions of Political Corruption: Implications for the Empirical Study of Political Ethics." *Corruption and Reform* 3:3–24.

Fair, Ray C. 1978. "The Effect of Economic Events on Votes for President." *The Review of Economics and Statistics* 6(2):159–73.

Fallows, James. 1994. *Looking at the Sun: The Rise of the New East Asian Economic and Political System.* New York: Pantheon Books.

Flanagan, Scott C. 1991. "Media Influences and Voting Behavior." In *The Japanese Voter,* ed. Scott C. Flanagan, Shinsaku Kohei, Ichiro Miyake, Bradley M. Richardson, and Joji Watanuki. New Haven: Yale University Press.

Flanagan, Scott C. 1996. "Media Exposure and the Quality of Political Participation in Japan." In *Media and Politics in Japan,* ed. Susan J. Pharr and Ellis S. Krauss. Honolulu: University Press of Hawaii.

Flanagan, Scott C., Shinsaku Kohei, Ichiro Miyake, Bradley M. Richardson, and Joji Watanuki. 1991. *The Japanese Voter.* New Haven: Yale University Press.

Fukuyama, Francis. 1995. *Trust: The Social Virtues and the Creation of Prosperity.* New York: The Free Press.

Giglioli, P. P. 1996. "Degrading in Public: Some Aspects of the Italian Political Corruption Trials." In *The Art of Persuasion,* ed. L. Cheles and L. Sponza. Manchester: Manchester University Press.

Hall, Peter A. 1997. "Social Capital in Britain." Presented at the Bertelsmann Stiftung Workshop on Social Capital, Berlin.

Hastings, Sally Ann. 1995. *Neighborhood and Nation in Tokyo, 1905–1937.* Pittsburgh: University of Pittsburgh Press.

Huntington, Samuel P. 1981. *American Politics: The Promise of Disharmony.* Cambridge, MA: Belknap Press.

Inglehart, Ronald. 1996. "Changing Values in Japan and the United States, 1981–1995." Presentation for Dentsu Institute for Human Studies, Tokyo.

Inglehart, Ronald. 1997. *Modernization and Postmodernization: Cultural, Economic, and Poltical Change in 43 Societies.* Princeton: Princeton University Press.

Inoguchi, Takashi. 1980. "Economic Conditions and Mass Support in Japan, 1960–1976." In *Models of Political Economy,* ed. Paul Whiteley. London: Sage Publications.
Iyengar, Shanto, and Donald Kinder. 1987. *News That Matters.* Chicago: University of Chicago Press.
Johnson, Chalmers. 1986. "Structural Corruption and the Advent of Machine Politics in Japan." *Journal of Japanese Studies* 12(1):1–28.
Kabashima, Ikuo. 1987. *"Kiken no kenkyū* [Research on rights]." Zasshi Senkyo.
Kinder, Donald R. 1981. "Presidents, Prosperity, and Public Opinion." *Public Opinion Quarterly* 45:1–21.
Kinder, Donald R., and D.R. Kiewiet. 1979. "Economic Discontent and Political Behavior." *American Journal of Political Science* 23:495–527.
Kinder, Donald R., and D. R. Kiewiet. 1981. "Sociotropic Politics." *British Journal of Political Science* 11:129–61.
King, Anthony. 1986. "Sex, Money and Power." In *Politics in Britain and the United States: Comparative Perspectives,* ed. Richard Hodder-Williams and James Ceaser. Durham, NC: Duke University Press.
Lewis-Beck, Michael. 1988. *Economics and Elections: The Major Western Democracies.* Ann Arbor: The University of Michigan Press.
Lind, E. Allan and Tom R. Tyler. 1988. *The Social Psychology of Procedural Justice.* New York: Plenum.
Lodge, Milton, Marco Steenburgen, and Shawn Blau. 1995. "The Responsive Voter: Campaign Information and the Dynamics of Candidate Evaluation." *American Political Science Review* 89:309–26.
MacDougall, Terry. 1988. "The Lockheed Scandal and the High Costs of Politics in Japan." In *The Politics of Scandal: Power and Process in Liberal Democracies,* ed. Andrei S. Markovits and Mark Silverstein. London: Holmes and Meier Publishers.
Markovits, Andrei S. and Mark Silverstein, eds. 1988. *The Politics of Scandal: Power and Process in Liberal Democracies.* London: Holmes and Meier Publishers.
McAllister, Ian. 1999. "The Economic Performance of Governments." In *Critical Citizens: Global Support for Democratic Government,* ed. Pippa Norris. Oxford: Oxford University.
McKean, Margaret A. 1981. *Environmental Protest and Citizen Politics in Japan.* Berkeley: University of California Press.
Meehl, P.E. 1977. "The Selfish Voter Paradox and the Thrown-Away Vote Argument." *American Political Science Review* 71:11–30.
Miller, Gary. 1992. *Managerial Dilemmas: The Political Economy of Hierarchy.* Cambridge, UK: Cambridge University.
Miller Gary. N.d. "Why is Trust Necessary in Organizations? The Moral Hazard of Profit-Maximization." Forthcoming.
Mortimore, Roger. 1995. "Public Perceptions of Sleaze in Britain." Special Issue on "Sleaze: Politics, Private Interests and Public Reaction," ed. Alan Doig. *Parliamentary Affairs* 48(4):579–90.
Muramatsu, Michio, Mitsutoshi Ito, and Yutaka Tsujinaka. 1986. *Sengo Nihon no atsuryoku dantai* [Pressure groups in postwar Japan]. Tokyo: Tōyō (Keizai Shinposha.
Nannestad, Peter, and Martin Paldam. 1994. "The VP-function: A Survey of the Literature on Vote and Popularity Functions After 25 Years." *Public Choice* 79:213–45.
Newton, Kenneth. 1997. "Social and Political Trust." Presented at the John F. Kennedy

School of Government Workshop on Confidence in Democratic Institutions: America in Comparative Perspective, Washington, D.C.

Newton, Kenneth, and Pippa Norris. 2000. "Confidence in Public Institutions: Faith, Culture, or Performance?" In *Disaffected Democracies: What's Troubling the Trilateral Countries?* ed. Susan J. Pharr and Robert D. Putnam. Princeton : Princeton University Press.

NHK. 1995. *A Bilingual Guide to the Japanese Economy.* Tokyo: NHK Overseas Broadcasting Department Economic Project and Daiwa Institute of Research.

Norris, Pippa (ed.). 1999. *Critical Citizens: Global Support for Democratic Government.* Oxford: Oxford University Press.

Nye, Joseph S., Jr., Philip D. Zelikow, and David C. King (eds.). 1997. *Why People Don't Trust Government.* Cambridge, MA: Harvard University Press.

Oh, John Kie Chang, 1999. *Korean Politics: The Quest for Democratization and Economic Development.* Ithaca: Cornell University Press.

Page, Benjamin I., and Robert Y. Shapiro. 1992. *The Rational Public: Fifty years of Trends in Americans' Policy Preferences.* Chicago: University of Chicago Press.

Peters, John G., and Susan Welch. 1980. "The Effects of Charges of Corruption on Voting Behavior." *American Political Science Review* 74(3):697–710.

Pharr, Susan J. 1998. "'Moralism' and the Gender Gap: Judgments of Political Ethics in Japan." *Political Psychology* 19(1): 211–36.

Pharr, Susan J. 2000. "Officials' Misconduct and Public Distrust: Japan and the Trilateral Democracies." In *Disaffected Democracies: What's Troubling the Trilateral Countries?* ed. Susan J. Pharr and Robert D. Putnam. Princeton: Princeton University Press.

Pharr, Susan J., and Ellis S. Krauss (ed.). 1996. *Media and Politics in Japan.* Honolulu: University Press of Hawaii.

Pharr, Susan J. and Robert D. Putnam (ed.). 2000. *Disaffected Democracies: What's Troubling the Trilateral Countries?* Princeton: Princeton University Press.

Putnam, Robert D. 1995. "Bowling Alone: America's Declining Social Capital." *Journal of Democracy* 6:65–78.

Putnam, Robert D. 1996. "The Strange Disappearance of Civic America." *The American Prospect* 24:34–48.

Putnam, Robert D., Susan J. Pharr, and Russell Dalton. 2000. "What's Troubling the Trilateral Democracies?" In *Disaffected Democracies: What's Troubling the Trilateral Countries?* ed. Susan J Pharr and Robert D. Putnam. Princeton : Princeton University Press.

Ramseyer, J. Mark, and Frances Rosenbluth. 1993. *Japan's Political Marketplace.* Cambridge: Harvard University Press.

Reed, Steven R. 1994. "Democracy and the Personal Vote: A Cautionary Tale from Japan." *Electoral Studies* 13(1):17–28.

Reed, Steven R. 1996. "Political Corruption in Japan." *International Social Science Journal* 149:395–405.

Richardson, Bradley M. 1974. *The Political Culture of Japan.* Berkeley and Los Angeles: University of California Press.

Richardson, Bradley M. 1997. *Japanese Democracy: Power, Coordination, and Performance.* New Haven: Yale University Press.

Rose, Richard, Doh C. Shin, and Neil Munro. 1999. "Tensions Between the Democratic Ideal and Reality." In *Critical Citizens: Global Support for Democratic Governance*, ed. Pippa Norris. Oxford: Oxford University Press.

Sandel, Michael J. 1996. *Democracy's Discontent: America in Search of a Public Philosophy.* Cambridge, MA: Belknap Press.

Schneider, Friedrich, and Bruno S. Frey. 1988. "Models of Macroeconomic Policy." In *Political Business Cycles*, ed. Thomas D. Willett. Durham, NC: Duke University Press.

Tarrow, Sidney. 2000. "Mad Cows and Social Activists: Contentious Politics in the Trilateral Democracies." In *Disaffected Democracies: What's Troubling the Trilateral Countries?* ed. Susan J. Pharr and Robert D. Putnam. Princeton: Princeton University Press.

Thurow, Lester. 1993. *Head to Head: The Coming Economic Battle Among Japan, Europe, and America*. New York: Warner Books.

Tsujinaka, Yutaka. 1986. *Rieki shūdan* [Interest groups in Japan]. Tokyo: Tokyo Daigaku Shuppankai.

Tsujinaka, Yutaka. 1996. "Interest Group Structure and Regime Change in Japan." Maryland/Tsukuba Papers on U.S.-Japan Relations 12–13.

Tsujinaka, Yutaka. 1999. "Japan's Mature Civil Society and Its Interest Associations," paper presented at the Annual Meeting of the Association for Asian Studies, Boston, March 11–14.

Tyler, Tom R. 1990. *Why People Obey the Law: Procedural Justice, Legitimacy, and Compliance*. New Haven, CT: Yale University.

van Wolferen, Karel. 1989. *The Enigma of Japanese Power*. New York: Alfred A. Knopf.

Vogel, Ezra F. and George C. Lodge, eds. 1987. *Ideology and National Competiveness*. Boston: Harvard Business School Press.

Watanuki, Joji. 1977. *Politics in Postwar Japanese Society*. Tokyo: University of Tokyo Press.

Yamamoto, Shinichiro. 1995. *Akarui senkyo suishin no tebiki* [Clean Election League guide]. Tokyo: T(ky(Gy(sei.

Zajonc, Robert B. 1980. "Feeling and Thinking: Preferences Need No Inferences." *American Psychologist* 35:151–75.

Part XIII

CORRUPTION TERMS, MEASURES, AND METHODOLOGIES

Introduction to Part XIII

More than most other concepts in comparative analysis, corruption confronts us with significant difficulties of identification and measurement. Over the years these have been visible in the literature in the form of protracted debates over definitions, and sweeping yet often unsupported claims about the comparative seriousness of corruption in some times and places versus others. The past decade's work has often gotten around the identification problem by ignoring it: many analysts to focus on "grand corruption," with the implication that this relieves us of the burdens of defining boundaries for the concept and dealing with tricky cases. Others have treated corruption as though it were a synonym for "bribery," an approach that facilitates formal modeling. But this greatly oversimplifies the phenomenon and may lead to theories, and reforms, ill-suited to less straightforward forms of corrupt activity and poorly adapted to the realities of changing societies.

On the measurement front, there has been considerably more progress, but again difficulties are apparent. Corruption scales abound, and over the past several years a variety of them have been consolidated in the Transparency International Corruption Perceptions Index, which now includes ratings for around ninety countries. These indices have helped produce a useful and provocative new generation of quantitative research. The problem, however, is that while most of the indices are based on perceptions—frequently, those of visitors from other countries—corruption remains a shadowy enterprise. Perceptions are subjective; they are based on differing experiences and comparisons, and may reflect the openness of corruption rather than its true extent or significance. Reducing complex cases to single numbers is risky business for societies such as Italy marked by significant regional contrasts. Most of the perceptions are those of international business people; while they may tell us something about the scope of bribery in a country's international commerce, they may say much less about the kinds of corruption affecting poor people and others who deal with petty functionaries.

When people say "corruption," are they necessarily talking about the same thing? After all, a seemingly straightforward term such as "policy" can have quite different meanings, even among European states sharing some common elements of history and political development. Holger Moroff and Verena

863

Blechinger show us how the discourse of corruption and the various informal terms used to describe its techniques do not just delineate categories of activity, but rather create a much richer semantic field. This discourse tells us not only what happens in the course of corruption, but also suggests the ways people understand these activities and the normative dilemmas they pose. Using a comparative dataset describing the ways corruption stories are covered in the news media of several democracies, Moroff and Blechinger show that comparisons of corruption using notions of culture only to equivocate about the normative status of particular actions are underestimating the complexity and subtlety of culture and corruption alike. In addition, various countries' journalistic reports on corruption place significantly different amounts of emphasis on various aspects of corruption. Reformers and analysts alike would be well-advised to consider linguistic evidence in greater depth; outwardly similar terms and concepts not only take on varying different shades of meaning, but also tell us a great deal about underlying conceptions of power and propriety.

Michael Johnston takes on the question of measurement in his discussion of the new corruption indices. The problem, he suggests, is not that they are necessarily wrong: it is difficult to contest the notion that Cameroun is more corrupt than Denmark, for example. Rather, the indices are incomplete, and are not systematically sensitive to change. Thus, a comparison of countries using most of the current index numbers may give a useful indication of relative levels of high-level bribery, but may not reflect other, less visible kinds of corruption, or the sorts of so-called "petty" abuses that in fact do so much to keep poor people poor. Moreover, a country that embarks on a significant anti-corruption effort is likely to find that international corruption ratings give little or no useful feedback on how much progress has been made. Indeed—paradoxically—progress in breaking up corrupt networks may well lead to *worse* ratings for quite some time to come. While no measure of corruption will ever be free of problems, and while the current scales have enriched the literature in major ways, there may be ways to improve our comparisons. Johnston proposes the use of multiple scales that merge reliable indicators of preconditions and consequences we have reason to expect, from theory, to be closely linked to corruption. This approach, while not yielding the single-number comparisons that have proven so popular in recent years, may (at least indirectly) tap into a wider range of corrupt activities, and may tell us more about opportunities for, and progress toward, reform.

44

Measuring the New Corruption Rankings: Implications for Analysis and Reform

Michael Johnston

I. Introduction

Other than the question of definitions, few issues have so thoroughly stymied the comparative study of corruption as that of measurement. Types and amounts of corruption vary among, and within, societies. Theory tells us that these contrasts reflect political and economic influences, history, and culture, and in turn affect societies and their development in important ways. But the difficulty of measuring corruption has long made it difficult to make such comparisons, to test hypotheses, and to build sound, comprehensive theories.

For many years, this problem was of concern mostly to academic analysts. But recently a variety of forces have put corruption back on the international policy agenda. These include, *inter alia,* the globalization and growing competitiveness of the world economy, and a resulting awareness within international aid and lending agencies, and on the part of private business, of the costs of corruption. Other influences include movements to ban international bribery by domestic legislation (the U.S. Foreign Corrupt Practices Act) or by international agreements (the OECD Anti-Bribery Treaty, and the OAS Anti-Corruption Convention); concern about the cost and efficacy of international development programs, and over the role corruption might play in perpetuating poverty; and the end of the Cold War, which reduced tolerance for corruption among ideological allies.

This long-overdue revival of interest has spurred innovative attempts at measurement. But many of these reflect the worldviews of the business and development interests that have brought them about, and while the resulting research has deepened our empirical knowledge of corruption it has also narrowed our understanding of it. "Corruption" as an operational concept is becoming synonymous with bribery, its impact judged increasingly in terms of economic development. Few would dispute the importance of those concerns, but they have fashioned a new orthodoxy about corruption mirroring the broader "Washington consensus" over trade, aid, and development. With that has come a tendency for rich comparative concepts and findings to be overridden by a narrower vision treating corruption primarily as a problem of political and economic liberalization. Not only does this vision disregard important variations, in the course of "explaining" corruption; as the momentum behind reform builds, there is a growing risk that scarce opportunities will be wasted because of policies that are insufficiently adapted to local realities, and to the complexity of corruption itself.

In this discussion I will consider the measurement issue on several levels. One concern will be the quality of the indices themselves—strengths as well as shortcomings. Another emphasis will be their impact upon the policy and analytical debates, with an emphasis upon definitions as well as upon analysis and reform. "Second-generation" measures, and ideas for further improvements, will also come in for discussion. Finally, I will survey the prospects for, and the needed connections between, better comparative research and a richer policy debate. The purpose of my critique is not to suggest that the new corruption scales are radically wrong; indeed, there is little reason to think they are. Nor is it to criticize the motives behind the various statistical indices. Rather, it is to emphasize the continuing need for a richly comparative and historical view of corruption built upon diverse kinds of evidence and theory.

II. What Makes Corruption So Difficult to Measure?

In principle, social scientists ought to be able to measure anything (Babbie, 1995: 110). But this is more easily said than done, and it is a long way from essential concepts and nominal definitions to the events or artifacts included in operational measures. Many concepts are categorizations of, or inferences from, phenomena that may, themselves, be difficult to identify and observe. Consider "democracy" (Collier and Levitsky, 1997): we know it when we see it, but the concept remains essentially contested (Gallie, 1965). Over time the concept has a way of "creeping" away from its starting point, necessitating a re-think of what it means (Collier and Levitsky, 1997). Reaching consensus over definitions, much less measurement, would be difficult. One result is that at times we study things mostly because they are easily counted. A more subtle danger is *reification* (Babbie, 1995: 116–118)—thinking about operational measures as though they were the concept itself.

Measurement becomes all the more difficult when that which concerns us is hidden. We know corruption exists, but direct witnesses are few; often, those with direct knowledge have an interest in keeping it secret. Where corruption is most serious the officials charged with control are themselves compromised; in such settings reporting corruption becomes an exercise in risk and futility. Violence or intimidation may be used to see off investigators and keep others quiet. Statistics on conventional crimes are notoriously inaccurate; how can we measure an activity that is usually clandestine?

The problem is even more complex because of an old problem—that of definitions. If we study corruption at a general level—particularly, if our concern is commonly repeated syndromes—it may make sense to examine the core cases and not worry much about cases the margins. But when it comes to counting and measurement the margins become critical—and there is much disagreement as to where those boundaries fall. Add to this the complex relationship between corruption and scandal (Moodie, 1980; Markovits and Silverstein, 1988): public reports and controversies may tell us more about the *appearance* of corruption—and thus, about political conflicts, or about journalistic practices—than about its actual extent.

Validity, Reliability, and Precision

Three attributes by which we judge any measurement are validity, reliability, and precision (this discussion draws heavily upon Babbie, 1995: 121–129).

Validity raises the question of whether our data actually measure what we claim they do. Concepts themselves do not exist in the real world, or have "real definitions" (Babbie, 1995: 116; see also Hempel, 1952). They are, rather, constructs useful for categorizing objects or events, and for drawing out attributes we think they share. Thus our empirical measures can never be better than approximations, and the literature abounds with "measurements" that draw on something in addition to, or other than, that which they claim to measure—or that are grounded in nothing at all. As Babbie (1995: 127–128) explains, we can assess the validity of a measure in several ways. Does it possess *face validity*—that is, does it have anything to do with the concept we have nominally defined? An index that excludes extortion while counting street crimes might return higher values for places we think are more corrupt, but it does not measure what we mean by "corruption". Does it possess *criterion-related* or *predictive* validity, in the sense of predicting changes in other variables that theory tells us should be linked to our concept? For example, corruption measures should statistically "predict" the credit ratings lenders give to various governments. Or, a measure might be related to other variables in ways that are consistent with what we know about those factors, even if it does not "predict" them—an attribute called *construct validity*. We might, for example, expect extensive corruption where institutions are of poor quality (Knack and Keefer, 1995) and ethno-linguistic fragmentation is severe (Easterly and Levine, 1996). A measure possessing *content validity* works well across diverse manifestations of a concept: corruption ratings ought to reflect the incidence of all the major varieties of corruption, not just one or a few. Finally, a concept might have *reference-group validity*—that is, be judged sound by people with extensive knowledge of whatever we wish to measure. This is of particular relevance to corruption measures, many of which draw upon the judgments of experts or international business people.

Reliability refers to the question of whether a particular measure returns consistent results. A corruption scale that rates Zimbabwe (say) as an 8 on a scale of ten one year, 2 the next, and 5 the year after that, is of little use: we have good theoretical reasons to expect that such wide variations are unlikely. No social-science measure will be completely reliable, but we can improve our results through careful construction of indices using good data, and by repeated testing.

Finally, *precision* refers to the fineness of the units in which our measure is expressed. In general, the more precision the better: we would have little use for a "yes/no" corruption variable. High-, medium-, and low-corruption categories would be better, and numerical rankings more precise yet. A related issue is *level of measurement*: some measures are *nominal*, grouping cases into categories among which there is no particular relationship (individuals' ethnicity, or the continent where a country is located, are examples). Others are *ordinal*, grouping cases into categories that can be ranked higher or lower in terms of some shared attribute. We might, for example, place countries into high, middle, and low GDP-per-capita groups; all in the "high" category would be more affluent than those in the "middle" group, but there would be considerable variation within groups and no assurance that the differences among groups are the same. *Interval*-level measurements array cases along some common dimension demarcated by units of identical size, but without a point indicating the complete absence of the attribute. The Fahrenheit scale is an example: its zero point is arbitrary, so that while a one-degree difference is identical across all values, a reading of forty degrees is not twice as warm as a reading of twenty. We might survey residents of several countries asking whether officials are venal or public-spirited, and express the results on an interval-level scale (say, +5 to—5). Such a measure could not, however, tell us a particular country has a total absence of public spirit or that it is twice as venal as some other. Finally, *ratio*-level data also array cases along a dimension marked off in units of identical size, but one possessing a true "zero point". Here, expressions of proportion are appropriate: a country with 50 million residents is twice as populous as its neighbor with 25 million.

Other things being equal, higher levels of precision and measurement are desirable. But there is such a thing as false precision: while it is more useful to know that a country's population density is 255 people per square mile than to say that it is moderate, it is neither useful nor statistically appropriate to express that measure as 255.348906346 people/mi². Paradoxically, one measurement can be more precise, but less accurate, than another: data telling us Country X's population density is 255 people/mi² may be less accurate than an ordinal ranking of "moderate" if the true figure is 75 people/mi². Level of measurement is an important statistical issue: it is tempting to treat ordinal data as interval-level, for example, but the results can be misleading.

III. The Indices: Notable Strengths, Continuing Weaknesses

First-Generation Measures

A variety of corruption measures, differing in breadth, methodology, and quality, are now available; still others are under development. Some of the longest-running efforts at measurement have been mounted by firms providing risk assessments to international business. These, some available on a proprietary basis only, include surveys by Political and Economic Risk Consultancy,[1] the Institute for Management Development,[2] Political Risk Services,[3] *The Economist* Intelligence Unit,[4] and Business International (now a part of *The Economist* group). Others are produced by advocacy groups such as the World Economic Forum[5] and Freedom House,[6] survey organizations such as Gallup,[7] publications such as *The Wall Street Journal,* and groups of analysts, sometimes working in affiliation with international organizations. Some rely upon sample surveys of the public at large, or of international business executives; others depend upon expert assessments. Not surprisingly, sample sizes vary widely. Some ask respondents to rate overall levels of corruption on a scale; others ask about bribes, extortion, or other irregularities in specific governmental functions; others tap respondents' own experiences of corruption. All are aspects of a particular country's corruption situation, broadly defined; what is less clear is whether different kinds of questions about a variety of countries, reported in different units, produce results that are broadly comparable.

Other sorts of data have also been used in the comparative study of corruption. In the United States, for example, the Public Integrity Section of the US Department of Justice regularly publishes data on corruption convictions in federal courts (see, for example, the article by Schlesinger and Meier in chapter 33 of this volume). Economists have used measures of economic problems that, while not offered as corruption scales per se, tap into closely related problems, such as data on "black-market premiums" or the quality of countries' institutions (Knack and Keefer, 1995). A different approach is the international compilation of criminal justice data by the United Nations Crime

Prevention and Criminal Justice Division.[8] These data encompass many countries and a long time span; on the negative side, reliance on official statistics raises questions of comparability across countries' definitions of corruption, court systems, and investigatory efforts.

Corruption versus Perceptions of Corruption. Most first-generation indices measure perceptions of corruption—comparisons among specific countries, or ratings on an absolute scale—and many depend upon the views of businesspeople. Given the lack of harder indicators, the fact that much corruption arises in the context of business deals, and the extent to which these people move about the global economy, this approach is a natural one. Moreover, perceptions of corruptness are significant in their own right, influencing foreign policy, aid, investment, and lending decisions. They also factor into political interactions, particularly as regards democratization issues. In other ways, however, appearances can be deceiving.

I focus here primarily upon Transparency International's Corruption Perceptions Index (CPI)[9]—the most widely used and, in many respects, the most ambitious effort to measure and compare perceived levels of corruption. The CPI—a kind of "poll of polls"—has won worldwide attention[10] and aided a variety of analytical studies (for a useful survey see Lambsdorff, 1999b). Coverage has expanded from 41 countries in 1995 to 99 in the 1999 version. Seventeen surveys are now used to calculate the CPI; databases for individual countries range from the minimum of three required for inclusion (11 countries) to thirteen for Hong Kong, Hungary, South Korea, and Russia, and fourteen for India. By contrast, in the first CPI (1995) there were no more than seven data sources for any country, and two—Colombia and Argentina—had but two ratings. CPI methodology has become increasingly sophisticated, and TI publishes a comprehensive "framework document" (Lambsdorff, 1999a) and list of data sources[11] on its website.

These ratings, and the scholarship and public debate they have spawned, have seemed to confirm much of what we had long suspected. Corruption rankings are worst for poor, undemocratic, and unstable countries. Multivariate analysis employing CPI data (and others) has produced solid evidence that corruption significantly slows and distorts economic development (see, for example, Paolo Mauro's analysis in chapter 20 of this volume) and reduces foreign direct investment (Wei, 1997). It is also linked to inflation (worse where inflation is high and variable—see Braun and DiTella, 2000) and weak political and administrative institutions (Knack and Keefer, 1995), and is marginally worse where political competition is weak (Braun and DiTella, 2000; Johnston, in chapter 40 of this volume). Corruption is worse, again, where ethno-linguistic divisions are severe (Easterly and Levine, 1996).

Like any social-science measure, the CPI has strengths and weaknesses. Its value in sparking new research and public debate is beyond dispute. So are the occasional misuses of the data, though that fault lies with users, not with those devising the scales: Transparency International has been careful to emphasize the CPI's limitations. The CPI's reliability has been commendable, as we shall see. Its precision and validity are more problematical; while difficulties in these areas are inevitable, they also identify challenges for improving our measures. A validity issue common to nearly all first-generation indices—a tendency to equate corruption with bribery, and to focus more upon high-level corruption than the so-called "petty" varieties—will come in for discussion later on.

Reliability. Reliability is the strongest point of the CPI. Rather than employing just one or a few indicators, the data reflect the views of thousands of individuals who encounter corruption in differing ways in a range of countries, and are gathered in a variety of ways.

Given the links between corruption and basic political, economic, and institutional processes, a reliable index should return broadly consistent values from one year to the next. And such is indeed the case. Table 44.1 presents the correlations among the CPI scales published to date. If these correlations were weak or inconsistent we would have reason to doubt the CPI's reliability, but the consistency across time is striking.

A few qualifications are in order, however. Coefficients could also be *too* strong: levels of corruption are likely to change, even if gradually, and to change in differing ways from one country to the next. A reliable scale should reflect these changes, too. Thus, is the coefficient of almost .94 between 1995 and 1999 scores, for example, too strong? There is no real way of

Table 44.1
Pearson Correlations among CPI Scales

	1995	1996	1997	1998
1996	.9770			
	(41)			
	P=.000			
1997	.9354	.9689		
	(42)	(47)		
	P=.000	P=.000		
1998	.9450	.9663	.9880	
	(42)	(53)	(52)	
	P=.000	P=.000	P=.000	
1999	.9386	.9594	.9820	.9933
	(42)	(53)	(52)	(85)
	P=.000	P=.000	P=.000	P=.000

coefficient
(cases)
1–tailed significance

knowing. Moreover, nine of the seventeen component measures in the 1999 CPI are actually three surveys taken in the same, or very similar, ways three years running (1997, 1998, and 1999). While this broadens the number of respondents, and does insulate the scores from short-term fluctuations caused by sensational scandals, this method might also magnify the errors and biases in particular surveys, thus undermining the CPI's responsiveness to real changes. Comparability is an issue too: scores for countries with thirteen or fourteen surveys must include most or all of the repeated measures—meaning that their scores reflect perceptions over several years—while those based on just a handful of surveys will not.

The correlations above cannot tell us whether year-on-year differences reflect changes in "real" levels of corruption, the addition of new data that improve the scale, or other methodological difficulties that weaken it. They give little immediate reason to doubt the CPI's reliability, but do raise the question of whether an *annual* index that, in early versions, extended ratings to two decimal places—as opposed, say, to a more general ranking published every three to five years—exaggerates the apparent significance of small variations of unknown origins.

Precision: The precision of the CPI and similar scales is difficult to evaluate. It is not obvious what units of measurement *any* corruption scale ought to use, or how we might expect observations to be distributed. While the many measures folded into the CPI contribute to its reliability, they yield results expressed in significantly different ways. Some produce perceptions of how corrupt a whole society is, while others deal with particular agencies or functions of the state. Various surveys ask about perceptions of the "problem," or of its "pervasiveness," "level," "number of cases"; CPI architects defend these as comparable assessments of the "degree" of corruption (Lambsdorff, 1999a: 7), but others might question this, particularly in differing linguistic settings. Some ratings are anchored on absolute scales, while others are ordinal comparisons only (judgments that Country X is more corrupt than others, or that there are "a lot," "a few," or "no" cases of corruption among particular officials). One—the Freedom House ranking—was not even expressed numerically in its original form. Sample sizes, ranges, and distributions vary considerably, and thus sampling distributions and standard errors are likely to differ as well. Rendering these data comparable—and specifically, averaging ordinal-level comparisons into an interval-or ratio-level overall ranking—inevitably produces results shaped by the assumptions of the statistician as well as by actual perceptions or events. One specific result of these difficulties is that while we[12] often treat CPI data as ratio-or interval-level, variations across all values—say, the difference between 5.0 and 6.0, versus 8.4 and 9.4—may not be consistent. The problem may be most difficult at the extremes—the high-and low-corruption cases that interest us most, and whose rankings draw most attention.

Closely related to this are the differing lists of countries to which various component measures apply. Ideally we would have the same large number of corruption measures for every country, but we do not. The architects of the CPI have, in recent years, required a minimum of three corruption sûrveys before a country can be included—an approach minimizing the error that might result from relying on just one or two ratings. But the missing data are not randomly distributed; countries with poor institutions and governance also tend to have the fewest scales available. Thus, those with the worst corruption might well have the least data, while others slightly better off, where at least *some* surveys have been conducted, may be wrongly viewed as the world's most corrupt societies (Kaufmann, Kraay, and Zoido-Lobatón, 1999a: 22–23). TI regularly warns against interpreting CPI results in that way, but variations in amounts and quality of data among countries raise validity and reliability issues—possibly reducing the former while artificially inflating the latter to some degree.

A different precision problem has to do with reporting results. CPI scores are reported on a zero-to-ten scale (with low scores referring to high levels of corruption, and *vice versa*) in tenths of points—and, for the 1995 through 1997 CPIs, in *hundredths* of points. It seems unlikely that this sort of implied precision is justified; at the very least, reporting only one decimal place beginning in 1998 was an appropriate change. What would be an appropriate level of precision? Since the CPI does not have a true zero point, and if we are not certain that variations are consistent across all values, an argument can be made that it is essentially ordinal-level, and ought to be reported in broad bands (perhaps "low," "low-medium," "medium," and so forth) rather than in numerical points.

Another precision issue, but one with validity and reliability implications as well, is the "single-number problem". Actual corruption varies in many ways: there are many forms—a validity issue discussed below—and contrasts within most societies. How much nepotism or patronage is equivalent to a certain level of bribery in road construction? Is that bribery comparable in significance to similar practices in arms contracting? No single national score can accurately reflect variations between northern and southern Italy, across Russia, or among Minnesota, Alabama, and New Jersey. Some countries have high-level corruption, others find it lower down the political or bureaucratic hierarchies, and still others see most abuses in electoral politics and patronage. It may be seen as a major concern even where absolute levels are likely moderate to low (as in New South Wales); elsewhere, corruption enjoys official protection. In some countries the problem centers around international trade, while in others it is home-grown. Obviously any account of corruption, be it a case study or a data point, will be a simplification, and the CPI's architects have no control over the interpretations that result. But we might still ask how much variation—quantitative and qualitative—*within* countries is obscured by assigning each a single number.

Validity. The CPI, and many of the measures upon which it is based, represent a clear advance over the anecdotal evidence and hypothetical cases that dominated earlier phases of research, and over the diffuse and emotional claims often marking public discussions. Its results are plausible: it is difficult to dispute the notion that Canada is less corrupt than Poland, and that Poland is less corrupt than Kenya. In addition, the CPI and similar scales relate statistically to others in ways that make theoretical sense—evidence for construct and predictive validity.

Problems arise, however, with the basic approach of using perceptions as our operational measure. Setting aside the difficulties inherent in measuring perceptions of *anything,* we must remember that perceptions are not the same thing as corruption itself. They may reflect the openness of corruption, rather than its actual extent. The two may differ considerably: indeed, Rose-Ackerman (1996) has observed that as corruption problems worsen in a country, the major dealings tend to become fewer in number, to involve higher stakes, and to take place closer to the top. We can easily imagine one country in which corruption takes place openly, in small-to-moderate transactions, and another with less frequent, but large, well-concealed deals at the top of the state structure—perhaps under the protection of the very officials and agencies nominally charged with bringing it to light. Where corrupt officials and their clients operate with impunity, informants and prying journalists might be silenced by intimidation. The few visiting businesspeople who do gain access to such dealings might quickly acquire a stake in keeping their true perceptions to themselves. Corruption might distort politics, the economy, and development, and yet this country might score better on the CPI that its neighbor, where less serious corruption is practiced more openly.

Other subtleties complicate the rankings. What is being perceived as more or less serious? Does "extensive" corruption refer to the number of cases, the sums changing hands, impact upon politics or the economy, or cases involving particularly important officials or programs (Rose-Ackerman, 1999: 4; Lambsdorff, 1999a: 7–8)? Perceptions could reflect general impressions, or ethical expectations, of whole societies—of inefficiency or official impunity, poverty, or a weak civil society—rather than knowledge of corruption as such. What appears to be corruption might actually be scandal stirred up by feuding factions. Some judgments might reflect culture shock (particularly if one's basis for comparison is a low-corruption society), language limitations,[13] or sheer dislike of a country or its regime. The perceptions of outsiders—even if they rest upon a shared definition—might tell us little about the *significance* of corruption: what it *means* in its context. A seemingly minor case might be freighted with significance lost upon outsiders or ordinary citizens unfamiliar with elite conflicts. Do we trust the honesty of visitors' reports? Some might be less than candid because of their firms' or agencies'—or their own—involvement in corrupt activities. Others who have not done well in business might exaggerate corruption to explain away their failures.

Another validity problem is similar to the "single-number" issue. League-table rankings effectively treat corruption as a single generic process or problem, inviting statistical analyses that impose a common model upon (and within) widely varying societies and cases.[14] Qualitative differences are reduced to matters of degree. Consider, for example, the changing calculus of daily life—and of reform—implied when corruption is the rule rather than the exception, is facilitated by well-organized groups holding political or economic monopolies (Johnston, 1998), or is backed up by force. Then, corrupt figures face few meaningful limits, and can practice extortion or outright theft more easily, rather than making *quid pro quo* deals. The losers from such corruption are more likely to respond in evasive or illicit ways (See Alam, chapter 42), rather than directly confronting it as they might where corruption is the exception and the rule of law is secure. Different models may be required to analyze such situations.

A "Bribery Bias"? If corruption indices tend to impose a single model upon corruption, what is it? To a significant degree it is that of bribery. Several of the components of the CPI specifically ask respondents to judge the extent of bribery, or of demands for bribes. Others implicitly emphasize bribery by sampling business people instead of, say, poor farmers. (In that connection, three component measures ask recipients the extent to which corruption harms the business environment—confusing measurement with the question of consequences and inviting connections between corruption and broader economic problems.) Nepotism, official theft and fraud, *political* corruption such as patronage, so-called "petty corruption" such as police shakedowns of stall holders at local markets, and election fraud may not fit the bribery model (or the daily experiences of business people) so neatly, and may thus be underestimated.

Again, qualitative differences are collapsed into matters of degree. Bribery may be the main form of corruption in international business, and may be what springs to most minds when "corruption" is mentioned, but in some respects it is a special case. In a strict sense, bribery is a *quid-pro-quo* on *comparatively* free and equal (if illicit) terms. It differs from extortion, where officials force deals that may be anything but free and are rarely equal. Bribery seems most likely to dominate where corruption is moderate to moderately high, illicit deals are a matter of course, and participants are not frequently punished. Where the risk of punishment is high, or (by contrast) where powerful officials act with impunity, things may be different: in the former, bribe payers may have to add a "risk premium," while in the latter they are at the mercy of officials. In some corruption exchanges, such as patronage and nepotism, considerable time may elapse between receiving the *quid* and repaying the *quo,* and the two may be difficult to link or compare to each other. And other forms of corruption—electoral fraud, embezzlement, or using official resources to operate an under-the-table business—are not exchanges at all. Respondents to the CPI's component surveys may be well aware of these variations, but their knowledge cannot be conveyed in any single rating.

Why Do These Problems Matter?

First-generation corruption measures have helped move the debate forward, and have framed new hypotheses for further work. None has been proposed as the final word on measuring corruption; and, to discuss their weaknesses is ultimately to return to the inherent difficulties of measuring corruption.

Still, the difficulties outlined above do matter. Existing indices likely help us least in the countries we care about most—those with the worst corruption problems. Even if country rankings make sense, causes, effects, and corrupt processes exist at several different levels of aggregation. Thus developing careful, nuanced accounts of corrupt processes remains a central task for comparative analysts. Without such foundations, the significance of any ranking is open to debate. A 1999 re-analysis of CPI data by TI representatives in Latin America and the Caribbean (TILAC, 1999), for example, emphasized the range of variation in ranking across the Americas, and compared scores for the *region* to those of other parts of the world—with results that made Latin American corruption appear not quite as exceptional, and the worst cases less typical of the region, than we might have assumed. Perhaps it makes most sense to say that corruption indices have definite uses, but are just one form of evidence among many others and may be more useful for framing hypotheses than for providing conclusive answers.

As noted at the outset, many of the current scales reflect the outlooks of international business, and of the aid and lending institutions that have put corruption back on the policy agenda. There is nothing wrong with this, and the field is richer today for the efforts of such groups. But theirs are partial visions nonetheless; knowing how corruption—conceptualized as bribery—affects development—expressed in GDP figures or in terms of governance indicators—is valuable knowledge, but there is much more to be said. Years ago, for example, Huntington (1968) proposed that corruption might be a preferable alternative to violence—in the process, making the important point that in judging its effects we must make comparisons to its real alternatives, not just to ideal processes and outcomes. Statistical indices cannot settle that sort of question by themselves; we will also need historical, linguistic, political, and cultural evidence, and knowledge of forms of corruption beyond the bribery paradigm. Classical concerns of theory—the nature of accountability and justice, the sources and benefits of good politics, the dynamics behind cooperation, the emergence of normative frameworks, and strong civil societies—are parts of that picture too. No index could be expected to reveal these subtleties, but they are no less important for being less easily quantified. These, again, are more than methodological niceties. Perceptions of corruption do shape important decisions, but the danger is that they will lead to an "echo chamber" problem in which officials and investors repeat what they hear from each other, in effect, and in which anecdotes and perceptions acquire false authority through repetition. Analysts can make good use of perceptions of corruption, but there must also be ways to anchor perceptions in less subjective information about societies.

IV. Back to Basics: Richer Comparisons and Policy Debate

It is unlikely that we will ever have valid, reliable, precise, subtle, and broadly comparable data on corruption—much less on all of its various forms. But even if we had, they would be only one aspect of the broader and richer comparisons that are needed both for analysis and reform. Understanding the varying forms of corruption, their links to deeply embedded causes, and their consequences requires many kinds of evidence, and theoretical approaches sensitive to a range of variations among societies. Reforms and more general development efforts need similar foundations. A number of attempts have been made to improve our measurements of corruption, and I will note a few of those below. But the real challenge for the next stage of corruption research is not just to improve our measurements, but rather to build a richer understanding of the phenomenon, and to show why such an understanding is essential.

Second-Generation Measures

The first-generation indices elicited strong reactions. Journalists pounced upon the CPI as a rating of the world's most corrupt countries, even though TI explicitly warned against that interpretation. International agencies and many scholars quickly put the data to work, while others were more critical. Governments joined the fray, some crying foul as negative ratings threatened their countries' images and economic prospects.

New "second-generation" measures have been part of the response. A variety of sample surveys, for example, have focused upon businesses, households, and individuals, and their experiences of corruption. Results can be difficult to compare, particularly across languages and cultures, but provide a wealth of detail. The most elaborate is the World Bank Institute's 1999 Business Environment and Enterprise Performance Survey (BEEPS) of twenty formerly communist states (Hellman, Jones, Kaufmann, and Schankerman, 2000; on methods, see pp. 1–8). BEEPS-style projects are formidably expensive, and while tapping a wider variety of corrupt practices than most other indices, still strongly reflect the views of business and lenders. Nonetheless, they are an extremely promising approach, and have already produced intriguing comparative results (Hellman, Jones, and Kaufmann, 2000).

In 1999 Transparency International, responding in part to criticism by countries rated negatively in the CPI, and in part to the growing realization, as the OECD anti-bribery treaty took shape, that *sources* of bribes also must be studied, devised a "Bribe Payers' Index" (BPI).[15] The BPI, based on Gallup surveys of business leaders in fourteen "emerging market" countries, ranked nineteen leading exporting countries in terms of their firms' propensity to pay bribes to "senior public officials". The results were quite different from the CPI: countries such as Sweden, Australia, Canada, the United Kingdom, and the United States came off much less favorably. The BPI has made headlines, but again questions are being raised. The new index does not appear to control for various countries' prominence (or lack of it) in trade, either overall or within particular regions. No distinctions are made as to the gravity of cases. It is not clear how respondents would assign blame for bribes paid by (say) an Indonesian employee of a Thai subsidiary of an Anglo-Dutch corporation that is part of a multi-national consortium bidding on a major arms contract. And again, there are all of the problems inherent in using perceptions to compare levels of corruption. To be fair, the BPI is a new measure; moreover, it raises an important issue, and Transparency International has been careful to document data sources and methods.[16]

Kaufmann, Kraay, and Zoido-Lobatón (1999a, 1999c) have constructed a sophisticated "graft" index within a broader assessment of the quality of governance. They use 31 component measures allowing the ranking of 166, 156, and 155 countries, respectively, on rule of law, government effectiveness, and graft (Ibid., 2; data are described in Kaufmann, Kraay, and Zoido-Lobatón, 1999b). An "unobserved components" model (Kaufmann, Kraay, and Zoido-Lobatón, 1999a, 1–2, 8–14; see also Greene, 1990: Ch. 17) treats country data as a linear function of governance—which remains unobserved, but is assumed to be normally distributed across countries—plus a "disturbance term". This approach, given certain assumptions, allows estimates of confidence intervals—but these turn out to be very large. While a handful of countries can be placed at the good- and bad-governance extremes, for most the data do not clearly show that probity, bureaucratic quality, and rule of law are particularly high or low—much less, allow fine comparisons (Kaufmann, Kraay, and Zoido-Lobatón, 1999a: 2, 15–19; for a critical evaluation, see Lambsdorff, 1999a: 18–20).

A different approach (Hall and Yago, 2000) gets at corruption by way of its correlates and consequences. It focuses upon "opacity"—the opposite of transparency—restrictions upon the open flow of information essential to efficient markets. Various forms, ranging from false accounting to intimidation, serve "to ensure the secrecy of corrupt or questionable practices" (Ibid.: 1). A statistical model, including CPI figures along with macroeconomic data and various measures of institutional quality, is used to account for the varying interest rates paid by governments as they float bonds on the international market. Those with poorer institutions and greater opacity pay higher costs— a "premium"—to borrow money. To estimate "the shortfall each country had from the perfect transparency score" Hall and Yago calculate an "institutions premium," a "corruption premium," and a "graft premium"—the latter based on the graft index calculated by Kaufmann et al.—for each of 35 countries (*Ibid.*: 5). Not surprisingly, poor institutions, corruption, and graft are linked to significantly higher costs of borrowing—estimated at over $130 billion per year for the 35 economies. Corruption itself remains difficult to measure, but this approach links perceptions to harder indicators. Construct validity, reliability, and precision are augmented by the fact that the various premiums reflect lenders' continuing evaluations of countries' economic performance and debt-service prospects. Building indices on reliable measures of variables closely related to corruption is a very promising strategy.

Better Research, Better Policy

Two major issues remain. One is a shortcoming with all of the measures now available. The other reflects the range of forces shaping the past decade's work.

As for the first: how much guidance do corruption indices give reformers? Can those fighting corruption in a society look to CPI scores for evidence of progress, and for guidance in shaping their strategies? In all likelihood they cannot. CPI data do exhibit impressive reliability, but as noted above we still do not know how well they track changes in levels of corruption. Perceptions may outrun, or lag behind, actual trends. Any comprehensive anti-corruption strategy will likely work better with some varieties of the problem than with others, and yet a single-number index will not be able to tell us much about those contrasts—and thus, much about which aspects of the strategy are working and which are not.

What is likely to happen to perception scores for a country that has begun to make meaningful progress against corruption? There are several possibilities: at the very least, progress will be uneven, and thus be recognized more quickly by some observers than by others. In that event, the uncertainty (variance, or standard deviation in some versions) of CPI scores might widen considerably while the scores themselves change in ways that would be difficult to interpret. More likely, a successful anti-corruption campaign would produce revelations of wrongdoing, convictions, and new allegations. This is all the more likely in a democratizing country with citizens, journalists, and opposition figures feeling more free to speak out, and contending factions using corruption allegations to settle old scores. In that setting, effective anti-corruption efforts would likely cause perceptions to *worsen* markedly, at least in the short run. Finally, a campaign that begins to break up corrupt networks may well lead to a short-term surge of overt, smash-and-grab corruption as elites, uncertain about their hold on power, take as much as they can, as fast as they can take it (Scott, 1972; Knack and Keefer, 1995). Once again, CPI ratings may worsen. Surveys, whether on the BEEPS scale or smaller, are probably the best way to gauge anti-corruption progress. But they are expensive, and may not reveal much about progress against the deeper causes of corruption, or *why* observed trends are occurring.

Can we devise relatively inexpensive measures that are still sensitive to changing levels of corruption, and can give useful guidance to anti-corruption efforts? One way might be to focus less on measuring corruption itself and more upon scaling its correlates. We have good reasons to think that a variety of conditions and phenomena are closely linked to corruption. Many of these have been measured at a considerable level of validity, reliability, and precision, and in ways that do not reify perceptions and anecdotes as broader trends. Serious corruption is deeply embedded, and causality can be difficult to disentangle; still, we might construct a pair of indices approximating causes and effects. Loayza (1996) has employed a similar approach in studying informal economies, a measurement challenge resembling corruption in many respects. On one side we could incorporate measures of major problems giving rise to, and sustaining corruption—poor-quality institutions, lack of political competition, a lack of openness in the economy, inflation, and weak guarantees of civil liberties and property rights, for example—as well as those that make corruption easier to conceal (such as Hall and Yago's measurements of "opacity"). A parallel index of consequences might include factors such as capital-to-labor ratios in key aspects of the economy, budget-composition indicators (see Mauro, chapter 20 of this volume), statistics on the efficiency of tax collection, "black-market premiums" in foreign exchange, trends in aggregate development, and so on. Both indices could be based upon an unobserved-components model; both could be tailored to include likely correlates of different forms of corruption. A focus upon specific countries or regions over time would reduce the risk of distortions caused by the differing data available in various countries. The result could be indices complementary to those now available yet sensitive to changes and to the deeper causes and effects of corruption.

There are some obvious problems here. Endogeneity and simultaneity make causes and effects of corruption difficult to separate: are ineffective tax collection or a "black-market premium" results of corruption, or incentives that cause it? This approach, while it might reveal distinctive aspects of corruption in particular societies or regions, would not produce "headline numbers" for broad cross-national comparisons, though as the discussion above makes clear, such comparisons face major difficulties to begin with. The statistical risks inherent in merging disparate indicators would remain. So would problems of reliability and precision: how, for example, should the components of such indices be weighted? Should we use a regression model that predicts CPI or other scores for some initial point in time and weight measures by their statistical power (along with control variables) to predict our "effects index," or changes in it? If so, how should we weight the components of the effects scale?

As with the CPI and other measures, there would also be questions as to how to report the results. Are annual results extended to decimal places appropriate? Would they raise expectations that cannot be met or, because of the long-term nature of basic reform, lead to disillusionment? Would reporting results in broader "bands" create the illusion that nothing is changing? On the other hand, if reforms really are likely to produce the *appearance* of increased corruption in the short-run, solid evidence that underlying changes are more gradual might be very valuable to anti-corruption agencies facing press and political scrutiny.

The second problem is a needless, and ultimately false, bifurcation in the corruption debate, generally expressed as a gap between "theory" and "practical" research. This too is linked to reform, but has deeper roots, reflecting the outlooks and interests that have shaped many first-generation measures and their uses. Usually the implication is that broadly comparative work—particularly that aimed at developing conceptual frameworks and broad-based explanations—falls into the former category, while the statistical approaches and reform orientation defining the "new consensus" embody the latter. Research and reform are indeed distinct enterprises, but the most troubling aspect of this bifurcation is the frequent implication that comparative research is irrelevant—or a positive hindrance—to "practical" insights about corruption.

This distinction, of course, quickly breaks down under critical examination: sound theory will always have to be tested against the best evidence available, while reforms or empirical research not guided by theory are pointless, and may do more harm than good. But it may damage both the analytical and the reform agendas. The scholarly tradition is distorted by an overemphasis upon the narrow range of factors included in the so-called "practical" arena—perhaps most clearly illustrated by the ways corruption indices reduce complex cases to single numbers and encourage cross-sectional statistical approaches that impose a single model upon widely divergent cases. Policymakers may lose sight of the historical origins of corruption, and thus of some of the forces and conflicts sustaining it; of the cultural and linguistic factors shaping the social significance of corruption as well as responses to reforms; and of the many opportunities—indeed, the necessity—to carefully choose policies and judge their effects in the context of local realities. In such a setting scholars—seeking "relevance"—may produce work that is atheoretical, ahistorical, and devoid of comparative insight—a collection of case studies without richness or context—while policymakers, rejecting the need for a subtle and contingent analytical framework, will support one-size-fits-all remedies or "toolkit" reforms that do not reflect the kinds of things comparativists have long known about the societies in question.

There is no valid reason why the theoretical/practical bifurcation should exist. Indeed, as emphasis shifts away from putting corruption back on the international policy agenda—a task for which indices such as the PCI have proven very well-suited—toward action against it, the need for theory, comparisons, and subtle, often qualitative sorts of evidence becomes greater, not less. Broad-based comparative frameworks merging quantitative evidence with qualitative knowledge, and with linguistic, cultural, and historical evidence, would serve both traditions well. Reform and analysis will always remain distinct enterprises, but as Hall and Yago's work on "opacity" suggests, the shortcomings of perceptual measures become less critical the more they are augmented with other evidence. Comparative frameworks may generate more precise hypotheses to the extent that they draw upon quantitative evidence. Here, in a way, the second-generation corruption measures help show the way forward: as they become more elaborate they are more and more dependent for their meaning upon complex models, and become increasingly distant from "corruption rankings". There is no reason why that trend cannot be carried further, with statistical analysis of corruption questions becoming one component in broader comparative frameworks that have linguistic and cultural subtlety, and qualitative and historical depth, along with the kind of breadth that cross-sectional statistical data can provide.

There is no doubt that the effort to measure corruption has been worthwhile. It has helped set to rest a variety of questions that had long kept the scholarly debate going around in circles, and has framed others in more precise and comparative terms. Even to devise a critique of the existing measures, and of the corruption-as-bribery paradigm underlying much of the recent empirical work, is to identify fresh comparative challenges. The potential of any research to produce rich *and* useful insights depends fundamentally upon careful design and honest application, not upon the apparent simplicity of its methods or results. The task now is to bring evidence of many sorts together into discussions of corruption that can match the comparative reach of most statistical indices with the complexity of corruption itself, and of the societies it affects most.

Notes

1. http://www.asiarisk.com
2. http://www.imd.ch

3. http://www.prsgroup.com
4. http://www.eiu.com
5. http://www.weforum.org
6. http://www.freedomhouse.org
7. http://www.gallup-international.com
8. See http://www.uncjin.org/Statistics/WCTS/wcts.html#globalreport and the agency's *Global Report on Crime and Justice* (Oxford: Oxford University Press, 1999).
9. http://www.transparency.org/documents/cpi; see also the very useful Internet Center for Corruption Research (http://www.gwdg.de/~uwvw/) established at the University of Göttingen by Prof. Johann Graf Lambsdorff, the CPI's author.
10. See, for the 1998 CPI, http://www.gwdg.de/~uwvw/PRESS98/Press98.html
11. http://www.transparency.org/documents/cpi/cpi_framework.html
12. I include myself in the term "we" here: see my article in chapter 40 of this volume.
13. On the subtleties of the language of corruption, see the articles by Genaux, and by Moroff and Blechinger, chapters 7 and 45 of this volume respectively.
14. I am particularly indebted to Mushtaq Khan for his comments on this point.
15. http://www.transparency.org/documents/cpi/bps.html
16. http://www.transparency.org/documents/cpi/bpi_framework.html

References

Alam, M. Shahid. 1995. "A Theory of Limits on Corruption and Some Applications." *Kyklos* 48(3): 419–35.

Babbie, Earl. 1995. *The Practice of Social Research.* Belmont, CA: Wadsworth, 7th ed.

Braun, Miguel, and Rafael Di Tella. 2000. "Inflation and Corruption.: Cambridge, Mass.: Harvard Business School, Division of Research, Working Paper 00–053.

Collier, David, and S. Levitsky, "Democracy with Adjectives: Conceptual Innovation in Comparative Research," *World Politics* 49 (April, 1997), pp. 430–451.

Easterly, William, and Ross Levine. 1996. "Africa's Growth Tragedy: Policies and Ethnic Divisions." World Bank, Policy Research Department, Macroeconomics and Growth Division, Washington, D.C.

Gallie, W. B. 1965. "Essentially Contested Concepts." *Proceedings of the Aristotelian Society* 56.

Greene, William. 1990. *Econometric Analysis.* New York: Macmillan.

Hall, Thomas, and Glenn Yago. 2000. "Estimating the Cost of Opacity Using Sovereign Bond Spreads". Working Paper, Capital Studies Group, The Milken Insitute, Santa Monica, CA 90401.

Hellman, Joel S.; Geraint Jones, and Daniel Kaufmann. 2000. "Seize the State, Seize the Day: An Empirical Analysis of State Capture and Corruption in Transition." Draft of paper prepared for the Annual Bank Conference on Development Economics. Washington, D.C.: The World Bank (April); http://www.worldbank.org/wbi/governance/working_papers.htm

Hellman, Joel S.; Geraint Jones, Daniel Kaufmann, and Mark Schankermann. 2000. "Measuring Governance, Corruption, and State Capture." Washington, DC: The World Bank (April); http://www.worldbank.org/wbi/governance/working_papers.htm

Hempel, Carl G. 1952. "Fundamentals of Concept Formation in Empirical Science." *International Encyclopedia of Social Science II* (7).

Huntington, Samuel P. 1968. *Political Order in Changing Societies.* New Haven: Yale University Press.

Johnston, Michael. 1998. "What Can Be Done About Entrenched Corruption?," pp. 149–180 in Boris Pleskovic (ed.), *Annual World Bank Conference on Development Economics 1997.* Washington, DC: The World Bank.

Kaufmann, Daniel, Aart Kraay, and Pablo Zoido-Lobatón. 1999a. "Aggregating Governance Indicators". Washington: The World Bank; August; http://www.worldbank.org/wbi/governance/working_papers.htm

Kaufmann, D., A. Kraay and P. Zoido—Lobaton (1999b), "Governance Matters." World Bank Policy Research Working Paper No. 2196, October (Washington D.C.: The World Bank); August version at http://www.worldbank.org/wbi/governance/working_papers.htm

Kaufmann, D. Aart Kraay, and Pablo Zoido-Lobatón. 1999c. "Aggregating Governance Indicators". Washington: The World Bank; unpublished (August).

Knack, Stephen, and Philip Keefer. 1995. "Institutions and Economic Performance: Cross-Country Tests Using Alternative Institutional Measures." *Economics and Politics* 7(3): 207–27.

Lambsdorff, Johann Graf. 1999a. "The Transparency International Corruption Perceptions Index 1999: Framework Document". Berlin: Transparency International (October); http://www.transparency.org/documents/cpi/cpi_framework.html

Lambsdorff, Johann Graf. 1999b. "Corruption in Empirical Research: A Review". University of Göttingen, Internet Center for Corruption Research (November); http://www.gwdg.de/~uwvw/

Loayza, Norman. 1996. "The Economics of the Informal Sector: A Simple Model and Some Empirical Evidence from Latin America." *Carnegie Rochester Conference Series on Public Policy* 45, pp. 129–162.

Markovits, Andrei S., and Mark Silverstein. 1988. *The Politics of Scandal: Power and Process in Liberal Democracies.* New York: Holmes and Meier.

Moodie, Graeme C. 1980. "On Political Scandals and Corruption." *Government and Opposition* 15(2): 208–222.

Rose-Ackerman, S. 1996. "When is Corruption Harmful?" World Bank, Washington, D.C.

Rose-Ackerman, S. 1999. *Corruption and Government: Causes, Consequences, and Reform.* Cambridge: Cambridge University Press.

Scott, J. C. 1972. *Comparative Political Corruption.* Englewood Cliffs, NJ: Prentice-Hall.

TILAC (Transparency International for Latin America and the Caribbean). 1999. "Another Form to Look at the TI Index: Latin America as an Example." Unpublished.

Wei, Shang-Jin. 1997. "How Taxing Is Corruption on International Investors?," National Bureau of Economic Research Working Paper 6030, Cambridge, Mass.

45

Corruption Terms in the World Press: How Languages Differ

Holger Moroff and Verena Blechinger

When the OECD put corruption on its agenda its officials learned that they also had to overcome linguistic barriers and the existence of diverse concepts of corruption in major languages. An example was posed by the recent OECD "Convention on Combating Bribery of Foreign Public Officials in International Business Transactions" which went into force in February 1999. When comparing the various versions of the text used by OECD members, one finds its French title to be "La Lutte Contre la Corruption," in Spanish it is the fight against *cohecho* (bribery of officials), Japanese combats *wairo* (bribery) and German fights *Bestechung* (bribery). It seems puzzling that the French version of the title uses the word "corruption" while the other titles quoted above refer to "bribery."

Does the absence of a French equivalent to bribery only confront us with a simple problem of translation, or does this difference in vocabulary also represent further difficulties regarding the connotative width of the terms used? Does the French term "corruption" relate to the same implied meanings as for example the term "corruption" in English or *Korruption* in German, both carrying morally charged undertones? One French negotiator explains the reasons for this wording: "During the three years of discussing these terms it was painful to me because in French we could not define the term [bribery] in a unique way. *La corruption* includes both small graft and huge corruption scandals. As cases are tried, the notion of what is corruption will become more clear, and we will see whether it is interpreted more as bribery or corruption."

Or, to address the question from another angle, does a rich semantic field on corruption terminology provide for a more differentiated discourse? This has been proven, for example, for political science's core terms, namely politics, policy, and polity—a differentiation that is not reflected in most continental European languages where only one term is used referring to those three English concepts.[1] Does the fact that there are similar variations for corruption-related terms indicate that different language communities cast corruption phenomena in different terminological molds; and does this influence the way they conceptualize and talk about the phenomena associated with corruption? Does a broader semantic field of corruption terms in a language further imply a more active discourse about the phenomenon or reflect a higher incidence of corruption? These questions do not only touch on lexicology or the mere word clusters at hand for speakers and writers of a particular language. Their answers might also offer means to see how far the argument of cultural relativism carries across languages. This study looks at the perceptual aspects suggested by language itself.

According to the linguistic relativity hypothesis we construct our understanding of the world through language,[2] recognizing that societies develop a more or less sophisticated vocabulary which reflects their particular physical and biological environments, and crystallizing around the kinds of activities they engage in for economic, cultural, and political self-organization. Language is thus not just a means to describe "reality" but it is to an extent "reality" shaping itself.[3] Without pushing the foray into deep epistemological waters too far, it is noteworthy that it has recently been shown how speakers of different languages had considerable difficulties distinguishing among colors for which their respective tongue had no separate terminological categories. This demonstrates that even sensory perceptions are modified by the language system in which we are used to thinking and acting.[4]

Blind spots of the "verbal eye" are scattered differently across the semiotic retina of individual languages and provide for translation and at times communication difficulties. Regardless of whether language "reflects" or "creates" reality, it surely mediates our experiences in one way or another, and it is likely that if a phenomenon is habitually talked about in a certain way, it will influence how one thinks and what one makes of it. Thus it is essential to discuss the semantic potential of different languages and the effects of systematic selections from this potential in actual language use. This presence/usage test not just of individual words but of lexical sets requires a descriptive-comparative as well as a descriptive-analytical methodology along the lines of *categorization* and *selection*.

In this study we aim at identifying the most pertinent terms relating to corruption and at quantifying how frequently they are employed in contemporary newspaper discourse. Thus, in the first part of the paper, we measure the relative importance of each term towards the others and point out parallels and differences in the make-up of the "terminological tool kits" and their connotative width available for dissecting corruption phenomena in English, French, German, Japanese, and Spanish. The second part of the paper addresses the changing levels of attention accorded to the topic in major newspapers in recent years. A look at these data will provide us with insights in the dynamics of corruption discourses in various countries and will give further information about the scope and focus of national corruption discourses. Newspaper coverage of corruption in all countries subject to this study is dominated by two core terminological concepts: one is represented by more generic, morally charged and connotatively broader terms including the English term "corruption," while the second group is rather focused on transactions such as the English term "bribery." Countries strongly differ, however, in the amount of attention given to each of the two concepts. While some national newspaper debates are dominated merely by transactional terms and thus suggest a public that addresses the phenomenon of corruption on a case-by-case basis, other discourses focus on terms with a broader connotative width and thus let us expect a rather systemic approach to corruption. These findings can be of key importance for the success of anti-corruption strategies and measures. The identification of key concepts in the discourses to be targeted is an important preliminary step before setting up public campaigns or planning strategies for the prevention and elimination of corruption.

The sources used to draw up the list of relevant terms are major one-language dictionaries, synonym and etymological dictionaries,[5] and the legal codes[6] of the countries that are part of our study, i.e., the U.S., Britain, France, Germany, Japan, and Spain. All these countries rank among the advanced industrialized nations. They are similar in their claim to a democratic political system with a separation of public and private spheres and a free press, and they represent three major geographical centers of political and economic activity and influence.

The terms we identify are first categorized and then analyzed for their importance in newspaper discourse. As an indicator of that importance, we refer to their frequency of usage as shown by the number of articles in which these terms have been employed in major national "quality dailies." As far as the electronic databases permit, we sketch the development of some core word groups for the last decade (and where possible beyond) and evaluate them in comparative perspective, thus showing changes in the frequency of their usage. From these data, we draw first preliminary conclusions about the relation, and possible changes thereof, between the two basic concepts we identify, terms with broad connotative width and transaction-oriented terms. In short, we ask: how does corruption terminology differ among countries? Does the difference in terminology lead to divergent concepts or reflect varying emphases? How do "discourse volumes" compare among the different countries and over time? And lastly, are there changes of this "discourse volume" and if yes, what does this imply for the understanding of corruption?

Three caveats come along with this study: First, public discourse about corruption does, of course, not only take place in national newspapers, but also, and maybe much more so, in magazines and tabloids, on television and radio, in public debates, speeches and policy papers, and in learned journals and books. Nevertheless, an analysis of corruption discourses in national newspapers seems an appropriate indicator for the subject's general and changing topicality and for its degree of differentiation and politicization. It can be argued that major dailies are likely to have enough "inertia" not to be carried away by periodic bouts of scandal harping by tabloids or sensationalist television stations. They cover corruption subjects in due relation to the importance of other topics, and they do not fight shy of it either, being themselves engaged, to varying extents, in sound investigative journalism and enjoying some agenda setting power. They thus can be seen as reflecting a balanced picture about the state and volume of public discourse on corruption. Second, one can not take newspaper language as a one-to-one representation of every day speech or written language. Internal editorial regimes for individual papers might exist, with certain words on black lists or clear instructions of how they are to be employed by in-house dictionaries and a less than proportional use of colloquial terms. All that said, however, newspaper language can still serve as a good approximation of common language and as we compare newspaper languages with other newspaper languages the same units of comparison are kept. Third, the computerized databases of the major dailies we used for this study limit our analysis, on average, to the period of the last ten to fifteen years. We are aware of the fact that this time is far too short to credibly suggest major changes in discourse volume. We also understand the risk for our conclusions from these data to fall victim of short-term inflation of newspaper coverage caused by major corruption scandals. However, even such a short time frame can provide useful information about the general characteristics of corruption discourse within a country. Even a ten-year time period allows us, for example, to characterize public interest in corruption as rather high or low, constant or changing. It also enables us to measure the relation between different concepts of corruption and the degree to which these concepts are present in public discourse. Furthermore, the transitional charts in this paper may provide a basis for future analyses to be conducted when databases will cover longer periods of time.

Overlapping and Diverging Conceptual Fields: Charting the Terminological Spectrum

The list of terms was drawn up with reference to dictionaries and legal codes, thus compiling lexical sets that cover a broad range of corruption phenomena and avoiding the use of synonyms. Given the manifold definitions of corruption put forward in a welter of relevant studies, which even warranted categorizing the various types of definitions, it is necessary to confine the number of terms included according to some criteria that are inherent in most of them. The basic definitional denominator applied here is derived from J.S. Nye and describes corruption as "behavior which deviates from the formal duties of a public role because of private-regarding pecuniary or status gains; or violates rules against the exercise of certain types of private regarding influences" (see Nye,chapter 17 in this volume). Beyond a violation of the laws or norms that mark the public/private borderline, terms must include an element of interpersonal exchange. This does not always have to imply a direct quid pro quo as in *bribery*. It can also refer to dependence in cases where autonomy might be expected, as for example with *nepotism* and *patronage*, or with other forms of obligation exchanges and bought pressuring such as *revolving door* and *influence peddling*.

Terms that are often linked to corruption are thus excluded because they lack such an exchange component, e.g., embezzlement, fraud, theft, mismanagement, conflict of interest, amassing of public offices, etc. Also excluded are terms for political exchange and constituency service with no direct private gain for the participating officials such as the concepts of logrolling (you vote for my legislation, I vote for yours) or pork barreling (the channeling of government appropriations into local electoral districts in order to please legislators' constituents).

The lexical sets as compiled below are far from being comprehensive and are limited to comprise no more than eight or nine terms for each language. Their aim is to render those terms that are most pertinent to corruption discourses in the languages concerned and to provide a basis for further analyses. Some terms were dropped from those sets on account of their limited practical relevance when they are not used at all in newspaper discourse and are marked as rare in the respective dictionaries or by native speakers.

Starting from relatively broad lexical sets we will narrow our focus by taking a closer look at the dominant terms as they emerge through our frequency count (Table 45.1). Individual terms are marked where they are also used and defined in legal codes (leg.), when they are used colloquially (col.), and where they constitute a somewhat idiosyncratic concept that has no exact equivalent in other languages and thus needs to be paraphrased (idio.). The terms are grouped in three categories, morally charged terms, transaction or action focused concepts, and morally neutral words that often describe particular kinds of corrupt practices. The first category consists, save for Japanese, only of the most generic term, namely corruption, under which most of the others could be subsumed but which also carries the strongest moral overtones and connotative width. The second category comprises terms that usually involve individual actions used with reference to a specific case and individual persons. Their attributive scope is limited to personal and mostly single transactions such as bribery or influence peddling. This attributive

Table 45.1
Lexical Catagories for Major Languages

Terms	morally charged generic	(trans)action focused	neutral and particular
Languages			
English (US)	*corruption*	*bribery* (leg), *influence peddling, venality,*	*graft, patronage nepotism, revolving door* (idio),*cronyism*
French	*corruption* (leg)	pot-de-vin (col, idio) [symbolic of a bribe] *trafic d'influence* (leg), *subordination* [bribing esp. of witnesses],*vénalité*	*patronage, nepostisme, pantouflage* (col, idio) [≈revolving door]
German	*Korruption*	*Bestechung* (leg) [bribery], *Vorteilnahme* (leg) [bribed to perform duty], *Schmieren* (col) [to grease]	*Filz* (col) [≈party book-administration], *Patronage,Vettern-wirtschaft* [≈mix of patronage & nepo-tism], Nepotismus,
Japanese	*fuhai* [corruption], *daraku* [corruption moral decay, decadence]	*wairo* (leg) [symboic of a bribe], *zôwai* (leg) [active bribery], *shûwai* (leg) [accept-ance of a bribe, passive bribery], *baishû* (col) [bibery], *settai* [wining and dining of official],	*oshoku* [as generic as corruption but less morally charged], *amakudari* [descent from heaven], *kone/paipu* (col) [graft]
Spanish	*corrupción*	*cohecho*(leg)[bribery esp. of officials], *sobornación* [bibery general], *mordida* (col) [symbolic of a bribe], *trafico de influencias* (leg), *venalidadad, untar* (col) [to grease]	*nepotismo*

scope is wider and less clear-cut with terms falling into the third category. They can describe systems of obligation exchanges as patronage and nepotism or refer to specific practices that can be prevalent systemic features within or of certain governmental institutions such as *Filz* (party book administration) or *amakudari* (descent from heaven, revolving door). The areas of overlap are prevalent. This is especially true for the first category of generic terms with strong moral connotations. It is just one term with the same Latin roots that is used in the four Western languages with Japanese offering a good equivalent to corruption. There is not much competition by other words that would qualify for this first category.

Divergences become apparent in the second and third columns. In all languages, with the exception of French, we find an equivalent to bribery that can be used either as verb or noun. It might then be differentiated further into passive and active, depending on who takes the initiative on the quid pro quo. Interestingly, what is called passive/active bribery in German, Japanese, and Spanish, is termed in English and more naturally in French, for its lack of a bribery concept, as active/passive corruption. Spanish and Japanese know two terms for bribery, one predominantly applied to bribery of an official and used in the legal codes (*cohecho* and *wairo*, respectively), while the other term is more generally used (*soborno* in Spanish and *basihû* in Japanese). This contrasts sharply with the absence of a bribery concept in its Romance sister language. Though the English word bribe derives from the Old French noun *bribe* (that once signified a morsel of bread given to a beggar), in contemporary French *pot-de-vin* is used as a somewhat euphemistic and symbolic concept of a bribe, evoking a small tip in form of a jar of wine. Both its colloquial nature and the fact that it does not lend itself to be used as a verb or adjective would make it seem unlikely to gain a wider currency. In this respect *pot-de-vin* is comparable to the Spanish/Mexican term *mordida* (literally the bite, meaning a bribe). Similarly to the Spanish *mordida*, which refers both to the act of bribing and the bribe itself, the Japanese *wairo* is used in everyday communication and in the legal context to describe both the bribe and the act of giving or receiving it.

Through other legal concepts, special terms have entered the different languages. Thus in German and in Japanese, we find special terms for bribing and being bribed to perform official functions within the official's duty and discretion (*Vorteilsnahme,-gewährung*, resp. *shûwai, zôwai*, both literally taking and giving advantages) and those actions that violate the official's duty (*Bestechung/wairo* bribery). But that distinction is neither made much of in every day language nor in newspaper writing. Quite the opposite is true for another legal term used in French and Spanish, namely the concept of *trafic d'influence* (influence peddling) that found its way into common and newspaper discourse.

The third category also shows some variety especially among the more idiosyncratic concepts, whereas the overlapping area covers concepts such as nepotism and patronage. However, patronage is a more ambiguous term in the Romance languages, since its derivatives are regularly used referring to employers, owners, a boss or general sponsors. They are therefore not predominantly associated with corruption. Spanish does not even afford such a term and has to paraphrase patronage as the abuse of the *control de nombramientos políticos*.

The three "idiosyncratic" concepts of *revolving door, pantouflage,* and *amakudari* (descent from heaven) are particular to their respective languages only in so far as they play on different metaphors for the phenomenon that former employees of a government department are hired by private companies regulated by that very department. A practice which is to an extent legally restricted and sanctioned in the United States, Japan, and elsewhere. The German concept of *Filz* or *Filzokratie* suggests impenetrably interwoven power relations based on party book and political patronage for which the term party book administration is a good estimation. The same concept can be associated with the Japanese terms *kone* and *paipu*. Both terms are derivatives from English terms, i.e., "connection" (*kone*) and "pipeline" (*paipu*), and refer to close relations to, and patronage by, the regulating bureaucracy which help to provide favorable treatment and any kind of advantages. The German term *Klüngel*, in contrast, refers to cliques of mutual support. It was originally used in reference to city administrations, but it is now applied somewhat euphemistically also to larger political entities. Another idiosyncrasy emerged during the last century in America with the term *graft* being applied not only to botany or medicine but also to dishonest and shady means by which to profit from government business. In its denotative range it is almost as generic as corruption, narrowed only by its implying a political setting and its potential for a connotative twist from the bad to the good. Through the concept of "honest graft" it can take on a less morally condemning color than the term corruption and warrants its being ranked among the more neutral or potentially neutral terms.

From Semantic Potential to Actual Use

The terms in Table 1 were subjected to quantitative analyses through a Nexis/Lexis® search and a search in the Nikkei Telecom database for the Japanese papers, providing information on whether and how often they have been used in major national dailies during the last decade. As an indicator we took the number of articles in a given newspaper in which the term is employed at least once.[7]

It was not wholly unexpected when terms belonging to the two core word groups of *corruption* and *bribery* emerged as the most frequent ones for all languages concerned. However, it was somewhat surprising that these terms and their equivalents consistently outnumbered any other term in their respective languages tenfold. Their overwhelming predominance warrants a closer look and a juxtaposition of language specific usages. Within the lexical pool of pre-selected words, discourse is cast to over 90 percent in terms of corruption and bribery. However, the relationship between these two concepts and the overall incidence level, or volume, varies greatly among the different countries. This is shown in figure 45. 1 below.

In Japanese and American newspapers, terms equivalent to corruption and bribery are employed in considerably more articles than in their European counterparts. This can only in part be attributed to the overall greater number

Figure 45.1

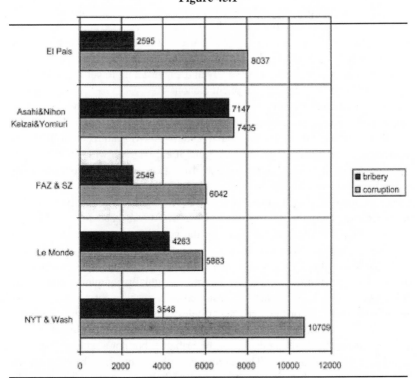

Number of articals over the seven years from Jan,1993 through Dec. 1999 in which indicated terms of equivalents are employed. Where more than one paper is used as source the combined average is taken (arithmetic mean). The bribery equivalent in Le Monde is *pot de vin*. For El Pais, *cohecho* and *soborno* take up an equal share in the bribery column. Both *fuhai* and *oshoku* are used as Japenese corruption equivalents, and *wairo*, *shûwai* and *zôwai* are used as equivalents to bribery. For the German columns the terms are *Bestechung* and *Korruption* (FAZ: *Frankfurter Allgemeine Zeitung*, SZ: *Süddeutsche Zeitung*, NYT: *New York Times*, Wash: *Washington Post*[8]

of articles carried by the U.S. papers. In Japanese newspapers, for example, although the *Asahi Shinbun* and the *Yomiuri Shinbun* are bi-dailies, the overall number of articles per day is considerably lower than in European or American newspapers.

Especially striking is the different relationship between those two core word groups. Whereas bribery (or equivalents) is used about half as much as the more generic term corruption in all Western language dailies, in Japanese ones this relationship is almost even with the more technical, transaction-centered terms for bribery lagging only minimally behind the terms related to corruption. This reversal would be more than complete if the morally charged *fuhai* were taken as the only true equivalent for corruption; then a mere 2,259 articles employing this term would be dwarfed by its juxtaposition to the more than 7,000 bribery articles. However, the more neutral but equally generic term *oshoku* has been included in the Japanese corruption bar of the above figure and it accounts for three-quarters of all the corruption hits. Both the prevalence of legalistic bribery terms and the morally less condemning corruption term seem to dovetail nicely and suggest a more sober and confining attitude of papers toward the phenomenon.

A special French peculiarity is the predominant use of *pot-de-vin*, which is taken as the only close equivalent to bribery and used for the *Le Monde* bar for that concept. Given its colloquial and figurative nature as well as its restricted use as a noun it is surprising that it enjoys such wide currency. An apparent lack of differentiation suggested by dictionaries is all but compensated by common usage, at least in newspaper discourse. On the other hand, usage in Spanish, which knows and defines in legal texts even two equivalents for bribery, namely *cohecho* and *soborno* (both used for the *El Pais* bribery bar), is dominated far more by the generic term *corrupción* than in any other language save English.

Of course, bribery and corruption do not stand for competing concepts and are certainly not mutually exclusive but rather mutually complementing terms in the sense that bribery can be subsumed as a specific form and concrete manifestation of a corrupt act. Nevertheless, the attributive qualities vary substantially. Mainly individual actors are usually called bribable in a specific situation, thus only a person can be bribable, but not a whole institution or even a political system. This contrasts with the much broader range of persons, groups, and institutions that can be labeled as corrupt. It is unlikely to read about a bribable planning department; instead it would sound less awkward to call it a corrupt planning department. Bribery and bribable are also concepts focusing on cases involving a specific quid pro quo. All in all, one might say that the bribe family of terms is confined to being assigned to concrete individuals and cases, and something that suggests, once it has become public, a controllable and corrigible flaw within an institution or system. In contrast, a corrupt system or institution suggests a structural flaw that is not easily amended. Thus for larger entities the potential of corruption terms to delegitimize is considerably greater than for bribery terms. The moral overtones of terms in the corruption group contribute their part to this as well.

What does this mean for public discourse? One might argue that a newspaper discourse that is cast mainly in bribery terms has a less delegitimizing impact on the whole political system than a discourse led mainly in terms of corruption. However, the case of Japan shows a somewhat different pattern. Over the last decades, the Japanese media have discussed incidents of corrupt behavior on a case by case basis, as is also shown by the high number of articles using transaction-related terms. By doing so, a more general discussion of the systemic causes of corruption or bribery did not take place except for a brief period of debates about political reform in the early 1990s, resulting in a loss of public trust in the political system and high levels of dissatisfaction with, cynicism about, and alienation from the political process that clearly becomes visible in the low voter-turnout at Japanese elections.[9]

Further below we try to sketch the dynamic development of these two core word groups over time, but first we turn to the static statistics on the other terms, which could be labeled peripheral on account of their secondary importance in usage. The data show how the remaining ten per cent of discourse "volume" is divided among the various peripheral concepts in the different "newspaper languages." (Figs. 45.2-6).

The trend of significantly higher incidence levels in the American and Japanese papers continues for the count of articles employing peripheral terms

Figure 45.2

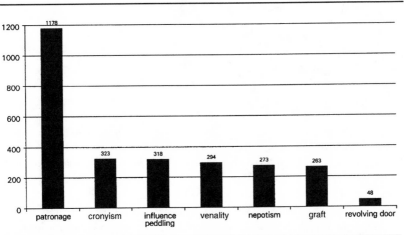

Usage incidence of peripheral terms as average of *New York Times* and *Washington Post* for past seven years (1993 through 1999,[10]

Figure 45.3

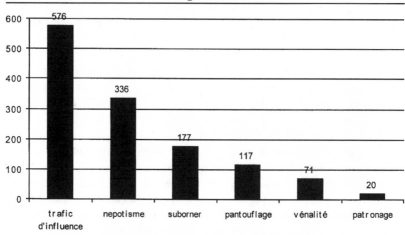

Usage incidence of peripheral terms in *Le Monde* (1993 through 1999).

Figure 45.4

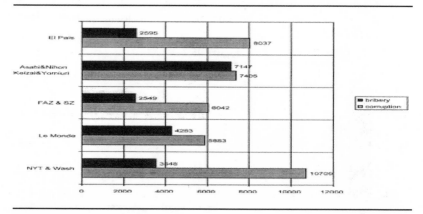

Usage incidence of peripheral terms as average of *Frankfurter Allgemeine Zeitung* and *Süddeutsche Zeitung* (1993 though 1999).

Figure 45.5

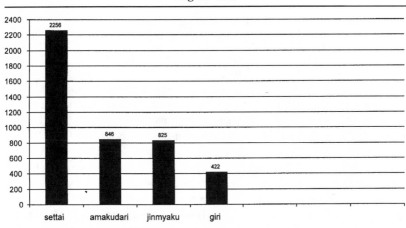

Usage incidence of peripheral terms as average of *Asahi, Nihon Keizai,* and *Yomiuri* (1993 through 1999). To balance the fact that two of the three Japanese newspapers used are bi-dailies, the number of hits was reduced by 25%.

Figure 45.6

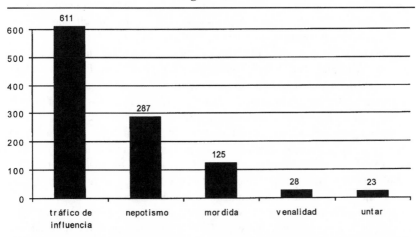

Usage incidence of peripheral terms in *El Pais* (1996 through 1999 extrapolated back to 1993).

as well. Six out of the seven pre-selected secondary American terms appear much more frequently than their equivalents in European papers and are used in a more evenly distributed mix, suggesting a greater degree of differentiation. However, compared to the high frequency of the core word groups, the American peripheral terms as a whole still play as minor a role in discourse as is the case for the other languages. For Japanese, the large number of articles using the term *settai* (wining and dining of public officials) might be caused by a series of scandals involving the wining and dining of bureaucrats that was disclosed during the time period covered in this study. While the number of articles using this term was constant at about 200 from 1991, it shot up to about 600 in 1995 and stayed at high levels since. The other peripheral terms do not reach significant numbers compared to what we identified as core terms, the equivalents to corruption and bribery.

Looking at the three most important, because most frequent, peripheral terms for each language it is striking how much they vary in contrast to the virtually identical core terms for the different "newspaper languages." Ranking among them are many terms marked as idiosyncratic, and for all five languages we find four different terms leading the list. For the two Romance languages the leading American term is conspicuous by its absence. The patronage family of terms is much too ambiguous in these languages and used regularly in discourses far removed from that on corruption; consequently it does not seem to lend itself naturally to be seen as constituting a prominent phenomenon in a corrupt light. Instead, the legal concept of *trafic d'influence* or *tráfico de influencia* is dominating in French and Spanish newspapers. It refers to a concept that can be linked more to bribery than to patronage, for it involves a concrete exchange and a clear cut, willful action among a definite number of persons, who do not need to be connected by personal friendship or family ties as is the case with patronage and nepotism. It appears that *trafic d'influence* is one of the few examples where an original and genuinely legal construct found its way into common discourse.

Turning to the more idiosyncratic concepts, we find that the French and Japanese equivalents of *revolving door* (*pantouflage* and *amakudari* respectively) are not as rare in newspaper discourse as their somewhat exotic status would have suggested. They seem to provide a good means to grasp and name the phenomena of governmental administrators switching sites, "selling" their services and insight knowledge to the regulated or contracted businesses as consultants or employees. For the Japanese case, the high number of articles mentioning *amakudari* might be related to the fact that the Japanese National Personnel Agency controls this practice and regularly publishes "White Papers" on *amakudari*, which are then quoted extensively in the newspapers. Since these phenomena are known and practiced in Germany and Spain as well, it would be interesting to see whether they receive less attention for lack of a sufficiently succinct concept that could be attached to it as an easily identifiable label. In turn, the same question could be raised regarding the non-existent or not well established concept of influence trafficking in the U.S., Germany, and Japan. It is certainly practiced, but is it called differently, running under a different label, or is it always described in its intertwined chains of influence exchanging, thus rendering it less graspable?

Filz is another leading peripheral term peculiar to Germany and maybe also to its political system. It refers to impenetrably intertwining power relations based on a party book administration that reaches down to local levels. These kinds of informal, party based support structures within the supposedly independent, disinterested, and impartial government administrations or even the judiciary, are, once again, known to other political systems as well. Nevertheless, it could certainly be an indicator for the fact that such informal structures are being especially pronounced in the German setting or many phenomena are cast in that conceptual mold in discourse. *Filz* does not refer to a specific exchange transaction as influence trafficking does, rather it is a quality attributed to a whole system or a larger entity. Though not as strong and morally charged as corruption, it has, through its assumption of being a pervasive trait wherever it is discovered, a much greater delegitimizing potential than *trafic d'influence* or even patronage.

Dynamic Developments of Core Word Groups

The overwhelming predominance of the terms corruption and bribery (or equivalents) in discourse warrants a further analysis as to how often they have been employed over time and across languages, thus moving from a static, synchronic comparison to a dynamic, diachronic one that will provide some depth of field (Figs. 45.7-10). Increases and changing relative importance of these two terms are documented in this way, and changes in the overall "discourse volume" will become apparent. We consider those papers for which data are available for the most part of the decade and where possible beyond.[11]

A sharp increase over the past six years can be ascertained for the French and German side, though a few fluctuations make the rise seem less steady, the current incidence levels are for both terms more than two times those of 1990 or 1992. However, they do not come close to the continually high levels in the American press. During the last nine years the *New York Times* and the *Washington Post* have used the term corruption on average twice as much as did their European counterparts, and only *pot-de-vin* in *Le Monde* could match *bribery* in frequency and actually overtake it since 1993. Japan, on the other hand, appears to have put corruption onto the dailies' agendas half a decade earlier. It experienced a foregrounding and politicization of the corruption discourse in its newspapers in the late 1980s much like the sea change

Figure 45.7

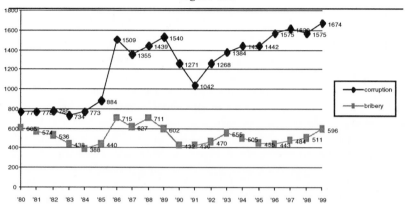

Number of articles in which indicated terms are employed since 1980 (average of *New York Times* and *Washington Post*).

Figure 45.8

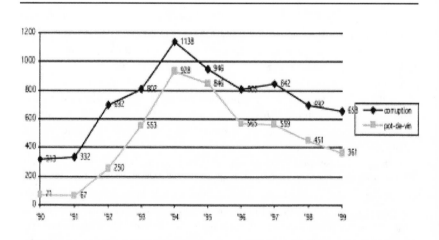

Number of articles in which indicated terms are employed since 1990 (*Le Monde*).

Figure 45.9

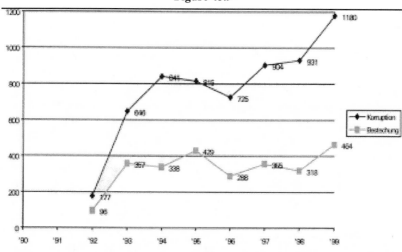

Number of articles in which indicated terms are employed since 1992 (average of
Frankfurter Allgemeine Zeitung and *Süddeutsche Zeitung*).

Figure 45.10

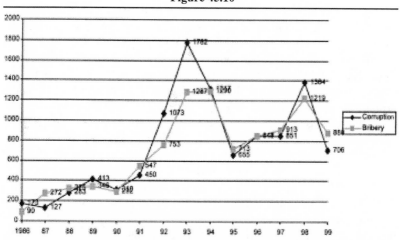

Number of articles in which *seiji osohoku* & *seiji fuhai* (corruption) and *wairo* & *zôwai*
shûwai (bribery) are employed since 1986 (average of *Asahi Shinbun, Hihon Keizai
Shinbun, and Yomiuri Shinbun*), the number of hits has been reduced by 25% to
balance the fact that two of the three Japanese papers used are bidailies.

in the U.S.'s dailies since the mid-80s. Great fluctuations are shown especially for the Japanese corruption terms, which seemed to gain in relative importance to bribery terms in the mid- and late 1990s. The peaks in the curves for both bribery and corruption terms might be attributed to a rising number of scandals that surfaced in the late 1980s and that brought about an intense debate on political reform in the early 1990s and on administrative reform in the late 1990s. Only after some years of heightened awareness and continuous reporting on bribery issues did the topic gain a broader base and in its wake a public debate about structural corruption and political finance set in, thus changing for a while the terminological composition of discourse in favor of *corruption*, which outnumbered bribery for a brief period and gained a significantly higher level of usage ever since. Still one has to keep in mind that the more neutral corruption term *oshoku* is used consistently three to four times more often than the morally charged corruption term *fuhai*. The figures for the U.S. papers show a disparate development first after 1985 when corruption terms increased over-proportionally in relation to bribery terms, though the trends remained the same. But since 1993 even these trends seem to have decoupled and are slightly contrary; while corruption usage is steadily increasing, bribery terms have somewhat decreased.

Even though the time series are too short to say something about a general trend of an overall growing newspaper discourse volume on corruption, it is possible to sketch recent developments and to point out possible trends. The twenty-year time period we can encompass for the U.S. suggests an overall and apparently lasting increase in usage particularly of corruption terms while the usage of bribery terms remained at a constant level. We also see a significant increase in the use of corruption related terms in European and Japanese dailies that strongly suggest a heightened topicality and politicization of the subject. Even if this is not due to a change in "press-appeal" and press exploitation of the topic but rather to truly event related reporting, the enormous fluctuations in usage are not matched by any other subjects or political buzz words such as "globalization" or "liberalization".

Conclusion

Commonalities in the make up of the various languages' terminological tool kits seem to outweigh their divergences. This is particularly true for the two key word groups of corruption and bribery. In this regard it is astounding that French has developed a colloquial equivalent to bribery which enjoys wider currency than most other "genuine" bribery terms in the other languages, whereas the Spanish *El Pais* makes little of the language's variety and casts its reporting mostly in terms of corruption. A rich semantic field does not always mean using it in actual discourse; on the other hand, a minor colloquialism can grow into a regularly used concept.

How are corruption phenomena talked about differently and what can be deduced from this for a more general outlook on the problem? Of course, the list of terms could be expanded (to cover such concepts as kickback, clientelism, *graisser la patte* (palm greasing), *jinmyaku* (obtaining advantages by using informal connections), to name but a few). However, a somewhat subjective pre-selection is necessary to limit the scope thus permitting a clearer illustration.

Firstly, the relationship between the key two word groups of corruption and bribery for the American, German, and Spanish newspaper languages is relatively constant in absolute terms and over time, bribery is used half as often as corruption. For the French *Le Monde* the rate increases and *pot-de-vin* is employed almost as often as *corruption*. In Japanese newspapers the curves for the two terms run almost in a parallel way, with corruption terms tending to outnumber bribery terms in periods of debate about genuine political reform. The parallel lines of the two curves for the Japanese terms suggests that in the Japanese media discourse, corruption is discussed in terms of bribery, pointing at a preference for a debate on a case-by-case basis, not as a systemic problem. This view is supported by the considerable fluctuation of the curves for the Japanese terms. The general increase in articles referring to corruption and bribery, however, can also be seen as a general trend towards a growing appeal of corruption terms in recent years.

Secondly, the overall levels of corruption and bribery articles combined differ markedly between the United States and Japan on the one hand and the three European countries on the other hand. Especially in the U.S. "corruption reporting" has remained consistently high, and for the early 1990s these concepts were invoked in more than twice as many articles as was the case for their European counterparts.

Thirdly, differences become apparent for the large pool of peripheral or collateral word groups. Leading concepts in this category differ among all languages save for French and Spanish, which both use their legal construct of *traffic d'influence* most frequently. *Settai* (wining and dining) outnumbers all other terms in Japanese papers; in German papers it is *Filz* (party book administration and patronage), and for the American ones it is patronage that ranks top. Maybe these various terms really describe varying phenomena, which could easily be argued for *settai* or *Filz*, but, it is equally likely that very similar phenomena in the countries concerned are cast in different conceptual molds and thus labeled differently. For French and Japanese we find that transaction-focused terms dominate usage in both spheres of core and peripheral word groups, whereas in the U.S. and Germany more generic concepts are playing a greater role in discourse, implying and connoting in many cases systemic features and flaws.

We have thus seen that there indeed exist linguistic borders between advanced industrial societies when it comes to corruption terminology. For possible anti corruption strategies this could mean that analyzing public corruption discourse and identifying key concepts in the lay of the countries is an important preliminary step before entering into and changing this very discourse through public campaigns or otherwise. Where pervasive corruption is talked about in terms of isolated events of single transactions or quid pro quos falling in line with governments' "containment" strategies once a corruption scandal surfaced in its ranks, then it becomes necessary to point to the underlying systemic features that make such behavior thrive.

Notes

1. Heidenheimer shows how this poses problems even to the research communities of different languages. For example, by lacking distinctions among politics, policy, and polity continental languages operate in less differentiated categories with political scientists trying to surmount this problem by adopting the English concepts. ("Politics, Policy and Policy as Concepts in English and Continental Languages," in: The Review of Politics, Vol.. 48, No. 1, pp. 3–30, 1986, Notre Dame, Indiana)
2. Whorf, B. *Language, Thought and Reality*, MIT Press, Cambridge, Mass., 1956. also Saunders, B.A. and van Brakel, J. *Behavior and Brain Science* vol. 20, pp. 167–228 (1997)
3. Though viewing cognition as dependent on language is one position among others. In contradistinction to this view Piaget argues that language is dependent on prior cognitive developments, or, running in a more supportive vein, the behaviorist school (Bloomfield) takes cognition simply for a kind of language on a subvocal speech level.
4. Davidoff, Jules et al. *Nature*, vol. 398, p. 203 (1999). This refutes in part Giovanni Sartori's (Guidelines for Concept Analysis, 1982, pp. 18–20) argument that languages which differ in the distinct naming of colors would not make the person using the more limited vocabulary color blind.
5. Of course, a critical evaluation of dictionary entries is warranted by the fact that they themselves might be of a normative and prescriptive nature rather than just reflecting common usage in a purely descriptive way. Nevertheless, the *Oxford English Dictionary*, the *Trésor de la langue Française*, the *Diccionario de la Lengua Española* of the Real Academia Española, the Japanese *Kokugo Daijiten*, and the *Deutsches Wörterbuch* by the Grimm Brothers subscribe to the method of etymological analysis and they derive definitions mainly through hermeneutic study of textual sources going back many centuries, and thus we assume them to be sufficiently descriptive.
6. Very helpful at identifying and locating legal terminology in France, Spain, and the U.S. was, among others, a study by the Max-Planck Institute for International and Comparative Studies of Penal Law (*Max Planck Institut für vergleichendes und internationales Strafrecht*) in Freiburg: Albin Eser, Michael Überhofen et al., *Korruptionsbekämpfung durch Strafrecht: Ein rechtsvergleichendes Gutachten zu den Bestechungsdelikten*, edition iuscrim, Freiburg, 1997.
7. For the search most terms were truncated so as to include all their variants, i.e., brib . . . yields all entries with bribery, bribing, bribe, bribable, briber, bribee, etc. Those terms that are also used in other contexts than that of corruption were filtered in such a way that the articles where they are used must also contain one

of the unambiguous corruption terms within one paragraph of the more equivocal term, i.e., graft has to be employed alongside corrupt . . . or brib. . . . and no term such as plant, organ or medical must be within that paragraph.

8. Newspapers were selected on account of national reach and coverage as well as their reputation of serious and sound reporting. In size and other "broad sheet" qualities they are sufficiently comparable. A further limiting factor is the extent to which electronic databases are available for each paper. Data for *El Pais* go back only untill April 1996; to provide for comparability the numbers were multiplied by a factor of 1.9 assuming equal levels of usage (thereby overestimating it somewhat) for the years 1993 through 1999. For Japan newspapers are *Asahi Shinbun, Nihon Keizai*, and *Yomiuri Shinbun*, as the Japanese papers are bi-dailies, the number of hits has been reduced by 25%. For the United States they are the *New York Times* (*NYT*) and the *Washington Post* (*Wash*). For Germany they are *Frankfurter Allgemeine Zeitung* (*FAZ*) and *Süddeutsche Zeitung* (*SZ*), for France *Le Monde* and for Spain *El Pais*.

   By meaning and frequency of usage the French *pot-de-vin* crystallized and is taken as the closest equivalent to bribery. As for Spanish, both *cohecho* and *soborno* are reference terms for the *El Pais* bribery bar. The corruption bar for Japanese is made up of both moral and neutral corruption terms *Fuhai* and *Oshoku*.

9. Krauss argues that with their focus on a case-by-case approach to corruption coverage and a rather reluctant attitude towards investigative journalism, the Japanese media do not sufficiently fulfill their function as the "watchdogs" of the political system, but rather have to be considered the "guard dogs" of the ruling elite (Krauss, Ellis: Japan. In: Mughan, Anthony, Gunther, Richard, and Paul Beck (eds.): *Media Technologies and Democracy*, forthcoming)

10. An intra-language comparison based on an analysis of the British quality newspaper the *Independent* brought the same results as the analysis of the above U.S. newspapers, except for much reduced use of concepts such as influence peddling and graft.

11. The graph for *El Pais* is omitted because the data base goes only back to 1996, which we consider insufficient for sketching even short term developments. We track the *NYT* and *Washington Post* back to 1980, *Asahi Shinbun, Nihon Keizai Shinbun*, and *Yomiuri Shinbun* back to 1986, *Le Monde* to 1990, *and FAZ* and *SZ* from 1992 onwards.

Part XIV

INTERNATIONAL EFFORTS TO CONTROL CORRUPTION

Introduction to Part XIV

The role of corruption payments by exporters in foreign countries has achieved unprecedented public attention as the rise of the global economy and the internationalization of markets have replaced the Cold War as issues of relevance to elites and masses around the world. The way this issue reached a high agenda position proceeded gradually over a quarter century. Examining corruption as an international policy problem, Kimberly Elliott emphasizes the role played in this process by the American Foreign Corrupt Practices Act of 1977, which for the first time criminalized bribery beyond the borders of the country passing such legislation.

Payoffs to officials and politicians in these countries often resulted in the winning of contracts. It was for this reason that other countries long declined to follow the American example, and it was only the shift to high level negotiations that led to the extensive use of international agreements to commit governments to monitor the behavior of their companies abroad. Such efforts made political sense, since corruption incidence has been found to be more positively correlated with how far governments intervened in the economy than with the relative size of public sectors.

In the first chapter of this part, Erhard Blankenburg carries us back to Europe to examine how the discovery of much greater levels of public corruption in many Western European countries was triggered by the increased activism of public prosecutors and investigating magistrates. These were national officials, but their activity engendered a network in which techniques of pursuing investigations were exchanged across borders. Whereas previously the activities of these officials had often been muzzled by politicians in national ministries, the groups of younger judges developed political know-how for unfolding their authority.

The study demonstrates how the fight for greater autonomy by public prosecutors was a prerequisite for the development and growth of the *mani puliti* revelations and prosecutions. The example of the Italian magistrates inspired attempts by their colleagues in France and Spain to assert greater independence in initiating actions that could lead to the indictment of public officeholders. Similar probes in Germany also came to have far-reaching consequences, insofar as they led to the revelations that the leading government party of the 1990's had secretly received illegal funding, which in turn forced replacement of that party's leadership.

At the international level, a framework for the analyses of the merging of national and international anti-corruption policies is provided by several key international organizations. Thus the role of the World Bank and the International Monetary Fund in reversing earlier positions of tolerating corruption that eroded the policy aims of their programs in developing countries is discussed in the context of priorities for international corruption strategies. As this strategy came to be implemented by the economic officials of the world's rich and developed countries, a certain specialization of labor emerged among the international agencies. Elliott contrasts the different opportunities that were developed both by worldwide organizations like the World Bank and the World Trade organization, and by regional groups like the Organization of American states.

One particularly important effort to coordinate international corruption standards and strategy is analyzed by Arnold Heidenheimer and Holger Moroff: the anti-bribery convention of the OECD. In the late 1990's this group of industrialized countries undertook to draft an agreement which would put the muscles of governments behind the effort to prevent companies competing for markets in developing countries, from obtaining contracts by paying bribes to officials or politicians. The authors analyze how the most important provisions of the convention came about in internal negotiations, in which initially some key European countries were loath to replicate the resort to criminal prosecution for which the American FCPA had set a precedent. They demonstrate how public pressure helped persuade both governments and business groups to accept commitments to combat international bribery. The convention committed signatory governments to adapt their national legislation, and provision was made for follow-up monitoring about how the rules were implemented.

46

Judicial Anti-Corruption Initiatives:
Latin Europe in a Global Setting

Erhard Blankenburg

The Latin countries of Europe—Italy, France, and Spain—have seen a wave of corruption scandals in the 1990s that deeply affected their political systems. This occurred as traditional ideological party loyalties broke down in the political arena as the need of the polarization of bourgeois parties to defend against the communist/socialist threat disappeared with the end of the Cold War. Hence, election campaigns have consequently become much more dependent on ever-new mobilization of voters, which, in turn, increased needs for party and campaign financing.

- The ideological and moral gap which resulted from these political changes was filled by the moral campaign of a few judges and prosecutors who in Latin countries enjoy a strong position in the criminal investigation process. Using preliminary arrests, search warrants and sometimes spectacular actions against prominent suspects, they managed to stage scandals with high news value. Even though guilty verdicts could not always be attained, investigations themselves became embarrassing enough to stop the careers of suspects and to lead them to look for pre-trial settlements.
- Increasing competition of mass media and their resulting investments in investigatory journalism helped escalate these scandals. In ever-new attempts at creating scandal sensations, the media developed their own moral entrepreneurship, testing innovative fields of moral sensitivity and public outrage.

Thus, scandalization became nationally divergent, using sex in some countries, police and terrorism in others, but corruption issues in all of them.

Finally, the international business community became activated against the trade barriers which corruption networks may constitute. Flourishing free trade in global markets presupposes universalistic and dependable legal rules. Hence, the World Bank has come to support anti-corruption drives of organizations like Transparency International.

Waves of Scandal

If ever there were a need to document the dependence of the attention patterns of political science on the agenda setting of politics, the literature on corruption would be a prime candidate. Scandals come in waves; a single pacesetter is often followed by many others. They announce changes in social and moral moods, often before academic discourses catch up to them. Therefore, it is worthwhile to read them as a moral mirror of the state of political regimes.

In this vein, the scandals around the bribing practice of Lockheed in the early 1970s can be read as an announcement of the economic globalization in our days; at the same time, they initiated global standards for the scandalization of corruption. With the Lockheed scandal rules of competition and fair trade in the weapons industry were claimed internationally, which shattered established financial empires and clientelistic patterns of a number of political regimes. Prince Bernhard of the Netherlands, President Leone in Italy and the Japanese Prime Minister Tanaka were accused of corruption. In Japan and Italy as well as in the Dutch royal house the elites were quite amazed that foreign media attacked them for behavior that in domestic terms had always been taken for normal. It was the American *Newsweek* magazine that used the bribe receivers for the political arena at home and—quite unexpectedly— unleashed scandals in the countries of the bribe payers. Up to then, the domestic arenas of the latter had been free of scandals, simply because their clientelistic practices had remained unchallenged.

History teaches that the definition of what is seen as corrupt changes with the regimes and especially their opposition.[1] It follows that before the analysis of any phenomena of corruption comes the analysis of those who define it as such. That involves more traps than might be expected. It is far too tempting to look only at those cases where the allegation has been successful in leading to scandal. As is the case with any behavior that is morally condemned, the dark field of outrage without consequences and of allegations without success is by far greater than that of full fledged scandalizing. Any theory of corruption, therefore, has to give an answer to the difficult question of non-events: why at what time which allegations of which definition of corruption led to scandals, while others did not?

This might be even harder to determine in observing corruption in our times as we have a hard time stepping out of contemporary moralism and its instrumentalization. Looking at our own experience as a fast-moving train of history might help. Ever since the initial event with its specific constellations of political interests and power plays like that of the Lockheed scandal, we find ourselves in the middle of collective learning processes of ever redefining what, according C.J. Friedrich, are to be considered pathological phenomena of politics.

Contemporary Arenas of Corruption Allegations

In the 1990s waves of corruption scandals shattered politics in Italy, Spain, and France, they swept over the cities of Berlin and Frankfurt, and they accompanied every change of ruler in Russia. Not that corruption had been new to them—it had usually been taken as a normal fact of politics, triggering some cynical gossip at best. It came as a surprise, however, that scandals unexpectedly led to prosecutions and impeachment with a real threat of escalating to changes in established regimes. However, the frenzy of scandals calls for caution: in pinpointing the crises of political systems in Indonesia and Russia, in Japan or Italy, allegations of corruption have played a role in shattering the legitimacy of the regime, but in none of these cases have they been sufficient to cause its breakdown. It takes more serious (mostly economic) calamities before a corrupt system effectively breaks down. In the turbulence of crises, however, the underlying weakness of regimes might be overshadowed by the escalating noise of scandals.

Most scandals start harmlessly. The case of Bettino Craxi in Milan, which triggered the collapse of the entire Italian party system, might serve as an example. It started in 1992 with the arrest of Mario Chiesa on a charge of embezzlement. In his capacity as administrator of a socialist housing corporation and orphanages he had been helping to secure votes for the Socialist Party and had collected financial contributions for the party. He got furious when the powerful party boss Craxi called him "a petty *mariolo*" and subsequently dropped him. Chiesa "sang" involving others in his affair. The investigation was extended to a network of minor Socialist Party officials, charging all of them with corruption. Only then did the party intervene trying to get Chiesa out of prison. Too late. The attempts only brought the bosses and Craxi himself into focus. To make things worse, their counterattack on the press and on the investigating prosecutors failed. The affair escalated into a full fledged scandal. Within a year the socialist party was delegitimized. Craxi fled to Tunisia in fear of criminal prosecution at home. Other parties only briefly enjoyed the breakdown of the Socialists. Once the scandalizing technique was in full swing, their clientelistic practice was accused of corruption, and within three years the entire Italian party system had broken down.

Figure 46.1

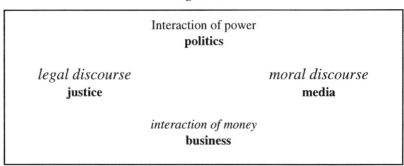

Interaction of power
politics

legal discourse   *moral discourse*
justice   **media**

interaction of money
business

Each of these arenas has changed since the 1970s, and this explains why corruption scandals spread in the 1990s.

It is fascinating to see how, concomitant with the escalation of a scandal, the arenas and the definitions of corruption are changing. It is the sequence of actors who determines the process of calling out "corruption!" which makes the difference. In Italy as well as in France the scandals of the 1990s are triggered by a new generation of investigative prosecutors and judges who went to law schools during the years of student rebellions; in Spain they came into office after the Franco regime. They are more active in using the legal powers which the increased autonomy of magistrates grants them, they dare to interact with the media and thereby some of their protagonists gain influence on political arena. While traditionally prosecution and courts had played a finalizing role legitimizing the scandalization which other players had let loose, the scandals in Latin countries of the 1990s were often initiated by investigatory judges and prosecutors. However, the arena of justice which is commonly used to legitimate moral judgments which are publicly tried out and discussed in the media cannot successfully scandalize without them. The legal process gains momentum by mobilizing the mass media, and these in turn use the courts of justice to form the stage of their scandalizing. While each of these arenas acts according to its own logic, it is only their interaction that can explain the likelihood of scandals and thereby the extent to which political corruption is said to prevail.

- It is often said that the fall of communist regimes in Middle and Eastern Europe ended an era of ideologically defined parties with a firm class basis among their members as well as voters. Their demise, however, has been observed as an ongoing process since the 1970s, in the Latin countries somewhat later than in welfare states of Northwestern Europe. Solid voter blocs gradually became supporters of single-issue movements changing according to the current political situations. Consequently, the place of political parties and trade unions polarized along the lines of class and religious denomination was taken by political campaign organizations, very similar to American party machines. Increasingly, politicians have to collect ever higher financial support for their campaigns. Depending on the number and organization of their sponsors they have to pay back in political currency after the elections, not only by fulfilling programmatic promise, but also by supplying sponsors with influential positions and prestigious office. In the USA such a "spoils system" is part of the traditional set of rules of democracy, which is only emphasized by the flood of regulations by which Washington tries to make "spoils" transparent. The structural problem of party financing of the American campaigns now reaches also European countries that so far had relied on rather stable, often publicly subsidized party financing. Politics has therefore become more prone to corruption, and thereby politicians more likely to become victims of scandalization.

- This scandalization is the job of the media. The increasing competition among an increasing number of media forces them to chase ever new sensations. Trying to win some advantage by exploiting privileged information over a short time, many political magazines and newspapers have built up teams of investigatory journalists, thereby explicitly following the example given by *Newsweek*, the *Washington Post* and *Der Spiegel* in the 1970s. Since the 1980s television companies and independent news agencies followed suit by investing in long term investigation projects, sometimes engaging in merciless *papparazzi* fights for successful scandals. The tone of their revelations qualifies them as moral entrepreneurs who, by often creative imagination, invent novel allegations, thus simply using trial and error to find out which topics might be suitable to arouse a moral panic.

- New to the game among the arenas is the prominent role of prosecutors and courts of justice. Scandals do profit from judicial procedures – especially those of criminal justice with their moralizing symbolism and their legitimation effects. Traditionally, however, they have come into the picture at a later stage when scandalizing had developed its full momentum. It comes as a welcome attribute that judicial procedures take time; even when fighting with obstacles to establish proof, this can be exploited dramatically, so that it might matter little, should they in the end be terminated by dismissal. The procedure is the punishment.

- In the Latin countries of Europe—Italy, France, and Spain—prosecutors and investigative judges have taken the lead in initiating scandals, a judicially active role in politics which was unimagined twenty years ago. First attempts were made in the early 1980s when an instruction judge arrested the owner of a factory for unfair dismissal of an employee and resisting a court decree of re-instatement, with the unions of the magistrates applauding the pioneer decision of a leftist judge. In Milano instruction judges, who had the offices and private homes of politicians searched, caused a public campaign of politicians against the courts of justice, with the latter winning the fight. The spectacular actions did not remain unnoticed by the media; they mobilized hundreds of *papparrazzi*—and even when the magistrates on subsequent press conferences held up the flag of innocent-until-verdict, the scandal had of course been let loose. Investigations turned into moral arenas, and a populist morality of scandal executed punishment

Theoretically, the analysis of arenas can be portrayed as the interplay of relatively closed systems, but for our understanding interactive links are more important than system boundaries. Depending on theoretical language they can be seen as discourses or as interaction systems. The different terms indicate the form in which power is seen to be exercised. Actors can try to step from one arena to the next by either judicializing politics or politicizing the arena of justice, instrumentalizing mass media for legitimation purposes or buying political decisions. Border crossing involves more or less dangers of legitimacy: using the media is easily portrayed in the interest of general transparency, bribing politicians has to be democratically masked while influencing judges can be done only subtly by throwing a long-term net of recruitment preferences, professional allegiances and reputational benefits.

Whatever could be called corruption in this web of border crossings depends on normatively desired constructions. In contrast to the literature of the 1950s and 1960s we would not dare to speak of corruption per se any more, but have to live with the concept as defined by the fabric of interactions and discourses themselves. The question to be answered analytically thus is not how corrupt a regime might actually be, but whether and under which circumstances the attempt to call a regime corrupt can be successful or not.

This leads us back to our original question under which conditions scandals can be successful, that is lead to the breakdown of a corrupt system. Recent cases of breakdown show that scandals can trigger off fundamental crises, but that they have to dwell on more fundamental moral and often economic weakness in order to substantially alter a system.

The high art of scandalous theatre is found in Italy. Since 1991 the system of political actors has substantially changed, but the behavior patterns of clientelism remained. What happened has been incredible in Italian terms: a petty, unusually puritan prosecutor had mobilized the entire Italian media world, the scandal falling in times of a major election campaign which leaves all of the dominant parties shattered, President Cossiga announces with the end of Cold War a new era of party democracy has dawned and resigns prematurely. The institutional change is stabilized by legislating a new voting law which deprives the established parties of their comfortable power bases.

A new cabinet under Berlusconi makes a desperate attempt to put themselves at the head of the campaign against the *mani puliti* by presenting strict anti-corruption regulations, though together with a decree for a general amnesty for allegations of past corruption. The new President Scalfaro, however, refuses to sign the decree, leading to resignation of numerous of cabinet ministers and managers of state enterprises.

The scandalous theatre makes prosecutor Di Pietro a hero of the nation, encouraging numerous imitators throughout the entire apparatus of justice. There was no lack of counterattacks: the prosecutors in Brescia investigated Di Pietro, accusing him of corruption and demonstrating thereby the degree of polarization within the Italian justice system. However, the procedure had to be terminated for lack of proof, and Di Pietro tried temporarily to serve in political office.

Also on the counterside businessmen who stand under suspicion of corruption enter politics. Berlusconi tries in 1994 to reform the party system but has to give up after a short and promising government period under the pressure of investigations and procedures directed at his own business enterprise. He has to face two verdicts for corrupt practices fighting them through possible appeals while a third investigation is already under way. He defends himself with the obvious argument that even a businessman with the most honest intentions could not help but give in to the extortion of civil servants, tax inspectors, and parties to pay the usual clientelistic contributions and outright bribes. According to him it is not the one who bribes but the claims of those who are bribed who have to be blamed for corruption. His media support his allegation that the system of justice is proving a "Marxist coup d'état."

To the foreign observer parliamentary scenes of verbal and sometimes physical polarization throw some doubt on the optimism that the new parties can stand the test of thorough party reform. What remains, however, is a fortification of the political role of the courts of justice, especially of the institution of investigating prosecutors. This continues the strengthening of the autonomy of justice which (even though already promised in the 1948 constitution) had been introduced at first in 1958 with the establishment of a *Consiglio Supremo da la Magistratura*. Even though this highest council has not been able to prevent the polarization of the magistrates in politically polarized camps, it has successfully shielded the recruitment and promotion of judges from direct interventions of the executive branch. According to the constitution the autonomy of the magistrates includes prosecutors who after the amendment of the penal procedural code in 1989 enjoy the same competence which had formerly been the power basis of investigative judges. The autonomy of criminal investigations more than ever forms the backbone of the definition power of the magistrates, enabling them especially to act in politically sensitive criminal investigations.[2]

France, too, has in the 1990s seen a breakdown of political clientelism, even though at first only in the provinces. Justice heroes such as van Ruymbeke, Halpern, and others became well-known names in the news in the country itself and beyond. Since 1992 the satirical magazine *Le Canard Enchainé* regularly took the initiative, since 1994 the most respected daily newspaper *Le Monde* has been listing more than a hundred politicians every year who were arrested and put under remand. Here, too, the investigatory competence is all decisive. The French prosecutorial office still being hierarchically subordinated under the Minister of Justice, politically sensitive procedures, especially in Paris, were often directed to nonsuit. Scandals in the provinces, however, escalated. Since 1997 when the President's office and government entered into open antagonism with the opposing parties, the national taboo on mining each other's hidden scandals has become precarious: the polarization of the co-habitation of a socialist government with a Gaullist presidency might render scandals possible among the political friends of the President (while he himself remains constitutionally immune from criminal investigations).

Judges, however, are independent in France, and as according to Latin tradition the criminal procedural code leaves investigation judges the authority to direct any criminal investigation themselves (which is even emphasized in appeal as competence of *"conseiller"*), these have developed a considerable potential for raising scandal. They can order a warrant of arrest and issue a writ of *capias* which in the case of prominent suspects cannot remain unnoticed by the media. In defense of their judicial autonomy, independent judges and hierarchically dependent prosecutors have been playing subtle games of judicial procedure.[3] In some scandals (such as those around the financial manipulations of the URBA corporation in 1991) investigative judges used their right of personal inspection and of issuing a search explicitly in order to shield their investigations against a hierarchical order of *nolle prosequi* by the General prosecutor. In such cases the support of the media disclosing information which has reached them without open breach of confidence can be a great help in effectuating criminal justice.

Even if they are careful not to actively alert journalists (as are those named above), an implicit amount of instrumentalization of the media cannot be denied. The investigation easily develops into public condemnation. Critics, especially among the suspects involved, therefore raise the allegation of a "coup d'état of the petty judges."[4]

In Spain, Judge Garzon played a similar role as the Italian and French justice heroes. As national investigation judge (*juéz central de instrucción* at the *Audiencia Nacional*) his competence reaches from the war on drugs and other forms of organized crime to fighting terrorism, high treason or crimes against humanity. Scandals under his investigation contributed significantly to delegitimizing the Gonzalez government in 1996,[5] and here, too, the collusion of investigatory judges with the media served inevitably as a means of public ostracism. The ambition of the Spanish judges did not stop at the country's borders: in prosecuting ex-president Pinochet (in the name of a Spanish and some Chilean victims of torture residing in Spain and against the defense of high-ranking political friends) they have been setting benchmarks for the emergence of an international legal order of human rights.

The constellation of politically emancipated magistrates opposing the patterns of traditionally clientelistic politics rests in all three countries on social changes among a new generation of judges and prosecutors, which is rendered even more acute by the growth of the personnel of the courts of justice. The three Latin countries in Europe had been used to historically close ties of the representatives of justice to the political establishment: twenty years ago, Spanish courts were still dominated by fascists, the Italian courts were polarized between Christian Democrats and leftist parties, and the French closely allied with regional and national elites. The delegitimation of these regimes and disestablishment of their elites gave the new generation a chance for establish institutions of autonomy for the magistrates as a third power in the *trias politica*. An expression of their independence is the establishment of "Supreme Councils of the Magistrate" in all three countries which reserve the right of recruitment and promotion of judges and of regulating the conditions of their work.

The politics of scandals, however, has always been the privilege of single judges and prosecutors, who managed to fight political corruption and tax embezzlement by raising the support of popular morals. The General Prosecutor Bernard Bertossa at Geneva invited the leaders of judicial protest in the Latin countries to formulate a common declaration. Their Geneva Appeal of 1995 understands itself as an attempt to form a common front of justice as a moral institution vis-à-vis the systems of illegal finance, corrupt politicians and tax evading business corporations.[6]

Of course, this evoked the countercharge of these petty judges lacking any democratic legitimacy.[7] The more effective judges play a political role, the more they have to account for standards of legitimacy. Therefore, any policy of active scandalization brings the profession into the arena of politics with its specific dependencies. Only tight control of all investigations and strict secrecy of the allegations would prevent the instrumentalization of judicial action outside the public hearings in the courtroom. German General Prosecutors try to do this by exercising tight control of all politically sensitive investigations in their offices. While this reflects, no doubt, a great measure of hierarchical control within the judiciary, it might as well be seen as a strategy of safeguarding professional independence. Being bound by statutory law and jurisprudence to the principle of mandatory accusation (*Legal-itätsprinzip*), the prosecution offices have in the Federal Republic managed to largely keep out of scandalous controversies. A few exemptions confirm rather than falsify the rule.

In the 1980s during the scandal around the tax exemptions granted to the *Flick* concern the disclosure of prosecutorial investigations became the topic of a major counter attack against the scandal-producing magazine *Der Spiegel*. The allegation that the judiciary in Northrhine-Westphalia, resorting under a Minister of the Social-Democratic opposition, had acted clandestinely against the collusion of Christian Democrats and Liberals in the federal government remained without proof, even though it was evident that information from the judicial files had been leaked contributing significantly to the final success of the scandal. The scandals around corruption and fraud in the 1980s led to a major breakdown of the financing system of the governing parties on the one hand, and to the bankruptcy of huge economic enterprises of the trade unions on the other.[8] They demonstrate that there are quite capable scandal entrepreneurs among the German media – even though they can hardly count on being popular heroes among the judiciary.

Activist prosecutors (like StA Schaupensteiner in Frankfurt) who tried to bring local corruption patterns into the public discussion in the early 1990s had a moderate success: as most of the investigations against local corruption had to be terminated because of lack of proof, the publications turned into a self-inflicted scandal blaming the ineffectiveness of prosecution rather than unveiling the corruption pattern itself.[9] That satisfied the goal of the scandal raisers, however: following a truly legalistic policy, they stuck to the inner-directed aim of enlarging their investigative competence which they satisfied in 1997 by an amendment of the penal procedural code.

Under exceptional circumstances, however, strict legalism can also lead to scandals, even in a hierarchically controlled German state such as Bavaria. As early as 1997 the Augsburg prosecutors' office opened investigations against some lobbyists of the German arms industry in relation to big transactions to party officials of the CDU, at the time the governing party under Chancellor Kohl (which, however, is not organized or represented in the State of Bavaria where the sister party CSU traditionally dominates). Augsburg prosecutors were competent for the investigations by the mere fact that the main suspect was registered in their district. Investigations lingered for more than three years, but the very correct and legalistic prosecutor would not close the file, especially as evidence was provided on his request by the prosecution office in Geneva, Switzerland (as we have seen, one of the centers of the European anti-corruption judicial activists). It took until November 1999 for an arrest warrant against the CDU financing official (the by-now retired honorable Dr. Leisler-Kiep) and the suspected lobbyist (Dr. Schreiber) to become public. As the latter was in Toronto, Canada at the time, he could prevent his arrest by staging a claim against extradition to the German judicial authorities. It gave the media free access to his stories that he disclosed piece-by-piece in order to threaten the German establishment and divert them from pursuing his case any further.

It was too late. Within the following four months one disclosure about party financing of the CDU after the other was unveiled by the media, by parliamentary commissions, and by the establishment of Kohl-followers among the CDU politicians themselves. It turned the party of former Chancellor Kohl upside down, destroyed part of his reputation and brought a new generation of party politicians to the fore (see Moroff, chapter 36).

The Global Dynamics of Scandal Industries

It is evident that each of the scandal stories bears its specific historical and cultural characteristics. But even though the collaboration of the system of justice with the media underlies national contingencies, it nevertheless takes part in processes of globalization. The popular, often vulgar morality of corruption scandals is easily instrumentalized for damaging political opponents, sometimes even for disqualifying them from the political arena altogether. Global learning and imitation have spread ever since the Watergate scandal demonstrated the power of media in American politics. All over the world daily newspapers, magazines, and television companies have invested in teams for elaborate investigations. Investigatory journalism has developed an outright scandal industry in the last twenty years.

Imitation of scandalizing can inflate the corruption issue, such as is the case in Russia where corruption charges are regularly used as political weapons. As here post-communism has transformed the late-communist barter system of the informal economy into a system of all pervasive corruption, such charges can be used as an easily mobilized norm trap. The current pattern of political fighting means that corruption charges will be instrumentalized by all political sides as a weapon against any political competitor.

Imitation of the corruption issue is also inflating scandals in the United States. When political scandals are drawn into issues of sex and crime, politico-judicial procedures and media exposure are used for scandals which in the European countries named above would be considered private affairs. A mix of political nomination and judicial proceedings renders the process a quasi-judicial image: if impeachment of the president or of a federal judge is involved, the Congress itself forms a committee that acts as highest judge.

The element of socially organized construction in scandals around corruption leads to the conclusion that the amount of scandals can in no way be taken as an indicator of any real extent of corrupt practices. The opportunity of triggering corruption scandals does not correlate with any measurable degree of corruption but rather with media competition, institutional competence, and power constellations in the interplay of the four arenas sketched above. That, however, does not mean that there are no differences in "corruptness" of regimes. In spite of all difficulties in measuring objectively the extent and form of corruption, there is no denying the observation that there are national (and also sectoral) differences in the degree of effectiveness of corruption networks.

That leads us to the fourth arena in the above scheme: the business world which increasingly tries to protect norms of fair competition and free markets by sanction impediments. They can count on international treaties which are on their side:

- such as the European Community which terminated many a tradition of national and regional protection by enforcing European merger control and the harmonization of tax and subsidy privileges;
- the international GATT regulations which allow national governments to insist on international tenders for national projects, such as did the American government in the case of the Narita airport near Tokyo which before had been a protected park-the pork barrel of high civil servants of the MITI department of commerce and technology.[11]
- or the pressures of the World Bank and IMF which tie their credit facilities in Indonesia and elsewhere to conditions by which they hope to end structural patterns of nepotism.

Notes

1. For a survey of the scientific literature in those days compare the first edition of Arnold Heidenheimer (1970) *Political Corruption*, with his more recent documentation together with Michael Johnston and Victor LeVine (1989) *Political Corruption*, New Brunswick: Transaction Publishers.
2. See for all of the countries here compared Carlo Guarnieri and Patrizia Pederzoli (1996) *La Puissance de Juger*, ch 1 du 2, Paris: Michalon.
3. See Violaine Roussel, "Les magistrats dans les scandals politiques," in: *Revue française de la science politique* 48,2 (1998) 245–273 who bases her analysis on systematic interviews with some twenty judges and prosecutors.
4. Cf. Denis Robert (1996) *La justice ou le chaos*, Paris: Stock
5. The instrumentalization of the press can be by *Il Mundo* as paper of the opposition against Gonzalez using investigatory information for scandalizing, just as *El Pais* is nowadays using them in opposition against Aznar.
6. See the documentation of Denis Robert, loc. cit.
7. The polemic *against* the increasing influence of judges as moral guardians is raised by Eric Zemmour, (1997) *Le Coup d'Etat des Juges*, Paris: Grasset.

8. See my contribution together with Rainer Staudhammer and Heinz Steinert in: Arnold Heidenheimer et al. (1989), *Political Corruption*, New Brunswick: Transaction Publishers. 913–32

9. Cf. Werner Rügener (1997) "Die deutsche Justiz und die Korruption," in: *Kritische Justiz* 30, 458–474

10. Cf. Brian Woodell (1996) *Japan under Construction: Corruption, Politics and Public Works*, Berkeley: University of California Press.

47

Corruption as an International
Policy Problem

Kimberly Ann Elliott

The number, variety, and importance of countries experiencing corruption
scandals highlight both the complexity of this phenomenon and its prominence as a global issue. When it is pervasive and uncontrolled, corruption
thwarts economic development and undermines political legitimacy. Less pervasive variants result in wasted resources, increased inequity in resource
distribution, less political competition, and greater distrust of government.
Creating and exploiting opportunities for bribery at high levels of government also increases the cost of government, distorts the allocation of government spending, and may dangerously lower the quality of infrastructure. Even
relatively petty or routine corruption can rob government of revenues, distort
economic decision making, and impose negative externalities on society, such
as dirtier air and water or unsafe buildings.

The spread of democracy and market-oriented economic reforms should
reduce corruption in the long run. In the short run, however, it has contributed to a "corruption eruption," some of which is real and some of which is
an artifact of increased scrutiny and openness. For example, the opening of
political systems may expose previously hidden corruption and create a perception of increased corruption, or it may allow newly empowered citizens to
voice disgust more openly. But imbalances in the pace and scope of political
and economic reforms may also introduce new forms of corruption or allow

Source: Revised and updated from Kimberly Ann Elliott, "Corruption as an International Policy Problem," in Kimberly Ann Elliott, editor, *Corruption and the Global
Economy* (Washington: Institute for International Economics, 1997).

more virulent forms to take hold. The privatization of state-owned enterprises, for example, is thought to have been distorted by bribes or favoritism
in many countries, Russia being the most prominent example. Real or perceived increases in corruption during times of transition threaten to undermine support for difficult reforms. Whether the political and economic opening that is occurring around the world is sustained may depend on the ability
of governments to do something about corruption.

More broadly, as economic globalization grows, so does the potential
impact of corruption on international flows of goods and capital. International
financial institutions and bilateral assistance agencies are concerned that resources intended to assist development in poor countries be used as efficiently as possible. The countries that were hit by the Asian financial crisis
quickly pledged to increase transparency and tackle corruption in order to
reassure international financial markets and restore inward capital flows. Less
developed countries are concerned that the perceptions of corruption will
cause them to lag even further behind as private capital increasingly displaces
official finance in many emerging markets . . .

Domestic Economic Consequences of Corruption

> *"[S]ure, there's some graft, but there's just
> enough to make the wheels turn without squeak-
> ing."* (Willie Stark, All the King's Men *(Robert
> Penn Warren)*

> *"Corruption leads to loss of much needed rev-
> enue and human talent for development, dis-
> torts priorities for public policy, and shifts
> scarce resources away from the public inter-
> est. . . . [P]olitical instability, corruption, and
> underdevelopment are mutually reinforcing."*
> (Stephen Ouma, Corruption in Public Policy and
> Its Impact on Development

While positive effects in some situations have been claimed for corruption,
most scholars agree with Ouma that widespread corruption is detrimental to
economic and political development. Even when relatively contained, corruption can cause inefficiency in the allocation of resources, greater inequities in
income distribution, and the loss of savings and investment due to the flight
abroad of proceeds from bribes (see Rose-Ackerman 1997). The consequences
in a given situation depend, among other things, on whether bribes are prof-
fered by the private sector or extorted by public officials, how prevalent
corruption is, and the degree of uncertainty associated with it.

The distinction between bribes that are voluntarily offered or extorted is similar to the distinction in Shleifer and Vishny (1993, 601–02) between corruption that involves theft and that which does not. In the latter case, the official turns over the full cost of the publicly-provided good or service (for example, a license fee) to government coffers but may be able to extract a bribe if he is in a position to withhold the service and, in effect, create an artificial shortage. If other officials can provide the service and are honest, competition among suppliers of public services will reduce the probability that bribes will be extorted. Among those most vulnerable to extorted bribes are firms with high fixed costs and without alternative production locations, producers or brokers of perishable goods, or uneducated taxpayers or other constituents in need of government services. Firms working under contracts with fixed deadlines and penalties for delays will also be vulnerable to bribe demands.

In the case of corruption with theft, the official accepts a bribe in exchange for lowering or waiving the price of the good (for example, a tax bill), thus depriving the government of its due. As Shleifer and Vishny note, "Corruption with theft is obviously more attractive to the buyers" and competition among buyers in this type of case will tend to increase the level of corruption (1993, 602; see also Klitgaard 1988, 87). The fact that the theft occurs also suggests that transparency and accountability in public service are inadequate, again making it more likely that corruption will be widespread.

The effects of corruption also depend on whether it is of the petty or grand variety (see table 47.1). Petty corruption generally refers to the routine government transactions typically overseen by middle and lower-level bureaucrats, such as tax payments, allocation of permits, and regulatory enforcement. At higher levels of the bureaucracy and among the political leadership, officials and politicians will tend to control more valuable assets or opportunities and have more discretion in their allocation. At this level, decisions are made regarding major procurements (including airplanes, military equipment, power-generating equipment, and telecommunications infrastructure) and major investment projects (including roads, irrigation projects, and dams). The greater the concentration of political power (i.e., the less accountable politicians and high-level officials are) the greater will be the opportunities to engage in corrupt behavior.

A cross-country study of administrative corruption in Korea, Malaysia, Nepal, the Philippines, Singapore, Thailand, and Hong Kong analyzes the prevalent forms and incidence of corruption in three government functions: taxation, expenditure, and regulation (Alfiler 1986) (see table 47.2 for a summary of the opportunities for and consequences of corruption). The study found that bribery was the most common form of corruption (compared to nepotism and "internal" corruption, basically defined as the theft of government property). As might be expected, it found that reduction of taxes owed was the primary corrupt objective in customs and other revenue collection

Table 47.1

Degree of distortion[a]	Voluntary bribes[b]	Extorted bribes
Petty	Paying to expedite a building permit for which seeker is eligible (speed money).	A licensing officer holds up building permit until a bribe is paid.
	Paying a building inspector to overlook a missing permit although the building is in compliance with all regulations (grease).	The building inspector threatens to levy a fine for not having a permit that builder is unaware is needed, unless a bribe is paid.
	Paying to get offspring who is on waiting list admitted to university.	The tax collector threatens to audit a company unless a bribe is paid.
	Paying the tax collector to lower your assessment and the customs officer to allow you to import steel beams duty-free.	When building is near completion, a high-level construction ministry official threatens to have it condemned as unsafe unless a large bribe is paid.
	Paying a building inspector to overlook deficiencies in building design or construction.	
	Paying a minister in exchange for the award of a contract to build a new hospital despite contractor's lack of experience and higher bid than competitors'.	
Grand		

a. These examples are intended to be illustrative. Whether a particular situation involves petty or grand corruption depends not just on the type of transaction but also on the size of the bribe and the level of the public official, which are likely to be positively correlated.

b. Voluntary does not necessarily mean enthusiastically, and, in practice, there may be a fine line between bribes offered and extorted.

agencies. With respect to government spending, the study found that over-pricing, substandard quality, and the theft of government property for sale on the black market were the most common consequences of corruption. In the regulatory area, most of the cases look at police departments, where the most common outcome of corruption was protection of illegal vice, such as prostitution and gambling.

As Scott (1972, 66) notes, "the pettiness of corruption refers only to the size of each transaction and not to its total impact on government income or policy." Indeed, widespread evasion of taxes, including customs duties, may seriously detract from the ability of the government to provide services. It is also likely to exacerbate the problem of low public sector wages and further spread the corruption virus. Finally, if the government is unable or unwilling

Table 47.2

Opportunities for corruption	
Vying for government benefits	Paying to avoid costs
Government procurement contracts, ranging from routine purchases of supplies to large infrastructure projects	Regulations
Purchases from or sales to state-owned enterprises	Taxes
Sales of state-owned enterprises (privatization)	Prosecution (for illegal activities such as prostitution or gambling)
Access to government-controlled or regulated supplies of goods (raw materials, luxury goods, etc.), credit, foreign exchange, import and export licenses, other licenses or permits	Delays, red tape
	Paying for official positions
Access to government services or subsidies, such as scholarships, health care, or subsidized housing	

Consequences of corruption	
Inefficiencies	Inequities
Misallocation of government resources due to award of contracts to less efficient bidders	Redistribution of assets from public sector to corrupt individuals
Distortions in allocation of government expenditure	Redistribution from relatively poorer to relatively wealthier individuals who are more likely to have access to government officials
Distortions in allocation of privatized enterprises	Undermining of political legitimacy
Inappropriate or poor quality infrastructure	
Undersupply of public goods such as clean air or water	
Incentives to create additional regulations or delays in order to collect bribes	
Lost national savings and lowered investment due to flight abroad of bribe "capital"	

Sources: Rose-Ackerman (1997), Johnston (1997), and Mauro (1997).

to reduce expenditures, revenue shortfalls due to widespread corruption could also have severe macroeconomic consequences.

Other potential consequences of petty corruption include

* negative externalities from unenforced regulations (environmental degradation, threats to worker or consumer health and safety),
* reduced government productivity when hiring is based on favoritism rather than merit,
* shortages of subsidized necessities (due to theft and smuggling), and
* misallocation of talent from productive to nonproductive rent-seeking activities.[1]

Of course, similar illicit activities can occur at higher levels of bureaucracy and the more that higher level officials condone or engage in such behavior themselves, the more pervasive corruption and its effects are likely to become.

Certain decisions, such as those concerning government procurement and infrastructure, can only be made at higher levels of government. Where such projects respond to genuine social needs, corruption may increase their costs, lower the quality, or lead to inappropriate choices of technology. Worse are "white elephant" projects that enrich officials and suppliers but serve little public purpose. While much of the corruption that comes to light involves white elephant projects or military procurement, data limitations make it difficult to move beyond anecdotal evidence and demonstrate that in general more corrupt countries spend relatively more on these types of projects.

Even though greater amounts of money will typically be required when individual transactions take place at the higher political and administrative levels, it is not clear that the aggregate effects of grand corruption are necessarily greater than those of petty corruption. The harassment element of extortionary petty corruption might be expected to have a broader negative effect on private economic behavior than would grand corruption, which is likely to be limited to fewer sectors. Rampant petty corruption may also be more politically corrosive over time because it directly affects more people on a regular basis.[2] In sum, although a little bit of high-level corruption may be more damaging to an economy than a little bit of low-level malfeasance, the cumulative effects of pervasive petty corruption can still be quite harmful.

Distortion of International Trade and Investment

The most serious consequences of corruption are those described above that afflict the countries where the corruption occurs. With increasing international economic integration, however, distortions to trade and investment flows have attracted growing attention. Most public statements about the evils of corruption by American policymakers and officials of international economic organizations include a reference to distortion of international competition. Former U.S. Trade Representative and Commerce Secretary Michael Kantor, for example, called corruption "a virus threatening the health of the international trading system" (Kantor 1996b).

For over two decades, the United States has had a particular interest in the impact of bribery on international transactions because of the belief that the Foreign Corrupt Practices Act (FCPA) presents a significant competitive disadvantage for U.S. firms competing with multinational firms from countries that do not penalize and may even implicitly encourage the use of bribes to win contracts overseas. These concerns have been ameliorated by the entry into force of the OECD Convention on Combating Bribery of Foreign Public Officials in International Business Transactions and an accompanying recommendation that countries prohibit the deduction of bribes as a business expense for tax purposes. The convention went into force only in February 1999 and whether implementation will be sufficiently vigorous to seriously dent the problem remains to be seen. The following sections examine the potential effects of corruption on trade and analyze the potential impact of the FCPA on U.S. multinationals.

Corruption as an Impediment to International Trade

While customs agencies are notorious for corruption in many countries, the net impact on trade is not always obvious. Impediments to trade will be increased if corruption is out of control, too costly, or primarily in the form of extortion. Impediments might be lowered, however, if corruption is a second-best response to high existing trade barriers or other distortions.[3] For example, a customs official who threatens to allow a shipment of bananas to rot on the dock unless a bribe is paid could reduce the level of imports if the importer is unable or unwilling to pay. But imagine an alternative scenario: suppose the importer of the bananas offers a bribe if the customs official will lower the duty owed. In that case, rather than reducing trade, corruption might actually increase it (while lowering public revenues). Since anecdotal evidence suggests that tax evasion is perhaps the most common motive for bribery, it seems plausible that corruption might increase trade at the margin (Klitgaard 1988; Alfiler 1986). In general, one would expect that, the more restricted trade is, the more likely it is that an *increase* in trade would result from corruption among customs officials.[4]

Either scenario could cause problems for firms prevented from offering bribes, whether from moral sensitivity or by the law. In the extortion case, exporters of similar highly perishable products would be most vulnerable, those selling specialized and technologically sophisticated products less so. Some big-ticket items, such as aircraft, are sectors with economies of scale and imperfect competition so that corruption may redistribute economic rents but have little effect on global welfare (Rodrik 1997). Finally, it is also possible that the effects of illicit payments that result in new trade barriers or illegal export subsidies can be addressed using existing rules.

In developing an appropriate international policy response, the impact on the policy of the countries involved also matters. Does corruption influence the formulation of policy and lead to discrimination against imports or foreign investment? Or does it subvert the government's declared policy and international commitments? In the first case, the injured WTO member may be able to use existing rules to challenge the discriminatory policy directly. For example, several U.S. steel companies recently asked the Clinton administration to file a complaint with the WTO claiming that Korean government subsidies to Hanbo Steel, allegedly influenced by bribes to government officials, had distorted world steel markets (*Journal of Commerce,* 21 February 1997, 3A). In other cases where corruption subverts government policy and particularly where it deprives the government of customs revenue, the government has an incentive to correct the problem and the problem may reflect inadequate government capacity rather than intent to discriminate. In that case, a trade remedy might not be helpful.

If corruption affects primarily the allocation of trade flows and not the volume and if any resulting discrimination among suppliers is due primarily to differences in treatment of transnational bribery among exporting countries, it might be more appropriate to analyze the problem as a potential export subsidy. As with other export subsidies, which are generally prohibited by the WTO, no exporter gains relative to another if equivalent subsidies (bribes) are available to all. The prevention of subsidy wars is in fact the major incentive for countries to negotiate agreements to constrain themselves. In this case, however, since the "subsidies" are off-budget, many governments have been less than eager to act and have done so only under intense pressure from the United States, whose exporters are unilaterally constrained by the FCPA.

The FCPA as a U.S. Export Disincentive

Following the corruption scandals of the 1970s involving illicit payments by U.S. multinational corporations to both U.S. and foreign politicians, there was some international discussion of bribery in the context of codes of conduct for multinational investors. However, these discussions did not result in much concrete action (Pieth 1997, and Heimann 1997). Only in the United States did the Congress pass legislation, signed into law by President Jimmy Carter in 1977, making it illegal for U.S. firms to pay bribes to foreign government officials.

From the beginning, some U.S. firms complained that the unilateral nature of the FCPA placed them at a competitive disadvantage relative to international firms based in other countries. In the 1988 Omnibus Trade and Competitiveness Act, Congress amended the FCPA with the objective of reducing the burden of compliance. In that spirit, Congress also added a provision calling on the president to negotiate an agreement with other OECD members addressing transnational bribery. Little action was taken on the latter provision until President Bill Clinton took office in 1993 (Larson 1997). The attention given to the issue by the Clinton administration raises two questions: why did international corruption suddenly appear so high on the list of U.S. trade priorities? And, how significant a competitive disadvantage has the FCPA been?

Why now? Not long after the Clinton administration entered office, Commerce Secretary Ron Brown launched a major export advocacy effort that eventually evolved into the "Big Emerging Markets" (BEM) strategy. For 1996, the Commerce Department identified Argentina, Brazil, Mexico, the Association of Southeast Asian Nations (Singapore, Indonesia, Thailand, Malaysia, the Philippines, Brunei, and Vietnam), the "Chinese Economic Area" (China, Hong Kong, and Taiwan), India, South Korea, Poland, Turkey, and South Africa as BEMs (U.S. Department of Commerce 1995). Comparing this list to the Transparency International Corruption Perceptions Index for 1996, one finds that the three largest BEMs, China, India, and Indonesia, along with the Philippines, were among the most corrupt of the 54 countries in the TI ranking. The TI rankings for Argentina, Brazil, Mexico, Thailand, and Turkey were also below the average score for the sample as a whole. The rankings for Taiwan and Korea were at about average while Malaysia, Poland, and South Africa received scores slightly above the average.[5]

The administration also identified "big emerging sectors," including energy, health care, information, and transportation, which are also sectors likely to have a large degree of state ownership or regulation in many countries. During an investigation by the U.S. Securities and Exchange Commission (SEC) of illicit payments in the 1970s, firms in several of these same sectors were reported to have made questionable payments to foreign public officials (Jacoby, Nehemkis, and Eells 1977, 141). (Although the FCPA had not yet been passed and these payments were not illegal under U.S. law, the SEC was investigating whether false reporting of the payments could have misled investors or deprived them of pertinent information.) Of the 63 health care, drug, or cosmetics firms responding to SEC investigators, 29 reported making "questionable payments." In addition, 31 percent of aerospace and 22.5 percent of air transport firms reported making such payments, while between 15 and 20 percent of the firms responding in office equipment, machinery, and electronics and electrical equipment admitted to making such payments. (Industry definitions can be found in Standard & Poor's "Classification of Industries" published at that time.) A cursory review of press articles over the past two years reveals that the big emerging sectors, and the military equipment sector, are also where corruption has been most often exposed.

But present levels of exports to these countries and in these sectors do not tell the whole story. These markets were selected not just because they were big but also because they were among the most rapidly growing. The size and rapid growth of the BEMs mean that their infrastructure needs are enormous. The U.S. Commerce Department has estimated that new infrastructure projects in Asia alone may be worth over $1 trillion over the next decade, with perhaps another $500 billion in such projects being launched in Latin America (U.S. Department of Commerce 1995, 22). With sluggish growth in much of the rest of the world, competition for exports to and investment in the BEMs was expected to be intense. This was why Secretary Brown in a 1995 report on the topic suggested that the U.S. and its major allies and competitors should consider developing

> [A] framework for keeping competition in which governments themselves participate within bounds. That would mean taking a look together at all the tools which are being used, and trying to develop some rules of the game in terms of financing (including foreign aid), illicit payments and other kinds of arrangements which are being used to win deals. (U.S. Department of Commerce 1995, 45)

How important a competitive factor is the FCPA? Although the growing importance of the BEMs in world markets has raised the profile of corruption as a potential distortion to international trade and investment, the magnitude of the impact on U.S. exports remains uncertain. For the FCPA to have an important overall effect on U.S. sales abroad, at least the following three things would have to be true: all or most of the large markets in which U.S. firms compete would have to be corrupt; evasion strategies would have to be difficult or nonexistent; and there would be no other offsetting factors.

Because of the nature of bribery, it is obviously difficult to estimate the overall magnitude of the cost of corruption. The U.S. Department of Commerce has estimated that bribes may have contributed to U.S. firms losing some $11 billion in contracts over the period from early 1994 to late 1996 (Trade Promotion Coordinating Committee 1996, 12). The department regards this as a low estimate, because this figure includes only the contracts that have come to light and because it excludes potential follow-on sales (for example, of replacement parts). There has been some confusion over the magnitude of these estimates, however, and it is difficult to evaluate their validity because the analysis on which they are based remains classified (see box 47.1).

Moreover, in evaluating the effects on U.S. exporters it is also important to keep in mind the *net* effects. As long as there are some situations where it is not necessary to bribe (because government officials are honest or other safeguards are in place) it is possible that bribes shift sources and destinations

Box 47.1
$45 Billion or $11 Billion (More or Less)?

According to congressional testimony by then-Secretary of Commerce Ron Brown in October 1995:

Since the OECD approved recommendations to limit illicit payments in [April] 1994, the U.S. Government has learned of almost 100 cases of foreign firms using bribery to undercut U.S. firms' efforts to win international contracts worth about $45 billion (Department of Commerce press release, October 12, 1995).

This testimony and a later speech by then-U.S. Trade Representative Michael Kantor that also cited the $45 billion figure received extensive press coverage (Kantor 1996a). The *Wall Street Journal*, for example, reported that "Mr. Kantor complained that U.S. companies...are losing some $45 billion annually to foreign companies that use bribes to win business deals" (7 March 1996, A2; on the same date, see also *Journal of Commerce*, 2A, and *Financial Times*, 5). Kantor repeated the figure in a July speech and then added, "Already this year we have learned of about $20 billion in additional lost contracts" (Kantor 1996b).[1]

Examination of the *National Export Strategy* report that contained the $45 billion estimate, however, shows that this is not the value of foreign contracts lost by U.S. firms. Rather, it is the value of the "nearly ninety cases" in which foreign firms are alleged to have offered bribes while in competition with U.S. firms for contracts (Trade Promotion Coordinating Committee 1995, 35). The report continues:

Of these ninety cases, the U.S. firms have already lost more than twenty contracts, worth almost $7 billion, *at least in part* because of the bribes paid by their competitors [emphasis added].

With regard to the sixty or so other contracts, worth $38 billion, apparently the reason the contract was lost is unknown or contract negotiations have not concluded. The 1996 *National Export Strategy* report alleged there were 139 contracts worth $64 billion where bribes were offered, with estimated U.S. losses in 36 cases worth $11 billion. The TPCC regards this estimate as low because "these figures represent only those cases which have come to our attention" (1996, 113).

Unfortunately, the *Foreign Competitive Practices Report* remains classified.[2] It is extremely difficult to judge the validity of any of these estimates without access to the underlying analysis or at least some idea of the methodology. Further complicating the issue, a preliminary (and apparently unpublished) Commerce Department summary of the review of bribery cases says that about half of them involved defense contracts. Given the political nature of most large sales of military equipment, it is even more difficult to determine the relative impact of bribes vis-à-vis other factors in these sales. It is also unlikely countries would ever agree to subject military sales to open, competitive bidding or that defense contracts will ever be decided on purely, or even primarily, economic grounds.

The raw figures must be put in context. Both the 1995 and 1996 reports conclude that firms offering bribes typically win 80 percent of contracts. But that figure is difficult to assess without knowledge of the percentage of contracts won by U.S. or other firms when no bribes were offered. To provide some sort of baseline, the U.S. share of total world exports in 1994 was about 12 percent; its shares of world exports of power-generating machinery and equipment (SITC 71) and aircraft and parts (SITC 792), two sectors thought to be plagued by corruption, were 21 percent and 40 percent, respectively (Statistics Canada 1996). The TPCC reports also emphasize U.S. government actions to overcome these problems: the 1996 report claims that U.S. government advocacy efforts over the previous two plus years had helped U.S. firms win 230 contracts worth $40 billion (88).

Notes

1. Kantor succeeded Brown as Secretary of Commerce following Brown's death on 3 April 1996.
2. According to the *Wall Street Journal* (12 October 1995, A3) the report was compiled with the help of U.S. intelligence agencies and contained "hundreds of examples of bribery and legitimate, often government-assisted, export promotion."

around without substantially changing global market shares. In a study of self-imposed export disincentives, Richardson (1993, 131) concluded that "Across-the-board regulatory burdens, such as procedures mandated for all businesses by the FCPA, seemed generally unimportant."[6]

Another widely cited study of the effects of the FCPA on U.S. foreign direct investment and exports of aircraft did find a statistically significant negative impact on these variables following passage of that law in 1977 (Hines 1996). But the analysis is of the period immediately following passage of the original FCPA so it would not capture offsetting effects following the 1988 amendments or other possible adaptations by American firms (see below). Using a more recent and possibly more reliable data set, Wei (1997) finds that corruption on average has a depressing effect on foreign direct investment. But he finds no differential impact on U.S. investors. Multinational firms in other countries apparently are just as cautious as are U.S. investors when it comes to risking their capital in nations where corruption is widespread.

Even if past competitive effects have been limited, however, some of the fastest-growing markets and most lucrative project opportunities are in emerging markets, many of which have also been judged relatively corrupt. Thus, there will now be more demand for corruption-prone types of exports and contracts in more corrupt countries. A second source of growing concern for U.S. exporters might be in the nature of the financing available for these projects. The World Bank and other official financial institutions, international and domestic, usually require international competitive bidding and the right to review contract awards before disbursing funds. A decade ago, the ratio of official development finance to foreign private capital flows for developing countries was 1.7 ($36.7 billion versus $21.4 billion). In 1995, that ratio had roughly reversed, with private capital flows exceeding official flows by 60 percent ($78.7 billion private versus $48.6 percent official). With a greater number of large projects being financed by the private sector, it is possible that the bidding process could become less transparent and more vulnerable to corruption (World Bank 1996, 35).[7]

Just the same, the prohibition against bribing foreign officials may not be as great a handicap for U.S. firms as has been claimed. Some firms have used the FCPA as a shield to protect themselves from extortion by corrupt foreign officials. George David, president and CEO of United Technologies Corporation, indicated at a meeting on ethics in 1993 that following a crackdown on illicit payments by a subsidiary in Mexico, not only were market share and profitability maintained, but the firm was "able to shorten [its] long, long overdue collection period on government receivables in one of the more notorious problem countries" (David 1994, 8). Just as a reputation for honesty may serve as a shield, a reputation for being willing to pay bribes may open one's firms to ceaseless demands for more. Some China observers note that whereas honest operations may be more challenging and time-consuming, they may avoid trouble in the long run (Ettore 1994, 21; see also Givant 1994). In another example, Colgate-Palmolive was reported to have used the FCPA as a shield to avoid paying bribes or being forced to engage in "nepotistic employment" practices while building a $20 million operation in Guangdong Province in 1992 (Pines 1994, 210–11).

Also, where bribes are an additional operating cost (as opposed to being offered to win a contract or other business), firms that can avoid internal corruption among employees and external corruption among suppliers, distributors, customers, and regulators should be relatively more cost efficient and competitive. Furthermore, if corruption is as common as alleged, the losers must be paying bribes for nothing, further raising costs. Pines (1994, 211–12) notes that, because they lack access to reliable information asymmetries, some firms may overpay or pay someone who fraudulently claims to have the "right connections." The perception that contracts can only be won through bribery could also result in reduced innovation and laziness on the part of some firms. Pitman and Sanford (1994, 18–19) argue that the FCPA could have offsetting benefits because it "mandates that [firms] find other, more effective methods to 'get the job done' when they previously may have thought bribery was their only option."

At the other end of the spectrum, some companies may decide to ignore the FCPA and risk getting caught. Lockheed Corporation (now Lockheed Martin Corp.), whose bribery of Japanese politicians in the 1970s brought down a government and contributed to the passage of the FCPA, pleaded guilty in 1995 to bribing an Egyptian official to win an aircraft supply contract (*Wall Street Journal*, 29 September 1995, 1). Two other large U.S. multinationals were under investigation in 1996–97 for possible violations of the FCPA, though formal charges were not brought (*National Journal*, 20 April 1996, 871). In March 1997, following settlement of another FCPA case with Triton Energy over questionable payments by its Indonesian subsidiary, the head of enforcement for the Securities and Exchange Commission, William McLucas, expressed concern that bribery of foreign officials might be becoming a significant problem for the first time since the FCPA was passed (*Bloomberg News*, 5 March 1997).

But there are also other, less risky methods of evasion. Among other changes, the amendments to the FCPA in the Omnibus Trade and Competitiveness Act of 1988 explicitly defined allowable facilitating payments for "routine governmental" services (licenses, permits, paper processing, provision of police protection, other government services) and created two affirmative defenses: that the payment is legal in the country where it occurs; or that the payment was for "reasonable and bona fide expenditure," such as travel or lodging for training or other trips abroad for government officials. According to a source at the U.S.-China Business Council, "You'd think

Disney World was a training site" (*Wall Street Journal,* 29 September 1995, 1; see also *New York Times,* 12 April 1996, A10). Wei (1997, 5n) also reports that conversations with Chinese businessmen and officials suggest more subtle, possibly legal forms of influence, such as study trips for officials to tour a foreign country, are more commonplace than outright bribes.

Finally, the aggressive advocacy and export promotion efforts of the Clinton administration provided at least partial and, perhaps temporary, offsets for any hypothetical disadvantage posed by the FCPA.[8] For example, although the Middle East is widely thought to be one of the most corrupt regions in the world and aircraft one of the sectors most vulnerable to distortion by bribery, President Clinton's personal intervention in 1995 helped to clinch the sale to Saudi Arabia of $6 billion in commercial aircraft for Boeing and McDonnell Douglas. At the time, presidential spokesman Michael McCurry was quoted as saying that the President was not at all hesitant in using his influence to "go to bat for American companies" (*International Trade Reporter,* 1 November 1995, 1824; *Wall Street Journal,* 18 December 1995, 1). The 1996 national export strategy report claimed that U.S. government advocacy efforts had helped U.S. businesses to make deals worth over $40 billion, nearly four times more than the value of contracts allegedly lost to bribery (Trade Promotion Coordinating Committee 1996, 89).

Whatever the current or anticipated impact, the Clinton administration has stepped up efforts to get other countries, particularly OECD member states, to take action against transnational bribery. In 1996, the Department of Commerce revised its "advocacy guidelines" to buttress the FCPA and to ensure that U.S.-based firms and especially subsidiaries of foreign-owned multinationals would not benefit from U.S. export promotion programs if they or any part of their worldwide corporate family engaged in bribery. The new requirements state that for U.S.-based subsidiaries or affiliates of foreign multinationals to qualify for U.S. government support when bidding on an international contract, the parent corporation must actively enforce a policy prohibiting the bribery of foreign officials (Trade Policy Coordinating Committee [TPCC] 1996, 119–122).[9] The Export-Import Bank (Exim Bank) and the Overseas Private Insurance Corporation (OPIC) also increased their reporting requirements for beneficiaries of their programs. Since U.S. subsidiaries of foreign-owned companies are already covered by the FCPA, the major aim of the changes in the advocacy guidelines is to put pressure on their overseas parent corporations to adopt stronger policies against bribery.

Some American policymakers have advocated even stronger unilateral action. One proposal, going beyond the augmentation of reporting requirements, would have explicitly conditioned eligibility for assistance from the Eximbank or OPIC on the adoption and enforcement of an antibribery policy by the corporate parent. That position was rejected as overly intrusive in the affairs of recipient countries who would also be party to the contract. Potentially more controversial were the oft-voiced hints dropped by Michael Kantor when he was Secretary of Commerce, and earlier as U.S. Trade Representative, that transnational bribery should be defined as an unfair foreign trade practice constituting grounds for retaliatory sanctions under section 301 of U.S. trade law (see for example, Kantor 1996a).

Despite all the attention, however, there is still little hard evidence that the FCPA has a major negative impact on overall U.S. exports. Without a doubt the impact on particular sectors is significant, and given the potential for more than $1.5 trillion in infrastructure projects in Asia and Latin America over the next decade, U.S. firms in these sectors have reason to be concerned about possible distortions from bribery. With globalization and democratization making corruption less and less acceptable around the world, however, U.S. firms that have been forced by the FCPA to become more innovative and aggressive should be well-placed to reap the benefits. The FCPA could also now be a competitive advantage in some newly democratizing countries where politicians or public officials concerned about negative publicity might prefer a U.S. firm because they can more credibly claim that no corruption was involved.

Notes

1. For an analysis of the effects of rent-seeking opportunities on the allocation of talent, and the follow-on effects on growth, see Murphy, Shleifer, and Vishny (1993).
2. I thank Michael Johnston for emphasizing this point. Also see Klitgaard (1988, 47–49).
3. It should be kept in mind that trade is a means to the end of improved economic welfare and not an end in itself. Thus, corruption that gets around trade barriers and increases import volumes is not necessarily welfare-enhancing.
4. See Wei (1997) for a discussion of the black market and the smuggling of cigarettes and other products into China.
5. The index and information on the methodology behind it can be found at http://www.transparency.org
6. This conclusion was based on an analysis of the impact of the regulatory costs of compliance with the FCPA, i.e., of the additional accounting and auditing costs of the disclosure requirements, and not the potential effects on competitiveness of being restrained from bribing in markets where competitors in fact do. Richardson's broader finding of little impact was based on the source-shifting behavior described above and on the fact that no firm interviewed by him mentioned the inability to bribe as a competitive disadvantage.
7. While the flows of private capital to emerging markets diminished sharply in the midst of the financial crisis in 1997, they were already starting to turn around in some countries in 1998 and 1999 as international investors searched for bargains.
8. Some American businessmen and government officials argue that the United States lags behind other countries in these other forms of export promotion, so there is little or no counterweight to the disadvantage posed by the FCPA. See the Trade Promotion Coordinating Committee's report on *National Export Strategy* (1996).

9. According to the TPCC report, government support in this context "can take the form of letters, representations, or other interventions by U.S. officials" (1996, 119).

References

Alfiler, Ma. Concepcion P. 1986. "The Process of Bureaucratic Corruption in Asia: Emerging Patterns." In *Bureaucratic Corruption in Asia: Causes, Consequences, and Control,* edited by Ledivina V. Cariño. Quezon City: JMC Press, Inc. for College of Public Administration, University of the Philippines, Manila.

Bhagwati, Jagdish. 1982. "Directly Unproductive, Profit Seeking (DUP) Activities." *Journal of Political Economy* 90, no. 5 (March): 142–47.

Congressional Budget Office. 1993. *Resolving the Thrift Crisis.* Washington: Congress of the United States, April.

Congressional Budget Office. 1992. *The Economic Effects of the Savings & Loan Crisis.* Washington: Congress of the United States, January.

David, George. 1994. "Notable and Quotable." *Corporate Crime Reporter* (November 21): 8–9.

Ettore, Barbara. 1994. "Why Overseas Bribery Won't Last." *Management Review,* 83, no. 6 (June): 20–25.

Heimann, Fritz 1997. "Combatting International Corruption: The Role of the Business Community." In *Corruption and the Global Economy,* edited by Kimberly Ann Elliott. Washington: Institute for International Economics.

Givant, Norman. 1994. "The Sword that Shields." *The China Business Review* (May-June): 29–31.

Hines, James. 1996. "Forbidden Payment: Foreign Bribery and American Business after 1977." NBER Working Paper No. 5266. Cambridge: National Bureau of Economic Research.

Jacoby, Neil, Peter Nehemkis, and Richard Eells. 1977. *Bribery and Extortion in World Business.* New York: MacMillan.

Johnston, Michael. 1997. Public Officials, Private Interests, and Sustainable Democracy: When Politics and Corruption Meet." In *Corruption and the Global Economy,* edited by Kimberly Ann Elliott. Washington: Institute for International Economics.

Kantor, Michael. 1996a. "Remarks Prepared for Delivery before the Emergency Committee for American Trade." Office of the U.S. Trade Representative, Washington, March 6.

Kantor, Michael. 1996b. "Remarks of Secretary of Commerce Michael Kantor before the Detroit Economic Club." U.S. Department of Commerce, July 25.

Klitgaard, Robert. 1988. *Controlling Corruption.* Berkeley: University of California Press.

Krueger, Anne O. 1974. "The Political Economy of the Rent-Seeking Society." *American Economic Review* 64, no. 3 (June): 291–303.

Larson, Alan. 1997. "U.S. Policy on Corruption." In *Corruption and the Global Economy,* edited by Kimberly Ann Elliott. Washington: Institute for International Economics.

Mauro, Paolo. 1997. "The Effects of Corruption on Growth, Investment, and Government Expenditure: A Cross-Country Analysis." In *Corruption and the Global Economy,* edited by Kimberly Ann Elliott. Washington: Institute for International Economics.

Murphy, Kevin M., Andrei Shleifer, and Robert W. Vishny. 1993. "Why is Rent-Seking so Costly to Growth?" *American Economic Review,* vol. 83: 409–14.

Ouma, Stephen. 1991. "Corruption in Public Policy and Its Impact on Development . . . " *Public Administration and Development,* 11: 473–490.

Pieth, Mark. 1997. "International Cooperation to Combat Corruption." In *Corruption and the Global Economy,* edited by Kimberly Ann Elliott. Washington: Institute for International Economics.

Pines, Daniel. 1994. "Amending the Foreign Corrupt Practices Act to Include a Private Right of Action." *California Law Review,* 82, 1 (January): 185–229.

Pitman, Glenn A., and James P. Sanford. 1994. "The Foreign Corrupt Practices Act Revisited: Attempting to Regulate 'Ethical Bribes' in Global Business." *International Journal of Purchasing and Materials Management.* 30, no. 3 (Summer): 15–20.

Richardson, J. David. 1993. *Sizing Up U.S. Export Disincentives.* Washington: Institute for International Economics.

Rodrik, Dani. 1997. "Comment" In *Corruption and the Global Economy,* edited by Kimberly Ann Elliott. Washington: Institute for International Economics.

Rose-Ackerman, Susan. 1997. "The Political Economy of Corruption." In *Corruption and the Global Economy,* edited by Kimberly Ann Elliott. Washington: Institute for International Economics.

Scott, James C. 1972. *Comparative Political Corruption.* Englewood Cliffs, NJ: Prentice-Hall.

Shleifer, Andrei, and Robert W. Vishny. 1993. "Corruption." *Quarterly Journal of Economics* (August): 599–618.

Trade Promotion Coordinating Committee. 1996. *Toward the Next American Century: A U.S. Strategic Response to Foreign Competitive Practices.* Fourth Annual Report to the United States Congress on National Export Strategy. Washington, October.

Transparency International. 1995. *Building a Global Coalition against Corruption.* Annual Report, Berlin.

U.S. Department of Commerce. 1995. *The Big Emerging Markets: 1996 Outlook and Sourcebook.* Washington.

Wei, Shang-Jin. 1997. "How Taxing is Corruption on International Investors?" Harvard University, Kennedy School of Government, February 25.

World Bank. 1996. *Financial Flows and the Developing Countries.* Washington: World Bank, May.

48

Controlling Business Payoffs to Foreign Officials: The 1998 OECD Anti-Bribery Convention

Arnold J. Heidenheimer and Holger Moroff

Introduction

Historians of the international economy may well identify the half century straddling the year 2000 as one marked by a very unusual degree of transformation in the way that political corruption was targeted by political and economic elites. The process commenced in the 1970s with the passage of the first national legislation criminalizing corruption abroad—the American Foreign Corrupt Practices Act, passed in the wake of revelations about bribery by large American companies. The 1980s then witnessed a vast expansion of private investment in the economies of the developing countries, and an unprecedented growth in world trade, accompanied by an explosion of bribery in the awarding of contracts. This was followed in the 1990s by the revival of governmental attempts to find effective ways of combating corruption in international business, an effort which culminated in a treaty in which over thirty of the advanced industrialized countries bound their governments to criminalize foreign bribery through the anti-bribery convention which came into force in the spring of 1999.

In this chapter we will utilize an analysis of the negotiations that culminated in the convention as a framework for discerning why the leading national governmental and business elites held varying positions about key economic and symbolic issues which cropped up. We will also seek to clarify why this convention with an unusually long-winded official title (Convention on Combating Bribery of Foreign Public Officials in International Business Transactions) got passed when it did, why the Organization of Economic Cooperation and Development became the venue for doing so, and what comparison with other international agreements made it seem worthwhile to expend so much diplomatic effort.

The attempt to develop an explanatory matrix to account for the success of U.S. anti-corruption effort must depart from an analysis of the OECD structures. Although its headquarters are not located on U.S. soil, the OECD's traditions are very much shaped by American influence. It is the successor agency to a late 1940s organization that was charged with implementing the American Marshall aid to Europe. Carryovers of that era are still evident today insofar as the U.S. delegation is the only one to have quarters in the main OECD building, located in the XVI *arrondissement* of Paris, where it occupies the entire top floor. Mainly the OECD is now concerned with helping governments to coordinate economic and trade policies, and to exchange planning expertise in areas like education and health policy.

OECD's member governments have encouraged the relative increase of private Western investment in developing countries, in contrast to investments there by public national and international organizations. That ratio changed from a public sector lead to a private sector predominance between l985 and 1995 (Elliott, 204). Many firms developed larger stakes in investments and sales. By the 1990s about one-third of the world's private productive assets were controlled by about 37,000 transnational corporations, with total sales of about $5.5 trillion.

Globalization of the 1990s has merely recaptured the relative international share of world trade which had been achieved a century earlier, prior to World War I. That high-water mark of international economic integration has been labeled as "the first global economy." The "second global economy" of the year 2000 differs from its predecessor both in its breadth, as indicated by the number of national markets, and in its depth, in terms of the density of interaction of trade and investment.

Why anti-corruption efforts have intensified is related to the tendency of national markets to lose their status as "principal entities" of the world economy. This became clear particularly for industries with globalized markets like the aerospace and weapons industries, where bribery revelations of the 1970s triggered the first massive resort to criminal penalties in national legislation. A more general tendency has been furthered by the way in which the liberalization of financial markets and the scale of technology has fused national markets.

The OECD Convention constitutes one of a number of efforts by transnational governmental organizations to put themselves on what was emerging as the "right" side of the corruption issue, or, more ambitiously, to enhance their capacity to discourage corruption. The World Trade Organization

(WTO) was like OECD a relative newcomer to this arena. However the WTO was poorly equipped to govern relations among businesses, so that transnational bribery could be controlled through the WTO, but not by the WTO (Nichols, 1997, 361–364).

Among international financial organizations, the World Bank had for many decades accumulated the most experience on what was to become the "wrong" side of the corrupt practices issue. For many decades it had studiously ignored very visible corrupt practices particularly by officials of the countries whose development efforts it largely financed. To reinforce its "blind eye" posture for most of this time it enforced internal regulation which inhibited direct reference to corruption in its own reports and publications.

These practices came under review with the ascent of James Wolfensohn to the presidency of the Bank. He gained insight into how internal politics inhibited effective bureaucratic corruption controls, by reviewing the activity of an independent inspection panel set up by the Bank in 1993. Some of the complaints brought to it involved corruption in World Bank projects, but when the panel found against the Bank management, it was often overruled. Among a sample of such cases, not even half were accepted by the panel. Among the other half the Bank's Board of Directors "fully backed the panel in only one case." Other observers echoed concerns about "ambiguities" between the Panel and the Bank's Board of Executive Directors. Even when Bank projects were withdrawn because of evidence of corruption, this generally occurred "without much publicity" (Rose-Ackerman 1999, 194–6).

This might suggest that the drafters of the OECD treaty found a niche of activity for which they had no particular experience, but for which other organizations had even less appetite or qualifications. As the new millennium opened national borders were still politically relevant, and even large firms were incapable of ignoring state boundaries in their organization of production. National states were still pursuing differing objectives in power contests with firms and other governments. It was because national boundaries continued to "create significant differentials on the global economic surface," that knowledgeable observers started to predict better chances for the effort made by the American government since the 1970s to have the OECD place the corruption issue on its active agenda.

Main Provisions and Contested Issues of the Anti-Bribery Convention

The Convention on Combating Bribery of Foreign Public Officials was signed by OECD Member States in November 1997 after being on the agenda, at American prompting, for three years, and after several rounds of intense negotiation. Many of its provisions mirror those of the American FCPA, which had been passed in 1977 at the height of the post-Watergate American reform wave, and we will here examine several key provisions from this perspective:

Criminal Sanctions: Overriding the objections of some European governments who wanted to curtail corruption through weaker civil law sanctions, the Convention followed the FCPA in criminalizing bribery of foreign public officials, whether appointed or elected, and including those working for public enterprises. It obliges the signatory countries to apply "proportionate and persuasive criminal penalties," and to prohibit off-the-books accounting devices that seek to hide such bribery.

The Convention Mode: Although the OECD usually culminated its agreements in terms of Recommendations to its member governments, the alternative Convention mode was strongly urged by European governments to assure a more universally binding effectiveness. The U.S. had initially backed the Recommendation mode, for fear that ratification of a Convention would be too drawn out, but accepted the compromise which inhibited delaying effects. Rules which curtailed the ability to delay enactment came to be exemplified by how the Convention went into effect in February 1999, after having been signed by fifteen of the signatory countries of whom five were among the world's leading trading nations.

Jurisdiction—National not Territorial: The Convention follows in the footsteps of the FCPA by surmounting territorial limits so as to make offenses punishable even if they were committed abroad. Also the German and other governments would be required to penalize natural and legal persons resident in Germany who bribed officials of any foreign country. This assumed that national legislators could build on traditions under which corporations and other legal persons were subject to criminal law penalties. Where this did not hold, as in the Italian case, special legal innovation was called for.

Active and Passive Corruption: The OECD Convention lines up solidly against bribers; but it does not require signatory governments to be even-handed in the punishment of bribers and bribees. This seems somewhat paradoxical, since in typical situations the bribers are private companies or middlemen, whereas the bribees are mostly officials who are public employees. Part of the explanation why "passive corruption" is treated less rigorously may be that bribed officials would in usual practices not be employees of the OECD signatory governments, but officials of developing countries. Another explanation of why the Convention omits penalties for the bribees is that "this would have posed insoluble problems of jurisdictional demarcation and might have led to accusations of violating national sovereignties" (Sacerdoti, 218)

Corrupt Intent: The Lockheed Aircraft Company was found guilty of bribing an Egyptian official in the late 1990s, even though it could not be demonstrated the she "misused her office." This was due to the American court's finding that it was the payer's intent, and not the recipient's actions, that constituted the controlling element in locating responsibility.

Sometimes the better handles available to one set of national prosecutors can help to compensate for the weaker ones of their peers elsewhere. Thus while Italian prosecutors had problems investigating some Italian companies for bribing Italian officials, some of them could be criminally prosecuted in the U.S. under the FCPA. Thus one Italian company whose issuing of financial securities in the U.S. made it subject to the FCPA was prosecuted by the U.S. Securities and Exchange Commission for mis-stating its financial condition by concealing huge bribe payments to Italian politicians. (Deming, 18)

National Bureaucratic Interests: When the OECD anti-bribery group began its recurrent meetings under its Swiss chairman, Mark Pieth, most of the national delegations differed from the American one in so far as they did not inherit developed and integrated national policy positions. The American delegation had a position paper in the shape of the FCPA, but in most of the other delegations, representatives of various ministries, had to work hard to develop and adapt their national positions in a series of meetings. Usually bureaucrats from the Ministries of Foreign Affairs and of Economics played key roles in the substantive negotiations, with their colleagues from the Ministries of Justice typically more concerned with problems of legislative formulation and implementation.

Which ministry chaired the delegations varied by country. For the Americans it was the State Department, with the Germans it was the Ministry of Economics. Although most of the delegates were lawyers, the majority of them had had little experience with international law and treaties. Since the OECD also lacked a precedent for negotiating an international treaty, the

---

Box 48.1
Key OECD Convention Provisions

The Offence of Bribery: Article 1 stipulates that "each Party shall take such measures as may be necessary to establish that it is a criminal offence under its law for any person intentionally to offer, promise or give any undue pecuniary or other advantage, whether directly or through intermediaries, to a foreign public official, for that official or for a third party, in order that the official act or refrain from acting in relation to the performance of official duties, in order to obtain or retain business or other improper advantage in the conduct of international business."

Criminal Penalties: Article 3 requires parties to sanction bribery of a foreign public official with "effective proportionate and dissuasive criminal penalties." If there is no provision for criminal penalties to legal persons, effective non-criminal sanctions shall be applied.

Enforcement: Article 5 requires that Prosecution shall not be influenced by considerations of national public interest, or the identity of the natural or legal persons involved.

Accounting and legal assistance: Article 8 requires countries to prohibit off-the books accounts, while Article 9 requires prompt legal assistance between countries, and prohibits them from asserting bank secrecy as a reason to deny it.

peripatetic meetings of the anti-bribery group could afford to be unusually flexible in their proceedings. This flexibility permitted the chairman to employ ad hoc techniques of inhibiting negotiation deadlocks. Thus at one crucial point leaders of five key countries met secretly at Gandria near Lugano to reconcile their key differences on the form and substance of the Convention.

An Anti-Corruption NGO: An important role in linking and activating the governmental, business and public opinion components of the anti-corruption coalition was played by Transparency International. Established with headquarters in Berlin in 1993, TI is hard to classify but it comes close to what the British call a Quasi-Nongovernmental organization, or Quango. It can hardly be labeled private, if only because its founder, Peter Eigen, spent most of his career in the public sector as an official of the World Bank, supervising Bank projects in Africa and elsewhere and because much of its start-up seed money was supplied by the German Ministry of Development Aid.

Eigen's initiative was originally presented as a protest against the complacency with which the World Bank had ignored or downplayed the Corruption issue. Thus TI joined a plethora of organizations which sought to critique and monitor the Bank's shortcomings on goals like poverty elimination. But with the coming of Wolfensohn, the Bank began to divulge and critique its own past record. In the iconography of the Bank Eigen was coopted from a position of an outside critic into a member of the Bank's own Hall of Fame. This recasting was reflected in an article by a senior *New York Times* journalist who wrongly described him as a predecessor of Wolfensohn as Bank chairman. (Schmemann, 1999)

As a consistent ally of the American anti-corruption effort, TI evoked much resentment in the Bonn bureaucracy due to its public criticism of German policies like those permitting the tax deductibility of bribes paid abroad. But TI's effort to mobilize additional groups extended beyond that of the diplomats and business reformers by capturing attention, not just of the economic journals but the mass media, and in then connecting the Western public to newly formed ones in the developing countries. It did this by founding national chapters in countries of Latin America and Asia, and later also in Africa. These have sisters on the World Wide Web and are drawn into the World Wide Network.

On the basis of such far-flung contacts Peter Eigen and his TI collaborators engaged in extensive public diplomacy with more or less open support by and in tandem with the U.S., and used this to put pressure on national governments. Thus in Germany it criticized business associations like the German Association of Industry and Trade (*Deutscher Industrie und Handelstag*) for its opposition to a federal "black list" of firms which were guilty of bribery practices. It also bemoaned that the criticisms by the German public accounts offices had not led to follow-up investigations by the public prosecutors except in only one of the fifteen Laender.

Infrastructure of Support Mobilization: From the time that the anti-corruption issue began to occupy a visible position on the international agenda of the political and business worlds, myriads of non-governmental, governmental and inter-governmental organizations came to be involved in discussing the terms of the Convention. Business leaders and organizations, some of whom had had the corruption issue on their agenda for several decades without much progress, played a crucial role. Thus the International Chamber of Commerce, which had dealt with trans-national bribery as early as 1977, yielded priority to the OECD effort. So did numerous other established and ad hoc groups linking American and European big business. Their efforts were reinforced by encouraging resolutions from groups like the International Bar Association and the Trans-Atlantic Business Dialogue. Typically the American business emissaries sought to convince the Europeans that U.S. regulatory legislation had provided both incentives and muscle which permitted firm and industry leaders to police their own ranks more effectively.

Where business groups were suspicious that the anti-bribery initiative would favor their larger international competitors, as was the case for companies and industries in France, Germany and some smaller European countries, the business association officials were reluctant to go out on a limb. Then the troops had to be rallied through visible exhortations by leaders of brand-name companies, as when heads of firms like Siemens and Asea Brown Boveri proclaimed support at the 1995 Davos Economic Forum. Some of the key firms had themselves been involved in recent corruption scandals, as Siemens in Singapore. After they too endorsed the Anti-Corruption theme, association functionaries like the Federation of German Industries secretary echoed that the economic '*Standort*' Germany could no longer afford to be linked to corruption scandals.

Actors and Props on a Moving Stage

If they had thought of commissioning a theatrical version, the OECD stage managers might have looked for scripting inspiration to dramas like "Seven characters in search of an Author," or "Snow White and the Seven Dwarfs." Audiences might have been clued in to the identities of the characters through notes in the program booklets which would read something like this:

Reborn Sinners: Compensating for preceding violations of "clean government" standards was what led the United States to become an initiator of tightened ethical regulations in eras such as the Progressive Period, about 1910, and once again the Post-Watergate period that led to the passage of the FCPA. It was not coincidental that the country which was most marked by periodic revivalist movements, and which viewed its economic and moral virtues as supporting its ascent to world leadership, had used diplomatic muscle to push the anti-corruption issue onto the OECD agenda. Changes in the world balance of political power, as well as the international economy, permitted greater lift-off opportunities in the 1990s than they had for preceding evangelizing endeavors.

Repentant Spenders: This category included national governments and international corporations whose earlier practices had violated reform goals or favored the tactical opportunities of bribe recipients. This included giant firms like General Electric (U.S.) and Siemens (Germany), whose agents had employed bribery to secure contracts in Asian countries. These companies added private financial and organizational support to those seeking to put teeth into the Convention. Also in this category were the public authorities of Switzerland, whose indulgence of bank secrecy had helped recipients of bribe money to escape prosecution through money-laundering and other techniques.

Fence Straddlers: Placing themselves in this category were national delegations whose home Ministries sometimes held differing positions on key policy issues that cropped up in the OECD discussions. In some cases low profiles in the negotiation process were due to fears that the export potential of important national industries would be unduly harmed. Countries which might be placed in this category were some whose companies were large actors in international trade, such as Japan and Great Britain, as well as some smaller ones, like the Netherlands. Many European national business associations could also be located here.

Reluctant Dragons: This category includes countries and industries which were anxious about losing their dominant position in particular groups of developing countries. France and Germany were worried about the competitive position of their firms in areas like West Africa, Southeast Asia, Latin America, and especially in the newly opened emerging markets of Eastern Europe. This coincided with concern that the legal ad-hocism might be difficult to reconcile with some judicial principles in these code-law systems where prosecutors and judges had less discretion in the initiation and handling of charges under criminal law.

Legal Basis for Effective Prosecution

Some European critics who were skeptical of American efforts to prescribe the FCPA as a model for replication asserted that the implementation history of the American statute itself demonstrated inherent limitations of its effectiveness. Thus they observed that over a twenty year period during which American companies executed foreign business worth trillions of dollars, a mere twenty-six American companies were successfully prosecuted for violations of the FCPA.

They were able to contrast the American record of less than two convictions per year with the record of Italian prosecutors in the *Mani-Pulite* investigations who at the high point of their activity were indicting hundreds of political, bureaucratic, and business officials for violation of various corruption statutes. (Dellaporta and Vannucci, chapter 37) A crucial difference between the two situations was that in the American case the public prosecutors had extensive latitude in deciding as to whether and when to prosecute. In Italy, they were acting under a legal tradition which obligated them to initiate prosecutions whenever evidence called for it.

Not only did the OECD negotiators have to draft Convention terminology which could surmount such crucial national differences in applying the law. They also had to look some years down the road so as to anticipate how international teams that would monitor and compare national implementation policies, would go about devising statistical and other measures of compliance and conviction.

Protection Arrangements: The relative size of both internationally active firms, and of national governments and their ministries, is very relevant for the way in which the OECD Convention seeks to link the legal internationalization of corruption offenses to the administrative feasibility of prescribed corruption punishments. Representatives of smaller OECD countries pointed to the difference between the information gathering capacities of American economic, diplomatic and intelligence agencies and those of their much smaller national equivalents. This view was buttressed by the partly classified Foreign Competitive Practices Report 1995, gathered by the U.S. Department of Commerce, which was compiled with the help of U.S. intelligence agencies and contained "hundreds of examples of bribery and legitimate—often government assisted—export promotion." (Wall Street Journal, 12 Oct. 1995, Elliott, chapter 47).

They also pointed out that American companies could to some extent procure official acknowledgment that intended actions would not violate FCPA prohibitions, and asked that the Convention allow room for techniques that would protect firms against extortion demands from officials. They also argued that while larger countries could use their political and economic clout to secure contracts for their companies abroad, small countries can not participate in that kind of pressuring especially where large defense contracts are concerned.

Pressures to end vulnerable practices by both industries and governments were countered behind closed doors by arguments that European business should not be shackled with yet additional control mechanisms and publicity requirements (Thomas Peltscher in Pieth/Eigen, p. 279).

Moral Imperialism: Observers from the developing countries sometimes noted off the record that the direction of the OECD efforts substantiated their fears that the selection of a nearly all-Western group like the OECD provided a forum that encouraged both public and private organizations to parade their own form of moral imperialism. Although the Convention would leave it to developing countries whether or not their native bribees would be prosecuted, it was arguable that through the Convention the developed countries were seeking to bind the poorer recipient countries to higher rules of behavior. Some regional groups like the Organization of African States were criticized for not giving the drive enough support.

To help counter such criticism the Western governments sought to pass parallel anti-corruption resolutions in more inclusive international organizations, especially the United Nations. Thus they encouraged the International Commission on International Trade Law to adopt a Procurement Law Model which sought to combat bribery within host countries. In 1996 this Initiative was taken a step further when the UN General Assembly passed a 'UN Declaration on Corruption and Bribery in Transnational Commercial Activity'. This Declaration, in the view of a U.S. State Department official 'provided the framework for true international cooperation on the OECD proposal, since it made it much easier to fend off the moral imperialism argument'. Subsequently the official title of the OECD Convention was extended to include the exact terms of the UN Declaration.

Legal and Conceptual Issues relating to the Convention Text

Public Officials: A key definitional issue in the negotiations was how to circumscribe the category of 'public official' on which the convention with the long winded name was centered. They came to be defined as including:

> ... officials in all branches of government, whether appointed or elected; any person exercising a public function, including public agency or public enterprise; and any official or agent of an international organization.

At issue here was whether one should build on a broader or a narrower definition. The FCPA had employed the broader definition by including those who held political party positions even if these were not combined with formal holding of a governmental office. Several OECD countries opted for a narrower definition which would not cover party office holders, and their views prevailed in the convention text.

A related problem concerned the 'violation of duty' concept which for continental countries built on a legal conceptual history not fully shared by the common law countries.

Legislators: Also at issue was if and how elected legislators should be included in the definition of bribees. In Germany and some other countries constitutional jurisprudence provides legislators with special immunities, which limits prosecution to cases where direct and crude forms of vote buying could be proven.

Party Finance: The question of whether payments to political parties in foreign host countries should be regarded as potential instances of bribery constituted one of the more long lasting issues, especially as between the American and the European negotiators.

A German participant reported that the Europeans were reluctant to follow the FCPA precedent of overtly including donations to parties. The Americans claimed that their calculations showed that about twenty percent of all bribes were forwarded through such party conduits and channels.

But the continental lawyers were reluctant to attempt to define offences that moved beyond quid pro quo exchanges to cover other situations "where there was a quid, but no pro quo." The outcome was that what the Germans call in peasant jargon, "the cultivation of the political landscape," or *'anfüttern'* was in effect removed from the roster of moving targets at which the OECD delegates could aim their shooting gallery weapons. (Deming, 33)

Facilitation Payments: Bribery as defined by the OECD convention relates only to payments made in order to retain or obtain business, which therefore excludes bribes paid to avoid taxes, customs duties, judicial or other regulatory obligations. This is seen by some as a weakness and possible loophole, though others argue that "small payments to low level officials to expedite routine approvals . . . [i]n places where [this] is customary practice, it may be better to provide some administrative flexibility than to ignore the problem." (Heimann in Elliott, pp.151)

Business Governance and Private Sphere Corruption Consciousness

One of the American arguments was that heavy handed policing of the convention's provisions could be minimized if other countries followed the American precedent of inducing firms to achieve higher levels of business governance based on more extensive public disclosure policies and internal monitoring standards. However, this legal device of a 'made in U.S.A' standard applied only to bribery of public officials, and plans to have the convention also apply to bribery among office holders of private companies did not get far.

Another obstacle here was that in the majority of American states, bribery that takes place exclusively in the private sector is not subject to criminal prosecution. Most of the delegates sympathized with the dilemma of their American colleagues, who were unable to contemplate asking their political superiors to lobby for the large scale revision of state statues which would have been a prerequisite for national implementation of such a broad convention's applicability.

American managers told the Europeans that they should not expect to be able to get their managers to impose tight anti-bribery rules overnight. Speaking on the basis of the U.S. experience since the 1970s, they advised that creating a culture of integrity required at least one managerial generation to get the roots of such company commitments established.

Tax Deductibility of Bribery Payments

Among national rules which proved most vulnerable to TI and press critiques of governmental integrity were the income and corporate tax law provisions in France, Germany and other countries which provided for the deductibility of bribes abroad as normal business expenses. In effect this turned governments into agencies that not only tolerated, but financially supported, bribery practices.

The finance ministry officials, who normally held the most prestigious positions, balked at the notion that outside moral pressure groups and foreign colleagues should attempt to sit in judgement on practices which had stood the test of time in the complex arena of international economic competition.

In the end the French and German finance ministries yielded ground by agreeing that when ratification of the OECD convention criminalized such bribery, this would be promptly followed by regulatory change prohibiting tax deductibility of bribery, at least in the more overt form in which it had been practiced. Other observers wondered whether legal ingenuity might not be able to circumvent much of the national legislation implementing the OECD convention.

Explaining the Timing (and Outcome) of the International Anti-Corruption Curb

In order to understand why the OECD convention came out the way it did at the end of the 1990s it is appropriate to contrast this effort with earlier ones to draft similar agreements. After all, this was not the first time the United States sought to urge other developed countries to follow its lead in outlawing corruption abroad. In the late 1970s the International Chamber of Commerce undertook such initiatives at American urging, and in 1979 the United States formally requested that the United Nations consider similar anti-corruption initiatives. These efforts went nowhere, and subsequently the officials of the Reagan and Bush administrations made no efforts to revive the issue.

Much has been made of the fact that the public opinion and media settings of the 1990s favored the American attempt to revive the corruption issue, but one should also ask whether the organizational vehicle chosen for this international thrust was also a significant contributing factor. Here one has to note that the OECD was quite inexperienced in this sector, both as regards the writing of a convention and as regards the focus of the regulatory intervention, let alone its first-time venture into the realms of international criminal law. Simultaneously with the anti-bribery convention the OECD launched a similar effort to standardize rules affecting international investment, the Multilateral Agreement on Investment (MAI). This effort came to be a setback for the OECD when its officials failed to demonstrate the necessary savvy to repulse coordinated attacks from developing countries, environmental groups, and trade unions. Among American agencies, the U.S. Trade Representative differed from the State Department in withholding political support. (Financial Times, Feb. 14, 1998)

Why did the anti-bribery treaty pose fewer problems? One reason is that objectors from the developing countries were not provided a platform, since they were not members of OECD. But public images were also projected more positively. Most OECD initiatives are, because of their typically technical nature, effectively insulated from public media attention, but the anti-bribery treaty proved to be an exception. This was mainly due to the fact that the media were led to see how the topic might have large readership appeal. Such an attitude was mainly achieved by linking the OECD negotiations to the news of domestic corruption which came to permeate the media in countries like Italy, France and Germany during the 1990s. It was not self-evident how control of foreign corruption in India was related to municipal corruption in Grenoble or Frankfurt, but ways of projecting the linkage were facilitated by the extensive publicity given to the international corruption index of Transparency International. The national bureaucrats and business association spokesmen who sought to impede the treaty found it impossible to recruit allies who might influence public opinion in the manner that TI was doing. There was no European equivalent to the coalition of U.S. public and private agencies and firms which increasingly drew allies from European officials and businessmen.

Consequently the elite attitudes toward the anti-corruption initiative began to undergo a change during the years leading up to the important 1994 Recommendation, which provided the content basis for the convention. Some member countries started to feel "embarrassed" to oppose the effort, and others realized that common action "was not so utopian after all." The issue became more visible in public discourse as "scandals made politicians realize that the general public was fed up with both domestic and international corruption." (Pieth, 1997 p. 123)

International Reform Sinews and Arteries

As noted above, the OECD *ad hoc* committee system provided the convention drafters with an unusual amount of leeway for compromises. But this also had the consequence that, apart from the persistent American nudging, there was a scarcity of platforms for favoring initiatives that cut across established turfs. Lacking such resources, the leaders sometimes sought to combat skirmish-fatigue among the troops by importing talents from adjacent bureaucratic turfs. Such a pool was made-up of the investigating judges and public prosecutors who were uncovering corruption in many near-by European countries. Mostly these scandals involved bribers and bribees of the same nationality, but some did involve corrupt exchanges across some European borders. At one juncture several of these prosecutors were invited to meet with the negotiators, and some of the dramatic cases involving the home countries of the negotiators helped induce the necessary zeal to break out of some negotiation deadlocks.

Leaders like Pieth also helped colleagues to aim for legislation with teeth by drawing on their experience in combating organized crime at the international level through the adoption of a tightened framework for international coordination in the effort to control processes like money-laundering. (Überhofen, 710)

Reform Motivation: Given that changing elite attitudes are an important factor, what time periods constitute the optimal units for understanding change in the longer term comparative perspective? Should one best think in terms of decades, or better in terms of centuries? Perhaps 25-year periods might be most suitable in the case of anti-corruption legislation. It was that kind of a time gap that separated the OECD action from the American initiative of the 1970s. If one goes back still another quarter century one can ask why an international anti-corruption initiative was not on anybody's policy or even theoretical reform agenda in 1950.

One can wander even more widely in comparing the sequential patterns with similar reform efforts in other arenas where private gain interacted with standards of public morality in primarily commercial settings. A renowned jurist has ventured to draw a parallel between efforts to control corruption with earlier international efforts to eradicate slavery. (Noonan, 684) This has led others to draw the historical analogy that "the 1990s could be to corruption what the 1850s were to slavery: a decade of irreversible change". The same authors also seek to persuade us that the 1990s constitute a "decade which is the first to witness corruption as a completely global issue" (Glynn, 1997).

Shifting perspective again, one could postulate that what most predisposed Western elites of 1950 against investing in control efforts was probably acceptance of the conventional wisdom which held that such efforts were inherently futile and a waste of time. Not only cynics believed that historical experience demonstrated it to be inevitable for the monitors of corrupt practices to become themselves corrupted. Moreover, both the American and European elites of 1950 had been politically socialized during an era when international reform goals had been particularly associated with the figure of Woodrow Wilson. If the American goal of "making the world safe for democracy" was naïve, what incentive was there to invest political capital to make parts of the world free from political corruption?

By the time of the turn of the millennium the adoption of the OECD Convention had come to provide what seemed like a workable instrument for the progressive reduction of corruption in developing countries. Some ob-

Box 48.2
U .S. Senators On Ratification of OECD Convention, July 16, 1998

Sen. Feingold (D, Wisconsin) It was just 20 years ago that Congress passed the Foreign Corrupt Practices Act, the FCPA. This landmark legislation, which I am proud to say was sponsored by one of Wisconsin's most respected public officials, Senator William Proxmire, was enacted after it was discovered that some American companies were actually keeping slush funds for making questionable and/or illegal payments to foreign officials to help land certain business deals.. . . .

But there has been, as I have been told by a number of business people, a price for taking such a high ethical road. In Germany, they even allow companies to take a tax deduction for bribes paid to foreign officials as a business expense. My business people in Wisconsin are always a little horrified when they hear that.

Sen. Hagel (R, Nebraska) I understand a German official stated recently that German companies spend an estimated $5.63 billion a year on bribes to foreign officials, most of it added on top of the contract price and then written off on their taxes. If this treaty is implemented, do you believe these kinds of bribes will be, can be eliminated?

Mr. Eizenstat. (State Department) Absolutely. They will be and they can be and I think that there will be very effective enforcement.

Sen. Sarbanes. (D, Maryland) I notice there are a fair number of fairly large economies around the world that are not participating in it.

Mr. Eizenstat. There are already five non-OECD countries who have agreed to ratify this, the fact that we already have so early on five non-OECD countries to go with the 29 that we have means that we will be covering with the 34 countries about 75 percent of all the trade in the world.

Sen. Robb (D, Virginia) Some view what we see clearly bribery as a cost of doing business. . . . Will this particular treaty make major inroads into changing the culture so that the international community does not have to continue to deal with something that is culturally ingrained and viewed differently than we see in very black and white terms here but is seen differently in some other nations?

Mr. Eizenstat. One of the prime reasons we have seen the Europeans come around on this is not only the bipartisan urging that we have had for a decade, but it is the fact that their own corporations realize that this is self-defeating. So, I think that there is a change in culture and that there will be, as a result, effective enforcement because the major corporations there recognize that they need an external constraint so they can say to the corrupt foreign official, look, our laws now prevent this, do not ask us. It allows them to put a shield up.

Sen. Helms (R, North Carolina): The Government of France not only failed to support U.S. antiproliferation efforts toward Pakistan, France tried to win the contract to deliver French-made fighter aircraft by giving a $200 million bribe to the husband of Madam Bhutto. . . . Now because the French bribe went to the Prime Minister's husband and not to the Prime Minister herself would that be prohibited by this treaty?

Mr. Eizenstat: When France ratifies this convention and enacts a criminal law against the bribery of foreign officials, such a transaction could be illegal then under French law, and that is the value of the convention.

Now with respect to the payment of an official spouse, although this would not be a *per se* violation either of our own Foreign Corrupt Practices Act, as it now exists, or of the convention, it would be covered under two circumstances.

Source: *Hearings Report, U.S. Senate Foreign Relations Committee, July 16, 1998*

servers were concerned that the costs of administering the controls on private business might induce a return to centralist controls: "The tone of OECD documents on bribery control is neutral, but accompanying materials make it clear that centralized control will result from adoption of the convention." (Anechiarico, 162) Others were concerned that it might provide something of a moral umbrella under which organizations with tainted records could seek to find shelter. Exemplary for this function was the attempt by the International Olympic Committee to disavow a record of corrupted decision making by affiliating themselves to the OECD's corruption control regime.

Toward the end of the year 2000, the ratification and monitoring process for the Convention seemed to be making good progress. Twenty -six of the thirty-four signatories had ratified it and most had passed implementation progress of member countries. This was completed for twenty-three countries, in seven of which serious shortcomings were noted. Thus France was criticized for envisioning a three year statute of limitations, which was regarded as too short. At this time, plans were also being developed for a second phase of country reviews, which were intended to examine how countries had complied with the accounting and auditing provisions of the Convention.

Note

We would like to acknowledge with great appreciation the assistance provided to us in the preparation of this research by Hillary Burke, Henri-Pierre Debord, Irene Hors, Carolyn Ervin, Laurence Giovacchini, Manfred Möhrenschläger, Mark Pieth, Giorgio Sacerdoti, and Thomas White.

Bibliography

Anechiarico, Frank. 1999. "Public Involvement at the Public-Private Interface," in L. W. J. C. Huberts and L. H. J. Vandenheuvel, eds. Integrity at the Public-Private Interface.. Maastricht: Shaker, 149–164

Cadot, Oliver. 1987. "Corruption as a Gamble," *Journal of Public Economics*, 33:223–224

Convention on Combating Bribery of Foreign Officials in International Business Transactions, December 11, 1997.

De George, Richard T. 1994. "International Business Ethics," *Business Ethics Quarterly* 4:1–9

Deming, Stuart H. 1998. *The Foreign Corrupt Practices Act and the Emerging International Norms*, Inman Deming law office, Washington, D.C.

Earle, Beverly, 1996 "The United States Foreign Corrupt Practices Act and the OECD Anti-Bribery Recommendation: When Moral Suasion Won't Work Try the Money Argument" *Dickinson Journal of International Law*, Volume 14, pages 207–239.

Eigen, Peter and Mark Pieth, Eds. 1999, *Korruption im internationalen Geschäftsverkehr: Bestandsaufnahme, Bekämpfung, Prävention*, Frankfurt: Luchterhand.

Elliott, Kimberly Ann, ed. 1997 *Corruption and the Global Economy.* Washington DC: Institute for International Economics

Flatters, Frank, and W. Bentley MacLeod. 1995. "Administrative Corruption and Taxation," *International Tax and Public Finance* 2:397–417

Glynn, Patrick, et al. 1997. "The Globalization of Corruption," in Elliott, ed. pp 7–30

Heimann, Fritz F. 1997. "Combatting International Corruption: The Role of the Business Community," Chapter 8 in Elliot, op. cit.

Hepkema, Sietze, and Willem Booysen. 1997. "The Bribery of Public Officials: An IBA Survey," *International Business Lawyer*, October 1997, pp. 415–422

Kobrin, Stephen J. "Beyond Symmetry: State Sovereignty in a Networked Global Economy".

LeVine, Victor T. 1989. "Transnational Aspects of Political Corruption" in: Heidenheimer , Johnston, LeVine eds. et al.: *Political Corruption—A Handbook,* pp. 685–700

Lundahl, Mats. 1997. "Inside the Predatory State: The Rationale, Methods, and Economic Consequences of Kleptocratic Regimes," *Nordic Journal of Political Economy* 24:30–50

Nichols, Philip M. 1997. "Outlawing Transnational Bribery Through the World Trade Organization," *Journal of Law & Policy in International Business* 28:305–381;

Noonan, John T. Jr. 1984. Bribes. New York: Macmillan,

Pieth, Mark. 1997. International Cooperation to Combat Corruption" in Elliott, ed. 119–132 *OECD Actions to Fight Corruption*, Paris, 1997.

Prasad, Jyoti N. 1993. *Impact of the Foreign Corrupt Practices Act of 1977 on U.S. Exports.* New York: Garland Publishing.

Rose-Ackerman, Susan. 1999. *Corruption and Government: Causes, Consequences, and Reform,*" Cambridge: Cambridge University Press

Rosenthal, Michael, 1989 "An American Attempt to Control International Corruption." In: Political Corruption: A Handbook, ed. A.J. Heidenheimer and M. Johnston, 701–715

Sacerdoti, Giorgio, Transparency International. 1995. "Building a Global Coalition Against Corruption," TI Annual Report, Berlin.

———. 1998. "Combating Corruption: Are Lasting Solutions Emerging?," TI Annual Report, Berlin

Schmemann, Serge. 1999. "What Makes Nations Turn Corrupt?" *New York Times.* August 28.

Überhofen, Michael. 1997. In Albin Eser et al., *Korruptions beKämpfung durch Strafrecht: Ein rechtsvergleichendes Gutachten zu den Bestechungsdelikten.* Edition iuscrim, Freiburg.

U. S. Congress "International Anti-Bribery and Fair Competition Act of 1998," enacted into law on November 10, 1998

Vermeulen, Gert. 1997. "The Fight Against International Corruption in the European Union," In Barry Rider, ed., *Corruption: The Enemy Within*, The Hague: Kluwer, 333–342

"World Bank Hires Auditors to Probe Its Own Spending; Possible Kickbacks, Embezzlement Cited." *Washington Post.* July 16, 1998.

"Helping Countries Combat Corruption: The Role of the World Bank," Poverty Reduction and Economic Management Network. Washington D.C. World Bank. 1997

Guide to Articles in Previous Editions of *Political Corruption*

Topic/Title	Author	Volume; Pages
Crime and Mobility among Italian-Americans	Daniel Bell	I 159–166
Patronage and Public Service in Britain and America	Samuel E. Finer	II 101–128
Social Perceptions		
Toward an Attitudinal Definition of Corruption	Kenneth M. Gibbons	II 165–172
The Rhetoric of Political Corruption	Bruce E. Gronbeck	II 173–190
Variations in Attitudes Toward Corruption in Canada	Kenneth M. Gibbons	II 763–780
Africa		
Corruption in the Public Services of British Colonies and Ex-Colonies in West Africa	M. McMullan	I 317–330
Nepotism and Bribery in West Africa	Ronald Wraith and Edgar Simpkins	I 331–340
Kleptocracy as a System of Government in Africa	Stanislav Andreski	I 346–360
Bribery in the Election of Ashanti Chiefs	K. A. Busia	I 447–452
Remuneration Levels and Corruption in French-Speaking Africa	Rene Dumont	I 453–458
Corruption and Self-Interest in Kampala and Nairobi	J. David Greenstone	I 459–468
Endemic and Planned Corruption in a Monarchical Regime	John Waterbury	II 339–362
Supportive Values of the Culture of Corruption in Ghana	Victor T. LeVine	II 363–374
Asia		
Sociological Aspects of Corruption in Southeast Asia	W. F. Wertheim	I 195–211
The "Sala" Model of Comparative Administration	Fred W. Riggs	I 212–219

Topic/Title	Author	Volume; Pages	
The Dimensions of Corruption in India	John B. Monteiro	I	220–228
The Peso Price of Politics in the Philippines	Albert Ravenholt	I	469
Corruption, Tradition, and Change in Indonesia	Theodore M. Smith	II	423–440
Singapore's Experience in Curbing Corruption	Jon S. T. Quah	II	841–854
Britain			
The Nature and Decline of Corrupt Election Expenditures in Nineteenth Century Britain	William B. Gwyn	I	391–404
The British Method of Dealing with Political Corruption	Madeline R. Robinson	I	249–258
Corruption and Political Development in Early Modern Britain	Linda Levy Peck	II	219–232
Socioeconomic Development and Corrupt Campaign Practices in England	John P. King	II	233–250
France			
How Government Won Elections Under Napoleon III	Theodore Zeldin	I	373–378
Paradoxes of Political Corruption: A French View	Jeanne Becquart-Leclercq	II	191–210
Germany			
The Decline of the Bureaucratic Ethos in the Federal Republic	Theodor Eschenburg	I	259–266
German Attempts at Legal Definition of Parliamentary Corruption	Theodor Eschenburg	I	404–409
Bureaucratic and Political Corruption Controls: Reassessing The German Record	Ulrich von Alemann	II	855–869

Topic/Title	Author	Volume; Pages	
Scandals			
On Political Scandals and Corruption	Graeme C. Moodie	II	873–886
The Mobilization of Scandal	Lawrence W. Sherman	II	887–912
Political Scandals and Corruption Issues in West Germany	Erhard Blankenburg, Rainer Staudhammer and Heinz Steinert	II	913–931
Assessing Effects			
Towards a Grammar of Graft	The Economist	I	489–491
Apologies for Political Corruption	Robert C. Brooks	I	501–509
The Contribution of Nepotism, Spoils and Graft to Political Development	Jose Veloso Abueva	I	534–539
Bureaucracy versus Kleptocracy	Sinnathamby Rajaratnam	I	546–548
The Effects of Corruption in a Developing Nation	David H. Bayley	II	935–952
Corruption: Its Causes and Effects	Gunnar Myrdal	II	953–962
The Political Consequences of Corruption: A Reassessment	Michael Johnston	II	985–1006

Contributors

M. Shahid Alam is Professor of Economics at Northeastern University, Boston.

Frank Anechiarico is the Maynard-Knox Professor of Government and Law at Hamilton College, Clinton, New York.

Ralph Angermund is Ministerialrat in the Education Ministry of Land Northrhine-Westphalia, in Düsseldorf.

Pranab Bardhan is Professor of Economics at the Institute of International Studies, University of California, Berkeley.

Erhard Blankenburg is Professor of the Sociology of Law in the Law Faculty of the Free University of Amsterdam.

Verena Blechinger heads the social science department of the German Institute for Japan Studies, Tokyo.

Thomas F. Burke is Assistant Professor of Political Science at Wellesley College in Wellesley, Massachusetts.

Donatella Della Porta is Professor of Political Science at the University of Florence.

Wayne DiFranceisco was a student in the Political Science Department of the University of Michigan.

Kimberly Ann Elliott is a Research Fellow at the Institute for International Economics, Washington.

Eva Etzioni-Halevy teaches in the Sociology Department of Bar Ilan University, Ramat Gan.

Carl J. Friedrich was Professor of Political Science at Harvard and Heidelberg Universities.

John A. Gardiner is Professor of Political at the University of Illinois, Chicago.

Maryvonne Genaux is a Fellow of the Institut Thiers, Paris.

Zvi Y. Gitelman is Professor of Political Science at the University of Michigan, Ann Arbor.

Ase Grodeland is affiliated with the Norwegian Institute of Urban and Regional Research in Oslo.

Yufan Hao is Associate Professor of Political Science at Colgate University, Hamilton, New York.

Arnold J. Heidenheimer is Professor of Political Science at Washington University, St. Louis.

Samuel P. Huntington is Eaton Professor of the Science of Government at Harvard University.

Paul Hutchcroft teaches in the Political Science Department of the University of Wisconsin, Madison.

James B. Jacobs is Professor of Law at New York University.

Michael Johnston is Professor of Political Science at Colgate University, Hamilton, New York.

Mushtaq H. Khan is a Reader in Economics at the School of African and Asian Studies in the University of London.

Jacob van Klaveren was Emeritus Professor of Economic History at the University of Frankfurt, Germany.

Tatyana Koshechkina was founder of SOCIS-Gallup Ukraine and is its International Research Director.

Sahr J. Kpundeh is a Consultant with the World Bank Institute.

Nathaniel H. Leff was Professor of Business at Columbia University, New York.

Colin Leys is Professor of Political Science at Queens University, Kingston, Ontario.

Tom Lodge is Professor of Political Science at Witwatersrand University.

Paolo Mauro is an economist in the Research Department at the International Monetary Fund.

Jean-François Mèdard is a Professor of Political Science at the African Studies Institute of the University of Bordeaux.

Kenneth J. Meier is Professor of Political Science at Texas A&M University, College Station.

William L. Miller is the Edward Caird Professor of Politics at the University of Glasgow.

Holger Moroff is a Fellow of the Institute of European Integration, University of Bonn.

Gunnar Myrdal was Professor of International Economics at Stockholm University.

Joseph S. Nye is Dean of the John F. Kennedy School of Government at Harvard University.

John G. Peters is Provost at the University of Tennessee, Knoxville.

Susan J. Pharr is Edwin O. Reischauer Professor of Japanese Politics, Harvard University.

Mark Philp is a Fellow of Oriel College, Oxford.

Veronique Pujas is a lecturer at the Institut d'etudes politiques at the University of Grenoble, France.

Jon S.T. Quah is Professor in the Political Science Department of the National University of Singapore.

Martin Rhodes is Professor of European Public Policy at the European University Institute, Florence, Italy.

Susan Rose-Ackerman is the Henry R. Luce Professor of Law and Political Science, Yale University.

Thomas L. Schlesinger teaches political science at the University of Wisconsin-Milwaukee.

James C. Scott is Professor of Political Science and Anthropology at Yale University.

Alice Sindzingre is a research fellow of the Centre National de la Recherche Scientifique, Paris.

Koenraad W. Swart held a Professorship in Dutch history at the University of London.

Alberto Vannucci is a post-doctoral fellow in political science at the University of Pisa.

Susan Welch is Dean of the College of the Liberal Arts at the Pennsylvania State University, University Park.

Simcha Werner is a lecturer in the political science department of Tel Aviv University, Israel.

Laurence Whitehead is a Fellow of Nuffield College, Oxford University.